The official history of the Bank of England from its foundation in 1694 until the Second World War is contained in the volumes by Sir John Clapham and Professor Richard Sayers, both distinguished economic historians. It has now been continued by John Fforde, a central banker by profession and a former Executive Director of the Bank. Mr Fforde has had unfettered access to the highly detailed material in the Bank's extensive archives covering the wartime and post-war periods, as well as the benefit of the oral evidence of some of those who held senior positions at the Bank at that time.

Beginning in the final phase of Lord Norman's long Governorship, the book goes on to cover that of Lord Catto and ten of the twelve years of Lord Cobbold's Governorship. It examines and appraises how Norman's very personal creation, set in statutory mould by the hurried nationalisation of 1946, moved on and led a vigorous though often frustrated life in the post-war years of recurrent external monetary weakness and persistent difficulties with both the content and the conduct of domestic monetary policy. The Bank's subordinate but restless relationship with the Treasury is central to the whole story; but Mr Fforde also examines the Bank's evolving and far from subordinate relationship with the UK financial community. The long story, some of it already familiar to students of the period, is related here from the viewpoint of the Bank for the first time and in detail; and the Bank's contribution to public policy is explained while the effects of its Constitutional position are assessed.

THE BANK OF ENGLAND AND PUBLIC POLICY, 1941–1958

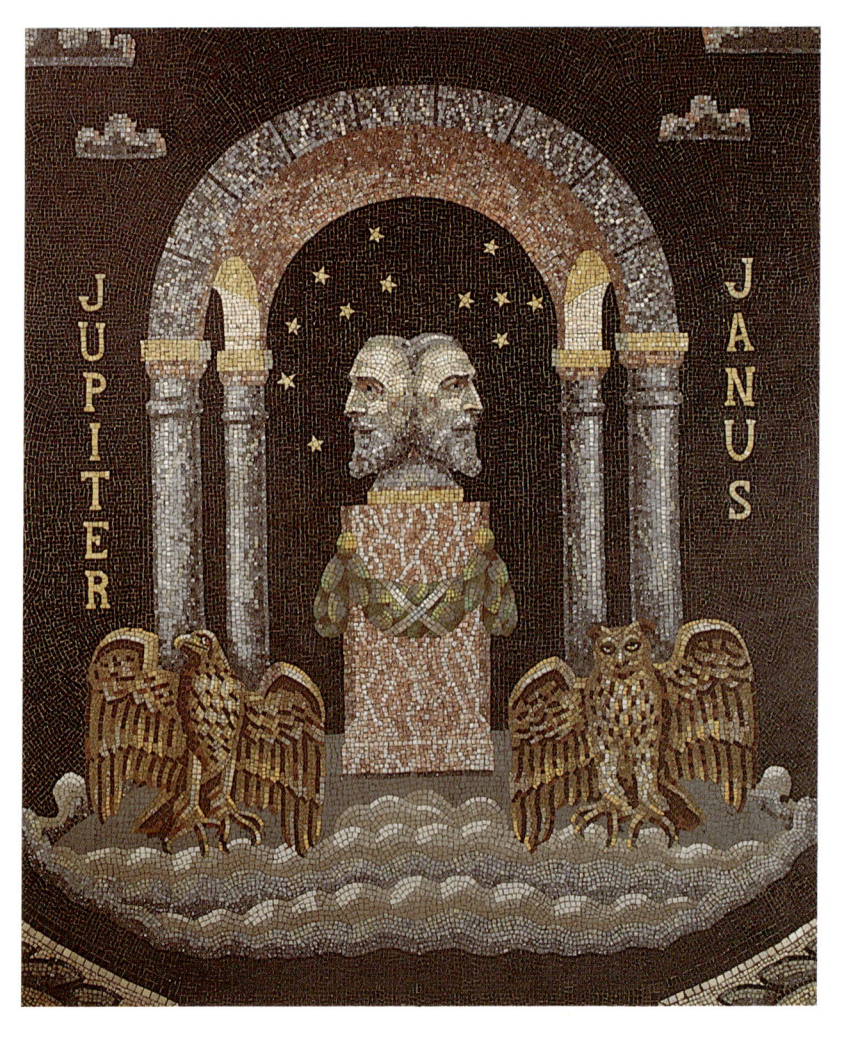

Bank of England: detail of floor mosaics by Boris Anrep

THE
BANK OF ENGLAND
AND
PUBLIC POLICY
1941–1958

JOHN FFORDE

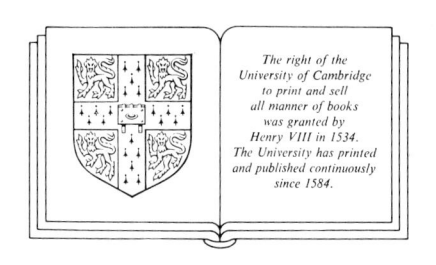

CAMBRIDGE UNIVERSITY PRESS

CAMBRIDGE
NEW YORK   PORT CHESTER
MELBOURNE   SYDNEY

Published by the Press Syndicate of the University of Cambridge
The Pitt Building, Trumpington Street, Cambridge CB2 1RP
40 West 20th Street, New York, NY 10011, USA
10 Stamford Road, Oakleigh, Melbourne 3166, Australia

© Cambridge University Press 1992

First published 1992

Printed in Great Britain by The University Press, Cambridge

British Library cataloguing in publication data
Fforde, J. S. (John S)
The Bank of England and public policy, 1941–1958
1. London, (City), Central banks: Bank of England,
history
I. Title
332.11094212
Library of Congress cataloguing in publication data
Fforde, J. S. (John S.)
The Bank of England and public policy, 1941–1958
p. ca.
ISBN 0 521 39139 3
1. Bank of England – History – 20th century. 2. Monetary policy –
Great Britain – History – 20th century. 3. Banks and banking.
Central – Great Britain – History – 20th century. I. Title.
HG2994. F46 1991
332.1′1′094109045–dc20   90-33131 CIP

ISBN 0 521 39139 3 hardback

CONTENTS

	List of illustrations and acknowledgements	page xi
	Preface	xii
	List of abbreviations	xvii
1	**The nationalisation of Norman's Bank**	1
(a)	Introductory	1
(b)	The Bill prepared	4
(c)	The Bill launched	17
(d)	The Bill's passage through Parliament	20
2	**Lord Keynes and the Bank: Bretton Woods and the Anglo–American Loan**	31
(a)	The setting: opposing forces	31
(b)	The first adoption of strategic views: 1941-1942	35
(c)	From the Mutual Aid Agreement to Bretton Woods: tactical alliance and strategic disagreement	49
(d)	The setting of the trap: from Bretton Woods to VJ Day	62
(e)	The Loan negotiations	73
3	**The false dawn and the crisis of 1947**	88
(a)	Determining a strategy for the sterling balances: 1946	88
(b)	Tying up the balances of the Sterling Area and Argentina: 1946–1947	95
	The Canadian Loan	97
	Australia and New Zealand	101
	Argentina	103
	India	108
	Egypt	114
	Appraisal	123

(c)	Europe not forgotten: 1942–1946	124
(d)	Preparing for sterling convertibility in Western Europe: 1946–1947	132
(e)	The dénouement: 1947	141

4 The four difficult years: from the crisis of 1947 to the Korean War — 166
(a)	Introductory	166
(b)	European payments problems	170
	Analyses, remedies, and the taking of positions: 1947	170
	The Ansiaux Plan and IEPC: 1948–1949	179
	The European Payments Union	193
(c)	Cheap sterling and the frontiers of exchange control: 1948–1951	219
(d)	The sterling balances: 1947–1951	249
	India and Pakistan	251
	Egypt	256
	Argentina	261
	London, Washington, and radical plans	267
(e)	Devaluation	276
(f)	Changes ahead: 1950–1951	304

5 Domestic monetary policy 1945–1951 — 314
(a)	Introductory	314
(b)	The lost alternative: 1943–1945	320
(c)	Cheaper money – preliminary moves	327
(d)	Cheaper money – mounting the assault on longer-term rates: 1944–1945	330
(e)	The road to the $2\frac{1}{2}\%$ irredeemable: 1946	339
(f)	1947: the retreat to 3%	355
(g)	Money supply, bank advances, and fiscal disinflation; 1948–1949	359
(h)	Direct credit control versus the interest-rate weapon	370

6 The watershed: 1951–1952 — 398
(a)	Clearing the decks	398
	The reordering of monetary policy	398
	The reopening of the exchange market	412
	Devising a longer-term plan for convertibility	417
(b)	Emergency action: the Robot plan	426

(c)	The breathing space and the genesis of the Collective Approach to convertibility	451
	Robot and intra-European trade and payments	452
	Robot and the Sterling Area	462
	Debate in Whitehall	465
	The rejection of Robot II and the birth of the Collective Approach	468
7	**The rise and fall of the Collective Approach: 1952–1955**	475
(a)	Introductory	475
(b)	The Commonwealth Prime Ministers' Conference, the row in Europe, and the failure of the first approach to the US	477
(c)	The reorientation of policy and the liberalisation of transferable sterling: March 1953–March 1954	492
(d)	Missing the tide, 1954, and the introduction of back-door convertibility in February 1955	505
(e)	The European Monetary Agreement, 1955, and the demise of Stage 2	528
8	**1956: The Bank and the Suez affair**	543
(a)	Prologue	543
(b)	The crisis	549
	Appendix: The mysterious telephone call	564
9	**Convertibility: the last act, 1957–1958**	566
(a)	The pound, the franc, and the Deutschmark: 1957	566
(b)	International liquidity and IMF quotas	572
(c)	The approach to Operation Unicorn: January – October 1958	585
(d)	Unicorn and the French connection: October – December 1958	595
10	**Domestic monetary policy 1952–1958: disillusion and debate**	606
(a)	The context	606
(b)	Thinking as you go: 1952–1954	613
(c)	The slide back to requests	632
(d)	Supporting the credit squeeze and supporting gilt-edged	643
(e)	The Macmillan style: 1956	652
(f)	Climax and aftermath: 1957–1958	669

11	**The Bank and the Square Mile**		695
(a)	Introductory		695
(b)	Janus in operation: the establishment of the FCI and the ICFC, 1943–1945		704
(c)	Further ventures in the public interest		727
	The Steel Company of Wales:1947		727
	The Commonwealth Development Finance Company: 1952		729
	The denationalisation of iron and steel: 1951–1955		733
	British Aluminium: 1958		743
(d)	Banking supervision		749
	Old style		749
	The pursuit of new-style supervision – the Credit Trading Bill and after: 1955–1958		761
12	**Envoi**		780
	APPENDIX A	The Bank and the commodity markets *J. F. A. Pullinger*	785
	APPENDIX B	Eastern Europe *J. F. A. Pullinger*	795
	APPENDIX C	The Anglo–American Loan negotiations: the US viewpoint *Corinna Balfour*	807
	Index		823

ILLUSTRATIONS

Janus mosaic	*frontispiece*
Chancellor and Governor, 1945	*page* 16
Montagu Norman, 1942	29
Cameron Cobbold as Executive Director, 1942	40
B. G. Catterns, Deputy Governor 1936–1945	46
An Argentine comment on Eady's success: 1946	107
Harry Siepmann, Executive Director 1945–1954	163
George Bolton, Executive Director, 1948–1957	197
Roy Bridge	217
Cameron Cobbold, Governor 1949	230
Dallas Bernard, Deputy Governor 1949–1954	239
Kenneth Peppiatt, Chief Cashier 1934–1949	319
Otto Niemeyer, Executive Director 1938–1952	337
Lucius Thompson-McCausland	419
Cameron Cobbold late in his second term, 1959	525
Maurice Parsons, Executive Director 1957–1966	584
John Stevens, Executive Director 1957–1964	604
Maurice Allen, Economic Adviser	619
P. S. Beale, Chief Cashier 1949–1955	627
Leslie O'Brien, Chief Cashier 1955–1962	634
Humphrey Mynors, Deputy Governor 1954–1964	682
The Parker Tribunal: a cartoonist's comment	703
Norman the Persuader, 1942	713
Lord Catto, Governor 1944–1949	726
Edward Peacock	734
Cyril Hawker, Executive Director 1954–1962	772

PREFACE AND ACKNOWLEDGEMENTS

Eight years ago the Governors asked if I would continue the official history of the Bank that had been begun by Sir John Clapham and carried a stage further by Professor Richard Sayers. Not being a professional historian I was at first reluctant to accept. But more than twenty years' experience of central banking, combined with an amateur interest in history, eventually overcame my reluctance. I began work in the spring of 1984 and completed the final typescript of a very long book in the autumn of 1989. It is, to repeat, the work of an amateur though its blemishes on that account may to some extent be compensated by the author's particular insight into the workings of the Bank.

It soon became clear that in the time available to me I could not attempt a complete history that would include a comprehensive study of the administration of the Bank as well as of its participation in public affairs. The former has accordingly been undertaken by another author, Mrs Elizabeth Hennessey, and will be published separately. My inability to undertake both tasks was mainly due to the sheer volume of material in the Bank Archive, material that had to be sifted and studied slowly and carefully (a professional might have been much quicker) so as to piece together in detail an often elaborate story that combined the technical complexity of central monetary affairs with their historically important politics. The official history of an institution, like one supposes the official biography of a distinguished individual, has to be as complete as possible. One cannot pick out the more entertaining and technically simpler bits while leaving the rest to the imagination.

The amount of material in the Archive, to which I was given unhindered access, underwent a quantum leap forward during the Second World War onto a new level that persisted in the post-war period. This may have been due in part to a greater inclination to keep policy records, an inclination that would have increased along with the Bank's closer association with Whitehall. But it was mostly due to the fact that life just became more complicated, particularly with respect to the external monetary affairs that commanded the lion's share of the Bank's contribution to public policy in the early post-war years. Indeed the history of sterling in that period, whether written from a Bank viewpoint or more widely, represents a daunting challenge both to the skill of the narrator and to the patience of even the most alert and assiduous reader.

Neither my predecessor nor myself have attempted, as a specific piece of work, a history of the Bank during the Second World War. In most respects Sayers ended his history in 1939. My own book is mostly about the Bank and public policy in the post-war period. Depending on the particular topic, however, it usually begins during the war years. For example, the Bank's contribution to discussions leading up to Bretton Woods, to the Anglo-American Loan Agreement and to post-war external monetary problems in general, begins as early as 1941. Again, the Bank's interest in post-war domestic monetary policy and also in the post-war financing of industry begins in 1943.

If the book often begins during the war, where does it end and why? The Bank's observance of the thirty-year rule governing public access to official documents, together with intended publication in 1991, suggested at first that I should take the story up to the end of Lord Cobbold's Governorship in June 1961. I later concluded, however, that the completion of various phases of policy in 1958 was more important than the change of Governor in 1961. The final resumption of sterling's non-resident convertibility, at the end of 1958, was one such completion. The termination of the 1950s 'credit squeeze' and the introduction of Special Deposits in July 1958 was another. Furthermore, within the Bank's relationships with the financial community, 1958 saw the end of the Bank's first attempts to solve the supervisory and credit-control problems thrown up by the newly emerging secondary banks. The book therefore finishes with these and other completions. It does not, for example, deal more than tangentially with the Radcliffe Committee and its Report, which belong more properly to subsequent history.

The structure of the book sometimes presents difficulties. For most of the time, the history of the Bank's participation in public policy divides itself into distinct and separable topics that often proceed contemporaneously but which can conveniently be treated in separate chapters or sections that stand on their own and which contain no more than a readily acceptable amount of cross-reference. For example, domestic monetary policy, despite its intimate linkage with external affairs, is treated as a subject on its own except in the account of the exchange crisis early in

1952. But on the external side, when policy divides itself into no less than four separate subjects that run concurrently during the four long years following the convertibility crisis of 1947, it would have been easier for the reader if these subjects could have been woven together into one continuous fabric. However, I found the task beyond me and retreated into four long and separate sections bolted together after a fashion by a common introduction and a common conclusion.

A history of the Bank's participation in public policy relating to the central monetary affairs of the UK must to some considerable extent be a history of that policy and those affairs. On the other hand it must also possess the nature of a biography, though in this case the biography of an institution rather than an individual. The right balance between these two ingredients is difficult to find. In searching for it one is partly guided by the material actually available in the Bank. The rest is a series of subjective judgements best described as following one's nose.

My principal sources have been the documents in the Bank's Archive. These often include copies of the relevant Whitehall papers; but I have occasionally resorted to the Public Record Office when this seemed essential to fill an obvious gap in Bank material or to obtain a Treasury slant on some particular episode concerning the Bank. In addition, a variety of biographies, memoirs and historical studies have been consulted and have been acknowledged in the text. Except in the case of the Anglo-American Loan negotiations, little recourse has been made to material outside the UK. Reliance on Bank files includes reliance on personal 'notes for record' by the Governor and others relating to particular meetings and conversations, mostly in Whitehall, which give a Bank's-eye view. Such notes necessarily contain a subjective element whose significance I do not assess but which I do not believe seriously distorts the story. More generally, Bank records on the development of policy tend to be more informal or intimate than do Treasury records. In Whitehall, it has been said, nothing prevails unless it is written down. Accordingly, what is written there must conform to that requirement. In the Bank, however, the spoken word retains, or used to retain, a higher status and the written word remained less formal.

I was fortunate in being able to supplement the documentary evidence by talking or corresponding with some of the survivors of the early post-war period. In particular, they provided me with valuable 'background' that helped to recapture the flavour of those times rather than challenge the accuracy of the written material. I must especially acknowlege the help given me by the late Lord Cobbold while thanking others from the Bank, all of whose contributions were of great value both individually and cumulatively. Those others were, in alphabetical order, Maurice Allen, Bob Barkshire, Hilton Clarke, John Kirbyshire, Sir Humphrey Mynors, Lord O'Brien, George Preston, Rupert Raw, Jasper Rootham, James Selwyn, Ernest Skinner, Geoffrey Tansley, Michael Thornton and Alan Whittcome. From the world outside Threadneedle Street I must thank Paul Bareau, Lord Caccia, Sir Alec Cairncross, Lord Croham, Sir Peter Daniell, Sir Frank Figgures, Charles Goodhart, Sir Donald MacDougall and Lord Sherfield.

With great patience, John Flemming found time to read the entire typescript and I am most grateful to him for his very helpful comments.

Throughout the preparation of the book, the Bank has looked after its official historian with customary thoughtfulness and generosity. In addition to accommodation and secretarial facilities, I have been provided with research assistance, given first by Corinna Balfour and latterly by John Pullinger. They appear in the text as authors of appendices. I am most grateful to both of them for all the help they have given me. The Bank's Archivist, Henry Gillett, and his staff have been unfailingly helpful in the pursuit of occasionally elusive material. Derrick Byatt helped with the proofs, as did Elizabeth Hennessy who also undertook to compile the index: my thanks to both of them.

Not for the first time, my wife has had to put up with the prolonged male pregnancy of my writing a book. Not for the first time, I must thank her for tolerating it and for providing her unique brand of encouragement.

JOHN FFORDE
November 1990

ABBREVIATIONS

AHC	Accepting Houses Committee
AIT	Association of Investment Trusts
ALCOA	Aluminium Corporation of America
AMC	Agricultural Mortgage Corporation
APU	Atlantic Payments Union
BA	British Aluminium Co
BBA	British Bankers Association
BIA	British Insurance Association
BID	British Industrial Development Corporation
BIS	Bank for International Settlements
CDFC	Commonwealth Development Finance Company
CEO	Chief Executive Officer
CIC	Capital Issues Committee
CLCB	Committee of London Clearing Bankers
CRND	Commissioners for the Reduction of the National Debt
ECA	Economic Co-operation Administration
ECSC	European Coal and Steel Community
EDC	European Defence Community
EEA	Exchange Equalisation Account
EEC	European Economic Community
EFTA	European Free Trade Association
EMA	European Monetary Agreement
EMF	European Monetary Fund
EPU	European Payments Union
ERP	European Recovery Programme

FCI	Finance Corporation for Industry
FHA	Finance Houses Association
FOA	Foreign Operations Administration
FRB	Board of Governors of the Federal Reserve System
FRBNY	Federal Reserve Bank of New York
GATT	General Agreement on Tariffs and Trade
GDP	Gross Domestic Product
HPTA	Hire Purchase Trade Association
IBA	Industrial Bankers Association
IBRD	International Bank for Reconstruction and Development
ICFC	Industrial and Commercial Finance Corporation
IDA	International Development Association
IEPC	Intra-European Payments and Compensations
IFC	International Finance Corporation
IMF	International Monetary Fund
ISHRA	Iron & Steel Holding & Realisation Agency
ITO	International Trade Organisation
LDMA	London Discount Market Association
LME	London Metal Exchange
MRP	Mouvement Républicain Populaire
MSA	Mutual Security Adminstration
NAC	National Advisory Council on International Monetary and Financial Problems
NATO	North Atlantic Treaty Organisation
NCB	National Coal Board
NDO	National Debt Office
OEEC	Organisation for European Economic Co-operation
PWLB	Public Works Loan Board
RTB	Richard Thomas & Baldwin Ltd

SCOW	Steel Company of Wales
SF	Stabilisation Fund
TDR	Treasury Deposit Receipt
TI	Tube Investments Ltd
UNRAA	United Nations Relief and Rehabilitation Administration

CHAPTER 1

THE NATIONALISATION OF NORMAN'S BANK

(a) INTRODUCTORY

FOR THE most part, this history begins during the Second World War while Montagu Norman was still Governor of the Bank. Norman is in charge when the Bank decides its attitude towards plans for a post-war international monetary order. It is Norman who sets the Bank thinking about domestic monetary policy in the post-war period. It is Norman who gets work done on the post-war finance of industry and sets about persuading the City to join the Bank in creating two new special financial institutions. It is Norman who ultimately commands the response of the Bank to initiatives on all these matters in Whitehall. Finally, it was under Norman that the Bank itself began to think about alterations to its constitution, alterations that were later to be made in great haste when the Bank was nationalised early in 1946.

These activities, at the end of his long and unique Governorship, were necessarily undertaken with the Bank that he had himself largely created. Onto a permanent staff mostly devoted to the efficient performance of regular tasks, Norman had superimposed an entourage or Cabinet of his own, either by special recruitment or by selection from the career staff. It was within this circle that questions of policy were discussed so that decisions could be adopted and put into effect. It was men from this group who represented the Bank at policy meetings in Whitehall and men from this group who helped the Governor maintain higher-level relationships with the City, with industry, or with central banks abroad. Besides the Deputy Governor, they were mostly Executive Directors, Heads of Departments, or Advisers. They were all people of high quality, some chosen for a combination of intellectual distinction and special experience, others for their knowledge and experience of financial markets, others still for a combination of administrative ability and some particular aptitude that the Governor wanted to harness. Their numbers were not large, perhaps no more than fifteen or twenty. They were more numerous on the overseas and foreign side. This was partly due to the advent of exchange control but mainly to the international status of sterling and to the relationships with overseas central banks that Norman had created in the inter-war period. The numbers concerned with domestic monetary policy were tiny, not more than five at the most. Economic advice was available as required, from two members of the profession. Industrial advice was also obtained. Finally there was a Press Officer.

Looking back in 1943, the Governorship and the above Cabinet had all developed as circumstances seemed to require and as Norman went along. Acts of Parliament had not had too much to do with it. The Gold Standard's revival and its later demise, the subsequent statutory institution of the Exchange Equalisation Account (EEA), and the Currency and Bank Notes Act, all in their way provided background. But the Bank itself, a chartered company, had become a central bank through evolved practice and remained with private proprietors and a Governor and Court self-chosen. Its relations with Whitehall and the City were clear enough in broad outline, but often informal, uncodified, and uncertain at the edges. Maintenance of the authority of the Bank, together with control over the direction in which it moved, therefore depended unusually on the supremacy of the Governor. The seeming autocracy in the Bank, at this time and later, was not so much due to despotic personalities at the top as to the need to prevent authority being dissipated and weakened by officials paddling their own canoes in poorly charted waters.

Norman himself has mainly come down to us as a strange but brilliant personality, one who combined exceptional charm with intuitive ability, but one who was prone to occasional depressive illness. He is a subject for the investigative biographer, unlike few if any of his associates and immediate successors. The Bank he created, with its uncertain edges, its informalities, its inner Cabinet, its somewhat mysterious authority, its studied public relations of supposed reticence, and its powerful Governor, was well suited both to his personality and to the surrounding circumstances. When serious illness forced his retirement early in 1944, at the age of seventy-two, his creation simply sailed on without him, trained to work as he had taught it. It is true that he was succeeded by a relative outsider, Lord Catto,[1] a shrewd and successful Scot, a man of

---

[1] *Catto, Thomas Sivewright, 1st Baron 1936, Bt, PC, CBE (1879–1959).* Educated Peterhead Academy, Rutherford College, Newcastle. Vice-President, MacAndrews and Forbes, New York 1908–14, Admiralty Representative on Russian Mission, New York 1915–17, British and Allied Food Missions, US and Canada 1917–19. Chairman and Managing

commerce and of humble origin. Not a full member of the City establishment, he was both an admirer of and admired by the Treasury. Already sixty-five years old, however, he sought no changes in Norman's Bank. Though occasionally liable to go down paths of his own, much of his regular work was devoted to encouraging and supporting Norman's team on issues of domestic and external policy. Norman's Deputy, B. G. Catterns,[2] carried on until the summer of 1945 when he was succeeded by Cameron Cobbold, who himself became Governor in 1949 and remained so until he retired in 1961. Though a very different personality to Norman, Cobbold maintained the latter's Bank substantially unchanged until the later 1950s and throughout the remainder of the period covered by this book. Only right at the end, with the Radcliffe Committee sitting, with some of the surrounding countryside altering, and with a new generation coming to the fore, did change begin.

Though they possessed the defects as well as the virtues of a small informal group surrounding the combined Chairman and Chief Executive, as the Governor in effect was, Norman's immediate successors withstood the pressures of the early post-war decades with great resilience. The tasks they had to pursue were usually difficult and seldom likely to meet with much positive success. They frequently had to serve masters in Whitehall with whom they did not have great sympathy, though often personal admiration. From time to time they harboured an alternative approach to monetary problems of the day, but often failing to convince Whitehall in private they had to keep it frustratingly to themselves. From time to time, too, they adopted radical ideas in preference to a customary pragmatism; only to see such ideas rejected. But though remarkably resilient, they could sometimes be too exclusive and in consequence too slow to adapt, thereby reducing their practical effectiveness. If Norman himself, as a creator, would not have fallen into that error, it would be asking too much of the lieutenants who came after him that they too should avoid it. Instead, Cobbold and his supporting cast stood up to pressures of crisis, anxiety, and continuing uncertainty at the edges of the Bank's responsibilities, which would in all probability have overwhelmed the sensibilities of their remarkable mentor.

Director, Andrew Yule, Calcutta 1919–28, Director, Yule Catto 1919–40, Partner, Morgan Grenfell 1928–40. Director, Bank of England 1940, Director-General of Equipment and Stores, Ministry of Supply 1940, Financial Adviser to the Chancellor 1940–4, Governor, Bank of England 1944–9.

[2] *Catterns, Basil Gage (1886–1969)*. Educated Trent College. Entered Bank 1908, HM Forces 1916–19, an Assistant Chief Cashier 1923, Deputy Principal, Discount Office 1923–5, Deputy Chief Cashier 1925–9, Chief Cashier 1929–34, Executive Director 1934–6, Deputy Governor 1936–45, Director 1945–8.

The whole story of those pressures, crises, anxieties and uncertainties is told in considerable detail in the many chapters that follow. The Second World War brought about an exponential growth in the Bank's documentation, growth that then ceased at a high level and persisted thereafter at that level. This leaves the historian with an immense mass of material relating to a very action-packed period. Though occurring chronologically later than the start of most other topics considered in this book, the story of the Bank's nationalisation is most conveniently told first. The Bank of England Act 1946 brought Norman's creation under public ownership while doing little to change it. So the introduction and passage of this Act constitute a convenient if lengthy supplement to these preliminary remarks.

(b) THE BILL PREPARED

The Bank of England Act 1946 has attracted little attention from historians. Its passage did not arouse great public interest or controversy. Until very recently there has seldom been any demand that it should be substantially revised. A very brief piece of legislation, clear and concise in most respects, it has not of itself been considered especially interesting. The Parliamentary Debates about it were often rather contrived. On one side were those in favour of placing practice beyond doubt by giving it statutory form. On the other were those who felt that the best thing to do with a satisfactory state of affairs was to leave it alone. Virtually nobody questioned whether the central monetary constitution of the United Kingdom, as it had mainly evolved over the preceding quarter-century, was in practice the best obtainable, fully fit for pouring into a statutory mould at the start of a brave new post-war world. Almost everyone just assumed it was so. Other countries had been obliged to enact legislation to set up central banks *ab initio*, often after prolonged public enquiry. In many cases the resulting institutions were accorded stated duties and responsibilities. In the United Kingdom no such need was felt. For the central bank was there already, the evolutionary product of growth over time.

For reasons lying deep in British habits of self-satisfaction, these circumstances of prolonged birth were widely presumed to endow the result with a special virtue, enhanced by a flavour of prestige, power, expertise and mystery. No matter that this flavour, together with much of the network of relationships between the Bank and the Government and between the Bank and the City, might reflect too much the dominance of a particular and unusual personality; such that at the end of the Old Lady's long journey into central banking it was difficult to distinguish between the desirable constitution of a central bank and the personal needs of its most famous and but recently retired Governor. No matter too that the country was about to adopt a new economic strategy, one that implied a persistent and prolonged inflationary undertow whose adequate constraint might in turn imply the need for a strong and specific monetary constitution. In 1945, exhausted but victorious in war, with a new and radical Government just elected with a massive parliamentary majority, British Ministers, officials, and legislators, were in no mood to stop and think, nor were they in a mood to question the wisdom of an apparently simple Act by which the Treasury merely acquired the stock from the Bank's proprietors, made arrangements for the Crown to appoint the Governors and Directors, and gave legal support firstly to the ultimate authority of the Treasury over the Bank in matters of policy and secondly to the authority of the Bank over the banks. The discretionary management of money, so as to avoid deflation and depression rather than to stop inflation, was seen as a political responsibility attaching to the Government of the day; for better or worse, but most assumed it was for the better.

The Labour Government took office at the end of July. The Manifesto on which it had fought the General Election contained the sentence: 'The Bank of England with its financial powers must be brought under public ownership, and the operations of other banks harmonised with industrial needs.' It did not take long for the incoming Chancellor of the Exchequer, Hugh Dalton, to decide that this pledge could easily be honoured through the enactment of a short Bill in the first session of the new Parliament. Its contents could be discussed, decided, and drafted in a mere few weeks. An outline plan was put to him under a covering note by the Permanent Secretary, Edward Bridges,[3] as early as 3 August. Its main authors were Herbert Brittain,[4] then a Third Secretary in the Finance Division of the Treasury, and Wilfrid Eady,[5] Second Secretary in charge of that Division

---

[3] *Bridges, Edward, 1st Baron 1957, KG, PC, GCB, GCVO, MC, FRS (1892–1969).* Educated Eton and Magdalen College, Oxford. Army 1914–18. Fellow of All Souls, Oxford 1920–7, 1954–68. HM Treasury 1919–38, Secretary to the Cabinet 1938–46, Permanent Secretary, HM Treasury and Head of Home Civil Service 1945–56. Chairman, Royal Fine Art Commission 1957–8, British Council 1959–67. Chancellor, Reading University 1959–69.

[4] *Brittain, Herbert, KCB, KBE (1894–1961).* Educated Rochdale Secondary School and Manchester University. Army 1915–19. HM Treasury 1919–57, Third Secretary 1942–53, Second Secretary 1953–7. Chairman, Iron and Steel Holding and Realisation Agency 1958–61.

[5] *Eady, Crawfurd Wilfrid Griffin, GCMG, KCB, KBE (1890–1962).* Educated Clifton and Jesus College, Cambridge. India Office 1913, Home Office 1914, Ministry of Labour 1917–38, Secretary, Unemployment Assistance Board 1934–8, Deputy Under-Secretary, Home

and one of the officials closest to the Bank. Brittain began with a description of the current state of affairs, including the comment that although changes in Bank Rate were legally the prerogative of the Bank, in practice no change now occurred without the closest consultation between the Bank and the Treasury. He then went on to note that the Bank had evolved over 250 years and that no one could say how it would evolve in future. From this he concluded:

> It is therefore very desirable to retain the present flexible set-up of the Bank as far as possible, and, in effect, to concentrate on giving statutory form to the present *de facto* position as regards (i) relations between Bank and Treasury and (ii) the traditional policy of the Bank to conduct its affairs in the public interest and not in that of the stockholders.

Dalton commented an emphatic 'yes', though he objected to one feature of Brittain's outline statute, namely the retention of private stockholders whose sole function was to provide legal cover for the appointment of five Directors, out of a proposed total of twelve, to remain with the Bank itself. In this Dalton was supported by Eady, who felt there was no sense in keeping shareholders with no real rights or functions. In a classic statement Eady went on to explain and justify the independence that would remain with the Bank under the proposed plan. Independence was:

> not to be exercised on major issues of policy; not to be exercised on appointment of Governor or Deputy, or in selection of Court. But on day-to-day business of internal management, and day-to-day relations with other financial institutions, there is everything to be said for viewing the Bank as a public corporation, subject to control on policy but not to interference in the running of the machine. The more the permitted independence on inessentials the easier will it be for the Bank to maintain its intimate relations with other parts of the financial system and with City interests. The reason for the high repute of the Bank, not only in this country but also, and the point is of very great importance, particularly under present conditions of our external finances, in foreign countries, is the degree of independence that the Bank has possessed. The general morale of the Bank and the power of speaking with complete freedom to the Chancellor and the Treasury are assets of the highest value. Under wise leadership these can be maintained fully within the general change of relations between HM Treasury and the Bank.

The Permanent Secretary judged the plan was workable, though he counselled close consultation with the Bank itself. But before any such consultation had occurred, and subsequent to a meeting between Ministers

Office 1938–40, Deputy Chairman, Board of Customs and Excise 1940–1, Chairman 1941–2, Joint Second Secretary, HM Treasury 1942–52.

and officials, a draft additional provision was submitted by Brittain. This was the origin of the controversial Clause 4(3) of the Act. It proposed that the Bank should have the power, where it thought it necessary in the public interest and with the approval of the Treasury, to make regulations governing the proportion of assets of different description to be held by the banks. With this draft provision included, the Chancellor wrote to the Governor on 14 August enclosing the outline proposals and suggesting a meeting to discuss them.

The outline took the form of draft heads of legislation and its main proposals were as follows. The Governors would be appointed by the Prime Minister and the Chancellor of the Exchequer jointly, that is to say the Treasury in its formal sense. It was suggested that there should be two Deputy Governors, one of whom would normally be chosen from the permanent staff. Instead of the existing twenty-four Directors there would be twelve, in addition to the Governors. All would be appointed either by the Treasury after consultation with the Court or by the Court with Treasury approval. The Directors would be part-time and there would therefore be no Executive Directors. Power would be taken for the Treasury to give directions to the Bank, but the intention was that this power would be used only in relation to major issues of policy. Subject to such directions, the management of the Bank's business was to remain the responsibility of the Court. Compensation to the stockholders was to be by way of perpetual non-voting annuity, charged on the profits of the Bank, in exchange for surrendered Bank Stock. The Bank would then issue special voting stock to the Treasury. Finally, a possible additional clause would give the Bank the powers, already mentioned, over the banks.

The new Parliament was opened by the King on 15 August. His Speech included the words: 'A measure will be laid before you to bring the Bank of England under public ownership.' But there was no mention of harmonising, by Statute, the operations of the other banks with industrial needs. In the Debate that followed, Churchill opened for the Opposition and declared that the national ownership of the Bank of England did not, in his opinion, raise any matter of principle. Foreign countries need not be alarmed at the prospect, for 'British credit will be resolutely upheld'. Later in the Debate Oliver Lyttelton, who thought the proposal unnecessary and unwise, continued for the Opposition and sought reassurance that the Bill would go no further than a simple transfer of ownership, with associated provision for Treasury appointment of the Court. Replying, the Chancellor told the House that to a large extent the proposal would do no more than 'bring the law into accord with the facts of the situation as they have developed'. After paying a generous tribute to Catto, and to the frank and friendly conversations that had taken place between them since the new Government had taken office, Dalton went on: 'I am happy to say that he has expressed his willingness to continue as Governor for a suitable period to manage the new regime which we propose to establish.'[6]

Neither the Chancellor's letter of 14 August nor most of its contents can have been unexpected by the recipient and his immediate colleagues. Apart from the discussions mentioned by Dalton in the Debate on the Address, and although there is almost no recorded evidence of other prior discussions on the subject between the Bank and the Treasury, it would be wrong to suppose that these had not happened. Lack of record may be attributed to mutual agreement to maintain total informality on so sensitive a subject. Lord Cobbold, speaking to the author in 1984, stated categorically that such discussions did happen and that they were thorough. There is also circumstantial evidence. An exchange of Treasury Minutes between Brittain and Hopkins[7], the then Permanent Secretary, as early as 1943 discusses proposals for altering the constitution of the Bank so as to satisfy public opinion without outright nationalisation or loss of operational independence. Hopkins was close to Norman, still Governor at that time. In February 1944, shortly after the latter had fallen ill but presumably with his earlier agreement, a note was submitted to the Bank's Committee of Treasury setting out changes that had been suggested from time to time 'from within or without'. All these suggestions were to be aired again in the following year, either during the preparation of the Bank Bill or during its passage through Parliament. They included firstly, a reduction in the size of the Court, provision for two Deputy Governors, Government appointment of some or all of the Court, fixed terms for members of the Court, and a provision for freezing the dividend at 12%. Secondly, and after pointing out that all the above would require legislation, the note for Committee of Treasury then listed suggestions for further changes that would not so require. These included a statement that the Chancellor was invariably consulted (or his approval obtained) before any change in Bank Rate, publication of a Profit and Loss Account, and

---

[6] Relations between Dalton and Catto were always cordial though perhaps not particularly close. Catto's own (privately published) memoirs stress the complete political impartiality with which he endeavoured to carry out his job; and this must have helped him with Dalton. It has also been said that Dalton, the Etonian academic and politician, was a little frightened of Catto, the experienced man of commerce with a humble background. But from references in his own diary Dalton seems to have been completely charmed by him, and always genuinely surprised that he was not rougher.

[7] *Hopkins, Richard Valentine Nind, PC, GCB (1880–1955).* Educated King Edward's School, Birmingham and Emmanuel College, Cambridge. Chairman, Board of Inland Revenue 1922–7, Controller of Finance and Supply Services, HM Treasury 1927–32, Second Secretary 1932–42, Permanent Secretary 1942–5.

provision of an Annual Report. Humphrey Mynors, then Secretary of the Bank, submitted a copy of this note to the new Governor early in June 1944. In May 1945, now an Adviser to the Governor, he prepared notes on two possible solutions to the problem of the Constitution of the Bank, the first of which was minimalist and the second of which was a straight outline of the one eventually enacted (excluding the provision for powers over banks). It is therefore likely that the Chancellor's main proposals of 14 August had already been accepted informally, besides being part of the understandings reached between the Chancellor and the Governor about the latter continuing in office.

But if the main features of the plan were acceptable to the Bank, there were various points of important detail that remained to be resolved. There was also the one feature that may have come as a surprise, namely the provision for statutory power of direction over commercial banks, a matter of some delicacy in terms of relationships both with Whitehall and with the City, and also a matter of public concern. In the ten days following receipt of the Chancellor's letter, and ahead of meetings between the Governors and senior Treasury officials on 28 and 31 August, Catto obtained written advice from the Deputy Governor,[8] from two of the Executive Directors, Niemeyer[9] and Holland-Martin,[10] and from Mynors. He had earlier replied to Dalton suggesting discussions at official level 'in regard to such points as do not affect questions of principle', these latter being reserved for subsequent discussion between the two of them.

Having already announced to maximum effect in the House of Commons that the Governor had agreed to stay on, the Chancellor was not now in too strong a position to resist the Bank on matters of important detail; and he did not like it. 'The Deputy', he noted on a Minute from the Permanent Secretary, 'has been trying to pull the Governor back by the coat-tails'.[11] But by 5 September he had agreed to a Court of sixteen Directors, including

---

[8] Catterns had given notice of impending retirement some months earlier and Cobbold had now succeeded him.
[9] *Niemeyer, Otto Ernst, GBE, KCB (1883–1971).* Educated St Paul's and Balliol College, Oxford. HM Treasury 1906–27, Controller of Finance 1922–7. Entered Bank 1927, Adviser to the Governors 1927–38, Executive Director 1938–49, Director 1949–52, Member of Financial Committee of League of Nations 1922–37, Chairman 1927, Financial Missions to Australia and New Zealand 1930, Brazil 1931, Argentina 1933, India 1935, China 1941, Fellow LSE, Chairman of Governors 1941–57, Governor 1958–65, Director, BIS 1931–65, Chairman of the Board 1937–40, Vice-Chairman 1941–64, Member, Council of Foreign Bondholders 1935–1965, Vice-President 1950–5, President 1956–65.
[10] *Holland-Martin, Edward (1900–81).* Educated Eton and Christ Church, Oxford. Executive Director, Bank of England 1933–48. Director, Bank of London and South America 1948–70, Deputy Chairman 1951–70.
[11] According to Cobbold, writing in 1977, the relationship between himself and Dalton (a fellow Etonian) soon became one of strong mutual dislike.

four Executives, instead of the Court of twelve with no Executives suggested by the Treasury. But the Bank had to accept Crown appointment of all the Court rather than of the Governors alone and had to accept that the Governors' term should be five years when it would have preferred seven. The powers of direction over the Bank given to the Treasury continued to be drafted in the most general terms, but they now included specific provision for prior consultation with the Governor, for which the Bank had argued. As to the financial provisions, it was now agreed that compensation should be by simple exchange of Bank Stock for Government Stock, rather than by perpetual annuity, and that the Bank should pay annually to the Treasury an amount sufficient to service the new Stock or such other sum as they might between them agree.

This left two questions remaining for decision. The first and lesser question was whether the Governor should in future have two Deputies instead of one. Whitehall preferred that there should be two, only one of whom would be a person promoted from the Bank staff. There had, officials averred, been criticism that the Bank was in the hands of its permanent officials. To meet this, the Treasury had originally suggested that there should be no Executive Directors on the new Court and it is possible that the same argument lay behind the proposal for two Deputy Governors. To the Bank this made no sense. As the Governor explained in the course of a letter to the Chancellor on 5 September, 'the proposal...raises some acute difficulties. The Governor and Deputy Governor are the chief executive officers of the Bank as well as the Chairman and Deputy Chairman of the Court of Directors. In the absence of the Governor all his powers devolve on the Deputy Governor. This is a convenient and efficient arrangement of internal management and in the relations of the Bank with the Treasury and the financial community. If there were two Deputy Governors the question would arise as to which one acted in the absence of the Governor: plainly only one could so act.' The Chancellor accepted this argument and the proposal for two Deputies was dropped. Another unstated reason for opposing it was the suspicion in Threadneedle Street that one of the two Deputies would turn out to be a Treasury official on temporary secondment from the Civil Service.[12] This would have been unwelcome to a Bank anxious to be seen preserving operational distinction between itself and the Treasury.

Finally there was the question of statutory powers over the banking system. Apart from Cobbold, who felt that some such general powers

---

[12] The Second Schedule to the Act disqualifies Civil Servants from membership of the Court, but only so long as they are in receipt of remuneration payable out of monies provided by Parliament.

would be welcome, the Bank disliked this idea from the start. In particular the Governor disliked it.

The Bank already possessed, or mostly thought it possessed, an authority over the banking system that was quite sufficient for all reasonable purposes. More than that, its prestige and standing in the financial community quite largely depended on the exercise of informal authority, often in private, by established custom. On this view, resort to statutory power would look like a clearly altered and actually diminished status, inconsistent with the underlying spirit of the Bill. Yet if the Bank were to press its objection too far, against a Government intent on ensuring that the banking system was brought within the legal framework of a planned economy, the only result might be that the Treasury itself took the powers the Bank did not want. Thus arguments were deployed to the effect that the powers were not needed, that they went beyond the purpose of the Bill, and that they might frighten depositors in the clearing banks. In response, the Treasury stood its ground on the principle while doing what it could to meet the Bank's arguments by devising the least objectionable form of words. Specific reference to regulation of the proportion in which various assets were held by the banks soon disappeared in favour of much more general wording. Draft penalties for infringement made a brief appearance and then vanished. The initiative for the exercise of the powers was placed firmly on the Bank, while the Treasury was left with the function of authorising the Bank to convert recommendations into regulations. But in a letter of 11 September Catto made a last effort to get rid of the offending clause.

To this end he even suggested that the powers be given to the Treasury, but in another Statute altogether, extending into peace the finance regulations of war. The Statute contemplated was the one that became the Control of Borrowing and Guarantees Act 1946. Inclusion of the banks within the scope of that legislation would have left intact and non-statutory the Bank's authority over the banks for all purposes other than those of credit control – broadly speaking those of a supervisory nature. This could have been worth having. In any event the Governor wrote as follows:

> You will recollect that from the first I did not like this as going beyond the purposes of the Bill, e.g., the acquisition of the Bank and the power of direction over it. These are important powers. It is true that the additional powers of 4(3) and (4) are indirect and through the Bank of England; and if you feel that Government policy requires these additional powers, then the wording proposed in paragraphs 4(3) and (4) is as good as can be devised. But I would be lacking in my duty to you if I did not tell you quite frankly

that I have grave doubts as to the wisdom of putting these additional powers into the Bank Bill. Surely they would be more appropriate in the Bill to extend into peace and perhaps make permanent the war financial regulations.

The Governor's doubts did not prevail and the Chancellor took an outline of the Bill to Cabinet on 13 September. It was approved subject to yet further amendment of Clause 4(3). This amendment was subtle and made a significant further concession to the Bank, one that the Governor had not in fact requested.[13] The earlier version had said: 'The Bank may either in furtherance of such directions [from the Treasury] or otherwise request information from and make recommendations to banks in regard to banking operations, and the Treasury may, if they think it expedient in the public interest, make such regulations.' The amended version dropped the reference to Treasury directions and reverted to the general form contained in the original outline of 14 August as follows: 'The Bank of England may, if they think it necessary in the public interest, request information from and make recommendations to banks and may, if so authorised by the Treasury, issue directions to any banker.'

Although enlarged during the passage of the Bill through Parliament, the Clause was now effectively in final form. It was to cause some confusion in the House of Lords, confusion that was only cleared up by the intervention of the Lord Chancellor. Some years later, in 1957, its import was to come as an unpleasant surprise to a Conservative Chancellor of the Exchequer. In a way, it was constitutionally confusing. The Treasury, deemed the ultimate authority in matters of monetary policy, could neither issue directives to commercial banks nor direct the Bank to do so. For in law nobody could be directed to judge the public interest in a particular way, nor could the Court of the Bank suddenly be dismissed if the Government disagreed with its judgement in the matter. On the other hand the Bank, having come to its judgement, could not issue directions without the approval of the Treasury. Responsibility was in fact to be shared between the two. The direct practical importance of these legal niceties can be overstressed. For instance, the authors of Clause 4(3) hoped it would not have to be invoked; and it never has been. But the Clause took the general shape it did because the Bank was an institution well aware of its tradition and concerned to preserve its customary authority. The wording of the Clause therefore gained considerable symbolic value and was seldom forgotten in the Bank during the early post-war decades.

[13] Sir Norman Chester in *The Nationalisation of British Industry 1945–51* (HMSO, 1975) attributes this to a desire in the Cabinet to lean on the Bank's customary authority in order to justify the absence of provisions for enforcement.

But if, in this respect, the Bank was left to judge the public interest, to whom or to what was it responsible in exercising that judgement? To the Treasury? To Parliament? Or to the public at large? And if in other respects the Bank was clearly responsible to the Treasury, how could it in this one respect, but in broadly the same field, be responsible to the general public? These questions are not raised to be answered, but rather to indicate how an existing ambiguity in the status of the Bank came to be reflected in an Act whose purpose was to give statutory form to the status quo. The Treasury could in practice already exercise authority over the Bank and had done so for some years. But it was not yet in a position to exercise much practical authority over commercial banks except in the clearly defined area of exchange control – and even then with the Bank as its agent. To be true to its purpose, therefore, the Act was obliged to underwrite the independent authority of the Bank in this latter field. By doing so it opened up the wider question of responsibility and accountability to which reference has been made. The Bank had already become adept at manoeuvre within this framework and was to remain so over the decades following its conversion to statutory form. But this did not necessarily ensure that all would be for the best in a monetary constitution whose central Act remained eccentrically devoid of any reference to the wider purposes and responsibilities of central banking.

Why was there no such reference? Why was the Bill drafted with scarcely any regard for central banking legislation in other countries? Both the Treasury and the Bank provided themselves with up-to-date information about such statutes in a number of countries, mainly the self-governing Dominions of the British Commonwealth. Moreover, during the inter-war period the Bank had been a very active adviser to authorities overseas who wished to set up their own central banks. A comprehensive brief on the statutes in Australia, Canada, New Zealand, South Africa, and the US was submitted to the Governor on 17 August by Mynors. In a further brief he pointed out that in the Australian case the central bank was statutorily responsible for pursuing a monetary and banking policy to the greatest advantage of the people of Australia, a responsibility that could however be legally assumed by the Federal Government in the event of an unresolved difference of opinion between the two. Mynors continued: 'The opportunity may be taken to declare by legislation the objects of the Bank. This may be thought undesirable or superfluous, but it would be well to be prepared with ideas.' His own draft heads of legislation then followed and included the sentence: 'The objects of the Bank will be within the limits of its power and in accordance with the policy of HMG from time to time to control the currency credit and banking system of the UK and to maintain and protect the external value of the pound sterling.' This wording perhaps posed more questions than it answered, but it was an attempt and the only known one. There is no evidence that it aroused the interest of anyone else.

In Whitehall, the Dominions Office had supplied the Treasury with a brief on central bank statutes in Australia, New Zealand, and India. It quoted Clause 8 of the Australian Act of 1945, which was on the point of receiving Royal Assent, and quoted it in full whereas Mynors had not. After 'the greatest advantage of the people of Australia' the Clause continued 'in such manner as will in the opinion of the Bank best contribute to the stability of the currency of Australia, the maintenance of full employment and economic prosperity and welfare'. This brief was passed to Dalton, who made no written comment on the Australian case.

There remains in the files just one other surviving reference to these wider constitutional issues. Early in September, when Keynes visited Ottawa to discuss the American Loan negotiations that he was about to conduct in Washington, he talked with the Governor of the Bank of Canada, Graham Towers,[14] who was closely interested in the nationalisation of the Bank. Towers was encouraged to put his views on paper. He did so and sent them to Keynes in Washington. On 25 September the latter sent Towers' note to Dalton and a copy of it, with separate covering letter, to Catto. In Canada, said Towers, the Federal Government and the Bank of Canada had a joint responsibility for monetary policy. There was nothing in their Act to absolve the Governor and Directors from full responsibility, and no provision for monetary policy to be determined by Government. The Canadian system of joint responsibility ensured that major differences of opinion were brought to the attention of Parliament and public. The Governors and Directors would resign rather than accept responsibility for a policy that they did not believe was in the public interest. Responsibility to the general public also gave the Bank of Canada a proper incentive to initiate and adapt. He concluded:

> The half-way arrangement under which the central bank is neither a department of government pure and simple, nor directly responsible to the public for its actions, may contain the worst elements of both worlds.[15]

[14] *Towers, Graham George Auldjo Ford (1897–1975)*. Educated St Andrew's College, Aurora, Ontario and McGill University. Army 1915–18. Royal Bank of Canada 1920–34. Governor, Bank of Canada 1934–54. Director, Canada Life Assurance 1955–73, Chairman 1961–9, Director, Canadian Investment Fund 1955–73, Chairman 1958–73, Director, Hudson's Bay Company 1955–70.

[15] As is recorded by Richard Sayers, Towers had in 1943 been seriously considered as a successor to Norman. He was held in especially high regard by the then Chancellor, Kingsley Wood. He was sounded out by Edward Peacock, a Canadian and a senior member of the Court, in the wartime journey described in Andrew Boyle's biography of

This reached London too late in the day and was anyway unlikely to command much attention. Dalton's response is not known. Bank of Canada records suggest Keynes himself did not agree with Towers. In Threadneedle Street, Catto's response was dismissive: 'There is nothing in Towers' memo that we did not know: in fact I think, considering the different circumstances, the proposed Bank of England arrangements are quite as good and in some respects better and more workable than the Bank of Canada arrangements.' The Deputy Governor agreed. But why did the Bank, an institution of such apparent power and authority, show such lack of interest in sharing general statutory responsibility for monetary policy in the way Towers suggested or in being given stated objectives like those of the Reserve Bank of Australia? Why did it confine its attention to the important but narrower question of statutory powers over banks? It may simply be that the political climate of the moment made any other course seem wholly impracticable, not even worth mentioning to the Chancellor. But there were other and deeper reasons.

During the preceding twenty-five years, including the very difficult period of the late 1920s and early 1930s, the Bank had not attempted, under private ownership as it was, to develop a position of public accountability for discretionary monetary policy. On the contrary, it had cultivated considerable public reticence while in private zealously building up its position as confidential monetary and financial adviser to the Government, its most important customer. Besides suiting Norman's personality, this part was natural enough for an institution whose experience and expertise in monetary policy, though deep, tended to be narrow and technical. It came easily too to Catto himself. He was a considerable admirer of Treasury officials, including especially Keynes, and had fitted easily into the Treasury as a financial adviser from early 1940 until his succession to the Governorship, with Government approval, in April 1944. The Bank as a whole instinctively held the view that while it should remain operationally and institutionally distinct from Government, regarding this as 'independence', it should accept Treasury control of 'policy'. 'I am an instrument of the Treasury', Norman told a gathering of Commonwealth central bankers in 1937. Moreover a penalty attaching to the private non-statutory relationship with Government, before nationalisation, was that it increased the risk of being cast in the role of scapegoat when things went wrong. So there was some disposition in 1945 not only to avoid public responsibilities that the Bank had not

Norman (*Montagu Norman*, London, Cassell, 1967) the latter for once not getting his way about Peacock's personal disguise. The Canadian Government was reluctant to let Towers go and the idea did not survive Kingsley Wood's sudden death during the autumn of 1943.

Chancellor and Governor at the Mansion House, 1945

hitherto sought but positively to welcome a Statute that placed overall responsibility on the Treasury where it had come to belong and where it could not thereafter be disowned.

A consequence of these attitudes was that the Bank did not pay much attention to the wider constitutional issues of central banking legislation. Instead, it readily accepted a form of nationalisation that allowed it in most ways merely to keep what little it had already got. Only Mynors, the former Cambridge economics Fellow, thought about the prime constitutional question and looked at the possibility of a different Statute with more clearly defined responsibilities being given to the central bank. His was a lonely distinction, but a considerable one.

(c) THE BILL LAUNCHED

The draft Bill was approved by Cabinet on 25 September and arrangements were set in hand for its publication on 10 October. Characteristically, great care was taken by the Governors to ensure that the Court of Directors, the Committee of London Clearing Bankers (CLCB), and the principal central bank customers of the Bank were reassuringly briefed.

The Governor explained the Bill in outline to the Court on 4 October. This was followed by a full discussion on the 11th. He emphasised that so far as circumstances permitted the Bank would retain its status and preserve its continuity. Regarding Clause 4(1), the Treasury's power of direction, he considered the provision for prior consultation with the Governor 'a most important concession'. Clause 4(3), the power of direction over the banks, continued a legal right that the authorities had had during the war and the practice of many years before the war. He approved the terms of compensation. The Bank was a continuing concern. It was not being liquidated. The proprietors must therefore expect compensation based on a perpetual fixed dividend and not on asset value. Among the Directors, Sir Alan Anderson voiced apprehension about the precedent that would be created by the initial Crown appointments to the new Court. The personality of the Governors and Directors was of extreme importance. The Governor assured him that no great changes were contemplated. Lord Kindersley[16] then protested that the stockholders were not to be told the value of the Bank's assets. The Governor reacted strongly, if rhetorically. Disclosure would lead to great complications and would be undesirable in the public interest and in the interests of the Bank as a running concern. Sir Edward Peacock put it more brutally. It would be most unusual to disclose asset value. If the Directors thought the terms of compensation were fair, the shareholders should be satisfied. For himself he judged the terms were indeed fair. But Lord Kindersley remained unconvinced. In the case of a forced sale, and the first of its kind, non-disclosure was a dangerous precedent. Court did not press the matter, but it was to surface vigorously at various points during the Bill's Parliamentary passage.

The principal overseas central banks were divided into two classes. The first received a personal letter from the Governor together with an explanatory note. The second received only a descriptive telegram. The first list contained the central banks of Australia, New Zealand, Canada, South Africa, India, France, Belgium, Sweden, Switzerland, and in the US the Federal Reserve Bank of New York (FRBNY). The Governor's personal letters to those on the first list emphasised the close collaboration between the Chancellor and himself in the drafting of the Bill and the prospect that

---

[16] *Kindersley, Robert Molesworth, 1st Baron 1941 (1871–1954).* Educated Repton. Partner, Lazards 1906–19, a Managing Director 1919–46, Chairman 1946–53. Director, Bank of England 1914–46, Governor, Hudson's Bay Company 1916–25, President, National Savings Committee 1920–46, senior British representative on the Dawes Committee 1924.

the Bank could continue to enjoy its traditional position. 'I have been consulted at all stages', he wrote, and 'whilst the Bill carries out in every way the Government's policy on public ownership, which is of course a fundamental change, it preserves to the fullest extent possible the continued existence of the Bank and its independence in the general conduct of its affairs.' The Treasury's powers of direction had, 'as a matter of fact in practice been the case for many years while the Bank's power to direct banks makes statutory a position which has hitherto relied on custom and tradition'. He felt that this section would prove more formal than real. Finally, the banking business would continue unchanged, a matter to which the Governor attached great importance as it meant relations between the Bank and the recipients of his letter would be 'as intimate and mutually serviceable as heretofore'.

For the rest, the clearing banks were seen by the Governor a few hours before publication of the Bill, while the Press Officer, Bernard Rickatson-Hatt,[17] was instructed to make as little comment as possible in response to enquiries from the press. If it proved necessary to say anything, he was to take the line that the Bill was the best that could be got and that it was in everyone's interest that it should go through Parliament with the minimum of fuss. Rickatson-Hatt attended a press conference given by Dalton on publication day and described the latter's performance as flippant and breezy. Catto responded by having a private word some days later with the editors of *The Times*, *Financial Times*, *The Daily Telegraph*, and *The Economist*. Finally, the Bank did not forget Norman. Curiously, neither of the Governors felt up to the task and it was left to Holland-Martin to write a brief personal note enclosing a copy of the Bill. It said: 'I think considering all things that it is about as satisfactory as we could have hoped, but…' No reply has survived.

The immediate public response to the Bill was favourable. With some reservations, those concerned were prepared to accept that it did little more than give statutory recognition to established practice, and did so in a sensible way, with fair compensation to the stockholders and with some useful safeguards against a possible abuse of public power replacing the possible abuse of private power. There was nonetheless some concern about the powers given in the Bill to direct the banks, even though the initiative in their exercise was to remain with the Bank and even though the continuity of the Bank's established nature was forcefully symbolised by the agreement of Catto to continue as Governor. On 10 October, Oscar

---

[17] *Rickatson-Hatt, John Bernard (1898–1966)*. Army 1915–25. Reuters 1925, Chief Correspondent, US 1926–31, Editor-in-Chief 1931–41. Entered Bank 1941, Adviser to the Governors 1941–58. Adviser, Bank of London and South America 1958–66.

Hobson,[18] the distinguished financial journalist, remarked that Clause 4(3) was the really contentious feature. 'At the minimum it is innocuous but at the maximum it could completely sap the responsibility of the commercial bank directors to their own shareholders and customers.' But two days later, reporting on City reactions to the Bill, his paper noted that the Clause was softened by the consideration that no departure from current practice was intended. Initiative lay with the Bank and not with the Treasury, and the key position was held by the Governor. The risk of ill-considered action was felt to be unreal, as that post should always be filled by one who enjoyed both the confidence of the Government and the banking community. The same concerns and reassurances were reflected in press comment generally, though there were sporadic references to considerations of coarser controversy. For example the right-wing *Daily Telegraph*, in a leading article on 11 October, described the Bill as irrelevant and a piece of political flag-waving. The established principle of collaboration between the Bank and the Treasury met all practical modern requirements and provided the nation with a central bank of indisputable experience working in close harmony with the central Government. But on the same day the left-wing *Daily Herald*, in a leader entitled 'Your Bank', said that henceforth there would be no real fear of the Bank pursuing a policy inimical to the interests of the community as a whole. In its broad outline the Bill was a simple and business-like measure that was fundamental to the efficient performance of Labour's programme. Earlier, in comment on the King's Speech, the *Daily Herald* had said: 'The forthcoming legislation affecting the Bank will give promise that the lives of our people shall never again be at the mercy of the restrictionist financial ideas which once ruled us so banefully.' Across the Atlantic, in the course of a leader entitled 'Socialising an Ancient Dame', the *Wall Street Journal* recalled the Webbs and their inevitability of gradualness and remarked that things were becoming more inevitable and less gradual.

Also from across the Atlantic came an enquiry from the President of the FRBNY, Allan Sproul.[19] He asked for clarification of Clause 4(3). Catto wrote back that although it was undoubtedly the most controversial bit, he felt the Clause was more formal than real. Sproul wrote again at the end

---

[18] *Hobson, Oscar Rudolf, Kt (1886–1961)*. Educated Aldenham and King's College, Cambridge. Financial Editor, *Manchester Guardian* 1920–9, Editor-in-Chief, *Financial News* 1929–34, City Editor, *News Chronicle* 1935–59.

[19] *Sproul, Allan (1896–1978)*. Educated University of California. Head, Division of Analysis and Research, FRB, San Francisco 1920–4, Assistant Federal Reserve Agent and Secretary 1924–30, Assistant Deputy Governor and Secretary, FRBNY 1930–4, Assistant to Governor and Secretary 1934–6, Deputy Governor 1936, First Vice-President 1936–41, President 1941–56.

of October confessing, 'the vague language still intrigues me'. He queried whether in reality the change was no more than formal. From Ottawa, Towers asked whether, if the Governor objected to a direction under Clause 4(1), the fact of his doing so would become public. Catto thought it would. Towers also asked, with regard to 4(3), how far informality could be pressed under the existing regime. Here Catto noted 'better not argue this in reply, just drop the point'. Among other recipients of the Governor's letter only Armitage of the Commonwealth Bank of Australia made any significant comment, drawing a pointed contrast between the Bank of England Bill and the more detailed Australian Act, which covered the rights, duties, and obligation of the Reserve Bank. He drew no riposte.

(d) THE BILL'S PASSAGE THROUGH PARLIAMENT

The Second Reading Debate was held in the Commons on 29 October. It was opened by the Chancellor, who explained the principal purposes of the Bill and went on to answer critics of Clause 4(3). Brittain's brief for him on this Clause, after remarking that the Bank stood Janus-like[20] between the Treasury and the banks, said that 4(3) 'gives formal recognition to the Bank's responsibility, under the Government, as the central monetary and financial authority of the country'. But Dalton wisely steered clear of these metaphysical rocks, stating simply that the Clause gave effect to the Government's undertaking to ensure that the operations of the other banks were harmonised with industrial needs, but that it could only be operated on the initiative of the Bank. He did not expect the powers to be used very often; they were more in the nature of a statement of principle. He welcomed a remark by Campbell, Chairman of National Provincial Bank and of the CLCB, that having read the Bill he considered that the good relations which had always existed between the Treasury, the Bank of England and the Joint Stock Banks, were likely to continue.

Dalton then went on to deny categorically that there was any intention of using Clause 4(3) so as to compel banks to reveal the private affairs of their customers to the Treasury through the Bank of England; and he was willing to propose an amendment to the Clause putting this beyond doubt. Thus it is clear that Dalton saw 4(3) as a provision needed for a specific

---

[20] A Roman God after whom the month of January is named, Janus was always portrayed with two faces, looking in opposite directions. The reason for this seems unclear. Some think it symbolised the need for a cautious look in both directions before taking action. That would suit the Bank. A less kind interpretation would be that Janus, though a God, was 'two-faced'. Today, Norman is represented in the Bank, on the author's own observation, by three pictures, a statue, a bust, and a mosaic. The last of these portrays Norman as Janus and was assembled when he was Governor. The expression on his face appears to be one of amusement.

purpose of monetary policy, namely the general or selective direct control of bank credit. He evidently did not see it as an instrument needed to support the Bank's supervisory responsibilities, as they would nowadays be called. The Bank had certainly sought to exercise such responsibilities over some parts of the banking system, informally and in secret, for many years and particularly since the Baring Crisis of 1892; and it was sometimes thought to have some rather vague responsibility for the health of the City generally. But the supervisory function, which was to come dramatically to the front of the stage thirty years later and to come to rest in the Banking Acts of 1979 and 1987, attracted no concern in 1945. The Government and the Legislature had nothing to say about it. Supervisory issues lay dormant at the time and it can be supposed that the Bank itself, having no wish to share this preserve with Whitehall, or discuss it there, was well content with the silence.

Since attack on the Bill by the Conservative Opposition had been rather blunted by their own leader during the debate on the Address some ten weeks earlier, Sir John Anderson, their opening speaker on 29 October, opposed the Bill mainly on the grounds that it was unwise to tamper with an unwritten constitution if it was already working satisfactorily. The point was developed by Isaac Pitman, recently a member of the Court. He said that the Bill was a waste of time, introduced to dispose of a bogey, and went on to mount a spirited defence of the Bank's behaviour in the inter-war period and of Norman in particular, whom he saw as a central banking St Sebastian.[21] Hugh Gaitskell cast doubt on all this. He did not accept that adequate control of the Bank, or of the Bank over banks, already existed, or could be relied on for the future without legislation. Robert Boothby, always a severe critic, thought that Norman was nearly always wrong and was moreover the embodiment of power without responsibility. He concluded with a rousing quotation from Abraham Lincoln: 'The privilege of creating and issuing money is not only the supreme prerogative of the Government, it is the Government's greatest opportunity. Money will cease to be master and become the servant of humanity. Democracy will rise superior to money power.'

The Bill was given a Second Reading without difficulty. It was then passed to a Select Committee of the House in accordance with the rules of procedure on 'hybridity', which permitted an aggrieved stockholder to petition against the terms of compensation. In fact none did. But the

---

[21] 'Previous Chancellors of the Exchequer, whom he served, have had a skilled adviser and an executive who carried out their policy regardless of whether the instructions agreed with the advice he tendered and his judgement. He has carried out those instructions, as I say, silently, taking all the arrows to himself, because he did not answer back.'

Committee was nevertheless obliged to hear evidence and decide whether the terms were fair. The Bank was a company incorporated by Royal Charter and published no accounts beyond the uninformative weekly Bank Returns. The proceedings of the Select Committee, to which the Governor would be required to give evidence, brought the possible disclosure of net worth very much to the fore. The matter was raised with some persistence during a procedural discussion on 31 October, when the Chancellor was reduced to playing for time by endeavouring to argue that some of the Bank's assets, such as the freehold property on Threadneedle Street, were not capable of exact valuation. Since the Committee was not to meet again until 20 November, there was time for the Governor to strengthen the position about disclosure that he had already adopted in Court.

First, Court itself resolved on 1 November that the terms were 'not unreasonable, and fair in the circumstances' and that they would accordingly not petition the Commons in Select Committee. Next, the Treasury was told that the Governor intended to take a firm line on disclosure and after a recent conversation with the Chancellor he assumed the latter would do the same. Meanwhile it was calculated that the net worth of the Bank might be some £70 million against a compensation value of £58 million. At the same time the Bank's solicitors, Messrs Freshfields, pressed the argument that since the stockholders could not liquidate the Bank, it could not be argued that net worth, rather than the fixed dividend, was relevant for purposes of compensation.

The Select Committee met on 20 November and in his opening speech Treasury Counsel, Cyril Radcliffe,[22] argued that compensation was fair on the evidence of Stock Exchange prices, on the *de facto* fixity of dividends, and upon the legal position supported by quoted authorities that a Chartered Company established under Statute could not liquidate itself without Parliamentary consent. Moreover Parliament would in no circumstances allow reserves to be distributed to stockholders in some imaginary winding-up. For his part, the Governor opened by describing the various functions of the Bank. In effect he followed established practice and defined the UK central bank 'in use', without stating broad objectives and responsibilities. He then went on firstly to confirm and underline the policy of the fixed 12% dividend and secondly to state categorically and at length his opposition to disclosure of the Bank's reserves. To suggest that disclosure was necessary in order to judge the fairness of the compensation terms was most unfair and most unreasonable. Hidden reserves were

[22] Later Lord Radcliffe; in 1957–9 Chairman of the Committee on the Working of the Monetary System.

essential to the strength and prestige of any great institution. But in the case of the Bank they were in no sense excessive considering the magnitude of the operations of so great an institution and the unique prestige and confidence that it commanded all over the world. Disclosure would be greatly against the national interest and might be very detrimental to the position of the Bank itself. Many people would think the figure very high, but not quite as high as they thought because of wild suggestions that had been made. The reserves were important, but he again assured the Committee that they were in no sense larger than was necessary.

Catto had certainly pulled rank with this *ex cathedra* utterance and he had risked cross-examination that could have been damaging. But nobody dared challenge the Governor to his face on what was then relatively unexplored territory. The Cohen Committee on Company Law had not yet been appointed and the subject of inner reserves was not yet a matter of much public debate. Moreover, the question was in truth rather irrelevant. Given the fixity of dividend and a presumption of continuing profitability, the value of Bank Stock was indeed independent of the level of reserves. It was fortunate that this was so, for the validity of the Governor's position was not beyond question. Twenty-five years later the Bank did disclose its inner reserves, following a like move by the clearing banks, which in turn followed the Report of a second Committee on Company Law and an intimation from Government that action would be taken to compel disclosure if the clearing banks did not do so voluntarily. But in 1945 the suggestion was clearly anathema to the Bank and an affront to its dignity. Disclosure would indeed have risked creating a decisive precedent, even though it was made in the special context of nationalisation. Other banks would have been apprehensive lest they too should be pressed to follow, the more so at a time when the political climate was unfavourable to them. Besides raising fears that the confidence of depositors might on occasion be disturbed by publication of true profits or losses, disclosure would have been heavily against established custom in a City where trust and repute, sometimes still applying to private partnerships rather than limited companies, mattered as much as the arithmetic of published accounts. Moreover the merchant banks, but not the clearing banks, did frequently disclose their true condition to the Bank, though only to the Governor or to the Principal of the Discount Office in person; and this formed part of the supply of confidential information necessary to the maintenance of the customary authority that, in 1945, the Bank was most anxious to maintain. Small wonder, then, that the Governor felt it necessary to stamp so heavily on suggestions that the Bank's reserves be exposed to view.

The Select Committee agreed the Bill without amendment. The ordinary Committee stage began on 17 December and was completed on the 19th. The Government duly carried its promised amendment to Clause 4(3), providing that no regulation should be made with respect to the affairs of a particular customer of a banker. Concerns were also expressed in the House, and in private by the clearing banks, lest directions should be issued without prior consultation and in secret. So Dalton agreed to introduce a further amendment giving bankers the right to make representations to the Treasury before a direction was issued. He was then pressed to make specific provision in the Bill for directions under Clause 4(3) to be published and laid before the House. In the end he agreed to consider a further amendment (to be taken in the Lords), which in effect assured publication unless the Treasury were to certify that the Official Secrets Act applied.[23]

Amendments apart, the Committee stage provided an opportunity for the Chancellor, in response to earlier requests by members, to give an undertaking that the Bank would in future prepare an Annual Report on its operations, a Report that would be laid before the House and could be debated. His intention was that the Report should give the maximum of information that would be consistent with the public interest and the reasonable requirement of operational secrecy, matters on which he would be disposed to be guided very much by the Governor. This was to prove a seedling that grew only slowly.

Finally, the Committee stage enabled Opposition members to make a determined effort to turn the Governor's flank on the matter of inner reserves. They felt that Catto's evidence to the Select Committee had been rather too favourable to the Government's case, and the argument was advanced that the security of the Bank, once nationalised, would depend on the Consolidated Fund and not upon the magnitude of its reserves. In that case the main argument against disclosure disappeared; and it was wrong for the Government to refuse to tell the House and the public the value of the assets it was proposing to acquire. This forced Dalton to retreat a little. He leant heavily on Catto's *obiter dicta*, but coyly averred: 'In the light of what I know, though I am not prepared to disclose it publicly, this is a good bargain for the State.' Later, in the Third Reading Debate, he

---

[23] Niemeyer pointed out in a Minute to the Governor dated 25 January 1946 that except in times of national peril this was all a mare's nest that had nothing to do with the Official Secrets Act or ordinary life. The issue of a Direction would be known to every bank and every branch of a bank, so that there could not possibly be any lack of publicity. The amendment would in fact result in putting a restriction where otherwise there would be none. They (the bankers) 'are nearly as bad at attempting to reduce flexibility to a statutory formula as the Chancellor is himself!'

went just a little further. After saying that for £58 million they were getting much more than £58 million, he offered the possibility of telling more after the Bill's passage through the Lords.

The Bill was given its Third Reading on 20 December and was passed to the Lords, who debated its Second Reading on 22 January 1946. Lord Pethick-Lawrence, who opened for the Government, ably expounded the case for a Statute that made clear beyond doubt that major decisions of monetary policy, domestic or external, were the final discretionary responsibility of the Chancellor of the Exchequer rather than of a Bank of England that was not responsible to any body of public opinion. He also emphasised the useful corollary that henceforth such decisions would be subject to Parliamentary questioning, a matter that was in doubt so long as any such decisions could be ruled by the Speaker as those of the privately owned Bank rather than those of the Minister. Lord Simon followed with the familiar line that statutory codification of the status quo was unwise and unnecessary. But in support of this position he stated that since the establishment of the Exchange Equalisation Account (EEA) in 1932 the Bank had simply been the adviser and executant in respect of monetary policy. 'The decision beyond all question is the decision of the Chancellor of the Exchequer. No other constitutional position is possible.' Lord Simon was a lawyer of great distinction. He had been Lord Chancellor as well as Chancellor of the Exchequer and Foreign Secretary. Yet some of his audience might have been a little taken aback at the ease with which he could oppose straightforward statutory codification simply by pronouncing both what the (unwritten) Constitution had come to be in the monetary field and by asserting that no other position was possible.

The Governor spoke in the Debate and expressed his contentment with the Bill as it stood without commenting on the principle of nationalisation. He concluded:

> Whether it is for good or ill will depend in large measure upon the spirit in which this Bill is administered, and particularly on the men chosen to be Governor, Deputy Governor, and Directors. For they must be men not only of wide experience in all branches of finance, commerce, and industry, but imbued with the spirit of service to the community.

A good deal of the remainder of the Debate was enjoyably occupied with the precise implications of Clause 4(3). Pethick-Lawrence was quite clear that it enabled the Treasury 'in effect' to give directions to the banks 'through the medium' of the Bank. There was no attempt 'to hide the fact that those directions will emanate originally from the Treasury'. Lord Swinton queried this, and sharply queried it when the Governor got up to state 'the initiative rests with the Bank'. Lord Piercy,[24] who in general supported the Bill and its apparent identification of Government as 'the locus of sovereignty' in monetary affairs, nevertheless considered that Clause 4(3) was subtly drafted so as to preserve 'some measure of autonomy' for the Bank in respect of directions to commercial banks. He argued correctly that the Bank could not be directed to think certain steps were in the public interest if in fact it did not so think. He thought it right in this context to lay upon the Bank the duty of considering the public interest. Lord Pakenham, replying for the Government, endeavoured to sidestep the point by saying that directions would be issued on the initiative of the Governor 'but of course with the sanction and in that sense the responsibility of the Treasury'. This did not satisfy Lord Swinton, who asked the Lord Chancellor, Lord Jowett, 'to tell us in this connection what the Bill really means'. The reply was as follows:

> The condition of the use of this machinery is plain. It is what the Bank think. Unless the Bank think it is in the public interest they cannot use this particular machinery at all.

With that the Government, their Lordships, the Bank, and the public had to rest content. Apart from agreeing the further amendment relating to publication of directions under Clause 4(3), the Lords had little more to say. They agreed the Bill on 6 February. The Commons accepted the Lords' amendments on the 12th and the Bill received the Royal Assent on 14 February.

Concern about the powers contained in Clause 4(3) had been powerfully and effectively voiced in the press ever since the Bill was published and particularly during its passage through Parliament. Noting that statutory control over banks was the significant feature of the Bill, a long article in November's *The Banker* considered that careful drafting was required because statutory powers could be left vague and undefined – like the Bank's sphere of influence in the past – and suggested that it be made clear that directions would be confined to the general purpose of controlling the volume and price of credit. *The Times* saw dangers in the wide nature of Clause 4(3) and the potential lack of constraints on its use. For good or ill, the Bill made the Bank 'the potential future dictator' of the banking system. Later, after the House of Lords Debate, it welcomed the

[24] *Piercy, William, 1st Baron 1945, CBE (1886–1966).* Lecturer, LSE, Ministry of Munitions and Inland Revenue 1914–18, General Manager, Harrison and Crosfields 1919–24, Director, Pharaoh, Gane and Co. 1925–33, Stock Exchange 1934–42, Export Credits Guarantee Department 1942–5, Director, Bank of England 1946–56, Chairman, Wellcome Trust 1960–5, Chairman, Industrial and Commercial Finance Corporation 1945–64, Director 1964–6, Chairman, Estate Duties Investment Trust and Ship Mortgage Finance Co, 1964–6.

reassurances given by the Governor and the amendments that had been made. The *Financial Times*, too, expressed suspicion at the motives lying behind 4(3) and, like other papers, reported the Chairmen of the Westminster Bank and the Midland Bank, whose annual statements both condemned the clause. 'Why', asked the former, 'are the activities of the commercial banks to come under the dead hand of officialdom?' There could be difficulties between banker and customer unless the powers were exercised with great care and restraint. Finally, *The Economist*, whose attitude to the Bill had been consistently uninterested,[25] fell into line with its contemporaries once it had been passed. Clause 4(3) went well beyond formalising the status quo. The declared intention behind it was the general or selective control of credit, which the Bank had not undertaken in the past. There was a danger of such controls running counter to profitability and of this leading to Government guarantees (and nationalisation) or to 'rule-of-thumb' banking. The amendments, and Lord Jowett's ruling on the Clause, were therefore to be welcomed as valuable safeguards.

There was of course never any doubt that the Bill would have a safe passage through Parliament. Yet the debates and discussions did bring a useful breath of fresh outside air into the rather close atmosphere that characterised the central banking status quo. While the Bank found that some members of both Houses were prepared to give it uncritical support, or even adulation, it also found others, and not just those who made the Bank a scapegoat, who were not prepared to accept at face value that its judgement was almost always wise and the high quality of its expertise beyond question. Nor did the authorities find ready acceptance of their view that they could always be trusted to administer the powers first set out in the Bill in so wise a manner as never to overrule the perceived natural rights of the victims. Despite the advice of officials to the contrary, three substantial amendments to Clause 4(3) had been conceded by the Chancellor in response to Parliamentary pressure, to representations made by the banks themselves, and to powerful voices in the press. No matter that the powers might never be put to formal use, their informal exercise would in future have to conform to the safeguards entrenched in the Act. But when all had been said, the fact remained that the UK had settled its monetary constitution in great haste and without public enquiry or debate. The wisdom of this course remained to be demonstrated. After forty-five years of almost uninterrupted inflation, some may judge that it still remains to be demonstrated.

On 1 March 1946 ownership of the Bank was transferred to the

[25] When the Bill was published, *The Economist* remarked that it would 'take a very nervous heart to register a flutter at what is contained in the Bill. Nothing could be more moderate.'

Treasury, the Governors and Directors formally took office under the new dispensation, and a new Royal Charter was granted. Catto was appointed Governor for the statutory five-year term; but he was already sixty-seven and was thought likely to retire once the new regime was well established. Cobbold was appointed Deputy Governor, but without indications that he would in due course succeed to the top post. Six Directors on the old Court were either over seventy or nearing that age. They retired on those grounds, while three others, whose main activities were a long distance from London, stepped down at their own request. Since there was already one vacancy caused by the retirement of Pitman in 1945, there was room for four new members within the new statutory limit of sixteen. These were Lord Piercy, the recently appointed Chairman of the Industrial and Commercial Finance Corporation (ICFC), George Gibson, Chairman of the Trades Union Congress and the first of successive senior trade-unionists to sit on the Court, Brigadier Robin Brook, a Labour sympathiser and an Olympic fencer who had a distinguished war record and was embarking on a career in the City, and lastly George Wansbrough, another Labour supporter with City experience.

The old Court did not disperse without appropriate ceremony. Late on Wednesday 27 February, the evening before their last meeting, they gave themselves and their former colleagues a dinner in the Court Room.[26] In the course of a short speech expressing the Bank's strong and continuing sense of corporate identity, of authority, and of a part to be played, the Governor said:

> It falls to me, not by merit or length of service, but by reason of my position as Governor, to preside tonight. It is an historic occasion – the end of one epoch and the beginning of another: And whether in the new epoch the Bank's position and influence will remain unimpaired, time alone will show.
>
> I am deeply appreciative of the manner in which all Members of the Court stood solidly behind me in this crisis in the Bank's history. A break in our ranks would have enormously increased the difficulties. The policy we adopted has proved its worth and gradually everyone is coming to realise that although the essential principle of Public Ownership had to be conceded, on all other matters, particularly those questions concerning the future of the Bank and its management and the protection of the Staff, we put up a fight behind the scenes and obtained every point we considered essential to the well-being of this great and ancient institution. If the Bill is administered in the spirit in which it was drafted, we need have few fears for the future. That future I cannot predict but I can say this, that there is nothing in the structure under the new Charter which would prevent the continued confidence, prosperity and prestige of the Bank.

[26] The drinks included Cognac distilled eight years before the Baring Crisis of 1892.

Montagu Norman, 1942
KARSH

He concluded:

> My Lords and Gentlemen, I will now give you the Toast of the evening and I couple that with the name of Lord Norman, for in very truth he has given all the best years of his life in pursuance of the object of this Toast. My Lords and Gentlemen with a full heart I give you the Toast 'Long live the Bank of England!'.

Norman's private diary for 27 February contains only the entry 'Bk. Goodbye dinner'. He was present and heard the toast. It is known that he replied and that the Governor told the Chancellor two days later that the reply was 'slightly pessimistic'.[27] Nothing else is known or now recalled. Enigmatic to the last, but with that one clue, Norman has left his valedictory to our imagination. But Per Jacobsson[28], of the Bank for International Settlements (BIS), had lunch with him a few weeks later and asked whether he thought the Bank was still the same place. Norman replied: 'They try to pretend it is the same place.'

SOURCES

Bank files
    ADM11/1–2   Nationalisation of the Bank: Charters, Statutes and By-Laws – Bank of England Act 1946 (May 1945 – February 1946)
    G1/261   Governor's File: Miscellaneous (1945)
    G15/19   Secretary's File: Histories of the Bank and Related Matters – Lord Cobbold's Notes of his Governorship (1949–61)
    G18/1–2   Lord Catto's Papers (August 1945 – July 1946)
PRO files
    T160/1408/1
    T241/5
Jacobsson diaries

[27] Recounted by Hugh Dalton in *High Tide and After* (London, Frederick Muller, 1962).
[28] *Jacobsson, Per (1894–1963)*. Educated Uppsala University. Economic and Financial Section of League of Nations Secretariat 1920–8, Secretary-General, Economic Defence Commission, Sweden 1929–30, Economic Adviser, Kreuger and Toll 1930–1, Economic Adviser and Head, Monetary and Economic Department, BIS 1931–56, Chairman of the Executive Board and Managing Director, International Monetary Fund 1956–63.

CHAPTER 2

LORD KEYNES AND THE BANK: BRETTON WOODS AND THE ANGLO–AMERICAN LOAN

(a) THE SETTING: OPPOSING FORCES

ON THE evening of 20 August 1947 the Chancellor of the Exchequer announced over the radio that external convertibility of sterling had been suspended because of an unacceptable drain on external reserves and the fast approaching exhaustion of available credits. Convertibility, at the fixed rate of $4.03 to the pound, had been introduced progressively over the months preceding 15 July, when it had to be made complete, in accord with Clause 8 of the Anglo-American Loan Agreement of December 1945. Now, six weeks later, it had been suspended and most of the Loan of $3¾ billion had gone. So ended in damaging humiliation the attempt to remove – within only two years of the end of the war – one of the main barriers to the full introduction of the peacetime international monetary order set out in the Bretton Woods Agreements. The British Government had been a needy but reluctant party to the adventure of the Loan Agreement. Many officials in the Treasury had regarded it with grave misgiving. The Bank of England had thought it very ill-advised, or even 'sheer madness', but had subsequently treated convertibility as a commitment that had first to be honoured before it could be abandoned. Keynes, who had invented the whole plan in the first place but had failed to get it agreed on terms he had earlier advised were vital to its success, had died shortly afterwards, worn out by overwork and ill-health. The Americans, who had driven too hard a bargain from a position of too much strength, had now been forced to realise that the economic and financial problems of recovery from the war were far more difficult than they had optimistically or even naively supposed. Already, earlier in the summer of 1947, the same Administration that had refused in 1945 to put to Congress any proposal for a grant-in-aid to the UK, and had terminated Lend-Lease with brutal haste, had become convinced that massive aid to Western Europe would be required before real progress could be made towards the vision of a multilateral world seen by the men of Bretton Woods.

Much has been written about this ill-starred voyage and all of it reflects the strong dramatic content of the story. For at its centre is the tragic sequence of the Loan negotiations themselves, held in Washington in the autumn of 1945. An Englishman of high and lasting international stature, but one whose only source of power was his own special genius and vision, suddenly found himself in a trap that he had feared but had hoped against hope he could avoid. Keynes could neither get what he needed nor withdraw to safety after admitting defeat. So he had to wear himself out in a fight on two fronts, to get a third-best outcome. In his own autobiography, written many years later, Lionel Robbins summarised it thus: 'Poor Maynard, how much trouble he had brought upon himself by his own rash impetuosity. And how utterly and devotedly he spent himself when the gorgeous vision was shattered and nothing but a *pis aller* lay ahead.'[1]

The Bank of England, with its operational knowledge of the Sterling Area and of external currency matters generally, was not asked to provide anybody to accompany Keynes to Washington in 1945. This was by then a little unusual. Thompson-McCausland[2] had been a member of the delegation that went with Keynes to the US in 1943 to discuss plans for the new monetary order. George Bolton[3] had been a member of the UK delegation at Bretton Woods in the summer of 1944. Later on, in the crisis of September 1947, the Deputy Governor was to be recalled from holiday and flown to join Treasury officials in Washington for urgent talks with the American authorities. Explanation of the Bank's absence from Keynes' small delegation in 1945 must be conjectural, for there is no trace of the matter being discussed at the time. It is likely that Keynes simply felt no need for a Bank expert, senior or junior. His immediate vision being what it was, he was not expecting to get involved in detailed negotiations with the Americans about the future of the Sterling Area or the evolution of

---

[1] *Autobiography of an Economist* (London, Macmillan, 1971)
[2] *Thompson-McCausland, Lucius Perronet, CMG (1904–84).* Educated Repton and King's College, Cambridge. Helbert Wagg 1928–9, *Financial News* 1929–34, Moody's Economic Service 1929–39. Entered Bank 1939, Adviser to the Governors 1949–65. Consultant to HM Treasury on International Monetary Problems 1965–8. Director, Tricentrol Ltd 1967–76, Chairman 1970–6, Director, Moodies Services Ltd 1968–75, Chairman 1970–5.
[3] *Bolton, George Lewis French, KCMG (1900–82).* Educated Leyton County High School. Helbert Wagg 1920–33. Entered Bank 1933, Deputy Principal, Foreign Exchange Section, Chief Cashier's Office 1934–6, Principal 1936–41, Adviser to the Governors 1941–8, Executive Director 1948–57, Director 1957–68, UK Executive Director, IMF 1946–52, UK Alternate Governor 1952–7, Chairman, Bank of London and South America 1957–70, President 1970–82, Chairman, Commonwealth Development Finance Company (CDFC) 1968–80.

monetary or payments agreements with countries in, for example, Europe or Latin America. Furthermore he was himself well briefed on these matters, having been immersed in discussions about them with the Treasury and the Bank since as early as 1941. But there was likely to have been another and more fundamental reason, namely that Keynes did not want to be accompanied on this hazardous mission by an opponent.

For although the Bank had repeatedly expressed support for Keynes' ultimate international monetary objectives, it had been a consistent and determined critic of almost all his practical proposals for attaining them. The Bank was at this stage no great enthusiast for the early restoration of the currency convertibility and non-discriminatory trade that was passionately advocated by the US Treasury and the State Department. Sometimes it also tended to reflect views of the American banking community hostile to the Roosevelt Administration and in particular to Henry Morgenthau,[4] Secretary to the Treasury and a man who detested central banks. It was throughout suspicious lest blueprints and formulae, much favoured at that time by particular economists, should get applied to circumstances that had turned out very differently to those that had been assumed, or to working monetary arrangements like the Sterling Area that lacked uniformity and were indeed conspicuous in their diversity. The Bank was suspicious, too, lest ambitious blueprints should be regarded as painless cures, diverting national attention from fundamental problems. Above all, the Bank was seemingly haunted by its own bitter experience of 1925–31 and fearful lest the British authorities should again undertake external monetary commitments, in particular the early resumption of external convertibility at a fixed rate of exchange, which they would find that they were unable to honour. A beneficial result of these suspicions and anxieties was that the Bank helped to ensure that the eventual blueprints contained practical safeguards. Prominent among these was the provision, in Article XIV of the International Monetary Fund (IMF), of a transitional period of some years, so that members could protect themselves against premature and unsustainable acceptance of the obligations on external convertibility set out in Article VIII. But another result was that the Bank became, if not a centre of opposition, a place where international monetary ideas alternative to those of Keynes continued to flourish. There was therefore a persistent underlying lack of mutual sympathy and understanding between Keynes and the Bank, even if their clashes in the Depression years

---

[4] *Morgenthau, Henry Jr (1891–1967).* Educated Cornell. US Navy 1918–19. Publisher, *American Agriculturist* 1922–33, Chairman, Governor's Agricultural Advisory Commission, New York State 1929–33, Conservation Commissioner 1931–3, Chairman, Federal Farm Board 1933, Acting and Under Secretary of the Treasury 1933–4, Secretary 1934–45. General Chairman, United Jewish Appeal 1947–67.

had mostly been put out of mind and Keynes had been made a member of the Court. Sometimes the Bank must have looked like a tiresomely independent technician with ideas beyond its station, while Keynes must have looked like a brilliant and erratic visionary lacking proper understanding of the world as it was likely to be.

In fact of course there was a good deal of the practical technician in Keynes and of the visionary in the Bank. In more normal circumstances there might have been some wise and effective higher authority to make the best use of both qualities in both. For the dispute between the two, as it developed, was not in reality very profound. Keynes was right to insist that the UK should support the establishment of a new international monetary system with new international institutions and with American backing. The Bank was right to insist on the need for proper safeguards for the UK and the Sterling Area during the first few post-war years and also right to remain suspicious of American intentions. But in the special circumstances of wartime, and of the early months of the transition to peacetime, higher authority may have tended to be preoccupied with other matters. As a consequence, and in view of his outstanding qualities – including a personality as magnetic and compelling now as Norman's had been fifteen years previously – Keynes came to establish in this field a position in the Treasury and with the Government that far outshone the other special advisers and the permanent officials.[5] His ascendancy also benefited from the relative political weakness of the Bank at that time. The Bank was widely thought to have been wrong during the inter-war years, while Keynes seemed to have turned out to be right. As regards international monetary strategy, neither Norman nor his successor had much influence with wartime Coalition Ministers. In such circumstances the Bank, still to be nationalised, was in most part an adviser only to Treasury officials and not to the Government in some wider sense. This subordinate role contributed to the ascendancy of Keynes.

His personal dominance carried inherent dangers. Prominent among these was the risk that the particular interests of the UK might, through an element of wishful thinking or over-optimism, become prejudiced through their subordination to the supranational objectives that Keynes

[5] As Otto Clarke wrote in his diary on the day of Keynes' death in 1946: 'His death leaves the Treasury in a terrible hole. Keynes has been the Treasury over the last few years; he has determined policy, spurred on the officials by criticism and help, conducted the major negotiations. This dependence on Keynes has been good for the Treasury in some respects; it has been bad in others for it has prevented the officials from developing an individual technique of thought. He has been the brains and the conscience.' (Richard Clarke, *Anglo–American Economic Collaboration in War and Peace 1942–49*, ed. Alec Cairncross, Oxford, Oxford University Press, 1982). Another observer of the Treasury at this time has described Treasury officials as either frightened or hypnotised by Keynes.

came to pursue and towards which the Americans were driving; just as, in the 1920s, British interests may have been prejudiced by Norman's pursuit of international monetary order at that time. The Anglo–American Loan negotiations exposed this particular danger. It can of course always be argued that some sort of external crisis would anyway have occurred in 1947 or that the special importance of convertibility, as a cause of that crisis, can be overplayed. But this does not alter the fact that a strategy adopted in 1945, and sealed by inter-governmental Agreement, ended in disaster.

The point of departure was much earlier than 1945 and was rooted in the discussions that took place in London prior to the Anglo–American Mutual Aid Agreement of February 1942. Into this agreement about war supplies there was inserted, at American insistence, a Clause 7 committing the parties, and other like-minded countries, to the elimination of all forms of discriminatory treatment in international commerce and the reduction of tariff and other trade barriers in the post-war world. This commitment, together with a variety of ultimate economic objectives (notably the maximisation of employment), was to oblige the American and British authorities to think through, and to agree upon, a framework of international monetary arrangements that would foster conditions under which free multilateral trading could be accepted and could flourish. Thinking through the monetary structure was to lead in turn to thinking about and eventually agreeing upon arrangements for a transitional phase, immediately following the war, during which economies would have to be reconstructed and reconverted and means devised for dealing with the financial aftermath. The Anglo-American Loan Agreement was one of the results.

(b) THE FIRST ADOPTION OF STRATEGIC VIEWS: 1941–1942

The Atlantic Charter was signed on 14 August 1941, nearly four months before Pearl Harbour and exactly four years ahead of VJ Day. Articles IV and V of the Charter declared support for access by all countries 'on equal terms, to the trade and raw materials of the world' and for the fullest collaboration with the 'object of securing for all improved labour standards, economic advancement, and social security'. There had also been discussions between the President and the Prime Minister about the terms and conditions of Lend-Lease, foreshadowing Clause 7 of the Mutual Aid Agreement already mentioned. This would commit the UK to enter into discussions with the US about progress towards the international economic objectives of the American Administration.

The British Cabinet responded to these developments by requesting the Treasury and the Board of Trade to consider post-war financial and trade policy with special reference to the expected Anglo-American discussions. The Treasury set to work promptly on its part of the work and on 16 September 1941 the Second Secretary in charge of the Finance Division, Richard Hopkins, wrote to the Governor proposing consultation with the Bank on post-war financial questions. As a first step, the Bank was then sent two papers, one by Keynes and the other by Hubert Henderson,[6] with the comment by Hopkins that he would 'like to concentrate first on thinking about what must be our policy in the immediate post-war period. I think we can give more leisurely consideration to the very difficult questions with which the second part of Keynes' paper is concerned.' This judgement about the phasing of the work was to prove very mistaken.

Keynes' paper, dated 8 September, set out a position from which he was not to deviate to any notable extent for the remainder of his life.[7] He was to develop and refine his exposition at various stages over the next few years, and tailor it to meet changing tactical needs, but its essentials, including its presentational dichotomy between alternatives, were to remain substantially unaltered.[8] He began with a cogent attack on international *laissez-faire*. 'To suppose that there exists', he wrote, 'some smoothly functioning automatic mechanism of adjustment which will preserve equilibrium if only we trust to methods of *laissez-faire* is a doctrinaire delusion which disregards the lessons of historical experience without having behind it the support of sound theory'. He went on to outline the grave economic situation with which the UK would be confronted after the war and to meet which a massive increase in export

[6] Henderson, Hubert Douglas, Kt (1890–1952). Educated Aberdeen Grammar School, Rugby and Emmanuel College, Cambridge. Fellow, Clare College, Cambridge 1919–23, Editor, *Nation and Athenaeum* 1923–30, Member, Committee on Economic Information 1931–9, Economic Adviser, HM Treasury 1939–44, Professor of Political Economy, Oxford 1945–51. Fellow of All Souls College, Oxford 1934–52, elected Warden 1951.

[7] He had visited the US during the early summer of 1941, mainly to sort out the financial administration of Lend-Lease. In the course of this visit he had talked with Secretary Morgenthau, Under-Secretary Dean Acheson, and White House adviser Harry Hopkins, and had been informed of the intention to demand acceptance of draft Clause 7 as 'consideration' for Lend-Lease. He is reported to have reacted violently against this but to have become convinced that it was likely, in effect, to be imposed. He then gave his mind to the problem of how to make the obligations implied by Clause 7 acceptable and workable. His Clearing Union proposals were the result, as was then his personal commitment to the international order contemplated by the US.

[8] Both Roy Harrod, in his biography of Keynes (*The Life of John Maynard Keynes*, London, Macmillan, 1951), and Lionel Robbins in his autobiography refer to the enigmatic ambivalence of Keynes' views at this time. He seemed to be both a bilateralist and a multilateralist. But the record suggests that while he felt he had to be prepared for either alternative he now strongly preferred the latter, though realising that creation of the necessary machinery would be a formidable task.

volume, compared to pre-war, would be inescapable. Overhanging this already difficult predicament would be the wartime accumulation in London of very large overseas sterling balances unmatched by external reserves. The US, in Keynes' view, had no adequate remedies to offer which could either overcome his general arguments against *laissez-faire* or measure up to the scale of Britain's own particular problem. So what was to be done?

One answer lay in making do with what was then likely to be available. The UK would end the war with a well-developed network of payments arrangements and payments agreements, including the Sterling Area itself; and this network, supported by continuing exchange and trade controls, would be vitally needed during the post-war transitional period (which itself might last five years) and could then be evolved into a permanent peacetime scheme. There was, however, an alternative. 'I attempt', Keynes wrote, 'in a separate paper to sketch an ideal system which would solve the problem on multilateral lines by international agreement. This is an ambitious scheme. But the post-war world must not be content with patchwork. If it can be accepted, several vital purposes will be served. But we have yet to discover whether those in authority in the world mean seriously their brave words about radical post-war innovation.' Keynes concluded by saying quite categorically that it was with this scheme that he favoured approaching the US. It was an attempt to satisfy their requirements. If not this, 'we can ask, what then? Now that you are fully seized of the essential elements of the problem, what alternative solution do you offer us?' There followed next day, in a further paper, Keynes' proposals for an International Clearing Union. Not only did these include quotas, overdraft rights, and disciplinary procedures affecting creditors as well as debtors. There were in addition outline provisions dealing with the international financing of post-war relief and reconstruction.

Henderson's paper was entitled 'The Nineteen Thirties', and he covered the economic history of this period in some detail. His analysis of the defects of *laissez-faire* were broadly similar to those of Keynes; but his final conclusions differed. Keynes was suggesting that radical reform of the international monetary system would enable a multilateral and non-discriminatory system of trade and payments to work satisfactorily, without prejudice to national economic goals about output and employment and indeed in greater furtherance of such goals. Henderson did not attack the proposed Clearing Union as such, but allowed no room for such things in his conclusion. 'I am convinced', he wrote, 'that a satisfactory system can only be rebuilt along lines which provide adequate scope for national policies of planning and control; and that in such a system quantitative regulation, exchange controls, and bilateral agreements, have a legitimate part to play.'[9]

In the Bank the subject was discussed between the Deputy Governor (Catterns), Cobbold, Siepmann,[10] Clay,[11] Bolton, and Thompson-McCausland. Norman himself was less closely involved. But he was certainly in control of the final decisions and a few weeks earlier he had set up a small committee, consisting of the latter four people and chaired by Siepmann, to consider on what lines exchange policy should be directed in the immediate post-war period and what modifications to exchange control might be required.

Among the Bank team the most prominent was Cameron Cobbold, both within the Bank and at meetings in Whitehall. The son of a Colonel in the British Army he was only thirty-seven, twenty years younger than Keynes. He had joined the Bank in 1933, initially as an adviser on the overseas side, and had quickly established a reputation for administrative ability, power of command, tenacity of purpose, and capacity for hard work. He was also a good linguist, with fluent French and Italian. In 1938, when still only thirty-four, he had been elected to the Court as an Executive Director. Like Keynes he had been educated at Eton and King's, Cambridge. But unlike Keynes, though like Norman himself, he had left Cambridge after only one year and gone into the City. Along with several of his senior colleagues in the Bank, he could make little claim to academic distinction. However, others in the Bank, notably Niemeyer, Siepmann, Clay, Thompson-McCausland, Mynors, and Kershaw[12] possessed first-class intellects on which a man of Cobbold's outstanding general ability could

---

[9] An enlarged version of this paper was prepared at the end of 1943. It was subsequently published, after Henderson's death, in *The Inter-War Years and Other Essays* (Oxford, Oxford University Press, 1955).

[10] *Siepmann, Harry Arthur (1889–1963).* Educated Rugby and New College, Oxford. HM Treasury 1912–15. Army 1915–19. HM Treasury 1919, Assistant to Finance Member, Viceroy's Council, India 1923–4, Adviser to National Bank of Hungary 1924–6. Entered Bank 1926, Adviser to the Governors 1926–32, Acting Chief of Overseas and Foreign Department 1932–5, Adviser to the Governors 1935–45, Executive Director 1945–54.

[11] *Clay, Henry, Kt (1883–1954).* Educated Bradford Grammar School and University College, Oxford. Lecturer for Workers Educational Classes 1909–17, Ministry of Labour 1917–19, Fellow of New College, Oxford 1919–21, Professor of Political Economy, Manchester University 1922–7, of Social Economics 1927–30. Adviser, Securities Management Trust 1930–3. Entered Bank 1933, Adviser to the Governors 1933–44, an Economic Adviser, Board of Trade 1941–4. Warden of Nuffield College, Oxford 1944–9.

[12] *Kershaw, Raymond Newton, CMG, MC (1898–1981).* Educated Sydney High School, Sydney University, and New College, Oxford (Rhodes Scholar). League of Nations 1924–9. Entered Bank 1929, Adviser 1929–35, Adviser to the Governors 1935–53. Member, East African Currency Board (1932–53) and several others. Adviser to CDFC 1953–55,

draw, so as to hold his own with senior Treasury officials and face Keynes without timidity or loss of confidence. Added to this backing was the strong technical support in the field of foreign exchange provided especially by George Bolton, also a young man and in his own way as prominent a personality. It was quite a formidable team.

In the event, the Bank turned away from the approach favoured by Keynes and proposed instead a much more step-by-step and try-it-and-see procedure. Its ultimate international monetary component would have been a development of the 1936 Tripartite Agreement for mutual co-operation between the exchange stabilisation funds of the US, the UK, and France. This set of ideas was not confined to the Bank and became known as the 'key-currency approach', to distinguish it from the new-institution approach of Keynes and others. A prominent American exponent was Professor J. H. Williams,[13] economic adviser to the FRBNY, the Bank of England's principal contact in the US.

Part of the Bank's initial opposition to the Clearing Union was instinctive. Central banks, particularly those presiding over large and sophisticated monetary systems, tend to dislike or even resent grand international and inter-governmental schemes dreamt up by economists who may seem, if only because of terminological differences, to be giving insufficient attention to the practicalities of the market-place. Moreover the Bank of England, and certainly its Governor, regarded international monetary matters as properly a main concern of the central banks of a few principal countries acting both as adviser to their respective Governments and as collaborative executants of agreed policies. This view was not to prove very wrong. But it was out of tune with the times in 1941 and especially out of tune with the situation in the US, where since 1934 international monetary policy had become *de jure* and *de facto* wholly the responsibility of the Treasury Department. A second strand in the Bank's opposition to the schemes first devised first by Keynes and later by Harry White[14] of the US Treasury was its suspicions of American interference

Chairman, London Board of Commercial Banking Co. of Sydney 1964–6 and of Bank of New Zealand 1963–8.
[13] *Williams, John Henry* (1887–1980). Educated Brown University and Harvard. Assistant Professor of Economics, Princeton 1919–20, Associate Professor of Banking, Northwestern University 1920–1, Assistant Professor of Economics, Harvard 1921–5, Associate Professor 1925–9, Professor 1929–33, Nathaniel Ropes Professor of Political Economy 1933–57. ECA Advisory Committee on Fiscal and Monetary Problems 1948–51. Vice-President, FRBNY 1936–47, Economic Adviser 1933–52, Economic Consultant 1956–64.
[14] *White, Harry Dexter* (1892–1948). Director of Monetary Research, US Department of the Treasury. Assistant to Henry Morgenthau 1941. In charge of Treasury's relations with US Army and Navy 1943. Assistant Secretary of Treasury 1945. US Executive Director, IMF 1946–7.

Cameron Cobbold as Executive Director, 1942

with sterling, a suspicion that was to prove well founded. The emergence of a closely knit Sterling Area, the pooling of dollar earnings in London, and the persistence of Imperial Preference were disliked by the American Administration and especially disliked by the State Department and the Treasury. The Bank, *per contra*, felt considerable satisfaction with the apparatus of war-time exchange control, which it had so recently created, as agent of the Treasury, and which it now began to see as a powerful instrument in peacetime for maintaining the exchange stability that had proved so elusive in the inter-war years. Allied to this admiration for control was a new-found confidence in the peacetime potentialities of the war-time Sterling Area.

In the course of a long paper on post-war exchange control, dated 25 September 1941, Bolton remarked that it was a waste of time discussing post-war schemes with Washington until the UK authorities were 'clear as to the scope and activities of our own post-war monetary arrangements'. He followed with an outline plan for a strengthened and integrated Sterling Area, a fixed sterling/dollar rate, the continued centralisation of foreign exchange and gold transactions through the Bank, the continued elaborate control of outward capital movements long and short, and the development of bilateral monetary agreements with non-sterling countries and currency areas. Bolton subsequently submitted a technical critique of the Clearing Union proposals, but remarked at the outset that the unknown length of the period of reconstruction made Utopian schemes such as the Clearing Union dangerously impracticable expedients that distracted attention from real problems and difficulties requiring solution. Siepmann, with support at this stage from Clay, did then try a different approach, expressed rather obscurely. He wanted the Bank to say it believed that a radical plan was to be preferred and should be pressed to the exclusion of any partial alternatives that dealt only with the symptoms of trouble. He had a strong preference for an automatic or self-compensating system as opposed to any system that depended upon the successful negotiation and renegotiation, under varying political pressures, of trade and monetary agreements. But he went on to argue that the Clearing Union would disrupt the Sterling Area. His general approach, sympathetic to Keynes, did not find favour in the Bank and Siepmann did not pursue it. Meetings and discussions continued throughout September and October 1941. The Deputy Governor wrote to Hopkins at the end of September, concentrating entirely on the problems of the immediate post-war period and suggesting that the principal task ahead was to convince the Americans that exchange controls, trade controls, and bilateral agreements had to be 'the framework within which our policy must be devised for a number of years after the war'. On 10 October Siepmann recorded that the Treasury was in substantial agreement with the Bank at that stage. Further, he wrote: 'They definitely assign to us the job of working out a plan and realise that this will take a long time.' On 17 October the Deputy Governor wrote again to Hopkins. He declined to give any quick answer to questions about whether and how the Sterling Area could be kept together after the war, but enclosed a memorandum that was mainly concerned to develop the case for freedom of action in respect of exchange and trade controls.

Keynes himself, who had coincidentally been elected to the Court, had had discussions with Bank officials and wrote to Catterns on 22 October questioning the discriminatory effectiveness of the Sterling Area post-war and raising the issue of the accumulating sterling balances. On 24 October the Governor had a chat with Hopkins 'on Keynes' long-term Utopia'. Finally, on 29 October Norman held a meeting with Catterns, Siepmann, Cobbold, and Clay. At the top of the agenda were three searching questions. Should the Bank press for early Ministerial decisions about the minimum amount of freedom of action that the UK should maintain *vis-à-vis* the Americans? Did the Bank approve that as a matter of tactics HMG should present an ambitious and far-reaching plan for discussion with the

Americans? Should the Bank as technical advisers to HMG endeavour to work out and give their blessing to a utopian scheme either by detailed criticism of Keynes' plan or otherwise? Against the first question Norman noted 'yes', while against the other two he noted: 'statement of ideals towards which we should like to aim if generally accepted (in place of Keynes plan)'. On the following day Hopkins sent the Bank a new Treasury draft on Post-War Monetary and Economic Policy. It still concentrated almost entirely on the immediate post-war disequilibrium and included only a bracketed sentence to the effect that an examination of the Clearing Union would be added later. On 4 November Catterns replied to Hopkins in accord with the Governor's decision of 29 October and enclosed the Bank's own skeleton draft of a memorandum for presentation to the US Administration. Two paragraphs of his letter deserve quotation in full.

> The discussions throughout have tended to assume two entirely different phases:
>
> (i) a transitional period and
> (ii) the final post-war period ('when things have settled down') when it may or may not be possible to introduce a completely new economic plan.
>
> This is, it seems to us, a somewhat misleading picture both for our own working and for presentation to others. The cardinal mistake and the greatest admission of defeat which we can make is to put up as a final objective something which we do not believe has a reasonable chance of coming about. We must set ourselves aims in which we believe and our policy must from the start be directed towards bringing them about. Progress can only be by trial and error but we must consciously strive to form and adapt our controls and our international economic relations with the ultimate goal always in view. We must never allow ourselves to contemplate a static transitional period and hope that on a given date one, two or three years after the war the heavens will open and our problems be solved.
>
> It has come to be assumed that exchange controls and trade controls are inevitably destructive and restrictive. On the contrary we believe that their intelligent use in co-operation with other countries is the only possible alternative to a regime of fluctuating exchange rates and speculative movements of funds, far more destructive of trade, and that if properly used they can be constructive and expansive: in fact, that without them the post-war world would inevitably fall back into the chaos of the Thirties.

The Bank's skeleton draft developed the views expressed in the letter and pointedly contained no reference to the Clearing Union or any similar plan. It remarked instead that the basis of the international monetary mechanism should in effect be the alternative Keynes had rejected, namely a co-ordinated series of bilateral agreements between the Governments responsible for the principle currency areas working through their central banking institutions.

The Bank's skeleton found no favour at all with Keynes and his supporting cast of like-minded economists, notably Roy Harrod and Dennis Robertson[15] but including also George Shackle, Robbins, and James Meade. During November Keynes had further talks with Bank officials and developed arguments that questioned the validity of the Bank's ideas about the Sterling Area; and in a note dated 9 November he linked these arguments with the Clearing Union proposals. Two weeks later Cobbold sent Keynes a note that sought to avoid technical argument and instead concentrate firstly on the common ground between the latter and the Bank with respect to ultimate goals and secondly on reiteration of the Bank's view, contrary to that of Keynes, that it was dangerous to 'paint in the foreground a detailed picture of what the eventual state might be... It tempts Government to suppose that they have only to set up an international bank when their troubles will be at an end'. Writing on the same day, Bolton also emphasised common ground between Keynes and the Bank, but agreed that while Anglo-American collaboration on an international scheme might buy assistance from Washington it would do so at the cost of antagonising the rest of Europe. There was next an intervention from Catto, then Keynes' colleague in the Treasury. He was by now a strong supporter of the former as well as a frequent visitor at the Bank and highly regarded by the Governor. He wrote to Norman at the end of November commending the Clearing Union and asking for a talk, which took place on 3 December.

He wrote again on 2 December enclosing a powerful note of his own. He found little actually to criticise in the Bank's skeleton draft because 'in fact it proposes only the maintenance and even extension of what we are doing now, it seems to be intended to meet difficulties as they arise and largely by trial and error to work out a more permanent system'. But he regarded this approach as largely palliative and as taking a short-term view. Keynes' proposals took a long-term view and were ingenious and constructive. If we were to accomplish anything at all and make a better post-war world than existed inter-war, 'we must aim high and have the courage and enterprise to strive toward something that will prevent the errors of the past. To let things drift would be a tragedy to ourselves and a profound betrayal of those who will come after us.'

[15] In a letter dated 27 November to Keynes, Robertson expressed 'a glowing hope that the spirit of Burke and Adam Smith is on earth again to prevent the affairs of a Great Empire from being settled by the little minds of a gang of bank clerks who have tasted blood (yes, I know this is unfair!)'

Two weeks later Keynes himself circulated a new version of his proposals and then made a determined personal effort to win over the Bank to his point of view. He wrote to Cobbold on 17 December and sent separate letters to both Governors on the 19th (twelve days after Pearl Harbour). To Cobbold he said he had got the impression that the Bank believed the Clearing Union proposals were inimical to maintenance of the traditional features of the Sterling Area. He went on: 'I feel, as you will see, exactly the contrary. It seems to be that the one chance of holding the Sterling Area together is a multilateral scheme which allows everything to go on as before.' To Catterns he wrote that even if his proposals proved too much for the Americans, 'shouldn't we be much better placed if we had *started off* at any rate by showing that we at least were ready to come into an international scheme for the benefit of the world at large?' Norman got the longest letter of the three. It embodied and enlarged the points made in the other two and made eloquent and respectful pleas that the writer's vision should be shared by the Governor. 'My proposal', he wrote, 'is *multilateral*. We might be forced to fall back on bilateral arrangements as a very bad alternative. But if we can get a multilateral system, I do not see how anyone in his senses could fail to prefer it. Therefore let us try for it.' His plan was: 'a bold bid to combine the great historical advantages of the XIX Century Gold Standard with modern ideas and the requirements of the post-war world'. He concluded: 'So I hope for your blessing and approval. I have received more encouragement for this from all quarters in Whitehall than for anything I have ever suggested.'

A man of Norman's complex sensibility, somewhat embittered by the past, was not to be captured by an approach of this sort. He was quite unmoved by it all. It is also likely that he was anyway not taking Keynes' proposals as seriously as he should. He was a frequent visitor at that time to Horace Wilson, Permanent Secretary at the Treasury and shortly to be retired, whose apprehension of what was afoot in the Finance Division seems to have been notably imperfect. On 10 December Norman recorded Wilson advising him that 'the post-war stuff with Washington is in cold storage'. On 30 December, after another chat with Wilson, Norman noted in his diary: 'JMK III? dead'. 'III' was the current version of the Clearing Union and it was on the contrary very much alive. Throughout January 1942 the Treasury was drafting its predominant share of a submission to Ministers on External Monetary and Economic Policy. This finally went forward on 12 March, running to 264 paragraphs and 3 appendices. The Clearing Union, with critique, occupied no less than 116 paragraphs. A mere 8 paragraphs at the end of the whole document were entitled 'monetary arrangements (more especially in the absence of a Clearing

Union System)'. They contained, unattributed, the Bank's suggestions for developing the principle of the Tripartite Agreement while adding, *inter alia*: 'It is not yet clear how such a plan can be made compatible with the arrangements of the Sterling Area'.

The Bank saw this paper in draft, as early as the end of January, and decided to make the best of it rather than stand out in flat opposition. The Deputy Governor, a man of considerable wisdom, wrote a long and accommodating letter to Hopkins early in February. He expressed general agreement both with the draft's exposition and with its structure; but on the Clearing Union itself Catterns wrote: 'We still feel this danger (of being regarded as a panacea) should be underlined, although we are in general agreement with your critical survey of the Clearing Union proposals and with your conclusion that they might usefully be put forward in general form, but not dogmatically, as a target for discussion as a possible contribution to a new monetary mechanism.' Catterns added later in the letter, with reference to the Bank's own suggestions: 'We would stress that the two approaches are not alternative but may well even be complementary: whatever form of international exchange clearing is adopted there will have to be direct underlying agreements between the various monetary authorities for day-to-day settlements, which would be dealt with by a clearing mechanism.' The prevalence of organised exchange markets and convertible currencies, through which and in which individual monetary authorities could conduct official business, could not then be assumed. In their absence there had to be some other means of operational linkage between one authority and another. Catterns wrote again three days later suggesting that the draft concluding paragraphs on planning and direction were presented too apologetically and without sufficient emphasis on the constructive uses to which bilateral or multilateral agreements could be put or on the dangers to the world economy involved in blind acceptance of the US State Department's theory of non-discrimination.[16]

[16] The Deputy's letter also referred to the curious sub-plot of this story known as the 'Hansen–Gulick proposals', originated in the autumn of 1942 by the two American Professors of those names (who visited the UK with State Department blessing). In essentials, the proposals were designed to apply 'Keynesian' full employment policies on an internationally collaborative basis (initially, Anglo-American) through an International Economic Board, an International Resources Survey, and an International Development Corporation. The Treasury treated most of this construction with the polite circumspection that it deserved, but saw merit, rightly enough, in the idea of a post-war international long-term lending institution. Roy Harrod, however, became much more enthusiastic and contributed, as an Appendix to 'External Monetary and Economic Policy', a complete plan for linking the Hansen–Gulick institutions with the Clearing Union. For good measure he added an 'Anglo–American Buffer Stock Control' for regulating commodity prices. Predictably, the Bank viewed this with the utmost reserve. 'In particular', wrote Catterns,

B. G. Catterns, Deputy Governor 1936–1945

Most unfortunately, this broadly conciliatory response was to have little or no influence on the main message delivered to Ministers. On 10 March the Bank was sent for the first time a draft of the vital covering note to the

> 'we regard the suggestion to link up the Clearing Union proposals with the Hansen–Gulick proposals as wholly premature and as being more likely to confuse both issues.'

massive main paper. It was in virtually final form, for comment within twenty-four hours. Its emphasis was much more long-term than short-term. The transitional period, and all the foreground that seemed so important to the Bank, was given relatively little space. The note concluded with a list of principal questions for Ministers to consider. Pride of place went to the Clearing Union. Should UK representatives put it forward to the US, perhaps as an illustration of a possible means of attaining the objectives, as a basis for discussion and exploration? No questions were put that specifically related to the problems of transition. The Bank did not like being bounced in this manner. So Hopkins received next day a hurt and memorable response from Norman, sharply distancing the Bank from the advice being offered and from the whole philosophy of aligning the UK with the external economic strategy of the Roosevelt Administration. The Governor wrote as follows:

> You sent us last evening copies of a 'summary statement' on post-war external monetary and economic policy. From the facts that you ask for comments on this fundamental document by midday today and that the document is a 'revised draft' to be considered at a 'final meeting' this afternoon, I assume that you do not expect the Bank to make any serious contribution. I will therefore confine myself to making three observations – two general and one particular.
>
> The general tone of the body of the note does not in our view give a balanced summary of the longer document agreed some weeks ago. The emphasis appears to us in several respects faulty and likely to suggest to an objective reader various conclusions from which we dissent, e.g.
>
> (a) That this country must, in theory, renounce all regulation of international trade and payments while finding excuses for not being able to put this policy into force at once.
>
> We believe in the need for constructive planning and control.
>
> (b) That the prime objective in forming British post-war policy must be to conciliate the present US Administration.
>
> We believe in setting our own house in order.
>
> (c) That the post-war economic world can be run as an Anglo-American syndicate without taking much account of other countries.
>
> We have not forgotten Europe.
>
> The general tone of the summary of questions for Ministerial decision also appears to us to give a misleading picture of the nature of the problems to be faced and of their relative importance.
>
> In particular, I must add that in our view paragraph 9, which has little relation to the paragraphs of the earlier note which it purports to summarise, is inaccurate and misleading and should be dropped.

There was a further brief exchange of letters two weeks later. Norman, having achieved no more than a drafting amendment to one paragraph, closed the correspondence as follows: 'I note that you did not find it possible to take account of the points raised in my letter of 11 March except for the alterations in para. 26 of the short note, which I fear I must regard as a rather meagre crumb.' On 31 March the Treasury papers were discussed by the Reconstruction Committee of the War Cabinet and recommendations in the covering note were approved by the War Cabinet itself in April, without substantial amendment.

It was an unhappy outcome, leaving behind it an unnecessary but menacing tendency to disunity at the heart of UK monetary administration. It had been unwise of the Bank to underestimate the wartime potency and imaginative force of Keynes' proposals, the power of his philosophy, the growing strength of his political influence in the evolution of Anglo-American economic relations, and the increasing financial dependence of the UK on the US. It was sad that Norman, now nearly seventy, was unable to adopt the role of elder statesman at this point. For it would have cost the Bank little or nothing to have responded with greater sympathy at the outset instead of trying to suppress the Clearing Union entirely, albeit with strong initial encouragement from Treasury officials. And it would certainly have been better if the Bank had given earlier acknowledgement to the likely post-war limits to a closely knit Sterling Area system. But it was also impolitic and short-sighted of the other side to ignore Catterns' olive branch, to pass up that opportunity of achieving unity of purpose, and to trample on the Bank so obviously, at the very end, for the presumably immediate tactical purpose of focusing Ministerial minds on Keynes' vision of the longer-term. For the Clearing Union had indeed come to look a little like a panacea and the formidable problems of transition had indeed been played down. The Bank may have been placing too great a faith in controls of all sorts, but its judgement, and that of many others, about the scale and time-span of the transitional problems was not to prove faulty, nor was to be its judgement that the machinery of the longer-term had little to contribute to their solution.

As things stood in the spring of 1942, the Bank was to continue its close association with the discussions about post-war international monetary arrangements and to contribute much fruitful advice. But its strategic position was to remain sadly and unnecessarily distanced from that of Keynes.

(c) FROM THE MUTUAL AID AGREEMENT TO BRETTON WOODS:
TACTICAL ALLIANCE AND STRATEGIC DISAGREEMENT

Nearly eighteen months were now to elapse before formal consultations took place with the American authorities about the post-war monetary system. Over two years were to go by before the Bretton Woods Conference itself assembled. During the intervening period there was much manoeuvring. The British sought with some success to gain international support for the Clearing Union, whether from Commonwealth countries, from Latin America, or from the London Governments-in-exile of European Allies. But the US Administration considered that the size of the potential obligation on the US would render the Clearing Union unacceptable to Congress. So the Americans put forward a plan of their own, for what eventually became the IMF and the International Bank for Reconstruction and Development (IBRD). As the American position evolved, the Clearing Union faded from view and the British negotiating effort was concentrated wholly upon securing indispensable amendments to the American plan. For its part, the Bank waged a vigorous and largely successful campaign against the objectionable features it saw in the American proposals. It also developed its thinking about the adaptation of existing wartime external monetary arrangements to a prolonged period of transition from war to peace. As a result the Bank established a strong defensive position, arguing that its suggested adaptations of wartime machinery would either be complementary to a longer-term international regime that might emerge from negotiations with the US or be necessary if nothing came of those negotiations. From this redoubt the Bank continued from time to time to argue against the early establishment of any new international monetary institutions, other than 'forums' founded on broad statements of objectives; and at one point the Bank rashly joined a political attempt to persuade Ministers to change course. But the increasing concentration of minds on the problems of transition brought with it the growing conviction in Whitehall, firstly, that direct American assistance to the UK would be required on a very large scale during the transition and, secondly, that this would not be forthcoming unless the UK acceded to the Bretton Woods plans. For this reason, if for no other, the opponents of this monetary machinery had little chance of winning the day. But the matter did not end there. Concentration on the transition, for which the Bank had all along argued, meant concentration on the increasing overhang of sterling balances in London held by countries both in the Sterling Area and outside it; and it came to be realised that this problem could hardly be kept out of sight during any negotiations for

American post-war assistance. Here, of all places, an identity of view between the Bank and the Treasury, in practice Keynes himself, was needed. But here again a divergence was to become apparent and to remain largely unresolved.

An important coincident factor in the evolving relationship between Keynes and the Bank was the change in the Treasury high command that took place in the spring of 1942. Horace Wilson retired and was succeeded as Permanent Secretary by Hopkins. The next in line, Frederick Phillips,[17] had already moved to Washington in the special wartime post of Treasury Representative. So Hopkins was succeeded as Second Secretary in charge of the Finance Division by a newcomer to the Treasury, Wilfrid Eady, a skilled and clear-headed negotiator who had had a long career at the Ministry of Labour until becoming Chairman of the Board of Customs and Excise in 1941. In his new post he had to steer his way, and his Ministers' way, through the complexities and stresses of external monetary affairs, with Keynes on one side and the Bank on the other. He did not possess the temperament that would have enabled him to establish effective command over either, let alone both, but neither was he the man to fall under anyone's spell. Since Keynes was by now more of a spellbinder than the Bank, this sometimes meant that Eady appeared as a supporter of the Bank when in reality he was endeavouring to hold the ring between the two.

Close relations between Eady and the Bank took time to develop and it was to Phillips, who was in London for some weeks during the summer of 1942, that Cobbold sent a private copy of an interim Report of Siepmann's Committee on Post-war Exchange Policy. This Report had been put together in some urgency after the Cabinet's approval of the Clearing Union proposals. When putting it forward to the Governors, Cobbold wrote: 'I do not think that it should be regarded as a rival to the Keynes Plan or any other plans for international settlement of balances. A great part of it would in my view survive as the underlying machinery for any more ambitious plan for international settlement.' The Report was mainly a refined and elaborated development of the ideas put forward six months earlier. It looked ahead to a world of widespread exchange controls and of separate currency areas, each with a monetary centre. The Sterling Area would be one of these groupings, which would be linked multilaterally or bilaterally by agreements for the maintenance of stable exchange rates, for

---

[17] *Phillips, Frederick, GCMG (1884–1943).* Educated Haberdashers' Aske's School and Emmanuel College, Cambridge. HM Treasury 1908–43, Assistant Secretary 1919–27, Principal Assistant Secretary 1927–32, Under-Secretary 1932–40, HM Treasury Representative in US and Joint Second Secretary 1940–3.

inter-area currency accumulations, and for the ultimate gold settlement of such accumulations. These agreements would be operated by central banks acting as agents for Governments. An essential preliminary, for the UK, would be special arrangements for reducing to manageable size the wartime accumulations of sterling by *non*-Sterling Area countries (notably in South America).

Phillips' response to this, in a personal letter to Cobbold dated 26 June 1942, was emphatic in its rejection of what he offensively termed the 'Schachtmann memoranda'. The world of separate currency areas, though conceivably realistic, was a profoundly depressing prospect, full of collisions and ensuing trouble; while agreements between areas, unlike Keynes' proposals, would make no proper provision for the orderly correction of balance of payments disequilibria by internationally accepted means. Faced with this reception, the Bank bided its time and waited for the American response to the Keynes Plan, which was shown to Secretary Morgenthau at the end of August. This version contained provision for the special needs of the transitional period to be financed through the Clearing Union.

But the American authorities had been quietly preparing plans of their own. Indeed Morgenthau had first asked Harry White, his Director of Research, for such plans as early as December 1941. An outline was forthcoming within two weeks and further developed in the following months. After favourable responses from the State Department and the White House in the summer of 1942, a copy of the plan was handed to Phillips privately in September. Phillips sent it to Keynes, who had a long private meeting with White in the American Embassy in London on 13 October. (White had travelled to the UK with Morgenthau, but on other business.) Among the issues raised at this meeting, as between the two plans, were the contrasting obligations on creditor countries, the widely differing provisions with respect to alterations in exchange rates, and White's proposal for two institutions (a Fund and a Bank) compared to Keynes' proposal for one (the Clearing Union). These private discussions were kept very secret. There is no evidence that the Bank was told about the White Plan at this stage and its existence was withheld from the group of senior Commonwealth officials who met with Keynes, Phillips, and other Treasury officials in London at the end of October to consider, *inter alia*, the Clearing Union proposals. Meanwhile the Bank was being firmly advised by Thompson-McCausland – whom it had sent on an exploratory visit to North America in the late summer – that the UK would lose all chance of constructive American co-operation in the post-war period if it pursued a mainly bilateralist approach to international monetary and trading questions. Later, at the end of the year, came a warning from the Economic Section of the Cabinet Office that the UK would face a substantial external deficit in the early post-war years even if exports grew rapidly to 150% of their 1938 volume, even if there was no net capital outflow, and even if there was no substantial build-up of stocks. All the more important, then, to secure American co-operation.

Early in February 1943[18] the latest version of the White Plan was conveyed officially to the British authorities. Surprisingly, this version contained novel additional proposals for the post-war funding of excess sterling balances through their exchange into obligations of the new international Fund and assumption by the UK of a long-term debt to that Fund. The Bank looked it over and quickly found some pragmatic merit in the concept of a limited fund for use by countries in the last resort. But it became puzzled and suspicious on other counts – especially about the likelihood of the fund actively dealing in exchange markets as a stabilisation fund in that sense – and asked for clarification. Furthermore, it soon concluded that White's proposals for meeting the problem of the sterling balances, taken in the context of his proposals generally, carried possibly dangerous implications for the future of the Sterling Area and were in any case likely to impose a heavier annual burden on the UK than might well otherwise be the case.

These worries were duly expressed in letters written to Eady on 18 February and 2 March. At the same time, at Cobbold's instigation, a revised, more persuasive, and more internationalist version was prepared of the Report that had been so summarily rejected by Phillips nine months earlier. This version was called 'Sterling after the War' and was sent informally to Eady early in April. It began by stressing that while the new international institutions suggested by Keynes and White could provide machinery that would help in clearing final balances between monetary authorities and in supporting countries whose balance was adverse, the daily business of the world would be conducted through other channels. A structure would therefore be needed to carry the settlement of day-to-day transactions; and until a new international organisation was in being this structure would have to stand on its own feet and provide its own discipline. Moreover, in the absence of early agreement on the establishment of a new organisation, broad agreement between the principal

---

[18] The Keynes and White Plans, after a phase of some inter-governmental confusion and exchange, were published together early in April.

nations on fundamental questions of policy should urgently be sought. These were stability of exchange rates (and no unilateral alteration of rates), prevention of disruptive capital flows, maximum possible convertibility of currencies for current payments, and the provision of special finance for early post-war reconstruction.

The paper went on to argue the case for endeavouring to maximise the international use of sterling and to that end the primary importance of appropriate domestic economic policy. Next came exposition of the principal features of a strong post-war Sterling Area, including special treatment of exceptional wartime accumulations of sterling by India and Egypt. Accumulations by other members of the Area were considered to be manageable without such treatment. There then followed a broad description of the bridges that could be built between the Sterling Area and the monetary areas of Holland, Belgium, and France through payments agreements. These agreements would contain 'policy clauses' in line with the general agreement on objectives mentioned earlier, as well as reciprocal arrangements about currency accumulations and their ultimate settlement in gold. The policy clauses could be replaced by the rules of an international monetary institution as and when it was established. New payments agreements would also need to be made with Argentina and Brazil, including provision for the funding of wartime accumulations of sterling. Other countries in Latin America could be treated as part of the US dollar area.

Finally the paper looked to a variety of agreements with the European neutrals, and eventually with the ex-enemy countries. In summary, the Bank looked to the early establishment of current-account transferability for sterling over a large part of the world, comprising the Sterling Area, the monetary areas of the Western European allies, and part of Latin America. Full current-account convertibility of such sterling would not be allowed but would constitute an ultimate objective. When this was reached there would be only two kinds of sterling, 'resident' and 'external'. The paper concluded by suggesting early talks at technical level with the Dutch, Belgian, and possibly French authorities in London.

The Bank was putting forward plans that could serve as a complement to those of Keynes and White, as an alternative to them, or as features of a prolonged transitional period. In the second of these roles they amounted to a further presentation of the key-currency approach, with its pragmatic monetary collaboration within a group of leading and like-minded countries working mostly at central bank level, and with its conspicuous lack of emphasis on global blueprints or formulae for the provision of credit internationally, for the regulation of exchange rates world-wide, and for the general maintenance of external convertibility. But in this role they stood little chance of acceptance in opposition to the seemingly simple and idealistic global plan of the Keynes or White variety with its special appeal to wartime yearnings for a brave new world.

Over the spring and summer of 1943, as the prospect of substantive talks with the US Treasury grew nearer, it became clear to Whitehall that there was nothing to be gained by pressing on with the Clearing Union against American opposition. The Canadian authorities, who were preparing a compromise plan of their own, gave useful advice on this point. They urged that much could be gained if the UK were to table a set of compromise proposals based upon the fundamentals of the White Plan, and that failure to do so would only encourage the Americans to get entrenched in the Plan as it stood while successfully rallying their Latin American and other allies in opposition to the British proposals. In response, the Treasury concluded that the 'subscription' principle of White's stabilisation fund had to be accepted. This meant dropping the Clearing Union and concentrating on improvements to the American plan. Now, for once and for this limited purpose, the Bank and Keynes became allies. Earlier on Keynes had already been persuaded that White's ideas for dealing with abnormal sterling balances through the Fund were misconceived. Early in July Cobbold set out the Bank's specific objections in a trenchant memorandum that was sent to the Treasury. Later in that month Keynes himself circulated a note setting out what he regarded as essential revisions to the White Plan. These included, firstly, much more elastic provision for changes in exchange rates; secondly, a prohibition on the Fund actively dealing in exchange and gold markets; and, thirdly, a provision limiting mandatory gold subscriptions to $12\frac{1}{2}\%$ of quotas. A few days later Cobbold wrote: 'Subject to one or two points I agree with Lord Keynes... If Ministers confirm the essential conditions... and these decisions can be firmly held, many of our anxieties would be removed.' A month later Ministers did confirm the essential conditions as part of the terms of reference of the UK delegation, headed by Keynes, which would go to Washington in September.

But despite the agreement with Keynes on major points relating to the White Plan, the Bank remained suspicious lest in practice Keynes should concede too much to the Americans in the course of negotiation. So it suggested yet again to the Treasury that an alternative approach should be considered. Here, the views of Norman himself came to the surface. His mood was now more mellow. In June Towers had sent him a message from Ottawa, enclosing a copy of the Canadian plan and arguing that an alternative and bilateralist approach was very dangerous. The Governor replied majestically a fortnight later. 'We here', he wrote, 'are bound to look at all such plans not only from the standpoint of the world as a whole but also from that of the British Empire and this country.' He felt it would be unwise to assume that international agreement on methods of organising the foreign exchanges would lead to positive results if there were any doubts, 'as I believe there to be', about policy. 'For my part', he went on, 'whilst applauding much in these proposals and setting an international organisation as the distant goal, I should prefer to be less ambitious and to start somewhat nearer the ground'. In exact accord with the Governor's preference, Cobbold wrote to Eady on 9 August setting out yet again the Bank's arguments in favour of an alternative approach. Attached to it was a rough draft of the heads of agreement between the US and British Governments towards which this approach pointed. The letter represents a definitive statement of the Bank's position as then established. It read as follows:

> I mentioned to you the other day the possibility of a rather new approach to currency discussions with Washington and you asked me to let you have our more considered views.
>
> Our general feeling is that the whole subject is in danger of being submerged in a mass of complicated technical and mechanical detail, a great deal of which is highly controversial and most of which is entirely incomprehensible to the general public. This view is strongly reinforced by the latest drafts of SF (Stabilisation Fund) and by the long memorandum of answers to the questions sent over by the US Treasury. From what we know of American detailed ideas it seems unlikely that an agreed scheme of technical mechanism can be reached except after long and perhaps acrimonious argument. If HMG once get involved in argument about mechanism they obviously run the risk of being forced for political reasons into mechanical arrangements of which they do not really approve; the alternatives of accepting proposals which do not really enjoy HMG's support and of having an open dispute with the American Government are both unattractive.
>
> Moreover, it is surely unwise to seek to impose on public opinion a detailed mechanism which does not inspire general confidence. We do not believe that from the present state of negotiations any technical mechanism can emerge which will carry the wholehearted support and approval of the business and general public here and in America.
>
> I understood from you that the present intention is to open more comprehensive negotiations with the US Government on post-war financial and economic policy as a whole. Would it not be consistent with this line of approach to lift the currency discussions away from details and mechanics and to try to agree first on certain general basic principles? If such agreement could be reached between the UK and US Governments and then be confirmed by the United Nations, an international institution on a brief

and easily intelligible basis, including long-term as well as short-term international lending under its wing, might at a later stage prove helpful in carrying out those principles.

In the preliminary stages it is surely Anglo-American agreement on principles that is really important. It becomes daily more evident that in the post-war world sterling and the dollar will be the only important international currencies and that the real concern both of the British Empire and the USA and of the rest of the world is to see Anglo-American agreement on principles and adequate working arrangements between sterling and the dollar.

Other countries will doubtless tend to group themselves in varying degree around sterling and the dollar; and we know enough of what is in the minds at least of the European allies and France to be sure that we shall meet with few difficulties from them in agreeing on principles.

I attach a rough draft of the heads of agreement at which an approach on these lines might aim; but, for the reasons given above, I make no attempt at this stage to go into mechanical details.'

The Bank's alternative, though it now incorporated suggestions for new international lending institutions *subsequent* to international agreement on basic principles of policy, found no more favour in Whitehall at this juncture than it had done earlier. The Bank's warnings were heard but the Government, the Treasury, and Keynes himself were now far too far down the road to Bretton Woods, and much too deeply committed to the US Administration in that respect, to draw back. 'Policy' and 'method' could be, indeed had to be, negotiated concurrently; and reliance had therefore to be placed on obtaining the concessions, in negotiation with the US, that the Treasury and the Bank had already agreed were vital. Disarmingly for the Bank, these concessions were effectively secured by Keynes during the negotiations that began in Washington at the end of September.[19] Much more elastic draft provisions for changes in exchange rates, appropriate to the correction of a fundamental disequilibrium, were now incorporated. The exclusion of the Fund from intervention in exchange markets (now known as Fund passivity) was assured. The problem of the gold content of subscriptions was on the way to satisfactory solution. 'Scarce currency' arrangements were taking shape. The draft provisions for dealing with abnormal wartime accumulations of foreign exchange were dropped. Finally, it was agreed that special provisions should be prepared to cover the immediate post-war transitional period. Cassandra, so it seemed, had been wrong and Keynes had again won the day.

---

[19] Thompson-McCausland was temporarily seconded to the Treasury for the purpose of attending these negotiations. He kept the Bank informed in a series of letters to Cobbold.

But Cassandra obstinately refused to be comforted. Despite Cobbold's earlier view that many of the Bank's anxieties would be removed, its opposition continued, partly through refusal to admit that all the concessions obtained in Washington, particularly the one regarding passivity, could be as good as they seemed and partly by shifting ground, firstly by concentrating once more on the problems of the post-war transition and secondly by questioning the viability of the adjustment process contemplated in the draft provisions of the IMF. In this latter context, the Bank was again associated with economists whose view of the proposed international monetary agreement was directly opposed to that of Keynes and his associates. This view was now propounded in the Bank by its economic adviser, Henry Clay, and again in the Treasury by Hubert Henderson. Clay was an industrial economist and a structuralist, or an interventionist variety of what would later be called a 'supply-sider'. He was among those who believed that the underemployment problem of the British economy in the inter-war years was predominantly attributable not so much to the application of nineteenth-century macro-economic method in circumstances of a Keynesian underemployment equilibrium, but rather to its application in an economy afflicted with a major physical problem of industrial adjustment to the irrecoverable loss of export markets for some of its principal products.

Clay had been closely associated with the Bank's work on industrial rationalisation in the 1930s and had indeed been recruited by Norman for advice in that context. Along with many other economists, he was now thinking about the problem of adjustment that would face the UK after the war due to the foreseen loss of invisible earnings, worsening terms of trade, and the consequential need to achieve a massive and sustained increase in export volume above the pre-war level. In his view, too early and hasty adherence to an international regime of non-discrimination, relying heavily on regulated alterations in exchange rates as a principal, but in his view quite unreliable, means of external adjustment to structural change, would risk disastrously repeating the inter-war experience. Henderson was of much the same mind and both these economists therefore supported officials of the Bank who were already suspicious, if for different reasons, of the direction in which the Anglo-American currency proposals were moving. They remained suspicious lest, in the end, too much would have to be conceded to the State Department and the US Treasury and lest the prominence given to international monetary plans should damagingly divert political and public attention away from concentration on the menacing structural problems of the British economy. Keynes and his supporters were aware of these dangers but offered four heavyweight points in reply. Firstly, there would be the protection afforded by the dispensations allowed during the transitional period, whose length remained to be negotiated. Secondly, there would be the great long-term advantages that a maritime trading nation could expect to gain from a workable and on balance expansionist multilateral regime supported by the US with its post-war economic dominance. Thirdly, the proposed regime would neither prevent interventionist domestic industrial policies nor stop the use of such devices as exchange control and quantitative import restrictions by countries in balance of payments difficulties, provided the restrictions were non-discriminatory. Fourthly, and clinchingly, there was by now no prospect of a negotiable midway option, of the kind suggested by the Bank, between effective collaboration with the US along the lines already begun and a reversion to antagonistic bilateralism.

In debating terms these answers were convincing. Paradoxically, as things actually developed later in the post-war period, something not very different to the kind of approach favoured by the Bank in 1943 did in practice come about. Far from becoming a supranational monster, the Fund developed as a flexible institution that retained the broad objectives of its founders but had to pay very close attention to the views and interests of informal groupings of key-currency members. But it is very doubtful whether this useful state of affairs could ever have been brought into being, and some intervening period of acute struggle and disorder avoided, unless first of all the opportunities offered by the American Administration, which led to the Bretton Woods Agreements, had been taken. The Bank, with its anxieties, its suspicions, and its well-founded concern for the transitional period, simply could not see this at the time. So in the winter of 1943–4 it relentlessly maintained its advocacy of an alternative approach, while working hard with the Treasury to secure from Washington satisfactory provisions for the post-war transitional period. In this vital latter task the Bank now got strong support from Catto. For the future Governor had by this time become sufficiently alerted by the analyses of Henderson and Clay to issue a loud and prophetic warning to his colleagues in the Treasury against the risks of hands being tied during the transition. Following preliminary discussions in the autumn and a long series of meetings at the Treasury beginning late in November 1943 and attended by Cobbold, Bolton, and Clay, an agreed set of draft provisions governing the transitional period were sent to White by Keynes on 19 December together with a persuasive explanatory letter containing *inter alia* a strong hint that the UK would need special financial help during that transition. No specific length was given to the period, but a member's retention of discriminatory practices for longer than three years would require consultation with the Fund. Early in January 1944 the US Treasury indicated acceptance of these draft provisions, with only minor amendments. In a note to the Governor dated 13 January, Cobbold stated: 'We must regard White's reply as reasonably satisfactory', but added: 'Actually it might have suited us better if he had argued about the transitional period and so drawn out the discussions.'

It was now Election Year in the US and the Roosevelt Administration was anxious to proceed as soon as possible to a full and formal international monetary conference that would secure agreement to set up the proposed new international institutions. In London this meant a fresh Ministerial decision whether or not to go ahead on the basis of drafts now broadly agreed with the US Treasury. In Threadneedle Street, without Norman, this meant a final slender opportunity to stop the whole plan. The Bank sailed into this opportunity, unwisely, for it had been driven into a corner from which it could only oppose the plan by the force and bluster that the other side could easily expose for what it was. The attempt even involved the Old Lady parading arm in arm with Lord Beaverbrook, of old one of Norman's bitterest critics. They must have made a very unconvincing couple.[20]

In his note of 13 January Cobbold openly voiced the Bank's deep suspicions of American interference with sterling, attributing dollar-imperialist and anti-London motives to the US Administration, while Clay concurrently opened a sweeping, angry, and telling attack with the sentences: 'The Keynes and White Schemes are among the most dangerous obstacles to a restoration of international trade. They have diverted attention from dealing with the needs of actual trade – framing commercial policy, providing finance for reorganisation and re-equipment etc. – to attractive but futile dodges such as varying exchange rates; this on top of successfully blocking any serious consideration of commercial policy for over a year.' A month later the Deputy Governor and Cobbold gave evidence to a Ministerial group chaired by the Chancellor of the Exchequer. In response to a short questionnaire sent to the Bank in advance they argued, firstly, that the Fund would work against the international acceptability of sterling because it would be gold- and dollar-orientated; secondly, that the exchange market passivity of the Fund and its exclusion from market transactions was not assured by present plans; and, thirdly, that, for several reasons, in particular the need to control all capital movements, the working of the scheme would make it necessary to

---

[20] The Bank and the Beaver appeared together in a cartoon by David Low the following summer.

impose damaging exchange controls against and within the Sterling Area. Two days later the Bank submitted a short note to the Ministerial group, setting out yet another version of the key-currency approach. On 1 March Cobbold saw Beaverbrook, a member of the Ministerial group, at the latter's request and with the Chancellor's consent. He argued that acceptance of the proposed legal obligation of fixed-rate convertibility would resemble a return to the rigidities of the gold standard, which Beaverbrook loathed, whereas under the Bank's own plan the UK would be free to alter in the light of events both the degree of *de facto* convertibility that it allowed and the rate of exchange. Beaverbrook subsequently put in a note of his own to the group, strongly supporting the Bank and looking 'with horror on the alternative Plan because it destroys the Sterling Area'.

With Beaverbrook dissenting, the Ministerial group recommended in favour of proceeding on the basis of the existing draft plans, though with an eye to points made by the Bank it expressed misgivings regarding Fund passivity, the position of the Sterling Area, and the draft arrangements for the transitional period. These recommendations were considered and accepted by the Cabinet on 24 February. On the previous day Keynes addressed a powerful Minute to the Chancellor, which was not copied to the Bank. He first dismissed the latter's technical objections, with some truth, as 'not much more than stalking horses' and then went on to demolish the case he considered underlay the Bank's alternative approach. It would mean going ahead without any confident expectation of transitional assistance from the US, while at the same time somehow achieving a visible external balance and maintaining a high level of discipline in the rest of the Sterling Area. The former would imply a level of austerity quite inconsistent with current Ministerial plans for post-war Britain. He concluded:

> The Bank is not facing any of the realities. They do not allow for the fact that our post-war domestic policies are impossible without further American assistance. They do not allow for the fact that the Americans are strong enough to offer inducements to many or most of our friends to walk out on us, if we ostentatiously set out to start up an independent shop. They do not allow for the fact that vast debts and exiguous reserves are not, by themselves, the best qualification for renewing old-time international banking.

In a letter to Beaverbrook on 8 March Keynes was even less restrained. 'You speak', he wrote, 'of the Bank having a plan. I have never seen anything from them which deserves this name. They could be described as having a prejudice in favour of an atmosphere. But as for a plan, it has never been produced... The Bank is engaged in a desperate gamble in the interests of old arrangements and old-fashioned ideas, which there is no possibility of sustaining. Their plan, or rather their lack of plan would, in my firm belief, lead us into yet another smash.' He concluded: 'the whole thing is sheer rubbish from beginning to end. For God's sake have nothing to do with it!' A little over two years later, just as the Bank feared, he was himself to engage in as desperate a gamble in a different cause but with like consequences.

The Bank had again lost, this time heavily, and Keynes had again won. A joint American and British statement by experts on the proposed IMF was issued as a White Paper in April and the principles contained therein were subsequently debated in Parliament and approved. Keynes himself spoke in the Lords' Debate on 23 May. Most of his speech was devoted to arguing the great positive advantages of the monetary system implied by the plan, but he also took this further opportunity to contradict those who either considered that joining the Fund would closely resemble a return to the Gold Standard or else that the scheme would undermine the Sterling Area. The Bretton Woods Conference was convened for July, with Keynes as a successful leader of the UK delegation. He was accompanied from the Bank by Bolton, who often regarded the procedures with amused detachment and sent back reports to Cobbold in London.[21] Threadneedle Street was down but not out. Catto (now Governor) wrote to the Chancellor on 7 June, arguing that the clause committing members unconditionally to external current-account convertibility after the end of the transitional period should be considerably softened. Not surprisingly, the new Governor failed in this endeavour, though he secured Treasury advocacy of useful clarificatory amendments to the relevant draft articles of the Fund. The Chancellor, replying to the Governor on 14 June, wrote: 'One of the main purposes of the scheme is to introduce some degree of certainty into international payments by a formal recognition that currencies are to be convertible, and your suggestion would, I think, be regarded by the Americans and others as cutting at the root of this obligation.'

Not before time the emphasis of thinking in the Treasury and the Bank now shifted away from Bretton Woods itself and onto the external

---

[21] The Conference itself became very congested. On 14 July Bolton reported: 'At the beginning of this week we were so far behind schedule that desperate measures were introduced. Keynes, who was made Chairman of the Commission concerning the IBRD, began a system of taking a meeting so quickly that no one could understand either what he was saying or to which clause he happened to be referring and by this means about half the clauses were referred to a Drafting Commission. The fun began after this process had been completed...'

financial problems of the transition. Indefatigably, Keynes had already set the ball rolling in a long paper dated 11 January 1944; and indefatigably the Bank had again taken issue with a large part of his thinking about the Sterling Area.

(d) THE SETTING OF THE TRAP: FROM BRETTON WOODS TO VJ DAY

Keynes' paper of January 1944 foresaw a total Sterling Area deficit (including that of the UK) of some £700–1,000 million over the first two post-war years. After allowing for a run-down of UK reserves, help from Canada, and some further run-up of sterling held by Latin American countries, he identified a need to obtain some £500 million (or $2 billion) of assistance from the US. This would be too large for the market, or the Federal Reserve, and would therefore need to be a Government loan at a special low rate of interest. An essential adjunct to this arrangement would be a deal with Sterling Area countries whereby the abnormal element in their London balances would be funded and their individual dollar outgoings restricted to the level of their individual dollar income. Keynes saw some danger that external financial arrangements on these lines would make life too easy for the UK, postponing needed adjustment; but the austere alternative would be even more awkward.

The Bank's initial response to Keynes' initiative was to accept his outline of the problem but to explain that uniform treatment could not be agreed with the diverse membership of the Sterling Area and could not be applied to the diverse nature of the sterling balances themselves. Instead the problem could best be met by the working out of informal understandings rather than the negotiation of formal rules. Concentration of the problem in the balances of India and Egypt was stressed. Predictably, Keynes in turn felt that in this context, just as in that of the IMF proposals, the Bank was overestimating what could be done with the Sterling Area through informal approaches. He then reworked his paper and a fresh version was circulated on 18 May. But some two weeks beforehand the new Governor had added his own voice, this time attacking the idea of a large US loan. Catto felt strongly that a large long-term loan, with fixed annual servicing, would lead once again to recrimination and default. He was, in his words, bitterly opposed to it and instead favoured either some continuation into peacetime of outright US aid or some form of secured interest-free credit on which the UK could draw as necessary and either repay in due time or else amicably forfeit the security. The Governor was to retain this personal view throughout all the subsequent episodes. His preference for aid rather than a loan was to be largely shared by Keynes and senior officials in the Treasury, but his suggestion of a secured credit was regarded as idiosyncratic and impracticable and was never a starter.

The revised version of Keynes' paper was not only a more polished and comprehensive treatment of the subject; it developed a sense of urgency and impatience with Whitehall attitudes that was unaccustomed music to ears in Threadneedle Street. On the point of departure for Bretton Woods, Keynes of all people was even able to write: 'Time and energy being given to the Brave New World is wildly disproportionate to what is being given to the Cruel Real World, towards which our present policy is neither brave nor new.' Further, with regard to borrowing from the US he argued against doing any such thing except on British terms. Within the Bank, Niemeyer, Cobbold, and Bolton immediately warmed to Keynes' attitude on these aspects of the matter, but presciently doubted whether it would prove possible to obtain money from the US in the form of a grant-in-aid. Congressional approval would be needed and after the war Congress would not be in a giving vein. Bolton in particular felt that it would not be possible to avoid borrowing by way of a loan at commercial rates and that it would be better to get this without strings on the New York market rather than through the political apparatus in Washington.

As to the arrangements to be made with the Sterling Area, the Bank and Keynes unfortunately continued to differ, if not on one aspect then on another. The Governor wrote to Hopkins early in July 1944, while Keynes was at Bretton Woods, setting out a fuller analysis of the diverse nature of the sterling balances and going on to suggest in greater detail than hitherto the informal understandings that the Bank had in mind. Firstly, members would agree not to reduce their sterling balances below the level reached at the end of the war except by agreed annual amounts. Secondly, members would agree to adopt house-in-order domestic policies. Finally, it would be agreed that accumulated balances should mostly be held in Treasury Bills, or on accounts at banks, bearing a very low rate of interest. There would, it went without saying, be no formal blocking of balances. On his return from Bretton Woods, weary but buoyed up by his personal success, Keynes viewed these suggestions with irritation. He contrasted them unfavourably with 'my plan'. They were too 'ad hoc' and would prove unreliable. Moreover, the proposal that agreement should relate to the post-war run-down of balances as such rather than, as he had proposed, to a combination of eventual agreed run-down and a restriction of each country's dollar expenditure in line with its dollar income, was in his view most misguided. On 13 August he sent to Treasury colleagues a terse memorandum to this effect, including an offensive paragraph[22] that disappeared in the version sent East. But the Bank now picked itself up and responded effectually to Keynes' argument. Firstly, it would be impracticable, inequitable, and contrary to the entire basis of multilateral collaboration within the Sterling Area if the dollar expenditure of each member were to be strictly related to its dollar income. Secondly, in the early post-war scramble for manufactures, a formal arrangement that discriminated strongly in favour of UK exports would in practice encounter supply constraints that would merely cause British exports that would otherwise have earned dollars or gold to be diverted to soft currency markets. Accordingly it would be much better to reply on informal and flexible 'gentlemen's agreements' to economise on dollar outgoings as need be instead of imposing a strict and formal rule in advance.

With his dispute with the Bank about the future of the Sterling Area unresolved, Keynes went back to the US in September 1944 and did not return until December. He was engaged in a series of complex but successful negotiations about 'Stage II', the foreseen interval between the end of the war in Europe and the defeat of Japan.[23] Lend-Lease on a reduced scale would continue and some permitted revival of British exports in preparation for Stage III would be accepted by the US, as would some further and substantial rebuilding of the British exchange reserves. But success with negotiating Stage II was now beginning ominously to undermine Keynes' judgement about the possibilities for Stage III, the period after the defeat of Japan. On 6 November he wrote to the Governor from Washington of his 'ever-growing belief that we are among friends here and that if only we can make them see the facts of the position as we

[22] It appears in the version published in *John Maynard Keynes: Collected Writings* (29 vols., Macmillan and Cambridge University Press for the Royal Economic Society, 1971–83) and reads: 'In substance the Bank's proposal is the same as that which they produced about six months ago and was fully discussed in Sir R. Hopkins' room with the Deputy Governor and Cobbold. We then produced arguments which we thought had shaken them. They now come back, however, without any reference to those arguments, or any attempt to meet them. Alas, one might as well speak to stone walls.' Perhaps he should have said 'a dialogue of the deaf'.

[23] For a time these were simultaneously and rather erratically conducted in tandem by Keynes and Cherwell (Professor of Physics at Oxford, but at that time Paymaster General, with a seat in the Cabinet, and personal adviser to the Prime Minister). Both paid court to 'Morgy', but with differing approaches. Some years later, in the aftermath of the 1952 'Robot' episode, Cherwell's junior staff (of which the author was a member) asked him: 'What would Keynes have said in this situation?' The Professor replied caustically and without any hesitation; 'Oh, *he* would already have changed his mind six times'; and he went on to add that by now Keynes would anyway have irritated everyone 'because he was so rude'. The Professor, himself without doubt one of the rudest men of his time, went on to recount as an example of Keynes' rudeness how they had both had a meeting with Morgenthau, at the end of which the latter had invited them both to the theatre. The Professor, anxious to please though easily bored to tears, had at once effusively accepted. Keynes had merely answered: 'What's the play?'

see them ourselves, they will reach the same conclusions'. He was now at the zenith of his power. Though formally no more than an adviser to the Treasury, his position had in practice become something akin to a monetary proconsul, with his own official, political, academic, and diplomatic network, and with freedom to speak in the Upper House of Parliament in support of external financial policies largely of his own construction. In the special field of Anglo-American wartime financial diplomacy he had achieved a personal success that disarmed criticism. His extraordinary intellectual capacity and stamina enabled him to produce long, complicated, and highly persuasive memoranda whose arguments, quantities, and proposals he could then propel almost unaided through successive phases of discussion, negotiation, and adaptation to apparently triumphant conclusions. Everyone else in the game, including the Bank of England, was by now a long way behind.

In March 1945 Keynes circulated his famous paper on 'Overseas Financial Policy in Stage III', which was to form the basis of his approach to the American Administration in the following September. A revised version was circulated to Ministers during May and at the end of that month the Bank was drawn into discussions about it in the Treasury. In the meantime the war in Europe had ended, Roosevelt had died and been succeeded by Truman, and in Britain the wartime Coalition had broken up and a General Election campaign had begun.

Keynes' great paper was long, magisterial, and lyrical. It sought to conjure up the vision of a grand financial settlement between the US, Canada, and the Sterling Area based upon a just division, among victors, of the burdens left behind by the war. This vision was termed 'Justice', in contrast to 'Starvation Corner' (making do without American help) and 'Temptation' (accepting American help on onerous American terms). Orders of magnitude had been transformed by prolongation of the war. The deficit in Stage III, foreseen a year earlier as up to $4 billion, could now be $6 billion or even as high as $8 billion. There would be some help from Canada and from a run-down of the UK's own reserves. But there would be little or no help from anywhere else except the Americans, *who would require a special quid pro quo in return*. Instead of the $2 billion suggested in February 1944, Keynes now proposed that, in exchange for a substantial grant-in-aid of $3 billion together with a $5 billion line of credit at a token rate of interest and easy terms of repayment, the UK would effectively undertake external convertibility, in the Bretton Woods sense, only one year after the end of the war.[24] Within that brief interval the UK would arrange settlements with Sterling Area countries so that

---

[24] At this stage, *formal* abandonment of the protection afforded by Article XIV of the IMF, after one year, was not proposed.

broadly a quarter of their balances would be written off (as a contribution to the cost of the war), a quarter would be left liquid and fully convertible, and the remaining half would be funded. The total of the balances to be so treated was estimated at £3 billion, or $12 billion. Members who refused to play would find their balances frozen.

Keynes then argued that Starvation Corner was not wholly impracticable but could lead to serious political and social disruption at home, to withdrawal for the time being from the position of a first-class power, to American hostility, and to defections from the Sterling Area. Temptation, he judged, would be beguilingly easy to negotiate but would mean a large loan at a commercial rate of interest, too heavy a burden of servicing, and the granting of external current-account convertibility from the outset, probably without a prior settlement of the sterling balances. Hard bargaining might elicit better terms so that Temptation would at least be better than Starvation Corner, but 'the sweet breath of Justice' between partners, in what had been a great and magnanimous enterprise carried to overwhelming success, would have been sacrificed to some false analogy of business. Even then Uncle Sam might quite likely remain under the conviction that he was Uncle Sap, a conviction which can only be removed by making him enter into the meeting-place by a different door'. This entrance amounted to a frontal and emotional assault in the name of Justice, in the confident hope that Uncle Sam would see it all Keynes' way.

But this poetic thought and phraseology, typical of the whole paper and its author, contained a tragic misjudgement whose effect was to be compounded by the unexpectedly early termination of Stage II.[25] The misjudgement was detected in the Bank, by the Treasury in London, and by the Treasury team in Washington. But with the end-war turmoil of tired relief at the moment of victory and the abrupt return to peacetime politics, Keynes carried all before him as the months elapsed and the need for Stage III negotiations grew closer. This process was assisted by the visit of a small high-level team that arrived towards the end of May from Ottawa and included the Governor of the Bank of Canada. With Keynes in the chair and the Permanent Secretary playing second fiddle,[26] the Treasury discussed Stage III with the Canadians over a weekend at King's College, Cambridge. Cobbold attended from the Bank. The visitors were informed from the chair, though informally, that British thinking (in fact,

[25] It is clear that throughout these months the policy makers in the Treasury had no inkling that a nuclear bomb might be used against Japan. If they had known, they might have made better policy.
[26] Hopkins was on the point of retirement from the top post, to be succeeded by Edward Bridges, Secretary to the War Cabinet.

Keynes' thinking) had moved away from the idea of a long transition because it would damage the development of world trade, damage the position of London as a financial centre, damage the prospects of sustained full employment, and lead to persistent friction within the international monetary community. They were then given an outline of Justice. The Canadians were themselves anxious to safeguard post-war markets for their exports outside North America and to this end were prepared to lend the UK money on generous terms. Accordingly they had no objection to Justice. Instead Towers warned against irritating the Americans by too heavy a presentation of Starvation Corner and suggested that loans on generous terms were as acceptable as gifts. He agreed with Keynes that selling Justice to the US would require great skill, but in no way warned that the attempt should not be made. As Catto recorded with disapproval two days later after Towers had called at the Bank: 'Towers thinks we should beg and borrow all we can and not worry about the consequences.'

A week later, at a meeting in the Treasury, Keynes was warned by Frank Lee[27] (from Brand's[28] staff in the Treasury Office in Washington) and by Gordon Munro[29] (from the High Commission in Ottawa) that Justice would be almost impossible to achieve in the climate now developing in Washington, especially in Congress, since the end of the war in Europe and since the change of President. Lee suggested an alternative. It might be better to go for some interim arrangement, along the lines of prolonging Lend-Lease, if VJ Day were to occur before a full settlement on satisfactory terms could be approached. From the Bank, Thompson-McCausland warned against attempting to coerce the Sterling Area into the drastic

---

[27] *Lee, Frank Godbould, PC, GCMG, KCB (1903–71).* Educated Brentwood School and Downing College, Cambridge. Colonial Office 1926–40, HM Treasury 1940–4, Treasury delegation, Washington 1944–6, Ministry of Supply 1946–8, Deputy Secretary 1947–8, Minister, Washington 1948–49, Permanent Secretary, Ministry of Food 1949–51, Permanent Secretary, Board of Trade 1951–9, HM Treasury (Joint) 1960–2. Master, Corpus Christi College, Cambridge 1962–71.

[28] *Brand, Robert Henry, 1st Baron 1946 (1878–1963).* Educated Marlborough and New College, Oxford. Fellow of All Souls College, Oxford, Colonial Service (South Africa) 1902–09. Partner, Lazards 1913–19, a Managing Director 1919–44, Director 1949–60 Member of Macmillan Committee on Finance and Industry 1930–1. Head of British Food Mission, Washington, 1941–4, Representative of HM Treasury in Washington 1944–6, Chairman, British Supply Council in North America 1942 and 1945–6.

[29] *Munro, Richard Gordon, KCMG, MC (1895–1967).* Educated Wellington and Royal Military College, Sandhurst. Army 1914–23. Helbert Wagg 1923–46, a Managing Director 1934–46. Financial Adviser to UK High Commissioner in Canada 1941–6, HM Treasury Representative in US and Minister, British Embassy, Washington 1946–9, UK Executive Director and Alternate Governor, IBRD 1947–9, Financial Adviser to Government of Southern Rhodesia and Chairman, Southern Rhodesia Currency Board 1950–2, High Commissioner for Southern Rhodesia in the UK 1953, HM Government Representative on Board of British Petroleum 1954–6.

surgery proposed. Threats of blocking would not be credible. Lee's opinion was identical with written advice sent by Brand himself in a succession of letters he wrote to Keynes at this time. This advice could not be ignored. In a reply dated 24 April, and written in a prescient interlude, Keynes said: 'I regard the difficulty of putting all this (Justice) across as quite enormous. What will finally come out is likely to be materially different, and it will be extraordinarily difficult not to be led into some unbalanced settlement which we shall subsequently regret. Various versions of Temptation will always be lying round the corner.' But he did not give up. He was able to take comfort from the prospect that VJ Day would not arrive until, say, early in 1946. This would postpone the day of financial reckoning and, if negotiations began in September 1945, give time for the Americans to be brought round to the real merits of Justice. He was even able to contemplate surviving an initial rebuff.

Three weeks later Thompson-McCausland circulated a paper in the Bank attacking Keynes' proposals on many counts. The Americans would not provide money to help the UK with the problem of the Sterling Area. In so far as they provided money to help the UK itself, the early-convertibility string attaching to it would be a dangerous hostage to the future. The plan for the Sterling Area was unworkable. The whole dramatic dichotomy between disastrous austerity and acceptance of massive American largesse was misguided. An alternative and better approach would be to seek agreements with the Sterling Area first – and in particular with India and Egypt, on whose behalf the bulk of the abnormal balances were held – before making an approach to the US that would aim to borrow up to $3 billion against the dollar needs of the UK itself over the ensuing four or five years. Parts of this were reflected, though in lower key, in a note sent by Cobbold to Keynes early in July. The Bank warned against linking discussions with the US to discussions with the Sterling Area, suggested that American help might best be related to the UK's own need for essential supplies from the US during the transitional period, and advised against attempting any uniform settlement with the Sterling Area.

At the end of July, as new Ministers were taking office, there were further meetings and further letters, while across the Atlantic Morgenthau left office and was succeeded as Secretary of the Treasury by Fred Vinson,[30]

---

[30] *Vinson, Frederick Moore (1890–1953)*. Educated Centre College, Kentucky. City Attorney, Louisiana 1913, Commonwealth Attorney, Kentucky 1921–4, Member of Congress 1923–9, 1931–8, Associate Justice, Court of Appeals for District of Columbia 1938–43, Chief Judge, US Emergency Court of Appeal 1942–3. Director, Office of Economic Stabilisation 1943–5, Vice-Chairman, US delegation to Bretton Woods Conference 1944, Director, Office of War Mobilisation and Reconversion 1945, Secretary of US Treasury

'an unknown quantity' as Bolton put it, though he had been helpful at Bretton Woods. On 23 July Cobbold attended a meeting held by Keynes at the Treasury at which the former's earlier note was discussed.[31] Keynes appeared to concede that uniform treatment of the Sterling Area was not feasible, that the Americans should not be a party to Sterling Area negotiations, and that it would be unwise to earmark part of the proposed US assistance for Sterling Area purposes. But he maintained that the UK would have to explain to the Americans in general terms what it was proposing to do about the Sterling Area. This was certainly correct, but the distinction between explaining in general terms and giving the impression of proposing uniform treatment was a treacherously narrow one that Keynes was subsequently unable to convey. On the vital question of the timing of external convertibility, Cobbold recorded as follows:

> This led to a discussion on the question of convertibility, during which Lord Keynes made it clear that in his view if the USA gave us the help proposed we should have to abandon the idea of a transitional period and accept the full Bretton Woods obligations from a fixed date, e.g. one year after VJ Day. Mr Brand expressed doubts whether the Americans would expect us to do this or whether we were wise in accepting the full obligations of Bretton Woods so soon. Others expressed doubts about the effect on our general payments arrangements of accepting full Bretton Woods obligations at an early stage and it was generally felt that this subject needed a lot of further exploration.

This record was sent to the Treasury on 24 July and followed by a letter to Eady on 26 July in which Cobbold fully expressed the Bank's increasing concern about the convertibility proposed in Justice. His concern was intensified by the realisation that Keynes was now proposing the worldwide external convertibility of sterling, in the full *de jure* Article VIII sense, and not just convertibility for Sterling Area countries. After developing an argument that the right to suspend convertibility if things went wrong would not in practice prove to be a worthwhile safeguard, Cobbold wrote[32] in characteristic vein:

1945–6, First Chairman, Board of Governors, IMF and IBRD 1946. Chief Justice of the US 1946–53.

[31] At least three records of this meeting exist. One, by H. K. Goschen (Treasury), one by Cobbold, and one by Siepmann (who was also present and thought that much of the discussion was confused). All recount Keynes conceding the Bank's main points regarding the Sterling Area, but only the two Bank records mention a discussion of the proposed timing of external convertibility and Brand's comment thereon. The omission of this from the Treasury record is surprising. In a reply to Cobbold on the 30 July, Eady said: 'We have only had a very short record prepared'.

[32] In a manuscript note to Bolton dated 25 July he said: 'Keynes has got it in his head that we should get rid of "transitional period" early – and HMT have some idea that we can rely on right to suspend convertibility.'

I believe that a great deal of 'non-discrimination' on current purchases could be arranged within the existing exchange control and payments agreement framework. I believe a move in this direction would be far safer than any undertaking 'to end the transitional period' at an early date, which would presumably mean abandoning the existing exchange control and payments agreement framework. I was interested to hear Brand's view that non-discrimination would probably satisfy the Americans and that they might think us rash to abandon our 'transitional period' rights too quickly. I believe that it would be rash in the extreme and that, on the contrary, if we are to fulfil our obligations about exchange rate stability, our best chance of doing so is by gradual development of our existing arrangements. In any case, I do not believe that we should place any reliance as a safeguard on an eventual right to suspend convertibility.

No written reply to this letter exists, though Keynes did apparently revert to the *de facto* convertibility of his earlier position. There was in fact little that could be said. Eady and others may have had their qualms. Brand, though a sympathiser with Justice, may have thought convertibility, *de facto* or *de jure*, 'a great leap in the dark' and 'a gamble, even if the world goes moderately well', as he had told Keynes in a letter written at the end of June. But the latter had now effectively locked himself into his vision of Justice such that his flexible mind could do little more than invent confident assertions to justify throwing away the key; for him there was simply no alternative. In a sharp rejoinder dated 9 July to Eady and Otto Clarke, who had prepared a fall-back plan against a failure to obtain Justice, Keynes put his reputation behind the rash judgement that there was little serious risk of an overall shortage of gold and dollars in the first three post-war years. Two days later, in a letter to Brand, he wrote: 'If in the course of the next two or three years we are able to overcome our overseas deficit then we shall certainly have been wise to have adopted convertibility and all will be well. If, on the other hand, we fail, then no alternative plan would have been in any degree better. No doubt convertibility would break down, but so would any conceivable arrangement.' The difficulty with this argument was the hidden assumption that the UK could overcome its external deficit in conditions where it would be bound by agreement to trade without discrimination or inconvertibility, in full competition with the US, while most of the non-dollar world would continue to be at liberty to discriminate against the UK. Thoughts of this kind, articulated differently, lay behind Cobbold's letter of 24 July.

The Bank had now delivered its last word on convertibility before Keynes moved ahead with his plan in the following month. On the next day the Governor himself wrote to the incoming Chancellor, arguing the case against a long-term loan and in favour of an interest-free secured credit of $4 billion. He also felt that in going for a grant of $3 billion, in addition to a loan, Keynes would be aiming altogether too high. He suggested $1½ billion would be better. It is not clear on what basis the Governor had arrived at a total of $5¼ billion, in a note that still referred in specific terms to the $8 billion in Keynes' original proposals for Justice, but he was perhaps unwittingly getting near a new number taking shape in Keynes' mind in response to advice and warnings from Washington.

This advice was powerfully reinforced early in August when Assistant Secretary of State Clayton[33] visited London, with two colleagues, for informal discussions at official level about, *inter alia*, Stage III. Keynes had all along been correct in his view that the Americans would seek to trade a large dollar credit in exchange for effective British abandonment of the Bretton Woods transitional period together with a radical treatment of the sterling balances. Clayton in the State Department and White in the US Treasury had both been arguing in favour of such a course, the former thinking in terms of a loan as small as $3 billion. So Clayton's firm advice to Keynes in London was that a gift by the US was most unlikely and that a loan in excess of $5 billion was not on the cards. Opinion in the Administration was thinking of $3 billion, at interest. Clayton also made it clear that in his view a drastic reduction in the transitional period, together with understandings about commercial policy, would be required in exchange for a loan. Keynes put up a spirited resistance to the notion that the UK could prudently and honourably concede so much for so little. He pleaded for an 'inspired solution', but Clayton gave him no encouragement. Hints that the UK would rather go down the bilateralist road than agree to so bad a deal with the US cut no ice. The Bank of England was not a party to these discussions and there is no evidence of its being informed about them.[34]

The Treasury was now getting boxed into an awkward corner. The numbers of American help contained in Keynes' earlier plan were clearly unrealistic and would have to be reduced. Yet a number as low as $5 billion, let alone anything lower, would be difficult to reconcile with those in the rest of the plan for the prospective UK deficit and other calls on

---

[33] *Clayton, William Lockhart (1880–1966)*. Left school at thirteen. Deputy Clerk and Master, Chancery Court, Jackson, Tennessee at fifteen. Court Reporter. American Cotton Co., New York 1896–1904, Partner, later Chairman, Anderson, Clayton and Co. 1904–40. Entered Government Service 1940. Coordinator, Inter-American Affairs, Deputy Federal Loan Administrator, Assistant Secretary of Commerce, Administrator of Surplus War Property, Assistant Secretary of State in charge of Economic Affairs, Under-Secretary of State for Economic Affairs.

[34] A paper by Clayton on a proposal to establish an International Trade Organisation, handed to UK officials on 4 August, was not received in the Bank until 23 October.

external resources. Worse still, there was the probability that interest would have to be paid on the sum borrowed. Thus there was a danger that something very like Temptation would have to be offered to a new Government whose dedication to the ideals of Bretton Woods could by no means be taken for granted. In response to this situation Keynes was preparing a new version of his plan in a form that might serve as a brief for an oral presentation of the British position at the proposed Stage III discussions in September. A first draft was circulated in the Treasury on 13 August and a revised version was submitted to a group of senior Ministers. Suddenly, on 14 August, Japan surrendered and on the 20th the British Government was informed that Lend-Lease would terminate with immediate effect. Stage III had begun, with nothing negotiated.

Keynes' revised plan conveniently substituted $5 billion for $8 billion as the measure of required assistance; but the projected UK deficit over 1946–8 remained $7 billion and the cost of early convertibility, for the Sterling Area alone, would not be negligible. Canadian assistance, use of half the UK reserves, and some early further run-up of sterling balances prior to convertibility, together with an assumption that sterling held by non-sterling countries would not fall, just filled the gap if $5 billion was forthcoming from the US. But this left no margin for contingencies and the UK would end up with reserves of only $1 billion. Anything less than $5 billion would clearly not suffice and on these numbers $5 billion itself was in fact too little. Nonetheless, the remnants of Justice remained. Despite Clayton's advice, the revised plan still proposed a grant-in-aid, for the whole $5 billion, rather than any kind of loan. The aim was 'to organise, so far as may be, a liquidation of the financial consequences of the war amongst all those chiefly concerned who have won a common victory by a common effort'. The plan was discussed at a meeting chaired by the Prime Minister late on 23 August. Keynes was present, as were Bridges, Eady, and Brand. Since the Governor had not been invited, the Bank's voice was not heard. Keynes' presentation was effective in a situation said to require an immediate decision. Ministers accepted his proposal to travel to North America as soon as possible and open negotiations on the basis of his revised plan, *ad referendum* to London as and when necessary. Keynes left London three days later, rather like Scott pressing on to the South Pole.

The trap had been set. Despite all the discussions, refinements, and misgivings, the negotiations were still to begin with a frontal assault by Keynes, in the unstated name of Justice, with virtually his entire position revealed, if not at the outset then very soon afterwards. Early abandonment of the transitional period and the undertaking to resolve the problem of the sterling balances within the same time-span were to be conceded at the opening, in the hope that a suitable mixture of statistical projections and eloquent appeal would then produce at least $5 billion in return. If the tactic worked, all well and good. If it did not work, there would be no alternative but to admit defeat, to regroup, and to negotiate Temptation from a position of unenviable weakness. It was an extraordinary gamble, of the sort Keynes often accused the Bank of wanting to take or of having taken in the past. Though well aware of the possibility of failure and very conscious of warnings about the changed mood in Washington, he seems to have thought that his spell could work and that he could still win. As for the Bank, it had been crying wolf for years past, ever since 1941. He would as usual, where necessary, pay attention to the Old Lady's technical criticism on points of detail. But her anxious opposition to prime features of the whole enterprise, in particular the commitment to early convertibility, could as usual be disregarded. Keynes was in charge.[35] But to adapt his own words, much of the differences between himself and the Bank had so far been about negotiating and agreeing plans for the Brave New World. Within those confines, Keynes had been successful, and apparently right, while the Bank had come to look wrong. Now it was a question of entering the Cruel Real World, in which Keynes' judgement had not recently been tested and the judgement of the Bank was more likely to be correct.

(b) THE LOAN NEGOTIATIONS

The Bank was kept informed, in part through Thompson-McCausland's contacts in the Treasury, of the rapid sequence of events following the Clayton visit and the termination of Lend-Lease. But there was nothing further to do until Keynes arrived in Washington and the main negotiations began. In the meantime Cobbold had succeeded Catterns as Deputy Governor, with no immediate successor as Executive Director, and both he and the Governor at once became immersed in the early drafting of the Bank of England Bill. Nevertheless a watchful eye was kept on the early series of telegrams between London and Washington. Keynes arrived in the American capital on 7 September and the Bank found cause for concern almost at once. On 10 September Bolton reported that the Treasury in London was at present very lightly manned on the Washington negotiations.[36] He went on to argue against a recommendation from

---

[35] In Washington the negotiating team was formally headed by the Ambassador, Lord Halifax. He played some part, at times a tactically important one, but Keynes was the effective leader.

[36] Eady was away on two weeks badly needed rest. But on 13 September he wrote personally to Cobbold from Eastbourne, concluding gloomily: 'We can now only await events. It may be that we can only fix the terms of the necessary US supplies for this year – or possibly

Keynes that acquisition of the Lend-Lease items in transit should be financed on the terms then offered by the US to all recipients, namely a thirty-year loan at $2\frac{3}{8}\%$, subject to review on the outcome of the wider negotiations then in prospect. The Governor shared this view and so informed Bridges. He thought it would prejudice the later negotiations for a $5 billion grant or non-interest-bearing loan. The Chancellor had already cabled his consent, though with great reluctance and provided Keynes felt that the wider negotiation would not be prejudiced. Fortunately, Keynes himself had second thoughts and succeeded in postponing the question until the main negotiations were complete.

In Washington, the first sign of future trouble, prejudicial to Keynes' bold tactical plan, occurred not in preliminary talks with the Americans but in an exchange with London over the handling of discussions on commercial policy. From earlier talks with Clayton, Keynes had concluded that his delegation would only be required to endorse general principles governing commercial policy and to go along with the American proposals for an international conference to be held in 1946 about the establishment of an International Trade Organisation (ITO). On that basis he felt he could handle the matter within his own grand design with the help of only one official from the Board of Trade, and that he should not be joined by a team of senior experts from London lest this should provoke the State Department into detailed discussions akin to the preparation of an Anglo–American commercial treaty. Officials of the Board of Trade, following talks with one of Clayton's subordinates after Keynes' departure, formed a directly opposite view and so warned the Washington Embassy. These officials were powerful people, quite outside Keynes' ascendancy. Keynes and Halifax appealed to the Chancellor, arguing cogently that they be allowed at least to start off on the lines originally agreed. But they were informed from London that Ministers had now decided that matters of commercial policy should mainly be handled by a special team of officials under Percival Liesching, who could not arrive until 28 September.[37] This must have undermined, to some notable degree, Keynes' already exposed tactical position. For it suggested the ambience of a prolonged commercial negotiation rather than the ready embrace of Justice.

the outline of the terms of a credit for 1946 of say $1 billion. Too little to clear up everything and...?'

[37] Among those accompanying him was Lionel Robbins, who recorded in his autobiography that Keynes left for Washington without any consultation with officials of the Board of Trade, 'having persuaded Ministers that he could secure a substantial grant in aid and at the same time settle the entire Article VII business on his own. It would be difficult to overstate the consternation which this aroused.' Board of Trade officials, Robbins relates, were convinced that the State Department would not allow commercial policy to be treated in this way.

Nevertheless, for the first few weeks the negotiations did not go too badly. By 20 September Keynes had completed his initial assault. The situation facing the UK had been explained in remorseless detail. The usual contrasting and alternative ways of meeting that situation had been cogently explained. In his presentation of arrangements that might be made with the Sterling Area, Keynes loyally displayed the heterogeneity of its membership before going on to set out unquantified proportions for write-offs, fundings, and convertible liquid balances. The required American assistance was put at $5 billion, on terms unspecified. Integral to the whole plan would be an undertaking that by the end of 1946 the UK would cease to avail itself of the concessions applicable in the transitional period under the fund Agreement (though formal abandonment of Article XIV was not proposed). His hearers seemed sympathetic. They welcomed the suggestions about the Sterling Area and about convertibility while appearing to consider that $5 billion was, from their side, on the cards. However, in the days that followed they continued to warn that an outright gift was unlikely to prove acceptable to Congress. Opinion reported in the press reinforced these warnings. Keynes accepted this and set about persuading London to fall back on an interest-free loan, although the signs were that this too would be difficult to get. The annual repayments of such a loan would cost $100 million, but in concept it would be consistent with Justice. An alternative would be a mixture of grant and interest-bearing loan, still costing not more than $100 million per annum. A commitment to meet such a cost might be mitigated by provision for waivers in the event of special difficulties.

Keynes wrote in friendly terms to Cobbold on 24 September, beginning with an account of progress on a plan to bring back to the UK the massive silver tankard bequeathed to the Bank by Pierpoint Morgan. He went on:

> We have been deluging you with 'Nabobs'[38] in the last few days which will at any rate prove that we have been working hard. On the whole, matters are not going too badly. But then we have not yet reached any of the real hurdles. I rather fancy that we are going to be made to mark time for the next week or so until the commercial talks can be brought abreast of the financial. In our case here the delay in starting the former has been rather a disaster.
>
> As you will have gathered from the telegrams, we have not yet broached the question of the terms of aid. I think that this, rather than the amount, is likely to be the difficulty. If we had no one to deal with but the Treasury and the State Department I should have good hopes for a Grant-in-Aid. But too much will turn, I am afraid, on their precarious judgement as to the way

---

[38] Telegrams from the delegation were code-named Nabob. Those to the delegation from London were code-named Baboon.

in which things have to be dressed up to satisfy Congress. I shall be sending Eady shortly a note about possible terms which he will no doubt be discussing with you.

But over the next few days the Bank found itself resisting a proposal from Washington that the numbers and fractions relating to the suggested agreements with the members of the Sterling Area, withheld in Keynes' oral exposition, should now be revealed to the Americans in writing. This would have meant putting forward a written outline plan without the heavily qualifying passages about the heterogeneity of the sterling balances. These had been included in Keynes' opening presentation but not in the memorandum, parts of which he now wished to hand over. Accordingly, while accepting that some written statment might be needed, both for the Americans and for Sterling Area members, Cobbold argued that it should indicate only general lines of possible settlements, which would vary greatly in different cases. 'We cannot emphasise too strongly that a plan on these lines cannot be applied in any sort of uniformity. In fact we believe it to be applicable in these sort of terms only to two or three countries. Any commitment to the US to apply it generally or uniformly can only lead us into violent trouble.' Further, it was essential that the final version should be seen in London before it was handed over to the Americans. But the Treasury evidently felt that Keynes had already gone too far for the situation to be met with a statement on 'only very general lines'. Yet how could the Government make a written proposal to the US Administration, including substantial write-offs of sterling balances, without any prior consultation with the holders? This awkward question had not been anticipated ahead of Keynes' opening statement and could not now be met except by dissimulation. With the support of the Prime Minister and the Chancellor, Eady telephoned Keynes proposing that he elicit from the Americans some suggestions along the lines he had himself made. He could then put back to them his own quantified ideas, in writing, which would then appear as a reasonable response to an American initiative. The text would need to be cleared with London.

Keynes took no immediate action, for he had become aware that White was preparing an American plan for the sterling balances that incorporated a direct link with American assistance to the UK. He learnt the details of this informally from White early in October and sent the plan to London for comment, suggesting it was worth serious consideration. White's plan, which was not approved by Vinson, envisaged firstly a loan of $3 billion to meet the UK's own deficit and secondly a purchase for dollars by the US of all of an assumed $5 billion of funded balances at a discounted value of $2½ billion. Of the remainder, $4 billion would be written off and $2 billion left liquid and convertible, though subject to minimum balance provisions. Despite all his supposedly detailed knowledge of the Sterling Area, and in particular its heterogeneity, Keynes apparently could not resist being attracted by White's elegant if abstract solution. In the Bank, the plan was heavily criticised by Thompson-McCausland in a note to the Deputy Governor on 15 October and by Rowe-Dutton in the Treasury on the same day. There was no way in which it could be successfully negotiated with the diverse membership, especially in a rush, and even if it could the result would be to convert the Sterling Area into a dollar area at a stroke. On 20 October the Chancellor cabled Keynes saying he hoped the White Plan would not reappear. For 'as we see it, it starts from the basis of presenting to Congress a specific agreement between us and the Americans for detailed and defined treatment of the sterling balances which the holders of those balances must afterwards be called upon to implement. It might also bring the Americans into our negotiations with the Sterling Area. I am sure you will agree that we cannot handle the Dominions like this, or indeed our other creditors.' There for the present the matter rested, leaving unresolved the question how to reconcile American demands for some clear-cut numerical plan to present to Congress with the practical need to approach each important member of the Sterling Area over the ensuing year and conduct a delicate negotiation case by case. However during October this important question of the sterling balances was subsidiary to the main issue of the total of American assistance and its cost. For it was over this that Justice was finally done to death and the British position fell apart.

During the first week of October the Treasury considered how best to respond to Keynes' request for guidance on the acceptability of a $5 billion interest-free loan, or alternatively a mixture of grant and interest-bearing loan, costing $100 million per annum to service but possibly with provision for waivers in defined circumstances of external difficulty. At the Bank, the Governors informed Eady of the obvious. They were apprehensive lest Keynes should now make a revised approach to the Americans, quantifying the amount of assistance needed and its terms, which would be interpreted as an opening bid and which the Americans would thereafter seek to alter in their favour. This well-founded worry, together with their fear of the UK slipping into commitments on the Sterling Area and on early convertibility, made them think it would be better if Keynes returned to London for consultations as soon as he had a definite idea of Washington's best offer.

After further advice from Keynes that there was no prospect of obtaining $5 billion without an annual cost of $100 million, the Chancellor finally sent him general guidance on 8 October that the Government would not accept a large loan at 2%, could not agree to service costs in excess of

$100 million, would prefer a mixture of grant-in-aid and a credit facility bearing 1% interest, but would not reject out-of-hand a loan of $5 billion without interest. Halifax and Keynes saw Clayton and Vinson on the following day only to be told that neither a grant nor an interest-free loan would be practical politics with Congress. Clayton then suggested, without demur from Vinson and in response to questioning by Keynes, a loan of $5 billion with a five-year grace period, $100 million per annum amortisation, $50 million per annum interest (rather more than 1%), and a waiver clause that would be triggered by reference to the level of UK exports.

Clayton next held a press conference at which, though without attribution to himself by name, the figure of $5 billion was stressed. This was widely reported in the newspapers as the amount the Administration intended to offer. Keynes then cabled London asking whether Clayton's outline proposal should be pursued and suggested it should not be rejected out of hand. This question was considered by senior Ministers on 12 October, with the Prime Minister in the chair. They decided that Keynes should stand firm on a maximum annual service cost of $100 million; but they did not rule out further consideration of a higher cost, depending on the response to the tactic agreed. The Bank, in discussion with the Treasury, supported the tactic and also argued that escape clauses would do nobody any good and could only lead to mischief. Keynes again wrote to Cobbold on 12 October. In the course of this he said, 'I think you may take it that the figure of $5 billion is now accepted', and later: 'There is not in my opinion any hope at all of a grant-in-aid. But my best bet would be that we shall get off with a service not exceeding $100 million a year protected by some escape clauses.' In a postscript he added: 'Since writing the above Harry White has told me that we must not yet regard the figure of $5 billion as firm. That is still a matter of controversy behind the scenes. He ought to know better than me. All the same I am quite clear in my own mind that all our recent private conversations with the top boys have been on the basis of $5 billion.' Keynes may have been deriving encouragement partly from Clayton apparently exceeding his brief and partly from American reluctance to reveal their hand before they were ready. Evidence from American documents suggests that they never seriously considered going above $4 billion once they had fully investigated the British case.[39]

Halifax and Keynes next saw Clayton and Vinson on 15 October. They made no progress at all and were told that the suggestion (it was termed an 'offer' in the telegram sent back to London) of $5 billion costing $150 million per annum, with waiver, was the best that could realistically be put

---

[39] An account of the negotiations from the American side is contained in Appendix C by Miss C. M. Balfour.

to Congress. The Americans were duly informed that in the last resort the British Government would accept an annual charge of $100 million. Keynes then recorded ominously that Clayton's mind now tended to move 'in the unpleasant direction of proposing a reduction of the credit below $5 billion while keeping the annual service at $100 million.' It was left that the American side would make a counter-proposal in the near future.

Ahead of this critical meeting Keynes and his colleagues made a strong attempt to retrieve the situation by endeavouring to persuade London to accept a loan of $5 billion on Clayton's terms, even though they feared that this might no longer be on offer. In their telegram of 18 October, six paragraphs acknowledged with eloquent sorrow that Justice was not to be done. They began: 'We came here in hope that we could persuade the US to accept a broad and generous solution...' and ended: '...we must think again, substituting prose for poetry. Our disappointment does not justify us in doing perhaps irreparable injury to our own body politic and economic or in shattering the basis of day-to-day Anglo-American co-operation. We must do the best we can.' After belatedly reminding London of its bargaining power – for the objectives of the American Administration regarding both the early setting up of the Bretton Woods institutions and early progress towards an International Trade Organisation would be thrown into confusion unless an Anglo-American financial settlement were agreed – the merits of the Clayton proposal for an interest-bearing loan of $5 billion were deployed. But the delegation in Washington was soon to learn that this game was no longer being played. Long before London could reply there was a further meeting with Clayton and Vinson at which the Americans offered only $3½ billion at 2% for fifty years, still on the condition that the British stood by their original proposals, made in pursuit of Justice, about the Sterling Area and convertibility. Their own calculations about the British balance of payments had persuaded them that $3½ billion was anyway enough, besides being easier with Congress. Disregarding his own (out-of-date) instructions Keynes then tried desperately to revive the original Clayton suggestion, only to be told that $5 billion was now believed to be too much for Congress. The Americans continued to be accommodating on the subject of waivers but held out no hope of more than a marginal advance on $3½ billion. This was Temptation with a vengeance. However Keynes and his colleagues were in no mood to advise that negotiations be suspended. One had to stay and make the best of a bad job. The American offer therefore deserved London's consideration.

If there was a moment when Keynes should have been recalled to London, this was it. His frontal assault in the name of Justice had failed, as he himself nobly admitted. In effect a new negotiation had to begin, and for this a new set of tactical dispositions needed to be made. A pause for reflection and redeployment was required, with all concerned located in the same place, London. Otherwise the British, with fast-growing fatigue, would be left split in two, communicating with each other cumbrously by telegrams and letters that risked constant misunderstanding on matters of increasing complexity,[40] while the Americans suffered no such disadvantage. Worse still, to continue the negotiations without an obvious break, and through the same leading personality, risked carrying through into 'prose' the concessions on the Sterling Area and convertibility that had been made only in the context of 'poetry' and had so far been judged appropriate only in that context.

However, neither the Chancellor nor the senior Treasury officials concerned seem to have been able at this juncture to contemplate so drastic and bold a step as either to recall Keynes for consultations or even to replace him. But in the Bank, as early as 10 October, Cobbold had noted: 'I think Keynes ought to come home.' He repeated this to the Governor on 19 October and also aptly warned against 'being soothed by the old tale that what Keynes and Halifax propose does not commit Ministers'. For his part, Thompson-McCausland noted on the telegram relating the offer of $\$3\frac{1}{2}$ billion: 'To one who has seen Lord K. in Washington this telegram displays familiar signs that his resistance is at an end. I fear that, if he is not strengthened by a return to London or other means, there is little chance of avoiding a fatal weakness at the very foundation of the international credit structure which must be built on the settlement between the US and ourselves.' Unfortunately, the Governor did not press this in Whitehall because he persisted in believing up to quite late in October that Justice could be revived if only Keynes were to represent it along the lines favoured by himself, that is, by laying considerable stress on a settlement of debt that was left over from the 1914–18 war and on which the UK had defaulted. With the Chancellor's agreement the Governor sent a personal telegram to Keynes along these lines as late as 19 October.[41]

---

[40] One of these was the vexed question of the waiver provision, under which the UK could in certain circumstances reduce or postpone service of the loan. It caused a great deal of heat and trouble, but proved to be of little subsequent importance and is not further dicussed.

[41] It is interesting to speculate whether Catto, the man of commerce with the Scots accent and with personal knowledge of the American business world, might not have played a better hand of Justice than the predominantly intellectual Keynes. Together they might have been unbeatable and their joint presence would have seemed quite natural to the Americans, among whose top three negotiators was the Chairman of the Federal Reserve Board (in whose Board Room the negotiations took place).

Keynes' reply of 22 October pointed out that the First World War debt was not a current issue and that a grant-in-aid was 'simply off the map'. More important, he argued against a break-off. The grounds would be unconvincing and negotiations would have to be resumed 'in a state of still greater emergency'. He would like to return briefly to London, but allowing for the sea journey[42] this would take three weeks and would 'hopelessly upset the timetable at which the Americans are aiming'. But there was in fact no immediate emergency. The UK external reserves had not begun to fall.

Though they did not recall Keynes, the Treasury and the Bank did immediately set about devising an entirely new set of proposals as a counter to the American offer. They correctly acknowledged Keynes' admission that the original approach, with its set of undertakings in exchange for a grant of $5 billion, or at least an interest-free loan, had failed. Very reasonably, their new package was tailored to Temptation. It was approved by the Ministerial group on 26 October and sent to Keynes and Halifax on the following day. In exchange for a loan of 2\frac{1}{2}$ billion at 1% (including the final settlement for Lend-Lease) together with an option on a further $2 billion free of interest (as backing for liberalisation of the Sterling Area), the UK would seek agreement with individual members of the Sterling Area about their 'appropriate contribution towards the rehabilitation of the whole situation', would recommend to Parliament adherence to Bretton Woods and, subject to satisfaction in the commercial policy discussion, would join in sponsoring the International Trade Conference. There was no specific mention of cancellation or funding of sterling balances and no mention of any date by which new arrangements would be completed or sterling convertibility introduced. The UK would go no further than agreeing to proceed as quickly as possible. If this package were to prove unacceptable to the US, then a version of Starvation Corner would be required, mitigated by a loan of up to 2\frac{1}{2}$ billion on purely commercial terms. There would be no liberalisation of the Sterling Area, no convertibility and ratification of Bretton Woods would be postponed. All this was set out in a Ministerial telegram to Washington, After describing the failed approach as a bold and constructive idea but a plan that had almost disappeared, the Chancellor concluded:

> All these might have been safely undertaken with $5 billion grant in cash or possibly on an interest-free basis, but they are neither safe nor a good bargain for $4 billion at 2%. The difference between that situation and the original plan is in our judgement not one of degree but of kind.'

[42] His health did not now permit long journeys by air.

On receiving these reasonable instructions, Keynes was reportedly furious. But he resisted an inclination to resign; instead he proceeded to challenge London. Austerity would be much worse than the Treasury thought, because nothing like $2\frac{1}{2}$ billion could be obtained on commercial terms or be afforded. In his view, moreover, its mere mention would infuriate the Americans rather than, as he had seemed to argue before, impress them with the UK's bargaining strength. He therefore argued that there was no point in putting it forward. The alternative plan suggested by London for a two-part loan would be put to the Americans, but it would be wise to begin considering what to do if it were rejected. Furthermore Keynes simply swept aside the concept of a fresh negotiation in a new situation that was different in kind to the original plan. He stated that the rather imprecise proposals for the Sterling Area contained in London's new package were inconsistent with his oral presentation at the outset of the negotiations, including liberalisation by the end of 1946, to which, he flatly asserted: 'We are certainly committed up to the hilt.' Shortly after this reply was sent, Robbins and Hall-Patch[43] returned to London in order to help explain the situation as it now appeared to those in Washington. Robbins was then head of the Economic Section of the Cabinet Office and Hall-Patch was an Assistant Under-Secretary in the Foreign Office (and formerly in the Treasury). The former had gone to Washington with the commercial party under Liesching; the latter had gone there with Keynes himself. According to Eady, in a conversation recorded by Cobbold on 2 November, they gave conflicting reports about the Washington atmosphere. None of it added much to what London already knew: 'that the whole thing had got embroiled in formulae and interpretation about Sterling Area, waivers, preference, options, etc., and that no two people, even on our side, see things quite from the same angle'. Eady himself contemplated going to Washington, but nothing came of this idea.

In due course London accepted Keynes' advice. The proposal for a two-part loan was then put to the Americans, who did not reject it out of hand but now made it clear, at variance with White's ideas, that they preferred a single homogeneous loan rather than an arrangement under which part of it was earmarked for meeting the needs of the Sterling Area. On the same day Keynes finally wrote to White, setting out what he himself conceived to be the UK proposals regarding the Sterling Area. This

---

[43] *Hall-Patch, Edmund Leo, GCMG (1896–1975).* Represented HM Treasury in China and Japan in 1930s, Assistant Secretary, HM Treasury 1935–44, Assistant Under-Secretary of State, Foreign Office 1944–6, Deputy Under-Secretary of State 1946–8, Chairman, Executive Committee, Organisation for European Economic Co-operation (OEEC), with rank of Ambassador 1948, Permanent UK Representative, OEEC, UK Executive Director, IMF and IBRD 1952–4. Chairman, Standard Bank 1957–62.

letter had been prepared after further and at times angry exchanges with Eady and contained grounds for a further and much more serious misunderstanding that was to surface two weeks later. For although Ministers eventually responded, on 23 November, to the American reaction to their proposal for a two-part loan by agreeing to accept a single loan of $4 billion if offered, they later rejected on 26 November the implications of an American draft agreement that had now become available. This first committed the UK to convertibility world-wide, by the end of 1946, and secondly made that commitment a binding one whether or not the new arrangements with the Sterling Area, or with other holders of sterling balances, had been completed. The US draft further entailed that the prior commitment would be made public.

The first of these implications, boldly committing the UK to extending convertibility to countries outside the Sterling Area by the end of 1946, had become known in Whitehall a week or so earlier and had caused a violent reaction. Ever since Keynes' first paper on Stage III, this had been a rather grey area. But it was now clear to the Bank that the safeguards of Article XIV, which it had fought so hard to secure, were being taken away with inadequate compensation. Cobbold minuted the Governor on 20 November:

> I am very unhappy about this. It is quite clear to me from the latest cables that the Americans are expecting us as the price of a 2% credit to renounce our 'transitional period' freedom in exchange matters after the end of 1946. Even if Keynes were to succeed in glossing the text of some of the clauses, there is no doubt in my mind that the Americans would continue to expect this and would regard us as having defaulted on our agreement if we acted otherwise.
>
> Even with a grant-in-aid I should have been chary of tying our hands in this way. With a repayment loan and more so with 2% interest I believe it is sheer madness.[44]
>
> I am bothered about the Bank's responsibilities because this is a field in which we have specialised knowledge and therefore special responsibilities for advising HMG. I suggest for your consideration that the Bank ought at this stage formally to advise HMG that a settlement on the lines now in view in Washington would be a bad settlement for this country.

Reporting on a meeting with the Treasury, he minuted two days later:

> I reserved our formal position but expressed the view, subject to confirmation by yourself, that we could not properly tie our hands in this way as the price of a $4 billion loan at 2%. I thought we should be running straight into a

---

[44] In like vein, Rowe–Dutton in the Treasury wrote: 'If I were an American deliberately seeking to destroy the British financial future, I could choose no better way of doing it.'

position where we would use up the dollars quickly and find ourselves so tied up that we had no alternative but to default on the loan or on the commitments or both. I also expressed the view that it is no use seeking a way round this fundamental difficulty by ingenious drafting which can only lead to misunderstanding and ill-feeling between USA and ourselves.

There is a personal telegram from Keynes to Bridges and Eady urging a quick decision and saying that he feels near the end of his physical resources.

From Washington Keynes now replied that it had been clear all along, and clear to the Americans, that the undertaking about the convertibility of current sterling receipts in the Sterling area was separate from undertakings to make agreements with members of the Sterling Area about accumulated balances; and he protested vehemently that no agreement was now possible without such a separate commitment. It may have become clear in Keynes' mind, and it may have been clear to the Americans, but there is no doubt at all that it had not at any stage been clear to the Treasury, the Bank, or the Cabinet in London. An inspection of the documents reveals the evolution of a pronounced ambiguity. With some considerable justification, the British in London could not imagine themselves agreeing in public to a prior commitment on early convertibility, on a specific date, just before entering a series of difficult negotiations with, for example, India and Egypt relating to their accumulated balances; and they interpreted the relevant texts accordingly. The Americans, anxious to secure a firm British commitment to convertibility by a specific date, interpreted them differently. The agreed Minutes of Keynes' oral presentation on 20 September clearly support the London interpretation. They contain no suggestion of separating the timing of convertibility from the conclusion of agreements governing accumulated balances or of a separate commitment on the former. But Keynes' letter to White of 7 November, prepared after the drafting tussle with Eady over the passages relating to accumulated balances, is definitely ambiguous and can be read either as implying such separation or not implying it. The Treasury in London, and the Bank, read it in the latter sense while the Americans picked up the ambiguity and removed it from the draft Agreement that they prepared so that the former sense was clear beyond doubt. Having, as they thought, pinned the British down on this vital question, they had no intention of letting go.

Keynes, who was by now nearing complete exhaustion, met this situation by flatly informing London that his delegation was committed to the American interpretation, that his integrity would be undermined if he had to go back on it, that the Americans regarded the point as having been conceded for weeks past, that no agreement would be possible without it, and that in any case a step-by-step approach to full convertibility, as agreements were concluded with other countries one by one, seemed nonsensical.[45] It was now too late for the British Government to adjourn the negotiations. They had already agreed to accept a loan of $4 billion and could only fight a rearguard action on convertibility. Attempts were made to abolish the separation of the undertaking on Sterling Area liberalisation from that concerning agreements about the balances, but without success. Attempts were also made to soften, or else postpone until the end of 1948, the commitment to extend convertibility to countries outside the Sterling Area, but with little result. Bridges was sent to Washington, in effect to take over from Keynes and to see whether any better terms could be obtained. But the Americans proved as adamant as Keynes had advised and would agree only to substitute 'twelve months after the Agreement becomes operative' for 'not later than the end of 1946' and to allow postponement of convertibility only in exceptional individual cases and even then only after consultation with the US. As to the amount, they were prepared to offer 3\frac{3}{4}$ billion together with $650 million for settlement of the Lend-Lease pipeline. Late on the evening of 4 December the Governor telephoned the Chancellor and urged that the Prime Minister should intercede with President Truman on the 'vital question of the transitional period and even regarding the rate of interest'. But this was to no avail; on the following day Ministers accepted the American terms.

So Temptation had won and Sheer Madness had come to pass. The British monetary authorities, from the Chancellor of the Exchequer downwards, found themselves committed to a course of action in whose success they had no confidence. They did not think that external convertibility could be sustained if introduced as early as specified in the Loan Agreement, and they were very doubtful whether in the interim they could achieve settlements of the sterling balances as favourable as the Washington negotiations seemed to require. In exchange for commitments of this debilitating nature, they had obtained, exactly as Eady had feared, a loan that was quite large enough to engender in the Government and the country a false sense of temporary security but not large enough, on any realistic British calculation, to finance the expected transitional deficit, let alone the extra strain of early convertibility. This was no good way for Ministers and their official advisers to start out on what was anyway going to be a very difficult journey. At best it could interpose an expensive false dawn before reality had to be tackled. At worst it would also expensively undermine both the confidence of the authorities in themselves

---

[45] But it was what actually happened, without mishap, to the monetary agreements with West European countries when these were amended seriatim during the run-up to July 1947.

and the confidence of foreigners that the British could be relied upon to honour their commitments. Only Keynes, writing early in the following January to the Chancellor, Bridges, Eady, and the Governor, still felt able to say: 'Unless we are sunk altogether, I cannot seriously conceive that we shall have difficulty in meeting our obligations: provided, that is, we make a reasonable settlement with the Sterling Area countries.' But the feasibility of conducting the required scale of major surgery on the sterling balances, by negotiation, had all along been one of the most doubtful features of the whole plan. The Americans had persisted in believing in it, and Keynes, himself a half-believer, had never succeeded in dissuading them.

For the Bank, the Loan Agreement epitomised what it did not want and what it had advised against. As for the Treasury, it now again knew, too late in the day, the perils of allowing itself to become dominated by a personality of great genius but fallible judgement. For it was Keynes who had advocated the frontal assault and stuck to it, despite the evident dangers. It was Keynes who had waved aside suggestions for a much more cautious plan that would have started with interim arrangements and would have remained entirely consistent with the Bretton Woods agreements and their ratification. It was Keynes who had pressed the assault, with almost all of his cards face upwards but without any properly prepared position on which to fall back if it failed. Finally, it was Keynes who had then responded to failure by driving on – at times ruthlessly and at times with unjustified faith that a serious dollar shortage would not develop – towards London's reluctant acceptance of the American terms as the only practicable course. But it was not Keynes' fault that the early momentum of the negotiations got lost through delays originating in London. Nor could he be held responsible for American illusions about the early post-war world in general or the British outlook in particular. Nor was it his fault that the Bank had earlier damaged its own effectiveness by a too persistent and at times obtuse opposition to the Bretton Woods vision. To a marked extent, the outcome of the Washington negotiations was the heavy price paid for the long-standing disunity in London.

It has sometimes been said that the relative failure of the Loan negotiations was in some significant part due to a clash of personality between Keynes and Secretary Vinson. But the documentary record does not require such support in order to explain the outcome. That they were in many respects two very different, even opposite, personalities is beyond doubt. They may well have irritated each other at times and said hard things about each other. The negotiations were difficult and became full of stress. But the Americans mainly emerge as rather straightforward people conducting a commercial negotiation with skill from a position of strength, though with extraordinarily misguided views about the early post-war prospect. It can be argued that they were in a position to impose any settlement they wished and that the British position was so weak that they had no choice but to throw themselves at American feet with an appeal for Justice. This argument can never be conclusively refuted. But it pays insufficient regard to the fact that a prior settlement with the UK was quite vital to American plans for a post-war international monetary and trading order. The British task was to meet that American interest in exchange for assistance on terms that they could accept with proper confidence. Had they tried to do so, instead of appealing at the outset for Justice, it is difficult to believe the outcome would not have been better than it was.

SOURCES

Bank files
  ADM20/30   Norman Diaries (1941)
  G1/16   Governor's File: John Maynard Keynes – Published articles, Memoranda, Letters, etc. (January 1941 – November 1949)
  G1/18   Governor's File: USA – $4000 Million Loan to UK (September 1945 – January 1946)
  G1/262   Governor's File: Miscellaneous Papers (1946–7)
  G18/3   Lord Catto's Papers (February 1945 – August 1947)
  OV38/1–11   International Monetary Fund (August 1941 – July 1945)
  OV58/23   Canada: Mutual Aid (September 1944 – January 1946)
  CBP376.02/1–9   USA: Anglo-US Financial Agreement Negotiations (August – December 1945)
PRO files
  T236/436–41
  T236/449–50
  CAB128
  CAB129
Writings of J. M. Keynes

CHAPTER 3

THE FALSE DAWN AND THE CRISIS OF 1947

(a) DETERMINING A STRATEGY FOR THE STERLING BALANCES: 1946

ON 30 November 1945, shortly before the Loan Agreement was signed, the Deputy Governor set up a small committee to consider how the obligations of that Agreement, regarding both convertibility and the accumulated sterling balances, should be carried out. Siepmann was Chairman[1] and the other members were Kershaw, Bolton, Mynors, and Thompson-McCausland. No time was lost. By meeting three times a week they were able to submit a draft report as early as 27 December. A final version, described as 'some first thoughts about Sterling Area negotiations', was sent to the Treasury on 9 January. An expanded version was circulated four weeks later. Application of the Loan Agreement to existing monetary arrangements between the UK and non-Sterling Area countries was taken more slowly. A draft on this aspect was available by mid-April, but work was then interrupted while contingency plans were prepared against Congress failing to ratify the Agreement. By the end of June this contingency had faded away and a final version of Siepmann's second Report was sent to Whitehall. But strategic decisions had effectively been taken earlier in the year in response to the first of the Bank's two Reports. These decisions were themselves preceded by a final instalment of the disagreements between Keynes and the Bank about external financial policy. In this finale it was the Bank's advice, firmly rooted in the prevailing external monetary, banking, and political relations, that at last prevailed and set the frame within which the ensuing negotiations were to be conducted.

---

[1] He had been made an Executive Director early in 1945, and after Cobbold's appointment as Deputy Governor in August of that year he was the only Director with exclusively overseas responsibilities until Bolton's promotion to the Court in March 1948.

Siepmann's Committee had first to take into account the complexities of the financial relationships between London and the rest of the Sterling Area. Balances held on official account included sterling held as cover for local note issues, or against approaching redemption of sterling loans or other special commitments, as well as unearmarked accumulations of external reserves. Balances held on private account ranged from the liquid assets of commercial banks to the working balances of trading enterprises or of individuals. The Bank did not seriously entertain the idea that this entire living structure should somehow be put into an abrupt receivership. Accordingly it did not argue whether, regardless of the grave political and economic consequences, balances should be blocked by unilateral British action on the morrow of Victory, mostly for cancellation or compulsory funding with the resulting array of specific difficulties and individual crises left to individual members to sort out. Nor, despite the exiguous level of the central reserves – some £500 million against liabilities of around £3,000 million to the Sterling Area alone – did anyone else in London persist with such an idea once they were confronted with the political realities of putting it into effect; though retaliatory action against an individual member who refused all reasonable co-operation was always considered a practicable option.

Against this background Siepmann minuted his Committee on 10 December: 'We have appointed ourselves to do a difficult and urgent job which really belongs to the Treasury. They ought to know what they have agreed and it is their business to tell us, so that we may translate it into action. But we shall have to discover for ourselves both what is to be done and how to do it.' Accordingly, the first report of the Committee began by emphasising that the convertibility of Sterling Area balances already existed *de jure*. The necessary wartime limitation of recourse to the central reserves in London was achieved by the exchange and trade controls of individual member countries working in voluntary co-operation with the UK and not by the operation of UK exchange control itself. US dollars were always provided on demand by the Bank, on behalf of the Exchange Equalisation Account, so long as the underlying transaction had local exchange control approval.

Thus Clause VII of the Loan Agreement, under which current receipts of sterling were to be made freely convertible for current payments twelve months after its ratification, meant simply that agreed trade discrimination should be terminated; member countries would then need to look only to their balance of payments overall and not to their balance with the non-sterling world as well. But in looking to their balance of payments overall, members would need to keep in mind that the obligations of Clause VII did not have to apply to accumulated balances, and accordingly that the aggregate of such balances should not persistently fall below an agreed minimum, after taking account of agreed releases under such funding arrangements as might be made. Members subject to reserves pressure would have to take prompt domestic measures to relieve it. They might also reconstitute their sterling reserves by, for instance, drawing on the IMF. The concept of an agreed minimum neatly disposed of any idea of 'drawing a line' between pre-zero and post-zero balances. But it did leave open the risk that an increase in capital outflow from the UK into the rest of the Sterling Area could inflate balances of the recipient countries above the minimum and allow further expenditure, some of which could fall on UK reserves. The Report considered whether UK exchange control should therefore be applied so as to contain such capital flows, but it concluded that new restrictions were inconsistent with the spirit of the Agreement and should not be imposed in advance of evident need.

The Report next considered how best to implement Clause X of the Agreement, on cancellation and funding. It looked first at Australia, New Zealand, South Africa, India, Egypt, and Iraq.[2] By deducting in each case normal currency cover, likely special calls on official balances for sterling debt redemption or for the net of various other special uses such as purchases of surplus military stores from the UK government, and all private balances, the Report derived a 'residue' of Government and central bank funds. This could be regarded as a measure of the threat arising from abnormal accumulation and of the amount that should accordingly be subject partly to negotiated cancellation, partly to funding, and partly to immediate release. The Report offered no view on the division between these categories, remarking that this was a political matter. Finally it considered the Colonial balances. Here there was a predominance of private funds, the majority representing the liquid assets of UK banks operating in the Colonies; official funds mostly consisted of the sterling assets of Colonial currency boards whose note liabilities, by law, required full sterling cover. The Report rejected as impracticable the idea that Colonial Governments should somehow be directed to conscript private

---

[2] It also looked at the substantial Irish balances. But these were mostly private balances largely representing the ordinary London funds of the Irish banks and of Irish citizens. The official balances were mostly currency cover. In fact the monetary relationship between the UK and Eire (which became the Republic of Ireland in 1948) was very closely akin to that of monetary union, and there seemed no sense whatever in trying to regard Irish balances as eligible for treatment along the lines set out in Clause X of the Loan Agreement. Siepmann's Report therefore confined itself to suggesting that the only way to meet the problem, if it threatened to become serious, would be to persuade Dublin to exercise restraint in its domestic economic policy.

Table 3.1. *UK gross sterling liabilities at 31 December 1945* (£ *million*)

	Official	Other	Total
Overseas Sterling Area			
Australia, New Zealand, and South Africa	265	40	305
India, Pakistan, and Ceylon	1,313	45	1,358
Middle East[a]	443	147	590
East, West, and Central Africa	128	77	205
Other	216	264	480
Total	2,365	573	2,938
Non-Sterling Area			
Western Europe	183	152	335
Latin America	159	7	166
North America	14	19	33
Other	44	86	130
Total	400	264	664
Grand total	2,765	837	3,602

[a] This comprised Egypt and Sudan, Palestine and Transjordan, and Iraq. The breakdown between official and other liabilities is approximate, as it is for Non-Sterling Area – Other.

balances, but it suggested that a quantity of official balances might be freed, and become available for 'adjustment' by cancellation or funding, through a uniform reduction in note cover to 80%. The Report also pointed out that a number of Colonial Governments had made interest-free loans to the UK during the war, which could be written down as part of a post-war settlement.

The result of this exercise was to confirm what had long been apparent, namely that the adjustable part of the Sterling Area's £3,000 million of balances, assuming no Area-wide blocking, was mostly concentrated in the accounts of India and Egypt, swollen by the heavy wartime military expenditure of the UK in those two countries. The derived residue of Australia and New Zealand together looked like being only some £50 million. South Africa, Iraq, and Eire were each special cases and could yield little that was adjustable. Colonial balances totalled nearly £800 million but the residue, comprising 20% of currency cover together with interest-free loans to the UK, came to only some £90 million. By contrast the Indian residue came to £430 million and the Egyptian residue to £235 million; moreover the Indian figure could be considerably larger, depending on how much of the total balances could be applied to Indian purchase of surplus UK Government stores and the capital funding by India of official pensions payable in sterling.

So the report went on to argue that the only way to tackle the overhanging balances was through individually agreed adjustments negotiated with, in the main, India and Egypt and through agreements or understandings that would prevent the balances of individual member countries, adjusted or not, from falling below a specified minimum. Negotiations with the principal holders would clearly be difficult and would not be made easier by the commitments made in the Loan Agreement. The British bargaining position was not very strong, and the ethical case for cancellation of war debts to India and Egypt was not accepted by local opinion. But the financial case for a programme of strictly limited annual releases from the balances of these countries was demonstrably compelling; and if the country concerned flatly refused all reasonable proposals on this score, the threat of *de jure* blocking and exclusion from the Sterling Area would become credible, because other members would be more reassured than alarmed by the expulsion of a member whose behaviour was clearly contrary to unwritten rules of the club.

The Bank's paper was well received by Eady but did not go nearly far enough for Keynes, who had always been attracted to the idea of drastic surgery even though he could sometimes be persuaded that uniform treatment was impracticable. He was now back in the Treasury after a short Christmas holiday spent resting after his ordeals in Washington and a brilliant defence of the Loan Agreement in the House of Lords. After a preliminary skirmish at a meeting in the Treasury on 15 January, he circulated a long note on 'Sterling Area Negotiations'. Pointedly ignoring the fact that the Bank had got in first, he said that his note was 'intended to start discussion and bring us to grips with the fundamentals to be settled'. It began by revising the Bank's method of calculating the residue in order to isolate figures for wartime accumulations and in other respects to identify a larger total than the Bank had done. He then outlined a rather complex variant, alterable to some degree in special cases, of the uniform approaches previously suggested by himself or by Harry White. But he added a section proposing devaluation of the Indian and Middle East currencies, whose overvaluation he put at around 30% and which would stimulate a flood of imports. The profit thus accruing to the sterling balances of those countries, if they were expressed in terms of local currency, could be used to write off a proportion of the residue, whose local currency value would thereby remain unchanged. Keynes allowed himself to think that this might help to make the effective cancellation of sterling assets seem less painful.

In the Treasury, Keynes' plan encountered a sharp rejoinder from David

Waley[3] in a note that concluded: 'I do feel strongly that if we try to reach a permanent and overall solution now we shall inflict such a blow on the prestige of sterling that we shall greatly add to our difficulties in seeing where the country's next meal is coming from, which is our present situation.' The strategic issue of imposed uniformity of treatment (Keynes) versus varied negotiations carrying consistency of intent (Bank) had now been joined; and the Permanent Secretary responded by setting up an Official Committee on Sterling Area Negotiations, with himself in the chair. This met for the first time on 30 January 1946. Keynes argued that protection of the UK reserves against sudden pressures arising from run-downs of working balances had to be settled in advance and that this required a uniform approach. The Bank disagreed, stressing the need to maintain the reserve-currency status of sterling and in that context emphasising the dangers of an imposed blocking.

Keynes also reiterated his arguments for the devaluation of Sterling Area currencies, but he met with little support. On 5 February he circulated a further short note that restated his position and was clearly intended to bring matters to a head. It would be wrong, he said, for any country to have an unrestricted claim on uncancelled sterling balances. Furthermore, the reordering of exchange rates must inevitably become part of the negotiations. It was essential to start out with a general formula, variable only in very special cases. The 'bankers ramp' of 1931 was mostly attributable to 'the reckless accumulation of liabilities in the immediately preceding years which we could not hope to meet when the tide turned. I think that we must ration ourselves this time on the extent to which we use the bankers' bluff as a means of supporting (temporarily) the prestige of sterling...I plead', he concluded, 'that this is not a case where we can muddle through without a drastic solution, grasping no nettles and just hoping it will be all right on the day.' One can see his point, the more so in view of his growing worry that the UK was undertaking excessive overseas expenditure on account of post-war relief and continuing military commitments. Conceptually, a 'drastic solution' could readily be regarded as integral to the logic and the quantities of the Loan Agreement. But it was an intellectual concept that Keynes had no hope of turning into reality. It was not practical politics. The UK could not begin its difficult post-war monetary voyage by declaring bankruptcy and imposing a settlement on its creditors. It had financed part of its wartime expenditure by taking in deposits from abroad, and it had no choice, in

---

[3] *Waley, Sigismund David, KCMG, MC (1887–1962).* Educated Rugby and Balliol College, Oxford, HM Treasury 1910–47. Army 1916–19. Assistant Secretary 1924–31, Principal Assistant Secretary, Overseas Finance Division 1931–46, Third Secretary 1946–7.

1946, but to steer its way through the resulting problems by negotiation and agreement rather than by diktat. Writing on the Bank's copy of Keynes' *démarche*, Kershaw commented: 'This is (nearly) hopeless; and consists largely in grasping a lot of imaginary nettles to add to the very real ones we have perforce to handle.'

Following a Ministerial meeting on 7 February, at which Keynes was present but at which the strategic issue was not fully revealed, Bridges held a decisive meeting of the Sterling Area Committee on 12 February. Besides himself, the Treasury was principally represented by Keynes and Waley. Meade attended from the Economic Section. Since Cobbold was in Ottawa, accompanying Eady on the Canadian Loan negotiations,[4] Siepmann led for the Bank and was flanked by Kershaw and Thompson-McCausland.

The Bank was well prepared and on 8 February had circulated the expanded version of its 'first thoughts'. There are two records of the meeting, the official Treasury record and the Bank record. Although they are consistent one with another, the Bank record is less formal. Keynes endeavoured to destroy the Bank's argument that adequate protection of the central reserves, after such cancellation and funding as could be negotiated, could be obtained by agreements on minimum working balances supported as need be by domestic measures and import controls by member countries. His main point was that most of the Sterling Area countries were in such fundamental external disequilibrium that quantitative restrictions would not adequately stem the tide of imports. Pressed to outline his alternative, Keynes advocated a 33% devaluation of Sterling Area currencies as a first step. In order to get this, he rashly proposed a unilateral blocking of virtually all the balances so as to give the UK control of the purse and provoke a crisis to which devaluations would be the only solution. Siepmann was asked for his view of this breathtaking proposal. The Bank record of the meeting says: 'Mr Siepmann said that he regarded India and Egypt as cases apart. There we would have to reckon with hostility and it might be right to face a row at the outset. But throughout the rest of the Sterling Area there was a great fund of goodwill towards the UK. To start off by forcing a crisis on our own good friends would be a devastating policy. Bridges appeared to agree with this and then turned the discussion to the question of individual countries.'

That, to all intents and purposes, proved to be the end of the matter. Keynes' writ, impaired by the Loan negotiations, no longer ran. The aim of a radical and uniform approach certainly lingered in some quarters and was clearly used in early and unsuccessful talks with Australia and New

[4] See pp. 97–101 below.

Zealand. Even the idea of Sterling Area devaluations was given some further thought. But the approach favoured by the Bank gained effective possession of the field. For the remaining weeks of his life, Keynes seems to have retired from this fray. He left London to attend the inauguration of the IMF and the IBRD at Savannah early in March. It was an unhappy and humiliating meeting that further weakened his precarious health. On his return he gave his mind to the financing of the Budget deficit and the furtherance of Dalton's policy of cheaper money. He was also contemplating a reduction in his Treasury commitments, though Harrod records that he continued to worry about the problem of the sterling balances. But late in April his heart finally gave way and his associates in Whitehall and Threadneedle Street were left to get on as best they could without him.

Tragic though it was, the death of Keynes did allow the negotiations on the sterling balances and the revision of monetary agreements with non-sterling countries to be conducted with a greater unity of British purpose. A period of very close harmony between the Treasury and the Bank now began. Yet the policy that they had been obliged by the facts of the case to choose was one more appropriate to their preferred course of a long transitional period than to the headlong plunge of the Loan Agreement. In this way the close harmony between the Treasury and the Bank became devoted to putting in place a set of arrangements that could be used after the Loan Agreement had perforce to be set aside.

(b) TYING UP THE BALANCES OF THE STERLING AREA AND ARGENTINA: 1946–1947

The broad strategy towards the sterling balances that emerged from Bridges' Committee was in due course accepted by the Chancellor. But his attitude towards treatment of the wartime accumulations remained severe. This was tactically correct at the outset, for the Loan Agreement was not formally ratified by Congress until July. But as time went on it also served as a counterweight to such softer views as might develop in other interested Departments like the India Office and the Colonial Office, and it may have served to stiffen the negotiating stance of officials in the Treasury and the Bank. Whatever the broad strategy, there was no doubt of the need to be tough on tactics. A variety of calculations made in the Treasury and the Bank during the spring of 1946 suggested that the UK could certainly not afford permitted releases from accumulated balances to exceed £100 million per annum over the ensuing five years and might well need to restrict them to £60 million per annum. After all the argument, and not a little theorising, in London and Washington, it was now time to seek agreement with countries that had not hitherto been consulted. They could be expected to hold out for the best terms they could extract, and most of them were very unlikely to look kindly on the idea that their external assets should be substantially scaled down, whatever the Anglo-American Loan Agreement might say. The story told in this section provides a striking contrast to the make-believe world of, for example, Harry White.

The first task was to decide on the order in which individual negotiations should take place. They had to be crammed into a period of some eighteen months and would have to be in the main conducted seriatim by a small team of senior Treasury officials supported by representatives from the Bank. It was an unusual instance of policy mostly originating in the Bank and execution falling mostly to the Treasury. For until renegotiation of monetary agreements in Europe came into view – at which point the central banks could play a principal role – the negotiations were bound to be inter-governmental. In addition the Treasury possessed in Eady an unusually able negotiator. His most difficult assignments were likely to be India and Egypt; but it was no use seeking early agreement with either of these countries, and especially the former, because their changing political situations and their special relationships with the UK had not yet reached a point where their responsible authorities would be prepared to enter unwelcome commitments about the use of their sterling assets. This impression was fully confirmed by Theodore Gregory,[5] Economic Adviser to the Government of India, at a meeting with Keynes late in February. Accordingly, attention shifted to Argentina, a prosperous neutral country whose turbulent domestic politics had turned during the war to an indigenous brand of populist nationalism that was about to get Juan Perón elected President. Though not a member of the Sterling Area, Argentina held at the end of 1945 some £105 million of gold-guaranteed but inconvertible sterling accumulated under a wartime payments agreement with the UK. This balance was expected to go on rising during 1946. Argentina supplied a substantial part of the British meat ration, under an agreement expiring as soon as August 1946, and harboured a British-owned railway system and other investments vulnerable to maltreatment.

Thus the ordering of negotiations tended to dictate itself. India and Egypt were consigned to 1947, to be preceded by Argentina in the summer of

---

[5] *Gregory, Theodore, Kt (1890–1970)*. Educated Owen's School, Islington and LSE. Lecturer, LSE 1913–19, Reader in International Trade 1920–7, Member, Macmillan Committee on Industry and Finance 1929–31, Professor of Economics, London University 1927–37, Economic Adviser to Government of India 1938–46, British Member of the Currency Committee, Bank of Greece 1946–55, Financial Adviser, British Economic Mission to Greece 1946–9.

1946. Decisions on what, if anything, should be done about the Colonial balances could be left for decision in Whitehall itself (in the end they were mostly left alone). Renegotiation of the monetary agreements in Europe, whose retention had anyway yet to be decided, would probably not present great difficulty and could begin later in the year. Relations with the Union of South Africa, the Sterling Area's main source of newly mined gold, were not particularly affected by the Loan Agreement. It sufficed to renew arrangements under which a large proportion of South Africa's gold output was sold in London for sterling, which the Union then used without severe constraint. This left Australia and New Zealand, both of whom held enough sterling for at least some of it to be regarded as eligible for cancellation or funding and with whom the UK enjoyed close and friendly relations. There therefore opened up the opportunity of seeking early and favourable agreements with them, at top political level, which might set a useful precedent when the time came to open the difficult negotiations in Delhi and Cairo. The opportunity was taken, but the outcome was predictably disappointing. Nor did the Canadian Loan negotiations, which began in Ottawa during February 1946, provide much support for the belief that a financial settlement with a friendly Commonwealth country would be especially favourable to the UK. These negotiations, in part a postscript to those held by Keynes in Washington and in part a forerunner of those relating to the sterling balances, find their proper place at this point in the narrative.

The Canadian Loan

Plans for 'Stage III' had always contained a settlement with Canada that would include a loan covering the UK's prospective deficit with that country during the first three post-war years. The first set of tentative proposals had come from Graham Towers when he met Keynes in Ottawa at the end of November 1944. In order to maintain Canadian exports to the UK at a reasonably high level during the transition, Towers suggested a loan of $Can. 1 billion, repayable after ten years at $50 million per annum but with provision for deferral if the UK reserves fell below a prescribed minimum. This would bear interest at 2% on $Can. 0·8 billion and at UK Treasury Bill rate on the rest. One condition would be current-account convertibility into Canadian dollars of post-war additions to the sterling balances. Keynes was reportedly very interested in these suggestions, which were the basis of unquantified proposals that were sent to the British Government in February 1945 and discussed at Cambridge[6]

---

[6] See Chapter 2, pp. 67–8.

in May along with Keynes' initial plans for American help during Stage III. The Canadians were supporters of those plans and Towers was very disappointed to find they had been scaled down when he saw Keynes in Ottawa the following September. At Keynes' request he went to Washington during October and did what he could to support the British case for a credit of $5 billion. He was critical of the sorry outcome in December, critical of British tactics, and worried about the future. He then recommended to Prime Minister Mackenzie King that the Canadian Loan to the UK should be interest-free, that a debt of $Can. 450 million arising out of the Commonwealth Air Training Scheme should be written off, and that some $Can. 600 million of interest-free debt owing to Canada under an Agreement signed in 1942 be allowed to run on and gradually be liquidated in amounts equal to private sales of Canadian securities owned by UK residents. But Towers' recommendations proved to be overgenerous.

A detachment from the Washington delegation stopped off at Ottawa in December 1945 on their way home to London and it was agreed that formal discussions would be held in the new year. Although the Canadians told the delegation that they thought the American Loan was smaller than it should have been and the terms too hard, they warned that those terms would restrict what they could themselves offer. The Liberal Government of Mackenzie King had an overall majority of only ten in the Canadian House of Commons and its Parliamentary strength was dependent upon seats held in Quebec, where support for the British connection was limited. The UK High Commission in Ottawa, headed by Malcolm MacDonald, advised London that although a loan of $Can. 1 billion remained feasible, the UK should not expect to get it on better terms than those agreed with the US. They added that although cancellation of the 1942 loan was not part of Canadian thinking, a write-off of the Air Training debt was a starter.

At meetings held in the Treasury during January 1946, at which Keynes was present, it was agreed to try for better terms than those secured in Washington, notwithstanding the advice from the High Commission in Ottawa. An interest rate lower than 2% would be sought on the new loan together with substantial cancellation of the war debts. The mission to Ottawa was headed by Eady, with Cobbold as his principal colleague. They left London in the second week of February and talks with Canadian Ministers began on the 11th. Eady's comprehensive presentation of the UK's external financial situation included the point that the negotiations were the second stage of a sequence that had begun with the American Loan and would end with agreements on the sterling balances.

He proposed an interest-free credit of $Can 1¼ billion, 1 billion being for the UK's needs and ¼ billion for the rest of the Sterling Area. Cobbold added further comments about the nature of the Area and went on to emphasise the importance of sterling to the recovery of continental Western Europe (another market for Canadian produce). In this context, the burden of British war debts would have to 'be adjusted so as not to impose an intolerable weight upon the people of the UK and upon the country's export trade'. Ilsley, the Canadian Minister of Finance, drew attention to the political difficulties of an interest-free loan and also raised the question of UK assets in Canada amounting to some $Can. 1½ billion. Eady replied that the UK's ability to obtain satisfactory settlements with the US, Canada, and the Sterling Area would determine its ability to carry out its objectives and, in the more limited field, to foster trade with Canada and absorb Canadian agricultural surpluses. If the Canadians insisted on too hard a bargain, the possibility of satisfactory settlements with the Sterling Area would virtually disappear. Dire consequences would ensue.

At the next meeting St Laurent, the leading French-Canadian in the Cabinet, put forward a quite different plan as a suggestion of his own. The UK would be granted a new loan equivalent to the value of the British-owned Canadian securities. The proceeds would be used to pay off the war debts and provide a modest amount of new money. The loan would be serviced by payments equal to dividends on the securities and amortised out of any sales of such securities that might occur in the ordinary course. As and when the UK needed more new money, Canada would be prepared to accumulate a substantial amount of sterling for eventual funding in two years' time. The British delegation was genuinely shocked by these suggestions and Eady went to great lengths to explain why they were unacceptable. Hypothecation of dividends on securities would worsen the problem of balance between the UK and Canada. The suggested terms looked as if they would be more favourable to the lender than those on the American Loan and therefore contrary to the Loan Agreement. They would also gravely prejudice the forthcoming negotiations on the sterling balances. Full valorisation of war debts at market rates was unacceptable and would prevent the UK from participating in an early return to multilateral trade. Cobbold then followed with a lively explanation of how, if necessary, 'the machinery of the Sterling Area could be used to achieve a Schachtian economy'.

St Laurent was not supported by his colleagues, who must have appreciated that his proposals could not possibly be accepted by the British Government. Accordingly, on 21 February, Ilsley came back with an offer of $Can. 1¼ billion new money on US terms, an extension of the 1942 loan for five years on existing terms, and cancellation of the Air Training debt provided the major holders of sterling balances conceded comparable relief. Eady replied that he thought these terms unacceptable and expressed particular objection to the condition attaching to cancellation of the Air Training debt. The whole matter was then referred to London and Cobbold returned there on 23 February. On the 26th, on behalf of the delegation, he sent Bridges an appreciation of the position in Ottawa. The Canadian terms were not likely to get much better; the balance of forces within the governing party would not permit it. Rather than risk an adverse Parliamentary response to an agreement containing better terms for the UK, Mackenzie King would adjourn the negotiations until the American Loan had gone through Congress. This would be dangerous, for an appearance of a breakdown in Ottawa could damage British prospects on Capitol Hill. If HMG therefore felt it better to try for an early settlement, the best hope would be acceptance of $Can. $1\frac{1}{4}$ billion on US terms, extension of the 1942 loan on existing conditions, and outright cancellation of the Air Training debt. An alternative possibility might be a loan of $Can. $1\frac{3}{4}$ billion at 1%, repayment of the 1942 loan, and cancellation of the Air Training debt. All this was then discussed at a Ministerial meeting chaired by the Prime Minister and attended by Cobbold and Malcolm MacDonald. It was agreed to try the alternative on the Canadians. If it failed, then the Canadian terms should be accepted, it having already been learnt from Ottawa that the proviso attaching to cancellation of the Air Training debt had been dropped.[7]

Eady saw Ilsley again on 27 February, but made no headway with the British counter-proposals. The existing provisions of the 1942 loan already included repayments equal to the sales, in any one year, of UK holdings of Canadian securities. Retention of this for the time being was politically necessary for the Canadian Government. London accordingly authorised acceptance of the Canadian terms. Outline agreement was reached on 2 March and the full text was published on the 7th. This contained a provision for consultation 'if in the opinion of either Government reconsideration of this Agreement is justified by the prevailing conditions of international exchange or by any change in the international financial situation which materially alters the prospective benefits and obligations flowing from this Agreement'. Fourteen months later the Canadians were to invoke this Clause so as to restrict UK drawings on the Loan.

The Canadian Loan was generous in amount, but its terms were no better than Temptation. No cancellation of the 1942 loan had been

---

[7] There were also miscellaneous claims and counter-claims arising out of the war and expected to produce a net UK liability. Ministers agreed to meet this up to a maximum of $Can. 150 million.

conceded and its favourable terms were to be reviewed after five years. But at least the Air Training debt had gone, whatever the French Canadian interest may have thought. After all that had happened in Washington, it was perhaps the best that could be expected. As an example of a Commonwealth attempt to substitute some element of Justice for the American version of Temptation, it did not have too much to commend it. As a signpost to negotiations on the sterling balances, it did not suggest an easy journey.

Australia and New Zealand

The Prime Minister of New Zealand, Peter Fraser, was in London during February 1946 and was invited to No. 11 Downing Street for a discussion about sterling balances. The Chancellor was flanked by his top officials and by Keynes himself, whose radical views clearly influenced the British attitude on this occasion. Fraser was invited to consider a proposal that no less than half of New Zealand's balances should be written off and the remainder released by instalments. All current earnings of sterling – and New Zealand was then in current-account surplus – would be free for use anywhere in the world. This proposal, if New Zealand agreed, could be put into effect almost immediately. Fraser was not to be bounced. He indicated in reply that while New Zealand might be prepared to make some sacrifice, he was doubtful if they could get by on only half their existing balances. He asked the Chancellor to put his suggestions in writing and undertook to bring the matter to the attention of his Cabinet in Wellington. He would then arrange for discussion to be resumed when Nash, his Finance Minister, visited London in May. The British proposals were included in an explanatory note that made no secret of the desire to make a favourable settlement with 'those nearest to us' before approaching India and Egypt. Fraser acknowledged this point in a letter to Dalton written towards the end of March, but remarked that: 'My first examination of the proposal does not indicate that what is suggested is possible without striking a severe, if not nearly fatal, blow at the economy of this country.'

Before resuming discussions with New Zealand, Dalton saw the Prime Minister of Australia, Ben Chifley, who was present in London early in May. The argument about India and Egypt was deployed even more strongly, particular emphasis being placed on the desirability of establishing with Australia and New Zealand 'some overall formula of wide application'. A 50% write-off of accumulated balances was mentioned, but was not put so crudely to Chifley as it had earlier been to Fraser. The Australian Prime Minister was accompanied by Dr Coombs[8] and between

---

[8] *Coombs, Herbert Cole (b. 1906)*. Educated University of Western Australia and LSE. Assistant Economist, Commonwealth Bank of Australia 1935–9, Economist to Com-

them they gave a cool reply. They stated that Australian balances would be drastically reduced over the next eighteen months, down to a post-war danger level of £80 million. Despite the sharp rise in imports that this implied, the Australian people would be making great sacrifices and the political difficulties of any sweeping gesture in favour of the UK would be insuperable. The most Chifley could offer was to think it over. After another plea for the evolution of some general formula, Dalton had to accept this situation. In a negotiation between friends, and with little or no deployable bargaining strength, he had not much choice. A week later he saw the New Zealand Minister of Finance, who took credit for having paid off in March £18 million advanced by the UK during the war to meet part of New Zealand's external military expenses. He expressed a willingness to discuss the question of sterling balances, and the Treasury subsequently proposed that £20 million out of a total of some £65 million should be written off, with agreed constraints on drawing down the remainder. In the end the Minister undertook to take this proposal back to Wellington for further consideration and also for discussion with Australia. But he warned that the approach of a General Election in New Zealand, timed for November, might delay a final decision. He asked for a full written statement of the British case. This was prepared and sent to Wellington and Canberra early in August. It relied heavily upon a concise explanation of the effect of the war upon the UK's external economic and financial situation, contrasting this with the much healthier position enjoyed by Australia and New Zealand. Very little direct weight was placed on the provisions of the Anglo-American Loan Agreement.

There the matter rested until early in the following year when the two Governments side-stepped the write-off proposals and offered outright gifts to the UK as a contribution to the costs of the war. These offers were accepted, Australia giving £A25 million and New Zealand £NZ12 million. The gifts were calculated in London to be roughly equal to write-offs of 15%. The question of subsequent reductions in remaining balances was left for bilateral discussion. Late in March 1947 Eady reopened the question with Nash and with Coombs, reporting them as being 'horrified' at the idea of any formal restriction. A further attempt was made in June, at official level, to persuade the Australians to enter a minimum balance agreement with the UK; but they would have none of it. So the appealing tactic of seeking first a favourable agreement with one's closest friends had

monwealth Treasury 1939–42, Member, Commonwealth Bank Board 1942. Director of Rationing 1942, Director-General of Post-War Reconstruction 1943–9. Governor, Commonwealth Bank of Australia 1949–60, Governor, Reserve Bank of Australia 1960–8. Chancellor, Australian National University 1968–76, Chairman, Royal Commission on Australian Government Administration 1974–6.

not been a success. It could perhaps be claimed that the principle of write-off had been established, indirectly. But for setting an example to India and Egypt it was more important to agree a restriction on run-down. In that respect, no progress could be claimed. It was not that Australia and New Zealand were unwilling to help the British. But they preferred to help by special gifts, or by a tightening of import controls, rather than by agreeing to restrictions directly affecting the banking facilities in London which they enjoyed as members of the Sterling Area.

Argentina

Far more encouraging were the negotiations with Argentina. Talks began early in July 1946, at Perón's invitation, and lasted until the middle of September. They were conducted by Eady,[9] with a supporting team that included F. F. J. Powell[10] from the Bank. He was also ably assisted by the British Ambassador in Buenos Aires, Reginald Leeper.[11] Eady's negotiating skills were displayed at their best. In a cable to London in September, after agreement had been reached, the Ambassador remarked: 'I have no hesitation in saying that their successful outcome is largely due to Sir W. Eady's patience, firmness and clear grasp of the subjects under discussion. During the final week when he had at last secured the initiative, his timing and handling of the discussions were masterly.' The main players on the Argentine side were Perón, his principal economic and financial colleague Miguel Miranda (then Governor of the central bank), and his Foreign Minister Bramuglia.

In bargaining strength the two sides were fairly evenly matched. Argentina had the meat and other produce that Britain badly needed; and under the Loan Agreement it had the attractive prospect of selling it to the UK for convertible sterling which would mostly be used outside the Sterling Area, in particular for the purchase of the American equipment required for Perón's programme of industrialisation. Argentina also had territorial possession of British-owned railways and other investments, largely controlled the profits of the former, and was now keen to see the

---

[9] It was not his first visit. He was born in Argentina in 1890, the son of a Civil Engineer working on railway construction.
[10] *Powell, Frederick Francis Joseph (1890–1975).* Educated St John's College, Finsbury Park. Entered Bank 1910, Assistant Chief, Overseas and Foreign Department 1932–5, Deputy Chief 1935–41, Adviser, Central Bank of Argentina 1935–6, Adviser 1941–6, Adviser to the Governors 1946–51.
[11] *Leeper, Reginald Wildig Allen, GBE, KCMG (1888–1968).* Educated Melbourne Grammar School, Trinity College, Melbourne and New College, Oxford. Foreign Office 1918–48, First Secretary, Warsaw 1923–4, Riga 1924, Constantinople 1925, Warsaw 1927–9, Assistant Under-Secretary 1940–3, Ambassador, Athens 1943–6, Ambassador, Buenos Aires 1946–8.

undertakings transferred in whole or in part to Argentine ownership. But Britain had territorial possession of the accumulated gold-guaranteed Argentine sterling, which in the absence of a new agreement could not be used outside the Sterling Area and which the UK could, in the last resort, freeze entirely. Expropriation of the railways without proper compensation could provoke such a move, which might not in that instance greatly damage the international status of sterling. Moreover the British, despite their great need, could be awkward over both the price and the quantity of meat imports from Argentina. There was obvious scope for agreement. But the Argentinians were inexperienced and over-confident. They overestimated their own strength and it took many weeks before they could finally be persuaded that Eady and his colleagues would truly pack their bags and return to London rather than sign up on Miranda's terms. They professed not to be interested in a British proposal that they use their accumulated sterling towards purchase of the railways and endeavoured instead to negotiate a phased release of their sterling balances on terms highly favourable to themselves; if conceded, this would have set the British an impossible precedent with India and Egypt.

Work began at a Presidential audience on 4 July, obtained reasonably promptly but only after a series of increasingly nettled Ambassadorial interventions with the Foreign Ministry. Eady made a long speech whose opening stanzas had been drafted in the Foreign Office and whose florid style he had earlier remarked, in a letter to Niemeyer, could be explained by the architecture of Buenos Aires. Powell, writing to Watson[12] in Threadneedle Street, remarked: 'No conclusions can be drawn at all from this meeting except that it was held in an atmosphere of "extreme cordiality" and that the great man stuck it out for more than an hour.' The President, who had himself little knowledge of external financial affairs, handed over the conduct of the negotiations to Miranda in the expectation that a favourable bargain would be struck. In the course of a frank telegram to London two weeks later Leeper noted that Miranda was effectively in charge of economic affairs. He was described as 'a tough ignorant know-all. Unfortunately he is more tough than Perón and less open-minded.[13] In the same telegram Leeper said Perón was boycotted by men of experience and education and had drawn round himself a 'rough,

---

[12] *Watson, Guy McOlvin* (b. 1905). Educated Dover College, Entered Bank 1924. Accompanied Sir Otto Niemeyer on Mission to Argentina 1933, Bank and HM Treasury Representative in Latin America 1939–46, Assistant Chief Cashier (Exchange Control and Overseas) 1946–51, Acting Deputy Chief Cashier 1951–4, Deputy Chief Cashier, Exchange Control 1954–7, Chief, Overseas Department 1957–9, Chief, Central Banking Information Department 1959–63, Adviser to the Governors 1963–5.

[13] He was in fact a successful capitalist, having made a fortune in the food-canning business.

raw and unscrupulous crew'. The best member of this was Bramuglia, 'quick, intelligent and well-meaning but nobody could call him a heavyweight'. Similar sentiments were expressed by Powell in a letter written to the Bank on 29 July. 'So far', he wrote, 'the idea of selling the railways has fallen very flat here – in fact it is like a red rag to a bull to Miranda. Without this "solution" our problems are, to say the least, difficult as we have little room for manoeuvre and these people's ideas about the position in Europe, etc., are so remote from reality and they are themselves so grasping, ignorant, and ridiculously inflated that ordinary argument makes no appeal whatever.' Eady himself did not find Miranda so objectionable. Writing to Cobbold eighteen months later, when told by the Bank that the Argentinian was ill, he said: 'As you know, I like the old ruffian and would rather do business with him than most of the other people I met out there.'

Without letting go of British insistence on an integrated agreement covering the sterling balances, the railways, and the meat, Eady patiently worked away at the Argentinian position on the first of these issues. They wanted $2\frac{1}{2}\%$ interest and sizeable annual releases. London, on being consulted, would not agree to interest above $\frac{1}{2}\%$ and was averse to any fixed programme of releases. Argentina then retaliated by suspending licences for meat exports to the UK and for good measure announced with a flourish that a public holiday would be held on 12 August in celebration of the reconquest of Buenos Aires from the British in 1806. But towards the end of the month the Foreign Minister began to take a hand and to give way on the demand for $2\frac{1}{2}\%$ interest while insisting that Eady make proposals for annual amortisation. The latter tried £10 million per annum on London but got the reply that this was far too much. Meanwhile Bramuglia had accepted the British position that any agreement on the sterling balances would be conditional on parallel agreements being reached on meat and on the railways. Since some eventual agreement now seemed to be in the wind, the Ambassador called on Perón and advised him that deadlock could only be solved by Presidential intervention. He stressed that wider considerations of Anglo-Argentinian relations were involved rather than a mere business deal. Could the President perhaps encourage Miranda, a 'comerciante', to be more like a 'diplomatico'?

Since this initiative did not at first produce much result, the British Mission pointedly crossed the River Plate for a short diplomatic visit to Uruguay. However, early in September Perón saw the American Ambassador,[14] who had been well briefed by Leeper. The President was

---

[14] Messersmith. He had been sent to Buenos Aires by President Truman to thaw out US–Argentine relations, which had become exceptionally bad during the war.

reminded of the very close links that had developed between the US and the UK during and since the war and of the dangers of underestimating British strength. Argentinians should appreciate British difficulties over sterling balances, but should also recognise their own difficulties if they failed to reach an agreement on meat. This helpful initiative also seemed at first unfruitful, for on 6 September Miranda produced his own idea of an integrated settlement. Eady had to reject this out of hand and began making tactical preparations for a breakdown, including ordering an aircraft from London to fly the Mission home. There was at first a hitch, the Mission being advised that the aircraft would be delayed indefinitely. Eady then sent a 'Most Immediate' cable to Bridges on 9 September asking for help, as 'we regard it as imperative for the situation here that arrangements should proceed for our departure as proposed'.

The following day he got a reply from the Foreign Office: 'Lancastrian [aircraft] leaves dawn Thursday arriving Buenos Aires 13th. Should be ready for return flight 14th. Details with Air Attaché.' Eady, recently complimented by Dalton 'for your patient resistance to outrageous Argentine demands', next obtained London's approval of a final offer. This offer included interest of $\frac{1}{2}$% on Argentinian balances, a release of £5 million per annum over the next four years, an arrangement for the railways to be taken over by an Anglo-Argentine consortium with a dividend of 4% guaranteed by the Argentine Government, and a four-year agreement to buy Argentina's exportable surplus of meat at a price, for the first two years, 45% above the pre-war level. This plan was launched on Miranda on 13 September, just as Eady's aircraft was leaving London. The initial response was unsatisfactory, but on 15 September Eady cabled London: 'We have done it!'; and so, but for giving an inch here and there, they had. Eady left for home on 18 September, to be received by a grateful Treasury, an admiring Bank, and a congratulatory Prime Minister. A critical cartoon published in Buenos Aires shortly after the Mission's departure depicted Eady walking off with the railways, the meat, and Miranda's trousers. But he earned praise in a nationalistic but friendly speech by Perón, who concluded by announcing an act of unexpected generosity. As proof of friendship 'to the noble British people so closely united to the Argentines on many occasions in their life', he had instructed the authorities to send three shiploads of meat to England in time to arrive, as a gift, for Christmas.[15]

[15] This caused instant head-scratching by UK Ministry of Food officials in Buenos Aires and a speedy cable to London. The gift was worth $\frac{1}{2}$ lb. per head. How could it be distributed? Selling it for the benefit of the Treasury would create a very bad impression. What about reducing the retail price of meat for one week, so that people got an extra $\frac{1}{2}$ lb. out of their ration of one shilling and fourpence? London's advice was urgently requested.

An Argentine comment on Eady's success: 1946

Early in October, when Eady was in Washington on his way back to England, Catto sent him a personal message of congratulation 'on the splendid success of your arduous South American mission which is not only of vital importance itself but will profoundly influence other similar negotiations'. The agreement on Argentinian sterling balances, both on the rate of interest and the rate of release, certainly deserved this praise. As important as the agreement itself was its demonstration that the UK could still drive a hard bargain against tough opposition. Neither the Anglo-American Loan negotiations nor the discussions with Australia and New Zealand had given any such impression. Catto's message to Eady also reflected a complete identity of view between the Treasury and the Bank throughout the negotiations in Buenos Aires.[16] Like the Treasury, the Bank fully supported an inflexible position towards Argentina's sterling until acceptable terms came into sight. Unity in London contributed to success in Buenos Aires. Commenting on a pessimistic note addressed to him by Siepmann on 23 July, when the Mission seemed to be getting nowhere, the Governor remarked:

> A funding loan is in my opinion quite impossible from our point of view and undignified. Unless some part of the balances are to be used for a deal with the Railways then they had better remain in their present form. But in spite of this I do not think the Mission should at this stage break off. Negotiations are only beginning and with South Americans patience is essential until a break becomes the only way of dealing with the matter. But we must first try to wear them down by sticking to our point of view.

India

The US Congress ratified the Loan Agreement in July 1946, thereby fixing 15 July 1947 as the date for sterling convertibility. The Bank then sent to the Treasury a final version of Siepmann's February report on the Loan Agreement and the Sterling Area. Following a meeting of the Sterling Area Committee, Waley then minuted the Chancellor to record progress to date and suggest, *inter alia*, the shape of approaches to India and Egypt. Neither of these countries seemed likely to offer any cancellation, but some agreement with them severely restricting their use of accumulated balances was absolutely essential. With the outcome of the Eady Mission to Buenos Aires then unknown, Waley concluded: 'Our strongest argument is that it is in the interest of all countries which hold sterling that the position of sterling should be maintained. Our weapon is that we can completely block the existing balances, but it is a weapon which it would greatly damage us to use, and the other countries will know this quite well. There is no disguising the fact that the next twelve months will be a very stormy time.'

The Governors noted Waley's Minute with approval. A few weeks earlier

---

[16] Significantly, the task of briefing the UK press on the details of the agreement was delegated to the Bank. Niemeyer duly held a press conference for twenty-six City Editors on 17 September.

the Bank had also seen a note written in the Treasury by Alec Grant,[17] who argued the case for attempting what Keynes had earlier termed the bankers' bluff instead of endeavouring to tie things up so tightly as to make the result scarcely distinguishable from blocking. 'Bankers', he said, 'like burglars can never sit on the fence: they are either in the big money or they are properly in the soup.' Siepmann, Kershaw, and others in the Bank were naturally sympathetic, but neither they nor Grant doubted the need to drive a hard bargain with India and Egypt as well as with Argentina. The possible shape of such a bargain with India, whose balances now totalled nearly £1,300 million and had yet to begin falling, was further discussed in the Bank during the early autumn. Kershaw suggested that it would be better to drop the idea of cancellation, which would serve only to sour the atmosphere in Delhi, and concentrate instead on tying up a large part of the Indian balances for release at an unspecified pace after 1950. The remainder would include the existing currency cover together with a freely convertible balance that would, by agreement, be used gradually and would enable India to get by until 1950. 'Tying up' might include using a proportion of the Indian balances to fund the country's sterling pension commitment (perhaps £250 million) and to acquire surplus military and other stores (perhaps £150 million). This accorded with advice given to the Treasury in July by Archibald Rowland, Finance Member of the caretaker administration run by the Viceroy (Lord Wavell) in New Delhi. It was also supported by intelligence from the Bank of Canada that recounted a conversation with an official of the Reserve Bank of India in which a freely usable balance of £150–175 million had been mentioned.

In the late summer of 1946 Wavell's caretaker administration was replaced by an all-party Interim Government of Indian Ministers. Nehru was Prime Minister and Liaquat Ali Khan, second-in-command of the Muslim League, was Finance Minister. The partition of India had not yet finally become a political necessity and it was still hoped that an all-India constitution could be worked out by a constituent assembly. Clearly it would take a little time before a new Government of an independent India could come into being. But the need to resolve the question of India's sterling balances was becoming increasingly urgent. Quite apart from the timetable of the Loan Agreement, there was the imminent prospect of India running a substantial external deficit in furtherance of plans for

---

[17] *Grant, Alexander Thomas Kingdom, CB, CMG (1906–88).* Educated St Olave's School and University College, Oxford. HM Treasury 1939–58, Under-Secretary 1956–8, Under-Secretary, Export Credits Guarantee Department 1958–66, UK Member on Managing Board, European Payments Union 1952–3. Secretary, Faculty of Economics, Cambridge 1966–71.

economic development. The intended size of this deficit, and the consequential run-down of India's sterling balances, could not be realistically determined in the absence of agreement with the UK. In November, therefore, the Indian Department of Finance proposed that negotiations should take place with the Interim Government in April of the following year, after completion of the Indian Budget. This was acceptable to London provided the formal negotiations were preceded by earlier substantive discussions at official level, with Eady and Cobbold representing the UK. Delhi agreed to this and the discussions were timed to start in January, with a Second Secretary in the Finance Department, Narahari Rao, leading for the Indians. At the same time it was made very clear in Indian Ministerial speeches, in extensive press briefing by the Finance Department, and in private discussion with the newly appointed UK High Commissioner in Delhi, Terence Shone, that the Interim Government would have nothing to do with cancellation, regarded itself as in no way bound by the Anglo-American Loan Agreement, and would concentrate on obtaining as rapid a repayment as possible of Britain's debt to India. The Finance Minister, speaking in the Central Assembly on 28 October, remarked that 'the sterling balances have been accumulated through the sacrifices, through the trials, sweat, and tears that the people of this country have gone through'. Nehru himself later remarked to Shone at their first meeting that Indian history and Indian conditions were extremely complex. However erudite one might be and however much study one might devote to them, 'one must never forget the emotional side'.[18] Finally, the Finance Department's press briefing ended by quoting

---

[18] The post of High Commissioner had been created ahead of, and in anticipation of, Indian independence. Shone had not been in India since childhood; nonetheless the courtierlike language of his initial despatch neatly recaptures the remaining imperial flavour of New Delhi during the last year of British rule. The following paragraph exemplifies:

'We continued our journey to Delhi on the 19th November in an aircraft kindly placed at our disposal by the Royal Air Force. On arrival at Delhi, we were met by the Military Secretary to the Viceroy, representatives of the Commonwealth Relations, External Affairs and Commerce Departments, a personal representative of Pandit Nehru, the Chief Commissioner and Lady Mackay, Mr Weil of the United States Embassy who greeted me on behalf of Mr Merrell (at present absent from Delhi), in addition to Mr Symon, Deputy High Commissioner, Mr Owen, His Majesty's Senior Trade Commissioner and the members of the staff of the High Commissioner who are already in Delhi. My wife and I then proceeded to the Viceroy's House where His Excellency and Viscountess Wavell had been so good as to invite us, and also Mr Bell and Mr Clowes, to spend our first few days. These have afforded an invaluable opportunity for making contact, not only with His Excellency and his staff, but also with the Commander-in-Chief and a number of Indian personalities whom Their Excellencies have kindly invited to meet us. Pandit Nehru, who was due to attend the meeting of the All India Congress Committee at Meerut on the 21st November, was unable to attend one of the luncheon parties at which I made the acquaintance of several other members of the Interim Government; and as I was given to understand that he was likely to be away for some days, I asked to call on him before he left Delhi. I enclose

no less an authority than Keynes, speaking at Bretton Woods in 1944: 'We are grateful to those Allies, particularly to our Indian friends, who put their resources at our disposal without stint and themselves suffered privation as a result...a settlement of these debts must be, in our clear and settled judgement, a matter between those directly concerned. When the end is reached and we can see our way into the daylight we shall take it up without any delay to settle honourably what was honourably and generously given.' To that there was no answer.

Eady and Cobbold set out by air at the end of January 1947, leaving England in the grip of paralysingly severe weather and on the brink of the fuel crisis. Descending into the invigorating climate and strenuous social activity of the imperial capital in winter, the Mission was warmly welcomed. 'Since Tuesday', Cobbold wrote back to Catto on 7 February, 'we have done no business but seen them all and every day at luncheons, cocktail parties, dinners etc....We have met Pandit Nehru and most of the other Ministers at two or three of the functions.' But the Mission had left London with a warning from the Viceroy's Private Secretary, George Abell,[19] that the prospects for an early settlement did not now seem good and that it might in the end prove necessary to go for a purely interim agreement that would last only until the constitutional changes had taken place. This warning proved only too accurate. For after a short series of meetings at which views were exchanged and the structure of a possible settlement along lines debated in London discussed, and after Eady had begun to consult London about the numbers that might be included in such a settlement, the Indians abruptly broke off the talks. They did so ostensibly on grounds that the gap between the two sides was manifestly too wide to justify further attempts to get agreement at official level; in fact it was because Liaquat Ali Khan saw no prospect of his being able to sell to his Congress colleagues any settlement that could be extracted from the British at that time.

It remained the intention to resume negotiations at Ministerial level in late April or May, but there was little expectation of success. This left the British increasingly apprehensive of an accelerating and unagreed rundown of Indian balances during the awkward period ahead. The Mission therefore warned the Indian delegation that provisional estimates of

a note of my first interview with him which was purely of a courtesy character and necessarily brief.'

[19] *Abell, George Edmond Brackenbury KCIE (1904–89)*. Educated Marlborough and Corpus Christi College, Oxford. Indian Civil Service 1928–47. Private Secretary to Viceroy 1945–7. Entered Bank 1948, Adviser 1948–9, Assistant to the Governors 1949–52, Executive Director (Staff and Premises) 1952–64. First Civil Service Commissioner 1964–7.

India's current account deficit for 1947 implied a drain of some £60 million on the UK. This could not be faced; the most that could be afforded was £30 million. The warning was heard, but as Cobbold wrote percipiently from New Delhi on 15 February: 'It is not easy to persuade them that they ought to take action, but even a limited success in persuading them is a very far cry from getting anything put into practice. I remain very anxious lest they will just go on and wait for something to happen and leave us to decide what, if anything, we are going to do about it.' He then travelled to Bombay for talks with the Governor of the Reserve Bank, Chintaman Deshmukh,[20] before rejoining Eady in Cairo. Deshmukh told him he did not think it would be hard to reach agreement on the rate of run-down of Indian balances. The real difficulties concerned 'adjustment' of the total – whether by purchase of stores or funding of pension liabilities – and the rate of interest. The British were insisting on $\frac{1}{2}\%$[21] when, overall and including their investment in gilt-edged stocks, the Indian balances were currently earning more than that.

After the Mission had returned to London, and as the weeks ticked by, it became increasingly clear not only that some short-term agreement on the rate of release was urgently needed but also that it was the only agreement that could be reached in the weeks now remaining to the Interim Government. Exchanges of telegrams between the new Viceroy (Mountbatten) and the Secretary of State ended with the abandonment of the Ministerial meetings scheduled for May or June. Indian Ministers had become wholly preoccupied with the transfer of power and the partition of the subcontinent, now scheduled to take place as early as mid-August. In London, the Treasury and the Bank were becoming almost equally preoccupied with the deteriorating external financial situation of the UK, the accelerating drawings on the American and Canadian Loans, and the imminence of convertibility. Part of this picture was the unregulated run-down of Indian balances. Beale,[22] who had accompanied Cobbold in Delhi, wrote to the Treasury on 24 April: 'Generally our feeling is that we must expect the balances to be drawn on fairly heavily between now and July

---

[20] *Deshmukh, Chintaman Dwarkanath, Kt (1896–1982).* Educated Elphinstone College, Bombay and Jesus College, Cambridge. Indian Civil Service 1919–33, Financial Secretary to Government of Central Provinces and Berar 1933–9, Secretary to Central Board of Reserve Bank of India 1939–41, Deputy Governor 1941–3, Governor 1943–9, Governor for India, IMF and IBRD 1946, Financial Representative of Indian Government in Europe and US 1949–50, Minister of Finance 1950–6.

[21] The prevailing rate on UK Treasury Bills.

[22] *Beale, Percival Spencer (1906–1981).* Educated St Paul's. Entered Bank 1924, Secretary, Reserve Bank of India 1937–9, Adviser, Bank of England 1946–8, Deputy Chief Cashier 1948–9, Chief Cashier 1949–55. General Manager, Industrial Credit and Investment Corporation of India 1955–8, a Managing Director, Samuel Montagu 1960–5.

whatever the Indians may do by way of taking heed of warnings which were given to them during our discussions in New Delhi.' The balances had in fact already fallen by no less than £90 million during the autumn and winter of 1946–7, and after a period of some stability they began to fall again at the end of May. By early July a further £41 million had been drawn. The Indian Government was reimposing import controls lifted in 1946, but their effectiveness and its timing were in doubt. Both sides then recognised that to leave matters hanging in the air during the throes of partition would risk a crisis in which the UK would have no choice but to block. A financial rupture between the two countries would then ensue. Accordingly Narahari Rao and B. K. Nehru[23] led a small delegation of Indian officials to London early in July, empowered to negotiate an interim settlement on the rate of release. This settlement would run for a few months before being replaced by separate agreements with the two successor Governments.

Meetings began on 9 July and continued until the end of the month. There was no serious disagreement. Early in the following month the Indian delegation accepted a British offer that £35 million should be released at once for use in meeting current payments anywhere in the world up to the end of the year, and that a further £30 million should be provided as a working balance. Out of the £35 million the Indians estimated they would need £15 million in US dollars, mainly for imports of wheat from Argentina. As to the remainder of the official balances, they were to be segregated in a No. 2 Account at the Bank of England, which could be used only for such purposes as the acquisition of surplus military and other stores owned by the British Government in India, the discharge of pension liabilities, and the financing of net capital flows between India and the rest of the Sterling Area.[24] As to the rate of interest, both sides accepted the status quo, the Indians agreeing not to alter the composition of their assets so as to obtain a higher yield.

The Agreement was signed on 14 August, in the last hours of British rule. Four short days later the UK High Commissioner in Delhi received 'Top Secret' telegrams from London warning him that convertibility was

---

[23] *Nehru, Braj Kumar* (b. 1909). Educated Allahabad University, LSE, and Balliol College, Oxford. Indian Civil Service, Member, Indian Legislative Assembly 1939, Under-Secretary, Finance Department 1940, Joint Secretary 1947, Executive Director, IBRD and Minister, Indian Embassy, Washington 1949–54 and 1958–62, Secretary, Department of Economic Affairs 1957–8, Commissioner-General for Economic Affairs, Ministry of Finance 1958–61, Ambassador to US 1961–8, Governor, Assam and Nagaland 1968–73, Meghalaya, Manipur, and Tripura 1972–3, Jammu and Kashmir 1981–4, Gujerat 1984–6.

[24] Calculation of the amount of such flows was to be agreed by the Reserve Bank of India and the Bank of England.

about to be suspended and containing the text of the message that he would deliver to the Minister of Finance.

The message included the sentence: 'We deeply regret that the drastic measures which have been forced upon us at short notice compel us to ask you, despite the recent signature of that Agreement, for the time being not to treat your No. 1 Account sterling as in practice freely convertible into American or Canadian dollars.' It went on to ask for cuts in India's dollar deficit for the rest of 1947 and for fresh agreement with the UK on a 'definite dollar target for the current period'. This message was delivered on 21 August and was at first received in relative calm. However, subsequent attempts by London to apply pressure on the Indian Government, itself caught in the trauma of partition, met with a firm and increasingly indignant refusal. Eventually, to threats that such refusal would drive the UK Treasury to impose an arbitrary ration of dollars on India, Delhi replied crisply that in that case India would regard itself as free to instruct exporters to refuse payment in sterling. At that point the British High Commissioner intervened on the Indian side with a telegram of such vigour that the Treasury thereupon desisted. On this telegram Beale noted: 'I feel the High Commissioner and his Deputy deserved a message of congratulation on this first-class telegram with which I agree entirely.'

Egypt

After leaving New Delhi, with its frank intimacy between the still governing and the soon to govern, Eady and Cobbold flew on to the feline complexities of Cairo and the barely concealed antipathy between the still occupying power and the unsteady regime of King Farouk and the Pashas. 'Cairo', wrote Eady some weeks later, 'arouses emotions in a visitor but not of a noble or generous character; it is as self-indulgent and pampered as Buenos Aires.' Cobbold, writing in 1977, contrasted Delhi and Cairo thus:

> In the Indian negotiations the atmosphere was friendly throughout, and though some hard things were said and arguments were forcibly pressed on both sides, there was never drama or bad-tempered confrontation.
>
> Although we pressed for outright cancellation, it was mainly a tactical gambit. Neither HMG nor the delegation believed that the Indians could ever accept it – nor indeed that, given the Indian war effort and the constitutional position of the Indian Government vis-à-vis HMG, there were very solid moral grounds for insisting on it.
>
> The Egyptian negotiations were a very different matter. Although surface politeness was mostly maintained, there was much bitterness not far below the surface, and on one or two occasions the atmosphere was ugly. I

remember permitting myself a very hot reaction on one occasion when Darwish (who was a clever but unpleasant character) had talked about the magnificent Egyptian contribution to the war effort.

Some of this emerges discreetly in the records, but my recollection is of a very much more unpleasant and hard-hitting negotiation – relieved only by the wonderful weather and swimming and tennis before breakfast at Mena House.

Throughout much of 1946 the British Government had been trying to renegotiate the Anglo-Egyptian Treaty of 1936, so as somehow to satisfy Egyptian demands for British military evacuation while safeguarding the maintenance of British bases in the Canal Zone and the right to reoccupy them in an emergency. These negotiations eventually foundered on another issue between the two countries, namely the Egyptian demand for sole sovereignty over the Sudan. Late in 1946 the Prime Minister, Sidki Pasha, resigned and was succeeded by Nokrashi Pasha. The new Government in Cairo took matters to the United Nations, without much success, while the British fell back on the unexpired 1936 Treaty. The Finance Ministry in Cairo then decided that the time had come to open negotiations with the UK in order to reach agreement about the use to which Egypt's balances could be put after the introduction of sterling convertibility. London agreed and it was arranged that the Eady–Cobbold mission should visit Cairo for preparatory talks on the way home from Delhi. Briefing by the Bank ahead of these talks advised that little would be gained by pressing the question of cancellation. It also warned that Egypt lacked the administrative machinery that would be needed to restrict a run-down of sterling balances within an agreed figure.

The need for a continuing British presence in Egypt was due firstly to the continuing strategic importance of the Suez Canal for British communications with the Persian Gulf, India, and the Far East and secondly to the special threat to the security of the Canal posed by increasing instability in the Middle East itself, especially in British-mandated Palestine. Against this background Egypt's bargaining position with respect to its £400 million of sterling balances was both difficult to discern and liable to shift. So long as the British remained militarily strong in the Eastern Mediterranean and were thought capable of using that strength to gain their ends, there was little by way of positive financial action that the Egyptians could dare to take. Nor could they stir up a great deal of civil unrest against the British presence on Egyptian territory, for this could as easily turn against the regime as against the foreigner. On the other hand, if the British tried to drive too hard a bargain on the sterling balances, they could unite opinion against themselves and make it more difficult to maintain their position on the Canal. There was therefore scope for a limited agreement on the sterling balances, though little scope for a permanent one. In the event an interim agreement was reached in July 1947, to expire at the end of that year. A peculiar technical consequence of this arrangement, arising mainly from the supposed restriction of sterling convertibility to current-account transactions, was that Egypt left the Sterling Area with the agreement and co-operation of the British authorities.

In Cairo, Eady and Cobbold were supported by the Treasury representative in the British Middle East Office, W. A. B. Iliff, by the Financial Adviser to the Embassy, W. J. Johnson,[25] and by the Bank's principal adviser on the Middle East, C. E. Loombe.[26] The Egyptian delegation was led by an Under-Secretary at the Finance Ministry, Mahmoud El-Darwish Bey or 'Darwish' for short. He was an able but difficult personality, a good negotiator and an accomplished operator in, as Eady put it, 'this city of political mysteries and personal intrigue'.[27] He strongly disliked formal sessions, preferring instead to thread his way through intense private talks, often with an intermediary rather than with Eady himself; and for this purpose he was frequently refreshed by his own comings and goings with Egyptian Ministers and the King's Chef de Cabinet. The British respected his ability, but in common with local Ministers and officials they often found his attitude of superiority objectionable; so, on occasions, did the Governor of the National Bank of Egypt, Frederick Leith-Ross[28] (otherwise known as 'Leithers', he had had a distinguished and varied Whitehall career). The National Bank was itself a complicating factor. It was a privately owned commercial bank that had gradually acquired central bank functions, including that of note issue. Its relationship with the Bank of England was close; and for some years prior to 1940 Niemeyer had been a member of its London Committee. It held over three-quarters of Egypt's

[25] 'The famous Johnson', as Loombe later remarked, 'who has put his foot in everything he has so far tackled.' But he had the reputation of possessing a rare talent for being able, somehow, not only to get on with the Egyptians but to get what he wanted from them.
[26] *Loombe, Claude Evan, CMG (1905–78)*. Chartered Bank 1925–41. Ministry of Finance, Iraq Government 1941–5. Entered Bank 1945, Adviser 1945–64, Adviser to the Governors 1964–5. Director, British Bank of the Middle East 1965–77, Chairman 1967–74, Member, Kuwait Currency Board 1960–9, Jordan Currency Board 1948–65, Sudan Currency Board 1956–60, Libyan Currency Board 1952–6.
[27] Ironically, he had also been a pupil of Dr Dalton at the London School of Economics.
[28] *Leith-Ross, Frederick William, GCMG, KCB (1887–1968)*. Educated Merchant Taylors' School and Balliol College, Oxford. Entered HM Treasury 1909, Private Secretary to the Prime Minister 1911–13, British Representative, Finance Board of the Reparation Commission 1920–5, Deputy Controller of Finance 1925–32, Chief Economic Adviser to HM Government 1932–46, Economic Committee, League of Nations 1932–9, Director-General, Ministry of Economic Warfare 1939–42, Deputy Director-General, United Nations Relief and Rehabilitation Administration 1944–6, Governor, National Bank of Egypt 1946–51, Deputy Chairman, National Provincial Bank 1951–66.

sterling balances, the remainder being held by other private interests. Thus the National Bank's sterling assets and the interest earned on them could be regarded, when it so suited the Egyptian argument, as private and commercial rather than Governmental. At other times and for other purposes the Egyptians would assert that the National Bank would shortly be nationalised and that its balances should be regarded as Governmental.

The Cairo talks did not last more than a few days. After a reasonably promising beginning, the Egyptian attitude mysteriously hardened. Darwish indicated that Egypt expected to be treated, in effect, along the same lines as Argentina. The sterling balances were not a 'war debt' but a commercial debt. Nor could Egypt agree to back-door scaling down by acquisition of surplus British material at an inflated price. Egypt's obligations to the UK were confined to those laid down in the 1936 Treaty and had been fully honoured. He went on to suggest that a proportion of the balances could be used to buy out the British shares in the Suez Canal Company and other UK assets in Egypt. In addition a small proportion should be converted into gold so as to improve the National Bank's note cover. The remainder should be subject to an exchange guarantee and released by instalments. While an interest rate of $\frac{1}{2}\%$ might be acceptable to the Egyptian Government, the relevant securities were in private hands (the National Bank) and earning more than $\frac{1}{2}\%$. In reply, Eady made it clear that an exchange guarantee could not be contemplated and that London was not interested in the sale of Canal shares or other British assets. He did however suggest, without getting a positive response, that a release of £10 million per annum for five years might be acceptable if Egypt could agree to a measure of back-door cancellation. This plan was put to the Treasury in London but rejected. The Chancellor, after referring to a hardening of British opinion on the question of cancellation and to the deteriorating external prospect, requested Eady to go no further. The Cairo talks were then concluded, both sides saying they would report to their respective Governments.

There followed two months of diplomatic activity in which the British tried to lure the Egyptians to a negotiating table in London and the latter endeavoured to extract prior conditions about the agenda. The Embassy in Cairo reported a variety of informal chats with Ministers, the Royal entourage, and with Darwish himself, while the question of the sterling balances, and the danger of their being totally blocked by the British, was well aired in the Cairo press. It was made clear that in the absence of any agreement Egypt's imports from all sources would henceforth have to be related strictly to her current receipts from exports or from such external borrowing as could be arranged. This was an unattractive prospect. So early in May, after a meeting between the British Ambassador and the Prime Minister in Cairo, the Egyptians agreed to enter negotiations in London without preconditions. These opened early in June. After the first meeting, which was attended by the Chancellor and by the Egyptian Ambassador, the delegations were again led by Eady and Darwish.

In the meantime, as the dollar drain on the UK was gathering speed and anxiety in London began to grow, the Treasury and the Bank became much concerned about the absence of Egyptian exchange control over sterling payments and the likely inability of the Egyptian authorities to impose an effective control in a hurry.[29] Even if a financial agreement were reached and outright blocking of sterling balances avoided, how could the Egyptians ensure that balances fell no further than the agreement permitted, and how could any one even pretend to know whether conversions of Egyptian sterling into dollars were restricted to meeting current rather than capital transactions? The solution to this problem favoured by the Bank and accepted by the Treasury was to extend British exchange control to all Egyptian sterling payments. This meant that Egypt would leave the Sterling Area for control purposes although continuing, certainly for the time being, to use sterling as its reserve and trading currency. Egypt would then be obliged to construct its own control of sterling payments that would complement and eventually make unnecessary any elaborate control from London. Once out of the Sterling Area, however, Egypt would be released from any obligation to accept sterling without limit in payment for exports or to provide Egyptian currency against sterling for UK expenditure inside Egypt. Clauses specifically maintaining these obligations would accordingly have to be included in an Anglo-Egyptian Agreement, paralleling the British undertaking to allow the convertibility of Egyptian accruals of sterling.

The decision to remove Egypt, by consent, from the Sterling Area may have been taken for good administrative reasons. But it had a substantial, if hidden, contingent cost to set against the gain in formal control over Egyptian balances. For if, as was very shortly to happen, the British unilaterally revoked the provisions regarding convertibility, the Egyptians would no longer be bound to accept inconvertible sterling without limit or to provide Egyptian pounds against it. They could then, if they so dared and if acutely short of convertible currency, request payment in dollars for the considerable local expenditure of the British forces in Egypt, unless the

---

[29] There was an Egyptian control of dollar payments, which enabled London to sanction conversions of sterling approved by that control, according to the ordinary Sterling Area procedure. But there was no control of sterling payments: so once sterling became convertible it could be used by Egyptians to make payments anywhere in the world without any local permission.

authorities in London agreed to release an adequate amount of Egypt's sterling balances for conversion into dollars. At the right moment, when renegotiating the interim agreement late in 1947, the Egyptians were to play this ace.

The London negotiations that began on 6 June lasted until the end of the month. They were uncomfortable and at times acrimonious. In his opening statement the Chancellor made no pretence at tact. He told the Egyptians that the British had saved them from conquest by Hitler and Mussolini. They had spent money in Egypt to keep out a brutal enemy of both countries. 'The graves of friends of each of us on this side of the table mark the price we paid. No one can repay us that price. Are we now to be told that there is a further price we must pay, in money or goods and in still further physical effort by our workers?' War debts were repugnant to good sense and justice. 'We can recognise this fact by Agreement now or we can leave events to force recognition later.' He asked for a substantial cancellation. In his reply, Darwish argued the contrary with equal force and emotion. The war had not been Egypt's war. She had been dragged into it because of her special position vis-à-vis Britain. It had not been fought to defend Egypt against the Nazis or the Fascists 'or any other sect'. Egypt had not been directly interested in the quarrel, but she had more than fully honoured the Treaty obligations. 'The hand generously and ungrudgingly extended by Egypt during the war seems to have been forgotten. The balances which had been hailed by British circles as reserves for difficult times to come have turned into war debts.' There was 'not the slightest justification on ethical, economic or legal grounds for scaling down the balances of Egypt.'

After a second uncomfortable meeting it was agreed that the question of cancellation would have to be put on one side if any progress were to be made. Darwish then informally explored with Eady and Iliff the possible structure of a two- or five-year agreement covering releases together with a once-over gold payment by the UK. But he suspected, not entirely without justification, that the British were playing for a breakdown that would enable them to freeze Egypt's sterling.[30] He therefore suggested an interim agreement running to the end of the year, by which time Anglo–Egyptian relations might have improved. Despite misgivings in the British Embassy in Cairo, the Treasury accepted the latter idea. An interim agreement, with 15 July approaching and the external situation darkening all the time, would be better than nothing and could be negotiated quickly. The atmosphere at once became more constructive. The question of a gold

---

[30] The Chancellor was by no means averse to this course. His antipathy to the Egyptians was manifest.

payment to Egypt was dropped in favour of a once-over release of £25 million to meet pre-zero commitments and provide a working balance. With this the British offered a further release of £5 million, for current expenditure, while Darwish demanded £10 million. Since he could not get this, he broke off the talks and returned to Cairo. Dalton then summoned the Egyptian Ambassador and issued an ultimatum. He offered a release of £8 million, a working balance of £12 million, and a further release to meet pre-zero commitments. But he required a reply within three days; if it was negative there would be an immediate blocking of all Egypt's balances. The Government of Nokrashi Pasha accepted this proposal and an Agreement was signed on 30 June. All balances other than an amount covered by the releases were segregated in No. 2 Accounts and Egypt ceased to be a member of the Sterling Area. As to the rate of interest on the balances it was agreed to leave the status quo undisturbed.

But that was not the end of the story and the sequel deserves recording. In the aftermath the British authorities were at pains to play down the departure of Egypt from the Sterling Area and to stress that it was brought about by agreement between the two Governments. In a cable to the central banks of member countries the Deputy Governor said: 'It will not detract from Egypt's ability to remain a member of the Sterling Area in the broader sense of maintaining the long-standing financial relations with the UK, of holding external reserves in sterling, and of using sterling machinery for financial settlements in other countries.' For their part, the authorities in Cairo set about enlarging their exchange control. To assist this process and to develop the necessary relationship with the UK control, the Bank arranged to send Loombe and Cunnell[31] to Egypt for two months. Their departure was however delayed by the development of a furious struggle in Cairo between the National Bank and the Ministry of Finance about executive responsibility for the enlarged exchange control. Leith-Ross expected his Bank to retain such responsibility, with the Ministry in final control of policy. Darwish, though on the point of moving to become Under-Secretary to the Council of Ministers, was equally determined that the Ministry should assume full control and that the British-tainted Bank should remain as an adviser only. Eventually a compromise was reached, with the Ministry and the Bank taking part in a kind of exchange control joint venture under a 'Supreme Committee' of Ministry officials and the Sub-Governor of the Bank. Leith-Ross cabled Cobbold: 'Arrangement

---

[31] *Cunnell, Rodney John* (b. 1911). Educated Wandsworth County School. Entered Bank 1929, Exchange Restriction Department, IMF 1952, Assistant Chief, Overseas Department 1954–8, Deputy Governor, National Bank of Libya 1958–60, Adviser 1960–70. Secretary, Reserve Bank of Rhodesia, London 1970–7.

should be workable provided committee and controller are officials of reasonable and not, repeat not, Darwish type.' 'Glad to hear things are clearing up a little', replied the Deputy, though he went on to express doubts about the compromise. He instructed Loombe, who left for Cairo on 31 July, to keep well in the background and away from direct participation in the Control. He was to be available only for advice to the National Bank and was to return home if his position was causing awkwardness or suspicion.

Loombe and Cunnell did not find much that they could usefully do in the disturbed ambience of Cairo. The Ministry of Finance was suspicious of their presence and the National Bank was nervous of seeking their advice. In addition they had to cope with the repercussions of a bogus press report, thought to be inspired by Darwish, of a supposed interview given by Loombe about Egypt's withdrawal from the Sterling Area. However, following a short visit to Khartoum,[32] Loombe was in Cairo when sterling convertibility was suspended on 21 August and lent a steadying hand during the following two weeks. Leith-Ross was away in Europe, leaving the National Bank in charge of Job, his Deputy. There was some risk that the Egyptian authorities might take fright and refuse to accept any more sterling. The risk was increased by some temporary confusion in London, which delayed the execution of Egyptian orders for the purchase of European currencies on official account against transferable sterling. Loombe was able to support Job, in opposition to subordinates, who waited patiently for the orders to be completed. He and Cunnell returned to London at the end of the month. Referring, in his report to Siepmann, to the seeds of revolution in Egypt he wrote: 'It is surely due only to lack of organisation that those fat pashas have not yet had their throats cut.'

Following the suspension of convertibility, Egypt was given a special ration of $6 million for the period up to the end of October. The Finance Ministry soon argued that this was not enough, stressing that Egypt had not taken any special advantage of convertibility during its six weeks of life and protesting that suspension had been both unilateral and without the consultation laid down in the Agreement so recently signed. The Treasury refused any increase on the $6 million, and in Cairo Iliff informed the Ministry that Egypt, being now out of the Sterling Area, must balance its

---

[32] The British-administered Anglo–Egyptian Sudan, as it then was, shared a common currency with Egypt. Accordingly, when the Anglo–Egyptian financial agreement came into force, the Sudan also left the Sterling Area and also had to extend exchange control. It was understood between London, Cairo, and Khartoum that the Sudan would not conduct affairs in such a way that it became a burden on Egyptian external reserves.

dollar payments as best as it could. The British authorities, on the initial advice of the Bank, were nonetheless aware of the ace that the Egyptians possessed if they were to require payment in dollars for local expenditure by the British forces. Both the Embassy in Cairo and Loombe in the Bank now further advised that the card would definitely be used unless Egypt's essential dollar needs were met. Nokrashi had returned empty-handed from the United Nations and needed to show success in negotiations with the British. He took over the Finance portfolio in November, shortly before negotiations on a second Financial Agreement were to begin.

The ensuing episode was inglorious for the British and satisfying for the Egyptians. In London, the Treasury decided, without much encouragement from the Bank, to sit tight and wait for the ace to be played. They would offer a further release of only £10 million of Egyptian transferable sterling for 1948, and in the last resort offer conversion of a mere £2 million into dollars. Negotiations began in Cairo early in December, with Iliff leading for the UK. He was joined by Menzies[33] from the Bank, who wrote from Shepheard's Hotel shortly after arrival in Cairo that: 'Iliff has no illusions about the strength of our hand and of our chief vulnerable point.' The Egyptian side was now led by Dr Rifai, another Under-Secretary at the Finance Ministry. He was a polite official who exercised competent persuasion without the highly stressed techniques employed by his predecessor. After several meetings and various informal talks the negotiations made little headway. London still refused to move towards Egyptian demands. In the Bank, Siepmann judged it safe to assume the ace was indeed up the Egyptian sleeve. In Cairo, Iliff asked the British Commanders-in-Chief Middle East for their assessment of the consequences of the card being played. He then decided to return to London for consultations. But just before he left, at a lunch party for the Egyptian delegation, Dr Rifai quietly made the point that if the two sides could not agree on a reasonable amount of Egyptian sterling being spent in hard currency areas, might it not be possible for HMG to undertake to cover part of their military expenditure in hard currency? Iliff advised, in an immediate cable to London: 'This is the first showing of claws and I take it as nothing more than a reminder that in certain circumstances we might expect to be scratched.' The effect on London was electrical, the full cost of the ace being estimated at no less than $76 million for 1948. Iliff returned to Cairo on Christmas Day with authority to increase the offered release to £23 million from £10 million and the dollar ration to £6 million

[33] *Menzies, Lawrence James*, Kt (1906–83). Educated Wandsworth School. Entered Bank 1925. Assistant Chief Cashier (Exchange Control and Overseas) 1943–52, Deputy Chief Cashier 1951–7, Adviser to the Governors 1957–8, 1962–4, Secretary, ECGD 1958–61.

from £2 million. The Egyptians then held out for more and with the British seemingly on the run they boldly recalculated their dollar needs upwards. Early in January the two sides finally agreed on a total release of £33 million (£21 million for spending, £11 million for an additional working balances) and a dollar ration of £7¼ million (of which £1 million was payable in gold to help with Egypt's subscription to the IMF). The policy of being tough with the unliked Egyptians, successful enough in the first Agreement, had failed in the second. There had been a shift in bargaining strength because the Egyptians now felt strong enough to exploit fully such financial muscle as they possessed. Their departure from the Sterling Area was certainly some help to them in this respect; however the principal factor was that the British could no longer use physical force to secure Egyptian compliance with their wishes but could not yet give up their military presence in the Canal Zone.

Appraisal

The complicated series of negotiations with Egypt, viewed alongside those with India, Argentina, Australia and New Zealand, had produced results that were a far cry from the surgical ambitions set out in the Loan Agreement with the United States. But in keeping with their policy of realism, the results were not so far from the aims set out by the Bank and agreed by the Treasury early in 1946. It is true that very little had been achieved by way of cancellation and that the war-debt argument had counted for little. But the dangerously large wartime accumulations of sterling had been successfully segregated into No. 2 Accounts, or applied to the local acquisition of British-owned assets, by negotiated agreement with the countries concerned.[34] There had been no resort to unilateral blocking, no impairment of the ordinary Sterling Area arrangements, and no lasting damage to the international status of sterling on that score. Initial releases from the No. 2 Accounts had been kept within the limits considered necessary early in 1946, before negotiations started. Disappointing was the failure to agree the terms of releases from Indian and Egyptian No. 2 Accounts for more than six or twelve months at a time; and the surrender to Egyptian demands in the second interim agreement showed how easy it was for strict control over releases to slip away. But

---

[34] In South America agreements were reached with Brazil and Uruguay, affecting balances of nearly £80 million, analogous to the Eady–Miranda Agreement with Argentina. Within the Sterling Area, agreements were made with Iraq, Ceylon, and Palestine (affecting balances of some £210 million) analogous to those reached with India, Pakistan, and Egypt.

much more disappointing and damaging was the failure to honour for more than a few weeks the undertakings on convertibility that were central to the first set of agreements. Those undertakings, arising from the Loan Agreement, had obliged the UK to reach agreements about the sterling balances by the summer of 1947. But by the spring of that year, with the dollar drain accelerating, the Treasury and the Bank were getting into a manifestly dangerous if not impossible position, from which it is sometimes argued they should have extracted themselves by postponing the date for convertibility. This argument, and the crisis of August 1947, is considered in a later chapter. First, the story of the supplementary monetary agreements with countries in Western Europe must be told.

(c) EUROPE NOT FORGOTTEN: 1942–1946

Beginning in 1942 with the 'Schachtmann memoranda', the Bank had always had in mind a network of monetary agreements linking sterling to the currencies of continental Europe. Over the longer term this was often seen as part of the working foreground to which the IMF and its rules would be the background. But in the short term it would be part of the monetary furniture of the transitional period, necessarily beginning with the reconstruction of monetary relationships destroyed by the war. As early as 1942 a Committee of Inter-Allied Experts was set up to consider post-war currency arrangements in Europe. This Committee met in London and was chaired by Waley of the UK Treasury, the Bank being mainly represented by Lithiby,[35] a principal adviser on European affairs. It was mostly concerned with the problems likely to arise over the resumption of sovereign national monetary systems as countries were liberated from enemy occupation. Prominent among these problems would be the issue of new legal tender and the cancellation, reduction, or replacement of inflated wartime issues. But the Committee also took note of the need for a procedure re-establishing exchange rates and other working relationships both between the new currencies themselves and between them and the outside world of the dollar and the pound sterling.

Early in 1944, as the Allied invasion of metropolitan France grew nearer and the fortunes of the Axis powers in Eastern and Southern Europe further deteriorated, the Treasury and the Bank began detailed planning of new monetary agreements with the European allies. They also began planning new agreements with the European neutrals so as to exploit the

---

[35] *Lithiby, John Stewart* (1892–1967). Educated Oxford. Worked in Paris 1919–40. Entered Bank 1940, Assistant Adviser 1940–4, Deputy Adviser 1944–6, Adviser to the Governors 1946–55.

improvement in British bargaining strength. Among those made with the Allies, the agreement with Belgium proved to be the prototype. A draft was sent by the Bank to the Treasury in March. Two months later a Belgian draft was sent to the Bank by Hubert Ansiaux,[36] a future Governor of the National Bank of Belgium and at that time attached to the Belgian Finance Ministry in London. Discussions ensued during the summer and included an intervention by a suspicious Keynes. He required to be satisfied that the Agreement would not run counter to the letter or spirit of Bretton Woods, at least during the transitional period for which it was in the first instance intended. The Bank managed to reassure him on this score and after further negotiation the agreement was signed early in October 1944, by which time the Belgians had resumed authority in Brussels. The Bank held a press conference at which Bolton explained the main points of the agreement. He indicated that it was intended to set the pattern for agreements with France, Holland, Norway, and others. Its principal features were as follows:

(i) The fixing of the rate of exchange between sterling and the Belgian franc, alterable only after mutual consultation;
(ii) A provision, without the exchange guarantee the Belgians wanted, for the Bank of England to hold up to the equivalent of £5 million as a working balance in Belgian francs and for the National Bank of Belgium to hold up to £5 million in sterling plus an additional sum equivalent to the total sterling holdings of the Belgian monetary area at the date of the agreement. Settlement outside these limits was to be in gold.
(iii) A provision for sterling held by residents of the Belgian monetary area (Belgium, Luxemburg, and the Belgian Congo) and for Belgian francs held by residents of the Sterling Area to be freely transferable within the two areas, and for such transferability to be extended to other countries or areas as suitable opportunity offered and as might subsequently be agreed. A consequence of this provision was to allow the 'additional sum' to be spent anywhere within the Sterling Area as well as in other countries that might later be added to the transferability list. There was accordingly no funding of accumulated Belgian sterling. But neither was there any right of convertibility into dollars.

---

[36] *Ansiaux, Hubert-Jacques-Nicolas, Baron (1908–87).* Educated Universitaire Libre de Bruxelles. Director, National Bank of Belgium 1941–54, Deputy Governor 1954–7, Governor 1957–71, Director, BIS 1957–71, Governor for Belgium, IMF 1957–71, Alternate Governor for Belgium, IBRD and IFC 1960–71, Chairman, Committee of EEC Central Bank Governors 1967–71.

(iv) A term of three years, subject to three-months' notice of early termination by either side, and subject to a special review if the contracting parties adhered to a 'general international monetary agreement'.

The agreement with Belgium was followed by an agreement with the French, who where chronically short of sterling, had no accumulated balances, and were granted £100 million credit. This was in turn followed by a new agreement with the Swedes, who agreed in secret to hold up to £40 million in sterling whereas previously they had held no significant quantity.

By early 1945 further negotiations were in progress or pending with Switzerland, Spain, and Portugal. But the prolongation of hostilities through the autumn and winter of 1944–5 delayed the conclusion of agreements with Norway, Holland, and Denmark. It also altered the Bank's view of the European monetary outlook. In a survey circulated on 26 April 1945, Bolton wrote that in 1943–4 UK policy had been developed on the assumption that, with respect to their external reserves, the Western European allies would end the war in a stronger position than the UK. But the prolongation of the war beyond September 1944 had had so destructive an effect that this assumption no longer held good, with the possible exception of Belgium. The damage to Western Europe was far worse than had been anticipated. Bolton saw dangers of an economic Balkanisation of Europe, or bilateralist *sauve qui peut*, and doubted the ability of the US to 'make any gesture outside the doubtful framework provided by the Bretton Woods Final Act'. He felt the UK could help by trying to persuade the countries with whom the UK had monetary agreements to use sterling between themselves multilaterally, underpinning this by close collaboration between central banks. 'This country', he added, 'cannot expect to remain a relatively peaceful oasis surrounded by neighbours in various stages of anarchy and dissolution.'[37]

[37] Information about conditions on the Continent at this time was available to the Bank from a wide variety of sources, including those arising from UK participation in the financing of United Nations Relief and Rehabilitation Administration (UNRRA) operations. Rather out of the ordinary was a letter from the Association of Pensioners of the Austrian National Bank and its predecessor the Austro-Hungarian Bank. Writing in English from Vienna in December 1945, this Association appealed to the Bank for food supplies in the following terms:

'There are in our association about 400 persons, most of them aged over 70 years, who, seeing that they are no longer able to do any productive work, are excluded from the common boards provided for working people. Since the kitchen formerly run by our association is no longer at the disposal of our pensioners, it is an almost unbearable task to provide the most necessary eatables for the households of old, and partly sick, people and especially so for single persons, so that hunger and misery are prevailing over many of our fellow-clerks.

Money cannot be of any use in this case, quite apart from the fact that the Fund

Bolton's idea of developing sterling as a means of transitional post-war intra-European payment was not then as misguided as it later became. It could work provided sterling remained largely inconvertible into gold or dollars, provided the necessary exchange control over non-residents remained effective, and provided trade discrimination by the participants in favour of each other was maintained. The effectiveness of exchange control was the weakest link in this chain, but evidence of this was not to appear for several years. Meanwhile, the whole episode of the Anglo-American Loan Agreement and the convertibility crisis, with its heavy damage to sterling's intra-European prospects, had first to be played through before the plight of Western Europe could be met with the Marshall Plan and later with the evolution of a specially constructed intra-European payments mechanism.

By the end of 1945 further monetary agreements had been made with Holland, Norway, Denmark, and Czechoslovakia and were nearing signature with Switzerland and Portugal. The latter included arrangements for the funding of £80 million of Portuguese sterling. From the Treasury a leading part throughout had been played by Hugh Ellis-Rees,[38] then an Assistant Secretary. Following the signing of the Loan Agreement with the US at the end of 1945 – an event that seemed to change the background against which these European agreements had been made – he circulated an eloquent memorandum which found its way both to Keynes and to the Bank. The monetary agreements and the associated development of close working relationships, he wrote, were part of a policy designed to draw the countries of Western Europe together in monetary and economic affairs, under British leadership: 'bearing in mind the advantages which would accrue to us all, not only economic but also

---

accumulated by our Association in the course of time and which was requisitioned by the national socialist government in 1938, would not help us in any way under the present circumstances even if it were still existent. We are therefore unable to relieve the distress of our former fellow workers by some action of our own accord.

In this emergency we beg to repeat our instant request to release us from our misery by sending us eatables. Whilst we beg to assure you of our heartfelt gratitude we also wish that God may reward you richly for your generous help.'

Siepmann consulted the Deputy Governor and another member of the Court; but it was reluctantly concluded that nothing could be done by the Bank. A member of the Overseas staff was asked to explain this when he travelled to Vienna. A somewhat similar appeal from the National Bank of Hungary was received early in 1946 and met with the same response.

[38] *Ellis-Rees, Hugh, KCMG, CB (1900–74).* Educated Tollington School and London University. RAF 1918–19. Inland Revenue 1919–38, HM Treasury 1940–8, Assistant Secretary 1943–8, Under-Secretary 1948, Financial Adviser to British Embassy, Madrid 1940–4, Member, UK Delegation to OEEC, with rank of Minister 1948, Vice-Chairman, Managing Board of EPU 1950–1, Permanent Delegate 1952–60 with rank of Ambassador 1954–60, Official Chairman of OEEC 1952–60.

strategic and political advantages, which are inseparable'. Integral to this policy, he continued, was maintenance of the Sterling Area as a walled city within which sterling was freely transferable but outside which transferability could be extended step by step, as circumstances permitted. Useful extensions had already been made on an administrative basis. But the Loan Agreement with the US had now intervened, with its commitment to the world-wide current-account convertibility of sterling sometime in 1947. This seemed to suggest that the monetary agreements would become redundant. What then would be British policy towards the countries of Western Europe whose economic predicament and external monetary arrangements would remain unaltered? Ellis-Rees continued: 'Geography, tradition, prestige, as the defender of Europe, and the general fellow-feeling among Europeans brings us close together and demands a positive policy on our part, and I do not think we can afford to pay lip service to the principle without making some effort to see that our practical policy conforms.' He advocated continuation of intra-European trade discrimination and maintenance of the close personal contacts that had already been made. As to the network of monetary agreements, how far could they be retained without conflicting with the Loan Agreement? He sought guidance. The Bank's response to this, fully consistent with the position it had taken during the lead-in to Bretton Woods, was to deny that sterling convertibility would render the monetary agreements redundant. 'We were laying foundations', protested Siepmann, 'not erecting huts.'

Bolton followed in full-hearted support of the monetary politique for Western Europe suggested by Ellis-Rees. In replying to the Treasury at the end of January 1946, Cobbold made clear that the Bank dissented from any view that the network of monetary agreements would not be needed for more than another year or so. He agreed, however, that their credit provisions might need modification. The Treasury reserved its judgement on this advice, while Keynes himself did not deploy any particular views on the subject or about policy towards Western Europe in the longer term. He did however register anxiety about a British tendency to set too much store by the American Loan, to be over-generous about immediate postwar relief in Europe and elsewhere, and to be extravagant over military expenditure abroad. He had always been worried on this score. Yet one of the main points he had used in selling the Loan to his colleagues in London was that it would enable the UK to preserve its great-power standing. Keynes was consulted by Waley about the Ellis-Rees memorandum and specifically about the sterling balances of non-sterling countries. But apart from special arrangements with Argentina, Brazil, and Uruguay, whose balances could be used to buy out British-owned utilities, he considered that the non-sterling countries should be treated on all fours with the Sterling Area – that is to say within the uniform approach that he was then advocating but for which he could not get support. Europe, as such, seems to have had no special place in Keynes' thinking at this time.

Whatever Siepmann might expostulate, continuation of the monetary agreements after sterling became convertible was not self-evidently necessary. Moreover, since full deployment of the case for their future required an exposition of technical issues that was made more complex by the difficulty of giving precise meaning to such terms as 'convertibility' and 'current transactions',[39] the second report of Siepmann's Committee, circulated at the end of June 1946, was not easy reading. It is, however, important to explain the Bank's reasons for advocating that the network of monetary agreements should be retained. For without its retention the crisis in 1947 could well have taken a decisively different course.

The issues are conveniently illustrated by reference to the regime then applying to the US dollar. There was, firstly, no American exchange control. Through the New York market the dollar itself was freely convertible into other currencies, for all purposes, while the dollar balances of foreign monetary authorities could also be altered by transactions in gold at $35 per ounce with the FRBNY acting as agent for the US Treasury. The market rates between the dollar and other currencies were for the authorities of those countries themselves to manage, by direct intervention either way in the New York market in support of a declared parity. Under this regime the US authorities did not themselves accumulate holdings of other, mostly inconvertible, currencies. They operated only in gold at the fixed monetary price, and passively. Nor were they concerned with the purposes for which currency conversions on the New York market were made. Nor, finally, was there any practical problem of ensuring that US exporters obtained dollars in exchange. They could either insist on payment in dollars direct, through dollar invoicing, or else be paid in foreign exchange that they could sell on the market at a rate which, under the Bretton Woods rules now coming into force, the country concerned undertook to support within narrow limits either side of parity.

The regime contemplated by the British authorities for convertible sterling was different to the American regime. Firstly there was the continuation of UK exchange control and secondly the continuing absence

---

[39] As Siepmann wrote in an unsent letter to Rowe-Dutton on 24 January: 'Both the Financial Agreement and the Final Act bristle with difficulties of interpretation which are all the more perplexing because the terminology is very often neither that of business nor of administration.'

of an exchange market in London. The former required that commercial receipts of foreign currency by UK residents should be sold to authorised banks for sterling, while the latter required the banks to sell accumulated foreign exchange to the EEA. The Account was therefore obliged to accumulate any surplus UK holdings of foreign currencies, including inconvertible currencies. The EEA could not, as things stood in 1946, then sell these latter holdings on the New York market because the exchange control of the country concerned would not permit the transaction to take place. It followed that arrangements for settling accumulations of inconvertible currencies could only be made through monetary agreements with the countries concerned. Through such agreements a link could be forged between sterling and, for instance, the Belgian franc. Thus the key question was: might the introduction of sterling current-account convertibility so alter things that UK banks and the EEA could avoid accumulating inconvertible currencies? For this change to occur, and accordingly for monetary agreements to become technically unnecessary, there would have to be a readiness by the authorities of inconvertible countries to mop up UK sales of their currencies, surplus to UK needs, by themselves selling sterling, dollars, or other convertible currencies in exchange in the New York market. In effect they would have to treat, for example, Belgian francs held on UK account as convertible, in much the same way as the UK exchange control treated sterling held on American account. Alternatively, the UK authorities would have to arrange, through exchange control, that all British transactions with inconvertible-currency countries should be invoiced either in sterling or in another convertible currency. While acknowledging that both these alternatives were technically feasible, the Bank strongly preferred retention of the monetary agreements and the system they represented rather than their abolition.

The reasoning of Siepmann's Committee on this point is not immediately clear to the reader of a mostly technical report some forty years afterwards, but it seems to have been as follows. Abolition of the agreements would in effect have meant that the UK would for practical purposes be joining the dollar area. Without an exchange market in London, all outstanding balances would be settled through the New York market, underpinned from time to time by gold transactions between the EEA and the Federal Reserve, or directly between the EEA and, for example, the National Bank of Belgium. To this the Bank offered four main objections. Firstly, it was felt that 'joining the dollar area', in the above sense and abolishing the mutual credit arrangements of the agreements would provoke the inconvertible-currency countries into active trade discrimination against the UK and more active discrimination in favour of each other. Yet the US Loan Agreement did not oblige the UK to accept this if it could be mitigated or avoided within the terms of that Agreement. Secondly, abandoning the monetary agreements would mean winding down the close collaboration between the British authorities and their continental counterparts, a collaboration that seemed so badly needed in the difficult early post-war circumstances. Thirdly, total reliance on New York for several years ahead would damage the restoration of London as a fully international financial centre. Fourthly, relying wholly on New York for day-to-day settlement would probably imply giving up any protection against convertible sterling being used for capital-account purposes outside the obligations of the Loan Agreement. In the much longer run, when an exchange market in London had been re-established and the immediate problems of European reconstruction passed into history, the network of monetary agreements could be allowed to lapse; but not yet, not in 1946.

The Bank may have left unstated another argument. The network of agreements would provide a ready-to-hand safety net if convertibility itself had to be abandoned in a crisis. Had the network been dismantled prior to convertibility, it could conceivably – and with great difficulty – have been reinstated in some way when convertibility was suspended. But another very different option would have presented itself, namely to have gone it alone without a suspension of convertibility but with a devaluation of sterling or, more likely, a period of floating against the dollar. Something closely akin to this solution did eventually present itself in the winter of 1951–2 and was very nearly adopted. Had this option been taken in 1947, and kept in place thereafter, British participation in the European Payments Union (EPU) would presumably not have happened and participation in the associated intra-European trade liberalisation would have been more difficult. Further pursuit of this might-have-been would not be useful; but there is no doubting the importance of the decision taken in 1946, largely in accord with the Bank's advice, to retain the network of monetary agreements. It was a decision the Treasury found easy to take. There is no record of any prolonged resistance to it. It meant, in effect, that while embarking on their brief and compulsory venture into the unrealistic world of the Loan Agreement, the British authorities did not sever the working links that would be required if a regionalist approach proved necessary after all – which it did.

(d) PREPARING FOR STERLING CONVERTIBILITY IN WESTERN EUROPE: 1946–1947

Having decided that the network should be retained, the Treasury and the Bank concluded that the monetary agreements should be amended so that they became technically attuned to convertibility. Waley minuted the Chancellor about this on 29 July 1946, remarking: 'Our aim will be to make sterling held by all these countries freely available for current requirements (subject to minimum balance arrangements where necessary) some time before the guillotine falls in July 1947. We want to avoid negotiating with an inconveniently short time limit.' Holidays, the Anglo–Argentine negotiations, and a visit by Dalton to the US and Canada then intervened. So it was not until October that the Bank resumed work on the subject. There were three points to be settled in each case. The first and simplest was that convertibility should apply only to sterling balances of central banks, net of Bank of England holdings of their respective currencies. This conformed to the concept of convertibility contained in the Bretton Woods Agreements and placed upon the central banks concerned some duty of ensuring that convertible sterling was not used to finance capital as well as current transactions. This in turn eliminated any need for the Bank itself to police sterling conversions effected by ordinary non-residents. The second point was to agree minimum balance arrangements, and this implied negotiations of varying degrees of difficulty.

The third point was more abstruse but just as important. It was necessary to ensure that when the UK authorities made sterling freely convertible, any barriers imposed by other authorities on such transferability would also be removed. For unless such barriers were removed, the general acceptability of sterling would be impaired; in addition the UK could find itself accumulating unwanted balances of inconvertible currency. Accordingly, all countries whose current sterling was to become freely transferable would have to agree to accept sterling from all sources in respect of current transactions. Looking back, such agreement might seem a mere formality, as surely no country was likely to refuse sterling in payment for current transactions if it was then freely convertible into dollars and, indirectly, gold. But the Bank did not take this view. It felt that many countries had become so bilateralist in their habits of thought that they would not automatically accept convertible sterling. Getting specific undertakings may therefore have been a wise precaution. But experience in negotiations with France[40] and Switzerland was to reveal a less

---

[40] France and the French monetary area was by far the largest unit with which negotiations took place. The ex-enemy countries were not yet on their feet, Germany itself being still under direct rule by the occupying powers.

palatable reason for seeking such undertakings, namely that sterling, even if freely transferable for current transactions virtually world-wide, would not automatically be regarded as if it were as good an asset as the dollar, or as good as gold.

The Bank's position on these matters having been clarified, the Deputy Governor wrote an explanatory letter to Eady on 4 November 1946, adding that he would himself shortly be travelling on the Continent and would like to open discussions with the central banks of Belgium, Holland, Portugal, and France. Following this letter, the discussions with the Treasury concentrated upon individual countries. There was no disagreement on general principles. With Holland, Norway, and Portugal no lasting problem seemed to arise. Norway's sterling balances were indeed large but could be almost eliminated ahead of July 1947 by advance payments to UK shipbuilders. By contrast, Sweden and Switzerland, but especially the former, had accumulated substantial balances since the end of the war and these would need to be tied up. This left Belgium and France among the important cases. At that time the former possessed official balances that did not exceed a likely debt of some £15 million to the British Government arising out of the war. Private balances however exceeded £20 million and the Treasury was concerned lest these should be transferred to the National Bank and subsequently converted. Belgium was now beginning to enjoy a period as one of the strongest economies in Western Europe, earning a substantial external surplus with its inconvertible neighbours but requiring convertible currencies for the purchase of primary produce in the Americas. It was therefore a potential concentration of danger to the UK reserves, both as a holder of accumulated but untied sterling and as a prospective heavy current earner of convertible sterling. The Bank may have seen these dangers but concluded, and so advised the Treasury, that nothing could be done except obtain informal assurance that the Belgian Government would repay its debt to HMG before converting any official holdings of Belgian sterling on a substantial scale. This advice was accepted and may have seemed well founded at the time it was given, when the world-wide dollar shortage was only beginning to become acute. But it severely underestimated the pace at which the Belgians would accumulate fresh sterling during the first half of 1947 (once they had agreed to accept it freely from all sources), their readiness to encourage the mobilisation of privately held sterling for use in international exchange, and their reluctance to repay the debt to HMG.

In sharp contrast to Belgium, France was chronically short of all foreign exchange, including sterling. Her monetary relationship with the UK and the Sterling Area had become very complex, evolving as it had from arrangements made early in the war (before the German occupation), through those subsequently made with the Free French authorities (first in London and later in North Africa), and on to the Anglo–French Financial Agreement of March 1945 and a Supplementary Agreement of April 1946. Under the former Agreement, the French quickly borrowed no less than £150 million from the UK; under the latter Agreement, they undertook to repay this over three years, partly in gold, partly by the transfer of French-owned sterling securities vested by the French authorities, and partly from requisitions of privately held sterling balances. These resources were also to be used to meet any further French deficit with the Sterling Area, for there was to be no further sterling loan. The French paid some £50 million in gold under the second Agreement, but in the autumn of 1946 their Prime Minister wrote to London asking for a renegotiation in order to relieve the pressure on French gold reserves. This request was granted and late in the year another Agreement was signed under which the debt to the UK was made repayable over ten years, beginning in 1950. In addition, the UK agreed to accept further transfers of vested securities in 1947 in exchange for sterling required by France for current transactions.

The series of negotiations in 1945 and 1946 had at times been difficult, with the result that in any further negotiations the French were inclined to look guardedly at any British proposal. Moreover they could not be expected to set particular store by an offer of sterling convertibility if there was no prospect of their accumulating (net) any sterling to convert. Yet the Bank was nevertheless keen to persuade the French, and with them the entire French monetary area, to accept sterling freely from all sources. Accordingly it proposed that the French might be offered convertibility of gross rather than net sterling receipts from outside the Sterling Area in exchange for agreeing to accept sterling freely, the quantities of such receipts being ascertained by the two central banks working in collaboration. The Treasury accepted this suggestion as the basis for discussion with the Bank of France.

The Deputy Governor obtained favourable reactions to all these ideas when he visited Brussels, Amsterdam, and Paris during November 1946. Supplementary Agreements with Belgium and Holland followed early in 1947, but by then the French had had second thoughts. Lithiby reported that though the Bank of France was very favourable to the spirit of the British proposal, they were insisting that nothing must commit the French to receiving less gold or paying out more gold than would be the case under existing bilateral agreements. He added that the French would accordingly not be willing to take sterling from countries with whom they had bilateral agreements and gold points. Guy Watson, in a note dated 20 February, referred to the gold-mindedness of the French, certainly no new phenomenon. However, Ellis-Rees made considerable dents in this position when talking to the French Treasury in March, though he also recorded the impression that 'if France did agree to accept sterling...they would have to push it out again quickly'. Some days later Paris agreed to accept sterling from all sources, and in London the Bank was asked to draft an agreement.

A Byzantine series of negotiations then followed, sometimes conducted in London, sometimes in Paris, sometimes between Ellis-Rees and the French Treasury, sometimes between Lithiby and the Bank of France. First, the French upset the British position by asking after all for an agreement giving world-wide transferability to their net receipts of current-account sterling from all sources while agreeing to safeguards restricting the conversion of sterling obtained from the realisation of French-owned sterling securities. The British could not refuse but replied that realisations of securities would in that case have to cease and would only be resumed after full consultations. The French turned this down and tended to go back to the original British proposals, though now refusing to accept sterling from countries with whom they did *not* have a monetary agreement. There was then another impasse, which in mid-June was once again resolved by Ellis-Rees. But the British then began to worry lest insisting that pre-zero accruals of sterling from the sale of securities should be usable only in the Sterling Area would contravene the Loan Agreement. Under the Agreement, such accruals could be blocked; but their transferability, unblocked, could not be limited. To get round this the Treasury proposed segregating French balances arising from security sales and gold payments – £34 million – in a 'Forward Commitment Cover Account' that could subsequently be used only to discharge commitments to the Sterling Area entered into prior to 15 July. At meetings held in Paris on 2 and 3 July the French replied, in a fine show of tactical indignation, that opening this Account would give the impression that they could not be trusted to meet commitments; and anyway it was unnatural to treat the counterpart of the gold payments as inconvertible. London then provisionally agreed with the French, somewhat in desperation, that an arbitrary £23 million of French sterling should be segregated, with a secret annexe to the effect that it could be used only in the Sterling Area. Bolton advised strongly against this covert breach of the Loan Agreement, whereupon the US authorities were asked at the end of July whether they would object to the earmarking of French balances against pre-zero sterling commitments. Washington offered no objection. However time had now run out because the acute phase of the convertibility crisis was beginning. The French became very restive, raising further snags; but by 13 August the UK Treasury had to decide that the negotiations be put on ice pending the result of the imminent wider talks with the American authorities. On 21 August Catto telegraphed Emmanuel Monick, Governor of the Bank of France, about the suspension of convertibility[41] and informed him that 'HM Government are forced most reluctantly to withdraw for the present their offer to permit transfers of sterling held on French account to the USA and other dollar countries'. Several days later Ellis-Rees wrote to Watson in the Bank about possible French membership of what was now the Transferable Account Area. 'I doubt', he said, 'if we should want the rather elaborate safeguards we were preparing to have before.'

The French could congratulate themselves on a lucky though possibly well-judged escape. By constant delays they had avoided agreeing to any segregation of their sterling balances in exchange for the convertibility of current receipts, and thereby avoided losing the latter within weeks only to find the British endeavouring to hang on to the former. They had, it seems, seldom been particularly anxious to conclude negotiations, never been particularly affected by the philosophy of the Loan Agreement, never been much impressed about the value of post-war sterling as a reserve and trading currency, and often been suspicious about British intentions. They had played things along, as the months went by, because they were short of sterling earnings and could not refuse all reasonable suggestions for adjusting their financial relationship with the UK to take account of the Loan Agreement. But as partners in a grand design for convertible sterling in 1947, it seems they had no more belief in its feasibility than, at heart, did the British themselves.

Among the many other telegrams sent by Catto on 21 August was one to the President of the Swiss National Bank. It contained no reference to any Anglo-Swiss Agreement and no request for further talks. Next day the Swiss authorities reassuringly announced that monetary relations between Switzerland and the UK remained quite unchanged. This unruffled response was due to the fact that the British had not succeeded in negotiating a Supplementary Agreement with the Swiss and had already accepted that the Anglo-Swiss Monetary Agreement of April 1946 should be allowed to run until expiry in 1949. The result of this arrangement had been that the Swiss would continue to hold up to £15 million, whose ultimate future would be negotiated when the Agreement ended, but

---

[41] This inter-central bank telegram, like others despatched round the world on that day, paralleled inter-governmental messages to the same effect.

would remain quite uncommitted to accept sterling from all sources. As Switzerland possessed a very desirable currency, its absence – along with that of France – from the virtually world-wide Transferable Account Area that the Bank had been seeking to construct for sterling was not entirely painless. It had come about because the Swiss remained very gold-minded, were very concerned to obtain adequate supplies of raw materials and food, and feared that ready acceptance of sterling would mean encountering an avalanche of it, in payment for Swiss exports, accompanied by a reduction in the availability of essential imports.

Wartime financial relations with the Swiss had been both complex and cool. Since a narrow Agreement, eventually signed in 1943, provided for all settlement between the two countries to be in gold only, the UK practised extreme economy in acquiring Swiss franc liabilities. When the war ended and an allowance of foreign currency for tourist travel was introduced, Switzerland was excluded from this arrangement. In the autumn of 1945 a Swiss delegation therefore visited London for preliminary talks about trade and payments between the two countries. Ellis-Rees and Bolton met them in the Treasury. Suggestions concerning a Swiss franc credit to the UK, or alternatively an exchange guarantee on such sterling as the Swiss might agree to accumulate, were firmly rejected by the British, as also was any idea that more than $\frac{1}{2}$% should be paid on such sterling. For their part the Swiss expressed willingness to accumulate a quantity of sterling in exchange for some liberalisation of UK imports from Switzerland and the removal of the UK ban on tourist travel to their country. The talks were very friendly and in November the Bank was asked by the Treasury to begin drafting an Anglo–Swiss Monetary Agreement of the Belgian variety, permitting the Swiss to hold an 'additional sum' not exceeding £10 million in addition to a basic £5 million. The ban on tourism would go. On this basis Ellis-Rees, accompanied by St John Turner[42] from the Bank, went to Berne early in February 1946 and negotiated a straightforward three-year Agreement with the Confederation, which was finally signed on 12 March. It included provision for review after one year, when unresolved questions, notably what should ultimately happen to Switzerland's accumulated sterling, could again be discussed. It also included an exchange of letters that acknowledged the existence of the then unratified Anglo–American Loan Agreement, but was unable to say what implications, if any, the latter might have for the future of the Anglo-Swiss Agreement and the treatment

---

[42] *Turner, Cyril William St John (1903–78)*. Educated Ipswich School. Entered Bank 1922, Assistant Adviser (Acting) 1946–7, Controller of Currency, Pakistan 1947–8, Adviser (Acting) 1948–58, Adviser 1958–63.

of Swiss sterling. Privately, Ellis-Rees and Turner both felt that the UK could not with any honour threaten to block such sterling, though they recognised that the Loan Agreement might oblige them to negotiate about its future long before the three-year term expired.

By November 1946 the Swiss had already accumulated £10 million, the limit for the first year, and were once more gaining gold from London. The Swiss economy was booming and the authorities were worried about inflationary pressures being aggravated by the internal monetary effects of a rising gold stock. They therefore reappeared in London with a request that the British should now restrict tourism in Switzerland below the level permitted by the £75 tourist allowance. This was met with the counter-suggestion that the Swiss should impose their own restrictions. They did in fact cut back on licences for exports to the Sterling Area and early in the new year they contrived an elaborate scheme designed to restrict expenditure by UK tourists in Switzerland. In London, by this time, the Bank was considering a Supplementary Agreement containing provision for the phased release of Swiss sterling after 1949 and Swiss acceptance of sterling from all sources after 15 July 1947. The Treasury agreed and Ellis-Rees and Turner went to Berne for negotiations at the end of February. But since the Swiss had nothing further to gain from world-wide sterling convertibility and were disinclined to negotiate in 1947 the fate of a balance that they had already agreed to hold until 1949, little progress was made. The Treasury was inclined to let the existing Agreement run on, but the Deputy Governor argued the importance of the Swiss agreeing to accept sterling from all sources and the need, under the Anglo-American Agreement, to come to some arrangement with them. The Swiss Embassy in London then indicated to the Bank that a settlement was now possible provided they were not pushed too hard on post-1949 releases. Soon afterwards, however, Watson reported that the Swiss were raising objections to accepting sterling from all sources; they feared it would prejudice their ability to extract supplies of essential imports from their trading partners. These objections persisted. An Anglo-Swiss exchange of letters in July acknowledged that the existing Agreement would continue unaltered. The Deputy Governor reported that Dr Keller (the Swiss negotiator) in the course of a long and full talk in Basle, had 'maintained firmly his dislike of a full transferability arrangement. The Swiss are clearly frightened of it and think it will mean both that sterling will be shot at them and they will have to take more gold in consequence and that their trade bargaining powers with neighbouring countries will be weakened.' For the Swiss, in other words, sterling was a weak currency that they did not wish to hold and which they judged to be over-plentiful.

Bitterly, the Swedish authorities must have come to the same conclusion when the Riksbank in Stockholm received its own telegram from Catto on 21 August. Only six weeks earlier they had reluctantly agreed, after a prolonged tussle, to a Supplementary Agreement that effectively froze, in exchange for the convertibility of current accruals, the £25 million of official sterling accumulated under the five-year Agreement of March 1945. They had done so when their own external situation was deteriorating, when they were enduring political criticism at home for their conduct of economic policy, and when they had hoped to make some use of what they had thought, and earlier been led by the British to believe, were liquid sterling reserves. They had endeavoured to obtain British agreement to set aside at least a proportion of the segregated balances for emergency use. London would have none of this and would agree only to an escape clause expressed in very general terms. In the end the Swedes had become very suspicious and endeavoured to obtain written assurances, which they said they had received orally (but which the Treasury denied), that whatever else happened the convertibility of Swedish sterling accruing after 15 July would be maintained for the remainder of the Agreement. This request was refused, and on 21 August the Swedes learnt that while sterling convertibility had been unilaterally suspended, without consultation, their £25 million remained immobilised in the Riksbank's No. 2 Account at the Bank of England. They had also virtuously accumulated £5 million in their No. 1 Account since 15 July, only to find it had now become inconvertible into dollars. They felt they had been fooled or betrayed. They would have done better to have followed the French example and held out for a few more weeks.

The Swedes were far from being gold-minded and were well disposed to the Bretton Woods system. Their Social Democrat Government was sympathetic to the economic problems facing the Labour Government in London and keen to overcome any ill-will left over from Sweden's wartime neutrality. Like the Swiss they were anxious to ensure supplies of essential materials and food; and like many other countries they were becoming very short of dollars while remaining long of sterling. So they were attracted by the prospect of sterling convertibility and ready in the end to strike a bargain over the segregation of their accumulated balance. Moreover, the two principal Swedish officials concerned with external monetary affairs were both men of distinction and admirers of the Anglo-Saxon mind. The first was Dag Hammarskjöld,[43] later Secretary-General of

---

[43] *Hammarskjöld, Dag Hjalmar Carl* (1905–61). Educated Cambridge and Uppsala. Under-Secretary, Ministry of Finance 1937–46, Chairman of the Board, Sveriges Riksbank 1941–8, Economic Adviser and Under-Secretary, Foreign Office 1946–51, Vice-Chairman,

the United Nations but then Under-Secretary to the Ministry of Finance in Stockholm and Chairman of the Board at the Riksbank. The other was Ivar Rooth,[44] Governor of the Riksbank and later Managing Director of the IMF. He had been Governor since the late twenties and was an old friend of the Bank of England. An anglophile, his son had served as a sergeant in the British army during the war. The more sad, then, that the Treasury and the Bank were obliged to treat their friends so badly.

The reader may be forgiven a sense of tedium after this foray into the largely forgotten world of bilateral monetary agreements and early post-war shortages. At least the parallel world of bilateral trade bargaining, with its endless lists of essential goods required but difficult to get, or inessential goods for sale but not required by the other side, has been left largely to the imagination. But the series of monetary negotiations between the UK and other Western European countries in the first half of 1947 have about them a recognisably depressing ring that is due neither to an inherent tediousness of the evidence nor to the futility of an exercise that was doomed to end in the embarrassments of 21 August. Rather is it due to the weakness of sterling and the absence of any Europeanist enthusiasm on the part of the British negotiators. The earlier enthusiasm shown particularly by Bolton and Ellis-Rees, which to some degree underlay the decision to preserve the monetary agreements themselves, does not find further expression. Instead there is a sequence of bilateral bargaining, not altogether successful or promising with respect to the intra-European use of sterling, in which the British seem motivated in the main by the need to obey an Agreement with the US that they did not like and by a desire to arrange for sterling to be managed in the narrower interests of the UK rather than in the interests of Western Europe generally. Monetary relations with the various countries are quite close and often cordial, though sometimes affected by mistrust or suspicion. The Bank was working hard to re-establish central bank relationships disrupted by the war and to build on them anew. But there is little vision of how Europe might develop and little sign of incipient British leadership in that regard. Unfortunately, neither the politicians in charge in Great George Street, nor the misjudgements entrenched in the Loan Agreement, nor the preoccupations with the Sterling Area, nor the growing menace of the

---

Executive Committee, OEEC 1948–9, Minister of State, Foreign Economic Relations 1951–3. Secretary-General, United Nations 1953–61. Nobel Peace Prize 1961.

[44] *Rooth, Ivar (1888–1972)*. Educated Uppsala. Solicitor of the Stockholm Handelsbank 1914–15, Head of Reimbursement Department 1915–19, Assistant Director of Swedish Emissionsaktebolaget 1919–20, Assistant Director and Solicitor, Inteckningsgaranti, Stockholm 1920–9, Governor, Sveriges Riksbank 1929–48, Director, BIS 1931–3, 1937–49, Managing Director, IMF 1951–6.

dollar drain were such as to encourage this kind of vision in British monetary officials at this formative time.

(e) THE DENOUEMENT: 1947

When convertibility was suspended on 20 August 1947, all but $400 million of the American Loan had been drawn out of the original $3,750 million. Suspension, and the whole panoply of crisis that went with it, was unquestionably a humiliation for the British Government and for sterling. The Loan had all but run out far sooner than originally intended. Agreements recently signed were unilaterally disregarded and the undertakings on convertibility were repudiated. The Bank, as principal financial adviser to the Treasury, did not escape criticism. But the handling of affairs over the six months preceding suspension was far from a monetary version of the Battle of Balaclava. A disaster had been feared in the Bank and the Treasury as long ago as December 1945, when the Loan Agreement was signed. By February 1947 the enemy guns could be heard both in Threadneedle Street and in Great George Street. In the ensuing months much thought was given to how they might be silenced, though to no avail. The difficulties or dangers of a prompt change of direction always seemed greater than those of going on unprotected down the track of pledged commitment.

An approaching shortage of dollars had become visible to the UK authorities in the autumn of 1946, when the forecasts for 1947 showed that a manageable external deficit overall was likely to be accompanied by a much less manageable deficit with the dollar area. Other countries were also becoming very short of dollars and the provision of early post-war relief by the US, for example through the UNRRA, was running out. The election of a Republican Congress in November did not encourage confidence in the resumption of relief and the ensuing decontrol of the US economy brought a sharp increase in the price of dollar goods. These developments in turn suggested that sterling convertibility might prove very expensive for the UK at a time when the British dollar deficit would itself be rising. The outlook worsened during the winter, and on 20 February 1947, in the middle of the fuel crisis, the Chancellor told his officials that he felt the Americans would have to be asked to postpone the date for convertibility.[45] Waley and Rowe-Dutton[46] advised emphatically against this on the

[45] Roger Makins, from the British Embassy in Washington, had told the Treasury that the Americans wanted advance warning of difficulties that might be encountered over the Loan.
[46] *Rowe-Dutton, Ernest, KCMG, CB (1891–1965).* Inland Revenue 1914–19, HM Treasury 1919–28, Financial Adviser to HM Embassy, Berlin 1928–32, to HM Embassy, Paris

grounds that postponement would be unlikely in practice to save many dollars. Countries that were short of sterling would have none to convert, while countries long of sterling, such as Argentina, would simply demand payment in gold or dollars for their exports to the UK unless their sterling was in fact made convertible. In short, a proclaimed continuation of inconvertibility would prove to be the start of a losing battle. But when informed of this advice, Bridges asked his officials to make sure that the Bank agreed. Rowe-Dutton accordingly asked for confirmation.

The Bank's reply, in a letter from Siepmann, agreed that the Chancellor 'would be ill-advised to enter a plea of *non possumus* at this stage' for three main reasons. Firstly, it was doubtful if the American Administration could of itself release the UK from a treaty obligation; and it was more than doubtful whether the new Congress, if consulted, would agree. 'We should have courted a refusal and exposed ourselves to all the damage of public admission, without the remedy'. Secondly, there was the argument already advanced by Waley and Rowe-Dutton about how few dollars would be saved. Thirdly, there would be the damage to confidence caused by suspension of negotiations already in train. 'To turn back now would give the impression that we are in really desperate straits already. Sterling as an international currency would be irretrievably damaged and the direct cost to us in dollars is not to be measured.' Furthermore the machinery of exchange control would be very severely strained by a reversal of engines.

Some of these arguments were much better than others. The first was a long way the best, the last a long way the worst. The others relied on judgements that could certainly be questioned. For example, if the whole enterprise seemed as ill-advised as the Treasury and the Bank had always thought, why should other countries lose confidence in sterling if they saw the UK taking steps to abandon it and revert to a step-by-step approach for enlarging the area of sterling transferability? To such a question the Bank would seemingly have replied at this time that confidence would be better maintained by other measures than the postponement of convertibility – effective steps to reduce the UK's own deficit, for example. Accordingly Siepmann's letter ended by suggesting the preparation of a wide-ranging programme 'in which convertibility is scarcely more than an incident no longer to be avoided'. Yet what confidence could the Bank have had that such a programme, supposing the Government were to agree to it, would

1934–9, HM Treasury 1939–51, Third Secretary 1947–51, UK Executive Director, IBRD 1949–51.

not in one or other vital respect prove quantitatively inadequate, unacceptable to Congress, or as damaging to the future of sterling as a postponement of convertibility? The Bank had in fact little ground for such confidence, either then or subsequently. So why did it tread so heavily on this first suggestion of postponement if it felt, as in fact it did, that convertibility was in reality rather more than an incident?

On 20 February, Bolton had circulated a long note entitled 'Economic and Industrial Crisis'. After an analysis of the prospects, it included the following apocalyptic passage:

> When the inevitable monetary crisis develops we shall find ourselves hamstrung without means to take measures to save sterling and the British Commonwealth from collapse. The effect of convertibility will be to add substantially to the drawings on the US dollar credit without giving us any offsetting advantages of any kind. The effect of non-discrimination in monetary and trade policy will largely prevent us from taking any kind of trading measures to enable us temporarily to acquire goods and services from those countries who owe us money and/or are willing to hold sterling. The international financial machinery worked out during the war has largely broken down. The only piece remaining in anything like working order being the IMF. This, however, can provide little or no relief and then only if the present timidity of the American Administration can be overcome by the threat of catastrophe to come.

He went on to propose renegotiation of the Loan Agreement, full restoration of the UK's rights to a transitional period under the Bretton Woods agreement, a tightening up of the Sterling Area, fresh discriminatory trade arrangements with Western Europe, and consideration of a 20% devaluation. 'If Washington refuses to negotiate', he concluded, 'we have no alternative but to leave the international institutions and repudiate our various obligations even at the expense of having to give up the unspent remainder of the US line of credit.' Postponement of convertibility seemed implicit in Bolton's argument that transitional rights should be restored. But if the rest of the wide-ranging programme suggested by Siepmann could be secured, then perhaps convertibility could after all be sustained and the standing of sterling, always in the forefront of the Bank's mind, enhanced. This thought certainly occurred to Bolton and Siepmann and possibly also to the Governor himself. In his unfinished memoirs,[47] written five to ten years afterwards, Catto stressed how central convertibility was to the entire Loan Agreement and how adamant the Americans had been about it. Therefore he could well have judged, early in 1947, that renegotiation of this particular provision would encounter

---

[47] *A Personal Memoir and Biographical Note*, privately printed by Constable, London, 1962.

the most resistance in Washington. Besides, the Governor was not only very much a man of his word but one who had throughout the negotiations been especially worried lest the UK should in some way repeat, after the Second World War, the failure after the First World War to honour financial undertakings given in 1914–1918. In later years Cobbold recollected the Governor's strongly held view that the commitment to convertibility, once made, should be honoured. At all events the wider viewpoint of Catto seems to have encompassed the rather narrower views of Siepmann and Bolton so as to produce the advice given to the Treasury in February 1947, with pride of place given to the foreseen American obstacles to a postponement of convertibility.[48]

Though mistaken on a longer view, this advice was not so obviously ill-founded when given. The crucial negotiations with India and Egypt were only just beginning, renegotiation of the monetary agreements was far from complete, and the dollar drain was not yet approaching the insupportable. It was, moreover, unquestionably right that the narrow issue of convertibility was only one part of the picture. The UK's own deficit, the dollar expenditure of the Sterling Area, and the commitment to non-discriminatory trading were together a good deal more important. There was therefore much to be said for treading on the idea of postponement, as an isolated move at that stage, at least until the shape and feasibility of 'an agreed programme on the whole complex of questions', as Siepmann put it, could be seen. The error lay in supposing that others, at home and abroad, would agree to a programme that was sufficiently strong – and in some respects painful – to support the maintenance of a convertibility that lacked political support or public popularity in the UK.

In the absence of further guidance from Whitehall the Bank next set about devising on its own the outline of a programme that the Governor could submit direct to the Chancellor. Towards the end of March a final version was ready for despatch. After stressing once again the dangers of unilateral blocking[49] in the absence of manifest compulsion, the paper went on to restate the arguments against seeking US consent to postponement of convertibility. But it went on to suggest that American opinion was beginning to change. Things had not worked out as the sponsors of the Loan Agreement had hoped. There was no sign of general equilibrium. There was a universal shortage of dollars and their provision

---

[48] Cobbold was away at this time, accompanying Eady in India and Egypt.
[49] The Chancellor had become irritated by the refusal of India and Egypt to consider cancellation and had asked officials to look again into the merits and mechanics of unilateral blocking.

by the US, far from increasing, was drying up. So it might now be opportune to seek American agreement firstly to a postponement, under Clause 10(ii), of the convertibility of releases from Indian and Egyptian accumulated balances (as opposed to the convertibility of current accruals) and secondly to some dispensation from the commitment to non-discrimination in UK import policy. The paper was shown privately to Eady, who had now returned from India and Egypt and whose own views were then set out in a long personal letter to the Deputy Governor. As a result the Bank's paper was given no further circulation. Instead the Treasury promised to prepare a paper of its own, in agreement with the Bank and in support of which the Governor would send a shorter note. Eady, who was still busy deterring Dalton from unilateral blocking, argued persuasively that Britain's dollar problem was but one part of a world dollar problem whose solution would require broad action by the US as well as continued austerity, trade discrimination, and, for many countries, inconvertibility. No early solution would come into sight unless the Americans could be persuaded that radical action on their part was required; and in that context it would be very inopportune to seek special Congressional approval to an amendment of one of the clauses in the Loan Agreement with the British. 'On this analysis', he wrote, 'it is unlikely that we shall be able to maintain convertibility, but to get out of it would involve changing the Loan Agreement at a crucial point.' On this analysis, too, postponing the convertibility of releases from Indian or Egyptian balances was not worth much and could prejudice the chances of worthwhile agreements with those countries. So Eady did not attach much value to it. As to non-discrimination, he thought the Loan Agreement already contained useful loopholes.

In retrospect this exchange was decisive in the development of policy towards the crisis ahead. It shows the head of the Finance Division of the Treasury reconciled not only to going ahead with convertibility but also to the likelihood of its subsequent suspension. It shows him prepared nonetheless to press on with agreements committing the UK to that convertibility and indeed to use it so as to help to gain British objectives for the immobilisation and phased release of accumulated balances. It shows the Bank firmly against proposing postponement of convertibility to the US, but without a convincing programme for maintaining it. It shows the Chancellor concerned in the main with the red herring of unilateral blocking. Both Bank and Treasury realised well enough that the problem was by no means just a British problem and by no means capable of early solution, though the Bank was later to put forward some rather wild ideas for attempting another Anglo-American plan for sterling. But neither yet showed much apprehension of an early and open sterling crisis in which they would lose control over the timing of their response. This seems crucial to an understanding of the advice given. It is as if they both contemplated a steady and controlled loss of dollars, which in due time they could arrest after due deliberation or even consultation.

It must be remembered that there had not been a run on sterling for sixteen years and none since the establishment of exchange control. Had the Bank or the Treasury thought in March 1947 that they would probably be losing $1,000 million during July and August, regardless of exchange control, they would have given much more serious consideration to postponement of convertibility, despite the disadvantages they saw in this course, despite its impact on the negotiations with countries in the Sterling Area and Europe, and however awkward it might be for Anglo-American relations. As it was, they continued with an approach that was in fact inappropriate to the unperceived time-scale within which they were working; and like most men devoted to carrying out a pre-set though apparently near-hopeless task, they no doubt gave way from time to time to a human optimism, a feeling that they might after all get away with it. Anxiety grew as July drew nearer and the dollar drain accelerated, but it was not until the end of June that serious contingency planning was begun to meet a crisis still feared only for the autumn.

Towards the end of April the Economic Section of the Cabinet Office circulated a note on the latest balance of payments prospects for 1947. These suggested a UK deficit of £450 million and a dollar drain of nearer £600 million, which would leave only £300 million or $1,200 million unused out of the American and Canadian Loans at the end of the year. The early conclusion of agreements on the sterling balances was advocated at some length, with blocking as a last resort. Further cuts in UK dollar imports were not pressed in this paper. But a few days later, on 23 April, the Governor himself wrote to the Chancellor about the external monetary position. He began by stressing the importance of maintaining confidence in sterling and the damaging effects that he judged would follow a postponement of convertibility or a resort to blocking which would be regarded as akin to repudiation of sterling debt. The right course was to arrange by mutual agreement with the most important countries concerned that the bulk of their balances should 'be frozen on some definite plan, with some releases, say, over a period of five years'. He went on to argue that when the five years had ended, and the burden of servicing the North American Loans had also to be shouldered, some further and more drastic action would be needed. He then revived an idea that had been was firmly rejected in 1945, namely that the Americans should take over some of this burden. Finally, in the course of a long concluding paragraph, he at last raised the central issue of domestic policy:

> Whilst in this letter I have confined myself mainly to the problem of the sterling balances with which, as agents for the Treasury, the Bank is primarily concerned, I should not wish you to think that, in fact, this is the most urgent or even the most important of our external problems, for it is, of course, only part of our difficulties. The hard currency deficit and the question of our import programme are the most urgent and important of our tasks...Unless that can be accomplished in an important degree, we are heading fast for exhaustion of our external resources and a crisis for which there will be no other remedy but ever-increasing economy in imports to a point that will make serious inroads upon the standard of living of our people.

This plea did not fall on deaf ears. Early in May the Chancellor proposed a cut of £200 million in dollar imports for 1947–8. But he failed to convince his colleagues that the prospect was as serious as he made it out to be. In the end, and not until June, he had to settle for a cut of only £100 million.

In the meantime the Bank's anxieties remained centred round the sterling balances, the difficulty of reaching agreement with India and Egypt, and the dangers of being driven to block unilaterally if no agreements emerged. In a note of 29 April entitled 'Convertibility and all that', Cobbold wrote: 'The more I think about this the less I like it, and I think we are in a jam. The fact that we foresaw this and warned the Treasury during the Washington negotiations is not much consolation...Things have moved against us even quicker than we anticipated and we are being forced into a corner.' The main trouble, as he saw it, was the Sterling Area negotiations. 'This has become a major political issue here and with the exchange position as it is and will be over the next months, we are and shall be on the defensive.' Pessimistic about the chances of successful negotiations with India and Egypt, he therefore developed the Governor's views and suddenly set out a plan for the sterling balances of these countries, a plan that bore a close resemblance to that put forward in Washington by Harry White in October 1945 and dismissed at that time. One-third would be frozen for five years and then funded, one-third would be acquired by the US in exchange for gold at local Middle East and Indian prices, and one-third would be cancelled. But such a scheme was as fanciful in 1947 as it had been in 1945, if not more so; and it seems to have been greeted with a discreet silence in the Bank.

It can be regarded as a counsel of desperation from a man who was going through the double agony of seeing his worst fears come true while being left with a senior executive responsibility for the conduct of events. However, the Governor was sufficiently impressed to write again to the Chancellor on 27 May, commending the plan as an imaginative and practical solution to the Indian and Egyptian problem. He added: 'There is of course great urgency for the time is short if we are to approach our American friends and ask their help and co-operation to rid us and the world of this octopus which unless dealt with now on a permanent basis will keep on increasing its stranglehold on our financial life.' Keynes had played with similar ideas. Others were to do so again in the future, including Cobbold. But such ideas were never practicable.

Urgency was indeed increasing. Earlier in May the Government in Ottawa, alarmed at the fall in Canadian exchange reserves and loath to take domestic measures of its own, had coolly requested through Eady that the UK should for the remainder of the year cease further drawings on the Canadian credit. After negotiation it was later agreed that the UK deficit with Canada should be settled 50% in gold or dollars and 50% by drawings on the credit. Concurrently, the working of the Supplementary Monetary Agreement with Belgium was giving cause for concern. Since the new year the Belgian authorities had readily accepted sterling from all sources. They had also stipulated that Belgian residents requiring sterling for use in the Sterling Area should first seek to obtain it from private holdings, thereby mobilising such sterling for international use. When the new Agreement was signed at the end of February, sterling held by the National Bank became convertible and by the end of May some $40 million worth had in fact been converted.

Meantime 'our American friends' were not showing much interest in British problems or in modifying the Loan Agreement. Their minds were fast opening to the magnitude of the world dollar problem, with its intensifying implications for American foreign policy in Western Europe and for the dangerously uncertain political prospects in France and Italy in particular. For example, at a dinner party held in Washington at the end of May for senior Canadian officials (including Towers), Under-Secretary of State Dean Acheson remarked that the piecemeal approach of fixing up one country after another would not receive political support and would have to be abandoned. Europe's problem would have to be tackled as a whole and an integral plan of economic co-operation would have to be worked out by Europeans themselves. As one aspect of such a plan, large-scale financial assistance might well be forthcoming from the United States. Several days later, on 5 June, Secretary of State Marshall delivered his Harvard speech and the idea of the Marshall Plan was publicly launched. On its own network the Bank received a letter dated 6 June from Bolton, who was on one of his visits to the IMF as UK Executive Director. 'As you are aware', he said, 'the vacuum caused by the collapse of the old policy is for the time being slowly filling up with tentative proposals for the integration of West European economies, thus both saving dollars and making Europe a more attractive risk to the US.' It was accepted that discrimination against US goods would have to continue. Bolton even allowed himself to think that the new US attitudes might foster new (old) ideas about American help with sterling balances. In fact, however, the immediate British problem had simply been bypassed by Marshall. Cruelly, the Treasury and the Bank in London were left facing the rough end of the collapse of the old policy at the same time as the Americans, who had forced that policy on them, had their eyes on new horizons.

Late in May the weekly loss of dollars exceeded $100 million for the first time and the situation was discussed on 6 June at a meeting between the Chancellor, senior Treasury officials, and the Governors. There was again agreement to go ahead with convertibility while trying to persuade the Americans of the need to allow continuing trade discrimination as part of a programme for meeting the world-wide dollar problem. Twelve days later, at a meeting between Treasury officials and the Bank, it was yet again agreed that to stop convertibility might be worse than to continue it. Mynors recorded: 'It was the one basis on which any trade in Europe was now on the move and to stop it meant the finish of sterling, and dollar invoicing for UK imports.' Both the Bank and the Treasury had now firmly dug themselves into this unreasoning judgement and had not yet considered in any detail what they might do if convertibility had to be stopped.

Several days later, on 23 June, Bolton circulated in the Bank a note that this time faced up to the fact that convertibility might have to be suspended unless further American assistance became available in time. But he saw such suspension as part of 'an economic Dunkirk' and still argued forcibly that failure to go ahead on 15 July would itself precipitate a crisis rather than avert it. Much more important, though in the context of suspension itself rather than of a preceding loss of reserves, he now drew attention to a critical danger that had not been mentioned when attitudes against postponement were hardening three months earlier. Together with other adverse factors, the onset of commercial leads and lags in payments, fully within exchange control rules in the UK and the Sterling Area, could bring on a speculative run that might make it impossible to hold the rate at $4.03. By the same reasoning, though Bolton did not say so, a run could make it impracticable to maintain convertibility, for such a speculative movement against sterling would both enlarge the payments deficit of the UK and the Sterling Area with the dollar area and cause an acceleration of current sterling transfers into central banks in, for example, Western Europe or South America, who were likely to convert the resulting accumulation into dollars.

Bolton's paper ended rather cryptically, with some suggestion that letting the rate go in a crisis might be preferable to suspending convertibility itself. Cobbold, writing a day later, supported Bolton's case against postponement in cooler language. But he too had now begun to look beyond 15 July and had discussed with Bolton, Kershaw, Mynors, and Thompson-McCausland the outline of a contingency plan for dealing with a crisis. An unsigned note entitled 'If there is no Marshall Plan' was circulated to this group on 24 June. It identified the exhaustion of the Loan as crisis point, rather than the development of a speculative run as such, and assumed this would be reached not later than November. It rejected both a floating rate and a return to extreme monetary bilateralism; instead it favoured a devaluation to $3.00 and an exchange control fence between American sterling and all other non-resident sterling. Rather than the finish of sterling, this meant withdrawing general convertibility into dollars but maintaining transferability of sterling within most of the non-dollar world. Ahead of the crisis itself, the note advised that there should be further cuts in imports, maximum diversion of imports from the dollar area, minimum releases of sterling balances, an approach to Sterling Area Governments to reduce dollar imports, and arrangements with South Africa that could go as far as exclusion from the Sterling Area and the consequential erection of an exchange control barrier between London and Johannesburg. The note ended: 'We believe it would be the Bank's duty to make clear the repercussions of domestic money policy on the balance of payments, and to point out that increasing money supplies at home must place greater and greater strain on all direct controls of the balance of payments, which the controls may not be able to withstand.' At a meeting with Bridges, Eady, and other officials on 2 July held to consider what to do if the Marshall Plan failed to materialise, the Bank aired all these ideas. A general exercise in contingency planning was then set in hand. Whitehall Departments were to draw up a shadow export and import programme, highly discriminatory on imports and possibly involving a controlled direction of exports. The Bank was to review external monetary arrangements and make proposals for the changes it judged would be needed. Questions about the exchange rate and about domestic monetary policy would be discussed between the Treasury and the Bank. It was agreed that the latest moment for reversing engines would be when the end of the Loan was in sight and before the reserves, amounting to some $2½ billion, had been touched.

The third week in July, immediately following full convertibility, produced a new record drain of $155 million. At the same time the Bank had begun to think about the monetary aspects of the European co-operation required by the US as a condition for Marshall Aid. Already at the end of June Bolton's fertile mind was thinking up schemes for a pooling of reserves and IMF drawing rights in continental Western Europe. This thinking was then tied into the contingency planning already set in hand by Bridges, and on 18 July Cobbold wrote suggesting that a continental bloc might be linked to the Sterling Area, with currencies transferable within the two blocs combined but not convertible into dollars. On the same day Bolton addressed his mind to another problem, namely that abrogation of any part of the agreements then concluded or still in negotiation, including the Supplementary Agreements about convertibility, would require three months' notice. In market terms, three months' notice of suspension of convertibility would be absurd. Yet a sudden unilateral suspension could be regarded as repudiation. To avoid this, Bolton hit on the idea of withdrawing the EEA from support of sterling in New York and confining official transactions in support of the official rate to London, mostly in gold. Conversion of sterling through New York would be deterred by falls in the exchange rate in that market and would not, he thought, simply be replaced by conversions in London. In this way the drain would be eased and a breathing space would be obtained for negotiations without *de jure* repudiation of any agreements.

In the second week of convertibility the drain fell back below $100 million. However it rose again to $115 million in the following week and to $124 million in the second week of August. Contingency planning moved ahead. On 31 July Munro, on a visit from Washington, called at the Bank and advised Cobbold that Marshall Aid would not begin until the spring of 1948 and that in his view convertibility would have to be suspended. On 1 August Cobbold showed Eady a private note in which he discounted Ministerial ideas that mere suspension would take away all the pain. But he now admitted that convertibility could not last:

I have always personally believed that the whole pack of cards of Bretton Woods, Washington Loan, ITO etc., was unsoundly or at any rate prematurely built and that it would collapse under 'transitional period' stresses. I agree therefore that convertibility as contemplated in the Loan Agreement (by which our hands are tied and which precludes us from using our trade, etc., negotiating weapons) must be modified.

He then went on to make use of Bolton's ideas for avoiding formal denunciation of convertibility, for the discriminatory reduction of dollar expenditure by the Sterling Area and Western Europe, and for the transferability of currencies within and between these two blocs.

There followed a final interval of ten days before the storm redoubled in fury and emergency action became impossible to avoid. During this period there was a debate in the House of Commons on the economic state of the nation. Both the Prime Minister and the Chancellor took part and both stressed the gravity of the external situation. But although the Government looked ahead to unpleasant remedial measures in the autumn, none were yet announced. Parliament itself then dispersed for the long summer recess. This Lear-like behaviour, together with the publicity of Loan drawings and market reports of heavy conversions, provoked a further exodus from sterling.

Earlier in the month preparations had at last been set in hand for an approach to the American authorities. Ideas subsequently approved by Ministers were brought together on 8 August at a meeting between the Treasury, the Bank, and the Foreign Office. Eady was to head a small delegation that would leave London on 15 August and report back not later than 25 August. He was to explain to the American authorities that the prospective exhaustion of the Loan, now predicted for October, would leave the UK in an untenable position unless the obligations of the Loan Agreement could somehow be relaxed. Formal suspension of the convertibility clause and of the commitment to non-discrimination was not to be sought. Instead, Eady was to suggest that the UK be allowed to modify these restraints in practice, through bilateral negotiations with the countries most concerned. The purpose of these would be to limit, by voluntary agreement, the amount of sterling converted into dollars. If the Americans proved receptive to this line of approach, it would be for them to decide, between several possibilities, how to arrange the necessary legal loopholes. Among these was the Scarce Currency Clause of the IMF, invocation of which could possibly override the Loan Agreement.

In parallel with these preparations, the Bank was developing plans for external monetary action to the point where they could be put into effect at short notice. This work was carried out by Siepmann and a group composed of Mynors, Lithiby, Powell, Beale, Grafftey-Smith,[50] Thompson-

[50] *Grafftey-Smith, Anthony Paul, Kt, CBE (1903–60).* Educated King's School, Ely. Entered Bank 1923. Army 1939–45. Assistant Chief Cashier (Exchange Control and Overseas) 1945–7, UK Alternate Executive Director, IMF 1946, Acting Adviser to the Governors 1947–8, Deputy Chief Cashier (Exchange Control and Overseas) 1948–52. Financial Adviser to Government of Southern Rhodesia 1952–4, to Government of Federation of Rhodesia and Nyasaland 1954–6, Governor, Bank of Rhodesia and Nyasaland 1956–60.

McCausland, and Rootham.[51] Bolton was on holiday, soon to be followed by Cobbold himself. As work went on various starters fell by the wayside. Not much more was heard either of the idea that sterling should be devalued to $3.00 or of the thought that domestic monetary policy should be altered. Next, the group turned down Bolton's proposal that support for sterling in New York should be withdrawn and that official-rate convertibility should be confined to gold operations in London. It was considered tantamount to a multiple-currency practice – contrary to the Bretton Woods Agreements – that would not in practice save many dollars but would certainly intensify a general sense of upheaval. It would therefore be necessary to disregard the provision for three months' notice contained in the Supplementary Agreements. The Bank also toyed with the possibility of improving international liquidity and easing the dollar shortage through a rise in the international price of monetary gold above $35 per ounce; but the Treasury had already concluded that it would be pointless to try this out on the Americans. Finally, the Bank was asked by the Chancellor to consider the emergency blocking of all sterling balances eligible for conversion into dollars. In a negative reply the Bank stressed that outright blocking would be in complete breach of recently concluded agreements, would cause extreme unpopularity abroad, and would make it very difficult for the UK to continue to obtain supplies against payment in sterling. These arguments were accepted.

Cobbold was at this time hoping that the pressure would soon begin to ease as the immediate rush to convert after 15 July subsided. Some of this hope was conveyed to Whitehall, but it proved ill-founded and on the afternoon of 13 August Siepmann set out to tell an alarmed and dismayed Treasury about the $161 million that had been spent over the previous six working days.[52] Just before this he had chaired a meeting of his group at the Bank. The members had by now assembled what was left of all the ideas that had been considered and had agreed upon a final plan. Against a general background of stricter economy in imports and intensified discrimination against dollar goods, emergency monetary action should

---

[51] *Rootham, Jasper St John* (1910–90). Educated Tonbridge and St John's College, Cambridge. Ministry of Agriculture 1933–4, Colonial Office 1934–6, HM Treasury 1936–8, Private Secretary to Prime Minister 1938–9, HM Treasury 1939–40. Army 1940–6. Entered Bank 1946, Adviser to the Governors 1957–63, Chief of Central Banking Information Department 1963–4, Chief of Overseas Department 1964–5, Assistant to the Governors 1965–7. A Managing Director, Lazards 1967–75, Director, Agricultural Mortgage Corporation 1967–77, Deputy Chairman 1973–7.

[52] Curiously, even though the EEA was a Treasury Account and relations with the Treasury were most intimate, the Bank did not at that time pass daily figures of its gold and dollar operations to Whitehall. The loss for the week ending 16 August came to $162 million and for that ending 23 August it was $181 million.

consist of a formal suspension of convertibility and its replacement by the division of external sterling into three broad categories: sterling held by American Account countries (the dollar area of, mainly, North and Central America); sterling held by Transferable Account countries (including the Sterling Area and Western Europe); and sterling held by a third group of mainly South American countries. The first would remain freely usable throughout the world. The second, provided it was not segregated and frozen by prior agreement, would be freely usable anywhere except the dollar area. The third category would be usable anywhere, but the amount becoming available for this purpose would be restricted by further bilateral agreement with, notably, Argentina. Some small 'ration' of dollars, it was agreed, would also have to be allowed to Transferable Account countries.

Siepmann's group considered that a scheme on these lines was the only possible one that would effect the necessary economy of foreign exchange without causing an international monetary seizure. The group still hoped that action could be postponed at least until the IMF Annual Meeting to be held in London in September, but it admitted that: 'We must be prepared for the eventuality that action would be forced on us in the meantime.' In fact, when he went to the Treasury later in the afternoon with the news that a further $161 million had been spent, Siepmann had himself concluded that there was now a general exodus from sterling.[53] In his record of this decisive meeting Thompson-McCausland wrote:

> The Treasury were alarmed at the rising trend. In the last few days the average loss was at the rate of some $100 million per week more than could be accounted for on UK current account. The politics of exhaustion of the credit at an unexpectedly early date by apparent capital movements were particularly touchy: (remember 1931). The Treasury asked whether the Bank had in mind measures to deal with such a situation. Mr Siepmann gave in broad outline the proposals which had been discussed at the Bank in the morning. The Treasury asked whether these could be put into effect on Tuesday 19th. The Bank deprecated fixing a date, pointing out that the urgency lay in having a scheme ready to put into operation at the shortest possible notice, not in deciding when it should be launched. It was agreed that the date should be fixed after the subject had been raised by Sir W. Eady in Washington.

The next day, in a carefully eloquent, convincing, and at times bitter memorandum, Siepmann exposed the situation of a speculative run in stark terms:

[53] In a personal and private letter to Cobbold written on 16 August, Eady wrote: 'Siepmann drew the inference that the avalanche was upon us and that everybody was finding ways of getting out of free sterling.'

The pattern of our losses suggests a general acceleration due to an attempt by holders of transferable sterling to take cover without delay. Many reported instances confirm that sterling has already ceased to be a currency which commands international confidence and there is some evidence that many of our own nationals would transfer their holdings elsewhere if they could. The conclusion to be drawn is that the dollar drain must be expected to continue, not only undiminished but probably at an accelerating rate, even if this means that present holders are left short of the means with which to meet their known obligations. The Argentine is a case in point: she is denuding herself of sterling in spite of the fact that in the comparatively near future she will have debts to meet which greatly exceed her present or prospective holdings of sterling.

Siepmann saw no merit in postponing emergency action any longer. There was nothing for which to wait. Since no new American money was in sight, the UK had no choice but to restore its freedom to restrict the external convertibility of sterling even though this meant repudiating written obligations recently incurred.[54] He then went on to argue the case for the plan that his group had agreed on the previous day and which had already been explained to the Treasury. His purpose was to head off suggestions for the suspension of virtually all transferability of sterling and a return to extreme monetary bilateralism. If that were to happen, 'all the advantages which we have sought by attempting (with some success) to re-establish sterling as an international currency would, for the time being, be lost and the world – already short of dollars – would be thrown back upon the use of local currencies for the finance of trade. If this were all we had to propose, we should not even be saving ourselves at the expense of others; we should be committing an act of sabotage on a world-wide scale and in defiance of our express engagements to all and sundry.' From this there followed the rationale of the plan being put forward, including the provision of dollar rations. He concluded: 'The programme would also need to be completed on the commercial side by recovering and using our liberty of action as regards non-discrimination; and on the supply side by a complete revision of import programmes and engagements to suit the new circumstances which would prevail over the next six months or so.'

It is likely that this paper was prepared partly as a brief for the Governor, who now participated directly in the resolution of the crisis and whom Siepmann accompanied to a further meeting with Treasury officials and

---

[54] An unsigned and unsuccessful note survives in the Bank files opposing immediate action and in favour of waiting until the Loan had gone and some fall in reserves had taken place. Its style suggests it was written by Cobbold just before he went on holiday. The author felt both that the pressure might ease and that repudiation of convertibility would be more acceptable internationally if postponed until exhaustion of resources were more obvious.

representatives of other interested Departments on the afternoon of 14 August. Catto subsequently wrote a diary of his own part in events and from this it is evident that the plan put forward by the Bank did not encounter resistance in Whitehall. A few days later, on 18 August, the Chancellor did suggest that the existing monetary agreements be virtually scrapped in view of the conditional gold obligations they contained. But he was persuaded by Bridges and Bolton that this would simply compound the damage.

At the Treasury meeting on 14 August, the Governor argued that there was no escaping the fact that unilateral suspension of convertibility would be a legal breach of the Loan Agreement. Unless, therefore, Eady could persuade the Americans to take a very sympathetic attitude, they were likely to impose an immediate freeze on the undrawn balance of the Loan. Depending on the timing of the suspension, this freeze could even include two drawings totalling $300 million for which notice had already been given. It was therefore most important not to rush a decision on timing, and tie Eady's hands in that respect, until some response had first been obtained from Washington, where talks were due to open on the morning of Monday, 18 August. This point was well taken in the Treasury and fully expressed in a note Bridges prepared for Dalton. The Governor continued to press it on these two during the weekend; but it was not possible to postpone a special Cabinet meeting called for Sunday evening. Worried and angry, Ministers were inclined to blame misuse of convertibility by countries to whom it had been granted. At first they wanted to suspend almost at once, on Monday evening, but the Chancellor persuaded them to delay until Tuesday night. This still gave Eady virtually no time to secure an agreement with the Americans and a satisfactory public exchange between the two Governments. He and his delegation had arrived in Washington on Sunday evening and were joined on Monday by Cobbold, whom the Governor had recalled from holiday in the South of France at the urgent request of Bridges and Eady. He flew back to London on Sunday, in time for discussions in the Bank and the Treasury, and left for Washington the same evening. In the Bank were the Governor, Niemeyer, Siepmann, and Bolton, the latter having also been recalled from holiday. An informal letter about this recall, written by Holland-Martin, provides a glimpse of the prevailing atmosphere:

> You will be here in the Bank by lunch-time, 1 o'clock at the latest on Sunday. The Governor and probably HAS and OEN will be lunching here and the Deputy Governor will join the party as soon as he can be brought from Croydon, whither a plane will bring him from Nice during the morning...WE [Eady] with PSB and LPTMcC are all off across the Atlantic

today, WE being in a sadly worn-out condition and anxiously awaiting support from the Deputy Governor...The Government are in these matters, as in all others, worried, nervy, and incapable of reaching decisions.

Eady broke the news to Secretary of the Treasury Snyder on the Monday morning. Concurrently, the Foreign Secretary briefed Ambassador Lewis Douglas in London, stressing that inaction would risk a collapse of sterling that would seriously damage international trade, particularly in Western Europe, and seriously damage the interests of US foreign policy. He met with a sympathetic hearing. But twenty-four hours was obviously insufficient time for agreement to be reached in Washington and for the modalities be settled. Eady, in a cable to the Treasury early on 19 August, and Cobbold in a telephone call to the Governor, urged that suspension be postponed until the evening of 20 August. Some hours later this request was granted. For his part the Governor had exerted his influence as best he could. As his diary records: 'I immediately motored to the Treasury, arriving shortly after 9 a.m., where I was told they were awaiting a cable from Sir W. Eady which had not yet arrived but which he had advised them was on the way. I said I wanted to speak to Sir E. Bridges because I had a telephone message from the Deputy Governor. I was informed that Sir Edward had gone over to 10 Downing St for a meeting of Ministers.' The Permanent Secretary was thereupon extracted from the meeting, told of Cobbold's message, and asked to pass it to Dalton. Not content with this, the Governor returned to the Bank and despatched the message and a covering letter to the Chancellor. 'Now it looks as if events are shaping themselves as I thought', he wrote, 'and that by the fences being rushed we are in danger of not carrying the Americans with us.'

In Washington, in the course of Tuesday 19 August, it became clear that the Americans were disinclined to exploit any legal loopholes through which a suspension of convertibility could pass. As had been predicted some months earlier, they felt that undertakings given to Congress had been too specific and that the Agreement itself had been too tightly drawn for the Administration to allow technicalities to be exploited and for a *de facto* breach to be condoned by Congress. In their view this meant that the undrawn balance of the Loan would have to be frozen. But they were prepared to be very helpful over the $300 million of drawings for which notice had already been given and about an appropriately friendly exchange of letters. They would also accept from the British a voluntary abstinence from further drawings. This would avoid declaring the UK to be in breach. Eady therefore proposed to London that the suspension of convertibility should be accompanied by an invocation of Clause 8(ii) of the Agreement, providing for consultations between the two countries, and by an undertaking not to request further drawings until those consultations had taken place. This was agreed and incorporated in an exchange of amicably face-saving letters that took place on 20 August, the date of suspension itself. The British Government reaffirmed its adherence to the long-run objective of full and free convertibility and described its action as 'of an emergency and temporary nature'. The American Administration noted this with satisfaction and went on to criticise speculation. The British action, it remarked, 'is deemed by you essential to afford the UK Government an opportunity for instituting measures to protect the system of convertibility from abuses which endanger its survival'. Finally, on a suggestion from London, Eady even obtained American assent to one last pre-zero notice of a further drawing of $150 million, leaving only $400 million for future discussion.

The 'Sheer Madness' of 'Temptation' was at last over. But another arduous chapter was about to begin. Some of the aftermath of 21 August, in relations with India, Egypt, and Sweden, has already been described; but there was of course much else. The dollar drain itself, though reduced to more manageable size, was not stopped by the suspension of convertibility. Use of the unspent balance of the Canadian Loan remained to be settled. Would it too be frozen or would the 50/50 arrangement still stand?[55] There was the IMF to approach as a new source of dollars. There were the Americans themselves to tackle, so that the position could be regularised and the remaining $400 million released. Further away, in the southern hemisphere, lurked Miguel Miranda, waiting to bargain his precious meat for as much British gold or dollars as he could get. A little nearer there was South Africa, the recipient, it was thought, of overmuch British capital and a big spender of hard currency. Could the Government of General Smuts be persuaded to deter some of this capital while also granting the UK a sizeable gold loan? Then, too, there was the rest of the Sterling Area, including the antipodean Dominions, whose members would require much persuading if they were to reduce their dollar expenditure. Finally, in this catalogue, there were the Belgians. Their multilateral earnings of sterling would continue to be large and recently they had been heavy converters. They were to prove notably difficult. In the first flash of anger at repudiation of the convertibility clause, the Governor of the National Bank was with difficulty persuaded not to stop

---

[55] By the end of 1947 the UK had drawn $Can. 974 million out of the $Can. 1,250 million agreed in 1946. Canada's external financial position became very difficult in the winter of 1947–8 and by agreement drawings were limited to $Can. 15 million a month. After mid-April 1948 no further drawings were allowed, a total of $Can. 1,020 million having by then been taken. Later on, drawings were resumed and a total of $Can. 1,185 million had been taken by the time service began in December 1951.

buying sterling altogether, and then only after the Bank of England had sought emergency help from Ellis-Rees who was able to arrange political pressure at the highest level. Thereafter there were prolonged negotiations, difficult at a number of points, which did not end until November when a new agreement was signed. The large Belgian external surplus with non-dollar countries meant that they went on accumulating sterling from the Transferable Account Area. Their holdings of sterling then quickly exceeded an enlarged limit provisionally agreed to take account of the Belgians' war debt to the UK, and the British became liable for gold payments in settlement of the excess. This was more than could be afforded at a time of acute dollar shortage and Belgium's position as a persistent non-dollar creditor was accordingly not reconcilable with full membership of the Transferable Account Area. It was therefore necessary, on an administrative basis, to restrict the transferability of sterling from third countries on to Belgian Account.

But just for the moment, in the late August days immediately following 'Operation Gearcrash', as suspension had been called in the Bank, there was room for thanks and congratulations. The operation itself had in the end been well conceived and well executed. The Lord President, Herbert Morrison, sent a congratulatory message to Bridges and to all concerned; Bridges in turn wrote a highly appreciative letter to the Governor and his staff. On Thursday, 22 August Catto explained matters to the Court. 'I also referred with great emphasis', he wrote in his diary of the crisis, 'to my pride in and gratitude to all in the Bank who had worked so long and so hard throughout the trying days of the past week and for the secrecy with which everything had been treated...I also circulated a Minute of appreciation to all concerned.'

For the exhausted Eady the crisis was the peak of his career. Before long his responsibilities were to change and to diminish in a reorganisation of the Finance Division of the Treasury into two separate Home and Overseas Divisions; and his close partnership with the Deputy Governor on overseas matters was to end. But for the present, in a letter written to the Governor from New York on 23 August, Cobbold expressed his unstinted admiration as follows:

> He has done magnificently here. Partly because of his own personality and partly because of the changes in the US Treasury he seems to me to have achieved for the first time since the beginning of the war a position of mutual trust on these subjects between the financial authorities. Hitherto one has always had the impression that each side is trying to see where the clever tricks of the other come in and that atmosphere seems to have been dispelled to a remarkable degree.

The crisis of August 1947 has come down to us with the name

'convertibility' attached to it. Its initial resolution consisted of suspension and its acute phase began shortly after 15 July. More generally, of course, the crisis marked the end of the Loan Agreement strategy. That some outcome of this kind, long feared, was going to happen in the latter part of the year had been foreseen in London for some six months. In the Bank, the memoranda by Bolton and Siepmann in February and March and the Governor's letters to the Chancellor in April and May had displayed an accurate appreciation of the prospect and of the various factors responsible for it. The dollar deficit of the UK itself, the dollar requirements of the rest of the Sterling Area, and the additional burden of convertibility at a time of acute world-wide dollar shortage were all correctly identified, and their respective quantitative importance was well judged. The effect of convertibility was to increase significantly the pressure on UK external resources, already very heavy, and to create expectations that an acute crisis, demanding drastic action of some kind, was fast approaching. The nature of these expectations must have been fatally worsened by the failure of Parliamentary statements early in August to announce any further measures to cut back the UK's own hard-currency expenditure. In the absence of such measures a crisis could be met only by allowing the exchange rate to move down or by restricting the use of external sterling, or both. The message was clear: anyone who could get out of sterling would be wise to do so.

In a post-mortem circulated early in September Cobbold himself traced the progressive loss of confidence in sterling. He judged it had begun in June and worsened in July and August; and he explained how a collapse of confidence could bring commercial leads and lags into play while inducing official holders of convertible sterling, whose balances would be suddenly increased by commercial sales, to convert whatever they could. But, as has been seen, there is little recorded evidence that the Bank gave clear warning to the Treasury or the Government that such a run was likely to happen. In the Bank itself, Bolton did not draw attention to the risk until late in June and then only in the wrong context of a suspension of convertibility. Earlier in the year, when sufficient action might just conceivably have been taken and when the decisive exchanges between the Treasury and the Bank took place, clear warnings of a confidence run do not seem to have been given, or been very current. Since the Bank was the Government's source of market advice, and since the Treasury had no market expertise of its own on which to rely, the Bank has to take the blame for this apparent failure. The timing of the crisis, in its final phase, took Whitehall by surprise. The sudden appearance of emergency measures during the holiday season, along with the dishonouring of agreements so recently made and the apparent squandering of the Loan, was a humiliation that angered the Bank's customers in Whitehall. According to Cobbold, in his post-mortem on the crisis, some people had thought that the additional cost of convertibility could largely be identified *ex ante* and be limited to the amount of agreed releases from pre-zero balances. They did not know about 'leads and lags' and the scope for a speculative run. They may have thought that the deity Exchange Control made this a relic of the past. They felt they had not been told that this was a mistaken view, and they grumbled. The lesson was well learnt in the Bank, perhaps even over-learnt. In future years it was more often criticised for crying wolf than for failing to warn.

As has been mentioned earlier, it is likely that Siepmann, Bolton, and others on the external side of the Bank did not themselves fully appreciate, until it became evident in the market, how great were the dangers of a run. It is also possible, indeed very probable, that like most hard-working executants of a policy imposed on them from outside, and against their own better judgement, they had perforce come to believe in at least half of their minds that it would after all prove workable. This is the more likely when 'it', convertibility, was in their eyes a most desirable goal.

How much difference would it have made if the Bank's warnings had been more persistent and their content much more urgent? Conceivably the Cabinet might have agreed to greater cuts in imports and agreed them earlier. But alternatively it might have dismissed the Bank's warnings as attempts to scare Labour Ministers into action favoured by the City. The Bank was not above suspicion in such matters. In any event, agreement to cut imports by £200 million instead of £100 million might have made little difference. The more important question is whether urgent early warnings would have obliged the Bank itself, and then the Treasury, to advise a determined approach to the Americans and whether, if so, the Government could have secured a prolonged postponement of convertibility and a full dispensation from non-discrimination without forfeiting the remainder of the Loan. It must be very doubtful if such an approach would have succeeded, or elicited much more than an unwelcome injunction to the British to set their own house in order. It was not until October, in very different circumstances, some time after the crisis itself and long after Marshall's Harvard speech, that the American Administration became seriously interested in devising ways of condoning a breach of the Agreement. Even if the US Treasury and the State Department had been privately convinced in April that the Agreement was going to prove unworkable, and it would have taken the full advocacy of the Foreign Secretary as well as that of the Chancellor to achieve this, they could not have conceded what was asked without going to Congress. It is most unlikely they would have been willing to try. The Democrat Administration of President Truman had been defeated in the Congressional Elections of November 1946 and had lost control of both Houses. Its fortunes were at a low ebb and the Republican Party was looking forward to winning the Presidency in 1948. Congressional opinion had yet to be persuaded that the problems of Europe, including Britain, were such as to require further American assistance. To go back to a more hostile Congress in response to a British argument for major relaxation of the conditions written into the Loan Agreement, less than a year after its ratification, would have been foolhardy both for the Administration and for the British Government.

Thirty years afterwards Cobbold wrote that the crisis of 1947 followed the Loan Agreement 'as night follows day'. It is difficult to fault this judgement. Whether or not the warnings given to the Government by the Bank in 1947 had been more urgent and timely, there was just no practical way out of the trap set in 1945. It forced the Treasury and the Bank to carry out an imposed and unwanted strategy based upon a terrible misjudgement. For this the Americans were mostly to blame, though Keynes cannot escape his share of it. Of course, by this curious route a great deal had actually been achieved. While ostensibly following a mistaken strategy the Treasury and the Bank did in the end gain several of the objectives of the better strategy that they had themselves preferred and were in large measure actually pursuing. Some features were anyway common to both. By the summer of 1947 the worst of the sterling balance problem had been at least neutralised for a time, without resort to blockings or repudiations. The transferability of sterling throughout a large part of the world had been mostly established, if on a precarious, mistrustful, and unsustainably liberal basis. With Western Europe the structure of monetary agreements and the associated processes of close consultation had been preserved and developed. The British economy itself, with the aid of the Loan, had made substantial progress and the need for further, more arduous, progress had now been recognised. But the cost of having to pursue the wrong strategy had been considerable. Agreements had been dishonoured almost as soon as they were made. Goodwill, not unlimited, had been sharply dissipated. Confidence in the management of sterling had suffered lasting harm. Too many dollars had been spent far too quickly. An unnecessary and humiliating crisis had needlessly damaged both the Government itself and the morale of its officials at a time when other and more necessary trials and tribulations, such as devaluation, grappling with the progressive breakdown of exchange control over non-residents, holding on to sterling immobilised in No. 2 Accounts, or solving the intra-European payments problem, were all to follow. The Americans would have found that their money had been much more wisely spent if it had been used to spur the British into a more orderly transition, using the more step-by-step approach that the British themselves mostly preferred and for which the Bank had always argued. When it was all over, the Deputy Governor, who must have felt, with complete justification, that it was he who had been right all along, took stock thus:

> We are back to the discussion which took place from 1941 onwards as to what policy we should adopt, but with the added difficulty of having made a false start. We have for the moment (*de facto* if not *de jure*) got out of the provisions of the Washington Agreement as to convertibility and as to limitation of our freedom under the 'transitional period' clause of Bretton Woods (which vis-à-vis the IMF we have never given away). But something must go in its place and we cannot expect to secure essential supplies for sterling unless we make sterling of some use to our suppliers. We should therefore seek to use both our gold and exchange resources and our export resources in the most useful and economical directions, doing our utmost to bring about equilibrium in our general balance of payments and re-adjusting our trade policy to reduce to the minimum our deficit with countries with which we shall be forced to settle mainly on a gold or $US basis.

Harry Siepmann, Executive Director 1945–1954

For Harry Siepmann the crisis of 1947 marked an unpleasant climax to a career in the Bank that did not end until 1954. Since the summer of 1945, when Cobbold had been promoted to Deputy Governor, he had been the sole Executive Director on the external side. Since Bolton was not appointed to the Court until March 1948, Siepmann, in some ways an eccentric intellectual averse to taking a decisive managerial lead, often found himself the rather reluctant occupant of a driving seat throughout the difficult and complex period between the signature of the Loan Agreement and the convertibility crisis. Although the policies formulated in the Bank on the sterling balances and the monetary agreements were not so much those of Siepmann personally, it was he who marshalled them coherently and often presented them successfully in Whitehall. Cobbold apart, there was no one else in the Bank who could have done this so well. It was Siepmann, too, who marshalled advice about convertibility in Cobbold's absence early in 1947, and it was he who directed the preparation of a plan of action to deal with the August crisis in such a way as to minimise international damage. With Cobbold and Bolton away on holiday, it was he (with the support of the Governor) who took the Bank into that action and took the Treasury with him. It was an achievement that he would not have wanted and one that seems to have hurt him emotionally. In the following years his interests narrowed and his attitudes hardened.

SOURCES

Bank files
- G1/101–3   Governor's Files: Exchange Policy – Economic Crisis 1947 (February – December 1947)
- G1/262   Governor's File: Miscellaneous Papers (1946–7)
- G3/99   Governor's Miscellaneous Memoranda (1947)
- OV31/99–101   USA: Anglo-US Financial Agreement (September 1945 – September 1947)
- OV43/6   Egypt: Country File (August 1947 – February 1948)
- OV43/40–1   Egypt: Financial (including Trade) Relations with the UK (January 1946 – December 1947)
- OV44/1   Sterling and Sterling Area Policy: United Kingdom – Sterling Policy (November 1939 – December 1947)
- OV44/49   Sterling and Sterling Area Policy: Sterling Area Exchange Policy (November 1945 – December 1947)
- OV44/55   Sterling and Sterling Area Policy: Dominion Sterling Balances and Exchange Policy (December 1945 – February 1948)
- OV45/66   France: Mutual Aid and General Monetary Agreements (December 1945 – August 1947)

OV46/1	Post-war Relief and Reconstruction: Europe and Far East (October 1941 – March 1946)
OV56/19	India: Indian Sterling Balances and Exchange Policy – Negotiations (January 1946 – April 1947)
OV58/9	Canada: Financial (including Trade) Relations with the UK (November 1945 – March 1946)
OV58/12–13	Canada: Financial (including Trade) Relations with the UK (January 1948 – November 1955)
OV58/23	Canada: Mutual Aid (September 1944 – January 1946)
OV63/5	Switzerland: Country File (May 1946 – July 1948)
OV63/9	Switzerland: Financial (including Trade) Relations with the UK (October 1945 – November 1948)
OV102/26	Argentina: Country File (November 1947 – August 1948)
OV102/178	Argentina: Financial and Trade Missions 1946 (May 1946 – April 1947)

Bank of Canada archives

CHAPTER 4

THE FOUR DIFFICULT YEARS: FROM THE CRISIS OF 1947 TO THE KOREAN WAR

(a) INTRODUCTORY

THOUGH MISGUIDED, the external monetary strategy pursued from the conclusion of the Loan negotiations in 1945 to the suspension of convertibility in August 1947 did have virtues of clarity and simplicity. Though dependent on American money and imposed as a condition of obtaining that money, it was the strategy of a monetary Great Power seeking to settle the aftermath of war so that the normal services of a reserve and trading currency could be resumed. After the crisis of 1947 the clarity and simplicity was lost and the Great Power appearance faded. Over the four following years the British authorities found themselves moving about from one problem to another and one episode to another, often being manoeuvred by the Americans or the continental Europeans, without reaching solutions that lasted very long. They were years of continuing anxiety and stress and were to be followed by yet another sterling crisis early in 1952. Adherence to Article VIII of the IMF remained an objective, but the strategy for reaching it became so pragmatic as at times to be scarcely visible. Convertibility was low on the list of priorities, a distant goal to be reached when the UK considered itself fully recovered from the war and when the world dollar problem had somehow been finally overcome.

The story of these four difficult years is a complex one, not least because the external monetary problems with which the Bank was concerned were overlaid by the cold war and the associated forceful conduct of American financial and economic policy in Western Europe during the period of the Marshall Plan. This is turn became closely interwoven with the integrationist movement in continental Western Europe that was to lead ultimately to the Treaty of Rome, but from which the UK stood aside. A brief preliminary sketch of the main themes of British external financial history over these four years is therefore needed to provide a framework for the ensuing chapters on the Bank's part in it.

For a start the problems of managing inconvertible sterling became much more difficult than had been foreseen. During 1948 and 1949 releases from No. 2 Account balances and sterling expenditure by colonial territories became too large, despite the greater authority of the Treasury during Stafford Cripps' Chancellorship. External political considerations overcame the supposed imperatives of external financial constraint, the more so at times when the UK external balance took a temporarily good turn. The Egyptian example has already been noted in an earlier chapter. India, in 1948, was to prove another. By late 1949 the Treasury was reporting to Ministers that the No. 2 Account procedure was proving ineffectual. This in turn aggravated the growth of unofficial markets in foreign centres where inconvertible sterling became a vehicle for obtaining scarce dollars through trade distortions and commodity shunting. Numerous varieties of inconvertible sterling were marketed at a substantial discount in New York and other free markets. This so-called 'cheap sterling' reduced the dollar income of the sterling countries. More importantly, it damaged the status of the pound as a reserve currency, damaged confidence in the official rate, and retarded the recovery of London as an international financial centre. This hit the Bank where it hurt. Moreover it proved impossible to bring the problem under any kind of control without perversely adding to restrictions on the use to which sterling could be put by non-residents. No sooner had this problem been contained, with difficulty, by further controls and by the external effects of the domestic adjustment achieved by Cripps' disinflation, than the American authorities became concerned lest the containment of the dollar shortage by the European Recovery Programme (ERP) should end by perpetuating a high-cost discriminatory bloc consisting of Western Europe and the Sterling Area. Accordingly, and in anticipation of Marshall Aid terminating by 1952, the Americans decided that a substantial devaluation of West European currencies would be required in 1949 if progress towards their own objectives was to be maintained. The cutting edge of this policy would be the devaluation of sterling, which would precipitate devaluations of the other European currencies. The Americans made no secret of their intentions and indeed promoted them in cool disregard of objections voiced in Whitehall and in Threadneedle Street. They were then assisted in their endeavours by the onset of their own recession, with its especially adverse impact on the external balance of the UK and the Sterling Area and, on a different level, by the resulting aggravation of the cheap-sterling problem.

The devaluation in the autumn of 1949 may well have been correctly judged in terms of American aims. Progress towards external balance in the first half of 1950, assisted by recovery in the US, was good. The dollar shortage eased. Cheap sterling rose near to the official rate. But the crisis of 1949, following the episodes of 1947 and 1948, did not improve the long-run view of sterling taken by individual national authorities in Western Europe and elsewhere. This made it the more unrealistic to suppose, as the Bank was still inclined to do, that greater use of transferable sterling could prove to be the monetary catalyst for a decisive liberalisation of intra-European trade from the prevailing bilateralism. Yet some such catalyst was not only desirable in itself but was ardently desired by the Americans. All along they had wanted to use the ERP as a lever for securing a substantial degree of West European unification. They were disappointed by the lack of immediate progress in 1948, but their attitude certainly encouraged the European movement that was gathering support on the Continent. It also played its part in the *rapprochement* between France and the emerging Federal Republic of Germany, an early sign of which was the Schuman Plan for a supranational European Coal and Steel Community (ECSC). Finally it helped achieve a solution to the problem of intra-European trade and payments that did not critically depend upon the positive support of the UK. The British Government deliberately kept its distance from the integrationist movement in Europe, preferring to rely on its Commonwealth connection and its 'special relationship' with the US to preserve what it conceived to be its world role and status. For this reason, but perhaps also because of their remaining vision of the international role of sterling, the British authorities tended to adopt a cool attitude towards continental or American schemes for an intra-European payments system. The British played a helpful part at technical level but were often reluctant in other respects, moving only so far as was necessary to avoid undue American displeasure. The eventual solution, the European Payments Union (EPU), proved outstandingly successful. But its negotiation in 1950, though at times marked by considerable tactical skill on the British side, required a downgrading of the reserve function of sterling in Europe. This did not improve self-confidence in Threadneedle Street, where underlying anxieties were being preserved at this time by the failure of another attempt to deal with the problem of the sterling balances.

Difficulties and frustrations with the management of sterling, including the management of the No. 2 Accounts, meant that the problem of the balances and the ultimate loyalty of the Sterling Area were seldom far from mind. Just as the onset of the first post-war crisis in 1947 stimulated Cobbold to advocacy of a special approach to the Americans for help in settling the problem, so also did the second crisis in 1949 provoke similar anxieties and suggestions. This time the Americans appeared somewhat receptive. At least they were prepared to discuss the matter, as part of a continuing consultative procedure that they offered the British as a sweetener for devaluation. After full treatment of the subject by a Treasury Working Party, the authorities in London responded with some modest practical proposals. But all they found, by mid-1950, was that Washington was no longer interested. Nonetheless, had the Korean War not intervened it is possible that the external financial problems of the UK would have progressively eased and the weakness of the sterling system would have become less apparent. Steady and relatively controlled progress towards adherence to Article VIII, alongside the other members of the EPU, might then have been achieved. As it was, the rearmament boom that followed the outbreak of war in Korea was followed by the onset of a third sterling crisis in the winter of 1951–2. All the now familiar features of falling sterling balances, a heavy discount on cheap sterling, an unsupportable external deficit incurred by the UK itself, the initial reliance on American help that then failed to come up to expectations, and the increasingly ulcerating prospect of reserves exhaustion were present in striking degree. It is not therefore surprising that the Bank then finally abandoned the whole evolutionary approach to convertibility that it had pursued since 1941, but had begun to doubt after the devaluation of 1949. Despite the election of a Government unwedded, for example, to the preservation of $\frac{1}{2}\%$ on Treasury Bills, the Old Lady seemingly lost confidence in the ability of the British authorities to manage an evolutionary approach any longer. She therefore saw close ahead a disorderly collapse of sterling precipitated by the exhaustion of external resources. There was then nothing left but to make a virtue of necessity, rather as Keynes had sought to do as long ago as January 1946. Early in 1952 the Bank joined the Overseas Finance Division of the Treasury in unsuccessful advocacy of a resumption of external convertibility, but this time at a floating rate of exchange, supported by a substantial blocking of sterling balances and involving UK withdrawal from full membership of the EPU.

However, the third crisis and the thinking that immediately preceded it belong to a different chapter of this book. First, with the help of this introduction, the themes of the four difficult years, namely intra-European payments, cheap sterling, devaluation, and the sterling balances, must be examined.

(b) EUROPEAN PAYMENTS PROBLEMS

Analyses, remedies, and the taking of positions: 1947

In the summer of 1947 the scramble to buy goods of all kinds from the Western hemisphere drained exchange reserves away from the countries of Western Europe. The sterling crisis made matters worse, by again restricting the uses to which the sterling earnings of Western Europe could be put. Marshall Aid was not yet available and was not to become available until the summer of 1948. Accordingly, the liquidity base of intra-European payments, including payments between Western Europe and the Sterling Area, tended to contract into the credit lines (in national currencies) contained within the prevailing network of bilateral monetary agreements. Each country then tried desperately to minimise any loss of gold or dollars, or maximise any gain, consequent upon bilateral credit limits being exceeded. A period of extreme bilateralism in trade and payments had inevitably to ensue unless arrangements could be made that permitted multilateral settlements to take place within the region and without sustained loss of gold or dollars. Within the Sterling Area such regional arrangements already existed, almost to perfection, sterling being freely usable without interference from UK exchange control. Of course, the other members could bring about an unacceptable drain on the exiguous central reserves of the Area, and arresting such a drain was in part a matter of bilateral negotiation between the UK and the member concerned and in part a matter of more general collaboration between all members. But within whatever restraints might be agreed on the extent to which a member might run down its aggregate reserves, the usability of available sterling within the Area remained entirely unimpaired. In Western Europe, by contrast, no comparable means of regional payment existed. It is true that sterling, after the crisis, remained transferable quite widely; but this could be maintained only so long as it did not bring about persistent accumulations of sterling in excess of bilateral credit limits and, in consequence, persistent pressure on UK reserves. There were also other difficulties affecting the suitability of sterling as a regional means of payment in Europe between monetary authorities. The crisis itself cast serious doubt on the reliability of British undertakings, while developments in 1948, notably the growth of cheap sterling, were to be of little help.

Creating a new regional payments system for use within Western Europe, though a clear priority in 1947 by any criterion and an even clearer priority within the American concept of a Marshall Plan that would assist West European unification, meant finding a solution to two obstinate problems. Firstly, arrangements for the creation of special additional regional credit, usable multilaterally, needed to be accompanied by an element of collectively agreed discipline where none at all hitherto existed. Otherwise spendthrift and politically less stable countries would quickly use all the credit and virtuous countries would provide it, after which there would be a reversion to the preceding bilateralism. Secondly, some European countries could argue persuasively that they were natural earners of a surplus with the others and that they ought to be able to convert this for making payments to the dollar area in exchange for essential supplies. Belgium was the outstanding example; and it was Belgium who therefore proposed that a proportion of Marshall Aid should be directed in such a way as to finance these conversions. Attempts to solve these problems met with only limited success until the ERP was well under way, until exchange rates against the dollar had been adjusted, and until the underlying dollar shortage had somewhat eased. At that point, in 1950, a clear-cut solution was achieved by the formation of the EPU. But in June 1947, just before the sterling crisis and just ahead of the Paris conference that prepared the European response to Marshall, this solution was a long way off. There were, however, initial analyses of the problems and initial suggestions about their solution.

At this early formative stage the monetary authorities in London were not at first lacking in imagination or ideas. But partly because of their growing and debtor-minded absorption in the crisis that was only a few weeks away and partly because of their evident disinclination to share in continental enthusiasm for creating some new regional monetary structure, their large-minded ideas did not prosper in Paris. Instead it was the Belgians, with increasing continental support, who gained the initiative; and over the ensuing months they constructed a distinctively European piece of monetary machinery with which the British were not fully associated. The machinery was not at first very important in itself. But its establishment against British resistance marked the beginning of a long trend. It is important to see how this came to happen and what contribution the Bank made to the outcome.

As early as the middle of June 1947 the Bank was well aware which way the continental wind was blowing and was not slow to inform the Treasury. The Deputy Governor, in the course of visits to Paris and Basle, had long talks with Monick of the Bank of France, Frère[1] of the National

---

[1] *Frère, Maurice (1880–1970)*. Educated Brussels University. Ministry for Economic Affairs, Ministry for Foreign Affairs, Chairman, Banking Commission 1938–44, Governor, National Bank of Belgium 1944–57. Director, Bank for International Settlements 1944–70, Chairman of the Board 1946–58, President 1948–58, Vice-Chairman

Bank of Belgium, de Jong of the Netherlands Bank, and Menichella of the Bank of Italy. He found all of them 'keen to get moving' and all of them in favour of at least part of Marshall Aid being provided 'in monetary form'. He then arranged for further informal meetings to take place in Threadneedle Street at the end of the month with representatives from Holland, Belgium, and France. Bolton, Lithiby, and Mynors attended these meetings from the Bank. Among the matters discussed were reserve pooling and the freeing of exchange control barriers between European countries so as to 'form in effect a European currency area'. Early in July Bolton circulated a note sketching preliminary ideas for a European fund containing an element of pooled gold reserves and IMF drawing rights. Cobbold, writing later in the month, concentrated instead upon the need for corrective measures within Europe, especially in France, and the need to build on the existing structure of monetary agreements and monetary areas. In the Treasury meanwhile, writing on the day after sterling began its brief journey as a convertible currency, Ellis-Rees remarked: 'Ignoring slight differences between one country and another, we can say there is established in Europe a mechanism for payments with the UK as headquarters.' He went on to suggest that the liquidity of that mechanism could be improved if credits granted within Europe since 1944 were now all funded, with repayment not to begin until 1952.

Five days later, on 21 July, Siepmann received from Hubert Ansiaux, now a Director of the National Bank of Belgium, the outline of a very different plan in which bilateral credits would be enlarged and balances in local currencies resulting from their operation would become transferable for current transactions within Europe through a central organisation set up for the purpose. These balances would all bear an exchange guarantee. Concurrently, as part of Marshall Aid, the US would assign gold or dollars to the central organisation. They would be made available in such a way that balances accumulating in excess of credit limits would be made convertible into dollars in the hands of the creditor country. The initial response of the Bank of England to these ideas was dismissive. Writing to the Treasury on 22 July, Bolton began by stressing, as had Ansiaux, the prior need for remedial macro-economic measures in France and Italy before any new developments in intra-European payments could usefully be discussed. But he then went on to support the ideas of Ellis-Rees. He thought, wrongly, that the Ansiaux Plan was based on an illusion. The Americans, he judged, would not part with gold in the manner proposed. However, Bolton came to realise that the Plan had attractive features, for

1965–70, Governor for Belgium, IMF 1946–57. President, Belgian–Luxembourg Foreign Exchange Institute, Member, Administrative Board, Brussels University, Chairman, Sofina.

he quickly devised an alternative one in which the intra-convertibility of European currencies, following corrective action by France and Italy, would be supported by the IMF while the rest of the existing system in Europe would be left intact. Alongside the network of bilateral credits and debits, each Western European country would agree to accumulate the currency of another up to a proportion, perhaps 50%, of the latter's quota in the IMF. The creditor country could then, if it wished, obtain repayment by obliging the debtor to draw the creditor's currency from the Fund. In this way substantial additional intra-European credit would be made available and intra-convertibility of European currencies would be sustained.[2] Concurrently Bolton now suggested the Americans might well agree to provide additional gold or dollars to Western Europe either by freeing the dollar resources of the IMF or by some other machinery more directly connected with Marshall Aid. In effect the IMF would be divided into two. One part would be used as a West European Fund supporting regional transferability while the other part would remain fully international and would include the dollar resources represented by the US quota. It was a simple and imaginative idea born of an imaginative brain working in the central bank of a reserve currency, a brain accustomed to authoritative improvisation. But the IMF was far too new and fragile an international plant to be rudely disturbed for regional purposes in the manner proposed by Bolton; and in any case something more narrowly European was demanded across the Channel. There was, moreover, an even more decisive objection. The proposals were both far too expansionist to be acceptable to likely creditor countries in Europe and far too favourable to the UK with its very large Fund quota. As it was, even the much more modest ideas of Ellis-Rees, for the long-term funding of accumulated intra-European debts, were to make no headway in Paris.

For the moment, however, the Treasury was inclined to accept Bolton's ideas as well as the suggestions put forward earlier by Ellis-Rees. They also viewed the Belgian plan with ill-judged disdain. Minuting Eady about it on 26 July, Playfair[3] wrote: 'None of us thinks this is a starter. M. Ansiaux has promised not to table it until he has talked to us...We propose to try to ride him off his scheme (to which he has given considerable publicity) but we must have some positive British contribution to make

---

[2] Austria, Portugal, Sweden, and Switzerland were not yet members of the IMF but would join the scheme as if they were.
[3] *Playfair, Edward Wilder*, KCB (b.1909). Educated Eton and King's College, Cambridge. Inland Revenue 1931–4, HM Treasury 1934–46, Control Office for Germany and Austria, 1946–7, HM Treasury 1947–56, Permanent Secretary, War Office 1956–9, Permanent Secretary, Ministry of Defence 1960–1. Chairman, International Computers and Tabulators 1961–5, Director, National Westminster Bank 1961–79.

ourselves. It is essentially a field in which this country should take the lead.' But the positive British contribution proved difficult to agree in a hurry, though it was indeed urgently needed if the opportunity of taking a lead was not to be let slip. At meetings with the Belgians on 28 and 29 July the Treasury lamely put forward an innocuous draft resolution about desiderata instead of an alternative plan. Ansiaux told Lithiby that he found the draft incoherent, unrealistic, and lacking any proper sense of urgency. He was not in the best of moods, having protested angrily to Hall-Patch in Paris that the British Treasury were treating him like a schoolboy.[4] The British attitude was also causing concern to Oliver Franks, Chairman of the Paris Committee for European Cooperation, who wrote to the Governor on 27 July pointing out that the Ansiaux Plan, or something like it, would be of value to the Americans as evidence of Europe's determination to help itself. Catto sent an emollient reply on the following day (which got lost in transmission) but attitudes in London did not change at all. In a letter to Playfair, Siepmann described a revised version of the Ansiaux Plan, which now included a link with the IMF, as 'evidently a composite document, hastily compiled and shockingly arranged. The drafting is villainous but this would not matter so much if the ideas were clear cut. Actually, they are vague and difficult.'

The Ansiaux Plan did in fact bristle with technical difficulties, but few in the Bank appreciated how conceptually attractive it was. Siepmann certainly did not, nor did Lithiby, the Bank's senior adviser on West European affairs. Yet the Plan's apparent offer of a mechanism for linking the liberalisation of intra-European payments to the special provision of a proportion of Marshall Aid told clearly and strongly in its favour. However it was in essence a creditor's plan, tailored very obviously to the perceived needs of Belgium; it was not at once attractive to likely debtors, none of whom had as yet any reliable indication of how Marshall Aid would be distributed in practice. Nor, quite apart from politics or *amour propre*, was it attractive to the UK authorities, who were in the throes of a rapidly developing crisis and in no mood to countenance any arrangement that might possibly increase the pressure on UK reserves. Nonetheless the Ansiaux Plan was the only runner and it formed part of the material for a protracted review over the following three months, a review that ended with two reports of a Payments Subcommittee of the main Paris Committee for European Economic Co-operation.[5] Up to the

---

[4] He was thirty-nine at the time, four years younger than Cobbold, and had been a Director of the National Bank since the early age of thirty-three.

[5] In the course of this debate the Belgians went as far as to scout ideas for a European central bank – then, as perhaps later, a somewhat provocative concept.

issue of its first Report this body was chaired by Waley and it was he who now belatedly attempted, as the convertibility crisis was reaching its climax, to devise an alternative and British plan that could be approved by Ministers and then sold in Paris.

It was Waley's last important task before retirement and it proved next to impossible. Segregating a part of the IMF, along the lines suggested by Bolton, was evidently considered out of the question; and anyway there were signs from Paris that other countries would not readily agree to diluting their dollar drawing rights in the Fund. But there were no other ideas, except variants of the Belgian Plan, for achieving intra-European regional transferability. Accordingly the British sketched out a plan for making all or most European currencies not only transferable within Europe but convertible throughout the world, in the same way as sterling had been made convertible. To that end Waley and Playfair proposed that the US be asked to grant gifts or loans in gold to European countries equal to their IMF quotas, additional to Marshall Aid itself, and conditional on each recipient then being fit to conform to Article VIII of the IMF. They also retained the proposal for the funding of existing intra-European credits. These ideas, wholly lacking in European vision and seemingly oblivious of the crisis rapidly overtaking convertible sterling, were approved by UK Ministers on 8 August and duly launched by Waley in Paris. There was opposition to the funding of credits and this proposal was dropped. The suggestion of 'convertibility loans' got a better hearing, as a variant of the 'stabilisation loans' of the 1920s, but only as an arrangement additional to the Belgian Plan rather than as a substitute for it. But especially after the suspension of sterling convertibility on 19 August, it came to be appreciated that large gold loans to Europe outside Marshall Aid were unlikely to get through Congress. This left variants of the Ansiaux Plan in sole possession of the field. As Mynors foresaw on 30 August: 'that the only teeth on offer are this ill-fitting plate by Benelux: that this is not generally favoured: but that the technicians are still to meet in September and that if no other set of teeth is on offer this one, though "killed" by Waley, will come to life again.'

There did in fact emerge one other set of teeth, this time from the Continent. It would have made transferable sterling the sole channel through which should flow the special Marshall Aid proposed by the Belgians. Sterling would be the means of intra-European payment and, as in the Ansiaux Plan, its convertibility at the margin would be underwritten by the US. But the British would have none of it. Presumably they feared that the aid would be inadequate and the inevitable American surveillance of the UK unacceptable. The Bank then came up with the only remaining positive option. Cobbold wrote to Eady on 19 September with proposals for anglicising the Belgian Plan. He proposed an enlargement of bilateral credit limits and a special tranche of Marshall Aid that would be used to take over no more than a predetermined proportion of the enlarged bilateral creditor positions emerging over a specified period. A degree of additional convertibility would thereby be provided, but one that did not make life too easy for creditors. Increased regional transferability was accepted as an aim, but it would come about as experience allowed and would not be automatic or integral to the Plan itself. There would, moreover, be no question of any of this coming into force ahead of Marshall Aid funds becoming available. Nor would there be any new European agency to administer the scheme, either as clearing house or as allocator of the Special Aid. Following the crisis and lacking enthusiasm for new European monetary institutions as such, the Bank and the Treasury were extremely reluctant to accept any new commitments on transferability or convertibility, or any surrender of freedom of action to a new regional body in Europe. In a note dated 24 September, Cobbold came out flatly against 'the folly of getting people tied up to commitments which the facts of life are likely to undo forcibly and untidily'.

But the Benelux countries had by then become firmly wedded to those aspects of their Plan to which the British objected. Attracted by the goal of a united Europe, one of whose most active and influential enthusiasts was Paul-Henri Spaak, the Belgian Prime Minister, they were much interested in the idea of automatic and full transferability. They were much interested too in the idea of a central agency that would be responsible for the periodic offsetting of each member's bilateral credits and debits. The Benelux countries, and especially the Belgians, were also attracted – as creditors as well as Europeans – to their idea of making overall net creditor positions convertible into dollars through the special provision of American Aid to a European fund administered by the central agency. Besides being thought over-generous to creditors, this feature, combined with the provisions for automatic transferability, remained unacceptable to the British who were anyway uninterested in the Europeanist features of the scheme. They persisted in fearing that the variety of European currencies ending up with, for example, Belgium or Sweden, would in practice consist of too much transferable sterling, whose convertibility would turn out not to be fully covered by the limited tranche of Special Aid.

The fear was excusable, the more so after the bitter experience of July and August. In 1947 and 1948 the use in Europe of a fully transferable reserve currency whose supply was not entirely throttled probably did mean that it more than any other currency was likely to accumulate in the hands of a persistent creditor; and Ansiaux failed to persuade the Bank that the convertibility of such accumulations would be offset by the British accumulating convertible balances in other currencies. In any case, at that point in the argument the subject became so complicated that reason was unlikely to surmount suspicion. The problem could only be resolved, in practice, by somehow eliminating members' national currencies from the final settlements between European monetary authorities. That would mean constructing an additional and artificial means of regional payment that could be used, in agreed proportion, alongside gold or dollars for the settlement of the aggregate net positions of each member country – in short by setting up a payments union. But in 1947 the conditions for this were not yet present. The creditor countries were, in a sense, too greedy and the debtors too needy, while the British would still have had in the back of their minds a recovery of sterling that would render any new regional machinery unnecessary. In addition, the vital link to Marshall Aid could not be precisely formulated before passage of the Aid legislation through Congress later in 1948.

When Waley's Committee met at the end of September, the British did not attempt to put forward Cobbold's anglicised version of the Belgian Plan. Though they realised that some version would probably be needed eventually, they preferred for the time being simply to refuse participation in the version then on the table. Ansiaux then sensibly allowed most of his Plan to be shelved until such time as American intentions about the distribution of Aid became sufficiently clear. Nonetheless the Benelux countries remained determined to make a start, however modest, with the construction of specific intra-European payments machinery operated by a central agency. They were supported by France and Italy; and, if need be, these five out of the eventual six signatories of the Treaty of Rome were prepared to go ahead on their own. There was a further meeting of the Payments Committee in Paris during October. But instead of Waley it was the official head of the French Finance Ministry, Guillaume Guindey, who now took the chair. The UK was represented only by two observers, one of whom was Lithiby. The upshot was an agreement between the five for the automatic offsetting, or 'multilateral compensation', of bilateral debits and credits where its effect would be to reduce existing balances. Where compensations would increase a balance, the consent of the parties was required. The ultimate convertibility of balances continued to be governed by existing bilateral agreements. The door was left open for the British and others, notably the Swiss and the Swedes, to join. They were invited to supply monthly information to the central agency and, if they so wished, to agree compensations as occasional members of the scheme. The agency itself was not to be some new-fangled creation in Paris but the BIS in Basle, the pre-war creation of European central bankers and of Norman in particular which had recently survived the attempt on its life written into the IMF Charter. Moreover it quickly emerged that a leading figure on the technical side would be F. G. Conolly.[6] A former official of the Bank of England, he had moved to the BIS before the war and his relations with former colleagues in Threadneedle Street remained close and friendly. The Bank, with the prior consent of the Treasury and in accord with the invitations sent out after the Paris meetings, agreed without fuss to provide the BIS with the necessary monthly information and full technical help. Towards the end of the year the UK formally joined the scheme, but as an 'occasional' rather than a 'permanent' member.

Not much was expected to come of it all and the prophetic significance of a Benelux monetary initiative actually getting off the ground in Western Europe, without British support and indeed against British opposition, was probably not appreciated in London. Nor was there any sign of its being appreciated, or regretted, in the Bank. The Governor seems to have taken no interest in this often abstruse field, while the Deputy Governor's support for an anglicised version of the Ansiaux Plan, produced at tactically too late a stage in the debate, exemplified the Bank's view of the whole matter. No memoranda seriously discussing the possible monetary implications of European unification, and the appropriate British response, survive from this period. No group was assembled to discuss these questions and report to the Governors; nor is there any evidence that the Treasury asked the Bank to dwell on matters that were now becoming the subject of keen attention and some personal dedication in Amsterdam, Brussels, Paris, and Rome. If anything, the crisis in the summer of 1947, which drained away so much of everyone's time and energy, drove the British monetary authorities back into their Sterling Area shell. It did not propel them towards a monetary component of the integrated Europe of which the Americans and others now had a compelling vision. This served to reinforce a developing attitude in the Treasury and the Bank that readily admitted the need to form good working relations with whatever 'Europe' might construct in the monetary field and even countenanced positive intervention in the process of construction so as to make eventual working relations easier or better, but which turned away from full participation in the vision and in the creative process.

---

[6] *Conolly, Frederick George (1899–1972)*. Entered Bank 1919. BIS 1932, a Manager, Monetary and Economic Department 1948–65.

This attitude was in accord with the general attitude of the Labour Government towards European unity. Under the leadership of the Foreign Secretary, the British typically preferred to build with such instruments as lay to hand rather than start laboriously constructing novel supranational machinery that would anyway interfere with British sovereignty. Treaties, alliances, and consultative Councils of Ministers were readily feasible. Constitutions for a United States of Europe were not. The early and critical phase of the cold war was approaching. The Russian grip on Eastern Europe was still tightening. In the West, the political stability of France and Italy was not yet assured and the political reconstruction of Germany had still to be settled. The year 1948 was to be the year of the Berlin blockade, the Brussels Treaty, and the final communist take-over of Czechoslovakia. For the time being, therefore, there was much to be said for the course of treaties, alliances, and councils that Ernest Bevin energetically and successfully adopted.

The Ansiaux Plan and the IEPC: 1948–1949

Although the machinery for multilateral compensation set up in Basle towards the end of 1947 may not have commanded much admiration in London, it did attract close interest in Washington. The Truman Administration secured passage of Interim Aid legislation through the Republican Congress in December and thereafter obtained introduction of a Bill for the full European Recovery Programme. This was scheduled for final passage in the summer of 1948, ahead of Presidential and Congressional Elections in the autumn. In the course of an official document published in support of the Bill, the Administration drew approving attention to the Basle machinery and to ways in which it could be supported through the provision of Aid in an appropriate way. Evidence of progress towards an agreed method of such support, with the Europeans securing collaborative agreement among themselves, was therefore going to be useful to the Administration in Washington. Accordingly two members of the American delegation in Paris attended the first two Basle meetings and stressed the political desirability of showing results at the first round of compensations. This took place at the third meeting, in January 1948. The Americans were disappointed at the very meagre results, only $1·7 million of compensations being effected. But they gave no indication that they wanted the machinery scrapped. Instead, they began to press for agreement on the mechanics of linking the compensation system to a proportion of specially provided Aid, a link that had, of course, always been a central feature of the Ansiaux Plan. Seeking such agreement was to be the principal task of the Paris negotiations on intra-European payments throughout the first half of 1948. Commenting on the January meeting, Lithiby himself wrote: 'If the stalemate continues, the inevitable result will be that European countries will become more and more embedded in bilateralism. So far as Marshall is concerned the result would be deplorable, as one of the few concrete examples of European self-help will have disappeared...It is now evident that even this measure of self-help cannot operate to a valuable extent without an injection of dollars to break the stalemate.'

But progress was not much helped, nor the active interest of top people in London encouraged, by the daunting complexities of the Basle machinery itself. Its workings had frequently to be expressed in terms of 'Compensation circuits', of 'Plafonds (non cumulables) des possibilités de compensation', or even of 'Possibilités de compensation de la deuxième catégorie, resultant d'une augmentation du solde de la relation-CLE'. In order to agree a method of calculation the delegates eventually had recourse to mathematical services provided by the Dutch. So it was perhaps not surprising that a small group of Treasury and Bank officials, formed in January 1948 to study questions of intra-European trade and payments, at first showed some disposition to go for wider horizons. These were more to the taste of the British who were still inclined to underestimate the Europeanist determination of the Americans.

Wider horizons had first been explored in the Treasury early in January by Rowe-Dutton, who had recently been promoted to Third Secretary in succession to Waley. He complained: 'We are all working too fast.' He foresaw a dollar shortage stretching into the indefinite future and with it the transitional period of Article XIV. To meet this contingency he in his turn wanted to rely on a rehabilitation of sterling so that it could serve as the international currency of the non-dollar world. But for the immediate future, in Europe, he favoured a regional monetary fund financed from the local currency proceeds of Marshall Aid. A copy of his note was sent privately to Siepmann. It attracted a notably personal and deeply pessimistic reply, which turned out to be its author's last recorded statement on the subject.

> Your reconstructed Europe on an honest sterling basis, with gold outlawed, seems to me to be the right conception, much as I deplore that we should be reduced to it; but I cannot see more than the first beginnings of this in 1948. Would it not be right to say that what we are short of is an international currency? The dollar never was that, because it was used either to settle a debt or to hold and keep, whereas a currency should be current. Sterling, which really was an international currency, is now so soiled and

unserviceable (this is what you seem to me to say) that it is fit only for the rag-bag and no longer for the washing basket. You want to get rid of it and start afresh, saving little more than the name. Now that we cannot make ourselves solvent, you hope we can survive a petition in bankruptcy, with our credit unimpaired. Perhaps that is not a fair way of putting it. You asked for something private and personal, and now you have got it. The remark I liked best in your paper was that 'we are all working too fast'. We have to because we are attempting too much. The prevailing sin is hubris – that over-weening self-confidence which tempts us to undertake the work of the gods. The consequences are well known and already apparent.

Rowe-Dutton's ideas were subsequently developed and adapted in the Treasury by Otto Clarke,[7] whose aptitude for devising bold schemes was second only to that of Bolton. He put to the study group an outline proposal for the total elimination of gold and dollars from intra-European settlement. Instead, countries would simply hold each other's currencies, accumulated balances being automatically funded when agreed limits were reached. All currencies would be transferable within Europe and the motive for bilateralism would thereby be removed at a stroke. A country that considered itself to be granting excessive credit would simply restrict exports to Europe and endeavour to increase them elsewhere. These proposals were received in the Treasury with excitement, but in the Bank Cobbold, Siepmann, and even Bolton all considered them to be quite unrealistic. Siepmann termed them 'hare-brained'. The Bank had in fact learnt its lesson from the bitter experience of 1947, including the dismissal in July of its own ideas for the creation of a large regional fund of European currencies. Actual or prospective creditors, who might even at some stage include the UK, would simply not agree to go on granting fresh credit in Europe on the open-ended scale suggested; and without their agreement no plan could prosper.

It no doubt required a considerable effort of mental adjustment in London, the centre of the sterling world, to accept that the tune should at this time be called by a minor power like Belgium. But that was how it was and the only effective course was to try to secure negotiation of a Belgian-type scheme on the most liberal terms that could be obtained. Towards the end of February the Treasury held the first of two exploratory meetings

---

[7] *Clarke, Richard William Barnes ('Otto'), KCB (1910–75)*. Educated Christ's Hospital and Clare College, Cambridge. *Financial News* 1933–9, Visiting Lecturer, Cambridge University 1935–6, Ministries of Information, Economic Warfare, Supply and Production 1939–45, Combined Production and Resources Board, Washington 1942–3, Assistant Secretary, HM Treasury 1945–7, Under-Secretary 1947–55, Third Secretary 1955–62, Second Secretary 1962–6, Permanent Secretary, Ministry of Aviation 1966, Ministry of Technology 1966–70. Chairman, Stothert and Pitt, Director, Courtaulds, EMI, GKN, Orion Insurance 1971–5, Guinness Peat Group 1973–5.

with representatives of France and Italy and the Benelux countries. Eady, who was being succeeded by Henry Wilson Smith[8] as Second Secretary in charge of Overseas Finance, took the chair. Always a prudent negotiator, he did not put forward Clarke's plan, although the likelihood of an enduring dollar shortage was discussed. The extension of non-dollar settlements within Europe was also mentioned, but only as a possible emergency measure ahead of Marshall Aid and ahead of some agreed version of the Belgian Plan whose energetic author had submitted a fresh version in advance of the meeting. The upshot was that this Plan remained yet again the front runner. In April, after the Belgians themselves had suddenly had second thoughts and briefly flirted with an entirely IMF solution to the whole problem, there emerged the 'Cripps–Ansiaux' agreement,[9] under which the UK agreed to participate in a suitable plan for enhancing the Basle compensation process by linking it to US Aid.

Over the following weeks further exploration of a link to Aid was not especially encouraging. In the Bank there was however a greater sense of urgency to see things through to a successful conclusion. Cobbold, Bolton, and Lithiby were closely involved, with encouragement from Niemeyer who wisely counselled: 'I think we should not look down our noses too much at this [the Basle machinery].' Cobbold replied, in agreement, that 'everybody is trying to build it into a West European and Marshall Aid Special Account structure'. But the attempts seemed to get bogged down and Ellis-Rees lacked firm guidance from London. Early in June, therefore, Cobbold and Bolton, with encouragement from Wilson Smith, revived the idea of a European Fund of local currencies, subscribed in proportions related to IMF quotas and, despite the Bank's dislike of such things, administered by a special European organisation. This, they argued, would demonstrate European self-help, would assist the working of the BIS Compensation Scheme, and could later be enlarged by infusions of dollar aid and in a manner to be decided by the US.

These ideas were much welcomed in the Treasury, where the need for a new British initiative in Paris had become apparent. The proposal for a European Fund was then further developed in the Bank and by 12 June

[8] *Wilson Smith, Henry*, KCB, KBE, (1904–78). Educated Royal Grammar School, Newcastle-Upon-Tyne and Peterhouse, Cambridge. GPO 1927–30, HM Treasury 1930–46, Under-Secretary 1942–6, Permanent Secretary, Ministry of Defence 1947–8, Additional Second Secretary and Head of Overseas Finance Division, HM Treasury 1948–51. Director, GKN 1951–72, Deputy Chairman 1962–72, Director, Powell Duffryn 1951–69, Chairman 1957–69. Director, Bank of England 1964–70.

[9] This was reached at a meeting of the Finance Ministers of the countries that had just signed the Brussels Treaty. At about the same time it had been agreed by the sixteen members of the Committee on European Economic Co-operation to set up a continuing organisation for such co-operation (the OEEC) alongside the ECA.

there existed a British Plan approved by the Chancellor and the President of the Board of Trade. But Ellis-Rees proceeded very cautiously in Paris, avoiding formal presentation of the Plan until confident of sufficient support behind the scenes. These tactics provoked considerable resentment in the Bank, where the originators of the Plan were waiting for results. Lithiby and Hamilton[10] were accompanying Ellis-Rees in Paris and the former was taken to task by Bolton for failing to table the British proposals at an early stage. Cobbold, writing on a note by Hamilton, remarked: 'The best way to take a lead is often to say what you think and not water it all down beforehand to suit your opponents' objections.' He felt that Ansiaux had overplayed his hand and that the British proposals, forcibly presented, would attract support. This judgement was probably wrong; but it was anyway not put to the test as little serious attempt was made to isolate the Belgians or to go ahead without them. The British Plan was finally tabled early in July, but it failed to gain the initiative. Its omission of a specific link to Aid told against it. Thus despite protests from officials in London Ellis-Rees allowed it to get submerged in the process of reaching an agreed settlement. The Chancellor, who had approved the Plan in the first place, was then obliged to go down this new road. His negotiator in Paris may have been somewhat of a law unto himself, but there was no denying his experience and skill in the particular field of European monetary arrangements, nor (after the events of 1947) his ability to judge the resolve of his superiors in London. Eventually, Ellis-Rees and Ansiaux reached an outline agreement at the end of July and this was approved by all the Governments concerned. It was not welcomed in the Bank and was indeed very close to the original Belgian Plan. The Basle machinery was to be revised so that all members became full members and all first category compensations became automatic. But instead of the European Fund favoured by the British there was to be a system of drawing rights in national currencies calculated according to forecast intra-European bilateral surpluses and deficits.[11] The provision of these drawing rights, and their use, was to be linked directly to a proportion of Marshall Aid.

The Bank now accepted the *fait accompli*. Lithiby and Hamilton were withdrawn from the Paris negotiations and replaced by P. S. Beale and

---

[10] *Hamilton, Cyril Robert Parke*, CMG (1903–90). Educated High School, Ilford and King's College, London. Entered Bank 1923, Assistant Chief Cashier (Exchange Control and Overseas) 1945–51, Acting Deputy Chief Cashier 1951–5, Deputy Chief Cashier 1955–63. Deputy Chairman, Standard Bank 1963–74, Vice-Chairman, Standard and Chartered Banking Group 1969–74.

[11] This was known as the 'Tomlinson method', after an American official of that name, and it seems to have been appreciated from the start that any scheme based upon exceptionally flimsy forecasts was likely to be difficult to work. It initially involved agreeing forecasts of no less than 170 bilateral balances.

Hilton Clarke.[12] Both were expert in the technicalities of international payments and exchange controls, the former pre-eminently so, and it was this expertise that was now required before the new scheme could be made ready for formal signature and inauguration. Beale flung himself into the discussions with the self-assurance of a technical virtuoso who knows his performance is going to outshine any of his rivals.[13] These qualities were reflected in very long letters dictated directly onto the typewriter and despatched to Grafftey-Smith in London, where they were suitably admired if at times imperfectly understood. Whether those same qualities endeared him to the other participants in Paris must be doubted.

Beale's main job was to see that the new Scheme was constructed so as not to damage the existing network of sterling monetary agreements, so as not to interfere with existing arrangements for sterling transferability, and so as not to commit the UK to automatic compensations that might lead to a loss of reserves. Gaining the first two of these objectives was not difficult though it required complex drafting. Gaining the third took longer. Automaticity of second-category compensations as well as first, leading on to what was now termed 'multilateral integrated compensation', was discussed at great length. But to Beale's satisfaction the 'theorists', as he liked to call his opponents, tended to get quite lost in technical obscurities of definition. In the end it was generally agreed that second-category compensations should not become automatic until more reserves became available. Beale and Clarke returned from Paris early in September, leaving Heasman[14] to hold the fort. The formal agreement for Intra-European Payments and Compensations (IEPC) was eventually initialled on 16 October. It was regarded as no more than a first stage. Article 25 bound the parties to review its working not later than 1 May 1949 and to consider whether it should be continued.

The Belgians had more or less got what Ansiaux had originally proposed, but the Europeanist attractions of the scheme had proved

[12] *Clarke, Hilton Swift, CBE (b.1909).* Educated Highgate School. Entered Bank 1927, Assistant Principal, Dealing and Accounts Office 1942–6, Deputy Principal 1946–50, Deputy Principal, Discount Office 1950–4, Principal 1954–67. Director, Charterhouse Group 1967–82, Chairman, Atlantic International Bank 1973–86.

[13] In a letter sent to Grafftey-Smith on 18 August he remarked characteristically: 'I cannot say that the members of Sub-Committee B are remarkable for their understanding of the technical problems. We are more likely to run into trouble over failure to comprehend than failure to agree.'

[14] *Heasman, Roy Ernest (1914–76).* Educated St Dunstan's College, Catford. Entered Bank 1932, UK Alternate, Managing Board of EPU 1954–5, UK Alternate Executive Director, IMF 1956–8, Adviser (Acting) 1958, Assistant Chief, Overseas Department 1958–9, Deputy Chief, Central Banking Information Department 1959–64, Chief, Economic Intelligence Department 1964–7, Chief Accountant 1967–70, Chief, Management Services Department 1970–3.

illusory in practice because of its technical complexity of operation and its perceived inadequacy of resources. It had not secured full multilateralisation of intra-European payments and it was not to be accompanied by much liberalisation of intra-European trade. At various stages since June 1947 the British authorities, notably the Bank, had had better ideas than the Belgian. They were simpler, more liberal, and not wholly dependent for their working on American Aid. But they failed to carry the day against the Belgian Plan, partly because of the manifest British weakness during and following the 1947 crisis and partly because of British disinclination or inability to put forward their ideas at the right moment or to dress them up in attractive European finery. By the time they were ready, in June 1948, to advocate a special regional European Fund administered by a special regional European organisation, their opportunity had passed.

However at the end of 1948 another opportunity appeared on the horizon. On 18 December, Conolly wrote from Basle to Niemeyer[15] in London, to Frère in Brussels, to Stoppani in Rome, and to Figgures[16] in the Secretariat of the OEEC in Paris. He listed the well-known defects of IEPC and suggested reforms. These included the abolition of drawing rights based on forecast bilateral surpluses and deficits and their replacement by some system, implicitly a quota system, based upon the realised monthly surpluses and deficits of each country with the other members as a whole. They also included settlement of such monthly positions, partly in gold or dollars and partly in 'European credit in one form or another'. A portion of American Aid was to be earmarked for European payments purposes in general and not for any particular country. Here, in just a few sentences, were the essentials of a European Payments Union, structured to the needs of the whole OEEC community of nations rather than to those of the Benelux countries and their sometimes reluctant supporters. Niemeyer passed the letter to Bridge for comment, and early in 1949 Conolly circulated a fuller version calling it 'Proposed New Scheme for Intra-European Payments'. It became known as the Conolly Plan. But its modest author had to wait some time before its ideas were taken up by those in a position to carry them out.

Early in 1949 the French put up a plan for securing the automaticity of 'Second-Category Compensations'. During January it was discussed in the

---

[15] He was a Director of the BIS as well as of the Bank.
[16] *Figgures, Frank Edward, KCB (1910–90).* Educated Rutlish School, New College, Oxford, Merton College, Oxford and Yale Law School. Called to Bar, Lincoln's Inn 1936. Army 1940–6. HM Treasury 1946–8, Director, Trade and Finance, OEEC 1948–51, HM Treasury 1951–60, Under-Secretary 1955–60, Secretary-General to EFTA 1960–5, Third Secretary, HM Treasury 1965–8, Second Permanent Secretary 1968–71, Director-General, NEDO 1971–3, Chairman, Pay Board 1973–4.

Payments Committee of the OEEC, chaired by Stoppani of the Bank of Italy. But it made no progress because various members, including the UK, feared it would entail excessive losses of gold. In the meantime the performance of IEPC itself was uninspiring. In an explanatory note circulated to its Branch Agents early in the new year, the Bank concluded that while it was still too early to pass judgement on the Scheme, the 'main obstacles to extensive success were the continued lack of balance in trade in Europe, the existence of one almost universal creditor (Belgium) which has granted drawing rights for amounts far less than its true export capacity, and the unrealistic value of many of the estimates of debtor/creditor positions agreed in Paris.' The Conolly Plan now had its moment of opportunity. It also had to be considered with some urgency because any scheme requiring consequential changes in ERP legislation would need to be presented to the Americans early in the spring. On 14 January Conolly circulated his outline to Belgian, Dutch, French, Italian, and British representatives for discussion at an informal meeting to be held by Guindey in the French Ministry of Finance on 19 January. The British recipient was the Bank, this time in the person of Roy Bridge.

Bridge[17] was now thirty-seven and an Assistant Chief Cashier. Late in the previous year he had been given direct operational responsibility for IEPC matters, including attendance at the technical meetings in Basle and assisting Ellis-Rees on the Payments Committee in Paris. He was to remain in this position throughout the life of IEPC and throughout the negotiations that led to its replacement by the EPU. Though a highly accomplished monetary technician, readily conversant with the intra-European monetary complexities, he was to prove far more than that. His appreciation of the wider policy issues was good, though at times a little muted in expression by his relatively junior status in the Bank's hierarchy. His grasp of evolving tactical situations was excellent. Dividing his time as necessary between London, Paris, and Basle, he provided his superiors with a constant stream of well-founded technical and tactical advice by telephone, letter, or memorandum. He had a strong and infectiously enthusiastic personality, spoke excellent French, and had developed an almost clinical interest in good food and wine. Though never able to induce in his ultimate superiors a fully positive attitude towards solution

---

[17] *Bridge, Roy Arthur Odell, CMG (1911–78)*. Educated Dulwich. Entered Bank 1929, Assistant to the Chief Cashier 1945–6, Assistant Chief Cashier 1946–51, Acting Adviser 1951–3, UK Alternate Director, Managing Board, EPU 1950–2, Principal, Dealing and Accounts Office 1953–7, Deputy Chief Cashier (Foreign Exchange) 1957–63, Adviser to the Governors 1963–5, Assistant to the Governors 1965–9. Director, Bank Julius Baer International 1970–8. President, Association Cambiste Internationale 1962–7, Honorary President 1967–78.

of the European payments problem, Bridge nevertheless acquired a powerful position in this field; and in the end this position helped him to nudge the Bank into accepting a solution contrary to its own inclination.

But none of these talents could at this early stage of their deployment drive the UK into support of the Conolly Plan; and without UK support it stood little chance. The Plan was designed for the Europe of the OEEC, not for some 'Little Europe' grouping, and the UK was far too important a member to be left out of a payments union. Bridge himself seems to have been sympathetic.[18] He sent a copy of the Conolly Plan to Ellis-Rees on 17 January, along with a moderately encouraging letter, while Bolton gave copies to Wilson Smith and Playfair on 18 January. Bridge's appraisal, in like vein, was sent to the Treasury on 22 January. But a covering letter by Bolton to Playfair, agreed with Cobbold, then threw a large bucket of icy water on the whole idea. It was 'an idea more than a plan', cloaked 'some fantastically difficult complications', and could serve as a basis only for lengthy discussion. It would moreover be dangerous to inject into Washington a new and perhaps more complicated approach to the European payments problem. The result might be 'a delay in the passage of the ECA Act'. If, however, the Treasury felt there was merit in Conolly's Scheme, it might be wise to find out informally from the Economic Cooperation Administration (ECA) whether a new approach to the European payments problem would be welcomed. Finally the Treasury were advised to treat Bridge's note 'with due reserve'.

Meanwhile, in Paris, Ellis-Rees had already indicated UK opposition to the so-called 'idea' on the flimsy grounds that the initial resources to be provided by the US would imply a cut in the amount to be provided in direct financing of deficits with the western hemisphere. He reported back to London that the French supported him, that the Benelux countries sat on the fence, and that only the Italians favoured the new scheme. But Conolly himself, who was present, reported to Bridge in London that Italy, Belgium, and Holland were all in favour. The French, as prospective debtors, were opposed because the scheme transferred some of the burden of adjustment onto debtors. The British were also opposed but nobody could understand why, since they were now creditors in Europe. It had, however, been agreed that the Americans should be approached by the Secretary-General of the OEEC (Marjolin)[19] to discover whether they might

---

[18] It is not improbable that he was himself an informal part-author of the Conolly Plan.

[19] *Marjolin, Robert* (1911–86). Educated Sorbonne, Law School, Paris and Yale. Joined de Gaulle in London 1941, Head of French Supply Mission, US 1944, Secretary-General, OEEC 1948–55, Professor of Economics, University of Nancy 1955–8, Vice-President, Commission of European Economic Community 1958–67, Professor of Economics, University of Paris 1967–9.

favour an allocation of Aid for Europe as a whole, untied to specific movements of goods. Conolly then offered to come to London to discuss his ideas with the Bank or the Treasury. But Bolton breezily dismissed this proposal: 'It would be a waste of time to come here until we know the result of the approach to Washington.' Three weeks later, on 14 February, Bridge minuted Grafftey-Smith that the Conolly Plan was said in Whitehall to be dead. 'This opinion', he wrote with some acerbity, 'probably arises from:

(a) Ellis-Rees' lack of enthusiasm – because he had nothing to do with it;
(b) Cold water from a high level at the Bank;
(c) The fact that Conolly's memo is not a Scheme but merely the idea for a scheme and no one (in Whitehall) has bothered to think it through to a conclusion.'

Conolly himself circulated a further note on 18 February after taking various observations into account. He eloquently concluded:

> The enormous advantages which would be provided by a net system of this nature with a minimum of estimates must outweigh hesitations and minor difficulties, and a real step would be made towards the goal set by ERP. No changes would be necessary in the present method of reporting, and the technical working is so simple that a smooth transition from the present plan would be assured.

But the Plan was indeed dead. Without British support it could make no progress in Paris, and at this stage the Americans were not ready to advocate the effective scrapping of IEPC after so much effort had been put into its creation. So Conolly himself, along with Bridge and others, had to turn his mind to improving IEPC without fundamentally changing it. The debates and negotiations in Paris quickly centred on the method of calculating drawing rights and the possibility of multilateralising their use, issues that were in the end to determine the minor modifications to IEPC eventually agreed for 1949–50. Along this road the Treasury was suddenly to produce a radical plan of its own when Clarke put forward a new version of his ideas for a non-dollar bloc. But this time his plan involved a monetary splitting of the OEEC, scarcely a starter; the initiative in this field, not grasped by London in the Conolly context, was not regained.

This little episode demonstrated the negative attitude taken at this time by those in control of policy in the Bank towards new intra-European initiatives. Dismissal of Conolly's ideas cannot be attributed to fears of excessive integrationism or supra-nationality; his scheme was markedly lacking in such qualities. Nor, so early in 1949, can it be attributed to a desire to batten down the hatches against the prospect of early devaluation. So where does one look for an explanation? One possibility is that the Bank had lost what little appetite it had for advocating new European schemes in Whitehall after the treatment meted out to its substitute plan for IEPC in the summer of 1948. Another possibility is that a 'big' scheme along the lines sketched by Conolly may have been felt to be a threat to the development of transferable sterling and to the network of bilateral monetary and payments agreements between the UK and the other members of the OEEC. Certainly, as the EPU negotiations were to show, there were real problems in linking sterling to a regional payments union, problems that were not encountered in UK membership of a limited compensation agreement; and it was clear then that the Bank preferred not to invite solutions to such problems until necessity prevailed. The records of early 1949 make no reference to this aspect of the matter, but Cobbold, Siepmann, and Bolton were all steeped in both the ethos and the mechanics of the sterling system, with its opportunities and its dangers. During 1948 they had been plagued by the problem of cheap sterling, by the difficulty of holding the No. 2 Accounts in proper check, and by the dual exchange rate practices of France and Italy. It is therefore hardly possible that they would have looked at Conolly's ideas without considering, almost as a reflex response, its implications for the sterling system. Perhaps this is what Bolton meant by the fantastically difficult complications of a plan one of whose principal merits was its apparent simplicity.

With the Conolly Plan cast aside, Bridge next argued several alternatives, the most important being that drawing rights should be calculated on the basis of each member's expected net surplus or deficit with the OEEC as a whole and should be usable multilaterally. Conditional and indirect aid could be applied through these estimated net positions. Bolton accepted this suggestion; the Treasury adopted it as a matter of tactics and tried it out on Ansiaux when the latter visited London at the end of March. Although he did not reject it, the proposal did not subsequently prosper,[20] in the main because of technical difficulties with the link to Aid. Since severing the link altogether, though technically easy, was not favoured, there emerged an alternative proposal. While most of the drawing rights should continue to be allocated and used bilaterally, a small proportion should be allocated to a pool for multilateral use so as to compensate for misforecasting of bilateral positions. The pool would be

---

[20] Interestingly, however, it was put forward in April by the West Germans.

supported by conditional Aid that would initially be unallocated but would be dispensed when a drawing was made on the pool.

These proposals were then greatly enlarged by the Americans, who now at last turned up with the answer to the question put to them earlier in the year in the Conolly context. They suggested that a much larger proportion of drawing rights should be allocated to the pool and a larger proportion of Aid similarly placed. They also suggested that a proportion of drawing rights should be fully convertible rather than transferable only within the OEEC. The thrust of American policy was now changing. They were seeking European devaluations and looking ahead to a less discriminatory European bloc and ultimately to the convertibility of European currencies. So they conceived the idea that a substantial proportion of Aid should be dispensed competitively through the operation of multilateral drawing rights. The British and others intensely disliked this proposal because it implied that their own estimated Western hemisphere deficits would not be fully covered by direct Aid. It was also thought in London that the risk to the UK reserves implied by the change to unallocated Aid would hold up plans for increasing the transferability of sterling. But European opposition to the American proposals was far from united and Bridge advised the Bank from Paris that the UK should urgently review its tactics. The Americans might accept multilateralisation restricted to 25% of drawing rights and in that event the British, as opposers, might find themselves isolated on the payments question as well as pressed from Washington to devalue.

At this point the Treasury momentarily lost its head. Having earlier rejected the constructive proposals of Conolly, it now found itself – not for the first time – in urgent need of an effective counter to the American plans. Under the influence of Clarke[21] it allowed itself to imagine that the UK could suddenly seize the initiative, isolate the Belgians (and Swiss), and

---

[21] At this time he was a convinced and even extreme Atlanticist, wholeheartedly opposed to more than limited UK participation in 'Europe', and an advocate of a union of some kind between the UK and the US, with the Commonwealth tagging along behind. He viewed continental Western Europe as a chronically weak and divided area, lacking in economic viability. These strategic misjudgements were poured out in a memorandum sent to the Permanent Secretary in September 1948. Subsequently, in a note of a discussion between senior officials of the Treasury, Foreign Office, and Board of Trade, he recorded as an agreed view: 'On merits there is no attraction for us in long-term economic co-operation with Europe. At best, it will be a drain on our resources. At worst, it can seriously damage our economy: British policy should be to assist European recovery without long-term politico-economic commitment.' If such was the view of very senior officials, and of the persuasive Clarke, it is not surprising that positive initiatives on intra-European payments were either adopted too late in the day or else were quite unrealistic (see R. Clarke, *Anglo-American Economic Collaboration in War and Peace 1942–49*, ed. A. Cairncross, Oxford University Press, 1982).

take the lead in forming a soft currency bloc from which the former would be excluded along with all settlements in gold or dollars. The Bank was wise enough at this moment not to be tempted by dreams of an enlarged Sterling Area and the Governor protested to Wilson Smith on 11 May that this was hardly the moment to pull everything up by the roots, split the OEEC into two, and collide head-on with the Americans. From Paris, Bridge remarked: 'Although it has attractions for us to take a realistic view and set up a hard and a soft world, I fail to see that it has attractions for OEEC countries to bring about any large measure of support for us.' Nonetheless on 16 May Treasury officials agreed to put the plan forward to the Chancellor with the recommendation that in the first place it be discussed bilaterally with the Americans behind the back of the other OEEC countries. While this was happening, the proceedings in Paris would obligingly mark time.

Stafford Cripps, however, was more clear-sighted than his officials and simply used the British plan as a tactical ploy rather than a serious proposal. He was unwilling to approach the US before first trying out the proposals on the Belgian Prime Minister, who was about to face a General Election. He was also unwilling to allow Ellis-Rees to exercise a veto in Paris if the majority of the Payments Committee favoured extension of IEPC for a further year without substantial change. Spaak came to London at the end of May. On being told of the British plan he said he was not prepared to consider Belgium's exclusion from the OEEC. The Chancellor then suggested to Ansiaux that there should be special bilateral arrangements to settle Anglo–Belgian payments problems outside the purview of IEPC. The latter reportedly replied that this was just another proposal for allowing the UK to procure the greater part of its imports from Belgium for nothing.[22] Weeks of bargaining ensued until a workable compromise was agreed early in July: IEPC was to continue for a further year, but 25% of drawing rights were indeed to be transferable (but not convertible) and supported by unallocated Aid. Alongside this, however, Belgium agreed firstly to a limit on the amount of drawing rights that could be transferred to Belgium and secondly to grant special credits to France, Holland, and the UK totalling $87½ million. In the course of these

---

[22] Bilateral trade negotiations with Belgium in 1948 had centred round supplies of Belgian steel and the Belgian insistence that the British took a quantity of 'inessential' goods along with the steel. Among such goods were potted winter-flowering azaleas, which the Belgians were peculiarly good at growing and which relieved the greyness of the English winter. In Whitehall, busy administering 'austerity', they were regarded as symbolic of frivolous luxury. But the British were at the same time trying to persuade Argentina to take Scotch whisky. As Miranda expostulated to them in Buenos Aires: 'You must get it out of your heads that you can make me buy what I don't want to buy. I don't want whisky. I want newsprint...'

negotiations the British secured adoption of a resolution in the OEEC in favour of a substantial liberalisation of intra-European trade, to be introduced over the following year. That the UK was able to do this despite her extreme sensitivity to gold or dollar payments in Europe was due to the emergence of an overall surplus in total Sterling Area trade with Europe.

Viewed on one level, the Chancellor had conducted a tough but successful negotiation, conceding on transferability and unallocated Aid while securing advantageous treatment of the Belgian problem. Viewed on another level, the failure of the British authorities to adopt a more positive attitude earlier in the year had repeated in 1949 the error of 1948 and made it necessary for them to conduct a difficult campaign at a late stage in order to safeguard their legitimate interests as best they could. As Bridge reported in a long letter written just before leaving Paris early in August: 'Our negotiating position has been dogged by suspicion on the part of all the other participating countries of the UK's activities. Our tactical position has throughout been bad in that we have all the time been fighting a rearguard action and then trying to cover up our retreat against pursuing opposition. I think you will realise that as a consequence we have found very little support for our efforts to write suitable safeguards to prevent transferability running riot.' He had come to admire the French, describing them as 'adept at sitting back and then at the tactical moment picking their own advantage out of other people's differences of opinion'. However, if the British were at times disliked, so at times were the Belgians. Three weeks later, Preston[23] (in Bridge's absence) was able to report from Paris that the Belgians had made themselves so objectionable that everyone else was once more friendly to the British.

Though IEPC, still essentially a development of the original Ansiaux Plan, was to continue well into 1950, the negotiations in the summer of 1949 served as a further demonstration of its underlying inadequacy and complexity. Other factors, too, were now combining to force another look at the whole problem of intra-European payments. With the devaluations of September 1949 and the appearance on the horizon of an end to the ERP in 1952, the Americans now wanted both a full liberalisation of intra-European trade and the introduction of much more effective payments arrangements that could pave the way to eventual convertibility. If moreover those things could not be achieved by the full membership of the OEEC, they perhaps could be obtained within a smaller grouping which

---

[23] *Preston, Leslie Thomas George (b.1908).* Educated William Ellis School, Highgate. British Overseas Bank 1926–39. Entered Bank 1939. Assistant Principal, Dealing and Accounts Office 1948–53, Deputy Principal 1953–7, Principal 1957–68. Director, Standard Chartered Banking Group 1970–9.

might anyway be able to make faster progress in other ways towards the ideal of unification. The creation of the Federal Republic of Germany in the summer of 1949, with Adenauer as Chancellor, and the greater stability in Italy under the Premiership of de Gasperi, added force to these thoughts. So also did the prospect of a *rapprochement* between France and West Germany under democratic Governments of the Centre or Centre-Right.

For their part, the British had by now firmly resolved to limit their own commitment to a European union. This excluded participation in a 'little Europe' with supranational institutions, but by no means excluded participation in a bigger Europe with collaborative arrangements for trade and payments. Meanwhile discussions in Washington prior to the devaluation of sterling had encouraged the British to believe that they could again look to the United States for special help with the problem of the sterling balances. Thus in the autumn and winter of 1949 the authorities in London were able to devise a more coherent and defensible policy on intra-European payments that enabled them to support, on certain specified conditions, the creation of an EPU. They were then able to negotiate from a position of some strength. As will be seen, the credit for this transformation must go to the Treasury. The Bank did not like the idea of a payments union in Europe, misguidedly rushed in with a purely sterling solution to the whole problem, fought with the Treasury over it, and lost. Though still very cool towards the idea, it then sensibly converted its objections to the EPU into conditions that had to be secured if membership were to be acceptable to the UK. This was a largely technical but very important matter of reconciling the sterling system – bilateral monetary agreements and all – with membership of a payments union. The Treasury agreed with the Bank about this and thereafter the two institutions worked in close harmony until the conclusion of the negotiations in the summer of 1950. Regrettably however, for the EPU proved very successful, the Bank remained unhappy about the outcome.

The European Payments Union

Immediately after devaluation, Bridge prepared a paper on 'Financial Relations with Europe', which he circulated on 29 September 1949. He noted the Government's policy of limited commitment towards European economic union and set this against American and continental attachment to it. He also noted the emergence of the 'Alphand Plan', under French sponsorship, for a Franco–Italian–Benelux Union (known later as 'Finebel') whose national currencies would trade at fixed rates against each other but quite likely float against the dollar. He did not then go on to discuss a successor to IEPC but instead developed an argument for relaxing UK exchange controls. The purpose was to increase the transferability of sterling in Europe in parallel with the liberalisation of UK imports from Europe. He considered that such a relaxation would be well received and would help to improve the low standing of the UK in the OEEC, a standing that had not been improved by the unexpected size of the sterling devaluation.

In the Treasury, Clarke's feet had returned to the ground and he had been applying his mind to the limited future of the ERP and the further progress that would have to be made towards the restoration of convertibility. He saw a need to reform the system of intra-European payments and introduce more appropriate incentives, along the lines advocated by Conolly nine months earlier. IEPC should be scrapped. Drawing rights should be abolished and be replaced by a simple system under which net surpluses or deficits would be settled half in credit and half in gold or dollars. Discussions then took place in the Treasury, at which the Bank favoured improving rather than scrapping IEPC and at the same time improving the transferability of sterling. A submission was then made to the Chancellor, who replied that he would like to see several schemes worked out before laying down any principles. The Treasury then asked the Bank to prepare a paper setting out alternative schemes. Bridge reported this request to Bolton, stating that there would have to be radical changes in the payments scheme in 1950, arguing that blueprints would as yet be premature, but asking whether the Bank should nevertheless comply with the Treasury's request. Bolton, in a remarkable diktat, replied that he had a rooted objection to hypothetical exercises 'particularly in the dangerous field of European payments schemes'. It was too soon after devaluation to get enmeshed in such debates and anyway the future of ECA was now itself very uncertain. He concluded: 'The Bank must therefore refuse to waste time and labour on abortive researches dependent upon an unknown political future. We must not say this in so many words to the Treasury but draw upon the usual fund of excuses for delay.' With these instructions, Bridge dragged his feet in the Treasury; but Playfair persisted with the remit from the Chancellor and argued that discussions in Paris on the form of next year's payments scheme could not be long delayed. At a later meeting, on 25 October, the Bank was advised that in addition to alternative payments schemes Ministers were now prepared to ask officials to consider the extension of sterling transferability within the OEEC area.

Bolton's eccentric reaction may partly be attributed to the ferment of ideas on European unity then bubbling away on the Continent. For example, Bridge reported on 26 October that Van Zeeland, the Belgian Foreign Minister, was advocating a supra-national monetary institution for Western Europe and that Marjolin, Secretary-General of the OEEC, was not very far behind. On 29 October Ellis-Rees excitedly told London that he had been 'aware of counsels of despair which lead to wild schemes of integration, supra-national organisations and the like'. On 1 November Bridge reported from Paris that the general form of next year's payments scheme would have to be decided over the next two months. He added: 'If the initiative is not taken by the UK, we may find ourselves fighting another unplanned retreat as we did in the summer of this year.'

In this heady atmosphere it was easy enough to fear that a new payments scheme, of the sort already sketched out successively by Conolly and by Clarke, would carry with it a new European monetary institution equipped with powers well outside the limits of British policy. By contrast, a different state of affairs, brought about by relaxations in UK exchange control so as to allow transferability of sterling throughout the OEEC for all purposes, might not only avoid new monetary institutions in Europe but could mark an accession of European monetary power to London, to the Treasury, and to the Bank. Ellis-Rees favoured some such development in his letter of 29 October, while the American authorities were known to favour an extension of sterling transferability as a useful European step on the long road back to convertibility. What was more, during the talks held in Washington prior to devaluation the Americans had encouraged the British to believe that there would be a continuing organisation of Anglo-American–Canadian co-operation and that they might be prepared to help solve the continuing problem of the sterling balances, provided the British for their part pressed ahead with worthwhile relaxations in exchange control. These possibilities had since become subjects of study in London. At the same time, it had been confidently if erroneously expected that devaluation would dispose of the problem of cheap sterling. Accordingly, Bolton thought he saw a glorious opportunity. In a memorandum sent to Wilson Smith on November he wrote that both Washington and Paris were agreed that IEPC was a failure. It neither met the objectives of the ECA nor did it introduce any real flexibility into the European payments system; and it was so complicated that it was doubtful whether it could be said to be technically workable. So after rhetorical allusion to 'the erection of glittering but empty facades of European unity designed to attract dollars from Congress', Bolton suggested embarking on a series of talks, beginning with the Americans, aimed at extending the Sterling Area into Europe. He had however to conclude that Belgium, Switzerland, France, and Italy could not at present be invited, 'the first two because they are on the gold standard and the others because they operate free markets in gold and dollars'.

George Bolton was now forty-seven and had been an Executive Director since March 1948. By the autumn of 1949 he had acquired a personal ascendancy in the Bank on most questions of external financial policy. His senior colleague on the overseas side, Siepmann, seems to have never fully recovered from the ordeal of 1947. Despite his long experience of European affairs in the pre-war period, he now took little or no interest in the post-war problems of intra-European payments and their related politico-economic issues. Since the winter of 1947–8 he seems to have had little to say and thus his experience and maturity were not readily available to counterbalance Bolton's often ebullient impetuosity. At the higher level, Cobbold's own control of Bolton may have weakened for a time after he became Governor in March 1949 and when his close concern with overseas matters became diluted by his other duties.

The effect of Bolton's ascendancy was influenced by his methods of work. Unlike, for example, Siepmann in 1946 and 1947, he had little taste for operating through working parties and committees. Instead, with his gifted turn of phrase, he liked discharging provocative written salvoes in various directions, modifying his views only in the light of the rather random responses that he got. He had very few, if any, close associates to whom he listened carefully on matters of policy. Given his authority in such matters, as a forceful Executive Director supported by personal experience in the field of foreign exchange, Bolton's method of working meant that his raw ideas were seldom subject to rigorous or systematic criticism in Threadneedle Street. This could be dangerous, because although he was a fount of often imaginative ideas on all questions within – or indeed without – his parish, Bolton's judgement was at times erratic and over-influenced by his personal opinions.[24] His note of 1 November 1949, on exchange policy and Western Europe, exemplified this danger.

Although the Treasury appears to have seen the force of what Bolton was saying, it took the obvious view that the only likely but by no means certain candidates for admission to the Sterling Area were the Scandinavians. This might be helpful as part of a putative 'Uniscan' grouping to counter the possibility of 'Finebel', but it certainly did not dispose of the wider intra-European payments problem; a UK plan was still required and

---

[24] His obituary in the Bank's house magazine, *Old Lady*, for March 1983 aptly recorded: 'No modest prose came from Bolton's pen: his word pictures were always painted in very bright colours for he was a man who believed.' It may be added that he stood well over six feet tall, had reddish hair, bright blue eyes, a round and cheerful countenance, a deep seductive voice, and all the agility of an exchange dealer. It must have taken skill, courage, and a stern heart to stand up to him.

George Bolton, Executive Director 1948–1957

the Bank had so far declined to provide one. The Treasury itself then toyed with the idea of a European Monetary Fund (EMF) but was warned by Bridge that access to the resources of such a body might be subject to considerable conditionality.[25] They also favoured some widening of transferability by relaxation of control rather than by new admissions to the Sterling Area, a course that the Bank (on technical grounds) was not disposed to favour. By mid-November Bridge was warning that plans for a successor to IEPC were going to crystallise in Whitehall 'forthwith', whether the Bank liked it or not. Should it therefore attempt to influence this process positively or should it go on maintaining no more than a watching brief? If the answer was 'yes', he himself favoured an EMF with maximum automaticity, and an ascending mixture of gold and EMF drawings to meet net deficits through the Basle machinery. But the answer he got was only a very qualified 'yes'. The Governor told Wilson Smith that he hoped the Treasury would stand firm against a new EMF organisation. After renewed debate Bridge recorded on 18 November that in the Bank's view the European payments problems should be met by an increase in bilateral credit margins and optional deferment for one year of the gold payments arising if the new margins were exceeded. During the deferment, deficit countries would draw on a pool of currencies subscribed on quotas based on their exports to Europe. If the pool proved impracticable, the Bank would favour a 'twilight period' in which, on expiry of credit margins, settlement would be half in further credit and half in gold. There would be no new European monetary organisation.

At meetings in Whitehall, Bridge and Hamilton argued this half-formed Bank plan against the Treasury, the Foreign Office, and the Economic Section, who clearly favoured either a regional Clearing Union or an EMF, either of which now seemed acceptable to the ECA. The Bank was granted another opportunity to put forward an alternative plan in writing, but this was foreshadowed by handing over Bridge's note of 18 November. In the meantime a neutral paper was to be put forward to Treasury Ministers. However, on the 27 November the Chancellor decided, on the basis of papers put forward by the Economic Section, to instruct Ellis-Rees in Paris to table a proposal for a Clearing Union. Bridges, who had been made aware of the difference of view, then called a meeting at which Bolton represented the Bank, the Governor being away in New York. He won a

[25] The Bank's attitude to the influence of creditors in an EMF may have been affected by a further instalment of the long-running serial of post-war Anglo–Belgian monetary relations. There was an unpleasant dispute about the exact amount of Belgian sterling to which an exchange guarantee, under the Anglo–Belgian Monetary Agreement, should apply as of the date of sterling devaluation in September.

stay of execution of the Chancellor's decision, provided the Bank's written views were forthcoming within twenty-four hours. A short paper was accordingly sent to Wilson Smith on the following day. Developing earlier themes, it first argued against any new system that both increased the amount of gold settlement and involved the UK in granting further credit. It then argued against setting up a quasi-permanent organisation when it was impossible to judge what circumstances would rule when ERP came to an end in 1952, and against setting up in Europe an institution that would be either a rival to the IMF or else over-subordinate to it. The paper went on to advocate maintenance of the existing network of bilateral monetary agreements, enlargement of the Sterling Area to include the OEEC members, creation of a new 'European Account' area for all those (except Belgium and Switzerland) who declined the invitation to join the Sterling Area, increases in bilateral credit limits, and lastly the suggestion for deferred gold payment and for an associated pool of currencies. Unallocated Aid would be used to ease payments difficulties of chronic debtors and to reimburse countries suffering additional gold losses through making their own currencies transferable.

The Bank's paper was considered at a further meeting held in the Treasury at which Bolton at last encountered effective criticism from officials who were anyway exasperated with the Bank's procrastination. His paper was given short shrift. As Grafftey-Smith ruefully recorded: 'It would be incorrect to say that there was any discussion of the Bank paper.' He went on to record that the reference to enlargement of the Sterling Area was ignored and that the exclusion of Belgium and Switzerland from the proposed European Account Area was regarded as a fatal flaw. Since arguments about the gold standard and about the undesirability of creating a new European organisation were simply set aside as points already taken in Whitehall, discussion turned naturally to the regional Clearing Union suggested by the Economic Section. After some vigorous opposition by Bolton the meeting ended by favouring a scheme known as the 'OEEC Currency Pool', which was to be operated by the BIS as agent, to be denominated in dollars, to use a system of fractional gold payments, and to include the right to impose remedial trade measures 'when the amber light showed'. The following day Bolton met Bridges and Wilson Smith to review the disagreement. It was explained that European currency schemes had to be put forward, under the pressure of political and other necessities. Major relaxations of exchange control, by contrast, would require Ministers to take policy decisions just when a General Election was pending. Treasury officials felt it was a waste of time trying to get such decisions taken ahead of that event. The quarrel between the

Bank and the Treasury was to be patched up by frank informal talks between the officials concerned.

On a reduced scale, this episode recalls the struggle between the Bank and Keynes during 1941–4. The Bank is once again beset by fears lest a new international institution should interfere in the management of sterling. It once again dislikes commitments to conduct international payments in some preordained manner, according to 'formulae'. Above all it once again earnestly wishes to preserve and develop, step by step, both the Sterling Area and the network of bilateral monetary and payments agreements. The manifest weakening of sterling during the three post-war years and the suspicion with which it was regarded, though well recognised by Siepmann early in 1948, is seemingly ignored. Devaluation, by endeavouring to retreat to a far more defensible post-war position, seems to have encouraged a sudden optimism; and the Bank's judgement of the politically practicable underwent a sudden relapse. Bolton, with the Governor's support, failed to interpret correctly the signals from Paris and also failed to appreciate the special political need for an improved and attractively packaged OEEC-wide payments scheme, as a European Payments Union would so clearly be. He therefore gave instructions to Bridge and others that a reply to the Treasury's request for ideas about a successor to IEPC should be deliberately delayed so as to give time for the Bank to put forward a patchwork plan that could in practice have no attraction for Whitehall. It was a very ill-advised move and served to muffle the British voice in Paris at a time when the initiative might have been regained and also to allow the lead in Whitehall on intra-European payments to pass for the moment to the Economic Section, where it did not properly belong. Subsequently it emerged that the Bank's vociferous objections to a European Payments Union were at root little more than a statement of the conditions that would need to be agreed before the UK could join. In short, they could readily be converted into a negotiating position, just as had proved to be the case with many of the Bank's objections to early versions of the IMF. Once this became clear, the Treasury and the Bank came together and the conduct of British policy began to improve out of all recognition. This happy turn of events was assisted firstly by the Belgians, who began by greatly overplaying their hand, and secondly by the Americans, who developed a serious division of view about the merits of an effective supervisory organisation in the EPU.

Following the decisions taken in the Treasury on 1 December 1949, the final drafting of the UK paper on the 'Currency Pool' was soon completed and Ellis-Rees was authorised to use it as a basis for discussion with the ECA in Paris. It accommodated the Bank on two points: firstly, that the

Pool should supplement rather than supersede the network of monetary agreements; secondly, that there should be no new monetary institution in Europe. But it came too late in the day. In Paris on 9 December the Americans themselves tabled a succinct draft of a straightforward payments union with automatic monthly settlements, partly in gold and partly in credit, full central bank transferability of member currencies, and complete liberalisation of intra-European trade. Some link to Aid would remain. Disregarding British ideas, the American draft stated firstly that bilateral monetary agreements would be 'obviated' and secondly that the union should be equipped with a powerful supervisory board. The latter would keep the development of each member's position under continuous review and consultation. This would intensify if a member came near to exhausting its quota (whether debit or credit) and would become prescriptive if a quota were exhausted and temporary additional credit had to be provided. Ellis-Rees responded by tabling the UK paper on 14 December. At the same time there was a resumption of ordinary working relations between the Bank and the Treasury at technical level. On 16 December Bridge wrote: 'Whether we ultimately have a clearing union or not, it seems certain the subject will be discussed at length and I believe we ought to forearm ourselves by working out some of the details.' On 19 December Bolton sent a heavy-footed letter to Wilson Smith, drawing his attention at rather obvious length to the objectionable features of the American proposals. Wilson Smith replied three days later that these points were already well taken in the Treasury.

The scene then shifted to Paris where a group of experts chaired by Ansiaux were engaged in preparing a plan of their own. It was circulated on 30 December and subsequently tabled for a Council meeting on 10 January 1950. It was received in the Bank on the 3rd but its full horror was not confirmed until 9 January, when Bolton and Niemeyer discussed it in Basle with Ansiaux and Frère. The Belgians explained that all existing bilateral agreements and credit margins would have to be cancelled, as the use of these in addition to the new credits in the new European payments scheme could be inflationary. By the same token all pre-existing resources in member currencies, notably sterling balances, would have to be frozen or funded, with annual releases carefully controlled; and it was even assumed that this applied in principle to the sterling balances of the Sterling Area as well as to those of countries in Western Europe. All currencies would then be made fully transferable within the OEEC and net positions would be settled automatically and multilaterally through the compensation machinery in Basle. Each member would have a quota, based on European trade. Initially a deficit position would be settled by drawing short-term credit from the new institution, repayable within twelve months. If the deficit proved more persistent, medium- or long-term credit would be drawn, up to quota limits and alongside a proportionate payment in gold or dollars; but the managers of the union would be able to impose conditions, requiring corrective action by the borrower. Incredibly, Ansiaux claimed that this construction had the full support of the British delegation in Paris, who had expressed only minor reservations of detail. Bolton told him abruptly that a very deep misunderstanding must have developed, and he promptly telephoned Grafftey-Smith in London, who alerted both the Governor and the Treasury.

On the following day Bridge attended a meeting of the Trade and Payments Committee in Whitehall. The Bank had clearly scored heavily as the bearer of accurate intelligence about Belgian intentions. Bridge recorded that the Treasury were severely shaken by the news from Basle. Appropriate instructions were at once sent to Paris, emphasising that any scheme on the lines visualised by Ansiaux would be quite unacceptable to HMG. A few days later the Governor himself intervened with a long letter to the Permanent Secretary. 'As you know', he wrote, 'the Bank have never been happy about the Clearing Union idea and would have preferred a less ambitious approach tending to build on what exists rather than to set up a new organism.' Subject to this qualification, he gathered that the Treasury and the Bank were generally agreed about the points in the latest drafts that must be protected. He then went on to set down the fundamental points so that there should be complete understanding about them before the clouds of technical complexity descended once more. These fundamental points were maintenance of existing bilateral monetary agreements, avoidance of a new European institution with powers over the domestic economic policies of OEEC members, and no prejudicial interference with the sterling balances. On the latter subject there would, however, be no objection to some statement of OEEC concern about the balances, for this might add urgency to Anglo-American discussions about them. In the Permanent Secretary's absence Brittain replied: 'We are, I think, entirely at one on these questions.' This new unity of purpose was further encouraged by reports from Washington of divisions within the American camp. The US Treasury was said to be unhappy about the proposals put forward by the ECA.

Battle lines were now drawn for a prolonged struggle whose first phase had to be settled within weeks. At the Treasury's request Bridge resumed his position in the Paris delegation, while officials involved at the Bank now had the Governor's 'fundamental points' as their clear guidance. At a meeting on 16 January, at which Brittain, Playfair, and others were treated to some flesh-creeping talk from Bolton about there being 'all the elements of a conspiracy to restore the essentials of the gold standard', the Treasury were disinclined to accept reassuring advice from Ellis-Rees about the state of affairs in Paris. On tactics it was confirmed that the delegation should state and re-state the British case and refuse to subscribe to any document that was not consistent with it.

Bridge then departed for Paris and attended a long meeting of the financial experts on 18 January, which, as he told Ellis-Rees, he found vastly disturbing. The Belgians, with support from the ECA, were bent on replacing the existing system of monetary agreements and on this fundamental point the British were on their own. He felt an early showdown was needed and reported back to the Bank in that sense, also commenting that Ellis-Rees' presentation of the British case 'lost the round on points through lack of punch'. This criticism was becoming widespread. Hammarskjöld, talking to Lithiby on 19 January, gave the impression that all the Scandinavian delegations in Paris longed for a firm line from the UK. Lithiby commented to Bolton: 'Knowing how friendly he is with ER, this means more perhaps than the broad hint you had in Basle from people whom we know dislike ER intensely'. Long accustomed to retreating, Ellis-Rees can perhaps be forgiven for being somewhat slow in appreciating that London at last meant business.

There followed a flurry of activity. The Governor wrote to Wilfred Baumgartner,[26] now Governor of the Bank of France, setting out the British point of view and adding that he now feared the IMF would wish to interfere with a new European monetary organisation and that this would be a road to confusion and strife. He also solicited the support of his old partner, Eady, now in charge of Home Finance. On the same day Bolton wrote a stiffening letter to Brittain in which he developed the point about the likely clash between the IMF and the powerful regional authority advocated by the Belgian and ECA factions in Paris. This clash was not simply a product of the Bank's imagination. The Managing Director of the IMF had already circulated a paper to his Executive Board stating *inter alia*: 'If it is found necessary or desirable to set up a regional organisation, the Fund should provide such an organisation.' Furthermore, the Bank was

---

[26] *Baumgartner, Wilfred Siegfried* (1902–78). Educated School of Political Sciences and University of Paris. Inspector of Finances 1925, Mission for the General Movement of Funds 1927, Chief of Cabinet, Ministry of Finances 1930, Deputy-Director, General Movement of Funds 1930–4, Joint Director 1934–5, Director 1935–7, President-Director General of Crédit National 1937, President, National Markets Office 1937–41. Member, General Council, Banque de France 1937–49, Governor 1949–60, Inspector-General of Finances. Director, BIS 1949–60, Governor for France, IMF 1949–60, Minister of Finance 1960–2, President-Director General, Rhône-Poulenc SA 1963–9.

shortly to receive a visit from the US Director of the Fund, Andy Overby. On 24 January he saw the Governor, who reported the conversation to the Chancellor. With a fine disregard for diplomatic solidarity Overby had denigrated the ECA, saying their ideas for an EPU were not supported by the US Treasury or the State Department, who were both highly suspicious of the way the OEEC was developing and saw the EPU both as a threat to their 'one-world' goal and as a threat to the authority of the Fund. In March the Fund despatched a Mission to Paris, but later lost interest in the subject as it became clear that there was after all not going to be a strong central authority in the EPU.

The discussions in Paris now moved to a state of deadlock. Ellis-Rees and Bridge entrenched the UK position and the final report of the financial experts, though still containing the bones of Ansiaux's original draft, reflected considerable confusion and disagreement. A meeting of OEEC Finance Ministers took place at the end of the month. In order to place the matter beyond all doubt, the Chancellor put in a paper of his own alongside the experts' report, with the support of his own officials and of the Governor. Differences of view about the powers of the new organisation or the credit structure it contained were not necessarily decisive, nor were they incapable of resolution through further negotiation. But the problem of integrating the existing sterling system within a European Payments Union remained wholly untackled. Despite threats from the ECA that things might go ahead without the British, Cripps made it quite clear that unless this problem could be solved in a manner fully compatible with the world role of sterling the UK would be unable to join. Writing on 3 February on his return to the Bank, Bridge advised that it was now up to the UK (and most likely the Bank) to take the initiative on this point if it wished progress to be made. Others would not do the job for them. The implied alternative was to risk the Union going ahead without sterling; and shortly afterwards he was to stress that another OEEC grouping would not find this difficult to achieve.

Over the next few weeks papers by the Bank and by the Economic Section on the integration of the sterling system within the EPU were discussed in the Treasury. Both accepted that sterling would have to be made fully transferable for settlement between member central banks, including Belgium and Switzerland, but that transfers to the rest of the non-dollar world would remain at the administrative discretion of the UK. Both agreed that some part of the sizeable sterling balances of Italy and Sweden would need to be tied up before the EPU commenced operation. Both then agreed that sterling should only be brought into the regular EPU settlements when existing bilateral limits were exceeded and gold would otherwise be payable. Both also agreed that a member country in serious difficulty should be entitled to 'deliberalise' its imports from other members and, at the same time, discriminate against creditor countries. But while the Economic Section felt that the UK should have a credit and debit quota like the other members, the rest of the Treasury, together with the Bank, felt it should have a credit quota only. The UK should provide credit but not obtain it. They were prepared to accept, as a consequence, a greater risk of gold loss in order to avoid the unwelcome attentions of the regional organisation, which they argued would be inappropriate to the world role of sterling. The Chancellor accepted the version favoured by Overseas Finance and the Bank. On 7 March, following their return to office at the General Election, the paper was accepted by Ministers. It was then sent to the ECA in Paris and to Ansiaux, as chairman of the experts, a few days later. Things now began to move in the UK's favour. Although the American response was very cagey, the Basle group of central bankers came round strongly against a powerful new supervisory board within the EPU. Frère, Governor of the National Bank of Belgium and President of the BIS, differed in this respect from Ansiaux, who had returned from a visit to Washington full of ECA support for a strong board. Cobbold wrote to the Chancellor on 14 March telling him of the developments in Basle. Cripps replied with due caution: 'We shall have to see what effect these views have upon the European Governments.'

The consensus in Basle owed something to a sub-plot that had been progressing throughout the winter. The Americans began it by voicing disquiet lest the strong supervisory board that they favoured should turn out to be located in Basle rather than Paris. Since this made Niemeyer and others suspect a renewal of the anti-BIS sentiment that had prevailed in Washington during and immediately after the war, they let it be known as forcefully as they could that the BIS itself would never wish to accept more than a technical banking responsibility for the EPU, whose board should be located elsewhere. More important, the American attitude would have alerted the continental central bankers, several of whom enjoyed much greater independence than the Bank of England, to the possibility of their own monetary policies becoming subject to interference from a political authority in Paris; hence, in all probability, their virtually unanimous opposition to such a board having strong powers. Minutes of the informal meeting at which this was agreed were circulated by Roger Auboin, General Manager of the BIS. A manuscript note by the Governor on the covering letter sheds interesting light on the status and nature of the BIS at this time. 'I have spoken to M. Frère', he wrote, 'and said that I assume this paper is domestic only and will not see the light of day. He assured me that this was so. I said I was entirely in favour of Governors using their influence with their Governments on these lines (which I have been doing for three months) but I thought it would be unwise for the BIS to take a position institutionally.' In other words, the BIS was in this instance a central bankers' club and should not, as such, take positions on behalf of its members. However this did not prevent Auboin and Conolly, as BIS officials, from promptly drafting a paper on an EPU that cut out the distinction between long- and short-term credits and disposed of any permanent supervisory body. Nor did it prevent them lobbying the French for support with these ideas.

The opposition of the central bankers, following the opposition of the British authorities and the likely clash with the IMF and the US Treasury, effectively killed off the idea of a strong EPU board, notwithstanding its powerful advocacy by the ECA. The Governor reported from Basle on 3 April on the general feeling, in which Frère fully participated, that the risk of a new institution with powers was 'pretty well dead and should be kept firmly dead'. At the same time the British proposals for reconciling sterling with a payments union gained the initiative by demonstrating that on certain conditions the UK would now say 'yes'. It was however suspected in Paris and Basle that the British might be seeking an unfair advantage that would enable them so to arrange matters through manipulation of bilateral agreements that they maximised their gold 'take' from the EPU when in surplus and minimised their gold loss when in deficit. The fact that two important agreements, the Anglo-Italian and Anglo-Swedish, imposed no gold point on official accumulations of sterling aroused particular suspicion. The question of sterling reconciliation therefore continued to be a subject of close negotiation. It was also the subject of suspicious consideration by the Americans. Early in April the UK Ambassador in Washington, Oliver Franks, was approached by Paul Hoffmann and Richard Bissell of the ECA. He was told that the British insistence on special rules for sterling was opposed both by the Americans and by the Europeans in Paris and that there was no room for compromise. The Ambassador subsequently advised Hoffmann that the position in Paris was not as the Americans had described and that 'if we could imagine the Americans withdrawn from the scene we should probably find acceptance growing before very long of something very like the ideas we had put forward'.

The progress of British ideas was next helped along by Frank Figgures, at that time seconded by the UK Treasury to the OEEC Secretariat where he was Director of Trade and Finance. Figgures called personally on the Governor[27] in Basle during the second week of April and suggested that the

---

[27] Among his many other talents, Frank Figgures was an accomplished wooer of the Old Lady. Unusually for Treasury officials, he would sometimes pay her an informal call when

proposed method of reconciling sterling with the EPU could as effectively and much more usefully be achieved by the BIS itself, as agent, at each monthly settlement rather than by the UK first operating the bilateral agreements. It was simply a question of furnishing the agent with the correct rules. This procedure would have the great political advantage that the UK could become a full member of a payments union that was equipped with rules governing the parallel operation of bilateral agreements between members in general, rather than become a special member with special rules applying to sterling in particular. Figgures followed this up in a letter to Lithiby and his ideas were subsequently supported by Bridge, who also argued that to allay continental suspicion gold points would have to be introduced into those bilateral agreements presently lacking them.

Most of this was now accepted in the Bank, whose views were made known in the Treasury. The Bank was next allowed to pursue some quite adventurous tactics in Paris, where the Americans were proving most reluctant to table another paper of their own and where Ansiaux seemed ready to accept a reconciliation with sterling broadly along lines worked out between Figgures and Bridge. The latter suggested that everything should be embodied in a Secretariat paper which, he personally hinted, the UK might then be able to accept. The Secretariat paper was drafted and became available on 21 April. However, it collided head-on with a separate and personal paper by Ansiaux, who was now pursuing some rather more adventurous tactics of his own. He had been constructing a new plan with which he was lobbying the 'Finebel' group, a plan that contained new proposals about the reconciliation of sterling and the co-existence of the bilateral network with the EPU. They were a good deal tidier than those put forward by the Secretariat yet still stood a chance of being acceptable to London. But at that point the acceptability of the new plan ended. For the other main purpose of its author was to ensure adequate discipline among EPU members now that there was no European support for a powerful supervisory board. Bridge described this part of the plan as a creditor's dream. All provision for medium- and long-term credit had been removed. Short-term credits, based on quotas related to trade and designed to meet only seasonal or accidental fluctuations, would bear interest at the creditor's Bank Rate and would be repayable, normally in

there was something afoot that he was concerned to influence and bring to an appropriate conclusion. He appreciated that without damage to the dignity of the Treasury he could often get a better appreciation of the Bank's thinking and a better reception for his own arguments by paying a timely call rather than by telephoning or waiting for the Bank to appear, fully briefed, in Whitehall. The Bank liked these calls, enjoyed Frank's vigorous and stimulating conversation, and felt suitably flattered.

gold or dollars, after twelve months' use. As a substitute for medium-term credit, there would be a modest initial ration of ECA dollars for each member and some continuing provision of the 'conditional aid' associated with IEPC. But more importantly, repayment of short-term credits could also be effected in part by the drawing of the creditor's currency from the IMF. These drawings would be repayable over two years. Finally, the facilities of the EPU would only be available to a member country so long as it respected the undertakings on trade liberalisation drawn up by the Union and renounced all discrimination in intra-European trade.

Continuing suspicion of British intentions, together with a sudden rather unconvincing and probably tactical resurgence of gold-mindedness on the part of the French, assured Ansiaux of apparently solid support for his plan from the Finebel group; and while ECA officials strongly disliked the illiberality of his credit provisions, they preferred his proposals about sterling to those of either the British or the Secretariat. As a result the redoubtable Belgian had regained the tactical initiative once more.[28] The victory was, however, a little hollow. The remaining disagreements about sterling, or even about emergency discrimination, were no longer of overwhelming importance. Despite suspicions to the contrary, the British intentions were at heart honourable and the solutions to outstanding questions were often in reality little more than matters of technical drafting. But the vital question of the balance between hard and soft means of payment in the monthly settlements of EPU remained substantially unagreed. Having lost their battle over the powers of a supervisory board, the Belgians and their supporters were now left to fight another, this time over the amount and term of automatic credit. It was a battle that they could not expect to win hands down against British, Scandinavian, and even American opposition, and during which it mattered little whose 'plan' was actually on the table. Bridge himself favoured the option proposal, explained below, which sought to achieve virtual interchange-ability between sterling and EPU credit; and in a powerful paper sent to the Governor early in May he described the EPU as a step towards the wider objective of an eventual return to convertibility. The EPU would itself increase the transferability of sterling in official hands, and now that the UK reserves were rising it might be possible to relax exchange control so as to increase the transferability of sterling in private hands. This, he felt was the way forward. One could not sit in bilateral trenches for ever. Moreover, the UK was publicly committed to complete transferability in the OEEC. The Ansiaux scheme, he concluded, 'makes sterling fully

[28] As a disconsolate Bridge wrote from Paris on 30 April: 'The Ansiaux paper turned out to be a Finebel plot.'

transferable within Europe, enables us to extend the day-to-day use of sterling, does not freeze any balances, and over a period gets rid of unwieldy European accumulations of sterling...In short, it is a move towards normal international financial relations and a logical step forwards from the dole system towards convertibility.' Whether enthusiastic about the EPU or not, and the Governor was decidedly unenthusiastic, the Bank agreed with Bridge about the merits of the option proposal; so did the Treasury.

Early in May, British Ministers decided their final negotiating position after a further round of consultation with their officials and with the Bank. Their attitude, and the attitude of the Governor, can best be described as one of constructive reluctance. The Ministerial view was typified by that of Gaitskell, now effectively the Chancellor's deputy. He circulated a memorandum full of an incipient nostalgia for a world of bilateralism, discrimination, and official settlement in sterling. The other world of the future – of multilateralism, non-discrimination, and the use of gold and dollars – seems to have had no real attraction for him, even in the regional European context. Nonetheless he was prepared to accept that American and continental pressures could not in the end be resisted. So it was a question of driving the hardest bargain, only giving up intra-European discrimination in exchange for the most liberal provisions on EPU credit.[29]

For his part, the Governor paid little heed to the excellent advice offered by Bridge. Instead, he re-emphasised the need to maintain the network of bilateral agreements against the contingency of the EPU failing, or proving so restrictive that the UK would be left with nothing but gold settlement in Europe once the ERP had finished. In a note to the Chancellor on 8 May, prepared at the latter's personal request, he opened with the remark: 'I have always disliked the EPU proposals and I still do. I regard them mainly as an attempt by some Americans (with strong support from Belgium) to force Europe (under threat of loss of ECA dollars) prematurely back to a form of gold standard.'[30] Schemes for mitigating this severe prospect resulted in highly complex formulae that might well not stand the test of practice. 'If it were possible to drop the whole thing and proceed on our own lines of gradually extending transferability I would be vastly relieved.'

---

[29] Gaitskell's memoranda, or those of them surviving in Bank files, were written with exceptional clarity and dialectical precision. But though they certainly express a point of view, they seem lacking in warmth. This no doubt belied his true personality, but one can understand Aneurin Bevan's epithet, 'desiccated calculating machine'.

[30] The use of the term 'gold standard' in the Bank at this time is puzzling. It is unlikely to have been used simply as a pejorative euphemism for the post-transitional Bretton Woods regime; more likely it meant a regime in Europe that abolished the bilateral network and thus ruled out the use of sterling as a reserve currency in that region.

But then came acceptance of political necessity and therefore the need to seek a compromise as little damaging to British interests as possible. The bilateral network should be kept intact, but some form of gold point in the payments agreements could be accepted. In the Ansiaux Plan the proposals for sterling were good and could be made better, but the plan as a whole, even if credit could be injected into it, 'pushes us too quickly into a gold standard world'. The Governor ended by saying that to the best of his knowledge his views were shared by the bulk of banking opinion on both sides of the Atlantic, 'which views with alarm the likely effect of these ideas on world trade and payments'. But on 11 May the Cabinet approved a memorandum by the Chancellor proposing UK entry into the EPU, provided bilateral credit arrangements could be maintained (though with agreed limits to holdings of sterling), and provided the Union contained adequate amounts of credit, which could remain outstanding as long as the scheme lasted. The UK was in general prepared to renounce intra-European discrimination, though it reserved the right to suspend trade liberalisation in an emergency and proposed principles that would allow discrimination in favour of extreme debtors and against extreme creditors.

Over a month was to pass before the Executive Committee of the Ministerial Council approved an outline of the EPU, which the Council itself accepted on 7 July; and a further six weeks elapsed before the definitive Agreement was passed by the Council on 18 August. Reaching an accord on the final shape of sterling's reconciliation with membership of the European Payments Union was accomplished without much difficulty in Paris, though with some divergence of view in London. In the main, the process consisted of Ellis-Rees gradually conceding that the proposals put forward by Ansiaux were broadly superior to those of either the British themselves or the Secretariat. In the final Agreement, countries that had accumulated sterling ('existing resources') under bilateral agreements were to be given an option. They could either agree terms with the UK, for repayment over a period of not less than two years and at an interest rate of 1%, or they could continue to hold the sterling against the contingency of their needing it to meet a deficit with the rest of the Union. In the latter option the balances would be brought into the clearing when the deficit arose and a gold payment would be avoided or reduced. If this caused the UK to lose gold that it would not otherwise lose, the ECA would provide the amount in question. These options settled the question of 'existing resources' but left open the question of the further use, within existing agreements, of bilateral credit. Here, the option method again applied. For example a member in deficit with the Union, drawing credit and paying gold in the agreed proportions and within its quota, could choose at the outset whether to use bilateral credit or EPU credit. But it could not use both, nor could it chop and change between the two. Moreover, in liquidation of the Union all bilateral credit would be replaced by EPU credit.

Reaching agreement on the size of the quotas, on the credit element within them, and on non-discrimination was rather more difficult. First and agreeably, now that the objectionable supervisory board had disappeared, the UK agreed to accept a debit as well as a credit quota. But against the creditor's dream put up by Ansiaux, containing no more than short-term credit, the British proposed quotas equal to 20% of trade turnover with a credit element of 15% usable over two years and current during the lifetime of the union. Almost everyone thought this would be far too large. It would, for example, have committed the UK to $1 billion of European credit and the Belgians to $450 million. Commenting to Wilson Smith on 15 May and to the Chancellor two days later, the Governor himself warned against adding heavily to sterling purchasing power abroad. Some people, he felt, were thinking too much of protecting UK reserves. Two years was a long time and things might well go in the other direction. The next positive move came from Ansiaux, who offered to drop his own proposals in favour of the British if quotas were cut to 10% of turnover and the credit element was cut to 5% (from 15%). Ellis-Rees rejected this offer. A week later the Americans privately suggested a compromise of 15% quotas and 9% credit.

Among the subsequent comings and goings was a lunch between Ansiaux and Bridge on 7 July. The former was inclined to favour the American compromise on quotas and also accepted that a deficit country nearing exhaustion of its quota should be entitled to deliberalise on a non-discriminatory basis. But he remained totally opposed to any rule providing for discriminatory restrictions against a persistent creditor, though he admitted that the possibility of discrimination had to be faced. Bridge recorded: 'We were both inclined to think that the ultimate solution might lie in providing for the Organisation to consider what action should be taken when a country's quota was exhausted. It would then be possible to deal with the situation sensibly in the light of the facts rather than in accordance with long-haired formulae written out in advance in the dark.' Two days later Gaitskell, for the Treasury, accepted the American proposal on quotas. The Belgians refused to accept and were rewarded with a smaller quota as a 'special case'. On 17 June the Executive Committee approved the EPU in outline. There was to be no provision for discrimination against creditors. Instead, when a creditor approached exhaustion of quota, there were to be discussions about the conditions under which the country concerned could remain a member. The ECA was expected to provide the Union with $350 million of working capital. As to the provision of conditional and indirect aid, this became associated with 'starting positions' in the EPU. The expected creditors were Belgium, Britain, and Sweden; the expected debtors were Austria, Greece, Holland, and Norway. The former agreed to start with debitor positions and the latter with creditor positions.

Surveying the scenery during July, top officials in the Bank were somewhat rueful. They had fought long and hard to preserve their much-loved network of bilateral agreements. But they had been forced to give up the idea of the EPU as a 'lender of last resort' and had been persuaded that technical objections to the UK being a full member of the EPU could quite easily be met. The final result was to link the Sterling Area to the EPU without according the UK currency any special privileges that ranked it ahead of EPU credit. The EPU Agreement did not even need to mention sterling. All it had to do was to lay down rules about member countries' holdings of each other's currencies. Moreover, the option provisions – combined with the rule that member currencies held under bilateral agreements (and not already funded) must be turned into European credit on liquidation of the Union – rendered the sterling bilateral network relatively unimportant for the duration of the Union. It retained its technical function of regulating inter-central bank working relations and it acquired the new but routine function of providing bilateral interim finance in the periods between EPU settlements. But its significant role as a provider of reciprocal credit between the UK and other OEEC countries was effectively subsumed within the EPU, and the chances of it easily returning to its former role, if required, on expiration of the EPU were diminished. This conclusion had to be unwelcome to the Bank whose Governor and senior officials had all along argued so strongly for preservation of the network, were keen on its active use, and certainly felt that its continuation provided some insurance against premature reversion to the 'gold standard' if the EPU should prove to be shortlived. Why, then, had the Bank offered little resistance to the option scheme in the negotiations?

The answer to this question is that the Bank did not intend to agree with the key provision that sterling acquired during the life of the EPU should be turned into EPU credit on liquidation. On 31 May Bridge drew attention to its importance in a note to Leslie O'Brien,[31] which recalled the Governor's

---

[31] *O'Brien, Leslie Kenneth, Baron (Life Peer) PC GBE (b. 1908).* Educated Wandsworth School. Entered Bank 1927, Deputy Chief Cashier 1951–5, Chief Cashier 1955–62, Executive

wish that the network should not be put into cold storage. O'Brien alerted Mynors,[32] remarking that there would be no incentive to hold unguaranteed sterling instead of European credit guaranteed in dollars. Watson wisely remarked that the value of sterling as an international currency depended on the use to which it could in fact be put rather than on the existence of a bilateral network. It is not hard to imagine the Governor's reaction to what was happening. There followed something of a row in the Bank, the development of a dispute with the Treasury, and a divergence of view between Ellis-Rees and London. The dispute centred round the interpretation of a draft paragraph on liquidation in the option proposals that were then current and had been agreed with ECA. Against written representations from Mynors and Ellis-Rees, who felt the ground disappearing underneath him, Playfair confidently insisted that the text had always meant that on liquidation sterling holdings would be exchanged for EPU units. He also argued effectively that the alternative interpretation (sterling holdings not so exchanged) would produce great complication to no good purpose and would furthermore involve the Treasury in an impossible burden of bilateral negotiations. But the decisive factor was the American interpretation of the paragraph, which they averred had been confirmed in May during a discussion between Cripps and Secretary Acheson. It was identical to that of Playfair. This was finally confirmed by the ECA in Paris towards the end of June, when the British tactical position was heavily affected by an approach then being made in Washington to the US Treasury and the State Department for help with the wider problem of the sterling balances. An attempt to retrieve the position by introducing yet another option, applying to sterling holdings on liquidation, then proved fruitless.

The Bank had lost. As Bolton lamented in a note to the Governor on 30 June: 'The special position of sterling has virtually disappeared.' It was then agreed to snatch some advantage from this defeat. O'Brien was authorised to propose to the Treasury that the existing network of intergovernmental bilateral agreements should simply by scrapped and a new network of straightforward inter-central bank arrangements substituted. The Treasury, in Playfair's absence, recoiled in shock from this sudden

Director 1962–4, Deputy Governor 1964–6, Governor 1966–73, Director, BIS 1966–73, 1974–83, Vice-Chairman 1979–83.

[32] Since April, Bolton had been absent in the United States, first on Fund business and then to participate in the abortive Anglo–American discussions on sterling balances. Even while Bolton was away, Siepmann continued to take absolutely no recorded part in the EPU discussions. Thus Mynors, with only limited experience of overseas affairs, had to fill the directorial gap. O'Brien was his principal assistant under Graffteey-Smith. The former was now aged forty-one, several years senior to Bridge, and was a fast-rising star in Overseas. As Deputy to Graffteey-Smith, O'Brien had the rank of an Assistant Chief Cashier.

about-face. The Bank had after all been telling them for years how necessary it was to preserve the network, if only as an insurance against future trouble. That advice had prevailed in 1946 and been proved correct in 1947. Furthermore, Bridge warned from Paris that so barefaced a confession of the truth would make the British look foolish. In the end it was agreed not to make sudden changes but to allow the new situation to emerge within the existing network. In a long explanatory letter on the EPU, circulated to Sterling Area central banks early in September, the Bank swallowed hard and summed it up realistically as follows:

> Each member of the European Payments Union has undertaken to grant all other members on request any temporary finance required between the operations of the Union. Also any balances in the currencies of other members accumulated during the life of the Union have to be given up on liquidation in exchange for an appropriate credit in the Union. On both these counts the credit provisions in the monetary and sterling payments arrangements of the UK with other European countries no longer have their former significance. The UK does not therefore propose to seek to include such provisions in her bilateral payments arrangements during the life of EPU. But should any of her bilateral partners prefer credit provisions with some upper limit on the old pattern, we should be willing to accept such an arrangement. In the main, however, bilateral agreements will in future merely carry into effect the EPU provisions for temporary finance, fix rates of exchange and continue the usual reciprocal undertakings regarding the availability of each partner's currency in the hands of residents of the other partner. It is felt that inter-Governmental agreement of this kind will serve a useful purpose and provide a foundation for new arrangements which might be required by a termination of EPU. All such agreements will be subject to three months' notice on either side and to review in the light of EPU developments.

The course of two loose ends suggests that the unintended fate of the bilateral agreements, together with the concurrent failure of the Washington discussions about the sterling balances, had left the Bank in none too nice a mood. The first was an argument with the Treasury, carried on by the Governor and Bolton, about whether a holding of EPU credit, or a liability to repay it, should be included in the EEA or in some other part of the Exchequer machinery. They argued in letters and in a special meeting with senior Treasury officials that EPU credit was not 'foreign exchange', that publicity given to EPU operations would stimulate pressure for greater information to be published about other operations of the EEA unless EPU credit was excluded from that Account, and that on liquidation of the EPU the EEA might find itself holding worthless currencies in exchange for credit held. In a letter dated 9 August the Governor was gently but firmly told by Edward Bridges that the Treasury was unable to accept any of the Bank's arguments and that Ministers had decided to include EPU credit in the EEA.

The second of the two loose ends concerned UK membership of the EPU Board. The Treasury was in favour of nominating an official of the Bank and agreed with the Governor that the nominee would be Grafftey-Smith, to be succeeded by O'Brien early in 1951. But after some discussion with Baumgartner the Governor agreed only on condition that the French also nominated a central bank official rather than a civil servant. In the event, for administrative reasons of their own, the French nominated Pierre Calvet, who had been (and was later to be) in the Bank of France but was currently working in the Ministry of Finance. Despite pleas by Playfair to Mynors and a telephone conversation between the Deputy Governor and Baumgartner – in the course of which the latter gave the impression that he viewed the matter with little concern – the Governor insisted on withdrawing Grafftey-Smith's name. Ellis-Rees was appointed alongside Calvet while both central banks undertook to provide technical assistance as necessary. In London this latter task fell naturally to Bridge.

The European Payments Union proved a striking success. Until the collective resumption of formal convertibility in 1958, the Union provided a technically simple mechanism of intra-regional settlement between the participating central banks. As such, it accommodated a massive increase in regional trade, while its consultative procedures enabled periodic and severe intra-regional imbalances to be adjusted without defections or collapse. The full post-war recovery of Western Europe and the transition to a period of rapid and durable economic prosperity and expansion were of course due to a whole variety of factors. But an efficient and easily understood payments system was assuredly one of them; and of all the systems considered from 1947 to 1950 it is hard to imagine any proving better at this job than a clearing union operating within the consultative procedures of the OEEC.

For the United Kingdom, the Union provided a considerable opportunity, without the commitments to 'integration' and supranational authority to which the British were so opposed. Together with the associated liberalisation of regional trade, the Union linked the whole Sterling Area with a region of rapidly expanding industry and commerce. With regard to the provision of financial services, the Union established regional transferability of member currencies at central bank level and placed no impediment on whatever development of sterling as a trading and investment currency the British authorities cared to permit and encourage. At the same time it terminated a set of bilateral arrangements within which the reserve role of sterling in Europe too often resulted in the build-up of balances that were held with reluctance and based on agreements reflecting politico-economic bargaining strengths in a bilateralist environment. By 1950 this system was disliked on the Continent. The crises of 1947 and 1949, together with the tenacious attachment of the British authorities to preservation of the system, made other countries suspicious of sterling and suspicious of British motives. The reserve role of sterling sometimes looked too much like a device that enabled the UK to pay for its imports by printing its own currency, without providing an adequate service in exchange for this privilege. Moreover, the usefulness of sterling as a trading currency in Western Europe was itself considerably reduced in 1948 and 1949 by the restrictions on non-resident accounts imposed by London in an endeavour to stop the traffic in cheap sterling. By greatly reducing the functions of the bilateral network, the EPU Agreement removed one cause of mistrust and established a working relationship between sterling and the Continent, at the level of official settlements, that well corresponded to the prevailing international standing of Britain's national currency.

The opportunity presented by the EPU was appreciated by relatively few in the Treasury and the Bank. Outstandingly, Bridge came to appreciate it and did his best to carry his seniors with him. In Overseas, O'Brien was quick to size up the favourable aspects of the situation, as was Watson in Exchange Control. In the Treasury, Playfair saw the opportunity, while Ellis-Rees, for all his exposure to argument in Paris, seems not to have done. But as has been seen, the Treasury Ministers, the Governor, and Bolton were curiously negative. At the end they were constructive, but they were most reluctant. Why did the Governor, whose strategic judgements had hitherto proved reliable, persist with this view? Why, still only forty-five himself, did he so clearly reject the well-argued view of his bright young man in Paris? There is no ready-made answer to these questions. As has been noted, the Bank devoted little systematic institutional thought and few resources to the issues of European union that surfaced on the Continent from 1947 onwards. Either, it seems, the Bank was not very interested or else, in respect of integrationist ideas, it was dismissive. Even in the EPU negotiations themselves, in which the UK did in fact successfully carry the banner for big rather than little Europe, the Governor remained firmly of the opinion that the EPU were better unborn but would have to be brought to life out of external political exigency.

In truth, the Bank did not set much store by transitional regionalism, as one-worlders in the Treasury were sometimes to call the EPU. Since it did not regard 'Europe' as a great British opportunity, the Bank was more concerned with the gnawing problem of sterling's survival, as a reserve

Roy Bridge

and trading currency, in the world that it saw ahead after Marshall Aid had ceased and when the commitment to Article VIII of the IMF might have to be honoured. By 1950, although the reserves were again recovering and despite some plans for extending the day-to-day transferability of sterling, the viability of a further long evolutionary step-by-step approach had begun to seem doubtful. The difficulties of running an inconvertible reserve and trading currency had been proved formidable. With concerns of this sort, the EPU was not very much help, especially if its own life was not expected to be very prolonged. Neither the EPU nor any of its proposed variants had much to offer the continuing problem of the sterling balances and the over-extended banking position of the UK. Nor was the EPU itself likely to add much weight to the Governor's repeated attempts to persuade the Government to change its domestic monetary policy, or its spending programmes, so as to help restore or sustain overseas confidence in the currency. Nor, though it did ensure an orderly official exchange-rate structure, could the EPU help with the problem of cheap sterling. For this was seen largely as a consequence of inappropriate domestic policies and of inadequate control over those sterling balances whose use had, by agreement, been formally or informally restricted.

Therefore it is not altogether surprising that worries about the future of sterling made the Governor nervous of the EPU and anxious to retain the bilateral network as an insurance against a breakdown, just as it had proved to be in 1947. Furthermore at this time he seems himself to have been using up mental capital, accumulated under the immense load of work sustained during his time as Executive Director and Deputy Governor, which was not being effectively replenished by considered and persistent advice from within his immediate entourage. Niemeyer, now concentrating on his Directorship of the BIS, played a helpful but at best a small supporting part. The new Deputy Governor, Dallas Bernard,[33] played no part at all in this area of policy. Siepmann, the senior of the two Overseas Directors and a man accustomed to systematic policy formation, mysteriously abdicated his interest in intra-European monetary arrangements soon after the crisis of 1947. The gap was filled by his junior colleague, Bolton, whose effective responsibilities became so diverse that his oversight of intra-European payments policy was intermittent. Given his methods of work and erratic judgement it would have been a lucky

[33] *Bernard, Dallas Gerald Mercer, 1st Baronet 1954 (1888–1975)*. Educated Royal Naval College, Dartmouth. Managing Director, Jardine Matheson 1922–8, Chairman, Hongkong and Shanghai Banking Corporation 1924, 1926–7, Director, Matheson and Co. 1928–1942. Director, Bank of England 1936–9, Executive Director 1939–49, Deputy Governor 1949–54. Director, Courtaulds 1954–64, Chairman 1962–4, Director, British Bank of the Middle East 1954–67, Chairman 1954–65.

accident if he had managed to point the Governor and the Bank towards a consistently less negative attitude in that field. Finally, the top officials did not challenge the ruling wisdom. Neither Grafftey-Smith nor Beale showed any inclination to do so. At a more junior level, Bridge certainly provided accurate reporting, reliable judgement, and a well-expressed challenge, all of which certainly reached the top of the Bank. But the views of an Assistant Chief Cashier on matters of high policy carried limited weight.

Ironically, the Bank's principal opponent, and in many ways the victor, was not some distinguished political economist or accomplished mandarin but none other than a fellow central banker, Hubert Ansiaux. For if Keynes be regarded as the architect of Bretton Woods, even though his own plan had to give way to that of Harry White, Ansiaux must be regarded as the architect of the intra-European payments arrangements. He was first in the field in July 1947 and carried the day later in that year and again in 1948 and 1949. His particular brainchild, the IEPC, was none too productive but was a lot better than nothing. It established the Basle compensation machinery and it paved the way for the EPU. The latter was not, in the first instance, his idea. Among others, Conolly and Bridge deserve credit for its origination. But Ansiaux took hold of it and developed it. Most notably it was he who invented the best way of reconciling sterling with membership of the Union. He was of course greatly helped all along by American support for his fundamental objectives. He was also helped by the creditor position of his own small country. But Ansiaux and the National Bank of Belgium deserve full recognition for their achievement. Their success is also a comment on the weakness of the UK and sterling in the early post-war years. Certainly London's tactical behaviour was weakened by a lack of European vision, but the negative attitude of the Bank of England reflected all along the defensive anxieties of a banker uncertain of his own future. The three other themes of these years – cheap sterling, the sterling balances, and devaluation – all accompanied the development of intra-European monetary co-operation and all affected the Bank's attitude to it.

(c) CHEAP STERLING AND THE FRONTIERS OF EXCHANGE CONTROL: 1948–1951

Though not generally convertible into dollars at the official rate, sterling remained widely transferable outside the dollar area after the crisis of 1947. It was therefore internationally usable for the financing of non-dollar trade. Successful maintenance of this state of affairs required that the barrier of exchange control between sterling and the dollar was properly preserved. For residents of the UK itself, this barrier was maintained by a combination of import and exchange controls. For residents of the Sterling Area it was likewise maintained by local controls whose policies reflected collaboration between member Governments and the British authorities. For 'non-residents', other than residents of the dollar area itself (whose sterling remained convertible), the policing of transferability and the enforcement of inconvertibility were effected by UK exchange control, accompanied by varying degrees of co-operation or consultation with foreign controls.

The need for non-resident inconvertibility reflected a persistent excess demand for dollars at the official rate of exchange. Controls operated from London were designed to prevent satisfaction of that demand by non-resident sales of sterling against dollars, gold, or other convertible assets. As time went on it was recognised in London that an increase in the flow of inconvertible sterling to non-residents, arising out of an adverse balance of payments of the UK and the Sterling Area with the rest of the non-dollar world, was likely to add to the demand for dollars and put greater pressure on the control barrier. Non-resident holders of inconvertible sterling could not, of course, exchange them for dollars with their own monetary authorities. All they could get was either their own currency or, depending on the precise rules, some other inconvertible currency. But in the prevailing conditions many dollar goods had scarcity value and could be sold in the non-dollar world at a premium over their dollar price expressed in local currencies at official rates of exchange. Therefore non-resident traders and merchants had a strong incentive to get round the UK controls even though this meant getting a rate of exchange for their sterling that was lower than the official rate. But although the control barrier was not thought to be watertight, there was in 1947 some assumption in the Treasury and the Bank that it would prove sufficiently effective to prevent leakages from becoming a serious problem.

This assumption was critical. Indeed the gradualist attitude to non-resident convertibility, in the forefront of Bank views about post-war external financial policy from 1941 onwards, necessarily relied on it. But it was not one that could be based on previous peacetime experience when such wartime aids as censorship of mails and state control of private industry and commerce were either absent or relatively minor. Controls operated in the inter-war period by, for example, the National Socialist regime in Germany were no reliable guide to the efficiency of controls on non-residents, controls that were needed for the management from a democratic society of an inconvertible but international currency in the post-war years of dollar shortage. Over 1948–51, however, the reliability of UK exchange control over non-resident transactions in peacetime was put to severe practical test and found to be poor. Despite a repeated tightening of the controls, unhelpful to the international standing of sterling, and despite repeated attempts to shore them up with supplementary controls over trade, serious avoidance developed whenever the dollar shortage was acute or the supply of sterling relatively plentiful. A flourishing cheap-sterling business grew up in free markets outside the UK, assisted by devices whereby Sterling Area trade with the dollar area was disguised as trade within the non-dollar world. Confidence in the official rate of exchange was weakened by this appearance of other, cheaper, rates. In addition, London was deprived of legitimate commercial business, the repute of British exchange control was diminished, and the dollar earnings of the Sterling Area were reduced.

It was never possible, in the nature of things, to establish in quantitative terms just how serious the leakage was. But it was certainly enough to discredit the control itself and to undermine the confidence of the officials who ran it. In the end this experience brought the Bank up against a strategic choice. On the one hand it could advise that the international functions of sterling be drastically reduced. Alternatively it could advise that those functions should be retained but that the gradualist approach should be abandoned in favour of an early restoration of convertibility. The Bank chose the second of these two. By 1950 it was keen to restore convertibility. In the crisis of 1952 it unsuccessfully supported proposals for a unilateral resumption of convertibility, but at a floating rate. Later, in the autumn of 1952, it supported a 'Collective Approach' to early convertibility, to be adopted through collaboration with the US, the members of the EPU, and the Sterling Area. This too was unsuccessful and in 1955, when the external payments problems of the UK had surfaced yet again, the nuisance of cheap sterling was finally eliminated by restoration of convertibility *de facto*, through official intervention in transferable sterling markets overseas. It is true that the experience with cheap sterling from 1948 onwards was not the only force propelling the Bank towards advocacy of an early return to convertibility. But it was a very powerful one, with a story of its own that requires telling.

First some further explanation is needed. The expression 'cheap sterling' was shorthand for a variety of financial manipulations that took two main forms, sometimes but by no means always directly related. The first form was 'commodity shunting'. This did not, by itself, involve any direct sale of sterling against dollars at a discount on the official rate. Instead, for example, a Dutch merchant might acquire a Sterling Area commodity, say rubber, that was readily saleable in the US. The rubber would be consigned to Rotterdam and be paid for in sterling from a Dutch transferable account. Since Holland was in the Transferable Account Area, no breach of UK exchange control was involved. The rubber would then be re-exported to the US, where it would be sold at a discount on the quoted New York market price, undercutting established traders. The dollar proceeds would then be used to buy dollar goods, which would be shipped to Holland and in their turn be re-exported to, for instance, Egypt and sold for transferable sterling at a substantial premium over their American price at the official exchange rate. The sterling profit on the second leg would normally exceed the loss on the first. But the feasibility of the entire shunt depended upon the country originally exporting the sterling commodity being unable or unwilling to control the ultimate destination of its exports, upon the merchant who bought the commodity being able somehow or other to retain the dollar proceeds of the re-export, and upon the 'Egyptian' control being prepared to allow imports from 'Holland', against transferable sterling, of premium-priced goods that were of obvious American origin.

The second form of cheap-sterling business typically involved the outright sale of transferable or even bilateral account sterling to an American resident for dollars at a discount on the official rate. The sale would be arranged in New York or in such other free markets as Zurich, Milan, or Tangier. The seller would use the dollar proceeds either to buy dollar goods for sale at a profit elsewhere or to acquire capital assets in North America. For his part, the buyer would use the sterling proceeds either to acquire Sterling Area commodities cheaply, shunting them to the US, or else to pay for shipping and other 'invisible' services provided by the UK or the Sterling Area. One could not easily shunt invisibles and did not need to, for these payments were imperfectly controlled in London. Thus, for example, French sterling could readily be used for settlement of an 'invisible' acquired from the UK even though the country receiving the invisible was not France but the US. But how could transferable sterling be sold in the first place to an American resident in the normal course without the permission (seldom given) of UK exchange control? The answer to this was that the sterling sold to the American buyer was not actually paid into his account but held on a transferable account of the seller while awaiting American instructions for payment to another such account or to an account in the Sterling Area. This was a straight avoidance, off-shore, of the UK control, but one of which the British authorities could not usually be aware and could not effectively stop without at the same time stopping almost all use of sterling in the countries concerned. Nor could they stop transactions that linked the shunting of commodities directly to dealings in cheap sterling. If the shunter did not want to use his dollar receipts to acquire dollar goods, he could sell the dollars for cheap transferable sterling instead. As a transaction between two transferable accounts, this would not attract attention in London.

It is not possible to say exactly how close was the linkage between cheap sterling itself, as quoted in New York, and the rate of exchange implied by simple commodity shunting. But it seems to have been accepted as sufficiently close for the free market rate in New York, or variety of rates corresponding to the numerous varieties of transferable and bilateral sterling, to be regarded as representative of 'the' discount of cheap sterling on the official rate.

Traffic of these various kinds began to attract serious attention in the late spring of 1948. But for some months beforehand the Bank had been aware of its potential dangers. This was shown by its intense interest in the multiple-currency practices of first Italy and then France; and by the action taken to protect sterling from their effects. In the very early post-war years of uncertain political stability, violent inflationary surges, intense import thirst, and constant pressure on sometimes imperfectly administered and leaky controls, the authorities in the countries most severely affected could seek some relief by permitting a free market in their own currencies against the dollar and by allowing certain categories of trade and financial business to be conducted there at the rates of exchange established. The official fixed rate was then retained for imports of essential supplies and exports of goods most in demand abroad. By this means the risk of an uncontrolled depreciation could be reduced. But multiple-rate arrangements of this or any other kind were contrary to the IMF Charter. Article XIV of that Charter allowed discriminatory exchange controls during the transitional period but did not allow multiple rates.

Italy, though a signatory to the Bretton Woods Treaty, delayed formally declaring an IMF parity for the lira until the currency had gained sufficient stability. In the interim, with effect from May 1946, a free market was allowed alongside an officially managed fixed rate. However, the British authorities were markedly unsympathetic to arguments justifying the introduction or retention of such practices. Instead, they saw the free market depreciation of the lira as a form of unfair competition affecting certain classes of exports, and they viewed the permitted free market as a direct invitation to dealings in cheap sterling. Initially in 1946 the sterling dollar cross-rate through the free-market lira had remained in line with the official parity, but during and after the convertibility crisis of 1947 it fell rapidly to $2·55. Repeated attempts to get the Italians to mend their ways proved unsuccessful. The Anglo–Italian Payments

Agreement of April 1947, negotiated on the assumption of early convertibility of sterling, made Italian membership of the Transferable Account Area conditional upon the elimination of multiple exchange practices and on the maintenance of orderly cross-rates. The Italians failed to meet this condition and their resolve to continue on that course was increased as the dollar famine worsened and as the British themselves unilaterally abandoned convertibility. However, London proved unrelenting and after further argument Italy was removed from the Transferable Account Area early in 1948. But the Italians succeeded in earning a substantial sterling surplus and the bilateralisation of Italian holdings of sterling did not prevent their use in the purchase of Sterling Area commodities or their sale, for dollars, between Italians (real or disguised) on the free market in Milan. Early in 1949, in the context of the first IEPC, Italy was readmitted to the Transferable Account Area.

Much more severe treatment was meted out to the French when they instituted a free market early in 1948 at the same time as carrying out a large devaluation. They had previously declared a parity to the IMF and their abandonment of a *de jure* unitary exchange system was the subject of intense prior discussion between London and Paris. The British authorities, in particular the Bank, feared that the deliberate defection of so important a constituent of the IMF as the French Monetary Area could endanger the whole Bretton Woods structure, so recently agreed, besides sharply increasing the scope for trading in sterling at a discount. Strong representations were made to the US Treasury and to the Managing Director of the Fund as well as to the French themselves. But in the critical cold-war winter of 1947–8 the American Administration was not prepared to force the issue in Paris. Therefore the Treasury and the Bank in London had to accept that the French might not be stopped and to consider how best to protect sterling against the consequences of a free market in Paris. At the end of 1947 French private balances in sterling amounted to some £33 million and it was judged essential to prevent these and any further accretions from being fed into that market. Accordingly, all the private balances were immobilised in No. 2 Accounts when the franc was devalued and the free market opened at the beginning of February 1948. Sterling on these accounts could be sold only for payment into the No. 1 Accounts of French authorised banks in exchange for francs and could therefore not be exchanged for dollars with another French resident at the free market rate. Simultaneously the No. 1 Accounts held by the French commercial banks and the Banque de France were bilateralised, that is to say made freely usable only for purchases from the Sterling Area and made unusable for transfer to a third country without permission from London.

It was hoped that these measures of protection against the free markets in Paris and Milan would serve to contain cheap sterling within manageable bounds. But early in May an alarm was sounded in the Bank by Thompson-McCausland. 'The dangers in this are serious', he wrote, 'friction with the reputable end of our trading community; loss of dollars; and growing criticism of exchange control. I think we must take it seriously.' His particular evidence came from the Hudson's Bay Company. Furs sold at auction in London for transferable sterling were being shipped to Tangier, Paris, Rotterdam, and Cairo for re-export to the US; or in one case there was a simple transhipment at Le Havre, for an American destination, of furs consigned to Italy. This was confirmed in the Bank by Exchange Control, who cited evidence supplied by London traders and bankers, some of it specific, some of it the general talk of the market-place. On 11 June, Bolton sent to Wilson Smith in the Treasury an explanatory memorandum that included descriptions of the commodity shunting and other cheap-sterling operations of traders and merchants in France,[34] Holland, Italy, Tangier, and Thailand. Commodities specifically mentioned, in addition to furs, were rubber, wool, tea, and pepper. Examples of the 'second leg' of a shunting operation were sales of American refrigerators, Swiss watches, and Brazilian coffee by Tangier to Egypt against payment in transferable sterling. The memorandum identified several factors responsible for the growth of cheap-sterling business: the growing dollar famine, the maintenance of either automatic or administrative transferability of sterling, the growth of free exchange markets, especially in Italy and France, and 'the growing pressure of traders in other countries to find a way through lax or incomplete controls where easy profits are to be made by using one or other of the many free exchange markets or by other methods which have similar effect'. But Exchange Control were as yet sceptical whether much could be achieved by a further tightening of their regulations. They therefore favoured an extension of export licensing in the Sterling Area so as to reduce the export of primary commodities to, for example, Holland or Italy to levels consistent with their domestic use in those countries. Nevertheless Tangier was removed from transferable account in August 1948 and its sterling was bilateralised.

During the late summer and autumn of 1948 cheap-sterling business continued to grow. Commodity shunting through Rotterdam was

[34] It appeared that French banks were sometimes prepared to accommodate such operations by, in effect, allowing holders of blocked No. 2 Account sterling to use No. 1 Account sterling for shunting purposes. This cast doubt on the efficacy of the measures taken earlier in the year. The measures applied to the French Monetary Area, which at this time included Syria and the Lebanon where leakages were more likely to develop than in metropolitan France.

especially prominent, despite reports that the Dutch control was requiring the dollar proceeds of re-exports to be surrendered for guilders at the official parity. London merchants, who were losing entrepôt business, asked the Bank for guidance but could be given no satisfactory answer. Senior officials under J. L. Fisher,[35] head of Exchange Control, again considered what might be done. On 23 November they submitted a memorandum to Siepmann, who had directorial responsibility for exchange control, suggesting this time that further restrictions should be imposed. Transferable accounts should be confined to the central monetary authorities of the countries concerned and fresh understandings should be reached with those authorities to ensure that transferability was used only for direct current transactions and not for purchasing prospective re-exports. At the same time privately held sterling in selected countries should be immobilised in No. 2 Accounts. The authors saw no comparable alternative except comprehensive export licensing by Sterling Area countries. The other course would be to join in the game, increase the number of transferable accounts, allow London merchants to participate, and in the end allow a two-tier market in sterling. These suggestions were discussed with Siepmann and an inconclusive note was forwarded to Cobbold. It was agreed that in certain cases a reduction in the number of transferable accounts might help, as might also a series of agreements confirming that transferability only applied to direct current transactions. But no conclusion was reached about the immobilisation of private balances or about radical alternative policies.

Siepmann himself clearly found the problem an agonising one. Temperamentally opposed to exchange control in any case, he was convinced it could only be operated successfully if the co-operation of the victims could be enlisted and maintained. He exerted all his influence to this end. So far as possible the control was run in a humane and understanding manner, as if it were an unpleasant but necessary activity conducted between friends. Cheap sterling strained that relationship by placing disabilities on British traders that could not easily be applied to foreign competitors. But being also devoted to the cause of sterling as an international currency, Siepmann was equally upset by the prospect of intensifying restrictions on non-residents in an often fruitless attempt to stop or reduce cheap-sterling business. In a brief note to Dallas Bernard,

---

[35] *Fisher, John Lenox, CMG (1899–1976).* Educated Liverpool University. RAF 1917–19. Entered Bank 1921, Assistant to Chief, Overseas and Foreign Department 1936–7, Assistant Chief 1937–9, Assistant Adviser 1939–46, Adviser to the Governors (Acting) 1946, 1947–8, Director of Operations, IMF 1946–7, Deputy Chief Cashier 1948–50, Adviser to the Governors 1950–9. Member, East African and West African Currency Boards 1953–9.

who had been approached about the shunting of Indian hides through Holland by American tanners, he lamented:

> There is no real answer, except that the pianist is doing his best. Cheap sterling and all the devious exercises to which it gives rise are our perpetual bugbear and we know well enough how many traders and merchants in how many markets are becoming exasperated beyond all bearing – and legitimately so, for they are helpless. So are we, unless gradually by agreement and cooperation with India and the Dominions, Holland, Belgium and all the South American republics, we can establish some kind of agreed order where at present there is chaos.

But the flow of unwelcome evidence continued uninterrupted. South African wool was being shunted to the US through Holland. Indian cotton was being shunted to Belgium through Holland. The broker market in cheap sterling in New York was reportedly growing; and the New York banks, who kept out of the business so as to assist the UK authorities, were getting restive. In the middle of January 1949, there arrived the first of many letters on the subject from Werner Knoke, Vice-President in charge of the Foreign Department at the Federal Reserve Bank of New York: 'Our latest information disturbs me', he wrote, 'new kinds of sterling have made their appearance, the Spanish account sterling being the latest dealt in here. Besides, some of our important banks now seem to be handling this business, and in substantial amounts. I have learnt for instance of a trade by one of them in French account sterling of almost £300,000.[36] The bank was emphatic, I understand, in making it clear that they acted merely as broker on a commission basis, without the sterling passing through the bank's account.' A copy of this letter was forwarded by Bolton to the Treasury. Meanwhile Bank officials had visited Amsterdam for talks with the Netherlands Bank and Dutch commercial banks. Although they had been assured of official Dutch co-operation, they came away with the impression that the Dutch control was weak while Dutch banks and traders were strong. Furthermore it appeared that Egyptian purchases of US goods for transferable sterling ostensibly paid to Dutch accounts were being arranged direct with parties in the US who disposed of the Dutch sterling in the free market in New York.

Late in January 1949 Exchange Control commented bleakly: 'We cannot see any prospect of checking the cheap-sterling business under present conditions. If all transferable account countries were to agree to use the accounts only for direct trade in each others goods, and at the same time we established a new rule here that the origin of goods must be given

---

[36] The reader is reminded that this would be some £5 million at 1989 values.

in EC forms, we might have some chance. We should still be at the mercy of the man who makes a deliberately false statement...'

These sentiments were strongly supported from another source. H. W. Gurney,[37] the respected manager of the EEA and a close associate of Bolton, was sent detailed evidence by the London office of the Guaranty Trust Company of New York. This drew attention to increasing cheap-sterling activity in the Middle East. Gurney forwarded the evidence to Fisher, with a covering note: 'From the tone of the correspondence it would seem about time some drastic action was taken to stop trading in cheap sterling in conjunction with merchandise.' In face of such pressure, and at the request of the Treasury, the Bank again reconsidered its policy. A fresh memorandum was prepared and circulated on 17 February 1949 along with a covering note that stated baldly: 'Though this business is still only a small part of all sterling transactions, it is growing, and already constitutes a threat to the whole basis of exchange control, stable exchange rates and, ultimately, the domestic stabilisation policy. Hitherto palliatives have been employed. More positive action is now needed.'

The paper began by rehearsing the measures already taken: exhortation of foreign controls, including the Dutch, 'but we have no confidence that fully effective action will result'; export controls in the Sterling Area, 'here again there is a limit to effective action'; limitations on the free markets in Paris and Milan, recently agreed, whereby the correct cross-rates would be maintained, 'but free markets survive in Tangier (though on a more limited scale than before), New York, Zurich, in several centres in the Middle East, and in the Far East. Moreover Dutch banks and merchants continue the business on a large scale through the operation of non-resident sterling accounts'; finally, attempts to ensure that countries did not license the import of goods that were obviously of dollar origin though invoiced in sterling, but 'Egypt is quite unaffected by it'. The paper went on to scout various further exchange control measures; the restriction of transferable accounts to central banks only, the substitution of administrative transferability for automatic transferability, or a general reversion to bilateral accounts. But it concluded firstly that none of these would be fully effective and secondly that they would incur criticism from Europe and the US while further exacerbating the feelings of British traders, 'as foreign traders found ways round them and captured the business'. What was to be done? As the paper tellingly remarked, in a Bank credo on the subject: 'Any fully effective solution by means of exchange restriction would require that we administer sterling as a

---

[37] *Gurney, Horace Walter (1890–1980)*. British Overseas Bank until 1939. Entered Bank 1939, Principal, Dealing and Accounts Office 1942–53.

domestic and not an international currency, as the Russians administer the rouble, never allowing it to pass out of domestic hands, and conducting all external business in other currencies. But we are committed to the Americans, both by the Loan Agreement and by reiterated statements, to move in the direction of making sterling more readily available for international trade; and even without such commitments the evidence of fact accumulates daily to stress the need for an international currency, while our own interest requires that we should continue to trade in sterling ourselves and to maintain sterling as the basis of the other currency systems which are founded on it. Extreme measures of exchange control are therefore ruled out.'

The matter had accordingly to be looked at in another way. The root of the problem lay in the excess of sterling in foreign hands and in the dollar famine. The UK authorities could do little more about the latter, but they could act to reduce the former. 'It must either be tied up or mopped up, or both.' The first thing to do was to hold to a minimum the amounts released from the No. 2 Accounts arranged in 1947. 'It is useless to exercise ourselves over the problem of free sterling and to multiply the restrictions on our own and other traders in the hope of curtailing it if at the same time great sums are being released to swell the supply.[38] The use of releases as a negotiating counter on which a few extra millions can be given to gain a point is in direct conflict with our main monetary policy.' Next, *all* non-resident accounts other than those of central banks and local authorised dealers should be immobilised on No. 2 Accounts that would be transferable only onto No. 2 Accounts at the central bank or authorised banks and only in exchange for local currency at the official rate. Finally the paper considered 'mopping up'. It argued firstly against the UK paying premium prices for non-dollar goods if this only served to swell the supply of sterling available for cheap-sterling business. It argued secondly against the doctrine that UK exports that merely served to repatriate foreign-held balances were not worth making. 'Exports which reduce the excess sterling now threatening the structure of exchange control and of fixed parities are as well requited as any which the Sterling Area makes.'

The paper remained with Siepmann for two weeks, during which time the Bank decided to conduct experimental undercover operations in the New York free market. Bolton wrote to the Treasury on 25 February saying it was proposed to use Ellerton of Barclays Bank as agent. The Treasury agreed. The move was timely, for on the following day a telegram arrived from Washington saying that the US Treasury was now becoming

---

[38] They were indeed being released (q.v. the immediately following section).

Cameron Cobbold, Governor, 1949

agitated. Secretary Snyder was said to be receiving an increasing flood of mail about the availability of transferable account sterling at cheap rates. Formal deputations of wool importers and woollen manufacturers were being received. Adverse Congressional reactions were feared, including a linking of cheap sterling with the emerging issue of the sterling–dollar parity. On 1 March, the first day of Cobbold's Governorship, Siepmann forwarded to him without amendment the policy paper on cheap sterling. In a short cover note he omitted direct expression of personal support. He remained a pessimistic realist on the subject. Judging from notes he wrote ten months later, he probably felt that almost any action would make matters worse, if not in one direction then in another. In that frame of mind there was little he could do but put forward to the Governor the proposals set out in the paper.

The Governor could support the proposals submitted to him and advise the Government to take a violent and probably irreversible further step down the road of exchange restriction. Or he could advise in effect a further period of make-do-and-mend, leaving strategic options open. The paper itself had tried to characterise the virtual blocking of private non-resident balances as something different from 'exchange restriction', an evasion that the Governor firmly rejected. In a markedly critical note addressed to Siepmann on 4 March he began: 'I realise the difficulties of concocting a memorandum about cheap sterling and I also realise that something has to be produced for the Treasury. I must confess, however, that I am not at all convinced by this product.' He doubted whether pressing the Treasury to take a firm line with India, Egypt, and others would bear much early fruit. As to the proposed extension of No. 2 Accounts, he wrote:

> I assume this means that the proposal is to block all private sterling accounts. Does this really make sense? It would obviously raise enormous difficulties and create frightful trouble (should we, for example, block private American accounts?) and when we had done all this would not a vast proportion of the money on private accounts have to be released for pre-zero commitments or normal working balances. Surely the bulk of excess sterling is in the hands of monetary authorities and authorised dealers which, I gather, under this proposal would be left free.
>
> I personally believe that there are only three alternatives:
>
> (a) to go on as we are for the time being, tidying up where we can;
> (b) to go to a full bilateral system and, if we are prepared to take such extreme measures, to go back on existing sterling balance agreements and unilaterally freeze balances down to the bone;
> (c) to change our whole concept and start thinking in terms of varying rates and supply and demand.
>
> If these are the real alternatives, let us say so bluntly to the Treasury.

The brief episode that followed exemplified both the authority of Cobbold as Governor and a trait of character which those who worked closely with him soon learnt to appreciate. He was a careful listener and a thoughtful reader. But he was not a lengthy debater. His meetings were inclined to be short and to the point. He was determined to maintain the authority of the Governor as the Chairman and Chief Executive of the Bank. He was certainly a commanding personality and was to exercise command in an almost military fashion for over twelve years. He was, however, sensitive to any questioning of the decisions that he was not slow to take but in which he may not always have had complete self-confidence. Once he had firmly declared a point of view he had as often as not announced his decision, or at least the general shape of it. Persuading him to change his mind was not impossible but was not a task to be taken lightly. In this instance it was in vain that Thompson-McCausland tried to argue that the No. 2 Account proposal was really part of the Governor's alternative (a); that there was no suggestion of blocking North American accounts or Sterling Area accounts; that extension to other European and Middle East countries of the treatment already applied to private French balances was not very revolutionary; and that private traders would be free to use sterling through authorised dealers' No. 1 Accounts. A meeting was held but the Governor was unmoved and gave instructions for the paper to be recast. He sent the new version to Wilson Smith on 18 March, saying he had recently had several talks on the subject with 'the Chancellor, Sir Edward Bridges and yourself'. He noted that the topic was highly inflammable and recorded an agreement with Wilson Smith that it would not be discussed in any wider forum until an entirely different document had been prepared.

The new paper contained rather more chapter and verse than its predecessor, but although it began with the same stress on the seriousness of the problem it went on to argue more strongly than before that the cause was as much the general dollar shortage as the excess supply of sterling. Next, No. 2 Account blocking and general bilateralisation were rejected in the same passage as the dismissal of administering sterling like the rouble. To bilateralise rigidly and to impose an extensive block on surplus balances 'would be neither practical politics nor in the national interest'. The paper then went on to suggest a wide variety of less daunting possibilities, described as palliatives. These included: minimising releases from balances already blocked; resistance to demands for premiums on the price of non-dollar supplies; greater recognition of the need to mop up excess sterling through exports to non-dollar countries; more export licensing of shuntable commodities; a reduction in the number of transferable accounts; altering the working of monetary agreements so as to lay down that automatic transferability be confined to direct current transactions; and enlisting the help of American Customs to hold up imports of re-exported Sterling Area goods on grounds of 'exchange dumping'. This latter idea came from Bolton and the paper concluded by putting forward another from the same source. Might it be possible to relax controls between members of the Intra-European Payments Scheme while putting an end to automatic transferability between that area and other transferable countries?

The Treasury mulled this over for some weeks while political pressures grew. The Chancellor was showing close interest. Parliamentary Questions on the subject were beginning to emerge and press comment continued. Some Commonwealth Prime Ministers, notably Chifley of Australia, had raised the matter during a recent conference in London. Meanwhile, Bolton had descended on Amsterdam late in March and threatened the President of the Netherlands Bank, Dr Marius Holtrop,[39] with the expulsion of his country from the Transferable Account Area. It was later agreed that the 750 Dutch transferable accounts should be reduced to about seventy and confined to authorised banks who would be instructed not to facilitate cheap-sterling business. It was also agreed that transferability should be used only for direct current transactions. But the Dutch qualified their agreement by stating they were not prepared to take unilateral action that would damage Dutch carrying and merchanting trade or cause existing trade to be transferred to other countries. The Netherlands Bank added that there was a political limit beyond which they dare not go and once this limit was passed the Dutch Government might find themselves supporting 'non-cooperative trading elements' in self-defence. Finally, the Bank's undercover operations confirmed all the other evidence. Ellerton wrote from New York: 'Up to the present we have demonstrated, unfortunately only too clearly, that we can deal here in various types of pounds up to very large amounts practically on the telephone. I have not operated quite as I intended for two reasons. Firstly, because we have proved a big market exists, there was no point in operating just for the sake of operating. Secondly, you will have understood that we have had to operate with the greatest care and caution for obvious reasons and we have had to disguise our operations in the most roundabout manner which is all most delicate, etc. But a free buyer could have operated quite easily in the shortest possible time.'

The Treasury did not greatly dissent from the views put forward by the Bank. But it did not fully accept that import-diversion in favour of non-dollar supplies should be reduced or abandoned or that the dollar export

---

[39] *Holtrop, Marius Wilhelm* (1902–88). Educated Amsterdam University. Vice-President, Shell Chemicals, San Francisco 1936–9, Managing Director, Royal Dutch Blast Furnaces and Steel Works, Ijmuiden 1939–46, President, Netherlands Bank 1946–67, Director, BIS 1946–67, President 1958–67, Alternate Governor, IMF 1947–52, Governor 1952–7.

drive should be weakened by special efforts to mop up excess sterling. Nor did the Treasury accept Bolton's ideas. Approaching the US Treasury for special help from the US Customs would simply provoke further discussions of the exchange rate (the American campaign for the devaluation of sterling and other West European currencies had already begun). As to relaxations of exchange control in a new European Account Area, the Treasury wanted to hear a lot more before expressing any view. Meantime the Bank had developed its ideas for additional export licensing in the Sterling Area and sent them to Whitehall. The whole subject was then discussed with the Treasury and the Board of Trade. After noting the action already taken on the financial side and recording that steps were being put in hand to reduce the number of transferable accounts, the officials discussed export licensing, which the Board of Trade was invited to examine with a view to formulating proposals for discussion with Australia and other Sterling Area countries. This two-pronged approach, combining financial and trade measures, was then put to Ministers and accepted by them. It was to remain the official policy on cheap sterling over the next three years and was at times pursued with a vigour that took UK Customs into an unfamiliar environment. The Treasury took overall command of its pursuit. It may be supposed that the Governor was content with this outcome. Drastic measures of exchange control had been discarded and some of the burden of containing cheap sterling had been shifted on to the Board of Trade. Strategic options remained open.

At about this point in the story, when the main lines of policy were being determined in London, a note was being written by a Mr J. G. Ribon in La Paz, Bolivia. It was entitled 'Sterling etc.' and three months later a copy was handed to Discount Office. Unusually and chillingly, it referred to the shunting of British manufactures; and as an engagingly frank example of the many pieces of evidence that accumulated in the Bank at this time, it deserves quotation:

> I received the visit of Mr Adolf L. Schrijver, of Albert de Jong & Co., 37 Wall Street, New York 5, NY.
>
> This firm specializes in foreign exchanges and foreign bonds and shares.
>
> Mr Schrijver mentioned to me that if we buy any appreciable amount of machinery and supplies in England, these can be obtained more cheaply by the following procedure:
>
> (a) Buy French sterling in New York at about $US3·25 per £.
> (b) Arrange with a French firm, for a small commission to buy the merchandise and have it shipped to some French port where it can be trans-shipped to destination. This merchandise remains 'in bond' or 'in transit' and does not pay duties in France.

This procedure is common practice and many agents specialize in this business, which is all arranged with the necessary licenses from the Bank of France and French Exchange Control. In this way purchases in England can be obtained for 15%–20% less than the cost if bought directly with American sterling (or dollars).

The firm of Albert de Jong is only interested in the foreign currency part of such business.

He mentioned that care should be taken to avoid buying by this method similar machinery and merchandise to that which can be obtained in France as this would arouse the suspicion of the Bank of England.

Mr Schrijver told me many other amazing details of what is being done in free and black markets on exchanges and buying and selling of commodities all over the world.

During the summer of 1949, as devaluation approached, cheap-sterling operations reached a climax. In the middle of June, H. J. Isner of Ullman & Co. came in to say that the scale of business in New York was very much larger than the British authorities seemed to think. Normal channels of information did not give a true picture. The inflow of European refugees into America during the war had established a new set of arbitrage operators in New York who had ample facilities, had made a lot of money during the war out of American exports, and were, in consequence, able to operate without bank assistance. They had long-established contacts all over Europe and Isner estimated that at least one-third of Sterling Area goods reaching America were paid for in cheap sterling. In Isner's view the root cause of the trouble was the amount of blocked sterling that had been released and the amount the UK paid abroad in premium prices for non-dollar goods. He further developed this case in a letter to Hamilton early in July, enclosing a copy of a letter from a New York contact who stated that many of the big banks had now entered the business either directly or through brokers. Guaranty,[40] Chase, City, and 'many others' were cited, as were several large brokerage houses including White Weld, Haydn-Stone, and Sutro. The flavour of this letter can be judged from the following extract: 'We have acquired one very powerful source (of transferable sterling), through the medium of Irving Trust, a Near East firm which is also established in Milan and here, and which is supplying large amounts of transferable pounds of Norwegian origin which can be transferred to Russian and other accounts.'

Another route through the jungle was meantime being explored by HM Customs. They were investigating irregularities in the export of rubber,

---

[40] But Mr S. D. Post, a Vice-President at their Head Office, wrote to London on 23 August: 'As far as we know, none of the larger banks in New York are handling any of these transactions at the present time, but some of the larger brokerage houses are, to say nothing of a multitude of smaller brokers.'

pepper, silver, and iridium, nominally consigned to China but actually going to the US for payment in Chinese sterling. The American firms concerned, among them the American Nile Corporation, appeared to maintain agents in Shanghai who ordered the goods and probably arranged the financing. Customs therefore asked the British Consul-General for information about several of the alleged consignees, namely David J. Gahtan, Moise Shammah, Sassoon S. Reuben, and the Hong Kong and Shanghai Trading Corporation. The Consul replied on 2 September. He had identified the named individuals, or their firms, together with some of their manifold international connections, but he could produce no evidence of irregularities. He concluded: 'I could make further enquiries from Iraqis, etc., with whom I am on friendly terms, but business and family ramifications of these kinds of people are so interrelated that to do so might merely result in disclosing your suspicions. I await your instructions.'

The Bank had not exaggerated when it had said that cheap-sterling business constituted a threat to the whole basis of exchange control. That business had now become something of an open scandal. Walter Fletcher, a Conservative MP, asked a series of Parliamentary Questions, to which the Chancellor could give no effective answer. Later, the authorities developed a hope that devaluation itself would greatly reduce the scale of the business. Speculative dumping of sterling would cease, the argument ran, and the free market rates for sterling would come much closer to the official rate so that the profitability of shunting would be cut. In the rather longer run, the general devaluation of European currencies would help ease the dollar shortage and reduce the scope for selling dollar goods at premium prices. These arguments were not without foundation, but they did not prove strong enough or quick-acting enough to prevent the problem from recurring in the autumn and winter of 1949. At this point, the UK authorities were particularly sensitive to anything that might reduce confidence in the new official rate of $2·80 to the pound; and it was this aspect of the matter that drove them to yet another, and this time final, review of policy and subsequently to further pursuit of the two-pronged approach agreed in the preceding spring.

On 4 October 1949, Henry Grunfeld of S. G. Warburg & Company called on the Bank with depressing talk that the Dutch and French were restarting cheap-sterling operations at $2·65 to the pound and the Italians at $2·50. Later in the month Siegmund Warburg himself called on Siepmann, but without anything that his host felt worth reporting. Warburg then had lunch with the Chancellor of the Exchequer and reportedly suggested that a small informal committee of bankers, merchants, and Government officials should be formed to help combat the cheap-sterling problem. Early in November he saw Stevenson[41] in the Treasury and said that the Bank was not fully in the picture. He suggested that a small group of bankers might call weekly on someone in authority, with all the latest information. A week earlier, the *Financial Times* had argued that the irresolute economic policy following devaluation had encouraged the re-emergence of cheap sterling and cast doubt on the new parity. The same paper reported in a mid-November feature article that the situation had deteriorated, that transferable sterling in New York was quoted at around $2·60, and that commodity shunting was restarting. Parliamentary Questions re-emerged. For its part the Bank had little firm evidence on the supposed renewal of commodity shunting and surmised that the new cheap-sterling operations were mainly associated with payment for invisibles.

In view of the strength of press reporting and the views expressed to them by a merchant banker, Treasury officials became distinctly restless. Warburg was, however, crossing wires. Kenneth Peppiatt[42] intervened to say so. The Bank then successfully resisted the idea of a special City group and obtained the Treasury's assent that in future the Bank should be the 'someone in authority' to whom information should be imparted by City sources. In December Warburg saw O'Brien. But he had in fact no hard evidence to report and was at some pains to soft-pedal his suggestion of an informal city group on cheap sterling (by his account of the lunch with Cripps, the group was to discuss the fundamentals of the economic and financial situation of which cheap sterling was nothing but a symptom). Although at this time the restlessness of the Treasury, in which the Warburg incident played a part, was mainly due to fears about confidence in the new parity, it was also due to friction with the Bank. The passage between Bolton and Playfair in November 1949 (over the formulation of policy on intra-European payments) has already been noted. This coincided with another ruction when the Chancellor suddenly announced that rewards would be paid to informers on exchange control offenders. Playfair had failed to consult Siepmann and the Bank had not been warned at any level. The Governor protested and the Permanent Secretary was obliged to write a letter of apology. Treasury officials, not themselves very

---

[41] *Stevenson, Matthew, KCB (1910–81)*. Assistant Secretary H.M. Treasury 1948–55, Under-Secretary, 1955–61, Permanent Secretary, Ministry of Power, 1965–6; Ministry of Housing and Local Government, 1966–70. Deputy Chairman, Mersey Docks and Harbour Board 1970–1.

[42] *Peppiatt, Kenneth Oswald, KBE, MC (1893–1983)*. Educated Bancroft's. Entered Bank 1911. Army 1914–18. Principal of Discount Office 1928–34, Chief Cashier 1934–49, Executive Director 1949–57. Director, Coutts and Co. 1958–69.

expert in exchange control but under strong Ministerial pressure, suspected with some justification that the Bank lacked enthusiasm for a further offensive against cheap sterling. But since the Treasury relied on the Bank for most of its information, Warburg was pushing at an open door. Stevenson went so far as to make two different reports of his interview with him: one was copied to the Bank and contained no criticism of that institution; the other was confined to the Treasury and reported Warburg hinting that the Bank was not grateful for information about cheap sterling nor indeed active in obtaining such information. Brittain then considered the idea of a City group that would meet with the Treasury and the Bank jointly. But officials turned it down, partly because the Bank was good at stifling discussion at tripartite meetings of that sort and partly because they now had confidence that O'Brien, recently appointed to the task, would provide effective liaison on cheap sterling between the City, the Bank, and the Treasury.

Meanwhile, towards the end of November, the Governor had gone to the US for informal talks with bankers and officials in New York and Washington. He found himself at the centre of complaint and interrogation from bankers about the poor condition of sterling and in particular about the resurgence of cheap sterling. He telephoned London for reinforcements and was joined by O'Brien on 30 November. In the meantime he cabled his Deputy saying that cheap sterling was damaging UK credit out of all proportion to the business done and that there was risk of another adverse confidence movement developing if matters were allowed to drift. He therefore wanted to consider with experts in the Federal Reserve Bank of New York whether some 'intervention and interference' might be advisable, even at some cost in dollars; and he requested that the Treasury be asked whether they might give him a free hand to arrange some experimental intervention. In his reply the Deputy Governor expressed the misgivings of senior officials in the Bank. Turnover in the New York market might not be very large, but if the rate there for transferable sterling were pushed up by intervention there would be further offerings by arbitrage from the various other free markets. Moreover, if underlying confidence was weak, a rate near parity might anyway simply provoke speculative sales. Assuming the Governor had a temporary demonstration in mind and not a continuing policy of intervention, a subsequent set-back might do more harm than the demonstration had done good.

In the Treasury, Wilson Smith was inclined to accept the Governor's suggestion. But the Chancellor refused to be rushed. He had hoped to get through to the end of December without too much trouble and rely on the end-year reserves announcement, which would benefit from the post-

Dallas Bernard, Deputy Governor 1949–1954

devaluation reflux, to bolster confidence. Besides he could not afford intervention on any large scale, nor any adverse publicity. He therefore asked the Governor to discuss the situation with Franks and Rowan[43] in Washington, after which all three would be able to advise him. After alerting Barclays Bank in New York to the possibility of a second experiment, the Governor then travelled to Washington. From there he sent a further cable to the Bank proposing that the policy agreed in May should be energetically pursued but should now be accompanied by intervention designed to keep the transferable sterling rate between $2·60 and $2·70. But on this occasion the team in Threadneedle Street stood their ground. They told him that the problem could be solved neither by control nor by intervention. 'We have gravest doubts', they cabled, 'as to

[43] *Rowan, Thomas Leslie, KCB (1908–72).* Educated Tonbridge and Queen's College, Cambridge. Colonial Office 1930–3, HM Treasury 1933–47, Assistant, later Principal Private Secretary to Prime Ministers 1941–7, Permanent Secretary, Office of Minister for Economic Affairs 1947, Second Secretary, HM Treasury 1947–9, Economic Minister, Washington 1949–51, Second Secretary, Head of Overseas Finance Division, HM Treasury 1951–8, Alternate, Board of Governors, IBRD and IFC 1957. Managing Director, Vickers 1962–7, Chairman 1967–71.

the wisdom of a demonstration. With the fundamental situation against us there is the possibility of being forced into permanent intervention, thus giving convertibility to those elements which least deserve it while taking the first step towards a fluctuating rate policy.' With courage, O'Brien strongly supported this in a note written to the Governor in Washington on 6 December: 'If we raise the rate substantially and continuously, a far greater volume of business than is now taking place is likely. How long could we stand a net drain of $2 million a week and how long would it remain so small particularly as it would surely be impossible to keep our action secret for long? It does not matter who does or does not deserve convertibility, the fact would be that anyone could have it for the asking. Could we possibly resist American pressure for formal convertibility in these circumstances?' He concluded: 'The more I think of this problem the more I believe that our people at home are right. It is incapable of solution by technical measures. Political decisions are necessary, which means that somehow or other the volume of sterling must be drastically reduced.'

Against this opposition Cobbold backed away from intervention, although transferable sterling stood at $2·50. Writing to Cripps from New York on 10 December, he reiterated his great concern about cheap sterling, which he had discussed with Franks, Rowan, and the Federal Reserve. But he confessed that he found solutions very difficult and concluded that he would take up the subject immediately he returned. The urgency had anyway been reduced by a change in the attitude of the New York bankers. Earlier in his visit the Foreign Exchange Committee, a liaison group between the New York banks and the Federal Reserve, had made representations about the cheap-sterling market and had made known their increasing reluctance to keep out of it themselves. O'Brien had accordingly been asked to call on the members of the Committee, to listen to their ideas and complaints, to explain the policy of the British authorities, and to ask them for their continued cooperation. He did this most successfully, the Chairman of the Committee telling him that 'the explosive frame of mind in which the banks were a fortnight ago has entirely evaporated'.

Before Cobbold returned to London, the Treasury and the Bank had conducted a fresh assault on the authorities in Amsterdam. The Dutch again accepted that the number of transferable accounts should be reduced to about seventy, undertook to adopt regulations preventing the sale of Dutch sterling in New York, and agreed in general that they would only re-export Sterling Area goods against payment in sterling. They also said that they would endeavour to ensure that sterling payments were in practice confined to direct current transactions; but they pointed out that their Customs did not take note, for exchange control purposes, of the country of origin of imports. As the Treasury commented: 'The efficacy of these arrangements will depend upon the Dutch authorities being able and willing to exert over their banking and merchanting community a degree of control which is not customary there.' Early in 1950 the Dutch Cabinet refused to accept the 'sterling for sterling' undertaking where it would prevent the on-sale of Sterling Area goods in Europe against payment in, for example, Deutschmarks. This left open another range of loopholes.

In the latter part of December the whole problem was again reviewed in the Bank. Thompson-McCausland circulated another paper, in which he came to much the same conclusions as he had done earlier in the year when he had contributed to the two-pronged policy accepted by Ministers in May. He complained once more that external monetary policy lacked coherence. The authorities were chasing their own tails. One arm of policy was attempting to operate an international but inconvertible currency; another was pursuing other objectives and allowing liberal releases of No. 2 Account sterling; another was fighting the dollar shortage with such zeal as to increase the supply of unwanted sterling in the non-dollar world; and yet another was trying to stop the resulting aggravation of the cheap-sterling problem by restrictions and requests that only made sterling less wanted and less usable as an international currency. He was strongly supported by Fisher and O'Brien. Nor had Siepmann changed his mind: 'Radical measures do not exist within the present structure of exchange control and nothing better than harassing tactics are available.' He was prepared to consider a limited amount of special aggressive action involving isolated blockings, black-listing, and sporadic intervention intended to unsettle the free markets. In a note dated 16 December, he delivered the last word on the whole subject:

> The organisation of business in cheap sterling is extremely widespread, detailed, intricate and varied, with the result that we can never hope to measure the extent of it. We see a selection of unrepresentative samples which happen to come our way, and they often astonish us because there is no general type of pattern. Wool, tin, rubber, spices or any other raw material of Sterling Area origin can form the basis. Shipment may be to any one of a great number of intermediate destinations. The ultimate outcome may be almost any sort of luxury export to a country which is short of dollars. The technique will vary according to the facilities offered in a wide choice of markets – Tangier and Beirut, Zurich and Amsterdam, with Paris as a co-ordinator. The degree to which laws and regulations have to be evaded or broken may vary from one extreme to the other. The boldness with which they are flouted is certainly increasing. Firms have been established in Genoa for the express purpose of organising this business and

nothing else. A number of American intermediaries are setting up on the Continent in order to specialise in it; and at least one American shipping company, interested in the freights, is lending the services of its ships' captains for the purpose of destroying or substituting documents. All this can and does go on without the help of any official connivance on the part of the exchange control authorities in most of the countries concerned. The Dutch merchants are as active as any, but the Netherlands Bank is fully as cooperative as we could expect.

The Governor reflected on this advice and on 2 January 1950 he issued his own conclusions. He had moved forward since the review of policy in the spring of 1949. He now saw that the only ultimate remedy was a general policy that would reduce excess sterling abroad, enforce appropriate fiscal and monetary policies at home, and permit a gradual move towards convertibility. But progress along these lines was unlikely to be made before the General Election (or, in fact, after it). In the interim he favoured some resort to the harassing tactics suggested by Siepmann, and he agreed that resort to any general No. 2 Account blocking or to intervention in the cheap-sterling markets constituted 'pretty desperate remedies and should be deferred until we see what we can do on other lines'. These conclusions were put to the Treasury by Bolton[44] on the same day and also to Bridges by the Governor. There was general agreement and an improvement in relationships. Shortly afterwards there was set up an informal Liaison Committee on cheap sterling, on which HM Customs were represented as well as the Treasury and the Bank. It met alternately in Great George Street and Threadneedle Street, with Stevenson chairing for the Treasury and O'Brien for the Bank. On 17 January the Governor wrote to Sproul outlining the policy that had been adopted and the arguments that lay behind it. Sproul replied on 30 January, advising against blacklisting or blocking of the accounts of individual firms where the evidence would not have stood up in Court. He otherwise accepted the general thrust of British policy towards 'a pocketful of fish hooks'. The only complete remedy lay in full convertibility; and he felt, wrongly as it turned out, that some Anglo-American package might be devised that would settle the problem of the sterling balances and allow convertibility to be restored.

Following the establishment of the Cheap Sterling Committee early in 1950 consideration was duly given to exemplary blocking. Private Chinese

[44] After the crisis of 1947 Siepmann seems to have given up representing the Bank in Whitehall. He was not popular in the Treasury; and although he had made the running in the Bank on this later occasion, it was Bolton who argued the policy 'at the other end of Town'. He too had his ups and downs in that quarter, but his engagingly pugilistic personality stood him in good stead and he was seldom down for long.

balances were indeed blocked, but specifically in the context of the communist take-over.[45] Next, Syrian and Lebanese sterling were examined, both countries having left the French Monetary Area, but no action was taken. The Treasury accepted Bank advice that freezing such balances would alarm the holders of sterling in the Gulf states, with resulting damage to a part of the Sterling Area that was growing in importance. Consideration was also given to blacklisting. One or two of the American banks in London were scrutinised with a view to withdrawal of authorised status, but again, possibly with Sproul's advice in mind, no action ensued. Nor were any steps taken against the several American brokerage houses who were known to be active in the New York market for cheap sterling. However, the Dutch firm of Fuhrmann & Company, thought to be prominent in the shunting of wool, was blacklisted by Exchange Control and their London office was given a vigorous diet of bureaucratic obstruction. In the meantime, HM Customs constructed a new form, the CD5, to be completed by exporters of goods destined for known centres of shunting activity. The exporter would be required to declare that the consignee was innocent of all shunting intent. The Board of Trade opposed this idea as inimical to exports and re-exports, for it would hamper the conscientious but let through those less scrupulous with their signatures. The CD5 does not seem to have been put to much use.

Rather more interesting was an expedition by Customs to Genoa, where the shunting of wool was believed to be particularly rife. They readily established that transhipment was a simple matter; but the Italian investigatory authorities refused to let them visit some twenty Milan

[45] Action was also taken at about this time to restrict the use of private sterling balances held by residents of Hong Kong. The Colony was nominally a member of the Sterling Area; but as a financial and trading centre in the Far East, with a flourishing entrepôt trade rebuilt since liberation from Japanese occupation in 1945, it had at first little or no effective exchange control. A free market in currencies had been allowed to grow up and flourish. In 1948, in order to stop the Colony being used as a route for the export of capital from the Sterling Area and as a centre where sterling could be acquired cheaply by non-residents, a local control had been imposed on all sterling transfers exceeding £500 to or from the rest of the Area. At the same time the authorities undertook to ensure that the full proceeds of Sterling Area goods re-exported from the Colony were surrendered at official rates. Local exchange control was, however, not fully effective, and the position became further complicated during 1949 by the flight of capital into Hong Kong from the Chinese mainland, caused by the Communist advance. There was a risk that the sterling balances of Hong Kong residents, freely available for use on the free market, would be sharply increased. One way this could happen would be through the direct conversion into sterling of the Hong Kong dollar notes that circulated widely in South China. In this situation, and bearing in mind that too unregulated a state of affairs in Hong Kong would weaken the British position in negotiations on cheap sterling with, for example, the Dutch, it was decided to segregate into No. 2 Accounts all Hong Kong sterling that was not held by authorised banks. Use of the No. 2 Sterling would be closely controlled from London. This measure was agreed in February 1950 and put into effect in June.

trading firms named in UK export declarations. HM Consul in that city subsequently wrote of some of these: 'I doubt if there is an honest trader in the building.' Throughout the period 1950–2 the Italian authorities were generally unco-operative. They took the view that it was up to the British to prevent sterling getting into undesirable hands and not up to themselves to restrict what was done with it when it arrived at such destinations; and anyway the British themselves refused, on valid grounds of banking confidentiality, to disclose to the Italian exchange control any details of the sterling holdings of private Italian residents.

The enquiry by Customs into Italian dealings in cheap sterling was paralleled by a Bank enquiry into the mysterious activities of the French.[46] How was it that French No. 1 Account sterling, confined to the accounts of French banks with London banks, could find its way onto the markets in New York and Zurich? An approach was made at Governor level to the Bank of France, and with the agreement of the Treasury a small group of Bank officials visited Paris at the end of January 1950. The central bank was concerned only with the routine mechanics. Exchange control was in practice administered by an agency of the Ministry of Finance, the Office des Changes. The visitors were well received at this latter institution, but they could detect no obvious loophole through which cheap sterling operations could be conducted. The mystery remained, though later in the year HM Customs unearthed a complicated series of transactions involving the export of gold to Egypt, at a free market price, for payment in Egyptian currency. This could be sold to a French bank (the French were short of Egyptian pounds) against No. 1 Account sterling at the disposal of the seller, who could in turn exchange it for dollars in New York or Zurich through the usual cheap-sterling channels.

And so it all went on. In February 1950 Siepmann found himself signing a long letter to Mr Ebtehaj, the Governor of the Iranian central bank, asking him to do what he could to prevent the shunting of Iranian opium to the US through initial sale to an intermediary who paid in transferable sterling obtained from the New York market. A little later he was advising that the problem of dual bills of lading (including 'optional' bills of lading, for ready use when switching destinations) might best be tackled by direct discussion with the principal shipping conferences. Such discussions duly

---

[46] It was an occasion for renewed friction with the Treasury. Playfair thought he had Bolton's assurance that one of the Treasury representatives in Paris would be kept fully informed and would accompany Bank officials to the Office des Changes. Nothing of the sort happened. Instead, Bolton waited for a full report from the Bank officials concerned before himself reporting to the Treasury that there was nothing to be followed up. Playfair had not been pleased. On learning that the Treasury's people in Paris knew nothing of the Bank's visit, he wrote: 'This is worse than outrageous, it is downright stupid.'

took place, both in London and Singapore, with possibly some limited effect.

One of the repeated complaints about cheap-sterling operations was that they diverted trade from normal channels and damaged the business of London merchants. As 'residents' for exchange control purposes, these merchants were either forbidden to participate in such operations or advised by the UK authorities not to facilitate their practice by non-residents. But such prohibitions or persuasions were not always easy to enforce. London diamond merchants, for example, habitually re-exported diamonds to continental destinations without knowledge of their ultimate destination. However, in September 1948 Customs seized three parcels of diamonds consigned to Tangier for payment in Tangier sterling but intended for immediate on-shipment to the US. The exporters, Messrs I. Henning & Company Ltd, one of the largest diamond brokers in London, were subsequently prosecuted by Customs, on the alleged grounds that they knew full well that the diamonds were actually being bought by one of their principal clients in New York. Their bankers were Hambro's Bank, who were also one of their shareholders; and Sir Charles Hambro, a Director of the Bank of England as well as Managing Director of the family bank, gave evidence for the defence. Sir Walter Monckton, no less, was defending Counsel. In December 1949 Customs won their case in the Magistrates' Court. Heavy fines were imposed and two individual defendants were given prison sentences. But on Appeal, heard in March 1950, they were exonerated of any intent to defraud. The prison sentences were quashed, the fines drastically reduced, and the diamonds ordered to be released. Customs in turn appealed, but without much success: all they got was the return of the diamonds to custody. The entire case took over eighteen months from initial seizure of the diamonds and its outcome can have given little encouragement to the authorities.

However in the summer of 1950 the clouds began to lift. The rate for transferable sterling in New York rose steadily and reached $2·70 early in June. At that level, though cheap sterling could still be used to pay for invisibles, commodity shunting was scarcely profitable. On the broader plane, the devaluations of the preceding autumn were taking effect. On a narrower front, following the British *démarche* of December 1949, the number of Dutch transferable accounts had at last been drastically reduced and the Dutch authorities appeared to have secured some restraint on the commodity shunting of sterling goods by their merchants and traders. In the latter half of 1950 the balance of payments of the entire Sterling Area greatly improved as a result of the 'Korean' commodity boom. Sterling at last enjoyed a fleeting period of scarcity and by early 1951 the balance of speculative opinion had swung right round. Upward revaluation, or even appreciation of a floating rate for sterling, were for a few months a feature of market expectations; and the rate for transferable sterling came close to the official parity.

As a result of these developments the Treasury slowly became less keen on the hot pursuit of operators in cheap sterling and more inclined to favour the opposite policy of exchange control relaxations that might usefully accompany the liberalisation of intra-European trade. With the precipitate fall in its Parliamentary strength the Government proved less keen to impose new controls. Though advised to the contrary by the Bank, it decided in the autumn of 1950 not to seek an amendment of the Act which would have brought payment for invisible exports under exchange control. Thus the work of the Cheap Sterling Committee fell away and in November the Bank was sufficiently sure of itself to circulate a long 'Empire Letter'[47] on the whole subject of cheap sterling. Its concluding paragraphs began: 'To sum up, we can say that the acute anxieties which beset us in the first nine months of 1949 and again at the end of that year no longer exist; and we can now see current cheap-sterling activities in a better perspective, i.e., as a small, albeit irritating, fraction of the sterling area's expanding trade and payments on a regular basis.' It was possible for adverse circumstances to recur. Some further action, especially against specific offenders, could not be excluded. 'But the broad picture before us now shows the main flow of our trade and payments moving through regular channels between embankments which are materially stronger than they were a year ago.'

Ten months later, in August 1951, the clouds came down again. In one of his regular letters from New York, Werner Knoke noted that transferable sterling had fallen from $2·59 to $2·55. A month later it was quoted at $2·53 and by 9 October had fallen to $2·42$\frac{1}{2}$ (a discount of over 13%). It fell to $2·39 just before the General Election at the end of the month but rose to $2·42 immediately afterwards. 'Churchill faces sterling problem', declared a headline in the *New York Times*. By January 1952 Exchange Control were reporting to Siepmann, Bolton, and Beale that cheap-sterling activity was now probably on a greater scale than at any time since the autumn of 1949. There was an urgent need for at least the appearance of further action; otherwise the situation would get out of hand and the co-operation of foreign and Sterling Area controls would crumble.

The evidence was indeed mounting. The Dutch seemed to be sinning again and yet another expedition to The Hague in December, led by the

---

[47] It was sent to the central banks of Australia, New Zealand, South Africa, Canada, India, Pakistan, Ceylon, and Southern Rhodesia.

Treasury, achieved little or nothing. The Italians were licensing the import of dollar goods shunted through Europe against payment in sterling. Increased activity in 'resident sterling' in New York suggested that some entirely new loophole had been opened in the Sterling Area, perhaps in the Gulf or in Nigeria. An MP submitted evidence that British goods were being consigned to the tiny colony of British Honduras for payment in sterling and being off-loaded in New York. Spanish exporters of textiles for payment in sterling were selling the proceeds in Zurich or Tangier to finance imports of US cotton. There was now Japanese sterling and Peruvian sterling to add to the already numerous varieties. One enterprising spirit in North America even tried to shunt thoroughbred horses from Norfolk to the US through Rotterdam, but was foiled by the exporter and his bank, who insisted on payment in American account sterling. Exchange Control could do no more than suggest another round of harassment, punitive measures against Holland, and the 'invisibles' amendment of the Exchange Control Act. However, at a higher level the Bank was no longer interested in such things. For the time had come for fundamental solutions and the only real remedy.

In mid-September 1951 the Governor asked that the merits of market intervention be re-examined. Nobody was enthusiastic. Only Siepmann was prepared to try it, but from a position of such nihilism as to make the policy unsaleable. 'I am against intervention', he wrote, 'just as I am against exchange control, for two reasons: it ought not to be necessary and it is almost impossible to manage with success.' Intervention to achieve parity with the official rate would amount to convertibility and would court defeat. Intervention to establish a fixed discount below par would be open to 'theoretical objections' and to tactical manoeuvres. Isolated raids would serve no good purpose. Therefore he propounded a policy of continuous intervention, without any declared objective beyond confusion of the enemy. 'Intervention', he remarked with an experienced cynicism, 'is never so effective as when it proceeds from no explicit or intelligible principle, so that the market is always uncertain of what to expect.' The Governor pondered over this cryptic message and replied that he would have another look at the subject at the end of October, after the General Election. On 31 October he received a long note from Thompson-McCausland, which this time began with a frontal attack on inconvertibility itself. The development of free markets since 1947 were 'a new fact outside the assumptions on which we worked in 1945–7'. Attempts to restrict the use of sterling in those markets had not succeeded in re-establishing inconvertibility and had had damaging consequences for sterling, for UK traders and merchants, and for the viability of exchange control. 'We have thus reached a point where we must recognise that inconvertibility is no longer possible for sterling in non-resident hands. A choice must be made between (a) making sterling a domestic currency with little or no international use and (b) retaining sterling as an international currency (and this country as a centre of international trade and commodity markets) – which means accepting convertibility for non-resident sterling.' This view was supported by Bolton and by the Governor. Indeed, some two years previously, they had acknowledged that convertibility was the only true remedy. But now – with another external emergency, another outburst of commodity shunting, and a new Government – the hour might have arrived. The change to convertibility would of course require the support of stronger domestic policies, but these were required in any event. When Maurice Parsons,[48] O'Brien's successor in Overseas,[49] forwarded the proposals of Exchange Control to Siepmann and the Governor on 4 February 1952, he remarked: 'If they [external holders of sterling] once begin to suspect that this Government, like the last, does not really mean business, I think we might find that the flood of cheap sterling which would then break loose might make the present state of affairs look like a mere trickle...When you ask me, therefore, for a practical conclusion on cheap sterling I must reply that the only place where you can usefully look for your answer is the Budget and the level of Bank Rate!'

By writing as he did, Parsons was expressing a view held by many people in Whitehall and Threadneedle Street at that moment. But to emphasise the importance of external confidence, together with imperatives of domestic policy, did not necessarily imply support for some early plunge into external convertibility. Nor did the cheap-sterling story amount to so conclusive an argument as to point inexorably in that direction. It was quite possible to hold, as indeed had the 'Empire Letter' a year before, that inconvertibility could be maintained more or less indefinitely, without unacceptable avoidance through the free markets, provided adequate support was forthcoming from domestic policy and provided the supply of sterling abroad was not rendered excessive by over-liberal credits or undue releases of No. 2 balances. Admittedly cheap-sterling operations became

---

[48] *Parsons, Maurice Henry*, KCMG (1910–78). Educated University College School. Entered Bank 1928, Private Secretary to the Governors 1939–43, UK Alternate Executive Director, IMF 1946–7, IBRD 1947, Director of Operations, IMF 1947–50, Deputy Chief Cashier 1950–5, Assistant to the Governors 1955–7, Executive Director 1957–66, UK Alternate Governor, IMF 1957–66, Deputy Governor 1966–70. Chairman, Bank of London and South America 1970.

[49] O'Brien had been appointed Deputy Chief Cashier on the home side shortly before the revival of monetary policy in November 1951.

intolerably large in a period of external deficit; but the solution was to correct the deficit, which was necessary in any case. There was no need to restore convertibility unless this was indicated for other reasons.

Yet in another way the cheap-sterling argument for early convertibility was unanswerable. For a start, the UK was indeed internationally committed to the restoration of convertibility in the not too distant future and was already under pressure in Europe to take steps to reduce the manifold but rickety restrictions on sterling transferability. Furthermore, these restrictions undeniably obstructed an objective of Treasury policy, the development of sterling as an international currency. Nobody had decided that sterling should, after all, be managed like the rouble. Quite apart from the damage done to the repute of exchange control and to the British trading community, the whole stance of policy against cheap sterling therefore pointed in the opposite direction to the declared external monetary strategy of the UK. This could conceivably be tolerated a bit longer if a sustained external recovery could confidently be foreseen, with restrictions being steadily dismantled as adherence to Article VIII of the IMF approached. But in the winter of 1951–2 this could not have seemed a realistic prospect to most of those at the top of the Bank who had survived the difficult years since signature of the Loan Agreement in December 1945. Instead they had to contemplate oscillations between external balance and deficit, with parallel oscillations in external confidence and a continuing exposed banking situation. On all the current evidence, exchange control over the current transactions of non-residents was being reduced to a degrading farce, wholly inconsistent with the desired international status of sterling and wholly offensive to a Bank deeply committed to accuracy and efficiency of administration. If, into the bargain, in pursuit of the strategic objectives, controls had actually to be relaxed during periods of fair weather and remain relaxed in foul, there could only be one conclusion: *de jure* inconvertibility was fast becoming *de facto* convertibility, but in a messy and inglorious way. Whatever others might judge or argue, the operational manager of sterling had by now no real choice left. Cheap sterling and the associated breakdown of exchange control propelled the Bank towards recommending an early restoration of convertibility. The difficult question that remained was how best to reach that objective.

(d) THE STERLING BALANCES: 1947–1951

Early in September 1947 the Treasury prepared a series of policy papers for Ministers in the immediate aftermath of the convertibility crisis. One of these was entitled 'Overseas Payments Problems' and its author was

Rowe-Dutton. He sketched out the main features of a trade and payments policy suited to conditions of inconvertibility, dollar famine, and low external reserves. Among the dangers that might wreck that policy were the amount of sterling balances that might still be drawn down and general overspending by the Sterling Area. Two years later, in a Cabinet paper on the sterling balances written in the aftermath of the second postwar sterling crisis, the Treasury was obliged to point out that the principal agreements on the wartime accumulations had not proved very effective. The segregation of official balances in the No. 2 Accounts had not achieved the desired results. Subsequent releases had been far greater than originally intended and although balances held by other members of the Sterling Area had risen in aggregate, the expenditure of releases from No. 2 Accounts had added to the external problems of the UK and exacerbated the problem of cheap sterling. So in this specific sense the problem of the sterling balances was unresolved. A substantial proportion of the wartime accumulation still remained and pressure for further over-generous releases was to be expected. The balances of India, Pakistan, and Egypt together still exceeded £1,000 million. Market opinion was in any case alert to the more general problem of the low level of UK reserves relative to external banking liabilities in sterling and apprehensive lest downward fluctuations in the latter should reduce the former to danger levels and provoke the speculative leads and lags that could precipitate a crisis. Excessive releases of No. 2 Account balances, especially if associated with the further growth of cheap-sterling operations, compounded these apprehensions. No wonder, then, that in the run-up to devaluation in 1949 and in his anxiety lest a new exchange rate should fall victim to an inadequate follow-through, the Governor urged the Treasury to reopen the special problem of the No. 2 Account balances with the American authorities and to seek their help in meeting the burden of apparently unavoidable releases.

The series of agreements reached in 1946 and 1947 – notably those with Argentina, Egypt, and India – had ensured that releases from segregated balances were contained within what the UK could safely accommodate at that time. But these agreements were either of very short duration or, in the case of Argentina, vulnerable to pressure for renegotiation following the suspension of convertibility. The first of the successor agreements was the twelve-month settlement reached with Egypt early in 1948 and described in an earlier chapter. The Egyptians had quietly threatened to demand payment in dollars for the local supplies and services provided to the British military forces present in their country under the Anglo-Egyptian Treaty of 1936. The reward was the release of

£33 million from the Egyptian No. 2 Account in 1948, over three times the sum originally offered, of which £7¼ million could be taken in US dollars, instead of the £2 million originally stated to be the most that could be afforded. The news of these generous terms broke just as a British mission was arriving in the Indian sub-continent to negotiate with India and Pakistan the successors to the interim agreement reached the previous August, on the eve of partition. Its arrival marked the beginning of a sequence of events extending over the next two years during which British policy was allowed to slip away into the ineffective state described by the Sterling Area Working Party in the autumn of 1949.

India and Pakistan

The mission to India and Pakistan was led by Jeremy Raisman, a much respected former officer of the Indian Civil Service and a former Finance Member of the Viceroy's Council. The Bank provided support in the person of Beale, whose technical skills were supplemented by a knowledge of India dating from two years spent as Secretary of the Reserve Bank before the war. Before he set out, Raisman had hoped to negotiate a comprehensive financial settlement with the two new Dominions, including agreement on the amounts they would pay to the UK for surplus British military stores and on the sums to be earmarked for the capitalisation of their sterling pension liabilities. However, the monetary partition of the sub-continent, including the share-out of official external assets, was being held up by the discord that had developed between Delhi and Karachi and took a further turn for the worse following the outbreak of hostilities in Kashmir. Accordingly Raisman found himself limited to negotiating, almost entirely with India, the terms of an extension until June of the interim agreement that expired at the end of January. Interim it may have been, easy to negotiate it was not. Although India's net loss of external reserves since the previous summer had in total not been out of line with estimates made when the first interim agreement had been negotiated, her net dollar expenditure had been more than double the $60 million indicated by Indian officials at that time. This had caused great anxiety in London and officials had made various attempts to find out why it was happening as well as to query the purpose of one or two specific transactions. Before this, the British authorities had sought to bring pressure to bear on Delhi to reduce dollar expenditure below the earlier estimate of $60 million; and, as related in an earlier chapter, a threat to impose a dollar ration unilaterally had been met with the retort that India would then be obliged to leave the Sterling Area. Renewed signs of interference by the former imperial power were therefore much resented. Indian Ministers and officials were grappling with a very difficult and disturbed internal situation[50] and had done their best, despite the need for food imports, to bring external expenditure under firm control.

The authorities in London were mindful of India's problems but since they could not contemplate another large and unpredictable demand for dollars, they pressed on the one hand for a detailed and continuing scrutiny of India's dollar import programme and on the other for an Indian drawing of dollars from the IMF. At the heart of the negotiations, though often unstated, remained India's membership of the Sterling Area. As an independent Dominion, India was prepared to agree some reasonable objective for her net dollar expenditure, along the same lines as might be agreed by Australia or by the UK herself. But there was a point beyond which India could not go. If asked to accept nothing but a token ration of dollars and if furthermore asked to submit to a degree of continuous surveillance of dollar outgoings by London, then it might be politically and financially better to leave the Area. Apart from the gold element in her statutory note cover, India had virtually no dollars of her own and no means at that time, as a member of the Sterling Area, of building up her own dollar reserve. The country therefore depended on London for dollars. If this source failed, India could do better by fending for herself outside the Area even though this might mean even greater immobilisation of the No. 2 Account balance. For the British authorities, the departure of India would have been a damaging blow to the standing and coherence of the Area and to the policy of maintaining close and friendly Indo-British relations. There was therefore a price the UK was prepared to pay for Indian membership, as well as a price so high that she could not agree to pay it without risking disaster to sterling. In the end, and after some trenchant telegraphic exchanges with Whitehall, Raisman was able to

---

[50] Beale wrote a long and worried letter to the Deputy Governor early in February. Many of the senior Indian officials concerned were due to retire or to move and adequate replacements would be difficult to find. This meant that the financial prospects for the second half of the year were gloomy and 'the sooner we get down to talking about them before all the people we know are dispersed and the second half-year is upon us the better'. As to the atmosphere in the capital, Beale wrote: 'Connaught Place is filled with refugee curbside dealers in all sorts of goods, either selling stuff they have managed to bring out with them or engaging in trades they are now entering as a means of livelihood. So long as the refugees remain in camps and in other overcrowded living conditions, generally with little money and nothing to do except talk about the atrocities which they have witnessed, the temperature will remain high and further disturbances must be expected unless Gandhi's peace efforts bear fruit – which is by no means certain.' Gandhi was murdered a few days after Beale's letter was written. The shock of his death helped to calm the communal strife he had been striving to cool.

agree a dollar ration of £10 million for the next half-year, instead of the £5 million with which he started. Alongside this there was a further general release of £18 million from India's No. 2 Account. For her part, India agreed to begin drawing from the IMF and also agreed on a monitoring procedure under which consultations would take place if her use of dollars looked to be going too fast for consistency with the £10 million ration. On his way home Raisman made an agreement with Pakistan that included a £6 million general release and a dollar ration of £3.3 million.

The succession of interim agreements was replaced in the summer of 1948 by three-year agreements negotiated in London with Ministers and officials from both the new Dominions. Preliminary soundings indicated that the Indians would press for a three-year agreement, with further releases from the No. 2 Account balance and some assurance of increased supplies of British capital equipment. It was also clear that they would continue to fight against the much disliked dollar ration. Early in June, in a Cabinet paper, the Chancellor advised against a three-year agreement, arguing that the UK could not afford the extra supplies of capital goods until 1952. He also pointed out that the balance on India's No. 1 Account had recovered sharply and now stood at £87 million. There would therefore be no need for any release in the year ending June 1949. Furthermore, India's net dollar deficit should be met by drawing on the IMF and borrowing from the IBRD. These ideas were tried out on the Indian and Pakistani delegations (led by their respective Finance Ministers) and were strongly resisted by the Indians, who made most of the sub-continental running. They argued for a three-year programme of releases, related to their new plans for capital development. During three weeks of Ministerial negotiations the British position steadily weakened, much to the dismay of Treasury officials. Eventually the Chancellor accepted a three-year agreement and the Indians settled for annual releases a good deal smaller than they had at first demanded. There was to be none in the first year in view of the large opening balance on the No. 1 Account, but if that balance fell below £55 million during the two subsequent years it could be topped up by a total of £40 million in each. India agreed to draw dollars from the IMF and the UK agreed to a dollar ration of £15 million in the first year, after which the situation would be reviewed. Agreement was also reached on the outstanding questions of military stores and pension liabilities. A comparable agreement was reached with Pakistan.

Although much more generous than the British had originally intended, the mid-1948 agreements were not far out of line with their two interim predecessors. For its part, the Bank made no demur. However, the agreements contained an additional understanding whereby the releases in the two later years could be anticipated in the first year if the No. 1 balance fell below £30 million. From the British standpoint, this proved a serious flaw. For in the summer of 1948, after the London agreement was signed, the Indians rashly relaxed their import controls on non-dollar goods. This was followed by a steep rise in imports. Despite Indian drawings of £17 million worth of dollars from the IMF, their No. 1 Account had fallen to £44 million by the end of the year and continued to drain away thereafter. Shortly after a British team had arrived in Delhi early in February 1949, for the regular consultations for which provision had been made in the mid-1948 agreement, the No. 1 balance had fallen to £31 million despite a further drawing of £6 million from the IMF. The Indians then indicated that they would have to anticipate the next year's release and would also need some bridging accommodation in dollars because their IMF drawings would shortly reach 25% of quota, after which a further application would be required. Neither the delegation in Delhi nor the Treasury in London were at first much perturbed by this, although Bolton did remind Wilson Smith that the Americans were likely to resist any idea that another Indian drawing on the Fund, above 25% of quota, should be regarded as automatic. As to anticipation of the next year's release, it seemed that much of India's additional imports were 'non-essentials', which Whitehall now considered the UK could supply without great difficulty. However, by early April the Indians were running out of the £40 million originally earmarked for the second year of the agreement and the Bank (as banker to the Reserve Bank of India) asked the Treasury whether the agreement would allow the second £40 million, earmarked for the third year, to be similarly anticipated. The affirmative reply was some days coming and on learning that all but £4 million of the first £40 million had gone, the Chief Cashier noted: 'Please make sure...that there is to be no breakdown in payments arrangements. We *must* be able to pay the cheques.'

Since the situation was running out of control, the Chancellor took advantage of Nehru's presence in London to propose a further round of discussions. The new Minister of Finance in Delhi, Dr Matthai, took some offence at this approach. Nonetheless he revoked all Open General Licences on soft-currency imports and argued for further releases from the No. 2 Account so as to finance the time-lag before these restrictions took effect. Talks took place in London during June 1949, while the Indians were exhausting the whole of the second £40 million and in Washington the Americans were opposing their application to draw a second $100 million from the IMF. The Treasury expressed grave disquiet at the 'spectacular' run-down of Indian balances and proposed that a very tough line be taken both on the dollar ration and on further releases. The burden on the UK was too great and had to be reduced. But in fresh understandings with the Indians, reached early in July, further releases of £50 million were agreed for 1949–50 and 1950–1 on top of the £80 million already 'anticipated'. In addition there was to be a special release of another £50 million to finance the time-lag. Finally, the hated dollar ration was discontinued. India attended a meeting of Commonwealth Finance Ministers during July and it was now considered impolitic to treat India differently to, say, Australia. The dollar ration went and best endeavours were substituted, though India's dollar deficit inclusive of the proposed Fund drawing was expected to remain at an annual rate of $100 million.

In effect, the Indians had used up in one year all the sterling resources that had been expected to last for three. This was treated as a bygone and releases were resumed at the enhanced rate of £50 million per annum with a transitional £50 million thrown in as well. British policy on the Indian balances, as agreed in mid-1948, had collapsed. To some extent this can be attributed to a lack of concern, in the Board of Trade rather than the Treasury, at the volume of 'unrequited'[51] UK exports to India. Then again, the provision for 'anticipations' in the mid-1948 agreement was a hostage to fortune. But at heart the collapse of policy reflected the fundamentals of Sterling Area membership. So long as India remained a member, and a friendly member whose continuing friendship was ardently sought, it was in the last resort impossible to deny it the banking facilities that went with that membership. In the absence of a long-term agreement the large No. 2 Account balance could not be made to behave as if it were funded debt; and if the Indians drew their No. 1 balance down below danger point, there was no practical alternative but to allow a further release from the No. 2 balance. The real brake on this process was the Indians' own need to husband their reserves rather than any British grip on those reserves.

Though becoming increasingly concerned about the wider problem of the sterling balances, the Bank had played no very active part in this particular episode. It had kept the Treasury informed about the fall in Indian reserves; it had participated in the negotiations between officials, though at a relatively junior level; and the Governor seems to have given moral support to Wilson Smith. But there is no evidence of his intervening directly with the Chancellor or other Ministers.

---

[51] Exports delivered in payment of overseas debt.

The Governor was however becoming heavily involved in the policy discussions, leading up to the devaluation of sterling in September; and in that context he was working on proposals that included a general solution to the problem of the balances, proposals described later in this chapter. Therefore on 15 July, when the negotiations were all but complete, Bolton simply pointed out to the Treasury what they presumably already knew, namely that Government policy on the Indian balances would increase pressure on sterling, make it the more difficult to convince the Americans that all necessary steps were being taken to put the UK's house in order, and fortify American critics who said that the British were encouraging exports to protected markets in the Sterling Area in preference to North America. The Governor then did intervene in support of Bolton, expressing his concern in conversation with Wilson Smith and again in a letter written on 26 July, which also referred to generous arrangements that appeared to be contemplated for Ceylon and Pakistan. He concluded: 'It is, as you know, our belief that one of the prerequisites for any general settlement which might arise out of the Washington talks is a settlement of the surplus sterling balances in a way which will remove some of the load on and threat to sterling. I do not quite understand the position about a review of the new arrangements [with India] but I trust that everything will be done to ensure that we can, without a charge of bad faith, review them and propose, if necessary, drastic modification in the light of the Washington talks.'

Egypt

Although experience with the Indian balances since the summer of 1948 had provided the most striking demonstration that No. 2 Account blocking was ineffective in practice, it was paralleled by further experience with the Egyptian balances and to some extent also by the evolving financial arrangements between the UK and Argentina. At the end of December 1948, after the Indian balances had begun their precipitate decline, the British authorities began the negotiation of a new agreement with Egypt; this agreement was to replace the twelve-month agreement of January 1948 in which the Egyptians had successfully blackmailed London into a generous release from their No. 2 Account and a sizeable dollar ration. During the course of that agreement Egypt had accumulated a balance of £60 million on its No. 1 Account (as a key supplier of expensive non-dollar cotton, her exports had flourished). At the same time Egypt had become a large importer of dollar goods through operations in cheap sterling. Accordingly, from the British financial viewpoint, there was no argument for a further straight release, some argument for a small dollar ration, and a strong argument for trying to tie the Egyptians down on cheap sterling, by threats of expulsion from the Transferable Account Area. It was expected that for their part the Egyptians would press for a further straight release and would respond to propositions about cheap sterling by arguing that the UK should increase the supply of goods available for export to Egypt.[52] Negotiations began in Cairo on 30 December but did not end until March 1949. The British delegation was led by Leonard Waight, UK Treasury representative in the British Middle East Office. In the opening stages he was accompanied by Loombe from the Bank, but the two disagreed and Loombe returned to London after no more than three weeks in Cairo. The leader of the Egyptian delegation was Emary Bey, an Under-Secretary at the Ministry of Finance and colleague of Dr Rifai who had negotiated the second agreement.

Relative bargaining strengths had changed since early 1948, somewhat to Egypt's disadvantage. Indeed at the end of the year the Government in Cairo was looking increasingly precarious. In the hostilities that had followed the British withdrawal from Palestine and the proclamation of the State of Israel, Egyptian forces had occupied the Negev. But in the late autumn they had been ignominiously driven out of all except the Gaza Strip by the Israelis, losing much equipment to their pursuers. The Israelis then crossed into Egyptian territory, opening up the ironic possibility that Cairo might have to rely on the British forces in the Canal Zone for protection. The British themselves were concerned to maintain land communications with Jordan and occupied Aquaba early in January 1949. Armistices between Israel and the various Arab states involved followed shortly afterwards. In the meantime, late in December, Nokrashi Pasha had been assassinated in Cairo by the Moslem Brotherhood and been succeeded as Prime Minister by Abdul Hardy Pasha, a relative unknown whose tenure was not expected to be prolonged. Egyptian elections were due in the summer of 1949 and the Wafd Party, under Nahas Pasha, was likely to win. Thus although the Egyptians were very keen, for domestic political reasons, to be seen extracting further financial concessions from the British, they were no longer in so good a position to force a showdown with London. But neither, on the other hand, did the British Government wish to impose on Egypt a financial humiliation that might drive the regime into a variety of anti-British measures that would do no good to either side. The cold war was now intense. The Berlin blockade was being met by the airlift whose effectiveness through the winter was in some doubt. The North Atlantic Treaty was in process of negotiation and thought was also being given to a Middle East treaty of

---

[52] Leith-Ross and senior officials of the National Bank of Egypt had no sympathy with the Bank of England over cheap sterling. The former told Loombe it simply reflected the fact that the sterling–dollar exchange rate was wrong.

alliance that could contain Soviet expansion in that disturbed area. So, distasteful though it might be, the Pashas would somehow have to be accommodated.

The question for either side was to discover the terms on which a bargain could in fact be struck. The answer was likely to be: on terms not much different to those agreed a year before. But since one could not get to this conclusion without a period of intense probing, the opening position of each side was extreme. Emary Bey demanded abolition of the No. 2 Account system; a gold guarantee on Egyptian official holdings of sterling; a share of the UK gold reserves and an increase in British exports of 'essential' goods to Egypt. An alternative to the last of these demands was a hefty ration of dollars. In reply Waight offered no release, no dollar ration, and precious little on essential supplies. But after a series of private meetings with Emary he advised London, accurately enough as it turned out, that agreement might be possible with a straight release of £10 million, a further release of up to £20 million if Egypt's No. 1 balance fell below £30 million, and a dollar ration of £3 million. He cabled: 'I cannot guarantee that the Egyptians will accept these terms. I believe that by patient efforts with Emary and Minister of Finance (who has only just been appointed) I have a reasonable chance of securing their acceptance in the end. It will not be possible to secure agreement on anything less than these suggested terms and if there is a failure it is likely that Egyptians will become very bitter with us. In that event dollar invoicing and a request for dollars for military expenditure loom up as probabilities in the near future whatever the political situation may be.' Loombe, together with Couldrey from the Board of Trade, thought that the terms suggested by Waight were needlessly generous and that it would be better to transfer the negotiations to London. They sent a dissenting cable to this effect. However, Waight was strongly supported by Ronald Campbell, British Ambassador in Cairo, who advised the Foreign Office: 'I do not share the view that owing to their present difficulties and embarrassments both internal and external the Egyptian Government are going to come running after us if only we stick out long enough. It is false psychology when dealing with Egyptians. They are, I think, more likely to become more bloody-minded regardless of ultimate consequences to themselves.'

In London, Loombe was supported by Cobbold and Siepmann. But the resulting Bank view made little impact on Whitehall. The Treasury opposed moving the negotiations to London and was concerned only with the tactics Waight might employ to secure marginally better terms than he had suggested in his cable from Cairo. Ministers agreed and Waight was advised accordingly. The Bank was annoyed by this decision, Siepmann lamenting: 'Egypt, Palestine, Iraq: all going, or gone, the same way for the same reasons. It is past praying for and we had better write off – how much?!' But while the Bank was clearly right to argue its own financial corner against, for example, the Foreign Office and the Ministry of Defence – neither of whom were directly responsible for handling the unpleasant monetary consequences of over-generous releases – its judgement of Egyptian psychology may well have been wrong. Loombe's own first-hand experience of the Middle East had been mostly confined to his wartime appointment as Exchange Controller and Currency Officer in Baghdad under the pro-British regime of Nuri Es-Sa'id. As his subsequent career was to show, he was very much at home with the Arab rulers of the Gulf and of Jordan. But he disliked the Egyptian rulers and regarded the Pashas with the greatest contempt. This led him to the view that extreme toughness in negotiation would succeed in 1949 just as it might have done in days gone by when the British Ambassador was a proconsul, with military force at his elbow, rather than a powerful diplomat. Waight, whose inter-war career had been in the merchant banking firm of Morgan Grenfell and who had had little experience of the Middle East prior to 1947 when he had been appointed to the Treasury post in Cairo, had a rather different approach to the task in hand. He viewed the officials at the Ministry of Finance with a respect that they certainly deserved as unusually shrewd negotiators. Furthermore, he not only had a good appreciation of the precarious stability of the Egyptian regime but also realised that in such conditions the threatened rulers could behave recklessly if cornered. Waight also appreciated that toughness in Cairo was in the end unlikely to be supported in London if a breakdown seemed imminent. Recalling the surrounding circumstances of the cold war, of Arab–Israeli conflict, and the need to preserve British communications with the Gulf, East Africa, and South-East Asia, it is difficult to fault the judgement of Campbell and Waight and difficult to quarrel with Whitehall's acceptance of it. Since Egypt did need to be treated with some care, perhaps Siepmann's lament is best interpreted as a grumble at the inevitable, written by a man who now realised that his policy of tying up the sterling balances could not in practice be followed through with adequate strength.

The negotiations in Cairo rumbled on for some weeks after Loombe's return to London. The Egyptians abandoned their extreme demands and began to discuss quantities for a further release and for a renewed dollar ration. The new Finance Minister impressed himself on Waight as pro-British. The latter stuck to his brief but was candidly informed by London: 'We greatly doubt whether given the political and strategic background we are in a position to stick to an ultimatum and we do not like asking you to put up a bluff in which we might not in the end be able to support you.' He came home for consultations in the latter part of February and at meetings in the Treasury proposed going up to a release of £30 million (half outright and half on the Indian model) and a dollar ration equivalent to £5 million, together with an exchange of letters confining the use of transferable sterling to payments for direct current transactions. The Bank thought these terms too generous and was further irritated by Wilson Smith, who refused to accept that the exchange of letters about cheap sterling should be a necessary part of any new agreement. Once again the voice of Threadneedle Street was heard, though not noticeably heeded. The Chancellor authorised Waight to offer an immediate release of £10 million, a further release of £20 million conditional on the No. 1 balance falling below £40 million, and a dollar ration not exceeding £5 million. The Treasury also instructed Waight to pursue the question of sterling transferability being confined to direct current transactions. After further talks with Emary in Cairo, Waight again asked London for authority to go up to £15 million for the direct release (reducing the conditional release to £15 million) and reported that the Egyptians were prepared to agree on an exchange of letters about the use of transferable sterling provided they got a reasonable dollar ration. His request was strongly supported on wider grounds by the Ambassador, who had had an encouraging talk with the Foreign Minister, Khashaba Pasha. The Treasury reluctantly assented and the following terms were agreed on 17 March: an immediate release of £12 million, a conditional release of £18 million, a dollar ration of £5 million, and an exchange of letters on transferable sterling. Judd Polk, US Treasury representative in Cairo, told Waight that he thought the terms were surprisingly generous. The US Ambassador in London was reportedly highly critical of their generosity. But the Bank, in a letter written in diplomatic terms by Grafftey-Smith to Tansley[53] in Washington, contented itself with the comment: 'Pressure from Foreign Office and War Office quarters on political and strategic grounds caused an early departure from the firm attitude agreed to by HMG.' He did however note with approval that the Bank's concern to combat cheap sterling had been helped by the exchange of letters over transferable sterling. But the help is unlikely to have been worth much. As for the Egyptians, they quickly spent their £12 million release. By the end of September the balance on their No. 1 Account, at £71 million, was almost back to the £69 million at which it had stood when the new agreement was signed.

[53] *Tansley, Geoffrey Howson* (b. 1910). Educated Finchley County School. Entered Bank 1928, Private Secretary to the Governors 1945–6, UK Alternate Executive Director, IMF 1947–50, Assistant Chief Cashier 1950–61, Agent, Law Courts Branch 1961–9.

Argentina

In addition to the malfunctioning of the third agreement with India and the inauguration of a third and generous agreement with Egypt, the spring of 1949 was marked by an unsatisfactory end to a second post-war agreement with Argentina. This latter was the so-called Andes Agreement, negotiated with Miranda by a British Mission led by Sir Clive Baillieu[54] and initialled in February 1948 on board the Royal Mail liner *Andes* shortly before its departure from Buenos Aires on a voyage to London. The outcome was unsatisfactory, partly because Argentine deliveries of meat to the UK fell appreciably short of the quantity agreed and partly because Argentine purchases of UK goods had gone ahead faster than planned. In one sense this latter development may have been useful. Since Argentina became very short of sterling and was to continue in that condition, the British did not have to worry about any more sterling releases and dollar rations. On the other hand, there were features of the Andes Agreement that encouraged overspending by Argentina, with effects on the UK similar to those of over-generous releases of blocked balances.

Three months after signature of the Eady–Miranda agreement in September 1946, the Argentine Government changed its mind about ownership of the railways. The proposed joint venture between the British companies and the Argentine state, with guarantees of revenue to the former, had been criticised as insufficiently nationalist and over-generous to the existing shareholders. The Perón Government therefore decided after all to give up the slow release of their accumulated sterling balances and instead spend all of them and more on buying out the railway companies.[55] Neither the boards in London nor the British Government were averse to such a deal, indeed had earlier preferred it; so early in 1947 a British Railways Mission in Buenos Aires agreed to sell for £150 million, subject to ratification by the shareholders and by the Argentine Congress.

---

[54] *Baillieu, Clive Latham, 1st Baron 1953 (1889–1967)*. Director, Dunlop Rubber Co. 1929–45, Deputy Chairman 1945–9, Chairman 1949–57, Central Mining and Investment Group Ltd 1945–59, Deputy Chairman 1959–65, Deputy Chairman, Rio Tinto Zinc 1962–5, Director Zinc Group 1924–49, Consolidated Zinc 1924–49, Deputy Chairman 1961–2, Director, New Zealand Loan and Mercantile Agency 1924–67, Midland Bank 1944–67. President, Federation of British Industries, 1945–7.

[55] For some unexplained reason Argentinian writers subsequently attributed the change to an American veto on the British side of the Eady deal, a veto applied because of an alleged conflict with the Anglo–American Loan Agreement. There seems to be no foundation for this idea. It is true that the Americans objected (without avail) to a clause in the Eady Agreement allowing Argentina to spend blocked sterling in the Sterling Area if she ran a deficit there; but that had nothing to do with the railways.

The former ratification was accomplished during the summer, but the latter had not taken place by the time the convertibility of sterling was suspended in August.

Buenos Aires then dismissed British arguments as casuistry and treated the suspension for what it was, a unilateral breach of the Miranda–Eady agreement. It had indeed dealt the Argentine Government a savage blow. Up to the few weeks immediately preceding suspension they had supposed that sterling would remain convertible and enable an Argentine surplus on trade with Europe to be used to buy manufactures in the US, whose protectionist agricultural policies effectively shut out most Argentinian products. This multilateralism was unusually valuable at a time when capital goods and other essentials were so scarce in Europe and so much more readily available in the US. It was all the more valuable to Argentina when its new populist Government was intent on rapid industrialisation under a five-year plan and its reserves of gold and dollars, accumulated during the war, were rapidly being spent. Yet suddenly the multilateral facility had gone.

Since Miranda's bargaining position was not strong enough to force outright payment in dollars for Argentine exports to Europe, he was faced with the task of bargaining sales of meat and other produce outside the dollar area against such supplies of essential goods, including oil and coal, as he could extract from the UK and elsewhere. The British needed Argentine produce, most especially the beef, but were reluctant to part with essentials in exchange and were not averse, at least initially, to Argentina accumulating a quantity of inconvertible sterling. Against this latter contingency, Miranda demanded that sterling on 'B' account should be given the same gold guarantee as the blocked balances on 'A' account. He argued that the decline in Argentina's gold and dollar reserves now made it necessary to include gold-guaranteed sterling within the currency cover required by Argentine law. But the whole of the 'A' account balance would be exhausted by the railway payment; accordingly it would be necessary to extend the guarantee to the 'B' account, whose convertibility had been stopped by unilateral British action. Miranda threatened to hold up ratification of the railway purchase and reopen the whole question of the price to be paid unless he got his guarantee. Neither the Treasury nor the Bank were in the least keen to concede this, but neither were they keen to unwind the agreement that had been laboriously put together with the railway shareholders. It was therefore conceded, on condition that the railway agreement was ratified. The Argentine Government then insisted that the guarantee should be included in a comprehensive agreement, covering trade as well as finance, that would replace the Eady–Miranda agreement. To negotiate this the British Government sent the Baillieu Mission to Buenos Aires early in December 1947.

In the negotiations that followed much of the time was occupied in bargaining over supplies of UK goods and sterling oil in exchange for a programme of UK purchases of meat, cereals, and other produce. But alongside this there took place equally important discussions about finance. In October 1947 Argentina's total sterling balances came to £132 million. They rose slowly during the winter towards the £150 million needed to pay for the railways but did not look like exceeding that sum. The payment itself would then have completely exhausted all Argentina's sterling and, such was the concurrent fall in her gold and dollar reserves, left the central bank with insufficient assets for its legal note cover. In effect, Argentina would need to borrow a small amount of sterling as a working balance and a much larger amount to maintain the note cover. This problem had been recognised in London before the Baillieu Mission set out. In the Bank, Powell was in favour of a loan of some kind because he judged that the railway settlement might otherwise be delayed or its terms reopened. Nor was the Treasury opposed to the idea. Encouraging the use of guaranteed sterling as note cover, in the conditions foreseen for 1948, was a means of immobilising Argentina's sterling surplus in that year and thereby postponing a day of reckoning when the surplus would either have to be eliminated by a reorientation of trade or met by a sale of dollars from UK reserves. In the Bank, only Niemeyer took the contrary view that Argentina should change or eliminate the note cover requirement and meet any temporary shortage of sterling by cutting dollar outlays.

Miranda explained his predicament to Phillimore[56] in Buenos Aires on 13 December, emphasising that his gold reserves were vanishing and suggesting that the Bank of England should make a sterling advance to the Argentine central bank. In London, the Bank of England rejected this idea, pointing out that it would anyway not help with the problem of note cover since the legal requirement applied to net rather than gross external assets. Since the next alternative, an inter-governmental loan, was thought to be contrary to the Anglo-American Loan Agreement, there emerged the idea of an advance payment for UK imports from Argentina. After the usual sequence of Anglo-Argentine exchanges, culminating in an ambassadorial *démarche* with the President and threats that the Mission would return to London, it was agreed that the Ministry of Food would make an advance

---

[56] *Phillimore, John Gore, CMG (b. 1908).* Educated Winchester and Christ Church, Oxford. Partner, Roberts, Meynell, Buenos Aires 1936–48, Representative of Bank of England and HM Treasury in South America 1940–5, a Managing Director, Barings 1949–72.

payment of £100 million against a list of specified imports during the year ending March 1949, plus a further £10 million in lieu of an increase in the price of meat. Argentina was then left with £117 million after paying for the railways. Repayment of the advance, after taking Argentina's expected surplus into account, was expected to leave Miranda with some £80 million at the expiry of the Agreement, all or most of which would be immobilised as note cover.

It was realised in the Treasury and the Bank that the Argentines might alter or abolish the law on note cover. But not much attention was given to this contingency, it being felt that Miranda would then somehow repay the advance earlier. Some in the Treasury were so confident that Argentina would continue to hold around £80 million of sterling that they were prepared to make Argentinian sterling on 'B' account generally usable outside the dollar area. At the last minute, however, when Miranda responded by demanding merger of the 'A' and 'B' accounts, other counsels prevailed. Both accounts were retained and both made usable only within the Sterling Area. Miranda seems to have accepted this with uncharacteristic calm. Perhaps he already knew full well that he was going to spend much more in the Sterling Area than the British thought.

Although the advance of £100 million was to be repaid over twelve months and was intended only to iron out an otherwise over-violent fluctuation in her external reserves, it greatly increased Argentina's immediate external liquidity. Without the loan, and ignoring the question of note cover, it would have started the year with a mere £17 million and would have had every incentive to go on earning a surplus so as to rebuild the balances to a more comfortable level. With the advance of £100 million Argentina was given the funds that enabled it to overspend in 1948 without encountering an acute liquidity constraint until 1949. As Argentina's domestic economic situation grew progressively more disorderly, such overspending took place. Inflation started to accelerate and the Government buoyed itself up with vain hopes, firstly that the Marshall Plan would provide dollars for European purchases of Argentine produce and secondly that a resumption of war in Europe would increase demand for that produce. During the term of the Andes Agreement, Argentine imports from the UK and the Sterling Area rose well above forecast while exports fell well below forecast, partly because deliveries of meat fell short of programme and partly because of loss of markets in the outer Sterling Area. By the first quarter of 1949 the country was actually in sterling deficit and balances fell below £40 million.

The note cover requirement was quietly breached in the autumn of 1948. Miranda professed that the central bank had discovered a loophole in the law; but he was well aware of an approaching external crisis, probably more aware of it than the British. He endeavoured to get some interim relief by holding up sterling remittance of various 'invisibles' and by slowing up exchange permits for imports, providing much work for Phillimore and Lomax (Commercial Counsellor), who were obliged to pester the authorities, including Miranda himself, to stop such manoeuvres. His longer-term plan was to negotiate another agreement with the UK and this time extort a massive increase in the price of meat. He frequently stated that he would travel to London for the purpose and as frequently postponed his departure. The Foreign Minister visited London in November without much result (though it should be noted parenthetically that he got a stern warning from Bevin that force in the Falkland Islands would be met with force). Eventually, in January 1949, it was agreed that another round of trade negotiations should take place in Buenos Aires. This time there was to be no British Mission. Instead, the Ambassador was to lead, supported by five experts from London, one of whom was John Stevens,[57] a rising star in the Bank. By the time they got to Buenos Aires, Miranda had been dismissed and had decamped to Punta del Este in Uruguay. He had had plans for a general devaluation that antagonised his colleagues, particularly Eva Perón. Either because he took papers with him or because he had kept things in his head rather than in files, it was to be some weeks before his successors could unravel what was happening, let alone begin meaningful negotiations.

Miranda never returned to office. He died in Uruguay in 1951. A commanding buccaneer of a man, UK Ambassadors found him distasteful. Reginald Leeper called him a tough, ignorant know-all. John Balfour, who succeeded Leeper in the course of 1948, referred testily to his 'spluttering sub-Catalan vernacular'. Others, like Eady, rather liked him. Phillimore, an experienced Argentine hand, was often on good terms with him and was a close observer of his explosive and sometimes clowning personality. There remain in the Bank files verbatim extracts of an interview he had with Miranda in September 1948. They deserve some quotation because they capture the personality and the atmosphere. They begin with Phillimore enquiring about the legal loophole and there being no need for sterling assets as note cover. In Phillimore's expert translation of Miranda's

---

[57] *Stevens, John Melior*, KCMG, DSO (1913–73). Educated Winchester. Solicitor 1937. Army 1939–45. Entered Bank 1946, Adviser 1946–54, Director, European Department, IMF 1954–6, Executive Director 1957–64, Director 1968–73. Head of Treasury delegation, Economic Minister in Washington, UK Executive Director, IMF and IBRD 1965–7. A Managing Director, Morgan Grenfell 1967–73, Chairman 1972–3.

Spanish the reply was: 'Exactly, and for that matter I've got practically no sterling left, as it is, with all the stuff I'm buying in England. You're all up in the air. There practically isn't any sterling.' Would the Governor of the central bank be successful in getting a dollar credit from Washington? 'Of course he won't. That's precisely why I had him sent up there, to discredit him. He's only making a fool of himself.' On Brazil, Miranda remarked: 'She seems to think her coffee is essential to us, but I could stop people drinking coffee tomorrow by starting a campaign telling them how bad it is for them. I could switch them over to maté instead.' About his own country: 'What a spendthrift country we are. You just can't stop an Argentine spending money. Do you believe there's any country in the world where people are better off than in Argentina today? Certainly they aren't in England. What is a rich man's income in England, for instance?' I told him a man had to be very rich to have a net income of £5,000 a year or, say, 100,000 pesos. 'And even then he can't buy anything without a ticket, can he? Do you know what my income is? Practically 50,000 pesos a day. No! This is a rich country all right. Even Perón can't bust it.' Miranda had this to say about British Missions: 'I am certainly not going to have any more British Missions here – a lot of stooges sitting around wasting week after week of my time and having to retire and telegraph London every five minutes. Now, if the British Government were to send out someone to negotiate with full powers, who could take decisions on the spot, like I can, that would be different.' As Phillimore was leaving, Miranda called after him: 'If you can, just put out a sounding quite privately, to see if there would be a chance of getting someone out from England. But not a Mission, mind you'.[58]

When they had at last pieced things together, Miranda's successors endeavoured to extract from the British the kind of terms he had himself favoured. They demanded a doubling of the meat price and a restoration of convertibility for their current earnings of sterling. But their position

---

[58] A similar account has been left behind by Lomax, who once found himself being used as a target for Miranda's rhetoric in front of a small audience from the meat-packing fraternity. Don Miguel, he wrote, 'employs the café debater's technique. After a long and wild harangue he waits two seconds for an answer and interrupts after the third word. When he does this I raise my voice, he raises his, and voices rise to a yell with noses a few inches apart, windmill gesticulation and a chorus of approving shouts from the butchers on the sofa...With their exit he was a changed man – mild, friendly and welcoming.' At another meeting, in January 1949, Lomax tackled Miranda with a list of orders for UK tin plate, for whose import the central bank was refusing to open the necessary letters of credit even though exchange permits had been granted. Miranda 'grabbed the list, stamped it with the word "approved" and initialled it. I thanked him but pointed out that he had initialled the same list a week before and that even so the central bank would not open the credit. "They probably lost the papers", he said, "they always do. Take it to them again."'

was weakening fast. Argentina's reserves were running out. Imports of essential raw materials were being held up. Inflation was accelerating. Wage increases as high as 60% were being granted and further devaluation was expected. Hopes of a large sale of meat to the US came to nothing and the ending of the Berlin blockade dispersed Argentinian ideas about a renewal of war in Europe. In Buenos Aires the British stood firm against convertibility, insisted on bilateral balance, and refused to concede anything like a doubling of the price of meat. Eventually, after negotiations marked as usual by tactics of the bazaar, including Argentinian exploitation of an alleged confusion between tons and tonnes, an increase of just under 30% on the Andes price was agreed at the end of May 1949. But the UK conceded nothing on convertibility and substituted a dollar for a gold guarantee on Argentina's sterling. The agreement was conditional on the prompt payment of commercial arrears. But months went by and this condition was not met. Argentina's shortage of sterling grew steadily worse and by the autumn the country was seeking a loan of £20 million. By that time, in the aftermath of sterling devaluation, London was coming to the conclusion that the Perón regime was incapable of carrying out the terms of any comprehensive agreement on trade and finance and this particular story need be followed no further. Although it had been solved in a manner that had added to the load on UK resources during 1948, the problem of Argentine sterling had by now disappeared while the largely self-induced weakening of that country's bargaining strength had latterly enabled the UK to avoid any loss of dollars on current Anglo–Argentine trade.

London, Washington, and radical plans

As has already been related, however, the severe problems of Indian and Egyptian sterling had far from disappeared; and in the spring of 1949, as a new agreement with Egypt was coming into force, as the existing agreement with India was falling apart, and as the problem of cheap sterling persisted, the Bank was coming to the conclusion that there was both the need and the opportunity to mount a full-scale attack on the whole problem of Britain's over-exposed external banking position. For in response both to the American pressure for downward adjustment of West European exchange rates and to a renewed loss of reserves, the Treasury was now giving serious consideration to devaluation. In this general context further bilateral talks with the US Administration, covering outstanding questions of post-war trade and payments, were foreseen; and it was this prospect that encouraged the Bank to consider root-and-branch ideas for wiping clean the whole post-1945 slate and making a fresh start, with further American help.

The initiative for a new approach came from the Governor personally. Not in appearance a restless radical by nature, Cobbold usually behaved in a manner typical of the institution over which he presided and where he had worked for sixteen years before becoming Governor. He was devoted to step-by-step adjustment of the existing system, or pragmatic evolution of what was to hand, alive and working. But once convinced that what was to hand was not working and could not be made to work properly, he would seize an opportunity to advocate demolition and reconstruction. Ahead of the crisis in 1947 he had toyed with the idea of seeking special American help over the sterling balances, but his initiative was out of time and unrealistic. However, on 12 May 1949 he included an attack on the problem of the balances among a variety of questions put to a new working group that he was appointing to consider the exchange rate and related matters. Following a lunch with the Chancellor on 1 June he recorded himself saying that he had some 'vague ideas in the back of my mind about whether we could not have a shot at some comprehensive settlement with the Americans this autumn to get some gold put up to deal with the excess balances and keep India, Pakistan, and Egypt off our backs for dollars for the next few years, making token payment of the old war debt and some regularised funding or deferment of the new war debt. This would have to be combined with pretty wide sterling transferability, though not convertibility into dollars.'

The Chancellor encouraged him to develop these ideas and soon afterwards, in a note circulated to senior colleagues, the Governor numbered action on the sterling balances as among the prerequisites of a successful devaluation (which he was not yet persuaded was necessary). Another prerequisite would be new arrangements with the US and Canada 'to take some of the rest of the world's demand for dollars off our backs'. If the prerequisites – which of course included adjustments of domestic policy – were not met, one devaluation would simply be followed by another; and it was within that framework that he elaborated some of his ideas in a note addressed to the Deputy Governor on 19 June. 'This may prove', he wrote, 'to be our last chance of clearing up the external position and getting things in hand instead of being battered by events.' It was necessary to think about the possibilities of some very radical changes. These included drastic blocking of all the sterling balances; making subsequent accruals transferable throughout the whole non-dollar world with some measure of convertibility into dollars; dismantling the distinction between the Sterling Area and the rest of the non-dollar world (a distinction he found 'out of date and bearing little correspondence to the facts of life'); and trying to get the US to take a 'big wad of the old balances off our back' in exchange for dollars on a one-for-two basis. He concluded: 'I realise that this is all very violent and ambitious and would cause every sort of administrative complication, but I think that if we do not do something violent and ambitious we are likely to bleed to death and I see no attraction in allowing the UK to starve in order to provide India with new railways.'

The Governor's immediate colleagues in the Bank were prepared to countenance something violent and ambitious, but they were not prepared to countenance complete blocking. As Siepmann pointed out, it would involve private as well as official holdings, would mean abrogating monetary and payments agreements, would constitute virtual default, and might well create such a shock as to render sterling wholly unacceptable thereafter. Moreover the balances now reflected post-war as well as wartime transactions, which would make the shock effect of blocking all the greater. The Governor appears to have accepted this truth and to have encouraged the development of an alternative plan in which blocking had no place but in which American help had accordingly to be much larger. The revised version was drafted by Bolton, but just as the earlier version seemed impracticable because of its reliance on unilateral blocking, so the revised version soon looked unrealistic because of the massive American assistance required to make it work. For while the external monetary predicament was not yet desperate enough for the UK to get away with unilateral blocking, the whole sterling system was no longer of such importance to American external economic policy as to justify massive special assistance. It is conceivable that the American attitude would have been different, or at least susceptible of persuasion, if the British Government had been prepared to make large cuts in its own expenditure, to bring short-term interest-rate policy out of its deep freeze, to adopt a much more positive attitude towards European integration, and to show greater earnest of its ostensible commitment to the resumption of convertibility. But as is recounted in the next chapter, the Government in London was prepared to do little or nothing that might have tempted the Americans into providing the funds for a reconstruction of the British external monetary position. The Governor's initiative therefore ran into the sand; though for the time being, in the run-up to devaluation, the problem of the sterling balances and its treatment with American help certainly remained on the agenda.

Bolton's grand slam version of the Governor's original plan included US help of some $4½ billion to write off the £1.45 billion of No. 2 Account balances in exchange for dollars at $3 to the pound and another $2.4 billion to bring the UK reserves up to £1 billion, which he judged to be an adequate defence against downward fluctuations in the remaining £2 billion of sterling balances. At the same time, the US would write off all the First World War debt together with the whole of the 1945 loan to the UK. This would amount to cancelling $6¾ billion of debt. Canada would be expected to act similarly. For its part, the UK would cancel all debts owing to it by France and other West European countries. The Sterling Area would then be merged with the rest of the world, outward exchange control would be imposed between the UK and existing members of the Area, and all sterling newly accruing to non-residents would be made fully convertible. All old untied sterling would be transferable anywhere except into currencies of the dollar area. Finally the ERP in its existing form, together with the IEPC, would be wound up and a smaller programme of Aid, for the continental members of OEEC only, would be substituted. Nobody could ever have accused Bolton of not producing grand plans when given the green light to do so.

The Governor criticised Bolton's plan on points of presentation and he also insisted that there should not be two kinds of sterling – convertible and transferable. All should be convertible unless tied up or cancelled. But Thompson-McCausland warned that unless the dollar shortage was overcome and other currencies made convertible, the UK would simply find itself in the same position as it was in 1947, with its enlarged dollar resources being used up by conversions. Nonetheless the bare bones of the plan were included in a Treasury paper that was submitted to Ministers early in July and which set out the various subjects to be discussed at the tripartite meetings with the US and Canada, now proposed for August and September. That was about as far as it got. When Secretary Snyder, together with the Canadian Finance Minister, paid a brief visit to London in the second week of July, he asked the Chancellor about the problem of the sterling balances but got only a defensive response about releases from No. 2 Accounts over the preceding two years. Shortly afterwards Cobbold abandoned any hope of getting the Americans to fortify the UK reserves but still persisted with the rest of the plan, now including some idea of *ad hoc* American help to underpin convertibility by buying sterling and holding it. But by the end of July officials of the Treasury and the Bank realised that there was no prospect of a strong package of domestic measures that would accompany a devaluation and could provide a firm platform from which to seek US help with the balances. The Government was not particularly interested, so it seems, in any noteworthy reconstruction of its external monetary position; at least it was not interested in such reconstruction at the price that it might have to pay in terms of domestic policy and external convertibility. The Treasury therefore began to favour a less ambitious approach. This was suggested to them in July by Oliver Franks and amounted to an adaptation of one part of the Governor's plan. The Americans would be asked to take over and write down, with the owners' consent, a proportion of the South-East Asian balances. The remainder, after writing down, would be exchanged for dollars, and the whole operation would be presented as a suitable means of channelling American aid to countries in that region, especially India, that possessed large quantities of tied sterling. The Treasury saw considerable difficulties with this suggestion, not least the difficulty of obtaining the owners' consent to writing-down. In the Bank, Mynors pointed out that the problem of the balances did not by any means wholly reside in the No. 2 Accounts. Uncontrolled and unpredictable repayments of untied balances, concentrated into a short period, could be a greater danger to the exiguous central reserves. But in default of any other remotely practicable proposal, the Franks Plan remained on the table, with the Governor himself emphasising the favourable effect its implementation could have on market opinion.

During the tripartite discussions in Washington the American and Canadian representatives listened attentively to a British presentation on the recent behaviour of the balances and approvingly accepted 'cold war' arguments justifying the very large releases of Indian sterling. They also dazzled British officials, including Bolton, by offering some continuing organisation in which matters of mutual concern could be discussed on a tripartite basis. It is doubtful if the US Administration took this offer very seriously, but the question of the sterling balances was nonetheless remitted to the new organisation; and in order to prepare the ground for substantive discussions the Treasury instituted a Working Party on the sterling balances early in October, the Bank being represented by Thompson-McCausland. It reported to Ministers early in November in a long and highly educative document on the post-war behaviour of the balances, the resulting burden on the UK economy, and the possibility of obtaining further American help. In the meantime, the Bank itself had gone over the whole ground once again, while Bolton was misguidedly proposing an enlargement of the Sterling Area as a key component of a solution to the problem on intra-European payments. The Bank's conclusions were set out in a letter from the Governor to Bridges on 18 October. He began by accepting there was no prospect of massive American help to fortify UK reserves or mop up the balances. But he went on to suggest that there might be some chance, in the context of the US

Aid programme, of the Americans underwriting the deficits of India, Pakistan, Ceylon, and perhaps also Egypt for a number of years. At the same time it might be possible to agree with Australia, New Zealand, and South Africa that they would 'keep off the UK reserves' for a similar period. There might then be a chance of negotiating a line of credit with the US to support a resumption of sterling convertibility. Although the Treasury may have been sympathetic to these suggestions, it judged that the Government would not accept any proposal involving an early resumption of convertibility. The Working Party's Report was therefore extremely cautious. It skirted round the various possibilities of linking American Aid to South-East Asia with the problem of sterling balances, adding both that the US was habitually suspicious of the Sterling Area and that the Indians and others might not like such linkage if it involved an element of cancellation. It also pointed out that a plan of that kind would require lengthy negotiation with all parties preparatory to obtaining Congressional approval. This meant there was no real prospect of action before early 1951. Its final conclusion was that an early approach to the Americans should confine itself to being educative and suggestive. If the response proved favourable, the holders of the relevant balances could be brought into the discussions; in the interim an effort should be made to slow down the rate of releases from No. 2 Accounts. If no American help was forthcoming, long-term funding, if necessary by unilateral action, should be considered. The Government accepted the advice contained in the Report and Leslie Rowan, who had stayed on in Washington after devaluation to help start the 'continuing organisation', was authorised to begin the approach to the US. His own view, expressed to the Governor during December, was that some help with the South-East Asian balances might be forthcoming but that concrete proposals would have to come from the British side. The Governor, whose eye was still focussed on a wider horizon, replied that concrete proposals had better wait until after the General Election (the Government's Parliamentary term was due to expire in the summer of 1950). He added that the Bank was hatching something else on the problem of the balances that could be put to the Treasury at that stage.

The 'something' turned out to be a plan for drastic unilateral action. This was thought out in January 1950 and refined during February, ahead of the Election that was held at the end of the month. It was called the 'freeze-and-offer plan' and owed a good deal to a redefinition of the problem of the balances, based on the argument that was put forward by Mynors in the previous August and developed by Thompson-McCausland in the new year. Now that the Indian crisis had faded into the past, and the sterling–dollar exchange rate had been adjusted, the problem of excessive releases from the No. 2 Accounts seemed less oppressive.[59] At the same time the intermittent but severe problem of cheap sterling, together with the low level of exchange reserves, focussed attention back onto the volatility of the No. 1 Accounts and of the untied balances generally. It was therefore concluded that the latter had to be reduced, partly by the UK running an external surplus and partly by some measure of forced funding. The need for a firmer fiscal and monetary policy was also stressed, as was some fortification of the reserves. So a new plan was devised for the balances which was intended to be final, clearing things up for many years to come. Siepmann, Bolton, Peppiatt, Mynors, Beale, and Fisher participated along with Thompson-McCausland and the plan was submitted to the Governor in outline on 27 January 1950. It was a plan for unilateral action, without dependence on the large-scale American help that all agreed was unobtainable.

All balances would be blocked and frozen for an initial period of one month. The holders would then be offered a long-dated $2\frac{1}{2}\%$ funding stock which would at first be unmarketable but which could be sold on the gilt-edged market after five years up to an annual maximum of 5% of the original holding. For every pound subscribed to this stock the UK would release a pound from the blocked balance and place it in a new account freely transferable throughout the non-dollar world. Concurrently, the Government would seek to liquidate its portfolio of dollar securities acquired from British residents during the war and use the proceeds partly to repay a secured wartime loan from the Reconstruction Finance Corporation and partly to fortify the UK reserves by some £200 million.

Although the rougher edges of this plan, such as the wholesale blocking of commercial balances, could be smoothed in a process of refinement and although the 'offer' aspect made it less Draconian than outright forced-funding, its radical and unilateral character meant in practice that the Government could only resort to it in a manifest emergency, however compelling the Bank might find the arguments for clearing things up for many years to come. In any other circumstances the nature of British relationships with the US, with the principal members of the Commonwealth, and with important holders of sterling outside the Sterling Area, were such that there was still in practice no alternative but to proceed by negotiation, whether initially with the US or with the principal holders of sterling. But as experience since 1946 had demonstrated, negotiation with

---

[59] The agreement with Egypt was prolonged in 1951, releases of £15 million per annum being contemplated for a further period of ten years. The agreement with India was similarly extended in 1952.

the holders meant abandoning uniformity of treatment and abandoning major surgery unless the whole plan could be made very attractive by exceptional American generosity. But this in turn, in 1950 as in 1949 or earlier, meant embarking on another expedition to Washington without any real prospect of success.

So 'freeze-and-offer' went the way of the other radical proposals that had preceded it. Attempts were made to turn it into a negotiated, multilateral plan to be put to a Commonwealth Conference in the first instance and, if agreed, put to the US for financial assistance. At the same time, the plan would be linked to a version of the earlier scheme for combining Aid to South-East Asia with a write-down of sterling balances. But negotiated radicalism was an illusion and in any case the result of the General Election, which left the Labour Government without an effective working majority in the Commons, implied that any sort of radicalism would be unacceptable to Ministers except in an emergency. The Governor remarked to Brittain on 1 March that 'freeze-and-offer' would have to be put on the shelf because the required political stability in the UK was now lacking. Though unstated, there must also have been the thought that full unilateral 'freeze-and-offer' would not sit well with the final negotiations for UK entry into the proposed European Payments Union. The only runner then left was the Franks Plan of July 1949, as developed by the Sterling Area Working Party, together with some rather vague and stale ideas for funding or cancellation. A memorandum on the subject was sent to Dean Acheson in the State Department during April, only to get a brusque reply early in May to the effect that the Administration was not interested in linking Aid to the problem of the balances.[60] So much for the 'continuing organisation' that had dazzled Bolton and others during the previous summer. All that was now left of the entire exercise were the vague ideas on funding; and on 8 June Mynors attended a meeting in the Treasury at which it was agreed that these boiled down in practice to going on with three-year programmes of releases with India, Pakistan, and Egypt. But the main problem of the balances had not gone away. Just as experience with cheap sterling had shown that the problem could be fully solved only by a resumption of convertibility, so the exercises on the sterling balances demonstrated that a bold solution involving blocking could be adopted only in an emergency. These two factors were to come together early in 1952.

Throughout these episodes in 1949 and 1950 the Bank had certainly

---

[60] The rebuff cannot have occasioned much surprise in the Bank. Bolton heard from Overby in January that in Snyder's view the sterling-balance problem would have to be solved largely by the UK itself.

not shown lack of concern over the dangerously exposed external banking position, whether the dangers were seen to come from excess releases of No. 2 Account sterling or from fluctuations in untied balances. Nor, after all its experiences since 1946, had the Bank remained reluctant to put forward radical proposals out of some overpowering affection for the Sterling Area. Quite the contrary, at the instigation of the Governor the Bank had taken the lead in formulating such proposals and canvassing them in the Treasury. But its willingness to countenance measures of that kind remained a close secret. In the nature of things, anything like the original 'freeze-and-offer' scheme could not conceivably be given any kind of public airing. So far as the financial community and the holders of sterling were concerned, the public stance of the UK authorities had to be that their bank remained open for business as usual and would so remain.

'Business as usual' included the established practice whereby members of the Sterling Area sold all their current earnings of foreign currency to the EEA in London. They were expected, in consequence, to hold their exchange reserves in sterling and not to accumulate separate reserves of gold or dollars. Some separate gold holdings did exist, for example those of India and Pakistan, Australia, and New Zealand, arising either from pre-war requirements of note cover or from an understanding that local output of gold could be retained. But these did not seriously compromise the established practice of the Sterling Area as a whole. However, after the devaluation of 1949 and during the Korean fluctuation in both the sterling balances and the UK reserves, there emerged some perceptible pressure for the diversification of members' external reserves. Australia had sold locally produced gold to the EEA since 1947, but ceased to do so in 1951 (ostensibly to improve Australian credit in the US). India, after the much-resented episodes of the dollar ration, built up a sizeable working balance in dollars through her Supply Mission in Washington. By 1951 it exceeded $70 million. Pakistan was allowed to purchase £4 million of gold from the EEA in 1951, ostensibly to increase the gold backing of the currency. In 1950 Ceylon was allowed to constitute a gold reserve of £4 million, by purchase from the central reserves in London. Diversification, even on this quite small scale, added a third dimension to the problem of the balances and one that could grow in importance if confidence in sterling continued to be fragile, or if it deteriorated further. By 1951 the first dimension, namely the releases of wartime accumulations, seemed to be under greater control. The second dimension, posed by the volatility of untied balances and the ratio of UK reserves to external monetary liabilities, was very prominent. The third was less prominent but full of potential menace if a third post-war sterling crisis were to occur.

(e) DEVALUATION

The preceding sections have been concerned with three interrelated topics, each with their own sets of problems, that commanded attention more or less continuously through the four years 1947–51. The same could also be said of the exchange rate, if the term is regarded as a euphemism for balance of payments problems; but the alteration of the rate in September 1949 is best regarded as an event on its own, as a break in continuity, and even as a new opportunity. It was not an isolated step but the prime mover in a general though not uniform realignment of Sterling Area and European exchange rates against the dollar. It had been widely expected and it had in considerable part been engineered by the American Administration, who judged that progress towards convertibility and non-discrimination during the second and final stage of the ERP would be very limited unless preceded by an exchange rate adjustment. It would indeed have been most surprising if such an adjustment, at some stage, had had no part to play in overcoming the dollar problem. An alternative solution would have been a deliberate consolidation into two separate trading worlds, with lasting discrimination against the US. Among many objections to this, one was overriding. It would have meant an open breach on a matter of vital importance with the country on whom Western Europe depended for economic help and for defence against the aggressor in the East. In practice, therefore, it was once again the Americans who determined the broad lines of policy within the international economic strategy to which their European allies, with varying degrees of enthusiasm, found themselves committed; and it was the Americans who then had to see that their policy was put into effect through pressures designed to induce their sovereign allies to take decisions of their own that conformed to the American design. For any one ally, it was then a question of whether to be pushed reluctantly into an otherwise unwanted action, whether to be active and exploit the situation, perhaps to obtain something more from Washington in return, whether to carry out some desired change in domestic economic policy, or whether to adopt some combination of these options.

The authorities in the United Kingdom were divided on these latter issues. Leading Ministers, who were within sight of a General Election, were not keen to face the domestic rigours of a devaluation immediately after the two years of austerity that had followed the crisis of 1947. They were on the whole passive and reluctant; their official advisers, by contrast, wanted to be active and to make good use of the opportunity that devaluation could provide. The Bank wanted to be particularly active, in the context both of the sterling balances and the growing traffic in cheap sterling. But Ministers had their way and the opportunity, such as it might have been, was let slip. Short-term political factors no doubt played a part in this. The fatigue and declining health of Stafford Cripps was another influence.[61] But there was a more deep-seated cause that became increasingly evident as the whole story unfolded. Whatever may or may not have been the achievements of the Attlee Government in social policy, in the adaptation of the British economy to harsh post-war realities, or in helping to organise successful pursuit of the cold war, it never thought out and developed an external monetary strategy of its own. It inherited the wartime thinking of Keynes and others, as embodied in the Bretton Woods Agreements, without great conviction. Next, in exchange for an urgently needed dollar loan, it accepted at the end of 1945 an American programme that it disliked and in which it did not believe. When this came to grief in 1947 it had no difficulty in adopting with some zest the renewed bilateralism, discrimination, and inconvertibility of the early period of dollar famine. But it then willingly accepted Marshall Aid from the Americans, whose underlying strategy, despite the set-back in 1947, was unchanged and whose pursuit of that strategy, though heavily modified, was no less determined and no less powerful. Beyond that, the policy of the British Government was largely passive. It accepted, when required to do so, that the UK remained committed to the world of Bretton Woods and the Loan Agreement, but was itself in no hurry to get there. It accepted, when necessary, that it had to play a part in intra-European arrangements designed to create conditions that would bring that world closer. But it took little initiative of its own and on the whole allowed others, American or European, to make the running, giving way only under pressure. As time went by, this passivity tended to bring it into disagreement with the Bank of England, whose growing worry over the country's precarious external monetary position led to a weakening of its gradualist approach, made it keen to seize any opportunity for decisively improving that position, and made it always prone to stress the vital importance of re-establishing and maintaining adequate overseas confidence in sterling.

It would of course have been difficult for the Bank, in 1949, to have advocated seizing an opportunity if it had simultaneously been a rigid opponent of devaluation itself. But equally it would have been unwise to press for devaluation at that time and court the risk that such a recommendation would help bring about the very conclusion that the Bank most certainly did not want, namely a devaluation on its own with

---

[61] Niemeyer told Jacobsson as early as December 1948 that Cripps now tended to rush from one question to another without giving himself time to study any of them profoundly.

little or no follow-through. Since experience with the 1947 crisis and its immediate aftermath certainly suggested that this risk was a serious one, the Governor was careful neither to get solidly entrenched into a position hostile to devaluation nor to go along with those who positively favoured it. Instead, and probably following his own instincts, he began by adopting the position that he was against it for the time being. As the crisis slowly developed, he shaded this into the position that although the case for devaluation was not yet proven, it could nonetheless provide an opportunity for a decisive restructuring of the external position, with American help. Finally, at the end of August he came to the judgement that it could not be avoided. This time-sequence of views corresponded fairly closely with those developed by the Chancellor and in its middle stages enabled the Bank to develop its case for seizing an opportunity, but without success.

Devaluation was first considered in the Bank as early as January 1948, when Niemeyer minuted Catto on the subject. He admitted that events might ultimately push sterling off $4.03. But it was one thing to yield to fate and quite another to welcome it. There were far too many people who talked as if depreciation of sterling was relatively unimportant or even a matter to be welcomed. 'My view', he wrote, 'would be the precise opposite. It would be intensely bad for us. Exchange depreciation in a modern world can never in any circumstances be of any lasting external benefit.' It would put up the price of imports without affecting their volume because they were already restricted to essentials; but with full employment, the consequent rise in the cost of living would precipitate an inflation of wage costs that would undermine whatever minor benefit, in a sellers' market, the depreciation might confer on UK exports. Neither, he argued, would the balance of invisibles improve. At the same time the task of managing sterling would be made more difficult as the confidence of holders would be damaged by a devaluation 'with no such excuse as actual war'. Temperamentally, Niemeyer would probably have opposed devaluation in almost any circumstances, but in the situation prevailing at the time his arguments would have commanded fairly wide agreement. Clarke, writing in the Treasury at the end of February 1948, did see some advantage in a devaluation that would help get the price mechanism working in the right instead of the wrong direction, namely, towards overcoming the dollar shortage. But Robert Hall,[62] writing in August

---

[62] Hall, Robert Lowe, Baron Roberthall (Life Peer) 1969, (1901–88). Educated University of Queensland and Magdalen College, Oxford (Rhodes Scholar). Fellow, Trinity College, Oxford 1927–50, Ministry of Supply 1939–46, Adviser, Board of Trade 1946-7, Director, Economic Section, Cabinet Office 1947–53, Economic Adviser to HMG 1953–61. Advisory

1948, made much the same case against devaluation as Niemeyer. So did the report of an ECA mission to the UK as late as November of that year. Even Per Jacobsson, a passionate advocate of decontrol, market freedom, fiscal rectitude, interest-rate flexibility, and external convertibility, was prepared at this time to regard adjustment of the sterling–dollar rate as premature, though probably necessary in the end.

Shortly after receiving Niemeyer's advice, Catto was informed that the Chancellor had asked for a war book on devaluation to be prepared, complete with arguments for and against, the likely effects, and the technical modalities. The Governor replied that the Bank would confine itself to comment on a Treasury paper, adding: 'I don't want it to be *our* draft!' Little difficulty was experienced with a draft on modalities, but the rest of the exercise lacked urgency or precision. It dragged on sporadically through most of 1948 without reaching any definite conclusion. In March Bolton circulated a note of his own, which amounted to a useful elaboration of the advice given by Niemeyer. During the summer he contributed to a discussion in the Treasury, with Rowe-Dutton and Hall, about the possible merits of floating the pound instead of devaluing to a new fixed rate. He readily secured agreement that a floating rate could not sensibly be regarded as an alternative option to fixed-rate devaluation and had instead to be regarded as a necessary consequence of all else failing. It would mean a repudiation of the Bretton Woods commitments and of the philosophy lying behind them, with unpredictable consequences for exchange stability throughout the world. It would also, though this was not necessarily a disadvantage, compel important changes in exchange control. The London foreign exchange market would have to be reconstituted so as to provide proper facilities in the UK for the hour-to-hour sale and purchase of foreign currency against sterling (in accord with exchange control permissions) and for forward cover.

Bolton had however given additional thought to the contingency of a *force majeure* float. For if the dollar shortage continued, or got worse, the Government might be compelled to devalue in the very circumstances to which Niemeyer and others had drawn attention. The devaluation would accordingly fail and involuntary floating would ensue. It would then be necessary to limit the damage, partly by restoring the flexibility of short-term interest rates in London and partly, he thought, by seeking to organise a non-dollar bloc, including the Sterling Area and as many countries of Western Europe as could be persuaded to join, whose currencies would be pegged to one another and float together against the

Director, Unilever 1961–71, Adviser to Tube Investments 1961–76, Principal, Hertford College, Oxford 1964–7.

dollar. Within the bloc, exchange controls would be relaxed. These ideas, which were to have a variety of echoes later on, were kept inside the Bank. They were refined by Roy Bridge early in 1949 and thereafter left in reserve. Very shortly afterwards there began an international debate on devaluation. This itself coincided with the onset of recession in the US and the consequential re-widening of the dollar gap, especially the Sterling Area's dollar gap. The two together were to bring about the devaluations of September 1949, in conditions more favourable than those prevailing in 1948 and therefore unlikely to precipitate a subsequent breakdown and an involuntary float.

The international debate was sparked by two documents, firstly a set of long-term programmes submitted to the OEEC by its members and secondly the Interim Report on the ERP published by the Secretariat of the OEEC at the end of December 1948. The clear message of the programmes and of the Report was that on current plans and forecasts a closing of the dollar gap by 1952, without further Aid, was unlikely to be achieved. One of the principal reasons seemed to be inadequate exports by member countries, especially exports to North America; and in numerous paragraphs the Report stressed that this could not be made good unless European export prices were reduced relative to those of competing American products, and reduced soon. The words 'exchange rate' were never mentioned, but the implication was obvious. It was seized upon in Washington both by the economic liberals in the Treasury, who were always suspicious that the ERP would unwittingly bring about a two-world solution to the dollar problem, and by the ardent Europeanists in the ECA who were becoming apprehensive lest progress on European unification should be seen to falter and Congressional criticism of the ERP should become overpowering.

As early as 14 January 1949 the UK Alternate on the IMF Board, Geoffrey Tansley, telephoned Bolton in London saying that the Administration and the Fund were both taking the OEEC Report very seriously. He expected the US Director of the Fund, Frank Southard,[63] to pursue the matter very actively in that forum. Sterling would not be exempt from the examination. Early in February, in a letter to Bolton, he repeated the

---

[63] *Southard, Frank Allan, Jr (1907–89)*. Educated Pomona College and University of California. US Naval Reserve 1942–6. Assistant Professor, later Professor of Economics, Cornell 1931–48, Chairman, Department of Economics 1946–8. Assistant Director, Monetary Research, Treasury Department 1941–2, Director, Office of International Finance 1947–8, Associate Director, Research and Statistics in charge of International Section, Board of Governors, Federal Reserve System 1948–9, US Executive Director, IMF and Special Assistant to Secretary of Treasury 1949–62, IMF Deputy Managing Director, Vice-Chairman, Executive Board 1962–74.

message at length and emphatically, remarking that the OEEC Secretariat had reaped a whirlwind. The UK Treasury was getting the same signals from its own representatives in Washington. Sydney Caine[64] reported the existence among important officials, especially in the US Treasury, of a feeling in favour of devaluation that was decidedly stronger than had previously been realised.

Finally, on 16 February, Secretary Snyder made matters quite clear to the House Committee on Foreign Affairs in a statement on behalf of the President's National Advisory Council on International Monetary and Financial Problems (NAC), which ended as follows:

> The Council believes that the exchange rate question should be reviewed with a number of the European countries in the course of the next year. The objective will be to explore with these countries the extent to which they can improve their balance of payments position with the Western Hemisphere, and whether or not changing the par value of their currencies will be conducive to this result. We recognise that this is an extraordinarily difficult problem which will require the most careful consideration, and the utmost secrecy in discussion. In years gone by, the United States Government generally took the position that the rate at which a country bought and sold dollars was primarily its concern. Now, however, when we are contributing billions of dollars to build up the European economies, it becomes a matter of grave direct concern to us insofar as the exchange policies which a country may be pursuing tend to retard its exports or misdirect its trade and increase its Western Hemisphere deficit, and thus indirectly increase its calls upon the United States for assistance. Where an exchange rate adjustment is indicated, a member country will be expected to propose a new par value to the International Monetary Fund.

The response of the UK was to play it all down and to emphasise that international discussion of exchange rate questions should as far as possible be confined to the Fund and kept out of the hands of the ECA and the OEEC. But opinion within the American Administration was hardening in favour of a devaluation of sterling. The ECA was in the van (and thought by the Treasury Department to be rushing fences). On 17 March Bissell[65] cabled Averell Harriman in Paris that he was convinced action

---

[64] *Caine, Sydney, KCMG* (1902–91). Educated Harrow County School and London School of Economics. Assistant Inspector of Taxes 1923–6, Colonial Office 1926–48, Third Secretary, HM Treasury 1948–9, Head of UK Treasury and Supply Delegation, Washington 1949–51. Vice-Chancellor, University of Malaya 1952–6, Director, LSE 1957–67, Governor, Reserve Bank of Rhodesia (London) 1965–7.

[65] *Bissell, Richard Mervin, Jr* (b. 1909). Educated LSE and Yale. Yale 1934–41, Assistant Professor of Economics 1939–41, Associate Professor, Massachusetts Institute of Technology (MIT) 1942–8, Professor 1948–52. Economic Adviser to Director, War Mobilization and Reconversion 1945–6, Deputy Director 1946, Executive Secretary, President's Committee on Foreign Aid 1947–8, Assistant Administrator, ECA Program 1948–51, Staff Member, Ford Foundation 1952–4, Special Assistant to Director, CIA

should be taken towards reaching realistic exchange rates between OEEC members and between those countries and the dollar. He added that the ECA regarded the sterling problem as the focal point, which should be examined at once. Shortly afterwards US Treasury officials also concluded that sterling should be devalued. In London, on 21 March, the new Governor noted in his diary:[66] 'I asked Bolton to get two or three people together and try and get down on paper the pros and cons of depreciation either of sterling or of European currencies generally on the dollar. I thought the gold price should also be covered. I am not anticipating likelihood or advantage in making a move in near future, but I think we are getting to the stage when we may be asked for considered views at any moment.' Earlier in March Professor Dennis Robertson had written to Mynors from Cambridge saying: 'Difficult and distasteful as it is the UK *must* now take the initiative in arranging a controlled devaluation, in the severally appropriate proportions, of all European currencies.' Early in April, however, Hubert Henderson told Cobbold the devaluation talk was silly. Robertson, whose views were echoed in *The Banker* magazine, was highly regarded in the Bank, particularly by the Governor, who had very recently been trying to hire him as Economic Adviser.[67]

The next American move was to secure an appropriate resolution in the IMF Executive Board. In discussion held at the end of March Southard developed the case deployed earlier by Snyder. His opponents reiterated the same case against devaluation that had held sway in 1948, while also attacking American protectionism. In addition they argued that the Fund had no right to initiate talks about a member's exchange rate. Southard then tabled a resolution to the effect that a review of West European exchange rates should be undertaken by the Fund in consultation with each member concerned. The prospect of a formal resolution, followed almost certainly by leakage of its contents, provoked a startled reaction in London. Tansley was told from the Treasury: 'We view this prospect with horror. The Chancellor considers it imperative therefore that whatever happens there should be no resolution passed by the Fund.' Franks was instructed to make a direct approach to Snyder and get the draft withdrawn. He made the approach, but to no avail. The Secretary bleakly reminded him that there was now very wide public interest in the subject of exchange rates, including Congressional interest. The acknowledged

---

1954–9, Deputy Director, Plans 1959–62, President, Institute for Defence Analyses 1962–4, Director, Marketing and Economic Planning, United Aircraft Corporation 1964–74.

[66] Catto had kept no regular diary other than a record of his engagements. Cobbold kept a brief record of his daily work, rather as Norman had done.

[67] See Chapter 5, p. 383 n. 35.

place to discuss the issues was the IMF and the correct conclusion to such discussions was a worthwhile resolution. Just as much harm would be done by failure to reach such a conclusion as by adoption of the draft resolution. It would simply throw the debate into the press and into Congress, whose debates on the renewal of the ERP were unfinished. Franks then advised London to face reality and the Treasury responded by offering a revised draft that omitted any reference to Western Europe and made it clear that the initiative for any discussions with the IMF on exchange rates rested with the members themselves. This attracted some European support, but in the end there was a compromise resolution that reinstated the reference to Western Europe while glossing over the question of initiative. Tansley accepted the compromise off his own bat, despite instructions to vote against a resolution that did not clearly meet the British position on the question of initiative. His courage was nonetheless personally commended by the Chancellor, a rare achievement for a relatively junior official. The Governor noted in his diary: 'There has been a lot of song and dance about the Monetary Fund decision. I think that in all the circumstances Tansley had no alternative but to act as he did and I have told the Treasury accordingly.'

It was understood that the Managing Director of the Fund, Camille Gutt,[68] would now embark on a round of informal visits to European capitals. The episode concluded on 8 April with Franks advising the Chancellor that over the next few months the UK should try to get a closer community of thinking with the Americans on the proper role of the IMF as well as, if possible, 'the matters of substance which are likely to arise from any further examination of the general monetary and balance of payments position in Europe'. A day earlier Wilson Smith, Hall, Clarke, Bolton and Mynors had met in the Treasury and it was agreed that a thorough review of the whole exchange rate question should be set in hand. Bridges, talking to the Governor shortly afterwards, said he now wanted to get into a position to show Ministers that the pros and cons of devaluation had been thoroughly considered.

During and after the episode of the Fund resolution the international debate became a bubbling ferment. The press, especially in the US, was full of it. From the New York Federal Reserve, Knoke reported to Bolton that

---

[68] *Gutt, Camille (1884–1971)*. Barrister and journalist 1906–14. Belgian Army 1914–18. Secretary-General, Belgian delegation to Reparations Commission 1919, Chief Secretary to Minister of Finance 1920–4, Assistant Delegate to Reparations Commission 1924–6, Assistant to Minister of Finance 1926–34, Minister of Finance 1934–40. In Belgian Government in London: Minister for National Defence and Transport 1940–2, Finance and Economic Affairs 1940–4. Minister of Finance 1944–6. Managing Director, IMF 1946–51.

the exchange market was much excited about it. In the OEEC in Paris there was some confusion at the prospect of Gutt's approaching odyssey. The Belgians were incensed about it and threatened, with support from the Dutch, not to receive the Managing Director at all.[69] But in conversation with Bolton in Amsterdam Holtrop gave good advice. He made it clear that he regarded the sterling–dollar rate as the key. If it moved, all would follow, though not necessarily to the same extent. If it did not move, none of the others would. In Basle, the French told Bolton that they were 'violently disturbed'. Next, Bissell returned unexpectedly to Paris in the middle of April, in part to urge progress towards convertibility and press for the liberalisation of the IEPC, in part to tell the British straight out, through Hall-Patch, that it would be a dangerous illusion to suppose that the US would remain silent for a year while London dragged its feet over the exchange rate. Discussions would have to proceed without delay because sterling was the key currency in Western Europe. They could either take place bilaterally in conditions of secrecy or else there would be continuous American pressure for distasteful discussions in a wide forum. This crude pressure was thought by the British to reflect rivalry between the ECA and the US Treasury, the latter being thought less hawkish. But it was probably no more than ordinary good advice. For when Bolton went to Washington and New York at the end of the month, shortly after Cripps had defiantly told a press conference in Rome that there would be no devaluation and that convertibility remained a distant goal, he reported by telegram: 'There is apparently some unanimity of opinion between ECA and NAC that devaluation of sterling is necessary and inevitable and that definite action should be taken in the near future.' He felt that the tactic of damping down excitement in the exchange field was now probably unworkable. In a letter written on 9 May he reported that: 'Depreciation of sterling has become the universal panacea; designed to bring about dollar balance, convertibility, and non-discrimination, etc., at one swoop.' Even Sproul in New York, a close friend and an opponent of early devaluation, warned that a negative defence by the British Government would not be acceptable. The only thing that might take the spotlight off the sterling exchange rate would be the initiation of 'constructive West European proposals such as extension of Transferable Account Area, relaxation in European exchange restrictions, and other steps leading towards economic integration of Western Europe'. This was,

[69] This got very rough. The Belgian Director on the Fund Board (de Selliers) wanted his dissent recorded fully in the Minutes, including not only a reference to Gutt being unwelcome in Brussels but also a statement that Frère (Governor of the National Bank) would not see him and that any non-Belgians who accompanied him would not be granted visas.

one supposes, cold comfort to the authorities in London. Although the Bank was sympathetic to an extension of transferability, the Treasury was at that moment resisting the liberalisation of IEPC and attempting to sell to the Chancellor its wild-eyed plan for a soft-currency bloc within which settlement in gold or dollars would be totally excluded. This could be construed as a move to integration, but certainly not in a form agreeable to Washington.

On 12 May, in response to these growing pressures and to signs of a gathering drain on the reserves,[70] the Governor formally appointed a small committee 'to consider and report to the Governors on the sterling–dollar rate and allied questions'. Niemeyer, though no longer an Executive Director, was again Chairman. In Bolton's absence in the US, the other members were Mynors, Kershaw, and Beale (now Chief Cashier). The Committee was furnished with a list of questions and asked to complete its work in three weeks. In addition to devaluation itself it was asked to consider 'fixed versus floating', the desirability of 'pulling as much of the non-dollar world with us as possible', any possible embellishments to make devaluation 'positive and not merely the result of pressure' (namely the Governor's ideas for dealing with the sterling balances, the dollar debts, and convertibility), and perhaps also simultaneous action 'on the domestic front'.

While Niemeyer and his colleagues were working on their report, and while officials in the Treasury were likewise occupied, the ground was being diplomatically prepared for the next phase of American policy. In Washington, Bolton had talks with the US Treasury while the Ambassador had meetings with officials in the State Department. They both found that a more moderate line was now being taken. At the same time the American Ambassador in London, Lewis Douglas, intervened. Himself less keen on sterling devaluation, he advised Washington that the public debate was damaging Anglo-American relations and could risk driving the British into a two-world redoubt. Confidential bilateral discussions were needed. These were next suggested by Caine in a telegram to London; and on 20 May Franks himself sent a long and eloquent telegram to Cripps in which he presented the American case for treating 1949 as a desirable year in which to turn away from the economics of reconstruction and towards peacetime normality. They had not fully thought this through, but neither had the British Government. So there was now an opportunity to reach some new community of minds with the US. If this

---

[70] They fell by £55 million in the second quarter of 1949, to £406 million. A level of $1 billion, or £250 million, would have been regarded as an absolute minimum working level.

opportunity were not taken and if the Americans continued to feel the British were being negative and defensive, then they would deliberately increase their pressure for devaluation. With a rare resort to hyperbolic vision, he concluded seductively: 'The present moment appears to present a real opportunity to establish in the economic sphere a parallel to the Anglo-American partnership in leadership which is already yielding fruit in the political sphere.' But the seduction of Cripps was beyond Franks' powers. The Chancellor agreed to an informal visit to Washington by Wilson Smith and Hall, as a means of playing for time[71] rather than preparing the ground for anything in the nature of some new Anglo-American leadership. On 30 May Franks reported that Snyder, who had earlier resisted such a visit on the grounds that London had nothing positive to discuss, had now been persuaded to agree to it. Wilson Smith and Hall left for Washington a few days later and returned in the middle of June.

At this stage the Governor could take some comfort from the widely publicised views of the Chairman of the Chase National Bank, Winthrop Aldrich, who was visiting London. He was unsympathetic to devaluation and very critical of the Administration's campaign on the subject. But at this time Cobbold also saw Baumgartner of the Bank of France. Although he found him hopeful that the position could be held for a few months, he also noted: 'He keeps an open mind about the autumn.' Soon afterwards there were reports from other sources that the French were playing a familiar game. They did in fact favour a modest devaluation of the franc against the dollar, but they were unwilling to do this ahead of a move by the British in case they would then be obliged to do it again. This position enabled them to agree with the Americans while blaming London for their own inaction.

Even less comforting for London was the manic behaviour of Maurice Frère, President of the BIS as well as Governor of the National Bank of Belgium, as recounted in a report supplied to the Bank in confidence by an American employee of Reuters[72] who had recently lunched with Frère in Brussels. Its author recorded: 'Given his official position, given also the very intimate relationship between European central banks, which excludes mutual criticism of one another's policies, I expected to find a diplomatic, if not evasive attitude, although I have known M. Frère very well for about twenty-five years. To my great surprise it was Frère himself

---

[71] He told the Governor on 24 May that he wanted to send Wilson Smith to the US so as to head off an early descent on himself by the Administration.

[72] Rickatson-Hatt, the Bank's Press Officer, had worked in Reuters before his recruitment by Norman.

who during the luncheon started the conversation on the pound sterling and did so with the opening sentence: "The pound sterling will be devalued within six months".' He had gone on to rehearse the familiar arguments for devaluation and the great pressure being brought to bear on the British Government by the Americans. 'Intentionally', the report went on, 'I brought up one argument after the other against the probability of an early pound devaluation; he brushed them all aside.' This influential Belgian opinion was paralleled by an article in *The Economist* that pointed to the rigidity of UK costs, the uncompetitiveness of UK export prices, and the ultimately untenable position of sterling at $4.03. Its editor, Geoffrey Crowther, had told the Governor privately some weeks earlier that he thought devaluation was inevitable. *The Times*, adopting a rather different line, warned the Government in a leading article that devaluation should only be rejected if disinflation in the UK were pushed further, if the amount of sterling made available abroad were cut, if further bilateral trade agreements for the exchange of high-priced goods were avoided, and if the external transferability of sterling were greatly increased. If these things could not be done, 'the strong case for putting off a decision about devaluation crumbles'. Unsurprisingly, Cobbold told Cripps on 1 June that he was 'a bit unhappy about the longer-term outlook. I was afraid that we looked to be drifting a bit and might find ourselves just pushed off our perch in some months' time onto another perch where we would be no better off.' For his part the Chancellor was 'very strong and sound against any move in sterling but is fearful of the effects of a prolonged talking campaign'.

Wilson Smith and Hall returned from Washington in mid-June. They were able to report a full exchange of views, but could not report any change in the now virtually unanimous opinion of US officials that sterling should be devalued. It had been agreed that further discussions, at a level to be agreed, should take place in July and September. By that time the exercise being conducted in Europe by the Managing Director of the IMF, pursuant to the resolution pushed through by the Americans in April, would also be completed. These prospects, together with a continuing loss of reserves, compelled the British authorities to sort out their ideas urgently and try to agree on a policy of some kind with which to keep the Americans at bay and get the loss of reserves under control. Treasury and Bank officials were at one in judging that tinkering, including further cuts in dollar imports, would not do. Some officials in the Treasury now judged that devaluation itself had become necessary, along with a tightening of domestic fiscal and monetary policy. But all were deeply concerned lest devaluation should be adopted as a relatively painless alternative to unpopular domestic retrenchment. It was a difficult if increasingly familiar question of tactics. If you sought to persuade Ministers to take firm domestic action in order to avoid devaluation, the risk was that they would respond with too little too late. If you sought to persuade them that devaluation was necessary but that it had to be accompanied by firm domestic action, the risk was that you would get a lot of the former and not enough of the latter. The tactical question was especially difficult for the Governor, who was developing his plan for setting right the external banking position of the UK with American help. He must have realised that such help would not be forthcoming without devaluation, yet in Whitehall he had to maintain, almost ex officio, a position of qualified opposition to it.

Niemeyer's Committee reported on 6 June. A copy was subsequently shown privately to Bridges, who returned it to the Governor on 17 June together with copies of a series of short Treasury papers on devaluation that had gone to the Chancellor. The Report began by disclaiming any sympathy for devaluation in the prevailing situation. It went on to rehearse the familiar arguments against floating and instead adopted the hypothesis of a straight devaluation to $3.25 or $3.00, which would be followed in whole or in part by most of the non-dollar world. Such a devaluation would have to be regarded as a once-for-all operation. It would have some beneficial effect on UK exports, but not much effect on imports. It would increase the cost of living by about 5% and touch off a series of offsetting increases in wages. It would not materially assist progress to the convertibility so wanted by the US authorities, because 'convertibility needs strong sterling, not sterling in convalescence after a major operation'. At this point a predictably dull report suddenly became interesting, almost certainly under the quiet influence of Kershaw, whose position on most issues was far less cramped than Niemeyer's position on devaluation[73] and whose slightly surprising membership of the Committee suggests that the Governor wanted a proper balance of views. The Report went on to refer to: 'a condition of economic change in which devaluation meets halfway other steps being taken to rectify the position. In short, the more flexible the economy the greater the opportunities presented by devaluation, a point which some American commentators realise.' Yet the economic organisation of the UK was in a singularly inflexible state. It had to become cost-conscious and set in hand cost reductions that might well become 'cumulatively uncomfortable if not met, *en route*, as it were, by a devaluation of the pound'. There followed a paragraph of enlightenment:

[73] Niemeyer submitted a note separate from the Report saying that he was more against even an eventual devaluation than the rest of his Committee.

If therefore the time came when devaluation had to be considered as a practical move, it would be essential, we feel, to aim at providing the conditions in which we could hope to maintain the new sterling rate. The danger of a rise in wages to an extent likely to affect seriously both the degree and the maintenance of any export advantage derived from devaluation is far greater than it was in 1931. The burden of public expenditure is much greater; the margin of private resources much less. Our net external resources are much smaller. The world attitude to sterling is much less confident and our dependence on the vagaries of Washington policies, both economic and other, much greater. We should need to do more than just shift the rate if the shift is to do any good. We must create a belief that on the new basis our economy is in order.

This means that we must provide a background such as:

(a) a balanced Budget at a level which allows for the formation of new capital – in other words, at a figure lower than the present;
(b) no increase or a very minor increase in the pre-devaluation wage level;[74]
(c) some reduction in home capital expenditure, particularly where it involves substantial demands on materials;
(d) a fairly tight monetary policy (*inter alia* to press out commodity stocks) and certainly no monetary inflation.

It is not for us to judge the political difficulties – particularly with a pending Election – of such a programme. But while circumstances might arise in which, combined with such a programme, devaluation might assist in restoring suitable relations between costs, prices, and wages, devaluation by itself, without such an adjustment, would not be a lasting solution.

As to the embellishments requested by the Governor – on the sterling balances, the UK's dollar debt, and convertibility – the Report was distinctly lukewarm. It discounted the chances of US assistance and confined itself to a brief discussion about an extension of transferability. The Governor was clearly dissatisfied. He omitted this part of the report from the copy sent to Bridges and two days later issued the broadside recounted earlier about being 'ready to think about the possibility of some very radical changes'.

Treasury officials were now divided. Bridges, Wilson Smith, and Eady took the high road of 'not yet', or not until the domestic conditions for success had been assured. Plowden,[75] Rowan, and Hall took the low road

---

[74] This is a rare example of Bank reference to wages policy. Since March 1948 the Government and the Trades Union Congress had collaborated on a wage-freeze with considerable success and were to go on doing so until the middle of 1950. But general opinion in the Bank seems to have regarded it without much confidence.
[75] *Plowden, Edwin Noel, Baron (Life Peer) 1959, GBE, KCB (b. 1907)*. Educated Switzerland and Pembroke College, Cambridge. Ministry of Economic Warfare 1939–40, Ministry of Aircraft Production 1940–6, Chief Planning Officer and Chairman, Economic Planning Board 1947–53. Chairman, United Kingdom Atomic Energy Authority 1954–9,

of 'do it now' and put the changes of domestic policy into place at the same time. The former group judged that devaluation would in practice be treated mostly as an easy escape. The latter group judged it would provide the only real opportunity firstly to take the necessary corrective measures of domestic policy and secondly to obtain American help in offsetting the external consequences of the recession. Less obviously, opinion in the Bank was also divided. Niemeyer represented the high road, remarking in a note to the Governor on 21 June: 'If it is necessary to get costs down, the only way to do so is to reduce them. Jiggling about with devaluation of dollar exchange will not help us.' Monetary and fiscal disinflation were the answers. Kershaw and Mynors, it seems, represented the low road, or at least the middle road. The Governor himself responded at once to the papers sent him by Bridges. In a note handed directly to Cripps on 18 June he began by saying that he had not formed a final view and went on to argue that there were three prerequisites to any consideration of a change in the rate: action on the UK cost structure through fiscal and monetary measures; action to deal with the sterling balances; and a new agreement with the US and Canada 'to help us by taking some of the rest of the world's demand for dollars off our back'. Only after these prerequisites had been met and the results had begun to emerge should devaluation be considered.

A few days later, on 23 June and after a series of meetings with the Treasury, the Governor wrote a long letter to Bridges and enclosed a new and revised version of the Niemeyer Report that had been drafted by Mynors. He was again careful at the outset to stress: 'I am, as you know, anxious not to express any final view at the present formative stage of discussions.' The rest of his letter, along with the new memorandum, contained a perceptible shift of ground. It was in fact a careful elaboration of a middle road, together with a firm statement of the need to reach agreement with the US about a solution to the problem of the balances. The need to take the corrective measures first, before considering devaluation, was again stressed, but the reference to letting the results emerge had gone. Nevertheless, the memorandum was at once criticised by Hall in a note to the Permanent Secretary (copied to Mynors personally). He argued that the middle road was unrealistic and lacked a sufficient sense of urgency. The low road was better: 'To sum up, I feel very strongly that there is nothing in our record which suggests that we can maintain the present sterling–dollar exchange rate, and I feel that there is little in our record to warrant the belief that we are likely to take

Chairman, Tube Investments 1963–76, Director, National Westminster Bank 1960–77, Chairman, Equity Capital for Industry 1976–82.

effective action either with the sterling balances or with monetary policy in time to produce any good effects.' On the same day Mynors wrote to Eady putting the case for raising Bank Rate to 3%, but stating it could only produce good results if undertaken in support of strong action on the level of Government expenditure.

The upshot of all this official advice was a paper put by the Chancellor to the Economic Policy Committee of the Cabinet on 28 June, to which was attached the Bank's paper of 23 June. The Chancellor agreed with the Bank about devaluation: 'I do not think this is the right time to carry it out, whatever the ultimate decision may be.' He had already proposed that a standstill be imposed on new commitments to buy dollar goods and that a new programme be worked out, amounting to a cut of 25%, for decision in September. He now asked for this to be agreed. Next he proposed that the expected excess of departmental spending over estimates should be offset by a cut in food subsidies, judging this would add as much as two points to the cost of living index. The Government should then try its utmost to preserve the wage-freeze. As to monetary policy, he felt that a rise in Bank Rate should be postponed. Long-term rates had already risen and this would suffice for the present.[76] Apart from a proposal to work out some means of giving a 'preferential award' to dollar exporters, no other adjustment of policy was put forward. Instead, considerable play was made firstly of consultations with the US and Canada 'to attempt to get their support for our reserves and for sterling' and secondly of an early conference of Commonwealth Finance Ministers 'to persuade them to economise in dollar purchases as we are doing, and to sell the greatest possible volume of their goods for dollars, as we shall attempt to do'. Finally, the Chancellor attached a draft parliamentary Statement embodying, as decisions, most of the proposals he had made.

However, since his colleagues were not persuaded of the need to announce anything at all about Government spending, the statement made in the Commons on 6 July contained no reference to it or to the need to reinforce restraint on wages. The Government, in public, was then left relying on dollar cuts, on talks with the US and Canada, on the conference of Finance Ministers, and on exhortations about industrial efficiency. Hugh Dalton, who must be presumed to have learnt something about the perils of ineffectual statements from his own experience in August 1947, was nonetheless among those opposed to any cuts in public spending.

The Governor had warned Bridges and the Chancellor personally that the statement would be bad for confidence. On being told by Cripps that no

---

[76] The Governor had favoured this line. The Bank did not think it worth wasting Bank Rate as an accompaniment to a minor change in fiscal policy.

deflationary policy was possible, he had replied that if the Chancellor was proposing to take the line that the only two solutions offered were devaluation or American help, he found it 'difficult to see how he could avoid being pushed into devaluation long before there was any possibility of American help. I also doubted whether the Americans were likely to play unless they saw evidence of our taking our own situation in hand.' At the end of their talk he reiterated: 'I thought financial opinion both here and overseas very much on edge and that if they got the impression that things were not being taken in hand, there might be quick and uncomfortable developments.' Cripps had no reassurance to offer him. At this point the campaign for the middle road was effectively lost and with it the opportunity that Cobbold had seen and explained. Whether they knew it or not, Ministers had decisively taken the lower side of the low road and were thereafter mostly concerned to minimise the domestic political damage. Treasury officials, along with the Governor, kept up the fight, but Ministers seemed deaf. They were also, it appears, deeply mistrustful of their official advisers.[77] Ministers either saw no connection between public expenditure and the exchange rate or else were paranoid in their attitude both to further cuts and to a resurrection of Bank Rate. All the ghosts of 1931 seem to have haunted them at this time.

By the end of June the Managing Director of the IMF had completed his tour of West European capitals and reported back to his Board. At lunch with the Chancellor and the Governor in London earlier in the month he had said that a realignment of European currencies would be premature. His hosts encouraged him to propagate that opinion in Washington; but his report did not do so. It bluntly admitted that European export prices were insufficiently competitive. Thereafter Gutt mostly confined himself to rehearsing the familiar arguments about devaluation and about the domestic conditions necessary for it to succeed. He came to no definite conclusion but noted that all eyes were on sterling, that nobody would move ahead of a change in the sterling–dollar rate, and that there had been more 'whens' than 'ifs' about such a change whenever the subject had arisen in discussions on the Continent. This was much more likely to encourage the Americans than deter them. But although convinced that a devaluation of sterling was essential, they were careful not to bring any more direct bilateral pressure on the UK. Ambassador Douglas still counselled caution, particularly following an interview with Bevin, who raised the spectre of a Sterling Area and West European bloc and pressed

---

[77] See Hugh Dalton, *Diaries*, ed. J. A. R. Pimlott (London, Jonathan Cape, 1983) and Philip Williams, *Hugh Gaitskell*, (London, Jonathan Cape,1979). Interestingly, Douglas Jay does not recall this in his autobiography, *Change and Fortune* (London, Hutchinson, 1980).

for American acceptance of British views about unemployment and deflation. Caution was also advised by the Canadians. Towers told Southard and Bissell in mid-June that there was nothing to be gained by needling the British over devaluation; pressure of events should be allowed to force action. So when Snyder and Harriman met in Paris early in July ahead of a visit to London, where they were joined by Abbott, the Canadian Finance Minister, they decided to take the line that they would seek British reaffirmation of the agreed basic objectives of convertibility and non-discrimination and encourage them to take these into account when proposing lasting solutions to their current problem. The Americans themselves would treat that problem as a British one and not attempt to propose solutions themselves.

In the ensuing talks that took place in London over 8–10 July the Americans had no difficulty in securing from the British a public reaffirmation of their adherence to the long-term policy of convertibility and non-discrimination. They also elicited from the Chancellor the admission that the UK must make its goods competitive and that the UK 'might have to be prepared to consider devaluation, not under present conditions, but as part of any general scheme designed to deal with the fundamental problems'. However, he had added that surplus countries would have to be prepared to reduce tariffs (and other obstacles to imports) and to encourage overseas investment. He also took credit for the UK proposals, now on the table in Paris, for liberalising intra-European trade. Finally the Chancellor proposed that there should be exploratory talks at official level, about long-term solutions, preparatory to another tripartite Ministerial meeting in September. This was accepted, but Snyder was not very impressed. Reporting later to the NAC, he wrote: 'It is difficult to see how any fruitful results can be obtained so long as the British refuse to take fundamental steps which will shake out the rigidities and make their economy more flexible. However, I believe we can make use of the forthcoming conversations to stress strongly that such steps are necessary if continued economic co-operation between our countries is to bear fruit.'

The talks with Snyder and Abbott were followed by a meeting of Commonwealth Finance Ministers, who agreed on emergency cuts in dollar imports. As to long-term solutions, the Finance Ministers generally supported the British position in the Anglo-American debate. But as July wore on and the drain of reserves was not checked, the Governor became increasingly pessimistic. In a note to Bolton about the need to scale down his ambitious plans for US assistance, he reverted to the theme that firm domestic action was needed in any event but was also needed to persuade the Americans to help. He added: 'As you know, I do not exclude devaluation as a part of comprehensive measures on these lines.' On 14 July he warned Bridges that the reserves looked likely to fall as low as £300–325 million by mid-September, when the Washington talks would be in full play. He also enclosed a separate note arguing that worthwhile cuts in Government expenditure would not amount to the general deflationary policy that Ministers dreaded. On 19 July he went to say goodbye to the exhausted Cripps, who was about to leave for several weeks complete rest in a Swiss clinic. He had nothing cheerful to tell him: 'I told him I was depressed about things in general and did not see how things could do other than decline either gradually or quickly. He thought things would go quietly until the end of August. I agreed this might be so but I did not feel too certain about it.'

Events in Whitehall moved quickly after the Chancellor's departure. Gaitskell, who effectively deputised for him, became convinced that devaluation was necessary. Douglas Jay, the Economic Secretary, had already reached that conclusion. On 26 July, on behalf of himself and his colleagues, the Permanent Secretary to the Treasury circulated a strong note to the Prime Minister in which he put forward a package of measures containing devaluation together with a slow-down of Government expenditure and a rise in short-term interest rates from $\frac{1}{2}$% to about $1\frac{1}{2}$% (in line with the Bank Rate of 2%).[78] Delay in the adoption of such a package risked an effective exhaustion of reserves and the loss of all room for manoeuvre. Decisions would have to be taken before the Washington talks opened if there was to be any hope of obtaining American help. This view was reflected in a draft steering brief, which advised that the cuts in public spending and probably also the rise in interest rates should be announced before the talks began. The brief also spelt out the sort of assistance that should be sought, in addition to help with the sterling balances. The Americans would be asked to resume official stockpiling of imported materials, to encourage lending by the Export-Import Bank, to agree to the unlocking of IMF loans to countries in receipt of ERP Aid, to agree to reciprocal cuts in tariffs, and to encourage outward investment.

The Cabinet met on 28 July and agreed that devaluation was now unavoidable. But Ministers were divided about Government spending. The majority, including the Prime Minister, were hostile to the announcement of cuts either ahead of devaluation or coincident with it. In 1931 the Labour Government had broken up in office while attempting to agree cuts

---

[78] In a note to Bridges, Eady recorded the Governor as being quite adamant that he would not agree to action on monetary policy without parallel action on public expenditure. He had advised Cobbold 'not to excite himself unduly at this stage'.

in spending designed to stave off a plunge in the exchange rate. Whatever else happened, the Attlee Government was not going to be manoeuvred into anything resembling that predicament, though it was prepared to make warning noises to the spending departments in private. After a fairly sharp tussle with Treasury officials, the majority view prevailed and a note was despatched by the Prime Minister to the Chancellor on 5 August. It recorded Ministerial acceptance of devaluation and duly reported unanimous official advice about expenditure cuts; but while not rejecting these outright it remarked that 'a devaluation, if desirable at a certain date on other grounds, should not be delayed in order to await further decisions on Government expenditure'. It concluded by canvassing possible dates from 28 August to 18 September.

The Governor, who had been kept informed by Bridges, wrote to the Prime Minister on 3 August, before the latter's note to Cripps had taken final shape. He gave general support to Bridges and his colleagues while, if anything, stepping back to the position that devaluation should not be considered until measures had actually been taken to reduce inflationary pressures and to relieve the weight of overseas sterling balances. But his main point was to warn of the dangers that would arise if world opinion were to regard the operation as the first of a series of devaluations. He also advised that if devaluation came about less as a matter of policy than as a matter of necessity, 'we should probably feel bound to recommend, always with the object of avoiding pressure for a further subsequent devaluation, a larger degree of devaluation than might be appropriate if it formed part of a general plan'. The Prime Minister confined himself to a terse if polite acknowledgement on the following day, saying that 'the matters to which you call my attention shall have my most careful consideration'. They may or they may not have done. Their effect is not discernible. The Prime Minister did not ask to see the Governor. Nor did Gaitskell. On the matter of devaluation, at this stage, central bankers were to be heard but not seen. So, after writing to Cripps that he would be back on 20 August and was leaving things in the hands of the Deputy Governor, Bolton, and Mynors, Cobbold left on 6 August for a short holiday in Austria.

While the Governor was away, the Bank was busy helping in the preparation of briefs for the Washington meetings and of notes on devaluation drill. Bolton, with O'Brien and Ainslie Darby,[79] were to accompany the official Treasury delegation led by Wilson Smith. Late in

---

[79] *Darby, Ainslie Charles* (b. *1907*). Educated Christ's Hospital. Entered Bank 1925, Assistant Principal, Statistics Office 1943–6, Deputy Principal 1946–9, Assistant 1949–50, Assistant Secretary 1950–9, Adviser (Industry) 1959–66.

July Bolton sent to the Treasury the Bank's *magnum opus* entitled 'The International Exchange Structure'. This had been in preparation since the Governor's request in June for some radical thinking. It stressed the limits of exchange control and the disadvantages of a two-world system of trade and payments. It then concluded that there was in practice 'little choice but to move towards a free system of trade and exchanges, the exchange policy that we adopt being dependent upon the success or failure of the forthcoming discussions in Washington. If the present loss of reserves continues and we fail to persuade the US to give additional financial assistance, in addition to drastic domestic action we might be forced into a situation similar to that of 1931–9. On the other hand, if it is possible to secure full American co-operation and assistance, we should endeavour to move towards a system of exchange stability combined with convertibility which would put an end to the difficulties associated with cheap sterling and bilateralism.' There then followed the grand design of American help with the balances, American underwriting of sterling convertibility (provided the UK kept in balance overall), unlocking of the IMF, and the merging, for exchange control purposes, of the Sterling Area with Western Europe. In a separate note the Bank also argued for a rise in the dollar price of gold from $35 to $50 per ounce. Though useful to have on the record, these papers could of course have no practical effect, for they were integral to the middle road that Ministers had rejected out of hand some weeks before.

Bolton also sent to the Treasury, at Rowe-Dutton's request, a note on floating. This was prepared in a great hurry and its author told the Treasury he was unhappy with it. Gaitskell, Jay, Hall, and Plowden had been toying with the idea of temporary floating as a means of feeling one's way to the correct fixed rate. Since a devaluation of anything up to 30% against the dollar was now being contemplated, this notion had some intellectual merit. But Bolton did not really address himself to it. Instead he responded with a hurried diatribe against systematic floating, which ended with the familiar dictum: 'Such a development could not be regarded as a policy but simply the inevitable result of an economic catastrophe.' The real if unstated objection to temporary floating was mostly technical. As had been set out in papers prepared a year earlier, it would have been very difficult to run a floating rate for sterling without reconstituting the foreign exchange market in London. There would also have been obvious difficulties with the operation of bilateral monetary and payments agreements, not to mention IEPC. Quite clearly, it would have been virtually impossible to carry through the necessary planning to meet these problems in the few weeks remaining before $4.03 was to be abandoned.

Equally clearly, putting the plans into effect would have greatly complicated the next phase and seriously risked damaging sterling during its critical period of convalescence. Perhaps the Treasury appreciated these points even though Bolton did not, in so many words, actually make them. In any event, little more was heard of the idea.[80]

While the British were preparing briefs for the Washington talks, the Americans were doing the same. They were more than ever convinced that West European costs and prices were substantially out of line with those prevailing in North America; and more than ever convinced that a realignment of exchange rates was essential. Devaluation of sterling was the key, the more so on account of the supposed post-war British propensity to indulge in over-full employment and persistent inflationary pressures. As to further help, the Americans tended to regard their recession as heralding a return to normal market conditions rather than a reprehensible lapse from full employment. They did consider a rise in the price of gold and an unlocking of the IMF, but rejected both as inappropriate or politically unacceptable. As to tariff reductions, simplification of Customs procedures and strategic stockpiling, they felt that progress was being made as fast as conditions allowed. Meanwhile, the Embassy in London was again counselling caution and tact. The British Government would acutely resent any hint of US interference in the internal affairs of the UK. 'The risk of irreparable damage to Anglo-American relations which could result from this meeting is so great that it is imperative to create and maintain a friendly atmosphere'. Be tactics as they may, it is quite clear the Americans were interested in devaluation to the exclusion of almost everything else. They might offer continuing talks on all manner of topics, but they had no serious intention of making important concessions of substance; and in the IMF they kept up the pressure through Southard, who initiated a series of seminars on exchange-rate adjustment.

Shortly after returning from holiday the Governor concluded that early devaluation had become necessary. On 26 August he wrote tactfully to the Chancellor, who had returned from Zurich in somewhat better health, that he was coming reluctantly to the conclusion that it would be difficult to restore confidence in the present rate now that the idea of devaluation was so deeply rooted all over the world. The loss of reserves had not increased, but neither were there any signs of it decreasing. If it was decided to devalue, it was vitally important not only to accompany it by

---

[80] Oddly enough, some American authorities were not wholly unsympathetic to temporary floating.

measures to restore confidence in the UK's internal finances and to deal with the sterling balances but also to make the change as part of a general realignment of currencies, 'giving it as much as possible the colour of a constructive international move rather than of an individual defensive retreat'. He went on to argue strongly against a floating rate, on much the same lines as Bolton, and advocated devaluation to a new rate 'where the world will think we are a little undervalued'. He suggested this might be in the region of $2.75. The letter was discussed between the two men on 29 August, and in a note to Bolton written on the same day the Governor remarked:

> I think the Chancellor personally stands very much where I do on the question of devaluation. He does not think it will do much good but, now that it has been talked about so much and so widely for six months, he does not see much hope of getting away without it. He is shocked by the idea of going below $3, but I restated the arguments which make me believe that that is necessary if they decide to make a move. The Chancellor does not see his way to do anything particular about internal finance and he seemed (rightly I think) pessimistic about much positive help at this time from the US.

The decision in principle to devalue had of course already been taken, but the decision to fix on $2.80 was not taken until 12 September, at a meeting held by Cripps and Bevin in the British Embassy in Washington. Ministers had not wanted to go below $3.00 but were persuaded to go lower by their officials and by Bolton.[81]

Not long after his arrival in Washington, Bolton travelled to New York for a full exchange of views with Sproul. Like Cobbold, the latter had now concluded that devaluation was inevitable and favoured a substantial cut so as to give some headroom thereafter. But he warned that despite the great fund of goodwill towards the UK, additional American help, short-term or long, would not be forthcoming unless the British Government curtailed its own expenditure, reduced capital investment in the UK and the Sterling Area, and further restrained the use of accumulated sterling balances. Sproul added, however, that American monetary policy, which – though basically easy – had tightened a little in 1948, was now being relaxed. Money rates were coming down to about 1%. This could be a useful context for a firming of rates in London. It might indeed have been.

On his return to Washington Bolton participated in the tripartite official discussions but reported in a letter to the Governor that they amounted to

---

[81] He had earlier been instructed by the Governor to record the Bank's formal dissent in writing if the Chancellor showed signs of deciding on a rate above $3.00. The Bank itself was prepared, with expressed misgivings, to accept $3.00.

no more than friendly shadow-boxing. The Americans, true to their brief, had nothing much to say about British policy and little to do except listen to Wilson Smith and his colleagues, who scouted their various ideas about helpful adjustments in US policy on tariffs, etc., who went through the story of the sterling balances, and who remained silent on devaluation. The only discordant note was the noise Southard was making in the IMF. Late on 6 September the Chancellor and the Foreign Secretary arrived in the US on board the *Mauretania*.[82] The Ministerial tripartite talks began on the 7th and on the second day the British told the others that it had been decided to devalue on 18 September. The amount was not disclosed and indeed was not finally decided until the 12th. But the Americans were delighted. Bolton reported on 11 September: 'A quite wonderful atmosphere of goodwill in Washington. The American and Canadian Ministers are falling over backwards to find means of helping, at the same time avoiding the necessity to go to Congress or the Canadian Parliament.' The means immediately offered consisted of a new committee which was to be the Continuing Organisation to look after the longer-term problems. Bolton then allowed his acuity of observation to be overcome by his natural enthusiasm for new visions. Rather as Keynes had written to Catto at the end of 1944 that 'we are among friends here', he now wrote: 'This of course represents a tremendous advance on anything that has gone before and, to some extent, parallels the Combined Chiefs of Staff Committee in the economic and financial field.' But he did go on to warn that the Americans were overdoing it, with the result that 'our people are becoming more reluctant that ever to face the real issues'.

The elaborate drill of a sterling devaluation under Bretton Woods rules now proceeded to its climax, like some lengthy royal ceremony. A host of telegrams to central banks were carefully prepared and despatched from the Bank by toiling officials, in correct form and order depending on the priority or trustworthiness of each recipient. Where no cypher facilities existed between central banks, personal emissaries were sent (to Rome, Copenhagen, and Dublin). Parallel procedures were carried out by the Treasury on the inter-governmental network. Late on 16 September

---

[82] It was still, just, the age of the Atlantic liner. Franks and Wilson Smith went out to the Ambrose Light by coastguard cutter to board the *Mauretania* so as to brief Cripps and Bevin. The devaluation drill was now working. The operation itself was called Rose. In telegrams between Washington and London all references to personalities, rates of exchange, etc. were disguised by code words. They were mostly biblical. The Chancellor was Obadiah and the Foreign Secretary, Ezra. There was no Judas. However, the Bank was Pilate – which suggested some Private Office sense of humour. The Chancellor's Private Secretary was William Armstrong, later Permanent Secretary and Head of the Civil Service.

Bolton attended 'an enormous cocktail party' at the French Embassy in Washington and, with the prior consent of Cripps, warned the principal West European central bankers that devaluation was to occur at the weekend. He even told Baumgartner the amount. Similar activities were undertaken by Wilson Smith on the Treasury's network. On the following day Bolton himself presented the British proposal to the Fund Board in his capacity as UK Executive Director. In the Bank, on Sunday 18 September, the Governor saw the Chairmen of the Committee of London Clearing Bankers, the Accepting Houses Committee, and the Stock Exchange to inform them that the pound would be devalued and to advise them that banks and markets were to be closed on Monday to give time for the dust to settle. In the evening, before the Chancellor's broadcast to the nation, the Governor assembled an informal meeting of the Court. He told them that devaluation by itself was never a solution; it was a recognition of a state of affairs. He went on:

> But as things are on 18 September, given the fact that HM Government have felt unable to take more drastic action in their policy in other economic fields, and given the continuing drain on our reserves, I do not personally think that devaluation could for long be avoided or could now wisely be delayed. Once it was decided to act, I feel sure that it was necessary, the more so because it has not proved possible to take more action to curb inflation, to make a heavy cut, and avoid any risk that world judgement might say we had not gone far enough. The one essential thing – and this I repeat and underline – is that devaluation can be done once but can and must not even be in question a second time unless there have been major events such as a world war in the intervening period. As I have said I do not wish to give you the rate – but the cut is heavy and on this point I think the Government have acted wisely and boldly.

Since July he had been keeping the Committee of Treasury[83] informed. They were shown the letter of 23 June to Bridges and the memorandum on devaluation that had accompanied it. They were shown and had approved the letter of 3 August to the Prime Minister and had been shown the latter's reply. On 31 August they were told that matters had been further discussed between the Governor and the Chancellor. Finally, on 14 September they were informed that devaluation was still under consideration and they approved a suggestion by the Governor that there should be an informal meeting of the Court to inform them of the decision, if it were taken, shortly before the public announcement was made. The Committee also supported a proposal by the Governor to advise the

---

[83] In addition to the Governors its membership was Ashley Cooper, Hanbury-Williams, Piercy, Sanderson, and Siepmann.

Chancellor, in the event of devaluation, that some small increase in short-term money rates was desirable. Later, on 28 September, they were told that the Chancellor had not accepted this advice. On none of these occasions was any discussion recorded.

Once sterling had moved there followed the general realignment that had all along been an American aim. Almost the entire Sterling Area followed the British, devaluing by 30% against the dollar. In Western Europe the pattern was more mixed. The Scandinavian countries and the Netherlands followed sterling. France and West Germany devalued by about 20%, the Belgians by 12%, and the Italians by 8%. On a trade-weighted basis the effective devaluation of sterling was less than 10%. The whole operation had gone remarkably smoothly, without leakage. Only the French were cross. They were about to announce with a flourish their plans for 'Finebel'. But devaluation of sterling got in their way and its extent was too large for their liking. Moreover, it looked too much as if a decision vital to Western Europe in general had been taken at an Anglo-American–Canadian caucus, behind everyone else's back and without consultation. The French Foreign Minister, Robert Schuman,[84] had actually been in Washington during the week immediately before devaluation for talks with Acheson and Bevin on a variety of matters and had not been let into the secret. But in fact the decision to devalue had been taken earlier by the Government in London and not as a result of the talks in Washington. Throughout the earlier months of the year the Americans had consulted very widely in Western Europe on the question of exchange rates and been told that sterling would have to go first. All their subsequent efforts had accordingly been concentrated on sterling. Tactically this meant bilateral (or tripartite) talks with the British and if necessary some exploitation of the 'special relationship'. This in turn may have meant infuriating the French, but that was a price that had to be paid.

Before returning to London from Washington at the end of September, Bolton wrote to the Governor about strong American hopes that devaluation would be followed by early signs of progress towards

---

[84] Schuman, Robert (1886–1963). Educated Universities of Bonn, Munich, Berlin, and Strasbourg. Barrister, Metz 1912, Deputy for Moselle 1919–63. Minister of Finance, Governments of Bidault 1946, Ramadier 1947, Prime Minister 1947–8, Minister of Foreign Affairs, Governments of Marie July 1948, Queuille September 1948–9, Bidault 1949, Pleven July 1950, Queuille March 1951, Pleven August 1951, Fauré January 1952, Pinay March 1952, Minister of Justice, Fauré Government February 1955. Leader, French Delegation, Third Session of UN General Assembly 1948. President, MRP 1945–9, President of Honour 1949–63. President, European Parliament, 1958–60, President of Honour 1960–3.

convertibility: 'I fully appreciate all the difficulties which may, from the stories reaching Washington, be increased by the possibilities of an early General Election. I hope you will warn Whitehall of the inevitability of new convertibility and/or transferability pressures coming from Washington.' He was right. Though devaluation was more successful than the Bank or Treasury officials had feared, the ordeals of sterling were not about to cease. Earlier sections of this chapter have related their persistence. The ECA, indefatigable as ever, was shortly to begin another year's campaigning, this time to force an appropriate solution of the problem of intra-European payments through the establishment of the EPU. Before long, too, the problem of cheap sterling was to recur. It was to occupy the close attention of the Governor and encourage the Bank to espouse more rapid progress to convertibility. Finally, there remained the sterling balances. Their future was to be discussed with the Americans, without much promise of worthwhile results, but the Bank went on nursing ambitions for their radical treatment.

Though it obstinately refused to countenance any restoration of flexibility in short-term interest rates, the Government did eventually agree on some degree of fiscal retrenchment and some further use of controls to cut back the investment programmes of the private sector. These measures, which amounted to £280 million in a full year, were announced at the end of October. Their actual effect was probably rather small. Far more important was an agreement with the Trades Union Congress to continue the wage-freeze for a further year, provided the cost of living did not rise by more than 5%. It actually rose by less than 3% in the year following devaluation. The trail then gets substantially lost in the dense macro-economic clouds that descended after the outbreak of war in Korea. But up to that point the external situation, helped of course by the cuts in dollar expenditure imposed before the alteration in the exchange rate, had greatly improved. The reserves, benefiting at first from the unwinding of adverse leads and lags, rose from some $1,300 million to over $2 billion by the summer of 1950. The American economy recovered rapidly from recession and US imports rose sharply. British exports to dollar markets responded well. One way and another it looked as if officials in the Treasury and the Bank might have underestimated the strength of the UK economy and the effectiveness, at least in the short run, of the policies – in particular, wage policy – that Ministers chose to pursue. That is not, however, to say that the officials were wrong to give the advice they did. On the contrary, given the disinclination of many Ministers to do much more than be pushed backwards into devaluation by American pressure and by market force, it was the prime duty of officials to go on hammering away at the need for domestic measures that would minimise the risk of a third post-war sterling crisis with all its ominous implications. Had they not so hammered, it is likely that the domestic measures actually taken would have been weaker than they were.

A more interesting question, from the Bank's viewpoint, is whether there really was an opportunity to restructure the UK's external balance sheet in 1949 and move much more rapidly towards convertibility. For, as has been related, the Bank's distinctive role in the crisis of 1949 was its judgement that such an opportunity was there and should be seized. Equally distinctive was the Government's disinclination to pay the price, though it seems in part to have accepted that the opportunity existed and that the restructuring suggested by the Bank would have been a great achievement. There cannot be much doubt that it would. By 1949 it was clear enough that the UK economy was most unlikely, in the then foreseeable future, to develop so favourable an external balance as to bring about the restructuring on its own. If that was so, then the exposed external banking position was bound to continue and bound to be a constantly debilitating and even erratic constraint, encouraging the stops and starts in macro-economic policy that were to become a feature of the landscape in the fifties and sixties. But if the Bank was clear-sighted in this respect, it may nonetheless have wrongly identified the opportunity. The story told in other chapters has indicated that this was probably the case. It was too late in the day, in 1949, to make another grand post-war financial deal on sterling, bilaterally with the Americans, on the basis that Cobbold and Bolton advocated. Even if the Government had been prepared to announce fiscal retrenchment in July 1949 together with some substantial extensions of sterling transferability, there is no evidence to suggest that the Administration and the Congress would have responded with the required financial assistance to the UK. The Americans were by then too suspicious of the British Government's intentions and too critical of its economic policies. In addition they were far more involved with their other European allies, and above all with 'Europeanism', than in the earlier post-war period. So they were by then unlikely to have seen convertible sterling and a restructuring of the sterling balances as the exclusive financial subsoil, along with the dollar, of the 'one world' for which they were working.

It is at this point that the absence of a clear and continuing British strategy becomes so evident. The Bank's advocacy of a fresh start, on an Anglo-American basis, was indeed advocacy of a strategic move. But nobody in Whitehall seems to have responded with the question: Yes, we agree with the aim, but are we sure the strategy is correctly shaped so as to attract American support? This was because the Government had no external monetary strategy of its own, or none worthy of the name; and, in truth, it could not have thought one out in a hurry, under pressure, in the spring and summer of 1949. Had it done so earlier, it might have adopted a very different and much more positive attitude towards the problem of intra-European trade and payments. This in turn could have made the Americans receptive to some of the Bank's ideas for helping the UK to make a fresh start with sterling. It would have meant the Treasury and the Bank, especially the latter, discarding some of their grander visions, or illusions, about the role of sterling in Europe. But a more perceptive Government, with a clearer analysis of the external monetary problem and clearer ideas about its solution, could have provided correct guidance. If one wanted a negotiated and multilateral solution to that problem, with US help, the keys lay in 'Europe'. The trouble was that nobody in London could agree soon enough on the right key, let alone turn it. The European initiative lay mostly elsewhere. Only after devaluation, when the moment of potential opportunity had passed and when American pressures continued, in the way Bolton reported they would, did the British (with little initial help from the Bank) turn their minds to a key labelled EPU. But even then the driving force was American, and the British position was essentially responsive rather than initiatory. The State Department and the US Treasury remained suspicious of British intentions and critical of the British attitude. On his return from a visit to the US in May and June 1950, Bolton reported that Acheson had told him over the dinner table: 'I am not interested in details. I want faith in European unity and an act of faith in blindly entering a broad stream of European consciousness of its inevitable destiny as a political unit.' He was not to get it.

(f) CHANGES AHEAD: 1950–1951

The four interrelated themes of the preceding sections, intra-European payments, cheap sterling, the sterling balances, and devaluation, cast a combined shadow over the beginning of the new decade. Together with the earlier episode of the false dawn and the convertibility crisis, they represented most of the Bank's post-war experience. As such they powerfully influenced its thinking as it looked at future progress towards agreed external objectives. For in the summer of 1950, as the storm in Korea was about to break, the external monetary situation of the UK suggested the approach of a climacteric. It was possible, though rather unlikely, that the country might proceed slowly towards a restoration of convertibility and non-discrimination without any intervening crisis and without any notable change in the various arms of policy. But if a third post-war sterling crisis did intervene, a contingency that the Korean War and the UK rearmament programme were to make virtually inevitable, notable changes of policy there would have to be. For the UK would seemingly enter the crisis without proper means of defence. Confidence had already been undermined by the crises of 1947 and 1949. The reserves remained inadequate. The problems of the sterling balances were still unresolved. The cheap-sterling traffic remained ineffectually contained. Short-term interest rates were still chained to the $\frac{1}{2}\%$ on Treasury Bills established in 1945. The budgetary situation, though well contained, seldom commanded adequate confidence abroad. The wages policy would shortly grow weak with age. Dollar imports were already severely curtailed by controls while an unsympathetic American Administration remained bent on driving the UK towards the convertibility and non-discrimination to which the British Government had repeatedly put its name. In Western Europe, it is true, the newly agreed Payments Union was a source of additional credit, but it was scarcely in any other respect a protection against crisis and it was of uncertain duration. It looked as though quite a lot would have to be altered if a third crisis was to be handled without descent into a disorderly collapse of sterling.

Judging by its thoughts and deeds, the Bank was becoming increasingly aware of the approaching watershed and increasingly apprehensive. As has been seen, it had tried without success to seize the opportunities it saw in 1949 and early in 1950 to deal with the problems of the sterling balances by radical measures, with or even without American help. It had by then also come to realise that the problem of cheap sterling, and the limits to exchange control that it represented, could not finally be solved except by restoration of the convertibility that the Government still saw as only a distant goal. As is recounted in Chapter 5, the Bank was losing no opportunity to urge Treasury Ministers to sanction an unshackling of short-term money rates, but it was making hardly any headway. Its influence on budgetary policy remained small, though it persistently nagged the Government about it. It was well aware of renewed American dissatisfaction with British policy towards attainment of agreed objectives and it observed that the Government was reluctant to respond. Some in the Bank began to fear that the UK was being driven into fixed-rate convertibility in conditions, both national and international, that would lead to economically undesirable and politically unacceptable consequences. This then led the Bank to consider the option of floating-rate convertibility in conditions very different to the 1930s and fraught with a new variety of dangers. None of this prospect can have been inviting to an institution that bore a major share of responsibility for the management of sterling yet was often denied managerial authority.

In March 1950, following the General Election and in expectation of renewed pressures from Washington, the trend of thought in the Bank about convertibility remained at first restrained and gradualist. Important memoranda circulated by Mynors and by Fisher emphasised a step-by-step reduction in exchange controls between non-dollar countries followed by phased reductions in trade discrimination against North America. Sterling convertibility would also require increased reserves, a lack of excessive sight liabilities in sterling, a healthy external balance overall, appropriate fiscal and monetary policies, and a reciprocal restoration of convertibility on the part of Britain's major non-dollar trading partners. It was also emphasised that the UK was committed only to current-account non-resident convertibility, not to the full convertibility of former times. Maurice Allen,[85] the newly recruited Economic Adviser, was more sceptical about the feasibility of any successful return to fixed-rate convertibility So was Bolton. In correspondence with Southard in Washington, who was as usual pressing the one-world case, he began to air doubts whether fixed-rate convertibility would prove workable in modern conditions. Short-term capital movements would, it seemed, no longer be reliably available to respond to acceptable changes in short-term interest rates and to correct temporary maladjustments of the external balance. Indeed, the exchange rate flexibility, or 'adjustable peg', of the Bretton Woods regime was inclined to encourage perverse rather than benign capital flows. Bolton wrote:

> If you want to reintroduce convertibility in the sense that means anything, you must explain with what machinery you propose to replace the automatic correctives in a world in which techniques of market management, exchange stabilisation funds, etc. have been developed which are designed to offset the inflationary and deflationary consequences; [which] would not include the stabilising influence of short-term capital movements; and in which deflation is associated in the public mind with widespread unemployment and political unrest. You cannot operate a system of convertible currencies by national exchange controls and frequent changes in import restrictions and tariff policy.

This well-pointed invitation did not attract a reply. But during the spring and summer of 1950 the American pressure increased. The British were

---

[85] *Allen, William Maurice (1908–88)*. Educated Dulwich and LSE. Fellow in Economics, Balliol College, Oxford 1931–48, Army 1940–5. Assistant Director of Research, IMF 1947–9. Entered Bank 1950, Adviser 1950–4, Adviser to the Governors 1954–64, Executive Director 1964–70. Visiting Fellow, Nuffield College, Oxford 1954–62.

warned in April that the US Treasury would now only discuss the sterling balances from the point of view of whether a particular solution would assist a move to convertibility. During a month's visit to the US in May Bolton was warned by Sproul in New York that the Treasury was highly critical of UK policy. Proposals about the sterling balances were unlikely to get far. It might therefore be unwise to put them forward because if, as was unlikely, they were accepted, they would provoke a demand for immediate convertibility. As related earlier in this chapter, the proposals did in fact get nowhere at all; and in June Assistant Secretary Martin[86] told Rowan that the US Treasury was not interested in the past of the Loan Agreement but only in future plans and an outline of the methods by which the UK hoped to attain convertibility and non-discrimination. A reaffirmation of broad policy-intent for 1952 and after, when the transitional period of the Bretton Woods Agreement would have expired, would not do. The Administration wanted plans. What, for instance, was to be done about the 25% cuts in dollar imports imposed in 1949? Were they to be reduced in steps, or abolished later in one move? Co-operation from the US Treasury would be much reduced unless the UK gave some sign on these matters. Entry into the EPU was not itself a reliable sign, for it could point either way.

The same ground was covered again in August, with Rowan gaining a point by arguing that the convertibility of sterling would need underpinning by reserves of at least $5 billion. Thereafter this particular pressure eased while questions of rearmament and its financing took over as the principal subject of Anglo-American economic and financial discussions. The reserves began their rapid but temporary 'Korean' ascent. On this latter account Marshall Aid to the UK was suspended early in 1951 at the same time as the Government agreed to a three-year programme of defence expenditure that was double the amount agreed a year earlier and a third higher than the first rearmament programme agreed in the summer of 1950. It was expected that some part of the obvious external pressure that would result from this heavy burden, itself compounded by the adverse movement in the terms of trade due to the boom in commodity prices, would be met by Defence Aid from the US. But virtually none of this

---

[86] *William McChesney Martin, Jr* (b. 1906). Educated Yale and Benton College of Law, St Louis. Federal Reserve Bank of St Louis 1928–9, Head of Statistics Department, A. G. Edwards and Sons, St Louis 1929–31, Partner 1931–8, Member, New York Stock Exchange 1931–8, Governor 1935–8, Chairman, Committee on Constitution and Secretary, Conway Committee to Reorganise the Exchange 1937–8, President 1938–41, Chairman and President, Export-Import Bank 1946–9, Assistant Secretary of the Treasury 1949–51, Chairman, Board of Governors, Federal Reserve System 1951–70, US Executive Director, IBRD 1949–52.

was forthcoming until the middle of 1952, when it amounted to some $340 million for the year,[87] the equivalent of just over 10% of that year's planned defence production, building, and stockpiling. In practice, though the Government may not have realised it, the UK was left on its own to cope with the combined effects of renewed and acute pressure on real resources, of renewed pressure on domestic costs and prices, and of very sharp fluctuations (as commodity prices boomed and then slumped) in the external income and expenditure of the outer Sterling Area.

Earlier in 1950 the Bank and the Treasury had endeavoured to meet some of the American agitation for progress towards convertibility. In July the Bank recommended that a West European Area should be instituted within which sterling would be fully and automatically transferable for all transactions, capital as well as current. In addition, inward transfers from transferable account countries outside Western Europe would be automatic for direct current transactions, though outward transfers would remain subject to administrative decision. However, the Treasury considered that these proposals went too far. It was thought that transferability on capital account would increase the supply of sterling in free markets, while greater transfers into Western Europe from, for example, Egypt would in practice end up in creditor countries like Belgium or Switzerland. Accordingly it was agreed only to enlarge the Transferable Account Area, complete with the restrictions imposed to hinder cheap-sterling operations, so as to include all prospective members of the EPU. These countries would in any case enjoy transferability at inter-central bank level because changes in official holdings of sterling could be brought into the monthly clearing. The Bank, through Bolton, protested that an opportunity was being missed to make sterling a more attractive international currency by sweeping away the paraphernalia of transferable accounts and allowing individual traders in Europe to use sterling for all intra-European payments without going through UK exchange control at all. But the Treasury refused to give further ground and the extension of the Transferable Account Area, complete with the paraphernalia, was set in hand. The result was distinctly discouraging, not to say humiliating. Nobody else wanted to join. Given the facilities they now enjoyed through the EPU, the countries concerned (including, notably, France) were unwilling to take on the duties of complying with UK restrictions on transferable accounts; and that was that. The Bank tried again early in 1951, suggesting to the Treasury a single area for all non-dollar countries

---

[87] This may be compared with the $400–450 million of Marshall Aid originally programmed for 1950.

with free transferability for all purposes. But there was no further response. Whitehall was becoming apprehensive of a renewed deterioration in the external balance of the UK. So the brief period of external surplus and of reserve accumulation had yielded precisely nothing in terms of the step-by-step approach to convertibility and had provided no encouragement to advocates of such an approach.

In the spring of 1951, however, another approach began tentatively to suggest itself. It arose from discussions in the Treasury and the Bank about the possibility of allowing sterling, which was still enjoying its temporary strength, to float and to appreciate. This move was seen as a defence against inflationary pressures arising from the world-wide increase in commodity prices; and it provoked a more thorough discussion than hitherto about the merits or otherwise of moving to a floating rate of exchange. In memoranda circulated in March 1951 Bolton and Fisher spelt out very clearly, and for the first time, that the Bank could not seriously contemplate a combination of non-resident *in*convertibility and a floating rate, at least not for an international currency like sterling. It will be recalled that the fixed-rate inconvertibility of sterling, with the rate administered according to IMF rules, was technically operated through the provisions of monetary and payments agreements, by the mechanics of EPU, by the unwritten rules of the Sterling Area, and by official intervention in the New York market by the EEA. Apart from the last two, none of these could be operated with a floating rate unless virtually all the non-dollar currencies were to peg on sterling, thereby participating in a joint float against the dollar. But this was thought a most unlikely contingency. Members of the Sterling Area, perhaps after discussion and negotiation, might indeed continue the fixed link with sterling. But most other countries would continue their fixed link with the dollar and their adherence in this respect to the IMF Charter. In addition, the floating of sterling would constitute a unilateral abrogation of the fixed-rate provisions contained in the monetary and payments agreements and in the Bretton Woods Agreement. A regime of floating-rate inconvertibility would in practice involve a variety of floating rates for sterling. There would be one rate against the dollar, for American account sterling, and a series of rates against other currencies, each with its own cross-rate against the dollar, depending upon how many different 'areas', each with its different treatment by UK exchange control, there happened to be. Official intervention by the EEA, to unify the cross-rates, would amount to restoring convertibility *de facto*. Accordingly, in practice, a decision to float sterling, with all the abrogations implied (not to mention the complications in the EPU), would either have to be accompanied by the restoration of non-resident convertibility or else by acquiescence in the appearance of a disorderly multiplicity of rates.

In a note sent to the Treasury on 22 March 1951 Bolton dismissed the idea of floating-rate inconvertibility. A disorderly multiplicity of rates, following an array of abrogations, could not be contemplated as a serious option for sterling. In his view: 'The only feasible method of organising a fluctuating sterling rate of exchange is to have a free exchange and gold market with no exchange controls [on non-residents], all pressures making themselves felt through the rate of exchange and the [sterling] price of gold.' But he then went on to warn against the strength of 'the convertibility pressure of sterling resources in the hands of non-residents' and the inadequacy of the reserves for purposes of market intervention. On the same day the Governor discussed this subject with the Chancellor who agreed that there could be no question of moving to a freely fluctuating rate though there might be some merit in shifting to a new fixed rate somewhere above $3.00 and holding it there by use of the EEA if necessary. But over the following weeks opinion in the Bank hardened against the idea of relatively frequent changes in a fixed parity, principally because of their probable destabilisation of confidence. On 19 April the Governor advised Gaitskell that the Bank 'had not found any arguments which shook our view that we had better stay where we are'.

But the idea of floating-rate convertibility had now surfaced in the Bank. Once it had done so, someone was bound to take a serious look at it as a possible way out of the stockade. If progress towards fixed-rate convertibility was proving to be an endless quest, and if a fixed sterling–dollar rate was anyway beginning to look fragile because, for instance, of instability in the US economy and difficulties in the processes of international adjustment, might not a floating rate be the right accompaniment to the convertibility towards which the UK was in any case being driven? An affirmative answer to this question was given by Thompson-McCausland, firstly in some comments on Bolton's view and secondly in a long paper circulated to the Governor and others early in May 1951. He had been impressed by the apparently favourable results of the 1949 devaluations. This led him to contrast a regime of relative exchange rigidity, accompanied by fluctuating use of trade controls, exchange controls, and gold reserves, with one of exchange flexibility and convertibility supported by some return to 'indirect controls', for example Bank Rate. The former tended to be ineffective and led in practice to the worst of worlds, one of 'adjustment by crisis' and periodic large devaluations. The latter could be both effective and relatively smooth in operation, particularly if supported by collaboration between the main non-dollar countries or even by a joint float. The exchange rate could either be fully floating, though affected at times by official intervention, or it could move by means of a 'crawling peg'. To the objection that this would mean a repudiation of Bretton Woods, it was argued that the original purpose of the IMF had already been undermined by the Americans, who had both restricted access to the Fund and prevented use of the Scarce Currency Clause.

This positive case for floating-rate convertibility encountered objections from Fisher (on confidence grounds) and from Allen. The latter was worried about the longer-run adverse effects upon overseas holdings of sterling, but he was mainly concerned to warn Thompson-McCausland and others against overestimating, on the experience of 1949 to date, the power of exchange depreciation as a means of external adjustment. Recent work in the IMF indicated that up to mid-1950 the devaluations were responsible for only a very small part of the turn-round in the US balance of payments. A floating rate, in Allen's view, would expose the UK to counter action from abroad and distract attention 'from the real jobs of carrying out the right measures inside each country'.

The Governors and Executive Directors read these exchanges but offered no written comment. It may be concluded that for the time being the view of the Bank, adverse to floating-rate convertibility, remained unaltered from the advice given by Bolton in March. It may also be concluded that views on floating-rate *in*convertibility, namely that it was a synonym for disorderly disintegration, remained unaltered. But Thompson-McCausland had provided a persuasive insight. For some countries fixed-rate convertibility might indeed be the right course. Sterling, however, was in a unique position. It was a reserve and trading currency, but one by now secondary to the dollar and to gold. It was supported by very inadequate reserves of these latter assets and by an economy whose competitive strength was declining. Floating-rate convertibility might in this special case be more suitable, though it would carry many difficulties of its own. Thoughts of this kind could be put to powerful use by Bolton if he were later to become convinced that the fixed rate for sterling could not be held and that a virtue had to be made of necessity. But they were entirely at variance with the received wisdom of the time. Looking back from the 1980s, after many years of floating rates, they might not seem very striking. But in 1951, when fixed exchange rates were not only embodied in international agreements but were also part and parcel of the Keynesian apparatus of domestic macro-economic management, floating rates were emotively associated with the disordered international trading conditions of the 1930s and were usually condemned on that account.

The development of the ideas and apprehensions described above, added to the frustrations listed earlier, more or less completed the mental condition of Threadneedle Street in the summer of 1951 as the third crisis approached. One other factor, adding to anxiety, deserves mention. The domestic political situation had weakened still further. Cripps had gone. Bevin was dead. His successor, Morrison, was not too well versed in foreign affairs and was having to deal with the crisis in Anglo–Iranian relations following nationalisation of the British Petroleum interests in Iran. Gaitskell's 1951 Budget, with its imposition of charges for National Health prescriptions, had been followed by the resignations of Bevan and Wilson. Since March 1950 the Attlee Government had lacked a reliable majority in the Commons; obviously it was in no shape to deal with another economic crisis. In September, as it became clear that the crisis was imminent and that no sufficient American rescue was in sight, Parliament was dissolved. In the ensuing Election the Conservative Party, under Churchill, was returned to office with a small but adequate majority.

SOURCES

Bank files

EC3/1	History of Exchange Control in the UK to circa 1963
EC5/1–7	Exchange Control Act: Cheap Sterling (May 1948–March 1952)
EC5/155	Exchange Control Act: General – Evasion and Possible Counter-measures (May 1947–April 1953)
G1/97	Governor's File: Exchange Policy (September 1939–December 1952)
G1/102–3	Governor's Files: Exchange Policy – Economic Crisis 1947 (August–December 1947)
G1/106–19	Governor's Files: Exchange Policy – Economic Crisis 1949 (January 1948–February 1950)
G1/120–1	Governor's Files: Exchange Policy – Economic Crisis 1951/52 (July 1951–March 1952)
G1/155	Governor's File: National Debt Office (November 1953–March 1980)
G1/264	Governor's File: Miscellaneous Papers (1949)
OV31/102–3	USA: Anglo–US Financial Agreement (October 1947–December 1951)
OV43/42–3	Egypt: Financial (including Trade) Relations with the UK (January 1948–March 1949)
OV44/1–7	Sterling and Sterling Area Policy: United Kingdom – Sterling Policy (November 1939–May 1951)
OV44/49–50	Sterling and Sterling Area Policy: Sterling Area Exchange Policy – General (November 1945–February 1952)

OV46/3–5	European Recovery Programme: General (April 1947–June 1949)
OV46/31–5	European Recovery Programme: Intra-European Trade and Payments (July 1947–May 1949)
OV46/37–9	European Recovery Programme: Intra-European Trade and Payments (September 1949–April 1950)
OV46/43	European Recovery Programme: Intra-European Trade and Payments (September 1950–January 1951)
OV56/20–2	India: Indian Sterling Balances and Exchange Policy – Negotiations (January 1946–June 1948)
OV56/23–7	India: Financial (including Trade) Relations with the UK (July 1948–July 1949)
OV56/55	India: Indian Sterling Balances and Exchange Policy – Briefs and Supporting Papers for Negotiations (November 1946–May 1948)
OV102/122–34	Argentina: Financial (including Trade) Relations with the UK (October 1947–August 1949)

PRO files
 T230/818
 T236/817

Bank of Canada archives

Jacobsson diaries

Foreign Relations of the United States, 1949, vol. 4

US State Department files

US Treasury files

CHAPTER 5

DOMESTIC MONETARY POLICY
1945–1951

(a) INTRODUCTORY

DOMESTIC MONETARY policy has been mentioned only occasionally in the chapters on external monetary affairs during the early post-war period. The subject is seen to surface briefly in the Bank during the convertibility crisis in 1947, but to no effect. It is glimpsed again during the summer of 1949, in the run-up to devaluation, but nothing happens and it is soon lost to sight once more. Later, following the General Election in 1950 and the outbreak of the Korean War in the summer of that year, the inflexibility of short-term interest rates at very low levels is seen as a source of deepening unease as the Bank looked ahead to a restoration of convertibility. Again, little or nothing happens. There is nonetheless an important story to be told.

The early post-war years are remembered for persistently strong inflationary pressures often accompanied by recurrent balance of payments difficulties and adverse pressure on the exchange rate. They are also remembered for the assumption of macro-economic responsibilities by Government, in line with the Keynesian revolution in economics, of a kind not hitherto undertaken. Foremost among such responsibilities was the commitment to securing full employment in a free society. So a whole new terminology of popular macro-economics had to be invented as democratic politicians sought to communicate the subject to their electorate. 'Too much money' chased 'too few goods', leading to 'inflationary gaps' and a failure to 'pay our way abroad'. 'Austerity' was enjoined on a restless population growing weary of permits and controls, of physical rationing, of levels of taxation never before seen in peacetime, and of currency restrictions on foreign travel. 'Short supply' and 'export only' marched hand in hand with the 'dollar shortage', while the complexities of external monetary relationships produced a range of expressions quite baffling to the layman. In a famous cartoon by David Low these were depicted as fantastic machines or weird animals: a group of 'soft-currency countries' were shown 'joy-riding in their price mechanism', and an inverted tiger-like creature was described as 'a convertible credit walking on a gold ceiling'. But conspicuous absentees from this catalogue were such phrases as 'keeping the money supply under control' or 'charging a realistic price for credit'. For monetary policy, in any ordinary sense of the term, played only a minor part in the range of policies designed both to resist inflation and to achieve external balance. So minor indeed that a small rise in Bank Rate to $2\frac{1}{2}\%$ in November 1951, after the return to office of a Conservative Government and at a time of clear economic overload with inflation running at some 8% per annum, was correctly heralded as a revival of monetary policy. What is more, during the first eighteen months of the 1945 Labour Government monetary policy was deliberately deployed in the reverse direction. Short-term interest rates, already very low, were further reduced. A determined if mostly opportunistic attempt was then made to lower the long-term rate of interest to a level scarcely reached in the Depression of the 1890s. The attempt achieved momentary success followed by an inglorious retreat.

In retrospect, the absence of an effective monetary policy in the UK during this formative period may be seen to have contributed to the decades of endemic inflationary tension, external weakness, and continuing relative industrial decline that were to follow. Like some other countries – but unlike, for example, West Germany – an element of macro-economic discipline was missing from the conduct of policy in the UK, and in the end no amount of ingenious substitution could reliably fill that gap. This may itself be regarded as a sad and even tragic failure in so far as an eventual resort to severe monetary discipline, some thirty years later, took place alongside an abandonment of the commitment to full employment.

Judgements about the long-term consequences of the relative absence of monetary policy during the early post-war years cannot, of course, be carried too far. They are not readily susceptible to conclusive justification by appeal to economic analysis or statistical evidence. They depend rather upon a political or sociological assessment of the long-run effects of a particular pattern of macro-economic policies upon the economic attitudes and behaviour of British politicians, Government departments, local authorities, nationalised industries, corporate enterprises, trade unions, and individuals. Such assessment is itself not only hazardous but beyond the scope of a history of the Bank of England. Yet it is undeniable both that the pattern of peacetime policies in the early post-war years was an exceedingly novel one and that it included an attempt largely to do without the use of a specifically monetary discipline that had been employed with few interruptions over the preceding century and more. It is also undeniable that in the decades that followed not only did a variety of weaknesses become gradually more and more manifest but monetary policy had to be moved progressively back towards the centre of the stage. It is therefore important to see how it came about that monetary policy played so persistently minor or even perverse a part after 1945 and how it was that the Bank of England, historically the administrator of monetary discipline, was able to exert little effective resistance to this state of affairs. The story is sometimes one of argument rather than of action, of what might have been rather than what was. But it would be wrong on that account to belittle its importance.

But first, what is meant by the words 'the Bank', in this context? In the chapters devoted to external monetary affairs during and immediately after the war, the Bank is seen as the two Governors, two Executive Directors, and a supporting cast of senior exchange controllers, exchange market specialists, senior overseas territorial advisers, and purveyors of economic advice. In Chapter 11(b) below, devoted to the formation of the Finance Corporation for Industry (FCI) and the Industrial and Commercial Finance Corporation (ICFC), the Bank is discernible as a powerful group comprising the two Governors, two Executive Directors, and several very senior officials including the Chief Cashier, the Economic Adviser to the Governor, and an adviser expert in the special finance of industry. In both cases the Bank is seen as an effective entity, capable of arguing and agreeing a preferred strategy, of mapping out policies designed to pursue a strategy (whether preferred or not), and of putting those policies into effect. In both cases the Bank is seen to be fully equipped to argue its case to the Treasury on the strategic or tactical level and, in most instances, to respond effectively to requests from the Treasury. And in both cases the organisation and top level staffing of the Bank was a product of the latter half of Norman's Governorship, when first industrial reconstruction and later the further elaboration of the Bank's international relations and exchange market presence absorbed much of his time. Domestic monetary policy, by contrast, which had been a source of so much pain during the years of the restored Gold Standard, had become relatively inactive after 1932 and had not required supporting with much new organisation in the Bank or with additional senior staff. Nor, with the abandonment of the Gold Standard and the subsequent adoption of exchange rate management through the EEA, had the Bank been left with responsibility for formulating and deciding such monetary policy as there was. Responsibility had passed *de facto* to the Treasury. In the Bank, therefore, the Chief Cashier, the Government Broker, and the Principal of the Discount Office retained only the executive responsibility for conducting official operations in the gilt-edged and money markets, often a matter of routine, and for tendering periodic advice to the Treasury about some new phase of Exchequer borrowing. Essentially this advice was concerned with market management and was tendered direct by the Chief Cashier to the Governors, who then conveyed it personally to the Treasury as required. Executive Directors, usually Niemeyer or Holland-Martin, occasionally became involved, as also did Clay, Economic Adviser until he retired in 1944. But there was no continuous monetary policy 'team' in the modern sense, with market operators working alongside specialist economists and statisticians.

This state of affairs persisted into and throughout the war. Accordingly, although the Bank was well enough equipped in 1945 to carry out the duties of issuing house and investment banker to its customer in Great George Street, it was less well equipped to formulate and to press on the Treasury some particular national monetary policy. Yet although it was not any longer responsible for deciding such policy, the Bank might still have considered itself responsible for advising the Treasury about it; and as will be seen later in this chapter, there was certainly an attempt, beginning in 1943, to form a Bank view about an appropriate domestic monetary strategy for the early post-war period, as well as to agree criteria for deciding on changes in interest rates within bounds circumscribed by a general consensus in favour of low rates. The judgements expressed, though not carried through into detailed prescription, stand up well enough to the test of time. But after the General Election in 1945 and the arrival of Dalton at the Treasury, this Bank view soon got lost to sight. Through the subsequent phase of cheaper money in the gilt-edged market, the Bank was overridden at an early stage and thereafter confined itself to giving technical advice in pursuit of the Chancellor's goals. Only later on, during the Chancellorships of Cripps and Gaitskell, did the Bank again begin to press a view on such matters as the level of short-term interest rates and the best way of securing a direct control of bank lending to the private sector.

The leading official on the home side was Kenneth Peppiatt, Chief Cashier until February 1949 and Home Finance Executive Director thereafter. Much liked and admired, he was a man of long experience in the gilt-edged and money markets, where his skills and judgement were undoubtedly good. He was, in addition, attached to straightforward principles of anti-inflationary debt management that were probably derived from the experience of European currency disorders following the First World War. These principles emphasised the need to avoid undue reliance on floating debt, a version of the 'printing press', as a source of funds for the Exchequer. But while certainly well able to advise on, for instance, the market implications of some suggested alteration in Bank Rate, Peppiatt would never have regarded himself as capable of arguing out a particular monetary policy in analytic terms with the university-educated mandarins in the Treasury, let alone with the distinguished economists imported into Whitehall during the war along with their differing theories about the rate of interest. Indeed it was well known that Peppiatt disliked attending meetings at the Treasury, preferring to deal with his customer by correspondence or over lunch in Threadneedle Street.[1] Meetings in Whitehall on domestic policy, with top officials or with the Chancellor himself, were therefore often left at this time to the Governors alone, neither of whom in the early post-war years was a technical expert in the subject. Not until 1948, following a Ministerial initiative, did the Bank's Economic Adviser begin to participate in discussions with the Treasury about monetary policy.

As will be seen in the account that follows, the Bank was at first uncertain and hesitant about its use of economic analysis and advice. The Governors and the Chief Cashier sometimes seem uncertain whether and to whom they should turn for such advice and uncertain about what to do with it when they get it. In his own special way, Norman had personally been able to use professional economic advisers and to recruit good ones. His immediate successors found this more difficult. Self-taught, Thompson-McCausland gave advice, but its impact was uncertain. Mynors, the professional economist, gave advice and was employed as an Adviser to the Governors, but seems at first to have had no clear terms of reference or regular occupation.[2]

The Statistics Office, attached at this time to the Secretary's Department, was almost wholly (and frustratingly) employed on balance of payments work. There were those in the Bank who were suspicious, even nervous, of economists and economic statistics, and perhaps even more suspicious

---

[1] In a Minute circulated in the Treasury during September 1945 Brittain referred to a discussion with Peppiatt. Against this the Chancellor wrote 'whoever is he?'. In April 1946 Jacobsson wrote in his diary: '[Peppiatt] speaks mostly in short abrupt sentences with a humourous glint. But he has intense feelings; he is an acute observer and no fool. In a way, he keeps himself to himself, but for those who like him he is a delightful companion.'

[2] Shortly after succeeding Clay in 1944, after the change of Governor, Mynors found a note on his desk written in Norman's familiar hand. It read as follows: 'I called to make you a bow. I hold that you have been side-tracked, where you will have little to do but very much to note.'

Kenneth Peppiatt ('KOP'), Chief Cashier 1934–1949
HANS WILD

of Keynesian economists than others. There were those too who felt not only that they could anyway get along quite well without professional economic advice but also that preserving the skills and influence of the Bank in the post-war era would depend overwhelmingly on market expertise, City intelligence, or skill with overseas financial diplomacy rather than on ability in applied economics. There was a good deal of truth in this,[3] but it was an attitude that neglected the uses of professional economic analysis and argument in the Bank's own special fields and paid insufficient heed to the growing influence of professional economists in Government, notably in the preparation of advice to Treasury Ministers. Under Norman's immediate successors, the Bank was slow to realise that it needed economists to argue with other people's economists, including those Ministers who were themselves economists. It was even slower to conclude that it needed the continuity of an economics section, with supporting statistical services, rather than piecemeal resort to one or two advisers with roving commissions. Although its use of economic advice became much more active after 1947, its failure to contemplate establishing an economics division in the early post-war years is likely to have weakened its voice in the Treasury on questions of macro-economic policy, including those questions of monetary policy that were notoriously an economists' battleground.[4] As it was, serious criticism of Dalton's policy, when it entered its critical phase in 1946, was developed by financial journalists rather than by the central bank.

It is therefore not much of an exaggeration to say that at the end of the war the British central banking function with respect to the formation of domestic monetary policy had come to rest almost entirely in a Treasury well enough versed in monetary economics, while its technical execution, of which the Treasury knew very little, fell to a Bank of England whose skills were confined to market management and whose dexterity in monetary economics remained little used outside Threadneedle Street. This curious apparatus was perhaps unlikely, at first go after the war, to produce good policy. Nor did it.

(b) THE LOST ALTERNATIVE: 1943–1945

Post-war monetary policy was considered in the Bank by a Committee on Post-War Domestic Finance, set up by Norman early in 1943 and chaired by Niemeyer. The main work of the Committee was a study of post-war industrial financing and the identification of problems whose solution lay in special new financial institutions (see Chapter 11(b) below). But it also

---

[3] Jacobsson remarked to Bolton in March 1948 that the BIS had only four or five economists whereas the IMF had forty-eight. 'That is your salvation', Bolton replied. 'Bernstein reads per day 8 to 10 notes and memoranda prepared by his staff. In addition he reads the newspapers etc; and he attends meetings. Often he has no time to sleep. It is a great physical achievement but it is not conducive to sound judgement.'

[4] Writing to the author in 1985, Sir Humphrey Mynors remarked: 'I should feel bound to concur if you took the view that the Bank ought to have set up a more professional unit, especially vis-à-vis Whitehall. To keep a guru down the end of the passage and give him just an occasional job, as a substitute, is not fruitful.'

took in a wider perspective. Although accepting that control of capital issues and the associated qualitative guidance to the banks about their lending policies would continue, the Committee doubted whether the full wartime apparatus of physical controls could be effectively maintained for long in peacetime and also doubted whether it would be wise to discard the use of higher interest rates as a restraining instrument of policy. In the latter context, there was concern that corporate sales of gilt-edged accumulated during the war would exert upward pressure on yields. It was feared that countervailing official purchases of gilt-edged would be inflationary unless budgetary provision was made for them. The Committee was very alert to the likely problems of post-war inflationary pressure and was at times divided over the respective merits of using monetary or fiscal policy to counteract them.[5] Henry Clay resolved this division by arguing that both these arms of macro-economic policy would be needed, that some rise in interest rates would probably be unavoidable, and that this would not, in the assumed conditions of excess demand, have an outright depressing effect on industrial expansion. The final Report remarked with percipience that the difficulty of reconciling the two policies of encouraging investment by low interest rates while seeking to keep prices down would be much greater after the war than in any previous period.

The Deputy Governor, Catterns, mulled over this wider aspect of the Niemeyer Report and became concerned about a likely problem of policy indicators in post-war conditions. In February 1944, when he was acting as Governor after Norman had fallen ill, he asked Thompson-McCausland for advice about this problem. The latter recorded:

> The Deputy Governor is uneasy at the prospect of our entering the post-war period without having any clear idea of what dials to watch in determining Bank policy. Under the Gold Standard there were well understood indicators. They were understood not only by the Bank, but by the informed public, and were set out and blessed by the Macmillan Committee. Almost immediately after the Report the Gold Standard was swept away. Since then we have

---

[5] Kershaw, for example, favoured using a higher Purchase Tax to restrain consumption. Niemeyer favoured a more active use of monetary policy. Unfortunately, for he clearly fought well, encounters of this kind did not suit Kershaw, who liked to shield himself from pressure whether physical or mental. The day after the Committee's Report was circulated he wrote to the Deputy Governor asking to be allowed to withdraw from this work. 'I think it is a mistake for me to be a member of this Committee; my work has lain, and lies, in other domains, and I feel that I cannot work either well or usefully in the controversial atmosphere that surrounds many of these domestic issues.' Niemeyer was made of altogether different material. An observer of him at the time recalls watching Otto walking up Threadneedle Street every morning from the Underground to the main entrance of the Bank. The expression on his face suggested that if he had come up against a brick wall he would have walked straight through it.

proceeded on a hand to mouth basis, learning much, lucky in not having suffered much, but not yet in possession of anything which could be called a system.

Thompson-McCausland, usually known in the Bank and the Treasury by his first name, Lucius,[6] was an Anglo-Irishman of considerable intellectual power and persuasive talent. But he was not a trained economist. After taking a double first in classics at King's College, Cambridge, he had worked first for the *Financial News* and then for Moody's Economic Service before joining the Bank as a 'Temporary Clerk' in Exchange Control in 1939. He quickly made his mark as a Bank representative on Whitehall committees. He was promoted to Assistant Adviser and in 1943 accompanied Keynes to the pre-Bretton Woods meetings in Washington. He had great confidence in his own intellectual powers, moved easily among senior Whitehall officials and economists, and regarded the exposition and indeed the further creation of monetary economics as within his capabilities. His performance in the latter respect must have impressed his superiors in the Bank, for in February 1944 Catterns sought advice from him, the self-taught, rather than from the Bank's two professional economists, Clay and Mynors. The latter was then Secretary to the Bank, having been moved from being Principal of the Statistics Office in 1938, but in the summer of 1944 was to be appointed Adviser to the Governors in succession to Clay. He had taken a double first in the Cambridge Economics Tripos and had later taught economics as a Fellow of Corpus Christi College. He had joined the Bank in 1933, at the age of thirty, to work in parallel with Clay but as an executive in the small Statistics Office rather than as an Adviser.

Aside from a liking for monetary economics, Lucius was also attached to the construction of ingenious schemes, as those who worked with him in later years on international payments problems were to know only too well. It was therefore not surprising that his response to Catterns, entitled 'Money after The Gold Standard', was not only idiosyncratic in its exposition of what he termed 'flabby' and 'taut' money but also proposed the creation of a new device, to be called the Money Equalisation Account, which would operate in gilt-edged in a price-stabilising fashion while somehow preserving taut money. Whether Catterns or Peppiatt, whose formal education had not included attendance at a university, made anything of all this is not recorded, but it is unlikely. Siepmann, himself a classically educated intellectual who had started adult life in the Treasury, was attracted to the diagnosis but wisely found himself technically

---

[6] At the time of the 'Robot' controversy in 1952 opponents in the Treasury altered this to 'Lucifer'.

unqualified to judge the quality of the solution. However Kershaw, a clear-headed Rhodes Scholar from Australia, had no such inhibitions. He termed the Money Equalisation Account 'a prestidigitationist solution' whose author was following the expansionists down the trail they themselves had blazed. Nothing more was then heard of it. But Lucius heeded Kershaw's criticism, rethought his approach, and a year later submitted a 9,000-word memorandum to the Chief Cashier entitled 'Cheap Money. A Criticism of Lord Keynes' Theory, and an Alternative View'. He also sent copies to Clay at Oxford, to D. H. Robertson at Cambridge, and to James Meade at the Cabinet Office. The criticism of Keynes' theory, though rather long-winded, was acceptable and not unfamiliar. Increases in the quantity of money could go on to affect the economy through portfolio adjustment (as it would later have been called) in favour of real assets as well as through the classical effect of a lower long-term interest rate upon investment. If the monetary authority supplied more money in correct response to some exogenous economic shock, the increase could become destabilising at a later stage, once the shock had passed. This delayed effect should be counteracted by appropriate alterations in short-term interest rates. Exposition of this latter process was again in terms of 'flabby' and 'taut' money and did not successfully establish a reliable means of identifying these concepts at work from monetary information. This defect was pointed out in replies from Clay (who suggested the paper should be published in a learned journal), Robertson, and especially Meade, all of whom seemed to find the critique of Keynes' theory itself acceptable and useful.

In the Bank, a copy of Lucius' memorandum was initialled without comment by Peppiatt, who must have found it very difficult if not impossible to digest. He may have noted, however, the attack on Keynes' theory of the rate of interest and the implications of such an attack for debates about the wisdom of seeking to reduce the long-term rate. The paper was also seen by Siepmann. But there is no evidence that it aroused any further interest. Instead, the Chief Cashier and others began to think about short-term interest rates, and about Bank Rate, in the specific context of the end of hostilities in Europe. This thinking was mostly completed just before the election of the Labour Government and before the intentions of the new Chancellor became evident, but in the knowledge that a broad continuation of cheap money would be wanted whoever was in power. It was also completed sometime before the Anglo-American Loan negotiations.

On 21 June 1945 Peppiatt circulated a Minute on Bank Rate, which began by noting that it had remained at 2% since June 1932, apart from a brief interruption at the outbreak of war in 1939. A rise was not yet indicated and was out of the question politically, although later it might well prove necessary. In the meantime a reduction might be considered. In the days of the Gold Standard the signals had been clear for all to read, but 'in these days the signals are either not flown or cannot be so easily deciphered'. He felt that a cut in the Rate to 1% would be followed by a fall in money and bill rates to around $\frac{1}{2}$%, by some fall in bank advances rates towards a maximum of 3% rather than 4%, and by some rise in the gilt-edged and equity markets. With exchange and capital issues control remaining, along with cheap money in the US, the external effect would not be adverse even though the underlying exchange position was weak. The effect on trade and industry would be small. During the next few years the financial demands of industry would be governed by productive capacity rather than by money rates. But the Exchequer would save nearly £17 million per annum of floating debt charges. Against this rather minor advantage, the Chief Cashier judged that a cut would be inopportune and looking a little further ahead to problems of inflation, downward pressure on gilt-edged prices, and external weakness, it seemed wrong to jump in now with a move designed to boost markets. Moreover: 'Against any political advantage there might be in lowering the Rate, there should be set the increased difficulty of raising it at the appropriate moment. It will not be easy, politically, to raise the Rate from 2% to 3%; but a rise from 1% to 3% would be even more difficult to achieve'.

Niemeyer, Bolton, and Mynors responded in writing to Peppiatt's note and all reinforced his opposition to a cut. Bolton, who wrote first, particularly stressed the need to maintain external confidence that 'we will manage our affairs efficiently'. There was, he felt, an underlying suspicion of sterling. The position was finely balanced and it would be imprudent to take any steps that would disturb it. A reduction to 1% would bring Bank Rate back into the limelight at a time when the unknown stresses of the transitional period would be growing. This would give the financial commentators and financial markets, such as New York, material on which to pass judgement upon the position of sterling and, in particular, on the fate of the dollar–sterling rate. Mynors, for his part, emphasised the approaching strains and stresses of the transitional period. He foresaw a growing public impatience with the speed of demobilisation and of the reappearance of civilian goods, higher prices for such goods as were available, and the need to retain controls longer than was hoped with more pressure for freedom to scramble for supplies than was feared. The effect of a cut in Bank Rate would mainly be felt through its effect on opinion. In the public mind it could be taken only as another indication that the way was clearing to the post-war world of peace and plenty, with full employment, social security, and the 'euthanasia of the rentier'. It was thus likely to accentuate the difficulties already mentioned. These considerations, Mynors felt, might seem to suggest raising rather than lowering the Rate: 'and that may come'. But for the present the important thing was to hold on to the status quo. Finally, Niemeyer summed it all up with characteristic brevity:

> I hold that it would be a great mistake at this juncture to reduce Bank Rate.
> While theoretically exchange control, etc., diminishes the exchange effect of a reduction, I agree with Bolton that the general repercussion abroad both vis-à-vis UK and in other countries themselves would be bad. Continentals are in fact very sensitive to what we do.
> At home the real effect would be very slight: but the psychological effect would be precisely that encouragement to the idea that all is now easy going and that plain living and high saving is no longer necessary: which we particularly want to avoid.
> I do not believe that the rate of interest is going much longer to be immaterial in the attraction of savings, or that it is a factor that can be lightheartedly neglected or replaced by other means.
> The way to keep relatively cheap money is not to provoke a forced and violent reaction in the opposite direction.

The views of the Governors are not recorded, but this whole exchange of notes, taken together with the other evidence preceding it, implies that the responsible senior officials of the Bank were looking towards the evolution of a flexible monetary policy involving the discretionary adjustment of short-term interest rates, up or down, and the maintenance of an orthodox funding policy in the gilt-edged market. Judgements about the desirable level of short-term rates would be made with reference to a variety of external and domestic criteria or indicators, with a typically strong emphasis on 'opinion', confidence, and expectations. An array of prices would figure in such judgements and would include those in the securities markets, the foreign exchange markets, and the markets for goods. There might also be reference to the pace of credit expansion, but it is unclear whether the growth of money supply, of bank advances, or of floating debt would be the measure preferred. Judgements would also have to be made with reference to goals or objectives. These appear mostly as avoidance of harmful monetary disturbance. Inflation, exchange instability, and speculative excesses in securities markets are bad. If there is an underlying deflationary tendency, cheap money is good. In short, senior officials were in favour of a commonsensical and discretionary monetary policy with a strongly 'banking school' tinge to it. In later years such a policy would at first come to seem a useful or even essential supplement to other areas of macro-economic policy. Later still, when 'monetarism' became powerful, such a policy would appear too weak and too insecurely anchored in objective monetary quantities. But in 1945, in a climate of euphoric idealism engendered by the return of peace, the approach was realistic. In so far as it contained a picture of the evolving UK economy, it was one of excess demand and inflationary pressure rather than an early tendency to underemployment of resources. In addition there is no special identification of the rate of interest as a key determinant, by itself, of the fixed investment that was widely thought to require special sustenance from Government policy. So there is no apparent predisposition in the Bank against a flexible interest-rate policy, nor any predisposition to favour driving interest rates lower whenever opportunity offered.

Apart from further minutes by Peppiatt and Niemeyer later in the year, in the context of debt management, the written exchange of views at the end of June was to prove the last of its kind for some time. The new Government took office at the end of July, bringing with it the early nationalisation of the Bank and the cheaper-money policy of the incoming Chancellor. The Treasury had meanwhile been doing its own thinking, without consulting the Bank, in an exercise called the National Debt Enquiry. This began in February 1945 with Hopkins and later Bridges in the chair. Principal members were Keynes, Eady, Brittain, Robbins, and Meade. The result was a Report, sent to the Chancellor at the end of October, that was sympathetic to the idea of securing a reduction in long-term rates below 3%. Concurrently the Chancellor was intent on securing an early cut in short-term money rates, back to the levels around $\frac{1}{2}$% that prevailed before the outbreak of war. The Governor evidently accepted this latter objective without much demur, though he did persuade Dalton that it would be better to achieve it by means other than a cut in Bank Rate. A few weeks later, following the cut in short-term rates recounted below, the Bank tried to gain acceptance of the view that 3% was more likely to prove a sustainable long-term rate than $2\frac{1}{2}$% and that an attempt to force the pace towards the latter would be ill-advised. But its advice was rejected and thereafter not repeated.

Accordingly the Bank's alternative, if it had ever been much in view, was lost to sight and monetary policy in the UK took a turning that had certainly to be wrong unless the whole apparatus of controls, supported by an adequately strong fiscal policy and adequate wage restraint, should render interest-rate flexibility unnecessary. The Bank did not judge that things would work out like that; and it was to be proved right. The near-term cost of taking the wrong turning is not measurable, any more than the very long-run consequences of having little effective monetary policy during the early post-war period. But it may have been quite large, for it contributed to a falling level of external confidence and a scepticism on the part of market opinion, for whose severe consequences the public had to pay.

Even if the Bank did not at this time feel itself responsible for initiating official views about national monetary policy, there must remain some surprise that the Governor gave the Government little warning about the risks of taking the wrong monetary turning in 1945 or of persisting with it in the gilt market in 1946, particularly in view of the enormous uncertainties hanging over the external prospects and, latterly, his own deep anxiety about the consequences of the Loan Agreement. It is possible, though unlikely, that he was personally more sympathetic to the Government's monetary aims than his colleagues. But the subject is not mentioned in his own brief memoirs and the fact that he did not seriously challenge Dalton at the outset is most likely attributable to the prior claims of the Bank of England Bill and the fear of direct Government control over the banking system. To get his way on these matters Catto had to cultivate and maintain good relations with Dalton, which he did. So he may well have judged it impolitic as well as fruitless to nag about the policy of cheaper money, a policy to which the Chancellor was enthusiastically and publicly attaching himself.

(c) CHEAPER MONEY – PRELIMINARY MOVES

The pursuit of a cheaper money policy was mostly but not exclusively confined to the Chancellorship of Dalton and had faded badly some months before his abrupt departure from the Treasury in November 1947. The policy was exercised in the main through official operations in gilt-edged. It was however accompanied by two other episodes, one concerning selective credit control and the other the lowering of short-term money rates. The first of these was completed before the change of Government in 1945. In addition, an earlier attempt to force the pace in gilt-edged had been made towards the end of 1944.

The apparatus of wartime controls included a strict control of capital issues. It was supported by the Defence (Finance) Regulations[7] and administered by a Capital Issues Committee (CIC) on which Niemeyer represented the Bank. The Committee worked under guidance issued by the Treasury, setting out priorities appropriate to time of war. In parallel

---

[7] Subsequently replaced by the Control of Borrowing and Guarantees Act 1946 and the Exchange Control Act of the same year.

with this control, but without resort to statutory Regulations, the clearing banks had been requested to administer a severe restriction on bank advances for non-priority uses. This request was contained in a letter written by the Chancellor to the Governor in September 1939 and subsequently agreed between the latter and the clearing banks. In August 1944 the Treasury began to consider modification of the priorities to suit the approaching transition from war to peace. With respect to bank advances, following a discussion between the Treasury and the Bank, it was agreed to rely mainly on a 'negative directive' rather than on a long list of priority activities. In May of the following year, after VE Day, the Chancellor wrote to the Governor accordingly. The banks were asked, and subsequently agreed, not to make unduly large advances for personal needs, not to grant facilities for speculative purposes, and not to make advances to anyone 'outside the ordinary course of their business' – that is to say, as a substitute for capital issues. On the positive side, the banks were asked to heed criteria set out in a new memorandum of guidance to the Capital Issues Committee.

No quantitative ceilings were imposed on bank advances, either overall or on advances to particular classes of borrower. Although the banks followed the guidance they were given, made easier by the outright physical shortage of, for instance, motor cars, money was freely available to borrowers whose activities were blessed by departmental licences or permits. In 1945, however, the control may have provided some dialectical support to arguments that a reduction in the cost of money would not be harmful despite the high pressure of demand in the economy. The wording of the Chancellor's letter, agreed in detail with the Bank in advance, also marked the onset of an exhortatory habit that was to persist over the ensuing decades and long after capital issues control itself had been reduced to vestigial importance. Successive generations of Chief Cashiers and their Deputies were to become masters in the art of touching-up the wording of directional guidance to the banks, guidance whose issue became a hallowed ingredient of each and every package of restrictive macro-economic measures.

After the reorientation of selective control in May 1945, the change of Government at the end of July, and the end of hostilities in the Far East, the Treasury lost no time in getting to work on a policy of cheaper money. Consideration was given to an early cut in short-term rates. On 21 August, in the Debate on the Address, the Chancellor said he was exploring future possibilities in the field of cheaper money. On 12 September Brittain, then a Deputy Secretary in the Finance Division, minuted the Permanent Secretary with a proposal to reduce the rates on Treasury Bills, Treasury

Deposits Receipts (TDRs),[8] and call money by $\frac{1}{2}$%. These, he wrote, were the only set of interest rates definitely higher than before the war and a large body of public opinion regarded them as excessive. He was sure 'that the overwhelming public reaction would be to welcome the reductions and not in any way to regard them as portents of dangerous Government policy'. Bridges advised that the wisdom of the move, and its timing, should be explored with the Governor. The Chancellor agreed, but added that he was sure that both short and long rates could and should be reduced and that an opportunity for action should not be missed. A few days later it was reported in the Treasury that the Governor agreed in principle to a cut in rates. The matter was discussed in the Bank on 24 September and it was confirmed that while a cut in Bank Rate itself would be unwise, it would be practicable to move rates down $\frac{1}{2}$% by administrative action on the TDR rate and by associated requests to the clearing banks and Discount Market on the call-money rate, the seven-day deposit rate, and the Treasury Bill rate. If, moreover, this method were adopted, there would be no reason for delaying beyond a few weeks and the operation could therefore be carried out so as to synchronise as closely as possible with the special Budget scheduled for 23 October. This was readily accepted by the Treasury and the cut in rates was discussed by the Governors with the clearing banks on 17 October. Their agreement was obtained, provided the cut in money rates could be presented as consequent upon a cut in the TDR rate, and the change was made known to the markets on the following afternoon. Next day, Friday, the operation was completed when the Discount Market brought the Treasury Bill rate into line. Dalton wrote a letter of thanks to the Governor in the course of which he said: 'I knew I could rely on your co-operation and I am very grateful to you for all that you have done.'

Though in part designed as the prelude to an assault on yields in the gilt market, the cut in short-term rates was presented as more in the nature of a technical adjustment[9] to the restoration of peace. The new structure, with Bank Rate remaining at 2%, was indeed the same as that prevailing before the outbreak of war. Catto, in explaining the proposal to the banks, went so far as to dissociate the change of Government from the change in rates, saying that the restoration of the pre-war structure would have been required in any case. In the Bank itself, arguments against proceeding by a cut in Bank Rate were not so strongly held against the alternative of proceeding by a cut in the TDR rate followed by requests about the call-

---

[8] Non-marketable three-month paper issued direct to the banks.
[9] Presenting something as a 'technical adjustment' to circumstances and not as a 'change of policy' was to become a central banking habit in the post-war world.

money and bill rates. Presenting it all as a reversion to the pre-war period, no matter that the surrounding conditions and prospects were totally different, may have made the medicine a little easier to swallow. It did not however cut much ice in the press, where the move was interpreted straightforwardly for what it turned out to be, a prelude to a cheaper-money drive in gilt-edged.

(d) CHEAPER MONEY – MOUNTING THE ASSAULT ON LONGER-TERM RATES: 1944–1945

In the main this assault consisted of the extension into peacetime of the wartime arrangements for financing the Exchequer and the active exploitation of these arrangements towards securing a lower longer-term rate of interest. The wartime arrangements were very simple.[10] In the gilt-edged market they consisted of raising funds through the offer of new securities, usually medium and long dated, on continuous tap. These operations were complemented by the buying-in of near-maturing stocks by the Government Broker for account either of the Issue Department of the Bank or of the National Debt Office (NDO) as manager of Savings Bank and National Insurance funds. In addition, the NDO would from time to time supply the Issue Department with long-dated securities from its existing portfolio, for sale in the market alongside the taps as a variation in diet, and invest the proceeds in special Annuities issued to it by the Exchequer. There was thus a well-oiled machine for the continuous raising of new money in the gilt market and for the continuous refinancing of maturities. The latter process was also assisted by the operations of the Discount Market, which could profitably run short-dated gilts financed on call money and therefore acted both as a trader in and a home for stocks that had become too short for their former owners, but still too long for acquisition by the authorities.[11] In accord with policy decided early in the war, the Government had been firm in its resolve not to issue stock yielding more than 3%. It had accordingly been prepared to meet any shortfall in funds, after allowing for its sales of gilts, for the inflow from National

---

[10] A detailed account of these and of their introduction during 1939–40 is to be found in R. S. Sayers' *Financial Policy 1939–45* (HMSO, 1956).

[11] By December 1944 the market's bond book totalled £170 million or about eight times the houses' capital resources. This was not without risk, but in May 1945 the Principal of Discount Office calculated that the market could just about stand a rise in bill rates to 4% and an associated fall in bond prices onto a yield basis of 4%. He accordingly considered the market adequately capitalised but without capacity to absorb further gilts. The Bank then proposed and the Treasury agreed that the houses be given capital issues consent to raise a total of £10 million extra capital over the next few years. This part of the machinery was thus kept in proper order and enlarged to cope with expected post-war sales of short bonds by industry and commerce.

Savings Securities, and for any other receipts, by selling floating debt to the banking system, either through Treasury Bills or through non-marketable Treasury Deposit Receipts issued direct to the banks.

The working of this machine, together with the maintenance of public confidence, had induced a slowly rising gilt market which enabled the maturity of the taps to be gradually extended. By the summer of 1944, the long-dated 3% Savings Bonds 1960–70 had been on tap for over two years, had raised over £900 million, and were due for replacement. In accord with the policy of not bringing a replacement on more attractive terms to the lender, and in line with the Bank's assessment of market conditions, a new 3% tap was brought maturing in 1965–75, five years later than the old one. The Treasury had wanted a 3% undated stock at this time but was advised that it could not be successfully issued at par. In the autumn, however, the Treasury took a more aggressive line, this time with respect to the replacement of the medium-dated tap, $2\frac{1}{2}$% National War Bonds 1952–4. This marked a first attempt to force the pace in gilt-edged by exploitation of the Treasury's virtual monopoly of borrowing in the capital market. It was not at all successful and served to confirm the Bank in its views about the unwisdom of such tactics.

The Chief Cashier had at first favoured a new stock maturing in 1953–5 or 1954–6 but had concluded it would prove unattractive. He therefore suggested, as something of a novelty, moving back down the yield curve and bringing a shorter loan. This would enable the coupon to be reduced to 2%. It could also stimulate sales of the 1952–4 bonds, the tap for which would remain open for a short time after the announcement of the new 1950 maturity. The Governor asked whether 2% might be too high, but was convinced by Niemeyer, Holland-Martin, and Peppiatt that it was right. He so advised the Treasury but found Eady and Brittain very keen to bring the stock at a rather lower yield, by issuing it at 101. Peppiatt protested as follows:

> The only reason for issuing above par would be a desire to give an upward twist to prices – and downward to rates. For some time past we have been anxious to do no more than maintain existing levels, in order not to add to our post-war financing problems. I hope and believe this is still our policy.

He added that a higher price might militate against the success of the issue. The Treasury then abruptly overrode the Bank. The Governor was told that the Chancellor had agreed to a 1950 maturity at par but had decided to cut the coupon to $1\frac{3}{4}$% even though existing stocks of comparable maturity yielded somewhat more. 'While we all realise that the lower rate involves a certain risk', Brittain wrote to Catto, 'I understand you are ready to agree that it is a reasonable risk to take.' The Governor may or may not have so agreed, but it is clear that the Chief Cashier had a very different view.

Announcing the issue in the House of Commons, the Chancellor (Sir John Anderson) made much of it commanding the lowest yield the Government had offered on any Stock Exchange Security during the war. In a foretaste of Daltonian tactics he asked for public support, adding that the new issue would not be on tap for long and that in due course the Government would revert to a medium-dated maturity. Although the announcement did succeed in stimulating sales of the old tap, the effect on the market was shortlived and the subsequent performance of the $1\frac{3}{4}\%$ tap was very disappointing. Sales to the public were well under £5 million a week when £20–25 million had been in mind. Under the continuous tap system a weekly creation of tap stock, representing the amount sold, was published in the Exchequer Return. A failure to sell through the tap was thus public knowledge unless it could be concealed by the authorities themselves subscribing, unidentified, for account of the Issue Department or the NDO. Such subscriptions, normally kept to about £0·5 million per week, were stepped up in November 1944 in order to present a better showing and encourage other buyers. But this manoeuvre, the ethics of which did not seem to worry the Bank or the Treasury, enjoyed only a modest success and the yield on the $1\frac{3}{4}\%$ bonds continued to compare unfavourably with that available on short-dated maturities in the market. The Treasury then suggested that the corner might be turned if additional funds were liberated by calling one of these maturities for redemption. But the Bank judged this too risky a tactic at this time. The appearance of the authorities forcing the pace might actually fail to breathe life into the tap, and in that event would too obviously bring about yet further resort to the floating debt. Chastened perhaps by its recent experience with the $1\frac{3}{4}\%$ stock, the Treasury agreed. Meanwhile that stock remained unpopular and by May 1945, unknown to the public, the Issue Department had subscribed no less than £150 million out of total sales amounting to £250 million.

The $1\frac{3}{4}\%$ tap was eventually closed early in June 1945 when the authorities reverted to a medium-dated loan, a $2\frac{1}{2}\%$ stock maturing in 1954–6. Preparation for this exercise prompted the Chief Cashier to circulate his views on Government borrowing during the transition. His note is the last Bank opinion on the subject to be written before the change of Government. It concisely expresses Peppiatt's position on questions of debt management at that time. He began by describing the policy pursued throughout the war as one of strict orthodoxy combined with simplicity.

Despite its virtual monopoly as a borrower, the Government had not attempted to force rates down. Except for a progressive slight improvement in term, the rate structure had been kept stable. Investors had come to accept that structure as reasonable and their acceptance had been reinforced by an expectation that gilt-edged prices would be maintained after the war. A natural trend towards liquidity had developed as hostilities in Europe were ending, but this had been fortuitously exaggerated by pitching the terms of the $1\frac{3}{4}\%$ bonds out of line with the market. So the floating debt had risen sharply, mostly through increased TDRs. This was not only inflationary but also unpopular with the banks, who were looking forward to resuming their normal lending business in peacetime. TDRs now amounted to more than £2,000 million, equivalent to over 40% of bank deposits, compared to advances of only £750 million. Looking ahead to the transition, Peppiatt foresaw a continuing large Government borrowing requirement together with the final maturity of some £700 million of central and local government bonds. Finance from National Savings would probably become negative, as would the supply of investible funds from industrial and commercial companies. It would therefore be prudent to have on tap the most attractive stocks possible within, for the present, the continuing constraint of the wartime rate structure. Even so, some increase in the floating debt would scarcely be avoidable. It therefore went without saying that voluntary repayment of bonds ahead of final maturity would simply aggravate the whole problem. From this assessment there followed the case for closing the $1\frac{3}{4}\%$ tap, replacing it with a $2\frac{1}{2}\%$ 1954–6, and possibly also creating and selling through the Issue Department additional tranches of two or three existing short and medium maturities. Peppiatt concluded as follows:

> In short, if during the next two or three years we are able to meet our very substantial commitments without undue reliance upon Floating Debt/inflationary borrowing and are, moreover, able to maintain a free market at reasonable prices in gilt-edged securities (which we shall not do without cost), I think that we should have done the utmost that is practicable; and that to attempt to do more would be to act in a manner contrary to the sound principles which should always govern British Government finance and which in the long run pay handsome dividends.

Following the change of Government in July the $2\frac{1}{2}\%$ National War Bonds 1954–6 and the 3% Savings Bonds 1965–75 remained on tap while the Treasury considered how best to put into effect the new Government's policy of cheaper money. The first step was the reduction in short-term rates already described. The second step was to be the bold announcement at the end of November that the two taps would be closed in December without any early replacement and that holders of two $2\frac{1}{2}\%$ stocks that had reached their first optional maturity in 1944 and 1945 would be offered the choice between cash repayment or conversion into further amounts of the short-dated $1\frac{3}{4}\%$ Exchequer Bonds. These moves were preceded by formative discussions as a result of which Dalton's adventure was decisively launched. The Bank argued for a more cautious approach, but its advice was rejected.

Discussion in the Bank began very shortly after the cut in short-term rates, when the $1\frac{3}{4}\%$ bonds rose nearly to par but showed little sign of gaining sufficient strength to enable the Issue Department to sell off any of its holding. Since it was judged that there was too much short-dated $2\frac{1}{2}\%$ stock in the market, Peppiatt now suggested calling the two $2\frac{1}{2}\%$ stocks, 1944–9 and 1945–7 for repayment in the spring of 1946, accompanied by an offer of conversion into more of the $1\frac{3}{4}\%$ bonds. Active buying-in of the two stocks by Issue, and the subsequent conversion of official holdings, would 'improve the appearance of the conversion result'. The Chief Cashier also suggested closing the 3% tap 1965–75 in December and replacing it with a new 3% stock '1985 or after'. The medium-dated $2\frac{1}{2}\%$ tap could remain open until February and a decision about its replacement could be taken nearer that time. Niemeyer expressed some scepticism, saying there would be a buyers' strike before long, but Peppiatt's ideas were accepted by the Governors and embodied in a note entitled 'Interest Rates' that was sent to the Treasury on 12 November. Its whole tone was cautious. The size of the future borrowing programme, the load of maturities, the already high level of the floating debt, and the danger of being misled by short-run speculative purchases of long-dated stocks were all stressed. It was essential to do nothing that would risk disturbance to the willingness of the investing public to buy Government securities. Very careful handling would be needed. In particular, an early attempt to float a long-term or irredeemable $2\frac{1}{2}\%$ stock would be unwise. The theory was often propounded that investors had to take what they were offered, but the failure of the $1\frac{3}{4}\%$ Exchequer Bond gave a recent example of the 'underlying fallacy of this theory'. Once a move was made to $2\frac{1}{2}\%$ for a long-term security, the market would consider that the worst had happened, would fight shy of the loan, and would await a move in the other direction – 'we should be regarded as having loosed off the last shot in our locker'. If all went well, it might be possible to improve on current long-term rates, but it was not safe for the moment to go beyond extending the date for a new issue of 3% stock. 'The long-term rates are more difficult to shift below what investors regard as a practical minimum.' Indeed they were.

The Report of the National Debt Enquiry was now available at the Treasury. It began with the caveat that specific action should not be undertaken without careful prior consultation with the Bank. But it then developed the argument that lower rates, if obtainable, would be advantageous in the slack economic conditions that were (mistakenly) judged likely to emerge once the transition was over. Lower rates would help stimulate the investment needed to absorb the savings coming forward at high levels of employment. They would also minimise the heavy fiscal burden of a National Debt swollen by war finance. The Report recognised the inflationary dangers of the transition but considered these would have to be met by a combination of high taxation and direct controls. A big rise in interest rates and a fall in bond prices would be very damaging, but if lower rates were to be pursued then there was need for caution in the choice of timing. The public would have to be convinced that lower rates would prove durable. However this was easier if the State was the main borrower and could therefore set the pace. Unlike the Bank, the members of the National Debt Enquiry saw no serious danger in a rise in floating debt held by the banks provided there were 'adequate understandings with the financial community' and provided the Government's policy was properly presented. The Report concluded by suggesting three new taps, $1\frac{1}{2}\%$ at five years, 2% at ten years, and a new 3% stock with a very wide maturity spread commencing at ten years.

This Treasury document, it will be recalled, had been prepared by Treasury officials and Whitehall economists. Astoundingly, in view of the intimacy of Bank–Treasury relations at this time, the National Debt Enquiry had deprived itself of any input from Threadneedle Street. Its Report did not reach the Bank until 20 October, after discussions had already been held at official level based on the Bank's note of 12 October. It was then heavily criticised by Niemeyer, whose comments were subsequently passed to Eady.[12] As an expression of influential Bank opinion directly opposed to that of the Treasury and its Chancellor these comments deserve extensive quotation:

> Except as a smoke screen at the time it was written, the Treasury paper is not a satisfactory document. Both its phrasing and its logic are very difficult to follow.
>
> It seems to me (a) to generalise far too much from particular moments in the past, (b) to underrate the stresses of the present (and future) and (c) never to have looked at all at the actual structure and market standing of the existing medium and long term debt.

[12] Cobbold wrote in manuscript to Niemeyer: 'We showed this (if I may say so admirable) note to Eady – I hope he may take some of it to heart.'

(a) The Treasury admit that low interest rates are not in themselves sufficient to cure depression. But they exaggerate the effects of high rates in preventing expansion. There may be moments when – with industry hesitant – a really high rate – say 6% – is decisive. But in a real prosperity boom even such a rate has very little effect. When rates are as low as 2–3% – which is in fact a cheap rate – the deterrent affect of the interest rate is very slight. I suspect this latter condition is the normal state and the 6% effect the exception. More than the actual rate, the movement to increase may be a deterrent (and vice versa): but no one at the moment is really contemplating that. And this psychological deterrent generally only functions when the patient's condition is already susceptible to a shock. It has no result in a boom.

Rates do not act, either way, like mechanical science; their effects vary with the presence or absence of a number of other factors and cannot be laid down *in vacuo* by a priori reasoning.

The Treasury ought to be much clearer than they are whether what they want is low rates or lower rates. Much argument is spent on the beauty of low rates – which we have had for years – or the desirability of avoiding 'a rise in the rate of interest'. But their conclusion jumps without any argument to the beauties of lower rates.

(b) They are still obsessed with pre-war fears of 'under investment', i.e., more saving than enterprise uses. Is this not a fantastic bogey after the wartime borrowing and savings campaigns? And wartime damage? The pre-war condition has entirely vanished and industry will now use all and more than anyone can save (assisted by controls and rationing) provided it is given security.

In my view the Treasury gravely underestimate both

(i) the increasing unwillingness of the public to save as war becomes remote and consumption goods more readily available; and
(ii) the pressure on the security market as industrial and other holders of existing Government Securities realise for their delayed quasi-capital needs.

New lenders will increasingly have (what they have not had during the war) other opportunities for using their money. With all the control in the world, these forces cannot be wholly eliminated.

Budget effects are the least important of the consequences of rate changes. If those changes are economically necessary, the Budget does not lose on them when all sides of the picture are taken into account.

Paragraph 16 seems to me to deal with appearances rather than realities. The real object of increasing money rates was not just to attract supplies of gold, but to shake out stocks of commodities carried on credit and to make prices more attractive to exporters. That resulted in a foreign demand for British goods and therefore produced exchange (Gold) but only as a

Otto Niemeyer, Executive Director 1938–1952

reflection of a deeper process. That process may still be necessary if we are to sell exports and acquire raw materials, quite apart from any Gold Standard question.

Paragraph 20 is a good instance of the delusions to which abstract theory may lead otherwise sane people. The argument that continuous borrowing gives the borrower command of the market can only be true if the borrower is able and willing to inflate *quant. suff*. This is in fact what 'adequate understandings with the financial world' really comes to.

It is unlikely that this attack found its way into Treasury circulation. Even if it had, its particular authorship would have made it unacceptable to the Chancellor. For Niemeyer in his own person typified another 'fantastic bogey', namely some relentless hard-money school whose influence the Government wanted to erase for eternity. Be that as it may, the Bank now found that the cheaper-money policy in gilt-edged was not for serious questioning and that its advice was being sought only on tactics. But of course the underlying divergence, which the Treasury had made little attempt to resolve, remained in place. As Cobbold had recorded some days earlier about the long-term rate:

> There is a fundamental difference of view in that we hold that HMG will be doing well if they can keep down to a 3% rate over a long period and that long borrowing at 3% is therefore good borrowing, whilst the Treasury hold that they have good prospects of doing better over a long period and that it is therefore a mistake to tie themselves up to 3% for longer than they can help.

In the end, and after a meeting on tactics between Chancellor and Governor, the Treasury were persuaded to drop their ideas for $1\frac{1}{2}$% and 2% stocks and to accept that the $1\frac{3}{4}$% bonds had first to be properly established in the market. They also dropped the proposal for a new 3% 1955–80, which they had been advised would prove a flop. But the Bank, in turn, had to give up the idea of a 3% irredeemable, which would have set the seal on that rate as the early post-war norm. Instead it was agreed firstly that the existing taps should be closed and secondly, ahead of a quarter in which the seasonal surge of revenue would temporarily almost eliminate the Exchequer deficit, that they should not be immediately replaced. This was announced at the end of November, together with the offer of additional $1\frac{3}{4}$% bonds in exchange for the $2\frac{1}{2}$% maturities. It was well received and the press response was generally sympathetic. For some months there had been a series of comments about the possible implications of a cheaper-money policy for the growth of bank deposits and floating debt; but there were not yet signs of alarm, much stress being placed on the retention of physical controls.

As for the Bank, it had begun the assault on the long-term rate with good tactical advice, in pursuit of a policy that it judged misguided and an objective that it did not think would prove sustainable if reached. It was perhaps partly for this reason that no serious consideration seems to have been given by the Treasury, before committing itself to a venture it acknowledged might well prove difficult, to what might be done if things began to go wrong. If under pressure, could or should the policy be enforced and preserved by a programme of deliberate and heavy market support, along lines later to be adopted (but ultimately abandoned) by the American authorities in defence of their $2\frac{1}{2}$% long-term rate? Would this creation of money really prove harmless? Would it be prudent in the British context, with sterling likely to be vulnerable to adverse confidence factors? If not, was it really worth facing the risk of an unedifying retreat that could well leave rates higher than they were at the start? Despite official faith in the efficacy of physical controls, questions like this would have been all the more pertinent when the Government was about to undertake obligations of external convertibility which the Treasury and the Bank were convinced would prove premature and bring trouble. Seemingly ignored, too, was the massive programme of nationalisation which would involve large-scale substitution of gilt-edged for equities in the stock market. But the Treasury, wedded to the wishes of its Chancellor and apparently satisfied it could deal with problems of confidence, was reluctant to discuss such questions with a very sceptical Bank that would beyond doubt have regarded heavy market support as a prescription for disaster and would have argued that the risk of its being needed was a conclusive argument for staying with 3%.

(e) THE ROAD TO THE $2\frac{1}{2}$% IRREDEEMABLE: 1946

At the long end of the market the response to the closing of the two taps in December 1945 was quite good. By the middle of January 1946 the yield on long-dated stocks had fallen below 3%. At the short end, however, and probably in part because of switching into longer stocks, the situation had not yet improved and the yield on the $1\frac{3}{4}$% bonds was still well below that obtainable on $2\frac{1}{2}$% securities of comparable term. However, encouraged and gratified by the fall in long-term yields, the Treasury was anxious to plan tactics for the next move and a meeting was held by Dalton on 17 January attended by Bridges, Hopkins, Keynes, Eady, and the Governors. Catto's written brief for this meeting, which was subsequently handed to the Chancellor, advised that $2\frac{1}{2}$% was not yet in sight at the long end and that haste should be made slowly. In particular it would be necessary for the authorities to bide their time until the results of the conversion offer became available at the end of February and the $1\frac{3}{4}$% bonds then had another chance to establish themselves at the short end of the market. Further issues of short bonds, at yields below $1\frac{3}{4}$%, were out of the question for the present. As to the succession of $2\frac{1}{2}$% maturities over the next decade, all with two- or four-year maturity spreads, it would be wrong to adopt any particular policy in advance. Decisions would have to be made stock by stock according to circumstances ruling at the time. This advice was fully discussed at the meeting and generally accepted. It was agreed to review the situation again nearer the Budget.

In the event, conversions by the general public into the $1\frac{3}{4}$% bonds proved rather small and by the close of the offer there remained outstanding for cash redemption nearly £180 million of the maturities. Conversions by the Issue Department and the NDO were quite large, making the overall result look respectable. But this brought total Departmental holdings of the Exchequer Bonds up to no less than £500 million and their market performance remained poor. Looking at this result and at the need to refinance a further £550 million of maturities in the coming year in addition to any other Exchequer requirement, Peppiatt suggested the early introduction of a new long tap, perhaps a $2\frac{1}{2}\%$ 22-year stock at a small discount. The running was then taken up by Keynes, who had left London towards the end of February to attend the Savannah Conference. On board the *Queen Mary* he gave his mind to the Government's borrowing programme for 1946–7 and the pursuit of cheaper money. He completed an eleven-page memorandum on the subject in mid-Atlantic and despatched it to the Chancellor after arriving in the US. A copy was then sent to the Governor.

Keynes began by arguing that on current estimates the Budget deficit for 1946–7, together with net extra-budgetary outgoings, might well be covered by receipts from National Savings and by the external borrowing or the run-down of reserves associated with the balance of payments deficit. It was therefore likely that no new money would be required from the market and that any new tap issues would prove to be part of a debt-funding programme rather than a borrowing programme. He then seemingly ignored the problem of refinancing maturing bonds and went on to point out that early and deliberate funding of floating debt, currently costing only $\frac{1}{2}\%$ per annum, would have little positive advantage to justify its cost. He then came to the central part of his memorandum, arguing that: 'Market conditions are likely to move in favour of the Treasury by the natural pressure of events unless that pressure is prematurely relieved by a long-term issue.' There were two reasons for expecting this pressure. Firstly, a large amount of short bonds had probably been held by investors who did not really need so high a degree of liquidity. These investors were now moving longer, in search of higher yield, because fears of dearer money had been dispelled by the Government. Secondly, the flows of current saving by individuals and institutions would favour investment in long-term securities, while dissaving by industry and commerce would involve disinvestment in short-dated securities. Appreciating that sufficient selling pressure at the short end of the market could so alter the shape of the yield curve that the buying pressure at the long end would be diminished, Keynes concluded that the technical problem at the moment was to find ways of getting 'at any rate all those who ought to be fairly liquid to hold bonds at a rate not exceeding 2% and if possible $1\frac{1}{2}\%$ or $1\frac{3}{4}\%$.

This will be extremely difficult to secure.' He therefore suggested that, in order to provide sufficient impulse towards cheaper money, the Chancellor's Budget statement might declare that the Government would not be needing to go to the market for new money and might then go on to include a bold debt-management package. This would contain reductions in the rates on National Savings and Tax Reserve Certificates, a declared intention not to bring a new long tap for the time being, and a new 2% medium-dated tap whose purpose would be to show official resolution on cheaper money rather than raise fresh funds. Keynes felt that a reduction in Bank Rate, which might help set the seal on all this, should also be considered; but he noted its possible effect on foreign opinion and added: 'It may well be that there is a case for doing nothing at the present time.'

Purely as an analysis of the short-term market prospects through the immediate phase of reconversion and their exploitation in pursuit of a lower long-term rate, Keynes' memorandum was difficult to fault even though at times he relied on optimistic judgement and even though he left out of account the problem of gilt-edged maturities. The latter, together with the unconverted residue of the two issues already called, amounted to £725 million; and their successful tactical handling would clearly be a vital part of debt management in the coming year. More surprising, however, was the absence from the memorandum of any note of warning, except as an aside in reference to Bank Rate. Keynes was at the time very worried both about Governmental extravagance, especially on expenditure overseas, and about the sterling balances. The American Loan was not yet through Congress and anyway its passage would ratify the undertakings already given on sterling convertibility. Yet his memorandum emphasised the special market circumstances of the transition and the opportunity they provided, without even a passing reference to the different conditions that might prevail at a later stage and to the long time it might take to establish $2\frac{1}{2}\%$ as a new norm. For someone of his distinction and experience these omissions cannot credibly be ascribed to shortsightedness. A more likely explanation is that his ceaselessly enquiring mind had become so intrigued by the short-run opportunities for official management of the market that he narrowed his terms of reference accordingly.

In the Bank, the Deputy Governor, Peppiatt, and Mynors were quick to stress both the need to refund maturities in order to avoid an upward jump in floating debt held by the banking system and, given the state of the short-bond market, the need to refund through a new long-dated stock as well as, perhaps, through sales from the official hoard of $1\frac{3}{4}\%$ Exchequer Bonds. They also looked rather further ahead than Keynes. 'We have tremendous maturities facing us over the next five or six years', wrote the Deputy, 'and we must anticipate a heavy borrowing programme. We cannot be sure that the market will remain in as healthy a state as it is now throughout that period...' Making hay while the sun shines can be a debt manager's temptation as well as his pleasure. But giving way to temptation in the spring of 1946 was no more than prudence. Thus on 14 March the Governor wrote to the Chancellor proposing a $2\frac{1}{2}$% 22-year tap priced at a small discount and only slightly above the market. He rejected a short-dated 2% stock as serving no useful purpose.

High level discussion between the Treasury and the Bank then continued for some weeks during the run-up to the Budget early in April. Keynes also participated after his return from Savannah, unwell and exhausted, towards the end of March. He continued to oppose the issue of a new long tap and an associated conversion offer to holders of the $2\frac{1}{2}$% bonds maturing in August. He argued instead for a more adventurous course, namely calling 3% Local Loans stock (an undated issue, redeemable at the Government's option since 1937) and offering a $2\frac{1}{2}$% dated stock in exchange. This meant leaving the maturing $2\frac{1}{2}$% bonds to be dealt with at a later stage and accepting some rise in the floating debt in the meantime. Since the Bank thought this would force the pace and risk a setback, the Governor, with strong support from the Chief Cashier,[13] continued to argue that a new long tap, along with a conversion offer in respect of the August maturity, should come first and that the conversion of 3% Local Loans should be left for later consideration. In the end the Bank prevailed, with support from Treasury officials, though the actual announcement of the new tap was left over until the market response to the Budget had been assessed. By that time, a few weeks later, Keynes was dead.[14]

Presented on 9 April, the Budget for 1946–7 contained an implied cash borrowing requirement of about £1,150 million compared to some £2,250 million in the preceding year. Since National Savings, still running strongly, were expected to bring in over £500 million and external borrowing was expected to be of the same order, the Chancellor could indeed declare that he would not need to go to the gilt-edged market for substantial new funds. This, together with the satisfactory contraction of

[13] On 2 April the Chief Cashier wrote: 'We here must have regard not to the snatching of some temporary and perhaps illusory saving in interest charges, but to the preservation of British Government credit over the years.'

[14] In an account of these discussions in *High Tide and After* (London, Frederick Muller, 1962, p. 124) Hugh Dalton wrote: 'This was my last discussion, indeed my last meeting with Keynes before his death on April 21st. Thus, contrary to what some have alleged, he was not weakening at all, at the end of his life, in his support of cheap money, or of the immediate steps required to cheapen it further. He had always been my mentor and stimulus on this subject.'

the deficit itself, the absence of a new long tap for the time being, and the Chancellor's continued attachment to cheaper money,[15] was well received in the market. Prices rose further and yields on long-dated stocks fell by over $\frac{1}{8}$%. At the short end even the $1\frac{3}{4}$% Exchequer Bonds at last found buyers; and the authorities sold over £170 million in the weeks following the Budget, mostly against purchases of the next maturity, while the yield fell by $\frac{1}{16}$% to $1\frac{5}{8}$%. Accordingly, at the end of April and ahead of announcing on 15 May the terms of a conversion offer to holders of the August maturity, the Bank again proposed that a new $2\frac{1}{2}$% long-dated stock should be issued, for cash as well as conversion, in order to take advantage of the better terms now available and press further ahead with a refinancing programme. The stock, maturing in 1964–7, could now be brought at par without forcing the pace. The Chancellor would have preferred a $2\frac{1}{2}$% undated stock but accepted that this goal was not yet quite within reach. He also queried the need for a tap but again accepted that this would be tactically correct and that a modest amount of new money, to help refinance the unconverted residue of the maturities, would be useful.

The issue was announced on 14 May. By then the market had risen further and the terms of the new stock had become conservative. Together with the orthodox appearance of the whole operation, this caused speculative selling and the market fell back. The official tactics, with their discouragement of frothy speculation, attracted favourable comment in the press, where analyses of the underlying implications of cheaper money were now beginning to appear. But they also induced some doubts about the limits to official ambition and in one case a criticism that the authorities had misjudged the market and missed an opportunity. The fall in the market also angered Dalton, who was not without private City advice and who now felt that he could have got away with better terms. He considered he had been wrongly advised by the Bank and in particular wrongly advised by Cobbold. In his memoirs[16] he said he was supported in this view by the Governor, who had been on holiday when the decisions were taken. It was even suggested that the Bank had got so immersed in the technicalities of the issue that it failed to notice the further improvement in the market before 15 May. But the mechanics of mounting a cash-and-conversion issue of this kind meant quite a long lead-time was required. For this particular issue 390,000 prospectuses and 650,000 application forms were to be printed, and final versions were

---

[15] Also evidenced by a reduction, to $2\frac{1}{2}$% from 3%, in the rate on National Defence Bonds (a National Savings non-marketable security) and to $\frac{3}{4}$% from 1% in the rate on Tax Reserve Certificates.   [16] *High Tide and After*, p. 125.

approved by the Treasury in proof on 8 May. The Bank had in fact informed Whitehall on 29 April that all details would have to be settled by 3 May if the 15 May deadline was to be met. When the terms were indeed agreed on 3 May, it was accepted that the programme could only be halted by 'violent' market change in the interim. In other words it could be halted or cancelled but not amended. In the event the rise in the market during the run-up was not sufficient to justify crash action. The Bank could of course be criticised for failing to foresee the further rise in the market; but it could as well be complimented for not indulging in a gamble when advising on the terms of a Government issue.

As things turned out, the market soon steadied and, although conversions by the public were small, the tap raised just over £400 million in cash by the time it was closed on 9 July. Together with official sales of Exchequer Bonds since the Budget, this meant that over £600 million had already been raised towards meeting a refinancing requirement of a little over £700 million.

It looked as if the Government's own prior needs, as seen at Budget time by the Treasury, the Bank, and informed critics, had largely been satisfied. Accordingly, the way seemed clear for the next and final step to a $2\frac{1}{2}\%$ irredeemable if the market so permitted. But fortune, on whose smile so much of the policy relied, now turned adverse. It so happened that a large and partly fortuitous increase in floating debt was about to occur, accompanied by the persistence of a rapid increase in bank deposits that had emerged in the spring. In addition, there was now in train a programme of modest but steady purchase of longer-dated stock in the market by the NDO, which was in search of an adequate return on Postal Savings and National Insurance funds. Though unpublished, these purchases were large enough to attract attention in the market, which then tended to magnify their size and in part mistake their motive. As a result of these two factors, the market and the financial commentators became suspicious on two counts: firstly that the abrupt increase in floating debt and the rise in bank deposits might not after all prove as harmless as the authorities liked to claim; and secondly that those same authorities were aggravating the process by surreptitiously buying in long-term stock so as to shorten the journey to a $2\frac{1}{2}\%$ irredeemable. So, although that final step could in the end be taken rather shakily in the autumn, it was done against an inauspicious background. The emerging pattern of Government financing during the first six months of the fiscal year 1946–7 is therefore critical to the whole story and requires some explanation.

After rough allowance for seasonality, the overall Exchequer borrowing requirement in the first half of the financial year was not out of line with the Budget estimates and averaged some £330 million per quarter. But the heavy net external borrowing forecast for the year as a whole had yet to materialise and did not in fact do so until the winter; for the time being, therefore, the whole of the borrowing requirement had to be financed at home. National Savings, relied on to provide over £500 million for the year, performed well in the June quarter but faded badly in the next. These developments accordingly undermined for the present the assumptions that had justified Dalton's declaration in April that little net new money would be needed from the gilt-edged market and that no undue increase in the floating debt would ensue. Over the July and September quarters borrowing on market Treasury Bills and TDRs came to £315 million. This growth of floating debt was equivalent to nearly half the borrowing requirement for the period. Moreover, it became highly concentrated in the September quarter when net borrowing through gilt-edged turned negative, mainly because of the incidence of stock redemptions in August. Concurrently the growth of deposits at the London clearing banks accelerated. From May to November the three-monthly rate of growth exceeded £300 million, and over two-thirds of this was matched by additional Government borrowing from the banking system. A rough allowance for seasonal factors would have suggested that bank deposits were growing at an annual rate between 15% and 20% and possibly faster. In 1945 they had grown by only 6%. As yet there had certainly been no acceleration in the real growth of the economy; rather the contrary. If, therefore, in the summer of 1946 anyone wished to argue, contrary to the new orthodoxy, that the money supply was being dangerously increased with adverse implications for the future, rather than being harmlessly boosted to satisfy a temporarily higher liquidity preference at lower interest rates, they had plenty of quantitative evidence with which to do it.

Such argument could not be deflected in 1946 by surrounding the publication of statistics with official argument about seasonal adjustments, front-end loading of the borrowing requirement, or the timing of external as opposed to domestic borrowing. For one thing, neither the Bank nor the Treasury possessed the monetary economics and statistical resources that could readily be used for such a purpose. For another – partly because of the Bank's intuitive concern, in the interests of market management, to preserve the secrecy of its day-to-day operations in gilt-edged – there were simply no published monthly figures of Government financing to which to refer, or at least none of the kind known since the statistical developments that followed the Radcliffe Report of 1958. Apart from annual information published at the time of the Budget there were only the weekly Exchequer Returns, whose form effectively concealed the overall borrowing requirement as well as the operations of the Issue Department, the NDO, and the EEA. Banking statistics by contrast, though they suffered from various imperfections and could not be tied in with meaningful Exchequer figures, were at least moderately reliable and were at least published monthly (by the banks). If these statistics showed that the growth of money supply was accelerating rapidly and if, as was the case, this was only in small part attributable to the rise in bank advances, then commentators were left to fumble with the authorities in statistical darkness for possible reasons why Government borrowing from the banks had accelerated. Absence of hard information served to create and fortify suspicion: perhaps the overall deficit was running higher than expected; if not, perhaps the authorities were monetising the National Debt by failing to refinance maturities fully, or even by buying in longer-dated stocks. The temporary absence of external borrowing, perhaps a mitigating factor, would be difficult to discern because although drawings on the North American Loans had to be published there was no reliable means of judging the operations of the EEA or changes in overseas holdings of UK Government Treasury Bills or gilt-edged. Nor were the authorities themselves much the wiser. Quarterly information on Exchequer financing in the early post-war years was not fully extracted from the statistical raw material until shortly before its publication in 1961.[17] In the late summer of 1946, for example, the Bank itself was only just beginning a first detailed mid-year forecast of the Exchequer's requirements for market finance over months rather than weeks ahead, the aim being to present a better case for this or that programme in gilt-edged. Up to then the Bank seems to have relied upon annual estimates supplemented by monitoring the growth of floating debt, a simple procedure that served well enough during wartime but was not appropriate to the more complicated and difficult world of peacetime debt management. Furthermore it was not until 1948, in response to a Ministerial initiative at the Treasury, that a serious attempt was made to link Exchequer financing data directly to banking statistics.

During the summer of 1946, the effect of the rise in floating debt and money supply on market and press opinion was compounded by the activities of the NDO in long-dated stocks. This development, already briefly mentioned above, was a consequence of the fall in market rates during the previous autumn and winter and an accompanying decline in the income of the Postal Savings Fund and of the funds held for the Trustee

[17] *Economic Trends*, December 1961.

Savings Banks. These funds had balanced portfolios containing a prudent quantity of liquid assets held especially against the contingency of post-war withdrawals. Thus the fall in short-term rates and the conversion of maturing stocks into lower-yielding Exchequer Bonds had an immediate adverse effect. In addition, the Chancellor feared he would compromise his cheaper-money policy if he issued special new long-term securities to these funds (terminable Annuities) at the old rates, which were above those prevailing in the market. Such issues, including the rate payable on them, would have had to be disclosed in the Exchequer Return. There accordingly opened up the possibility of a deficiency emerging in the Savings Bank fund which, as the law stood, would have to be met from a special Parliamentary Vote. One obvious answer to this, and one favoured by the Bank[18] would have been to lower the rate of $2\frac{1}{2}\%$ paid on Postal and Trustee savings. But the Government, for political reasons of its own, refused to do it. Nor on the other hand did the Treasury like the idea of a deficiency vote. The Controller of the NDO therefore argued that he should be allowed to buy stock in the market, including long-dated stock, with newly accruing funds and also, when advantageous and when available, acquire longer-dated stock issued through a tap or in conversion of maturities.

These proposals entailed modifying the set of arrangements that had been constructed during the war so that the Funds could both obtain adequate income and serve the operational needs of gilt-edged market management. Under those arrangements the NDO had not been a net buyer of gilt-edged in the market, though since 1943 it had assisted official debt management by buying accumulations of near-maturing stock from the Issue Department against sales to Issue of longer-dated stock, acquired before the war, which Issue in turn on-sold in the market. The Office also subscribed to tap issues on behalf of the Unemployment Insurance Fund. But by far its largest source of new money were the Postal and Trustee Savings Banks, whose accruals were lent direct to the Exchequer either through 3% Annuities specially issued for the purpose or, to provide liquidity, through Ways and Means Advances at 1%. In the winter of 1945–6 the Bank was not averse to some modification of these arrangements because it felt that modest net purchases by the Office, if appropriately timed, could help to shield the market from the full effects of

---

[18] The NDO was formally answerable to the Commissioners for the Reduction of the National Debt (CRND), who include, by Statute, the Chancellor of the Exchequer and the Governor or Deputy Governor of the Bank of England ex officio. In the early post-war period the Controller of the NDO paid due regard to formalities and addressed policy memoranda to the Chancellor and the Deputy Governor. In reality the questions at issue were handled by the Treasury and the Bank in much the same way as any other questions of debt management, the final decisions resting with Whitehall.

selling pressures that might arise from industrial and commercial liquidation of gilt-edged acquired during the war. But at the same time the Bank was anxious to retain its use of the NDO both as a source of additional stock for sale in the market and as an additional buyer of early maturities. The Treasury, while not dissenting from these views, carried the argument an important stage further and was prepared to allow the NDO to buy longer-dated stock in the market – up to agreed limits – even though the market trend was upwards, provided the effect on prices was not too visible. The Chancellor himself, who saw such market purchases as a useful auxiliary in his cheap-money drive, readily concurred. Towards the end of May 1946 the NDO was accordingly let off the leash. Over the ensuing eight weeks, during the issue of the $2\frac{1}{2}\%$ 1964–7 stock, it bought over £20 million of longer-dated stock, mostly Savings 3% 1965–75. A further £23 million of stock, more widely spread, was bought between mid-July and mid-September. In the meantime it had acquired £272 million of the new issue, £260 million by conversion and the rest by cash subscription.

The market purchases by the NDO were conducted through the Government Broker, but at this time apparently without close control by the Chief Cashier. This degree of operating autonomy was unfortunate. Despite their formal secrecy, untypical official transactions in stocks that were neither on tap nor approaching maturity were always vulnerable to being noticed by keen-eyed market participants. They were the more vulnerable when no issue was on tap and there were no large-scale switching operations associated with it. In the event, because the NDO was anxious to complete a previously agreed programme of acquisition within reasonable time on a rising market, its purchases do indeed seem to have been spotted. Totalling so far some £45 million, they were not very large in relation to the £400 million raised by the Government in June and July through the $2\frac{1}{2}\%$ 1964–7 tap. But they were quantitatively significant in market terms. Their presence was evidently felt; and in the statistical mist surrounding Exchequer operations they were large enough to increase suspicions about the causes of the rapid growth of bank deposits. Early in September the Bank became alarmed at what was happening and complained that the buying operations of the NDO were interfering with the long-established official technique of selling stocks into a firm market against acquisition of early maturities. On 4 September the Deputy Governor complained to Bridges that the NDO was now 'continually in the market for longs to the exclusion of everything else' and that there was a risk of a firm but very narrow market being artificially forced up to dangerous levels. The Treasury then agreed that the NDO should refrain from pressing their purchases in such conditions; but the damage to market opinion had by then been done. Unease in the press, provoked at first by the banking figures, had begun in the *Financial Times* early in August and developed further in September. *The Economist* published a long and far from reassuring leading article entitled 'Cheap Money and "Unfunding"', while on 9 September the *Financial Times* referred directly to the NDO buying up Government stock. It would have been better if the opportunity presented by the threatened deficiency in the Savings Bank funds had been seized with less gusto and handled with greater care.

The poor reception given to two Local Authority loan conversions in early August and early September reinforced the impression that the market, though at first outwardly firm, was narrow. Prices then fell back and purchases by the NDO were allowed to resume. A further £10 million of longer-dated stock, mostly 3% 1965–75, was acquired in the ensuing three weeks. It was against this indifferent background that the Bank had to begin thinking about a new issue in the gilt-edged market during the autumn or winter. On 19 September the Chief Cashier minuted the Governors to the effect that the low yields prevailing would now suggest converting 3% Local Loans, of which the public held £323 million out of £429 million, into a $2\frac{1}{2}$% irredeemable. A week later he followed this with a full analysis of Exchequer requirements over the remainder of the financial year and concluded that the conversion operation should be accompanied by an issue of £300 million for cash.

The analysis had been prepared by Roy Bridge, then an Assistant to the Chief Cashier working on the Exchequer and money market desk. His work was endorsed and acclaimed by Mynors and marked a timely innovation without which rational mid-year discussion of post-war Exchequer financing was becoming almost impossible. Bridge set out full estimates of the Exchequer's overall cash requirement alongside estimates of its financing through NDO Annuities, External Debt, and National Savings. The resulting residual financing through floating debt was then adjusted to take account of the EEA (changes in reserves), NDO Ways and Means Advances, and changes in overseas official holdings of Treasury Bills. The final residue was then an estimate of the change in market-held floating debt. This amounted to an increase of about £300 million from mid-September through to the end of March 1947 and formed the basis of Peppiatt's suggestion of a cash issue of gilt-edged stock.

The Chief Cashier's proposal was fully discussed in the Bank and with the Government Broker. There was some doubt about the wisdom of bringing a $2\frac{1}{2}$% irredeemable. But Mullens strongly advised that to bring a $2\frac{1}{2}$% dated stock in replacement for the undated 3% Local Loans would represent a degree of unfunding and would be ill-received by a market that was already losing momentum. Mullens considered that, in contrast to the situation prevailing earlier in the year, the market lacked speculative support and that an appearance of official hesitation in the drive towards a $2\frac{1}{2}\%$ irredeemable would be interpreted as a sign that the policy had reached its limit and that the time had come to sell. This advice being accepted, the Chief Cashier's proposals were set out in a note that was discussed by him and the Deputy Governor at a meeting with senior Treasury officials on 29 September. It was agreed to go ahead, subject to market developments and subject to the views of the Chancellor and the Governor on their return from the first annual meetings of the IMF and the IBRD then under way in Washington.

During the first ten days of October the market situation became somewhat worse. Opinion was disturbed by a public warning about the risk of a fuel crisis during the coming winter. The market also had to digest another apparent failure of a Local Authority issue and another round of sceptical press comment centred on an article by Wilfred King[19] in the October issue of *The Banker*, entitled 'Gilt-edged and the Volume of Money'. Commentators remained apprehensive about the rise in money supply and, as they detected, the absorption of gilt-edged into official hands. They also began to doubt whether the authorities themselves would be prepared to tolerate the inflation of bank deposits for much longer. In the market, prices fell back and yields crept up a little, thus making a new $2\frac{1}{2}\%$ irredeemable look 'above the market'. On 9 October, in a note for the Governor on his return from the US, the Deputy recorded that both Mullens and Nivisons[20] reported heavy and unsettled markets and that 'with sentiment as it is today they could not advise us to go ahead with this operation'. The two brokers met again with the Governors and the Chief Cashier on 14 October, ahead of a decisive meeting at the

---

[19] King, Wilfred, CBE (d. 1965). Educated LSE. *Financial News* 1929–40 (short time with *The Daily Telegraph* during this period). Ministry of Supply 1940–5, Assistant Editor, *The Economist* 1945–6, Editor, *The Banker* 1946–65. Honorary Fellow, LSE, Vice-President, Royal Economic Society. Author, *The History of the London Discount Market* (London, 1936).

[20] The senior partner of this firm, Lord Glendyne, had been close to Norman, who consulted him as well as Mullens on important market questions. This practice persisted for some years after Norman's retirement but was later abandoned, although Nivisons continued to enjoy direct access to the Chief Cashier when fixing terms for Local Authority stocks brought by themselves as brokers to the Authority concerned. Shortly after the author became Chief Cashier in 1966 the practice was explained to him, without evident enthusiasm, by the then Government Broker, Peter Daniell. In due course I was visited by Lord Glendyne himself, then over ninety, and by John Boscawen, his number two. One welcomed this alternative window on the gilt-edged world; but by that time Nivisons tended to come to the Bank to get advice rather than offer it.

Treasury on the same day. Although no decision was reached, the general view was rather averse to going ahead. However, the authorities had now wandered into a position where postponement carried considerable risks of its own. The Government appeared to need money and was under criticism not only for failing to raise it in the gilt-edged market but also for buying its own securities in that market. Postponement might have served to make this criticism the more credible. Deliberate resort to the creation of floating debt was an option the authorities could not now dare to take, did not in fact consider, and one that the Chancellor himself had implicitly rejected in his Budget Speech when presenting his argument that the Government would not need to raise new money from the gilt market. An alternative to postponement might have been to retreat on to possibly safer ground, perhaps abandoning the Local Loans operation and reverting to a $2\frac{1}{2}\%$ dated tap for cash. But this would in turn have risked a major readjustment in the market and the unacceptable defeat of a loudly proclaimed policy. In the absence of a decisive market argument to the contrary, the only effective choice was to press on regardless, gambling without very much confidence on an outright win and hoping that failure would not be too severe or humiliating.

This choice was duly taken, with rather more gambling enthusiasm in the Treasury and rather more hope for only a mild failure in the Bank. At the critical meeting on 14 October the attitude of Treasury officials was exemplified in the advice given by Hopkins. He argued that the Chancellor was in practice publicly committed to establishing a $2\frac{1}{2}\%$ long-term rate and that it would be wiser to take the plunge boldly, now, rather than wait for a better opportunity. Any other course would give the impression that the Government was losing its nerve. For his part the Governor expressed considerable doubts about the chances of success if the operation was launched straight away. But neither could he advise with any confidence that a better opportunity would present itself in the future. Thus if the Chancellor wished to try to establish a $2\frac{1}{2}\%$ rate, he (the Governor) could not definitely advise against going ahead. Catto spoke to a brief that was carefully prepared by Cobbold and succinctly expressed the predicament of an officer who fears he is pushing into an untenable salient under a general who still thinks he is heading for a breakthrough. It read as follows:

> A draft plan has been worked out between the Bank and the Treasury, whilst you were away, for a new move to be announced this week if it is thought appropriate and if Market conditions permit. The plan is to call 3% Local Loans for redemption and to issue simultaneously a $2\frac{1}{2}\%$ Stock 1975 or after. In some ways we might have preferred to issue a stock with a long final date

but it is felt that it would be unsound, when calling a loan on which the Government has an indefinite option, to substitute it with a loan with a definite date. The Market advise that issue of a dated Stock to redeem Local Loans would be widely criticised on principle and would also be regarded as an admission that the $2\frac{1}{2}\%$ rate cannot be definitely established.

We are undoubtedly getting near the end of the story. There has in fact been a definite turn in Market atmosphere during the last three weeks. Markets as a whole have been hesitant and there has been a great deal of talk in the City about the bottom [in yields] having been reached and about heavy official buying which it is alleged has been necessary to keep interest rates as they are. New York markets have been weak and prospects there are obviously uncertain. Although New York may not have the same direct influence on London as it used to, there is no doubt that weakness and uncertainty there have sentimental and psychological repercussions here. Statements about the coal situation have underlined the general uncertainty and uneasiness.

We cannot feel at all certain or advise confidently that in present Market conditions an issue on the lines proposed would attract much money or be particularly successful. In fact it is quite possible that the response might fall well short of the amount necessary to redeem Locals. Yields are approximately on a $2\frac{1}{2}\%$ basis, but there is little activity in the Market and there is a growing reluctance to buy gilt-edged on the present interest and tax levels. We doubt therefore whether much money will be forthcoming and we fear that the new stock might go to a discount if things do not pick up during the winter.

On the other hand we cannot be at all certain that conditions will be more favourable later on. If therefore the Chancellor is anxious to make this move in the interests of establishing a $2\frac{1}{2}\%$ rate, he may prefer to try it now rather than to put it off, in spite of the risks.

For reasons which have been given more fully in a note prepared for the Treasury, we should regard the issue of a short or short medium at this stage as quite out of the question.

It is felt that it might be a help if some brief, but categorical, comment could be made by the Chancellor, possibly in his Mansion House speech, rebutting the Press allegations about official support for Government securities. A denial would have to be quite brief and should not enter into any detailed figures or argumentation.

The issue was announced by the Chancellor in the House of Commons on 16 October. He concluded: 'A landmark has been reached. For the first time in the history of the National Debt, HMG are able to issue for cash an irredeemable security yielding $2\frac{1}{2}\%$ at par.' Dalton followed this up with appropriate promotional passages in his speech at the annual Mansion House Dinner for the Chancellor and the Governor on the evening of the same day. He included a display of some insouciance about the rise in money supply and a none too convincing denial that the authorities had been indulging in large-scale support of the market. The initial response, as reported in the press, was no worse than cautious. It was expected that investor resistance to the Government's terms would be greater than hitherto, but it was nevertheless felt that redemption of the Local Loans 3% stock would directly or indirectly create a substantial reinvestment demand[21] for the new 2½% stock. However, *The Economist* remarked that investors were being asked to give a 'complete hostage to the policy of ultra-cheap money for more than a generation'; and early in November Wilfred King published a second article in *The Banker* entitled 'The Modern Goschen'. After reporting a City reaction of astonishment, surprise, and incredulity, he exemplified these by remarking that investors were being asked to assume that cheap money was here to stay, together with successful reliance on the capital controls entailed, a willingness on the part of the authorities to buy in stock as necessary, and perpetual avoidance of the use of interest rates as a policy instrument.

Attitudes of this kind were not improved by the announcement, later in November, of the terms on which railway securities would be exchanged into new Government stock on the effective date of nationalisation – then over a year ahead. In addition to creating a technical demand for railway stocks standing below their gilt-edged exchange value, the announcement served as a sharp reminder of this prospective increase in the total supply of Government securities. In the end the issue of 'Daltons' was not a total failure; but it left the market very vulnerable to further adverse developments. The result was certainly not the success on which the Treasury had gambled. Despite official attempts to drum up support before the tap was closed, and despite the use of very misleading figures[22] to that end, the entire exercise left the Government short of over £80 million instead of raising a worthwhile amount of new money. In addition, the NDO continued to acquire long-dated stock in the market, thus adding to the total of unfunding. Over the six months ending in March 1974 this latter came to £147 million. Out of the £429 million of Local Loans outstanding, £118 million was redeemed for cash in the hands of the public. A further £102 million was acquired from the public for cash in the

---

[21] Local Loans stock was a liability of the Local Loans Fund. As such it was not in law a liability of the central government Consolidated Fund and holders could not therefore be offered conversion into a Government stock. Since they could however be invited to reinvest their redemption moneys by subscription to the 2½% tap, every holder was sent such an invitation along with the notice of redemption, and the 'conversion' of Local Loans stock was effected in that way.

[22] Stating in December that 'already we are almost home and I shall not keep the tap open much longer', the Chancellor gave figures of reinvestments and tap subscriptions which tacitly included those of the NDO and the Issue Department. By then it was of course well known that such figures gave no useful clue to reinvestments and subscriptions by the public.

normal course of the Issue Department buying in the maturing Loans. Against this expenditure of £220 million the Government raised £137 million in cash through the tap, leaving a net outlay of £83 million. As to the new stock, £479 million was created, of which only £248 million was acquired by the public (cash £137 million, 'conversion' £111 million). Of the remaining £231 million, the NDO held £135 million and the Issue Department £96 million (for future sale, if possible). But if all this was a qualified failure, other developments, tantalisingly, were more favourable. Fortune's smile began to recover from its eclipse, but too late.

Anyone charged with responsibility for debt management in the UK soon learns that the Government's own borrowing needs frequently defy accurate prediction. Forecasts have to be acted upon but can prove by turns cruelly or happily misleading. The winter of 1946–7 seems to have been no exception. The figures are difficult to reconcile, but it looks as if the borrowing requirement over this period was some £300 million less than the Bank had been expecting. In any event, during the fourth quarter of 1946 the requirement fell from the levels reached in the summer and the Exchequer achieved a seasonal surplus in the first quarter of 1947. Meanwhile, external borrowing gathered pace while National Savings recovered. Thus even though unfunding in gilt-edged continued, the rise in floating debt held by the public was only some £85 million in the fourth quarter compared to over £300 million in the third. In the first quarter of 1947 such debt fell by some £80 million. Concurrently, Government borrowing from the banking system first decelerated and then turned negative. The growth of bank deposits behaved likewise, despite some upturn in bank advances.

But, to change metaphor, the Seventh Cavalry had arrived too late, and possibly even at the wrong location. Wrapped in a statistical fog, whose obscurities the Chancellor had at times actively tried to exploit, the authorities were in no good position to claim credit from new developments that could be clearly seen only if the entire fog suddenly dispersed. Market confidence, already bruised in the run up to 'Daltons', was unimpressed by developments in Exchequer financing and money supply that were only partly visible. Instead, opinion continued to concentrate on the credit expansion of 1946, to worry lest the Government should allow it to resume, and to ally these concerns to growing unease about inflationary pressures at home, about the external deficit, and about the approach of convertibility. The exceptionally severe winter and the associated fuel crisis added to this unease. So the market tide turned adverse. In response, the authorities stood by and watched. Funds available for investment by the NDO fortuitously fell away, but the Bank itself made no attempt to intervene decisively. Although there is no evidence of such a course being considered at the time, a policy of heavy intervention would most likely have made matters worse, particularly in the absence of an ability to claim advantage from such favourable developments as there were. To have been seen doing something to which opinion was by now very hostile – and which had been denied when done previously – would have been to invite selling pressure rather than deter it. To maintain the policy it would then have been necessary to increase intervention and, in effect, openly peg the market.

The effect that pegging might have had on confidence generally, including overseas confidence, is a matter of historical speculation, but it is unlikely to have been good at this time. The question is, however, unusually academic. As has already been noted, determined intervention was not an option that the Treasury or the Bank had yet considered as a practicable response to a sharply falling market. The whole policy of attempting to bring down the long-term rate was opportunist in character, relying on the exploitation of market opportunities rather than on any radical change of practice. Once the doubtfully favourable opportunity had passed, there was nothing to do but wait and see. By early April, ahead of the new Budget, Daltons had slithered to around five points discount on their issue price of par and were yielding about $2\frac{5}{8}\%$. Only a major revival of confidence would enable the lost ground to be regained. It was not to happen.

(f) 1947: THE RETREAT TO 3%

Over the spring and summer of 1947 the gilt-edged market became oppressed by the growing external crisis, by the growing realisation that remedial domestic measures would be needed, and by doubts whether such measures would be taken. These doubts were at last partly dispelled by Dalton's November Budget and by his sudden replacement as Chancellor by Stafford Cripps. But investors then became disheartened by the prospective appearance of £1,000 million of rail compensation stock in the new year. At no stage, however, was the market burdened by another issue of Government stock for cash or conversion. The underlying cash position of the Exchequer had greatly strengthened. The borrowing requirement for 1947-8 ended up as low as £204 million compared to nearly £850 million for 1946-7. Receipts from external items, predominantly the US and Canadian Loans, came to a massive £902 million, leaving nearly £700 million for the net repayment of domestic debt. *Ex ante*, things were not expected to work out quite like that; but as the situation evolved tentative plans for a new issue, including a conversion offer to holders of 3% Conversion Stock 1948–51, could be shelved without much embarrassment. Furthermore, some degree of discreet market support could be provided during the worst phase, and normal buying in of the next maturity could proceed, without the accompanying steep increases in floating debt and money supply that had been so evident a year earlier.

At the outset, just before the April Budget, the Bank had tentative plans for bringing a $2\frac{1}{2}$% dated stock during the summer in order to fund some of the floating debt created in the previous year. But the Governor and the Chancellor agreed to wait and see how markets behaved. In any case, the Issue Department owned £95 million of 'Daltons', that could be sold if demand recovered. The Chief Cashier looked at the matter again early in June. Although markets were no better and none of the 'Daltons' had been sold, floating debt was being reduced by external borrowing. The Chancellor therefore readily agreed with the Governor that no action should be taken. The convertibility crisis then intervened. The gilt-edged market fell very heavily and yields rose $\frac{1}{2}$% or more. By 3 September 'Daltons' had fallen from 95 to as low as 86. Their yield was approaching 3% and indeed reached that point two weeks later as nervousness continued in the long run-up to the November Budget. During this period the Bank again kept out of the long market but intervened on a modest scale to steady the short end. Over the September quarter the Issue Department bought some £30 million of under-ten-year stock as well as £52 million of the next maturity. In addition, the NDO bought over £20 million in accord with a modified investment policy agreed earlier in the year, with less emphasis on maximisation of yield.

The débâcle in gilt-edged reflected the fading of confidence in the Government's conduct of economic policy. It attracted a good deal of sour comment about the vaunted policy of cheaper money and the seemingly light-hearted official attitude to credit expansion in 1946. Feelings in the Bank were also a little sour. Complaint about the indecisive drift of current policy came well to the surface. Both Kershaw and Peppiatt circulated notes arguing for a sharp tightening of fiscal policy in order to produce a convincing overall fiscal surplus. Peppiatt referred to the prevailing uncertainty and lack of confidence in the gilt-edged market and to the need for a 'stable solid jumping-off ground in place of what appears to the public to be the present shifting sand'. Without this solid basis, any attempt to stage a revival by greater intervention would be futile. He and Cobbold were now fearful of pressure being brought to bear on the Bank to force the market up artificially ahead of the issue of Transport stock in the new year so that the latter could be brought with a $2\frac{1}{2}$% coupon; and it was clear that Dalton would, if possible, want to avoid the personal defeat of a return to a 3% coupon. The Bank was therefore at pains to argue that creation of money by increased intervention would run directly contrary to the presumed aims of the forthcoming autumn Budget, would risk another defeat ahead of the Transport issue, and would make the aftermath of that issue even more difficult to handle than was in any event likely to be the case. The right way to tackle the problem was through a sound autumn Budget and this would have far more effect than any market intervention. The Bank should therefore confine itself to continued buying-in of the next maturity and to levelling out in a small way where it seemed appropriate. All these arguments were deployed at a meeting with the Chancellor and his senior officials early in October. It was then agreed that for the time being there should be no change in Issue Department operations but that the continuing investment programme of the NDO should be concentrated in the twenty-year area, where the Transport stock was likely to be brought.

The autumn Budget was introduced early in November. Indirect taxes were increased and expenditure cuts announced. On the following day, as a result of a wholly inadvertent 'leak' of Budget information to the press, Dalton resigned and was replaced by Cripps. The latter, who had previously been President of the Board of Trade, had taken up the newly created post of Minister of Economic Affairs at the end of September. This Ministry had been set up to fill the co-ordinating role in macro-economic policy previously performed, inadequately, by the Lord President, Herbert Morrison. It was now merged with the Treasury and that Department thereby acquired the central role that it had previously lacked. But neither the fiscal nor the Ministerial changes engendered much revival in gilt-edged, where the approaching £1,000 million of Transport stock was now the dominant feature. Under the terms of the Act, the Treasury were obliged to issue this stock on 31 December 1947, strictly in line with market values. Although they could choose the term, they could not take liberties with the price and yield appropriate to that term. Complicating the tactical situation was the approaching first optional maturity in March of 3% Conversion Stock 1948-53, of which £187 million remained outside official hands at the end of October. If the stock was to be redeemed at first option, in accord with the Government's policy of treating 3% maturities in that way, an announcement to that effect together with the terms of any conversion offer had to be made by 1 December. Since the Bank was anxious to mount a conversion operation, in the interests of avoiding a resumption of recourse to floating debt, it first proposed that a further issue at par of $2\frac{1}{2}$% Funding Stock 1956-61 should be made for the purpose. But by the end of November the market had fallen back to yield levels that made this plan impossible. A $2\frac{1}{2}\%$ issue for an even shorter term remained feasible but would look like a weak move, while the issue of a higher-yielding stock would have prejudiced what chance remained of bringing the Transport stock below 3%. So on 26 November the Governor advised the Chancellor that a conversion offer should not after all be made. Refinancing of the maturity should therefore be left on one side until the Transport issue was out of the way. If necessary a new tap stock could then be brought. Cripps and his officials accepted this advice and continued to hope that the Transport operation could at least be undertaken at $2\frac{3}{4}\%$. But it was not to be. Final terms were settled on New Year's Day and 3% Transport Stock 1978–88 came into being. On the following day the Treasury quickly and quietly completed the burial of its former policy by increasing the rate on Government loans to Local Authorities to 3%, in line with the market.

Over the next two years, until the maturity of $1\frac{3}{4}\%$ Exchequer Bonds early in 1950, the Government made no new issues of gilt-edged stock. A substantial cash surplus in 1948–9 continued on a smaller scale in 1949–50. Furthermore, since there were large receipts from external items, including Marshall Aid, floating debt was reduced and official operations in central government stocks were quite small until the buying-in of Exchequer Bonds began late in 1949. But within this welcome background there emerged operational problems arising partly from the need to raise finance for the newly nationalised industries, through periodic issues of Government-guaranteed stock, and partly from renewed difficulty in accommodating the investment needs of the NDO within the wider interests of debt management. However, with the Exchequer in surplus and the attempt to preserve $2\frac{1}{2}\%$ recently abandoned, there was now much less political and official concern with long-term interest rates. Attention shifted instead to other aspects of monetary policy. First, in 1948, the Treasury and the Bank became closely interested in the relationship between the fiscal surplus and the course of bank advances and bank deposits. Next, in 1949 and later, the level of short-term interest rates came under scrutiny and the wisdom of clinging to the structure established in 1945 was finally called in question.

The Bank is likely to have embarked on this new phase with its self-confidence enhanced and its confidence in its masters diminished, even though the arrival of Cripps must have to some degree mitigated its disillusionment with Whitehall. Alongside the disaster of convertibility, the fate of the cheaper-money adventure in gilt-edged was admittedly of lesser account, though no doubt it made some contribution to the general loss of confidence in the summer of 1947. But the Bank had done its loyal best to carry out the policy that the Treasury had decided. Within the limits of unchanged technique, straightforward opportunism, and somebody else's strategic misjudgement, it had in practice given good tactical advice. In particular, its judgement ahead of the decision to launch 'Daltons' had been almost exactly correct. Looking back early in 1948, the Governors, the Chief Cashier, and others concerned could therefore have felt that their strategic views, overridden in 1945, had been amply vindicated and their tactical expertise confirmed. With the Bank settling down under the Act of 1946, this increase in self-confidence would make it easier for the Old Lady to play a more aggressive part in the formulation of monetary policy. But it might also serve to confirm some intuitive prejudices. The cheap-money policy, like the framework of external monetary undertakings enshrined in the Anglo-American Loan Agreement, could be regarded primarily as a policy of political economists. Their theories, their judgements, their goals had ruled. The less sophisticated but nevertheless powerfully expressed views of 'practical men', whose experience was rooted in financial and commercial markets, had been set on one side. Those men had then been used as little more than technical assistants. Now it looked as if they had been right after all. A prejudice against interfering academics would seem to have been justified. But if it be the case that monetary policy, domestic or external, is best formulated and executed by a close combination of market skills, economic analysis, and statistical expertise, this confirmation of a Bank prejudice would not prove an unmixed blessing.

(g) MONEY SUPPLY, BANK ADVANCES, AND FISCAL DISINFLATION: 1948–1949

The Treasury was reorganised following the change of Chancellor in November 1947 and the absorption of the Ministry of Economic Affairs. The Finance Division was split in two, with Eady in charge of Home Finance and Wilson Smith in charge of Overseas Finance with Rowan and Clarke. At the same time the Economic Section under Robert Hall, though still remaining nominally part of the Cabinet Office, moved into Great George Street along with the newly created Central Economic Planning Staff under Plowden. In order to complement these acquisitions and assist with macro-economic policy, a second Junior Minister was appointed with the title of Economic Secretary. The first holder of this post was Douglas Jay. Later a senior Minister in the Labour Government of 1964–70, he was a Fellow of All Souls, Oxford, an experienced financial journalist, and had been a wartime Civil Servant. His literacy in economics was undoubted and he had been appointed Economic Adviser in No. 10 Downing Street in September 1945. He had entered Parliament at a by-election in July 1946 after giving early warning to No. 10 about the impending fuel crisis. These changes in Whitehall meant that the Bank, as earlier described and still unaltered, would encounter a different range of personalities at the Treasury when questions of domestic monetary policy were up for discussion. In particular, the new range would include a working unit of professional economists, together with an Economics Minister, where since the death of Keynes there had been none (other than Dalton himself). It was not long before the change made itself felt.

The new Treasury Ministers and their advisers were determined to reduce the inflationary pressure they saw in the economy and to bring the external deficit under greater control. To this end they began planning for a substantial overall Budget surplus in 1948–9. But the Economic Secretary soon became concerned lest the disinflationary effect of this surplus should be offset by an expansionary monetary policy. He therefore turned the Government's previous reasoning upside down. In his view the credit expansion of 1946–7, in part caused by the cheaper-money policy in gilt-edged, had in turn had inflationary consequences through the capital gains associated with the rise in security prices. Even though that policy had faded away, the banks were now expanding their lending to the private sector. In 1947 bank deposits rose 6% while advances rose 18%. At the prevailing very low rates of interest this expansion of advances could accelerate and might well do so if borrowers sought in that way to offset the effects of a tighter fiscal policy on their spending power. This thinking was in terms of saving and investment. The fiscal surplus, acting to reduce bank deposits, would increase aggregate saving and reduce some investment. A countervailing expansion of bank advances would have the reverse effect. So in one way or another it would have to be prevented. In the background there of course remained the apparatus of direct controls on private expenditure, but it was now accepted that these were not fully effective unless supported by firm fiscal and monetary policies.

After initial discussion in the Treasury, during which it was questioned whether a policy of reducing bank deposits should be carried to the point of raising interest rates, the views of the Bank were sought. A letter raising a series of searching and for those days unfamiliar direct questions was accordingly sent to the Chief Cashier. Did the Bank agree that a reduction in bank deposits should be the objective? What factors were responsible for the recent increase in deposits? To what extent did bank deposits contribute to the inflationary pressure? What technical means were available to the Bank to assist in deflating deposits? Would the Bank consider, in this context, the relative merits of open-market operations, Bank Rate policy, changes in the banks' cash ratios, and voluntary restrictions on bank lending? The Chief Cashier appears to have been a little perplexed by this about-turn and somewhat at a loss to know how to respond to questions requiring a prolonged excursion into monetary economics and central banking technique. Two years previously one group of politicians, officials, and economists had not thought it worthwhile consulting the Bank on these fundamentals of monetary policy. Now another group, working for the same Government but with apparently different ideas, had sent the Old Lady 'at technical level' a very wide-ranging questionnaire that the Bank was not well equipped to answer at length and with speed. Yet a convincing response was required, partly because the Minister was himself showing a sophisticated interest 'at technical level' and partly because the suggestion of direct control of bank lending raised sensitive issues about relations between the authorities and the banking system, and about the position of the Bank itself in that context.

There ensued some discussion, in which Niemeyer and Mynors participated. The latter pointed out the dangers of thinking that one could deal with an inflationary situation solely by a Budget surplus at a given level of interest rates; one had also to reconsider some cherished ideas about cheaper money 'even to the point of not minding if it gets a tiny bit dearer'. But for his part Niemeyer blamed the rise in money supply squarely on past fiscal deficits and stated boldly: 'When that ceases, bank deposits will cease to rise. When there is a surplus, they will fall.' The Governor agreed with Niemeyer, saying: 'In a word, a *real Budget surplus* plus reduction in floating debt which that would make possible, is the *true* remedy.' With this hasty and dogmatic guidance, together with his own technical knowledge of central banking, Peppiatt wisely avoided trying to reply in writing to the Treasury's questions and instead persuaded the Governor to invite the Economic Secretary and Eric Bamford (Deputy Secretary, Home Finance) to lunch on 30 January 1948, to be followed by a talk with himself and Mynors. At this talk the Bank stressed the need for a true Budget surplus overall, argued rather surprisingly that a rise in Bank Rate would not achieve much beyond disturbance to gilt-edged, and stated that a more rigid control of bank lending would break down in practice and would in any case be unnecessary. Furthermore, as floating debt and bank deposits fell in line with the fiscal surplus, the cash base of the system would contract pro rata in accord with the Bank's policy of 'keeping the banking situation as tight as may be consistent with financing the Government's needs'. This helped allay Jay's fear that the banks would find themselves with surplus cash and would then respond by expanding their lending.

Nobody, except possibly Mynors in his comment about the rate of interest, seems at this stage to have raised the obvious point that if the banks, within their qualitative lending guidelines, wished to expand advances and deposits, they could readily and automatically keep their cash ratios in line by selling floating debt to the Bank as need be, at the prevailing fixed interest rates. In fact, by reassuring the Economic Secretary that *excess* cash would not accumulate, the Bank had hastily and rashly invited him to believe either that *new* cash would somehow not be forthcoming or else that he need not worry about the demand for advances. Whether Jay was convinced by these after-lunch propositions is not clear. But he decided that the Bank should be held to its advice. On 7 April, following the introduction of a disinflationary Budget that contained an overall surplus, the Chancellor wrote to the Governor: 'Under the Finance Bill, the Budget surplus will be applied, as it accrues during the year, to redeem floating debt, and I look with confidence to the Bank to ensure that this process is in turn reflected in a substantial fall in the level of deposits in the clearing banks, and is thus made effective in counteracting inflation.' Enclosed with the Chancellor's letter was a memorandum drafted by the Economic Secretary that set out the mechanics of cash reduction and stated that the contemplated mild fall in bank deposits, amounting to some £600 million, ought to be sufficient to ease slightly the pressure on physical controls without implying any rise in interest rates or any undesirable deflationary symptoms.

Evidently realising with some apprehension that the Bank was implicitly being asked to commit itself somehow to holding bank advances steady without any agreement on the means of achieving this result, Mynors had endeavoured without success to stop this letter being sent. He felt it was exactly the way to provoke future misunderstandings and proposed that in his reply the Governor, while welcoming the fiscal surplus and foreseeing some fall in bank deposits, should avoid precise commitment. In the event, Catto sent a very short reply, saying merely that he was in 'complete agreement with the general objective of your letter and the memorandum'. A few weeks later Mynors wrote that bank advances were likely to go on rising but that criticism would not be justified provided the banks were observing the qualitative guidelines. He went on to observe: 'As long as the price-weapon, i.e. the rate of interest, is forsworn, there is no other criterion.' Meanwhile the Treasury were monitoring events. The Economic Section circulated bi-monthly reports on the economic situation and the

Treasury Accountant, Chadwick, began to produce detailed figures of Exchequer financing which, with help from the Bank, could be set alongside the monthly banking figures. However, exact linkage was not obtained because the Exchequer figures still related only to calendar months, while the banking figures related to third Wednesdays (the bank make-up days).

During the summer of 1948 it began to look as if bank advances were indeed continuing to grow and that there were as yet few signs of disinflation in the economy. The usual statistical shortcomings and the absence of proper seasonal adjustments served to obscure the trend until later in the autumn, but this did not prevent the Economic Secretary from addressing an emphatic warning to the Chancellor during August. Inflation of bank credit had more than offset the budgetary deflation. The one important cause of the continued rise in the cost of living, the continued fall in unemployment and a new wave of wage demands, was the inflation of credit. It could be argued that higher advances were needed to finance higher prices, but this was no more than the classical argument of a banking system justifying its part in a steady inflation. The Bank was not taking the necessary resolute action. It must now be told firmly that there must at least be no further rise in advances and secondly that there must be some fall in deposits.

This message was conveyed by Eady direct to the Deputy Governor in the Chief Cashier's absence. Cobbold then sized up the situation clearly and realistically. There was no means, he bleakly replied, of restricting the banks through operations on their cash ratio 'without a pretty violent assault on the rate structure'. The only alternative was by a direct approach to the banks asking them to keep advances down, but this would need very careful handling and could not be set in motion until late September when the Governor and the clearing bank Chairmen would be available. In the meantime, Mynors should keep in close touch with the Treasury about the level and nature of bank lending. Eady accepted this advice and in due course the Governor began informal consultations with the Chairmen of Midland and Lloyds, Lords Linlithgow and Balfour, who were at this time also Chairman and Deputy Chairman of the CLCB. Early in October a further increase in lending became known and caused considerable concern in Whitehall. Soundings of the banks then served to confirm what the Economic Secretary had said. Directional guidance was being obeyed and the rise in advances was no more than a reflection of, *inter alia*, the higher cost of inventories. Naturally enough the Treasury was not comforted by this; and early in November Mynors reported that Hall and Plowden were accusing the banks of promoting inflation and asking for drastic action to control them. The statistical and economic basis of this accusation was, as usual, doubtful and the Bank, as ever, was in no mood to conform to the rather volatile opinions of successive Treasury economists about the remedy to be employed. But neither could it prevent the Treasury from examining the proposal for action and putting forward a considered recommendation. Over 1948 as a whole bank advances grew 14%, equivalent to about three quarters of the $4\frac{1}{2}$% rise in deposits.

There is little doubt that the Bank detested the idea of imposing advances ceilings on the banks, though the precise reasons for this were not well articulated at this time. To some extent the Bank, as spokesman or sponsor for the banks, may have wished to protect its constituents from an objectionable imposition damaging to their long-term efficiency. Another reason may have been that the imposition of ceilings would have required a formal directive, or something very close to it, an action the Bank wanted to avoid. But in the main the Bank's attitude seems to have reflected both a deep-seated practical scepticism about direct banking controls as such – a scepticism that was to prove well founded in later years – and a growing conviction that excessive public spending combined with the very low rate of interest were at the real heart of the problem. As for the Treasury, both officials and Ministers seem at times to have regarded the absence of quantitative controls on bank lending almost as an anomaly, or even as an affront. They felt that the banks should behave as instruments of Government policy and that direct controls ought to achieve this aim. In these years such considerations as the long-term effect of base-period rationing on the efficiency of the banking system never seem to have entered the Whitehall mind. Be that as it may, in the closing months of 1948 the Bank successfully fought off the proposal by at last effectively combining the voices of its practical men with those of its economic advisers and also by exploiting the Government's own deep-seated fear of overdoing monetary restriction. But at only one moment did the Bank reveal that it was to some degree playing its traditional part of Janus, leaning on the banks where it could while protecting them from a Draconian directive and persuading the Treasury that so drastic a move would be dangerous. This one moment came when the Treasury suggested that the 'central monetary authorities' had powers to direct the banks. It was promptly reminded that under the 1946 Act such power rested solely with the Bank, acting in the public interest though with the consent of the Treasury.

The Bank's challenge to the arguments of the Treasury economists came first from Mynors and later, while the former was travelling on Bank business abroad, from Thompson-McCausland. Mynors, in a long letter to Eady and Hall in the middle of November, excused his unfamiliarity with post-Keynesian terminology and argued that the rise in bank deposits was attributable to planned savings falling short of planned investment. But he then drew attention to the hit-and-miss effects of restricting advances. In some cases alternative finance might be available without much difficulty, for example by delaying tax payments. In other cases cut-backs in investment might occur but could be wasteful (uncompleted projects otherwise officially approved) or unwelcome (projects in development areas). In addition there were alternative ways of reducing bank deposits, if that was desired, and possibly also of increasing savings. Funding operations on more attractive terms could be undertaken. So why not attack the problem on several fronts rather than one? As far as the banks were concerned, they were well aware of the interest being taken in their activities and were already taking due account of it. Hall replied to this in a letter to Lucius a few days later, making the point that a deficiency of planned savings could be met by the activation of idle deposits rather than the creation of new ones and that this would cause a useful disinflationary cut in liquidity. He was not too concerned about the hit-and-miss effect of credit restriction but was concerned and very uncertain about the consequences for interest rates.

Ten days later Lucius responded with an enquiry into the velocity of circulation. Always more interested than Mynors in the money supply itself, he argued that the fiscal disinflation deriving from the Exchequer's surplus would, at first, mainly affect demand deposits, whose former owners would indeed then seek greater accommodation from their bankers. It had also, as it happened, coincided with a fall in the note issue. However, the Exchequer had paid out large sums in redemption of maturing gilts and this was likely to have inflated time deposits and financed the rise in bank advances. In fact, although total deposits and advances had indeed gone up, the rise in the former was largely concentrated in time deposits. The rise in demand deposits had been quite small and less than the cut in the note issue. Lucius saw all this as the first stage in a process of monetary disinflation, which was accordingly consistent with a rise in money supply.[23] The second stage would come because there would be pressure to reduce bank advances back to normal; and at that stage total deposits would fall. 'All this', he wrote in his mock-

---

[23] The money supply he had in mind corresponded with the 'M3' of later years, and his reconciliation of a rising M3 with monetary disinflation may bring a smile of recognition to those interested in similar pursuits thirty or forty years later.

pedagogic style, 'amounts to a preliminary re-shaping of the qualitative money structure from which deflation can better be carried through to the final stage in which the deflation is also quantitative.' The idea of the 'final stage' was little more than wishful thinking, but it enabled Lucius to argue that to take fresh measures to increase the pressure on borrowers would risk going too far. 'The effects of a severe shock, once administered, must take their course and cannot be turned off at will.' Accordingly, why not let the existing medicine go on working, helped along perhaps by administered cuts in licensed investment programmes? In addition, the rise in money supply could be helpfully reduced by an increasing volume of corporate funding through new issues on the Stock Exchange.

Hall first talked this through with Lucius and then replied in writing on 1 December. Confessing that he was slowly getting more educated about this difficult problem, he went on to concede many of the points that the latter had made; but he left open for further discussion the question whether the pressure on borrowers needed increasing and, if so, how severely. Here the running was now being made by Eady, probably after private discussions with Cobbold. He had already rejected a general ceiling on bank advances. It would be arbitrary and unselective in nature. Moreover, 'a widespread restriction of credit... would bring into action latent deflationary influences on a large scale. Deflation like inflation gathers momentum and is very difficult to correct promptly if it threatens to go too far.' Instead, the existing selective guidance to the banks should be quietly reinforced by the Governor speaking to the Chairmen. Matters then hung in the balance for a week or two. The Economic Section still favoured an advances ceiling and it was at this point that the question of a directive to the banks was raised by the Treasury. Though unwell at the time, the Governor himself then intervened energetically in a letter to the Chancellor 'dictated from my bed'. He aligned himself forcibly with the position taken by Eady, expressed concern that the question of directives and powers had been raised, and enclosed a personal memorandum violently opposing the imposition of a ceiling on bank advances. Catto was now approaching seventy. His forthcoming retirement at the end of February 1949 had been announced in October and the succession of Cobbold to the Governorship had been confirmed. (Cripps first offered the job to John Hanbury-Williams,[24] Chairman of Courtaulds and a much respected member of Court, who turned it down after discussion with

[24] *Hanbury-Williams, John Coldbrook, Kt (1892–1965)*. Educated Wellington. Courtaulds 1926–52, Director 1930–5, Managing Director 1935–40, Deputy Chairman 1943–6, Chairman 1946–52. Director, Bank of England 1936–63, Executive Director 1940–1.

colleagues at the Bank. Cripps then told Cobbold that the Governorship was his.) This did not prevent Catto from entering the fray with characteristic bounce. Writing to Cobbold in manuscript from hospital he expostulated: 'This pressure from the Economic Section on financial and banking matters must be dealt with forcibly otherwise you will have no peace in the future; and it is better and indeed my duty to deal with it, and that has the advantage of not disturbing your personal relations with any of them, for you will have to live with them... Please go over my memorandum and make what deletions or additions you and the boys, especially OEN and KOP, may think advisable. But unless such corrections are fundamental, leave it as I have written it which has at least the virtue of brevity.' His memorandum, which included some imaginative exaggeration of the supposed ill-effects of an advances ceiling read as follows:

1 There is probably little doubt that the country's economy is geared beyond our resources, but how much it is difficult to assess.
2 Such a programme is bound to be inflationary but on the whole not more than was to be expected from the great industrial effort which the country is making.
3 One of the evidences of the inflationary tendency is of course high bank deposits and high bank advances.
4 I understand the Economic Section of the Treasury are disturbed by this and at a recent meeting put forward suggestions about a ceiling for deposits and advances.
5 I view such a suggestion with the utmost alarm: it is not practical and would land us in a mess of violent deflation. It is contrary to two fundamental principles of sound banking and finance:
(a) that money must never be made unobtainable. The banks must always be willing lenders; and
(b) that disinflationary action through the banking system can only be by pressure on the borrower.
6 In the past, pressure on the borrower has been applied by raising money rates to a point when the borrower reduces his borrowing: but with a vast Government debt such as exists today and with our present highly geared economy that remedy cannot be used effectively because the margins of profit of the average industrial borrower are such that he would not be deterred in his borrowing by any normal rise in money rates, and any important rise in money rates is out of the question because of the enormous additional interest cost to the Exchequer on floating debt, and conversions looming ahead in the future.
7 How then, can pressure of a sound disinflationary nature be applied? Plainly only by:
(a) a Budget surplus which will automatically reduce floating debt and gradually have its effect on bank deposits; and

(b) by reduction of the pressure at its source by the planning authorities impressing on the Government Departments concerned to be more selective in their granting of permits and licences of all kinds.

That is where the trouble starts, for once a permit or licence is obtained and the holder goes to his bank for an overdraft to finance it, then the bank manager, very rightly, thinks he is helping the national interest by providing the money. Do any of the appropriate Government Departments, in granting permits or licences, ever check whether the client is over-stocking or over-trading and whether in fact granting the permit or licence simply means further pressure on the banks for advances in excess of the necessities of the case?

8 It is an entire fallacy to suppose that pressure from the Bank of England on the banks could rectify inflationary pressure which comes from over-gearing the country's economy. Plainly what is needed is to be more selective in the gearing. The Bank of England can of course give the banks guidance on specific lines, such as to curtail their facilities on hire purchase, dealings in property and real estate, Stock Exchange loans, etc., etc., and I also gave a pretty general all-round warning in my Speech at the Mansion House on October 19th 1948. Indeed, the Chairman of our largest bank said to me as I sat down: 'Thank you Mr Governor, we have had our warning!' In the form of guidance there are perhaps further specific things the Bank of England can bring to the attention of the banks and they are always most co-operative in accepting guidance on these matters in the national interest.

9 My considered judgment, therefore, is that any suggestion of a ceiling for bank deposits and advances is entirely unpractical: it would be violently deflationary and dangerous to the Chancellor's policy of maximum production and rehabilitation within our resources which he has put before the country with so much inspiration and success. The only practical ways of dealing with the problem are those I have indicated in paragraph 7.

10 A time may come in the near future, when possibly some slight adjustment upwards of short-term money rates may become advisable for technical reasons and to indicate our continued control of the market and that money rates may not always remain as low as they are now: but that would not have any appreciable effect on bank advances, and would require the most careful consideration because even a very slight increase in short-term rates would cost the Exchequer a good many millions.

The Chancellor replied at once in his own hand:

Thank you for your letter of the 17th and its enclosure. Let me just say how much I hope that you are better and that all has been found well in the hospital.

I will go into your paper with my advisers.

You need not trouble about the relations between the Bank and the Treasury. We all greatly appreciate the willing and helpful co-operation we always receive from the Bank.

Four days later, when the dust had settled a bit, the Deputy Governor called on the Chancellor and the Economic Secretary. There was a long discussion about bank advances. It was finally agreed that no ceiling should be imposed. Instead, the banks were to be informed that a further reduction in floating debt was in prospect and that the Chancellor was hoping that the consequent reduction in deposits would not be offset more than absolutely necessary by a rise in bank advances. To the extent that the clearing banks could, without causing disturbance, co-operate in achieving this result, it would be extremely welcome. Early in the new year the Deputy Governor conveyed this message to Lords Linlithgow and Balfour. He stressed the informality of his approach and the absence of any written request. Both bankers replied that instructions already issued in their own banks were fully in line with the message received; but both said that some rise in advances was likely to prove unavoidable. They readily conveyed the Deputy's message to their members and its contents were duly recorded in the Minutes of the CLCB. This was the first such request to be made since the Bank of England Act 1946 and it had been made in exactly the manner that the Bank preferred. There was no directive, not even a letter. The Deputy had, it is true, handed the bankers a brief *aide-mémoire*, which 'they could take away if they would like', but otherwise there was nothing in writing. There had been awkward moments in the debate with the Treasury. The Bank had begun by appearing to give rash assurances that it had no agreed means of honouring. It had later been assailed for failing to honour them. But it had then fought its corner well, not least by suddenly mobilising the resources in monetary economics of which it had so far made little regular or systematic use. The Treasury had then been persuaded to do things the Bank's way and not to press a policy of credit restriction further than that route could readily accommodate. The bankers, in turn, found themselves being asked to do what, from previous hints, they had already begun doing for themselves. Right or wrong, Janus had certainly preserved his identity.

But the Bank was not so unwise as to believe that the question of advances ceilings had been shelved for the foreseeable future. It was indeed to prove a recurrent bone of contention for over twenty years; while for the immediate future, for so long as short-term interest rates remained frozen at their inappropriately low level, for so long as further restrictive macro-economic measures might well be needed before too long, and for so long as some monetary component of such measures was likely to be wanted, a tightening of direct controls on bank lending was bound to remain on the agenda. The next battle, still over advances ceilings, was to be fought at the time of sterling devaluation in the autumn of 1949. But early in that year the Bank sought to prepare for trouble by examining ways of unfreezing short-term interest rates as at least a part alternative to a tightening of direct controls. Some preliminary thought had been given to this early in December 1948, shortly after Oscar Hobson had raised the matter in the *News Chronicle*;[25] and on 24 January 1949 Cobbold asked for a report on the subject from a group composed of Niemeyer, Peppiatt, Beale (now Chief Cashier designate), Mynors, Bull (Discount Office), and Thompson-McCausland.

(h) DIRECT CREDIT CONTROL VERSUS THE INTEREST-RATE WEAPON

In his memorandum sent to the Chancellor before Christmas 1948 the Governor had made two points about money rates. His first was that a level high enough to deter borrowing would prove prohibitively expensive for the Exchequer. His second was that there might nonetheless be some advantage in a slight upward adjustment. In making these points he was reflecting a Bank view that had come to be held towards the end of 1948 and which formed a prior assumption of the group appointed by Cobbold early in 1949. A rise in Bank Rate to, say, 4% would in fact have cost the Exchequer some £160 million per annum in floating-debt charges, or some £120 million net of additional tax receipts, with more to come if maturing bonds had to be refinanced at higher coupons. There would also have been a considerable balance of payments cost, possibly some £70 million, though the extent of this would have depended upon consequential negotiations with, for example, India about the rate to be paid on Treasury Bills held in No. 2 Accounts and the rate of release from those Accounts. Net of additional income tax receipts, and assuming some success with overseas holders, the cost would seemingly not have been entirely prohibitive if the disinflationary benefits of higher rates had been thought very great. Total expenditure by the central government at this time was about £4,000 million. But there is no doubt, as became apparent later, that the argument of cost was constantly stressed by a Government that was in any case strongly predisposed against the use of 'dear money' in macro-economic policy.

But ruling out a substantial increase in Bank Rate did not necessarily mean keeping money market rates at the $\frac{1}{2}$% to which they had been misguidedly reduced in 1945. They could be raised to 1% or $1\frac{1}{2}$% within the existing Bank Rate of 2%. In the Bank such a move seemed as if it might be within the bounds of practical politics and possess a number of advantages that would be at least some help both with overseas confidence

[25] 'Bank Loans too High', 1 November, and 'Back to Bank Rate?', 29 November.

and with the state of expectations at home. Accordingly, the Governor had suggested in his note that a slight upward adjustment could be useful; and indeed it might have been. But, as is told in the pages that follow, political resistance to even this slight change was to prove insurmountable while the Labour Government remained in office, right through the devaluation crisis in 1949, and again through the renewed inflationary surge in 1951. Some minor adjustment to commercial bill and advances rates was eventually tolerated. But neither Cripps nor his successor Gaitskell could be persuaded to allow a rise in money rates generally, including especially the Treasury Bill rate. When pressed into a corner, they both pleaded political impossibility. But they were also inclined to make use of the debating fork that while a large rise in money rates seemed to be in nobody's mind, a small one was unlikely to achieve anything worthwhile to justify its budgetary and external cost. The truth was that a disinflationary interest-rate policy was unwelcome to the political and economic Left, while Dalton's gilt-edged experiment must have further dulled Ministerial appetites for any adventures in that direction. The effects of interest-rate policy in the heyday of Cripps' Treasury seemed either nebulous or malign, and their exposition seemed beset with mystique or 'mumbo-jumbo'. The effects of fiscal policy, by contrast, appeared both readily quantifiable and beneficent. There was a strong element of irrationality or even hysteria about this opposition to any use of the interest-rate weapon. High interest rates were blunt and antiquated crudities associated with the traumas of the 1920s and early 1930s. They belonged to the restored Gold Standard, to depressive deflation, and to heavy unemployment. They also belonged to Norman's Bank, many of whose leading lights still inhabited their windowless fortress in the City and still attempted to lure the hapless politician back to the bad old days with smooth talk of 'technical adjustments'. High interest rates, even slightly higher interest rates, and most of all a restoration of Bank Rate were not supposed to be part of the new enlightenment that had dawned in 1945. Considerations of this kind probably grew stronger rather than weaker as the political fortunes of the Labour Government declined and its internal unity came under growing pressure. By the summer of 1949 the Government found itself with another severe external crisis to be surmounted; this time with a General Election only months ahead. Later, in 1951, it was obliged to cope with the violent economic stresses following the war in Korea, when its majority had been reduced to single figures, when several Ministers resigned in disagreement with some of the fiscal measures taken, and when another election could not be long postponed.

Against this unpromising background the Bank could but persist with arguments that were becoming increasingly self-evident. Niemeyer's group began this process with a brief report submitted early in February 1949. They recommended that the 2% Bank Rate be made effective, partly by gradually raising the rates at which official operations in the money market were conducted and partly by occasional lending to the market at Bank Rate itself. By these means the Treasury Bill rate would be raised to $1\frac{1}{8}$% or a bit higher. Rates on bank advances would probably not change. Arithmetically this would achieve little more than restoration of the pre-Dalton structure of money rates. But the group felt that the psychological effect would be worthwhile. There would have been a decisive break with the recent past and there would follow some expectation that further moves might be made. The banks might then be a little less ready to lend and customers a little less ready to borrow. Moreover the rise in bill rates 'would tend to correct the extreme anomaly of our present rates for foreign credits which are substantially below foreign, e.g. American, rates (and in the circumstances of this country quite ridiculous)'. In addition there might be some favourable effect on overseas opinion. More generally the group saw the proposed changes as a first experimental step in the restoration of a flexible monetary policy. The merits of further steps could be properly assessed only after the first had been taken. Cobbold, who had now taken over as Governor, discussed the Report with the Group early in March but concluded that 'it would not be wise or appropriate to put forward proposals on these lines at the present time'. The banking figures for January and February were very satisfactory and Mynors had reported a much less aggressive tone in the Treasury regarding bank lending. Disinflation in general was now judged to be proceeding according to plan. There were even some signs that Ministers were beginning to worry lest it should be carried too far.[26] There was therefore little point in the Bank agitating for an upward move on interest rates. Furthermore, the case had already been put in public by the Chairman of Lloyds Bank, whom the new Governor might not have wished to echo in private with the Treasury.

With the change of Governor there came changes in the resources devoted by the Bank to domestic monetary policy. Though staying on the Court, Niemeyer retired as Executive Director and was henceforth mainly occupied with his directorship of the BIS and with his continued membership of the Capital Issues Committee; but for several years he remained available as an active adviser on domestic policy. Dallas Bernard, formerly Executive Director in overall charge of staff and premises, now

[26] Early in May 1949 the Treasury even got as far as considering monetary measures to combat incipient slump. The short-lived recession in the US was by then apparent. But thoughts of monetary re-expansion soon vanished in face of the renewed external crisis.

became Deputy Governor. There were therefore two vacancies within the four Executive Directorships allowed under the Act, the two already in place being Siepmann and Bolton. To fill one of these Peppiatt, now aged sixty, retired as Chief Cashier and joined the Court.[27] To fill the other, Mynors was promoted from his post of Adviser to the Governors. The former became the first of the Executive Directors whose specific duties were confined to matters of Home Finance. The latter took on the housekeeping job but retained his function as an economic adviser and remained the sole professional in that role until the recruitment of Maurice Allen in 1950. To succeed Peppiatt as Chief Cashier, the Court appointed P. S. Beale, with his outstanding technical ability. To mark these changes the Governor instructed the new Chief Cashier to submit a written weekly home finance 'story' for discussion every Friday morning. This may not seem a very startling innovation, but it is a fact that no such written story had hitherto been provided. The intention of these changes was to strengthen the small group at the top of the Bank concerned with domestic policy, yet without creating a supporting unit of economists and statisticians.

In his new post, less beset with exacting daily routine, Peppiatt set out to improve the Bank's direct knowledge of the commercial banking situation. He instituted regular private talks between himself and the chief general manager of each clearing bank, thus complementing the Governor's periodic discussions with the Chairman of the CLCB. The first round took place in the spring of 1949. The bankers reported some signs of stress in parts of the building industry and in light engineering but in general felt that the growth in advances would continue at a rather slower pace (in fact advances grew 11% in 1949 compared to 14% in 1948, while the growth of deposits came to a complete halt). Apart from a request to the banks to take note of some revised guidance issued to the Capital Issues Committee by the Chancellor in April, there were no further developments until the summer, when the Treasury and the Bank began urgently to consider how they should respond to the onset of the second post-war external crisis. There was unanimity among Treasury officials that further restrictive measures would be needed if the external deficit was to be corrected, whether or not there was a devaluation. Such measures, they agreed, would need to include a tightening of monetary policy, which would in turn imply both a direct restraint on bank advances and a willingness to allow interest rates to rise. Copies of the relevant papers were handed by Bridges to the Governor, who set about preparing

---

[27] It is said that he was offered the post of Deputy Governor but refused it; and that the unexpected elevation of Dallas Bernard was the result.

an early response on the main issue of devaluation.[28] But at the same time, on 19 June, he asked Peppiatt, Niemeyer, Mynors, and Beale for advice about the monetary component of a package of domestic measures. Two days later they submitted a note favouring a rise in Bank Rate to $2\frac{1}{2}\%$ or 3% and market operations to make it effective. A gradual tightening of rates with Bank Rate unchanged, as suggested in the previous winter, was no longer felt to be suitable because 'it would not greatly strike the attention of the man in the street' and because it would look overly hesitant for the situation that was in mind. Nor was it now felt practicable to negotiate a special continuation of the $\frac{1}{2}\%$ Treasury Bill rate with large overseas official holders. As to direct controls, the group felt that the banks were already watching advances very carefully and that, in addition to the rise in Bank Rate, all that would be needed would be a reminder about the objectives of Government policy and a request for continued cooperation.

The Governor discussed this advice with Eady, emphasising that firm recommendations could not yet be made because they would have to depend on the relation of monetary action to any other proposed action. Such other action, at this stage, proved to be little more than an administered cut in dollar imports over the ensuing twelve months coupled with a Parliamentary Statement flatly denying any intention to devalue. So, at the Governor's own instigation the proposal to raise money rates was mentioned, only to be rejected, in a comprehensive paper circulated by the Chancellor to the Economic Policy Committee of the Cabinet early in July. The gilt-edged market had now started to fall and the Chancellor averred that this sufficed, as a self-tightening of policy, for the present. But the underlying thought in the Bank was that, if possible, politically limited monetary ammunition should not be wasted in ineffectual support of inadequate measures in other areas of policy. Both at a meeting with Treasury officials on 25 June and at a meeting of the Economic Secretary's Working Party on 4 July, Mynors stated flatly that the Bank would not advocate a change in Bank Rate except in support of cuts in public spending. The point was repeated, this time by the Governor, in a talk with Eady at the end of July.

This exchange marked an early example in a very long series of package-assembly exercises in which the Bank endeavoured to bargain its compliance with restrictive monetary measures in exchange for adequate or commensurate severity in other fields of macro-economic policy. It also marked the onset of a more aggressive attitude on the part of the Bank in Whitehall, an attitude associated in part with the new Governor himself

[28] See Chapter 4(e) above.

and in part with the renewed and dangerous darkening of the external monetary outlook. Cobbold was by temperament more inclined than his predecessor to assume *de facto* responsibilities to the public at large as well as to the Treasury. But the more aggressive attitude, exemplified by this early attempt to strike bargains over monetary policy, was unlikely to have much impact in 1949 because the Government was not anxious to impose a restrictive monetary policy as a make-weight in an otherwise weak package. In the longer run, however, the tactic was often a useful one. The Bank could not itself dictate policy. It lived in justifiable fear of its masters in Whitehall indulging in half-measures, including the imposition of ineffectual controls on banks or half-hearted increases in interest rates. Half measures would then leave the Bank with yet another external crisis just round the corner – for whose even more unpopular resolution it would often be saddled with a share of the blame. Accordingly, in an imperfect world, there was usually much to be said for resisting specific proposals for a tightening of monetary policy until the rest of a package was near completion.

In the summer of 1949, however, completion never happened. During the remainder of July the Governor continued to argue unavailingly for cuts in public expenditure, even suggesting that for the present these would by themselves suffice and would not need the support of a disagreeable monetary policy. The Chancellor replied that a deflationary policy was out of the question. Political attitudes to a higher Bank Rate remained very hostile and the Economic Secretary, in his Working Party on the banking situation, again went round the course in search of usable direct credit controls. He was eventually convinced that an additional and detailed selective control of bank lending would be impracticable and that the most that could be done was for the Governor to issue a further request to the banks for general restraint. He also suggested that bank deposits might be reduced if the banks could be persuaded to sell giltedged; but it was pointed out that this was scarcely a feasible tactic in an already weak market. In the meantime the Bank had become alert to the awkwardness of calling on the banks each week to take up six-month TDRs at fixed rates if money rates began to move up and might be expected to move further. It was, accordingly, thought better to reduce the quantity of TDRs and replace them with additional Treasury Bills for sale at the weekly Tender. This process of replacement was begun quietly in mid-July, after the Treasury had been informed and agreed.

With the reserves continuing to fall and no rescue in sight either from domestic measures or further North American help, the British authorities resigned themselves to the inevitable. On 19 September sterling was devalued by 30%, from $4.03 to $2.80. Apart from a consequential rise in the price of bread[29] (implying a refusal to increase food subsidies), there were at the time no accompanying fiscal or monetary measures. There was instead a powerful voluntary wage freeze, implying a fall in real personal incomes, which the TUC agreed to maintain unless the retail price index rose by more than 5%. The Bank, with the support of the Home Finance division of the Treasury, had at the very end reverted to earlier ideas and proposed that money rates should be eased up into a closer relationship with the 2% Bank Rate immediately following devaluation. A particular argument in favour of this could be seen in the further recent rise in gilt-edged yields. At one end of the market, $2\frac{1}{2}$% Consols now yielded nearly $3\frac{1}{2}$% and had fallen eight points since the early summer. At the other end, $1\frac{3}{4}$% Exchequer Bonds 1950, with only five months to run, yielded nearly $1\frac{1}{4}$%. The yield of $\frac{1}{2}$% on three-month Treasury Bills was therefore all the more anomalous; and the Chief Cashier was concerned lest a worried Discount Market should itself raise the Bill rate at the Tender, whatever the Bank had advised. However, the Governor expected and received political resistance to any change in money rates. At a meeting on 22 September the Chancellor flatly refused to accept the Bank's modest proposal. Mynors recorded him as saying that it was politically out of the question in face of difficulties with the TUC over wages and the cost of living. Economically, he (Cripps) could not feel convinced it would be effective. At any rate the proposal would have to go to Cabinet and he was not prepared to take it there at this stage. Later he remarked that it was impossible to increase the profits of the Discount Market in the present state of opinion about wages.[30] The Economic Secretary argued a case for more controls, but the Governor replied that without some increase in interest rates he could do nothing more with the banks by way of advice or request and hoped he would not be asked to do so.

Three weeks later, when the Treasury was preparing cuts in public expenditure programmes, the Governor was again asked (this time by the Chancellor) for suggestions about how to tighten credit without any accompanying rise in money rates. The Governor gave much the same answer as before but undertook to discuss the question with the representatives of the clearing banks. The banks again opposed the idea of an advances ceiling or of tougher selective restriction. But they agreed it might be useful if the authorities were to send them a letter 'in general

---

[29] Made more acceptable to the trade unions and the public by restoration of the white loaf, unavailable since early in the war.

[30] There was little reason to suppose such profits would have increased. Initially there would have been a fall.

terms' and if this letter were published. They also agreed to join the Governor at a further meeting with the Chancellor. This took place on 19 October. It was agreed firstly that the letter 'in general terms' should be drafted and secondly that the clearing banks should prepare a note, in consultation with the Bank, setting out the practical and technical objections to a more formalised limitation of advances. The agreed letter was sent to the Governor on 24 October. It requested 'that, in their general policy in regard to credit facilities, they [the banks] will use every endeavour to ensure that inflationary pressures are held in check'. The Chancellor informed Parliament about the letter on the day it was published, 26 October. At the Governor's suggestion, he further clarified matters by saying that no increase in money rates was in prospect.

The clearing banks duly submitted a memorandum entitled 'Growth of bank advances since the end of the war', which was passed to the Chancellor by the Governor on 7 November without significant alteration by the Bank. It constituted a definitive reply to advocates of advances ceilings and began by arguing that some rise in bank lending was an inevitable consequence of the switch-over from a wartime to a peacetime economy. Unless a healthy flow of new capital issues could be established[31] the rise in the sterling cost of many primary commodities following devaluation was likely to cause a further increase in advances. An attempt to stop this by the imposition of ceilings, whether in aggregate or on particular groups of borrower, 'would encounter great practical difficulties and would be inimical to the economic interests of the country'. Since there was no normal or regular relation between trade turnover and the amount of bank finance required to carry it, the application of a particular ceiling could have no rational basis and would be quite arbitrary. Trying to apply it to an overdraft system, with its agreed contractual limits normally exceeding the amount drawn by a large amount, would merely provoke heavy precautionary drawings along with the padding-out of requests for renewed facilities. Those borrowers who were actually deprived of the finance they needed would either be forced to such expedients as the realisation of gilt-edged or would resort to non-banking

---

[31] This was a familiar thread running through the unending arguments about bank advances. Capital issues by UK industry and commerce, negligible in 1945, had risen to £240 million in 1948, but fell back sharply to £115 million in 1949 before rising to £308 million in 1950. A large part of the fluctuation was attributable to the nationalised industries, who borrowed heavily from the banks ahead of a market issue. Private sector issues fell less sharply to £112 million in 1949, but would probably have increased if the stock market had been in better shape. Share prices (Actuaries Investment Index – December 1950 = 100), which had reached a peak of 121 in the Dalton period of credit expansion, fell 18% in the first half of 1949 and had made little recovery by the end of the year. The associated dividend yield, $3\frac{1}{2}$% in mid-1946, rose from $4\frac{1}{2}$% to $5\frac{1}{2}$% during 1949.

sources of credit that could not be regulated in accordance with official policy. Banker–customer relations would be seriously damaged and healthy competition between the banks would be inhibited. The ceilings would, moreover, have to be applied to acceptance facilities, with damage to the international use of the Bill on London. Accordingly, the authorities should continue to rely on the co-operation of the banks to apply selectivity in their own way and without rigid quantitative limits. 'The screening of advances', they wrote, 'in accordance with official policy has been carefully carried out hitherto, indications of Government policy have been kept constantly in mind and every effort has been made to withhold facilities for anything in the nature of speculation or for any type of transaction which would conflict with officially expressed statements of principle.' Their continuing co-operation would be readily forthcoming in terms of the latest communication from the Chancellor.

It was not easy to reject this well-reasoned and co-operative paper; if anything, it could be criticised for offering something not very different in practice from what it so cogently rejected. So near, in fact, that the Minutes of a meeting of clearing bank Chief Executive Officers held on 20 December included the following fateful item: 'Agreed that no Clearing Bank will take an account from another Clearing Bank involving loan or overdraft facilities because such accommodation has been refused by that other bank in compliance with the directive of the Chancellor of the Exchequer.' Bank advances had not yet begun to rise in response to devaluation, though they were shortly to do so. Over the three months ending mid-November advances to the private sector hardly grew at all. The Governor and Eady were therefore able to agree ten days after the despatch of the clearing banks' memorandum that 'if the economists etc. could be kept quiet we had much better say no more about any of this for quite a time'. But a week later the Deputy saw Bridges and recorded that the Chancellor was still being 'badgered by people on the subject of credits and advances'. The result of this badgering was a draft letter to the Governor, dated 23 November, which lurked uneasily in the Treasury until 19 December when Bridges showed it privately to its intended recipient. Without any mention whatever of the rate of interest, the draft stated, *inter alia*:

> If, however, the aggregate of advances is left to the discretion of the Clearing Banks, then the total volume of deposits, and thus of money, is also left to them. In my view it is the primary and indeed the essential function of a Central Bank to determine the total volume of money, and I do not see how I, or you, could accept any other view. For the Clearing Banks will judge the requirements of industry in the light of the price level, and thus tend to vary their advances upwards or downwards according to whether prices are

rising or falling. If they do this, the monetary system will interpose no checks against inflationary tendencies and the internal situation will be inherently unstable. I do not suggest, of course, that the Clearing Banks would in practice carry this to extremes, but I do think that as a matter of principle we should not have to rely on their discretion, and thus abdicate our own primary purpose.

The Governor told Bridges that he felt it would be better if the letter were left unsent. He repeated this early in the new year, remarking that it would be unfortunate to have on record a letter to which he would be bound to reply rather sharply. Bridges concurred and the letter was not sent. It would indeed have been ridiculous to instruct the central bank that its primary and essential function was to 'determine' the total volume of money, while categorically refusing to allow that same central bank to raise the short-term rate of interest above its near-zero level. As Mynors remarked in the course of a note to the Governor in mid-January 1950: 'The present trouble is in fact only the application in the monetary field of the principle familiar elsewhere, that you can control price or quantity but not both: that if prices are to be fixed, some system of rationing or allocation will be necessary. We are accused of an inadequate system of rationing or allocation.'

However, during the first half of 1950 there came something of a lull in the 'present trouble'. The external reserves were rising and the external balance seemed to be responding well to the new exchange rate. Exports and export orders were buoyant and the American recession seemed to be over. At home, the wage freeze was holding and inflationary pressures seemed to be sufficiently contained. True, bank advances began to rise rapidly, partly in response to the rise in the sterling price of many imported commodities, but they did not at this stage attract Governmental criticism. Furthermore in December 1949, following a very bad phase after devaluation, the Treasury and the Bank had mounted a successful conversion operation in the gilt-edged market. The famous $1\frac{3}{4}$% Exchequer Bonds, whose issue had caused so much difficulty in 1944-5 and again in 1946, matured in February 1950. The sum of £786 million was outstanding, of which over £500 million was already in official hands, having mostly been acquired over the preceding year or more – partly against official sales of other stocks, including the Issue Department's holding of Dalton's irredeemable. Of the £269 million of Exchequer Bonds remaining with the public, £235 million were converted into $2\frac{1}{4}$% stock, 1955, at par, leaving only £34 million for cash redemption. The Exchequer achieved a small surplus in 1949-50, to which were added receipts from extra-budgetary funds and from external items. The resulting repayment or repurchase of debt held by the public exceeded £300 million and consisted of market purchases of the maturing Exchequer Bonds net of official sales of other securities. Thus the successful conversion operation came in useful: it avoided any significant increase in floating debt.[32] An attempt to repeat this success, in June 1950, was not so rewarding. A cash-and-conversion offer of 2½% stock 1956–61 was made so as to begin dealing with the final maturity in 1951 of 2½% National War Bonds 1949–51, of which the Issue Department and the NDO already held a large amount. The results were disappointing and over £200 million of the maturing bonds were still in private hands when a further offer, this time of 3% stock 1966–8, was made in the autumn.

At the General Election held on 23 February 1950 the Labour Party's large overall majority in the Commons was cut to single figures and the chances of the new Parliament serving anything like its full term were clearly small. Political uncertainties and sensitivities were therefore increased rather than reduced. At the Treasury there was a further uncertainty. The Chancellor, on whose high standing and reputation so much depended, was not well. After a stay in a Swiss clinic during the previous summer he had made an apparent recovery, but it was not to prove long-lasting. In his absence Hugh Gaitskell, Minister of Fuel and Power, had acted as his deputy and after the February Election he was moved into the Treasury as Minister of State. Two months later he became in effect Minister in charge of overseas finance and 'Chancellor-in-Waiting'. A professional economist as well as a distinguished politician, he was to continue the tussle with the Bank over interest rates and credit controls that had been initiated two years previously by Douglas Jay. The latter now became Financial Secretary, with the onerous Parliamentary duties attaching to that post, and had less time to spare for surveillance of the domestic monetary situation.

The lull in the Bank's 'present trouble' did not last through the summer. South Korea was invaded by the North on 24 June 1950. American intervention in support of the South followed within days and with United Nations authority. Following as they did the earlier succession of cold war episodes in Western Europe and China, the hostilities in Korea provoked

[32] Beginning in 1948–9 the Bank became closely involved in the issue of Government-guaranteed stocks for the nationalised industries. This involvement continued until the mid-1950s when such issues were terminated in the interests of improved debt management. But they were not of great monetary significance during the Cripps period. New issues of guaranteed stocks came to £137 million in 1948–9 and £82 million in 1949–50. Their sale to the public, either on issue or subsequently out of the Issue Department (which effectively underwrote them) had monetary effects similar to the sale of ordinary gilts, but was normally associated with a funding of bank advances to the public corporations concerned rather than a repayment of Government floating debt.

the United States into a programme of rearmament that soon implied a doubling of American defence expenditure. A world-wide boom in commodity prices quickly set in. The UK, partly under pressure from Washington, decided to increase its own defence expenditure by 50%, or some £400 million per annum over the ensuing three years. These developments, to which would later be added a further increase in the defence programme to a level double that planned before the outbreak in Korea, abruptly undermined the post-devaluation balance of the economy. Furthermore the wage freeze had come to an end on 30 June.[33]

Instead of looking forward to steadily rising output, with external balance and without undue inflationary pressure, the electorally precarious Government had now to contemplate a resumption of shortages and bottle-necks, renewed price and wage inflation, the imposition of greater fiscal austerity, and the threat of renewed external weakness. It is therefore not surprising that Eady warned Mynors on 25 July that there was likely to be a resumption of discussions on credit control, with Ministers continuing to lack confidence in the informal control operated by the Bank but perhaps this time prepared to contemplate some small adjustment of short-term interest rates. The rise in advances that had attracted little criticism during the winter and spring now had to be regarded in a quite different context; and credit control had now to be viewed as a positive instrument for helping secure a large transfer of resources into defence production. But rather than simply tread over all the old ground about advances ceilings, the Treasury now tried another tack. Writing to Mynors on 16 August, Burke Trend[34] sought the Bank's views on what might be achieved 'by purely technical measures of the kind which various continental countries have undertaken since the end of the war with different degrees of success'. He also asked what more could be done 'in the more general non-technical field' to control advances on a more selective basis to help transfer resources to defence production.

By the expression 'purely technical measures', Trend was referring in general to ratio controls, whether incremental or not, whose intended effect was to restrict a bank's ability to expand a particular class of assets,

---

[33] The index of wages rose less than 1% over the year ending June 1950; the retail price index rose by $3\frac{1}{2}$% and import prices by 17%.

[34] Trend, Burke St John, Baron (Life Peer) 1974 (1914–87). Educated Whitgift and Merton College, Oxford. Ministry of Education 1936–7, HM Treasury 1937–55, Principal Private Secretary to Chancellor of the Exchequer 1945–9, Under-Secretary 1949–55, Office of the Lord Privy Seal 1955–6, Deputy Secretary of the Cabinet 1956–9, Third Secretary, HM Treasury 1959–60, Second Secretary 1960–2, Secretary of the Cabinet 1963–73. Rector, Lincoln College, Oxford 1973–83.

namely lending through advances. Gaitskell himself was interested in such controls and earlier in the year the Economic Section had written a paper about them. They were later to have a long though far from respectable history in the UK. With a tightly-knit banking system operating a cartelised regulation of rates both on advances and on interest-bearing deposits, ratio controls had, at first sight, some considerable attractions in the Treasury as a means of achieving restriction without either an increase in interest rates or any tiresome and possibly ineffectual voluntary understandings between the Bank and the banks themselves. On closer examination these attractions tended to diminish, so that in practical operation a ratio control was either ineffective or else looked little more than plaster decoration on what was in reality an advances ceiling. But it is not evident that this particular point was fully taken in the Bank in 1950. For instead of answering the Treasury's question, the Old Lady confined herself to providing information and comment on the technical measures used in other countries, while not failing to point out that the measures had usually included increases in money rates. No plan for the use of ratio controls in the UK was even sketched in the Bank at this time.

Such a negative response could not have been made without instruction from the Governor who, it became clear, regarded the idea of ratio controls as a red herring designed to detract attention from what he saw as the main issue for monetary policy in the new and darkening context of 1950–1, namely the short-term interest rate. He may well also have seen their advocacy at this time as an attempt to undermine the independent authority of the Bank over the commercial banks. 'Requests' by the Bank, voluntarily accepted after informal discussion with the banks and prior negotiation with the Treasury, were in accord with that authority. Altering a mandatory ratio, at arm's length, would look and probably become much more like simple obedience to a Treasury demand. Cobbold was very concerned to preserve both the authority of the Bank and such independence as the 1946 Act allowed. Having begun by skilfully adapting the established method of proceeding by discussion and request, he was not the man to look kindly on an early change to ratio controls. In his record of a conversation with Trend on 15 September, the Governor wrote:

> We had a word about credit control etc. I said that I was not anxious for memoranda to go out from here setting out exactly the whys and wherefores of possible action in relation to action taken overseas. I thought this would be likely to start a number of hares and I had very definite ideas about what was and what was not practicable. I was of course delighted that he should discuss the question with Mr Mynors and Sir K.O.P.

Two weeks later Mynors reported a private talk with Trend at which the latter said he was committed to writing a paper both on ratio controls and on interest rates. After making clear he was in no way committing the Governor, Mynors explained that 'higher compulsory reserve ratios would in the end be effected by our increasing bankers cash'. Trend undertook to send him a draft of his paper, but (if sent) it does not survive in Bank files. The Treasury, through Eady, then made two more efforts later in the autumn to coax a paper on the subject out of the Bank, but to no avail. The Chief Cashier did however commission a draft paper, in case of need, which was to go slightly further than anything written hitherto. The author was Maurice Allen, who had arrived at the Bank as an Economic Adviser earlier in the year.[35] After a full analysis of ratio controls and suchlike in other countries he concluded, without need for further argument, that: 'The substance of the various regulations used abroad to keep the amount of commercial bank credit below what resources and liquidity permit does not seem likely to be more restrictive or more selective than may be realised by current arrangements in the UK.' The paper was sent to Beale as a draft and went no further. As to a tightening of selective credit control, Mynors sent a note to Eady late in August explaining yet again that money

[35] Maurice Allen, formerly a Fellow in Economics at Balliol College, Oxford, had come to the Bank from the IMF, where he had been Assistant Director of Research under E. M. Bernstein. Since 1948, and before the appointment of Mynors to the Court in March 1949, the Bank had been looking for an additional professional economist to act as adviser in similar mould. Earlier, in the summer of 1948, the Governor had tried very hard to entice Dennis Robertson into the Bank as an additional Adviser to the Governors. But after several months' hesitation Robertson declined, preferring to spend the rest of his working life in Trinity, Cambridge. In his reply to this refusal Cobbold sought Robertson's advice about what he should do next. 'My own feeling', he wrote, 'and I think Mynors shares it, is that there is nobody else at, if I may use the phrase, "the top of the profession" who would quite fit in here. My own mind turns therefore towards looking for a first-class younger man to fit under Humphrey Mynors and somewhere alongside Thompson-McCausland. The latter has, as you know, all the drive and a lot of knowledge but he is short on the academic and analytical side of which we stand in great need...I think it really important from the national point of view that we should have the best men available here...Would you have a think about this and let me know whether I can write to Clay and Henderson and ask them to get in touch with each other and you to see what you can jointly suggest.' Advice was duly sought from these two and their first choice was Richard Sayers, who declined. The post was then offered to Allen, who accepted in November 1949 and took up his duties in March 1950. He was to serve the Bank for twenty years, first as Adviser and later as Executive Director. The author first met him in Paul Streeten's rooms in Balliol in the spring of 1949, whence he had been invited to tell me about the career possibilities in the IMF for economics graduates. I remember the experience vividly. Maurice did not really enter the room. His short and slender frame suddenly and quietly materialised in it. He then sat down on a sofa and gave me, with absolute clarity and impartiality, the briefing that I wanted. Shortly afterwards, as suddenly and quietly as he had arrived, he vanished through the door leaving only a memory of smartly patterned socks. I was to meet him again later in the 1950s, when he became a Visiting Fellow of Nuffield College and not long before I followed him into the Bank.

lent by bank advances was not like a commodity whose physical rationing would have a roughly uniform effect on each user. Its impact depended on the financial situation of the borrower, which had no necessary correlation with the 'priority' accorded the borrower's activities by the Government. Some worthwhile selective restraint was being achieved under present arrangements. Letters of guidance to the Capital Issues Committee could always be altered and the banks informed of the change. But it would not be sensible to press selectivity further than that. Eady tended to agree with this advice, as indeed he had done in 1949. Opposition to it came from Ministers and from the Treasury economists.

While keeping ratio controls and suchlike at bay, the Governor was preparing a further assault on the Treasury's position on interest rates. Earlier in the year, at Peppiatt's suggestion, he had asked Niemeyer, Mynors, and the Chief Cashier to see whether there was any workable means of getting round the Treasury road-block by somehow reducing the budgetary cost of a rise in short-term rates. The only way to do this would have been to agree with the banks, and possibly also some of the large holders of sterling on No. 2 Accounts, that a proportion of their holdings of floating debt should be segregated and should continue to bear interest at only $\frac{1}{2}$% when rates generally were raised. It was more than doubtful if overseas holders would agree, and it would not be possible to segregate from the money market the large volume of Treasury Bills that the banks needed for liquidity purposes and traded from day to day. It might be possible to agree that the remaining £500–600 million of TDRs be frozen at the prevailing rate of $\frac{5}{8}$%. But the saving would not be very great and would have to be set against the adverse effect on 'opinion' of what might appear to be a forced loan at an artificially low rate. In a classic statement of the truth, Niemeyer summarised the whole issue and put it into broad context as follows:

> The Treasury always lay too much stress on the purely Budgetary aspects of this question. (No doubt short financing generates short views!) The importance (and effects) of the problem are far wider. Its neglect may easily produce economic results far more costly to the nation than any Budget cost of a remedy. People abroad mistrust Sterling. They know that we continue to inflate, and are well aware where this will lead us, particularly when Marshall Aid ceases. We cannot counter this want of confidence by arguments about Budget cost – indeed that line only intensifies doubts about our resolution to secure sound finance; and these doubts are very expensive to us.
>
> I see nothing to be gained by clever tricks to avoid the natural course. They will not carry conviction either at home or abroad. I believe they would even do us more harm than having to wait until we can carry the right policy.

The Governor accepted this firm practical advice. By the autumn of 1950, when he again asked his officials for views about interest rates – this time in the changed and much more inflationary context of the commodity boom and the rearmament programme – ideas for shielding HMG from the cost of a rise in rates had been set aside.

On 30 October 1950 a report was submitted by Niemeyer, Peppiatt, Mynors, and the Chief Cashier. General inflationary pressures and risks were now seen to be much greater than a year before and there seemed no early prospect of their being significantly reduced by policy outside the monetary field. Nor did an edging-up of rates within the existing 2% Bank Rate any longer seem an appropriate response. So the group once more turned to a rise in Bank Rate, this time to $2\frac{1}{2}$% as a 'signal', together with some modest associated rise in market rates and in the cost of bank advances. They judged that this break with the past would have a useful psychological effect, notably on the 'urge to hold commodities' and 'some of the more doubtful projects for which bankers are pressed to provide advances'. They added that present circumstances differed fundamentally from those of the 1920s and that there was no risk of unemployment resulting from the moderate monetary steps proposed. Niemeyer, now aged sixty-eight, was again their most forceful exponent. In the course of a note sent to the Chief Cashier as early as 17 September he wrote:

> It is also a fact that we have the lowest Bank Rate in Europe except Switzerland: and that Belgium, Holland, Sweden, USA, and Canada have recently put up their rates, while Western Germany has raised the minimum reserves.
>
> Why do all these countries take this action? Clearly not for fun: but because they see no other way to exercise some control over costs and prices.
>
> Is the UK position really different? Direct physical controls are breaking down: and in any case never applied to (a) wages (b) the more important raw materials, e.g., metals, wool, cotton, oil, etc., which are governed by world prices. International discussions on these prices seem in practice more concerned in fixing minimum prices for producers than in achieving lower prices for consumers.
>
> We are, therefore, progressively getting into a position where if we do not use the money control – incidentally simple and inexpensive in administration and flexible – we shall drift, with little or no effective control at all into a position of steadily rising money prices and steadily decreasing real earnings, both for exports and in internal life.
>
> The argument about increased Floating Debt charge – never very impressive unless all thought of funding is to be abandoned – does not really weigh against this prospect. Wage increases alone cost the economy far more.
>
> Whether the unemployment argument against deflation derived from the 20s is valid or not for that period, it is not applicable to present conditions.

With full employment we have a shortage of manpower, now to be enhanced by (a) the increased numbers required for the Forces, and (b) the extra hands required for increasing armament production. There is no likelihood for a number of years ahead of an over-supply of labour – unless this arises from inability to pay for imported raw material, which is the ultimate real danger.

Otherwise the problem for the next few years is not to find employment, but to divert it to the more productive trades and away from the less productive and the parasitical.

If we do not do this, particularly as Marshall Aid declines and payment of debt to USA (£55 million p.a.) starts, we shall lose trade to more effective European competition, including Germany.

Niemeyer showed this note to Jacobsson, who read it on a train between Basle and Frankfurt, and received a sympathetic response. Jacobsson was pursuing a personal crusade for progress towards restoration of the external convertibility of the main currencies and the resumption of free multilateral trade. To this end he regarded the restoration of domestic monetary flexibility as useful, if not essential, and felt it would be 'doubly dangerous' for London to be left behind in such a movement. For his part, the Governor found a firm supporter in Baumgartner, Governor of the Bank of France, a close friend and colleague over many years.[36]

The upshot of it all was a letter from Cobbold to Bridges on 3 November enclosing a shortened version of the Niemeyer group's Report. In the spirit of the 1946 Act, the letter ended formally as follows: 'I would be grateful if you would let me know in due course whether it would meet with the approval of HMG if the Court were to make an alteration in Bank Rate as proposed and if we were to take the other measures proposed in the short-term market.' These latter were to include edging up the Bill rate to $\frac{7}{8}$–1%.

Shortly before the above letter was sent, and consistently with its purposes, the Government had announced a new issue in the gilt-edged market, this time a 3% stock maturing in 1966–8. £250 million was

---

[36] A friendship that became particularly important during the 1950s, as will become apparent in later chapters. In some undated personal notes, a copy of which he gave to the author and which are quoted here with the family's permission, Lord Cobbold recalled: 'Our "convergence" as a family with the Baumgartner family has been a very happy and an unusual item in our lives. We were both married early in 1930, Susan was born within a few months of their elder daughter, the same with David and their son, and again with Rowland and their younger daughter. I first met them at a Bank of France reception in 1934 and I came in touch with him a good deal over the later 1930s. After the war he was made Governor of the Bank of France three months before I became Governor. We worked very closely together for 11 years until, after having earlier persuaded de Gaulle to leave him at the Bank, he was dragooned into becoming Minister of Finance a year or so before my retirement. Hermione and Christiane have always liked each other and we have often stayed with them, and they with us.'

offered for cash and the stock was also offered in conversion of the remaining balance of 2½% stock 1949–51. Together with the earlier issue of 2½% stock 1956–61, the cash offer marked the end of the wartime and early post-war tap system, the restoration of former arrangements for Issue Department underwriting of a public offer of a stated amount, and the Department's subsequent discretionary sale in the market of stock not taken up on issue. In the autumn of 1950 the Treasury did not need to go to the market on account of domestic budgetary requirements, but it did need cash to help finance the heavy sterling expenditure of the EEA without recourse to the banking system. Before the adverse impact of rearmament and of yet higher import prices on the UK balance of payments, and while the Sterling Area countries were earning the surplus of dollars they were later to spend, the UK reserves were rising very rapidly. A stock issue that would help offset their domestic monetary effect was therefore a sensible orthodoxy. It was also advantageously low-key in political terms, which would certainly not have been the case with an increase in Bank Rate, even one of only ½%. But the result of the issue was not very good. The public subscribed £48 million in cash and only £7 million in conversion. The Departments took up the rest of the cash issue and a further £81 million by conversion.

The Chancellor's health had not responded to a further stay in Switzerland and in mid-October he had been obliged to resign. Gaitskell, who succeeded him, had to face the daunting problems of rearmament and renewed inflationary pressures without the authority of Cripps and in face of the fragile Parliamentary balance. Though a skilled economist, or perhaps because of it, he distrusted any reliance on the 'psychological' effects of monetary manoeuvres and was either suspicious or mildly contemptuous of those who advocated them.[37] In that frame of mind he was unlikely to face the certainty of political protest on the Left at a small rise in Bank Rate in exchange for the uncertainty of its psychological impact. Though he survived to know it was gathering force, he did not stay in office long enough to have to combat the full fury of the post-Korean external storm and its threat of a third post-war alteration in the status or exchange value of sterling. Had he done so, it is possible that his attitude to the effects of a higher Bank Rate, and especially the effects on overseas opinion, might have been forcibly altered. As it was, the combination of a political tightrope, of personal conviction, and of the absence of immediate external compulsion facilitated the retention of that attitude during the whole of his brief Chancellorship.

[37] See Philip Williams, *Hugh Gaitskell: A Political Biography* (London, Jonathan Cape, 1979), p. 241.

After some clarification by correspondence between Eady and Peppiatt, the Governor's letter and memorandum of 3 November were discussed at a meeting with Bridges and other senior officials, including Plowden, on 1 December 1950. At the end, the Permanent Secretary said the official Treasury was prepared to support the Bank's proposal and on 7 December the Governor sent him a short note for the Chancellor to accompany the official Minute. Early in January 1951 Gaitskell discussed the whole question informally with the Governor and stressed the great difficulty of negotiating expenditure cuts with his colleagues if he were to put up short-term interest rates and as a result pay out more money to the banks. Against this perceived drawback he saw no conclusive advantage in a course of action whose effects were admitted to be mainly psychological. Nor was he particularly keen to tighten up on the cost or availability of bank advances, since it might be unwise to discourage the holding of stocks in the prevailing near-war conditions. The Governor stuck to his point of view. In the course of his replies, and stepping slightly outside the spirit of the 1946 Act, he stressed that the Bank would be taking great responsibilities in not raising Bank Rate at a time when it felt a dangerous situation was threatening. He held his position at a meeting with Ministers and officials on 5 January, again with support from the officials concerned, now including Hall. But Ministers remained very reluctant. The Chancellor asked whether the Bank Rate weapon was not outworn and suggested that new techniques needed to be introduced. Finally, on 17 January, he wrote to the Governor, in reply to the Bank Rate proposal, rejecting the advice of his own officials as well as that of the Bank. He rehearsed the points already made at the meetings and went on:

> I must make it plain that I am not opposed to using the monetary instrument where it can be appropriately employed without entailing an extra burden on the Exchequer. I hope, therefore, that the Bank and the Treasury will continue to co-operate on this basis and I should like there now to be consultation about the possibilities of action of this kind – in particular, I think we should seek the co-operation of the banks in restricting the increase in advances and I should not be averse to some increase in the rate of interest charged on them if it is felt that this would be helpful. Then too we have agreed that long term rates should be allowed to harden somewhat.

His letter concluded: 'I am however opposed to a change in Bank Rate and the Treasury Bill rate, because this would impose a heavy burden[38] on the budget without any guarantee of results which would justify it.' The

---

[38] The Bank had estimated this to be £25 million per annum less an offsetting increase in tax revenue from banks and similar holders of floating debt.

Governor acknowledged this tactical defeat on 19 January. He went on to suggest that guidance to the CIC and the banks might be usefully reviewed and that thought should be given to an increase in advances rates.

Deposits at the London clearing banks grew by about 5% in 1950–1 and advances and commercial bills by 11%. Lending to the central government rose modestly, hardly any of it through floating debt. Compared with 1949–50 the growth of advances had in fact slowed down, though there were signs of reacceleration early in 1951 as the impact of the commodity boom was felt. The main change between the two years was that substantial net repayment of Government debt to the banking system had come to an end and had been succeeded by moderate net borrowing. This was in turn due not to any significant change in the budgetary situation but to the massive change in receipts from external items. These were slightly positive in 1949–50 but were heavily negative (£613 million) in 1950–1 due to the steep but temporary increase in the external reserves. Over the fiscal year 1950–51, though still in surplus on budgetary account, the Government therefore needed to raise some £350 million after allowing for its heavy expenditure on the external reserves. Some £180 million of this had to be raised on Treasury Bills and TDRs. However, virtually all came from overseas lenders and virtually none from the banks. In the Budget presented on 10 April 1951 the striking increase in defence outlays was only partly offset by increases in personal and corporate taxation. At the same time a marked but supposedly manageable deterioration was foreseen in the external balance, from hardly-won surplus to moderate deficit. This Budget arithmetic was to prove much too optimistic both about the external balance and about the course of domestic demand, particularly of consumer demand. But even so it was clear at the time that the pressure of aggregate demand would remain high, that the pressure on the engineering industries would be very high indeed, and that with the sharp further rise in import prices feeding through into retail prices the problem of securing adequate wage restraint was going to be difficult. Nor was this likely to be made easier by the Ministerial resignations that followed the announcement in the Budget that prescription and certain other charges were to be introduced in the National Health Service. It is therefore not surprising that attention was soon being paid once again to a possible tightening of monetary policy, over and above a fresh request made to the banks at the time of the Budget and associated with revised guidance to the CIC. By the middle of May the press and the City were seriously debating whether the combination of fiscal policy, direct controls, and wage restraint might require support from a more active monetary policy, including a rise in short-term interest rates.

By the end of May the Governor was once more returning to the charge on this issue.

In a preliminary note on 29 May, prepared in consultation with Niemeyer, Peppiatt, Beale, and Allen, Mynors drew clear attention to the powerful if varied nature of the opposition to 'dearer money'. Misguidedly in present circumstances, higher interest rates were associated with unemployment. They would also be thought a confession of failure of the planned economy. 'In the present regime', he wrote, 'both Ministers and officials see the economy as "manageable" by central decisions which are in substitution for "the blind forces of a money economy" etc.' According to this school of thought any needed change in monetary conditions should be brought about by direct controls. Finally, the theoretical structures used by the present regime could not admit of large 'psychological' effects. Thus the results of a $\frac{1}{2}$% rise in money rates would be judged very small and not worth the budgetary and political cost. Nonetheless it would be worth approaching the Treasury yet again. The prevailing short-term rates were encouraging a rise in foreign borrowing in London. Long-term rates were again edging up, towards 4%, and private borrowing from the banks rather than the capital market was thereby being encouraged. Furthermore, the Budget arithmetic had already been upset by the threat to oil supplies posed by the nationalisation of the British oil assets in Iran. All this now pointed to edging up money rates within the 2% Bank Rate rather than raising the Rate itself. The Governor wrote to the Chancellor two days later emphasising the fragility of the rate structure. Since press discussion, City debate, and market rumour were undermining this structure, there was again a risk that the Treasury Bill rate would rise of its own accord. It would therefore be better to retain the initiative and encourage a modest rise in money rates in co-operation with the Discount Market. He had in mind a Treasury Bill rate still under 1%. The case was also presented, with an eye to the Chancellor's own thinking, as experimenting with an alternative technique to the use of Bank Rate itself.

This initiative fared little better than its predecessors. At a meeting with the Governor early in June the Chancellor was prepared to contemplate some rise in private borrowing rates, but he was not willing to move on the Treasury Bill rate and favoured some special arrangement that would isolate the latter from other short-term rates. Gaitskell had in fact set out his own views very clearly in a note dated 2 June and entitled 'Credit Policy'. This was at first circulated only in the Treasury, but later in June Eady was authorised to send it to the Governor. This was done on 19 June. Cobbold handed an informal reply to Eady two days later.

The Chancellor's Minute began by noting firstly that the long-term rate had been allowed to rise and secondly that it was generally agreed between the Bank and the Treasury that there ought to be some tightening up of credit. It was however extremely important that 'we should understand clearly what we mean by a stricter credit policy and what purpose we wish it to serve'. In the Chancellor's view, it was through changes in the banks' assets that credit policy affected the economy. A reduction in advances was then identified as the desired aim. How was this to be achieved? The Bank was proposing withdrawal of the $\frac{1}{2}\%$ regime in the money market and the creation of uncertainty regarding the price at which cash would in future be supplied to the banks. To this the Chancellor replied uncompromisingly as follows:

> The objections to this are that it is by no means clear why this very slight change in the present procedure would necessarily lead to a reduction in advances. That it would cause a general firming-up of short-term rates is no doubt the case. But this is not the ultimate object and in itself is not likely to be very important. The other objection is, of course, that it would increase the burden on the Exchequer – even a rise of $\frac{1}{4}\%$ involving £16 million a year more in interest charges.
>
> There is another simpler and more effective way in which the Bank of England could secure control of the credit structure. If the whole business of lending on short-term to the Government were put on one side and the banks and the discount houses were told that things would go on just as before, that they had to continue to take the same amount of Treasury bills as before at $\frac{1}{2}\%$, there really is no reason why credit restriction should not operate on the remainder of the banks' assets. Thus, supposing the Bank of England sold bills, which the discount market and all the clearing banks were obliged to take up, the balances of the latter at the Bank of England would be reduced – always remembering that they would not be allowed to re-discount bills – and the clearing banks would then be obliged to restrict credit in other directions. It is true that they might decide to sell long-term investments. But, as a group, they would probably be far from anxious to create a further fall in gilt-edged.
>
> The same result could no doubt be achieved if the Banks were simply told that they had to provide in TDRs whatever funds the Government required. Once they had been told this, then in all probability, they would continue to make sure that the discount market had enough money at call to buy Treasury bills. Again, if, in these circumstances, credit were contracted, the Banks would be forced to restrict credit in other directions.
>
> Finally, it might, of course, be simpler merely to give them direct instructions about the level of advances, with perhaps some guidance as to the particular borrowers who should be cut – and adjust their cash reserves accordingly.

As to which of these various methods is most appropriate, this is partly a matter for the banks themselves and partly a purely technical issue. The two essential points are

(a) that advances should be reduced – and not any other of the banks' assets;
(b) that there should be no increase in the rate at which the Government borrows short-term.

These proposals amounted either to a form of ratio control or to an outright advances ceiling. In his reply Cobbold accepted that the aim of policy was to influence bank advances but went on:

> The main thought in our mind is that having gone a long distance, with considerable success, in keeping down advances by co-operation with the banking system, what is needed is something which will also influence the attitude of the potential borrower. It is true that no action will bite heavily and violently, short of a rise of a point or two in interest rates generally which would appear impolitic on general grounds at the moment. The effect of a smaller firming up of interest rates on the general mentality of the commercial community cannot be assessed by any rule of thumb and must be a matter of judgment. It is certainly possible that we are wrong but the consensus of opinion at the Bank is definitely that a small firming up on the lines proposed would have a material effect and would well justify the increased charge on the Exchequer.

As to direct regulation of the banks' holdings of short-term Government debt, the Governor argued that the introduction of such forced lending would do serious damage to British Government credit. It seemed vital, in the current and foreseen circumstances, to do nothing that would adversely affect the acceptability of Government debt. Any suggestion that short-term Government securities were frozen and illiquid, or were being forced on unwilling holders, would have an immediate and violent adverse effect.[39]

The disagreement between the two men remained unresolved at a further discussion held on 3 July and recorded by the Governor on the same day. The Chancellor had reaffirmed his position and added for good measure that he found the Bank's proposals impossible politically. Putting them into effect would make his position with the trade unions untenable. The Governor continued:

---

[39] Some years later, when the Bank finally agreed to a form of ratio control, great care was taken to avoid any appearance of a forced loan to HMG. The Special Deposits Scheme interposed the Bank between the banks and Government debt and was described as a 'monetary instrument'.

I replied that on the political side he must be the judge and I was not disposed to argue. On merits, it was a question of judgement. I had a definite view which was in disagreement with his. His arguments might be right politically and I was not competent to argue the case on economic doctrine but I was pretty certain that from a financial and practical angle I was right. We agreed therefore to differ and to let the matter stand as it is until the autumn.

Neither side in this exchange paid much attention to the one factor that might have made a decisive difference to the argument, namely the approaching external crisis. It seems in fact that neither side was fully alert to the severity of the storm that was to break only two months later. In the Treasury, where a paper circulated early in September was dramatically to declare the onset of the worst external crisis yet experienced, the Budget-time forecasts still ruled. In the Bank, although the external outlook was judged to be threatening, Treasury forecasts were not effectively challenged or criticised, though viewed *per se* with some scepticism. An *ad hoc* critique by Mynors or Allen – and especially one by the latter, who was well-versed in such skills – would no doubt have been prepared if requested. But it was not requested, and as yet there was seemingly no disposition to do so. This was a pity. A cross-check on Treasury forecasts, undertaken by a respected critic, was badly needed. An established economic section in the Bank would have provided one as a matter of course; but the Bank still preferred, not altogether without reason, to rely much more on its own speciality, market intelligence, than on any 'academic' forecast. However in the summer of 1951, when a precipitate change of external fortune was about to occur, market intelligence was no better than Treasury arithmetic. Not until mid-September did Bolton, never one to pass up a chance to prophesy disaster, announce from the crow's nest that the iceberg was directly ahead.

There is little more to be told. Following his exchange with Gaitskell earlier in June the Governor had encouraged the banks and the Discount Market to edge up advances and commercial bill rates while leaving the Treasury Bill rate undisturbed. Over the summer advances rates rose $\frac{1}{2}\%$, to an average of $3\frac{1}{2}-4\%$. On 5 July Cobbold again met the clearing banks. He told them that the inflationary dangers were now very great and that the balance of payments again looked threatening. The Government was opposed to a general increase in money rates and the authorities faced a choice between continued voluntary restraint or more direct action on bank lending. The latter had been set aside for the present, but only if the former could be intensified. The Bank had fought for maintenance of the voluntary system, but this meant it had to be fully confident of its effectiveness, in spite of difficulties of competition between banks and of relations with customers. The bankers replied that the main inflationary influence lay outside their control, but they assured Cobbold of their co-operation and promised 'to have another go' at restriction. The Chancellor was so informed; and later in the month he explained his position both on the Treasury Bill rate and on bank advances to the House of Commons. Finally, at the end of August, the Governor again discussed the whole question with the Chancellor. Despite the ominous change now evident in the external situation, he found Gaitskell generally unmoved. Advances continued to rise rapidly and the Chancellor felt that the request to the banks might be put even more strongly. Some further increase in advances rates might also be appropriate; but there must still be no increase in the Treasury Bill rate. That marked the end of the story. On 19 September a General Election was called for 25 October. Early in October the Bank began preparing advice on monetary policy against the contingency of a change in Government. On 26 October that contingency became fact and a new phase had begun.

Thus ended three years of almost continuous argument between the Government and the central bank about domestic monetary policy. The argument had primarily been about short-term interest rates; but this issue had got enmeshed with an argument about direct credit controls, which concerned the status and authority of the Bank as well as the instrumental efficiency of such controls themselves. It ended, too, more than six years of underlying disagreement about the appropriate place of monetary policy in the post-war world, a disagreement dating from the suppression of the 'lost alternative' in 1945 and the subsequent rejection of the Bank's strategic advice about the long-term rate. It had been muted at first during the high tide of post-war Socialist optimism and while the Bank was finding its feet after the constitutional change incorporated in the Act of 1946. But disagreement got stronger and more open later on, especially after the accession of Cobbold to the Governorship, the onset of the second external crisis, and, still later, the onset of renewed pressures following the outbreak of war in Korea. The six years also contained the initial British experience with Keynesian macro-economic policies and within that framework the discretionary management of money. That management had been mostly exercised from Whitehall, and by politicians and economists rather than administrators. But it had mostly been executed by the 'practical men' in the Bank who had strong ideas of their own about the proper exercise of discretionary policy, were sensitive to the external dangers of mistaken policy, and had access to economic advice that was sceptical of the prevailing new orthodoxy.

The result of this argument and disagreement was a kind of stalemate, or frustrating compromise, some of whose debilitating features were to persist over the years that were to follow. The Government had failed to get its way with the long-term rate and had clearly been unwise to make the attempt it did in the way it had. Later, the Government failed to get its way with the Bank over advances ceilings or ratio controls, even though the former might have proved more effective, for better or worse, than the less formal voluntary arrangements constructed by the Bank with the banks. But though preserving in that way its customary status and authority in the banking system, the Bank in turn largely failed to extract from the reluctant Government any agreement to institute a flexible money-rate policy, which remained tainted by association with the mass unemployment of the inter-war period. Furthermore, the exercise of credit control through voluntary co-operation and unquantified requests suffered many of the same long-term disadvantages – by suppression of competition and the diversion of business to uncontrolled channels – as formal ceilings or ratio controls. There is no doubt that constructive compromise can be virtuous: it is often thought to be a British talent. But compromise can also bring the worst of both worlds, or the vices of being neither one thing nor the other; and the compromise on monetary policy, so it appears, constituted a stalemate rather than a constructive process.

The evolution of this particular institutional stalemate had at times been featured by clear thinking on both sides. But it also encouraged an element of wishful thinking. Over the last three years of the Attlee Government the Bank was obliged to undertake a role of manoeuvre and argument, but within a very confined space. There were City limits to the severity of credit controls on the one hand and there was the Government's emotional hang-up about short-term interest rates on the other. It was therefore easy enough and tactically useful for the Bank to go along with the view that a decisive revival of interest-rate policy, for example a 4% Bank Rate, was simply not to be considered by sensible people. It would be much too harsh on the economy, much too expensive for the Exchequer, and a drain on the balance of payments. In consequence such a policy was never subjected to thorough consideration or analysis, although in 1949 and again in 1951 it might well have been the correct one to pursue. Instead the Bank had to argue for an easing of the $\frac{1}{2}$% strait-jacket, sometimes by advocating a small rise in Bank Rate and sometimes by proposing that the 2% Bank Rate be made effective; and in both cases the consequential rise in the Treasury Bill rate was usually to be limited to around $\frac{1}{2}$%. In pursuing this line of approach, and perhaps to combat the strong political resistance thereto, the Bank persuaded itself that just a little rise in rates would have a big 'psychological' effect. This was never very convincing. The immediate market impact of so striking a change in policy might indeed have been considerable, but a durable psychological effect on the economy at large was much less plausible. By the same token, the Government's opposition to higher interest rates, itself lacking much analytical foundation as applied to post-war circumstances, induced Treasury Ministers to persuade themselves that quite small, directly controlled alterations in the pace of bank lending would prove to be of valuable macro-economic importance. Neither practical argument to the contrary nor monetary analysis could make much headway against this belief in the partial control of money.

The evolution of the stalemate, with its resulting weakness in central policy, owed a lot to the division of responsibilities entrenched within the settlement of 1946. Indeed the reality of that weakness and division was clearly demonstrated by what happened over 1948–51, and in particular by the way in which Cobbold presented his case on interest rates to the Chancellor and was overridden; by the way in which he successfully resisted the Treasury's approach on ratio controls; and by the way he developed, at first in partnership with Catto, the Bank's authority over the banks in the field of credit control. The Governor was exercising the customary and statutory responsibilities of the Bank to the fullest extent possible, while having to concede to the Treasury its authority over the shape of monetary policy in general and over the short-term rate of interest in vital particular. He had to do this while realising that in its own constituency, or even beyond it, the Bank could not wholly escape attribution of a share in the responsibility for clinging to the short-term rate of $\frac{1}{2}\%$ in apparent defiance of the laws of gravity. Over the years to come, the stalemate was to be eased and the compromise to be made more constructive, sometimes more so, sometimes less. But its framework was to remain intact and the attitudes engendered by it were to persist unaltered.

SOURCES

Bank files

ADM14/14   L. P. Thompson-McCausland's Papers: Post-war – Domestic Money, etc. (April 1942–February 1953)

ADM14/16   L. P. Thompson-McCausland's Papers: Cheap Money – a Criticism of Lord Keynes' Theory (March–April 1945)

C20/1   R. A. O. Bridge's Papers: Miscellaneous   (November   1935–September 1948)

C40/438   Chief Cashier's Policy Files: Government Borrowing – CRND Investment Policy (January 1944–April 1948)

C40/449	Chief Cashier's Policy Files: Government Borrowing – 3% Savings Bonds 1965–75 (June 1944–March 1976)
C40/450	Chief Cashier's Policy Files: Government Borrowing – $1\frac{3}{4}$% Exchequer Bonds 1950 (October 1944–November 1945)
C40/465	Chief Cashier's Policy Files: Government Borrowing – Small Savings (January 1947–June 1948)
C40/472	Chief Cashier's Policy Files: Government Borrowing – $2\frac{1}{2}$% Savings Bonds 1964–7 (January 1946–December 1962)
C40/476	Chief Cashier's Policy Files: Government Borrowing–3% Conversion Stock 1948–53 (October 1947–August 1948)
C40/686–7	Chief Cashier's Policy Files: Monetary Policy – Advances and Control of Inflation (1949–1952)
C42/1	Chief Cashier's Personal File: Interest Rates (June 1945–October 1951)
C47/30	Discount Office (Markets Supervision) Files: Discount Market – General (April 1927–November 1949)
G1/69–71	Governor's Files: Financial and Monetary Policy – Exchanges of views at Governor/Chancellor/Clearing Bank Chairman level (October 1932–December 1951)
G1/120	Governor's Files: Exchange Policy – Economic Crisis 1951–2 (July 1951–January 1952)
SMT2/307	Securities Management Trust Files: Chairman's Papers – Postwar Financing of Industry (March 1943–May 1944)

CRND/Issue Department records

PRO file
    T166/1408

CHAPTER 6

THE WATERSHED: 1951–1952

(a) CLEARING THE DECKS
The reordering of monetary policy

FOLLOWING the announcement in September 1951 that a General Election was to be held on 25 October, the Governor moved fast since the Conservative Manifesto contained a reference to the more active use of monetary policy including variations in the rate of interest. Two papers were prepared for him by Mynors. They described the external and internal conjuncture, indicated the dangers immediately ahead, and suggested a range of remedial action. On 14 October the Governor asked him to draft a third paper, putting the first two together in a form suitable for despatch to the Treasury. Cobbold added some forceful passages of his own at the beginning and end of this new draft and sent the combined version to Whitehall in a letter to Bridges:

> I am writing to ask that you will bring to the attention of His Majesty's Government, when a new Administration has been formed, the views of the Bank of England on certain aspects of the present financial situation. Much of what I set out below does no more than repeat advice which has been tendered by the Bank from time to time during recent years, but I feel it appropriate that our views should now be restated.
> I must begin by saying that the dangers to the currency, both at home and abroad, seem to us most threatening. At home there is evidence of a creeping distrust of the currency (and consequently of Government and other fixed-interest securities) as a means of saving. We do not suggest that fear of inflation has yet taken hold of the public in the sense in which that fear is felt in continental countries where runaway inflation and disappearance of savings have been experienced. But the slope is slippery, and unless present doubts can be relieved, the movement might gather pace quickly. Even now the general disinclination to save, and the general feeling that the value of money is in continuous decline, are creating

practical difficulties in the financing of public and private investment programmes.

Abroad, all the information which reaches us gives a grave view of the future of sterling, and the discount on forward and free sterling rates has lately widened to an alarming degree. The figures of the overseas balance of payments (both for the United Kingdom and for the sterling area) are known and estimates for the coming months are disturbing. It is perhaps less generally appreciated that a real loss of confidence in sterling could result in very much heavier and quicker inroads on our reserves than are contemplated in the estimates of current payments. There was experience before devaluation in 1949 of what can happen when payments to the sterling area for goods and services are held back whilst payments by the sterling area to the rest of the world are anticipated. This movement is again gathering force, and pressure on our gold and dollar reserves could rapidly become almost overwhelming.

We may look for remedy first in action which directly affects the overseas balance of payments, and secondly in action in the domestic field which affects directly the internal position of the currency and indirectly the balance of payments.

The possibilities under the first heading are:

(a) A further *devaluation* of sterling. I assume that it would be generally agreed that this could only add to our difficulties and must be out of the question unless we were to be finally driven to it by failure to take other action.

(b) A cut in *imports*, particularly from dollar areas and, in the light of current developments, from Western Europe. Something must clearly be done in this field, both in the United Kingdom and in the Sterling Area. But there is a definite limit, beyond which a reduction of imports into the United Kingdom will disproportionately damage our production. And we must reckon with a strong feeling by other members of the Sterling Area that they are being asked to cut dollar expenditure again (whilst many of them are earning dollars on balance) because the United Kingdom is not keeping its own house in order.

(c) The pressure to increase *exports* must obviously be maintained. But prospects of a large further contribution from this source are not good. Sales resistance and competition have increased since the last export drive was launched, and much industrial capacity has been switched over to armaments. Moreover the yield from Sterling Area exports of raw materials depends mainly on international events outside British control.

(d) *Invisible income*, an important item in the balance of payments, must be maintained and if possible increased. The United Kingdom's earnings from banking, insurance, marketing and similar services depend on the view which is held of sterling abroad and on the degree of service which the United Kingdom can offer. The best way of improving earnings from this source will be to maintain sterling as a currency which the world wishes to hold and to give as much attraction and freedom as possible to overseas traders and investors in this market.

(e) Expenditure in foreign currency might be curtailed at some points by a tightening of *exchange control restrictions*. But we have frequently expressed the view, to which we adhere, that a tightening of restrictions would at the present stage only increase the incentive to evasion and make sterling still less serviceable and attractive to overseas holders. In our view the objective of policy must be in the other direction – towards making sterling an increasingly useful and desirable currency on its merits, with convertibility, at least for current transactions, as the target. Cuts in the import programme and encouragement of exports and invisible earnings are certainly necessary. But direct action in this field will prove ineffective if not combined with measures in the domestic field. Over-spending, over-consumption and over-investment in the United Kingdom are the prime cause of the threat to both internal and external value of the currency.

Under this second heading:

(a) *Government expenditure* should be cut or deferred wherever possible. This will have a greater effect than any other measure on the facts of the situation, on sentiment at home, and on sentiment abroad.
(b) *Private consumption* should be cut by fiscal and monetary methods.
(c) *Investment* should be cut – in the public sector by deferment of projects which, however desirable in themselves, the country cannot afford now, and in the private sector by fiscal and monetary methods.
(d) To achieve a reduction of consumption and of investment in the private sector, fiscal policy should be supported by a tighter *credit policy*, involving a general increase of short-term money rates and possibly some increase in the long-term rate. Such monetary action can however only serve to supplement a tighter fiscal and budget policy, and will serve little purpose by itself.
(e) It needs no emphasis that *production* is the core of the problem; and that, particularly for the export market, production *costs* are becoming daily more important. On a longer view fresh incentive and higher reward for hard work at every stage will be necessary; but the first step must be to secure the value of the currency, without which new incentives and rewards will prove illusory.

Finally I wish to emphasise the urgency. Every month which passes without adequate action will make action more difficult and will demand even more drastic action in the end. Even if some of the necessary measures cannot be made effective at once, the safety of the currency requires that a comprehensive programme should be announced, and all possible measures taken, without delay.

Several of the continental currencies are under pressure, and there are dangerous inflationary pressures in the Sterling Area and elsewhere. Inflation and depreciation are infectious. A strong and early lead by the

United Kingdom in taking the action necessary to maintain the value of the currency should have a stabilising effect throughout the world. It would also greatly improve the prospects of cooperation in domestic and external policy by other members of the Sterling Area.

Assessment of the political practicability or expediency of particular lines of policy is no part of the Bank's function. The Bank consider it their duty to set out for submission to His Majesty's Government, on formation of a new Administration, the very serious view which they take of the situation and the general lines of action which, without regard to political considerations, they judge necessary to protect the currency.

I am of course at your disposal for discussion in due course of any of the points raised in this letter.

In addition to the preparation of this *démarche* the Governor had been working on yet another set of plans for restoring the flexibility of short-term interest rates. On 17 October he told Bridges he was pretty certain that he would in any event recommend an increase in Bank Rate within the next few weeks. Several days earlier he had seen, but not liked, a paper by the Chief Cashier entitled 'Inflation and Bank Rate', which covered a good deal of philosophical ground but confined its practical suggestions to a new idea for dividing the money market in two and moving up short-term rates on private sector borrowing while leaving the Treasury Bill rate unchanged. Writing in manuscript from Basle, the Governor asked for something more ambitious and comprehensive. He felt that the first two months of a new Government (particularly if it was Conservative) would give a chance and 'perhaps last chance, of drastic measures to clear up this position and free our hands on rates'. He then put forward some ideas of his own that included an initial rise in the Treasury Bill rate to around 1% combined with a funding operation that would convert a large quantity of Treasury Bills into short-term bonds yielding $1-1\frac{1}{4}\%$. This operation would be undertaken in agreement with the clearing banks, the discount houses, and the Bank's central banking customers. He concluded characteristically: 'I don't know whether any of this makes sense or is practicable – but *we must do something* to clear this up and *free our hands* to use interest rate and this is *our only chance*.' He added that he had 'arranged with Hugh Kindersley that he will be available to help us with this over the next two weeks' and wondered whether the advice of Ellen, former General Manager of the Union Discount, could be obtained on the same basis.[1]

The Chief Cashier soon came up with the answers that the Governor had requested, while himself keeping a firm grip on the finer technicalities. He

---

[1] It is not recorded whether Kindersley actually provided any help. Mr Ellen was duly seen by Peppiatt and by the Governor. He was thanked for his helpful advice, but there survives no record of what it was.

suggested that Bank Rate should be raised from 2% to $2\frac{1}{2}$% and made effective at a fairly early stage. But the consequential rise in the Treasury Bill rate would be limited by the Bank announcing, along with the rise in Bank Rate, that it would be prepared to lend to the discount houses against the security of Treasury Bills at a specified rate below Bank Rate. This would be followed by a funding operation of the kind mentioned by the Governor, subscriptions to the new bonds being payable through the surrender of Treasury Bills. The clearing banks and other institutions affected would be encouraged to subscribe, but there must be no suggestion of forced funding. The bonds would be for one, two, or three years at $1\frac{1}{4}$%, $1\frac{1}{2}$%, and $1\frac{3}{4}$% respectively. The banks might subscribe for £500 million, bringing their liquidity ratios down towards a normal 30%, and the Discount Market for up to £100 million. With central banks subscribing perhaps £300 million, the total might come to about £900 million out of the £3,200 million of Bills outstanding in these institutional hands.

Beale's formulation was accepted by the Governor, it being agreed that the proposed Lending Rate against Treasury Bills should be 2%. Bringing the market into the Bank would be an occasional event whose frequency would depend on the needs of the moment. Ordinarily, shortages in the market would continue to be relieved by open market operations in Treasury Bills acquired at market rates. It was thought that the new arrangements, with Bank Rate at $2\frac{1}{2}$%, would probably establish a Treasury Bill rate between $\frac{3}{4}$% and 1% and a commercial bill rate of $1\frac{1}{2}$% (up $\frac{1}{2}$%). The funding operation, besides usefully reducing the liquidity of the banks, would thereafter isolate an appreciable part of the pre-existing floating debt from the immediate effects of further movements in short-term rates. This isolation was indeed its primary purpose, intended to reduce Governmental resistance to subsequent proposals for movements in short-term rates that would increase the budgetary cost of debt service.

Beale had the plan ready by 24 October and it was included in a letter handed to Bridges by the Governor on the 30th, R. A. Butler's second working day as the Chancellor of the Exchequer. Before explaining the plan, the Governor recalled the Bank's previous attempts, from 1949 onwards, to break out of the $\frac{1}{2}$% straitjacket and asserted the great need in present circumstances to take 'a definite step and to get away from the rigidity which ties our hands in operating on the volume of credit'. After explaining the plan, he stated that: 'requests to the banks in the matter of selection of credit would remain in force (and I should propose to stress this point when explaining new measures to the bankers)'. It was impossible to quantify the positive results of the proposed measures; but they would, in conjunction with others, 'certainly contribute to stabilising the value of the currency'. Finally, while stressing the urgency of the situation, the Governor included an important paragraph about responsibilities. He and his immediate advisers, Peppiatt and Beale, were concerned lest the Treasury should start to interfere with the daily management of the money market. The Governor wrote:

> The Bank of England must take the responsibility for the technical market questions of Bank Rate and allied Bank of England rates. I do not want to bother the Chancellor of the Exchequer to any greater extent than by asking for his assurance that these moves would be in line with his general intentions in other financial fields (without which they would be fruitless) and that he would approve a tightening of credit on these general lines.

He also gave Bridges a much shorter note, for himself and the Chancellor only, making three points, as follows:

> Monetary measures by themselves, however savage, will not restore confidence in the currency unless accompanied by heavy cuts in expenditure and investment programmes.
>
> The proposals are made as a first step with the main objective of getting away from an impossibly rigid situation which ties our hands on credit policy. The proposals do not represent drastic or shock tactics. The whole machinery is rusty, circumstances are new and these proposals are intended as experimental to find a path over unmapped territories. Moreover the mere indication that the negative attitude towards this subject is being replaced by a positive attitude will undoubtedly have a good effect at home and abroad. Continuance of the negative attitude would be most damaging.
>
> Monetary policy will not really bite directly on inflation unless it goes much further. It would begin really to bite and bite hard with Bank Rate at 4% and upwards with the shake-outs and upsets which this would cause. This may well prove necessary before confidence in the currency can be fully restored. An alternative policy would be to go direct to these violent measures but it would have to be recognised as a leap in the dark with extremely uncertain but drastic consequences.

Bridges and his colleagues supported the Governor's proposals. Indeed senior Treasury officials had all been in favour of a rise in short-term rates since the previous January, when they had been overruled by Gaitskell. The Governor saw the new Chancellor for the first time on the evening of 30 October. They had a wide-ranging discussion, based on the two letters to Bridges and the short additional note. They also discussed relations between the Bank and the Treasury and arrangements for regular meetings between themselves. A few days later they agreed to have regular weekly meetings, supplemented as required. This marked the beginning of a closer relationship than Cobbold had enjoyed with Cripps or Gaitskell.

Then, relations had been cordial, correct, but slightly distant. The Governor had been treated more like a senior Civil Servant than some special being who could be treated more like a colleague. With Butler it was different, as indeed it was to be with Macmillan. The Governor must at once have felt he was more in the swim than he used to be and, encouraged by his talks at the Treasury, he took the opportunity of a routine meeting with the CLCB on 1 November to warn the clearing bank Chairmen that early changes were in the wind, that rusty machinery might need to be restored to working order, and that their close support and assistance might well be required. On the following day, Friday, at a further meeting with the Chancellor and Bridges he was told to expect the go-ahead early in the following week for action later in that week.[2] On Monday 5 November he was asked whether a move to 3% might be better. He advised that $2\frac{1}{2}$% remained the right choice for a first step and as a signal that the authorities were now prepared to resume the use of short-term interest-rate policy in support of other measures. A figure of 3% would achieve little more in this respect and might well upset the funding operation that was to be launched shortly afterwards. Once it had been decided not to 'proceed at the moment to a drastic rate of 4% or 5% we see advantage in doing the minimum necessary to achieve the flexibility objective'. This advice was accepted and the rusty machinery for changing Bank Rate and the structure of short-term rates was set in motion.

The Governor, Peppiatt, the Chief Cashier, and their supporting officials worked hard with the necessary oil. On Tuesday the Chairman of the CLCB and his Deputy, Lord Balfour of Burleigh and Mr Tuke, were given an exceptional 24-hour warning by the Governor. Shortly after 3.00 p.m. on Wednesday the Chancellor began his statement, which included the announcement of import cuts, a reduction in the foreign travel allowance, postponement of new building work, and a foreshadowing of cuts in

[2] It was to be the first of many occasions when Parliamentary and political considerations had to be properly meshed with Bank formalities and market management. Butler wanted to make a statement to the House of Commons on the afternoon of Thursday 8 November, which would include his announcing that Bank Rate was being raised. But it was pointed out that he could not do this on a Thursday because the Bank, following its long-established routine, would have had to announce 'No Change' (in Bank Rate) to the public and the markets during the meeting of Court that same morning. If, on this occasion in 1951, the Court were to take no decision, and make no announcement ahead of the Chancellor's statement, markets would be brought to a confused standstill. Accordingly, the Chancellor agreed to make his statement on the afternoon of Wednesday 7 November, coincident with a special meeting of Court and a special Bank Rate announcement. The Bank did not like its Thursday routine being overridden in this way, but it frequently had to put up with it at times of crisis when a package of measures was being announced by the Chancellor. Nowadays, when neither Bank Rate nor its contrived successor Minimum Lending Rate survive, these particular problems have passed into history. Others may have taken their place.

Government expenditure. At 3.30 the Court assembled in the Bank for a special meeting to register formal approval of an alteration in Bank Rate, after twelve years of 'No Change'. At 3.45 the Chancellor announced the change to the House and the world, in words carefully chosen to conform with the division of responsibilities between the Treasury and the Bank. 'After the most careful consultation with the Governor of the Bank of England' he had concluded it was 'necessary to depart from the arrangements in force... The Bank of England are today, with my approval, raising the Bank Rate by $\frac{1}{2}$% to $2\frac{1}{2}$%... Bill rates may be expected to increase somewhat and to fluctuate according to supply and demand, subject to day-to-day operations by the authorities... I propose at the same time to take the complementary step of bringing the Floating Debt into more manageable proportions by a short-term funding operation...' Concurrently the Bank sent full explanatory telegrams to all the principal central banks abroad, the Governor himself sending a personal message to Allan Sproul in New York. The Scottish and Northern Irish banks were also sent explanatory telegrams.

Meantime the messengers in the Governor's corridor were busy shepherding visitors. At 3.30 p.m. he saw the Chairman and Deputy Chairman of the London Discount Market Association. He told them he hoped the market would not go for more than £50 million of the new funding bonds and suggested that the next Treasury Bill Tender might suitably produce a rate of about $\frac{7}{8}$%. They were followed by the Chairman of the Stock Exchange at 4.00 p.m. and next by no less than fifteen financial journalists,[3] who crowded into the Governor's room at 4.30. The Bank was represented by Peppiatt, Beale, and Rickatson-Hatt as well as by Cobbold himself. After stressing the identity of views between the Bank and HMG, sketching out the various alternatives – doing nothing, taking drastic action, flag-waving without effective content, or a first step getting away from rigidity – and explaining what had actually been done, the Governor asked his visitors to emphasise firstly 'the move away from rigidity and towards flexibility and reality' and secondly that the Chancellor's speech, including the monetary measures, 'demonstrate an intention to take hold of the situation and do what proves necessary to put it right'. On the following day the Governor spoke to a special meeting of the CLCB, emphasising that the requests made to them earlier in the year, about the selective restriction of advances, remained very much in force. The banks should if possible intensify their efforts to restrict inessential credit. To Tuke, who said it would not be easy for them to put up lending

---

[3] Among the better remembered were Oscar Hobson, Paul Bareau, Richard Fry, Harold Wincott, Sydney Gampell, Frederick Ellis, and Gordon Tether.

rates again, so soon after the round of increases carried through in the late summer, the Governor replied that he wished the rise in Bank Rate to be regarded as a definite encouragement to stepping up charges for inessential and marginal borrowing. After speaking to the Chairman of the Accepting Houses Committee in the same sense, he saw the Discount Market again on Thursday afternoon and encouraged them to go for a Bill rate of $\frac{7}{8}$% rather than anything higher at this early stage. As to the funding bonds, his earlier suggestion of £50 million was intended as a top limit. If the Market wanted to take less, he would not at all mind though he thought it would be useful for them to have a certain amount for dealing purposes. Lastly, to complete the whole operation, the Governor handed a manuscript note to his Deputy, Dallas Bernard. It was not a mere formality. Cobbold was sparing with his compliments and when he made them he meant them. The note read:

> I should be glad if you would have conveyed to those concerned in the various Departments of the Bank my thanks and admiration for the efficient and secret handling of yesterday's arrangements, in their preparation and execution, and in the cabling and filing services.

At the Tender on 9 November the rate on Treasury Bills rose to just under $\frac{7}{8}$% and a week later it rose to just over that rate. The funding operation also went according to plan. Overseas central banks subscribed £293 million (of which India, Pakistan, and Egypt accounted for over £200 million), the London banks took £500 million, the discount houses £40 million, and the Bank itself took £167 million, partly for subsequent sale in the market by Issue Department and partly as an investment for the Banking Department. The total came to £1,000 million. The bonds were called Serial Funding Stock. £450 million matured in November 1952, £200 million in November 1953, and £350 million in November 1954. The liquidity ratio of the clearing banks fell from 39% to 32%.

For the markets, the commentators, and the public the whole operation came as no surprise. Given the reference in the Election Manifesto, together with what *The Economist* described as a crisis of solvency and a desperate situation, it would have been astonishing if Bank Rate had not been raised as soon as possible after the new Government had taken office. Before the Election, *The Economist* had argued for a Bank Rate of 4% and it therefore expressed some disappointment at the rise to only $2\frac{1}{2}$%. But this did not prevent it from remarking, in the course of a long article on how the new policy might be expected to work, that the whole operation was 'a well balanced and closely integrated programme of change, and one of its principal merits is that it carefully avoids giving the impression that these moves towards tighter money are necessarily final.'[4] Other writers in the quality press made similar comments.

During the interlude that ensued between the restoration of flexibility in November and the increase in Bank Rate to 4% early in the following March, all the machinery, whether old and rusty or already in post-war use, was given some additional polish. British monetary policy then became set in a mould that was to last for many years, notwithstanding the introduction of technical modifications following the deliberations of the Radcliffe Committee in 1957–8. Overall responsibility for policy rested with the Treasury; responsibility for advice and execution rested largely with the Bank. The ingredients of policy were firstly a flexibility of short-term interest rates administered cautiously and in large part with an eye on the performance of sterling; secondly the frequent use of direct qualitative and quantitative control over bank advances exercised by the Bank without formal directive and through a mostly cartelised banking system; thirdly a special statutory control over consumer instalment credit executed by the Board of Trade; and finally the use of gilt-edged funding operations to limit bank liquidity and, it was held, reinforce control over lending. The money supply itself received little or no attention. Until the post-Radcliffe reforms there was no increase in published statistical information and until the mid-1950s there was little increase in unpublished material. The reactivation of interest-rate flexibility in November 1951 is therefore best regarded in the way it was presented at the time, namely as the overdue removal of an absurd anomaly within the existing framework of monetary policy rather than as the inauguration of an entirely new approach.

The first application of additional polish did however consist of an attempt to identify the change in control over the volume of credit that the restoration of interest-rate flexibility could bring about. In an exchange with the Treasury over the drafting of a brief for the Chancellor to use in the Debate on the King's Speech, the Chief Cashier resisted too bold and confident a reference to restoration of control over the cash base of the banking system. But he did allow a reference to this way of looking at things and to the possibility of jolting the banks into a change of behaviour. The brief included the following sentence: 'The knowledge that the Bank of England are once more in a position to apply pressure on the credit base, even if this leads to some increase in interest rates, should itself have a restraining effect on the banks in making advances; and although we cannot at present foresee the precise effect this will have on the rates

[4] Under the editorship of Geoffrey Crowther, *The Economist* was at this time enjoying a period of greatness as an influential journal of political and economic opinion.

of interest charged by banks to their customers, the tendency will clearly be for lending rates to increase with consequent discouragement to borrowers.'[5] Too much should not be read into that sentence. But it seems to place its author somewhere in between the position later held by advocates of 'monetary base control', at the time of the monetarist ascendancy in the early 1980s, and those who argued that such a method added nothing (except intellectual confusion) to the control of monetary conditions through official manipulation of interest rates. It is however doubtful whether the banks were in fact at all jolted by the restoration of flexibility in 1951. As will be seen, the Bank had some difficulty persuading them to make any increase at all in their lending rates following the rise in Bank Rate to $2\frac{1}{2}\%$.

After this brief foray into the intellectual quicksands, the Bank took steps to ensure that official talk of flexibility was not mere words. Trinder, Manager of Union Discount, reported to Peppiatt on 15 November that the money market seemed to be settling into a new structure of rates that already looked as rigid as its predecessor. Accordingly on the following day the Governor obtained Eady's agreement to the 2% Lending Rate being made effective and his acceptance of a consequential further rise in the Bill rate. Bridges and Butler were so informed, and on 19 November two discount houses were forced into the Bank for a modest £1·6 million for seven days. At the Tender on the following Friday the Bill rate rose to nearly 1%. Concurrently, requests from the Treasury for more detailed regular information were resisted. Within agreed lines of policy, the Governor regarded day-to-day official tactics in the money market as the Bank's affair. The Chief Cashier declined to provide Trend, Under-Secretary in Home Finance, with a mass of market data but agreed to have regular talks with him about the way things were going, a procedure that was to last for many years.

As to the machinery of direct credit control, the Governor did not have an altogether easy passage with the clearing banks. Their advances were rising fast and in fact grew by some 16% in 1951 although deposits, affected by the large external deficit, actually fell slightly. Advances rates had been raised during the summer and now averaged $3\frac{1}{2}$–4%. In talks with Peppiatt during October the Chief Executive Officers (CEOs) said they expected the rise in advances to continue, though perhaps rather more slowly, despite the utmost attention being given to the official request. They stressed that the rise in the 'personal and professional' category had been halted. Nonetheless, at the time of the increase in Bank Rate to $2\frac{1}{2}\%$,

---

[5] A brief for Lord Swinton, for use in the Lords' Debate on the King's Speech, went rather further in the direction of base control.

both the Chancellor and the Governor asked the banks to intensify the restriction of credit for inessential purposes. On 12 November the Governor followed this up in a meeting with Balfour and Tuke, asking for a further rise in lending rates to reflect the rise in Bank Rate. He suggested that for individual cases the increase might range from $\frac{1}{4}$% to 1%, depending on the essentiality of the borrower's business and the purpose of the loan. He also asked that over the next six months the clearing banks should provide, in confidence, monthly as well as quarterly figures of advances analysed by category of borrower. The banks responded to this through a note submitted to the Chairman by the CEOs collectively. They were most reluctant to embark on a further increase in rates when this could not be justified either by the $2\frac{1}{2}$% Bank Rate[6] or by an increase in running expenses and would accordingly be seen as an unwarranted addition to their profits. Furthermore, they queried whether rises of up to 1% would in practice serve to discourage borrowing. As to rate-discrimination against borrowing for inessential purposes, they stated with dignity: 'The application of a particular rate of interest to an account must always be based upon the credit-worthiness of the borrower and not upon the category of the industry in which the customer is engaged. We do not feel able to depart from this principle.'

The CEOs discussed these matters again two weeks later. They stuck to their principle but agreed to some flexibility in its application. As facilities came up for renewal, careful consideration would first be given to the possibility of reducing limits and secondly to increasing the rate of interest by $\frac{1}{2}$% or more. Justification for the latter would be compliance with Government policy in support of a general restriction. This, the banks stated, should be 'one of firmness, tempered with gradualness, as any panicky or precipitous measures would be harmful to the general economy'. On 29 November the Chairman and Deputy Chairman of the CLCB wrote a letter to *The Times*, warning bank customers that credit was going to become more difficult and asking for their co-operation. On 4 December, Treasury guidance to the CIC was once again reinforced. All applications in respect of 'projects for the production of inessential goods, especially where these are intended mainly for the home market and consist largely of metal using projects', were to be discouraged. A copy of the new guidance was sent to the Governor by the Chancellor, who added: 'It is already understood, but I wish to emphasise that banking facilities should not be given for the speculative buying or holding of securities, real property, or stocks of commodities; that finance for hire purchase should

---

[6] The ordinary top rate, agreed in letters between bank and customer was Bank Rate varying plus 1%, i.e. $3\frac{1}{2}$% in November 1951.

be limited; and that notwithstanding the statutory exemption [from CIC control] of borrowing made [by banks] in the ordinary course of business, bank advances should not in general be made for capital expenditure.' The various banking associations were sent copies of this letter and duly assured the Governor of their co-operation. Early in the new year the growth of advances slowed down. In the spring of 1952 they actually fell. To what extent this was due to officially imposed restrictions rather than to a decline in demand associated with the fall in commodity prices and an autonomous easing of pressures on the economy, it is impossible to judge. But it was tempting to attribute a fair proportion to the restrictions themselves, one of which remains to be described.

Amongst the detail agreed between the clearing banks was an intention to give six months' notice to hire-purchase finance companies that their facilities would be reduced first by 10% and then by another 10% six months later. Since these companies also ranked among the lowest in the priorities of the CIC, they were clearly being subjected to the severest discrimination. But as is normally the case with monetary controls that do not apply to the whole market and can be avoided by recourse to other channels of finance, it could be argued that such discrimination was both inequitable and ineffective. Even in its lesser form, before this latest intensification, it had begun to cause trouble. At the end of 1950 the accounts of the newly nationalised electricity authority had shown a substantial increase in the hire-purchase of durable consumer goods retailed through the authority's showrooms. Great Universal Stores Ltd showed a similar growth. The gas boards were soon to follow. In neither case had the additional instalment credit been financed by bank loans made for the purpose. An even greater potential threat was the ability of the finance houses to take deposits on their own account, wholly outside any official constraint, voluntary or statutory. As early as February 1951, at a meeting of the clearing bank CEOs, it was stated that funds were being raised in this way. In May Bank officials concluded that further financial controls of the kind then employed would be ineffective or unfair. Therefore it would be better to go for a statutory control, operated by the Board of Trade, over the actual terms of instalment credit. In October the Treasury formed an inter-departmental group, which included the Bank, to review the subject. Taking note that control over instalment credit terms had recently been reintroduced in the US, the Board of Trade favoured its use in the UK. After a pause, discussion was resumed early in 1952. At the end of January an Order was promulgated, under surviving wartime powers contained in successive Supplies and Services (Extended Purposes) Acts. Cookers, furniture, and solid fuel heaters were exempted from its provisions, but hire-purchase terms[7] for motor cars and most other durable consumer goods were restricted to a minimum deposit of $33\frac{1}{3}\%$ and a maximum repayment period of eighteen months.

The existing controls over finance houses, exercised through the banks and the CIC, were nonetheless retained in their full rigour. This belt-and-braces approach was probably due to the economic emergency of the time and to a feeling that financial controls could help restrain a widening of the market for consumer credit, which terms control on its own could not prevent. The authorities must have been well aware of a pent-up demand for motor cars and other durables. But persistence with stringent financial controls, in an area that was becoming markedly competitive and profitable, strongly encouraged the growth of a grey market in finance where the Bank's writ simply did not run. In a few years' time this was to prove a considerable and intractable problem (see Chapters 10(c) and 11(d) below).

With the introduction of hire-purchase terms control the reordering of domestic monetary policy was complete. The mould, as was noted earlier, had been set into a combination of interest-rate flexibility and direct controls. But there had been no new official investigation either into the proper place of monetary policy in the task of macro-economic management or into the best way of operating such policy and monitoring its progress. The Bank's own views on the role of monetary policy had, it seemed, changed little since the deliberations of Niemeyer's Committee on Post-War Finance in 1943. The two economists, Mynors and Allen, both thought on 'banking school' lines and attached great importance to the effect of changes in monetary policy upon expectations, particularly when such changes were supported by other alterations in macro-economic policy. Changes in Bank Rate were especially significant, affecting expectations about the rate of exchange as well as about the course of domestic activity and profits. These psychological factors reinforced and at times overshadowed the direct effects on aggregate demand exerted by changes in the cost and availability of credit. It followed that monetary statistics, such as they were, provided information of limited value. Outside the specific field of hire-purchase, they were often more a guide to the conformity of the banks with official wishes than to the economic effects of policy. Assessments of the latter were therefore heavily judgemental and conspicuously reliant on qualitative, even anecdotal, information. The gathering of economic and financial intelligence was as important as the collection and compilation of statistics. Views such as

---

[7] All this was long before the growth of unsecured personal loans repayable by instalments. Accordingly hire-purchase was the predominant form of consumer instalment credit.

these fitted readily enough with those of other senior people in the Bank, whose experience and expertise rested upon a knowledge of the markets in which the Bank operated and whose judgement was continuously nourished by market information.

Critics of these views usually argue that they lead to policy weakness and lack of clear public presentation, particularly if the central bank is subordinate to the Government of the day; though in 1951 there were other critics, on the political left, who argued that the resurrection of Bank Rate represented a threatened return to blind forces of monetary deflation. But looking forward in the new year of 1952, these were issues to be settled pragmatically. Monetarist arguments, and the causal use of the quantity theory, were scarcely to be heard. There was not, in short, too much new thinking to be done in the unfashionable field of monetary economics. Nor was there yet much to think about with respect to a monetary technique that continued to rely heavily upon direct, if ostensibly voluntary, control over the banks. As has been related in Chapter 5, during the years immediately following nationalisation the Bank had succeeded in retaining its authority in this field at a point midway between Whitehall and the commercial banking system. But competition between the banks, already limited by restrictive practices, was further stifled by this official imposition of credit rationing through gubernatorial requests backed by the Chancellor's wishes. In the longer run, underlying forces of competition and financial innovation were to render this system inoperable. But in 1951 the issues of competition and regulation were for the future. There was the economic emergency to be overcome and experience with interest-rate flexibility to be gained. Only after that might it be possible to begin thinking about monetary technique and its possible modification.

The reopening of the exchange market

Discussions in the Bank in early 1951, about a floating rate for sterling and the link between a floating rate and the restoration of convertibility, had pointed out that it would be necessary to reopen the London market in foreign exchange. But the possibility of a floating rate, considered an unlikely contingency at that stage, was by no means the only argument for reopening the market. In 1947, during the brief period of convertibility, tentative plans were worked out for authorised banks in London to deal in US dollars against sterling with each other, with New York, and with the public at rates inside the official upper and lower limits. The objective was to enable London to compete on equal terms with New York and redevelop a source of invisible income; but the plan died with the suspension of convertibility. Three years later, in the autumn of 1950, the issue arose in another form when Bolton became concerned about the use being made of the official provision of forward exchange cover. Under arrangements that had been in force since the outbreak of war, forward cover in respect of approved transactions in the main currencies could always be obtained by the banks directly from the EEA at a fixed cost of 1% per annum. In a letter sent to Wilson Smith early in November 1950 Bolton drew attention to the currency risk to which the EEA was becoming exposed. With sterling strong and the dollar weak, the EEA had passively acquired through its provision of cover an overbought forward position of $240 million. Furthermore the official provision of forward cover was not confined to residents of the UK. American importers of sterling goods were permitted to buy the sterling forward from the EEA at 1% per annum if buying such cover in the New York market, the dollar being weak, was more expensive. Bolton considered it wrong that the EEA should be obliged to take currency risks of this kind and that near-speculative activity should be encouraged by the provision of 1% cover regardless of the circumstances. Yet the EEA could not itself vary the cost of cover without being seen to pass judgements on the strength or weakness of the currencies concerned, an activity that would get it into political hot water. It would accordingly be better to reopen the forward market, take the EEA right out of ordinary forward business, and allow forward rates to be determined by supply and demand.

Bolton's views encountered some opposition within the Bank, for example on the grounds that the EEA would not in practice be able to get rid of its currency exposure. For when exchange rates were under pressure it could well find itself having to intervene heavily in the market so as to maintain tolerable conditions. But the Governor supported Bolton and a letter sent to the Treasury in November 1950 suggested that the forward market be reopened and that official intervention be reserved for conditions when 'rates for one reason or another tended to move to an abnormal extent'. Treasury officials, headed by Wilson Smith, were sympathetic, but Ministers proved reluctant. Douglas Jay, now Financial Secretary, argued strongly that there was in fact no risk in the EEA holding dollars, spot or forward, and that the appearance of wide forward premiums or discounts in London would simply encourage rumours and expectations that the sterling–dollar parity was going to be changed. Bolton replied that the New York market already allowed this to happen and that reopening in London would make little difference. The Chancellor (Gaitskell) remained unpersuaded and asked for a note on the technical operation of forward exchange markets. This was prepared in the Bank and sent to the Treasury early in February 1951. But despite a reminder sent in March there was no further response.

During the summer of 1951 the Bank's case was further strengthened by the appearance of a device known as 'double tirage', whereby French importers of Sterling Area goods normally invoiced in sterling, for example rubber and tin, could in effect obtain forward cover from the EEA in London, at $1\frac{1}{4}$% per annum, instead of from the Paris market at up to 5% or even 10% per annum.[8] By the autumn of 1951 the EEA had in this way acquired an exposure in French francs equal to £6 million, with every prospect of further growth. The Bank did not like this exploitation of cheap forward cover in francs, did not like two sets of bills being used to cover the same transaction, and did not like the franc invoicing of sterling goods.

Following the change of Government at the end of October and the resumption two months earlier of downward pressure on sterling, Bolton returned to the charge. This time he argued in favour of reopening the London market for spot as well as forward transactions, the official limits on the spot rate against the dollar being widened to two cents either side of $2.80 instead of the existing half-cent. He again encountered some opposition inside the Bank. Fisher doubted whether in practice the banks could make much of a spot market even within the wider spread and also whether a wider spread would have any dampening effect on speculation. In the same fashion he doubted whether freeing the forward rate in London would be helpful. A heavy discount on forward sterling would increase pressure on the spot rate and provoke large-scale official intervention, leading to a last state no better than the first. If this were so, what was the point in penalising the sound trader by forcing him into a heavily depreciated forward market? Fisher ended his note with the pointed comment: 'I am wondering if the proposal is not in fact moving towards floating rates.' But the Governor again supported Bolton and had already spoken to the Chancellor on the matter. Accordingly on 5 November a letter was sent to Rowan firmly recommending that the market be reopened as soon as possible. This time, with sterling under pressure spot and forward,[9] Bolton laid great stress on the current growth of open positions in foreign exchange through the operation of commercial

---

[8] Double tirage required the Sterling Area exporter to invoice in French francs, draw a 90 or 120-day franc bill on the French importer (which was accepted by him), and cover the francs forward with the EEA. The importer would pay francs to the exporter on maturity and the proceeds would be used to meet the forward contract with the EEA in exchange for sterling. This would then be used to repay a sterling bill that the exporter had drawn on the importer at the outset, under an acceptance credit, and had discounted for cash in London. The cost of the forward cover with the EEA was met by the importer, by adjustment to the face value of the franc bill.

[9] The EEA had been $210 million overbought forward at the end of June 1951. On 5 November it was $36 million oversold. It was also heavily oversold in Belgian francs, to the tune of the equivalent of £40 million.

leads and lags. He argued that these were encouraged by the present arrangements, under which, in the event of expectations being reversed, an open position could always be covered forward at very low cost or else closed by a spot purchase at minimal loss. Freeing the forward market and widening the spot spread would change this and therefore help reduce the growth of open positions against sterling. As a supplementary measure, Bolton proposed that the exchange control rules governing credit facilities for the movement of goods between the UK and non-sterling destinations should be tightened.

The Bank's proposals were discussed with Rowan and Brittain on 20 November and Bolton's arguments were reinforced by an explanation of 'double tirage', which was still growing. Despite some worries about the psychological impact of allowing the forward rate to go free, Treasury officials agreed to recommend to the Chancellor that the exchange market be reopened in the way the Bank had proposed. A decision about the tightening of credit facilities was deferred, in view of opposition from the Board of Trade. The case for reopening was then explained to the Chancellor in a Minute from Brittain. He mentioned also that neither Treasury officials nor the Bank thought that freeing the forward rate would suggest to the market that the authorities were thinking of floating the spot rate. There would anyway be a clear understanding that the Bank would keep a close watch on the new market and intervene if it showed signs of getting out of hand. In a conversation with the Governor on 23 November the Chancellor agreed with the proposals in principle, though he had some reservations about their political impact. But he saw the Governor again on the 30th and agreed that the market should be reopened on 17 December. Official publicity would treat the move as a technical and not as a political matter. Following this meeting Cobbold alerted the Chairman of the CLCB and arranged for preparations to be made between Bolton and Ellerton[10] of Barclays Bank, the latter being Chairman of the Foreign Exchange Committee of the British Bankers' Association. This Committee, and its executive sub-committee, was the banking system's representative body in all discussions with the Bank on questions relating to exchange control and to exchange markets.

The Bank had been preparing a 'Draft Notice to the Market', which was discussed with Ellerton and two of his colleagues on 5 December. Bolton made it clear that arrangements would be made by the Bank, with authorised banks individually, agreeing strict limits on the open positions

---

[10] Bolton had already had a preliminary talk with Ellerton on 20 November, as had the Governor on the 23rd.

that they could run overnight in foreign currencies and on the total of foreign exchange they could hold as cover against net forward sales. The bankers, in their turn, advised that the existing number of foreign exchange brokers (four) was likely to prove insufficient. Preparations, which included the drafting of telegrams to central banks overseas, then went ahead without any serious hitch, the banks being assured that the EEA stood ready to nurse the market during the initial period. In the event little nursing was needed. Early in the new year Bolton was able to report: 'In my opinion the authorised banks have done amazingly well in view of the short notice we gave them, their lack of equipment, and the shortage of expert staff, to have developed a market which works smoothly on narrow dealing margins...' The spot rate against the US dollar had tended to fall towards the lower limit of 2.78, but official intervention on any substantial scale had been needed on only two occasions.[11] In the forward market, the premium on three-month dollars had narrowed from three cents down to one and no sizeable intervention had been needed. The Treasury was well satisfied and neither in the markets nor in the press were there laments at the passing of the old system.

The reopening of the exchange market was amply justified on the arguments used. In a world of exchange volatility and rapidly fluctuating expectations, with the protection of exchange control eroded by growing resort to 'leads and lags', it no longer made sense to provide traders with spot exchange at a tiny spread around parity and forward cover at 1% per annum. Quite apart from the encouragement given to quasi-speculative operations, the old system must have damaged confidence simply by looking out of date. But there can be little doubt that the Bank had other arguments in mind in addition to those actually deployed. It was giving much thought to the restoration of convertibility, though until the end of January 1952 this was still seen as a longer-run rather than an immediate objective. Thinking about convertibility meant thinking about its technical operation, including the question of a fixed or a floating rate. There is little evidence that the possibility of the latter was taken very seriously during the last quarter of 1951, though there are signs of it being in the back of the mind. But convertibility in, say, 1953 would require a London foreign exchange market in any event, whether the exchange rate was fixed or floating, though in the latter case it was a technical necessity whereas in the former it was an obviously desirable complement. So reopening the market in December 1951, along with the restoration of flexibility in the

---

[11] This was not a good guide to the concurrent movement in UK reserves. Foreign exchange ordered by Bank customers, mainly central banks and HMG, was usually supplied directly by the EEA and not put through the market.

money market six weeks earlier, did indeed constitute a successful clearing of the decks.

Devising a longer-term plan for convertibility

The exchange reserves, including an accumulation of credit in the EPU, rose by £680 million in the twelve months following the outbreak of war in Korea. Sterling balances rose £570 million during the same period, almost entirely in the Sterling Area. The turnround was dramatically fast. In the September quarter of 1951, the reserves fell by £215 million and EPU credit by £90 million while the sterling balances started their descent with a fall of £65 million. In the December quarter the reserves fell £335 million and EPU credit by £190 million while sterling balances fell £270 million. Over the whole fifteen months right through to September of the following year the reserves and EPU credit together fell by no less than £1,120 million and the balances by £715 million.[12] The UK's own current account deficit exceeded £400 million. At the outset, at the end of June 1951, the published reserves amounted to £1,380 million and the sterling balances totalled £3,795 million. By the end of March 1952 the reserves had melted away to only £600 million or $1,680 million. But in October 1951 and over the remaining months of that year, neither the Treasury nor the Bank contemplated crash action. They certainly did not belittle the seriousness of the situation, but they judged that it could be kept under control. This would be achieved firstly by a series of measures beginning with those announced by the new Chancellor early in November and ending with a strict Budget in March 1952, and secondly by complementary action in the Sterling Area to be agreed at an early meeting of Commonwealth Finance Ministers and their officials. There seemed therefore to be time and opportunity to prepare plans for a new approach to the United Kingdom's external monetary problems, including a new approach to convertibility: time, because crash action was not immediately necessary; opportunity, because of the reordering of economic policies under the new Government and the readiness to look at external monetary problems with a fresh mind. In addition it was felt that the independent members of the Sterling Area would not remain fully loyal if they were confronted at the forthcoming Conference with the same old request for import cuts and no new ideas for the future.

However, as had always been the case with ambitious solutions to Britain's external monetary problems, those who constructed them found

---

[12] The run-down of Australian, New Zealand, Indian, and Pakistani holdings exceeded £715 million. Other balances showed some net increase.

themselves like the squirrel in the proverbial cage. At one end was an apparently attractive exit marked 'Grand Multilateral Solution'. Through this exit one proceeded by negotiation and agreement with the Sterling Area, together perhaps with Western Europe, and went on to an agreement with the US for the provision of large financial underpinning for convertibility and exchange stability. But whenever it was examined more closely, this exit sooner or later turned out to be blocked by the expected behaviour of the US Congress, if not of the Administration, the scale of whose help was likely to be sadly inadequate. So back the squirrel went to the other end of the cage. Here was an exit marked 'Unilateral Trapdoor'. Through it one froze the sterling balances without warning, simultaneously declared convertibility, and, if need be, floated the exchange rate. But when this exit in turn was examined, it was seen to be blocked by the damage it would do to external monetary relations and by the evident macro-economic dangers of floating the rate with a fully loaded economy and without adequate reserves. It was therefore marked 'For Emergency Use Only'. Finally the squirrel would go to the middle of the cage, to an easily opened and hauntingly familiar exit marked 'Temptation'. Through it one proceeded by negotiation and agreement leading to the restoration of fixed-rate convertibility without adequate underpinning and without adequate restraints on the sterling balances. In reality, the choice usually turned out to lie between 'Temptation' on the one hand and proper use of the 'Emergency Exit' on the other.

In the Bank, at the end of October 1951, Thompson-McCausland opened the debate with a rough sketch of a grand multilateral solution that left open the question of fixed versus floating exchange rates. Repeating familiar arguments deployed six months previously and earlier, he began by explaining that the development of free markets abroad and the periodically booming business in cheap sterling made it impossible to enforce the inconvertibility of non-resident sterling at the margin and would, in the end, make it impossible to retain the loyalty of UK traders. In the absence of any desire for a policy that would terminate the international functions of sterling, a return to the *de jure* convertibility of non-resident sterling had to be accepted. But convertibility was unlikely to be accompanied by exchange stability, even though the UK's own house was in good order. Fluctuations in the US economy, with their associated recurrent dollar shortages, would induce recurrent devaluations of non-dollar currencies. The UK, because of the international use of sterling, was particularly vulnerable. The exchange reserves were already too small to absorb these ebbs and flows and *a fortiori* much too small to absorb them in conditions of convertibility, non-discrimination, and trade liberalisation.

Lucius Thompson-McCausland

Accordingly, in exchange for measures correcting the UK and Sterling Area deficit and an undertaking to restore convertibility, the Americans would be asked to adopt a wide range of good-creditor policies. On the monetary side this might mean liberalising access to the IMF and enlarging its dollar resources. On the trade side it would mean tariff cuts, reductions in agricultural subsidies, and the reform of Customs procedures. It would also be necessary to reach agreement on the sharing of rearmament burdens and on the future of the EPU. At this point, as if he appreciated that these ambitions were unrealisable, the author took a quick look at 'Temptation' and added rather mysteriously: 'Even if the mission fails to secure all that it wants, the plunge to convertibility should nevertheless be taken on the grounds that inconvertibility is now more dangerous than convertibility'. There was no mention, at this stage, of a floating rate.

These ideas were next taken up by Bolton. In a private and personal note to Lucius dated 8 November, he said: 'I would like you to consider with me a new approach to our whole foreign exchange policy.' Exchange control had moved beyond the limits of efficiency, strains on the Sterling Area were accumulating, UK invisible earnings could not be maintained without a change of external financial policy, and the old system of bilateralism and planned imports and exports had irretrievably broken down. The restoration of interest-rate flexibility and the prospective restoration of a free market in forward exchange 'suggests we are now free to reconsider foreign exchange policy without regard to the fears and inhibitions of the past'. The upshot of his collaboration with Lucius was a long draft on 'External Economic Policy' (a final version was never prepared), which borrowed the latter's rationale and added a judgement by Bolton that the policies and practices of the past six years seemed to be ending in unendurable strains and friction in the administration of trade and foreign exchange. It followed that there was no alternative to a policy of progressive convertibility accompanied by a rapid discarding of much of the methods and practices employed since 1939. 'Our liberty of action', he went on, 'is however curtailed by the existence of the Sterling Area, large sterling balances in the hands of other central banks, a balance of payments deficit, trade discrimination against the dollar area, the lack of an effective price system at home owing to the food subsidies and the absence of commodity markets, and inadequate gold reserves.' Furthermore, since international payments problems were now worsened by the servicing of post-war indebtedness to the US and Canada, Bolton's multilateral solution included an agreed moratorium on these debts as well as a range of proposals along much the same lines as those sketched by Lucius. Instead, however, of direct financial assistance from the US, requiring Congressional approval, he proposed raising $1 billion from US commercial banks – using as security the EEA's dollar portfolio and the independent gold reserves of Sterling Area central banks – and raising up to another $2·4 billion through the IMF. He concluded with a familiar flourish: 'If the diagnosis is accurate that bilateralism has failed, and we are faced with either enforced convertibility through the collapse of administrative practices or a conscious acceptance of limited convertibility, there is no time to argue about details and difficulties. It is essential to obtain agreement on policy before circumstances take charge and leave us with the worst of both worlds.'

A further note by Lucius, dated 26 November, sought to add polish to his earlier paper and to Bolton's draft. He again relied heavily on the likelihood of recurrent dollar shortages arising from instability in the US, however virtuous the domestic policies of the UK and the other principal non-dollar countries. Continuing inconvertibility and trade discrimination, quite apart from avoidance through cheap-sterling operations, were no longer much help. They served merely to blunt the competitive power of UK exports in the dollar area or, outside it, in countries that were strong dollar earners. Their principal effect was to delay an inevitable devaluation, which then occurred in a major crisis. Therefore, unless American co-operation could be secured, along the lines set out in Bolton's draft, it would be better to accept a unilateral move to convertibility and adopt a positive policy of exchange rate adjustment. This latter, he asserted, would defend the UK both against such discrimination *vis-à-vis* sterling goods as might be a consequence of convertibility and against periodically aggressive sales of dollar goods in third-country markets.

Although Lucius did not say so specifically, his arguments added up to a case for floating-rate convertibility. Bretton Woods considerations apart, periodic prompt downward adjustments of a fixed parity would obviously have been impossible to handle in the case of an international currency with very inadequate reserves. A floating rate would have had its own dangers but could have been a superior operating technique in such conditions.

Elsewhere in the Bank, enthusiasm for convertibility was not shared by Kershaw or, a little later, by Mynors. The former was bothered by the 'plugging' of convertibility, doubted whether adequate American help would be forthcoming, ignored the arguments about a unilateral move, and stressed the need for domestic adjustment. 'The main-spring [of sterling] is the monetary and economic position of the UK. Every measure, therefore, which tends to redress the position here will make it ultimately easier and less expensive to give wider convertibility. It is a question of where one begins. It may well be that we are entering upon one of those corrective phases which seem apparently inescapable in the nature of the human attitude to economic activity.' Mynors was a rather more outspoken critic. 'Of course inconvertibility is unwelcome and troublesome', he wrote, 'but it is certainly not unreal. I think we should cease dreaming and try to formulate a better policy than we have had, taking the inescapable inconvertibility for granted.' To argue, as Lucius had, that a downward move in the exchange rate was itself an instrument of adjustment could only be described as 'non-sense', even with appropriate domestic measures. 'Devaluation sets up all sorts of pressures on costs and prices: its virtue, when it has any, is that it makes it easier to operate on costs and prices: if the operation is unsuccessful, you devalue again. How many times? What are the prospects of retaining convertibility of a currency which has a fine record of successive depreciations?' Mynors concluded, like Kershaw, that domestic adjustment should have first priority. 'It seems to me quite unreal to canvass the virtues of convertibility until we have done something about the familiar list of things which ought to have been associated with the devaluation of 1949 and would have been its justification.'

The Governor himself heeded the advice of Kershaw and Mynors rather than get carried away by the headier mixture of rhetoric, market insight, and self-taught economics proffered by Thompson-McCausland and Bolton. On 28 November he wrote a private and personal note to Rowan, enclosing copies of notes by his own advisers and emphasising that he had not yet reached a final conclusion. He agreed that: 'We ought to have an *aim* about convertibility in the light of present conditions, accept the fact that the wartime exchange control pattern is not the ideal policy for today or tomorrow and move in the direction of our aim wherever possible.' But he could see neither the underlying solvency nor adequate exchange resources for attempting an early move. 'Instead', he wrote, 'we must concentrate, and quickly, on our own (and Sterling Area) internal position. This means urgent action to take the overload off our economy...' However, as the weeks went by and the briefs for the Commonwealth Finance Ministers' Conference were prepared in Whitehall, Cobbold shifted his ground. For it became apparent that the Treasury intended to offer the Conference a mixture containing some nine-tenths of short-run fiscal and monetary austerity and only about one-tenth of tentative ideas about the longer term, including in particular the restoration of convertibility. The Governor felt, correctly as it turned out, that this would not suffice and he feared that the Conference would accordingly fall dangerously flat. He therefore drafted a note of his own, for direct submission to the Chancellor. Although he showed it to Bolton, Fisher, Kershaw, and Lucius and paid some regard to their comments, the version sent to No. 11 Downing Street on 3 January 1952 and discussed with Butler on the following day was substantially unaltered from the first draft.

The Chancellor's response was encouraging and he asked for a shortened version to be prepared. This was duly sent to him on 7 January. In its Conference context, it of course contained no hint whatever of an early move to convertibility from a position of weakness and no hint of a floating rate of exchange. These were possibilities that may have been in the back of the mind in Threadneedle Street, but they mostly related to the different contingency of Emergency Action. The note in fact contained an outline plan for achieving a multilateral solution based upon 'houses in order', upon a coordinated programme of Commonwealth Development[13] calculated to strengthen the area as a whole, and upon a restoration of convertibility supported by US assistance in forms that included a stabilisation credit and a review of the whole position of post-war international indebtedness. The Governor suggested that this outline be discussed privately with the Finance Ministers. If they agreed and if the Conference was a success, lines might subsequently be opened with the US Administration and the technical issues might be further explored with Sterling Area central banks. There might then be a further meeting of Finance Ministers towards the end of the year 'with the idea of having something concrete to discuss with the [new] US Administration[14] early in 1953'. The plan might encounter insurmountable difficulties and come to nothing. But this should not inhibit exploration with the Commonwealth and later with the US. Vigorous action on the immediate front would lose half its effect unless the Commonwealth could be persuaded that 'we have faith and ideas about the longer term and that we want to work out future arrangements *jointly* with them'. In view of subsequent events, one particular paragraph deserves quotation in full.

> It is obvious, for a variety of reasons, that no big long-term plans involving a new approach to sterling–dollar relations can be put into operation in 1952. Even if further large-scale aid were in sight, it would do no good for the Sterling Area to undertake new commitments before their internal inflationary positions have been corrected and their current balance of

---

[13] The Bank's espousal of this cause was slightly out of character. The record suggests that it may have been influenced by the ideas of Sir Edgar Whitehead, then Finance Minister of Southern Rhodesia, whose Economic Adviser was Sir Gordon Munro, an old friend from earlier post-war episodes. Whitehead/Munro ideas for a Commonwealth Investment Corporation were sketched in a long telegram from Salisbury to the Commonwealth Relations Office dated 20 December 1951.   [14] 1952 was Presidential Election Year.

payments put into reasonable shape. Without internal stability and the prospect of current balance of payments equilibrium, ideas of convertibility, stabilisation loans, etc., are premature. Moreover this is clearly a difficult year in which to hope for a fundamental new approach from USA. In 1952 the Sterling Area must therefore concentrate on putting its various houses in order.

The Commonwealth Conference opened in London on 8 January. A series of meetings between officials lasted until the 11th and was succeeded by Ministerial discussions that lasted until the 21st. From the outset it was clear that the visiting delegations would not be content with concentration on short-term measures for meeting the immediate balance of payments problem. They demanded discussion of longer-term remedies for the tendency of the Sterling Area to run into recurrent crises. The Australian officials, supported by the New Zealanders and blessed by the Canadians, argued for an outline programme on rather the same lines as that submitted to the Chancellor by the Governor.[15] First of all, houses must be put in order and kept in order. Secondly there would have to be a concurrent approach to the US for financial assistance to underpin a restoration of convertibility and for long-term development capital. A convincing programme of this kind would re-establish confidence in sterling and open the way to inflows of private capital from outside the Sterling Area. The Ceylon representatives went further and proposed replacing the informal mechanism of the Area with a sterling payments union, complete with quotas, rules, and an initial distribution of the central reserves among the members. The Rhodesians pressed their demand for a new organisation for Commonwealth development.

At the beginning of the Ministerial meetings the Chancellor went a long way towards accepting the Australian proposals, though he stressed the absolutely vital importance of short-term corrective action. Subsequent talks endorsed the views expressed at official level and led to the formation of two working parties, one on development and the other on convertibility, which were to report within weeks and lay a basis for continuing work. At the penultimate session Sir Arthur Salter[16] (UK Minister of State for

---

[15] This was not a coincidence. The Governor had developed a close acquaintance with the authorities in Australia and New Zealand. Important official visitors from those countries usually called to see him when in London. Earlier in 1951 he had attended a meeting of Sterling Area Governors in Sydney and had also had discussions in Canberra and Wellington. He was therefore in a good position to form accurate and up-to-date judgements about antipodean attitudes to the future of sterling. He would also have benefited from Kershaw's long experience.

[16] *Salter, James Arthur, 1st Baron 1953, PC, GBE, KCB (1881–1975)*. Educated Oxford High School and Brasenose College, Oxford. Director, Economic and Finance Section League of Nations 1919–20 and 1922–31, Gladstone Professor of Political Theory and Institutions,

Economic Affairs) spelt out the now familiar preconditions for restoring convertibility and added, unexpectedly, that it would also be necessary at some later stage to decide whether restoration should be accompanied by a fixed or floating exchange rate. A fluctuating rate with the support of the EEA might be the best solution.[17]

In the two weeks immediately following the Conference the Governor pursued his ideas for a 'Commonwealth development body', with some support from visiting Ministers who called on him in Threadneedle Street (e.g. New Zealand's Holland). He also kept an eye on the working party on convertibility chaired by Salter. The report of this group was signed on 9 February. It expounded at greater length and with much less clarity the outlines already explained by the Australians and, earlier, by the Governor. On exchange-rate policy it was obscure, though it contained a pregnant sentence to the effect that circumstances could arise in which 'a decision has to be taken...on the immediate action necessary to deal with a sudden emergency, and it is possible that in such circumstances prior consultation may not be practicable'. However, the views of the Bank on exchange-rate policy, *taken in the context of a multilateral solution*, remained hostile to a floating rate. In a paper sent to Salter and Brittain on 25 January, with the Governor's approval, Bolton argued as follows:

> There is, however, one price which must not be brought under the general principle of free market movements; that is the sterling–dollar rate. The crisis of inconvertibility is basically but one of the manifestations of the ebb in public confidence in the money system throughout the world. The effects of this in more advanced degree can be observed in France and elsewhere in the collapse of capital formation and the sterilisation of savings in secret hoards. We feel that the interests of the UK and of the Commonwealth will best be served by a sterling convertible into all foreign currencies at rates based on $2.80 = £1. Indeed, it is questionable whether all present

---

Oxford University 1934–44, MP (Independent), Oxford University 1937–50, Parliamentary Secretary to Ministry of Shipping 1939–41, Joint Parliamentary Secretary to Ministry of War Transport 1941, Head of British Merchant Shipping Mission, Washington, 1941–3, Senior Deputy Director-General, UNRRA 1944, Chancellor of the Duchy of Lancaster 1945, Chairman, Advisory Council, IBRD 1947–8, MP (Conservative) Ormskirk 1951–3, Minister of State for Economic Affairs 1951–2, Minister of Materials 1952–3. Fellow of All Souls College, Oxford.

[17] Salter was shortly to prove a firm opponent of the Robot plan for emergency action that included floating-rate convertibility; so who persuaded or allowed him to suggest a fluctuating rate, admittedly in the longer-term context, at a plenary session of Commonwealth Finance Ministers? As Otto Clarke must by then have been drafting his pre-Robot paper on floating-rate convertibility (circulated on 25 January), it may be that he and Rowan had been talking to Butler and Salter on the subject. The idea of a floating rate had also been raised in Cabinet earlier in January. Its origin may have been Lyttelton, Colonial Secretary and a strong supporter of floating rates.

members of the Sterling Area would be prepared to maintain their membership if sterling were subject to wide fluctuations in terms of the US dollar. If sterling is to avoid following the same course as the French franc (whether under convertibility or under nominal inconvertibility), maintenance of a stable exchange rate must be recognised as a prime object of high policy.

As late as 4 February, in the record of a conversation with Salter about the draft Report on convertibility, the Governor wrote: 'I noticed that the sentence about maintaining fixed rates had been dropped from the Report. I thought that some reference to the importance of stability was necessary.' But the context was now undergoing a sudden tidal change. The Treasury was drafting a paper on Emergency Action and the Bank was on the brink of making proposals for the crash introduction of floating-rate convertibility and the blocking of sterling balances.

A second Commonwealth Conference, held in the late autumn of 1952, agreed on the outline of a Collective Approach to convertibility, this time including the other members of the EPU. The formulation of that approach benefited from the dramatic episode described in the next section and from the ensuing Whitehall debate. But its basis had been laid a year earlier as a result of debate in the Bank rather than the Treasury and as set out in the Governor's note to the Chancellor of the Exchequer early in January 1952. It belonged to the category of grand multilateral solutions, which in the event prove impossible to achieve in full. But along with the reordering of domestic monetary policy and the reopening of the exchange market, the Governor's outline plan and its acceptance by the Chancellor completed the clearing of the decks. The frustrating world of the tired and dispirited Attlee Government was already a fading memory. Cobbold must have felt he had at last entered into his rightful inheritance.

(b) EMERGENCY ACTION

On 4 January 1952 Lord Brand sent to Arthur Salter a confidential Report on Sterling Area Policy prepared by a study group at the Royal Institute of International Affairs (Chatham House), a group set up on Salter's own initiative. Brand himself had been the Chairman and the members had included Professor Robbins, Geoffrey Crowther, Professor Paish, Professor Mansergh, and J. R. Cuthbertson (head of economic intelligence at Lazards). The contents of its Report were unexcitingly orthodox, except for a recommendation that the Treasury should draw up a contingency plan in case orthodox remedial measures to deal with the current difficulties proved too little or too late. The blocking of the balances of the Sterling Area or the abandonment of a fixed rate of exchange were highly disagreeable to contemplate; but the 'degree of disadvantage' should be considered in advance so as to avoid an unconsidered decision at the eleventh hour. This was good advice. But the Treasury did not respond until the end of the month, when it concluded that the emergency was already close at hand.

A copy of the Chatham House Report found its way to the Bank and the suggestions about blocking and floating were discussed by Fisher in a note circulated on 24 January. Unilateral blocking would amount to repudiation and would 'destroy sterling as an international currency for reserve and trade purposes'. In his view, therefore, blocking would have to be done by consent. Owing to the severity of the crisis, it might have to be accompanied by a floating of the exchange rate and a prolonged depreciation, unattractive though this would be for the international status of sterling. The floating rate would also entail non-resident convertibility. Fisher concluded, with useful insight: 'Crisis measures postulated above might wreck the ship if adopted too soon, while on the other hand they might be useless if adopted too late, and result merely in the quicker demise of sterling as an international currency.'

Though in the meantime the Chancellor asked his officials for thought to be given to emergency action, the Chatham House Report was followed on 25 January by a seminal Treasury paper on convertibility, written by Otto Clarke and addressed only to Rowan and to other colleagues in the Overseas Finance Division of the Treasury. No copy survives in the Bank, nor any written reference to it. Whether it was shown to Bolton or Lucius there are no means of telling, but in essence it adopted and adapted most of the positive reasoning previously deployed by the latter, but not accepted in the Bank, in favour of floating-rate convertibility. A two-world solution, based on sterling, was no longer practical politics. Other countries, including the independent members of the Sterling Area, would not agree to it. Nor could the present set of arrangements be preserved for long. Cheap-sterling operations, together with the need to increase the invisible earnings of the UK, made it necessary to restore convertibility. Yet likely storms over the years ahead made it unrealistic to suppose that progress towards an objective of fixed-rate convertibility could be both steady and sufficient. Clarke then suggested that fixed-rate convertibility for non-residents could be restored if the sterling balances of non-sterling countries were firmly blocked (except for genuine working balances) and if sterling credit was made very tight indeed. Quantitative restrictions on imports of non-sterling goods would continue but would become non-discriminatory. By implication, discrimination in the UK's favour by non-sterling countries would also cease and UK exports would be exposed to the full force of US, Japanese, and German competition. Until British exports became fully competitive there would be a heavy loss of reserves. This might suggest a big loan from the US to tide the UK over; but such a loan would be of no use because it would in practice be squandered. In addition to this particular problem there was a terrible dilemma posed by the Sterling Area. One possibility was, in effect, to wind it up and treat its members exactly the same as everyone else – with blocked balances, outward exchange control by the UK, and full convertibility. This, however, would imply the loss of a very large protected market, adding greatly to the already heavy burden of adjustment forced on the British economy. Yet the alternative, retention of the Sterling Area status quo, meant the Area 'working 100% with us and making big adjustments voluntarily, which would be very painful and difficult'.

At this point floating the rate came to Clarke's intellectual rescue. For it seemed to get round the problem of the inadequacy of reserves while at the same time enabling prompt variations in the exchange rate to set up equilibrating pressures on the UK and the other members of the Sterling Area. Like Lucius, he made much of the contrast between prompt adjustment encouraged in this way and the delayed adjustment-by-crisis that was in practice a feature inherent in a fixed-rate regime. 'We can', he lamented, 'lose $1,500 million of gold without anybody noticing it at all – and no adjustment until the Government decrees it; and then it is the Government's fault, imposing artificial restrictions, and the *real* conditions of life go on as before.' If the rate had been floating down during the preceding six months, 'we should now have been in great pain, but adjustment would have been going on'. Clarke admitted to formidable difficulties that had to be set against the advantages of floating. Firstly, Sterling Area economies had such deep-rooted structural problems that the exchange rate might fall very low indeed and create 'internal instability on a self-defeating scale'. Secondly, the continued existence of exchange controls was likely to produce a poor and unstable exchange market. Thirdly, there was the risk that the Sterling Area would fall apart because some members would stay with a fixed parity against the dollar and consequently float against sterling. Nonetheless, Clarke concluded that it might be possible to get together a scheme for floating-rate convertibility that could be put into operation at a fairly early date. 'There are terrific risks in all this, but if we have blocked balances effectively, and are adopting a *really* scarce money policy, and the Sterling Area is taking it all seriously, it might be a starter. It may be technically quite impossible. On the other hand, I cannot see how we can hope to get convertibility with a fixed rate within a measurable time, and there are very good reasons to suppose that the Sterling Area cannot continue for a very long period with sterling inconvertible.'

It was one of those papers that fairly deploys all or most of the relevant arguments and hits out at the reader with great rhetorical force, but relies for its conclusion on the personal mood of the author. Clarke was in a pessimistic and heroic mood. Things were not going to get any better by themselves, new Government or not. The external monetary status quo, meantime, would progressively weaken or disintegrate. Better, then, to break out into entirely new ground, with all the undoubted risks involved, than sit about waiting for the walls to fall in. Maybe people would then behave better. Revolutions are sometimes worthwhile and no good revolutionary worries too much about what happens afterwards.

In this case the revolutionary cause was assisted by the unexciting conclusions of an otherwise stirring paper entitled 'Emergency Action', which Clarke also drafted and which Rowan forwarded to the Chancellor on 8 February. It had been prepared in consultation with Bolton and, very late in the day, with Robert Hall. The paper predicted that the reserves would fall below $1,600 million by the end of March and below $1,400 million by April, with little prospect of much early recovery. If the short-run payments objectives of the UK and the rest of the Sterling Area were achieved and if internal policy measures succeeded in restoring confidence, it might be possible to ride out the storm. But the paper warned that if these favourable factors did not prevail: 'We should be in a desperate situation. The exhaustion of reserves would then depreciate the pound under the most unfavourable conditions. This would inevitably mean the dissolution of the Sterling Area and the end of sterling as an international currency. In this situation, without effective reserves, we should have to say that there could be no more drawing on the reserves and that everyone would have to fend for themselves as best they could. We should ourselves be faced with a major disruption of the economy...Facing such risks, we clearly cannot allow events to take their course, in the hope that fortune will favour us.' The paper went on to reject devaluation because of the wrecking effect on confidence of a second downward step within three years. Also rejected was any blocking of sterling balances. Further import cuts, including cancellation of commitments, might be possible but were not much favoured. External borrowing would be a possibility only if one could be sure that the emergency would in all its essentials be overcome by other means; and in any case only a relatively small amount could be borrowed from the IMF (requiring American consent), while the EEA's dollar portfolio ought not to be pledged or sold except *in extremis*. Direct American assistance, as recent experience showed, could not be relied upon. Therefore all really depended upon domestic policy, meaning a very tough set of measures in the Budget and a tightening of monetary policy. This could be followed by drawing on the IMF and obtaining an Export–Import Bank credit from the US. The paper also particularly stressed the need for further cuts in defence expenditure, for curtailing the Government's plans for the expansion of residential construction, for cutting food rations, and for the adoption of a programme to reduce fuel consumption and increase fuel production.

The drafter of this paper was already a convert to floating-rate convertibility. Hence, presumably, its unappealing advocacy of standing firm, in a redoubt of politically unpalatable domestic measures, against the threat of an imminent and ultimate catastrophe described in brief but frightening terms. In reality, as all disaster managers come to realise, the ultimate economic disaster almost never occurs. There is almost always some way through. It might have been appropriate in this case to present a two- or even three-stage plan of flexible response. The first stage might have been construction of the redoubt. The next stage might have been a fall-back, if the redoubt were about to be overcome, and could have been some form of floating-rate convertibility. The third stage might have been a programme of negotiations through which the US, the independent members of the Sterling Area, and the continental Europeans sought somehow to restore order and bring the UK back into the fold. But although traces of such a flexible response appear in proposals subsequently put forward by the Bank and by the Treasury, they were not well presented and the Government was not advised to manage the disaster in that way. Rowan and Clarke were in fact on the brink of opting for revolution, for making virtue out of necessity. They were about to offer floating-rate convertibility both as a solution to the external emergency and as a basis for making an entirely fresh start with external financial policy and with macro-economic policy generally. This was bound to have some political attraction, especially for Churchill. It would be novel and exciting and not just an intensified version of stale Crippsian austerity, even though it itself entailed a heavy dose of that treatment.

Since the Treasury had, so to speak, declared a state of exchange emergency, the Bank was duty bound to respond with a plan for appropriate external monetary action. It duly did so, presenting an operational case rather than a set of macro-economic arguments. On 6 February 1952, while Clarke's 'Emergency Action' was still being revised in the Treasury, a single unsigned page containing eight brief numbered items was circulated in the Bank. The recipients were the Governor, Bolton, and the Chief Cashier, but its contents reflected much of the thinking that had taken place in the Bank over the previous two years. Its authorship is unknown,[18] but it sketched the bare bones of a plan for the restoration of non-resident convertibility accompanied by a tightening of monetary policy, the blocking of 80–90% of all sterling balances followed by their long-term funding (except for use in financing approved Commonwealth development), the merging of the Sterling Area with all other areas for exchange control purposes, the widening of the spread around the $2.80 parity to $2.40 to $3.20, the pledging of the EEA securities as collateral for a dollar loan from commercial sources, and an attempt to persuade the Americans to put IMF resources at the disposal of the UK. On the evening of the same day the Governor recorded in his diary: 'I had a talk with Sir Leslie Rowan about his memorandum on emergency action and more drastic ideas which were circulating in our minds. I told him I was going to have a talk with the Chancellor and that we should probably be talking to them further in the next week or so.' On the following day the Governor had a private talk with Bridges about Budget plans and also about the sterling situation generally. He then talked with the Chancellor 'at home after dinner', and it was left that the Bank would try to 'produce some ideas (rather than recommendations) about sterling in general some time next week'. On the next day, 8 February, he saw Deshmukh, (now Indian Minister of Finance), and recorded: 'We agreed that the outlook was awkward and that beyond a certain point there was no advantage in sitting still and waiting for the deluge.' Bridges was seen again on the 11th and Rowan on the 12th, when the latter was shown a draft note for the Chancellor. This had been written by the Governor himself and met with Rowan's emphatic approval. A final version was handed to Bridges on 13 February for onward transmission to Butler.

Of the papers written in favour of floating-rate convertibility at this time, Cobbold's note to the Chancellor was the most cool and level-headed. He began by reviewing current policy and by emphasising the need to form a judgement within the next few weeks, in the light of Budget plans and all other relevant factors, whether there was reasonable hope that the sterling system could survive the next eighteen months on the basis of that policy. He went on to stress that forming such a judgement and taking any necessary action had to be a UK responsibility. 'We have', he wrote, 'a fiduciary responsibility towards overseas holders of sterling. This responsibility is particularly clear in relation to colonial territories whose

---

[18] From subsequent circulation lists it can be inferred that the author could have been Fisher, Parsons, or Thompson-McCausland. His later collaboration with Bolton and the technical breadth of the outline suggest that the author was Fisher, writing under instructions from Bolton.

policy we direct and to a somewhat lesser extent in relation to independent members of the Sterling Area who keep their reserves in sterling and who by and large have played in with our general policy.' If the judgement were negative, it followed that the UK authorities had a duty to take early action to protect the currency 'however radical such action may seem'. The first thing to do in any event was for the UK and the other countries in the Sterling Area to put their houses in order. This objective covered the whole field of domestic policy and the Governor assumed that the forthcoming Budget, together with action in the rest of the Commonwealth, would work towards it. But would this be enough? Unfortunately, sterling was under a cloud for several reasons other than the prevailing balance of payments deficit. Firstly, overseas sight liabilities were far too big in relation to UK reserves. Nobody would really believe that sterling was immune from recurrent crises until either the sight liabilities had been cut or the central reserves had grown to a figure that could clearly cope with them. Secondly, inconvertibility made sterling unwelcome to non-resident holders, encouraged the growth of cheap-sterling operations, and clearly threw 'continuous and growing doubt on our ability to maintain our official rate'.[19] Thirdly, there was straightforward scepticism about the UK's ability to hold the $2.80 rate. If, accordingly, a negative judgement were to be reached about the viability of the sterling system as currently organised, a determined effort would have to be made to deal with these matters, and this would be in addition to the internal measures that were in any case required. 'This would be a most disagreeable process for us and everyone else, but is greatly to be preferred to waiting for worse disasters to be imposed on us and them by the facts of life.' There followed a short list of the essential features of the disagreeable process, along the lines sketched in the unsigned note of 6 February. Firstly, there would have to be a freezing or funding of 80–90% of all sterling balances, subject to arrangements being made, particularly in the Sterling Area, to allow banking machinery to carry on. Provision might also be made for Sterling Area frozen balances to be released over a period to help meet the sterling content of Commonwealth development plans. Secondly, unfrozen and subsequently accruing sterling in the hands of non-residents of the Sterling Area and of monetary authorities in the Sterling Area should be freely transferable throughout the world 'and thus enjoy some degree of convertibility'. Thirdly, and with qualifications, the sterling–dollar rate might be allowed to move over a much wider range. Fourthly, ways and means would have to be sought to strengthen the reserves (presumably

---

[19] Principal cheap-sterling rates at this juncture were averaging round $2.40, or 15% discount on the official parity.

through a credit from US banks and possibly also by a drawing on the Fund).

The Governor's assent to a policy of limited floating, in contrast to his recent opposition to it, was expressed as follows:

> The sterling–dollar rate (and consequently sterling gold price) would have to be reviewed. For reasons given elsewhere devaluation to a new fixed rate has been ruled out as a contribution to our difficulties. For similar reasons we have hitherto always stood out against a floating rate for sterling which, until the fundamental troubles are being firmly dealt with, could only mean progressive depreciation. If however a New Deal could be envisaged, including determined internal measures in the United Kingdom and throughout the Sterling Area, and also radical changes in our exchange system on the above lines, a sterling–dollar rate floating over a much wider range than at present around a fixed parity might prove the best solution and might be a necessary protection for the degree of transferability and/or convertibility envisaged.

Before concluding with an important passage about the timing of the operation, Cobbold again warned about its dangers. The difficulties, both political and technical were 'prodigious' and nobody could predict its outcome. 'If, however, we form the judgement that the alternative is a wasting disease, we ought to face the difficulties, take the decisions and do our best to carry the Commonwealth with us.'

As to timing, a comprehensive plan could not be prepared and agreed with the Sterling Area Dominions in time for presentation along with the Budget on 4 March. Presentation with the Budget would also mean an almost impossible overload both for the presenter and for the recipients. The best course, therefore, would be to carry through the domestic measures first and immediately afterwards present to the Dominions the picture as it then looked, together with the proposals for drastic action. If the immediate impact of the Budget were favourable, this would give a good opportunity for taking action between the Budget date and the publication early in April of the reserves loss in the first quarter. This last date had now to be regarded as an uncomfortable zero hour and 'we must look to the publication of those figures with grave concern unless action in every possible field has been taken before that date'. The Governor did not concern himself with the possibility that the response to the Budget might be sufficiently favourable to render drastic external action unnecessary, or at least untimely or impolitic. Yet if that response did prove favourable, it was not very likely that the Government would pursue, to use Cobbold's words, a prodigiously difficult and most disagreeable course whose outcome nobody could predict.

It is important to note that the Governor's plan contained wider spreads around a fixed parity, not the abandonment of a parity. In subsequent discussions with the Chancellor, Cobbold placed great emphasis on this, arguing that the objective must be stability and that the wider spreads were not to be used as a cover for progressive depreciation. He evidently saw them in strictly operational terms. Research has not revealed any written debate in the Bank about the merits or otherwise of very wide spreads around a fixed parity as a technique of exchange-market management in conditions of convertibility. As was related in the section on the reopening of the London Exchange Market, there was indeed some debate in November 1951 about the merits of going to the two-cent spreads from the prevailing half-cent, the argument in favour of the former being that it would help combat the build-up of large open positions either way. Between the successful reopening of the market in December 1951 and the discussions on emergency action in February 1952, the Bank seems to have extended the argument in the context of convertibility and concluded in favour of *un*published spreads as wide as 15% either side of parity. This brought the managerial argument for such semi-floating into the same ground as the macro-economic argument for greater exchange flexibility as an aid to the process of adjustment. But that did not mean that advocates of the former agreed with the latter; and the confusing division between the two did not help the subsequent presentation of the plan to Ministers.

An extended version of the plan outlined in Cobbold's note was drafted by Bolton in collaboration with Fisher and with the Governor himself. It included such refinements as the reopening of a free gold market in London together with that of other commodity markets. More important, any idea of imposing exchange control on the Sterling Area and merging it with all other areas for control purposes had been dropped. The new version was given to Rowan on 16 February and circulated in the Bank to the Governor, Bolton, Beale, Parsons, Fisher, and Lucius. Neither Mynors nor Allen, the Bank's two professional economists, seem to have been consulted.[20] On 19 February the Governor talked the matter over first with Bridges and later with Butler, referring also to Budget proposals and to a move in Bank Rate. He then went on to a fateful dinner with the Prime Minister, the Chancellor, and the Leader of the House of Commons (Crookshank). There was some agreement that emergency action along

---

[20] By his own clear and emphatic account, sent to the author early in 1989, Allen was not informed of the plan until 25 February. Hall's diary, however, records him being informed as early as 21 February (*The Robert Hall Diaries 1947–53*, ed. Alec Cairncross, London, Unwin Hyman, 1989, p. 205).

the lines suggested by the Governor was probably necessary.[21] Equally important, however, was the Prime Minister's insistence, supported by Crookshank, that reference would have to be made to the plan in the Budget so as to make it part of a comprehensive solution. This necessarily meant announcing it in the Budget Speech as a set of decisions with immediate effect. As it had already been announced that the Budget would be brought forward to 4 March, from early April, the Prime Minister's insistence required the scrapping of the Bank's suggested timetable – action in April – and its immediate replacement by a crash programme for unilateral action on 4 March. This was in fact wholly impracticable; and a few days later the Budget had to be postponed to 11 March in order to allow even minimal time for this crash programme to be carried through. But it still meant that Cabinet approval would have to be obtained by the end of February, after prior discussion among a group of Ministers most closely concerned. This in turn left no proper time for full elaboration of the plan, for the customary thorough discussion at official level under the chairmanship of Bridges, or for the subsequent submission to Ministers of a considered view on the bald proposals that had been originated in the Bank, had been accepted by Overseas Finance, and were admitted to be revolutionary and highly controversial. The inevitable result was a period of confusion in which the advocates of Robot, as the plan was now code-named, appeared as plotters of a revolutionary coup that could be stopped only by mobilisation of support from any available quarter.[22] The Economic Section under Hall and the Central Economic Planning Staff under Plowden were both astonished, not to say outraged, that Ministers should be considering so radical a plan, affecting the heart of macro-economic policy, without full professional economic advice. They were supported by Salter and were shortly to be joined by MacDougall, Economic Adviser to Lord Cherwell, Paymaster General, and the Prime Minister's personal adviser on economic subjects as well as, for example, nuclear energy.

Not for the first time the Bank's case was to suffer from lack of professional economic input in Threadneedle Street and from exposure to the full blast of professional criticism, this time almost impromptu, from a group of Whitehall economists whose appreciation of the Bank's particular operational concerns was imperfect to say the least. On this particular

---

[21] Cobbold recalled in later years that Churchill was attracted by the idea of 'setting the pound free'.
[22] Donald MacDougall. *Don and Mandarin: Memoirs of an Economist* (London, John Murray, 1987). Edwin Plowden, *An Industrialist in the Treasury* (London, André Deutsch, 1989), and *The Robert Hall Diaries 1947–53* tell a story of intensive lobbying by the opponents of Robot, while the revolutionaries themselves relied upon surprise, secrecy, and the inherent authority of the Chancellor.

occasion, moreover, the Bank's case was damaged by the way in which the Overseas Finance Division of the Treasury presented the supporting economic as well as operational arguments to Ministers. Furthermore, the Bank itself, running to the Governor's initial timetable for action in April, had not had sufficient time to work through the technical details of its own proposals. Perhaps also because of its tendency to underestimate the politico-economic importance of the EPU, the Bank had only just begun to think through the European implications of its plan and the complex technicalities of UK disengagement from the Payments Union whose credit had recently proved so valuable a supplement to the disappearing exchange reserves. These implications were hurriedly considered during the last week in February and a plan for a very short transitional continuation of UK participation in the EPU was agreed. There also emerged a set of ideas for splitting Western Europe in two and forming a sterling-oriented club out of one part. But these were still in a formative stage at the end of the month and were not put to Ministers. Clarke, using to the full his experience as a journalist and drafting at breakneck speed a seventeen-page Ministerial paper for the Chancellor to circulate to his colleagues, simply put his head down and charged through the European difficulty with sentences typical of the level to which excited officials were now reduced by the lack of adequate time. 'Both the EPU and the liberalisation of intra-European trade are in any case near to collapse, but our becoming convertible would kill them altogether. Indeed, with sterling on a floating rate, each of the European countries would have to reconsider its fundamental economic policies, and new alignments would probably result. This process would be bound to create the need for adjustments of a painful kind while the transition was taking place, and this would have some political and military importance.'

Nor, by the time the Treasury started drafting its paper for Ministers, had the Bank become wholly clear about the proposals it had put forward for the Sterling Area. It had been agreed with the Treasury that the machinery of the Area should so far as possible be retained intact. There would be no extension of UK exchange control that would place a barrier between the UK and the Scheduled Territories. Without such control there could be no legal blocking and no forced segregation of balances into blocked accounts and convertible accounts, a procedure that it was intended to apply to 90% of all the balances of non-residents (except US and Canadian holdings). Instead it would be necessary to devise a plan for the voluntary but prompt further tying-up of some identifiable part of the official balances of Sterling Area countries, amounting to 80% of the total. Use of the untied portion would be subject to the same understandings as before, while private balances would remain freely usable within the Area. To make the operation look more convincing to foreign opinion ('tying-up', as has been recounted, had not got a very good record) there would also be a funding of Treasury Bills held, for example, by the Commonwealth Bank of Australia, into short-term bonds. In the version of Robot put to Ministers on 22 February it was stated that the independent members of the Area would be asked to agree to 'immobilise' 80% of their official balances and to maintain a fixed exchange rate with sterling. In the absence of agreement they would have to leave the Area and become subject to the new arrangements, including blocking, to be imposed on non-residents. All this would be followed in a matter of weeks by a fresh Commonwealth Conference, specially summoned to sort things out. In subsequent discussions with the Treasury the Bank continued to favour the funding proposals, but it seems to have had second thoughts about a uniform 'immobilisation' supported by threat of expulsion. It realised that in practice there would inevitably ensue some kind of country-by-country negotiation, at political level. This would not have been feasible in the time available, particularly in view of the imminent Conference. In the timetable subsequently constructed the countries concerned were to be given five days in which to agree or not agree. The most that might then have been achieved in practice, given British political objections to expulsion on the one hand and Commonwealth political objections to 80% immobilisation on the other, would have been some very interim understandings. But in the event Robot was cancelled before these familiar questions could be resolved.

Clarke's draft was circulated by the Chancellor to a small group of Ministers, including Cherwell, on 22 February and was discussed by them on the same day. It frequently resorted to the striking and often emotive phraseology of the sort quoted above. In structure it was in effect an amalgam of Clarke's own paper on convertibility circulated in Overseas Finance a month earlier and the operational plan put forward by the Bank in Cobbold's note to Butler and in the longer paper subsequently sent to Rowan by Bolton. To this Clarke added the suggestion of another Commonwealth Conference for the end of March. This was to be followed by a London Conference with the US, Canada, and the other members of the OEEC 'in order to consider world economic policy in the light of our decisions'. Parts of the amalgam alarmed the Governor. He had come round to accepting wider dealing margins as an appropriate operational technique for managing sterling in conditions of convertibility without large reserves. But he had not bought the supposed positive economic merits of a floating rate as an equilibrating force operating on the economy at large. He therefore did not like a phrase in Clarke's paper about taking the strain on the rate instead of the reserves and noted on his own copy (22 February): 'I told the Chancellor that I thought the argumentation good, but that there was much too much "floating". We must have a high degree of stability.' Two days later he made his position quite clear in two further notes to Butler and Bridges. 'The wider limits (2·40–3·20, but not publicly announced) must be supported by every possible measure to strengthen the real and psychological position of the currency. If not so regarded and so supported, a "floating rate" is a polite name for progressive devaluation and would be even worse than devaluation to a new fixed rate... An international currency must have a high degree of stability. Unless we make this objective clear, we are wasting our time in trying to make sterling acceptable internationally by giving it a degree of convertibility... It is most important that a decision to float the rate should be presented in this way, both for home opinion, US (and IMF) and foreign opinion generally, and not least for the Sterling Area, who will not be attracted by a currency which looks likely to fluctuate all over the place and to "take on the rate" any absence of necessary action in other fields.' So much for the benign equilibrating force that Lucius in the Bank and Clarke in the Treasury found so alluring.

Opposition to the Chancellor's proposals, in the Treasury and elsewhere, now began to take shape rapidly. The Economic Section, in its turn working at top speed,[23] admitted that it was impossible to take the risk of continuing with present arrangements completely unchanged and drafted an alternative scheme for emergency action, which was designed to take care of the sterling balances without at the same time moving to floating-rate convertibility. The economists felt the consequences of the latter would be an abandonment of commitments made in the 1944 White Paper on Employment Policy and the abrogation of external commitments embodied in the Bretton Woods Agreements. It was a recipe for disaster. No store was set by Clarke's proposed Conferences. Because of continuing dollar shortage, floating-rate convertibility would cause discrimination against UK exports and unemployment in the UK. The exchange rate would move sharply downwards and risk serious domestic, financial, and political instability, which would in turn worsen the external problem. Abroad, the likely consequence would be a mutual cutting of imports and a downward spiral in world trade. It was accordingly essential to maintain the exchange rate at $2.80. To this end, the Economic Section strongly

---

[23] Robert Hall recorded later: 'On Saturday 23rd February I prepared with the assistance of 5 members of the Economic Section a memorandum and gave copies of this to Armstrong for the Chancellor, Strath (Plowden's Deputy) and Rowan with a copy for Bolton.'

supported the range of domestic measures set out in the Treasury's earlier paper on Emergency Action and added a set of proposals for sharply reducing rather than increasing the existing degree of external convertibility. The balances of non-sterling countries would be blocked and new accruals would be expendable only in payments to the Sterling Area. This would mean leaving the EPU; but with fixed exchange rates it would be possible 'to form a new Union based on credit margins with no gold points'. Sterling Area balances would not be blocked but together with fresh accruals would be made expendable only within the Area. To start them off, the independent members would be given a small working balance of dollars from the central reserves. These suggestions found little or no favour outside the Economic Section. They amounted to a two-world solution that would have rendered sterling virtually unacceptable as a means of international payment and done considerably more damage to the Sterling Area than the voluntary immobilisation and the floating-rate convertibility proposed by Overseas Finance and the Bank.

Nothing more was heard of this alternative plan at this stage and Hall next joined forces with Cherwell, Salter, and Plowden to constitute an informal grouping that argued and lobbied against any emergency action on the balances, the exchange rate, or convertibility and advocated reliance on a tough Budget, a high Bank Rate, and if need be a modest drawing on the IMF. There was also the Foreign Office to be taken into the reckoning. Since Eden was at a NATO conference in Lisbon, Brittain of the Treasury and Berthoud of the Foreign Office were sent out on 22 February to brief him about the plan.[24] Difficult and delicate negotiations had been proceeding for some months, within the framework of NATO, between the US, the UK, France, and West Germany concerning the relationship between the British armed forces and those of the proposed European Defence Community (EDC). An important objective of policy at this time, in the context of the cold war, was to gain French acceptance of the rearmament of West Germany; and the proposed supranational EDC, rather like the ECSC in its special field, was to be the chosen means to this end. The UK, following under Churchill and Eden the policies of limited commitment to new European institutions that were adopted under Bevin and Attlee, made clear its intention not to join the EDC but undertook to guarantee a close relationship with it. The delicate question was whether such a guarantee would satisfy the French and help secure ratification of the EDC treaty by the difficult and unruly French Assembly. Although Eden had little knowledge of economic policy, he must have viewed with

---

[24] Plowden, an opponent of Robot, attended the Conference but returned early, on 24 February.

surprise and alarm a set of proposals for unilateral action by the UK whose own authors advised that it would suddenly destroy the arrangements for intra-European trade and payments that had been so laboriously constructed in 1950. In the context of his negotiations about the EDC such action could hardly have seemed more inappropriate. In any event, he firmly opposed the plan on his return to London and his opposition may well have been a decisive factor in the Cabinet's rejection of it.[25]

But if it was Eden's influence that finally swung the balance, it was Cherwell who levelled it beforehand. Like Churchill himself, though twelve years younger, 'the Prof' was getting tired. He had not wanted to leave, once again, his comfortable life as a Professor of Physics at Oxford. But since he was a courageous man with a deep sense of public duty and a deep attachment to Churchill, he had returned to the Cabinet and had brought MacDougall back to London with him as his economic adviser and assistant. He was made a member of the Economic Policy Committee of the Cabinet and in that capacity was shown the Chancellor's draft memorandum on 22 February. He at once voiced opposition. Temperamentally averse to unquantified economic arguments expressed in emotive and rhetorical terms, he was even more averse to them if they were deployed by high Civil Servants, about whose intellectual habits he could be acid.[26] It was indeed his duty, as special adviser to the Prime Minister, to be a clear-headed and suspicious quantifier; not for nothing was he sometimes called in Whitehall 'The Prime Minister's Adder'. In this particular case the Prof was confronted by a paper that proposed revolutionary external action on the basis of an alarming but necessarily flimsy set of predictions and of a set of arguments that were expressed in a manner that could hardly have been better calculated to arouse his hostility. Worse still, from the Prof's point of view, was the support given to the Chancellor's proposals by the Bank of England. Cherwell was an

---

[25] In his memoirs: *Full Circle* (London, Cassell, 1960) Anthony Eden made no reference to Robot in a chapter entitled 'The Pangs of EDC'. Nor does R. R. James in his *Anthony Eden* (London, Weidenfeld & Nicolson, 1986). Cobbold's own recollection was that he understood at the time that Eden's intervention was the decisive factor.

[26] Early in 1952, as a junior member of his economics staff, I was summoned to his presence and abruptly asked in his best Roman senator style: 'Why do our electricity people build expensive cathedrals round their generators?' I confessed I did not know and was rewarded with a short homily to the effect that large sums of money could be saved by the erection, in substitution for 'cathedrals', of cheap structures that sufficed to protect generators from the weather. He had seen examples in California. I was instructed to look into the matter. I duly did so. But discussions with friendly officials in Fuel and Power were not very helpful and I reported back to the Prof with a number of objections. I was again summoned and this time fixed with a mysterious smile. 'You know what's happening to you, don't you?' 'No Sir', I replied. So he told me, with a sibilant hiss: 'You are getting like one of those c-civil s-servants.'

intellectual and social snob, sometimes to the point of an eccentricity[27] that was endearing to some and enraging to others. Towards bankers he affected an aristocratic disdain. A rich but financially careful man, he can seldom have had much to do with them. They were tradespeople, well enough versed in their commercial pursuits but otherwise ill-educated and not to be trusted with much responsibility in the field of national economic policy. Central bankers were not very different, in his mind, to commercial bankers. He knew little of them and was not disposed to make much effort to understand what they were trying to say. Besides, as he ignorantly told Jacobsson, he thought they were 'not cultivated people'. He never saw the Governor's careful note of 13 February to the Chancellor and he judged, wrongly, that Cobbold was fully identified with the whole of Clarke's draft.[28] He then seemed to imagine that in a blinkered and nostalgic way

[27] The endearingly farcical side was to the fore in his journey to the atomic energy installation at Calder Hall in Cumberland sometime in 1952 or 1953. Telegrams were sent in advance to suitable Dukes who could be relied upon to provide lunch or overnight hospitality for the Prof and his entourage (Private Secretary, Personal Servant, Chauffeur, and emergency supplies of vegetarian food) as they lumbered north and back in his prewar black Packard – cramped in front, cavernously roomy in the back. The Duke of Westminster obliged at Eaton Hall, the Duke of Portland at Welbeck. The Chauffeur lost his way near the latter and it looked as though they might actually be late for lunch. A passing policeman was asked for directions but did not know where Welbeck was. The Prof was outraged. Raising his voice and pointing with his umbrella he said to his secretary: 'Tell him he's a disgrace to the Force.' On another occasion, the Prof's smaller car, a postwar Austin, broke down while motoring near Oxford. His Secretary had the courage to suggest they return to Oxford by bus rather than wait a long time for a hired car. Cherwell recoiled at the very idea, remarking plaintively: 'But if we do that I shall have to get in with all those people.'

[28] In his memoirs, *Don and Mandarin*, MacDougall relates how he and Cherwell used the former's contact with Maurice Allen, his tutor at Balliol in the 1930s. Allen dined with MacDougall at the Reform Club on 25 February, at the latter's invitation, and accompanied him afterwards to No. 11. There, according to MacDougall, he gave him the impression that the Bank was divided over Robot and that the Governor had been persuasively sold the plan by Bolton and Lucius. This purported information, with names omitted, was passed to the Prime Minister by Cherwell on the following day. Allen was an exceptionally discreet man, with a keen appreciation of the loyalty expected by the Bank from its staff. In the course of his talk with MacDougall he was invited to see Cherwell but refused. In his own account of the episode, sent to the athor early in 1989, he relates how he chatted with the former confidentially, economist to economist. He had only recently become aware of the Robot plan and was indignant that it had got to so advanced a stage without adequate discussion, as he saw it, of the economics involved. His inclination was to oppose the plan; and he must have given this impression to MacDougall, who inferred that opinion in the Bank was divided. But Allen was not yet sufficiently established in the main counsels of the Bank to be a reliable observer of them. The documentation of the plan does not record extensive debates about it in Threadneedle Street; and there survives no evidence of divided opinions beyond Allen's own dissent. It is possible, judging from the exchanges recorded at the end of 1951, that Mynors and Kershaw would have been less enthusiastic than Bolton or Lucius. But there is little evidence of their being much involved in Robot. As to the Governor being persuaded by Bolton and Lucius, the record establishes firstly that he did not need persuading once the emergency had been declared by the

the Bank was somehow again seeking to restore past glories of the Victorian era.[29] Accordingly, with MacDougall's help, he proceeded to undermine the Chancellor's plan.

It was not a very difficult job. The Robot memorandum made no secret of the plan's revolutionary intent and of the drastic and painful internal and external consequences that were supposed to follow once it was put into effect, further Conferences or not. For those who did not share the revolutionary ardour, its justification seemed to rest entirely upon the presumed external emergency and the need to act suddenly and unilaterally before the situation slipped further out of control. Accordingly, once that justification was effectively challenged, if only through the convincing offer of a stay of execution, Robot was unlikely to be accepted by a Conservative Cabinet with a small Parliamentary majority,[30] a strong tendency towards consensus politics, and a disinclination to throw unnecessary rocks at the delicate fabric of West European collaboration. Cherwell did in fact challenge it on two main grounds. Firstly, he argued that there was no need to panic. A combination of tough fiscal measures, a Bank Rate of 4%, further import cuts, modest external borrowing, and Sterling Area restraint should in his view suffice both to sustain confidence and to bring the external accounts into balance. Secondly, he argued that the expected depreciation of the exchange rate would make matters worse rather than better. The amount of domestic adjustment required would be increased and the risks of runaway inflation enhanced. In a Minute sent to the Prime Minister on 26 February, supplementing a Cabinet Paper circulated the previous day, he concluded:

> If we follow this policy resolutely I believe we can round the corner, earn universal respect and get a chance to start the long steady task of building up our reserves and making Britain strong again. The other plan proposed, with its floating rate of exchange for the pound and all the dangers implied

Treasury and secondly that he actually did not buy the macro-economic arguments for a floating rate used by Lucius and Clarke. Be all that as it may, the point remains firstly that Cherwell knew so little of the Bank that he had to rely on MacDougall's report of what Allen had said privately and secondly that he did not hesitate to pass such uncorroborated intelligence to No. 10. Allen, who was unaware that Cherwell was drafting a Cabinet paper, reported his own part in all this to the Deputy Governor. The latter approved his refusal to see Cherwell and said: 'He is a Cabinet Minister. If he wishes to receive advice from the Bank he can easily ask for it.'

[29] He certainly used this idea in seeking to influence the Prime Minister against Robot. When Chancellor of the Exchequer, Churchill had heeded the advice of Norman in agreeing to the ill-starred restoration of the gold standard in 1925. But Churchill was very friendly to Cobbold, with whom he had a family connection.

[30] The Conservatives had an overall majority of only sixteen and had actually polled slightly fewer votes than the Labour Party at the Election in October 1951.

in convertibility, means a reckless leap in the dark involving appalling political as well as economic risks at home and abroad in the blind hope that the speculators will see us through.

Robot was discussed at three Cabinet meetings during 28 and 29 February. Ahead of these, the Governor attended a meeting with the Prime Minister, the Foreign Secretary, the Chancellor, and Bridges. He took the opportunity to reiterate the views he had put forward to the Chancellor two weeks earlier but had later modified to take account of the shorter timetable that had been imposed. Tough domestic measures, though essential in any event, would not suffice to hold the situation for very long unless action were taken to reduce the weight of overseas sterling liabilities and to introduce a substantial measure of convertibility accompanied by exchange-rate flexibility. On the point of tactics and timing, the Governor had now accepted that it would be unwise to take the domestic measures first and hope that they would in practice prove to be sufficient, or at least create a less critical situation. For such a procedure carried the evident risk that Robot would then have to be introduced in circumstances of renewed emergency and would imply admission that the earlier measures had failed. It would therefore be better to do both operations at once and to be, as the Governor put it, constructive as well as restrictive. In notes prepared ahead of the meeting he wrote: 'I would hazard a purely personal opinion that while Governments everywhere would be bound to protest, everybody who understands this, particularly in the countries whose life-blood depends on sterling, would heave a sigh of relief.'

But it was not to be. The majority of the Cabinet were men of caution and they were confronted with a gambler's choice. The political and economic risks, domestic and foreign, inherent in Robot were not worth taking if there was a sporting chance that domestic measures would see the Government through the immediate crisis and enable the Bank's special concerns to be considered more thoroughly at greater leisure. Since the Prof and his allies were saying with clarity and conviction that there was such a sporting chance, they won the day. However, the Treasury and the Bank did not lose the war. Ministers seemingly[31] endorsed the view that the Sterling Area could not be preserved indefinitely on a basis of inconvertible sterling and agreed that no opportunity should be lost of moving towards the ultimate goal of convertibility. They also agreed that

---

[31] One says 'seemingly' because the Secretary to the Cabinet recorded them as doing so in an 'uncirculated record' that was not subsequently incorporated in the formal Cabinet Minutes, though it was seen by the Treasury. Whether Cherwell ever saw this record, or agreed it, is not entirely clear. The record would not have been seen in the Bank, though its sense may well have been explained to the Governor by the Treasury.

some action on Robot lines might be taken at a later stage, either if the circumstances became more favourable or if a continuing loss of reserves compelled the Government to take urgent action to protect the currency. For his part, the Governor wrote to the Chancellor a few days later to take note of the Cabinet decision, to express the Bank's hope that the Budget measures would succeed, and to record the Bank's opinion that 'in view of the level of our reserves and the various pressures on the currency, an improvement resulting from the Budget should only be regarded as a breathing space for urgent consideration of comprehensive and constructive measures in the overseas sterling field'. *A fortiori*, if the Budget failed to restore confidence, comprehensive action would immediately be necessary to avert a major disaster. Cobbold followed this up by asking the Prime Minister to allow him to bring a deputation of three non-executive members of the Court 'to lay before you the grave view which is taken, not only by the Court of Directors of the Bank, but also by industrial and commercial circles in the City, of the state of our exchange reserves and the consequent threat to the economic and social life of the country and Commonwealth'. The Prime Minister granted this request and the deputation (Hanbury-Williams, Sanderson, and Piercy) called on No. 10 on 6 March. Introduced by the Governor, who tastefully referred to the Court Minutes of 8 October 1795, when a deputation had called on the younger Pitt in analogous circumstances, they duly delivered their message and stayed talking with Churchill for about an hour. In particular they urged that if the Budget brought about some improvement in external confidence in sterling, this should be taken as an opportunity for further action and not as a reason for delay. Cobbold recorded: 'The Prime Minister appeared to take the points.'

Out of the programme of Emergency Action originally put forward by the Chancellor, there now remained only the Budget measures themselves, including a fresh exchange of telegrams to the principal Sterling Area countries asking for further import cuts consequent upon a further deterioration in their external prospects, a deterioration itself attributable to a further fall in their export prices. The Bank played some part in drafting the appropriate telegrams and doubted whether the response would be favourable. In fact the response was reasonably satisfactory. The countries concerned were now as anxious to conserve their own external reserves as they were to collaborate with the UK to protect the central reserves. Aside from this exercise, and from its crescendo of advocacy in favour of toughness, the Bank's main function was to advise about Bank Rate, carry through the agreed change, and help the Treasury draft the relevant passage in the Budget Speech.

The reordering of monetary policy, described in an earlier section, was still attracting considerable attention. In the financial markets, yields on long-dated gilt-edged stocks had risen nearly $\frac{1}{2}$% by the turn of the year, to $4\frac{1}{4}$% and more. Debenture yields had risen to nearly 5% and new issues had become difficult. The yield on ordinary shares had risen to 6% by January 1952 and the market was depressed by the appearance of several large new issues thought to be brought as a consequence of pressure by the banks on large borrowers with access to the new issue market. An influential article by Wilfred King in the *Financial Times* explained how the reduction in bank liquidity achieved by the special funding operation, together with the scope for engineering further reductions in more orthodox ways, had opened up the possibility of stronger official influence being brought to bear upon bank lending, with consequential effects upon the capital market. This factor, in his view, was in part responsible for the considerable psychological impact of a change in policy that had itself contained only a small rise in short-term interest rates. The other factor responsible for that impact was the simple 'announcement effect'. Notice had been given that a further tightening should be expected if the situation were to require a further tightening of macro-economic policy in general. Since it was evident that the pressure on sterling was continuing and that a strong package of measures was going to be required at the time of the Budget, a further rise in Bank Rate was among the measures that had to be contemplated. Commenting on the trade deficit and the loss of exchange reserves, the *Financial Times* remarked on 12 January that it was 'impossible to overstate the urgency of the situation'. A few days later the Chancellor asked the Governor whether he felt it would be right to raise Bank Rate at the end of the month to coincide with the announcement of hire-purchase controls and of additional import restrictions. The Governor replied that a rise to 3% would merely create further uncertainty about a subsequent move. It would be better to leave the Rate alone until the Budget, when a rise to 4% or $4\frac{1}{2}$% might be recommended. In the meantime the measures already taken should be left to 'work themselves through'; and during the current quarter, when the seasonal Exchequer surplus was augmented by sterling receipts from the EEA (reflecting the reserves loss), the Bank intended to maintain pressure on the liquidity of the clearing banks.[32]

By mid-February, when the plans for emergency external action, at that

---

[32] This looked like being so severe that the Bank actually set in hand a programme of accelerated buying-in of the next gilt maturity. But in the event the Exchequer surplus proved to be smaller than forecast and clearing bank liquidity did not fall below 31·6% against a conventional but flexible minimum of 30%.

stage contemplated for early April, were taking shape, the Governor decided to offer a provisional recommendation about Bank Rate in the context of the Budget then timed for 4 March. He did so in a note sent to the Chancellor on 13 February, the same day as he delivered his main paper on floating-rate convertibility. A week or so earlier he had asked Niemeyer for an opinion on the subject and received in response a single page of distilled thought. Discussing a move in Bank Rate within a general framework of interest-rate flexibility was at this time something of a lost art. Neither of the Governors nor any of the Executive Directors or senior officials, with the possible exception of Peppiatt, had had any close involvement in the Bank Rate discussions that went on prior to the long period of 2% that began in June 1932. Niemeyer, still on the Court though non-executive, would have had such experience and it was characteristic of Cobbold to tap it. Another source of Nestorian wisdom was Peacock, who was no longer on the Court but was still available for occasional advice. This veteran of the 1931 crisis was consulted about Robot and wrote to the Governor on 29 February from his room at Barings: 'Unless the action is taken I understand that creeping paralysis is almost inevitable. Creeping paralysis is practically incurable, so although the operation involves serious risks, the situation would seem to demand it.'[33]

Niemeyer first considered timing and impact. He was clear that a move should be made and that it should be coincident with the Budget – 'One howl instead of two: and each will help the other.' He then went on to the amount: 4% might look like the top, which would be good and might make subsequent cuts easier. Moreover the $1\frac{1}{2}$% rise would be unusual and this would have psychological value. But $3\frac{1}{2}$% would look more normal and would be less likely to disturb long rates excessively. It would look less like a gift to bankers at the Treasury's expense, 'and so for what it is worth less vulnerable to political attack' and should not risk being thought to herald the 7% and 6% of 1920. It would also be appropriate in relation to the US rate of $1\frac{3}{4}$% and continental European rates of 4% and more. On balance, Niemeyer favoured $3\frac{1}{2}$%.

The Governor, who had the exchange emergency more in mind, was inclined to favour 4% after discussion with the Deputy Governor, Peppiatt, Mynors, and the Chief Cashier. He wrote accordingly in his letter to the Chancellor, making considerable use of Niemeyer's tactical exposition while resorting to a certain amount of mysterious talk about the way current policy was working. Judgemental monetary policy has often been

---

[33] The Chancellor of the Exchequer consulted Lord Waverley (formerly Sir John Anderson) and Richard Hopkins about Robot. Both were in favour. He also consulted Lionel Robbins, who thought the time had not yet arrived for such desperate measures.

expounded in terms of imagery. Norman sometimes used the railway image – waving the green flag – while Cobbold often favoured motoring – giving a green light. Later still, in the period of aggressive monetarism, the resort was to carnal words like posture, stance, and thrust. But there has probably always been the medicinal imagery; in February 1952 the Governor wrote: 'The disinflationary effects of the November measures are still working gradually through the economy. If left undisturbed they will probably have had their full effect in about one or two months' time.' This obscurely persuasive statement was juxtaposed with the point that the money market would turn easier after the end of the revenue quarter and liquidity pressure on the banks would be relaxed. There was therefore an argument for keeping up the disinflationary pressure by a rise in interest rates, which this time would discourage borrowing and perhaps also help to encourage the public to become savings-minded again. For the rest, the Governor employed Niemeyer's arguments but came out in favour of 4%, mainly on the grounds that the exchange situation was so dangerous that the authorities could not neglect any action that might help remedy it. There was no consideration of $4\frac{1}{2}$% or 5%, simply a flat judgement that 4% would be regarded as the probable top. But Cobbold himself would then have had in mind his own plan to bring Robot into action early in April and the contingency that a further rise in Bank Rate might have to be considered at that stage.

The advice given to the Treasury in favour of 4% was not altered after the rejection of Robot; and the Rate was duly raised to that level on Budget day. The special rate for advances against Treasury Bills was retained and raised to $3\frac{1}{2}$%. Concurrently, the banks were asked to extend to Sterling Area borrowers a range of restrictions that had recently been imposed, through exchange control, on non-residents. The most important of these was the reduction of the maximum usance of drafts under acceptance credits from 120 days to 90. Finally, the Bank took care to keep its special friends overseas properly informed. Almost all the text of the Governor's note to the Chancellor, about 4% versus $3\frac{1}{2}$%, was sent to the Commonwealth central banks, to the Federal Reserve (Sproul and Martin), to Rooth at the IMF, to Brennan in Dublin, and to all the Scandinavians. Other Europeans were omitted from this list, but Cobbold wrote a private and personal manuscript letter to Baumgartner in Paris a week before the Budget. It was followed by a private meeting. Baumgartner spent the night of 15 March at Knebworth and Cobbold recorded: 'I had a long talk with him about the French situation and also gave him a hint in very general terms that we were thinking about exchange questions here.' As is related in the next section, this French connection was to play an important part in the evolution of Treasury and Bank attitudes to the EPU in the context of a further attempt to set Robot in motion.

The Budget itself included increases in indirect taxes and a cut of £160 million in the retail food subsidies, which were regarded abroad as symbolic of fiscal laxity. The saving achieved by the latter was then used to reduce Income Tax through an increase in allowances. Butler also announced another cut in import quotas, the third since he had taken office. Supported by the 4% Bank Rate and, ironically, by the absence of any alteration in the exchange rate – word of a floating rate had leaked into the market[34] – the Budget succeeded in halting the loss of reserves. There was some unwinding of speculative positions. By exploiting the new but limited flexibility prevailing since the reopening of the London market in December 1951 the authorities allowed the rate to bounce up from $2.78\frac{1}{4}$ to nearly $2.81, within a few days. The Treasury Bill rate rose from just over 1% to just over $2\frac{1}{2}$% but little further. The yield on short-dated gilts rose by nearly $\frac{3}{4}$% to $3\frac{1}{8}$%, but that on long-dated stocks hardly rose at all, by $\frac{1}{8}$% to a little over $4\frac{1}{2}$%. The immediate emergency was over and the breathing space had begun. It turned out to be a good deal more than that. Not until the autumn of 1954 was sterling to come under pressure once more. But in March 1952 this was difficult to foresee and both the Bank and the Treasury continued to fear an early resumption of pressure and a consequential need for action. As will be seen in the following chapter, the Robot plan was refined and modified in the spring and summer so as to improve its acceptability both to the Sterling Area and to the other members of the EPU. But it remained at heart a British plan for mainly British action rather than a plan for collective action preceded by negotiations.

The Bank and the Treasury (Overseas Finance) were severely bruised by the mauling of Robot. They were seen as having rashly attempted to engineer a change of economic and monetary strategy without proper consideration or consultation in Whitehall. They were thought to have tried to exploit the procedures of Budget secrecy so as to prevent or stifle opposition[35] and to have relied much too much on persuasive rhetoric. They fought on their own expert ground, yet they lost the battle and in so doing greatly enhanced the reputation of their opponents, who were seen as gallant knights saving the country from a group of misguided

---

[34] In the *Financial Times* of 8 March, 'Lombard' reported that such rumours 'continued to circulate in most of the world's foreign exchange markets yesterday'. Bridge reported from Paris that similar gossip was current in official OEEC circles.

[35] MacDougall records how the Chancellor endeavoured to gather up all the copies of his draft Robot paper at the conclusion of the initial Ministerial meeting and how the Prof clung resolutely onto his.

conspirators. All this gravely damaged the underlying merits of their case. In doing so it may well have damaged the future development of British external monetary policy, with adverse consequences for the conduct of economic policy generally. For there can be no doubting the importance of the questions at issue, underlying questions that were independent of the special emergency prevailing in February 1952.

A return to external convertibility could not be put off indefinitely. International commitments, pressures from the Sterling Area, and the crumbling of exchange control over non-residents compelled such a return. That being so, how could things be managed successfully, without a dangerous tendency to recurrent crisis and loss of confidence, so long as the external banking position of the UK remained so exposed and the resulting problem of the sterling balances remained unresolved? Next, was it wise to suppose that the management of an international currency, but one secondary to the US dollar and unsupported by an unquestionably strong economy, could be well conducted at a rate of exchange fluctuating only 1% either side of a parity that could in practice only be changed in a crisis and only through the procedures of the IMF? Sterling was beyond question in a unique category and this problem of management had, after all, not been considered at Bretton Woods and had nothing to do with anti-floating arguments about pre-war currency chaos and competitive depreciation. Even if it had, was it right in the light of post-war experience to persist with exchange rate arrangements that arguably delayed rather than expedited the processes of international economic adjustment? Lastly, was it any longer right to believe, as Cherwell, MacDougall, Hall, Plowden, and others believed so strongly, that a resumption of sterling convertibility in 1952 would be followed by a collapse of the discriminatory trading arrangements that were integral to containment of the remaining dollar shortage? Were they right to argue that UK exports would themselves be the subject of discrimination once sterling became convertible? Were their opponents right to accept this rather than challenge it? Or had the machinery of European economic co-operation been so well developed since 1947 that considerable trade discrimination could have been preserved by negotiation despite a resumption, for special reasons pertaining to it alone, of sterling convertibility?

In the light of subsequent history the answers that suggest themselves are not obviously favourable to the judgements of Cherwell and others in 1952.[36] This subject will be discussed again in later chapters. But in

---

[36] This thought finds an echo in Frank Lee's foreword to *A Banker's World: The Revival of the City, 1957–70: Speeches and Writings of Sir George Bolton*, ed. Richard Fry (Bank of London and South America, 1970). Lee, then Master of Corpus Christi College, Cambridge, wrote:

February 1952 the mistake of the Treasury and the Bank was to suppose that they could gain adoption of a newly formulated strategy through a hastily prepared crash programme in a crisis; and in particular a programme that seemed to throw away UK participation in the system of intra-European trade and payments for evidently no better reason than lack of time to think through a workable solution to this obviously vital problem. The lack of time was critical to the failure of the whole enterprise. Both the Treasury and the Bank were slow to set in hand a contingency-planning exercise for an exchange emergency. Four more weeks of thorough debate would have made a world of difference. The Chatham House Report, which was sent to Salter as early as 4 January, recommended that a contingency plan be drawn up and specifically mentioned both blocking and floating. But perhaps because of preoccupation with the Commonwealth Conference, it was not until the end of the month that the Treasury began to prepare 'Emergency Action' and not until early February that the Bank started work on Robot. With the experience of 1947 and 1949 behind them and the work of the Conference ahead of them, the beginning of December 1951 would not have been too early to begin planning against an open exchange crisis and for the customary debate among officials under the aegis of Bridges. Even with the delay until the end of January, all might not have been lost if it had been possible to stick to the two-stage procedure favoured by the Governor in his note of 13 February, a procedure that separated the timing of Robot from the timing of the Budget and would have allowed time, perhaps plenty of time, for its roughest features, notably the lack of adequate consultation with the Commonwealth and the lack of a plan for meeting the European problem, to have been properly fined down. But Ministers, especially the Prime Minister, ruled otherwise without any proper appreciation of what they were doing. For them, the plan had to be part of the Budget. The Treasury officials and the Governor accepted this ruling and thereby effectively sealed the fate of the plan itself.[37] Perhaps they were a little

'He [Bolton] thought me a timid bureaucrat. I thought him a reckless adventurer. I felt that his judgement of what policy we should follow on economic matters too often had only emphasis to commend it. The one thing which I never doubted was the splendid and unfailing competence which he showed in carrying out whatever policy was adopted, whether he had opposed it or not. Looking back I feel now that we did not really differ about fundamentals but about timing. We both wanted to see an economy as free as possible from restrictions where enterprise, risk-taking and expertise would have full scope and a fair reward. His faith in our ability to move quickly to such a state of affairs was always more robust and optimistic than my own. I now think that for the most part he was probably right and I was wrong.'

[37] In the course of a note for record prepared as early as 4 March 1952 Robert Hall remarked: 'In my view the main difficulties arose because of the decision reached on the evening of 19 February to try to get the plan through before the Budget. As telegrams would have

hypnotised by Churchill and by some instinctive desire to achieve the impossible if he asked for it to be done (Bridges and Rowan had worked closely with him during the war). Some may also have underestimated the likely opposition and become intoxicated by the excitement of the course on which they were embarked and the extraordinary procedure they were now obliged to adopt. But by agreeing to combine Robot with the Budget they stepped over the line between the possibly right and the definitely wrong tactical way of bringing about the strategic change to which they had suddenly been converted by the immediate crisis. This made them sitting targets for the opposition that developed, and rightly so. The Governor was carried along with the rest in this swift current.

(c) THE BREATHING SPACE AND THE GENESIS OF THE COLLECTIVE APPROACH TO CONVERTIBILITY

At the end of March 1952 the exchange reserves totalled $1·7 billion, some $200 million or more above the presumed point of open crisis. More important, the improvement in confidence was being maintained and now seemed unlikely to be upset by publication in April of the end-March figure for the reserves. But the situation remained very precarious. Balance of payments forecasts, together with the fragility of confidence, suggested that the loss of reserves could easily be resumed and that the emergency could reappear. In the event, there was virtually no change in the second quarter and the position was successfully held throughout the third, after which the reserves at last began to recover. But looking ahead in the spring and early summer, the Treasury and the Bank could not dare to foresee anything more than a short breathing space. This could nonetheless be used to go through the ordinary procedures of debate and refinement, which in the case of Robot had so far been omitted. Thus it was that from March through to the end of June there was a debate within the Treasury and the Bank about external economic strategy. It was accompanied by the construction firstly of plans for meeting the intra-European problems inherent in the floating-rate convertibility of sterling and secondly of means whereby the impact of 'immobilisation' on the sterling Commonwealth could be greatly softened without leaving the problem of the sterling balances unresolved. A revised version of Robot

> had to go to Commonwealth countries about a week before, this left an impossibly short time for discussion and the time was very short even after the decision to put the Budget a week later. I myself felt, however, throughout the discussions that the procedure was quite different from anything to which I have been previously accustomed.'

was then presented to Ministers early in July for action later in that month. It was very different to its February predecessor and no longer directly related to an actual and acute crisis. But it was so tainted by association with the February plan that it stood little chance of acceptance. It was considered by a group of Ministers but never got as far as the Cabinet. Its rejection was followed within a few weeks by a further and wider Whitehall debate about convertibility, which was conducted as part of the preparations for a November Conference of Commonwealth Prime Ministers. A memorandum entitled 'Steps Towards Convertibility' was circulated at the end of August and reported a majority view in favour of an early 'Collective Approach' with the principal European countries, the US, and Canada. The aim was to reach convertibility by the second half of 1953, still with the floating rate to which Overseas Finance and the Bank remained firmly attached once they had accepted it in February 1952. A minority opposed even this scheme, believing it would be both possible and advisable to maintain inconvertibility and a fixed rate of exchange until the world dollar problem had demonstrably been solved and convertibility could be safely undertaken.

Robot and intra-European trade and payments

Following the March Budget first thoughts in the Bank were given to altering the manner in which Robot had been presented. Lucius suggested a more positive tone that would stress the merits of convertibility and contain 'none of the deplorable apologetics which appeared in the first Treasury drafts'. Bolton then circulated a revised plan that reduced the proposed unpublished float to 10% either side of parity instead of 15% and referred to the 'funding' of official Sterling Area balances rather than to their 'immobilisation' and to 'severe restrictions' on the use of pre-zero non-resident balances rather than to their blocking or freezing.[38] Encouraged by a report received from Max Stamp[39] about the attitude of

---

[38] Ninety per cent of all balances were still to be frozen *ab initio*. But official balances below £1 million would be excluded and would become convertible. Ten per cent of higher official balances would be released at once, as a working balance in convertible sterling. The remainder, including private balances, could be used to meet all pre-zero commitments; fresh accruals would be credited to convertible sterling accounts. The residue would have to remain invested in the UK.

[39] *Stamp, Arthur Maxwell (1915–84).* Educated The Leys School and Clare College, Cambridge. Army 1939–45. Financial Adviser, John Lewis Partnership 1947–9. Entered Bank 1950, Adviser (Acting) 1950–3, UK Alternate Executive Director, IMF 1951–3, Director, European Department, IMF 1953–4, Adviser to the Governors 1954–7. Director,

the Managing Director and others in the IMF, Bolton now proposed seeking a $650 million stand-by credit from that institution in support of convertibility. He concluded that it would all be presented 'as a combined effort of Commonwealth, West Europe, and, we would hope, the USA to clear up the wreckage of the post-war period and restore international unity in the monetary and economic field'. But the West European element in Bolton's revised plan was still no more than a dream. European countries were to be regrouped, and a club was to be formed with those who joined the UK in floating against the dollar. Members of the club would agree to continue joint discrimination against the US on non-essentials and to encourage a revival of East–West trade. On withdrawal from the EPU, the resulting UK debt to the Union, amounting to some £215 million, would be treated as 'old sterling', the name that was to be given to the severely restricted non-resident balances. Lucius continued to entertain similar ideas of a sterling-based club whose members cleared through London and with each of whom there would be agreed a small two-way bilateral credit. If a credit were exhausted, there would be an immediate settlement, through the EPU agent if the Union somehow survived, wholly in gold or dollars if it did not.

Bolton and Lucius, like Clarke in the Treasury, were both afflicted by the kind of Euro-blindness that had affected the Bank's thinking on various occasions. The EPU and the associated trade liberalisation codes could not in reality be waved away just because the British had decided on sudden unilateral action to meet a uniquely British problem. Their politico-economic importance was much too great. Why, too, in these circumstances should members link their fortunes to an already somewhat discredited currency whose managers had simultaneously placed very severe restrictions on pre-zero non-resident balances? Would the floating-rate convertibility of newly accruing sterling be such a great prize in such conditions? As has been related in the preceding chapter, Bolton and Lucius in the Bank and Clarke in the Treasury brushed aside such points by boldly asserting that the EPU was anyway on the point of collapse. Despite sympathetic whispers from France, where the monetary authorities were also facing an exchange emergency and the exhaustion of their EPU quota, this was a complete misjudgement.

The EPU was admittedly going through a difficult passage. Firstly, the particular conjuncture of large creditor and debtor positions – with the UK and France predominating among the latter and the Belgians in the van

Hill Samuel 1958–76, Triplex Holdings 1963–75, Olympic Holidays 1981–3, Chairman, Maxwell Stamp Associates 1962–79. Member, Council of Foreign Bondholders 1950–3, 1955–7.

among the former – was threatening to exhaust the Union's working capital of convertible currency. Belgium's quota had been exceeded and her familiar problem-status as a persistent creditor in Western Europe had returned. In addition to these monetary problems, the two large debtors had undertaken a substantial deliberalisation of their imports from other members. But there was plenty of political will in Western Europe to resolve such questions. It was to prove quite easy to overcome the deficiency of working capital by suitable adjustments to the proportions of gold and credit in the structure of credit and debit quotas. As to the Belgian problem, it occupied some of the most well-trodden ground in postwar financial diplomacy. After the customary struggle, the Belgians, still among the most ardent political supporters of the European movement, were to accept a formula that settled what they were owed while obliging them to give more credit in the future. Finally the French and British deliberalisations would diminish in the course of time. The likelihood of these various developments must have become apparent to the Treasury during March. For Rowan remarked at a meeting with the Bank on 17 March that the treatment of Europe and the EPU might well be a crucial point when Ministers came to a fresh decision on Robot. The attitude of the Foreign Office to that plan, and particularly to its European aspect, had to be kept in mind. Its profound misgivings were firmly restated by Makins[40] at an interdepartmental meeting with Rowan on 24 March.[41] Moreover at the OEEC Council on 20 March the Chancellor confirmed UK support for that organisation, accepted extension of the EPU for a further year after 30 June, and suggested that the problems of working capital and of the persistent creditor be remitted to the Managing Board for discussion and resolution. He could hardly now proceed with Robot, without encountering accusations of perfidy, unless he could at least offer a workable plan for minimising its disruptive effect on West European monetary arrangements. Bolton's suggestions about splitting West Europe in two

---

[40] *Makins, Roger Mellor, 1st Baron Sherfield 1964, GCB, GCMG, FRS (b. 1904).* Educated Winchester and Christ Church, Oxford. Fellow of All Souls College, Oxford 1925–39 and from 1957. Entered Foreign Office 1928, Assistant Under-Secretary 1947–8, Deputy Under-Secretary of State 1948–52, Ambassador, Washington 1953–6, Joint Permanent Secretary, HM Treasury 1956–9. Chairman, UK Atomic Energy Authority 1960–4, Hill Samuel Group 1966–70, FCI Ltd 1973–4, ICFC 1964–74, EDIT 1966–73. Chancellor, Reading University from 1970.

[41] Lucius recorded Makins as arguing that the plan entailed repudiation of agreements, blocking of balances, and the destruction of the EPU. It changed the whole structure of international relationships. At the same time the international economic situation was deteriorating. Although that would have happened anyhow, now all would be blamed on the UK. He therefore wanted to be convinced that the move was absolutely essential, that there was no alternative, and that it would work. Otherwise HMG would have to 'crawl back'.

would not meet this specification. Something else had to be devised and Bridge was at hand to devise it, working closely with E. R. Copleston,[42] Under-Secretary in Overseas Finance alongside Clarke. The EPU was within Copleston's field of responsibility and he was in close contact with Ellis-Rees in Paris.

Hitherto, Bridge had mainly been thinking through the technicalities of UK withdrawal from the EPU and the introduction of alternative payments arrangements. He continued this work during March. One possibility would be to delay the institution of convertible-sterling accounts for residents of member countries, including their central banks, and for the UK to remain in the EPU for a transitional period lasting until 30 June. This would soften the blow and allow time for discussion about successor arrangements. Another possibility would be to apply Robot in full from the outset but for the UK to continue in the EPU and continue to provide interim finance for a very short period of, say, two weeks. A third possibility was to withdraw altogether at zero hour but thereafter grant sterling credit bilaterally, *ad hoc*, until new arrangements were agreed. The Bank preferred the last of these three options, as technically the safest, but was prepared to accept the second if politically necessary. After discussion the Treasury decided on the second. Despite its political attractions, a delayed withdrawal seemed too hazardous. With sterling floating there would arise vexatious problems about the calculation, in EPU units, of surpluses and deficits. If moreover some of the others floated too, these problems were seen to be insoluble. As to private traders, they might well use the transition both to avoid the effects of blocking and to anticipate a continuing depreciation of sterling. In both cases pressure on the reserves would be aggravated. An early withdrawal, with a two-week transition, seemed preferable despite its apparent brutality (outright withdrawal seemed altogether too brutal). It was therefore all the more important to devise proposals that were more in tune with the statement about the EPU that the Chancellor was to make to the Council of the OEEC on 20 March.

Bridge duly came up with an answer. The UK would withdraw from the monthly settlements, but all or part of the accumulated UK debt to the EPU would be added to the working capital of the Union instead of being divided up and repaid bilaterally in monthly instalments spread over three years, as laid down in the provisions for withdrawal contained in the EPU Agreement. At the same time sterling would, at least in part, be made acceptable as a means of discharging 'gold' payments to the Union by the

---

[42] *Copleston, Ernest Reginald*, CB (b. 1909). Educated Marlborough and Balliol College, Oxford. Inland Revenue 1932–42, HM Treasury 1942–57, Under-Secretary 1950–7. Deputy Secretary, University Grants Committee 1957–63, Secretary 1963–9.

remaining members at the monthly settlements. The Managing Board, on which the UK would retain a seat, would undertake a new responsibility for recommending special sterling credits, out of its increased capital, to members who were both in deficit with the Sterling Area and had very low reserves. A Monetary Agreement with the EPU on these lines would be accompanied by a parallel agreement under which OEEC trade rules would continue to apply, in whole or in part, to trade with the UK. In contrast to attitudes prevalent in other quarters, Bridge wrote:

> Although we should avoid the normal repayment obligations of £6 million a month on our EPU debt, this contribution [to the capital of the Union] would be of great value to Europe since it would at the same time solve the problem of EPU's inadequate capital and provide a means for the granting of temporary sterling finance to EPU countries under joint European supervision. That would widen EPU's scope and make it effectively more European in outlook and function; it should also remove friction with the USA over the working capital fund.

He had devised a means whereby the British could put Robot into effect and at the same time play a constructive part in the EPU as an associate member. The plan would not work if other important members were to float their currencies while still others remained on fixed rates. Europe would then inevitably be monetarily divided. But if the rest wanted to maintain fixed rates and to maintain the EPU, then Bridge's proposals would be workable.

Although there is no evidence that Bolton greeted them with enthusiasm, he himself put these ideas forward to the Treasury where they were accepted with gratitude by Rowan and Copleston. Later in April the latter sent a note explaining and commending them to Ellis-Rees in Paris. Copies were sent to the Foreign Office and the Board of Trade and comments were requested. Ellis-Rees warmly welcomed the proposals. Cohen at the Board of Trade was also supportive, though he warned that some reduction in favourable discrimination might have to be accepted. Berthoud, for the Foreign Office, was more distant and fully reserved his position. But even he felt that 'something on these lines' was worthy of further study and would go 'at least some way in the direction of doing our best to avoid infringing our obligations'.

As time went by, however, the Treasury and the Bank came to think that the likelihood of other European countries following the UK into floating-rate convertibility had markedly increased. This in turn enabled them to infer that the acceptability of the proposed British action had also risen since March. Bridge's ideas thus faded into the background in favour of plans for a short transition that would be followed by unspecified but supposedly friendly discussions in Europe about the monetary and trading relationships that would follow the likely termination of the EPU.

In view of the continuing doubts of the Foreign Office and the obvious awkwardness of suddenly scrapping the EPU within weeks of its successful renewal, how was it that the Treasury and the Bank were able to judge that other member countries would be likely to follow sterling with relative equanimity? Bank memoranda recall, in general terms, a widespread debate about exchange policy and convertibility that was taking place in Western Europe at this time. All kinds of possibilities were in the air. But the source of the judgement seems to have been a sequence of private discussions between the British and French authorities and especially between Cobbold and Baumgartner. The latter was close to the new Prime Minister, Antoine Pinay, a conservative who had taken office early in March and who subsequently embarked on a novel programme of domestic monetary stabilisation.

As early as 15 February Lithiby had reported from Paris on a conversation with Baumgartner at which the latter had expressed dislike of the EPU. France, he said, had always disliked the whole concept but had been led to accept it so as not to appear to drag its feet.[43] 'There is no doubt', Lithiby advised, 'that Baumgartner looks forward to a much closer collaboration in trade and monetary matters with the Sterling Area – with a view to creating a normal and not artificial mechanism through which West European economies would function.' On 7 March, in the course of a reply to the Governor's private letter of the 6th, Baumgartner told Lithiby that he did not think the EPU in its present form would last much longer. A few days later he told Bolton that he was most anxious to identify a French financial reform with steps taken by London. He would not wish the French to move in isolation; but he could not wait much longer because of the threatened exhaustion of French exchange reserves. He subsequently told Cobbold, who so informed Rowan, that he could hold out until the end of April or mid-May. Meantime, on 12 March, Lithiby was reporting that at lunch with Felix Gaillard, Secretary of State for Finance in the Pinay Government,[44] the latter had expressed grave doubts about the continuation of the EPU and was very receptive to the idea of

---

[43] In 1949 and 1950 the then French Governments were supporters of a little Europe – 'Finebel'. They played no very definite role in the EPU negotiations but may have disliked the 'big Europe' concept underlying them. This was a far cry from Baumgartner's position in 1952, when he favoured a closer bilateral link with sterling. But the balance of forces in the French Assembly had changed at the Elections held in July 1951, in favour of the Right, at the expense of the Socialists and the Mouvement Républician Populaire (MRP), within whose ranks were the main supporters of European integration.

[44] Pinay himself was Finance Minister as well as head of the Government.

close Franco-British collaboration. As a result of various measures, including the announcement of a gold-guaranteed Government loan, the franc exchange rate improved during April. But ideas for collaboration with the British nonetheless took further root. On 15 May, from Basle, Bolton reported that Baumgartner had told him that the French would like to link the franc to sterling at about 1,085 francs to the pound, somewhat lower than the prevailing rate, and would then like both currencies to float against the dollar and both to be convertible for non-residents. The Frenchman had also referred to some approaches being made to the Belgians. These ideas had been concealed from the French and Belgian experts on the EPU. If, however, the EPU were a political necessity, it was thought to remain workable if all members jointly floated against the dollar while retaining fixed rates between each other.

On 22 May the Governor recorded that arrangements were being made for him to accompany the Chancellor to Paris on 6 June for a private meeting with Pinay and Baumgartner. A few days later Bolton provided the Governor and the Treasury with some preliminary ideas about Anglo-French collaboration. There is no Bank record of the meeting on 6 June, but by the 12th the Chancellor was asking his officials for advice about the implications of various possible French moves. On 19 June Bolton recorded that at a meeting held by Rowan the general feeling was 'that the circumstances were now such that it was much more likely than six months ago that other European countries, e.g. France, Belgium, and even West Germany, would become convertible on a floating rate, in some cases perhaps regardless of whether or not the UK were to set an example'. On 21 June Rowan minuted the Chancellor about the timing of new-style Robot and referred to the desirability of prior consultation with France, Belgium, and the Scandinavians. On 27 June the Governor recorded that the Chancellor had authorised him to talk 'pretty freely' to Baumgartner about the new plan. A timetable prepared on the same day allowed for France and Belgium to be informed, for discussion and decision, as much as nine days in advance, and for West Germany, Holland, and the Scandinavians to be informed four days in advance. On 30 June the Governor sent the Chancellor a note recording further discussions he had now had with his French counterpart:

> M. Baumgartner repeated his view that concerted action in July would be wise. The Bank of France take the view that the French ought to take action themselves before the end of July, irrespective of action elsewhere. M. Baumgartner thinks it uncertain whether or not the French Government would move by themselves, but that they would certainly move with us if we did something. For his part he thinks it would be wise to act in July (he would

greatly prefer 20th to 27th), as he is fearful of a new crisis developing over August/September and anticipates every sort of rumour over the Mexico City period. He is most anxious to make a move while the Government have the initiative and not wait until they are forced into precipitate action.

The convertibility issue is not serious for him, as the franc is not held substantially overseas. But he would be quite prepared (as a comparatively meaningless gesture) to allow overseas holders of francs to buy any currency in Paris (i.e. the same treatment as we propose for external sterling).

He thinks they could work on about the same pattern of opening rates as we have provisionally in mind, the franc opening at a rather lower rate on sterling and therefore somewhat more heavily depreciated than sterling on the dollar. We agreed that we should try for an experimental period of, say, two months to keep a steady cross-rate and stable rates between £ and franc without any formal link.

He is not worried about our proposals for freezing balances as they now stand (i.e. banks working balances to be freed) or about our gold proposals.

He is a little anxious about possible American attempts to impose conditions for their acquiescence.

We talked about EPU and rest of Europe but agreed we must wait for decision of principle before going into detail.

He asked me to tell Mr Rooth privately about our conversation.

On 3 July the Governor informed Baumgartner by telephone that Robot was no longer running. On the 7th Bolton had a talk with him at Basle and recorded that while their external outlook remained poor, there seemed little chance of the French taking any independent and isolated action. Nevertheless Baumgartner would 'continue to develop a plan similar to those discussed in London during the last six months'. He would also try to keep Pinay interested in that subject, particularly in view of a probable recurrence of pressure to devalue the franc. He would keep the Bank of England informed.

It is possible that the authorities in Paris were in part using the central bank network so as to monitor British intentions and avoid being put into the situation that had so infuriated them when sterling was devalued by 30% in 1949. But such speculation apart, there seems no reason to doubt either the sincerity of the Governor of the Bank of France or the attraction, to him, of floating the franc downwards rather than devaluing it. Robot was an opportunity to achieve such an aim while placing some of the responsibility on London. However there must be some doubt whether, come the day, he and his allies in the Ministry of Finance would have won in Paris a battle analogous to that fought and lost by the Treasury and the Bank in London. It is true that the Pinay Government was less Europeanist in complexion than its immediate predecessors, having shed Socialist support on the left while gaining support from Gaullist deputies on the right. But Pinay's majority in the Assembly still depended upon the votes of the MRP, with its strongly Europeanist element. Robert Schuman, one of its most prominent leaders, had retained the Foreign Ministry when he joined the Pinay Government. The ECSC, which had now been approved by all the legislatures of the Six, came into being during the spring of 1952. The treaty setting up a European Defence Community was signed in Paris at the end of May but had still to be ratified. Joining the British in a dash for floating-rate convertibility would have meant collaborating in measures that would have disturbed existing arrangements for intra-European trade and payments, made technical operation of the ECSC and EDC considerably more difficult (in the likely absence of a joint European float against the dollar), and indirectly damaged the prospects of obtaining ratification of the EDC from a reluctant Assembly. These would have been vital considerations for the MRP, whereas the achievement of floating-rate convertibility would not have been so vital a matter for the conservatives and Gaullists. That being so, and the Pinay Government having held office for little more than four months, the MRP Ministers could well have gained the day and stopped French alignment with Robot. As for the Belgians, they would no doubt have adapted themselves readily enough to some new state of affairs if the EPU had disappeared. But they remained keen supporters of European unification and it is unlikely that they would have actively assisted that disappearance. Nor does there seem much reason to suppose that the West German and Italian Governments, both Christian Democrat in orientation, would have been keen to follow a British lead into floating-rate convertibility. Attitudes adopted later in the year on questions of convertibility and exchange rate flexibility, showed almost unanimous continental support for retaining the EPU for at least a further year or two.

The Treasury and the Bank may have been too easily led by their private discussions with the French into believing firstly that several important countries would indeed follow sterling (and withdraw from EPU), secondly that they would do so with some enthusiasm rather than in anger at what the British had done, and thirdly that all this would be a good thing. But perhaps they wanted to be led in this direction. For whatever reasons, whether it was dreams of a sterling-led system of European payments with a joint float against the dollar, indifference to goals of European unification, outright opposition to such unification, inadequate appreciation of American interest in it, or straight misjudgement about the practical durability of the EPU, the UK monetary authorities had remarkably little inclination to preserve the intra-European system of trade and payments that they had reluctantly helped to construct. Had they been so inclined they would have retained the plan supplied by Bridge and would have recommended that the other members of the EPU should not be encouraged to follow sterling. Only when Robot had been effectively killed and only when the Treasury had to open up the whole field to interdepartmental debate and agreement, in preparation for the autumn Conference of Commonwealth Prime Ministers, did their attitude towards Western Europe undergo a change, this time in favour of a mostly collective rather than a mostly unilateral approach to convertibility and one that would include the Europeans at an early stage. Even then as subsequent events were to show, the change was rather more apparent than real.

There is no evidence that the Foreign Office knew what was going on between the Bank of England and the Bank of France. Had it known, it would surely have attempted to put a stop to it. After much diplomatic activity, the EDC Treaty had been signed and had been accompanied by an Anglo-American declaration guaranteeing support of the Community in event of aggression against it. The final hurdle was to get the Treaty ratified by the various legislatures, by far the most awkward of which was the French Assembly. Here, ratification was dependent on the votes of a divided centre that was providing, in varying degree and complexion, an essential element in the unstable Ministries of the Fourth Republic. But there were those in the French centre, inside and outside the Assembly, who baulked at the idea of surrendering military sovereignty in Western Europe to a supranational authority in which the West Germans would have an increasingly important voice and from which the British were absent. Bearing in mind that the stability of French Governments at that time was also weakened by increasingly grave and increasingly expensive problems in the overseas territories (first in Indo-China, later and fatally in North Africa) as well as by persistent fiscal difficulties arising from growing domestic expenditures and inadequate taxable capacity, it is no wonder that ratification of the EDC was always seen as most difficult to secure. In the end, in 1954, the Assembly was to reject it.

There can accordingly be little doubt that the Foreign Office in London, and Eden personally, would have resisted the secret diplomacy with the French monetary authorities that was being conducted by the Treasury and the Bank. Had Robot actually been put into effect with French collaboration, and had it not been followed by a joint European float against the dollar, it would have reorientated French external economic policy in Europe so that it pointed in the opposite direction to the French defence commitment, which all the efforts of Anglo-American diplomacy were being directed to secure. Whether the Treasury and the Bank paid much attention to these foreign policy considerations is doubtful. They receive only very general mention in Treasury memoranda and almost no mention in those written in the Bank. It was, however, a responsibility of the Treasury to weigh such considerations when deciding among the alternative means of handling the problem of Robot and the EPU. What is astonishing is the apparent absence of any Treasury consultation with the Foreign Office, a state of affairs that seems to have had its parallel in Paris.

Robot and the Sterling Area

Alongside the evolution of these ideas for meeting the European snags, there developed a softening of Robot's Sterling Area features. This was in turn followed by exploratory talks with the Prime Minister of Australia, Robert Menzies, when he visited London at the end of May, and with the Governor of the Reserve Bank of New Zealand in mid-June. Both sets of talks were encouraging.

Already, during the pre-Budget discussions, the Bank had half persuaded the Treasury that outright and uniform *de facto* blocking of official sterling balances held by members of the Sterling Area would not in practice happen. For compelling reasons of Commonwealth and Sterling Area co-operation, some kind of negotiation with each of the countries concerned would prove unavoidable in 1952 just as in 1946 and thereafter. Yet experience of such negotiations had been discouraging. By the end of March, when it looked as if another meeting of Commonwealth Finance Ministry officials might be held in June or July, the Treasury had itself come round to this point of view. But what then was to be done if funding was very difficult to negotiate and likely anyway to be hedged with escape clauses allowing a funded balance to be used in an emergency? It would perhaps suffice if each country made a declaration that identified a hard core of balances that would not be drawn down except after prior consultation with London. It was estimated that by this expedient some £800 million of balances could be rendered more or less harmless for purposes of foreign opinion. The idea was set out in a draft Cabinet paper dated 4 April.[45] Towards the end of that month the matter was again considered, this time in the context of the forthcoming visit of Menzies, with whom the Chancellor intended to discuss the subject of floating-rate convertibility. Ahead, too, of a further meeting with Commonwealth officials and of the September meetings of the IMF and IBRD in Mexico City, there was the question of what, if anything, should now be said to other members of the Sterling Area. Should a senior Treasury official be sent off

---

[45] The paper was prepared in case Robot was to be proposed at this time; but the Chancellor decided not to carry things further.

to tour the Area? The latter idea was opposed by the Bank on the grounds that the official would be unable to say much and would accordingly give the bad impression that the UK had nothing to say. The tour did not take place, but the discussion with Menzies went ahead and the proposal for declaratory identification of hard core balances was included in the Chancellor's briefing for this occasion. The Governor saw Menzies on the morning of 10 June and again, this time with Butler, on the same evening. He recorded:

> Without in any way committing himself and whilst saying that the technical aspects would need a lot of consideration, Mr Menzies was clearly in favour of a step on these lines and would probably favour it sooner rather than later. It fits with his general conception that the Commonwealth should take positive steps along a definite road and put themselves in a position to negotiate jointly with the USA on a constructive basis...The whole of the conversation was, however, on a constructive and positive basis and the Robot proposals were envisaged as a step on the road and not as an unwelcome alternative to threats of early disaster.

With the Chancellor's authority, the Governor talked about Robot to Fussell, Governor of the Reserve Bank of New Zealand on 13 June and recorded:

> Mr Fussell thought the ideas sensible and constructive. He would see no difficulty about a statement that New Zealand regarded the bulk of her balances as a minimum reserve. While he cannot commit the New Zealand Government, he is practically certain that they would follow the UK rate policy.

In the paper put to a group of his colleagues early in July in which he proposed early implementation of the revised version of Robot, the Chancellor said: 'The main difference is that I have decided not to propose any formal funding of Sterling Area countries' sterling balances.' Later, he went on to explain the proposal for declaratory identification of minimum balances. Rather longer time would be given for Commonwealth Governments to consider the whole plan and the Chancellor hoped he would be able, come the day, to announce that the scheme carried their full support.

So far as they went, these developments were promising. Declaratory identification of minimum balances, at a time when total balances had already been heavily run down towards minimum working levels, should not have been difficult to achieve and would have been helpful internationally. The task would then have been to ensure that a recovery in the balances attributable to a rise in net earnings of foreign currencies was well supported by a rise in the central reserves in London and not dissipated by increased UK expenditure outside the Area. Encouraging too was the fact that neither Menzies (who was accompanied by the head of the Australian Treasury) nor Fussell reacted with shock or dismay either at the prospect of floating-rate convertibility or at the plan as a whole. Bearing in mind the concurrent attitude of the French monetary authorities, misleading or not, the Bank and the Treasury could properly derive considerable comfort from the fact that none of these overseas soundings had provoked the kind of horrified denunciation that the first version of Robot had encountered from critics nearer home.

Equally comforting was the response of Ivar Rooth, Managing Director of the IMF, in the course of a private talk with the Governor on 2 July. His initial reaction was not unfavourable. He thought that the suggested step would be regarded as a major measure consistent with the objectives of the IMF and seemed less worried than Cobbold had expected about the floating rate. He felt that the IMF would wish to ask some questions about financial policy generally and he thought it absolutely essential that a step of this kind should be accompanied by firm measures in the field of investment programmes and public expenditure. Without firm assurances on these points he would feel considerable doubt about the success of the operation and the reactions of the IMF Board. Also, Canada and possibly the US might raise questions of trade policy and discrimination. But, as the Governor recorded: 'Subject to these points, his personal and preliminary view is that if we could make a good story about general financial measures there should be reasonable prospect of substantial IMF support, both morally and materially.' On 22 July Rooth wrote at length to Cobbold, spelling out and emphasising the need for additional and firm domestic measures, in good time, both in the UK and in the other countries of the Sterling Area. He also foresaw pressures from non-residents to convert as much as they could. 'You will understand', he wrote, 'that we will ask questions and that you will have to convince us that there are good chances for avoiding an experiment à la 1947.' None of this would have been objectionable to the Bank; it would have been positively helpful. Rooth was elaborating his initial response; he did not counsel against the whole enterprise.

Debate in Whitehall

The construction of plans to deal with the impact of Robot on Western Europe, to soften the proposals for immobilising the balances of the Sterling Area, and to take soundings abroad where possible, would have been otiose if the Chancellor himself had accepted the February defeat as final and regarded the post-Budget improvement in sterling as a reason for dropping the idea of floating-rate convertibility altogether. In the event he did not do so, but there was considerable debate within the Treasury, in which the Bank participated, and there was at times some doubt about where the Chancellor actually stood. The Bank itself never weakened, though on 18 March the Governor received a written warning from Niemeyer, whom he had now asked for advice. He was firstly warned against blocking non-resident balances. 'Will they [non-residents] not say the block is certain: the continuance of freedom [convertibility] is uncertain. We were had once in 1947. Once you have begun a block, the mania is infectious: and how do we know you will not do it again before long? Such a feeling would destroy confidence in free sterling: convertibility from strength is one thing: convertibility starting with the advertisement of weakness is quite another.' Cobbold was also warned about the presentation of exchange flexibility: 'Obviously any talk of "floating" (except in privately varying your gold points) would defeat any hope of confidence. I should fear even the 10% margin would leak out and become a bear point.' How far would the plan depend on American support in the IMF and the maintenance of existing US aid? Was it at all realistic to suppose that such support would be forthcoming in an Election year? Finally, Niemeyer did not suffer from Euro-blindness. Among reasons for doubting a favourable response from Washington was 'the destruction of EPU, which many of them think the only sign of United Europe'. Niemeyer was for waiting and seeing: 'I am not yet entirely convinced that it [the Budget] may not be sufficient without these complicated manoeuvres, which will be difficult to present and will almost certainly be misrepresented.'

Another advocate of delay, this time in Whitehall and therefore a full participant in the debate, was Plowden. He was not averse to a floating rate but was fearful of the effects Robot would have on trade discrimination and on the repute of the UK. In his view the trading world would end by being split in two (more severely than it already was) and the UK would find it had to suspend convertibility a second time, with a depreciated exchange rate. The inability of the US to act decisively in Election Year would make this more likely. Accordingly, HMG should rein in its ambitious housing programme, allow greater exports of coal, cut dollar imports even more, stand ready to increase Bank Rate above 4%, borrow dollars both against the EEA portfolio and from the IMF, and propose a voluntary funding of Commonwealth sterling balances.

Cherwell and MacDougall also belonged to the general category of waiters; but the latter was not invited to take part in this particular debate and the rest of the ground was occupied by Robot one-worlders (Overseas Finance) and emergency two-worlders (the Economic Section). The latter now put forward, at much greater length, a revised version of the proposals they had first aired during the February battle. The dollar shortage was going to persist, the Americans were not going to adopt adequate good-creditor policies, and the only way to protect the sterling countries and the other members of EPU from a general reduction in output and employment was to reinforce the existing discriminatory arrangements in trade and payments. To this end, the credit element in the EPU should be greatly increased while the existing degree of convertibility of Sterling Area balances should be withdrawn. To make this palatable, the central reserves of the Area should be shared out and each member should be left to balance its dollar account bilaterally. Occasional devaluations might be necessary in order to avert the emergence of too great a gap between the two worlds. The economists saw many difficulties in their plan but argued it would produce better results than the attempted crash adjustment through Robot. With a display of alternative statistics, Overseas Finance argued in reply that the remaining dollar shortage was mostly attributable to poor performance by non-dollar economies, in particular the UK, and very little to poor behaviour on the part of the US. Adjustment would be painful but not unendurable; and the floating rate would help. The two-world alternative was unrealistic and wholly contrary to obligations undertaken by the UK at the end of the war, in the Bretton Woods Agreements and the Anglo-American Loan Agreement. Few countries would want to follow the UK in that direction. Furthermore the economists' proposals for the Sterling Area would effectively break it up.

These criticisms were strongly supported by the Governor in a denunciatory note handed by him to Butler on 27 March. Maurice Allen, himself probably in the same camp as Plowden, was equally critical of the 'visionary world' constructed by Hall and his colleagues. They had, in fact, no supporters; and the effective choice lay between Robot and waiting. Plowden's position, which would have commanded support outside the Treasury, was in fact a strong one, and given the measures he put forward it was not easy to attack him for risking another emergency. His weak point was his reliance on help in 1953 from a new US Administration. With a clarity of vision that it had subsequently to suppress when agreeing to the Collective Approach, Overseas Finance remarked: 'We think it wrong to place reliance on a long-term policy which depends upon US Governmental action in the financial and commercial policy field, *and which starts by negotiation* [author's italics]. There is no ground for expecting that the new US Administration will be willing or able to do what we should want...' At the end of a long paper Overseas Finance advised that Robot should be put into effect as soon as it had been decided on the best means of overcoming the twin hurdles of what to do about the other members of the EPU and how to present the plan to the Sterling Commonwealth.

There followed a period of some indecision. Treasury Ministers evidently gave no clear response to the voluminous literature just described. By early May the Governor, for one, was becoming impatient. The Chancellor told him that the odds against early activation of Robot had lengthened and that he was beginning to think more in terms of a move in the autumn. Cobbold judged that matters were beginning to drift now that the compulsion of immediate emergency had for the present been lifted and that negotiations for the renewal of the EPU were well in hand. For his part, the Chancellor may have begun to feel that the Governor's judgement on emergencies and his appreciation of political factors was not as good as he had thought. At any event, relations were such that Cobbold wrote in a note to Butler dated 6 May:

> At the moment no definite decision has been taken between convertibility as a real and early objective (which must mean a tight credit policy internationally as well as domestically) and the opposite objective of building up areas of 'soft' trade on a structure of credit and inconvertibility. Arguments can be adduced for either horse, but no argument can favour riding both horses at the same time or alternating between one and the other. In particular relation to Mr Menzies visit...it is surely essential, even if it proves impossible to propose a particular plan or timetable, to be able to state a definite line of policy, at least to the extent of saying whether our aim is the North Pole or the South Pole.

An answer, of a sort, appeared in a paper on economic policy circulated by the Chancellor to his colleagues on 17 May. In a paragraph on external financial policy his position on the exact course to be followed was carefully reserved, but he went on: 'We cannot continue indefinitely with an inconvertible currency and with sight liabilities which are not adequately limited having regard to the weakness of our gold reserves.' Convertibility had to be an early objective. But the rest of the paragraph was consistent with waiting, of the Plowden variety.

The rejection of Robot II and the birth of the Collective Approach

At dinner with the Chancellor on 22 May the Governor again urged that matters should not be allowed to drift. As time went on, the favourable response from Menzies and Fussell, the continuing signals flashing across the channel from the Bank of France, and the approach of the August and September danger zone brought the Chancellor round against delay. The Governor wrote to him formally on 21 June, following a conversation earlier in the day. He asserted that the signs were all pointing to a gradual reappearance of the pressure on sterling. World financial opinion was beginning once again to believe that sterling was a risky currency to hold and that a short position was unlikely to lead to loss and might well lead to profit. It would therefore be very unwise to leave things unaltered over the rest of the summer and through the Fund and Bank meetings in September. But a further rise in Bank Rate would not suffice and might only cause alarm. Further cuts in public spending would not by themselves be enough to reverse the trend against sterling. 'I therefore suggest', he went on, 'that you may think it opportune again to consider the possibility of adopting changes in the external sterling structure, in concert with measures in the field of public expenditure.' External borrowing would in present circumstances be imprudent, 'but if a plan were adopted on the lines earlier discussed, it would be an advantage to strengthen our reserves with some additional line of credit'.

The machinery of writing a Cabinet paper, preparing supplementary briefs, drafting telegrams, and working out timetables swung into action once again. Robot II, to be introduced on 21 July, was to be accompanied by the announcement of cuts in public spending and, if possible, by a stand-by from the IMF. In the first place it would be presented to the Cabinet as a wise precaution ahead of renewed emergency. But it would also be presented to the Cabinet and to the public at home and abroad as a positive and constructive step, not as a move from weakness. However, as Cobbold noted twenty-five years later, the Treasury and the Bank were flogging a dead horse. The Economic Policy Committee were hostile and the Chancellor took the matter no further. However modified the plan itself, however favourable the soundings taken, whatever the risks of waiting, Ministers had no stomach for a still radical plan, involving further unpleasant domestic measures, which had been unsuccessfully pressed on them in so different and strident a manner four months earlier. They were once more easily convinced by the arguments of Cherwell that the plan was both reckless and unnecessary and by the continuing opposition of the Foreign Office. The Governor had to accept defeat; though he warned the Chancellor on 4 July that it was even money on an autumn crisis and that he would have to consider his personal position if the reserves got as low as $1.4 billion and there had still been no action.

Robot II could have been better constructed and better presented. The support, or at least the neutrality, of the Foreign Office might have been obtained if Bridge's plan for dealing with the EPU had been adopted instead of the alternative course of secret collaboration with the unreliable French. Given, too, the response from Rooth and the likelihood of a Fund stand-by, it might well have been possible to reduce the blocking of non-resident balances while retaining the hard-core declarations from the Sterling Area. The floating-rate convertibility of sterling, with the long-run advantages claimed for it by Overseas Finance and the Bank, could then have been introduced without unacceptable risk of an international or intra-European disaster. It would thereafter have been the job of the British and their Sterling Area partners to manage it in such a way that critics' fears of a dangerous and recurring depreciation proved groundless. As it was, due to the unfortunate trauma of Robot I, to the strong and even bitter differences of view that persisted thereafter, and to the defective handling of the European aspect, the opportunity was finally missed. In consequence, the Treasury and the Bank were driven once again to the other end of their cage and obliged to devise a quite different plan, this time one for a negotiated multilateral solution that necessarily precluded from the outset any possibility of decisive unilateral action by the UK. As Overseas Finance had already warned and as post-war experience had hitherto demonstrated, this abandonment of bargaining power was likely to mean that the so-called solution would prove to be obtainable only on other people's terms for gaining other people's objectives, while the peculiar British problems would be left unresolved and simply left to be endured in the hope that they would fade away. The fixed-rate convertibility, without special fortification of the reserves, which finally came to pass in 1958, was to prove as difficult to manage and as vulnerable to recurrent crises as the advocates of Robot had foreseen, and for the reasons they had stated.

The mood in Threadneedle Street was by now weary and irritable. Bolton and various other players seem to have taken refuge in silence and it was Lucius who now represented the Bank on Whitehall groups that discussed external policy. He also worked with the Governor on a further *démarche* that was sent to the Chancellor at the end of July. Cobbold appealed for a strong and constructive policy with which the UK could give a lead at the November Conference, acquire solid Commonwealth support, and 'open up with the new American Administration as a strong partner on the basis of achievements and solidarity'. He excused himself for trespassing on political ground, remarking: 'I have lived very close to this for a number of years and have had the backwash of no little disillusion from some earlier conferences and discussion.' He enclosed with his own short Minute an unsigned note by Lucius that was hectoring and minatory in tone, both about Government finances and about indecision over external policy. Butler was upset and let it be known that he thought the Bank was being unfair. On that note, many of the top players dispersed on holiday, the Governor going to Scandinavia for most of August.

In his absence new plans were discussed and developed by an interdepartmental Working Party chaired by Brittain and composed of other Treasury representatives, the Economic Section, Cherwell's office, the Foreign Office, the Board of Trade, the Commonwealth Relations Office, the Colonial Office, and the Bank. Lucius attended for the latter, with Jasper Rootham as his alternate. The Working Party was set up following a Report on External Economic Policy prepared by the same interdepartmental grouping. This Report had endorsed 'one-world' as the ultimate goal but had left open the crucial and controversial question about the pace at which the goal should be approached. It was accepted by Ministers as the basis of policy to be put to the November Conference. On that foundation various other reports were to be prepared and among these was one on steps to convertibility. But before Brittain's group had met, Cherwell influenced its effective terms of reference by circulating to his colleagues the outline of an Atlantic Payments Union[46] (APU) to be formed from the EPU membership, the US, and Canada. Its principal selling point was the participation of the United States in regular and relatively informal monthly discussions of the kind undertaken by the EPU Managing Board. Fixed exchange rates, inconvertibility, and discrimination against the US would remain at the outset and would be incorporated within the operational rules of the new Union. But it was argued that participation of the US, of the great convertible with the many inconvertible in the same continuously working mechanism, would powerfully assist gradual orderly progress towards one-world on terms fair and acceptable to all. This romantic vision instantly appealed to the Prof's colleagues. Officials on Brittain's Working Party were accordingly instructed to give it full consideration. The Bank at once subjected it to rigorous scrutiny.

The Working Party toiled long and hard throughout the August weeks. It met in a basement room in the Treasury, often late into the evening. The APU emerged severely battered and with its best features extracted by the Treasury and adapted for use in a different plan. The proposed Union proved full of technical difficulties arising from the need to accommodate as a full member one very large country (the US) whose currency was convertible and who was expected to be a persistent creditor. It involved a special gold tax on settlement with that creditor and a variety of provisions, seemingly including special controls imposed by the US, that would be needed to prevent misuse of the dollar credit to be provided through the US quota. Furthermore, it seemed clear that the Americans could not join a quasi-permanent institution, involving complex rules and

---

[46] According to MacDougall (*Don and Mandarin*) this idea originated from a private discussion he held with Marjolin, Secretary-General of the OEEC, earlier in the summer.

controls and the provision of credit on a large scale, without an Act of Congress whose early passage seemed most unlikely. In addition to such problems it was not easy to see how the proposed Union could properly be described as a step towards convertibility, except by its authors who were known to oppose restoration of convertibility until a Greek calends when the world dollar problem had been finally solved.

For these reasons Cherwell's plan attracted little support. It did however serve to open up a debate about how the Commonwealth, Western Europe, and North America might in practice collaborate in an appropriate forum so that the principal inconvertible currencies could all become convertible at the same time and at a fairly early date. For without a plan for such collective action the Treasury and the Bank had nothing worthwhile to offer except yet another version of Robot and nothing in prospect save yet another episode of rejection. It was probably Figgures,[47] recently returned from the OEEC, who then hit upon the idea of going all the way back to the 'key-currency' ideas favoured by the Bank and others during the war, at that time as an alternative to the Bretton Woods proposals. Why not form a nucleus of countries whose currencies were internationally important and use it to promote early convertibility, at a fixed or floating rate according to choice, for those now inconvertible? To this end, the US could be asked to provide a large support fund for use by any member in the group needing balance of payments assistance. The nucleus could also agree to discriminate against any member, that is to say the US, who was recognised as a persistent creditor. Apart from such discrimination, all import quotas between members could be eliminated and reimposed only in conditions of extreme emergency. The nucleus that suggested itself contained the UK, the US, Canada, France, West Germany, Belgium, and Holland. The Sterling Area could be associated with the nucleus through its link with the UK; other countries could be associated through their membership of the IMF and the General Agreement on Tariffs and Trade (GATT). Finally, the nucleus countries could meet regularly and informally, so as to constitute the 'forum' that all of Britain's group agreed was needed. These ideas were subsequently elaborated, named a Collective Approach to Convertibility, and supported by a large majority. Their only opponents were the Economic Section and Cherwell's Office, the former because of remaining two-world inclinations and the latter because they did not believe that the suggested trade rules and support fund would

---

[47] He was then an Assistant Secretary and drafter of the Working Party's Report. Manuscript notes by Thompson-McCausland, written during one of the meetings, attribute the 'key-currency' revival to him.

provide adequate safeguards against the dangers they perceived in early convertibility.

The Bank had no difficulty falling into line with the Whitehall majority. Once unilateral action had been ruled out, some kind of collective approach had to be accepted. This being so, an approach that concentrated on the key currencies and allowed maximum scope for informal consultation and for meeting difficulties *ad hoc* was bound to be welcomed in Threadneedle Street, whatever doubts may have been felt there about its actual feasibility at the time. The Governor saw the Working Party's Report in draft when he returned from holiday. On 29 August he wrote to the Chancellor about it, beginning by reiterating his concern that a definite policy should be settled before the Conference. He felt the Report covered the ground well and he was glad to see that emphasis was placed on the necessity of firm domestic policies. He shared the view of the majority that early steps towards convertibility were necessary. To that end he was prepared in principle to support the Collective Approach. But he warned that it was sterling convertibility that counted, not Deutschmark or French franc convertibility. This meant that the UK must keep the initiative and not get too tied up in committees and rules. He warned also that any fresh dollar assistance must be treated as a stabilisation reserve and not spendable like Marshall Aid.

Contrary to the Governor's fears there was no early emergency. The breathing space had already extended from weeks into months and was now to extend into years (though not much more than two). Ministers agreed to the UK embarking on a strategy of Collective Approach to Convertibility, to be conducted through collaboration with a 'nucleus', an idea that foreshadowed the groups of ten, five, seven, and so forth that were to emerge in the 1960s, 1970s and 1980s. The Approach contained no grandiose ideas for the extension of the sterling system or for an Anglo-American monetary hegemony. It was indeed silent on such matters. Nor, whether by accident or design, did it rely on any particular resolution of the problem of European unification. In those respects it was a well-founded strategy, finally replacing the shapeless dispositions that had prevailed since 1947 and sensibly seeking to modify the grand machinery of fully international monetary government contemplated by the founders of the IMF. But far-sighted strategies may be unable to solve the urgent problems of their author if they depend upon the support of those for whom the problems are less urgent and for whom existing arrangements seem to be working quite well. The Collective Approach depended upon large-scale help from the Americans and active support from the Europeans, neither of whom were to regard the general problem of convertibility as urgent or the existing arrangements, especially the EPU, as unsatisfactory or outdated. On those counts the Approach was likely to prove yet another rapidly fading vision. Furthermore, although some blocking of non-resident balances was still contemplated, earlier emphasis on the sterling balance problem had now disappeared and in doing so had made the scale of American assistance all the more important. But for better or worse, after ten months of Conservative Government, the watershed was now over. New policies had been formed and a new strategy for sterling agreed.

Sources

Bank files

ADM14/30	L. P. Thompson-McCausland's Papers: Robot (October 1951 – July 1952)
ADM14/33	L. P. Thompson-McCausland's Papers: Commonwealth Economic Conference (August 1952 – January 1953)
ADM14/34	L. P. Thompson-McCausland's Papers: Committee on Preparations for Commonwealth Economic Conference (July – December 1952)
ADM14/35–7	L. P. Thompson-McCausland's Papers: Further Current Papers (December 1952 – May 1954)
ADM14/38	L. P. Thompson-McCausland's Papers: EPU (October 1953 – July 1954)
ADM14/39–40	L. P. Thompson-McCausland's Papers: Collective Approach Committee – Bank and Treasury memoranda (May 1954 – October 1955)
C40/687	Chief Cashier's Policy Files: Monetary Policy – Advances and Control of Inflation (1950–2)
C42/2–3	Chief Cashier's Personal Files: Interest Rates (October 1951 – April 1957)
C43/105–8	Gold and Foreign Exchange Files: Foreign Exchange – Exchange Dealings and Forward Exchange (August 1949 – December 1952)
C55/118	Discount Office: Diaries (1951)
EID4/74	Home Finance: Statistical Series – Macmillan Figures (1934–58)
G1/71–2	Governor's Files: Financial and Monetary Policy – Exchanges of Views Principally at Governor/Chancellor/Bank Chairman level (January 1951 – January 1955)
G1/97	Governor's File: Exchange Policy (September 1939 – December 1952)
G1/120–3	Governor's Files: Exchange Policy – Economic Crisis 1951–2 (July 1951 – July 1969)
G3/4	Governor's Diary (1951)

G3/16 Governor's Notes of Conversations (January 1951 – December 1952)
G3/57 Governor's Duplicate Letters (September – December 1952)
G3/108 Governor's Miscellaneous Memoranda (1952)
OV44/50–1 Sterling and Sterling Area Policy: Sterling Area Exchange Policy – General (June 1949 – September 1952)

PRO OF files
Jacobsson diaries

CHAPTER 7

THE RISE AND FALL OF THE COLLECTIVE APPROACH: 1952–1955

(a) INTRODUCTORY

ALTHOUGH THE strategy and the presentation of the Collective Approach were 'one-world' in character, its origins have been seen to lie firmly in the predicament of the UK and the Sterling Area. Its primary purpose was to resolve the recurrent problems of sterling, as perceived by the Treasury, by the Bank of England, and by Commonwealth Governments. Yet although the UK authorities often spoke and wrote as if the special interests of sterling could be identified with those of the international monetary system as a whole, this was not now so apparent to countries outside the Sterling Area. It was therefore no longer the case that a presentable one-world plan for trade and payments that included some solution of the sterling problem could readily obtain financial support from the US or the willing collaboration of Western Europe. Consequently, negotiating a plan whose fulfilment was conditional on such support courted rebuff if the plan required those other countries to do things they did not want to do, or found politically awkward, and if a rebuff could be administered without fear of retaliation. As it turned out, the principal countries of Western Europe proved resistant to ideas for an early return to convertibility and highly resistant to any plan for the early termination of the EPU, the more so if floating exchange rates would follow. They also proved very suspicious of any British tactics that suggested an attempt to occupy a privileged position in discussions on trade and payments with the US. Concurrently, the slow-moving and financially cautious Republican Administration that took office in January 1953, after twenty Democrat years, was to prove as receptive as its predecessor to views expressed by continental Western Europe and as little concerned to provide any more resources for some supposedly speedy resolution of the problems of sterling. Consequently it was to have no inclination to approach Congress for financial support for the Collective Approach. Publicly committed as they were to such an approach, in which unilateral action was renounced, the British Government therefore risked from the outset encountering opposition against which they would have no effective reply.

Obvious enough with hindsight, this risk was also there to see in the autumn of 1952. In a note to the Chancellor submitted on 1 September along with the Report of his Working Party on convertibility, Brittain stated 'no one is under any illusion about the difficulties of bringing such a scheme to pass'. As Treasury officials were well aware from their experiences in 1950 and 1951, and had already warned, seeking special American financial assistance in support of sterling could be an unrewarding task; while the experience of 1945 had decisively demonstrated the dangers of a one-tactic, cards-face-upwards encounter with Washington. Above all, experience since 1947 had shown that the Americans would not respond favourably to approaches on trade and payments unless these were supported by West European countries collectively, and unless they furthered the goal of European unification without seriously damaging the long-run objective of a multilateral system of trade and payments world-wide.

As to Europe itself, the British authorities had been closely involved with the OEEC from the start and also closely involved in the whole long sequence of international negotiations about intra-European payments that began in the summer of 1947 and had continued at frequent intervals ever since. The Treasury and the Bank, as well as the Foreign Office, were well informed about the variety of attitudes and sensitivities across the Channel, whether through bilateral diplomatic contacts, the Basle network, the EPU Managing Board, or the OEEC itself. In the person of Sir Hugh Ellis-Rees, now UK Minister to the OEEC, the Treasury possessed a senior official whose experience of financial relationships between the UK and continental Europe was second to none. Accordingly, if the authorities in London had been determined to apply the experience of the recent past to the tactical problems of successfully negotiating an early implementation of the Collective Approach, they would have had to conclude that prior agreement within Europe (following agreement with the Commonwealth) was a necessary condition for a successful approach to the US. Obtaining such agreement might well have required a *tour de force* in financial diplomacy that would in any event have been altogether beyond the capacity of the Treasury and the Bank. But the exercise was not in fact attempted. Instead, the Collective Approach was launched in a manner that could hardly have been better designed to ensure that it was blocked. The European aspect was badly mishandled, causing anxiety, criticism, and resentment, which was at once made known to the Americans. They in their turn saw the Approach as a British initiative for British purposes, an initiative that they judged risky and premature and which could safely be deflected without fear of any disruptive response from London.

Those in the Treasury and the few in the Bank who were close to the OEEC and EPU saw what was likely to happen – as did the Foreign Office, but to no effect. The Government, advised by the Treasury and supported by misleading advice from American sources via the Bank, began by ignoring the risks of a unilateral approach to Washington. Just before discussions were opened with the new Administration, the Treasury did at last become alert to the gravity of the European aspect and with help from the Bank it did devise a plan for dealing with it. But this came too late in the day. The ensuing rebuff in Washington was humiliating to London, though comparatively harmless internationally. Because the Collective Approach was an answer to a British problem and not a response to urgent international demand, its rejection simply left the British back where they started, committed to a collective approach of some kind but with the responsibility for somehow solving their own particular problems at or before such time as those problems once again became acute. Thus by the end of March 1953, almost immediately after the return of the Chancellor and the Foreign Secretary empty-handed from Washington, Bolton was once again thinking about unilateral action – but this time beginning in the field of exchange control rather than in the management of the exchange rate.

(b) THE COMMONWEALTH PRIME MINISTERS' CONFERENCE, THE ROW IN EUROPE, AND THE FAILURE OF THE FIRST APPROACH TO THE US

Early in September 1952 there was at first some doubt whether the Government would agree to the Collective Approach being put to the preparatory meeting of Commonwealth officials scheduled to begin towards the end of the month. The plan, which of course included the floating-rate convertibility that had already been rejected in two versions of Robot, had a poor reception at a Ministerial meeting on 5 September. Only the Chancellor supported it, with the Foreign Secretary sitting on the fence. Cherwell was a leading opponent and remained attached to a complex variant of his Atlantic Payments Union. The Governor then became worried lest the Conference should be given no clear lead at all, and he wrote in that sense to the Chancellor on 11 September. However, the plan got a much better reception at a Ministerial meeting on the 15th and was cleared for presentation to Commonwealth officials. Though Cherwell and MacDougall continued a rearguard action that was intended to hold the Treasury in check, Rowan outlined the plan in an opening statement to the preparatory conference on 23 September. Bolton was present and reported that the UK initiative had caused a buzz of excitement. In the meetings that followed the plan was challenged on a number of points but not enough to threaten its survival. Convertibility for non-residents had little intrinsic attraction for Sterling Area members but could be accepted as a necessary step along the road to greater exchange freedom for all. The floating rate aroused considerable suspicion from all except the Canadians, but that suspicion could be allayed by British assurances that although the aim was stability, considerations of market management and cyclical disturbance required exchange-rate flexibility. Next, the idea of a stabilisation fund run by a nucleus of key-currency countries was objectionable to India, Pakistan, and Ceylon; but their objection could be met, as the Canadians soon suggested, by reconstituting the proposed 'forum' as a joint Committee of the IMF and the GATT, on which a wider range of countries would be represented. Financial support for convertibility would then fall to be provided through the IMF, with enlarged resources, instead of through a newly created stabilisation fund. Finally, there was disquiet, especially from India and Pakistan, at the proposal to dismantle all quantitative import restrictions except those on dollar goods; but this proposal could be watered down without much difficulty.

The preparatory conference dispersed early in October and at the end of that month a suitably modified version of the 'Collective Approach to Multilateral Trade and Payments' was annexed to a memorandum put to the Cabinet by the Foreign Secretary ahead of the Prime Ministers' Conference timed for the end of November. In a key paragraph headed 'The Nature of the Approach', convertibility and its financial support were to be put in place *first* and were to be followed by a concerted *long-term* policy for the removal of quantitative restrictions on trade and 'the progressive removal of discrimination as the world dollar problem is solved'. Other main elements were good creditor policies on the part of the US and modifications to the IMF and the GATT, including formation of the newly proposed Joint Committee. After the Conference, discussions would be opened 'with the United States and leading West European countries to secure agreement on a course of action'. Astonishingly, neither the OEEC nor the EPU were mentioned anywhere in this document. Nor was there any reference to the blocking of non-resident balances, a course of action that was rapidly fading from view and becoming confined to the possibility of negotiated restraint on the use of official balances by at most four principal holders (Italy, Japan, Sweden, and Thailand).

If the prospects for Commonwealth support were now reasonably good, preliminary signals from the Continent were not promising. In the OEEC, the Ministerial Council had asked the Managing Board of the EPU to prepare a preliminary report on 'the questions and problems raised by the convertibility of currencies for payments on current account'. By the end of October early drafts of this report had been prepared by the OEEC Secretariat and were strongly against early convertibility, a conclusion that attracted substantial support. The UK representatives, bound by the secrecy then attaching to the Collective Approach, could make no effective contribution, but various other members feared that convertibility would either lead to an increase in trade restrictions or to heavy depreciation of European currencies against the dollar. They preferred to stay with the EPU and with the associated intra-European trade rules. The French – commenting during October on an expert's report to the OEEC on internal financial stability and broadcasting on a very different frequency to the one they had used in July – took much the same view, adding that convertibility by itself would have little point if it obliged countries to tighten trade restrictions and discriminatory practices. Furthermore no less an authority than Ansiaux, at a lunch with Ellis-Rees on 10 October, said his views had changed radically; for much the same reasons as those being advanced by the Secretariat of OEEC, he felt that in present conditions it would be a great mistake to contemplate a move to convertibility.

All this was reported back to London, by Grant to the Treasury and by Portsmore[1] to the Bank, while on 4 November Roll[2] reported to both

[1] *Portsmore, Frederick John* (b. 1906). Educated Strand School. Entered Bank 1925, Assistant 1949–53, Adviser (Acting) 1953–9, Adviser 1959–65, UK Alternate Executive Director, IMF 1953–5. Vice-President and London Representative of the Crocker-Citizens National Bank 1965. Respectively UK member and alternate member on the EPU Board.

[2] *Roll, Eric, Baron* (Life Peer) 1977, (b. 1907). Educated Birmingham University. Professor of Economics and Commerce, University College of Hull 1935–46, British Food Mission to North America 1941–6, Assistant Secretary, Ministry of Food 1946–7, Under-Secretary, HM Treasury (Central Economic Planning Staff) 1948, Minister, UK delegation to OEEC 1949, Deputy Head, UK delegation to NATO, Paris 1952, Under-Secretary, Ministry of Agriculture, Fisheries and Food 1953–7, Executive Director, International Sugar Council 1957–9, Chairman, UN Sugar Conference 1958, Deputy Secretary, Ministry of Agriculture, Fisheries and Food 1959–61, Deputy Leader, UK delegation for Negotiations with EEC 1961–3, Economic Minister and Head of UK Treasury delegation, Washington, Executive Director for UK, IMF and IBRD 1963–4, Permanent Under-Secretary of State, Department of Economic Affairs 1964–6, Director, Bank of England 1968–77, Deputy Chairman, S. G. Warburg 1967–74, Chairman 1974–83, Joint Chairman 1983–7. Chancellor, Southampton University 1974–84.

institutions that a number of continental European representatives in the OEEC had begun to fear that the organisation was likely to be bypassed by a unilateral British approach to the US. On the same day, Conolly of the BIS warned Portsmore that the Secretary-General was doing all he could to obtain support for a joint European approach to the US through the OEEC, provided there was a consensus in favour of an early move. Portsmore, reporting Conolly's warning to the Bank, added: 'I have not yet heard anything here to contradict it.' Bolton passed this information to Rowan at the Treasury, suggesting it would be better if further preparation of the Managing Board's Report were postponed until after the Commonwealth Conference when the UK representative would be in a proper position to contribute to it. Next the Governor told the Chancellor he was unhappy about this situation and felt that some empire-building was going on in Paris. The Bank then successfully went into action in Basle. While the central bank Governors did not feel the Report could be postponed, they did agree that it should as far as possible become purely technical, with no political element and no specific conclusions. In the end the Report was indeed technical and was not formally circulated. It was mainly concerned to demonstrate in great detail that convertibility and full EPU membership were incompatible.

These clues to the likely reception of the Collective Approach on the Continent were received just before the Treasury and the Bank had to put forward provisional recommendations about the procedure to be followed after the Commonwealth Conference. The Europe section of Overseas Finance, headed by Copleston, boldly suggested that the next step should indeed be a joint initial approach to the US and Canada by the UK and its prospective European partners. But this was rejected in favour of an initial British approach to the US and Canada on the one hand and 'selected Europeans' on the other, together with a general statement of UK intent in the OEEC. But although simultaneous, the approach to Washington would in fact, as Lucius bluntly put it, 'be the main negotiation'. At this stage the British authorities were still pursuing the idea of a key-currency nucleus and had developed relatively few thoughts on what was to happen to the non-nucleus, or unselected members of EPU, when that institution ceased business. The nucleus itself was to include only the UK, France, Benelux, and perhaps West Germany. The OEEC as a whole, of which the UK was then in the chair, was to be left on the monetary sidelines. Both Bolton and Rowan were uneasy about the suggested procedure. What seemed to be needed was a quick agreement in principle, from both the US and the selected Europeans, after which a whole variety of details would need to be worked out in a whole variety of separate forums. The danger was that details would get discussed too early and in the wrong place. But there was no easy way round the danger, there being no ready means of ensuring a quick agreement-in-principle.

Shortly before the Prime Ministers' Conference attention shifted to the US, where Eisenhower was now President-elect and the appointment of Foster Dulles as Secretary of State and George Humphrey as Secretary of the Treasury had been announced. In the third week of November the Governor visited New York, Washington, and Ottawa. On his return to London he wrote direct to the Chancellor recording the main impressions he had gained. Firstly, the Administration would take a lot of convincing that enough had been done in the UK and the rest of the Sterling Area to provide a secure foundation for any new arrangements in which the US might be asked to participate. That was nothing new. But the second message was both more specific and tactically much more important, though misguided. Its principal sources seem to have been the recently appointed Chairman of the Federal Reserve Board, McChesney Martin, Allan Sproul in New York, and Towers in Ottawa. Cobbold recorded it as follows, with his own endorsement:

> Great importance would be attached in responsible circles to the method of approach. It is felt most strongly that there should be an early contact between yourself and the new Secretary of the Treasury, to be followed up at high level between the UK and US Treasuries to see if there can be some meeting of minds before discussion gets into a wider circle or any Round Table Conference is arranged. I received similar advice from Mr Towers, Governor of the Bank of Canada, and I concur most heartily with it myself. We must of course take care not to neglect our European friends, but I should have thought it should prove possible to keep the most important of them privately informed of what we were doing and why we were doing it in this way.

Very similar advice was given to Bolton by Lincoln Gordon, the representative of the Mutual Security Administration (MSA) in London. He said that the approach to the US should be entirely informal and be made by the UK alone. He also recommended that any approach to European countries should be direct to the countries concerned and not through the OEEC. But the trouble with all this advice, to which the Bank was bound to give considerable weight, was that it did not take nearly enough account of the strong possibility that many of the Europeans would be very suspicious of a unilateral British approach to the US, would be inclined to oppose British ideas for early convertibility, and would themselves tell the Americans this directly. There was in any case no real possibility of opening discussions with the US privately, in secret, under cover of some general exchange of views. For the Commonwealth Conference was bound to issue a communiqué that included some reference to the Collective Approach and to the consultative procedures that were to follow. In any event too many people knew what was afoot.

In the meantime various details of the plan were being put into place in London. The IMF Board, guided by Rooth, had recently agreed the modalities of stand-by facilities and an adaptation of this procedure was fitted into the Collective Approach. A very large stand-by of up to $2·5 billion was thought to be needed to support sterling. Since only $1·3 billion could be obtained from the existing UK quota, some $1 billion would be needed from a special ex-quota facility. The entire amount would be drawable over any twelve-month period. Drawings would nominally be repayable over three to five years but in practice would be repaid earlier. In addition to the large UK stand-by, further funds would be needed to provide stand-bys for the 'selected Europeans'. As a result the Fund's dollar resources would be drained off and the drawing rights of the rest of the world impaired. Accordingly the Fund would have to borrow from the US, which meant persuading the US to lend. Very much a second best to borrowing from the Fund would be for the UK to embark on a barrel-scraping search for dollars from the Federal Reserve, the US Treasury Stabilisation Fund, the Export-Import Bank, and US commercial banks. Most of this would need the approval of the Administration, who would also have to agree to any large UK stand-by. Alongside the facility would be the new joint IMF/GATT Committee of Twelve. The nucleus countries, namely the US, UK, Canada, France, West Germany, and Benelux would be permanent members. The remaining membership would rotate and might initially include Australia, India, one Latin American country, one Middle East Country, one non-nucleus European country, and Japan. There would be two plenary meetings a year, attended by top officials from each country; but there would be provision for *ad hoc* meetings in case of need. During intervals between meetings, alternates would meet frequently or even continuously. It was in this forum that discussion would proceed on 'the whole complex of finance, trade, and associated problems' (words used in the Cabinet memorandum of 31 October).

All this was to prove an elaborate castle in the air. But for its part the Bank was now embarking on a rather different and more earth-bound venture. Although only a small part of the Collective Approach, it was one that found a mention in the final communiqué of the Conference and was to have a worthwhile life long after the Collective Approach itself had been forgotten. This venture was the Commonwealth Development Finance Company (CDFC). All along, since the earlier Conference in January 1952,

Commonwealth development had been a lively topic. Whether developed or underdeveloped, the independent members of the sterling Commonwealth were concerned to attract foreign investment capital. Indeed one of the arguments for the restoration of convertibility and the rehabilitation of sterling more generally was that it would improve the flow of, for example, American capital into Australia. The other side of the coin was the development of additional production that could help replace hard-currency supplies. Like sound internal policies 'worthwhile development' was a concept to which it was not difficult to secure ready assent. Worthwhile action, which often depended upon the removal of deterrents in the capital-importing countries themselves, was not so easy. But early in October 1952 Cobbold mentioned to the Chancellor that he had ideas about a Commonwealth development loan. The UK had always been a source of capital for the Empire and there were no exchange control impediments to UK investment in the Sterling Area. Nonetheless there might be room for additional facilities provided they did not overstretch the limited resources of the UK. By the end of October the Governor had dropped the idea of a loan and was thinking instead of a City organisation that would start in a small way and perhaps form a link with the IBRD. The Chancellor gave him encouragement and during the first ten days in December, while the Conference was sitting, much of his time was spent in negotiation with City and industrial interests and in preparing an announcement about CDFC[3] that coincided with the final communiqué on 11 December. In the same context the UK Government undertook to facilitate the financing of schemes in other Commonwealth countries, which would contribute to the improvement of the Sterling Area's balance of payments. One way of doing this would be by making sterling available to the IBRD for the support of such schemes.

The Conference itself ran into only one serious difficulty. The delegations of India, Pakistan, and Ceylon refused to commit themselves to retaining the fixed link with sterling if and when the latter floated against the dollar. They wanted to reserve the right to peg on the dollar and float against sterling. If exercised, this right would have been incompatible with membership of the Sterling Area: in practice it would have meant the countries concerned being free to build up their own gold or dollar reserves for use in maintaining the fixed link with the dollar. The issue was brought to Cabinet on 4 December and it was agreed that the Collective Approach could not go ahead unless the Asian Dominions conceded. At the request of the Chancellor and in consultation with Rowan, the Governor then

[3] A brief description of the negotiations is related in Chapter 11 below.

intervened with the Indian Finance Minister, Deshmukh. He was an old friend, first as a senior official in Delhi and later as Governor of the Reserve Bank of India. Together they worked out a compromise that, by implication, would give the Indians the option of pegging on the dollar if sterling were to be floated at a time of UK emergency and was confidently expected to depreciate heavily. This gave them what they really wanted, without notable damage to the British position. In a Minute agreed personally between the two and subsequently also with the Finance Ministers of Pakistan and Ceylon, the key passage read:

> If it were generally thought, at the time when the operation was undertaken, that the prospects of success and of reasonable stability were good, it would be convenient for all Sterling Area currencies to keep in step with sterling. But it would be for the Sterling Area countries and other countries associated with the Collective Approach, in the light of the conditions then ruling, to decide on the precise techniques to be adopted.

In the Bank, this solution was challenged by Parsons. 'I feel sufficiently disturbed', he wrote to the Governor, 'to put my misgivings on paper.' The key passage seemed to him 'to be open to the charge of seeking agreement at the cost of clarity'. Would it not be much better to face the whole problem squarely now and explain to the Indians during the Conference just where their present train of thought was likely to lead them? The Governor, though not a man ordinarily given to ingenious compromises, was far more experienced than Parsons in negotiating with the sub-continent. He firmly rejected the advice offered. One might talk frankly to the Indians in private 'but without threats and *not* in Conference. If Mr Menzies and Sir C. D. are allowed to shout at each other, we should get a hardening of positions we shall never get back from. We shall be much wiser to get the best expression we can of *their* intention to play with us.'

The communiqué was issued on 11 December. In a section entitled 'International Action' the Conference recorded its agreement 'to seek the co-operation of other countries in a plan to create the conditions for expanding world production and trade. The aim is to secure international agreement to the adoption of policies, by creditor and debtor countries, which will restore balance in the world economy on the lines of "Trade not Aid" and will, by progressive stages and within reasonable time, create an effective multilateral trade and payments system covering the widest possible area.' Under the heading 'Finance', the Conference agreed that an integral part of any effective multilateral system was the restoration of the convertibility of sterling. Its achievement, however, depended upon successful action by the sterling Commonwealth countries, upon appropriate trade policies on the part of other countries, and upon adequate financial support 'through the IMF or otherwise'. No mention was made of exchange flexibility nor of the convertibility of other currencies. Finally, under the heading 'Procedure', the Conference proposed 'to seek acceptance of this plan by the Governments of the United States and of European countries, whose cooperation is essential, and to work as far as possible through existing international institutions dealing with finance and trade'. The close ties between the Commonwealth countries, the US, and the members of the OEEC were emphasised in a concluding paragraph.

Although the communiqué left open the precise order in which further consultations were to be held, the British Government had already made up its own mind about it. At a Cabinet meeting on 4 December it was accepted without argument that the plan should first be put to the US. The initial approach to the incoming Administration should be an informal one through the British Ambassador. If this went well, it would be followed by Ministerial talks. At a further Cabinet meeting shortly before Christmas the Chancellor reported that together with the Foreign Secretary he had spoken privately in Paris to representatives of the US and the main European countries about the work of the Conference. He felt this had gone reasonably well, though there were signs of future difficulty in handling Italy (not a nucleus country but a member of the EPU, the ECSC and, prospectively, the EDC).

Another document to appear in December 1952 was the Fourth Annual Report of the OEEC. It acknowledged that discussions about convertibility were taking place but argued pithily that so long as the dollar problem persisted and the gold and dollar reserves of West European countries remained low, 'attention must be directed towards increasing the usefulness of existing institutions such as the EPU and the IMF, and of arrangements such as the OEEC code of liberalisation and the GATT'.

Although the Chancellor thought his talks in Paris had gone reasonably well, it soon became evident that European reactions to the Conference communiqué and to British intentions about prior consultation with the US were as hostile as Ellis-Rees and others had warned they would be. On 22 December Portsmore reported to the Bank that most members of the EPU Board were very doubtful whether early convertibility of sterling or other currencies would hold any advantages for European countries and felt it was important to consolidate the progress already gained through the EPU. Early in the new year Ellis-Rees wrote to the Treasury warning that unless the procedure were reversed – so that European countries were fully consulted before the Americans – the former would make their own representations to the US and British leadership in the OEEC would be prejudiced. In fact, he advised, the proposed procedure risked destroying the Collective Approach.

Robert Marjolin, Secretary-General of the OEEC, gave similar advice when he visited the Treasury on 16 January. He thought that the proposed order of events was the worst possible. A quick decision from the Americans was most unlikely and the period of uncertainty through ignorance was therefore likely to be prolonged. European anxieties were threefold: fear of an Anglo-American *fait accompli*, fear of restrictive trading by the Commonwealth, and fear of a collapse of the EPU with nothing effective to take its place.

In Basle, the central bank Governors were less hostile, though most were concerned about the future of the EPU and did not, as Cobbold recorded, 'want to see it shaken until they were certain that there was something that suits them better'. The Governor was however warned about a rumpus being generated in Paris. He passed this information to Treasury Ministers, suggesting that some quiet talks with the principal Governments, dispelling any suggestions of a bounce, would suffice to meet the difficulties. Meanwhile the Bank of France was again keeping as close to the Bank of England as it could. Baumgartner expressed understanding of British tactics. He felt sure that the Governor would keep him informed and that the British would play in with the French as soon and as closely as they could. He nevertheless warned that René Mayer, who had just succeeded Pinay as Prime Minister, was somewhat perturbed, under pressure from Monnet and Marjolin. He suggested that a quiet chat between Mayer and the Chancellor would be helpful, a suggestion that Cobbold duly passed, with his own support, to Butler.[4] Meanwhile the storm continued. On 26 January Portsmore reported that the other members on the EPU Managing Board, with minor exceptions, were united in opposition to the UK. On the 25th, at a meeting in the Treasury, the Foreign Office expressed great concern about European reactions to the Commonwealth Conference and took its turn in arguing that Europe should be fully consulted before the US. But the Treasury refused to give in, suggesting instead that the imminent announcement of the visit of Eden and Butler to Washington, beginning at the end of February, should be preceded by a mollifying and reassuring communication to European Governments.

The Eisenhower Administration had now taken office. At the end of January Secretary Dulles, accompanied by Harold Stassen, the new Director of MSA (shortly to be renamed the Foreign Operations

---

[4] Mayer visited London during the first half of February.

Administration), left for a brief introductory tour of NATO capitals. They began in Rome, where they were pleased both by Italian support for European unity and by the moderation of Italian requests for US financial assistance. But the Prime Minister, de Gasperi, expressed concern over the UK attitude to the OEEC and the EPU. The Americans must have been well aware that this concern was widespread. On 3 February, at a meeting with OEEC delegates in Paris, Dulles went out of his way to refer to the question of forthcoming international economic talks. He assumed this was very much on the minds of European countries and gave an assurance that the US would enter into no commitments with the UK without full opportunity for consultation with the OEEC. He pointed out that the US had no knowledge of the contents of the UK proposals and might simply reject the lot; but certainly no agreement would be reached without full consultation. Earlier, at a gathering of US representatives in Western Europe, Dulles emphasised the close Congressional interest in progress towards European unity and the link between such progress and the provision of further Aid. Congress, he remarked, had felt for some time that they had granted money for European Aid on the basis of vague, and unfulfilled, promises of European unity.

Though the wave of continental protest did not succeed in altering the British choice of a prior approach to the Americans, it was not without effect on British thinking. Belatedly, as on so many occasions since the problems of intra-European payments were first considered in the summer of 1947, it was realised that rather more was needed than generalised undertakings to work out the details of any new intra-European monetary relationships at a later stage, after the rest of the Collective Approach had been agreed with the Americans and the principal members of EPU. During January 1953 the Treasury was busy drafting a memorandum on the Collective Approach for the US Administration. The paucity of ideas about the European content of the plan was all the more apparent now that continental views were becoming known and that the underlying arguments for an early move to external convertibility at a floating exchange rate – before rather than after the eventual dismantling of discriminatory trade restrictions – could not suitably be deployed in front of the new audience. These underlying reasons were peculiar to the external monetary problems of the UK and had little attraction for other countries in Europe, who normally saw convertibility coming after rather than before the freeing of trade. The underlying reasons could be discussed with the Sterling Area; and they could be understood and be agreed in that forum. But they could not very well be put to Washington or Paris without revealing that the Collective Approach was mostly a British plan for solving British problems. The eventual UK paper circulated to the US was indeed notably devoid of reasons why convertibility had first priority. It was therefore all the more important to devise a convincing plan to meet European worries about the monetary relationships that might follow the early termination of the EPU.

The Bank was asked to provide such a plan and did so in ideas that foreshadowed some of the features of the European Monetary Agreement signed in the summer of 1955 and activated at the end of 1958. Thompson-McCausland was at this time developing ideas about the special part to be played by a Fund stand-by in providing the proposed underpinning for sterling convertibility. He argued that an entirely new facility would be required. Ordinary drawings would be inappropriate, for they would usually require negotiation, would carry conditionality, and would be repayable over three to five years. Sterling convertibility, by contrast, required the support of a banking facility on which drawings could be made unconditionally at any time but would be repayable within twelve months with the option of one renewal. The facility would in effect constitute a direct reinforcement of the first-line liquidity provided by the reserves. But these ideas, although paralleled to some degree by thinking in the Fund itself, were ahead of their time. They were more suited in the first instance to arrangements that could be made through central banks rather than through the IMF; and they pointed the way to the swap networks and the Basle Agreements (for support of sterling) that became a feature of international currency management in the 1960s. Whether they would have gained ground in 1953 if the Americans had supported the Collective Approach is difficult to judge. But ahead of the negative American response they could at least provide a proper reply to European critics. Special IMF stand-bys, access to which would be automatic and unconditional, would be granted to the principal members of the EPU and could reasonably be regarded as compensation for the abolition of EPU credit. Concurrently, the EPU Managing Board could be preserved as a forum in which any outstanding questions of intra-European payments and exchange rates could be monitored and debated.

These proposals were accepted by the Governor and passed by Bolton to the Treasury, where they were well received. Clarke in particular was attracted by the idea of compensating the members of the EPU for the loss of credit rights. In his view, Ministers would be greatly influenced in their whole attitude to convertibility by the willingness of Europe to follow the UK. On 21 February the Treasury circulated a Cabinet paper entitled 'Europe and the Commonwealth Conference Proposals', which opened with the rueful sentence: 'The Americans will be well aware of the anxiety already displayed in most European countries about the conjectured content of our proposals.' There followed, at long last, a candid and realistic statement about the whole problem. The Americans would want to be assured that the disappearance of the EPU would not be followed by any deterioration in the freedom of intra-European trade and payments. They would want to establish whether the UK proposals would help or hinder progress towards their goal of European political and economic unity. There was genuine anxiety in Europe about the consequences of terminating the EPU, anxiety that was accentuated by the special factors arising from the workings of the ECSC and, prospectively, of the EDC. Since it would be useless to turn a blind eye to these European difficulties or hope that they would in time go away, the UK would have to make clear to the Americans that 'we fully recognise both the serious and far-reaching effects of our proposals on the European economy and also the genuine difficulties which other European Governments may have in accepting them. But we have in fact given the matter a great deal of thought and have some tentative suggestions to make as to the broad lines of a possible solution.'

There followed an explanation of the proposals that had originated in the Bank, as well as the important additional suggestion that the new Managing Board should have at its disposal, for lending to weaker members, a fund comprising the capital subscribed to the EPU by the US. The proposals, in shorter outline, were also included in a paper that was sent to Rooth in Washington along with a copy of the main paper on the Collective Approach that had been circulated to the US Government. This latter document, dated 10 February, contained appropriate general expressions of concern about the European problem but no reference to specific proposals for dealing with it. (These had not yet been agreed in London.) At preparatory discussions with American officials – headed by W. Randolph Burgess, a distinguished banker who was now Under-Secretary for monetary affairs at the US Treasury – Makins and Hall-Patch stressed that London was thinking hard about the European problem and had no intention of proposing abolition of the EPU without replacing it with something better. Burgess acknowledged that the Americans had received an initial blast of European criticism about the supposed British intentions but said that things were now quieter and that some countries had taken a more favourable view of the possibilities of convertibility.

The stage was now set for the Foreign Secretary and the Chancellor to leave for the US on 26 February and for talks with Dulles and Humphrey to begin on 4 March. The Bank was not formally represented in the UK delegation, but the Governor sent Parsons to the US on 19 February. The

Governor himself was open-minded about the prospects of success with the Americans and fairly sanguine that the storm in Europe would blow over without much lasting damage. In a letter sent to Baumgartner on 6 February he strongly defended the decision to carry out an initial exploration in Washington ahead of talks in Europe. He was sure the exploration would 'give some idea of the lines which it may be worth pursuing and of those which are not – and that we shall then have to do some hard thinking together on this side of the Atlantic and try to hammer something out. At the moment I have not the slightest idea where we shall get to, or when or how. I should be more bothered if I felt that there was any fundamental difference about the direction in which we want to go – but I do not think there is.' He next wrote a personal letter to Sproul, which he sent on 11 February along with one to Rooth. After recording with approval that the emphasis had shifted away from convertibility as an end in itself to more general objectives of a one-world economy, he stressed that despite doubts and hesitations on particular points there was a remarkable solidarity of view in the Commonwealth that the general line of policy was right. He then considered the European problem and the prospects for the Anglo-American talks:

> We have run into some heavy weather with the Europeans. This is mainly on political and procedural grounds. There is a good deal of empire-building within the OEEC organisation, and some genuine nervousness that they may find themselves pushed into more of a free and competitive economy than they think they can stand – and of course always a state of nerves when we seem to be more preoccupied with Commonwealth than with Western Europe. On the whole our central banking friends seem much less bothered than the political people, and I am hopeful that after the Washington talks this may all settle down.[5]
>
> As I see it the possibility of progress depends almost entirely on the attitude of your people. Things having improved here and with sterling looking healthy at the moment, our people will certainly make no move unless they get the feeling that there is a real desire for a new look at all this on your side. I am very glad RAB and Humphrey are going to meet – this seems to me the only conceivable way of finding out whether it is worthwhile trying to take all this further this year or not.

The answer was not long delayed. After three day of talks Parsons cabled the Governor on 6 March that the temperature was exceedingly cold. The UK proposals had been greeted as wholly laudable, but doubts had been expressed whether the UK economy was yet strong enough for their

---

[5] A few days after this letter was sent the Governor spent a day in Paris. Baumgartner agreed with him that the British need not be too concerned about the EPU fuss and that the storm would soon blow over.

introduction. It seemed that the Administration was in any case very averse to approaching Congress for the proposed financial assistance or for necessary measures on the trade side. He concluded bleakly: 'In my estimation, the plan in its present form is unlikely to go forward for at least another twelve months.' Neither the Minutes of the meetings, nor the anodyne communiqué issued when the talks had finished, nor the telegram sent by the Chancellor to the Prime Minister, nor Rowan's despatch to Bridges differed much in substance from Parsons' telegram. The Eisenhower Administration was not ready to decide upon any comprehensive plan for freer trade and payments. But it was in any event disinclined to look seriously at a plan that contained notable risks, did not enjoy firm European support, and whose need did not seem to be very urgent. There was, for instance, little need to fear disruptive unilateral action by the British. For the time being, therefore, it was best to leave well alone, allowing time for prolonged reflection and for the existing arrangements, including the EPU, to continue their satisfactory work.

The Anglo-American talks in March 1953 effectively killed the Collective Approach as conceived in London in the autumn of 1952 and as subsequently developed. The corpse remained unburied for some time; several attempts were made to resuscitate it; and in London its name survived as a description of different plans that were later developed. But the Americans never showed any enthusiasm for it, however much thought they gave to the development of international trade and payments. Nor, once the threat of an Anglo-American *fait accompli* and any threat of unilateral action by the UK had been removed, did the original British plan attract so much attention in Europe. There survived a more lively appreciation that the eventual winding-up of the EPU, the introduction of such continuing intra-European arrangements as might be needed, and the resumption of external convertibility by West European countries, should be undertaken by collective agreement. There also survived some reluctant recognition that sterling convertibility might need special help from the IMF and might need to be accompanied by a widening of official dealing spreads. But there remained little acceptance of the view that convertibility should come early and should precede rather than follow a gradual dismantling of discriminatory trade restrictions. If the UK, for reasons peculiar to the management of sterling as an international but inconvertible currency, felt unhappy with this order of priorities, then it had somehow to find a way of ameliorating its own problems without breaking the understandings about intra-European trade and payments. In this respect the situation was not unlike that already reached in July 1952 when the second version of Robot was rejected, the difference being that the then obvious alternative way out of the cage, a grand multilateral solution, had now once again been blocked.

The Old Lady was not the mother of the Collective Approach; she was more like its aunt. The plan was a Treasury invention that had to be accepted as a tactical necessity at the time. Its original 'key-currency' features, although largely lost as the plan was developed and adapted in response to overseas criticism, were attractive to the Bank. But although at times its strong supporter, the Governor always viewed it with some scepticism. With ample justification, he feared that it would either tie the hands of the British authorities or weaken their resolve over decisions about sterling, decisions that were a British responsibility and could not properly be shared with others;[6] and as he told Baumgartner and Sproul in February 1953, he had some doubt whether the plan would in practice prove the vehicle in which international progress would be made. Then, too, the Bank more generally was never very comfortable with solutions that entailed frequent political and bureaucratic interference, often through cumbersome international institutions, in matters of the market place. In this way the stalling of the Collective Approach, following the blocking of Robot, provided the Bank with an opportunity to devise a low-key market solution to at least some part of the sterling problem. The trouble with the schemes that had been blocked was that, in their different ways, they had been much too high-key and dramatic. Largely through Bolton's combination of insight and technical knowledge, this time productively constrained within a rather narrower framework than usual, the Governor was able to make some use of the opportunity that now began to be offered.

(c) THE REORIENTATION OF POLICY AND THE LIBERALISATION OF TRANSFERABLE STERLING: MARCH 1953 – MARCH 1954

On 10 March 1953 Sproul wrote in a personal letter to Cobbold that the UK should not be too disappointed at the negative outcome of the Washington talks, which he attributed to 'the immediate aches and pains of our new Administration'. 'If you can keep on the upgrade', he wrote, 'and not lose the impetus gained from the Commonwealth Conference, and your own past actions, I don't think we should be discouraged, even

---

[6] Per Jacobsson wrote in his diary for 1 March 1953: 'Cob said to Auboin (General Manager of the BIS), "When we are ready in London we shall take our steps without asking Jacobsson or you, Auboin, or the OEEC in Paris for that matter." That is the spirit. It seems fine but it is not altogether a healthy spirit since it means the British want international consultations only for the others.'

though we might like to get ahead faster than seems likely.' Warning against losing the initiative, he remarked: 'If we wait until everybody is ready, willing and able, however, without the spur of positive action by the two great trading and financial areas, we are likely to wait a long time, or forever.' This advice accorded closely with the Governor's mood and he wrote to the Chancellor on 13 March mentioning Sproul's views and saying how important it was to retain the initiative. To this end the immediate task was to mend fences across the Channel where, he wrote optimistically, 'I think we now have an opportunity of mobilising a lot of support for our objectives in Europe (particularly from quarters to which the present US Administration will listen).' The Treasury was of the same mind and the Chancellor himself had been encouraged by the Americans to keep up the momentum of his policies. Accordingly, on 23 March he made a conciliatory statement to the Council of the OEEC. It was received well enough, but Butler told his officials he was convinced that the Europeans as a whole did not go along with British ideas about convertibility. Three days later, in an unprecedented display of official Treasury concern for European goodwill, Rowan and others talked for eight hours with the Board of the EPU and the OEEC Steering Board for Trade, about the Collective Approach whose details were now exposed virtually in full, including the exchange-rate flexibility. But Portsmore reported that the atmosphere was no more than 'reasonably good'. Ansiaux was sympathetic and the Scandinavians seemed favourably disposed, but the French and the Dutch expressed doubts and the Germans, Italians, and Swiss said nothing. At bilateral talks held in Paris towards the end of April, the French, without showing their hand, asked Rowan a number of familiar questions about the future relationships between those currencies that became convertible and those that did not and also about the future of trade discrimination.

Meanwhile Cobbold was becoming impatient. He continued his frequent correspondence with Sproul, a feature of this period. Early in April he stressed the need to keep the initiative in joint Anglo-American hands for fear that matters would otherwise be let drift. Keeping up momentum was not easy. 'I am not sure whether your people fully realise how difficult this is over here. Anything that can be done to give the impression here that your people are working seriously on all this and putting it high on their agenda will be very helpful.' Sproul replied on 20 April. He too was becoming impatient. 'There is a possibility, which has seemed to increase a little lately, that these matters may drift into the hands of Study Commissions or become involved in Conferences of so broad a nature as to impede progress.' Rowan corroborated this on return from a brief further visit to Washington. The Administration had asked Lewis Douglas to prepare a confidential report on the British plan and was also setting up a commission of enquiry into US external economic policy.[7] Burgess had even used the word 'demise' in reference to the Collective Approach. Rowan concluded that the Americans would not acquire much enthusiasm for the British proposals and would look instead for half-way houses.

The Governor himself then visited New York and Washington, reporting back to the Chancellor at the end of May. He talked with Martin and Sproul in the Federal Reserve and with Humphrey and Burgess at the Treasury. When he pointed out that time was slipping by and momentum was in danger of being lost, he got much the same message as Rowan. The Collective Approach was unacceptable, according to Burgess, 'because there were too many things in the box'. The Governor concluded that the Americans had given very little further thought to the whole subject, were hoping it could all be left to Lewis Douglas or to the Randall Commission, and had little idea what to do if the hopes were not fulfilled. They wanted to lend support to the UK initiative but would favour a bit-by-bit approach rather than an early assault on Congress. 'Bit-by-bit', ironically enough, included an American suggestion made a few weeks earlier that modestly wider spreads for sterling should be introduced without a concurrent restoration of convertibility. This had to be given another airing in Whitehall before it was again rejected, except as a remote possibility in a crisis. The question of exchange rate policy then became immersed in a special Treasury-Bank exercise about the likely effects of an American recession, now judged to be in the offing, and the right policy responses to them. This proved to be something of a reprise of the Robot controversy, with the Bank and Overseas Finance favouring floating-rate convertibility and 'the planners' (as Thompson-McCausland called almost everyone else in the Treasury) favouring the maintenance of activity in the non-dollar world through discriminatory trade restrictions, appropriate domestic policies, and IMF drawings.

The implications of all this were not lost on Bolton. As early as the end of March, in the course of a letter to the Treasury, he had said: 'I am convinced that specific action in the technical field is a necessity, not only to keep the major policy alive but also to gain experience of the consequences of fewer restrictions.' He suggested hardening the EPU settlements, widening the transferability of sterling, dismantling the restrictions on transferable accounts in Western Europe (the restrictions imposed to hamper cheap-sterling operations), and allowing authorised

---

[7] The Randall Commission. It was not finally appointed until September 1953.

banks to conduct arbitrage operations in the main EPU currencies so as to facilitate the multilateral clearing of commercial payments through London. The Treasury was reportedly sympathetic, except on the hardening of the EPU, and the Bank was left free to develop Bolton's ideas. The arbitrage proposal was later accepted and put into effect during June, but little else was changed at that stage. Early in the same month, however, Bolton argued that a much greater change of policy was likely to be needed before long. Declaring it obvious that the Collective Approach had reached a condition of stalemate, he concluded: 'On the assumption therefore that by September the Americans will have failed to decide what part they should play internationally in the field of trade and payments, London probably has no alternative but to seek a means of putting Commonwealth economic policies into operation through methods that may differ substantially from those included in the Collective Approach.' The Governor indicated agreement and an exercise began 'to see if we can agree on the line of a new campaign'.

Laurence Menzies began the exercise with an outline plan for unifying and freeing all non-resident sterling outside the dollar area. There would be a single Transferable Account Area within which transferable accounts could be opened by all. Balances on those accounts would be transferable for any purpose, capital or current, within the entire non-dollar world. Control on payments to the dollar area would remain. In addition, the London gold market would be reopened and residents of the Transferable Account Area would be allowed to deal if they opened special 'gold sterling' accounts fed from initial sales of gold or dollars. Menzies accepted that the unification and freeing of non-dollar, non-resident sterling would substantially increase the ease with which cheap-sterling operations could be undertaken. The seriousness of this problem depended both on the intensity of dollar shortage and on the state of the Sterling Area's balance of payments; but on reflection Bolton himself regarded it as a major defect of Menzies' proposal and advised the Governor accordingly. The latter agreed that unification should not be pursued at this stage. An alternative that was not, at least in logic, open to the same objection would be to enlarge the Sterling Area; but Bolton now doubted whether this old and familiar idea had anything to recommend it. Further examination reinforced that scepticism. However the proposal to reopen the London gold market was a different matter. It would be in line with the policy of reopening London commodity markets, subject to exchange control safeguards designed to prevent their use as an indirect means of conducting currency speculation. Reopening the gold market would bring back business lost to other markets, notably Zurich, and would help to keep

South Africa more content with continuing membership of the Sterling Area and with the sale of substantial quantities of newly mined South African gold to the EEA.[8] It would, however, be an entirely free market in which the price, as in other free gold markets, could depart from the US monetary price of $35 per ounce. This price applied only to transactions for monetary purposes between the US Treasury and approved overseas monetary authorities. The US Treasury did not intervene in free markets and since the war prices ruling there had shown a premium over the monetary price. Gold producers, including South Africa, had come to sell an increasing proportion of their output on these markets. This state of affairs was not welcome to the US, whose own citizens had not been allowed to own gold since 1934. It was felt that the premium markets encouraged private gold-hoarding and cast doubt on the validity of the monetary price. The reopening of London, the biggest market in pre-war times, therefore risked American displeasure and was unlikely to be contemplated so long as the Collective Approach seemed a runner. If it were no longer a runner, however, this objection could fall to the ground.

At the end of June 1953 Lewis Douglas completed his report for the President and a copy was made available to the authorities in London. It analysed the importance of sterling in world trade and of the restoration of convertibility as part of the move to freer trade and payments. It complimented the British Government on the progress made towards a stronger and more competitive economy but judged that the UK was not yet strong enough to stand the strains and stresses of convertibility without risk of repeating the ill-fated experiment of 1947. It urged that the US 'commence to remove from our own policies the impediments to freer trade and currencies'. Though helpful, the report did not take the Collective Approach much further and during July Sproul wrote to the Governor: 'Reluctantly I must confess that I was overly optimistic last Fall as to the speed with which a new Administration might take up the problem and grapple with it constructively, and that I was almost equally awry on the Lewis Douglas study which seems to be winding up...The only likely thing in prospect is for little steps which it is hoped will be in the right direction.' Cobbold replied: 'I am inclined to share your rather gloomy feelings about all this. In the meantime we are getting on with easing up a bit here and there, getting commodity markets going, etc., so as to keep things moving along in the hope that your people will get round to the subject in due course.' He added that he sensed the beginnings 'of some

---

[8] Dr Steyn of the South African Finance Ministry had talks with the Treasury and the Bank during June 1953. He was very disappointed with the lack of progress on the Collective Approach. He also raised the question of the gold market, hinting that they might open a market in Johannesburg.

questioning in Whitehall whether there is any real hope of your Administration tackling these subjects seriously at all'.

Early in September, after talking to Bolton who had travelled to the US ahead of the Fund and Bank meetings, Sproul wrote about the appointment of the Randall Commission. 'It is a mixed group, the public members on the whole being liberals in their approach to our foreign economic problems and the Congressional group containing some pretty rock-ribbed individuals. I think it is fair to say, however, that unless some of these latter people can be brought around, by study, discussion, and persuasion, to a clearer recognition of our position in the world, the outlook will be dim.'

The Collective Approach was again discussed in Washington in September, concurrently with the Fund and Bank meetings. But it was once more made clear by Secretary Humphrey that there was no prospect of additional dollars being made available to the IMF for the support of sterling convertibility, at the very least until after the mid-term Congressional elections in November 1954. Nor was there any prospect of decisions on US trade policy until well after the Randall Commission had reported in six months' time. Bolton, writing back to London, added that lack of any agreement in Europe about the Collective Approach was making matters worse. 'The pace is being dictated by the pace of the slowest, e.g. the French. Washington is forced to wait on all the European Governments, OEEC, and EPU before it can begin to tot up the bill, quite apart from acting as umpire in conflicting policy arguments. Unless we can change our tactics to an attack in force with genuine and acceptable Allies (Germans and Dutch with Canada actively associated on the side) on specific objectives we are going to get nowhere.'

The bad news from Washington was confirmed by Lewis Douglas when he visited London at the end of September. He agreed with the Governor that all was going terribly slowly and that nothing could happen until after the Randall Commission had reported. So Cobbold was now prepared to explore a complete change of course and he told Rowan on 29 September that he thought the main possibilities for the next month or two lay in the fields of sterling transferability and the gold market. On 5 October Thompson-McCausland sent a note to the Governors drawing attention to progress that had been made on the trade side during 1953. Most imports of raw materials and food into the UK had been returned to private hands and discrimination had been abandoned. Consumer rationing was disappearing. More commodity markets were being reopened, and the usefulness of sterling was thereby being enhanced. But monetary arrangements were lagging behind. Non-resident inconvertibility and the consequent survival of 'cheap-sterling' markets was inconsistent with the freeing of trade that had taken place. The UK should therefore press ahead with convertibility, unilaterally if need be. The Collective Approach had served a worthwhile purpose by provoking widespread debate that had 'served to implant the idea of a good creditor in America, of some approach to central reserve lending by the IMF, and of a phase beyond EPU in Europe'. If advance was to be made beyond the point now reached, it would only be through unilateral action by an individual Government.

Two weeks later Bolton declared that the Collective Approach had served its purpose and that nothing could be gained by 'pursuing in detail this series of tentative proposals'. Discarding the caution he had shown during the summer, he now suggested sweeping changes in exchange control over non-residents, amounting to non-resident convertibility and a widening of the sterling–dollar dealing spread to $2·74–$2·86. But in a note entitled 'An Outline of Foreign Exchange Policy', circulated on 21 October, he had quickly modified this plan by dividing it into two stages. The first, which could be introduced in advance of a meeting of Commonwealth Finance Ministers in Sydney, would consist of the unification of all non-dollar, non-resident sterling and the abandonment of the administrative restrictions designed to discourage cheap-sterling operations. The second stage could be discussed at Sydney and would primarily include abolition during 1954 of the barrier between the Transferable and American Account Areas (that is to say the resumption of convertibility) hopefully supported by stand-by assistance from the IMF, a banking credit in New York, and some parallel action by the Germans, Swiss, and Dutch. In the event of subsequent trouble, recourse would be had to the combined use of the reserves, Bank Rate, and a fluctuating rate of exchange.

The Governor wrote to Sproul once again on the same day as he received Bolton's 'Outline': 'any definite move on the technical side on the lines put forward by RAB to Humphrey is well and truly bogged down and will never emerge from the hordes of "experts" in IMF, EPU, and XYZ. Is it, or is it not, worth trying to think up a bit of a short cut, and, taking advantage of the sympathy with objectives which seems to exist, giving a push into some deeper water without waiting for all the weather to look fine – it never will – and the climate will not stay favourable for too long.' As the Governor was well aware, the UK reserves had risen by $700 million to only $2·5 billion over the preceding twelve months while sterling liabilities had risen by $600 million. The recovery was fragile and the external banking position had hardly strengthened. The Collective Approach had got nowhere. What, then, was to happen if the breathing space came to an end and sterling came under renewed attack?

Sproul replied sympathetically on 13 November; but already on 30 October the Governor had sent a long note to the Chancellor, which he discussed with him privately 'at length and in some detail'. As a result the note was turned into a long formal letter which was sent on 4 November. It drew on the ideas of Bolton and Thompson-McCausland, added the Governor's own thoughts and judgements, and squarely set out the policy that the Bank was to advocate for the next two years. It was one of his best letters, drawing clear lessons from his experience since the change of Government in 1951 and charting a practicable course within which there was plenty of room for tactical manoeuvre and flexible response:

> I have mentioned to you in the last weeks my belief that the time has come when we should have a new look at our exchange policy.
>
> I would, in retrospect, divide the 'Collective Approach' proposals into two sections:
>
> (a) The statement of policy and objectives. This seems to me to have been useful and successful. It has achieved wide support in the Commonwealth, in Europe after initial troubles, and in many influential circles in USA. It has helped to improve the general climate, it has given UK the initiative and it has provided a pattern within which it has been possible to make some progress towards the objectives.
>
> (b) The technical proposals – i.e. what we should do about sterling and what we should expect others to do. As things have gone over the past year, particularly in USA and in EPU, this section seems to me completely bogged down. I do not believe that this plan in this form can now come to anything and I do not think that anything is to be gained by tinkering with it or amending it.
>
> I think that HM Government's policy of freeing things up, removing controls and allowing the price system to work has now (perhaps just in the last months) crossed the Rubicon. Our exchange control arrangements are still geared to a controlled economy and are running behind our commercial and commodity arrangements. This means that we are in some ways getting the worst of both worlds. If things continue to go fairly well we shall not derive full benefit from the commercial freedoms. If things take a turn for the worse we shall be in a dilemma – we shall either have to reverse engines about physical controls, rationing etc. (which, though you will know much better than I, does not look easy except in war conditions) or else make a dash for freedom on the exchange side in the worst conditions. On the longer view I do not believe that our present exchange pattern, based on close administrative and technical cooperation between the independent members of the sterling area and on a ring fence between sterling area and the rest, can survive indefinitely – it is showing progressive signs of strain.
>
> From the US, IMF and 'support' angle I do not believe there is now any possibility in the foreseeable future of getting Congress or even the Administration to take any formal commitments to provide definite support

funds or credit facilities on the lines envisaged in the 'Collective Approach'. On the other hand there is much sympathy with what we are trying to do and they might well do their best to give us encouragement and support, both moral and material, if we took action on our own responsibility without asking for commitments in advance.

From the Commonwealth and European angle, if we let the present position stagnate we shall lose the initiative and leadership we have built up over recent years. I believe there might be considerable support from the most important European Governments if we felt able to take a further step on our own initiative provided that it did not *in practice* upset rate stability or kill EPU.

I suggest, therefore, that, as world events are developing, adherence to the present time-table will involve risks either of losing initiatives and advantages or of having to scurry for cover in disorder in a storm. If this assessment is right, there are strong arguments for considering, in advance of the Sydney talks, whether, whilst maintaining the policy and objectives of the 'Collective Approach', we cannot find some technical means of speeding up the time-table.

As a first step consideration might be given to a general simplification of exchange control practice towards non-resident sterling other than on American account, with a view to allowing a regular market in a single transferable sterling to develop in overseas markets alongside official sterling. With the present strength of sterling and with the shortage of sterling in various countries, and given reasonable political stability, there is little reason to think that the transferable sterling rate would drop – it might even improve in the early stages and we would consider the possibility of occasional intervention to narrow the spread between transferable and official rates.

This would bring us nearer to, but would still leave to be faced, the next step of free transferability between American and other non-resident sterling. 'Convertibility' has become an issue which arouses passions national and international, and which is completely misunderstood by the public, who think it means that they could travel where they like and remit what they like and who would be greatly upset when they found it did not. It would help objective discussion of the problem if the term 'Convertibility' could be firmly put in the background.

But the free transferability of non-resident sterling (which is what has been meant by 'Convertibility' in these discussions) is a stated objective of HM Government and is an increasingly necessary complement to HM Government's policy in other fields. Here again, in the new market conditions, there are technical possibilities of a further advance which merit study in relation to the general political and economic picture.

If it would be convenient I shall be glad to arrange for our representatives to discuss these matters with representatives of HM Treasury, to see whether any concrete proposals could be worked out for your consideration.

The Chancellor, who was anxious to arrange a positive agenda for the Sydney Conference, replied on 6 November that he fully agreed that the letter should be discussed between the Bank and the Treasury. Bolton's 'Outline' had been sent to Great George Street the day before, with the additional proposal of official intervention in the transferable market during Stage 1, designed to help bring the transferable and official rates closer together. But while the Treasury was willing to consider most of Stage 1, including the gold market but without the addition of intervention, it was not willing to make any commitments to the Bank about Stage 2. Despite the far-sighted ideas formulated earlier in the year, the Treasury was still far from clear about intra-European monetary relations under convertibility and wider spreads. In particular it was rightly uncertain how it would be possible to collaborate on exchange policy with other European countries without giving up freedom of action. Nor was the Bank very reassuring on this question. Bolton and Thompson-McCausland had abandoned hopes of European currencies being pegged to sterling and now made detailed reference to the very informal but nevertheless effective Franco-Anglo-American Tripartite Agreement of September 1936. They even recirculated a note on the subject written by Siepmann in August 1937. This began: 'The great value of the Agreement is not due to its terms but to the fact that it is regarded as a pledge of co-operation. The exact scope of this cooperation is all the better for not being understood.'[9] This might have been all very well in 1937 or 1987 but it would have taken a lot of swallowing in 1953, in a Western Europe now very much conditioned to formal agreements and written rules. In the Treasury, where Brittain and Clarke in Overseas Finance had now been replaced by Playfair and Arnold France,[10] officials were distinctly puzzled. Nor had they entirely given up hope of obtaining promises of American assistance before taking the plunge into Stage 2. Humphrey was coming to London in December and there was the Randall Report scheduled for the late winter.

Cobbold was not too disheartened by the Treasury attitude and began to exploit the tactical flexibility of the Bank's new course. He wrote to the

[9] The Governor was in full agreement with the line being taken. In a manuscript comment on a note by Bolton early in 1954 he said: 'When I negotiated the Tripartite Agreement with M. Fournier I repeated like a parrot, "Ni accord, ni entente, uniquement coopération journalière", until it became a joke between us. We ought to go on the same basis and work for as much *de facto* stability as possible. We should neither expect nor give commitments about future behaviour of currencies in unforeseeable circumstances. I don't think it will serve any useful purpose to argue about all this with the Europeans in advance of the next round on convertibility. What will interest them is whether we keep stable and look like staying stable.'
[10] *France, Arnold William, GCB (b.1911)*. Educated Bishop's Stortford College. District Bank 1929–40. Army 1940–3, Deputy Economic and Financial Adviser to Minister of State in Middle East 1943–5. HM Treasury 1945–63, Assistant Secretary 1948–52, Under-Secretary 1952–60, Third Secretary 1960–3. Deputy Secretary, Ministry of Health, 1963–4, Permanent Secretary 1964–8. Chairman, Board of Inland Revenue 1968–73.

Chancellor on 27 November, suggesting that Stage 1 be put into operation before the Sydney Conference and be followed by a 'bridge period' of uncertain but not indefinite length during which there would be official intervention in the market for transferable sterling designed to bring the transferable rate closer to the official rate. If this succeeded, the UK could then seek a general blessing from the IMF and the US for widening the official spread – *unofficially and informally* (author's italics) to $2·75–2·85. The two rates might then coalesce, though transferable and American account sterling would still be formally separate.[11] This would 'leave any more formal commitments to a day when positive international action became more possible'. But again the Treasury was not to be rushed. It accepted the unification of non-dollar, non-resident sterling but would give no commitment on intervention or on the informal widening of spreads and would not agree to any action before the Sydney Conference. There next descended another heavy shower of cold water from the US. In talks with Treasury Ministers and officials in London during December, Secretary Humphrey said that he thought the only result of the Randall Commission would be to preserve the status quo and avoid steps in the wrong direction. In response to a suggestion from Butler, which he attributed to the Prime Minister of Australia, Humphrey said he saw no chance of the US being persuaded to call a world economic conference. They went on to discuss IMF stand-bys, but the Americans were worried about unconditionality. As to their financing, Humphrey again made it quite clear that the Administration would not go to Congress for money to increase the Fund's resources. He also showed some aversion to the idea of the Fund obtaining fresh resources by borrowing. The Chancellor ended the discussion by appealing for an American 'Act of State' comparable to Lend-Lease; but it may be doubted if his audience were listening.

The Sydney Conference proved a quiet one. Menzies told Butler, who agreed, that convertibility was at least a year off. Members generally reaffirmed their support for the Collective Approach and noted that some progress had been made in the lifting of restrictions in the UK, in increasing the Sterling Area's reserves, and in talks with the IMF, but they recognised the lack of progress with the US and Western Europe and the continuing inadequacy of the UK reserves and of Fund resources to support them. The Finance Ministers were consulted about Stage 1 and indicated assent, though with some reservations on the gold market. Parsons, whose star in the Bank was firmly in the ascendant, accompanied the British delegation and wrote back to Bolton: 'The discussions so far on

---

[11] He reminded Rowan a few days later that the current strength of sterling made coalescence a strong possibility. This favourable opportunity would not last indefinitely.

the Collective Approach have certainly lacked any sense of urgency or even reality and convertibility seems to be more and more regarded by officials in all delegations, except the Canadian, as a pipedream.' The Canadians were indeed pursuing their interest in multilateral trade with a positively Belgian tenacity. Rasminsky (later Governor of the Bank of Canada) told Parsons that the UK was in danger of missing the boat on convertibility and that Southard, American Executive Director of the IMF, thought that a stand-by of $2 billion was on the cards. Finance Minister Abbott objected to the reopening of the London gold market on the usual grounds of American objection but was tartly reminded by the Chancellor that as Canadian gold production could already be sold on free markets it was difficult to see why they should oppose reopening of the market in London.

The Report of the Randall Commission was published in Washington at the end of January 1954. Though moderate and helpful in tone, it did not carry the debate on convertibility very much further. Sproul wrote to the Governor on 25 January: 'In our particular field, however, there seems to have been no difference of opinion and a way to further progress may have been opened.' But in his reply Cobbold wrote: 'I confess that I am a little disturbed by what seems to me the absence of a sense of urgency.' The paragraphs on convertibility, which had been drafted by Professor J. H. Williams, advocated a gradual and controlled approach, hand in hand with the removal of restrictions on trade. A dash for convertibility at a freely floating rate was not favoured, though some degree of managed floating was acknowledged to be useful. But the EPU should not be dismantled before there was something better to put in its place. The Commission then acknowledged that sterling was a key currency in which about 40% of world trade was financed, but it judged that UK reserves were insufficient to sustain its convertibility. The Report accordingly concluded that the reserves should be supplemented by more active use of the existing resources of the IMF and perhaps also through lines of credit with the Federal Reserve. Williams, talking to Parsons in New York on 17 February, pointed out that Randall had become a Special Adviser to the President and argued that the Report was more positive than it seemed. Progress might now be possible on several fronts, including fortification of the UK reserves. However, Sproul wrote again to the Governor on 15 March, warning that in practice the Federal Reserve would not grant any line of credit to the UK without the strong recommendation of the US Government. There was, he said, no current prospect of this being made.

In the meantime the Bank and the Treasury were quietly going ahead with Stage 1. On his return from Sydney via Washington, where he had obtained the US Treasury's assent to the proposed reopening of the London gold market, Rowan saw Bolton on 4 February and agreed that a plan of action should now be put to the Chancellor. On the 17th he again saw Bolton and told him that the recommendations for 'unification' were being put forward, though there were a number of dissentients. The Chancellor held a meeting on 2 March with his senior officials, the Governors,[12] Bolton, and Parsons. Cobbold was asked by Butler firstly whether unification would prejudice in any way the timing of a decision on convertibility and secondly whether it would remove some of the available defences against a US recession. The Governor answered both questions in the negative, though he remarked that he had never made any attempt to hide his opinion that unification was a further step in the direction of convertibility. Hall, on the other hand, suggested that the operation be deferred until the economic climate looked rather more settled. The US was at this time going through a mild recession and there continued to be some anxiety in parts of the Treasury, and in particular the Economic Section, lest the external balance of the UK and the Sterling Area should be adversely affected.

The Chancellor thought it over for a further twenty-four hours and then agreed that unification, together with the reopening of the gold market, should take effect from 22 March. Telegrams were quickly agreed with the Treasury and put into final form for despatch to overseas central banks. The clearing banks were quietly given advance warning, by Bolton to Ellerton. On 15 March the Governor wrote personally to Rooth and sent appropriate extracts to Sproul in New York and to Towers in Ottawa. The tenor of all these communications was low-key and technical, the changes being presented as a further step within the general policy of removing restrictions where possible and of moving towards a freer and more multilateral system. In his letter to Rooth, Cobbold noted that the reopening of the gold market had the blessing of the US Treasury and that all the Commonwealth Governments had been informed at Sydney. As to the general nature of the policy being pursued, he wrote:

> I would not like you to draw any particular conclusions from these changes which, although substantially technical, will attract a considerable amount of public comment. They are consistent with all the other steps which we have taken over the past few years to get rid of unnecessary and hampering restrictions but they do not represent any more rapid advance towards the convertibility of sterling. This, as you know, depends to a large extent upon decisions which have to be taken in Washington.

Graham Towers cabled 'Congratulations' when he received the Governor's

[12] Mynors had succeeded Dallas Bernard as Deputy Governor on 1 March.

telegram. Stage 1 of the Bank's programme had been achieved. Stage 2, including the 'bridge' of intervention in transferable sterling, had now to be approached.

(d) MISSING THE TIDE, 1954, AND THE INTRODUCTION OF BACK-DOOR CONVERTIBILITY IN FEBRUARY 1955

Stage 2 was to prove far more difficult. At various points along the road the Governor again endeavoured to persuade the Treasury that *de facto* convertibility and wider dealing spreads could be achieved unilaterally without precipitating monetary disorder, European political upset, or adverse trade policies. Coalescence of the official and transferable rates would come first, encouraged if need be by intervention in support of the latter. Next would come a widening of the official dealing spread and acquiescence in this unilateral move by an IMF reassured by British professions of virtuous intent. But the formal exchange control distinction between transferable and American account would remain. Although in practice transfers between the former and the latter would be allowed, convertibility *de facto* would not have become convertibility *de jure*. This, Cobbold argued, would provide a cover under which EPU and the liberalisation codes could continue while agreement could be reached about such continuing intra-European monetary arrangements as were thought to be required post-convertibility, about the phased elimination of discrimination against dollar goods, and about IMF stand-by support for sterling and other newly convertible currencies. But the Chancellor and his officials never accepted these arguments. The cover, in their view, would be so transparent as to put them in the untenable position of unreasonably denying that they had gone ahead to convertibility without first satisfying the preconditions laid down in the Collective Approach. In practice this meant that official intervention in support of transferable sterling, *without* coalescence, was the absolute limit to unilateral action.

Intervention in transferable was introduced early in 1955, when the breathing space had at last ended, when sterling had again come under pressure, and when cheap sterling was again giving serious trouble. But the subsequent inability to proceed any further with Stage 2, together with the onset of a period of renewed external weakness that lasted until 1958, meant that the UK was dragged by the nose towards *de jure* fixed-rate convertibility without substantial fortification of the reserves in order, severally, to placate European opinion, to avoid accepting a large Fund stand-by on the wrong terms, and to avoid risking the domestic political awkwardness of sterling falling to the lower end of a wider spread.

The unification of March 1954 was well received in the markets. Sterling continued firm and the reserves went on rising. At the end of March the official rate was $2·81$\frac{9}{16}$, while transferable was quoted in New York at $2·77$\frac{3}{4}$. By the end of April, a month in which the reserves rose by as much as $135 million, these rates had risen to $2·81$\frac{7}{8}$ and $2·79$\frac{1}{4}$. Transferable was now within the 1% dealing spreads either side of the official parity. So eyes in the Bank naturally turned towards some early move towards Stage 2, including Fund acceptance of wider spreads, and to negotiation of a large stand-by at the autumn Annual Meeting that would support the final move to convertibility somewhat later.

The omens across the Atlantic, misleading as they so often were, seemed at first to be quite good. In mid-March, at a meeting of the joint US and Canadian Committee on Trade and Economic Affairs, the Canadians had urged the Americans to take a more positive attitude towards the Collective Approach, having concluded at a preparatory meeting of officials that the Administration had not formulated a coherent attitude towards it at Cabinet level. Indeed the Foreign Operations Administration (FOA), the most active agency in this field, was thought to favour a strengthening of regionalism in Europe and to be exercising its influence against a positive American response to the British proposals. In reply, Secretary Humphrey changed tack and encouraged the Canadians to believe that the Administration would now be prepared to agree a large Fund stand-by for the UK, in support of convertibility, provided the British Government 'felt sufficient assurance in their own situation to move ahead'. The stand-by would be a charge against the Fund's existing resources and might amount to the total British quota of $1·3 billion. These encouraging noises were relayed by the Canadians to the UK Embassy in Washington, and in detail by Towers to Cobbold a few days later. Concurrently, twenty-eight closely typed pages on sterling convertibility, including the suggested stand-by, were circulated in the Fund by its Director of Research, Eddie Bernstein of Bretton Woods fame. Though in fact a bad omen, and a foretaste of excessive bureaucratic concentration on the details of a UK stand-by on the part of every interested party in Washington, this epistle served to reinforce an impression that the whole subject had now become alive.

Bolton set to work once more and suggested, as a first step towards Stage 2, getting Fund and American acceptance of wider spreads and an effective but unofficial range, to which there would be no lasting commitment, of $2·75–2·85. Within this, and if necessary with the help of intervention, transferable and official would be allowed to coalesce. Then, in the autumn, a stand-by would be agreed. Both Parsons and Thompson-

McCausland were quick to point out the crucial tactical aspects of the developing situation. As transferable had appreciated without assistance to $2·79¼, it was realised that there could in practice be no going back to the days of large discounts without courting a serious relapse of confidence. So intervention could hardly be avoided if the transferable rate fell back appreciably. It was also realised that coalescence within the existing spread of $2·78–2·82 risked over-confidence and a temptation to look again at the fixed-rate convertibility which the Bank and Overseas Finance still regarded as unwise. But it proved as difficult to persuade the Treasury to take positive action on wider limits when sterling was strong as it would later when sterling was weak. Bolton deployed arguments about defending the money market against a sterling boom by allowing the rate to rise above $2·82, but they cannot have carried much conviction. His final paper on the subject was sent to Rowan at the end of April. The Governor supported him in a letter to the Chancellor; but the Treasury was not keen. Officials had their eyes on the autumn meetings and the fairer winds from North America had renewed their interest in pursuing the multilateral road of the Collective Approach, or what remained of it.

A Collective Approach Committee, no less, was now formed. Gilbert,[13] Bridges' Deputy, was its Chairman,[14] with Rowan and other officials representing the Treasury. Caccia represented the Foreign Office and Frank Lee the Board of Trade. Bolton (with Lucius as his alternate) attended for the Bank and was asked at the Committee's first meeting why the Bank were now saying that intervention in transferable was unavoidable when, allegedly, they had previously advised the Chancellor that unification did not commit him to intervention. The record does not precisely substantiate this latter claim. At the time, the Governor had advised that unification would not prejudice the timing of convertibility though it did represent a further step along that road. Bolton replied on 21 May, saying simply that the rates had now come close together and could not, for familiar reasons, be allowed to diverge much in the future. His proposals were then considered by the Chancellor and turned down. Butler was in a cautious mood and the Treasury judged that intervention in transferable and a widening of the official spread would in practice risk, as Rowan put it in a letter to Bolton, 'sliding prematurely into convertibility' without the

[13] *Gilbert, Bernard William, GCB (1891–1957).* Educated Nottingham High School and St John's College, Cambridge. HM Treasury 1914–17. Army 1917–18. HM Treasury 1918–56, Joint Second Secretary 1944–56. Member, Restrictive Practices Court 1957.
[14] Treasury documents suggest that Rowan wanted to take the chair and did not expect Gilbert, to whom he put the proposal, to take it himself.

preconditions of the Collective Approach being satisfied. But, he asked, was there building up a technical situation that would deprive the Government of choice in the matter of intervention? Bolton replied at some length, pointing out how bad it would look, after the progress of the past few years and the repeated declarations of external economic policy, if transferable sterling reverted to a heavy discount and cheap-sterling operations were to flourish once more. The choice would remain with Whitehall, but the arguments would all point towards intervention. He concluded by advising that the question of early intervention be kept open, to be reconsidered if the run-up to the IMF meeting seemed promising. But at about this time the signals from Washington, previously so enticing, began to assume a familiar harsh tone.

Some weeks before, Sproul had twice written to Cobbold warning him on the first occasion that 'this business of convertibility and stand-by credits is still not in the forefront here' and on the second that 'nobody seems to be in much of a hurry over here'. Yet Under-Secretary Burgess, in the course of a long talk with the Governor during a visit to London early in May, confirmed outright that the Administration was now ready for further progress and would like a good deal to be done at the September meeting. He said the same thing in the Treasury while the long-serving Southard repeated it to Bolton, emphasising that the US Treasury was now taking convertibility seriously and had got to get somewhere by September. He did not think there would be difficulties over the stand-by, but the US Treasury would require considerable reassurance about the UK's proposed exchange policy. However, he also mentioned the continuing differences of view between the Treasury Department and the FOA about the merits of persisting with the EPU. Hall-Patch reported from Washington a fortnight later that while expectations of action in September were gathering way, Southard was beginning to talk ominously about the contents of a letter of intent which the UK would have to sign. A few days later he wrote that the US Treasury was losing control and that all Washington would be brought into the drafting of this document, with each interested Department seeking to get conditions written into it. There would be confusion and delay. Rickett[15] wrote to Rowan from Washington a week later, warning that trade discrimination was the principal American interest. In the Bank, the Governor expressed concern to Rowan by aptly

---

[15] *Rickett, Denis Hubert Fletcher KCMG (b. 1907).* Educated Rugby and Balliol College, Oxford. Fellow of All Souls College, Oxford 1929–49. Principal Private Secretary to Prime Minister 1950–1, Economic Minister and Head of UK Treasury and Supply Mission, Washington 1951–4, Third Secretary, HM Treasury 1955–60, Second Secretary, 1960–8. Vice-President, IBRD 1968–74. Director, Schroder International 1974–9.

referring to the possibility that the 1954 stand-by negotiations might get into 'a 1945 Loan negotiation position'. He warned Rooth, during a brief meeting at London airport, against too much American interference in the stand-by terms.

While the westerly winds were once again beginning to blow cooler, the Bank and the Treasury had begun to give closer constructive attention to one of the other preconditions of the Collective Approach, namely that satisfactory arrangements should be made with the other members of the EPU before convertibility was restored. Ever since the spring of 1953 there had been discussions on this subject in the OEEC and in the Managing Board of the EPU. But they had served to clarify attitudes and to identify problems rather than to arrive at negotiated solutions. Marjolin had again visited London in June 1953, arguing with Rowan that some special intra-European mechanism would be needed, post-EPU, in which convertible and inconvertible currencies could both participate. There would be a transitional period between the resumption of convertibility and the abandonment of trade discrimination. During that transition some kind of modified EPU would be needed. The Council of Europe, in a report issued in the same month, had expressed concern lest convertibility should damage intra-European trade. But the EPU Board failed to get to grips with these problems, the French and the Belgians arguing that this would be premature. Finally, Rowan attended another joint meeting of the EPU Board and the Steering Board for Trade at the end of June 1953. He told them that the UK had put its cards on the table at the earlier meeting and that it was now up to the other members to think the matter through and respond in constructive terms. But at a meeting of the EPU Board at the end of September no such response was forthcoming. The Belgians, French, and Italians worked successfully to shelve the British proposals, to wrest the initiative back from London, and to open up the field for other ideas. Meanwhile the UK was reliberalising its trade with Europe and on that account not keen to see an early hardening of the EPU terms of settlement. Next, the Germans and the Belgians, at political level, began to argue the merits of full convertibility, for residents as well as for non-residents, and to belittle the non-resident convertibility advocated by the British.

By the end of 1953, when Stage 1 was in the offing and Stage 2 hopefully not far distant, the Bank had become concerned at the impasse in Europe; concerned because it recognised the great reluctance of British Ministers to take any steps towards convertibility that would break the EPU before proper agreement about what was to succeed it. After considerable debate between Parsons, Thompson-McCausland, Rootham, and Watson, a complicated outline of a 'Revised EPU' was circulated early in December. It was an important outline because, for the first time, it contained ideas for maintaining a clearing mechanism, with some provision of interim credit, that would enable convertible and inconvertible currencies to co-exist in an intra-European system. These ideas, in one technical form or another and for one reason or another, were to persist. As will be recounted later, they were to have decisive side-effects on the far more important issue of British exchange-rate policy.

No further progress was made in Paris during the first few months of 1954 while the UK went ahead with Stage 1 and the American Administration was making encouraging noises about sterling convertibility and a Fund stand-by. In order to lift the subject of post-EPU arrangements out of the EPU Board and of OEEC Committees of officials, a special Ministerial Group under British chairmanship was established to deal with it.[16] In that context the Collective Approach Committee in Whitehall asked the Bank to prepare a series of papers. The EPU itself had now been renewed for a further year and there was some presumption growing in London, in view of the expected progress of the discussions in Washington, that it might come to an end in the summer of 1955. So the Bank, duly produced a further note on the suggested European Fund for the needy (for example Greece and Turkey) to be financed out of the EPU's dollar capital, augmented perhaps by the principal European countries and administered by the OEEC. It also produced a new paper entitled 'European Central Bank Co-operation Post-EPU' and suggested that this subject be referred by the Ministerial Group, shortly to meet in London, for consideration between the central banks themselves and not by the EPU Board. Apart from discussing exchange guarantees on balances arising from the provision of automatic credit within a membership some of whose currencies had more flexible rates than others, the paper effectively proposed the continuation of a payments union but with 100% gold or dollar settlement at the end of each specified period. Within those periods interim finance would be made available, just as in the EPU but only up to agreed limits. The Bank did not explain why anyone should want to participate in such a union; but it believed that what was wanted in Europe was a means of avoiding *daily* settlements in gold or dollars (particularly the former), an assumption supported by Cochran, Rooth's Deputy, when he visited the Bank on 3 June after travelling on the Continent. The author of the Bank's paper was Bolton, who ended by

---

[16] Its members were UK, Belgium, France, West Germany, Greece, Italy, the Netherlands, Sweden, and Switzerland.

remarking, with wisdom born of hard experience, that the temptation to promote sterling as the main currency of European settlements should be resisted. He felt it would be a mistake for HMG or the Bank to put forward proposals of that kind. 'It would seem preferable to continue to develop the efficiency of all London international markets and to rely upon these to cause a natural gravitation towards the use of sterling and sterling markets.'

The Bank's ideas about a continuing intra-European payments mechanism, ideas which found their way to the Ministerial Group along with the suggested European Fund, caused some excitement in Paris and Basle. Bolton reported that enthusiasm for an early move to convertibility had grown and that Marjolin was now a keen supporter. An expectation was mounting that at the autumn meetings the Chancellor would propose a timetable as well as a policy and tactics. But alas he had no such intention. At precisely this critical moment of full tide, with the European aspect at last going well, British resolve was crumbling. On 3 June, at a meeting with the Governor, Bolton, and senior Treasury officials, Butler suddenly expressed great concern lest the initialling of a Fund stand-by in September should publicly commit the Government to introducing convertibility within a few months thereafter. Such a commitment, he said, would be very difficult politically. The Governor could but agree that announcement of a stand-by would increase expectations of an early move and, as such, would improve market confidence still further. But failure to move, or prior failure to make progress in September, would make people think that things were going wrong. Confidence would then weaken. It might be possible to avoid formally agreeing a stand-by in September, but the terms were bound to be discussed and some favourable statement would have to be made if informal agreement on the terms had been reached.

Probably unknown in detail to the Governor, the resolve of the British Government was now beset with uncertainty about the timing of Churchill's retirement from No. 10 and how soon thereafter his successor might call a general election. Senior colleagues expected that the Prime Minister, who had suffered a stroke in July 1953, would retire during the summer of 1954. In the end however he decided to carry on through the winter. There also seems to have been some understanding that Eden would go to the country soon after succeeding to the Premiership. The Conservative campaign would seek to capitalise on the successes of the Government's economic policy and aim to increase the Party's tenuous majority in the Commons. Since an early move to convertibility would not be without risk and could provide the Opposition with further ammunition, there was evidently taking root in the Chancellor's mind a presumption that the final move to Stage 2 could not be undertaken this side of the election.[17]

As this political indecision grew, the American attitude to a Fund stand-by continued to harden. Hall-Patch reported that the Administration was gradually imposing conditions. Burgess was now arguing that countries becoming convertible should be required to adopt Article VIII of the Fund Charter rather than continue for a time under Article XIV. This would mean, in effect, the abandonment of all discrimination hand in hand with convertibility, a view confirmed by Burgess and Stassen when they attended a meeting of the OEEC Ministerial Group in July. This American attitude increased opposition in Whitehall to Stage 2. The Economic Section, under Hall and Little,[18] argued that there should be no convertibility until discrimination had gradually disappeared. A few weeks later they raised another issue, saying that there was a world rather than a UK shortage of reserves (outside the US), which the IMF might be unable to fill. International liquidity needed to be restored to the levels of the 1930s; and a new 'Automatic Credit Union' in Europe might help towards this objective.

Meanwhile Rowan told the Governor that he expected UK Trade Ministers to oppose convertibility if it meant abandoning discrimination. At a moment when the outlook for the UK and Sterling Area balance of payments had anyway begun to deteriorate to the point where there was little margin to spare, unfavourable calculations began to be made about the effect of non-discrimination on UK exports of manufactures. Even Lucius, an indefatigable advocate of convertibility, advised Bolton of the need to continue discrimination in manufactures during a post-EPU transition. On 28 June Cobbold wrote again to Sproul, who was himself becoming increasingly gloomy:

> It seems to me we have got about as far as we can technically on 'Convertibility' – it is now in the political machine and we shall have to see what grinds out of the European meetings in July and the Washington meetings in September. The political side of all this is not easy over here any more than it is on your side. I am keeping up a little mild encouragement on Whitehall friends (on the theme song that there is a tide which might be

---

[17] The Chancellor's nervousness about convertibility may also have been due to his being constrained by the setting up of a special Cabinet Committee on External Economic Policy. However, it met only twice and was dissolved in November 1954.

[18] *Little, Ian Malcolm David, AFC* (b.1918). Educated Eton and New College, Oxford. RAF 1939–46. Fellow of All Souls College, Oxford 1950–2, Fellow, Nuffield College, Oxford 1952–76, Deputy Director, Economic Section, HM Treasury 1953–5, Professor of Economics of Underdeveloped Countries, Oxford University 1971–6, Special Adviser, IBRD 1976–8.

missed) but I do not think it wise to try to push too fast just now. If we can keep the 'market' boat steady for the next few months something may emerge.

When however he returned from holiday on 1 September, the Governor found awaiting him a report from Bolton saying that official sterling had weakened to $2·80\frac{1}{4}$ under seasonal pressures, though the market was calm. But by the end of the month the rate had fallen to $2·79 and the EEA had begun to intervene in support. The Governor wrote to Sproul that he was not concerned but added: 'Looking ahead a bit, I am more bothered by the risk that sentiment towards sterling may change a bit if the idea gets about too much that the move towards convertibility is off the map.'

To add to all these growing difficulties, the French Assembly finally rejected the EDC Treaty in August 1954, thereby appearing to inaugurate a period of uncertainty and confusion in the politics of European unification that would be likely to affect attitudes towards the winding up of the EPU. In one of his wilder, Cassandra-like moods Bolton warned of the likely disintegration of Western European 'political policies' and began to think aloud about the external monetary policies that might follow, including the removal of the virtual European veto on UK exchange policies which he felt had arisen from the tactical way the Collective Approach had had in the end to be handled by the British Government.

The scene then shifted briefly to Washington, where the corpse of the Collective Approach was hurriedly re-interred. British Ministers made it clear that political difficulties would prevent an operation being mounted for at least another year. The Americans, for their part, now said they would insist on the UK entering a *unilateral* obligation to abandon all discrimination when the proposed Fund stand-by came into operation. This overbearing requirement, heavily reminiscent of 1945, was quite unacceptable to the British. Even worse, Secretary Humphrey suggested to the Chancellor that US tariffs were too low and might have to be raised. 'I do not think anything further will emerge from these meetings', Bolton wrote back to Cobbold, 'that will in any way change the impression in the minds of the Chancellor and the other members of the Delegation that the Collective Approach, certainly in its present form, is dead.' He added, over-optimistically, that Hall had been won over to the Bank's proposal for intervention in transferable, 'thus slowly moving by degrees from a fixed controlled system into a convertible and fluctuating system'. From Washington, the Chancellor wrote to the Governor in like vein: 'This [his talk with Humphrey] does not mean that we are hopeless but it does mean that we walk on political ground which in this country is even more uncertain than it is at home.' Writing early in October, Sproul summed it up: 'I suppose the Chancellor pretty well convinced our public that final convertibility has been put in the cooler for the moment, but I hope not in the deep-freeze.'

Shortly after Butler's return from Washington the Governor impressed on him yet once more that the momentum of policy had somehow to be kept up even though formal convertibility was not on the cards until well into 1955. The interval should be used 'for getting ahead constructively and quietly with the things *we can do* without anybody's permission and with support from our Commonwealth and European partners (but keeping our policy firmly in our hands and not putting it in theirs)'. There could be further exchange control relaxations. The EPU might be adjusted onto a 100% gold and dollar basis ahead of convertibility. Experimental intervention in transferable could again be considered. But none of this had much appeal. In the Bank, Lucius was again pointing out that an experiment was impracticable if it meant a trial run. Either one intervened so as to secure coalescence and proceeded thereafter to Stage 2 or one intervened so as to stop transferable going to an unacceptable discount. In either case the move would prove irreversible. He wrote when the underlying condition of sterling was deteriorating and when confidence had been impaired by the lack of progress in Washington. Expectations had been created but not fulfilled, and to the markets it looked as if something must have gone wrong. As the year drew to a close it was becoming clear that the tide had indeed been well and truly missed. By early December official sterling had fallen to $2·78½ while transferable had fallen away to $2·70½, a discount of nearly 3%, and the reserves were falling. There could now be no question of moving from a position of strength. There was instead the situation over whose prospect the Governor had fretted for some little time, a situation requiring an answer to the question: What was to be done if a phase of renewed weakness began before convertibility had been achieved? Finding and agreeing the answer was to occupy the first two months of the new year.

'Momentum' of a special and very important sort was, however, being kept up in Europe and was to occupy much of the stage during the autumn and winter. Early in September, before leaving for Washington, Bolton and the exchange dealers (now headed by Menzies and Bridge) had put forward further ideas for central bank co-operation post-EPU. Instead of a payments union with interim finance and 100% gold settlements, why not have an inter-central bank swap network? The maximum size of the swaps would be fixed by agreement and each facility would be usable at any time, for three months extendable for one further month up to 30% of the original deal. Balances would bear interest at the applicable rate for Treasury Bills.

One virtue of exchange swaps was that they solved the problem of exchange guarantees on intra-European official balances in the most simple fashion. A network, Bolton suggested, would assist orderly exchange management and provide a machinery for daily settlement in currency between central banks. This proposal was tried out on several of the continental central bankers whom Bolton met during the Fund/Bank meetings. The response was mixed but friendly; and the proposal, with refinements such as a link between repayment of swaps and drawings on the European Fund, was running in the Bank during October. Early in the following month Bolton mentioned the network to Koszul of the Bank of France during a wide-ranging exchange of views that took place in Threadneedle Street. The meeting took place on the initiative of Baumgartner, who was aware of some renewed perplexity and suspicion in Europe about British intentions[19] now that the Collective Approach seemed to have been abandoned and sterling had weakened. In London the Treasury, whose principal concern was the prospective negotiation of the European Fund, remained content to leave the payments side to the Bank for informal discussions in Basle. Politically, too, the completion of post-EPU arrangements was attractive to the Chancellor, and on the initiative of Cobbold a two-day meeting of experts was held at the BIS in mid-November. Bolton took the chair; France was represented by Bolgert and Koszul, Germany by Emminger, Italy by Baffi, Belgium by Ansiaux; Holland by Professor Posthuma, and Sweden by Lundgren.

Bolton began by giving assurances that British exchange rate policy would be one of stability but within a somewhat wider dealing spread. His audience welcomed this general assurance and a discussion ensued about how wide was wider. It was felt that to go from 2% to 3 or 4% would be all right, so long as any special arrangements for multilateral compensation provided adequate cover against exchange risks incurred by central banks, but that anything wider would give rise to serious uncertainty. Nobody other than the UK wanted to adopt wider spreads in any case. The meeting then turned to Bolton's proposal for a swap network. The discussion that followed was again friendly, but inconclusive. It was also, with hindsight, unreal. Inter-central bank gold settlements, on a daily basis, would certainly be cumbersome and extravagant in the use of limited gold resources. But they would also be quite unnecessary if individual central banks held working balances in dollars or sterling and intervened in exchange markets, as required, to maintain exchange rates within the prescribed margin either side of parity. The experts meeting in

---

[19] Another source, Conolly of the BIS, told Parsons in October that a 'fog of suspicion' greeted any British initiative in the EPU Managing Board.

Basle knew this perfectly well; and in the event, when the EPU was finally brought to an end four years later, the central banks mostly found that they had no need to use the special intra-European mechanism for multilateral compensation that was then provided. Exchange market intervention through dollars or sterling, supplemented by occasional gold movements, sufficed. But in 1954 and 1955 there was insistence, at least by some members of the EPU, that a special mechanism would be required. The Bank itself was not unsympathetic to the argument about avoidance of daily gold settlements. As manager of a reserve and trading currency it had no liking for them. Others, for reasons that will be explained, also thought they saw the retention of a special intra-European system, post-EPU, as a safeguard against reversion to bilateralism and as a useful continuing contribution to the process of achieving European unity. More important, they also saw its negotiation as a means of nailing down the British on exchange-rate policy.

As Heasman was to explain in a note circulated in February 1955 but which the Bank seems not to have appreciated hitherto, the bulk of intra-European commercial payments *other than* those with the UK (and with it the entire Sterling Area) had been effected through the networks of bilateral payments agreements that had grown up in Europe early after the war and had continued after the construction of the EPU. The system of multilateral compensation built into the EPU had thereby acquired a special importance, even a mystique. Without it, some feared, there would follow a tendency on the part of the weaker and low-reserve countries, France included,[20] to draw back into their bilateral networks and revert to a bilateralism of trade as well as money. Even in the Bundesbank (at that time the Bank Deutscher Länder), in a country now far from weak, there were professed fears of a resurgence of 'Schachtian' practices.[21] Hence, quite apart from the specific desire to avoid daily settlement in gold, there was a widespread wish to retain an intra-European system of settlements together with the essential ingredient of interim finance between settlement days. The Bank had come a long way since its own passionate attachment to the UK's bilateral network in 1950 and did not like

---

[20] The French attitude to intra-European monetary questions was none too clear to the Bank at this stage. Baumgartner was as usual friendly and sympathetic, but his Deputy on the external side, Calvet, was pleased that convertibility had been postponed, anxious about French external prospects, and determined to secure a further prolongation of the EPU.

[21] Vocke, President of the Bank, made this point to Cobbold at Basle in January 1955. Emminger, talking to Bolton a month later, went much further and said the British should not overlook the fact that the bulk of the existing German officials had trained under Nazi philosophies and had absorbed Schachtian methods. He therefore hoped that a realistic agreement would be reached on methods for maintaining European co-operation after the adoption of convertibility by some of the leading countries.

prolonging a set of arrangements that could hinder an increase in the use of sterling and the services of the City. But it had to acknowledge the European argument, deployed as it was in a set of negotiations that the UK authorities wanted to be brought to a successful conclusion. It also had to recognise that the mystique of EPU-type arrangements had a significant Europeanist and liberal political content at a moment when progress towards unification had been set back by the collapse of the EDC.

Accepting these continental constraints entailed acknowledging the incessant emphasis placed by several European central banks upon the importance of exchange guarantees on the currency balances they might hold. It also meant acknowledging the related insistence by some countries upon ultimate settlement in gold rather than convertible currencies. The emphasis on guarantees arose in part from their customary and justifiable inclusion in bilateral monetary agreements drawn up during the early post-war period of exchange-rate uncertainty. But it was also due, within the Basle fraternity, to the fact that several continental central banks (France and Italy were exceptions) held their countries' external reserves in their own balance sheets, a practice that made some of them highly averse to undertaking currency exposures of any kind. This sensitivity to currency risks, which sometimes extended even to the US dollar, contributed firstly to the retention by some countries of gold as the primary reserve asset and secondly to fondness for intra-European arrangements containing built-in guarantees.[22] It also contributed to the more general European reluctance to accommodate within such arrangements dealing spreads much wider than the 2% allowed by the IMF. For some wanted it both ways; not satisfied with protection when they were creditors against depreciation by the debtor, they also wanted protection when they were debtors against appreciation by the creditor (that is, protection against 'loss' if a borrowed currency, having been spent, appreciated in the market and had to be bought in for repayment at a rate higher than that at which it was originally acquired). Ordinary exchange swaps or other such procedures could not provide this latter protection. Thus while a spread of 4%, or even 6%, might be accommodated within an EPU-type system of settlements if accompanied by assurances that stability was the aim, anything wider was not acceptable to a number of the Basle group of central banks.

The implications of these somewhat abstruse, sometimes emotional, and frequently tactical considerations proved critical for the future of British

---

[22] The UK itself held its reserves mainly in gold, justifying this practice on the argument that the central reserves of the sterling system should not be held in a national currency that was capable of depreciation against gold, as had happened to the dollar in 1933–4.

exchange-rate policy. They amounted to this: if the UK wanted to emerge from these negotiations with an agreement that was satisfactory to all concerned and with some kind of intra-European successor to the EPU – a successor in which it would be a full member – it could not at the same time altogether avoid *de facto* commitments on exchange policy that were inconsistent even with 'stability without commitment' (as informal and unofficial wider spreads were now called in London) let alone with unqualified floating. It did not matter that a special successor system of intra-European settlements was almost entirely unnecessary. The continentals could go on insisting that it was badly needed and by doing so could keep the UK tied down on exchange-rate policy.

After its experience with Robot and the Collective Approach and its constant trouble with the European factor, the Bank was now at last prepared to give ground and argue in favour of a greater degree of commitment on spreads rather than face yet another loss of momentum – this time attributable to differences in Europe over British exchange-rate policy – that would damage sterling at a time when it was already weakening. But the Treasury was at first reluctant to agree. Writing to Bolton on 15 December[23] after reference to the Economic Secretary, Rowan emphasised that UK policy remained 'stability without commitment'. While accepting that specific dealing margins would in effect mean 'abandoning our flexible rate policy', as Rowan put it, Bolton nonetheless noted in manuscript, 'co-operation with Europe is not possible on the basis of fully floating even only in theory'. Just before Christmas, with the Governor's specific authority, he replied in the course of a letter to Rowan:

> As things have become more stable (since the crisis of 1952), particularly in Europe, I think our minds have moved gradually more in the direction of *de facto* stability, both in our own interests and in the interest of securing a Collective Approach by a number of partners. We here continue to regard violent fluctuations in the rate as a measure to be resorted to in conditions of crisis...and we should still wish to keep our hands as free as possible (i.e. stability without commitment) to deal with such conditions. But in conditions as they are developing...we cannot in practice look to widely

---

[23] Bolton's statement at the November meeting of experts had been misunderstood by some of those present, who took it to mean that the UK had definitely shifted from floating to a commitment on wider spreads. Whatever his private thoughts at the time, Bolton had not gone as far as that. However, reports to the contrary were relayed by some of the experts to Ellis-Rees in Paris. He was unbriefed and complained to the Treasury. Hence, it may be supposed, Rowan's concern to get matters straight with the Bank.

fluctuating rates as a policy. In our own interests it will be essential for our traders and those who trade with us to have the assurance of reasonable stability. From the point of view of our partners in the Collective Approach it is now quite clear that we shall not have the support of the Sterling Area, of Europe or of America for a policy which does not promise, by one means or another, a high degree of day-to-day stability.

The subject was further debated in the Bank during January 1955. Parsons and Thompson-McCausland developed Bolton's argument, drawing attention to the Government's greater willingness (since 1951) to use Bank Rate, to the reduction of instability in the USA, and to the European rejection of floating exchange rates. But they drew the line at a public commitment to a specified spread, preferring to rely on informal collaboration with the Sterling Area and Western Europe about exchange rate limits. Bolton, for his part, while reaffirming his belief that sterling could not be managed in the world as it now was within a margin as narrow as 1% either side of parity, remarked that flexibility was now 'a matter of degree'. The issue was also being raised in Paris, first during a meeting of the Ministerial Group and later at a meeting of the EPU Board. The French, Italians, and Swiss were firm supporters of a continuing intra-European system of settlement (including interim finance), mainly in order to get what they wanted on exchange-rate policy. So at the end of the month, looking ahead to further meetings in Basle and to the growing weakness of sterling, the Governor decided that the Bank now had no choice but to go to the Government for fresh guidance. He accordingly wrote to Rowan in unusually bald terms.

The next Basle meeting of experts could not avoid discussing the 'likely exchange-rate framework on which the settlement machinery will have to be based'. Since each of the others was planning to retain a fixed-rate structure, the Bank would have to set out the British position quite clearly. 'Stability without commitment' would not suffice. There remained three alternatives: Firstly, the present regime, with its 2% spread, could be maintained post-EPU and administered through market intervention, with daily settlement between central banks in gold, dollars, or other convertible currencies. Alongside this, for use by those who wished, could be arrangements for deferring daily settlement, through swaps or suchlike, with final settlement in gold or convertible currency. In the Governor's view the other members of the EPU would be quite content with such arrangements. He felt that they would also be content with a second alternative in which there would be a moderately wider spread for sterling alone, which would either be publicly announced or be made known in confidence to the other participants. The third alternative would be one in which sterling floated without commitment on limits. The Governor advised that in that case European central banks would need guarantees on any sterling they held and that sterling would not be held widely or used commercially without full forward exchange facilities. As to special intra-European payments arrangements, he felt that the UK would probably find itself excluded. So which of the three alternatives should be pursued in Basle, consistently with what the Treasury would be saying in Paris during discussions about the European Fund?

The Treasury, at Ministerial and official level, had to answer this awkward question at the same time as it considered another set of recommendations from the Governor (sent on 20 January and discussed below) about intervention in transferable and further progress with Stage 2 in response to the growing weakness of the pound. The uncertain political situation, including the timing of a General Election, made decisions no easier, and the Chancellor's own ability to take them was impaired by the long illness and recent death of his wife. After a long talk with the Governor and a meeting with the Permanent Secretary, at which the Governor was present, Rowan now finally concluded that 'stability without commitment' was after all no longer viable as a statement of policy. Failure to go to a commitment on dealing limits meant abandoning the monetary lead in Europe that the UK had seemingly regained and being seen to do so on the issue of fixed versus floating at a time when sterling was under pressure and, if free, would float downwards. He therefore suggested to the Chancellor that the Bank should take the line at Basle that at the appropriate stage the UK would seek the agreement of the IMF to a dealing spread of some 5–6%. This would be publicly known, but the UK would reserve the right to change it at some time in the future if circumstances required. Ahead of a General Election, however, the Chancellor was not prepared to go quite that far. He and his colleagues wanted to avoid so clear a decision and also avoid a break in Basle or Paris. Only two weeks earlier Butler had met Burgess in London and assured him that the UK wanted to make a success of the related negotiations in Paris about the European Fund. The Chancellor therefore authorised the Governor to continue the negotiations on the 'working hypothesis' that if HMG were to be taking action now, involving convertibility and the supercession of EPU, it would apply to the IMF for acquiescence in a dealing margin of 5–6%. But the Governor was to make it clear that this was no more than a working hypothesis and that it did not in any way bind a future Government. It was agreed that use of this procedural device would in practice to some extent prejudice the Government's freedom of action in the future. But it was acknowledged that the whole movement of thought and opinion had been towards greater stability and that securing agreement to complete freedom of action was no longer practical politics. The Commonwealth were to be informed about the 'hypothesis' as soon as it had been explained in Basle.

The Governor duly followed these instructions at the monthly Basle meeting in mid-February and reported: 'I would say that this was generally well received. There was certainly a feeling that this somewhat closer definition of what we might mean by 'stability without commitment' was reassuring and greatly facilitates consideration of the practical problems which would arise on convertibility…For what it is worth these talks have served to maintain our initiative in this field and we shall be in the Chair at the expert discussions.' He added that his colleagues in Basle shared a view that argument about fixed versus floating rates, in academic as well as official and political circles, would damage them all if it went on through the spring and summer. The next meeting of experts was fixed for early March and the Basle Governors agreed that they should now concern themselves solely with the technical problems of settlement, etc., post-EPU and arising from the British hypothesis. They would cease to argue about the merits of fixed or floating rates or wider spreads.

Having settled the problem of exchange policy in the Basle context, at least for the time being, the Bank and the Treasury had next to decide on action that might actually arrest the pressure on sterling and hold the situation until the political uncertainties and inhibitions had been resolved. Bank Rate had been raised to $3\frac{1}{2}\%$ on 27 January, but this was regarded only as a warning shot. Discussion on further measures was already well under way and had been opened by the Governor in a private meeting with the Chancellor on 20 January, when he tabled a note on exchange policy that he later circulated to Bridges, Gilbert, and Rowan. He acknowledged that the preconditions of the Collective Approach could not be realised for at least another year and recognised the temptation to sit tight. But he argued: 'We are now drifting into a position where our own exchange system is beginning to work against us and will make completion of the Collective Approach more rather than less difficult.' The root trouble was the re-emergence of a multiple rate structure for international sterling, with transferable quoted at a substantial discount.

> Once again the strength of sterling is being sapped away, materially because payment to the Sterling Area is increasingly made through cheap sterling and psychologically because of the existence of an active market in cheap sterling at a considerable discount. Once again a two-price system for sterling goods is appearing, and our traders are at a disadvantage (about which they are becoming increasingly vocal).

The free markets abroad were now more broadly based than in the 1940s and before the unification and simplification of March 1954. The cheap rates were accordingly less vulnerable to violent fluctuation, but by the same token payments were increasingly passed through the cheap markets. The world movement away from bilateralism made it impossible to use the palliative remedies that had previously been adopted. So the Governor again suggested a move to Stage 2 through a widening of the official dealing spread, intervention in transferable, coalescence of the two rates, and a move towards 100% gold settlements in the EPU; but he did not propose formal abolition of the exchange control barrier between American and transferable accounts. All these objectives, he wrote, could be attacked either piecemeal or at one bound.

The immediate response of Treasury officials was that these proposals so closely resembled *de facto* convertibility that they collided with the Cabinet view that it was impossible to introduce controversial matters affecting trade and payments before or during an election campaign. Treasury Ministers agreed. But early in February they and their officials were confronted with an adverse balance of payments forecast, suggesting that the weakness of sterling in the second half of 1954 had indeed been more than a seasonal phenomenon. Forecasts for 1955 showed the Sterling Area as a whole in current-account deficit with the rest of the world, a sharp deterioration on the out-turn for 1954 almost entirely attributable to a worsening in the position of the UK itself. Allowing for capital flows, including servicing of the North American Loans, this all pointed to an uncomfortable loss of reserves which risked sudden and dangerous aggravation by confidence factors that were already being undermined, according to the Bank, by disappointed expectations of convertibility and the widening of the discount on transferable. Something had to be done. If Stage 2 was politically impossible – and now in addition looked as if it would definitely be a move from a position of underlying weakness – there remained to consider some kind of holding operation that would leave the main issues for decision until after the Election.

There ensued a brisk debate between Whitehall and Threadneedle Street, with the former stressing the need for internal measures to correct the balance of payments and the latter the need for external measures to restore confidence. The Bank was closely questioned about the market in transferable but held its ground. So in a long paper put forward on 15 February Rowan finally concluded that the best means of holding the line would be a combination of internal measures and intervention in transferable without any widening of the official dealing spread. The purpose of intervention would not be to bring about coalescence but 'to keep the rate at a figure in relation to official sterling which made it less profitable to deal'. No approach to the IMF would be needed. Fund rules did not prevent the EEA dealing in transferable at rates outside the official dealing margin, provided the transactions were conducted in overseas markets and not in London. Rowan admitted that intervention without wider spreads might create some presumption that sterling convertibility, when it came, would be at a fixed rate. But he did not attach decisive importance to this point, particularly in view of the 'working hypothesis' just expounded by the Governor in Basle.

Cobbold may well have realised at this point that intervention, once successfully undertaken, would to a large extent let the Government off the hook of convertibility. The sting of cheap sterling would have been removed, *de facto* non-resident convertibility at a small discount would rule, and that might be that for some time (in the event, for nearly four years). The Bank would itself have achieved a very worthwhile objective only to find that the final prize, including the wider official spread and the fortification of the reserves, had eluded it. At any event, at a meeting with Butler on 15 February the Governor made a last attempt to get agreement to Stage 2, or a modified version of it. They would begin in February with intervention in transferable together with some tightening of credit and of controls over hire-purchase. Then at the end of March they would raise Bank Rate to $4\frac{1}{2}\%$ and publicly announce that the 1% spread had gone. They would not then aim for coalescence but would endeavour to keep official and transferable about 1% apart from each other. The attempt did not succeed and on 18 February the Governor admitted defeat in a note left with Edward Bridges. Coming round to the course recommended by Rowan – while protecting another flank with the remark, 'I am certain that Bank Rate alone or with hire purchase, but without anything in the exchange field, would be ineffective and would be a waste of heavy artillery' – he recommended that intervention should be started in the following week accompanied by a $4\frac{1}{2}\%$ Bank Rate and positive steps on hire-purchase.

The atmosphere had become tense. Differences of view, and even animosities inherited from the struggles over Robot, began to surface. At a meeting in the Treasury on 15 February, held by the Economic Secretary (Maudling) and attended by the Deputy Governor and Maurice Allen from the Bank, there was some support for taking domestic monetary action first and postponing intervention until later. The Deputy stressed the desirability of concurrent domestic and external action. The Economic Secretary, evidently a novice in the subject, wanted to know why cheap-sterling business could not be stopped by European exchange controls. There was resistance to the unpleasant truth that HMG's choice of policy and its timing could be largely determined by foreign opinion. Two days later Allen circulated a chilling note in the Bank about the risks of treating confidence too lightly when it was already impaired by a worsening balance of payments and by disappointments about exchange policy. The following day he had a long talk in the Treasury with Hall, who complained that a crisis atmosphere was being made and said he did not believe an exchange crisis would develop any more than he had believed similar reports in 1952. The economic situation did not justify a lack of confidence. Overseas visitors that he had met seemed very content with the UK's economic condition. In any case, how could a crisis be averted by so technical a measure as intervention in transferable? He was assured, moreover, that it was not now politically practicable for the Chancellor to authorise intervention. Anyway, scarcely anyone outside the City wanted convertibility, and certainly not industry. If the external situation did worsen substantially, it would not be insuperably difficult to regain control.

There followed three critical meetings on 21, 22 and 23 February, between the Chancellor, senior officials, the Governors, and Bolton. Cobbold opened the first by remarking that if a crisis existed (the reserves looked like falling $60–100 million in February), it was a technical one. A small turn for the worse in the fundamental conditions had put a match to it. This had been predictable, and predicted, ever since Robot had been turned down. He then stood his ground on Stage 2, in the form recommended a month earlier; but the main debate concerned whether to take domestic monetary measures on their own, at least as a first step, or whether to combine them with intervention in transferable. The running, according to the official record, was mostly made by the Chancellor and the Governor with occasional interventions by Rowan and Bolton. Against repeated questioning the Bank maintained that domestic measures alone, including a $4\frac{1}{2}$% Bank Rate, would not suffice. The markets would expect external action. If they did not get it, and even if the domestic measures had an immediate favourable impact, there would be a relapse requiring further and more drastic steps (including intervention) at a later date. The Chancellor was at first reluctant to agree. He felt intervention would commit the Government to taking the further step to full convertibility. It would therefore be a decisive and irrevocable move that would need a Cabinet decision. This would be difficult to get. His colleagues would say that the internal situation should be put right before any move to convertibility was taken. However, by the second meeting he had come round to the Bank's point of view and at the third meeting, on 23 February,

Cameron Cobbold late in his second term, 1959
IDA KAR

he was able to say that the Prime Minister would support an increase in Bank Rate combined with intervention in transferable. The Cabinet agreed late the same afternoon and action followed the next day, a Thursday.

On Tuesday the Governor had called a meeting of Committee of Treasury, augmented by Kindersley and Vivian Smith,[24] and obtained their agreement to the tactics he was pursuing in Whitehall. On the afternoon of Thursday 24 February the Deputy Governor, Bolton, and Peppiatt spoke individually to representatives of the press,[25] without departing from the general line being taken by the Chancellor in the House. Evidence of renewed inflationary pressures had been growing.

---

[24] *Smith, Randal Hugh Vivian, 2nd Baron Bicester (1898–1968)*. Educated Eton and Sandhurst. Army until 1920. Managing Director, Morgan Grenfell 1930–67. Director, Bank of England 1954–66. Director, Vickers, Shell, Associated Electrical Industries, Chairman, Royal National Pension Fund for Nurses 1963–8.

[25] This was becoming the custom on such occasions. Mynors saw Oscar Hobson (*News Chronicle*), Frank Wright (*The Times*) and Gordon Tether (*Financial Times*). Bolton saw

The external position did not look quite as good as hitherto. Consumption, encouraged by the growth of hire-purchase, was tending to become excessive. While not a cause for alarm, these symptoms required precautionary measures. So Bank Rate had been raised to $4\frac{1}{2}$% and hire-purchase terms control was being reimposed. In addition, the journalists were told that the recent weakness in sterling was partly attributable to the abnormal conditions created by the co-existence of the market in official and the market in transferable. The combination of increased turnover in the latter market and the widening of the margin between the two was resulting in a fall in the supply of dollars to the market in official and a distortion of trade. A technical weakness in the system needed to be put right. The Bank was therefore now including operations in the transferable sterling markets as a part of their general management of the sterling exchange. It was a small further step along the road pursued for the past three years but, the journalists were told, it had no greater significance.

Ahead of time, the Bank and the Treasury had agreed the tactics that might be employed. If sterling was weak and the discount on the official rate was widening, strong intervention should be used to prevent the discount exceeding 2%. If the pound was strong, transferable should be allowed to go as high as $2·78. In the event, sterling recovered somewhat in the weeks following 24 February. By the end of March official had risen to $2·79$\frac{1}{4}$ while transferable had risen sharply from $2·72$\frac{1}{8}$ to $2·76$\frac{5}{8}$ and the discount reduced to about 1% at a cost of $48 million in intervention. Thereafter, though the currency continued under intermittent pressure, there was less need to intervene and a discount of at most 1% was maintained without difficulty.

Although the Governor had had to mount a sustained offensive in order to get intervention included within the measures taken on 24 February, he can seldom have done so from a stronger position. He had many times warned about the consequences of missing the tide. Now, early in 1955, those consequences were plain to see. External weakness had recurred and overseas opinion had swung round just when the old defences against external crisis had been dismantled but before new ones had been put into place. A return to strict import controls and to the '57 varieties' of external sterling that had prevailed prior to the unification of March 1954 was plainly going to be a political impossibility, as well as a policy that would finally destroy overseas confidence in the British Government's

Whitmore (*Telegraph*), Fry (*The Guardian*) and Nasmyth (*Reuters*). Peppiatt spoke to Wilfred King (*The Banker*), Norman Crump (*The Economist*) and Williams (*Daily Mail*).

external monetary dispositions. Yet the floating-rate convertibility and reserves-fortification of the Collective Approach had either been negotiated away to almost nothing or else proved unobtainable. At this juncture the Government faced an early general election and the need, as the Chancellor must by then have had in the back of his mind, for a popular Budget to precede it. So although there were arguments for postponing intervention in transferable and the implied *de facto* restoration of non-resident convertibility at an exchange rate quite close to the official one, they stood little chance of prevailing. Whether the Bank's judgement was good or bad, there was a clear risk that domestic monetary measures by themselves would hold the position only for a brief period, after which transferable would again go to a heavy discount. Confidence would then be even more fragile, the election even nearer, and a popular Budget would be unacceptably dangerous. Intervention in transferable, alongside a $4\frac{1}{2}\%$ Bank Rate and the restriction of consumer credit, was the obvious answer, even though it might be expensive and even though it was certainly a further big step towards convertibility. It both improved the prospects of the holding operation of 24 February serving its purpose and, ahead of the Budget and the election, set up a defence against reimpairment of confidence that would drive the transferable rate to an ugly discount and risk starting up the processes that would lead to a full-scale exchange crisis. It would have been rash indeed to ignore the Governor's advice on this occasion.

External convertibility had therefore largely arrived, by the back door, unofficially, and notably unacknowledged by its sponsors. At long last the whole miserable problem of cheap sterling, which had so powerfully affected the Bank's thinking about external policy since early 1949, had been swept aside. But although it was a great deal better than nothing, entry by the back door necessarily precluded a concurrent front-door move to a wider dealing spread for official; and it did not provide any obvious occasion for the reopening of negotiations for a Fund stand-by to underwrite front-door convertibility by strengthening the UK's external banking position. At the same time it removed a significant part of the element of compulsion that had in practice propelled the British authorities towards *de jure* convertibility since the closing months of 1951. By removing that degree of compulsion it encouraged further delay if, for other reasons, delay were in any case attractive to Whitehall. The longer the delay, the more likely that the UK would in the end reach *de jure* convertibility saddled with a fixed rate of exchange, a 2% dealing spread, and inadequate liquidity. On that account the Bank was concerned to argue that Stage 2 should be implemented as soon as the election was out of the way. But its great bargaining card, cheap sterling, had gone for ever and the Bank was to find that the election would be followed by yet another set of reasons for still further delay.

(e) THE EUROPEAN MONETARY AGREEMENT, 1955, AND THE DEMISE OF STAGE 2

Looking ahead in early March 1955, after the measures of 24 February, how stood the preconditions for *de jure* convertibility? The pursuit of the Americans for approval of a large fund stand-by and the adoption of 'good creditor' policies had largely been abandoned. Exchange-rate flexibility, in the form of 'stability without commitment', had been circumscribed in the cause of collaboration with Western Europe and was vulnerable to further constraint for the same reason. The renewed weakness of sterling had been checked by the tightening of monetary policy and by decisive official support of transferable, but a position of strength had by no means been regained. Further measures of domestic adjustment would be needed and their early prospect, ahead of a general election or after it, was highly uncertain. Only in Europe of all places, given the history of that topic, did it look as though agreement could be reached on a collaborative procedure for restoring convertibility and providing such intra-European arrangements as were felt to be needed after termination of the EPU. Construction of the European Fund looked like being relatively straightforward. Reaching agreement on a continuing but largely purposeless system of monthly settlement and multilateral compensation, together with the associated and far from purposeless questions of exchange-rate policy, would no doubt require the customary combination of robust negotiation and, for many people, technical unintelligibility; but the necessary political will was present and in the end an agreement could be achieved.

The UK would then be left with the choice whether to proceed as soon as practicable to *de jure* convertibility along lines agreed in Europe or whether to postpone until one or more of the other 'preconditions' were satisfied. But in the event the weakness of sterling reappeared and the reserves continued to fall, towards danger levels. Monetary policy proved inadequate and fiscal policy weak. So postponement of *de jure* convertibility was the inevitable choice. The Bank had to accept this, but throughout the summer of 1955 – the fourth since the rejection of Robot in February 1952 – it fought one last running fight for its own version of convertibility via Stage 2, insisting that adoption of wider spreads, the encouragement of coalescence, and an administered withering of the exchange control distinction between American and transferable account could all be done step by step, without necessarily triggering the end of the EPU or bringing about a precipitate dismantling of all discrimination against dollar goods. But the Treasury, including the Chancellor, flatly refused to move. The Bank refused to concede. A disagreement was recorded.

The whole tangled and by now distinctly stale subject was then allowed to drop for a bit while the Treasury slumped into increasing gloom about the external economic outlook. Early in 1956 Rowan circulated a long paper entitled 'Can the UK Pay its Way?'; Butler left to become the Prime Minister's understudy as Lord Privy Seal while Harold Macmillan was obliged to leave the Foreign Office for No. 11. Not until April of that year did the Governor take up the question of external financial policy with the new Chancellor, with little positive result. Throughout almost all his four years at the Treasury, Butler had maintained a personal commitment to the restoration of external convertibility and the policies associated therewith. Though much more a man of decisive action than Butler, Macmillan came to the Treasury without any such commitment and was prepared to look at the issues anew. In June 1956 Rowan therefore circulated a defensive paper called 'Why Convertibility?', on which Cobbold noted with some degree of justifiable exasperation: 'A lot of good reasons for doing the things we ought to do and a lot of good reasons for not doing them until a lot of things happen, which never will happen.' Rowan's own position in the Treasury was declining. Both Bridges and Gilbert were to retire in the autumn of 1956, the former after a decade in the top job. Although Rowan was among the front-runners to succeed him, his personal commitment to the external policies pursued by Butler and frequently opposed by the Economic Section evidently did not stand him in good stead with Macmillan. So Roger Makins, then UK Ambassador in Washington, was brought in from the Foreign Office to take over from Bridges at the Treasury.

Apart from the change of Chancellor and the prospective change of Permanent Secretary, the strategic ground of external economic policy was anyway beginning to shift underfoot. Continuing American disinterest in sterling convertibility was accompanied by a new and momentous departure in Western Europe, namely the run-up to the Treaty of Rome that followed the Conference of the Six at Messina in July 1955. This was to deflect attention away from external monetary affairs and on to vital long-term questions of external commercial policy. Next, the UK became engulfed in the Suez affair, the consequent exchange crisis, and another Ministerial change, this time including the Prime Minister as well as the Chancellor. All this constituted the earlier stages of another distinct phase in the history of sterling, a phase of crisis and temporary retrieval that lasted until the move to *de jure* convertibility at the end of 1958. The special story of the Bank of England and external policy, which began with the change of Government in 1951 and went on through Robot and the Collective Approach, effectively ended with the signing of the new European Monetary Agreement in July 1955 and the inability in London to proceed any further at that time. But the last instalment of that story, the sequel to intervention in transferable, still remains to be told.

Early in March 1955 thought at once began to be directed towards the next steps along the road. Thompson-McCausland, over-impressed by the favourable initial response to the February measures, suggested that the idea of a large IMF stand-by could safely be dropped. There would remain the gold and first credit tranche, together amounting to some $500 million and virtually obtainable on demand. But this was making a virtue of necessity. As the Governor reminded him, the stand-by had been dead for at least six months past; and the Treasury soon confirmed that the matter was not to be raised again in Washington. Further thought by a group numbering Parsons, Thompson-McCausland, Stamp, Menzies, and Hamilton started from the point that the next stage would have to include the widening of the dealing spread on official sterling. This, they went on, would require a sympathetic response from the IMF. In order to get it, convertibility would have to be somewhere in the shop window, if not absolutely out in front. Once the official spread had been widened the two rates would virtually coalesce and there would be neither logic nor administrative reasons for retaining the separation between transferable and American account. *De jure* convertibility would follow in short order. 'On the assumptions stated', they wrote, 'there are no useful intermediate measures.' The group advised that the authorities would do well to press ahead as soon as the Election was over. Concurrently, all necessary measures should be taken to 'ensure the stability of the economy'. The substance of this level-headed advice was embodied in a note sent by Bolton to the Treasury on 30 March, but the distinction between *de facto* and *de jure* convertibility was made less sharp and it was acknowledged that early action would entail some reordering, to say the least, of the negotiations taking place in Paris and Basle. Fisher, commenting in his usual role as a critic, suggested that an intermediate stage of *de facto* convertibility would after all be practicable and useful. The Governor, who had earlier advocated such a course in Stage 2 and was to do so again after the Election, was inclined to agree but remarked that 'we must leave this to the political end pro-tem'.

Early in April Churchill finally vacated No. 10 and Eden at last succeeded him. Shortly afterwards the General Election was called for the end of May. A Budget was then introduced whose principal features were an optimistic assessment of the macro-economic prospects and a reduction in Income Tax. The Government was returned at the Election with its majority increased to a comfortable sixty. One set of political uncertainties, which had affected the conduct of external financial policy for the best part of a year, had been removed. But another set of uncertainties promptly took its place. Due to the proximity of the Election, the Government was not fully reconstructed when Eden became Prime Minister and there was therefore an air of provisionality about his Ministerial team. This extended to the recently bereaved Chancellor, who was in his fourth year at the most strenuous departmental post in Whitehall and badly needed a change of air, especially at a time when the economic situation, now marked by growing industrial trouble (notably in the railways and the docks), required close political attention. Matters were not improved by the new Prime Minister's unfamiliarity with economic affairs, by his lack of self-confidence in that field, and accordingly by his inability to provide the leadership that should have compensated for the Chancellor's fatigue.

The provisionality of the Cabinet was not ended after the Election but persisted right through the summer and autumn. When the reconstruction finally took place at the end of December 1955, the Treasury certainly obtained in Macmillan a forceful and ambitious leader. But he had not wanted to move from the Foreign Office after only nine months in a post he regarded as senior to the Treasury, and his relations with the Prime Minister were not good. Eden's premiership, quite apart from its tragic dénouement in the aftermath of Suez, was an unhappy one and it did not provide the political background favourable to the long-term decision making that might normally be expected of a Government newly elected with a comfortable majority.

But at the end of March 1955 these later and unexpected uncertainties were in the future. The immediate uncertainty was electoral and it was in that context that the UK monetary authorities had to handle the continuing negotiations in Paris and Basle about the renewal of the EPU and the arrangements for its eventual replacement. These negotiations had already come a long way and had to be brought to a constructive conclusion, a fact of practical politics that was bound to bear upon the timing and content of any further specifically British move to convertibility.

At first the negotiations about a post-EPU system of settlement and associated questions of exchange policy went unexpectedly smoothly. A second meeting of experts, held in Basle under Bolton's chairmanship early in March, resulted in an Agreed Minute of altogether refreshing clarity drafted by Parsons and Koszul. It was submitted to the Governors attending the monthly meeting ten days later. The British 'hypothesis' of a 6% spread, with the aim of a 'maximum degree of stability', was noted and accepted. Most of the others present thought they would stick to a 2% spread, though some thought their countries might want to consider the possibility of wider margins if, in the event, that course were adopted by the UK. Next, the experts readily agreed that under convertibility, 'the bulk of international settlements would take place naturally through the markets, with each central bank intervening as necessary within its declared fixed limits'. Close co-operation between central banks would be essential and through such co-operation there would be a possibility of measures of mutual assistance, including short-term swaps; but these would be a matter for detailed discussion between individual central banks. The whole question of a special continuing system of intra-European multilateral settlement was put on one side, though the possibility of continuing the EPU for a transitional period on a 100% gold basis was considered. Bolton expressed an open mind on this suggestion. The Agreed Minute was taken by the Basle Governors at their March meeting and accepted by them without difficulty. In particular they reportedly agreed with Cobbold that the experts had fully covered the ground about the technical arrangements for multilateral settlement under convertibility and that it was not necessary or advisable to go over that ground again in Paris.

A few days earlier Rowan had made the same point to Ellis-Rees but was later warned that keeping the subject out of the Managing Board, whose members represented Governments rather than central banks, might prove difficult. It certainly did. For when the Board met on 23 March to consider a draft Report on the renewal of the EPU and the establishment of the European Fund, Ansiaux exploited the opening in the Basle Minute and insisted that the whole framework of the EPU should continue after convertibility, with monthly settlements 100% in gold. He was strongly supported by the French, the Italians, and the Swiss, while the Germans and the Dutch were sympathetic. Only the Danes (on behalf of the Scandinavians) supported the British view, patiently argued by John Owen[26] of the Treasury, that maintenance of the EPU framework would represent an unnecessary piece of machinery since all that was required could be done through the exchange markets. He added that such machinery would encourage countries to remain inconvertible. A storm ensued. The British were roundly accused by the French of brutality

---

[26] *Owen, John Glendwr, CB (1914–77).* Educated Bedford School and Balliol College, Oxford. War Office 1937–8, HM Treasury 1938–42 and 1945–73, Under-Secretary 1959–73. Treasury Historical Section 1973–6.

towards the EPU and of attempting to deny other countries the right to organise their own system in Europe (without the UK) if they wished. Ansiaux, for Belgium, stressed with some degree of menace that countries were quite free to opt out and, if they wanted, attach themselves to the Sterling Area. He and his allies did however drop a demand that the EPU should be hardened to 100% gold settlements straight away, at the June renewal. 75% would do and was acceptable to London.

This Belgian attempt to foster a European monetary bloc, excluding the UK and the Scandinavians, was misguided or at the very least premature. The British and their central banking friends in Basle were correct in arguing that continuation of the EPU framework would be unnecessary and probably unhelpful; and it was unwise of Ansiaux to base a campaign on the maintenance of a piece of machinery that would quickly become redundant. Things soon cooled down. At the end of March Cobbold wrote to Baumgartner that he did not really understand what he had heard. Could the Bank of France perhaps prevent any definite position being taken up by the French Government until the British had emerged from their electoral uncertainty? As usual he got an encouraging reply from his close friend in Paris: 'Nous verrons plus tard, quand les circonstances auront mûri, s'il est possible de mieux faire.' In Whitehall Cobbold counselled the Chancellor against conceding too much to the Belgian initiative and was soon rewarded by signs of considerable divergences of view among the continentals. Bolton reported from Basle that Ansiaux had exceeded his instructions, was at loggerheads with Frère, and was probably playing Europeanist politics under the influence of Spaak. Heasman reported from Paris that no detailed plans for a post-EPU clearing system had yet been worked out by the opposition.

By the middle of April, when further discussions had taken place in the Managing Board, it was clear that no solid little-European front yet existed. The Germans and the Dutch were lukewarm about preserving the EPU machinery, though the latter felt that some arrangement for interim finance would still be needed. The Italians conceded that preservation of the machinery would be no more successful in preventing a return to bilateralism than would a system of market intervention. The French seemed to have lost their outright enthusiasm for preservation. The Swiss and the Belgians remained in favour, though the latter were known to be divided among themselves; and at the end of the month Ansiaux himself travelled to London for talks with Bolton and Parsons. He made it very clear that the Belgian attitude to the EPU was dictated by Spaak, in the cause of European unity. The latter, however, was less interested in the EPU as a technical mechanism than as a base upon which some supranational monetary authority might be built at a later stage. If, accordingly, it were possible, post-EPU, to set up a high-level committee that would meet regularly in Paris to monitor and discuss European trade and payments, much of the Belgian opposition to suspension of the EPU would fade away. This proposition was repeated to Ellis-Rees a few days later, after the Managing Board had agreed a Report that was even-handed between preservation and abolition. Rowan, who attended a meeting of Ministers' Deputies in Paris early in May, then tried it out in private discussions with the Germans, the Benelux countries, and the Swiss. He got support for the proposed 'forum' but found that the idea of somehow preserving the EPU mechanism, or something close to it, was still running. Indeed he reported to the Governor that he found himself alone (apart from the Scandinavians) in opposing the latter and was concerned about how to protect the Chancellor from encountering the same position at the Ministerial meeting in June. Cobbold now agreed that it was urgent that further thought be given to the whole question. He still felt that in the end it would prove unimportant, but he agreed that it mattered a great deal during the run-up to an agreement.

The results of the British General Election became known on 23 May. Thereafter, the monetary negotiations in Paris came to a head and subsequently became interlocked in London with a resumed debate between the Treasury and the Bank about the next steps to convertibility. At a meeting of the Ministerial Council of the OEEC held in mid-June it was agreed to renew the EPU for a further year, with settlements at 75% in gold and dollars instead of 50%. It was also agreed to include a break clause enabling the Union to be terminated during the year if members representing at least half the total quotas so voted. But this clause was made subject to certain conditions about the post-EPU regime, conditions to be agreed by the end of July when the renewal of the Union (postponed for one month) would then take effect. These conditions were firstly the continuance of an intra-European clearing system, secondly the constitution of the European Fund, and thirdly the provision of rules in support of continuing intra-European trade liberalisation. The UK had again argued that the first of these was unnecessary and probably impracticable, though the Dutch had now put forward a scheme which they argued would meet the situation without cutting across British interests. But the point had to be conceded if agreement to the break clause was to be obtained; and this in turn meant further discussion about exchange-rate policy. As Rowan and Bolton told Overby and other visiting US Treasury officials, attempts were being made to tie the UK down on exchange policy and London was not going to fall for it.

The Council of Ministers referred the issue of a system of settlements and associated questions of exchange-rate policy to a joint assembly of the EPU Board and the central bank experts. It was to be chaired by Calvet of the Bank of France, the French representative on the Board, and was to complete its work within a month. Reporting on the June Basle meeting, Cobbold told Rowan that there was still an almost mystical desire to retain the EPU as a protection against bilateralism. Since some concession to this emotion might prove useful, Rowan suggested that it might help if the aggregate result of all these negotiations were named the 'European Monetary Agreement' (EMA).

It is not necessary to follow the esoteric discussions of the Calvet assembly about the Dutch scheme, which involved the provision of interim finance secured on a prior deposit of gold in the new 'union' and its repayment in gold or dollars at the end of each settlement period. In its eventual form, as included in the EMA, the prior gold deposit had disappeared and the scheme itself bore a close resemblance to the swap network, with prior agreed limits, that had been suggested by Bolton and the Bank's exchange dealers in September of the previous year. But the real importance of the discussions, as had been the case all along, related to the exchange-rate strings that might be attached to membership of any new scheme. Ever since March the British had stuck to their 'hypothesis' of a 6% spread. But with the passage of time this had come increasingly to resemble a commitment, or at least a firm intent.

On 21 June the Governor wrote to Bridges suggesting that the hypothesis be taken a stage further and a 6% spread acknowledged in the relevant text as the maximum acceptable within the new intra-European payments arrangements. But the long-suffering Overseas Finance Division would have none of this. It was not prepared to make what it felt would be seen as a public renunciation of its remaining freedom of action in exchange-rate policy, however vestigial it already was, for the sake of securing agreement to a scheme that seemed to have little practical value. Nor was it prepared to concede that such a renunciation would be needed to secure agreement to the break clause in the EPU renewal. The issue was discussed at a meeting with the Chancellor on 24 June. The Governor saw the force of the Treasury's argument and indeed accepted it; but he was increasingly worried lest insistence on freedom of action, within general assurances about exchange stability, should appear to be a lead from weakness and arouse suspicions about intended British responses to a renewal of pressure on sterling. The official rate, which had stood at about $2·79\frac{1}{2}$ both before and immediately after the Election had fallen back to $2·78\frac{3}{8}$ by the end of June, and the fall in the reserves had been resumed. There were frequent outbreaks of rumour, sometimes emanating from Paris, about a sterling devaluation and also about a widening of the dealing spread to 6% or even 10%. In these circumstances the Governor began to argue in favour of pre-empting the outcome of the Paris negotiations by adopting Stage 2 forthwith, before the end-July renewal date for the EPU, and subsequently declaring a new and wider dealing spread without long-term commitment. The question of a further move to convertibility was in any case due for renewed discussion now that the inhibition of a general election had come and gone. The Chancellor, though fussed by difficulties of timetable, agreed to reconsider Stage 2 while giving firm instructions that there should in the meantime be no concession in Paris on dealing spreads.

Over the ensuing two weeks the Governor had a number of informal meetings with the Chancellor, Bridges, Gilbert, and Rowan individually. Views were clarified but little agreement was reached. On 6 July he wrote a long letter to the Permanent Secretary, very much for the record, setting out the content of the informal talks and making the Bank's position quite clear. It was common ground that while internal policy was the most important of all, it was in the UK's interests to pursue a policy of moving towards greater freedom of exchanges and towards what had generally been termed convertibility. But there was disagreement about the timing of the next move. The Treasury, though earlier favouring a move after the Election, now seemed to want to defer it. The Bank wanted to go ahead without delay and felt that deferment could only give an impression of uncertainty. There was also disagreement about the content of the next move. The Treasury favoured going all the way to formal convertibility in due course. The Bank favoured a further technical step – the most obvious one being coalescence plus a wider spread. As to the negotiations in Paris, the Bank felt they should not be completed before the UK had made a further move on its own; otherwise that move, when it came, would be constrained by a new legal text, a factor that would probably work in favour of further delay. As the Governor put it with awful clarity: 'We should then slip further and further into *de facto* convertibility at the present narrow spreads...and should find ourselves tied up to something very like Gold Standard practice at fixed rates and narrow margins.' This prospect was heightened by the indifferent outlook for sterling. Expectations of a further move towards convertibility were again being aroused by British insistence on a break clause in the renewal of EPU; and it had become widely known that HMG were insisting on their right to introduce greater exchange flexibility. But the outlook for the balance of payments was not comforting; the period of seasonal weakness was approaching, as was a further round of international meetings and conferences. There was therefore a likelihood of further pressure on sterling, and this in turn would make a further move to convertibility more difficult. 'The Bank hope therefore that HMG will consider the possibility of making an early move (with appropriate consultations with the Commonwealth, in Paris and in Washington) on the lines of the proposals put forward on 20 January last...' Such a move, he concluded, should be linked to an appropriate statement on internal policy.

The Chancellor and the Permanent Secretary met with the Governors on 7 July 1955. The Bank was told that it was politically impossible to inject into the Paris discussions the immediate move to Stage 2 put forward by the Governor. But an attempt would be made to make the link between the EPU break clause and convertibility sufficiently elastic to make some such move possible at a future date without involving the consequences of formal convertibility. Any such move would require Commonwealth agreement and might be discussed during the Fund and Bank meetings to be held in Istanbul in September. In the course of his reply Cobbold repeated his view that the eventual effect of the Government's decision might be convertibility on lines as inflexible as those of the old Gold Standard.

Disagreement in London, which was to continue, did not prevent agreement being reached in Paris. The Calvet group met again on 11 July for a meeting lasting several days, this time with Von Mangoldt of the Bank Deutscher Länder in the chair. On the crucial question of exchange policy, the Treasury had won the day and the UK was not pressed to agree in advance to a specified maximum dealing spread. In particular the French, who were probably now not quite so worried that the UK would resume convertibility at an early date, were able to 'mieux faire' and were clearly anxious to avoid prolonging a dispute whose echoes in the press and in the markets would be harmful to the franc as well as to the pound. Calvet therefore told the meeting that the Board should recognise that the UK had already gone a long way to meet them, by a moral commitment to keep their margins as narrow and stable as possible and should not insist on more. The Board willingly agreed. Even the Swiss were in a mood to compromise on this issue while the Belgians kept quiet. There was not much further debate. On 22 July Baumgartner telephoned Cobbold to say that he thought the Paris talks were drawing to a successful conclusion. On the 29th the Council of Ministers approved the text of the European Monetary Agreement, which prolonged the EPU until June 1956 (with the break clause), settled the terms of the European Fund, provided for a continuing system of multilateral compensation, confirmed that the liberalisation code would continue after convertibility, and made provision for the consultative committee or 'forum' that Ansiaux had suggested in April and the British had readily accepted at that time. The preamble contained suitable words about the desirability of dealing margins being kept as limited and stable as possible.

In its way the EMA was a minor triumph of good sense and able negotiation. It did not tie the UK down on exchange-rate policy quite so severely as the Bank had feared or had at one time been prepared to concede. That the UK did not subsequently make any use of the limited freedom allowed for wider dealing spreads was entirely its own choice and one that owed little to continental pressure. Yet the negotiating linkage between exchange-rate policy and a post-EPU system of settlement was at first insufficiently appreciated in London, while British insistence on the break clause handed negotiating leverage to those on the continent who wanted to ensure that exchange-rate flexibility was as limited as possible. Come the point, the break clause was not used in 1955–6 because of the continuing weakness of sterling, and it may be doubted whether its inclusion in the renewal of the EPU was ever as necessary as the British had thought. Underlying these aspects of British policy in the EMA negotiations was a growing uncertainty of British purpose about a strategy for sterling and a growing concentration on the dictates of the short term. One way or another, as the Governor was now clearly warning, the UK was moving towards fixed-rate convertibility without fortification of the reserves, with its external banking position unimproved, and with a balance of payments lacking in underlying strength. Neither Robot, nor the Collective Approach, nor any modification of these had considered such an outcome as anything other than a description of a condition that ought to be avoided.

The disagreements between the Bank and the Treasury over 'Stage 2' were not altogether concealed from public gaze. On 11 July the *Financial Times* published a leading article entitled 'Two Voices'. This contrasted the voice of the Treasury, which spoke of convertibility as 'still a far off hypothetical thing', and the voice of 'those who have the actual day-to-day management of Sterling and of the world-wide financial transactions in which Sterling is involved'. This latter voice spoke of unifying the official and transferable rates and thereby making sterling convertible at a single floating rate. Continental holders viewed this with apprehension. Clarification of policy was required, for the uncertainty was contributing to the weakness of sterling. The Chancellor, prompted by Rowan, was upset by the article and telephone Mynors to say so. Bolton told Rowan that the Treasury had been warned that a newspaper campaign was inevitable. He added, in a comment to Mynors: 'There is no leak. All the material is available to any intelligent observer.' A few days later there was an exchange in the House of Commons when Gaitskell and Roy Jenkins pressed the Chancellor both about convertibility and about exchange flexibility. Butler side-stepped their questions, but at the end of the month he made a statement in the House intended mainly to reassure public opinion about the Government's domestic resolve. It included a strong declaration that the parity of $2·80 would be maintained. Sterling, which had been supported through the late part of July at $2·78$\frac{3}{8}$, recovered to $2·79 with transferable at $2·76$\frac{1}{2}$. But continuing adverse trade figures, the formulation of fresh wage demands, and speculation about the reason for Cabinet meetings early in the Recess, soon brought about a relapse. By mid-August sterling was again being supported by the EEA at around $2·78$\frac{1}{2}$ with transferable at $2·76$\frac{1}{8}$.

These developments in the exchange market confirmed that public uncertainty about the Government's intentions regarding the management of sterling had to be resolved, one way or the other, as soon as practicable and not later than the Istanbul meetings. A dangerous situation was developing, with the possibility of the reserves falling to $2 billion or lower. The authorities could move to Stage 2, as recommended by the Bank; they could move to formal convertibility, as preferred by the Treasury if a move were made at all; or they could make no move and announce that they had no intention of making one for some time ahead. As early as 19 July the Governor was undauntedly advising the Chancellor to announce a variant of Stage 2 at Istanbul. 'We *must* put this anxiety and uncertainty to rest soon. You will have all the Finance Ministers there. I do not see another easy date.' This particular variant included as options a 4% spread and a 6% spread. Although Stage 2 would not automatically invoke the EPU break clause, the Governor suggested that the EMA should nevertheless be brought into force during the winter. The proposal was duly considered at a meeting with Butler and his officials. The Chancellor himself was sympathetic to a half-way house between the existing situation and full convertibility. But his officials again argued that no such resting place could be found and that in practice the Governor's proposal amounted to full convertibility, with inevitable consequences in the IMF, the GATT, and the OEEC. All agreed that the internal economic situation required close attention; otherwise a move to wider spreads would be regarded simply as a measure of devaluation. The Chancellor concluded that he should make as strong a statement as possible to the House and that further consideration should be given, ahead of Istanbul, to any steps that might be possible short of full convertibility.

In response, and despite some voices within the Bank suggesting that a 4% or 6% spread was hardly worthwhile, the Governor made a final attempt to get what he wanted, this time with a 4% spread instead of a 6% spread, coalescence within it, and no rush to disband the EPU if the other members did not want to disband. Even if the spread were to remain at 2%, an attempt should still be made to encourage coalescence. Whatever was decided, 'sterling policy should emerge from Istanbul *settled* and *definite* for a long period ahead'. Treasury officials continued their opposition to proposals of this kind. Coalescence was still tantamount to convertibility and there was no avoiding it being publicly and politically treated as such. Consultation with the Commonwealth and with the Europeans would be required and could not be completed before Istanbul. In any case, it would all be seen as a move from external weakness, and the effects would be severely compounded by the likely dismantling of discrimination against dollar goods at an estimated balance of payments cost to the UK of £300–400 million per annum. Finally a 4% spread would prejudice a later move to 6%. For its part, the Bank continued to deny these objections. In particular, the Governor questioned the Treasury's view of discrimination. Why should the US and Canada want to make UK policy more difficult by trying to rush everyone into Article VIII because official and transferable sterling had come together? As to the admitted move from weakness, things would only be made worse if the Government was seen, once more, to back away from convertibility after all the careful preparations leading to signature of the EMA. The Chancellor read the papers and listened carefully before deciding to reject the Bank's advice. He was publicly committed to moving to convertibility from a position of strength and had renewed that commitment in the House at the end of July. This, together with the need for Cabinet consent and discussions overseas, made it impossible to accept the Governor's proposals. The discrimination aspect reinforced this view. The Governor warned that the Government would be risking an autumn crisis, but the Chancellor replied that he was prepared to run that risk and rely upon a clear holding statement at Istanbul together with pursuit of a firm internal policy. The next move might be in the spring of 1956 and might lead to full and formal convertibility.

The holding statement at Istanbul was duly made and the UK's good intentions about internal policy were emphasised in private discussions with the Americans. At home there were further fears of an approaching crisis and official pressure was building up to persuade Ministers to take substantial countervailing measures without delay. Bolton reported to the Governor: 'I have seen Rowan and Caccia frequently and there have been meetings of Permanent Secretaries about the situation. They are unanimous in advising Ministers that definite action must be taken and announced before end-September and I now feel certain that something useful will be done.' An autumn Budget, reversing the one brought before the Election, was in the offing. Early in October the markets began to anticipate it and sterling recovered to $2·79 and above. It improved further after the Budget of 26 October, in which Purchase Tax and Distributed Profits Tax were increased and public sector investment programmes cut. In November sterling rose above $2·80. The crisis had been averted, as had front-door convertibility or any version of Stage 2. The much-debated entity remained firmly at the back entrance, successfully eliminating the heavy discount on transferable that had caused trouble twelve months earlier and had given the Bank so much influence in the Treasury at that time.

The disagreement between the Bank and the Government over external policy was a disappointing outcome to all they had been through together since 1951. The Treasury, putting the best gloss on it that it could, described it as a difference about timing rather than about the substance of policy. To some degree this was true. The arguments in favour of postponement, until the underlying situation had been put right, were strong; and the UK was under no pressure from Governments in North America, Western Europe, or the Commonwealth to make an early move. Postponement, as the Bank argued, would admittedly be a sign of weakness; but the weakness was already there for all to see and any additional sign would merely emphasise a need for corrective measures, a need that was anyway becoming manifest. But a prior move to Stage 2, with a declared dealing spread of 4% (or perhaps 6%), would have been unlikely of itself to inspire confidence and would most likely have added to the pressures on sterling and the pressure for corrective internal measures. The Governor's arguments in favour of Stage 2, including denials that it was indistinguishable from formal convertibility, were indeed a little ragged and his warnings about a crisis occurring if it were not put into effect seem a little strident. So why did he personally persist in a course which, certainly by August, invited defeat and disagreement in the face of better arguments on the other side? Two reasons may be advanced. Firstly the Bank, along with many in Whitehall, may have begun to lose confidence in the ability and resolve of the Eden Government. If this were so, the Bank would have seen it as its duty to keep up the pressure on the Government to carry through to a proper conclusion an external policy agreed in 1952 and since confirmed on various occasions. Keeping up the pressure, alone if need be, meant enduring tactical setbacks and deploying vulnerable arguments, but in a good cause. Secondly there is no doubt that by the summer of 1955 the Bank was acutely aware that the original strategy of the Collective Approach had all but failed: no large stand-by or other help, no floating rate, no strong balance of payments. Almost too late it began to warn the Government where all this was inexorably leading, though the Bank itself had earlier been willing to concede more on 'stability without commitment' than the Treasury. Accordingly, the unease of the Bank, and the particular unease of the Governor, may well have made it persist with advocacy of Stage 2 as a last hope of achieving some degree of exchange flexibility through unilateral action. Once obtained this flexibility might have increased at a later date.

SOURCES

Bank files

ADM14/34	L. P. Thompson-McCausland's Papers: Committee on Preparations for Commonwealth Economic Conference (July – December 1952)
ADM14/35–7	L. P. Thompson-McCausland's Papers: Further Current Papers (December 1952 – May 1954)
ADM14/38	L. P. Thompson-McCausland's Papers: EPU (October 1953 – July 1954)
ADM14/39–40	L. P. Thompson-McCausland's Papers: Collective Approach Committee – Bank and Treasury Memoranda
C8/6	Foreign Exchange and Gold Markets: Dealers' Reports – Regular External Reports (February 1955 – December 1957)
G1/98–99	Governor's Files: Exchange Policy (January 1953 – February 1958)
G3/5–7	Governor's Diaries (1952–4)
OV44/51–2	Sterling and Sterling Area Policy: Sterling Area Exchange Policy – General (March 1952 – December 1953)
OV44/59–65	Sterling and Sterling Area Policy: Sterling Area Exchange Policy – Collective Approach to Convertibility (October 1952 – December 1957)
OV46/59	Post-war Reconstruction: EPU Managing Board Discussions (July 1952 – February 1953)
OV46/65–8	Post-war Reconstruction: European Monetary Agreement (June 1954 – May 1959)

Foreign Relations of the United States

CHAPTER 8

1956: THE BANK AND THE SUEZ AFFAIR

(a) PROLOGUE

WHEN MACMILLAN moved to No. 11 at the end of 1955, the UK reserves were smaller than those of either West Germany or France and amounted to $2.12 billion or some £750 million (compared to a nadir of £600 million during the crisis in 1952). The sterling balances stood at about £3,750 million of which £800 million was held outside the Sterling Area. In order to contain the risks inherent in such a position it was judged that the UK needed to run a surplus on external current account averaging at least £300 million per annum. In 1955, however, there had been a current deficit of £100 million and only a small surplus on the part of the rest of the Sterling Area. The reserves had fallen accordingly, by £230 million. As has been related earlier, confidence had weakened sharply and the possibility of another devaluation was frequently canvassed in the markets whenever some item of bad news or market intelligence made sterling a subject for speculative attention. Following the failure of the Collective Approach as originally conceived, the implications were only too apparent to the Treasury and the Bank. On 3 January 1956 Leslie Rowan concluded a gloomy but well-founded survey for the new Chancellor as follows: 'In these circumstances, one is bound to conclude that, on the basis of present trends, policies and moods, we are *not* capable of meeting our *existing* commitments (other than with the help of physical controls and Aid) *without the probability or even certainty of continual crises which may well undermine our total policies and will certainly undermine the sterling system*' (author's italics). The Bank concurred. Nearly a year later, in the immediate aftermath of the Suez crisis, the Governor in his turn summed up Britain's external financial predicament and wrote to Macmillan:

Whatever longer-term effects Suez may prove to have on the economy, it has certainly had the immediate effect of laying bare to the public eye, both at home and abroad, some of the weakness of which we have long been conscious.

You and I have, I think, both felt that the measures of the last few years, including the credit squeeze and various fiscal adjustments made by your predecessor and yourself, have helped to move the economy towards an uneasy equilibrium but have left some basic problems untouched. We have over the last five years been able to maintain our position on a see-saw, retaining just adequate confidence in the currency by a slender margin. After the events of the past few months I do not believe this is good enough.

At no stage during 1956 did the Bank or the official Treasury take any brighter view of the underlying situation, though the reserves did recover by $265 million over the first six months. Nor, following the seizure of the Suez Canal at the end of July, did they view with anything but alarm the likely effect upon sterling of a military confrontation with Egypt and the possible interruption of Middle East oil supplies. In the view of the Bank and of senior Treasury officials, such a confrontation would be likely to precipitate a severe exchange crisis unless accompanied by financial assistance on a large scale from the IMF or directly from the US. The Chancellor, as a member of the inner group of Ministers known as the Egypt Committee, was by all accounts an ardent supporter of the use of force against Egypt. He was also the Minister responsible for assessing the external financial constraints that could interfere with the pursuit of such a policy and even become dominant at a critical point along an obviously dangerous road. The reserves fell $50 million in the third quarter of 1956 and would have fallen by $230 million were it not for the fortuitous receipt of $180 million from the sale of Trinidad Leaseholds Ltd to Texaco. But Macmillan was prepared to gamble on getting sufficient assurance of financial support from his old friends in the US to insure sterling against the heavy short-term pressures likely to result from a resort to force, which, on another gamble, would succeed very quickly. Clear weather would then follow. His colleagues, including the Prime Minister, were accordingly ill-prepared for the exchange crisis that blew up when the double bet was lost and the Government found itself at the financial mercy of a confused and angry Administration in Washington.

The Government was then obliged to give way to American demands while ensuring that the US Treasury was treated to some recital of the awful consequences that the Chancellor asserted might follow a collapse of sterling. Impressed by the demonstration in the Middle East that the British were after all capable of kicking over the traces, the Americans then prudently decided to take no chances with sterling. Humphrey the tortoise suddenly became Humphrey the hare; and Macmillan found himself the recipient of monetary help on a scale that in a better cause had entirely eluded his predecessor. The UK was allowed to draw the first two tranches of its IMF quota and was granted a stand-by for all the rest. At the same time the Exim Bank offered a credit of up to $700 million for the purchase of dollar oil supplies, the Suez Canal being blocked for the time being. Looking all the way back to 1952, this was dramatic confirmation that the Americans would quickly give way to compulsive unilateral action what they would deny to reasoned argument. Perhaps Robot, if put into effect with French collusion, might have resembled some kind of financial Suez; though what strings the Truman Administration might have attached to American goodwill on that occasion must remain anyone's guess.

But early in 1956, when the Suez affair was still well down under the horizon, the UK authorities paid some heed to the precarious situation described by Rowan and introduced a further series of corrective measures. On 6 January, after the change of Chancellor, there came a speech by the Economic Secretary, Edward Boyle, reaffirming the maintenance of the $2.80 parity and hinting at further supportive measures to come. Sterling rose to 2.80\frac{5}{8}$, but at the February Basle meeting the central bankers reported to Bolton that markets remained frightened about the probability of devaluation. At the end of February, as related in Chapter 10, Bank Rate was raised to $5\frac{1}{2}$% and hire-purchase controls were tightened and extended. There were also modest cuts in investment allowances, in the remaining food subsidies, and in public sector investment programmes. In his April Budget the Chancellor increased the tax on distributed profits to 30%, cut subsidies still further, increased the tobacco tax, and introduced more attractive savings instruments, including the prize bonds (Premium Bonds), which Macmillan introduced with a characteristic panache that foreign opinion found unconvincing. Over the first six months of the year the reserves rose by $265 million, but seasonal factors, including servicing of the North American Loans due in December, suggested that at the end of the year they could well fall back to where they started ($2.12 billion) or below.

Complementary to the above alterations in domestic policy and contributory to their rationale there was further official debate about external monetary arrangements. A fresh Sterling Area working party of Treasury and Bank officials, chaired by Rickett, had been set up in the autumn of 1955 at the suggestion of the Governor following a debate within the Bank prompted by Bolton. It reported in the late spring of 1956.

Of particular concern were further signs of reserves-diversification in the Area and the approaching independence of African colonies with large sterling balances. Confidence had once more been sapped by the conduct of UK economic affairs over the preceding eighteen months as well as by the prolonged debates about convertibility and wider spreads. But after the customary tour around this particular course it was concluded that there was little to be done beyond conducting economic policy in such a way that inflation was controlled and that an external surplus averaging £350 million per annum was achieved. The Bank agreed with this conclusion without much confidence that any such surplus was on the way. Alongside this review there was some revival of the debate about convertibility itself. In the Bank, Bolton had for the moment run out of worthwhile ideas. It was to be his last year as an Executive Director; and the younger generation, represented by Maurice Parsons (his successor) and Max Stamp, were disposed to accept the negative outcome of Robot and the Collective Approach. They then concentrated upon how best to live with fixed-rate convertibility, exiguous reserves, and oppressively large external liabilities. This was to make Parsons more than ever a dedicated opponent of sterling devaluation and a puritanical apostle of domestic economic disciplines. Like Bolton with the ideas of the early fifties, he too was destined to go down to defeat. But that was over ten years ahead.[1] For now, he could confidently write:

> The steady erosion of the domestic purchasing power of the pound and of the reserves have between them undermined the confidence in the currency to an alarming extent and have thereby made problems of technical management much more difficult. The primary remedy for this, however, will not in my view be found by improved techniques but by more realistic policies as regards consumption and investment.

Stamp, commenting on a note by Bolton, questioned the whole basis of the

---

[1] Parsons was now in his mid-forties. His spare frame was over six feet high and like Bolton he had a deep and compellingly resonant voice, but persuasive or at times ponderous rather than seductive. He was a lay preacher (nicknamed 'the parson' by Norman, with whom he worked as Private Secretary) and there were those of us who felt latterly that at times it gave him an unfair moral advantage in debates about the obligations attaching to the management of sterling. The post of Executive Director, in succession to Bolton, was probably a strain on his underlying capacity, a condition that was for some years concealed by the apparent validity of the principal position he adopted but was confirmed by his reluctance to work with more than a very few chosen lieutenants at any one time. During 1964–6 the author was a member of his immediate entourage and worked closely with him on the negotiation of the first Basle Agreement on the sterling balances as well as on other international monetary questions. I found him a most considerate, constructive, and effective leader. But later, as Deputy Governor, he became frustrated, morose, difficult, and altogether past his best – perhaps a portent of the mental illness that subsequently overwhelmed him.

argument for early convertibility. Unless the balance of payments had definitely passed its worst, a move would not help confidence, could well make matters more difficult, and in the event of future trouble would be made a scapegoat. What was more, the system of *de facto* convertibility with dual exchange rates that had been running since February 1955 could run on for another year without dire consequences. 'The world is now used to it, and on the whole accepts it, as a sensible system in our present situation.'

The Governor listened to the debate and was inclined to make the best of the situation as he found it. On 12 April he sent a short note to the Chancellor, for discussion following the Budget. Its occasion was the need to decide whether to renew the EPU for a further year, with the same break clause providing for the activation of the EMA during the year. 'This', he wrote, 'raises the whole question of convertibility, collective approach and all that. I do not myself think it would be wise or profitable to go over past history on all this or, so to speak, to seek to reopen collective approach negotiations.' Since February 1955, he continued, sterling had in practice been convertible for non-residents, subject only to a very small and almost constant discount on the official rate of exchange. The practical points for decision were firstly whether to stay put or to bring the rates together and secondly whether, if the rates were unified, 'do we do it inside the $2.78–2.82 bracket or do we insist on wider spreads?' Going backwards, by letting transferable run to a wide discount, was not a viable option. 'In the event of disaster our course would be to bring the rates together and allow them to float.' But the existing situation, with dual rates, was never designed to be a semi-permanent condition, though it could probably last another year or so, becoming all the time more inconvenient and unreal. One inconvenience was that the UK banks were not allowed to deal in transferable. The next move was bound to be a forward one. It was only a question of timing; and here the two most important considerations were to act early in the life of a Government and to act when 'things have been worse and look like getting better.' Objections to a move came mainly from those who feared it would lead too quickly to abandonment of discrimination against dollar goods; but the Governor again argued that this need not happen if the move were properly conducted in low key. As to wider spreads, he gave up the struggle, not without bitterness:

> My personal view is that we have missed the boat for a flexible rate or wider spreads. If we had done it some years back and been content to pick up the bits afterwards, I think we should have got away with it and derived some advantage. Even a shorter while back, I think we could have got away with

rather wider spreads, which would have been technically useful. After more recent events and, in particular, the palaver last Summer, I do not think we could get away with wider spreads without doing much more harm than good: few other currencies would follow us and it would generally be regarded (now, I fear, at home as well as abroad) as a first step to further devaluation.

In any event the one thing we must absolutely avoid is further discussion or negotiation on the rate question. Sterling just will not stand it. We have discussed all this *ad infinitum* with Commonwealth, USA and Europe. We need now to decide what we want to do, and do it.

On 24 April the Chancellor, accompanied by Bridges, Gilbert, Rowan, and Hall, met with Cobbold, Bolton, and Parsons. The discussion amounted to a stale re-run of the debates that had taken place in the previous summer. The Bank again wanted to move and judged it could be done quietly. The Treasury officials again disagreed, adding that the position would now be worse than that contemplated in the Collective Approach, for there would be no wider spread and no guarantee of IMF support. Someone even asserted that convertibility at the official rate would of itself cause central banks in the Transferable Account Area to sell their sterling for dollars and that a considerable proportion of the £800 million of such balances would therefore be converted.[2] The official record concluded: 'The Chancellor of the Exchequer said he would like to think over these matters before reaching a decision.' Some debate evidently continued. Rowan circulated a paper entitled 'Why Convertibility?' early in June. But the decision was negative. The EPU was renewed for a further year. The Chancellor himself was more interested in the British response to the approaching Treaty of Rome, on which there was now much debate in Whitehall, Bolton reporting on 3 July that 'the Treasury are split from top to bottom between adherents of a closer economic union with Europe and a group who reject any doctrines that are not included in the Collective Approach'. Rowan was reportedly numbered among the latter. True to character, Bolton attempted to involve the Bank in this debate. The 'strange insight', which Norman had long ago had to admit, did not fail him at this turning point.[3] The American sun was dimming, he wrote. The post-war world was on the

---

[2] This was nonsense, as Parsons explained in a letter to Rowan a few days later. Total sterling holdings of all non-sterling central banks amounted to only £285 million of which some £110 million was on Egyptian No. 2 Account. Of the remainder, £24 million was on Egyptian No. 1 and £85 million was held by the Bank of Japan. Neither of these holders was likely to be deterred from converting into dollars by the existing differential between transferable and official.

[3] Recounted in Jacobsson's diary for 26 March 1950 as follows: 'Norman never believed in Bolton's judgement – "not balanced, but often a strange insight, I am willing to admit to that."'

move. The British had 'no alternative but to develop more effective relationships between Western Europe and the Commonwealth, unless they are to drift aimlessly while events take their course. Such a relationship involves new procedures, mechanisms and a creation of personal relationships which at present do not exist.' The Governor, though not hostile to this line of thought, was more cautious. Writing to Macmillan early in August, he counselled circumspection from the beginning about any financial counterpart to new trade arrangements with Western Europe. Hands must not be overtied. Sterling and the Commonwealth had to be kept in mind. There had to be maintained 'a degree of independence for sterling policy, which is not essential to Western European countries without international currencies' – a proposition as true in its way at that time as it was in different circumstances thirty years later. By this time, however, the Suez crisis had broken and the ordinary threads of policy formation were severed.

(b) THE CRISIS

The direct involvement of the Bank in the Suez affair may be likened to that of a warship's engineer before and during a naval engagement. It was from time to time given instructions, which it carried out. From time to time it emerged to advise or to warn that its instructions needed revision or were having unexpected or unwelcome consequences. It was also called upon to help Treasury officials advise about what would happen to its machinery, sterling, if the engagement were to become notably hotter and if valuable allies were to turn away. Towards the end, when it looked as if the machinery might be overwhelmed, it gave advice about essential running repairs. When all was over, it resumed its ordinary role when the Governor wrote to the Chancellor about the need to tackle basic problems responsible for the proven weakness of the sterling machinery. But the Bank was never involved, and had no need to be involved, in the actual preparations for armed conflict, save in the minor matter of currency notes for use by an occupying force. The preparations with the Israelis and the French were necessarily undertaken by a small Ministerial Group working in the utmost secrecy. As Cobbold clearly recalled in 1977 and as is confirmed by the Threadneedle Street archives, the Bank was kept completely in the dark until the evening of 30 October, twenty-four hours after the Israeli attack on Egypt. Then, just after the ultimatums had been sent and the Prime Minister had informed the House of Commons, Macmillan saw the Governor and, as the latter noted in his diary, 'sketched existing decisions and some possible courses of events'.

The crisis had begun as long ago as the evening of 26 July when President Nasser announced the immediate nationalisation of the Suez Canal Company following the failure of negotiations with the Americans and others about the financing of the High Dam on the Nile at Aswan. The Egyptian action was denounced from virtually all sides in the House of Commons on the following morning. The Cabinet then agreed that HMG should seek to secure the reversal of the Egyptian action, by the use of force if necessary. Immediate consultations with the US and France were to be set in hand and the Egypt Committee of senior Ministers was established. As matters of consequential detail, exports of military equipment were to be banned and Egyptian balances in the UK were to be blocked.[4] On the same afternoon Exchange Control notices were hurriedly issued removing Egypt from the Transferable Account Area and prohibiting all payments off any Egyptian sterling accounts without prior permission of the Bank on behalf of the Treasury. Shortly beforehand the Governor advised the Deputy Chairman of Westminster Bank not to allow any unusual payments out of the account of the Suez Canal Company without first consulting the Bank.

Over the next few days Exchange Control was busy sorting out the administration of the block on Egyptian balances. A supplementary notice was issued on 31 July, allowing payments off Egyptian accounts to UK and Sterling Area residents in respect of pre-zero transactions relating to exports of goods to Egypt. The precise definition of pre-zeros, this time applying to invisibles as well as goods, was liberalised and refined over the following ten days and payments off Egyptian accounts to transferable accounts, for pre-zeros, were also allowed. No post-zeros were allowed at all, the Governor making the point to Bridges and Rowan that any attempt to impose a financial blockade on Egypt would soon be rendered ineffective once post-zeros of any sort were permitted. The intentions of Ministers were not very clear, except that they did not want to be seen retreating from their original and hurried decision to block. But a financial blockade was unlikely to achieve very much and all too likely to cause as much or more damage to the UK as to Egypt. UK exports to Egypt would be lost to competitors in other countries for lack of payment in sterling. Sterling Area countries would become restive if Egypt refused to accept sterling (on

---

[4] Earlier in the year the Governor had asked Exchange Control for advice about action that might be taken if events were to take a more serious turn in the Middle East. Blocking of Egypt's No. 1 Account was considered and the procedure for doing so brushed up. The Treasury was informed and a memorandum was circulated to the Chancellor by Rickett on 11 April. It advised against blocking unless the reason for doing so was manifestly justifiable to financial opinion. Even then it would be better if supported by parallel US action. Closure of the Suez Canal was thought to be a justifiable reason for blocking.

to blocked account) in payment for supplies of, for example, cotton. The Gulf States, mostly members of the Sterling Area, would be restive if Egypt was unable to pay for their oil because of the block on Egyptian sterling reserves. These latter comprised some £20 million on the No. 1 Account and £110 million on the No. 2 Account that had been blocked since 1947 and was being gradually run down by annual release. The only way a financial blockade could become effective would be its application by all major trading nations as well as by the UK. But there was never any prospect of that happening. Soundings were taken by the Treasury early in August and the response was discouraging. The Governor then told Macmillan that the unilateral blocking could only be regarded as a holding operation, for a few weeks. But the Chancellor did not want to be seen retreating and he allowed the situation to run on into September and October, hoping for an early solution to the whole crisis.

At the end of August Leith-Ross, now Chairman of the Standard Bank, wrote to Bridges in appropriate terms of ex-Civil Servant severity.[5] He pointed out the absurdity, as he saw it, of blocking private Egyptian balances (blocking of Government accounts, he thought, was justified as cover for the Suez Canal shares until compensation was paid). 'It is of course the case', he wrote, 'that all economic warfare measures hurt the country that applies them as well as the country to which they are applied, but I do not recollect any other case in which the damage to the country which applies the measure so outweighs any damage (or rather inconvenience) that may be caused to the "enemy" country. So I should like to know what the object is.' After consultation with Bolton, a short reply was sent that included the sentence: 'The existing freeze admittedly hurts innocent parties, including British exporters and private residents of Egypt, but the measures will either be withdrawn if agreement is reached, or changed in character if the situation gets worse.'

But in the absence of any settlement of the quarrel with Egypt the freeze began to fester. Complaints grew and were relayed by Tansley, now in Exchange Control, to an Egypt Working Party that had been set up in the Treasury. Parliamentary Questions were feared to be in the offing. The problem of Egyptian payment for Gulf oil grew more urgent. The Governor complained to Rowan, concluding that trade between Egypt and the Sterling Area was tending to re-establish itself after the initial impact of the freeze, but in currencies other than sterling. This tendency would increase unless in the near future it proved possible to put the present temporary

---

[5] He had earlier told the Deputy Governor that Nasser was an Ataturk rather than a Hitler.

arrangements on to a more adequate and permanent footing and to gain the support of the other great trading nations. 'Unless this is done we may well find ourselves making one exception after the other... with the result that the only lasting damage that is done is to sterling. I believe that our whole policy about the freeze will need early reconsideration.' There was no response. Macmillan had other fish to fry. By 14 October the Prime Minister and the Egypt Committee were becoming enmeshed in Franco–Israeli plans for military action against Egypt. On 24 October the secret Sèvres Agreement was signed by the UK, France, and Israel; and the Israeli attack was timed for the 29th. Minor muddles, like the increasingly discredited freeze on Egyptian sterling, could be pushed to one side.

Two other engine-room issues may be mentioned. The first concerned the payment of Canal dues. It could of course be no part of British policy to be seen trying to obstruct passage through the Canal – the vital international waterway carrying vital supplies – by interfering with such payments. The most the Government could do was avoid any new arrangements in the UK that could be construed as recognising the new Canal Authority being set up by Cairo. Accordingly, on the Governor's advice, the Government instructed the Midland Bank not to accede to an Egyptian request to open an account in London in the name of the Authority. As to the dues themselves, Ministers finally conceded that shipowners should either continue to pay them in sterling to the old Company in London or, if that was their custom, pay through local agents and apply to the Bank for the necessary foreign currency. It was recognised that the Egyptian authorities could insist on payment in Egypt, that they could refuse payment in sterling to blocked account, and that foreign currency would have to be provided in such cases.

The second of the two other engine-room issues was the provision of currency for use in Egypt by the armed services in the event of a successful invasion. Related to this was the provision of financial advice to an occupying force. The Governor raised these matters with Rowan early in August, saying he would ask Michael Babington Smith[6] to act as adviser if an occupation seemed imminent.[7] Later in the month, on Ministerial instructions, £2 million of British Military Administration currency notes, part of a store held in the Bank since 1945, were released to the War Office and despatched to Limassol in Cyprus.

---

[6] *Babington Smith, Michael James*, CBE (1901–84). Educated Eton and Trinity College, Cambridge. Director of Finance, Supreme Headquarters of the Allied Expeditionary Force (SHAEF) 1943–5. Deputy Chairman, Glyn Mills 1947–63, Director, Bank of England 1949–69, BIS 1965–74, Compagnie Financière de Suez 1957–74, Chairman, London Committee of Ottoman Bank 1975–82.

[7] He was in fact seen by the Governor on 31 October and asked to make himself available.

These were all minor matters compared to the central problem of sterling itself. As early as mid-August the Governor, with Rowan's support, was advising the Chancellor to meet any additional strain by firm intervention in the exchange markets. Going backwards on convertibility, or letting the transferable rate go, would do far more harm than good. Three weeks later, with no settlement in sight, Bridges held a meeting in the Treasury, at which Mynors and Bolton were present, to discuss the sort of action that might be taken in the event of war with Egypt. He reported its conclusions in a Minute to Macmillan dated 7 September. Two hypotheses were considered: firstly, if the UK had overt support from the US and elsewhere, and was acting in accord with UN wishes; secondly, if the UK was acting with the support of only the French and one or two others, without overt American support, with a divided Commonwealth, and probably also with a divided public opinion at home. In the first case, all would be well with sterling. Business-as-usual would be indicated. In the second case, it would not be possible to predict the timing or magnitude of the strains to which sterling might be put. At the worst, however, the strains might be so great that whatever precautionary measures were taken it would not be possible to maintain the exchange rate. Bridges concluded magisterially and memorably: 'What this points to therefore is the vital necessity from the point of view of our currency and our economy of ensuring that we do not go it alone, and that we have the maximum US support.'

The Chancellor, meanwhile, was toying with the idea of allowing the transferable rate to fall a little, partly because it was under pressure from Egyptian sales arising from a Chinese sterling credit; but he was advised by Rowan, himself acting on advice from Bolton, that this would only upset confidence to no good purpose. The Deputy Governor repeated this advice at a meeting held by the Chancellor on 14 September. The Bank was supported by the official Treasury, and Macmillan dropped the subject. He and Rowan then left for Washington to attend the Fund/Bank meetings, in the course of which the latter warned him that confidence in sterling was unlikely to recover even if hostilities in the Middle East were averted. In their absence Bridges, now in his last month at the Treasury,[8] asked Rickett to work out in collaboration with the Bank a preliminary view about action that might be taken if the drain on the reserves continued. Following a meeting with Parsons and others on 25 September, Rickett reported back to Bridges, with the Governor's approval. For

---

[8] Makins left the Washington Embassy in September and took several weeks' holiday before taking over at the Treasury in mid-October.

familiar reasons, a return to direct controls and bilateral agreements was regarded by the Bank as the worst of all possible alternatives. As to exchange-rate policy, the only satisfactory course was to defend the present parity. This in turn meant adherence to firm domestic policies. But if, despite every effort, the parity could not be maintained, then the Bank would prefer a floating rate to a devaluation and would recommend unification of transferable and official. The effect on the Sterling Area would be bad and could not feasibly be mitigated by offering exchange guarantees on sterling balances. Among temporary measures to defend the parity, the obvious front-runner was a Fund drawing; and it was felt this should be actively considered if the reserves fell near to $2 billion (they were already down to $2.34 billion).

Early in October the Governor agreed that Bridges should speak to the Chancellor on the lines of Rickett's report with the reservation, noted in his diary, that it was 'most important not to regard the courses of action outlined as other than remote and undesirable'. In the middle of the month he wrote to Macmillan about discussions he had had with eight Commonwealth central bank Governors who had visited the Bank on their way back from the Washington meetings. Several of them had expressed the view that a further devaluation of sterling, which the Suez dispute could render more likely, would mean the immediate break-up of the Sterling Area and would destroy sterling's international position, at once as a store of value and rapidly as a trading currency. In reply Cobbold had said that HMG were determined to maintain the existing parity, adding that earlier ideas of wider spreads were now no longer running. Macmillan acknowledged this on 24 October, the day the Sèvres Agreement was signed, saying: 'I need hardly say that I entirely agree with the line that you took.' The Sterling Area Governors were probably overstating their case. It is not recorded whether the Chancellor believed them; but they had provided him with some ammunition for later use when begging the Americans for help.

When he saw the Chancellor with Makins and Rowan on the evening of 30 October, to be told of imminent Anglo-French hostilities against Egypt, the Governor said he had given instructions that any unusual orders for the transfer of sterling funds held at the Bank by Arab countries should be referred to him before execution. In any case of a doubtful nature he would consult HM Treasury; but, so far as possible, it was agreed to avoid any outright blocking. As to the markets, it was agreed (in the Governor's record) 'to dig our toes in on the whole exchange front'. The Chancellor said he felt it likely, as things developed over the next few days, that the question of an IMF drawing and of applying to the US for a waiver of interest on the post-war loan would need to be reviewed. Rickett, working with Treasury officials and with Parsons from the Bank, then put together a note on emergency action which he sent forward to Rowan on 2 November. He concluded that a Fund drawing would be the right step. Domestic measures could come later, depending on the results of the Suez operation and, in particular, its effect on oil supplies. However, the drawing was not required immediately and Treasury officials accepted the Bank's advice that the Fund should not be approached just yet. If possible the UK should wait until there had been some improvement in sterling. Rickett pointed out that access to the gold tranche was virtually automatic and access to the first credit tranche normally given with very few questions asked. He added, however:

> In present circumstances we cannot assume that we shall get a drawing without difficulty. It is conceivable that the US might oppose a drawing by us, particularly if in the meantime the General Assembly had passed an adverse resolution. We considered what bearing this might have on the timing of any approach to the Fund. On the whole, the arguments seemed to be in favour of delaying it as long as possible in order to give tempers time to cool all round. There is obviously nothing to be gained by an immediate approach since we could not in any event hope to forestall action in the General Assembly.

The reserves had fallen by $84 million in October. Between noon on 30 October and noon on the 6 November, the day the Cabinet agreed to a cease-fire, both official and transferable were heavily supported by the EEA at the cost (all for value in November) of nearly $100 million. But $74 million of this was lost between 30 October and 2 November, the pressure in the ensuing days being much less and totalling $24 million. Nevertheless, after allowing for the end-year loan service amounting to $180 million it was clear by the 4th or 5th that the reserves would fall below the presumed 'action level' of $2 billion by 31 December, and possibly a long way below unless confidence somehow returned. There was now little immediate prospect of any such favourable development. The Egyptians had succeeded in physically blocking the Canal and thereby interrupting and delaying the flow of Middle East oil to the UK and Western Europe. American opposition to the Anglo–French action had become all too obvious to everyone, first through the Security Council and next in the General Assembly of the UN. It was also clear that opinion in the UK was deeply divided and that the Government was coming under intense pressure. But there was still no immediate need to embark on any preliminaries to a Fund drawing. Pressure on sterling had in fact temporarily eased. There is no record in the Bank of any further discussions with the Treasury about the exchange situation between 2 November and 6 November, though telephone conversations at official level would certainly have taken place. On 7 November, after the cease-fire, Bolton circulated a full policy note, which was sent to Makins by the Governor on the 8th. It recommended, *inter alia*, a Fund drawing of at least $1 billion, the preliminaries to be set in hand as soon as the time was appropriate. It did not propose an immediate approach to the Americans, any more than had Rickett's note of 2 November.

According to Macmillan's own published account of the events of 6 November, he began the day by telephoning the United States to enquire whether the Administration would support a UK drawing from the IMF. The reply, he says, was delayed and came through after the crucial Cabinet meeting had begun. It amounted to a refusal, unless the UK conformed to the UN Resolution ordering a cease-fire. Since the authenticity of this story is doubtful – for reasons explained in the appendix to this chapter – it is here assumed that the telephone calls did not take place and accordingly no judgement is made about the wisdom of so surprising a tactical move on Macmillan's part. What is not in dispute is that the Chancellor told his Cabinet colleagues about the pressure on sterling and its dangers. Opinions, as recorded in memoirs or biographies, differ regarding the effect that the news about sterling had upon the Cabinet when it finally came to decide, early in the afternoon, whether to order a cease-fire for midnight on the same day or whether to postpone until further ground had been won by British and French forces and, in all probability, the entire Canal Zone had been secured. Had it been secured, the subsequent position of the British and the French, not least over clearance and control of the Canal, would have been far stronger. Rhodes James, in the authoritative account given in his biography of Eden, says the run on the pound and the negative response from Washington were decisive for Macmillan though not for the Cabinet as a whole. The latter, in his own memoirs, denies this and rightly points out that neither in the immediate exchange situation nor in the alleged American attitude to a Fund drawing was there a decisive argument for an immediate cease-fire rather than a delay of, say forty-eight hours. In actual fact there was little or no adverse monetary argument bearing upon this particular question. In so far as confidence in sterling might have been improved by Anglo-French capture of the Canal, the monetary situation pointed *against* a cease-fire. Perhaps the most that can be said is that the external monetary constraint was a factor of some importance, varying in its effect upon individual Ministers, on whom the pressures of the crisis had become intense and for whom the news of a run on sterling came as a sudden additional shock. They had not been warned about it and at this late stage may well have been frightened by the Chancellor's sudden revelation of its potential force.

The early cease-fire left the British in the weakest possible position: with oil supplies reduced, without any control over clearance of a Canal still largely in Egyptian hands, and with a sharply reduced credibility, which the Prime Minister's sudden departure to the West Indies on 23 November, for urgent reasons of health, did nothing to improve. Accordingly, the pressure on sterling was virtually certain to continue and its scale would become apparent early in December when the reserves loss for November had to be announced. An open exchange crisis would then be imminent; and unless the Government was prepared to respond with a sharp tightening of domestic policy, which it was now in no good shape to do, it would have no alternative but to get full-scale external financial assistance on whatever terms the United States demanded.

Agreement with the Americans was not finally settled until 3 December. In the preceding weeks, after the cease-fire at midnight on 6 November, the Bank continued its part as ship's engineer while losing no opportunity for suggesting, to no effect, that the occasion of the crisis might be used to bring about the unification of official and transferable sterling. Bolton's note of 7 November was sent to Makins by the Governor on the 8th. Dismissing such expedients as removing support from transferable or reimposing abandoned exchange controls, the note argued that maintenance of the sterling system required maintenance of the parity, together with support for transferable so that the discount did not rise much above $1\frac{1}{2}\%$. It also argued in favour of intervention in support of security sterling because 'a big discount on security sterling weakens transferable sterling through techniques which have been developed in Kuwait, Hong Kong etc.'[9] Its principal consequential recommendations were a Fund drawing of not less than $1 billion and a mobilisation of the EEA dollar portfolio so as to raise $750 million. The full co-operation and support of the Commonwealth was to be sought before an approach was made to the US. The Governor himself saw the Chancellor on the evening of 8 November and Makins early on the 9th. In his own note of record he said it was agreed with Macmillan that the right course continued to be 'to hold the position firmly through these critical days or weeks, not bothering over much about any specific level of reserves'. He went on to advise that later in the month, 'when the dust has settled a bit and some of our international friendships can be restored', a major salvage operation should be considered 'to show our determination to hold the existing rate

[9] See Chapter 9, p. 568.

structure'. A Fund stand-by confined to the gold tranche or even this together with the first credit tranche would not suffice. More would be needed, including perhaps an Exim loan to cover additional supplies of dollar oil. To Makins he added that unification of the rates 'might also fall to be considered as part of a major operation' and that 'I should regard it as essential that ... HMG should take action in the domestic economy to offset the damage done by Suez and to show that we mean business about holding the rate'.

During the next two weeks the Treasury and the Bank discussed a two-stage plan for managing the worsening situation. The first stage assumed no early support from the US and consisted of mobilising such few resources as were to hand for reducing the November reserve loss to some $150 million, thereby lessening the risk of an open crisis. The second stage assumed a resumption of American goodwill and constituted the salvage operation mentioned by the Governor to the Chancellor on 8 November. But as the days went by and the loss of reserves continued, the prospect of a successful first stage receded. By 16 November the reserves loss had risen to $200 million. By the 19th it looked like becoming $300 million or more. The suggestion had been made in the Treasury that a Fund drawing of the gold tranche should be sought, despite likely American[10] opposition; but the Bank argued against using up some of the limited resources needed for the eventual salvage operation in this way. Instead, the Governor advised that the November loss should if possible be reduced to less than $200 million by a certain amount of juggling by the EEA, including the sale in the market of $65 million of short-dated US Government securities held by the Account but not included in the reserves. The entire situation was reviewed on 19th November at two meetings held at the Treasury by the Chancellor. The Bank was represented by the two Governors and by Bolton. It was quickly agreed that the right course was to maintain the stability of the currency and take any action necessary to maintain it. A 'catastrophe course', as Cobbold put it, of free floating was rejected. It was also agreed to reduce the November loss by selling the US Government securities and by other minor expedients, without publicity. Finally, it was agreed that a comprehensive statement should be made on 4 December when the reserves loss would be published. It would announce the Government's intention to support sterling, indicate the assets available, and, as the Treasury record put it, list 'the various steps that were under consideration to maintain an adequate level of reserves'. Internal measures would also be announced. The record

---

[10] The French, unaffected by romantic notions of special American friendship, had wisely taken the precaution of drawing theirs early in October.

concluded, euphemistically: 'It would be desirable to discuss the substance of the statement in advance with the US Government and the Commonwealth.' Discussing the substance with the Americans meant seeking their support for its contents. This in turn meant being prepared to accept their terms.

There can have been little doubt about the American attitude. In a long letter to Rowan (copied to the Bank and preceded by telegrams) that arrived in London on 21 November, Harcourt[11] made the situation quite clear. 'We meet a brick wall at every turn with the Administration. They remain extremely friendly on a personal basis but are not prepared to discuss any serious business. I think the attitude of the Administration can best be summed up by: "you have got yourselves into this mess, now get yourselves out of it"'. As to the Secretary of the Treasury himself, Harcourt wrote: 'Humphrey is profoundly worried at the overall effects on our economy, but is still unwilling to move. He remains convinced, however, that the most important thing is the rebuilding of the Atlantic Alliance and in the end I think we shall get help but we shall only get it when things are really desperate and only at about one minute to twelve – they look on the present as being about 11 o'clock[12].' The Chancellor and his officials then decided to open informal negotiations with Humphrey by playing on his reportedly profound worries. On 26 November the new UK Ambassador, Harold Caccia,[13] forwarded to him a personal message from Macmillan. This emphasised that the trouble with sterling was overwhelmingly due to confidence factors and concluded as follows:

> I know that there has been a deep division between our two countries in the action which we and the French took in Egypt. We took that action in the

---

[11] *Harcourt, William Edward, 2nd Viscount, KCMG, OBE* (1908–79). Educated Eton and Christ Church, Oxford. Army 1939–45. A Managing Director, Morgan Grenfell 1931–68, Chairman 1968–73. Minister (Economic) HM Embassy, Washington and Head of Treasury Supply Delegation, US 1954–7. Member Radcliffe Committee, 1957–9 and Plowden Committee on Overseas Representational Services 1962–4. Chairman, Legal and General Assurance 1958–77, Chairman, Rhodes Trust 1975–9.

[12] In a subsequent telegram the UK Ambassador said evidence was accumulating that Humphrey was the most intransigent and vindictive member of the Administration over the British action against Egypt. He added: 'This may stem in large part from his belief that we went into Suez without due thought for the economic consequences and that these consequences will almost certainly lead to demands on the US which will seriously affect his already precariously balanced budget.' The Secretary's subsequent behaviour suggests that he soon overcame his ill-temper.

[13] *Caccia, Harold Anthony, Baron (Life Peer)* 1965, (1905–1990). Educated Eton and Trinity College, Oxford. Foreign Office 1929–65, Assistant Under-Secretary of State 1949–50, British High Commissioner in Austria 1950–4, Ambassador, Vienna 1951–4, Deputy Under-Secretary of State 1954–6, Ambassador, Washington 1956–61,Permanent Under-Secretary of State 1962–5, Head, Diplomatic Service 1964–5. Provost, Eton College 1965–77.

belief that it was not only in our own but in the general interest. I can only hope that time will show that we were not wrong. The undermining of sterling would of course hurt us, but that would be far from all. It would do irreparable damage not merely to sterling but to the whole fabric of trade and payments in the Free World. This would be a major victory for the Communists.

This was powerful rhetoric, enhanced by the tragic outcome of concurrent events in Hungary; but on 24 November the UN General Assembly resolved by sixty-three votes to five to censure Britain and France and demand their immediate withdrawal from Egypt. The US was among the sixty-three. On 27 November Humphrey told Caccia and Harcourt that the US was powerless to act in support of sterling until HMG had shown, in a way the world could accept, that the UK was conforming to rather than defying the wishes of the UN. He did not in any way dispute the British assessment of the sterling position and he told his visitors that the US would go along with the UK as far as they could as soon as the latter made it possible for them to act. A substantial Fund drawing and an Exim loan were mentioned. An announcement by the British Government of a phased withdrawal from Egyptian territory, which would be accepted by the majority of nations as a pledge of good faith might, Humphrey advised, enable the US to act. Over the next few days the Chancellor argued strongly in Cabinet for acceptance of the American terms. With varying degrees of reluctance his colleagues eventually agreed. The State Department, through the US Treasury, then endeavoured to pin the British down to announcing a precise date for withdrawal, even though the UN Secretary-General and the Egyptians were both prepared to accept something less precise. But the Ambassador was authorised to stand firm and at the last minute, late on 3 December and after the Foreign Secretary had made his statement on withdrawal to the Commons, Humphrey told Harcourt that the point would not be pressed. On the following day the Chancellor announced a reserve loss of $279 million (this was after receipt of some $30 million from the sale of US Government securities). About a Fund drawing he was able to say: 'We are making an immediate approach to the IMF with a view to drawing on part of these resources.' As to other borrowing, notably secured borrowing from the Exim Bank, he mentioned the EEA portfolio (amounting to $750–1,000 million) and was allowed by the Americans to say: 'I am assured that, if requested, support in the form of a loan against these holdings will be promptly available for dollar requirements from the appropriate agency of the US.' He also announced, with prior approval from Washington, that the UK was applying for a waiver of interest due on 31 December on the US and Canadian Loans (together totalling $104 million). Finally, he announced a substantial increase in the tax on petrol.

Next day all was sunshine in Washington when Harcourt had a further talk with Humphrey and proposed that the UK draw the first two tranches of its quota from the Fund and be granted a stand-by for the third and fourth. Humphrey said he had come to the same conclusion. There would also be the Exim facility of $700 million, making a total of $2 billion in support of sterling. The same weather prevailed when Macmillan met Humphrey at the Talleyrand Hotel in Paris on 11 December after the application to the Fund had succeeded. Both were attending a meeting of NATO finance Ministers. The Chancellor was congratulated on his statement. The erring ally had indeed returned and been handsomely rewarded. Macmillan's part in bringing this about may not have been a very edifying one, but there was little else he could responsibly have done. By 19 November, when the decision to begin negotiations with the US was taken, the prospect was daily becoming more dangerous. There was no guarantee that the first phase of the two-stage plan would succeed in containing the November reserves loss sufficiently to avoid an accelerating run. To have held out against American demands, or failed to negotiate at all, must have seemed an increasingly dangerous gamble. This would only have been worth taking if some supreme objective were at stake. But now, following the cease-fire on 6 November, there was no supreme objective beyond avoidance of further humiliation. As it was, Macmillan got everything the UK needed, in exchange for a surrender that could not anyway have been long postponed.

The Bank took no further part in all this after 19 November, save the provision of technical support with the approach to the Fund. But it re-entered the fray after the crisis was over. The Governor himself left for his usual annual trip to Canada and the US on 27 November. Writing to Harcourt from New York on 13 December, he said he talked to a lot of people 'about Suez, Israel–Arab etc. being now firmly on the UN/USA plate and high time they did something effective about it. A lot of sympathetic noises but not much confidence about effective action.' Back in London, on 6 December, after talking with Mynors and Bolton, Rowan circulated a note on 'Policy if we do not succeed in holding the rate'. It advocated a 1956 version of unilateral floating-rate convertibility and was described by Mynors as 'the thoughts of an utterly exhausted but indomitable TLR [Rowan] rather than a record of our talks at the Treasury'. But it had been overtaken by events and soon passed into obscurity. More apposite was a note by Parsons circulated to the Governors on 17 December. Its message was that nothing had been done to change the attitude that gave rise to the underlying weakness on which the confidence crisis was built and that there was every indication that the market was still regarding sterling with caution. 'This will only be altered, I believe, when measures are taken by the UK Government which demonstrate that we are determined to cut the demands on the economy to a level which it can bear.'

The Governor needed little encouragement before writing to the Chancellor on 20 December in the same vein as Parsons and beginning in the terms mentioned at the beginning of this chapter. It was one of his most forthright letters but to all appearances one of his least effective. He argued for early and radical action to correct the underlying weakness of sterling – 'dramatic, far-reaching and convincing measures in 1957, to be initiated in the first three months of the year'. He saw no advantage in a higher Bank Rate or a tightening of credit restriction. What was needed was an overall Budget surplus achieved not by increasing the already stifling level of taxation but by reducing expenditure. He expressed the feelings of market and overseas opinion in very blunt terms:

> The feeling of the markets both here and abroad is quite clear and I had ample evidence of it last week in Canada and America. The markets are prepared to believe that we mean what we have said about using and mobilising reserves to defend the rate. They do not anticipate early devaluation but they have been shocked by the weakness exposed by recent developments and they have their eyes very firmly fixed on what they regard as three questions marks; our willingness to live within our means, our overseas commitments, and our productive capacity (or will to work). Until these questions are answered to their satisfaction, the underlying pressures will remain against us and will become stronger. And I sensed in the US, in the two very different climates of Washington and New York, an ominous feeling that it was just worthwhile helping us out this time but that if we could not now make ends meet we should not be worth bothering about.

The letter concluded by asking the Chancellor to show the letter to the Prime Minister and proposing that at some convenient time it should be discussed with them both. As related in Chapter 10 (f), an inconclusive meeting ensued early in the new year. But by then the Prime Minister's health had again deteriorated and he resigned on 9 January 1957. On the following afternoon Macmillan succeeded him at No. 10 and shortly afterwards Peter Thorneycroft moved from the Board of Trade to the Treasury. A period of political healing and recuperation then began; and Macmillan was certainly not the Prime Minister to begin it with 'dramatic, far-reaching and convincing measures'. The underlying weakness was to continue. The Suez crisis, lasting from 30 October to 8 December, had cost $450 million of reserves. The end-year debt service had cost another $180 million. Second-line reserves, represented by drawing rights in the Fund, had had to be mobilised. The Governor's suggestion that this reinforcement should be accompanied by the unification of official and transferable had got lost in the turmoil of the final weeks. His uphill task was to resume.

APPENDIX: THE MYSTERIOUS TELEPHONE CALL

LATER IN November 1956, when US help for sterling was being negotiated in exchange for British agreement to an early withdrawal from Egyptian territory, it is more than likely that telephone conversations took place between UK Ministers and senior members of the American Administration. In his own memoirs Butler recounts one such talk; and it is possible that Macmillan's recall, years later, of a conversation on 6 November (cease-fire day) was a confusion of memory. A search of the Public Record Office and enquiries of the US Treasury reveal no trace of such a talk on that day. Another author working on the Suez affair has looked into the papers of Humphrey and Burgess, with equally negative results. The memoirs of Eden, Butler, Selwyn Lloyd, and Maxwell-Fyfe do not mention Macmillan referring to the telephone call at the time. Alistair Horne and Rhodes James both refer to it in their biographies of Macmillan and Eden; but both seem to be relying on Macmillan's memoirs. Neither Lord Sherfield nor Lord Caccia, whom the author consulted, had any recollection of the call having taken place; though both thought it possible that Macmillan could have made such a call, in the very peculiar circumstances prevailing, without informing the UK Ambassador in Washington or the Permanent Secretary to the Treasury in London. It is possible that Macmillan privately telephoned Lord Harcourt, who then got in touch with the American authorities and called back. But Harcourt left no private diaries or notes relating to his time as a UK Minister in Washington.

To the absence of supporting evidence there can be added inherent implausibility. Is it likely that at so vital a moment the Chancellor would have shown the Americans a trump card that they probably did not yet know they possessed, when the UK exchange situation was not yet critical, when official advice was against such an approach, and without apparently consulting any of his colleagues? Is it likely, in any case, that he could or would have got hold of, for example, Humphrey in the very early hours of the morning (US time) of Election Day? The implausibility is not wholly conclusive. Macmillan's later recall of so traumatic a day should have been good. His biographer states that diaries and notes on Suez were made but that they were destroyed early in 1957; so absence of surviving written record can be explained.

On balance it has seemed best to assume that no call was made on 6 November, though the possibility remains that evidence to the contrary may still emerge.

SOURCES

Bank files
- EC5/356 Exchange Control Act: Exceptional measures contemplated or taken in relation to Egypt during various crises in the Middle East culminating in the Suez Crisis of 1956 (October 1947 – August 1956)
- EC5/357 Exchange Control Act: Exchange control policy concerning Egypt during the Suez Crisis and its aftermath (August 1956 – April 1957)
- G1/99 Governor's File: Exchange Policy (March 1955 – February 1958)
- G1/124 Governor's File: Exchange Policy – The Suez Crisis (August 1956 – June 1959)
- G3/9 Governor's Diary (1956)

G3/72	Governor's Duplicate Letters (July – September 1956)
G3/72	Governor's Miscellaneous Memoranda (July – December 1956)
OV44/30	Sterling and Sterling Area Policy: Sterling Area Working Parties (September 1955 – January 1956)
OV44/33	Sterling and Sterling Area Policy: Sterling Area Working Parties – Report on Problems of the Sterling Area (July 1956 – October 1957)
OV44/65	Sterling and Sterling Area Policy: Sterling Area Exchange Policy – Collective Approach to Convertibility (March 1955 – December 1957)

CHAPTER 9

CONVERTIBILITY: THE LAST ACT, 1957–1958

(a) THE POUND, THE FRANC, AND THE DEUTSCHMARK: 1957

FOR ALL the pessimism occasioned by the Suez Crisis and for all the convincing talk of underlying structural weakness, the position of sterling some two years later was to seem very much brighter. During 1958 the UK ran an external surplus of £344 million on current account. Inflation had fallen to 2% while unemployment had risen only marginally (to 2%). The reserves, less than $2 billion at the height of the Suez crisis, had risen to over $3 billion by September 1958. This was admittedly reduced to $2.36 billion if the post-Suez drawings on the IMF and the Exim Bank were taken into account; but, against this, sterling balances had fallen over the period by the equivalent of $440 million and the ratio of external monetary assets to liabilities had improved. Confidence, so shaken at the time of Suez, had returned and the sharp American recession of 1957–8 had not had any of the adverse international monetary consequences that had so often been feared. Lastly, and partly in response to an initiative undertaken by the UK Treasury with the American Administration, there was in hand an agreed increase of 50% in IMF quotas which would increase the UK's second-line reserves by another $650 million. Euphorically, the Treasury was able to write as the opening sentence of a note on external assets and liabilities: 'The present external monetary position of the UK is stronger than at any time since the war.' At the end of 1958 the *de jure* convertibility of non-resident sterling was at last declared, the EMA was put into force, and the EPU was terminated. The tide had again come in; and this time, under the Chancellorship of Heathcoat Amory, it had been caught. Although he was busy reflating the economy, with the full support of the Prime Minister and other colleagues ahead of a general election that was to be called and won in September 1959, his favourable tide took a little time to ebb. Not until 1961, when

Cobbold gave up the Governorship of the Bank and just after he had helped inaugurate the epoch of central bank co-operation through exchange swaps, did another external crisis occur along with a revival of all the worries about structural weakness. By then Heathcoat Amory had retired, Selwyn Lloyd had succeeded him, and Lord Cromer was taking over in Threadneedle Street.

The favourable tide had needed some encouragement. It did not begin to flow until the winter of 1957–8 and after yet another serious run on sterling. This was overcome, and the favourable phase of the cycle commenced, by measures that included raising Bank Rate to 7%, a level not seen since 1920. Seven per cent formed part of the strange interlude of early-day monetarism that faded rapidly after Chancellor Thorneycroft and his two principal juniors (Enoch Powell and Nigel Birch) had resigned from the Macmillan Government in January 1958 following a Cabinet dispute over public expenditure. The Bank had been a strong supporter, even the initiator, of a 7% Bank Rate; but it had found itself concurrently involved in a considerable tussle with the Government over an accompanying tightening of controls on bank advances, a tussle that raised all the questions about the Old Lady's powers and responsibilities in this field that had been left by the Act of 1946.[1] This issue fell within the terms of reference of the Radcliffe Committee, which had been appointed in the summer of 1957 following dissatisfaction with the results of domestic monetary policy in 1955 and 1956. The Bank's evidence was to occupy much time over the ensuing year. All this exposure was dramatically increased by the proceedings of the Parker Tribunal,[2] which enquired into alleged leakages of prior information about the 7% Rate and which required detailed evidence from Bank Directors and their public cross-examination. These matters are discussed in other chapters but are mentioned here as background to relations between the Bank and the Treasury during this period, relations that were not always as harmonious or intimate as they had been. Furthermore, the Governor himself was beginning to tire of his job. The second of his two five-year terms, themselves following seven arduous years as Executive Director and nearly four as Deputy Governor, was due to expire in February 1959. Though by then still only fifty-five, he would not wish to continue for much longer. He was to stay and see the Bank through the immediate post-Radcliffe years but then go off to pastures new, in Buckingham Palace as Lord Chamberlain.

---

[1] See Chapter 10 (f) below.   [2] See Chapter 11(a) below.

Early in 1957, having failed in the immediate aftermath of Suez to persuade the Government of the need for 'dramatic, far-reaching, and convincing measures', the Governor was far from reassured by a rather dull Budget and by a slow recovery of only $140 million in the exchange reserves during the first half of the year. At the end of May 1957 he wrote a gloomy letter to Thorneycroft, saying that anxieties about the long-term future of sterling were spreading rather dangerously in the country at large and that there was an underlying feeling that demand remained excessive and costs were continuing to rise. 'This leads people to wonder whether any Government is going to be able to reverse these tendencies and how they are going to do it.'

Gloom about the domestic outlook was accompanied by another breakdown of exchange control, somewhat akin to the former cheap-sterling phenomenon but this time involving residents of the UK and the Sterling Area. The traffic was known as the Kuwait Gap, though Hong Kong and Bahrain were also involved. Exchange control in Kuwait was limited in scope and Kuwaiti residents were free to use dollars to purchase American and Canadian securities. They could then sell the securities to UK residents against sterling, at the substantial premium prevailing in the London market due to the restrictions imposed on the direct acquisition of dollar securities by UK residents. The sterling thus acquired was then sold to residents of the dollar area at a discount and used in payment for Sterling Area invisibles (to which the Exchange Control Act still did not apply). The end result was that the UK acquired additional dollar securities and paid for them through invisible exports from the Sterling Area at a depreciated rate of exchange (typically around $2.55). The cost to the UK reserves, principally due to export of capital that would not otherwise have taken place, could be substantial. The gap began to be exploited on a large scale in the latter half of 1956 and the flow became a flood in the first half of 1957; at one stage it was estimated to be running as fast as $500 million a year and to be in large measure responsible for the very slow recovery of the reserves post-Suez. One solution was to impose a special control between the UK and the Sterling Area so that dollar securities could be acquired only by one UK resident from another instead of from any resident of the Sterling Area (for example a Kuwaiti). In the end this solution was adopted by the Treasury and put into effect early in July. The Bank had not liked the idea, regarding it as a backward step likely to damage confidence and likely to provoke exploitation of other loopholes. It had favoured the opposite course: intervention in support of resident sterling. But the pressure was too strong and in the end the Governor did not resist imposition of the new control. Thereafter he did not have to wait long before anxieties about the long-term, fortified by the recent flow through the Kuwait Gap, became exchange speculation in the short-term.

Early in August, after the Bank had received some prior warning from Baumgartner, the French franc was devalued *de facto*. This was followed by speculation on an upvaluation of the Deutschmark occurring some time after the West German elections due in mid-September. The backwash at once fell on sterling. Devaluation talk revived and the inadequate reserves began yet again to drain away. In the last three weeks of August they fell directly by as much as $203 million, back to $2.14 billion, with a further loss of $137 million through the EPU due for settlement in September. True, over $1.2 billion of the post-Suez facilities with the IMF and the Exim bank, totalling $1.8bn,[3] remained undrawn. But it would have been dangerous to be seen making use of them if 'confidence' had already become unimpressed by their existence. The storm had broken in the middle of the holiday season. The Governor himself was due for a break and went away from 23 August to 14 September. In his absence Mynors was in charge.

Before leaving, however, the Governor discussed the situation with Mynors, Hawker[4], O'Brien, Thompson-McCausland, Rootham, Menzies, and Raw.[5] He also contacted Bolton. Parsons and Stevens were absent on holiday. It was clear that pressure had somehow to be brought to bear upon the German authorities so that German domestic policy was made less restrictive, or the exchange rate for the Deutschmark adjusted upwards, or both. The Deutschmark seemed clearly undervalued. While sterling was not clearly overvalued, there was everything to be said for a set of domestic measures that would suffice to allay the long-term anxieties about which the Governor had written to Thorneycroft earlier in the summer. In the circumstances of a renewed run on sterling, only eight months after the Suez crisis had been resolved and after $560 million had been borrowed under the facilities then agreed, the British Government would this time need little persuading of the need for prompt domestic

---

[3] Comprising the IMF quota of $1.3 billion and an Exim credit of $0.5 billion. The $2 billion originally agreed with Secretary Humphrey was later reduced, after sterling had recovered, to $1.8 billion. Of this, $560 million had been drawn from the IMF.

[4] *Hawker, Frank Cyril*, kt (1900–91). Educated City of London School. Entered Bank 1920. Deputy Chief Cashier 1944–8, Chief Accountant 1948–53, Adviser to the Governors 1953–4, Executive Director 1954–62. Chairman, Standard Bank 1962–74, Chartered Bank 1973–4, Standard and Chartered Banking Group 1969–74.

[5] *Raw, Rupert George*, CMG (1912–89). Educated Eton and Brasenose College, Oxford. War service in Scots Guards, Control Commission, Germany 1946–8. Finance Director, OEEC, 1952–5. Entered Bank 1955, Assistant Adviser 1955–7, Adviser 1957–63, Adviser to the Governors 1963–72, Alternate Member, Board of Management, BIS. UK Director, European Investment Bank 1973–81, Deputy Chairman, Italian International Bank 1973–6, Chairman 1976–9.

action. The argument would be about its nature and extent. But persuading the German authorities to do anything at all, let alone promptly revalue, was an altogether different task and one that the machinery of West European economic co-operation was not yet equipped to tackle. The situation was indeed quite novel. No previous post-war sterling crisis, if crisis this was, had been associated with the clear overvaluation of a major continental currency.

The initial response of the Bank to this problem belonged far more to the Cobbold–Bolton era of intermittent radicalism than to a later phase of stern orthodoxy. It was briefly sketched in a note sent by the Governor to Makins on 22 August. This looked to co-operative international action being discussed, and its outlines agreed, after the German elections and during or shortly after the Fund/Bank meetings in Washington at the end of September. There would be five main objectives: maintenance of the $2.78 floor; successful persuasion of the Germans; IMF support for whatever was agreed; further action by the deficit countries of Europe (mainly the UK and France); and maintenance of either the EPU or the EMA. In pursuit of these aims there seemed two principal alternative policies. Firstly, there could be a policy of maintaining the existing structure of exchange rates at all costs. This meant relying wholly on domestic measures, but with assurances of support from the IMF, which could if necessary borrow Deutschmarks for the purpose. Direct collaboration between the central banks concerned, through exchange swaps, was not considered on this occasion. Secondly, and combined with domestic measures, there could be a policy of exchange-rate adjustment, effected by removing the existing top dealing limits on European currencies while retaining the floor limits. There could either be no new top limits or a set of considerably higher ones – a spread of some 7% was suggested, with sterling fixed at $2.78–3.00. At the same time official and transferable sterling would be unified and the EPU would give way to the EMA. The Governor queried whether the first alternative was practicable, but thought the second 'might do the trick'. However he emphasised that the Germans would be very difficult to move. 'It looks likely we may get into an absolutely first-class row with Germany, in which it would be vital to have the USA (and IMF) on our side and if possible having their own row with Germany.' In a letter to the Chancellor, sent on 22 August, just before leaving on holiday, he wrote: 'We have a difficult time ahead. The Germans are going to behave like Germans, it looks like a new boomlet internally, and round the corner there are some hints of a drying-up of international liquidity, which all indicates that we should be ready to take any necessary steps in the autumn and go into 1958 at least with our own affairs in good order.'

The idea of readjusting top limits was an interesting one, containing as it did a means of appreciating the Deutschmark while providing a potential for greater operational elbow-room in the market management of sterling. In a form applying to sterling only, it was an idea that was to surface again during debates in the following year, when it was strongly supported by Bridge. But at no stage did it attract worthwhile support outside the Bank. On 10 September the Treasury circulated a paper on sterling in the course of which a readjustment of top limits was briefly considered. It was judged unlikely to be negotiable with the Germans and only too likely to bring increased pressure for reduction in the lower limits. Nor was it thought that the unification of sterling rates and the introduction of the EMA would be particularly strong bargaining counters in a negotiation about the adoption of good creditor policies by Germany. It was therefore concluded that the UK interest would best be served by maintaining the existing exchange parity and exchange arrangements. Pressure should certainly be brought to bear on Germany, but at senior political level and related to considerations of European unity. When he returned from holiday the Governor accepted this conclusion with little demur. There was in fact no real possibility of quickly negotiating a change in European exchange-rate arrangements from a position of weakness and with people whose aversion to anything resembling floating rates was already well established. Nor anyway would it be safe for the UK to start hares running in this field, a development that would soon become known in the markets where sterling was under strong pressure. The Governor had previously abandoned hope of a floating rate or wider spreads in his letter to Macmillan in April 1956. His readiness to revive the idea in August 1957 showed his customary imagination; but it was clearly out of its time, despite some press discussion of wider spreads.

The reserves continued to fall in September. By the end of the month, after the fall had been arrested and after the August EPU deficit had been settled, they totalled only $1.85 billion (gross of the $560 million of medium-term debt incurred after Suez). So in discussions held in mid-September, after the Governor returned from holiday, it was readily concluded that strong, even dramatic, measures would have to be announced before the Washington meetings if a statement there by the Chancellor was to carry credibility. On 19 September Bank Rate was raised from 5% to 7%, putting into the shade a tightening of credit controls and renewed assurances about restraint on public expenditure. Writing personally to Jacobsson[6] in the IMF, the Governor remarked:

[6] Now Managing Director of the Fund. See p. 573 n8.

> I do hope you will use your influence on the Germans to ease up a bit internally and let their rates down. If the present position persists, Germany is just going to suck money out of the rest of Europe and we are in for bad times – and now nobody can say that we have not played *our* part in this story.
>
> And this cannot be repeated again. Unless the Germans want to bust Europe and start off a world deflation they must take action soon.
>
> You (following Monty Norman!) taught them to build up their strength – quite rightly. Now it is up to *you* to teach them how to be a sensible creditor.

To Vocke in the Bank Deutscher Länder, he wrote:

> I am happy to see the announcement today of your reduction of rates [from $4\frac{1}{2}\%$ to 4%]. I need hardly say that any further steps which you feel able to take in this or other ways will be most welcome! If we can between us make some contribution towards stopping this absurd speculative movement, I think it will be of great help to Europe.

After a period of hesitation sterling began to recover. By 23 September the rate had risen to $2.78\frac{7}{8}$ and the drain had halted. In October the reserves rose above $2 billion[7] and in the following month the rate rose above $2.80. The favourable tide had begun to flow. But the September crisis had unnerved the Prime Minister. He was temperamentally out of sympathy with high Bank Rates, was apprehensive of an approaching US recession, and faced the task of rebuilding the electoral fortunes of the Conservative Party in time for an election in 1959 or, at the latest, 1960. External problems could get in his way. So he complained to the Treasury that the policies needed to handle the problems of sterling and the Sterling Area made other economic policies very difficult to pursue; and he asked questions about the future of the Sterling Area. He got a long and dusty answer from Rowan. Firmer resolve was needed, year in year out, to give priority to the required external surplus; nor was there any way of peacefully winding up the Sterling Area. It was conceivable, but unlikely, that the Americans might help with a facility that funded periodic falls in sterling balances. Some relief might however be afforded by international measures that increased liquidity all round. A rise in the price of gold was very unlikely, but an increase in IMF quotas might not be impossible and the Treasury was working on this question.

---

[7] There was an underlying rise, attributable to the recovery of sterling in the market, of just over $120 million. This was enough to finance in October the EPU settlement for September. In addition, the Government now drew $250 million of the $500 million Exim credit arranged after Suez.

(b) INTERNATIONAL LIQUIDITY AND IMF QUOTAS

Rowan's reference to IMF quotas drew attention to the topic known as 'International Liquidity', which appealed to Macmillan and which was to attract much interest and protracted international argument and negotiation over the following decade. The first phase occupied 1957 and 1958. It resulted in the all-round increase of 50% in IMF quotas and in some measure became associated with the final move to external convertibility at the end of the latter year. The Bank, alongside the Treasury, became closely involved but displayed in this first phase a marked uncertainty of analysis and judgement. This may in part be attributed to the Governor's preoccupation with the Parker Tribunal and the Radcliffe Committee and in part to the shake-down of senior personnel that followed the resignation of Bolton as Executive Director in February 1957, the concurrent move of Hawker to Home Finance in succession to Peppiatt, and the appointment of Parsons and Stevens as Executive Directors on the external side.

In accord with a more liberal lending policy and some temporary recurrence of an American external surplus, drawings of dollars from the IMF became quite heavy during the first half of 1957. In addition, there had been the UK drawing in December 1956 and the large UK stand-by. The Fund accordingly began to supplement its limited dollar resources by sales from its limited stock of gold. Questions then began to be asked about its prospective liquidity. Per Jacobsson, who had succeeded Rooth as Managing Director of the Fund in November 1956,[8] met Rowan in London during May of the following year and remarked that while an increase in the price of monetary gold was hardly a starter, steps would be needed to increase international liquidity if the outflow of dollars from the US were

---

[8] The succession to Rooth had occupied a fair share of the Governor's time since early in 1955. The first name to be approached was Graham Towers, who had recently retired from the Bank of Canada (to be succeeded by Jim Coyne); but he turned it down. Further discussion within the international monetary fraternity of treasuries and central banks eventually focussed on the Governor of the Bank of France, whose candidature was firmly supported by Cobbold. But Baumgartner refused, after several approaches, in April 1956. He was unwilling to leave his post in Paris at a time when the difficulties of the Fourth Republic were deepening. A variety of other names was then considered, both among central bankers and civil servants, without any agreement. Eventually, Jacobsson's name was suggested by Under-Secretary Burgess and gradually gained support. Cobbold regarded him as a man of undoubted, if particular, merits. Though no administrator, he had charm, good sense, and was a friend. Since Macmillan was ready to risk this unusual appointment, UK support was assured; as, after some debate, was the support of the 'continentals'. On 10 September 1956 the Fund Executive Board agreed to invite Jacobsson, who had earlier let it be known that he would accept provided he had general support. Rooth left for home on 9 October and his successor arrived early in the following month, just in time for the Suez crisis of sterling.

reduced. Guy Thorold,[9] who had succeeded Harcourt as British Economic Minister in Washington, wrote to the Treasury and the Bank early in July and drew attention to questions about the liquidity of the Fund. There could be implications for the UK stand-by, due for renewal in December. The matter was not immediately urgent but should be kept in mind. In the Bank, following Jacobsson's visit, thought had been given firstly to Fund drawings in inconvertible currencies and secondly to a tightening of the Fund's lending rules accompanied by an increase in the cost of accommodation. An increase in quotas was not thought to be a promising approach. It would, as Portsmore[10] put it in a note to Parsons and Stamp, be a thinly guised request for an American interest-free loan. US lending to the Fund under Article VII (relating to scarce currencies) would be a better bet. But Parsons seems also to have received advice, probably from Stamp, that the threatened shortage of liquidity in the Fund could be a warning symptom of a much bigger problem of international liquidity generally. So in a letter to Rowan on 18 July he took both lines at once, following Portsmore's advice about making Fund lending more short-term and more expensive but adding:

> Indeed if the Fund liquidity problem continues to grow, it may be an indication of a fundamental world problem which is on a much bigger scale than a mere question of Fund liquidity. The problem of international liquidity – the maintenance of an adequate increment to the world's reserves of gold and dollars to sustain an ever-growing volume of international trade – may well be a problem for which international action is required. To attempt to treat this useful warning symptom rather than the cause of it would be a mistake.

It may have been this thought that lay behind the Governor's remark, in his letter of 22 August to the Chancellor, that 'round the corner, there are some hints of a drying-up of international liquidity'.

By the time of the Fund meeting in September 1957 the Treasury was coming round to the view that some means was going to have to be found of improving international liquidity, and that HMG would accordingly be obliged to support an increase in Fund quotas if that were to be suggested. In the event, Jacobsson did no more than refer to the question in his inaugural address to the Board of Governors. Relatively little discussion

---

[9] *Thorold, Guy Frederick*, KCMG (1898–1970). Educated Winchester and New College, Oxford. Army 1917–19. Ministry of Economic Warfare 1939–45, Assistant Secretary 1944–5, UK delegation to OEEC, Paris 1948, Head of Treasury Delegation and Economic Minister, Washington, UK Executive Director, IMF and IBRD, 1957–9, Director, Agricultural Mortgage Corporation 1963–8. Director, A. W. Bain, Sons and Bevan Ltd, President, Corporation of Insurance Brokers.

[10] Portsmore had become one of Parsons' close collaborators and remained so until he retired from the Bank in 1965.

followed, but at the end of the meeting it was agreed that the Fund itself would undertake a study of international liquidity. Next, on 2 October in the Bank, Stamp circulated a long paper entitled 'Future Arrangements for International Payments'. It was now beginning to be widely recognised, he began, that present arrangements might not be sufficient in the future to secure an uninterrupted expansion of trade. The solution to the problem was vital to the UK:

> because our position as a banker with inadequate reserves means that pressures resulting from inadequate world liquidity will be felt earliest by the UK. The recent run on sterling when our current account is in a healthy position is a symptom... There must be something wrong with a situation in which intense pressure is put on the UK, when its current account is healthy, simply because the US has temporarily ceased to add to the World's dollar supply and the German current account surplus, though impressive, is something which ought to be quite absorbable by the rest of the World. It is because international liquidity arrangements are unsatisfactory that speculation has reached such large proportions and has made the whole problem more severe.

Failure to solve the problem could bring abut a real danger of trade contraction and a reversion to trade restrictions. But a combination of gold production and likely dollar outflow would not suffice. Nor could the UK contemplate an increase in sterling liabilities. Something else would have to be devised. A rise in the price of gold was open to serious objections (American opposition and long-run damage to the dollar). An increase in Fund quotas would be resisted by the US Treasury on budgetary grounds and would be open to the additional objection that the Fund would be lending more and more money, unsecured, to doubtful borrowers. Finally the use of currencies additional to dollars and sterling, as reserves, would be inhibited by exchange risks.

These arguments, some of which were stronger than others, enabled Stamp to embrace the cause of a World Central Bank. This entity would create a structure of credit based on gold and dollar capital subscribed by member countries, who would undertake to accept the Bank's liabilities as a means of payment between monetary authorities and to hold them as reserves equivalent to gold or dollars. The amount of credit created each year, according to some perceived need, would compensate for 'the shortfall in new gold production and any tendency of reserves to be inadequate because of maldistribution and the growth of world trade'. There would be a consequential problem of how to distribute the credit, other than through an ever-increasing quantity of unsecured lending. At this stage Stamp had no ready solution to offer but he was later to include one in the Stamp Plan, as it came to be known, according to which the credit would be distributed as Aid to developing countries and spent in the developed countries, thereby increasing their reserves. Stamp's paper was notable for its presentation of the argument in support of a world liquidity shortage. But his advocacy of a World Central Bank was much too romantic and unlikely to appeal in the Bank. It also displayed a liking for the type of Anglo-American monetary scheme-mongering that took a dismissive view of monetary attitudes prevalent in continental Europe. Be that as it may, Stamp was to make no further contribution to thinking in the Bank. He wrote a letter of resignation to the Governor on 16 October and left on the 31st, later joining the merchant banking firm of Philip Hill, Higginson (later Hill Samuel).[11] He had been contemplating a move for some months, feeling he had no further to go in the Bank since the appointments of Parsons and Stevens to the Court earlier in the year.

In the absence of Parsons in the US, Stamp's paper was forwarded to the Governor by Stevens, who distanced himself from the suggested solution. He did, however, agree that the problem of international liquidity certainly existed and proposed that it should be studied by a group of Advisers and by the Head of the Overseas Department (Watson). Nothing seems to have come of this. It would not have been to Parsons' taste to pursue a topic in that way and the whole subject was allowed to cool off during the following months. Nor did the Fund study make much progress, though Heasman reported from Washington that Bernstein was opposed to an all-round increase in quotas and in favour of the Fund being given new borrowing powers which it would use in pursuit of a more liberal lending policy. Portsmore noted 'Bernstein's thinking is on similar lines to our own'.

The Treasury, however, was much more active and on 21 January 1958 Rowan sent Parsons copies of two papers on international liquidity, one analytic and the other prescriptive. Just before this, Oliver Franks sent the Governor an advance copy of his annual speech to the shareholders of Lloyds Bank. This included a passage about international liquidity and a suggestion that the IMF might 'move in the direction of becoming a super-central-bank', along much the same lines as those sketched by Stamp three months earlier. For its part, the Treasury had concluded that a world shortage of liquidity was approaching, aggravated by maldistribution of the existing supply. Its second paper ran through a whole series of possible remedies, or combinations thereof, including the use of inconvertible

[11] A little later, under the aegis of Philip Hill, he formed a small consultancy firm, Max Stamp Associates, which developed a successful business advising the Governments of newly independent developing countries about aid-financed projects.

currencies by the Fund, use of borrowing powers under Article VII, a grand sterling–dollar swap arrangement (and other swaps), a rise in the price of gold, additional Fund borrowing powers, and an all-round increase in Fund quotas. This last would require legislation in the United States (and elsewhere) and would most likely entail a proportionate increase in gold subscriptions that would have to be met from the often inadequate national reserves. Nonetheless, the paper concluded: 'In spite of these difficulties it does seem that in the longer-term an all-round increase in quotas would be the most satisfactory way of increasing liquidity.' In his letter to Parsons covering these papers, Rowan said: 'Ever since the Bank and Fund meeting we have been thinking here about the problems of world liquidity and I believe that in the Bank also thought has been devoted to this question. I think the time has come for us to bring together the results of all this thinking.' He accordingly proposed an early meeting, mentioning that it was intended to use the second paper as background for talks with Commonwealth officials in February. Five days later he sent the Bank a copy of a letter to Lee at the Board of Trade and enclosed a paper entitled 'World Economic Problems'. This included a passage on liquidity that in turn included the statement: 'The recurrence of these [balance of payments] crises, seen in the light of the undoubted decline in the ratio, leads to the conclusion that there is now a definite shortage and maldistribution of liquidity.' The letter to Lee began: 'As you know, it is proposed that we should have informal talks with the Americans in the near future, following the discussions held by the Prime Minister and subsequently by Sir Robert Hall, in Washington.'

The Bank appears to have had no idea of what was afoot. In particular, the Governor seems to have been kept in the dark, for on 28 January he asked Parsons to arrange for Franks' paper to be looked at rather urgently by, among others, Thompson-McCausland, Menzies, and Fforde.[12] He made no reference to the Treasury exercise and seems to have been unaware of it, remarking instead: 'I think the international liquidity question will become of first importance. I have had some talk with Per Jacobsson and am proposing to send Thompson-McCausland to Washington in early spring.' Parsons replied to Rowan about 'World Economic Problems' on 31 January, just as consideration of the Franks paper was getting under way in the Bank. Abruptly reversing his response of the previous summer, he made only a very negative reference to international liquidity: 'I think it would be fair to say that the major cause of inadequate reserves has been excessive liquidity in terms of domestic money and that the first task in

---

[12] I had joined the Bank as a junior economic adviser early in 1957.

dealing with the reserve problem is to prevent the over-liquidity problem from continuing and getting worse.'

The Bank had now to make up its mind. Was it to go along with views expressed earlier by Stamp and by Parsons himself in the summer of 1957, or was it to go along with the alternative view already expressed by Parsons to Rowan at the end of January? There was some debate. Menzies and Fisher both concluded that inflation was the heart of the problem and that additional international liquidity would simply encourage a rake's progress. Thompson-McCausland argued that to talk of a world shortage of reserves was a dangerous and misleading over-simplification: it led to the presumption that an increase across-the-board would be a good solution when it might simply miss the point. What was needed instead was a combination of greater policy co-ordination between the main countries and better means of channelling 'internationally valid money', on a short-term basis, between the haves and the have-nots. Adaptation of the IMF through special borrowing under Article V and extra-quota lending under Article VII would be a good way of helping to achieve these improvements. There was no need to go for a world central bank with discretionary powers of credit creation. In a long paper circulated on 5 February, Fforde expressed it rather differently. The 'redistributional cure' was a possibility but was probably impracticable. 'The burden, including that of new or prospective indebtedness, on the have-nots may prove too great and the pressure upon the haves not strong enough. For all the progress of the last few years, reserves have become less adequate, not more. There is a serious risk that a deflationary disturbance in the US and Europe will compel a general and disastrous retreat from liberalisation of trade and payments some time before any redistributional *trend* can reassert itself. Economists have cried this wolf far too much but nevertheless I do not think we can, in the present international outlook, afford to support the taking of such a risk in the cause of anti-inflationary policies, even though there is the other risk (to my mind the lesser) of encouraging further inflation.' He favoured a moderate increase in the price of gold together with an enlargement of IMF quotas.

Fforde stuck to his guns but was in a minority of one.[13] A revised and strengthened version of Thompson-McCausland's note was sent to the Deputy Governor by Parsons with support from Stevens. With the Deputy's approval it was then sent to Rowan, but there was no response

---

[13] Later in February, after the Bank view had crystallised, he wrote a dissenting note to Parsons arguing that Lucius' solution was too idealistic about the practical possibilities of better macro-economic management and too cramping. It would be better to bring about an improvement in international liquidity by an all-round quota increase than by special Fund borrowing and lending.

prior to the latter's departure for the US on 14 February. The Treasury was of course already committed to the more expansionist point of view and was unlikely to take much notice of the Bank's judgement that: 'Merely to increase the aggregate (by e.g. a higher gold price or higher IMF quotas all round) would only prolong inflation and postpone the day when mistaken policies of both debtors and creditors would again produce maldistribution with repetition of the present threat. And it would be strongly opposed by the USA for this and other reasons.'

The Rowan–Hall talks with an array of senior Administration officials (including Anderson, who had succeeded Humphrey as Secretary of the Treasury) were held towards the end of February and seemed at first to confirm the views expressed in London by the Bank. The Americans completely disagreed with the view that there was a general shortage of liquidity.[14] They admitted there was a problem of reserves distribution but considered this needed examination case by case. They were, however, concerned about the possible effects of their still-deepening recession and agreed to receive further British work on the whole subject of liquidity and to resume discussion at an early date. On his return to London Rowan set up a Working Party on International Payments Problems, with himself in the chair, to carry things a step further. The Bank was now fully associated with the exercise: Parsons became a member of the Working Party, with Thompson-McCausland as alternate. The latter had previously divided this territory with Stamp, but he now took sole possession and was to remain there, despite occasional challenges, until he retired from the Bank in 1965.

The signals from Washington soon became less discouraging. Thorold reported on 11 March that Saulnier, Chairman of the Council of Economic Advisers, had told him that the UK was rushing its fences. There was a need for a more thorough diagnosis. He thought there might well be a problem of maldistribution, though perhaps no overall shortage, and was concerned lest a prolongation of the recession should provoke trade restrictions. The US would provide help if this threatened and it would be better if an appropriate method were thought through in advance. Against this background the Bank undertook to supply the Rowan Working Party with a note showing in what way it would wish to modify the paper on international liquidity that the Treasury had prepared in advance of the February talks in Washington. This was done in a paper sent to Rowan by

---

[14] Mynors, who visited New York and Washington shortly afterwards, reported that the Americans were puzzled and somewhat suspicious of the UK approach. Was it another attempt to get US help for the UK? He recommended that Thompson-McCausland's visit should be postponed until the end of March, which it was.

Thompson-McCausland on 21 March. It was intended to serve two purposes, firstly to satisfy the remit from Whitehall and secondly 'to give you an idea of the general line we [the Bank] think might be put to Per Jacobsson in Washington'.

The Bank's paper was vintage self-taught Lucius, irritating or convincing according to taste. Its opening theme was that the international payments problem was akin to those encountered in nation states when modern monetary systems were evolving out of 'the original coin structure'. This way of looking at things was held to justify a view that there was, or could be, no shortage of the 'international credit base' itself – enlargement of which by a rise in the price of gold or further expansion of reserve currencies was anyway impracticable or unwise. An increase in IMF quotas, which would considerably increase UK external liquidity ahead of any final move to convertibility, was completely ignored. It was all summed up as follows:

> The problem which faces the world in its international money structure is thus not widely different in kind from that encountered in national money structures before the functions of a national central bank had been fully developed. There is no demonstrable shortage of the international credit base itself but there is demonstrable risk that shortages may occur in specific places at specific times with grave consequences to the whole international money structure. It is in these specific shortages at specific times that the problem lies and the solution is to be sought. If means can be found, and can be manifestly seen to be available, to tide currencies over a period of stringency while the necessary remedial measures are applied (under pressure, if necessary, from the lending institution), some approach to a solution may be in sight.

This led easily to renewed advocacy of special borrowing and lending by the Fund, a subject 'which was envisaged by Lord Keynes and the British Delegation in the preparatory talks with the American Treasury before the Bretton Woods Conference'.

The Treasury, which had now learnt with some surprise of Thompson-McCausland's intended trip to the US, reacted with indignation and alarm to this differentiation of the Bank's approach from its own. On 24 March, immediately before his departure for the US, Lucius was put on the proverbial carpet by Rowan. He was reminded that the approach put to the Americans in February had been approved by Ministers even if it had not been fully cleared with the Bank and that a very difficult situation would arise if it appeared from anything the Bank might say in Washington that it was thinking on different lines to the Government. Lucius attempted to back-pedal, protesting that his note was really about a practical solution to practical problems as they arose and avoiding a sterile debate about the adequacy of reserves. But Rowan was not to be mollified. He re-emphasised firstly that great damage would be done if it appeared that the Bank and the Government were taking different lines and secondly that so far as the IMF was concerned neither the Treasury and the Bank together nor, more importantly, Ministers had yet reached any conclusions about the particular system or systems that would be most appropriate to deal with the problem. Rowan sent Parsons a copy of his record of the meeting.

The Governor then endeavoured to cool the situation, telling Rowan that he did not think Thompson-McCausland's visit to Jacobsson could or should be interpreted as indicating any divergence between Bank and Treasury. But Parsons was not in a mood to cool anything; nor was he in any way prepared to doubt his own judgement of American attitudes. Writing on 28 March to Lucius in Washington, he recounted a 'rough time' at a further meeting with the Treasury, saying: 'At least I think we have got them off their over-simplified analysis of the general problem which I warned them would in no circumstances be accepted by the Americans, who would regard it as being merely an attempt to push them into a corner where, in order to escape, they would have to accept Keynes' Bancor Scheme!' As to the Governor's talk with Rowan, he wrote: 'The upshot is that we are all agreed that we want to avoid any suggestion of a rift between the Government and the Bank but that the Governor does not accept that your visit to Washington *and the kind of things that you would propose to say there* [author's italics] need be interpreted in that light.' This was verging on the foolhardy.

Fortunately for everyone concerned, the fuse was in the end put out by the Americans themselves; otherwise there could have ensued a damaging row between the Treasury and Bank. For Lucius began his talks in the US by explaining his own ideas to Exter[15] and Roosa[16] in the FRBNY. Writing to Parsons on 1 April, he reported that he had introduced the subject by saying that while the Bank was at one with HM Treasury in its concern with problems of international liquidity, it 'would perhaps present them rather differently'. His listeners had given him

---

[15] Exter, John (b. 1910). Educated Fletcher School of Law and Diplomacy and Harvard. Teacher, History and Economics, Western Residential Academy, Tufts College, Harvard 1934–43, Radiation Laboratory, Massachusetts Institute of Technology (MIT) 1943–5, Economist, Acting Chief Far East, FRB 1945–50, Adviser, Central Banking, Philippine and Ceylon Governments 1948–50, Governor, Central Bank of Ceylon 1950–3, Chief, Middle East Division, IBRD 1953–4, Vice-President, FRBNY 1954–9, Vice-President, First National City Bank of New York 1959–60. Senior Vice-President 1960.

[16] Roosa, Robert Vincent (b. 1918). Educated University of Michigan. Teacher of Economics, Michigan, Harvard, MIT 1939–43, FRBNY 1946–60, Vice-President, Research Department 1956–60, Under-Secretary for Monetary Affairs, US Treasury 1961–4, Chairman, Board of Trustees, Brookings Institution 1975–86, Partner Brown Brothers Harriman and Co. 1965–, Director, American Express Co. 1966, Texaco Inc. 1969.

encouragement. They mentioned the scepticism of Washington about an overall shortage, the unfavourable initial impact of the Rowan–Hall visit, and their desire to 'think about solutions which might have a chance of acceptance', Exter reportedly remarking that a rise in the gold price or a general increase in quotas was out of the question. Writing again a week later, Lucius went further and advised Parsons to try to stop Rowan from sending a technical party to Washington in advance of the resumption of high-level talks lest it should get in the way of the solutions favoured by the Bank, which he judged the Americans would accept. 'Since this is, in essentials, a banking matter not a Treasury one,' he wrote grandly, 'it would be easy for technical discussions to take a Treasury party into fields where they were unsure of themselves and to drive them into stating positions again rather than discussing them.' But on the following day, in another long letter to Parsons, he reported a viewpoint among his contacts in Washington that was very different to the one gleaned in New York. Discussions with Jacobsson, Southard, and Marget (Federal Reserve Board) about means of dealing with 'a shortage of reserves when and where it may show itself in particular cases' had revealed that these three thought 'quite easily and happily' in terms of a general increase in Fund quotas, with some but not much qualification about a tightening of conditionality. Jacobsson was thinking of an increase of 40%, in line with the inflation of the dollar since 1946, Southard of 50%, Marget somewhere between 40% and 100%. The official position of the US Treasury was still heavily reserved, but Lucius felt that the Administration would be sympathetic to argument about strengthening the Fund provided they were not at the same time asked to accept that there existed a world shortage of liquidity. The UK Treasury was duly informed and felt encouraged. The potentially interminable argument about whether or not there was a general shortage of liquidity, a maldistribution of an adequate total, or an absence of proper machinery for optimising use of what there was, could now be moved into a minor key. The Chancellor of the Exchequer, winding up for the Government in the Budget Debate, remained firm in declaring that a problem existed but avoided provocative phrasing or commitment to any particular solution. In mid-May Rowan and Hall made a second and tactful trip to Washington. While the Secretary of the Treasury warned them that the Administration was not yet ready to take a firm decision, his officials made it quite clear that the favoured solution, when the time came to decide, would be an all-round increase in Fund quotas.

During the summer the Administration made up its mind. In an exchange of letters between the President and the Secretary of the Treasury it was agreed to support both an increase in Fund quotas and the creation of a new affiliate of the IBRD, the International Development Association (IDA), which would lend money to developing countries on easier terms than the IBRD itself. There was no difficulty with Jacobsson, who visited London early in August and told the Bank and the Treasury that he favoured a 50% increase in quotas. At the Fund's annual meeting at the end of September, held this time in New Delhi, the Americans proposed that the Executive Board should examine the adequacy of existing quotas and report. The necessary resolution was duly passed and a report recommending an all-round 50% increase was prepared. Following ratification by the US Congress and by the appropriate procedures in other countries, the revised quotas came into effect in the autumn of 1959.

Late in May, after the second Rowan–Hall discussion in Washington, the Governor had felt able to write: 'This all suggests to me that LPTMcC's visit was very useful and rescued things from the flop of the earlier Treasury visit.' But he was overstating the part played by the Bank and underestimating its lucky escape from an embarrassing situation. It might indeed have been helpful, at the formative phase of American thinking on the subject, for the British to have had someone in New York and Washington who was not crying 'world shortage of liquidity' at everyone he met. It might, too, have conceivably been helpful to have someone there who not only positively denied a general shortage but proposed a solution to particular shortages that, on close examination, bristled with practical and political difficulties. An all-round increase in Fund quotas could then have presented itself as the obvious exit. However there is no evidence to support so positive a view of Lucius' visit. Moreover, the Treasury in London was kept well aware, through Thorold, of the way American minds were moving. The best that can be said is that luckily the visit did no harm.

Small in itself, this episode illustrated the dangers of the Treasury keeping the Bank at arm's length, especially at a time when its sensitivities were likely to be easily aroused and its behaviour, following changes of senior staff, was likely to be unfamiliar. Between the summer of 1957 and early 1958 the Bank was clearly in two minds about international liquidity. Following the Fund meeting in September 1957, and the preceding difficulties between the Bank and the Government over the control of bank advances, the Treasury went ahead with its own studies of reserves shortage, consulting Ministers when necessary but without even informing the Bank. This was a snub. When at last consulted, the Bank was confronted with a ready-made Treasury view on a subject with which it had of necessity to be vitally concerned. Its natural temptation to

Maurice Parsons, Executive Director 1957–1966

respond with a different view was then enhanced by the evident desire of Parsons to establish a strong position as Bolton's successor and by the desire of Thompson-McCausland to occupy the ground left by the sudden departure of Stamp. These two then combined in a position different to that of the Treasury, but one that suited the particular attitudes of the former and the idiosyncratic intellectual tastes of the latter. Having combined, they then fell into the error of ignoring the immediate interests of the British Government (an increase in external liquidity) and of flatly asserting, as the purported judgement of the Bank, that the Americans would not agree to any of the solutions favoured by the Treasury, including an increase in Fund quotas. The Governors seem to have observed what was happening without seeing fit to intervene. The

Governor brought his new, but junior, economic adviser into the debate; but to no effect. The Bank was fortunate that in the end no great damage resulted and that it could decently withdraw under cover of an American-inspired solution for whose adoption the UK Treasury must take a substantial share of the credit.

(c) THE APPROACH TO OPERATION UNICORN: JANUARY–OCTOBER 1958

Talking to the Governor early in January 1958, the Permanent Secretary said he had an open mind about unifying official and transferable sterling. Cobbold responded with an undertaking to take up the whole issue once more. Nearly twelve months later, on 27 December, unification at last took place, the EPU was discontinued, and the EMA was brought into effect. It might be thought that after all the preliminaries, culminating in the signature of the EMA in 1955, the actual transformation would be a simple matter requiring a straightforward decision by the British Government and some straightforward mechanics of UK exchange control and of intra-European payments arrangements. Quite the contrary: the final act was preceded by yet another round of full debate between the Treasury and the Bank, by yet another phase of disagreement before the Treasury came round to the view that the time was at last right, by a very deliberate and cautious approach by the Chancellor (closely watched by the Prime Minister), by the most meticulous sounding-out of official American and European opinion, and at the end by a most elaborate procedure of prior communication with the principal countries concerned. The show was greatly enlivened at the very end by another exciting appearance of the French. For the last time in the regular post-war series, they were engaged in a devaluation of the franc. Pinay was back as Minister of Finance under de Gaulle while Baumgartner was still Governor of the Bank of France. The unification of sterling had to be timed to coincide with the French devaluation, without either side appearing to lose face or to be acting under pressure from the other. This time, unlike in 1952, the Baumgartner–Cobbold connection proved reliable and all was well. This was important, for the operation took place at a moment of great tension in intra-European politics. The negotiations for a European Free Trade Area, linking the six countries of the EEC to the UK and others, broke down late in 1958 and the provisions of the Treaty of Rome were due to come into force on New Year's Day 1959. A currency row between London and Paris was the last thing anyone wanted.

There was also an unexpected diversion at the start of the year. The

Governor's response to his talk with Makins was delayed a little by the sudden resignation of the Chancellor of the Exchequer and his two principal lieutenants. Heathcoat Amory, a kindly, able, cautious, and careful man, not a party politician in any ordinary mould, was promoted to the Exchequer in place of Thorneycroft. The period of early-day monetarism had been terminated; but Bank Rate remained at 7% and sterling was unharmed. The official rate rose during January to 2.81\frac{5}{8}$ and the reserves rose by $130 million, to $2.4 billion. On 4 February the Governor sent a long letter to Makins in which he argued that another favourable opportunity was at hand to end the unsatisfactory dual-rate system of *de facto* convertibility and to complete the process that had been interrupted since the summer of 1955. As usual, he argued that the opportunity be seized in case adverse developments should supervene and compel floating-rate unification from a position of weakness. The measures taken in September 1957 had helped restore confidence, but 'the present state of our exchange system is not conducive to confidence'. To have a multiple-rate structure was not a satisfactory state for an international currency. It was also costly and anomalous: costly because, for example, the EEA had recently been selling sterling in the transferable market at a discount, in order to avoid coalescence, only to find itself having to buy more sterling at par through the EPU; anomalous because a large part of the total market for sterling against dollars had to be made in overseas centres rather than in London. This not only damaged London's position as an exchange centre, it also reduced the operational visibility available to the managers of the EEA. Unification would admittedly entail the termination of the EPU and some reconsideration of trade discrimination; but were these factors as important now as they had seemed several years previously? Finally, though not wishing to 'reopen the question of wider margins or anything which might cast doubt on our determination to hold the present sterling parity', he remarked that the Bank still felt there might be technical advantage, at the right moment, in removing the top limit of $2.82 while retaining the floor.

The Governor's letter did not appeal to Rowan, who was anyway devoting much of his time to the question of international liquidity. At a meeting on 7 February, attended by Parsons, the latter found him 'in his most miserable mood; he had made up his mind and was searching only for the disadvantages'. Rowan felt that the time was still not right – internal stability was still not assured, world trade prospects were darkened by another recession in North America, and support for the reserves was inadequate. Moreover, since the Governor's proposal seemed too unilateralist, help from, for example, America, Canada, or Germany would not be forthcoming. In the context of an approach to the Americans on international liquidity, an early move to sterling unification would indeed have been oddly timed and might have served to confirm suspicions that the argument presented about liquidity was a screen for trying to get help for the UK. But the Governor knew his Treasury and kept up the pressure. He spoke to the new Chancellor on the subject and wrote to him early in March, enclosing a copy of the passage on convertibility with which he had opened the subject with Macmillan in April 1956. Heathcoat Amory held a meeting but no decision was taken, the Chancellor later telling both Governors that various and conflicting considerations were not yet resolved in the minds of himself or his advisers. A firm answer would be deferred, perhaps until after the Budget. This decision was repeated by Makins in a letter sent to the Governor on the following day. He added that: 'The Prime Minister has asked that two memoranda should be prepared: one setting out the pros and cons of bringing the official and transferable rates for sterling together and the other discussing the arguments for and against a floating rate.' The Treasury would be in touch with the Bank about their preparation. The Permanent Secretary declined to take charge of this exercise himself and left it to Rowan and Hall. Together with Arnold France they formed a Treasury team opposite Parsons and Hamilton from the Bank. At their first meeting, on 12 March, they agreed to anticipate disagreements by commissioning separate drafts from the Treasury and the Bank on both the questions raised by the Prime Minister. In particular, on unification the Treasury was to produce the 'cons' and the Bank the 'pros'.

The Bank drafted quickly and sent its two papers off to the Treasury. It repeated the case for unification already deployed by the Governor, adding that the emerging weakness of the dollar, together with the start of discussions in Europe about a Free Trade Area (FTA), strengthened that case. The Treasury, in its own paper, argued resolutely to the contrary: the publicly stated preconditions for unification had not been completely fulfilled; the effects of the US recession on free-world trade and payments could not yet be adequately judged; and the UK reserves, net of drawings on the IMF and Exim Bank, remained too low. All in all, therefore, it would still be better to wait. However on the eternal question of fixed versus floating rates, the two institutions were much closer together. With an eye on temptations that might be lurking in No. 10, both were pointedly concerned to argue against the use of exchange depreciation as an adjustment to inflationary policies by a debtor country, the more so if that country possessed an international currency with low reserves and much larger monetary liabilities. The Bank added that a fully floating rate for sterling, contrary to IMF rules, would bring the 'whole world structure of exchange rates into question'. Both institutions then examined the familiar managerial case for wider dealing spreads in the special case of sterling. Both agreed that it had force. Both next agreed that to widen the spreads above and below $2.80 in the near future, to an extent managerially worthwhile, would be to run too great a risk of upsetting the holders of sterling balances. The Bank then considered with some sympathy the idea first mooted by the Governor in August 1957: of retaining $2.78 as the lower limit while raising or removing the upper limit of $2.82. But it pointed out that IMF consent would be needed and warned that raising the upper limit might upset confidence in a future period of adverse pressure because people might think it a prelude to lowering the lower limit. The Treasury was less sympathetic. In addition to the risk mentioned by the Bank there was the objection that the proposal would not work unless the rate appreciated to around, say, $2.88. This was either very unlikely to happen or would damage the UK's competitive position if it did.

The debate continued for a little longer. The Treasury, on Rowan's insistence, sharpened up its draft against early unification. The phraseology became shrill. Unification was an irrevocable step and 'a major event in the post-war economic developments and will attract comment and scrutiny from all over the world'. A repetition of 1947 (it was now 1958) would be a major disaster for the 'whole sterling system and therefore for the West'. Therefore: 'We must be able to convince home and world opinion so clearly that we have moved from strength that no-one will doubt that we can hold the position.' The Treasury could offer no assurance that the position could be held. Inflation in the UK had not yet been clearly halted; the US recession still loomed large; the problem of the German surplus remained; and the cyclical position of the Sterling Area was not strong. The termination of the EPU would be unwelcome to France and might therefore prejudice the FTA negotiations. Furthermore, the unification of rates would 'be regarded at home as a major step and will certainly arouse acute controversy – not divided entirely perhaps on party political lines'. How could the Government argue that it was moving from strength when its 'whole economic policy is based on the opposite hypothesis – that inflation is still the main target (this may change but until wages have been settled it is obviously an open question) and that though we have started well on the road to improving our external monetary situation we still have a long way to go'. Judging by this hyperbolic blast it would appear that Treasury officials were frightened that their Ministers would not listen to them. But as the Bank gently pointed out in the final version of its own paper: 'Although admittedly the amalgamation of rates would be, in our view, an irrevocable act, it would be no more irrevocable than the present situation.' Contrary to the Treasury's assertions, the moment was quite favourable – as the Governor had first argued six weeks earlier. If it subsequently became very unfavourable, the UK would be no worse off with a single rate than it would in practice be with a dual rate. Indeed it would be better off because the risk of being forced to amalgamate the rates in a crisis would have been eliminated. The paper concluded:

> The one thing we must not do is to imagine that other people will have confidence in our currency if we manifestly exhibit no confidence in it ourselves. If no action is taken now the conclusion may well be drawn that what has been the policy of HMG for ten years or more, namely convertibility of the pound sterling, is now no longer the policy but only a far-distant objective. If this assumption became general it could only have the effect of producing conditions disadvantageous to us and likely to make any further advance in the direction of unifying the rates that much more difficult.

The debate about a floating rate also continued for a little longer and was sharpened by another Minute sent by Macmillan to Heathcoat Amory on 21 March. This suggested that the former was coming round in favour of floating the pound. Asking for a paper on the constitutional and technical processes needed for a move to a floating rate, the Prime Minister wrote:

> I think this ought to be put in hand at once. I imagine that we had it ready in case we had to do it out of weakness last Autumn. We had equally better be ready to do it out of strength when we judge the right moment has come; of course for the purpose of this exercise I am assuming that we would want to do it when the moment comes. At any rate, the study should be made in this spirit. I do not want an argument as to whether we ought to do it. I want a presentation of how to do it if we decide to do it.

Both the Treasury and the Bank again suspected that No. 10 was flirting with the idea of a fully floating rate as a soft option that would allow domestic policies to be loosened. There was press gossip that the Bank and the City were in favour of floating while the Treasury was hostile. Accordingly, in papers sent to the Chancellor by Rowan on 2 April – comprising the final versions of the two opposing papers on unification and a new version of the agreed Treasury/Bank paper on exchange policy – the case against full floating was argued heavily and at length. Robot now belonged to another universe. A few days later the Governor sent the Chancellor a note on the subject by Bolton. It was sympathetic to the theoretical arguments in favour of floating but argued against it on familiar grounds of practical politics. He had concluded: 'It would be prudent to organise monetary policy both at home and abroad, on the probability that something like a unified floating-rate policy is inevitable but to make no attempt to force the pace until it becomes more acceptable to the Western world as a whole.' Cobbold commented to the Chancellor that he shared Bolton's view that floating was not a starter at the present time, adding that, in any case 'we should find ourselves bound in practice to keep very stable rates: neither the USA nor the rest of the world would stand for our monkeying sterling about all the time against the dollar'.

This official onslaught on such heresies as may have been entering Ministerial heads in Downing Street was successful. Nothing more was heard of floating the pound. On the other question, unification, the Chancellor and the Prime Minister eventually agreed in May to take no early action but to consider the matter again in the autumn. Makins remained an ally of a disappointed Governor, telling him on 30 May that he feared they had missed the bus, that he personally thought it a pity, but that he had been unable to get any support from Ministers or other Treasury officials.

But what had happened to the still important issue of wider spreads? The Bank had in fact given way to the Treasury, seemingly in the interests of presenting a united front against full floating. The surrender was vigorously opposed by Bridge,[17] who recorded his dissent in a strong note to Parsons and the Governors. He began by criticising the relevant passages in the agreed paper for the Chancellor as inadequate, partisan, and wrongly argued. He went on to restate the case for using wider spreads as a means of reducing the volume of speculation and consequently of reducing fluctuations in the reserves. Market opinion, he added, was behind him. 'There is an influential and increasing body of expert opinion, particularly in the London and New York markets, which has become convinced that the narrowness of the existing margins increases speculation when the pound is under pressure. This conviction is based upon knowledge and observation of the behaviour and mentality of commercial clients, be they importers or exporters or alternatively foreign corporations with interests in the Sterling Area.' Bridge agreed that the underlying strength of sterling depended upon sound internal polices but concluded: 'But that is surely true irrespective of what margins are practised in the exchange rates. I do not believe that the present narrow margins afford any protection at all; on the contrary, as I have indicated earlier in this memorandum, I am persuaded that the truth lies in the

---

[17] He was now Deputy Chief Cashier in charge of gold and foreign exchange operations; George Preston was Principal of the Dealing and Accounts Office.

opposite direction. In my opinion, it is of considerable importance that we should have the added protection to the reserves of a wider margin...before the next general election takes place and that this should be achieved without any change in the support rate of $2.78 but through the raising of the official upper limit above the present figure of $2.82.' In reply, Parsons made no attempt whatever to argue with Bridge on his own expert ground. Instead, he resorted to political assertion. 'In my judgement', he told the Governors on 21 April, 'it would have been fatal to have attempted to argue that we want a fixed rate but wider margins. This would have been too subtle a distinction for Ministers and also, in due course, for public opinion.' The Governor acknowledged this message without written comment.

So summary a dismissal of considered advice given by its chief of exchange operations, and the failure to use that advice with the Treasury, was unusual conduct for an institution responsible for advising the Government about market management. It was all the more unusual when the particular proposal under discussion had been suggested to the Treasury by the Governor twice in the preceding eight months and when the whole issue of wider spreads had been argued exhaustively with the Government during the period preceding the signature of the EMA in 1955, with the Bank always arguing in favour. But Parsons was not interested in attempting to improve the performance of sterling by alterations in operational technique, as he had told Bolton shortly before the latter's retirement as Executive Director early in 1957. He took the same view in 1958. For him, it was domestic policy that mattered. Clever changes in market management would only serve to weaken that policy, just as all-round increases in international liquidity would only serve to promote further inflation. So it would be fatal to argue in favour of wider margins. No good could come of it. It was therefore right to disregard the opinion of the Bank's leading expert in foreign exchange and also right to abandon the views on wider margins long held by Bolton. Both were more concerned with the better management of sterling in a very imperfect world than in exploiting a fixed-rate narrow-margin system in order to enforce greater discipline on the Government. Parsons' view was certainly straightforward. It was difficult to contradict in a climate of opinion that was becoming increasingly cynical about British macro-economic policy. But it was based upon the judgement or the belief that narrow margins, fixed rates, and low reserves would durably engender the required discipline. There was no solid foundation for this belief, as Parsons himself was to discover in the 1960s. Although by 1958 wider margins would have been very difficult to obtain, despite the fact that they were allowed within the EMA, it might have been better if the Bank had remained true to its own proper trade and continued to argue in their favour. As it was, however, the topic simply passed out of view.

By the end of July 1958 the reserves had risen to nearly $3.1 billion, despite a large fall in the sterling balances. The external current account was in substantial surplus. Bank Rate had been kept at 7% until a reduction to 6% on 28 March. A further cut to $5\frac{1}{2}$% was made on 30 May and another to 5% on 27 June. Inflation had fallen to 2%. Externally, no dollar problem had emerged and the US economy had begun to recover from its sharp recession. Finally there was the prospective increase in IMF quotas, which could help offset the fall in international liquidity that would result from the termination of the EPU. Even the Treasury, so fearful three months earlier, concluded this was too good an opportunity to be missed. Unification could not be postponed forever. Moreover, a general election was likely to be called during 1959 and it was desirable, ahead of that event, both to renew the Fund stand-by and to make satisfactory arrangements for gradually repaying the Suez drawing. Unification could help with both. Accordingly, on 15 August Rowan minuted the Chancellor recommending that unification be put into effect before the end of the year and be combined with a three-year extension of the stand-by coupled with a three-year repayment of the drawing. The Governor supported Rowan, although warning that leaks might compel earlier action. Early in September the Chancellor minuted the Prime Minister along the lines proposed by Rowan but in rather more cautious language. He did not ask for any definite decision ahead of the Commonwealth Trade and Economic Conference to be held in Montreal later in the month or of the Fund/Bank meetings to be held in New Delhi early in October. But he suggested that he should have exploratory talks with Secretary Anderson, Per Jacobsson, and others. Authority for this was given at a meeting of those Ministers who were directly concerned.

At a lunch in New York on 27 September the Chancellor told Anderson that he hoped it might be possible to take the final step to convertibility[18] in a few months time, perhaps within six months. The Treasury record added: 'If this was to be achieved, it would be necessary for the UK to secure a renewal of the IMF stand-by for a three-year period. On that basis the UK would probably wish to start repayment of its drawing from the

---

[18] Use of this word worried Cobbold. On 29 September, in a note handed to the Chancellor, he said: 'I am somewhat bothered by the way the word "Convertibility" is being bandied about again. I have always tried to kill it because nobody knows what it means.' He hoped unification would be described only as a 'further step along a road'. It was certainly an important step, 'but in my judgement of less practical importance (though perhaps more formal importance) than the decision in 1955 to support the transferable rate'.

IMF at the beginning of 1959 rather than in 1960.' Anderson, who was reported to be well pleased by a British announcement in Montreal of further reductions in discriminatory trade restrictions, welcomed the prospect of unification and referred to it as a most hopeful step which would assist the economy of the whole free world.

The scene then shifted to Delhi where, in the course of the Fund/Bank meeting, at which the enlargement of quotas and the foundation of the IDA were set in train, the Chancellor discussed unification with the Managing Director. The latter had been profoundly impressed, perhaps overmuch, by the 7% Bank Rate and its aftermath. He told the Chancellor that the attitude of foreign banks towards sterling had completely changed for the better. He also told him that unification, by the end of the year, would be the correct course.[19] In its absence people might begin to think that the Government lacked confidence in the economic prospect. But he impulsively shied away from the suggestion that the UK stand-by be renewed for three years as an accompaniment to unification. He felt it would be a great mistake to put it forward. It would constitute a major exception from usual practice; the Fund would not like it and it would have a bad effect on other countries. It was unnecessary and would detract from UK credit. Finally, he said, some members would not like it because they would interpret it as a move to underwrite the possibility of a Labour Government. On the other hand a renewal for one year would be no problem and if another facility, or another renewal, turned out to be needed thereafter, he was sure the Fund would respond.

The Chancellor was accompanied by Makins, Rickett, Thorold, Parsons, and Portsmore. They were all impressed by the conviction with which Jacobsson had spoken and apparently saw no advantage in attempting to rally support against him. To do so, it may be supposed, would have risked creating a dispute that might not have gone in favour of the UK and might have spoiled the ground for unification. Moreover, the UK quota might have increased by 50% by the time a one-year renewal of the stand-by had expired. Officials therefore advised the Chancellor to drop the proposal for a three-year extension, which he did.

In a letter sent to the Governor on 8 October Parsons reported: 'The weather here is unreasonably hot and humid and there is a great deal of delicate health. So far I have survived.' Perhaps, therefore, it was a combination of adverse climate, gastro-enteritis, travel-weariness, and the weight of Jacobsson's personality that prompted so hasty an abandonment

---

[19] The Chancellor also got a favourable response from Dr Erhard. As soon as the UK made sterling convertible, West Germany would follow suit. Erhard added that the move was widely expected in Europe and that he hoped it would not be too long delayed.

of the previously held position. There was, after all, no need to decide in Delhi; and the Managing Director's arguments were flimsy to the point of triviality. To say that making an exception for the UK would be an undesirable precedent was to ignore exceptional features that surrounded sterling and were acknowledged by all concerned. To say that a three-year extension would detract from UK credit and, by implication, that a further renewal after a one-year extension would not so detract seems no more than off-the-cuff rhetoric. Likewise, to say that a three-year extension was unnecessary was to judge a case before hearing it; and the remark about underwriting the possibility of a Labour Government was unworthy of a senior international official. No doubt the Managing Director was finding the meetings in Delhi a heavy burden and a drain on his physical resources. A surprise British proposal, even if only exploratory, could well have made him conjure up a series of irksome difficulties and respond in a spontaneously negative manner.

In the end, however, dropping the proposal for a three-year stand-by was to prove no bad thing for the UK. The ideas for really substantial fortification of the reserves that had prevailed in the early days of the Collective Approach had long since been abandoned. The Suez stand-by, arranged to meet the specific crisis of December 1956, was on a smaller scale and already nearly two years' old. As it turned out, to have extended it for a further three would have been an improvisation that would not have been much use until it was on the point of final expiry in 1961. Something rather different was going to be needed if outright fortification of the reserves on a large scale was impracticable. Central bank swaps and, eventually, a central bank facility directly related to adverse movements in the sterling balances, were more to the point. In the meantime the UK had to make do with what it had, together with an enlarged IMF quota.

While Parsons was in Delhi, the Bank was advising the Treasury about the detailed procedure to be adopted for combining unification of the sterling exchange rates with the termination of the EPU, the activation of the EMA, and the renewal of the Fund stand-by. This in turn brought the Bank into the careful planning of what was to become an unusually complex operation. Previously code-named 'Moonshine', it was now christened 'Unicorn'. The whole exercise was set in motion by Rowan on 2 October and a week later the Bank sent a paper to the Treasury advising against starting with unilateral unification and then proceeding to discussion in Europe. A more collaborative procedure was required, one that at the same time minimised the risk of leakage. This involved secret prior consultation at central bank level with the Germans and French followed by Governmental and central bank consultation with all the principal members of the EPU. If all went well, there would then be a weekend announcement by the Chancellor and the EMA would come into force on the Monday. A refinement to this procedure would be to intervene in the market, in order to bring the rates close together, if there turned out to be a delay of a day or more between the British announcement and the activation of the EMA. Intervention of this kind might also be needed if the negotiations failed and the UK was obliged to start the procedure of withdrawal from the EPU. After discussion with the Treasury, a programme on these lines was agreed and included in a paper sent to Treasury Ministers on 17 October. The covering note acknowledged abandonment of the three-year stand-by and advocated an early move, in advance of formal application for a one-year renewal of the Suez stand-by.

Rowan now left the stage abruptly and for good. Passed over for the top job in 1956, he had no further to go in the Treasury and was not keen to move to another Department. Although he had only just turned fifty, he had been a second Permanent Secretary for over ten years. He accepted an offer to join Vickers Ltd as their Finance Director and left the Civil Service altogether. Denis Rickett, a less outspoken and more diplomatic character, succeeded him in the Treasury.

(d) UNICORN AND THE FRENCH CONNECTION: OCTOBER–DECEMBER 1958

France was at this moment absorbed in the transition from the Fourth Republic to the Fifth. The new constitution was submitted to the people by de Gaulle in the autumn of 1958 and was approved in a referendum. Under a new electoral law allowing for two ballots, a general election was then called for 23 November and 30 November, to be followed by a Presidential election ending on 21 December. In the meantime there were the negotiations for a European Free Trade Area, to which the French were opposed, ahead of the inauguration of the Common Market in the new year. As if these political complexities were not enough, there was the French economic situation to take into account and the large French debts to the EPU,[20] whose repayment would need to be settled if the EPU were terminated. De Gaulle and Pinay had appointed an advisory committee chaired by the right-wing economist Jacques Rueff which was expected to recommend a further devaluation of the franc and a liberalisation of French imports from OEEC countries as part of a stabilisation programme.

---

[20] Out of a consolidated EPU debt of $460 million, repayment of only $72 million had so far been arranged. There was also a special credit of $150 million of which $105 million had been drawn and was due for repayment by instalments beginning in 1960. France had also drawn $393 million from the IMF, repayable in 1960 and 1961.

The developing situation on the Continent demanded tact and caution in London. By the end of October and early November the signals coming to the Bank from the EPU Board indicated the necessity of obtaining prior French approval for the timing of Unicorn if the operation were to be a collaborative success. Mackay[21] of the Netherlands Bank told Stanley Payton[22] that the other members of the Six had no idea how to deal with the French, who were the dominant influence in the EEC Commission. However anxious other Governments of the Six might be to make a move to convertibility and the EMA, they would not move without the French. Everything would therefore depend on how the latter reacted. If they blocked a move, the rest of the Six would stand by them. But Mackay added that the French would have good reasons for not blocking it. In particular, a devaluation of the franc was becoming unavoidable and the commencement of the EMA could be the cloak and the opportunity. A recent meeting between Adenauer and Pinay, at which further help for France had been mentioned, was encouraging on this score. Similar reliable intelligence must have been reaching the Treasury and it was then decided to seek further guidance through the central bank network, at high level. The Chancellor accordingly agreed with the Governor that the latter should speak to Blessing[23] and Baumgartner in Basle, and the results of their meetings were sent by Cobbold to Makins on 11 November.

Baumgartner indicated that although his remarks were private and personal he had no objection to Cobbold mentioning the gist of the conversation to the Prime Minister and the Chancellor for their personal information. He welcomed an assurance that the UK would make no move before the French Elections and said he would himself prefer a move between then and the end of the year rather than later. But this time, unlike in the summer of 1952, he made it clear that the French Government could take a different view. However, Cobbold himself was confident that his French counterpart would do his best to obtain the support of de Gaulle for a move soon after the Elections. Blessing, for his part, said he would welcome a British move and assured the Governor that Germany would follow at once and would support the change from the

[21] Baron Mackay was a director of Netherlands Bank and a descendant of a member of the Scottish clan of that name who had been a soldier in the Netherlands army of William III.
[22] *Payton, Stanley Walden CMG (b. 1921).* Educated Monoux School. Fleet Air Arm 1940–6. Entered Bank 1946, UK Alternate on Managing Board of EPU 1957–9, Governor, Bank of Jamaica 1960–4, Deputy Chief, Overseas Department 1965–72, Adviser 1972–3, Senior Adviser 1973–5, Chief of Overseas Department 1975–80.
[23] *Blessing, Karl (1900–71).* Educated High School of Economics, Berlin. Official in Reichsbank 1920–37, Director 1937–9, Adviser, Ministry of Economic Affairs 1934–7. Director, Unilever Group in Germany 1939–41, 1948–57, Chairman 1952–7. Director, Daimler Benz, Dresdner Bank, etc. 1941–57. President Deutsche Bundesbank 1958–69.

EPU to the EMA. He had the definite agreement of Erhard to this and felt confident that they could resist any opposition that might develop in the Six. In Paris, however, von Mangoldt was repeating to Ellis-Rees that the Germans would not follow a British move against the wishes of the French.

A few days after these quiet words in Basle, the Free Trade Area negotiations were suspended. Baumgartner telephoned the Bank on 17 November. As Cobbold had left on a short visit to the Far East, Mynors took the call and recorded: 'In a very guarded conversation he said that his plans were in train but "would take a long time"; and he is much troubled by the present state of relations arising from the collapse of the FTA talks. I infer that he was pleading that we should do nothing to exacerbate relations for the time being: but he will be writing.'[24] UK Ministers were rather of the same mind. Maudling wanted to postpone Unicorn, feeling it would only worsen the Anglo–French situation. But Treasury officials warned that this would come near to giving the French a veto and the Chancellor wisely played for time. In the UK delegation to the OEEC there was at first considerable gloom, but this gave way to a brighter mood when von Mangoldt shifted ground and said that he did not think the French would block the change to the EMA if the other members of the EEC were in favour. In London, the Bank was anxious lest the tide should be missed after all, so leaving disappointed expectations and an awkward passage for sterling in an election year. So the Deputy Governor therefore suggested that Stevens be sent to Paris for talks at the Bank of France, which Makins thought might be a starter. On 28 November the Treasury revised the Chancellor's draft Cabinet paper to take account of the French difficulty, arguing that it could and should be overcome through German influence and British persuasion.

The pace now accelerated. On 2 December the Chancellor sought and obtained the Prime Minister's approval for Thorold to approach Anderson and Jacobsson about renewal of the stand-by for which formal application would follow within days. They were to be told privately about the UK's intentions but warned that events might be held up by the difficulties in Europe. By this time the Chancellor and his officials were becoming resigned to postponing Unicorn until early in the new year. In a note sent by Parsons to the Governor on 4 December, timed for the latter's arrival in the US on his way back from Japan, it was reported that Ministerial feet were very cold. The Ministers doubted whether they could depend on German support against French wishes. But at least there was no hold-up in Washington: Thorold and the Governor saw Anderson on the 8th and

---

[24] If he did, the letter has not survived.

received a favourable reception. The Secretary appeared ready to support renewal of the stand-by, was keen on an early move, and had discussed the European difficulty with various continental authorities. But there were limits to the pressure he could bring to bear and he accepted that a short postponement might well be necessary. However, while the Governor was joining in the talks in Washington, Stevens was attending the monthly meeting in Basle where unification was the main topic of conversation. He reported that the Germans, Swiss, Belgians, Dutch, and Swedes were all in favour and anxious to move; only the French and Italians had reservations. Stevens had talked it over with Baumgartner, whose problem was mainly one of timing. The franc was now under strong pressure, but no decision on devaluation could be taken until the expected victory of de Gaulle in the Presidential Election on 21 December. Rueff would recommend devaluation, but the decision would be for the General to take; it was not a foregone conclusion. Stevens acknowledged the French problem but warned that market forces were on the move in London.

Stevens' report was sent by Mynors to the Treasury, where there was at once an appreciation of the risk that instead of refusing to follow a move by the British, the French might actually move first, devaluing and declaring the franc convertible at the same time, which would be damaging to sterling. Accordingly the Chancellor, urged on by his officials, was minded to go ahead with unification before the year-end. He was to attend an OEEC Ministerial meeting in Paris on 15 December and would tell his French and German counterparts of that intention. But before getting Cabinet authority for this he wanted to know whether the Bank would ascertain the precise intentions of the French Government. At a meeting on 11 December he was told that Baumgartner had telephoned the day before to say that a date 'after Christmas' would be agreeable to him. France would be ready to follow a British lead on unification, but there had been no mention of devaluation. The Chancellor was then advised that it would confuse matters if a further approach was made from London to the Bank of France unless HMG had itself taken a firm decision. Accordingly, the matter was now at last put before the Cabinet, who agreed only that they would be prepared to unify the rates either simultaneously or after a French move. It there were any question of moving ahead of the French, further reference to the Prime Minister would be required.

Instructed to attempt once more to elicit French intentions, Stevens met Baumgartner at his house on Sunday 14 December. He was assured that the French would make no difficulties over Unicorn provided it was done at a mutually convenient time, and simultaneously with parallel action on their part. Assured that the UK would not move before Christmas, Baumgartner said it would be very welcome if the British move also coincided with devaluation of the franc; but he again said no decision on the latter could finally be taken until after 21 December. He enquired whether it might be possible to continue the EPU on a 100% gold basis instead of activating the EMA, but he was told this would be technically very awkward.

Although both Baumgartner and Stevens were in favour of continuing their talks the stage was now set for discussions between the Ministers meeting in Paris. Erhard told the Chancellor on 14 December that he hoped the UK would be moving very soon, that Germany would follow straightaway, and that the French would also follow suit. To this end, he was prepared to offer the French financial assistance up to $300 million and would tell de Gaulle about this on the following day. To suggestions that the UK might either approach the French or else enter into tripartite talks with them and the Germans, the Chancellor gave a cautious reply. Perhaps Pinay would care to make the first step? Mindful, no doubt, of past difficulties with the General, the Chancellor remarked that he was always prepared to do his best to keep the French happy but did not want to be blamed for it afterwards. This message evidently made its mark, for at dinner on 16 December Pinay was very friendly and responded positively to a suggestion that action in Paris and London should be synchronised. Action in Paris would include devaluation and a date between Christmas and the new year would be acceptable. Pinay added that it would help the January discussion on European co-operation if, as the Chancellor reported later to Macmillan, 'We had this piece of co-operation behind us'. The German Finance Minister (Etzel) joined the conversation and again confirmed that they would follow a British move. Pinay assured the Chancellor that de Gaulle supported the suggested procedure.[25] Heathcoat Amory then proposed that if the three Governments agreed, the three central banks should be asked to work out the technical steps. This was accepted by Pinay, who said he was aware of the contacts between the Bank of France and the Bank of England. In London, the Prime Minister now agreed that the operation could go ahead and the Bank was authorised to pursue its technical discussions, the Treasury directing that New Year's Day should be the assumed target date.

Apart from a final agreement on timing there was now only one important point to be settled. It was known that the French wished to re-

---

[25] The Chancellor, cautious to the last, later obtained confirmation of this from Etzel, who had himself spoken with the financial adviser on the General's staff.

examine that part of the EMA that made provision for the European Fund because circumstances had greatly changed since 1955 (in particular, the Treaty of Rome had come into being). Accordingly, they did not wish this part of the EMA to come into force automatically when the EPU was terminated. However, apart from the $113 million to be transferred from the EPU, none of the Fund's capital could in practice be called up without the unanimous consent of its members. So there was room for a formula. After consultation with the Treasury, the Bank proposed that there should be an *aide-mémoire* recording that the $113 million would be transferred and that no further capital would be called until a comprehensive re-examination of the provisions of the Fund had been made, but that sympathetic consideration would be given to the possibility of an *ad hoc* multilateral credit if any member country should find itself in serious difficulty before any modifications to the Fund had been settled.[26] This formula was agreed first with the Bundesbank by Rootham, who travelled to Frankfurt on the 19 December. The Germans also agreed that the whole operation should take effect on Monday 29 December instead of 1 January. The former date was now preferred in Threadneedle Street and had been accepted by the Chancellor on the Governor's advice. Stevens then went to Paris for talks with Baumgartner and Calvet on 21 December. He found that the French also preferred the 29th, would go along with Unicorn whether or not they finally decided to devalue, and were prepared to accept the British formula on the European Fund. The French also asked for a swap facility of £20 million. Since Cobbold had expected this request and had already obtained the Chancellor's consent, Stevens was able to meet it.[27] With the UK stand-by at the IMF safely renewed for a year as of 19 December, everything was now ready for the operation to proceed.

Allowing for the shut-down over Christmas and Boxing Day, there were only three working days left before the public announcements would be made over the weekend of the 27th and 28th. The multitude of telegrams were finalised and the remaining European emissaries sent on their way: Stevens went on to Rome from Paris; Crick[28] went to Brussels and

---

[26] Virtually all the $113 million to be transferred from the EPU was already needed to support the multilateral clearing for which the EMA provided.

[27] The French had for some time window-dressed their EPU position by temporarily gathering in the foreign currency balances of the French banks at the end of each month. When this 'ratissage', as it was called, terminated along with the EPU a once and for all drain on French end-month reserves was expected.

[28] Crick, Leslie Frederick (1908–85). Educated Colfe's Grammar School, Lewisham. Entered Bank 1928, Assistant to Chief Cashier (Exchange Control and Overseas) 1948–50, UK Alternate Executive Director, IMF 1950–1, 1953, Adviser (Acting) 1954–6, Adviser 1956–7, Deputy Chief, Overseas Department 1957–9, Adviser 1959–67, Adviser to the Governors 1967–8.

Amsterdam; Raw went to Oslo and Stockholm; Rootham remained in Frankfurt. In Rome, Brussels, Amsterdam, and Stockholm all was plain sailing, but in Frankfurt and Oslo there was trouble. Rootham found himself caught in a fine tangle of communication between the Federal Government, the Bundesbank, the Bank of France, the Bank of England, the UK Treasury, and the UK Embassy in Bonn – further confused by the inexplicably faulty circulation of Foreign Office telegrams. The Germans had suddenly become suspicious that the French wanted to kill the European Fund and in so doing leave a previously agreed EPU 'rallonge' for Turkey uncovered by a prospective drawing on that Fund. Their suspicions were groundless, but the formula had to be amended, in agreement with the French, before the Germans were satisfied and prepared to accept the text. Rootham had to work very hard indeed to get everyone into line.

In Oslo on 23 December Raw got a very frosty reception. Brofoss, Governor of Norges Bank, thought the timing was wrong. He thought that a valuable weapon of pressure on the Six, and particularly on the Germans, was being thrown away by an initiative that would oblige the Scandinavians to settle their accumulated deficit in the EPU in full, in gold or dollars. Worse was to come from Skaug, the Minister of Commerce. He had had no prior warning of Raw's message because the UK Ambassador had been unable to get hold of the Foreign Minister and had not delivered the British message to anyone else. Skaug, Raw reported, 'was highly incensed and emotional'. He had been a keen supporter of the UK in the FTA negotiations and regarded this lack of consultation as a betrayal. He felt he would have to resign. More to the point, he said that the termination of EPU credit would wreck their balance of payments programme for 1959 and that they might have to cancel orders for ships. Furthermore they would have to start repaying $86 million of EPU debt. Raw gave no indication that the UK might be prepared to help but carefully explained the formula about the European Fund. Before he left on the following day Brofoss told him that the damage could be mitigated if he or Getzwold (Ministry of Finance) were invited to London for talks in January. In his report to the Governors Raw advised that they be well treated and that the UK should urge the Germans to grant Norway generous repayment terms. He was right. The British tended to be careless with their solid Scandinavian friends. The Swedes had been very badly treated in 1947, and in 1958 the Norwegians had every reason to expect more consideration than they got (even if the Foreign Office message had not gone astray).

There were no further hitches. The French took their decision to devalue and the Bank of France suspended its foreign exchange dealings on 26 December. London followed suit for the Saturday morning session on the 27th. At 5.50 p.m. on that day the Treasury announced that unification would take effect from 9.00 a.m. on Monday 29 December. Recalling the evolution of policy since 1952 and emphasising that 'this is part of a coordinated European move', the text concluded as follows:

> In the light of conditions in the exchange markets in recent months and of discussions in Montreal, New Delhi and Paris, the Government has decided that the time has come to merge Transferable and Official sterling. The authorities will take steps to merge Transferable, American, Canadian and Registered Accounts which will, in future, be known as External Accounts. It follows that sterling for Overseas Account will in future be dealt in a single market in London.

Three Treasury press conferences on 27 December were taken by Rickett with Bridge in technical support. In the Bank, a succession of leading financial journalists had interviews with Parsons. There were few problems.

On 29 December Makins sent the Governor a warm letter of thanks for the work put into Unicorn by the two Overseas Directors and by the Bank staff concerned. 'We feel', he wrote, 'that, largely as a result of their efforts, this has been a very satisfactory combined operation.' The Governor wrote on the same day to Baumgartner, Blessing, Menichella, Ansiaux, Holtrop, and to Brofoss inviting him to London in January. His personal letter to Baumgartner marks the end of the French connection in this story. It read:

> Now that the first phase is over I should like to thank you and Calvet for all the help you gave to Stevens over the last few weeks and also to congratulate you on the firm measures which I know owe much to your inspiration and perseverance.
>
> As you know, I have never wavered from the view that the real things that matter in Europe are a strong economy in the UK and France and real co-operation between UK, France and Germany. If the Central Banks, with the support of the Treasuries, have as I hope made a real step towards breaking down the ridiculous and dangerous situations which were developing it is something we can be very pleased about. We can only pray that it works out well.

It is to be supposed that Baumgartner replied, probably in his own hand and in French. But since the reply does not survive in Threadneedle Street, perhaps Per Jacobsson, long the most devout apostle of convertibility, should have the last word. In a letter of thanks for the telegram that the Governor had sent him, he wrote:

Thank you for your telegram since it makes us very happy here to know that we have been at least in some measure helpful at this juncture when such important steps have been taken along lines which have for long been dear to the hearts of both of us. I am, of course, exceedingly glad that it came off before the end of the year and that the operation was carried out in close cooperation with the French and the other continental countries. I am sure, as I told you years ago, that your great knowledge of the French mentality will prove useful in the relations of your country with the continent.

As the curtain came down on the long and often depressing chronicle play that had started in 1950, if not earlier, and bore the title 'Convertibility', the actors deserved several curtain calls. In the last act the principal players had demonstrated an impressive talent for effective financial diplomacy in Europe. Officials in the Bank and the Treasury had collaborated effortlessly and efficiently to gain their agreed objective. Despite frictions that had occurred since the Suez crisis in 1956, there is every indication that in this operation the Treasury had complete confidence and trust in the Bank and every indication that the Bank kept the Treasury very fully informed of all it was doing in Paris, Frankfurt, or Basle. At the critical phase Mynors, Stevens, and their advisers played their part to perfection, while the Governor's long and close attention to friendship with his European colleagues, most especially with the Governor of the Bank of France, proved invaluable. But a special round of applause would have been deserved by that unpolitical politician, the Chancellor of the Exchequer. Seemingly unconcerned for himself, he never interfered more than was necessary, never put himself on stage until he judged the time was absolutely right, and never put a foot wrong with the Prime Minister. The Bank and the Treasury were lucky to have him in No. 11 at that moment.

Nonetheless, few members of the audience would have allowed their judgement about the play to be dimmed by the brilliance of the final performance. All that had happened, give or take the local difficulty with the French, was that the UK had taken advantage of a favourable and probably fleeting opportunity to remove the anomaly of the two rates for converting sterling into dollars. The underlying problem of sterling remained. As long ago as 1950, following the crises of 1947 and 1949 and when the breakdown of exchange control over the current transactions of non-residents had become undeniable, the Bank had begun worrying about how sterling could be managed in conditions of convertibility without periodic crises that would progressively destroy its inherited functions as a reserve and trading currency. Not until the end of the period, and even then out of a conviction born only out of apparent

John Stevens, Executive Director 1957–1964

practical necessity, did the Bank stake almost all on the uncertain performance of the UK economy and the uncertain reliability of its management. Earlier it had tried all it could to obtain additional protection from crisis by a special fortification of the reserves, by some measure of greater exchange flexibility, and, at one stage, by substantial further immobilisation of sterling balances. But whether through opposition in Whitehall, disinterest in Washington, or the gradual surrender to continental interests, its efforts had been in vain. Perhaps the Bank, since 1946 a subordinate institution, was not always the best of advocates, not always tactically wise, and no clearer about Europe than anyone else. Yet its strategic vision about sterling was more correct than most and less obscured by optimistic attitudes about what the British economy could achieve in respect of its external commitments and domestic social goals.

The Bank also saw more clearly than most that unpopular unilateral action could not always be avoided if the UK was to get its way in international negotiation. The internationalism to which the British were attracted by their fading Great Power status could not in reality be relied upon to deliver everything or, in the case of sterling, deliver anything very much. But that was how it was, and in December 1958 an opportunity had been taken and an anomaly terminated. The special problem of sterling remained to tax abilities in Threadneedle Street for another two decades.

Sources

Bank files

G1/99	Governor's File: Exchange Policy (March 1955 – February 1958)
OV38/52	International Monetary Fund (April – December 1957)
OV38/54–5	International Monetary Fund (July – November 1958)
OV44/11	Sterling and Sterling Area Policy: United Kingdom – Sterling Policy (May 1957 – June 1958)
OV44/21–4	Sterling and Sterling Area Policy: Unification of all Non-Resident Sterling (July 1956 – December 1958)
OV53/1–3	International Monetary Reform (January 1958 – November 1960)

CHAPTER 10

DOMESTIC MONETARY POLICY
1952–1958: DISILLUSION AND DEBATE

(a) THE CONTEXT

THE RAISING of Bank Rate from $2\frac{1}{2}$% to 4% in March 1952, related in Chapter 6(b), was intended to demonstrate that the cautious dusting-off undertaken in October 1951 was no bluff. Four per cent was thought to be a high rate, well charged with psychological currents that would inspire confidence abroad and a change of expectations at home. Its undoubted novelty by comparison with official practice since 1932 and its fortunate association with the disinflationary after-effects of the Korean commodity boom combined to ensure its acceptance as a successful act of policy. But viewed in isolation from its favourable context, the 4% Bank Rate had done no more than confirm the modest element of interest-rate flexibility that had been added to a monetary policy hitherto reliant mostly on direct controls administered through requests to the banks. Though high by some comparisons with the past, and certainly a bold break with Governmental interest-rate attitudes of earlier post-war years, 4% was not high in relation to prevailing levels of private sector profitability; in real terms it was very low, or negative. Nor, accordingly, was it likely for long to weaken expectations of continuing full employment and high demand for goods and services. Its message was likely to fade with the passage of time. Yet monetary policy had been brought closer to the centre of the macro-economic stage. Besides being essential to the protection of sterling, it was part of the Conservative Government's alternative to a policy of planning and controls, an alternative that was to allow greater freedom while maintaining the bipartisan commitment to full employment in a free society. So monetary policy as now refurbished, was in future going to have to be used positively, alongside and in support of fiscal policy and as an everyday instrument. As such, it would need to get the desired results and obtain them in a more systematic and reliable manner than that provided by the once-over impact of a Bank Rate revival on a generation that had anyway mostly forgotten the circumstances of its long-departed golden age. Yet the framework that was completed in 1952, without much prior thought and at a time of crisis, was flawed by serious internal defects that were to become very apparent as time went on and were to dog the conduct of British monetary policy for two decades if not three.

Central to these defects were the remaining inhibitions surrounding the use of interest rates as the cutting edge of policy; inhibitions apparently shared by most of those concerned in the Bank and accepted without serious argument. Scattered references in policy files mention the substantial restrictive effect on private sector expenditure that was likely to be caused by short-term rates as high as, for example, 10%. But such rates are usually mentioned only to be dismissed as out of the question. In September 1957, it is true, Bank Rate was raised as high as 7%; but this was justified by the special and temporary economic conjuncture that was judged to be present and by another mood of desperation about external confidence in sterling. It was, moreover, accompanied by a tightening of direct controls. A 7% Bank Rate was used again in 1961 and 1964, while 8% was reached during the 1967 devaluation and again early in 1969, but always accompanied by direct controls over bank lending.

Since the issue was never thoroughly debated in the years leading up to the Radcliffe Report, it is not easy to isolate the various reasons for these interest-rate inhibitions. The hostility to higher interest rates on the political left has already been noted in earlier chapters. It derived in part from an emotive association of high Bank Rates with the politico-economic traumas of the inter-war years, but it also owed a good deal to post-war macro-economic fashion. This fashion had no regard for a restrictive policy instrument that was not positively selective in terms of domestic policy priorities; was thought indeed to be bluntly and perversely selective in so far as it restricted industrial investment or private housing rather than private consumption; was expensive for the Exchequer and the external balance; had effects that were almost impossible to quantify in advance; and risked upsetting expectations in so violent a fashion as to endanger full employment. To a quite considerable extent this hostility was carried over into the political centre or half-right, which governed the UK from 1951 to 1964 and conformed to the so-called 'Butskellite' consensus on economic goals and macro-economic method. This consensus always excluded control of the statistical money supply as a separate or 'intermediate' objective of policy. Accordingly there was no separate monetaristic role for the rate of interest, which continued to be regarded as simply another tool of demand management, like taxation or hire-purchase controls, albeit one with special external and expectational connotations but also with special domestic disadvantages if pressed beyond moderate use. Once the Bank had won its point about Bank Rate in October 1951 and March 1952, mainly with its eye on external opinion, it broadly conformed to this consensus about interest rates. Neither the Governor, nor his senior officials, nor his closer colleagues on the Court, dissented from it. There is some evidence to suggest that Mynors had rather different views but, as Deputy to Cobbold from March 1954, he did not press them.

Within the consensus the Bank of course occupied its special sterling-orientated perch. But it was no longer a dissenter; and much of its energies on the home finance side, were devoted to a succession of circle-squaring attempts to devise an effective domestic monetary policy that paid no close attention to the money supply as such; placed only limited reliance on manipulation of the price of money; and had therefore to rely heavily on trying to influence private expenditure by inducing changes in the availability of bank advances. It could not however rely indefinitely on 'requests' to banks or other financial institutions to restrict or reduce their lending without in the long-run destroying their nature as competitive private enterprises and provoking the growth of a parallel credit market on a scale that undermined the controls themselves. It therefore had to search for some other way of inducing changes in availability. The ultimate or even immediate fruitlessness of such a quest would have been clear enough if it had then been working with a financial system, in particular a banking system, that was markedly competitive in structure and practice. But this was far from the case. It has again to be remembered that for purposes of monetary policy the UK banking system consisted at that time of cartelised deposit banks – English, Scottish, and Northern Irish – whose published results were rendered obscure by reason of changes in the hidden reserves that the banks were permitted to maintain pursuant to the Companies Act 1948. Interest rates paid on term deposits, which were virtually all at short notice, were fixed by agreement between the banks and bore a conventional relationship to Bank Rate. There was no wholesale money market in the sense known in the 1970s and 1980s. Except through advertising and other product-differentiating means of cultivating the goodwill of customers, 'liability management' did not occur. Somewhat similar conditions prevailed in the provision of advances. But the banks were still very underlent, for during and immediately after the war they had built up large investments in British Government securities, amounting to about one-third of their total assets. Here no convention or rule applied and there was no interbank agreement. So 'asset management', involving the run-off or market sale of investments and application of the proceeds to increasing advances, could readily take place unless it became seriously unprofitable. Asset management could also occur if the liquidity of the banks comfortably exceeded the 30% ratio they customarily observed. Outside the clearing banks, there were the accepting houses, the Discount Market, the British overseas banks, and the foreign banks in London. But in the 1950s none of these were of much importance as lenders within the UK; and though uncartelised (except for the discount houses) they did not in practice constitute any kind of free market operating alongside the clearing banks.

A markedly uncompetitive system, together with the provisions of the Bank of England Act 1946, certainly made the banks responsive to 'requests' from the authorities regarding both lending priorities and quantitative limitation, provided the requests did not compel them to bear down too hard on individual customers or to break contractual agreements with them. In carrying out such requests the banks were for a time content to apply a no-poaching rule in order to prevent customers going to a second bank for an advance denied by the first. But this rule was disliked and it made the system of peacetime restrictive requests, first brought fully into being under the Labour Government in 1948, look too obviously what it was, namely the conversion of bank managers into administrators of a Government-imposed system of non-price credit rationing. Was there therefore some other means of exploiting the rules and conventions of the cartel so that a restriction of lending could be induced by the official creation, through the market, of the required balance-sheet pressures, reinforced by Bank Rate signals and messages? In this way restriction would not need to be accompanied by a no-poaching rule or by any official guidance other than a list of priorities derived from those in force for the CIC. It was obvious that balance-sheet pressures could be exerted by bringing pressure to bear on the 30% liquidity ratio through official funding operations in Government Debt; and if the banks were to respond by selling investments rather than restricting advances they might find that they could only do so at an unacceptable loss. But application of pressure depended upon the funding capabilities of the Bank and the Treasury. These were in turn affected by the size of the Exchequer deficit and by the state of the gilt-edged market, the latter being vulnerable not only to expectations of heavy official funding but also to expectations of heavy sales by the banks. So inducing restriction through market pressures was most unlikely to be an easy task. Nevertheless the Bank was bound to advise trying it. Despite Treasury indifference to the long-run competitive efficiency of the banks and a Treasury thirst for the apparent simplicity of lending ceilings, the Bank could not ignore the longer-run implications of such controls. Quite apart from the future of the banks as private enterprises, there was the risk that their co-operation with the Bank would diminish over time, thus leading to formal directives and an ensuing mass of avoidances engineered by the banks themselves. Furthermore, constricting the cartelised system through direct controls risked forcing the growth of new free-market credit institutions outside the Bank's jurisdiction. Such growth would weaken the effect of the controls and would still further undermine the co-operation of the banks. Successful use of induced balance-sheet pressures whose effect relied upon cartelised behaviour would itself be vulnerable to some of these untoward consequences. But it seems to have been thought that the vulnerability would be less than with outright credit ceilings.

Against this background the history of monetary policy in the 1950s, from the introduction of the 4% Bank Rate in 1952 until the Radcliffe Report in 1959, represents an encounter with dilemmas. These led first to disillusion with reliance on the Bank's desired 'market pressures' approach to credit restriction, secondly to the reimposition of a prolonged credit squeeze operated mostly through 'requests', thirdly to attempts to extend the scope of requests beyond and outside the banking system, and fourthly to a debate about new technical devices that could make the Bank's preferred approach less vulnerable to failure. Finally the dilemmas were resolved for a time by the combined use of a 7% Bank Rate and credit ceilings which helped to bring about an easier economic situation in which the controls over bank advances and consumer credit could be abandoned. With the approval of the Radcliffe Committee these were replaced by a combination of Bank Rate flexibility and ratio controls, the latter through a newly invented variant called Special Deposits. This was to last until the remaining inhibitions surrounding the former and the limitations inherent in the effectiveness of the latter compelled a reversion to 'requests' (alongside another period of 7% Bank Rate) when macro-economic difficulties recurred in 1961 and again in 1964–5. On the latter occasion the requests were altered so as to govern a formal system of quantitative ceilings or base-period rationing that was to grow in elaboration as attempts were made to stop avoidance while allowing at least some movement to occur in the structure of the banking system. Its numerous and growing disadvantages were to lead to it collapsing in its turn in 1971, during a temporarily favourable economic conjuncture, as part of the monetary revolution called 'Competition and Credit Control'.

Yet another set of dilemmas was to follow in the later 1970s, when the authorities sought to restrict 'liability management' on the part of the now uncartelised and competitive banking system by imposing incremental penalties on the growth of interest-bearing deposits. This was abandoned in 1980 during the early phase of monetarist policy and following the abolition of exchange control. During the whole post-war period, right up to 1980, direct credit controls of one kind or another were always regarded as a readily usable policy option, welcome to some and distasteful to others but nonetheless there to be used. When reimposed, they invariably provided a phase of temporary relief, real or imagined, which was invariably followed by mounting difficulties and discontent. The first full cycle, in the 1950s, was no exception.

An introductory explanation of the context within which the enhanced domestic monetary policy was debated, decided, and operated during this period would not be complete without reference to the administrative structure on the home side of the Bank and its prevailing relationship with the Treasury. Earlier chapters have recounted how these had been developed under the post-war Labour Government. They were to continue broadly unchanged throughout the pre-Radcliffe years even though monetary policy had acquired far greater importance. One of their central features was the continuing primacy of the Governor, supported by the Court, as the arbiter of Bank policy and the person through whom policy decisions were finally determined between the Bank and the Treasury and through whom requests were debated and agreed with the banks. Lying behind the Governor's position with respect to the Treasury was the formal position of the Court with respect to Bank Rate (subject to the Treasury's powers of statutory direction) and the formal position of the Bank with respect to powers of direction over banks. On the external side, by contrast, where the Bank managed the EEA and ran Exchange Control as agent for the Treasury, the power of the Governor remained very great but depended rather more upon the Bank's managerial, intellectual, and technical weight and rather less on such formal independence as remained to it.

On the external side, the relationship of agent and principal and the great complexity and range of the subject matter produced working relationships between the Bank and the Overseas Finance Division of the Treasury – below Governor or even Executive Director level – within which both debates on policy and discussions 'at technical level' took place. On the home side, the reverse was the case. The ambiguous formal relationships entrenched in 1946, together with a strong Governor and the administrative (though not intellectual) simplicity of the subject matter, encouraged a relative paucity of relationships below Governor level and discouraged debate with Whitehall about policy or about the whole subject of monetary policy – how it worked and how it should be operated.

Furthermore, none of those at first principally concerned – Peppiatt, Mynors, Beale, and Allen – showed a personal inclination to work for a modification of this state of affairs. The experience of 1948, when the Bank joined the working party on credit control chaired by Douglas Jay, was not repeated. Not until 1956, following the policy troubles of 1955 and before the setting up of the Radcliffe Committee, did the Chancellor and the Governor agree that a review of monetary policy be undertaken by a small group of their respective senior officials. Nor for its part did the Treasury attempt to involve the Bank at all closely in its own macro-economic deliberations. Not until after Radcliffe did the Bank participate in Budget discussions or in the preparation of official national income forecasts. It had participated in balance of payments forecasts for many years, but only because it produced much of the statistical information.

During these years, therefore, the normal practice of the Governor was to call for policy advice from individual members of the small home-finance team and for the most part adamantly to disallow prior discussion by his officials with Treasury officials, except 'at technical level'. Having held a meeting, made up his own mind, and more often than not written his own brief, he would then argue the Bank's case personally with the Chancellor or the Permanent Secretary, on occasion making what tactical mileage he could out of the Bank's formal position and his own public status. All of this was a procedure for resolutely retaining some worthwhile degree of independence and authority for the Bank and resisting encroachment from Whitehall. But in the absence of any usable declaration in the 1946 Act of public duties and responsibilities of the central bank and its Governor, and given the element of legal subordination to the Government contained in that Act, this was bound to be a task of increasing difficulty and tension as monetary policy became a matter of increasing political interest and concern. Nevertheless, Cobbold tackled it with some success and with all his customary determination and ability, believing as he did that he and his colleagues bore some responsibility to the public at large as well as to the Government of the day.

But he continued to tackle it with very limited resources. The Governor himself bore a very heavy and diverse burden of work while having no pretensions to skill in monetary economics and no early training in the management of markets.[1] His Home Finance Director, Peppiatt, was not the man to advocate or preside over an expansion of resources devoted to monetary policy. He remained a first-class market man, but not much

---

[1] These limitations made him a nervous witness before, for example, the Radcliffe Committee. Like Norman before him, he was well aware that economists on such bodies could easily lure him into an argument that soon took him out of his depth.

more. Nor was Beale, as Chief Cashier, interested in enlarging an empire that already made too many claims on his time. O'Brien, his principal Deputy and an expert delegator, was to appreciate the need for more resources and in particular the need for more intense and systematic use of statistical skills and economic advice, but he was not effective in this respect until some time after he succeeded Beale as Chief Cashier in 1955. Mynors, who became Deputy Governor in March 1954 in succession to Dallas Bernard, does not seem to have resisted the home finance status quo in the Bank at that time, whatever may have been his underlying opinions about the adequacy of the Bank's economic and statistical services. Nor did Allen, as Economic Adviser, resist the status quo until his own increasing workload suggested that another economist should be recruited. (After one false start, this was accomplished early in 1957.) Furthermore, the highly expectational, psychological, and non-quantitative approach to monetary economics favoured by both Mynors and Allen – quantification being confined to such exercises as short-run predictions of Exchequer financing or bank liquidity ratios – did not encourage the enlargement of the Bank's statistical and economic services, an exercise which was not set in hand until after the Radcliffe Report in 1959.

The upshot in the earlier 1950s was a small and efficient piece of machinery that provided the Governor with well-ordered advice on immediate policy questions at very short notice. It could likewise produce a brief critique, usually and rightly negative, of proposals for improving the technical mechanism at the authorities' disposal. But though sometimes capable of enunciating, usually very briefly, the elements of a monetary strategy, it was much less good at debating strategy and questioning the conventional wisdom. This made the Bank vulnerable to error that was rather more than tactical; and error in turn made the Bank vulnerable to encroachment by the Treasury. As mentioned earlier, the Bank's preferred approach to monetary policy in these years suffered from serious technical difficulties. This too made its relationship with the Treasury an awkward and unstable one.

(b) THINKING AS YOU GO: 1952–1954

On 18 March 1952, a week after Bank Rate had been raised to 4%, the Chief Cashier addressed the annual meeting[2] of the Branch Agents in tones of triumph. Reliance on physical controls and taxation to restrain inflationary tendencies in the private sector had been proved inadequate.

---

[2] Then held at Head Office in March of each year. It included, on the relevant Thursday, the annual Agents' Lunch given by the Governors and Directors in the Court Room.

Restraints on the supply of money through successive requests to the banks had also proved inadequate. The new Government had therefore decided to use the interest-rate weapon and the results were already there to be seen. The Bank was no longer powerless; it did not have to provide whatever cash the banks needed. At the same time, the banks' liquidity ratios had been sharply reduced by the Serial Funding operation of November 1951, thereby greatly helping the operation of the new policy. Advances rates had risen and the aim was to eliminate unnecessary loans. The restriction of credit 'would damp down unnecessary expenditure – particularly capital expenditure – and it was hoped this would release labour and resources for production and for export'. The Chief Cashier concluded by stressing the interaction of domestic and external problems. What was needed was a change in the general attitude and sentiment towards sterling. Aided by credit policy, this would be achieved by limiting the supplies of sterling so as to make it a wanted currency.

Beale was a monetary technician and an administrator, not an intellectual and not an economist.[3] His views at this time reflected realistically enough the novelty of a 4% Bank Rate and the potentialities of the interest-rate weapon, whose powers would be transmitted to the economy through a mixture of cost effects and availability effects. But later, when the familiar domestic and external problems were returning at the end of 1954 and when Beale himself was about to leave the service of the Bank, he was almost alone in roundly declaring that in the absence of direct controls the whole apparatus of monetary policy could not be made to work without much higher interest rates than those then contemplated. For the present, however, triumphalism ruled. Responding at the end of May to a request from the Governor for views about the merits of moving Bank Rate up to 5%, Beale declared that the new policy and the 4% Rate were producing the expected results. 'On all sides one sees that money is recognised as being no longer freely available for the asking, with the result that in some directions prices are being depressed through curtailment of demand.' That being so, a rise to 5% would simply look panicky. Moreover, it was not indicated by any upward pressure on rates in the money market and its probably depressing effect on the gilt market would make it more difficult to bring pressure to bear on bank liquidity through official sales of stock. It should be kept in reserve against a resumption of external crisis.

The Governor's question had been addressed to Peppiatt as Home Director and was occasioned by, as he put it, 'a good deal of talk about a

---

[3] When asked in May 1952 to talk to Lord Brand about the new monetary policy, he prudently declined and suggested that the task should fall to Allen.

further increase in Bank Rate' and by continuing anxiety about the external situation. It was the period of urgent official debate about external monetary strategy following the first rejection of Robot and the likely need for early action was still very much in the Governor's mind. Accordingly, he asked Peppiatt for his opinion and for the views of others directly concerned, whom he listed as Beale, Allen, Mynors, Niemeyer, Bolton, and Parsons. Although each added his own special slant, the unanimous view of the latter five, from which Peppiatt himself did not dissent, supported the Chief Cashier. Allen, who felt that immediate action was needed to reduce public spending, was content to sit tight with 4% for the present so long as bank advances were held at their recent level (they had in fact begun to fall) and did not need to be restrained by a further interest-rate demonstration or a stepping-up of official funding. Mynors felt that 5% would be no good substitute for the cuts in public spending that he too felt were needed. In his view it was the absence of further cuts that made it appear as if HMG were relying only on monetary policy and, because of the continuing external dangers, caused talk of a further rise in Bank Rate. But 4% was working well and it would be best to leave things alone unless and until the situation again deteriorated 'before other things were done', when they would be 'forced upon the Government hurriedly, probably accompanied in the circumstances by a rate of 6% or 7%'. Niemeyer, in seven lines of typescript, was of a like opinion. Bolton felt that in the context of inconvertible sterling and exchange control a higher Bank Rate would not of itself attract more foreign funds. It could have a favourable confidence effect, but this would become 'an ephemeral emotion' if unaccompanied by a movement of funds on interest-rate grounds. Moreover, the economic climate was becoming deflationary and a higher Bank Rate would make this worse and thus irretrievably damage the Bank Rate weapon for future use. It should therefore only be considered 'in connection with some short-term and limited protective objective arising out of, say, the introduction of sterling convertibility'. Parsons, whose particular concern was the restriction of overseas borrowing in London, preferred a rise in Bank Rate to any further tightening of direct control. But he agreed that this was not the time to hoist a storm signal. Finally, Kershaw, whom the Governor brought in for an additional opinion, agreed closely with Mynors.

Cobbold held his own counsel but gave no indication of dissent from the advice given. On his instructions, the exercise had been carried out very quickly. Apart from Kershaw, who was not consulted until the rest of the advice had been given, all members of the team responded within forty-eight hours. Although by some of the standards of later decades the arguments were notably bereft of quantification, they had all been marshalled and all been used to present firm judgements. It was perhaps not a very difficult task on this occasion, especially when the new policy was clearly benefiting so much from its shock effect on the private sector; but the expeditious way in which the exercise was carried out and the nature of its contents showed that the Bank was fast learning the new Bank Rate game. As an example of that game, this instance was not very different in its outlines from other examples that could be taken from the history of the following twenty years.

Over the following months, as the external tension gradually eased and domestic pressures subsided, thoughts of a 5% Rate receded. The encouraging overall downward trend of bank advances continued. In the six months up to May 1952 they had fallen by £12 million, compared to a rise to £212 million in the corresponding period of 1950–1. In June and July the special monthly figures, which had been continued for a further six months, showed further falls in advances and the Chief Executive Officers of the clearing banks told Peppiatt in July that this was likely to persist. Advances to retailers, to the textile industries, and to the personal and professional category were all reported to be falling, while those to higher priority borrowers in engineering, chemicals, and steel were all rising or expected to rise. Meanwhile, however, the Governor was telling the Chancellor that credit restraint in the private sector was only part of the story and emphasising the importance of keeping public spending within the limits of what the country could afford. Late in August the Bank began to devote more time and systematic attention to Government Debt operations and the liquidity of the banks. Here, the outlook was less promising and attitudes were far from triumphant.

At the end of August 1952 the Deputy Governor wrote to Edmund Compton[4] in the Treasury expressing the Bank's concern at the rise, only partly seasonal, in Treasury Bills and the sharp recovery of the liquidity ratio to 35·9%. 'Pressure on bank advances', he wrote, 'is the key point of our present credit policy, but the pressure on their advances cannot be kept up when their holdings of floating debt get out of line with other assets.' The outlook for the remainder of the financial year was poor. Even allowing for successful refinancing in November of the maturing one-year Serial Funding Bonds and for substantial conversion of $2\frac{1}{2}$% National War Bonds 1951–3, it looked to Allen as if clearing-bank liquidity would be as high as 36% in March 1953. Furthermore, he judged that: 'There is

[4] *Compton, Edmund Gerald GCB, KBE (b.1906).* Educated Rugby and New College, Oxford. Assistant Secretary, HM Treasury 1942–7, Under-Secretary 1947–9, Third Secretary 1949–58, Comptroller and Auditor-General 1958–66.

enough slack in the present supply of money to permit a most undesired expansion both of home investment and of consumption if provocations to spend more develop from an eased supply of investment goods and from higher wages. If we count on these provocations occurring, then I think we must also expect that we will not be able to put up enough resistance to them.' Allen had begun to take a close interest in the projection of Exchequer financing and its associated effect on the banking system, with special reference to the seasonal minimum in deposits and liquidity that occurred every March. He became a considerable expert without being able to improve the accuracy of forecasts, which he sometimes liked to rename 'illustrations'. Such accuracy was a goal that was to elude generations of Bank officials; but the projections continued to be made, even though it was always agreed that the uncertainties inherent in the task were ineradicable.

On this first occasion his forecast proved too pessimistic. Although the Exchequer out-turn was a good deal worse than estimated, funding operations were far more successful. The maturing Serial Funding Bonds and National War Bonds were more than fully refinanced through new bonds maturing in 1953, 1954, and 1955, partly by subscriptions on issue in November and partly through subsequent official sales through the market. The banks themselves felt able to reduce their first-line liquidity and were net buyers on a large scale, their investments increasing by some £225 million in the last quarter of 1952, a sum equivalent to over 3% off their liquidity ratio. Market conditions remained favourable in the new year and a small new issue of stock, 3% Exchequer 1960, was made at the end of February. It brought in £30 million from the public, the rest being sold by Issue over the following few months (it had all gone by early June). The liquidity ratio of the clearing banks came to 32·9% at mid-March, which gave a better appearance then 36% might have done. But, as Beale pointed out at the time, there had been no squeeze. A ratio of 32·9% was comfortable and had been achieved by the choice of the banks themselves. The whole experience gave little encouragement to the belief that bringing pressure to bear on bank liquidity through official operations in the gilt market would prove a reliable weapon of policy. In the meantime, Allen himself remained uneasy and his unease was shared by the Governor, who wrote to the Chancellor early in January urging a reduction in Government borrowing and fiscal changes designed to encourage more saving.

These forebodings may have been well founded in the longer term, but in practice there was little cause for immediate concern. Bank advances, as the Chief Executive Officers told Peppiatt in March, were likely to run level. Bank deposits were rising at less than 3% per annum. Sterling remained firm and the external prospect was satisfactory. The Chancellor was able to reduce Income Tax in his Budget. Things were at last getting better. The yield on long-dated gilt-edged, which had risen above $4\frac{1}{2}$% in July 1952, fell below 4% in April 1953, while the dividend yield on ordinary shares had fallen from 7% to 6%. In June a further tranche of Exchequer 3% 1960 was well received, nearly half being taken up on issue by the public. Yet Bank Rate remained stuck at 4%, the level to which it had been driven by the exchange crisis in March of the previous year. What was to be done with it? Wait until the breathing space came to an end and then move higher still? Or move down in the interim, even though the domestic situation might not call for it? Another new exercise in policy advice had become timely. On 30 June 1953 the Governor asked Peppiatt, Beale, Mynors, Allen, and Niemeyer to consider the wisdom of a move in Bank Rate in September 'if things run on an even keel over the summer', adding that he was still 'bothered by the weight of the debt charge on HMT over against short-term debt in particular'. He also asked for advice about a possible funding operation in the autumn and whether any modifications should be made in credit directives. At the same time the Bank was actively considering some relaxation of the controls on banking credits to non-residents, controls that had been tightened early in 1952.

This time, the response to the Governor's question revealed important differences of approach and of opinion, exemplified by the views of Niemeyer on the one side and Allen on the other. Niemeyer thought it important to show that Bank Rate was flexible and could be moved down in response to the strength of sterling and the trend of rates elsewhere without signalling a return to cheap money and without any alteration in credit directives. He recognised that a reduction might convey a wrong message to those engaged in wage bargaining and recognised that it could look wrong alongside 'the Chancellor's obvious unwillingness even to contemplate, let alone to carry out, real restrictions in Budget expenditure'. But he thought these factors were outweighed by the others. He favoured a move in July rather than September and added, for good measure, the argument of *reculer pour mieux sauter*. Allen, writing a week later and at much greater length than Niemeyer's customary single page, argued that 'with a more deliberate endeavour to control domestic activity, policy may now require to be unresponsive to traditional tests of improvement in the external strength of sterling and lowering of rates abroad'. This view, he added, 'reflects a diminution in the role of international capital movements and the fact that direct controls and foreign aid make changes in reserves (perhaps especially when favourable) a less useful test of the country's real

Maurice Allen, Economic Adviser

international position'. As to the maintenance of flexibility, he argued that this did not require frequent movements in the Rate so much as 'a conviction by all concerned that they must not get themselves out on a limb in case credit should be tightened'. Armed with this approach to the Governor's question, Allen considered the domestic economic situation and the balance of payments outlook, judged that neither were out of the line with the Budget strategy, and concluded: 'In brief, I see nothing but the Treasury Bill argument [cost to the Exchequer] to initiate a proposal for lowering the Rate at the present time.' A cut might become appropriate in the autumn, but as a stimulus to the economy it would be better to relax control of overseas lending connected with UK exports. 'Such measures may well prove at least as effective a stimulus as a change of Rate and most probably are a step in a better direction.'

The Governor, who discussed these differing views with the home finance team on 15 July, was sympathetic to both sides. He certainly did not want to engage in any significant relaxation of policy. But neither did he want to be pegged to 4%, which he thought a comparatively high Bank Rate in itself. There was also a special technical problem arising from the persistence of the dual Rate (Bank Rate 4%, Bank Lending Rate against Treasury Bills $3\frac{1}{2}$%). Market rates for Treasury Bills had fallen, to $2\frac{3}{8}$% or less from nearly $2\frac{1}{2}$% in the spring of 1952. The Bank had not resisted this development. The commercial bill rate, however, had remained at the 3% that had been agreed between the Bank and the Discount Market in March 1952. The rigidity of this 3% was attracting the criticism that it was out of line with the market and unnecessarily hindered the development of bill finance for overseas trade (within the limits allowed by exchange control). But 3% could not simply be abandoned, and the rate allowed to fall, without leaving the 4% Bank Rate clearly out of line with market rates generally. So why not unify the two rates at $3\frac{1}{2}$%, by reducing Bank Rate to that level and abandoning the special rate against Treasury Bills? Commercial bill rates would drop sharply, to a level below $2\frac{1}{2}$%, but this could be presented as helping the finance of overseas trade, while the cut in Bank Rate would be presented as mainly a technical adjustment. At the same time, if the Treasury were to accept a set of proposals put forward by Bolton (principally including restoration of the 120-day maximum usance for bills drawn under acceptance credits in favour of non-residents and in respect of UK exports), there could ensue the relaxation of controls over overseas lending favoured by Allen. All the points at issue would then have been met. The Governor wrote to the Chancellor accordingly on 16 July. Attached to the letter was a draft passage for inclusion in a Parliamentary Statement, which would seek to make it abundantly clear that there was to be no general relaxation of policy. Both Butler and Bridges accepted the technical arguments but were now hesitant about timing and presentation, Cobbold referring in his diary to 'the Chancellor's delicate position at the moment'.[5] There were further meetings, but at the end of July the

---

[5] It was the first of several moments when Butler got near to the Premiership. Churchill had been ordered to take a complete rest following a stroke suffered late in June. Eden was recovering in the US from major surgery and it was, for the time being, doubted whether

Governor was told that although the exchange control relaxations could go ahead, a cut in Bank Rate would have to wait.

By mid-September the Chancellor's special difficulties had subsided and he was ready to agree to a Bank Rate of $3\frac{1}{2}\%$ and abolition of the dual rate. The change was made on 17 September, the Bank announcing that Bank Rate and the special Lending Rate against Treasury Bills had been unified at $3\frac{1}{2}\%$. This, the press and public were told, would 'allow more freedom in the day-to-day operation of the market and will facilitate the flexible use of Bank Rate in either direction as circumstances require'. Reading between the lines, this meant that the problem of the commercial bill rate would be eliminated, that 'Bank Rate' as unified would be more in touch with prevailing market rates, and that going to $4\frac{1}{2}\%$ (say) from $3\frac{1}{2}\%$ would be easier than going from 4% to 5%. A press briefing, telegrams to overseas central banks, and letters sent by the Governor to all the banking associations in receipt of his request, all emphasised that the change did not involve any alteration of monetary policy. Existing requests remained in force. Following the change, the Treasury Bill rate fell a little, to $2\frac{1}{8}\%$, while Commercial Bills fell from 3% to $2\frac{3}{16}\%$. Rates on bank advances were cut by $\frac{1}{2}\%$, a technical result of the fall in Bank Rate but a real one nevertheless, whatever the associated official message.

The heavily negative presentation of the change reflected in some part the coincident slight and seasonal weakening of sterling, which fell to $2.80\frac{1}{4}$ in September 1953, but also a sharper warning tone contained in a joint note by Mynors and Allen. The domestic grounds for reducing Bank Rate seemed rather weaker than they had done in July and the external situation was not quite so good. In the longer run, they wrote, 'insufficient progress is being made in reducing Government expenditure and in raising the whole status of export trade as a part of national activity, while the level of industrial investment (relative to that elsewhere) is perhaps still too low'. The inference was that monetary policy could not play a very active role for the time being. 'There are no present grounds for further stringency, while to lower rates might intensify a feeling of complacency which is not justified.' Nonetheless the economists now went along with the technical arguments for $3\frac{1}{2}\%$ while warning against relying too much, in presentation, on the technical nature of the change. It was not really the case, they said, that the market was influencing the Bank. The situation tolerated rather than warranted a lowering of the Rate.[6] When Bank Rate

---

he would be fit to sustain the burden of No. 10. It fell to Butler and Salisbury, the next two senior Ministers, to keep the Government running.

[6] They could have added that it had at least in part arisen because of the Bank's own open-market tactics.

was raised, they added, people were told to take monetary policy seriously. It was not then open to the authorities to tell people when their actions should be taken seriously and when not. A lowering of rates, though small, could lead to a change in the climate of bank borrowing even though 'requests' were unchanged. These and other considerations afforded ground for misgiving. Nonetheless the risk should be taken 'in order to avoid the greater risk of finding the weapon of monetary policy again unusable'.

There may have been something in the argument that the all-round improvement in the situation since March 1952 deserved some acknowledgement from the monetary arm of policy, through use of the instrument whose restored flexibility had been so loudly proclaimed. Yet, as the economists had pointed out, the situation did not require any stimulus. The level of interest rates, though reached during a crisis, was not too high. Closer examination would rather have suggested it was too low. But the economic advice was framed very much in terms of expectations and of the message a change in Bank Rate might convey. Against that advice, it could be argued that the abolition of the dual rate and the reduction in Bank Rate to $3\frac{1}{2}\%$ would not do much to stimulate optimistic expectations; if it did, these could be offset by official messages that there had been no change in policy. If the cost of credit was indeed not acting as a significant restraint on expenditure but if, for other reasons, it was desired to lower it slightly, the natural if rather crude outcome was simply to supplement the change in Rate by issuing an accompanying message so as to avoid encouraging undesirable expectations. Mynors and Allen had warned against muddying the waters by this special labelling of particular Bank Rate changes and would presumably have preferred official admission that a fall of $\frac{1}{2}\%$ in the Rate was indeed a slight easing of policy. But the Governor, whose grasp of the subject was practical and administrative rather than intellectual, seems to have taken no notice, to have heeded his advisers' warnings about the economy, and to have proceeded without difficulty to the use of a countervailing message.

This procedure could serve well enough on a particular occasion when special technical reasons were present. But if used repeatedly it risked discrediting the instrument of Bank Rate itself, undermining the rationale of its resurrection in 1952, and reinforcing the need to rely on direct controls. Yet it was used again, though less forcefully, in May 1954, when Bank Rate was cut to 3%, a move whose wisdom was later doubted by Cobbold himself. The motivation for the cut appears to have been external rather than domestic. In the US, the Federal Reserve discount rate had been cut to $1\frac{3}{4}\%$ from 2% in February 1954, following a fall in the US

Treasury Bill rate to 1%. The Bank of France also cut its rate and there was considerable talk about interest rates at the Basle meeting in February. In London, Bill rates tended to fall a little and the Bank offered no resistance. The gilt-edged market remained quietly firm. The exchange rate was also firm, with sterling averaging $2.8194 in April and the discount on transferable (newly unified) falling to $\frac{7}{8}$%. There was talk of an inflow of short-term funds to London, prompted by a covered arbitrage margin favourable to investment in sterling. In his advocacy of an early further move towards convertibility, Bolton was arguing that the inflow of funds, partly 'hot' money, could become excessive and misleading. The reserves rose steadily, by over $460 million in the first five months of the year, and were approaching $3 billion. But neither the domestic economic situation nor the domestic banking situation looked as if they needed another lowering of short-term interest rates. Industrial and commercial confidence had further increased. Profits were good. The Budget had introduced fiscal incentives to fixed investment. The fall in bank advances had come to an end and the banks were telling Peppiatt that they expected a slow rise over the months ahead. They were under no balance-sheet restraint. Liquidity was a comfortable 33% in March and the ratio of investments to deposits was as high as 36%, the banks having further increased their holdings of gilts during a funding operation in October 1953, which had converted maturing Serial Funding Bonds into further bonds maturing in 1954 and 1957 and which had also included an issue of 3% stock 1962–3 for cash. Despite this operation and despite an offer early in 1954 to holders of $2\frac{1}{2}$% National War Bonds due on 1 March to convert into a $3\frac{1}{2}$% stock maturing in 1969, Treasury Bills in market hands grew by £173 million over the financial year, closely in line with the growth of bank deposits.

Peppiatt and Mynors (now Deputy Governor) both drew attention to the risks of a cut to 3%. The former, though listing the external arguments, noted among contra-indications high business activity, low unemployment, rising bank advances, an active stock market, and rising commodity prices. A cut to 3% would produce a saving for the Exchequer and, in Peppiatt's view, bring Bank Rate into close touch with market rates; but such arguments were somewhat make-weight. Mynors began by remarking: 'The most important aspect of the Bank Rate in these days is the line which it is thought to give on the attitude and expectations of the authorities.' Given the latest reports from the US, a reduction to 3%, would not be taken to indicate official fears of a recession. It might instead be 'interpreted to mean that we are content to follow the US line of ultra-easy money, with inflationary possibilities...Whatever public statements were made (and it would be desirable to say even less than on the last occasion) there would be a risk of stimulating some latent inflationary forces at home.' However, the Governor was more impressed by the external arguments, including presumably the fear of a large hot-money inflow, and obtained the Chancellor's approval for a cut of 3%, which took place on 13 May. Cobbold personally drafted both the text of the telegram to the principal central banks and the guidance to the press. The first began: 'Bank Rate movement today is a routine adjustment to new conditions and has no special significance.' The second began similarly and continued: 'Many factors have to be taken into account, including market conditions at home and overseas and general developments since the last change in Bank Rate. All in all it is considered that the new Rate is more appropriate to present conditions.' According to Reuters, the City, took a rather different view. The cut was regarded as yet another expression of confidence by the Chancellor of the Exchequer about Britain's economic situation. Some hot money might be withdrawn, but in the longer run the cut would give added confidence to overseas investors. Reuters' report ended: 'In addition it will no doubt encourage big business to extend its activities and give industry further grounds for confident expansion.' The Bill rate fell to $1\frac{5}{8}\%$ and bank advances rates steadied at around $4\frac{1}{2}\%$.

The cautious but confusing policy of reducing interest rates while describing each downward move as routine, or as indicating no general change of policy, was now to encounter a foreseeable hazard. On 14 July the Board of Trade Order of February 1952, imposing control over the terms of hire-purchase agreements, was revoked and not replaced. There remained only the background monetary control exercised by the banks and the CIC over lending to hire-purchase finance houses. Nobody could credibly describe the abolition of terms control as a routine adjustment and for its part the Bank had warned the Treasury that the background monetary control, already under strain, would in consequence have to be relaxed. This was done a few weeks later, the Treasury having agreed that it would be better to avoid so expansionist a message as would be implied by doing both operations at the same time. On 19 August the CIC was advised by the Chancellor that it need no longer exercise a rigid ban on issues by hire-purchase companies; and simultaneously the Governor advised the banks that he would not object if they abandoned the 10% cut in facilities to such companies agreed in 1952. It was abandoned on the following day.

The possibility of relaxing or suspending hire-purchase controls had been raised in Whitehall as early as May 1953. The Bank had opposed it, Allen remarking: 'I think it is still at least a bit early to talk of easing hire-purchase restrictions.' In the autumn of 1953 strong representations were made to the Treasury by the Society of Motor Manufacturers and Traders, who argued for removal of the monetary control on hire-purchase finance houses and for a relaxation of terms control over purchases of commercial vehicles. They were of the opinion that terms control was itself a sufficient control. The monetary restrictions either limited finance-house competition or else encouraged a multiplication of small companies that could be capitalised under the £50,000 minimum written into the Control of Borrowing Order. From the Bank a letter was sent to the Treasury arguing that the case for easing terms control was unproven and that there was no reason to relax. There the matter stood until June 1954 when the Board of Trade suddenly proposed complete suspension of terms control, mainly because of increasing avoidance. Hire-purchase sales were in fact booming. Contracts for motor vehicles were running one-third higher than a year before. At the same time small hire-purchase firms were proliferating while large firms had reportedly begun to take short-term deposits so as to sidestep the restrictions imposed by the Bank and the CIC. The Treasury was minded to accept the Board of Trade's arguments. The Bank, surprisingly, did not oppose them and confined itself to securing some parallel if limited relaxation in the monetary restrictions themselves. It seems likely that the Governor was beginning to worry about avoidance of those controls. For example, he reacted strongly against the acquisition of a deposit-taking finance house by the Commercial Bank of Scotland.[7] Although the economic situation hardly warranted it, the relaxation of controls over consumer credit may not have seemed unattractive to the Bank in so far as it enabled 'monetary controls' to be relaxed as well. The more reason, then, to have gone more slowly earlier on with reductions in Bank Rate, however labelled. Within weeks of the suspension of hire-purchase controls the barometer began to fall. Sterling fell by over a cent in August and below $2.80 in September. The reserves fell slightly. The restoration of convertibility, widely expected abroad, was again postponed and the discount on transferable began to widen. As the autumn wore on, it became increasingly evident that monetary policy would have to change course.

At the end of September Allen sent the Governor, Bolton, and Peppiatt a note on the current economic position. After an examination of wages, productivity, commodity prices, new orders, consumer demand, public current spending, domestic investment, and external trade he concluded: 'Something of a demand inflation seems to be arriving, quite substantially

---

[7] See Chapter 11(d) below.

on export account, but as a whole not yet so marked as to suggest results worse than lengthening order books. At the same time, prospective cost increases may easily exceed concurrent economies and demands may be quite strong enough to encourage passing costs on in higher prices.' The immediate objective was to deter both labour and business from 'over-exploiting their success', but curiously Allen did not think monetary action was yet needed.

At the annual Mansion House Dinner a few weeks later both the Chancellor and the Governor referred to inflationary tendencies in the economy, a message endorsed by Oscar Hobson in the *News Chronicle* at the end of October. The bankers, meanwhile, told Peppiatt that there were no signs of any slackening of the high rate of business activity and that in consequence they looked for a further rise in advances, though not on any 'spectacular or dangerous' scale. Although a rise was indeed very evident from the latest figures, the Governor, talking to the Chancellor early in November, advised that a change in Bank Rate was unlikely to be needed before the end of the year. However, it was subsequently agreed between them that market rates should be firmed up a little by bringing the Discount market into the Bank when the opportunity offered. Sterling had fallen to $2.78\frac{5}{8}$ by the end of the month and the Treasury Bill rate had begun to rise slightly (by the end of the year it had reached $1\frac{7}{8}\%$ from a low of $1\frac{5}{16}\%$ in October). The yield on long-dated gilts also rose, from $3\cdot35\%$ in October to $3\cdot64\%$ in December. Writing in the *Financial Times* on 30 November, Roy Harrod, the distinguished economist, drew attention to rising order books, lengthening deliveries, and growing labour shortages. Modest early action was needed, comprising a rise in Bank Rate and a more restrictive request to the banks, if much more painful treatment was to be avoided at a later stage. Hobson, writing a week later, went further. Taxes were too high and should be cut, while Bank Rate should be used 'boldly and resourcefully'. He thought the Governor was 'inclined to assess the powers of Bank Rate too modestly'.

Looking ahead to a period of renewed restriction, the Bank now debated the effectiveness of its armoury. Unfortunately this particular debate was largely about an irrelevance. In mid-November, after reading an article by W. T. C. King in *The Banker* entitled 'Flexible Money and Full Employment', the Governor had started the debate by asking his advisers for views about King's suggestion that changes in the exchange reserves should be allowed to have a more automatic impact on the credit base and hence on domestic monetary conditions. This was a subject in which the substance was well mixed up with the technicalities. But in a paper sent to the Governor early in January 1955 the Chief Cashier had little difficulty

P. S. Beale, Chief Cashier 1949–1955

demonstrating that an automatic link between Bank Rate and changes in the reserves would be out of place in the world of Bretton Woods, Butskellism, and the Sterling Area. He was supported by Peppiatt, Allen, and Fisher. As Allen put it: 'The leading problem of monetary policy with full employment is only obscured by talk of "natural" movements or of rules for credit policy. The main issue is whether monetary controls are to be used to resist external deficit and inflation due to rising wage costs. Precautionary monetary action against many causes of inflation coming from the private side – speculative inventory and investment booms, unduly high consumption out of a given income – should not injure but protect the stability of activity and employment.' These thoughts constituted good advice but did not address themselves to the question that was worrying the Governor. 'Are we sure', he replied, 'that we do not need to furbish up our weapons or look for new ones, e.g. spreading Exchequer movements more evenly over the year, arranging for a varying cash ratio?'

Underlying the Governor's unease may well have been the Chief

Cashier's warnings about the difficulty of bringing effective pressure to bear upon the clearing banks other than by direct requests. Beale saw this quite clearly and did not hesitate to say so. As early as the previous July, when monetary control over finance houses was being discussed, he had postscripted a note to the Governor: 'We must not overlook the possibilities of an indiscriminate increase in bank advances, with the clearing bank ratio of advances to deposits at 28% compared with a pre-war maximum of 50%.' In a note to his Deputy (O'Brien) written early in the above debate, he said: 'We must make the points in my early draft about the position of the bankers in present circumstances, viz. that not only is their advances ratio very low but despite our funding operations they are still possessed of large amounts of maturing short-terms bonds...Therefore a very large increase in rates would be needed before any effective cut in bank advances could be expected to take effect.' The same point was made, though less forcefully, in the paper sent to the Governor early in January, which attracted general support. It was an awkward point, focussing on the central difficulty of policy.

It is a matter of speculation how subsequent discussion, throughout 1955 and after, would have proceeded if Beale had remained at his post. But that was not to be. He was only forty-eight and might have expected to succeed Peppiatt, who was due to retire as Home Director early in 1957. But he had made powerful enemies in the Bank and was not popular in the City. He was widely considered arrogant and his treatment of subordinates who did not come up to his high standards was often resented. His remarkable technical and administrative abilities could not make up for these obstacles. Nor was Beale popular with the Treasury, whose officials found him a reluctant provider of operational information. So he was encouraged to leave. In the autumn of 1954 a new special financial institution, not dissimilar to the Finance Corporation for Industry, was being set up in India with the approval of the IBRD. It was to be called the Industrial Credit and Investment Corporation of India (ICICI) and the post of first General Manager was to be filled from abroad. Beale, who had served as Secretary to the Reserve Bank of India for a period in the 1930s, was persuaded to take the job, having been discouraged from believing that he would in due course be appointed to the Court. On 3 December it was announced that he was resigning as Chief Cashier, with the approval of the Bank, in order to take up a post of great importance, namely the general managership of the ICICI.[8] Not long afterwards it was announced

[8] In the course of a research project sponsored by the IBRD, the author met Beale in Bombay in October 1955. Far from his oak-panelled sanctum in Threadneedle Street, he was to be found in a makeshift office at one end of a large empty upper-floor room above a

that he would be succeeded at the Bank by O'Brien. At the same time, in order to keep him level with O'Brien, Parsons was promoted from Deputy Chief Cashier to Assistant to the Governors. Beale stayed in India for three years; he then returned to the City and joined Samuel Montagu, later acquiring a number of industrial and commercial directorships.

O'Brien, who took over from Beale shortly before his forty-seventh birthday, had been first Deputy Chief Cashier on the home side since 1951 and had been associated with the revival of monetary policy from the start. Notwithstanding the bleak opinion of his departing predecessor, he felt that the restrictive policy that looked like being needed before long should, at any rate in the first instance, be pursued through Bank Rate messages combined with the exertion of official pressure on the liquidity of the banks. As it happened, the prospects of achieving the pressure that had been absent over the two previous years now looked rather good. The cash needs of the Exchequer had been sharply reduced, partly on budgetary account, partly on account of less lending to nationalised industries and partly by the turn-round in the fortunes of the EEA. As a result, receipts from National Savings, together with the normal rise in the Note Issue, looked like covering most of the Exchequer's remaining cash requirement. Thus even if funding through gilt-edged were small,[9] the rise in financing through Treasury Bills would not be large. There were, moreover, indications that these Bills were being bought on an increasing scale by non-bank investors. Ever since the unpegging of autumn 1951 they had yielded more than seven-day bank deposits, the margin in December 1954 exceeding $\frac{3}{4}$%. All in all, with bank advances now rising quite rapidly, it was possible to predict with some confidence that liquidity ratios would fall sharply. In Allen's view, conveyed to the Governor via Peppiatt on 21 December, the average ratio would be reduced to little more than the 30% minimum by the end of March. It must have seemed that if pressure could be maintained thereafter, there might possibly follow some favourable change in the behaviour of the banks. But presumably this itself would

---

department store. He treated me to a brilliant and humorous exposition of the hazards of establishing new industrial enterprises in developing countries. I recall no trace of the qualities that had led to his departure from the Bank.

[9] In June 1954 there had been a cash and conversion operation in which 3% National Defence Stock 1954–8 had been called and 2% Conversion 1958–9 issued. In July there had been a conversion offer of $2\frac{1}{2}$% stock 1963–4 or $3\frac{1}{2}$% 1999–2004 in exchange for $1\frac{3}{4}$% Serial Funding Bonds maturing in November. Finally, in December, holders of a $2\frac{1}{4}$% stock maturing in February 1955 were offered in exchange 2% stock 1960 or a further tranche of 3% stock 1966–8. Throughout, there were also issues of guaranteed stock by nationalised industries. The net result of the operations, together with the normal operations of the Issue Department and the National Debt Office, had been good up to the summer but thereafter were indifferent. For the fiscal year 1954–5, funding through gilt-edged came to only £30 million.

depend in part upon official messages; and it was to this aspect of the matter that the Governor turned early in the new year.

He had been in no hurry to address this subject, having warned in his Mansion House speech that Bank Rate could not perform miracles. He preferred to get market rates up and allow Bank Rate talk to get around before moving the Rate itself. By mid-January the situation had matured, Bill rates having moved up towards 2%. With the exchange still weak and with ideas for the unification of official and transferable sterling within a wider dealing spread being put to the Treasury, there was no point in further delay. The Chancellor agreed and Bank Rate was raised to $3\frac{1}{2}$% on 27 January. Writing to Allan Sproul, Cobbold said that a rise of $\frac{1}{2}$% had been largely discounted and was not expected to have much effect. But a rise of 1% would have been too drastic and 'left our hands less free for a later move in either direction'. He evidently had in mind a subsequent increase of 1% and was worried less 5%, rather than $4\frac{1}{2}$%, would prove politically difficult to get. A general election was in the air. The markets were given the message that $3\frac{1}{2}$% was a mild warning signal. Bill rates then rose to $2\frac{3}{4}$% and advances rates by $\frac{1}{2}$%. Gilts continued to weaken and equity prices fell back. But sterling remained at the support level of 2.78\frac{1}{2}$ and in February the reserves fell to $2.68 billion (from the peak of just over $3 billion reached in the previous June). Bank advances, including advances to retailers, to hire-purchase companies, and to the personal and professional category went on rising. Early in February the Governor warned the clearing banks that the rapid growth of hire-purchase needed careful watching. Further policy action was not far off and the Governor, already worried about the armoury of weapons, asked the home side to consider methods of tightening credit conditions as part of a comprehensive programme to correct the weakness in sterling and arrest inflationary tendencies.

O'Brien replied in a note dated 15 February and written in close consultation with Allen. They agreed that credit should be tightened so as to check the growth of domestic spending, improve overseas confidence, and restrain overseas borrowing in London. But Allen again warned that monetary policy was not as well placed as in 1952 and could not now secure in short order a higher rate of saving, nor a change of attitudes on wages, nor greater effort at work. Moderately tighter credit conditions would probably not be taken as a warning that seriously adverse conditions were round the corner. O'Brien then went on to reject such suggestions as raising the banks' cash ratio, asking the banks to observe a higher liquidity ratio, reintroducing Treasury Deposit Receipts, or selling Issue's gilt portfolio at whatever price was necessary to find takers. He preferred 'a sharper application of the traditional methods' plus the reimposition of hire-purchase controls and some renewed tightening of exchange control over credits to non-residents. The traditional methods would include a rise in Bank Rate to $4\frac{1}{2}\%$. When this came, on 24 February, along with hire-purchase terms control and intervention in transferable, the press was told that the rise in Bank Rate to $3\frac{1}{2}\%$ on 27 January had been accompanied by a tighter credit policy. The rise to $4\frac{1}{2}\%$ would further tighten all kinds of short-term credit and bring a substantial increase in its cost. In addition, it should exercise a general restraint and would be reinforced by the reimposition of hire-purchase controls.

That was the message this time. As a message, it had a look of clarity about it. But would anybody take much notice? In particular, would the banks and their borrowing customers pay attention to it or would they behave as Beale had predicted or as Allen had warned? Probably all those concerned in the Bank, from the Governor down, were alert to these questions and none too sanguine about the answers. Since the autumn of 1951 they had all learnt the tactical modalities of altering Bank Rate and attaching a message of explanation on each occasion. They all knew that 1955 was very different to 1952. But they had no new ideas for making monetary policy as effective now as it had apparently been three years previously. Advances ceilings imposed through renewed requests were undesired, while pushing interest rates up to a point where they became a potent force in themselves was out of the question. So the Bank largely resorted to the only remaining expedient, which was to pass the parcel back to Whitehall. Monetary policy, it argued, could make only a limited contribution. Responsibility for the main effort lay elsewhere. On the afternoon of 24 February, after the $4\frac{1}{2}\%$ Bank Rate had been announced, the Governor adopted the very rare course of writing a formal letter to the Chancellor on behalf of the Court. Its principal paragraphs read as follows:

> 'First, they wish to emphasise their view, to which I have given expression from time to time, that the possible contribution of credit policy to a balanced economy should not be overestimated. The earlier rise in Bank Rate to $3\frac{1}{2}\%$ had a considerable warning effect and in the last week or two the inflationary boom in the Stock Exchange has been shaken out. It is to be hoped that this new move will materially assist in strengthening the 'disinflationary' climate. But the inflationary pressures which have threatened to develop in recent months have their origin much less in the monetary than in the cost and wages structure. Whilst monetary policy can be of assistance, it is the Court's view that the battle against inflationary tendencies must mainly be fought in the wider fields of economic policy.
>
> Secondly, the Court feel that $4\frac{1}{2}\%$ is a comparatively high Bank Rate in the circumstances of to-day: it is a rate which they would not wish, in the

monetary conditions at present ruling in the world, to exceed except in moments of crisis, and which they would not wish to maintain for too long. A rate at this level, if continued for a long period, is bound to have undesirable as well as desirable effects. It is the Court's hope that the results of the general economic policy of HM Government will make possible some relaxation in credit policy at a fairly early date.

The Chancellor was asked to regard this as a formal letter from the Bank to the Government and he agreed to lay it before the Cabinet. He replied formally and politely on 25 February; but the letter's contribution to Government policy was slight. In fact Whitehall took no notice. Within weeks there would be a popular pre-election Budget and a declared increase rather than decrease in reliance on monetary policy. Within weeks, too, the Governor would be talking to Lord Aldenham, Chairman of Westminster Bank and current Chairman of the CLCB, in order to open up private discussions with the banks about credit restriction. Within months, published 'requests' were to be back with a vengeance.

(c) THE SLIDE BACK TO REQUESTS

When Bank Rate was raised to $4\frac{1}{2}\%$ on 24 February 1955 and hire-purchase terms control was reimposed only seven months after its complete suspension, the banks were once more asked by the Governor at the request of the Chancellor to limit the provision of finance for hire-purchase. The CIC was likewise requested. A few days later the London clearing banks agreed that they would grant no new facilities for financing hire-purchase and no increase in existing facilities. No other request was made at this time, reliance being placed on a sharper application of traditional methods. The banks were becoming subject to the liquidity pressure that had earlier been forecast. The ratio was down to 31·3% in February and sales of investments by one or two banks had been necessary to keep above 30%. But the Chief Executive Officers reported to Peppiatt that trade was active and flourishing. There was likely to be a further rise in advances even though a $4\frac{1}{2}\%$ Bank Rate might prove some deterrent. In the month to mid-March average liquidity fell to 30%, with some banks falling below that minimum. Advances rose further and there were additional sales of investments on a falling gilt-edged market. But if the desired pressure was present, evidence of a restrictive response to it on the part of the banks was not forthcoming. The Treasury, sharply on the lookout for such evidence, suggested to the Bank that the banks be asked to provide figures of classified advances monthly instead of quarterly. But the Deputy Governor told Compton it was not worth the extra work.

However, on 22 March the Governor asked Aldenham[10] whether borrowers were being discouraged or lenders looking twice. He was told that while General Managers had become more alert to liquidity it was doubtful if there was any change of attitude in bank branches. Perhaps some borrowers were less eager to borrow, but not many. The Governor replied that it was obvious that the authorities were trying to bring about a change in the trend of advances, especially in advances financing consumption. Since he was not keen to write letters or to solicit new directives from the Chancellor, he wanted to discuss how the official message could best be brought to the attention of the banks. Aldenham agreed to speak informally to his colleagues. At Peppiatt's instigation, the Bank was meanwhile examining various ways of keeping up the pressure when the seasonal factors turned unfavourable to the authorities, as they would do after April. The Governor noted: 'I am most anxious to keep up pressure so far as possible both on cash position and liquidity ratio during the next three months.' He felt that reliance on normal methods would not suffice. Perhaps some new arrangements should be put in hand. The Chief Cashier forecast 32% by mid-May, which the Governor thought 'too high for 1955'.

On 18 April the Governor had a further talk with Aldenham and with his Deputy, David Robarts,[11] Chairman of the National Provincial Bank. They said it was difficult to select the victims of restriction and they grumbled about the lack of restraint by nationalised industries. Cobbold said the Bank's object in raising Bank Rate and operating on the liquidity ratio was to induce a more negative attitude to bank advances. However, since gossip had it that little or nothing was happening, something else might have to be done. They discussed the possibility of a statement by the Chancellor that the banks could use to justify restriction to their customers, but it was agreed to leave things alone until after the pre-Election Budget. Peppiatt, in an annotation descriptive of the dominant view then prevailing in the Bank, remarked: 'If they want HMG (present and future) to run their business, this is the way to go about it. The banks should read the signals themselves and act accordingly.' The Budget Speech, when it came

---

[10] *Aldenham, Walter Durant Gibbs, 4th Baron (1888–1969).* Educated Eton and Trinity College, Cambridge. Army 1914–18. Director, Anthony Gibbs and Sons (Chairman 1939–65), Westminster Bank (Chairman 1950–61), Chairman, CLCB and President, BBA 1954–5.

[11] *Robarts, David John (1906–1989).* Educated Eton and Magdalen College, Oxford. Chairman, National Provincial Bank 1954–68, National Westminster Bank 1969–71, Director, Robert Fleming 1944–76, Chairman, CLCB and President, BBA 1956–60 and 1968–70. Church Commissioner 1957–65.

Leslie O'Brien, Chief Cashier 1955–1962

a few days later, was little help to the bankers but Aldenham obtained the Governor's agreement to defer any further discussions until the CLCB meeting in May, when the April figures would be available.

In the meantime O'Brien had responded to demands for the reconsideration of alternative arrangements in a note on credit policy circulated on 18 April. This opened with a statement on objectives, which placed some unfamiliar emphasis on money supply as well as bank lending. It read:

> The principal object of credit policy at the present time is, as a brake on an undue growth of money incomes, stockpiling and exuberant spending generally, to restrain as far as possible any further expansion in the supply of money and perhaps even, in case of need, to achieve some contraction in it. All other objectives are incidental to that aim. In practice, this means seeking on the one hand to induce a reduction in bank advances, and hence in bank deposits, and on the other to draw down deposits directly by some form of funding. The level of bank advances can be affected both by deterring borrowers, by pushing up interest rates and raising doubts about the continued availability of credit, and by deterring lenders, through pressing down the banks' liquidity ratio towards the conventional minimum of 30% and through evidence of our intentions as to policy.

The note went on to reject such devices as a revival of Treasury Deposit Receipts (and their exclusion from the banks' liquid assets) and roundly declared:

> Our examination of these possibilities has forced us to the conclusion that the only means by which a reduction in the money supply can be achieved are either an Exchequer surplus or the sale of securities (by a funding or by open market operations) to the customers of the banks; and that new techniques have little assistance to offer towards the achievement of this aim.

For his part, Peppiatt noted that the present methods were achieving the Bank's objective, subject to the slow reaction of the banks, and seemed capable of doing so for the next few weeks. After that, methods might need to be reconsidered. This proved to be the case.

Both the April and May figures indeed showed that clearing-bank deposits were falling. Seasonal factors apart, one influence working towards this end were the official sales of gilt-edged. But in other respects the statistics were not at all reassuring. Advances rose £44 million in April and another £36 million in May, while the banks sold investments of £64 million and £76 million in order to maintain liquidity at $30\frac{1}{2}\%$. These sales, together with those by the Bank (averaging some £50 million a month), were successfully pressed on a generally falling market. The yield on short-dated gilts rose from 3·43% at the end of March to 3·96% at the end of May and 4·02% by end-June, a level higher than the peak reached during the crisis months in 1952. But clearing bank investments still amounted to nearly one-third of their assets and the switch into advances yielding 5% or more remained attractive and competitively appropriate to individual banks; and it was the rise in advances rather than the fall in deposits that attracted the concern of the authorities, notwithstanding the views of the Chief Cashier about the importance of money supply. At the CLCB meeting in May – held when the April figures were to hand but ten days before the General Election – the Governor said that although the external response to the February measures was all right so far, he was less satisfied with the internal response. He reiterated that 'a somewhat more critical attitude to advances would be in line with official policy'.

In his attempt to chivvy the banks into a restriction of advances without recourse to a public request, the Governor was supported by evidence of the continuing pressure on bank liquidity and by the advice he was getting from Peppiatt. He may not have set much store by the movement in bank deposits and O'Brien's views on money supply, but he could draw some support from the latter's admission about the importance of 'evidence of our intentions as to policy'. In any event he knew how difficult it could be to maintain the momentum of funding and he knew well enough that the Treasury considered bank advances to be the primary target. Furthermore, thanks to the absence of debate in the past, he was in no position at this stage to open up a fight with Whitehall about the fundamentals of monetary economics. As for the Chief Cashier, the effectiveness of his opposition to alternative arrangements could not readily survive a succession of bad advances figures; and his position with the Governor was not strengthened by the fact that these figures were consistently worse than forecast.

At the end of May Aldenham endeavoured to obtain from the Governor some softening of the official message, so as to justify any increase in advances that might result from the imminent railway strike. But Cobbold refused and there was no further dialogue for several weeks. The Bank kept up pressure in the money market, forcing the discount houses into frequent borrowing at Bank Rate, and the Treasury Bill rate rose from $3\frac{3}{4}\%$ at the end of March to just under 4% in June. The dialogue recommenced at the end of that month, with the banks complaining that the gas and electricity industries were drawing up to the limit on their advance facilities when they ought to be going to the long-term market for money with which to repay those drawings. Furthermore the banks wanted the facilities reduced. This matter was eventually settled by the industries being temporarily given higher limits in exchange for an assurance that they would go to the market as soon as conditions permitted and for the Governor's agreement to some deviation of liquidity below 30% so long as advances to the two industries continued to rise. The bankers also suggested that they should write a letter to *The Times*, much as they had done in 1952. The Governor was agreeable to this, again stressing the importance and indeed the necessity of keeping up pressure on advances. The letter was subsequently cleared with the Chancellor and published on 30 June. It referred to the well-known policy of the Government to restrict bank advances, to large and small customers alike and however reasonable those advances would be in normal times. The letter concluded: 'The banks therefore hope that their customers will understand that the present stringency is a matter of public policy and will co-operate with the banks by keeping their credit requirements as small as possible.'

Cobbold was now becoming increasingly concerned about the economic and monetary prospects as well as about the Government's seemingly heavy reliance on monetary policy to bring things round. He was getting advice from Thompson-McCausland (alarming) and Allen (less alarming) that creeping inflation was threatening to undermine the whole fabric of macro-economic policy. Now was the time, early in the new Parliament, for effective action to be taken. Allen argued that the problem was one of only a small but persistent excess of demand. He had persuaded himself that if this could be put right by monetary policy, without much rise in unemployment, if bank advances were tightly held. The Governor showed this advice to the Chancellor on 5 July along with a supporting note of his own that also stressed the need for restriction in the public sector to complement a firm monetary policy. It was, he concluded, important to get principles agreed and stated before the summer holidays. On the same day, in accord with the wish of the CLCB, he gave a lunch in the Bank for the Chancellor, the Economic Secretary (Edward Boyle), Aldenham, and Robarts. The bankers told the Chancellor that they needed a more helpful climate of opinion. Adverse responses to their letter in *The Times* showed that customers saw no reason why their business should be curtailed when public expenditure showed no signs of economy and Ministers made optimistic speeches about investing in prosperity. The Governor gave them support, arguing forcefully for a Government statement about the need for all-round restraint. The Chancellor remarked disarmingly that the majority of his advisers had placed exaggerated faith in the efficacy of monetary measures and were correspondingly disappointed. He then suggested that Treasury officials might meet the bankers for enlightenment, and it was agreed that the Bank should arrange this.[12] Aldenham later told the Governor that he did not find the lunch party very reassuring. Nor was it, for the Chancellor said nothing specific about action in the public sector.

The banking figures for June (from mid-May to the end of the half-year) became available to the Bank on 15 July. Though deposits were now £65 million lower than a year before, advances had continued to rise and further sales of investments had been made. Liquidity was only 30·1%. Gilt-edged prices had again fallen, to a level more than 7% below that prevailing at the end of 1954. Though this development did not seem to be having much effect on the policy of the banks towards advances, it did encourage them to look about for fresh sources of liquidity. Information from the exchange market during June revealed that the Midland Bank had been bidding for dollar deposits and switching them into sterling for employment as liquid assets. The cost, including forward cover, was about 4% per annum and it looked as if Midland had increased its liquidity by about 2% in this way. After some debate it was concluded that there were

---

[12] The Bank was quick to spot the dangers in this suggestion. The Governor later agreed with Aldenham that the Deputy Governor should chair such a meeting supported by O'Brien and Allen. The banks would be represented by Robarts and the Chairman of the Chief Executive Officers' Committee. In a note to Aldenham the Governor remarked: 'We should all be on our guard against allowing casual contacts on these matters to develop between individual CEOs and individual Treasury officials, which would get us in a mess!'

no good grounds for stopping this through exchange control. Moreover, since the exchange reserves and the market for spot sterling both benefited, it was decided to take no further action, though the knowledge that liquidity was being fortified in this painless way (UK Treasury Bills were now yielding almost 4%) must have further weakened the Governor's confidence in traditional methods. He saw the Chancellor on 15 July and was told that the Government was proposing to make a Parliamentary statement about further restraint in both the private and the public sectors.

Whatever his own view on the matter, in practice the Governor now had no choice but to accept the final step in the reversion to requests, or *de facto* directives. All that could be saved was his position as intermediary between the Chancellor and the banks; though even this did not amount to much in practice. The pass had been sold by the banks themselves two days earlier, when Robarts and Thornton[13] (Chief Executive Officer of Barclays Bank) had at last come together with Gilbert, Brittain, and Hall of the Treasury at a meeting held in Threadneedle Street by the Deputy Governor supported by the Chief Cashier and Allen. The latter recorded Robarts as follows:

> He could not too strongly emphasise how difficult it would be to apply the credit squeeze further unless it were made clear in a very serious statement by the Chancellor that HMG recognised the situation called for a deferment of some of their projects; that industry should do the same; and that the banks should support this policy of curtailment. On the other hand, only yesterday the Chancellor had spoken in the House of the need to maintain investment at as high a rate as possible.

Thornton spoke in full support. It was impossible, he said, to take sufficient action without the co-operation of the public, who, at present, just did not understand. They heard that there was no crisis and that they needed an expanding economy with a maximum rate of investment. They could not see why this meant that they had to accept credit restriction. The banks wanted the Chancellor to help them help him, and what would suit them was more gloom. For the Bank, the Chief Cashier was left to argue that the tight monetary policy of the preceding four months ought to have sufficed and that they ought to discuss whether in present-day conditions it could be expected to have its traditional effect.

---

[13] *Thornton, Ronald George*, Kt (1901–81). Educated St Dunstan's College, Catford. General Manager, Barclays Bank 1946–61, Director 1961–2, Vice-Chairman 1962–6, Director, Bank of England 1966–70, Chairman, Barclays Export Finance Co., Director, Friends Provident and Century Life Office, United Dominions Trust 1962–71. Member, Committee of Inquiry on Decimal Currency 1961–2, Export Council for Europe 1960–4.

But O'Brien was left alone with these central banking thoughts. The Treasury was interested only in getting advances down by direct control and the banks were interested only in being told to do so by the Chancellor. It is possible that they were pleading for a request in order to avoid facing up to individual decisions, in a competitive market, to cut back on lending instead of continuing to sell gilt-edged at unattractive prices; but there is no evidence to support this conjecture. The banks were in a mood to get close to the Treasury and the Bank would have been excused if it had said to itself 'God protect me from my friends'. The meeting had been set up at the Chancellor's request, ostensibly so that Treasury officials should be enlightened about the way the banks conducted their lending business and the practical difficulties of limiting it. Robarts had instead used the meeting to address the Treasury directly on a matter of high policy. Yet not many months would pass before the banks were back in the Governor's room complaining about the very regime for which they had so abjectly asked. Robarts could be a tough and skilful negotiator when he wanted. He was to be such in September 1957, when controls on bank advances had again to be agreed with the Bank and the Government. But he could be rather short-sighted, concentrating only on the matter immediately in hand and directly on the focus of authority.

There remained to discuss the Chancellor's proposed statement and agree the terms of his letter. This process was extended over ten days, with the Governor arguing all along for a strong statement that bore down on public-sector spending and on the need for an all-round rephasing of capital programmes as well as an intensifying of the credit squeeze. The bankers supported him. Together they had some success and in addition managed to block any public quantification of the fall in advances that was requested as well as any reference to the 30% liquidity ratio. The statement was made on 25 July. It included announcement of a tightening of hire-purchase terms control and proclaimed that the banks would be asked to achieve 'a positive and significant reduction in the total of bank advances outstanding'. Action in the public sector was imprecise but indicated that some capital spending by local authorities and nationalised industries would be postponed or rephased. In the course of his letter to the Governor the Chancellor averred *ex cathedra* that 'the necessary reduction in demand is unlikely to be achieved unless the total of bank advances is reduced below its present level'. It was left to the banks to decide how this should be done. The Governor spoke to the CLCB on 16 July and told them an initial and material reduction in advances should be achieved by October and a further cut by December. He did however, add that he regarded the request as a support for 'technical credit policy' rather than an alternative. Technical pressure would be maintained. He concluded by saying that steps ought to be taken at once, before the Chancellor's statement went stale, and that a new self-denying ordinance should be considered. He was assured of the banks' co-operation, though they grumbled at the imprecision of restrictions on the public sector. 'They wish to point out', Robarts wrote to the Governor on 28 July, 'that the policy of restriction of bank credit cannot by itself be expected to cure the present excessive consumption at home of the country's resources. It must be accompanied by energetic and effective measures of retrenchment in the public sector of the economy.' The Governor was asked to forward this to the Chancellor. The latter replied on 8 August, giving some reassurance, but only in general terms.

The other banking associations were sent the request and all agreed to comply. The British Insurance Association (BIA) also received the letter and expressed a desire to co-operate. However, the Chairman of the Finance Houses Association (FHA) replied: 'It is hoped that the Chancellor's letter will result in some restrictions on those concerns, not members of this association, who have been transacting a large volume of hire-purchase business but who to date have been untrammelled by restriction.' This was an opening shot in a long campaign, in the main about the growth of the market in finance-house deposits and how, if at all, it could be controlled.

The clearing banks acted decisively and without delay. They agreed the self-denying ordinance for a period of six months, agreed that the aim should be to cut advances by 10% by the end of the year (excluding repayments by Gas and Electricity), agreed to reduce finance-house limits by 15%, agreed to reduce all other limits wherever practicable and as soon as possible, and agreed that new applications for advances should be examined with even greater care. Unless specifically required for exports, import-saving, necessary seasonal commitments, or essential requirements of the defence programme, they would be turned aside. Advances to the personal and professional category would be given particularly close scrutiny. Having obeyed the authorities with such alacrity, they were distinctly nettled to read that the Chancellor had told Gaitskell in the House that existing investment programmes would not be affected. Aldenham, on holiday in Connemara, wrote to Robarts in protest and asked him to see the Governor. 'I do not think you or I would have tolerated without protest the positive and significant reduction...if we had realised that the slowing down of existing investment programmes was to be cancelled.' Robarts duly told the Governor, who wrote to Bridges expressing considerable concern. The Chancellor said he felt wounded by an imputation of bad faith but took no action. In truth, the banks had been over-eager and a little naïve in their negotiations with so accomplished a player as Butler.

The Treasury, meanwhile, had been feeling both introspectively depressed and guilty because its policy had gone wrong. It had been intended that the stimulus of the tax cuts announced in the Budget should be offset by the tighter monetary policy introduced in February. But the latter had apparently failed to deliver, much to everybody's embarrassment. What had gone wrong? Was it that the Bank had failed to warn the Treasury that months would elapse before any results became visible? Or was it that the Bank's preferred method of operation, through Bank Rate and liquidity pressure, was ineffectual? Robert Hall wrote a long memorandum in these terms to Bridges, who forwarded it to the Chancellor and added: 'We were entitled to rely on the (admittedly rather general) but nevertheless very positive assurances given by the Governor that all was well in hand and that he wished to be left to handle the matter in his own way.' The Chancellor replied that if anyone was to blame, he himself was. He added 'The Governor told me that the Bank's action in the early stages saved a worse inflation'.

Bridges then tackled the Governor, saying that the Treasury and the Chancellor felt they were not close enough to the working of monetary policy. They wanted closer contacts with the Bank and wanted to know a good deal more about what the banks were doing. They also wanted further occasional meetings like the one chaired by the Deputy Governor and attended by clearing bankers and Treasury officials. In a successful rearguard action Cobbold stood his ground. Operational responsibility belonged to the Bank, subject to agreement at the top about policy. The Treasury could have more information on market operations if they wanted. He agreed that regular meetings between the Chief Cashier and the Treasury might be useful, but he recorded: 'I made it clear that would not be the appropriate place for any discussion of policy.' As to relations with the clearing banks, he was not prepared to agree to any departure from the accepted method of dealing with Whitehall relations with the banking community, 'at the top level through the Governors of the Bank of England'. He was prepared to bring the Chairman of the CLCB to see the Chancellor or, exceptionally, to arrange a large meeting. He would also continue to keep the Chancellor and the Permanent Secretary informed about such matters as bank advances and liquidity ratios; and over the next phase would provide them with some kind of monthly report. But he would not agree to any regular meetings chaired by the Bank and attended by clearing bankers and Treasury officials. Such matters would cast doubt on the whole method of relations and sooner or later get everyone into difficulties. 'I regarded this as a matter of high policy and of cardinal importance in the relations between HMG and the City and I was not prepared to move.' Bridges accepted this for the moment, with some reluctance, as did the Chancellor after a talk with Cobbold on the following day; and that was that for the time being. In mid-August the Governor agreed with Aldenham, in his capacity as Chairman of the British Bankers Association (BBA), that the members of the BBA would provide monthly figures of classified advances for the next few months. In addition the Chairmen of the Big Five would each call in from time to time for an individual chat about bank lending. The Treasury was not informed about the additional statistics. They were not to be published and were to be given only to the Bank and to the members of the BBA.

Mistakes had been made. The ambiguous institutional arrangements, put into statutory form in 1946 and developed thereafter, had themselves contributed to this. The whole enterprise was a novel one, undertaken in conditions markedly different from 1952. The Bank, as has been argued earlier, was obliged to try out its preferred approach in an overheating and over-confident economy without much more than a moderate increase in interest rates and with a very underlent banking system. Beale had warned that it would not work and the Governor obviously lacked full confidence in it. Peppiatt wanted to try it, but seemingly only as a form of extended message to the banks. O'Brien, more alert to the long-run dangers and disadvantages of alternative methods, was keen to stick to the preferred approach and was certainly able to pursue it with great vigour. It achieved a fall in money supply, but nobody else was interested. The Governor, for his part, did not delay in repeatedly warning the banks about the need to restrict. But he had to work against a background of high confidence which Ministers were doing their best to encourage ahead of a general election, and his personal authority was inadequate to the task. Policy, after all, was Government policy not Bank policy; and the banks, reluctant to disappoint their customers, could with every justification point to Government policy generally and complain that they were being given no help in carrying out the task that they were told was theirs by the Governor.

In the Treasury, the principal economic adviser, Hall, seems to have expected a restriction of bank advances as the cutting edge of monetary policy (rather as he had done in 1948) and to have expected such restriction to begin very soon after the February measures. In the absence of any thorough prior discussion on the whole subject between the Treasury and the Bank, this was not an unreasonable point of view, though it showed an unfamiliarity with the facts of monetary life. But in any case how could he have confidently advised the Chancellor that he could cut taxes and rely on monetary policy when, fundamentals apart, there had been no discussion with the Bank about the magnitude, in terms of aggregate demand, of the task allotted to monetary policy and no discussion at all about the amount of the cut in bank advances that was thought to be needed? Even if there had been, it is doubtful whether anyone had any means of judging the relationship, if any, between bank advances and the gross domestic product. The 'positive and significant reduction' requested in July, and identified as 10% by the banks with the acquiescence of the Bank and the Treasury, had no sophisticated origins. Nor was its subsequent effect easy to discern.

But despite all the mistakes and misjudgements about the longer haul, the February measures, including most importantly the intervention in transferable, did achieve their vital immediate objective of halting the fall in the exchange reserves and holding the position over the change of Prime Minister, the Budget, and the General Election; and they did this without disturbing public opinion. In those respects they were extremely successful. To have achieved the longer-run macro-economic results subsequently demanded of them, they would have had to have been much rougher at the outset, with a higher Bank Rate than $4\frac{1}{2}$%. Expectations would have had to be changed and business confidence diminished. But that could have damaged the Government at a most inopportune moment; and it was the Government and not the central bank that was ultimately responsible for policy. Butler was partly right and not simply being courteous when he told Bridges and Hall that the blame was his, not theirs.

(d) SUPPORTING THE CREDIT SQUEEZE AND SUPPORTING GILT-EDGED

When he told the banks on 25 July 1955 that technical pressures would be maintained alongside the direct request to restrict advances, the Governor would have had in mind discussions that had recently taken place both about Bank Rate and about future funding operations. The Chief Cashier had advised on 18 July that funding should be increased in order to keep up pressure on bank liquidity. He felt that the banks would not, if they could help it, realise any more investments. On the following day he submitted advice about Bank Rate. He admitted that $4\frac{1}{2}$% had had insufficient effect on expectations and on bank advances: $5\frac{1}{2}$% might do better. If it did, there would be a useful secondary effect in the gilt-edged market and on funding. But one would have to go to 7% or 8% to achieve any appreciable effect on borrowers. Tacitly, this was not a feasible option. Furthermore, the uncertainties over exchange policy (during the run-up to the EMA, with rumours of wider spreads for sterling) might cause a rise in Bank Rate to be misinterpreted as heralding a return to convertibility or, alternatively, an exchange crisis. On balance he was against a change. On 21 July Cobbold consulted the Committee of Treasury together with Hambro, Kindersley, Smith and Keswick. He said he was firmly opposed to an increase and would ask for a directive if the Chancellor nevertheless insisted. The Directors present supported him, several confirming the view that a rise in the Rate would be seriously damaging to sterling. The Chancellor, though advised by the Economic Secretary to favour a rise on psychological grounds, accepted the Bank's view and the matter was not pressed.

But Bank Rate remained on the agenda. Sterling did not respond well to the July measures or to the assurances given at that time that no change in exchange policy was contemplated. The rate fell to $2.78\frac{1}{2}$ in August and the reserves continued to fall, by £31 million after dropping £48 million in July. The gilt-edged market continued to weaken, the yield on short-dated stocks rising to 4·6%. However, the rise in bank advances, excluding advances to nationalised industries, slowed abruptly. Bank sales of investments subsided, and before going on holiday later in the month Cobbold left a private note with Butler advising strongly against a rise in the Rate. Throughout this whole phase of policy nobody in the Bank was prepared to argue that the opportunity be taken to obtain a rate of interest that would be high enough to deter borrowing and deter expenditure. The Bank chose instead to accept a return to requests and to press the Treasury to tighten fiscal policy. The Governor therefore pursued with the Chancellor the now familiar argument that Bank Rate would put the emphasis on the wrong place and distract attention from the real problem. 'Financial opinion at home and abroad', he wrote, 'is now focussed on wages and the public sector. It is here that the next round of attack should be directed and seen to be directed.' Bank Rate should be kept in reserve. Meanwhile, the Chief Cashier was lobbying the Treasury from his side. He wrote to Brittain on 17 August, pointing out the desirability of keeping up the pressure on clearing bank liquidity and saying how difficult this was becoming with a consistently weak gilt-edged market and large Exchequer outlays 'below-the-line'. He put forward the suggestion that all Local Authorities of any size should be obliged to go to the market for money instead of to the Public Works Loan Bond (PWLB).

Whitehall was itself now coming to the conclusion that the July measures were not going to be enough. An autumn Budget was going to be needed to increase taxes and cut spending. In Cobbold's absence the Deputy was warned about this by Bridges through Compton on 1 September and told about it by the Chancellor on the following day when he was asked where Bank Rate might fit into such a policy package. Mynors doubted whether it would be useful if the rest of the package had real value and also doubted whether it would be needed to strengthen the gilt-edged market. The merits of an earlier rise in the Rate, as a holding operation, were also considered, the Deputy saying he would prefer to avoid it but recognised that markets might compel it. He also warned that a much higher Rate would, in his words, 'hurt some of the market machinery'. The Bank could and would look after this if it was necessary in the general good but would on that account have to be the more certain that a much higher rate was required.[14] The Deputy saw the Chancellor again on 8 September and found that any enthusiasm for a rise in the Rate had waned. In the event, markets did not compel a move and the Bank returned to the business of operating the credit squeeze with an unchanged $4\frac{1}{2}$%. The Governor went ahead with his progress reports and Peppiatt with his talks with the Chief Executive Officers. The Chief Cashier concentrated on funding. The Treasury waited impatiently. For them, progress with the positive and significant reduction proved disappointingly slow and its effects uncertain. In the end they returned to the charge that they were not being kept adequately informed.

Advances fell steadily if rather slowly. Between July and November the clearing banks had cut by $4\frac{1}{4}$%, the BBA figures showing that about 40% of this had occurred in the personal and professional category, retail trade, and hire-purchase finance. Net deposits had fallen 3%. In October Peppiatt saw the Chief General Managers of the Big Five and of two of the smaller clearing banks. He reported that all were making a big effort to reduce advances, though it was uncertain whether the 10% target would be met. Limits were being cut and there was a marked falling-off in the granting of new credits. There were no serious casualties. Liquidity averaged 33·5% in October, not a high level for the time of year. Investment portfolios remained reasonably liquid despite the heavy sales of short-dated stock.

---

[14] The capital and reserves of the discount houses had been seriously depleted by the depreciation in gilt-edged (see Chapter 11(d) below). Consequently they were short of margin on their secured borrowing. Peppiatt therefore proposed to the Governors on 12 September that (as a temporary and exceptional measure) the Bank should cut its own required margin from 5% to 2% where market advances were secured on Treasury Bills and very short-dated gilts. 'For what it is worth', he added, 'I have in mind that we took somewhat similar action in 1931.' The Governor held this over for two weeks and then agreed. The London Discount Market Association (LDMA) was so advised by the Principal of Discount Office and was instructed that no publicity was to be given to the change.

The Governor, talking to bank Chairmen, got much the same impression as Peppiatt but was also told that the demand for fresh advances had fallen, probably because it was known that many applications would be refused. Early in November he told the CLCB how important it was to maintain the pressure of the credit squeeze unabated. He expressed the opinion that it would have to be maintained well into 1956 and that technical pressures would be kept up for that purpose. He reported this in a letter to the Chancellor, saying he was satisfied that every one of the clearing banks was making a very real effort to get as near as possible to the 10% target by the end of the year. Butler replied saying that failure to meet the target would imply that the credit squeeze had no further to go, which would be a 'most unfortunate result'. He agreed it would be wrong to give any impression that the squeeze would end or be relaxed at the end of the year.

Keeping up the technical pressures was the concern of the Chief Cashier. In a note to the Governors written on 1 September he warned of difficulties ahead. The turnround in the trend of advances would itself improve bank liquidity, while the continuing weakness of gilt-edged made it unlikely that Issue could sell stock on the scale reached earlier in the spring and summer. Yet there was the Exchequer deficit to meet, a deficit swollen by the requirements of the nationalised industries (the Bank had had to take up most of two recent issues by Electricity and Gas), together with the November maturity of £524 million of 3% Serial Funding Bonds, only 20% of which was in official hands. Further ahead, £824 million of $2\frac{1}{2}$% National War Bonds fell due for repayment in August 1956. O'Brien suggested that a new short-dated stock be issued partly for cash and in exchange for the November maturity. Early in October he put forward specific proposals for the cash issue of £250 million 4% Conversion Stock 1957–8 at $99\frac{1}{2}$, to yield just under 4%, and a conversion offer of the same stock to holders of the Serial Funding Bonds. The Governors agreed and the Treasury accepted the proposals without discussion or demur. After the operation was announced on 10 October, the public subscribed £$65\frac{1}{2}$ million to the cash issue and converted £$96\frac{1}{2}$ million of the November maturity. Allowing for conversion of official holdings this left just under £100 million for cash redemption. The Treasury was pleased, Compton writing warmly to O'Brien: 'With characteristic modesty you don't mention that the result is within 1% of your forecast, and I should like to congratulate you on this as well as on the success of the operation itself.' Something was going right for a change.

But if the cash and conversion operation had gone as well as expected, funding operations in aggregate proved unsatisfactory. Further issues of

Guaranteed Stock were made and largely taken up by the Bank. Over the whole December quarter there was net disfunding of nearly £50 million and clearing bank liquidity rose unexpectedly to $37\frac{1}{2}$% at the end of the year (it had been $34\frac{1}{4}$% at the end of 1954). Though the exchange rate had improved following the autumn Budget and the fall in the reserves had been checked, the gilt-edged market enjoyed only a very brief recovery. Prices fell back in November and the market became ragged. Peppiatt, in consultation with the Chief Cashier and the two Government brokers, Derrick Mullens and Peter Daniell, judged it would be right and safe to intervene. The Governors agreed and a change of tactics was adopted on 11 November. The Treasury was kept informed. Contrary to its usual practice, the Bank was prepared cautiously to buy stock outright (ignoring purchases of the next maturity) and also to take in longer stock against sales of shorts. In a report submitted on 23 December Peppiatt said that the undertone had remained bearish but that a higher level of prices reached immediately after the change of tactics had been maintained. The operation had not involved a net cash outlay over the whole period and in Peppiatt's view it had prevented prices from going several points lower (in which case two Local Authority stock issues, for Liverpool and Glasgow,[15] could not have been brought). The Bank had however been a net seller of shorts and a buyer of longs. Its intervention does not seem to have been spotted, though the *Evening Standard* reported on 25 November that a mystery buyer was around. 'This Mr X operates carefully. His brokers never bid for stock. But there are days when they take big lines of those that suit his fancy.' With the agreement of the Treasury the Bank reverted to its normal practice early in the new year, the aim being, in Peppiatt's words, to operate 'with the objectives of (a) being cash in hand on balance and (b) only effecting exchanges to suit our book and not, as more recently, to meet the wishes of the Market'.

Though successful within its own limited purpose, the above operation in gilt-edged was followed by a further fall in prices towards the year-end and into the new year, the yield on long-dated stocks reaching 4·87% at the end of February compared with 4·64% at the end of November. Its success also constituted a profound temptation for the future. If the Bank and the Government broker could operate to underpin the market with the knowledge of the principal jobbers but without any investor knowing what

---

[15] Both were customers of the Bank and Mullens. The ethics of grooming the market ahead of these issues could have surprised some observers had they known what was happening. But they would not have worried the Bank. Market intervention would have appeared justified by the wider public interest.

was going on and without the excuse that they were acquiring stock for the National Debt Office in the normal course, they would be tempted to nurse the market whenever the needs of Exchequer financing and debt management made it seem expedient to do so.

From intervening only when the market could be judged to be demoralised and irrational, it could then be but a short series of steps to frequent and systematic intervention, whose existence would be public knowledge and which would be justified as underpinning the liquidity of the market and maximising the attraction of gilt-edged to large investors. From then on the authorities would be committed to intervention, with considerations of monetary policy affecting the tactics of intervention day-to-day rather than its exceptional use. Withdrawal would then constitute a change of strategy, only to be undertaken as part of a change in the technique of monetary policy as a whole. In later years, beyond the scope of this book, temptation and the voracity of the Exchequer proved too great. Systematic intervention became the everyday practice, until it was stopped in April 1971. Peppiatt, who remained at the helm as Home Director until February 1957, was only too well aware of what would happen if the authorities gave way to temptation and embarked on systematic intervention. He had already warned the Governors about it in a rare statement about market management submitted early in 1952. The occasion was a debate about the threatened inadequacy of jobbers' capital and what to do about it. In a *locus classicus* on the whole subject he wrote:

> The suggestion has been made from time to time that in order to prevent wide fluctuations in prices we should operate in the Gilt-Edged Market far more freely than we do at present – in fact that we should 'job'.
>
> Broadly speaking, the existing practice is to confine our activities to the following:
>
> (a) to buying the next maturing stock in order to facilitate conversion/redemption; and to selling, over a period, stocks left with us as a result of such operations:
> (b) to acting as involuntary 'underwriters' of cash issues to the public by HMG and/or by nationalised industries; and to selling stocks thus left with us:
> (c) to assuring a market (short term) at the time of issue of compensation stocks (e.g. Coal) by purchase and subsequent sale as opportunity offers:
> (d) to smoothing out any relatively small technical troubles which may at any particular time be embarrassing the Market:
> (e) most exceptionally, to making a demonstration such as we made in November 1949 when clearly stocks had fallen to an unduly low level: also, very occasionally, to giving some moderate year-end support for balance sheet purposes:

(f) to assisting funding, in a general way, by a willingness always to sell longs in exchange for shorter Government securities.

Such activities are, in my opinion, both necessary and proper.

As the Central Bank we have a duty to control the volume of credit. But we have, I should maintain, no such duty to control the price of Government securities – even if we could (cf. USA). In fact, it would be difficult, if not impossible, to achieve both these objectives at the same time; because, when we are restricting credit, securities tend to fall and if we were to seek to reverse this movement it would involve pumping large sums of money into the market, thus defeating our primary purpose.

Moreover, if we were to job actively, we should tend to amass a large portfolio of securities, usually at unfavourable prices on a falling market (we could not act on the 'bear tack') and my belief is that had we so acted during the recent fall we might have found ourselves with a further £50/100 million stocks at prices most of which would now look absurdly high. We should become the target for criticism and pressure by both Whitehall and the public. And, above all, we should soon create a situation where we were in fact THE jobber and should thus destroy the very market which we were trying to maintain.

The Gilt-Edged Market at present functions on the whole satisfactorily, though the enormous volume of securities now dealt in and the difficulty experienced by the jobbers of accumulating capital certainly raise problems (see attached article in to-day's *Financial Times*). But the answer to any problem which may arise is, in my opinion, to be found in consultation between ourselves and the Chairman of the Stock Exchange with a view to strengthening the position of the jobbers, as may from time to time become necessary, by the following means:

(1) by encouraging a greater flow of capital in their direction, e.g. from Insurance Companies, Investment Trusts:
(2) by fiscal remedies:
(3) by persuading the Banks to give favourable terms to gilt-edged jobbers for carrying stock

or by a mixture of all three. In short, we should, if and when the need arises, take such action as would tend to support and strengthen the machinery of the Market and not to destroy it.

The Chief Cashier (Beale) noted his agreement with this approach, as did the Governor. The opinion of this author, who had to operate the technique of systematic intervention in its later flowering, is that it would have been better if the Bank had stuck to Peppiatt's precepts through thick and thin. But that is for a future historian to judge.

The indifferent performance of official funding and the concern lest the banks should not reach the target of a 10% cut by December 1955 both emerged while the Bank once again thought about the future of credit control and the Treasury again attempted to get closer to the administration of the credit squeeze and closer to the banks themselves. At the end of October the Governor asked the Home Finance team for advice about credit policy in the first half of 1956. He did not think anyone would want another request for a further cut in advances. It would be better to rely on technical measures 'supported by such private guidance about our aims as seems appropriate' and to hope that the banks had by now learnt enough to avoid public requests from the authorities. If the Bank's technical arrangements were inadequate, some new ones would have to be constructed. What, Cobbold asked, might these be? A discussion with the recipients of his note suggested that bank liquidity in March 1956 might, with good fortune, be close to 30%. But Cobbold pressed for a paper on additional ratio controls in case such weapons were needed after all. A few days later, at the November meeting of the CLCB (with the Governor present) Oliver Franks[16] said he disliked the self-denying ordinance and wanted to return as soon as possible to a position where the banks conducted their business on a free enterprise and competitive basis, without being outposts of the Treasury. He received general support. The Governor replied that he had always been in favour of using the technical methods but that avoidance of Government requests in the future would only be possible if the clearing banks were able to react somewhat more quickly to Bank Rate changes and other technical pressures than they had done early in 1955. The Bank would want to maintain these pressures through the opening months of 1956. If this proved difficult to engineer, he would want to discuss with the banks what technical measures might be introduced so that pressure could in fact be maintained.

Examination of additional ratio controls by O'Brien and Allen again revealed no easy road to salvation. Allen, who correctly defined the problem as how to do without direct requests and with the least possible recourse to raising interest rates, considered that supplementing the 30% ratio with a revival of the TDR was the least unpromising among a variety of alternatives. But he saw that although the total of non-liquid assets might be controlled by this means, their distribution between investments and advances would not. The only solution he could see to this problem, if it was advances that especially needed controlling, was a fiercer application of pressure. O'Brien, who replied to the Governor on 17 November, still saw little or no attraction in any of the alternatives (cash ratio, liquidity ratio, TDRs). A variable cash ratio would be useless unless the whole system were altered, making access to the Bank more difficult

[16] Then Chairman of Lloyds Bank.

and allowing for much greater variations in short-term interest rates, which was not wanted. A variable liquidity ratio meant substituting compulsion for prudent banking practice and would set up all kinds of avoidance. A revival of TDRs would be less objectionable but would be open to the criticism that the Government, as a result of its own failure in other fields, was resorting to forced loans from the banks. The Governor was in broad agreement with the Chief Cashier but, in case of accidents, asked nonetheless for more detailed work to be done on variable liquidity ratios. Peppiatt's view was that 'nothing attractive emerges from this interesting study'.

O'Brien submitted an additional technical note on variable liquidity ratios at the end of the year. It was not encouraging, for it examined awkward new questions about powers, penalties, coverage, definition, and application, on the assumption that all banks would need to be brought in and not just the London clearers. Converting a banking practice into a machine for mandatory control was by no means straightforward and, once done, invited the ingenious to devise every possible means of avoidance. Such means as the taking of competitively bid sterling deposits, a practice already adopted by finance houses, or the taking of dollar deposits and switching them into sterling must have come to mind. The Governor read it all and noted: 'Useful to have handy – hope it will not be needed.' So far, the whole exploration was resembling a walk up a cul-de-sac. As Macmillan took office as Chancellor at the turn of the year, the Bank had nothing to offer except continuation of the existing squeeze, supplemented, if market developments permitted, by orthodox pressures on the banks.

At this stage the Treasury was gloomy about the prospects of cuts or deferments in the public sector. It had also just had another brush with the Bank about the conduct of the squeeze, a brush that had on this occasion ended in a draw. Early in November Gilbert told the Deputy Governor that there would be bouts of worry in the Treasury about the efficiency of the squeeze until the battle was clearly won. At the end of the month, while Cobbold was absent in the US, Bridges and Compton tried to persuade Mynors and O'Brien to arrange another meeting between the clearing banks and Treasury officials. O'Brien minuted the Deputy that he heartily disliked the idea.[17] It would indeed have been a second blow with the thin end of a sizeable wedge; and on 6 December Mynors told Bridges he could not accept the proposal. He did however agree to transmit a list of Treasury

---

[17] Peppiatt commented: 'I could not agree more – let HMT do their job and leave us to do ours.'

questions to the banks and to solicit replies, which would be collated by the Bank. He was sent the questions by the Permanent Secretary on the following day. The Treasury wanted qualitative evidence to supplement the statistical information: How were branch managers tackling the job of restriction? What kinds of overdraft had they been attacking and with what success? Where were they meeting resistance and what did they do when they did? To what extent would results be delayed by the need to negotiate new agreements? In the opinion of the banks, what factors would govern the operation of credit restriction in 1956? How important were liquidity prospects? The Treasury also asked the Bank to ask the FCI, the ICFC, and the AMC whether they were experiencing additional demand on account of credit restriction by the banks.

A stately exercise was now put in hand. At the request of the Deputy Governor, the Chief Cashier consulted the Chairman of the Chief Executive Officers, Thornton of Barclays. Together they produced a paper, which was drafted in the Bank. This was then cleared with Aldenham and with the Governor. A final version was sent to Bridges on 13 December and was politely acknowledged on the following day. It was couched in a particular language of forced dignity and careful qualification. The paper noted that the degree of understanding and co-operation shown by the banks' customers had been remarkable; but resistance had to be expected as the squeeze got tighter. It went on to advise the reader that 'the progress made towards restraint cannot be judged simply by the figures of positive reductions'. One reason given was that without restraint advances would have grown. This simple thought was expressed as follows: 'Allowance must also be made for the probably unusually large amount by which advances would otherwise have risen over this period which from the outset contained forces making for abnormally high activity.' As to the Treasury's specific questions, the paper explained in its sonorous English that while most pressure had fallen on borrowing for consumption, advances for capital expenditure had been especially discouraged and provisions for repayment of seasonal advances had been strictly enforced. Medium-sized companies had been hit more than large ones, who had other sources of finance. Further pressure on the former might well compel reductions in activity. Resistance would grow – especially from small traders, who would be hard hit, either directly or indirectly, by a shortening of trade credit. Beyond that, the banks did not have very much to say, though they did aver: 'Bearing in mind that what has been called for was a moderate not a drastic cut-back, the action taken when difficulty is encountered is usually based on compromise. Generally action takes the form of the reduction being postponed for a short time.' For the future, the banks saw a very heavy suppressed demand for accommodation and were unable to foresee much further fall in advances. As to liquidity, they expected to survive the revenue quarter without great difficulty. Liquidity pressure, they remarked dutifully if circumspectly, 'provides its own incentive to obtaining reductions in advances'. Finally enquiries of the FCI, the ICFC, and the AMC had yielded little of any significance. Bank records do not relate whether the Treasury was happy with this stodgy fare. But it had to put up with it, though tempers in Great George Street were not improved by the accidental discovery in mid-December that the Bank was getting monthly figures from the BBA and had not told Whitehall.

(e) THE MACMILLAN STYLE: 1956

At the above conjuncture of fidgety nerves over the policies of 1955, edginess between the Treasury and the Bank, and unease about 1956, Butler at last left the Treasury and Harold Macmillan moved unwillingly into it. On 2 January he had his first official meeting with the Bank. The Governors and the Chief Cashier attended and on his side the new Chancellor was flanked by Boyle, Bridges, and Brittain. The Governor outlined the disappointments of 1955 and advised that there should not yet be any relaxation in monetary policy. He explained how the restriction of advances was working, whom it was hitting and whom it was not, on much the same lines as reported earlier by the banks themselves. The downward pressure would have to be maintained. To this end he advised against tampering with the 30% liquidity ratio and in favour of increased funding operations in gilt-edged. But the market was poor and the Bank, having intervened to steady it during November and December, was now minded to let it find its own level, even though this might lead to a higher Bank Rate. One of the problems was the large and regular issuing of long-dated guaranteed stock by the nationalised industries; it might be better if this ceased and the industries borrowed direct from the Exchequer so that the combined needs of the Government and public corporations could be managed centrally by the Treasury and the Bank. It would be better still if the capital programmes of the corporations were reduced. The commercial and banking world would not believe that inflation could be stopped by the credit squeeze alone; and supporting action on public-sector investment was required.

The new Chancellor was in general agreement with the Governor's view of the outlook and reassured him about public-sector spending. He went on to develop his consensual and corporatist views. The economic problems of the country could only be solved by the co-operative effort of all who believed in freedom. The Government, the Bank, the City, and Industry should work together within a common plan, criticising each other in private but presenting a solid front in public. It was 'important to get the right mood across', both in Ministerial speeches and, he hoped, in the annual statements of bank chairmen. Two days later the Governors gave a lunch for the Chancellor, the Economic Secretary, Aldenham, and Robarts. The bankers agreed to continue the squeeze, though with a slower fall in advances and the warning that a squeeze by them without 'a corresponding squeeze by him' would not restore the position. For his part the Chancellor tried to coax them into refraining from reading him lectures in their annual speeches, saying this would enable him to make cuts without being told he was obeying the bankers. Such a tactic, persuasive in his skilled hands, was typical of the Macmillan style. Aldenham thought the lunch 'so encouraging'.

Before Christmas, and ahead of these exchanges with Macmillan, Allen had offered fresh advice to the Governor. He saw a need to moderate industrial investment, in both public and private sectors, in order to free further resources for export in the engineering and metal-using industries and relieve the general shortage of labour. 'Financial discouragement' in the private sector would have to be increased. Large companies with ample resources could be discouraged if interest rates were raised and the higher level was expected to last. They could be attracted into gilts instead of fixed assets; but raising the yield on the former would probably require a rise in Bank Rate – a better method than trying to press stock on a falling market. Medium-sized companies could only be discouraged by greater restriction, for no practicable rise in rates would deter such borrowers. If greater restriction could be achieved through the existing request, then no rise in Bank Rate was needed, though it would be needed if more pressure on the banks was required. As to small businesses, they were probably hit too hard as it was. Allen then recited the usual arguments against a rise in the Rate: Exchequer and balance of payments costs, effects on the politically sensitive mortgage rate, and the risk of failure leading to discredit of Bank Rate itself. He also emphasised the necessity of parallel action in the public sector. But he nonetheless accepted that a rise in Bank Rate should be part of a policy package affecting both sectors. The Chief Cashier supported him and the Governor accepted his advice, which had now moved slightly away from the highly expectational tone of preceding years. It relied rather more upon the direct, if unquantified, effects of credit-rationing and higher rates. But, in the absence of reliable evidence, it was as usual all a matter of judgement or opinion. In 1955 monetary policy had not lived up to its earlier promise. It had been slow to act. When, more at the insistence of the Treasury than the Bank, it had at last achieved a reduction in bank advances, its effects seemed inadequate and rather haphazard. The road to the Radcliffe Committee had begun. But first, in 1956, there was to be a further extension of the scope of requests. At Macmillan's insistence, this was at last accompanied by a joint review of monetary policy on the part of the Treasury and the Bank. It was also accompanied by the first signs of serious avoidance, through the growth of the competitive market in finance-house deposits.

Macmillan's oversight of monetary policy was marked by the breezy charm of manner that served to soften the impact of his tactical skill and determination. Unique among post-war Chancellors, he often engaged in an informal correspondence with the Governor in addition to frequent meetings with him. On 3 January, after their initial meeting, he wrote: 'I was particularly cheered by your determination to continue the credit squeeze and to keep the graph of the level of advances downwards at the angle of the last six months.' The Governor, however, had not committed himself to any such angle. In his reply he described the downward inclination as a curve rather than an angle and asked that the Minutes of the meeting be amended to read 'continue the downward pressure on bank advances with something like the same force as during the last six months'. He followed this up with some suggestions for the Chancellor's first public pronouncement, amounting to a renewed plea for complementary action, in support of the credit squeeze, in fields directly under Government control. With firmness Macmillan retorted: 'I am sure our common purpose requires that the downward slope of the curve from now on will not be very different from the July – December angle.' Ten days later he invited the Governor to a dinner party in No. 11. His letter began: 'Having now been Chancellor long enough to get some idea of the main problems which face us, I am beginning to consider what we ought to do about them. As you know, I have never been ashamed of picking other people's brains and I want to do so now.'[18]

The Chancellor had been bequeathed a precarious position. After the annual servicing of the North American Loans, the exchange reserves had fallen to just over $2.1 billion at the end of December. The rate against the dollar exceeded $2.80, but markets were nervous. The monthly trade figures were not very good and the pressure of home demand remained high. Unemployment was very low. The wages round was setting firmly into a 7–8% pattern and inflation was running at 5%. An expansionist at heart, Macmillan nonetheless appreciated that he would have to begin

[18] The other guests were Franks, Brand, and Percy Mills from 'outside', and Boyle, Bridges, and Hall from the Treasury.

with all-round retrenchment. This meant on the one hand keeping a firm hold on the Bank and the banks while on the other hand persuading his reluctant colleagues to agree to cuts in spending even though estimates for 1956–7 had already been settled. On 20 January he held a further meeting with the Bank at which he hinted at a package of measures to be announced in February. The Governor approved the timing and now said he would consider an accompanying rise in Bank Rate provided the rest of the package was strong enough. He rejected a suggestion that the clearing banks' minimum liquidity ratio be increased but agreed to review this question once more. He again pressed for reductions in borrowing by nationalised industries. On 2 February both the Governor and the Chancellor spoke to the CLCB. The former told them there must be no let-up whatever in policy towards advances and that he might have to ask for liquidity to be kept higher than the traditional minimum of 30%, much though he disliked tinkering with ratio percentages. The Chancellor followed by thanking the banks for their co-operation and offering veiled assurances about cuts in public spending.

Bank Rate was raised to $5\frac{1}{2}$% on 16 February. It was welcomed by the Chancellor when, on the following day, he announced a tightening and extension of hire-purchase terms control, cuts in bread and milk subsidies amounting to £38 million, suspension of the investment allowance for private capital outlays, and a cut of £70 million in the investment programmes of state industries and the central government. Macmillan had experienced some difficulty in obtaining his colleagues' agreement to the cuts in expenditure, but the Governor and the Court were satisfied that enough was being done to warrant the inclusion of $5\frac{1}{2}$% in the total package. They were anyway under fire in some quarters for alleged timidity over the Rate. Oscar Hobson, in a *News Chronicle* article entitled 'Macmillan should insist on higher Bank Rate', had written in January that long experience proved that proper control of the money supply was the only way to stop cost inflation. The recent use of Bank Rate and credit controls had been half-hearted. 'The neglect to use the Bank Rate with decision has been a deplorable mistake...Macmillan's first action as Chancellor should be to overcome the inhibitions of the Bank of England – for all their lip service to flexibility – against raising their Rate above the present very moderate level. I cannot see that he is going to get far with his fight against inflation unless he does.' Whatever the Governor and his colleagues thought of this, they stuck firmly to their guns in telegrams and press briefings, about the change to $5\frac{1}{2}$%. A rise of 1% was 'normal' and was to be seen as a wise accompaniment to the other measures. Anything more dramatic would have suggested a crisis when none existed. In a very private note to the Deputy Editor of *The Times*, Maurice Green, Cobbold confirmed the Court's view that monetary policy had been at risk of being overloaded. The Bank would not have been willing to go to $5\frac{1}{2}\%$ unless it had been satisfied about the adequacy of the accompanying measures. Much would have been gained if the week's decisions could bring about a 'new feeling that credit policy in the private sector is being used in harmony with financial policy in related spheres'. The initial reaction of markets was in fact rather grudging and the Chancellor was left in the position of having to do more in his Budget if opinion were to be fully convinced.

In the meantime the Governor had been exploring possible extensions to the scope of official requests or, as Macmillan might have phrased it, extending the co-operative effort of all those who believed in freedom. One idea, which started running at a meeting with the Chancellor on 3 February, was to appeal directly to large industrial companies whose own financial resources were big enough to make them immune from credit-rationing by banks. The appeal, to be made by Macmillan, would be for restraint in capital expenditure. As a start, the Bank undertook to compile a list of such companies. Another idea was to obtain the co-operation of the BIA so as to close a gap in the apparatus of control operated by the banks and the CIC. Earlier in 1955 the Treasury had been worried about insurance companies directly undertaking commercial property development for subsequent leasing. There was also the growth of sale and lease-back transactions. But the Bank had advised that a request to such companies would not be sufficiently effective. However, at a lunch they gave the Governor on 24 January, the Committee of the BIA encouraged him to think that they were anxious to be co-operative. Early in the next month the Chairman of the BIA, J. A. Pollen of London Assurance, called at the Bank and asked the Governor whether he would be prepared to speak informally and privately to insurance general managers about the monetary situation and policy. He also volunteered a draft note containing a set of guidelines that the Governor might indicate would not conflict with official policy. Cobbold gave these ideas a cautious welcome. He could not dictate a course of action to insurance companies and did not wish to be seen trying to do so. But he was certainly ready to support the credit squeeze by endorsing a BIA initiative designed to restrain the companies from responding to new business which the squeeze on bank lending was pushing in their direction. After consultation with the Treasury, where he was given encouragement, he agreed the guidelines with Pollen, who circulated them to his members. He also spoke informally to general managers. The guidelines were four in number: not to make loans for purposes directly counter to Government wishes (e.g. hire-purchase); to go slow on finance for industrial and commercial companies or for property development; to defer building plans where reasonably possible; and to look with favour on propositions approved by the CIC. This example of an auto-directive, whose effects could not in practice be policed, was supplemented by a Parliamentary Answer in which the Chancellor sought to discourage sale and lease-back of commercial property. It is not known how successful he was. As to Pollen's guidelines, he reported back to the Governor in April saying that the exercise had gone quite well but that he had had difficulty with two large members of the BIA.

In mid-March the Bank returned to Whitehall with its promised list of large industrial companies and it was agreed that the Chancellor should seek their co-operation by inviting a series of groups to No. 11 for drinks. This corporatist essay in extended requests did not get very far, if anywhere. Nor did a request to the British Overseas Airways Corporation asking them to desist from selling airline tickets payable by instalments. BOAC replied that although they would cease advertising the facility, they had no practical choice but to match their competitors. There was however a much more serious cloud overhead. The Bank had been worried for some time about the growing avoidance of monetary controls by finance companies. Some of the larger ones had been taking competitively bid deposits for some years. They had now been joined by a multitude of small companies whose initial capital was below the CIC minimum of £50,000. A secondary or fringe banking system was in the making, with its implied dangers both to the integrity of official monetary controls and to the safety of depositors. As is related in Chapter 11(d), the Bank had given close thought to this problem during the winter of 1955–56 and concluded that legislation would be needed to provide for the licensing and supervision of deposit-taking finance houses. Preliminary discussions had been opened with the Treasury and the Board of Trade. But for the present it was avoidance of the credit squeeze that most worried the Governor. In February the Manchester Branch reported that 'industrial bankers' had no difficulty raising money at 8%, which they on-lent at 11%.[19] A few days later Lombard Banking Ltd, a leading finance house, reported a sharp rise in deposits, a rapid growth in its balance sheet, and record profits. The Governor was angry and remarked: 'These people are sabotaging our

---

[19] In April 1930 the Bank began to obtain regular quarterly reports from its Branch Agents on the local state of trade. The material so provided was incorporated in a quarterly Industrial Report prepared by Statistics Office. The frequency of both reports became monthly in March 1951 when the Industry Report, with a covering note by the economic adviser, began to be taken at monthly meetings with the Governors.

policy and the sooner we get after them the better.' But the Chief Cashier had to tell him early in March that there was no quick and ready way of doing this. The matter was brought up at a meeting with the Chancellor, at which the Governor said that fresh legislation was required. Shortly afterwards, on the basis of a Report submitted by the Treasury, the Board of Trade, and the Bank, Ministers decided that a full licensing Bill would have to be prepared. It was bound to be a lengthy process; and when it was eventually prepared the Government was to decline to introduce it.

The squeeze was now showing decided signs of wear. On one side it was obliging the authorities to try extending requests into territory where compliance was both less reliable and less observable. On the other, it was forcing the growth of a competitively organised parallel market in deposits,[20] with obvious dangers to the regime of credit control, which could only be properly reached through new and complicated primary legislation. As to the banks themselves, the downward trend in advances came to a halt in February and March, contrary to the Chancellor's wishes about the angle of decline; and the Chief Executive Officers told Peppiatt that it was becoming increasingly difficult to achieve further reductions, despite the further rise in Bank Rate. They added, however, that the general atmosphere had become much more restrained and that in many directions there were undoubted signs of a slow-down in investment. But the 'technical pressures' on the banks were not strong. The liquidity ratio at mid-March was as high as 33%, despite a better gilt-edged market after the February measures and net official stock sales of nearly £90 million during the first quarter of the year. (£300 million of a new short-dated stock, Exchequer 5% 1967, was issued early in March and £104 million was sold at once.)

It was therefore not surprising that Macmillan began to get uneasy about monetary policy. On 20 March he told Cobbold that while he was resisting pressure to appoint a Committee to conduct a public enquiry into the monetary system and monetary policy,[21] he was beginning to favour an internal enquiry. He soon got beyond that stage and began exploring the possibility of early action. 'You and I are buffeted about on the waves of chance', he wrote to the Governor in vintage style on 23 March, 'the

---

[20] The full organisation of such a market, with deposit brokers emerging as intermediaries, was further facilitated by the growth of Local Authority deposit-taking, in the form known as Temporary Money. In the autumn of 1955, in the interests of diversifying public sector borrowing, the access of Local Authorities to the PWLB was restricted and at the same time the ban on local authority 'mortgages' of less than seven years' original life was removed. The subsequent growth of the temporary money market and of associated money-broking business was a result.
[21] The source of this pressure was a deputation led by Bob Boothby.

press is demanding more and more toughness...I have to try and do this in a Budget and you in the conduct of monetary policy... but as you well know, if you put more taxes upon the mass of people they demand more wages; and if you put it upon the higher earning classes, you depress them to a point that they will stop earning.' After relating how he was making a big effort to get large cuts in expenditure at a later stage, he asked whether, as a public gesture of real value, he might announce in his Budget Speech the imposition of a variable liquidity ratio on the banks. The purpose was to help him, 'not merely by what you are doing but by getting the full benefit of everyone knowing what you are doing. For it is not only what we are, but what we seem to be that matters in this psychological sphere.' The Budget would have to succeed in reinforcing the February measures, 'So we must not neglect any weapons, however distasteful or contrary to our traditions'.[22]

The Governor talked this over urgently with the Home Finance team and with Niemeyer before replying on 26 March in a letter that was agreed individually with members of Committee of Treasury. He reminded the Chancellor that he had already warned the banks that he might ask them to move temporarily to a higher liquidity ratio. This, he thought, had had a useful effect. But publicly prescribing a higher ratio would be a very different matter. It would look as if he were forcing the banks to hold more Treasury Bills, which would in turn look like an admission of defeat over funding and of disorder in Treasury financing. Furthermore it would not have much effect on the banks, who could top up their liquidity by failing to convert their holdings of the next maturity. It was far more important to reduce the financial demands of the public sector and improve the climate for funding than to intensify the already tough squeeze on private-sector credit. The Governor went on to defend the banks and the existing methods of control, which in his view had worked well and deserved praise rather than blame. Macmillan replied: 'I entirely agree with you. The British way of running the banking system has much to be said for it. Unfortunately, much is being said critical of it – not all from outside. For this reason anything I say on this subject must not confine itself to general praise but must make it clear how the "authorities" go about their business.'

Over the next few weeks, ahead of the Budget on 17 April, there followed a tussle between the two men about the relevant passage in the

---

[22] In 1977 Cobbold wrote: 'I have often been asked which Chancellor I though the best or the worst. I have never been willing to go beyond saying that Cripps had the most acute mind (and, contrary to general belief, a warm if shy personality) and Macmillan was the most fun to work with.'

Speech. Macmillan wanted to suggest that introduction of a variable liquidity ratio was a policy option under consideration. Cobbold wanted him to suggest that it was no longer being considered; in addition he wanted him to compliment the banks on their efforts to comply with requests. In the end it was the Governor who came out on top by pressing home the point that public hints of positive action would bring confusion and uncertainty rather than give an impression of creative resolve. But it was made clear to the Governor in private that the Chancellor had himself come to no conclusion and wanted to keep open the possibility of introducing a variable ratio, particularly because of the internal review that was getting under way and is described below. The Governor next endeavoured to pre-empt matters by proposing that he should bring pressure on the banks to reinvest their holdings of the August maturity – with an implied threat that refusal would hasten the onset of mandatory and variable liquidity ratios. But Macmillan was not to be rushed into a novel exercise in persuaded balance-sheet pressures and wanted the review to be completed first. Meanwhile, he had agreed to the issue for cash of a further tranche of Treasury $3\frac{1}{2}$% Stock 1979–89 at 81, to yield 5%. It brought in very little from the public on issue and remained to be sold through the secondary market when conditions allowed. Through the whole June quarter, however, there was no net funding. The market recovered briefly after the Budget and before the new issue was announced; but it drifted down again in May and June, yields rising to $5\frac{1}{4}$% and more while the exchange rate fell back below $2.80.

It was evident that the Budget had not served to establish market confidence and early in May the Chancellor felt that it was necessary to see the clearing bankers again and add his support to a renewed request from the Governor that the squeeze be continued. Macmillan referred to 1956 as a test year in which failure to control inflation by the present methods would entail a return to full *dirigisme*. In private, the Governor warned Robarts and Franks[23] that a variable liquidity ratio could not be ruled out. The internal review was not finally completed until the end of June, when a Report entitled 'Monetary Organisation' was submitted to the Chancellor and the Governor. It had been commissioned in April and the first meeting of the 'Four Wise Men',[24] as they were called, took place on 2 May. The initiative had come from the Chancellor, who asked Compton and Hall to prepare a report in consultation with the Bank. When he learnt about this, O'Brien (with the Governor's encouragement) set in hand a preparatory review that would include some examination of techniques employed

[23] Robarts had succeeded Aldenham as Chairman of the CLCB. Franks was now Deputy Chairman.   [24] Compton, Hall, O'Brien, and Allen.

elsewhere, especially in the US. He also obtained the Governor's approval for himself and Allen to collaborate with Compton and Hall. But the approval was heavily qualified: 'It must be very much to see how far there is a meeting of minds and very much *ad referendum*. Many points of policy may arise where differences of view may have to be considered at Governor and Court level.'

O'Brien wanted the review to suggest answers to some very difficult questions. To what extent could monetary policy be said to have failed over the preceding fifteen months? Was failure due to bad timing, to lack of severity, or to lack of statistical and other information? To what extent were the present weapons of policy inadequate or ineffective under present conditions? He also noted the Governor's particular concern, shared by Peppiatt, that prolonged use of a high Bank Rate placed a heavy burden on the Exchequer, including the payment of large sums in interest on the sterling balances. Compton, in the Treasury, was asking much the same questions, and the whole debate about monetary policy was enlivened by articles by Manning Dacey[25] and W. T. C. King in *Lloyds Bank Review* and *The Banker*. Neither of these authors favoured variable liquidity ratios. Both were advocates of more energetic funding. But Allen and O'Brien, while certainly supporters of bigger and better funding, now took a generally sceptical view of the scope for an effective monetary policy in the absence of requests and in the absence of either a cut in public-sector borrowing or some autonomous rise in savings. In memoranda written at the end of April the direct effect of practicable increases in short-term rates was again dismissed as unimportant. Movements in Bank Rate were a necessary adjunct to changes in the direction of policy, but they did not need to go as high as 5%. Pressure on bank liquidity could be effective in inducing a restriction of advances and a cut in deposits. However it was a hit-and-miss affair at the best of times, as 1955 had shown, and was in any case vulnerable to avoidance by bank sales of gilt-edged or by the running-off of maturities. Allen could see no answer to this latter problem other than asking the banks not to let their investments fall. Both he and O'Brien turned instead to the long-term rate, which they thought should be kept high so as to encourage saving rather than discourage investment. O'Brien added that sufficient saving might not be forthcoming without the forced saving of a Budget surplus. Neither saw any advantage in mandatory

---

[25] Dacey, W. Manning (d.1964). Educated London School of Economics (LSE). *News Chronicle* 1935–8, Leader Writer, *Financial News*, Editor, *The Banker* 1938–46, Assistant Editor, *Financial News*, Financial Editor, *The Observer*, Assistant Editor, *Financial Times*. Economic Adviser to Lloyds Bank 1946–64. Author, *The British Banking Mechanism* (London, Hutchinson, 1951). Honorary Fellow, LSE.

liquidity ratios. There was also a long paper by Fisher that included an account of recent experience in other countries; but he had no more to offer than the other two.

The Wise Men met on three occasions during May and at the last of these commissioned Allen to draft their Report. A first version was ready by the end of the month and was shown to the Governor at that stage. He noted that it had been a most useful exercise and was delighted at the prospect of agreed conclusions between Treasury and Bank representatives. But he again opposed the inclusion of any policy recommendations in the final version, setting out his position as follows:

> I do not think that a document of this sort is the place for recommendations about future policy in such matters as interest rates and discussions with the clearing banks. In fact I think this would tend to reduce the value of the report, which is at present an agreed objective review of historical fact and estimates of figures.
>
> The Bank's policy for the future depends largely on the course of events; the essence of monetary policy is flexibility. It would not be convenient to the Bank to deal with future policy questions in a joint report of this nature. The Bank's policy on these matters is under constant review by the Governors and the Court and is discussed regularly and frequently between Treasury and Bank in the ordinary course of business. At any time the Treasury wish to have the Bank's view on any of these future policy matters, the Bank are of course ready to give it. This has in fact been given very recently in discussions and will doubtless remain under close discussion in coming months.

With Cobbold's permission, this note was shown to Compton by the Chief Cashier. The former accepted it as a reasonable statement of the Bank's position but reminded O'Brien that the Chancellor was expecting a more policy-orientated report than the present draft. They agreed that the best course (and one frequently adopted on like occasions over subsequent years) would be to keep the Report more or less in its existing form and cover it with a separate Treasury Minute containing views about future policy. The Governor's sensitivity on matters of policy, though familiar enough, was increased at this time because the draft Report contained tentative estimates of the Exchequer and banking outcome for the remainder of 1956–7. These indicated that adequate balance-sheet pressure on the banks was unlikely to be achieved, at least not until right at the end of the period. The long-term policy issues thus raised, including the early introduction of a variable liquidity ratio, were obviously awkward and not one that the Governor could countenance being debated to a final conclusion by the Wise Men. Indeed, during June the Bank further considered the merits of an advances ratio, at the Governor's request, even though the draft Report had explained its inherent difficulties and disadvantages. The Bank also considered the possibility of ironing out the large seasonal fluctuations in bank liquidity by the issue of short-term securities that would mature in the revenue quarter and would be excluded from the liquidity ratio itself. Neither proposal survived criticism. A uniform advances ratio, imposed when uniformity of practice did not exist (the more so with the non-clearing banks) would not be feasible. Individual ratios would be getting close to individual ceilings and the strait-jacket this would entail. Evasion, through customers' bills or reclassifying advances as investments, would be easy. So in one way or another the Bank would be drawn into the detailed regulation it did not want. As to smoothing out seasonal fluctuations in liquidity through the issue of special 'non-liquid' securities, Peppiatt dismissed the idea as 'palpably bogus', which in reality it was, and not essentially different from the variable liquidity ratio which he also disliked.

In the end the Wise Men produced no new and distinctive wisdom. Monetary policy influenced spending by altering the availability and cost of borrowing and by changing business confidence. The latter was more difficult to dampen now that Governments were committed to full employment and high levels of activity. Increases in the cost of borrowing had less effect than before due to high taxation.[26] Anyway, 'conditions in money markets abroad and considerations of exchange policy restrict the range within which it is suitable for the authorities to try to keep interest rates, particularly short-term rates'. It was therefore necessary to rely rather heavily on influencing availability, though even here a restriction could be offset by an increase in velocity as previously idle balances were activated. Nor was a restriction itself easy to achieve through pressure on bank liquidity – for reasons that were now well-known, including the ability of the banks to sell investments, an activity that was itself more likely to absorb inactive deposits than reduce spending. Since mandatory ratios had their familiar disadvantages, it all came back to co-operation between the authorities and the banks, which meant preserving good relations with the latter. The Report concluded:

> In our view the most practicable and most flexible way to influence banks in this country remains that represented by existing techniques. It is a combination of the balance sheet pressures that can be exercised when the

---

[26] Sir Dennis Robertson was shown the Report privately by Compton. He was in general agreement with it. But regarding taxation and interest he remarked: 'Many have noticed this, but no one seems ready to draw the inference – that a 9/- in the £ would have to get used to larger, rather than smaller, swings in Bank Rate than a 2/- in the £ would find necessary'.

floating debt is under control and of relations between the banks and the authorities such as enable requests successfully to be made to the banks not to press the possibilities of a situation to limits that embarrass policy. The prospects now ahead are, so far as we can see, compatible with such organisation.

The Wise Men had nothing to say about the avoidances already worrying the Treasury and the Bank, nor had they anything to say about the long-run effects upon the efficiency of the banking system that would be inherent in a regime of persistent restrictive requests. The most that could be said for their Report was that it did not frighten those who received it. They were not asked to embark on some new and untried venture. The Governor found it convincing and 'considering the subject, a remarkably readable document'. In the course of a generally approving letter to Bridges, he wrote that the main lesson of the Report was that monetary action could not be effective unless fully supported by general Government policy. But to his lasting credit he added a powerful reservation about the dangers of maintaining a severe squeeze for too long:

> The efficiency of the banking machine, the normal relation between banker and customer, and a proper degree of competition to provide the best service to the public are all bound to suffer. There is a stage (I am not suggesting at what date it comes) when a credit squeeze does more harm to the country than good.

Bridges agreed that the character of the squeeze and the heavy reliance on requests was indeed likely to have such effects. But neither he nor the Governor had any monetary prescription for avoiding it. With greater use of the interest rate still ruled out, the only solution was to rely more heavily on fiscal policy, a course blocked by political resistance. All that was left was to carry on with the squeeze as best one could.

Sterling slipped below $2.80 in June 1956 and the reserves had stopped rising. Yields on medium- and long-dated gilt-edged continued to edge up, the latter to $5\frac{1}{4}\%$. In the middle of the month the Governor spent several days talking with industrialists in the Midlands and the North. He was told that the credit squeeze was holding and that small- and medium-sized firms had become more cautious about new commitments. But the very large firms and the nationalised industries were going ahead as if little or nothing had happened. He found much resentment against the latter, who were thought to be virtually immune from cuts and to be setting a bad example on wages. Writing about this to the Chancellor on 18 June, Cobbold said he thought there should be further cuts and that undertakings should be made about a stiffer attitude to public-sector wage claims. The Chancellor should then see twenty or thirty leading industrialists (as the Governor had suggested earlier in the year, to no effect) and seek their co-operation both on wages and on capital expenditure. There was little response. Macmillan was more interested in reinforcing the credit squeeze within the context of the Wise Men's Report. Accordingly, on 27 June the Governor wrote to Bridges, proposing that the banks should be asked to maintain the full force of the squeeze and in addition so to manage their policy on investments that the incidence of the August maturity and other factors did not produce an excessively high liquidity ratio. If liquidity did become clearly excessive, the authorities would be forced to consider a higher and mandatory liquidity ratio. These proposals were accepted, along with the Wise Men's Report, at a meeting with the Chancellor and officials on 4 July, and the Governor spoke accordingly to Robarts and Franks on the following day.[27] He was supported by a Parliamentary Answer in which Macmillan said the Government was anxious that the full force of the credit restrictions should be maintained. On 6 July it was announced that holders of the August maturity would be offered a new six-year $4\frac{1}{2}\%$ stock in exchange. The offer was to be closed on 20 July. For their part the banks noted what had been said to them about liquidity and agreed to continue their existing restrictive policy on advances, but they warned that it might not lead to any further substantial cut in the total.

At the meeting on 4 July it had also been agreed that the Chancellor should meet the bankers again, but not until after the close of the conversion offer. A meeting at the Treasury was subsequently arranged and this time representatives of all the leading banking associations, not just the London clearing banks, were invited to attend. Furthermore, the Chancellor insisted that it be followed by a communiqué whose terms would mostly be agreed in advance. This proved difficult. The underlying movement in bank advances during June proved to be upwards and, in response, Macmillan wanted a communiqué that pressed for a further reduction. The Governor argued that this would give the unfortunate impression that HMG were again placing excessive reliance on monetary policy, just as they had done a year earlier. In the end, the communiqué avoided an explicit request for a further cut, though it did contain a request for 'the contraction of credit' to be resolutely pursued; at the meeting both Macmillan and Cobbold expressed the hope that the downward trend in advances would be resumed. The banks got little in the way of assurance

---

[27] He subsequently became worried lest his message might later be said to have got less clear in transmission. On 16 July, with Robarts' concurrence, he circulated it in writing to each Chairman.

that there would be any further cuts in public spending and were again exhorted to avoid the possibility of a mandatory liquidity ratio by suitable support of the Government's funding operations. Quick on the draw, they replied that uncertainty about the liquidity regime made them want to maintain a higher ratio than usual.

At this point in the story the Suez Crisis intervened and the Chancellor's interest in the conduct of domestic monetary policy was reduced. Accordingly the Bank and the Home Finance division of the Treasury were left rather more to their own devices. The banks did redouble their efforts and the fall in advances was resumed. Excluding lending to nationalised industries, the total outstanding lending by the clearing banks in September had fallen by 10% since June 1955. But liquidity, at nearly 37%, was in the Governors' reckoning barely tolerable. The banks, particularly the Midland, had not reinvested all their holdings of the August maturity; their investments had fallen by £75 million in that month, but they did buy gilts on a modest scale in the following months. Although Macmillan was annoyed at their initial defiance on this point, the time for further threats of imposed ratios was past now that the Middle East had become the Government's preoccupation. The whole idea of managing the liquidity ratio through official requests made to the banks in private, so as to give an impression that the 'technical methods' were working as well as the direct request to reduce advances, was in any event, to use Peppiatt's phrase, 'palpably bogus'. It was a makeshift devised by the Governor in order to head off the strong Whitehall demands for a mandatory and variable ratio, demands that were part of the scenery during the first six months of 1956 and which he feared would be strengthened by the special coincidence of the August maturity. As a piece of technique, usable over a long period, it had nothing in its favour. Given the block on full use of the interest-rate weapon, there was something to be said for applying pressure on bank balance sheets as much and as often as was possible or desired. Given the hit-and-miss nature of that process, a nature enhanced by the underlent position of the banks, there was also a lot to be said for direct requests about advances. But there was nothing to be said for requesting the banks themselves to bring pressure to bear on their own balance sheets as well as asking them to restrict advances directly. Accordingly, in the closing months of 1956 the Bank again devoted considerable time to examination of the Exchequer requirements, their monetary implications, and the task of funding them satisfactorily both through ordinary operations in gilt-edged and through the issue of special securities designed to smooth out the seasonal fluctuations in the Exchequer's cash flow. But examination of the monetary implications of

Exchequer requirements had hitherto been hampered by the fact that clearing-bank figures (except at half-years) related to balances outstanding on the third Wednesday of each month, whereas the Exchequer figures related to calendar months. At long last, in August 1956, it was agreed that the latter would be provided by the Treasury Accountant on third Wednesdays so that accurately dovetailed 'Exchequer and banking figures', as they were termed, would become available.[28]

Early in October O'Brien and Allen looked into the future once more. They concluded that contrary to first impressions, and abstracting from the crisis in the Middle East, the prospect was not such as to warrant the prescription of liquidity ratios or advances ceilings. The economic situation was a little better. In particular, the external current account had returned to surplus. On the monetary side, advances were falling, the August maturity had passed, and the gilt-edged market was looking to a fall in Bank Rate early in 1957. If the Suez crisis were surmounted, the prospects for further funding seemed quite good. Since official sales in October were substantial (over the whole Suez quarter they came to £150 million) no further action was needed. For the remaining months of the year, this advice held good. Early in December, when Macmillan announced that the UK was applying for a Fund drawing in the aftermath of Suez, he was content to reaffirm existing monetary policy rather than announce any further tightening.

During the interlude provided by the combination of the Suez crisis and the abatement of bank advances, O'Brien and Allen came to final conclusions about the merits of issuing special securities so as to smooth out seasonal fluctuations in Exchequer cash flow. This idea had been rejected by Peppiatt earlier in the year. But in November 1956 Thornton[29] circulated a draft note arguing that financing seasonal deficits by the issue of liquid assets (Treasury Bills) was bad policy if nobody could ever reliably tell what part of the accumulating deficit was seasonal and what was not. There was a constant risk of the banks misjudging their liquidity in, say, September and adopting an undesirably easier policy on advances. It

---

[28] Early in January 1956 Michael Thornton had joined the Chief Cashier's team, in part as an adviser and analyst in monetary statistics. This increase in the human resources devoted to Home Finance in the Bank was long overdue and the improvement in Exchequer and banking figures was one of the results. Thornton later played a leading part in the general improvement in financial statistics followed the recommendations of the Radcliffe Committee.

[29] *Thornton, Michael James, CBE, MC (1919–89).* Educated Christ's Hospital and LSE. Entered Bank 1938, Assistant to Chief Cashier 1955–7, Deputy Principal, Statistics Office, 1957–9, Principal, Home Intelligence Office 1959–62, Assistant Chief, Central Banking Information Department 1962, Deputy Chief Cashier 1962–7, Chief of Economic Intelligence Department 1967–78.

would therefore be wise to try to iron out seasonal fluctuations in liquidity by issuing 'Revenue Bonds' that would be excluded from the banks' liquidity ratio. The aim would be to issue the bonds alongside ordinary funding so as to fine-tune the ratio at or near 30%. O'Brien was sceptical. 'Shall we not look rather foolish if we produce a new mechanism which only tidies up the present position without altering our underlying difficulty?' Nor was Allen keen. He thought it was difficult to overcome the objection that Revenue Bonds would be a bogus way of reducing liquidity and little better than direct requests. He also thought it would be unreliable. It would be difficult to judge how many bonds to sell and difficult to sell the right amount. So the idea came to nothing and the year ended with a requested credit squeeze which in its own terms was 'working', but with all the longer-term problems no further on the way to solution. Accordingly, in his post-Suez letter sent to the Chancellor and the Prime Minister on 20 December, the Governor again relied on the argument that monetary policy was being asked to do too much while fiscal policy was doing too little. He did not believe they could look to the credit squeeze for more help. Bank advances were 10% below the level of June 1955 and actually lower than they were at the end of 1951. 'In fact', he wrote, 'I think that bank advances are now as low as they should be and that an efficient private economy requires that they should begin to mount a little.' As to Bank Rate, he saw no advantage in a rise and for some months had been looking forward to the opportunity for a cut. The time was not yet ripe, but a strong Budget and clearer evidence of a flattening-out in the economy could provide the right environment. He wanted an overall Budget surplus, which he was not to get.

(f) CLIMAX AND AFTERMATH: 1957–1958

Early in January 1957 the Governors saw the Prime Minister, the Chancellor of the Exchequer, and the Lord Privy Seal (Butler) at No. 10. The meeting had been arranged in response to Cobbold's letter of 20 December, in which he had sought to use the economic aftermath of the Suez crisis as a base on which to argue for decisive domestic measures that would result in an overall Budget surplus and, he judged, a return of domestic and overseas confidence in the currency. The discussion was long and inconclusive, the Ministers doubting whether an overall surplus was practicable or desirable. A week later Eden had resigned and been succeeded by Macmillan. The resulting vacancy at the Treasury was filled by the promotion of Peter Thorneycroft from the Board of Trade. Enoch Powell became Financial Secretary and Nigel Birch, Economic Secretary.

The new Chancellor was unlike Macmillan or Butler. Intellectual subtlety and persuasive charm were not his style. He preferred clarity, simplicity and the issue of clear instructions rather than carefully phrased requests. He preferred statutory authority to less formal methods of getting his way and was frightened rather than encouraged by a long-standing credit squeeze that relied more upon co-operation than compulsion. He was rightly nervous of losing control of events, a nervousness that was by no means misplaced after the unimpressive record of economic policy since the winter of 1954–5 and the consequential weakening of the Government's authority, a weakening intensified by the Suez affair and the fall of Eden. Nor did the record of 1955–6 predispose him to rely only on Treasury economists for professional economic advice. In the late summer and autumn of 1957 Thorneycroft paid close attention to the opinions of Professor Lionel Robbins. Following the rise in Bank Rate to 7% in September, a struggle with the CLCB about lending ceilings, and the short-lived adoption of strict money supply control as a key objective of policy, Robbins even joined a Treasury and Bank working party, chaired by the Economic Secretary, on the problems of monetary policy.

In the end the attachment of these Treasury Ministers to a firm clarity and simplicity, together with a refreshing conviction that blurred edges spelt weakness, led to their collective resignation early in January 1958. Since the Prime Minister and other members of the Cabinet had refused to accept in their entirety the cuts in estimates needed to hold public expenditure level, the Chancellor and his two colleagues preferred to go. Thereafter, the conduct of policy returned more to the British norm. This left monetary policy in a state of part reform with its dilemmas only partially resolved. Largely on the belated initiative of the Bank, but also in the absence of any other worthwhile option, Bank Rate had suddenly been restored to a position where it could be used to achieve decisive results. But the authorities seem to have lacked full appreciation of their own achievement. Seared by the preceding struggle between the Government and the banks and reluctantly concluding that some continuing special means of controlling bank advances remained a political and practical necessity, the Bank finally gave way to Whitehall demands. It accepted that a ratio control would have to be put into place if quantitative requests and self-denying ordinances were ever to be eliminated. The upshot, endorsed by the Radcliffe Committee, was Special Deposits. This scheme was introduced in the summer of 1958 and misled people into believing that there had been fashioned a new and effective weapon that both replaced direct controls and made exclusive reliance on Bank Rate unnecessary. The upshot later on was an insensate mixture of Bank Rate, seldom if ever used decisively, of ineffectual Special Deposits, and of rigid lending ceilings that bred evasion and discontent. Thus the events of 1957, though certainly an interesting and lively climax to the sequence begun early in 1955, ended in a kind of watery false dawn that heralded no lasting sunlight for the Bank.

But as the new Prime Minister took office and the new Treasury Ministers arrived, the Governor allowed himself some modest optimism. In a manuscript letter of congratulation and thanks sent to Macmillan on 10 January, he again advised drastic measures on public expenditure, using this time an unfamiliar personal argument calculated to appeal to its recipient. 'My bugbear has always been that if we strain all our resources, do a lot of non-productive and semi-productive capital expenditure and spend too much money in the years when employment is over-full, we shall be left with nothing up our sleeves to fight unemployment when things turn the other way... The more brickbats you have thrown at you in the next two months, for being tough all along the line, the more the country will follow you and the more they will thank you in the end.' The Prime Minister's reply was cordial and encouraging and included the sentence: 'I was very interested in what you wrote and with your permission I shall show your letter to the new Chancellor.' Encouragement came also from the markets. Sterling moved up to 2.79\frac{3}{4}$ in January. Gilt-edged recovered. Funding operations were resumed on a substantial scale and raised official hopes of liquidity pressure on the banks. The Treasury Bill rate began to fall and the Bank did not resist. The banks renewed their self-denying ordinance for only a further three months, but Cobbold did not object, believing there was some hope of getting away from it during the summer. By the end of the month he judged that the time had come to get Bank Rate down a little. In keeping with the message-tagging developed in 1953 and 1954, it would of course be presented as only a technical adjustment, not to be taken as a sign of easier policy; but it could encourage the gilt-edged market, which might otherwise run out of steam, and it would avoid an appearance of getting stuck on a near-crisis Rate of $5\frac{1}{2}\%$. The Chancellor was at first doubtful, but early in February he agreed to a move and the Rate was reduced to 5% on 7 February. Outward telegrams to central banks mirrored press briefing and stated: 'It will not be an indication of any easing of monetary policy but rather of the flexible use of existing weapons in the maintenance of a restrictive policy the need for which is not ended.'

The move to 5% was misjudged. It had been widely expected in the markets and largely discounted. It was also followed immediately by the issue of a second tranche of £300 million of $3\frac{1}{2}\%$ Funding Stock

1999–2004,[30] virtually all of which was taken up by the Bank for sale in the market when opportunity offered. The new year optimism at once subsided. Sterling rose no further. Gilt-edged fell back a little and official sales of stock were halted. Bank advances rose sharply and disconcertingly in February, an enquiry by the Deputy Governor eliciting from Robarts the bleak reply that the demand for credit for essential purposes of national importance was immense and increasing. With advances for non-essential purposes already severely curtailed, a rise in the total had to be expected. Looking afresh at the economic prospects for 1957, Allen advised that domestic demand, especially in the public sector, was too buoyant. It would be very difficult to hold down the level of bank advances yet again; but the attempt would have to be made. However, it no longer looked as if any restraint on the banks would be forthcoming from liquidity pressure. With funding halted and various random factors turning adverse, the ratio in March and April looked like being 32% and more.

It was against this darker background that on 15 March the Bank had its first full encounter with the new Chancellor, who was now busy formulating his budgetary and monetary policy for 1957–8. On the table was a joint Treasury and Bank paper entitled 'Monetary Measures', which had been prepared as a supplement to the earlier Report of the Four Wise Men. It advocated maintenance of a high (for example 5%) long-term rate because its authors judged that this would be effective in attracting investors into government debt. It advised against aiming for high short-term rates. Movements in Bank Rate were useful in affecting expectations, in influencing overseas views about sterling, or in conveying official messages. Downward moves, $\frac{1}{2}$% at a time and with the Bank following rather than leading the market, were usually 'technical', upward moves, 1% or more at a time, were usually 'policy'. But there was 'not much point in having a high short-term rate for the sake of its direct effect on borrowers' because the classical function of discouraging the borrower had been very much weakened by high taxation and full employment. As to control over bank credit and the associated need for an effective and resolute funding policy together with an Exchequer surplus, the paper again pointed out the well-known difficulties of exerting sufficient balance-sheet pressure on the banks and the resulting need for 'requests'.

By this time it had been decided, the Governor not dissenting, to announce in the Budget Debate that a Committee of Enquiry into the monetary system would be appointed. However, two years might elapse before it reported and the Chancellor was in no mood to wait that long for

---

[30] A first tranche of £139 million had been issued in July 1954 as part of a conversion offer in respect of 1$\frac{3}{4}$% Serial Funding Stock 1954.

an answer to the nagging problems of credit control. He was worried and upset by the rise in bank advances in February. Though warned of the difficulties by Mynors, he was convinced that the rise must be halted, whether or not this meant a restriction of lending to high-priority borrowers. The Government could help by aiming for an Exchequer cash surplus. Opportunities for successful funding should also be taken. But in any event the banks should be asked to hold the level of advances at about the end-1956 level. The Bank was told to discuss this with the CLCB, whom the Chancellor would himself wish to meet before final Budget decisions were taken. There could also be some tightening of the guidance given to the CIC. Shortly after this meeting the Governor returned from a trip to Southern Africa to be greeted by a curt letter from Thorneycroft saying that the rise in bank advances left him with the uncomfortable feeling that the economy was slipping out of his control. 'It is not so much that I think we ought to apply the brake any harder at the moment; but I do want to know that we have a brake that works.'

Cobbold fought his corner when he wrote back on 21 March. It would be unrealistic to suppose that advances would not rise perceptibly in 1957 and it would be wrong policy to attempt to prevent that rise. The banks, who were behaving sensibly, should be allowed to accommodate priority needs and he did not think their doing so would present any real problem. A more promising course might be to devise some outright monetary check on development expenditure in areas where the Government footed the bill and where at present there was no financing impediment. These arguments were pressed when the Governors and the Chief Cashier attended a meeting with Thorneycroft and officials on 25 March. Cobbold adding that the banks were getting restless with the self-denying ordinance and the denial of all competition. A credit squeeze might be all right as a short-term instrument, but if it was necessary to prolong it for a long period something fundamental must have gone wrong elsewhere. The Chancellor then paid attention to the Bank's advice and accepted that some increase in the level of advances might result from the provision of bank finance for purposes of the highest priority, for example medium-term export credit. On this basis, agreement to maintain the squeeze was reached with the CLCB and other banking associations and announced in the Budget Speech on 7 April. But the Governor had written to the Chancellor again on 4 April, drawing attention to 'the general feeling in the banking industry that maintenance of a voluntary credit squeeze and of agreements not to compete for business becomes increasingly difficult as time goes on'. The monetary passage in the Budget Speech referred *inter alia* to the widest differences of opinion among the best qualified people in a difficult field about how best to attain agreed objectives of monetary policy. It concluded by announcing the appointment of a Committee 'to enquire into the working of the monetary and credit system, and to make recommendations'.

The Budget was restrictive but not decisive. After relatively minor tax concessions, the projected overall deficit, £125 million, was low; but the Governor had failed to persuade the Government that drastic measures should be taken and an overall surplus established. That would not have been Macmillan's style and the new Chancellor had yet to establish himself as a dominant force in economic policy making. Accordingly if the Bank was correct in its judgement, confidence was likely to remain low and sterling was likely to remain vulnerable to every passing shower. However, for a few months there was an uneasy pause, a fortunate one because the Bank and its opposite numbers in the Treasury were hard at work preparing written evidence for the Radcliffe Committee. Bank advances, which had risen sharply in February and March, quietened down. Sterling kept steady just above $2.79 and the reserves rose a little, reaching £850 million at the end of June compared to £781 million in January. Over the same period the Treasury Bill rate fell a little, to below 4%. Early in May O'Brien began to consider a further cut in Bank Rate. In the gilt-edged market, initial responses to the Budget were favourable and the Bank at first made good progress with further refinancing of the June maturities.[31] Official sales of stock were appreciable and the issue early in May of a further tranche of £100 million $4\frac{1}{2}$% Conversion 1962 attracted public subscription totalling £62 million. But conditions subsequently deteriorated, yields at the long end of the market rising above $5\frac{1}{2}$% by the end of June. A period of low morale, beset by despair and exasperation about seemingly perpetual inflation, was setting in. At the end of May the Governor wrote in very gloomy terms to the Chancellor about growing anxieties over the longer-term future of sterling, growing doubts whether any Government would be able to reverse the inflationary drift that seemed to beset the UK economy, and the consequential growing difficulties with Exchequer financing. Demand, particularly consumer demand, was again rising and recent wage awards of up to 5% (associated with a 7% rise in earnings) did nothing to help. Drawing on impressions from a variety of sources, he believed there to be a strong and growing current of gloomy opinion and he asked that his letter be shown to Macmillan and Butler. Nothing happened and the uneasy pause continued.

The Governor continued to worry and sought advice about what should

[31] £300 million of 5% Exchequer 1957 and £101 million of $2\frac{3}{4}$% Funding 1957.

be done from a wide range of his advisers. Allen, Fisher, Menzies, Raw, Rootham, Stamp, Thompson-McCausland, and Fforde were all asked for their individual views. Allen managed somehow to avoid replying, at least in writing, while none of the others came up with anything very fresh or appetising.[32] Jack Fisher was perhaps nearest the mark when he advocated a hefty package that would include imposition of a general sales tax, a higher Bank Rate ('even exceeding 6%'), a compulsory variable liquidity ratio for the banks, a tightening of exchange control on credit to non-residents, and a much stronger exhortatory lead from Ministers. Cobbold listened to it all and held his own fire. Towards the end of July, as the exchange rate eased ominously to 2.78\frac{1}{2}$ and the reserves fell slightly, he again turned his attention to Exchequer financing. Funding in the June quarter had been slightly negative and although this could in part be attributed to a seasonally high Exchequer deficit and to the redemption in June of maturing stock that remained in private hands, the market was poor and the outlook unpromising. Moreover a further £500 million of gilt-edged ($2\frac{1}{4}$% Serial Funding Bonds) was to mature in November. O'Brien and Allen were arguing that the overall deficit for the year looked like being carried on Treasury Bills (as it turned out, a correct judgement). The Governor then wrote to the Chancellor, pointing out the probable awkwardness of mounting a conversion offer for the November maturity if there was still little demand for medium- or long-dated stock and when an offer of short-dated stock would very visibly add to the already heavy load of maturities in the next few years. Some refinancing could of course be achieved if there were opportunities for selling stock already in the Issue Department, but the Bank was left with the general impression that in current conditions out-payments below-the-line that were not met from a surplus above-the-line had to be financed on floating debt, mostly from the banks. If bank financing was thought to be dangerous when undertaken to meet a deficit in the private sector, as the Government held, was it not equally dangerous if done by the public sector? Was this not an argument for looking again at the overall deficit itself?

To complete the picture of domestic gloom, the Governor was again made aware of the banks' restiveness over the self-denying ordinance. It had been reluctantly renewed for a further three months in April, the Chief Executive Officers unaminously agreeing that 'banking as a whole suffers when the element of competition is withdrawn. Initiative and enterprise become stifled in such conditions and relation between the banks and their

---

[32] Though Thompson-McCausland, who was developing heterodox monetary theories of his own, advocated a vast and special funding operation in order to reduce the inflationary forces that he saw adhering to the monetary and securities 'structure'.

customers suffer.' With similar reluctance, self-denial was renewed for a further three months in July. On 1 August the Governor met the CLCB and offered them no cheer. Restriction would have to continue. Asked about the ordinance, he said he shared the bankers' dislike for it as a permanent or semi-permanent arrangement. His private view was that if restrictions on bank lending had to go on for a long time, which he hoped would not be the case, some other method would have to be found so as to dispense with voluntary self-denial. Perhaps the Radcliffe Committee would come up with the answer.

The uneasy pause came to an abrupt end in August. Sterling came under attack after the *de facto* devaluation of the French franc on August 10[33] and the reserves suddenly fell by over £80 million (down to $2.14 billion). The Bank, and with it the Treasury, was now getting into a tight corner from which the various expedients employed since 1955 no longer provided an assured escape. Moderate restraint in fiscal policy had been tried repeatedly, with insufficient results in terms of domestic and overseas confidence or of chronic inflationary tendencies. The credit squeeze imposed in the summer of 1955 had been maintained with similar inadequate results and was showing signs of increasing wear and tear. External borrowing had been undertaken after Suez, but the breathing space provided had not been used to best effect. More recently, Exchequer financing seemed to be approaching a state of inflationary disorder that alarmed the Bank. Nothing had been done in July, before the Parliamentary Recess, to guard against an autumn crisis. The Chancellor had alternately issued warnings about inflation and made encouraging remarks about the state of the economy. The Government had announced the formation of a three-man Council on Prices, Productivity, and Incomes to dispense wisdom in the jungle, a well-meaning but unconvincing contribution.[34] Yet within weeks the exchange situation had turned sharply adverse and the chances of avoiding an autumn package were small.

On earlier occasions in his career the Governor had shown himself ready to change ground quickly once he had concluded that existing policies using existing methods were no longer working and could not be made to work in short order. August and September 1957 provided another such

---

[33] Baumgartner came to London for the day on 22 July and a change in the franc exchange rate was mentioned. Cobbold telephoned him on 7 August but was told that a move was now less likely. The French authorities attempted to avoid *de jure* devaluation by a series of import surcharges and export subsidies, but exchange markets responded by quoting the franc as if it had been devalued by 20%.

[34] Its highly distinguished members were Lord Cohen, Sir Dennis Robertson, and Sir Harold Howitt (a judge, an economist, and an accountant).

occasion. The Bank was truly boxed in and an attempt had to be made to get out, by violence if need be. On 22 August, before leaving on a badly needed holiday, Cobbold sent the Chancellor a memorandum sketching out a possible package of measures that would include a drastic increase in Bank Rate. The note was very much his own work, though agreed in discussion with Mynors, Hawker, O'Brien, and Fforde and put together after another quick canter round the familiar course of ratio controls, etc.[35] It relied very little on the deteriorating exchange situation and concentrated instead on the domestic outlook. Demand was growing and inflationary pressures were building up, not as bad as in 1955 but just as dangerous because confidence had been so impaired in the meantime. If these signs were confirmed in September, measures would have to be taken. 'They should be sharp and comprehensive, and (bearing in mind various doubts on the international horizon and possibilities that the tide may turn) they should so far as possible be easily reversible.' For reasons that had already been stated many times the Governor argued that the credit squeeze was played out[36] and that no new device would be worthwhile. Accordingly 'the only candidate left in the monetary field (apart from maintaining existing requests to bankers) is a drastic increase in Bank Rate either in one move or in quick stages. The objections are obvious and by itself further Bank Rate action could well do more harm than good. We should, however, consider it seriously if we judged that in conjunction with a general programme it would have quick effects and that very high rates need not be maintained too long.' The rest of the memorandum was mainly concerned to scout a variety of general fiscal possibilities, both on the expenditure side and on taxation. It concluded by noting that the immediate exchange prospects also pointed to a sharp disinflationary package. The Governor discussed his note with Makins and Compton and was strongly discouraged from believing that any short-order cuts in public expenditure were feasible.

The Governor was on holiday in Sardinia until 14 September and it fell to Mynors to steer the Bank through the first part of a veritable mine-field. He began by seeking further advice from the Home Finance team in the Bank, asking for a review of possible further monetary measures designed to restrict expenditure in the private sector. The Chief Cashier argued

---

[35] It included an examination of 'Special Deposits' matching and therefore neutralising increases in bank liquidity. Niemeyer, invited as usual to contribute wisdom at such conjunctures, regarded them as 'just another dodge', and concluded: 'I am rather frightened of adventuring on the north face of the Eiger with a rather threadbare rucksack and not many crampons.' He was right.

[36] Mynors, commenting by letter, thought that concentrating on bank advances was 'escapism' and that Bank Rate deserved more thought.

against imposing a ceiling on bank advances by a direction under the Bank Act, for he judged it would be exceedingly difficult to apply. A variety of loopholes would have to be stopped; it would operate arbitrarily and harshly in particular cases; and it would be a step down a long road of detailed control. He therefore advocated a different approach. CIC control should be tightened. Hire-purchase terms control should also be tightened and in addition be followed by simple legislation bringing deposit-taking finance houses within the official net. Finally, there should be a fierce rise in Bank Rate, which 'might have quite different consequences from the gradual intensification which has so far been the policy'. It could convince 'opinion', stop the drain on the reserves, and turn the gilt market. The consequences might be sharply deflationary, but the exchange situation left the authorities with little alternative. Fforde, only recently recruited and acting in the absence of Allen on holiday, took the argument a stage further. Since July nothing had emerged regarding the domestic economic situation to justify further measures in keeping with the Government's declared policies. Nor had there emerged any change in the balance of payments prospects, which had recently been favourably assessed. Admittedly the exchange situation had deteriorated, but this was due to the European currency tangle and did not of itself justify drastic measures in the UK. Nonetheless, the drain on the reserves could compel the Government to take such action, regardless of other arguments to the contrary. The order would then be to do something drastic first and sort out the consequences afterwards. This was a temptation and an opportunity. In his judgement the internal situation was probably much more vulnerable than before to any further steep increase in monetary stringency:

> With one abrupt move there is the vision of:
>
> (i) Halting inflation in its tracks while preserving full employment in the future.
> (ii) Creating, after a short period of confusion, a 'rebound' in the gilt-edged market and a restoration of confidence in fixed-interest securities generally – lower rates therefore being sustainable in the future.
> (iii) Restoring external confidence in sterling and, over the years, greatly improving its strength.
>
> I think, as I will argue below, that there is only one method of carrying through such a policy in the present context – namely, a fierce rise in Bank Rate.

Fforde went on to support, reinforce, and add to the Chief Cashier's arguments against relying on a ceiling on bank advances and in favour of a steep increase in Bank Rate. But the latter 'would not be any ultimate use if it failed to achieve its primary objective, the quick halting of internal inflation. There may be a danger that it would too successfully convince foreign opinion and prospective purchasers of gilt-edged; and that there would then be overwhelming domestic pressure to reduce the Rate before it has done its work internally. A few weeks may, I suggest, really mean a few months.' With the Governors already convinced that the credit squeeze was played out and with the Chancellor heeding advice about getting the money supply under firm control, the vision seen by O'Brien and Fforde was to prove attractive.

But if the Bank was coming round willy-nilly to advocacy of a sharp rise in short-term interest rates, the Treasury was not. The Chancellor, now persuaded that further measures were going to be needed, turned the other way and embarked on yet another direct onslaught on the banks. He wanted them to commit themselves to a ceiling on advances, if not a specified reduction. To this end he was prepared to use as much tactical pressure as he could, including threats of compulsion and of new statutory powers. Bypassing Treasury economists and apparently acting on advice from Professor Robbins, he combined this Draconian approach to the banks with the sudden adoption of a simple monetarist presentation of policy. Inflation would be halted by stopping the increase in money supply that financed it. The Government would stop its own borrowing from the banks by the simple (though by no means watertight) expedient of stopping the growth in its own expenditure. The private sector would be stopped from such borrowing by the equally simple device of directing the banks not to allow any growth in their advances. On the face of it, Bank Rate had no place in such a scheme; and in a draft paper to the Cabinet written early in September the Chancellor said as much. But, for the time being, the freeze on public expenditure turned out in practice to mean no more than placing a ceiling on public-sector capital expenditure at the 1957 level, while the ceiling on bank advances became qualified in the course of negotiation. In the end, when the exchange situation was even more pressing, the Chancellor heeded reiterated advocacy from the Governor and accepted that a 7% Bank Rate would be useful. But in the interim much energy had been spent, some might say wasted, in a collision with the CLCB, which at one stage threatened to become public and which also raised in stark terms the position of the Bank under Clause 4(3) of the Bank of England Act.

At a meeting with the Chancellor on 4 September Mynors was informed that the Government was thinking of a formal quantitative limit on bank advances and was asked to speak to Robarts and Franks about it. He did so on the following day and received the response he expected. The banks could not commit themselves to any particular level, though they were willing to maintain their existing restrictive policies. The way they ran their business, through the overdraft system, made commitment to a rigid and restrictive figure impossible without risking the dishonouring of obligations to customers. They added, very pertinently, that things were getting to the stage at which a rise in interest rates would have a real effect on borrowers. The Deputy then told the Chancellor that the banks could not commit themselves to an advances ceiling though they were prepared to discuss the question with him if he wished.

On 9 September Thorneycroft and his officials met Mynors, Robarts, and Franks. The banks were told bluntly that the Government wanted to *impose* a limit on bank credit in parallel with the proposed limit on public expenditure. Robarts replied, equally bluntly, that the banks had already restricted advances to the point where any further cuts must frustrate exports and other essential activities. A specific limit would be both unwise, leading to dislocation and loss of confidence, and unworkable. He offered an agreement to maintain or perhaps intensify present restrictive policies if they were assured that the Government would cut its own spending. The Chancellor repeated his demand for a ceiling on advances, saying that it was for the Government rather than the banks to take responsibility for the consequences. Robarts refused to comply with the demand and was supported by Franks, who expressed considerable scepticism about the supposed cuts in public spending and suggested that any restrictive action by the banks should be supported by a rise in the cost of borrowing. The Chancellor said he did not rule out dearer money as a supporting measure. He was also ready to consider exempting export finance and other special commitments from the ceiling. But Robarts still refused to accept a quantitative limit, using this time the very bad argument that the banks must be allowed to respond to the need for a higher level of advances to finance the same volume of trade at higher prices. The meeting ended in deadlock and with the Chancellor saying he would like to meet the entire CLCB on 11 September. During the discussion Thorneycroft had threatened to impose an advances limit by Act of Parliament.[37]

The Deputy Governor's hour had come. He moved quickly so as to make it quite clear to the Chancellor where the Bank stood on the vital issue that

---

[37] This was omitted from the Minutes. At Robarts' instigation, Mynors mentioned the omission to Compton but suggested that perhaps the record were better silent on the point.

had been raised. He knew what the banks were and were not prepared to offer. He knew the Chancellor was in a mood to impose on the banks a limit that they could not voluntarily accept and to which they might well take exception in public. He also knew that the only statutory powers in existence were those contained in the Bank of England Act and that they could not be used unless the Bank considered it in the public interest; and he knew that judging the public interest, in this context, was reserved by law to the Governors and their colleagues on the Court. The Treasury could not order them to make a particular judgement. The unexploded bomb dropped by the Act was in danger of going off. Mynors must have spent some anxious hours before deciding what advice, as acting Governor, he should give the Chancellor ahead of his meeting with the full CLCB. But his conclusions were bold, clear, and decisive. The dangers of a public collision between the authorities and the banks, with the Bank itself a party to the imposition of statutory compulsion quite contrary to its long-established practice, far outweighed any supposed benefit to the monetary policy the Government was wanting to pursue. Accordingly, it was extremely doubtful whether the Court would judge the issue of a formal directive to be necessary in the public interest; and on 10 September Mynors so informed the Chancellor, in a letter ranking as important as any ever written by a Deputy Governor. He began by arguing that a formal ceiling, whether workable or not, was unnecessary and was unlikely to secure the results expected from it. There was no evidence of laxity in the granting of new overdraft limits, which might justify imposition of an advances ceiling. Moreover a formal limit 'by no means necessarily hits the people you wish to influence and can to an incalculable extent be evaded by a redeployment of existing bank deposits'. Mynors the economist had never been an admirer of currency-school thinking. The letter continued:

> I expect that the clearing bankers will be willing to give you a renewed assurance that they will continue their present restrictive attitude for a further period. I judge that I can secure a similar assurance from other bankers. I do not expect, for the reasons given you by their Chairman and Deputy Chairman, that they will voluntarily accept a formal limitation. It would not serve the purpose in view if you were publicly to express a wish to which they felt in honesty bound to demur: or indeed to which they found themselves in fact unable to conform.
>
> The question then arises of powers, if not of sanctions. The only existing powers reside in the Bank Act 1946. Without having consulted my colleagues, I feel bound to advise you that I much doubt whether they would think it 'necessary in the public interest' to seek your authority for issuing a direction under that Act, by which a formal limit of the kind under

Humphrey Mynors, Deputy Governor 1954–1964
TOM HUSTLER

discussion was imposed on the clearing and other bankers. To take fresh powers is not only out on the present timetable: but I need hardly say that it would raise the gravest questions of the relations between the government and the banking system. It is not necessary to plead the existence of the Radcliffe Committee as an excuse for not pursuing this subject: one look at the exchange situation is enough.

Whether they liked it or not, Treasury Ministers now knew that compulsion was not practicable for the present. They had to do their best without it, by negotiation. After the Deputy Governor and all eleven members of the CLCB had trooped into his room on 11 September, Thorneycroft (who was on this occasion joined by Birch as well as by officials) began by again proposing a ceiling on advances as part of a policy to control the money supply. He received the same answer as before. The banks could not commit themselves to a quantitative limit; the CLCB was unanimous on this point. To the argument that he was only asking the banks to do what they would have to do anyway if the authorities could exert sufficiently liquidity pressure, Franks replied that their response would be to sell investments and that they had no experience of a situation in which they would be obliged by such pressure to reduce advances. He went on to argue that even if some means were found to bring advances down, they would be replaced 'by unsecured deposits and other forms of non-bank credit'. Thorneycroft then made a number of concessions. The limit would apply to the average level of advances in the ensuing twelve months compared to the average level in the preceding twelve. He would announce this as his objective and the banks might respond with a statement that they would use their best endeavours to meet this limit. He was also prepared, reluctantly, to consider exemption of medium-term export credit (and perhaps other special advances) from the calculation of the objective. Nonetheless he intended to monitor progress very closely. If results were not adequate, the Government would have to consider fresh legislation. It was left that the banks would consider these revised proposals.

The Governor returned on Saturday 14 September and went straight to the Deputy Governor's house. By the morning of 18 September all decisions had been taken, the intervening period having been one of intense activity. The Governors saw the Chancellor with the Economic Secretary and the Permanent Secretary on Sunday evening. A draft statement was on the table. Cobbold spoke to a note he had prepared that day arguing that the package was not yet adequate; it was not strong enough on public expenditure and paid far too much attention to bank advances. People would think that focussing on bank advances, which were and had been well contained, was evading the main issue. The most effective monetary action would be a sharp increase in Bank Rate. But the Bank would wish to be confident that very high rates would not have to last for long; and this meant Bank Rate being supported by fiscal measures and by the restriction of finance available for hire-purchase. He was not yet sure that the Rate needed to be moved immediately. As to the draft statement, which contained an announcement about credit restriction accompanied by a threat of new legislation, he advised very strongly that it should not include any such threat. Present methods had proved effective and could be advantageously continued for a further period. In the longer run legislative changes might prove desirable but would need to have behind them the weight of an independent enquiry (Radcliffe). An attempt to rush this fence would damage overseas confidence and cause disruption in the banking system. For his part the Chancellor argued that a rise in Bank Rate, if agreed, should take place on 19 September so as to coincide with his statement. The Governor accepted that there were strong arguments in favour of such timing and undertook to consult his colleagues and come back with a firm Bank view within twenty-four hours. He also undertook to consult the clearing banks about the proposed reference to bank advances in the statement.

On the following day, 16 September, the Governor and Robarts agreed a form of words acceptable to the banks and omitting any reference to additional powers. With that exclusion the banks were now prepared 'to use their best endeavours' to achieve the results the Chancellor wanted. The Governor at once informed Thorneycroft about this in a letter that repeated earlier arguments for a stronger fiscal component. They met the same evening and the Treasury agreed to reconsider its draft about bank advances. The Chancellor also accepted the force of the argument for cuts in current expenditure in the public sector but did not see what he could do about it at that stage. As to Bank Rate, the Governor said it was becoming clear that the Court would favour an increase to a minimum of 7% and would strongly oppose a smaller increase. The Chancellor indicated some personal preference for 7%; but he made no commitment and asked for a written version of the Bank's case. Treasury officials were more doubtful, being anxious lest so high a Rate should have to be maintained for a long period.

On the morning of 17 September, the Governor prepared a telegraphic-style note on Bank Rate in consultation with the Deputy, the Chief Cashier, and Allen. By 10.30 it was on its way to the Treasury. It was a note that carried conviction because it placed full emphasis on the positive merits of going to 7%, purely as an act of monetary policy, and had virtually abandoned the usual arguments about it only being a move in support of other elements in a package. The Governor had now fully realised the strength of the weapon the Bank was proposing to use and also realised the strengthening of his own advocacy that would result from his readiness to advocate a 7% Rate on its own merits. If the fiscal side remained weak, then 7% would just have to be maintained all the longer. The note is worth quotation in full:

> It would show determination to take strong action in this field in support of objectives of draft statement.
> It would give a jolt, show that the exchange position is serious (which will anyhow become painfully evident at end-month) but that the Bank propose to fight for the pound by determined use of their weapons.

A rise of this sort would have a considerable effect on borrowers, and is likely to cause deferment of spending plans. It would, in our view, be at this stage the most effective contribution on the monetary side to restriction of spending in the private sector – much more effective than any pressures or directives on the banks.

After initial phase it should, if other action is convincing enough, help to settle gilt-edged market, which is likely to think it is the top.

It would strengthen our arguing position with the Germans in international forum, and remove accusation that it is we and not the Germans who ought to change policy.

Technically it would put London rates more where they should be in comparison with other centres and with the relative strength and weakness of currencies. It may or may not (according to the *general* programme and the conviction it carries) attract funds to London, but it will certainly discourage overseas borrowing.

If no firm Bank Rate has been taken by the time September exchange figures come out, overseas opinion and perhaps domestic opinion would judge that we were not prepared to act firmly and would have increasing doubts of our determination to hold the value of the pound.

The objections are the obvious ones of cost to budget and interest on sterling balances – but the main objectives are now so important that these should not be overriding.

Our main hesitations have been whether action on other fronts will be sufficiently strong to persuade the world (together with proposed move) that we mean what we say and are going to carry it through. If action in other fields is not strong enough and does not carry conviction, it may be difficult to reduce fairly early (as would be desirable) to a more normal rate. The effectiveness of the move will be greatly strengthened to the extent that the statement can be strengthened in other directions, particularly on current public expenditure.

Reasons why we should not contemplate a smaller move:

It would be regarded as a routine move in view of exchanges and without much significance.

When September figures come out it would be criticised as inadequate, and there would be discussions about further moves, with continuing unsettling effect on gilt-edged market.

It would have nothing like the same impact on borrowers and spending plans and would make little contribution to disinflation.

In our view, it would involve additional cost for little advantage.

Later in the morning of 17 September, after the note on Bank Rate had reached Whitehall, the Governor was informed by Makins that the Chancellor could not persuade his colleagues to accept the form of words on credit restriction that was acceptable to the banks. They had reverted to the previous draft. Cobbold advised Makins that if Ministers so persisted, the result would be a public and quite unnecessary collision between the

Government and the banks. At his suggestion, a meeting was arranged for 2.15 p.m.

The Chancellor and the Permanent Secretary faced the Governor and the Chairman of the CLCB. Robarts, who later described the meeting as 'fairly frigid', confirmed the Governor's advice and urged the Chancellor to think again before throwing away, to no useful purpose, the excellent co-operation between HMG and the banking system. The Governor, with the prior agreement of Robarts, then told the Chancellor that they would both wish to see the Prime Minister before any final decision involving a public collision was taken. Thorneycroft agreed to this and also agreed to reconsider with his colleagues the passages in dispute. Robarts then left the meeting and the Governor returned to the question of Bank Rate. All members of the Court now agreed that 7% was the minimum. Some wanted to go higher, but the Governor himself favoured 7%.[38] The Chancellor said he too was moving that way but thought that the Prime Minister would need a good deal of convincing. The Governor said he would want if necessary to have a word with the Prime Minister about the Rate. A meeting at No. 10 was then arranged for 9.00 p.m. Before it began, Thorneycroft showed the Governor a new draft that he thought should be acceptable to the banks. It was shown to Robarts, who agreed to it at a brief meeting held late in the evening after the others had emerged from No. 10. There had been a long discussion during which the Prime Minister showed a reluctance to use the 7% Rate if, as he feared, sterling could later be overwhelmed whatever was done. In the end he agreed to sleep on it and talk to the Chancellor in the morning. The next day he agreed to 7% and the Governor was so informed at 11.45 a.m. on 18 September. The change was announced twenty-four hours later, along with the freeze on public-sector capital expenditure and the target ceiling on bank advances to which the clearing banks would do their best to conform. A press briefing and telegrams to other central banks emphasised the Chancellor's determination to maintain the exchange parity of $2.80 to the pound, noted the heavy speculative pressure, and concluded: 'It has therefore been thought appropriate to make an exceptional rise of 2% to the unusually high Rate of 7% to demonstrate beyond question that the full vigour of monetary measures will be employed in support of other action taken by the Government to maintain the value of the currency.'

The rise to 7% came as a complete surprise and shock to the financial markets and to industry and commerce; and it gave credibility to the

---

[38] Discussions with various of the part-time Directors were held by the Governor on the 16, 17 and 18 September. Earlier, Mynors had sought their preliminary views.

sudden and at first sight eccentric change in the presentation of macro-economic policy, in favour of controlling the money supply. The exchange market soon recovered, the EEA began to recoup lost dollars, and the gilt-edged market regained its poise. Long-term yields had reached 6% at the end of August but had fallen to $5\frac{7}{8}\%$ at the end of September and to $5\frac{5}{8}\%$ by the end of the year. By then sterling had risen to nearly $2.81 and Bank Rate remained unchanged at 7%. Assisted by a fall in commodity prices and the onset of a sharp though brief recession in the US, the prospects, expectations, and anxieties in the UK gradually moved away from those prevalent in the summer. At the turn of the year Allen submitted a progress report to the Governor, a report the latter required for a discussion with the Chancellor. Despite Board of Trade reports somewhat to the contrary, the Economic Section in the Treasury judged that the upward trends in private investment, consumption, exports, and employment were all faltering. Allen himself was mildly sceptical about this but reported that the banks were seeing a distinct change in customer attitudes, particularly towards inventories. Further ahead, if the recession in the US continued and world trade fell slightly, the next wage-round in the UK could be very moderate and the rise in retail prices could be halted. And, for a time, it was indeed halted. The part played by the Bank Rate in bringing this about can be endlessly disputed; but it will be admitted that it served to disturb well-rooted inflationary expectations and to force attention on the cost of borrowing at a moment when cyclical factors were about to shift downwards. Robert Hall, talking to Allen early in January 1958, placed considerable weight on the effectiveness of 7% and argued that there should be no early relaxation, 'no green light anywhere'.

Whatever 7% did or did not achieve, there is no doubt about what the Bank intended it to achieve. The Governor's final note before the change made this very clear and in the course of his annual Mansion House speech delivered a few weeks later he remarked: 'Occasionally there are times when the general climate, and parallel action taken by Government in other fields, suggest that a sharp increase in interest rates can have decisive effects in the domestic economy...The immediate protection of sterling and a prospect of decisive results were both present when Bank Rate was raised to 7% three weeks ago.' The operative word was 'occasionally'. Like the memoranda written in the Bank before 19 September, the speech argued that the particular circumstances provided a particular opportunity. The proper use of Bank Rate in other circumstances had not been reconsidered. By implication it would just go on being used in the way it had been used since 1953, in a supportive and message-giving role. There were some who hoped that the decisive results expected in September 1957 would be so durable that monetary policy would not need to be returned to centre stage and that the problems of its use would accordingly become minor. But it was no more than a hope and one that proved ill-founded. It is doubtful if the Governor or the Treasury placed faith in it.[39] Accordingly, if Bank Rate could only occasionally be put to decisive use, official influence over the availability of credit rather than its cost would have to remain a key ingredient of policy. For this reason, as well as the obvious need to resolve the acute difficulties that had arisen between the Government, the Bank, and the clearing banks, official attention after 19 September was again almost exclusively concentrated on how best to induce and maintain a restriction of credit.

The Chancellor felt bruised by his encounter with the Governors and the CLCB, while Robbins was telling him that the authorities had lost control of the credit base. He was not prepared to tolerate this situation and wanted to be provided with the outline of a workable solution by the time he returned from North America in the second week of October. In a Minute beginning 'we are not in control of the credit base' he assigned this task to the Economic Secretary and a working group consisting of Treasury and Bank officials and Robbins.[40]

Losing no time, Birch held the first meeting on the afternoon of 19 September. The Bank defiantly tabled a short and unsolicited note. It roundly declared that since the problem of checking bank advances could now be considered in abeyance for a year, discussion of steps needed to get control of the credit base meant discussing means of limiting Government recourse to the banking system. For good measure it added that it was now necessary to consider 'the grey market in credit that is already with us,' one of whose effects was to cause a diversion of funds away from Government paper. Birch parried this by declaring that 'funding at all costs' was not a starter and by agreeing that work on the possible regulation of deposit-taking finance houses should be resumed. The Bank later put in a paper on the grey market, but by that time the Working Party had come to the end of its work; and despite this and other diversionary

---

[39] Shortly before the Rate was raised, the Governor told the author; 'I want to stop this nonsense [creeping inflation], once and for all.' But a week or so after it was raised I was summoned to his presence and rather nervously asked: 'Do you think it's going to work?' Equally nervously, I said I had convinced myself that if this did not work nothing would. 'Hmm', was the reply and he changed the subject, remarking: 'I'm spending far too much of my time on this damned leak business.'

[40] In addition to Birch and Robbins, the members were Padmore, Hall, Compton, Mynors, and Fforde. The Secretary was Jack Downie, a very able and percipient member of the Economic Section (whose sudden death in 1959 was a severe loss).

tactics, the Bank could not stop the group from devoting almost all of its time to alternative methods of controlling the banks, usable statutory powers being assumed throughout. After discussing a long paper from Robbins, who favoured a fixed, mandatory liquidity ratio combined with mandatory holdings, as required, of Treasury Deposit Receipts[41], a draft report was written and sent to the Chancellor on 8 October together with a clear-sighted covering Minute by Birch. He explained the favoured scheme, in which TDRs were now called 'Stabilisation Bills', and drew attention to various attendant problems. The enabling legislation would look as if the Government were taking powers to raise forced loans from the banks, which would be unfortunate. A statute might have to apply to all banks, when a uniform liquidity ratio was only applicable to the London clearers and the Scots. Compulsion could lead to detailed interference. Effective control over the banks would further encourage the grey market. The question of the supply of money could not be divorced from that of its price. In addition he informed Thorneycroft that the Bank reserved their position on the whole draft Report. But at this point the Group's work was finished; the Governor intervened, with the help of the Permanent Secretary, to sort things out directly with the Chancellor.

Cobbold had now concluded that the Chancellor and his colleagues could not be fought off by the tactics hitherto employed. He saw a real danger of the Government introducing fresh legislation that would give the Treasury powers of direct control over banks – and who knows what else besides. The existing system of credit control had in fact got to the point where it was liable to be overturned by angry or exasperated Ministers in an emergency. It followed that the Bank would be unwise to rely on it much longer. Speaking privately to the clearers in June of the following year, when he was urging them to accept the Special Deposits scheme, Cobbold said he was absolutely satisfied that 'if we run into another crisis, for whatever reason, or in any way get to a position where clamping down is necessary, a Government of either main party would

---

[41] It was a paper built on the unstated assumption that variations in Bank Rate would not suffice; and that the credit base, seemingly a synonym for money supply, had accordingly to be controlled by funding or by direct controls. He did not think funding could do the job reliably in the disturbed conditions prevailing. Accordingly, an 'extraordinary expedient' was needed until conditions returned to normal. He disliked advances ceilings because they would lead to detailed official interference, to evasion, and to objectionable self-denying ordinances. Among alternatives he preferred the liquidity ratio plus TDR as being the most flexible. He did not mind too much if the banks sold investments to their customers instead of cutting advances. Either way the credit base would be limited and he did not think that customers who bought the investments could in all cases be said to be activating idle deposits.

insist on the introduction of some new instrument rather than rely entirely on informal co-operation'. He had been through this for ten years and since the previous September had been convinced that things had to change. There had 'very nearly been a blow-up'.

If the Government could not be fought off, it could very likely be bought off. Why not offer them the kind of new instrument favoured by Professor Robbins, suitably adapted and to be agreed voluntarily between the Bank and the banks? Some such scheme had been discussed within the Bank time and again over the preceding years. There were various objections to it, but the Governor had never closed his mind to it; and the Radcliffe Committee was bound to consider the whole question and seek evidence from the Bank about it. So why not pre-empt both the Government and the Committee by constructing a Bank version of the scheme favoured by Robbins and selling it to both? This is what the Governor now began to do. He saw Thorneycroft on 8 October, the same day as the Birch Minute was circulated, and wrote him a very long and discursive letter on the following day. In it he defended the record over the post-war years and argued that it was quite wrong to assert that the authorities had in practice failed to control the money supply. In particular, bank advances to private borrowers had increased by only 5% over the past six years and were likely to be held steady for a further year. The problems of Exchequer financing were more obdurate and the merits of the existing system, whereby the Government's needs could always be met by an automatic increase in Treasury Bills, were open to question. He then warned that fresh legislation, giving the Treasury direct control over the banks, would make the UK the only leading democracy where the Treasury had such powers, including powers to force the banks to lend to itself. It would radically alter the powers and responsibilities of the Bank (a matter of grave concern to the Court) and there would be serious effects on confidence in the British banking system and in sterling. 'Above all', he concluded, 'I am anxious that no step should be taken which would interrupt the dawning improvement in the exchanges and the domestic economy, or would prejudice the very fruitful co-operation which exists between the Treasury, the Bank of England and the commercial banks.'

Thorneycroft replied on October 14 in terms that Makins had squared with the Governor on the 11th. He opened the door to a settlement: 'I do not wish at this stage', he wrote, 'to take a decision, even of a provisional character, on policy, still less on changes in the relationship between the Treasury and the Bank of England or the banks. What I do want is to have a plan worked out.' He then proposed that their respective officials should proceed immediately to work out a plan of action 'in the event of it being subsequently decided that it was necessary to take some action on the lines suggested in the draft report of the Economic Secretary's Committee'. The Governor readily accepted this proposal, adding that the Bank had done a lot of preliminary work on a paper on alternative techniques for submission to the Radcliffe Committee. This would soon be finished and he proposed that it form the starting-point for the discussion proposed by the Chancellor. The Treasury accepted this and made no attempt to interfere with the Bank's paper before it was submitted independently to Radcliffe during November. At the end of that month the discussions between Treasury and Bank officials were started; and the Special Deposits Scheme, which in the Bank's paper to Radcliffe had been judged the least objectionable among many, was refined and eventually agreed with the banks in the summer of 1958.

By December 1957 Thorneycroft was becoming absorbed in the struggle over public expenditure, a struggle that was to end with his resignation early in January 1958. The question of fresh legislation in the monetary field then faded from view and the Special Deposits Scheme was put into place within the framework of relationships that the Governor was so determined to preserve. The principal difference between the scheme itself and the previously suggested 'liquidity ratio plus TDRs' lay in the interposition of the Bank between the banks and the Treasury. Instead of subscribing to TDRs the banks were to place Special Deposits with the Bank, who would then on-lend them to the Treasury. Calls and releases of Special Deposits would be made by the Bank in much the same way as changes in Bank Rate, with the Government's approval. In this manner the scheme was constructed as a monetary or central banking instrument. So far as possible it did not look like an instrument for raising forced loans from the banks. In all other respects it was open to the same objections as had hitherto been raised to such schemes and was to have a far from glorious future. Its principal and perhaps only virtue lay in the circumstances of its birth; for it enabled the dangerous impasse of 1957 to be resolved to the satisfaction of the Government and the Bank and it enabled the credit squeeze to be terminated in 1958 without appearing to leave the authorities empty-handed. It was, however, only an appearance. When the truth became evident some years later, six years of 'voluntary' lending ceilings followed.

One other consequence of September 1957 remains to be discussed. The Report of the Bank Rate Tribunal (Chapter 11(d) below) in January 1958 drew attention to the 'difficult and embarrassing position' in which part-time Directors of the Bank might find themselves if they had foreknowledge of a likely change in Bank Rate. The matter was then referred by the

Government to the Radcliffe Committee, which reported in the summer of 1959. In November of that year, following full consultation with the Governor, who had in turn fully consulted the Court, the procedures for changing Bank Rate were altered. The Court delegated to the Governor standing authority to settle changes in the Rate with the Chancellor. The agreement between the two would be recorded in a formal exchange of letters on the day before the change was made. The Court would be informed on the day of the change itself and formally approve it. The change would then be announced in a formal statement by the Bank, which would include the phrase 'with the approval of the Chancellor of the Exchequer'. Explaining these new procedures to the House of Commons, the Chancellor (Heathcoat Amory) said that when framing the view of the Bank as to the level of the Bank Rate, the Governor would be free to have discussions with the Committee of Treasury and with other part-time Directors of the Bank. But he would not put specific proposals before the Committee of Treasury or the Court. The practical effect of this latter change was to remove the part-time Directors from prior discussions about changes in the Rate and relieve them from the 'difficult and embarrassing position' to which the Parker Tribunal had referred. In future the Governor could no longer call the views of the Court in aid when discussing a change in Bank Rate with the Treasury. It is possible to see this as a formal change of minor practical significance. But to the extent that it deprived the Governor of a tactical weapon that was quite frequently used in Cobbold's time, it signified some loss of independent authority.

There we must leave the story. The actors walk off this particular stage and on into the future. Ministers, Treasury officials, Governors, Directors, Chief Cashiers, Economic Advisers, and clearing bankers will go on arguing, negotiating, and managing their way through the thickets of dilemmas and discontents that surrounded UK monetary policy after the part-reforms of 1957 and 1958; for fundamental questions had been left unresolved. The last word, as is sometimes suitable, must remain with the principal member of the cast. Cobbold had been closely concerned with domestic monetary policy ever since he became Deputy Governor in the summer of 1945 and even more so since he assumed the Governorship in 1949. It was not a subject in which he ever felt particularly at home, but neither was it one where his duties could easily be delegated to others. Difficult questions of the Bank's responsibilities and its relationships with the Treasury on the one hand and the banks on the other touched it at too many points, and latterly too often. It is therefore not surprising that when he saw early versions of the Bank's paper for Radcliffe on 'Alternative

Techniques' he found their content unsatisfying. In a note circulated on 21 August 1957, which well shows a combination of powerful insight unsupported by expert analysis, he wrote:

> I think the trouble is that these are really only different forms of the same *fundamental* technique, which is that our present system requires that the banking system will always provide the cash necessary to meet Government requirements, by indirect recourse to the Bank of England if necessary and up till then by creation of inflation in the banking system. The only influence the Bank can have on this process is by gearing up interest rates a bit, which has no effect on Government borrowing and only a limited effect on private borrowing. So long as we maintain this fundamental technique, and with the present relationship in the banking system between investments and advances and between longer-term and shorter-term securities, I doubt whether any technique can possibly control the level of bank advances except by either persuading or directing the banks to keep a certain level of advances. Must we not consider how we are going to put to the Committee and with what policy slant, the *real* technical alternatives?

These thoughts led the Governor into the over-radical realms of rediscount quotas (rationing central bank credit) rather than into greater use of Bank Rate, though one economist in the Bank was not slow to point out the connection between the two. But one way or another, whether because of the immediate urgency of the crisis in relationships with Whitehall or because the majority of his advisers could anyway see little merit or sense in pursuing fundamentals at this time, Cobbold's request came to naught at the very moment when Bank Rate was being put to decisive use. He was, so it seems, too easily persuaded into arguing that such use could be only very occasional in practice. He was also no doubt readily persuaded that rediscount quotas and suchlike were too outlandish to be propounded from Threadneedle Street. Perhaps, too, the chance exigency of the 'leak' enquiries absorbed too much of his attention at the critical moment. But he must be saluted for asking the fundamental questions.

SOURCES

Bank files
  C40/452   Chief Cashier's Policy File; Government Borrowing – 3% Exchequer Stock 1960 (1953)
  C40/453   Chief Cashier's Policy File: Government Borrowing – 3% Exchequer Stock 1962/63 (1953–63)
  C40/479   Chief Cashier's Policy File: Government Borrowing – 4% Conversion Stock 1957/58 (September 1955 – January 1957)
  C40/480   Chief Cashier's Policy File: Government Borrowing – $4\frac{1}{2}$% Conversion Stock 1962 (May 1956 – November 1957)

C40/488	Chief Cashier's Policy File: Government Borrowing – 2½% Exchequer Stock 1963/64, 3½% Funding Stock 1999/2004 in Exchange for 1¾% Serial Funding Stock 1954 (1954–68)
C40/659	Chief Cashier's Policy File: Local Authorities and Public Corporations – Local Authority Loans (July 1953 – December 1972)
C40/688–91	Chief Cashier's Policy Files: Monetary Policy – Advances and Control of Inflation (1953–6)
C40/704	Chief Cashier's Policy File: Monetary Policy – Advances and Control of Inflation (1957–8)
C40/720–1	Chief Cashier's Policy Files: Monetary Policy – Advances and Control of Inflation (1937–56)
C40/917	Chief Cashier's Policy File: Radcliffe Committee – Some Possible Modifications in Technique (May – September 1957)
C42/3–4	Chief Cashier's Personal Files: Interest Rates (January 1952 – April 1959)
C42/12	Chief Cashier's Personal File: Monetary Situation, Including Gilt-edged Market (November 1954 – October 1959)
G1/72–3	Governor's File: Financial and Monetary Policy – Exchange of Views Principally at Governor/ Chancellor/ Clearing Bank Chairman Level (January 1952 – January 1955)
G1/75	Governor's File: Financial and Monetary Policy – Exchange of Views Principally at Governor/ Chancellor/ Clearing Bank Chairman Level (January – December 1957)
G1/78	Governor's File: Financial and Monetary Policy – Economic Secretary's Working Group on Credit Control (September – November 1957)
G1/79	Governor's File: Financial and Monetary Policy – Governors' and Advisers' Assessments of UK Economic Situation (November 1956 – February 1965)
G1/80	Governor's File: Financial and Monetary Policy – The Economic Situation at End–1957 (December 1957 – January 1958)
G1/81	Governor's File: Financial and Monetary Policy – Miscellaneous Correspondence and Reports.
G3/10	Governor's Diary (1957)
G14/152	Committee of Treasury File: Interest Rates, Monetary Policy and Credit Control – Bank Rate and Related Matters (October 1921 – March 1947)
G14/156	Committee of Treasury File: Interest Rates, Monetary Policy and Credit Control – Arrangements for the Determination and Announcement of Bank Rate/MLR (December 1957 – June 1978)

CHAPTER 11

THE BANK AND THE SQUARE MILE

(a) INTRODUCTORY

PRIOR TO the Second World War, to nationalisation in 1946, and to the adoption of comparatively interventionist macro-economic policies by British Governments, continuing relationships between the Bank and the financial community were mostly a product of banking responsibilities, typically with respect to the accepting houses and the discount houses. Only occasionally did these extend to the clearing banks and the British overseas banks. To these relationships were added others, of varying duration, associated either with some new central banking interest, for example in the field of industrial rationalisation, or with some City need to make use of the Bank's ability to advise or mediate, an ability increased by the change in the Governorship accomplished by Norman. In modern parlance, though now remote from modern practice, the function being performed was often supervisory; but it was exercised through the Bank's evolved power as central banker *de facto* and not through specific powers granted it by statute. It was also being exercised by a Bank that remained in private ownership with some ultimate accountability to its private proprietors, even though it was very ready to acknowledge the public interest and to consult with Government when required. For its own part, the financial community had over the years organised itself into a variety of trade associations or clubs, each with rules and agreed procedures. These clubs were useful to the Bank as channels through which information could flow, collective negotiations be pursued, or standards of behaviour be maintained. They were complemented by the indispensable channels of communication with individual banks and other individual constituents of the financial community who sought the Bank's advice or acknowledged its suzerainty. The Governors, the Executive Directors, and other members of the Bank's inner grouping, including in particular the

Principal of the Discount Office, were always available for confidential consultation.

The Bank's authority, though considerable, was very far from absolute, even over members of the banking system. Norman had developed and strengthened a feudal monarchy, reliant on custom rather than statute, parts of which were far more submissive than others. He had not transformed it into a modern state and was averse to obtaining, so to speak, the support of imperial legislation from Whitehall. It followed that the Bank could exercise effective power only so long as its behaviour and its rulings conformed to accepted current practice as seen by practitioners. It could persuade or cajole, but it had to be very careful about giving orders. The rather ramshackle monarchy over which it presided could not accommodate much discontent without courting disobedience to the monarch and a damaging decline in the standing of the central institution, as the Bank was sometimes called. So despite an abundance of laudatory mystique and the occasional receipt of self-interested flattery, the Old Lady stood in reality at the apex of a self-regulatory system of which she was as much the prisoner as the sovereign.

The changes precipitated by the war intervened to alter and enlarge the functions of the Bank. They also, but to a limited extent, altered the basis of its power. However, the structure of the financial community was virtually unaltered and was to remain so throughout the first post-war decade. But at the end of the decade, when a multitude of new deposit-taking finance houses grew up in avoidance of the official credit controls, the structure began to crumble at the edges and to present a problem that the Bank's customary methods were powerless to solve. Likewise the unregulated growth of competitive take-over activity in the London market presented self-regulatory problems that could not be solved by the regular use of customary authority in Threadneedle Street.

The first change, brought by the war itself, was the imposition of statutory exchange control. The Bank constructed it and administered it as agent of the Treasury, often with the help of staff specially recruited from the banking system; often too with the active assistance of that system, to whose members the Bank delegated much of the day-to-day work and on whom, by virtue of the surrounding self-regulatory ethos, the Bank could rely provided the control itself was administered in a flexible and humane way. Thanks to Siepmann and many others, it was so administered. The Bank never forgot its prior underlying relationships with the City and its need to preserve them in spirit if it was not to degenerate into an unimaginative bureaucratic machine beset by rival lawyers interpreting the text of innumerable orders in different ways. Thus, for example, it was the Bank that devised means of reopening the London commodity markets after the war in such a way as to prevent their being used by UK residents as a route for taking positions against sterling. As is related in Appendix A, it was some years before the reopening of most of these markets was allowed by the Treasury. But there was never any doubt of the Bank's intentions in the matter, always provided the overriding requirements of exchange control could be met. Likewise, with the progressive breakdown of exchange control over non-residents' current transactions, a story related in Chapter 4(c) above, the Bank was able to minimise covert City participation in cheap-sterling business by the use of persuasive argument that relied heavily on goodwill towards Threadneedle Street. In the postwar decades, moreover, exchange control over residents, as opposed to non-residents, was relatively free from evasion and avoidance, or at any rate sufficiently free to retain public confidence in its integrity. In some other countries this was not so, despite the liability of offenders to prosecution. In short the British control, together with the collaboration between it and Sterling Area local controls, was a tribute to the application of the Bank's customary method to an elaborate statutory task. It also provided the Bank and its staff with a new source of financial and commercial intelligence; and although individual items of this intelligence, under the rules governing its provision, could not normally be used for purposes outside exchange control, they must have greatly improved the background knowledge with which the Bank approached questions of external financial policy.

The advent of exchange control, and its continuation after the war, had the further consequence of bringing the Bank closer to the Treasury and making clear that in this field it was part of the machinery of central government. The nationalisation of the Bank in 1946 further extended that status. But unlike exchange control, the Bank of England Act contained no provisions at all for the enforcement of directives or the punishment of offenders. By implication therefore, and in the practice developed over the following years, the Bank was left to get its way with the banks by the informal methods employed hitherto. Whether these methods were strengthened by the change in status brought about by the Act is a very moot point. On the one hand the underlying authority of the Bank, as an instrument of Government, may have been enhanced by the Act. But that authority may have been in practice reduced by the degree of statutory subordination of the Bank to the Treasury. Informal methods that are effective when dependent upon powers inherent in central banking and upon the persuasive strength of leadership still exercised (at least formally) from within the private sector can become weaker if they are seen to be simply a means whereby Treasury authority can be made effective without statutory powers of enforcement.

In the administration of exchange control the Bank could go on using its self-regulatory heritage to good effect in support of fully enforceable statutory powers. At the other extreme, the Bank could go on practising its self-regulatory functions in the field of banking supervision, such as it was, where its authority continued to rest on inherent financial power and where the Treasury did not wish to interfere. The Bank could also continue to advise and mediate on such City matters as came to its attention. In the spring of 1947, when the financing of the Steel Company of Wales was being arranged, the Bank in the person of the Governor became involved in settling differences between merchant banks on a matter touching the public interest. In the winter of 1958–9, during the battle for control of British Aluminium, the Governor intervened with the aim of establishing a truce followed by round-table talks. In his view, this would have been in the public interest. He was able to start negotiations for a truce, but things had already gone too far; the bid for British Aluminium could not be withdrawn and the negotiations came to nothing.

In between these extremes of exchange control at one end and old-established, self-regulatory activity at the other lay the whole new field of credit control, where the Bank was required to exercise authority partly on behalf of the Treasury and partly on its own account in pursuit of domestic monetary policy. As has been seen in chapters devoted first to the monetary policy of the Labour Government during the Chancellorships of Cripps and Gaitskell and secondly to the credit squeeze of the mid-fifties, this proved a thankless task. Armed with the power of directive reserved to it under the Act and with the self-regulatory authority derived essentially from other and different functions, the Bank began by successfully establishing itself as a powerful intermediary between Government and banks and one that worked through informal requests instead of detailed quantitative controls. But especially under the Conservative administrations of Eden and Macmillan, the Treasury made a habit of wanting more precision than the Bank could readily deliver. Officials and Ministers frequently chafed at the self-regulatory method. Even the banks themselves, on at least one occasion, preferred direct consultation with the Chancellor to indirect negotiation through the Governor. When in 1957 the Bank warned that it would decline to issue a formal directive to the banks, it was at once threatened with amending legislation. In short, nationalisation increased the power of 'the authorities' in the field of credit policy while in practice reducing the self-regulatory authority that the Bank might otherwise have wielded in that area. The result was an unhappy ambiguity, almost a degree of pretence and make-believe, which did little to enhance the Bank's relationship with the banking side of the City or its relationship with the Treasury.

The greater degree of Governmental intervention in the affairs of the Bank and the City was not confined to exchange control and domestic monetary policy. There were other instances where the Bank found itself engaged in tasks that derived at least in part from Governmental pressure. Much the most notable of these, in the years covered by this book, were the negotiations leading to the establishment of the FCI and the ICFC early in 1945, an exercise of self-regulatory authority that took place prior to nationalisation and in which the Bank demonstrated its successful occupation of a middle ground between Whitehall and the Square Mile. Another example, the establishment of the Commonwealth Development Finance Company (CDFC) in the winter of 1952–3, was both more impromptu and less demonstrative of the Bank's authority in the City. But at about the same time the Bank was required to assist with the denationalisation of the steel industry, a task that entailed obtaining the voluntary support of City institutions and overseeing a series of complicated operations. The task was carried out with singular success. In all these instances the Bank was furthering Government policy. In some it had itself participated in the formation of the policy. But it worked through the exercise of a customary authority that in these fields was both unaffected by nationalisation and in no way directly dependent on the power of a lender of last resort. The Bank was instead performing a function that no other City institution and no Government Department could perform. It was providing a service for which there turned out to be a demand – even if the City was not fully aware of it until persuaded. Though they were not always entirely successful or popular in the City, the Bank was often at its happiest when conducting exercises of this sort. They were constructive activities that stretched an inherited talent possessed by no one else.

The same could not be said of the Bank's response in the mid-fifties to the mushroom growth of the new bank-like activity, outside the Square Mile, that inexorably followed the use of financial controls against established finance houses and against the banks themselves. The Bank was stung by the growth of this grey market in credit that threatened seriously to undermine the integrity and effectiveness of its informally requested credit squeezes. It was also aware that the proliferation of small, inexperienced, and unsupervised deposit-takers carried with it the risk of failures and the spread of contagious mistrust in finance houses generally. It knew that bringing all the small fry within the net of City associations and customary authority would be a next to impossible task, at least in the conditions of the mid-fifties' credit squeeze. So the Bank quickly opted for new legislation, unfortunately without adequate prior thought about its purpose. It assumed from the start that the Act would be administered by the Board of Trade rather than by the central bank and it seemed from the outset far more interested in getting at the grey market for consumer credit in particular than in the prudential supervision of fringe deposit-takers in general. The Board of Trade's preference, more soundly based, was to place prudential supervision first. The unsurprising result was a draft Bill that provided neither for new credit controls nor for comprehensive supervision of deposit-taking and suffered from unresolved problems of definition. The Government declined to introduce it. Then, when it was too late, the Bank discarded its previous approach and developed ideas for a modest single-purpose Bill for the supervision of deposit-takers, still by a Registrar in Whitehall rather than by the Bank itself. But the Government remained unwilling to move and the Bank turned back to the possibility of extending its customary authority outside the established boundaries, a possibility that looked less daunting when the credit squeeze was terminated in the summer of 1958 and, shortly afterwards, the clearing banks became major shareholders in large finance houses. But an adequate extension of the feudal boundaries through adaptation of the Finance Houses Association proved unobtainable. As is related in section (d) of this chapter, it was a story that exposed shortcomings in the way the Bank itself was run as well as the inability of customary authority to cope with important changes at the periphery of the banking community. A start could have been made with a useful Banking Act in 1957, but the opportunity was fumbled and lost. Norman's Bank was not designed for such a purpose; and another event at this time, here the subject of a short digression, served to confirm its obsolescence.

The Parker Tribunal was set up in November 1957 to investigate allegations of a Bank Rate 'leak' that arose mainly on account of after-hours selling of gilt-edged on 18 September, the day before the Rate was raised to 7%. The Tribunal concluded that there had been no leak. But the enquiry cast an unexpected and penetrating light on sales of gilt-edged on 17 and 18 September by Lazards, Jardines, and Royal Exchange Insurance, firms in which two part-time Directors of the Bank, both with some foreknowledge of the Rate change, were directly involved. The Tribunal completely cleared the two men, Lord Kindersley and Sir William Keswick, of any impropriety, but pointedly remarked that part-time Directors might on occasion find themselves in 'a difficult and embarrassing position'. Its Report went on: 'This raises a general and very important question of policy with which we are clearly not concerned.' However, before the Tribunal reported, the Governors and the Court had debated the question of policy. They persisted in supporting retention of the established practice of consultation with individual Directors prior to a change in Bank Rate. They either could not or would not concede the point of public credibility.

Before the change, Keswick had been personally concerned in responding from Mathesons in London to a request for advice from Jardines in Hong Kong about the sale or retention of gilt-edged. In view of his position at the Bank, he had felt it necessary to disclose the matter to the Deputy Governor before cabling Hong Kong on 16 September and advising a sale, which took place on the 18th. The Deputy had agreed that the advice was entirely proper in the circumstances. At that stage Keswick had not been consulted about a move to 7% on 19 September, but he had earlier been given indications that a rise in the Rate might be in the offing. Kindersley, as a Managing Director of Lazards and Chairman of Royal Exchange Insurance, had formally been a party to gilt sales by both these firms late on 18 September. But although he had not been an active party to the relevant decisions in either firm, he had been consulted by the Governor on 16 September about an increase to 7% on the 19th.

In addition there was the 'Gallagher episode', as it may be called. W. N. Gallagher, in 1957 an assistant master at Mill Hill School, was a former member of the Indian Civil Service and had worked in Lazards for about a year during which, in November 1951, Bank Rate had been increased. His employment there was not a success and had been terminated by Hugh Kindersley, as he then was. Gallagher's subsequent behaviour could be described as grudge-driven or as public-spirited, according to the point of view. But what he had to say could not be brushed aside. He wrote to the Governor on 28 September 1957 that Lazards had sold all their gilts prior to the 1951 change in Bank Rate and had subsequently bought them back at lower prices. He considered that they had had a tip-off and that Kindersley's position at the Bank was responsible. He said he had written to the Chancellor early in 1952 arguing that Directors of the Bank should be required to give up their private interests. At first Cobbold did not respond. He had recently written to the Prime Minister to tell him that he had consulted the Court, the Chairman of the Stock Exchange, the Government Broker, the Chairman of the CLCB, the Chairman of the LDMA, and, individually, Kindersley and Keswick. All had supported his own judgement that there had been no leak. But Gallagher wrote again two weeks later, arguing that he should be invited to the Bank for a talk. The Governor then wrote to Norman Brook, Secretary to the Cabinet, who confirmed that the then Chancellor had received a letter from Gallagher in

1952 and who advised that he be seen. He was then interviewed by Abell and repeated that Lord Kindersley's 'two hats' had been responsible for Lazards' gilt sales in October 1951. He was next seen by Kindersley himself and was confronted with evidence to the contrary, which obliged him to withdraw his allegations; but he wrote in again, this time to Abell, at the end of October and again on 13 November. Gallagher accepted that he might have been wrong about 1951, but he continued to assert that staff in Lazards thought that someone had been tipped off and to argue that the potential conflict of interest between being a Director of the Bank and, for example, a Director of a merchant bank was unacceptably strong.

Gallagher then went further and put in a statement to the Tribunal, which had been set up pursuant to a Resolution of the Commons on 13 November. His statement was not published, but he reportedly reverted to his allegations about Lazards' gilt-edged sales in October 1951. The Tribunal's response was to ask for details of Lazards' dealing in gilts in the period before and in some cases after every change in Bank Rate from November 1951 onwards. The information was duly supplied. It confirmed sales before and purchases after the change in 1951 and revealed sales on the day before the change in February 1955. But it was stated that on neither occasion had Kindersley been consulted.[1] Judging by its complete exoneration of Kindersley with respect to any suggestions of impropriety in 1957, the Tribunal must have accepted this.

Despite the activities of Gallagher, not to mention the intense glare of publicity caused by the Tribunal's investigation into the gilt-edged sales of Lazards and Jardines in September, the Governors and the Court held their ground on the issue of consultation with Directors prior to a change in the Rate. Nor did they take much notice of private advice from *The Times*, *Financial Times*, and others, conveyed by Lord Brand, that some alteration of the existing procedure was now unavoidable. Accordingly, the Governor put in a special additional statement to the Tribunal, defending the status quo on the grounds firstly that prior consultation (long established) was both useful and necessary, given the Court's responsibility for agreeing a change in the Rate, and secondly that the integrity and *savoir-faire* of Directors was beyond question. The Tribunal, as noted above, did not entirely agree with the Bank. The position of Directors, it said, could at times be difficult and embarrassing. As related in Chapter 10 above, the question was referred to the Radcliffe Committee, who reported in favour

[1] The Secretary to the Bank reminded the Governor of his approach to Kindersley in mid-October 1951 asking for help in the discussions then current in the Bank about ways of unpegging short-term rates and agreeing with him that he could stand out of any investment question in his own business without embarrassment. There is no record in the Bank that this information was passed on to the Tribunal.

The Parker Tribunal: a cartoonist's comment
(*Manchester Evening News*: 23.1.58)

of a change in procedure. This was put in place late in 1959 and prior consultation ceased. The old arrangements, perhaps typical of the inner City of Norman's time and further back, had been judged out of date.

The above digression apart, some aspects of the relationship between the Bank and the financial community with respect to exchange control over non-residents and to domestic credit control have already revealed themselves in chapters relating to external financial policy and to domestic monetary policy; and these have been the subject of further comment in these introductory pages. Some other aspects, also the subject of comment, are considered in greater detail in the remainder of this final section. Enough has already been written to show that the relationship was far from simple, far from autocratic, and one that naturally tended to vary according to the function being performed or the service being provided. The Bank carried out a variety of different tasks with a variety of different powers; but it had a strong inherited preference for carrying them all out, so far as possible, in the same informal, persuasive, and self-regulatory way.

(b) JANUS IN OPERATION: THE ESTABLISHMENT OF THE FCI AND THE ICFC, 1943–1945

On 23 January 1945 the Bank held a meeting in Threadneedle Street with twenty-two senior financial journalists. Its purpose was to brief them about two new financial institutions, in both of which the Bank itself was to be a shareholder and whose imminent birth was being announced that day in the House of Commons by the Chancellor of the Exchequer. The Governor was in the Chair, flanked by Niemeyer, by his special adviser on industry, Ernest Skinner,[2] and by his Press Officer, Bernard Rickatson-Hatt. The meeting had the appearance of a press conference, but the journalists were told it was an informal meeting, strictly private and off-the-record. Specifically, they were told not to quote the Governor by name. If necessary, remarks could be attributed to 'a high City authority'. In its customary Normanesque fashion the Bank was securing press publicity for its own views about the Finance Corporation for Industry and the Industrial and Commercial Finance Corporation. To this end, Catto stressed that their purpose was to supplement and not replace the ordinary channels of finance, that they were evidence of the financial community intending to play its part in post-war reconstruction, and that they could be adapted if they did not meet the requirements of developments as yet unforeseen. For his part, the Chancellor of the Exchequer told the Commons:

> These two companies are being created on the initiative of the banking, insurance and investment sections of the business community of the country and in the opinion of His Majesty's Government they will constitute an important and helpful step in the post-war finance of industry. For these reasons I welcome these two projects as being directly in accord with and calculated to help in an important degree the Government policy of full employment.

The launch got a favourable reception. It represented the culmination of nearly two years' hard work, spent first in arguing out and deciding what was going to be needed and secondly in bringing the result to life. The whole project had been initiated by Norman and, apart from the question

---

[2] *Skinner, Ernest Harry Dudley, CBE (1892–1985).* Entered Bank 1911, Governor's Secretary 1929–32, Deputy Secretary 1932–5, Assistant to the Governors 1935–45. General Manager, Finance Corporation for Industry 1945–8, Chairman, Northern Division, NCB 1948–50, Chairman, Durham Division, NCB 1950–7, Member, Colonial Development Corporation 1958–60.

of his own succession, had been his main creative activity during the closing months of his long Governorship. It had then been taken up enthusiastically by Catto, assisted by Norman's own team. The new Governor did not belong to the inner City but his range of contacts in industry and commerce was very wide and his negotiating skills in Whitehall and the Square Mile proved quite equal to the task. The story provides a detailed and clear insight into the way the Bank then thought both about immediate post-war issues of macro-economic policy and about associated problems of industrial financing. It also provides a detailed case study of the way the Bank went about the business of overcoming reluctance in the City while calming a degree of over-enthusiasm in Whitehall. Finally, the story shows the ease with which the caravan moved on, little changed, after Norman's departure. For all these reasons it has a historical importance greater than any that attaches intrinsically to the two institutions concerned.

On 2 March 1943 the Prime Minister broadcast to the nation about a four-year economic plan for the transition from war to peace. Churchill talked about social security and education, about safeguarding the value of savings, about the new role of state enterprise, about the rebuilding of exports, and about the need to 'revive at the earliest moment a widespread healthy and vigorous private enterprise without which we shall never be able to provide, in the years when it is needed, the employment for our soldiers, sailors, and airmen to which they are entitled after their duty has been done'. In this context, on 26 March the Governor set up a Committee on Post-War Domestic Finance, whose terms of reference were:

> To report on the methods that could best be adopted in the immediate post-war period to ensure effective co-operation between HMG and the Bank of England, the banks, the market, and other lenders, in meeting the financial needs of the community – both long and short-term – and having regard, *inter alia*, to the necessity for:
>
> (a) initiating and administering effective control;
> (b) establishing some means of judging the validity of demands, especially for new industries;
> (c) co-ordinating allocation of capital with the allocation of materials;
> (d) dealing with the needs of industry in such a way as to encourage maximum employment and the extension of research.

Niemeyer was Chairman and the other members were Holland-Martin, Peppiatt, Kershaw, and Mynors. Skinner and Bolton were available as required. Mynors left the Committee in July 1943 and was replaced by the Bank's senior Economic Adviser, Henry Clay.

As related in Chapter 5(b), the Committee began by reviewing the likely development of the post-war macro-economic situation and the policy instruments that might be used to guide it. It then went on to consider a quite different set of problems. Instead of concentrating on methods of restricting the supply of finance in accord with Treasury priorities, the Committee focused on ensuring that all approved and deserving borrowers would in practice be able to get the money they needed. Accordingly Niemeyer turned his attention to the machinery of the capital market. Gilt-edged could be adequately sustained by using, as the need arose, the liquid resources of the Issue Department and the National Debt Commissioners. With a viable gilt market, an industrial market should follow and could then itself absorb a large volume of industrial new issues provided they were marshalled to ensure a smooth flow. But there would be misfits whose needs would have to be met in some other way and whose importance, both economic and political, might be considerable. Niemeyer accordingly wanted the Committee 'to consider how we can organise either through ourselves or more indirectly, as far as may be to the exclusion of direct Government finance, for these misfits, i.e. to whom should they go for finance: who should vet them: and what technical forms should their issues take?' He concluded: 'If we arrived at a view on these questions we should then have to consider how to secure financial co-operation from lenders: and how to sell our ideas to the Treasury.'

At this point the Committee sought help from Skinner, formerly Private Secretary and latterly a special adviser to Norman. He had been closely associated with the Bank's endeavours to assist rationalisation and to improve the provision of finance for industry in the 1930s. His knowledge of industry and its personalities was considerable and he had already developed ideas of his own for shaping and controlling capital expenditure in industry and linking that control to the provision of finance. Except for a few very large companies, like Imperial Chemical Industries, he considered there should be no access to the new issue market for individual companies. Instead, consents for borrowing would first be arranged through industrial trade associations acting in concert with a Whitehall 'Priority Committee'. Finance, by loan or equity, would then be provided by trade association finance corporations, who would themselves draw on a central finance corporation. This latter, with capital subscribed by the City and by Government, would finance itself from the market. In addition to this very corporatist structure, with its strong element of self-dirigisme, Skinner judged that some special organisation would be required to meet the needs of small businesses and provide guidance through the difficult period of reconstruction.

Skinner's ideas owed much to his pre-war experience. He had little confidence that left to themselves, even with the Government setting the priorities, markets would produce the right industrial answers for the long term. But he had even less confidence that these answers could be obtained from Whitehall. So he thought there should be some machinery of planning or rationalisation run by groups of industrialists themselves. This would first decide the right physical development of an industry and then go on to ensure that finance was provided for that development and for none other.

The Committee gave the idea a very lukewarm reception. Apart from its complexity and the difficulty of getting enough of the right people to run it, there was the obvious unpopularity of trade associations and the restrictive practices associated with them. In general, the Committee had much more faith in competition and markets than did Skinner. His scheme was turned down and attention concentrated on a simple plan put forward by Peppiatt early in June. This kept the Capital Issues Committee in place, allowed for ordinary use of the new issue market and the banks by industrial borrowers, retained the Agricultural Mortgage Corporation for agricultural borrowers, and added an Industrial Finance Corporation as a long-stop for Niemeyer's 'misfits', large and small. Its capital would be provided by the Bank, the banks, and other City institutions.

Everyone on the Committee favoured either one new institution or alternatively two, one for large firms and one for small. But there was at first some familiar division of emphasis between those who saw the 'long-stop' as such, namely a passive recipient of occasional special cases, and those who saw it as a more active concern. Kershaw was an eloquent advocate among the latter, saying it was essential the new institution should 'not be a mere resting place for the discarded scraps of the market. An ineffective body...would do more than merely pass into early oblivion; it would disappoint the public and tend to provoke more sweeping and possibly less controllable measures at a later date. To some extent, therefore, it is inevitable and even desirable that the corporation should be a competitor with existing channels of lending.' Possibly with an eye to ideas current in Whitehall, the Committee seems to have allowed this issue to remain open and on 24 June the Chairman was ready for a draft outline Report to be prepared. On the same day Skinner returned to the charge in a Minute addressed to Niemeyer and copied to the Governor. 'Without proper guidance the City can do much harm', he said. 'The subject is a big one, but I hope you will say that the City cannot attempt to judge of the physical aspects of applications, and that wherever the responsibility rests, it is not with the City. I still think that the Trade Associations can and ought to be constructed so as to take this responsibility, but the idea does not commend itself to you and I can see that for the moment at any rate it is politically difficult.' Norman pencilled on his copy 'Controversial: should like to discuss', but seems to have gone along with the Committee's views. Later, in July, he reminded Niemeyer that the banks would require some persuading before they would agree to give support to a new institution. But when the Committee's Report was submitted to the Governors in October, it concluded: 'It would seem to us that there will be many cases – far more than in pre-war years – to which the existing machinery of financial issues, even when buttressed by the considerable number of other financial agencies already existing, will not be well adapted. We think it will be necessary to provide further machinery.'

There followed the proposal for an Industrial Development Corporation, with authorised capital of £50 million and with the Bank, the clearing banks, insurance companies, and investment trusts as proprietors. HMG would subscribe a modest reserve fund. With a bow in Skinner's direction, some positive role for trade associations was not ruled out.

At about this time the Bank obtained a copy of a very much longer memorandum by the Board of Trade covering the whole field of post-war industrial policy. It included an Annex on 'Finance for Industry', which referred with approval to a Treasury view that there might be room for a new finance corporation to provide funds for smaller enterprises. The memorandum was also interested in finance for industrial rationalisation, but felt this should be provided by a public-sector body. In sharp contrast to the Niemeyer Report, the Board of Trade document was not exclusively concerned with the transition period from war to peace, but rather with a new peacetime normality. It therefore tended to look back more deliberately to the inter-war period, to the Macmillan Report of 1931, and to the 'Macmillan gap' in the capital market. Its suggestions for additional financial machinery were presented in that context, the Board of Trade taking the view that the various pieces of machinery constructed before the war, and in which the Bank had had a hand, had not fully solved the problems to which they were addressed. The Bank, by contrast, considered that the arrangements made in the 1930s, including the Bankers Industrial Development Company (BID) and Credit for Industry Ltd, had adequately filled whatever gap might then have existed. At this stage the Niemeyer Committee's proposal for a new Industrial Development Corporation looked entirely to a new set of problems, or new gap, which it foresaw emerging in the immediate post-war phase of reconstruction, and did not link its proposal to the Macmillan Report. The Bank maintained this position throughout the subsequent negotiations leading to the formation of the FCI and the ICFC. Whitehall probably viewed things differently and the Macmillan legend proved a powerful one.

The Niemeyer Report was circulated to Committee of Treasury on 25 October. Two days later Norman received a minute from Skinner dissenting from the proposal to set up a large, single development corporation. Existing machinery, including the gap-fillers of the 1930s, was probably enough. There was not sufficient proof that more was required and it could be unwise to rush ahead without any experience of post-war conditions. The Corporation's purpose, evidenced by its title and the proposed size of its resources, was over-ambitious and it could be unwise for the City to be seen to be taking such heavy responsibilities, only to get the blame if things went wrong. As an alternative, Skinner suggested that a new and privately-owned company might be formed for the finance of small business, while for bigger firms there should be an enlargement and resuscitation of the Bank's now dormant joint venture with the clearing banks, the BID, but with the new capital being subscribed entirely by the Bank. Niemeyer's own answer to this was that the scheme put forward for a single corporation was illustrative rather than final, but that a large scheme would be needed if Whitehall was to be kept from introducing machinery of its own. Shortly afterwards the Governors were informed that the Board of Trade was pressing for such machinery to be devised but that the Treasury was resisting, would much prefer a City arrangement, and would like the Bank to suggest one.

It was now clear that pressure from Whitehall was being applied and that Ministers would soon want to know what the Bank and the City could offer. Norman did not delay. Soon after receiving the Niemeyer Report, if not before, he had made up his mind that new machinery of some sort would be needed and that this would require him personally to mount an initiative with the banks and other City institutions. At the age of seventy-two, after some years of relative boredom and inactivity, he had at last landed a new part with a script that was both interesting and familiar. He set about his task, through the established City channels. On 1 November he saw Campbell, Chairman of the CLCB, about post-war finance of small businesses. On 5 November he saw one of his private City contacts, Clarence Sadd of the Midland Bank, on the same subject. He asked him to think about a possible scheme for a bankers' company to help small businesses. The Governor took no soundings at this stage about a parallel scheme for large firms and was probably still unclear about the wishes of Whitehall on that score. But it is likely that he was already thinking of a separate company for this purpose, with capital subscribed by insurance companies and investment trusts as well as the Bank itself. His earlier experience would have inclined him against the commercial banks being involved in long-term industrial lending, either directly or through a company whose capital they subscribed.[3]

The Governor was unwell and away at St Clere (his country house in Kent) during the second half of November. When he returned, he found awaiting him a strong note from Niemeyer. It began by tactfully denying that his Committee's Report was in any way inspired by the Treasury or written with any knowledge of what the Treasury had in mind. 'In fact', he wrote, 'a great deal of it was directed to devising some means of discovering whether the Treasury had any ideas, in the hope of influencing those ideas before they became fixed.' Moreover, the Board of Trade's memorandum on help for industry had arrived at the Bank after Niemeyer's Report had been circulated. But Niemeyer felt everyone was now convinced that the financial needs of large and small businesses in the immediate post-war period would greatly strain the existing system. Only the banks would have money to spare, but it would not be right for them to lend long. There would therefore be a gap, and consequently an opportunity for the City to make constructive proposals or else see the lead pass elsewhere. At about the same time Skinner was advising that the various schemes for Government assistance and control of industry, set out in the Board of Trade paper, constituted a 'bureaucratic monster'. Next came discussions with Eady, who wrote to the Governor on 7 December and mentioned schemes for both large and small businesses. Norman did not wait any longer. On 9 December he told Frazer, Chairman of the Investment Protection Committee of the BIA, that he wanted £10 million from the insurance companies towards capitalisation of a finance corporation for large industrial businesses. On 15 December he saw Crichton of the Association of Investment Trusts (AIT) and noted in his diary: 'I appeal for £10 million, which he receives well and will submit to his Committee after Christmas.'

The Governor was now engaged on all fronts. Sadd, who had sent in a note outlining a plan for a small business loan guarantee corporation (a seed that was not to germinate for some thirty-five years), had been seen on 9 December and kept in play. Campbell had come back on 6 December and agreed to wait for further developments. Goodenough (Barclays Bank) was seen on 10 December and Wardington (Lloyds Bank) on the 17th. On 20 December the Governor called in the Niemeyer Committee and told them he was sounding out the bankers about a finance company for small businesses and finding them *'difficile'*. He also told them he was

---

[3] In reply to an enquiry from the author early in 1985, Ernest Skinner (then aged ninety-one) made this point.

approaching the insurance companies and investment trusts about a £20–30 million company for the larger firms. Campbell was seen again on the 22nd, both about a £20 million bankers' company for small business and a £30 million company for large firms to be capitalised mostly elsewhere. Norman recorded: 'We discuss both. He melts. I agree to meeting five clearers in new year if he can square Christopherson. He promises support.' Meantime Frazer, of the BIA, had returned with various points to put on behalf of himself and Crichton of the AIT, chief among which was a request for assurance that the proposed company would do sound business and would not simply be a home for lame dogs. He was seen by Norman on 17 December and told 'no intentional lame dogs'. The company's loans 'would be intended for repayment by issue on the market sooner or later'.

Looking again to Whitehall, Norman had met and seemingly captured Lord Woolton, the Minister of Reconstruction, immediately after his initial exchange with the Treasury. The Minister wrote to him two weeks later in appreciative terms. 'My conversation with you a fortnight ago gave me not only pleasure but encouragement in this difficult work that I have recently undertaken. It is a comfort to me to know how practically, as well as sympathetically, you yourself are viewing the industrial end of it.' He enclosed a draft statement about the proposed new financial machinery that he would have liked to make early in the new year and asked for Norman's comments. The next day, 23 December, Eady returned to the charge in a letter to the Governor and a conversation with the Deputy. The letter enclosed a long note on finance for industry, which had been attached to the Report on Employment Policy that was being submitted to Ministers. Eady was anxious to impress on the Bank that the suggested new machinery should be equipped with adequate human resources as well as money and should be prepared to collaborate both with a suggested statutory 'Industrial Commission' and with Whitehall Departments. Some prominent Ministers were sceptical of the ability of the City to provide what was needed and would need little persuading to opt for Governmental machinery instead, a solution to which the Treasury was strongly opposed. Norman replied on 29 December and enclosed an outline of the small business scheme. This embodied a choice between a guarantee corporation and a company that would itself lend. The former had been suggested by Sadd and also, in mid-December, by Peppiatt. Norman preferred it as being 'cheaper and simpler in every way'. But the Treasury did not agree. It preferred the alternative and Eady so informed the Governor on 31 December. Norman gave way. In a letter to Sadd early in January he enclosed a copy of a scheme from which the guarantee option had been omitted. His letter, with its unusual but characteristic phraseology, repays quotation. It covered other ground as well as industrial finance.

> As a meagre return for your letter of the 30th December,[4] I offer the following remarks: I note with relief from pages 316 and 317 of 'Agenda' that the writer thinks there is little ground for requiring any further extension of control over the Central Bank or any structural changes in the commercial banks. I regret his remark that at some future date it may be desirable to lay down a definite requirement about the minimum ratio. Personally, I am opposed to any further legal regulation of banking. I believe the bankers should by custom establish good behaviour and good policies and that this custom would come to have the strength of law and, if necessary, be enforced by public opinion. This is not to say that Bank A should not adopt a minimum ratio of 10% any more than that Bank B should not vary between 8% and 12%. But once we urge legislation to make us good we shall get no end of it – perhaps too much.
>
> As to the Conference of Chairmen, I may point out, between you and me, that this is being done by request as to a date, time and attendance and, for your private eye, I enclose a copy of the prospectus designed for its discussion. This prospectus is most disappointing, chiefly because it avoids your admirable and economical method: it claims money from the bankers but stints them in representation and it is extravagantly conceived. But while this is admitted, to your private ear, there seems to be no present alternative; this draft has the blessing of Whitehall and nothing short of it has (although there may perhaps be room for some compromise): my purpose is to satisfy Whitehall: to keep them out of the banking business and free of malevolence towards the bankers.
>
> This is all I can say after several days on the sick list and a mind which needs Aquinas and Erasmus more than medicine out of a bottle...

On 10 January the Governor wrote to Woolton, telling him how far he had got and advising against any public statement at that time. His letter read:

> I have not overlooked the letter you wrote me on the 22nd of last month nor the fact that a few days later you said an answer was desired by the January 14th. So let me explain how we stand about funds for post-war.
>
> I am trying to establish two funds: one to finance approved small businesses which can materially increase employment and can provide some backing of their own, and the other to help, where necessary, with the reconstruction of certain industries.
>
> As to the first, I am still in discussion with the bankers. As to the second, while I have made certain suggestions to other parties, I have had no sort of answer. I therefore am not in a position to support any such statement as

---

[4] Since the letter was sent to the Governor personally and has not survived, it is not known to what the first paragraph of his reply refers.

Norman the Persuader, 1942
KARSH

you had in mind, nor do I know when I may be in that happy position. Moreover, you will allow me to question whether at this stage it would be wise for you to make any statement as to the provision of money for small business or for industry, because I should fear that the immediate result would be a catechism by all the newspapers, claims by many small and large concerns, and an attempt in some quarters to force the provision of moneys and the decisions as to their allocation into Whitehall. This would be dire!

I hope for your agreement and remain,
    Yours sincerely,
        M. NORMAN

The Minister replied, concurring, on the following day. But Norman was to play his part no further. A few days later he fell dangerously ill and was never to return to the Bank as Governor. On 1 March, when he was past the worst of his illness, Catterns wrote to him 'about one or two matters you were dealing with exclusively yourself, including the provision of capital for small and large business post-war' and asking whether he might take this over as things were rather on the boil. Norman, whose relations with his Deputies were seldom easy, replied with nobility: 'My dear B.G. You must certainly go ahead and deal with these urgent questions as they arise and in whatever way you think best.' If he felt any anxiety about the delegation of authority, he had little cause for it. For he left behind a talented team well able to look after themselves.

By the end of 1943 the Bank and the Treasury had each become clear in their minds about the 'bankers' company for small business'. They knew what they wanted and it was then left mostly to the Bank to carry through the necessary negotiations with the clearing banks. But the same was not yet true of the suggested 'reorganised BID for the larger firms'; and with Norman's sudden departure from the scene there ensued a period of reflection and argument. Was the new institution to have an active or relatively passive role? If the former, to what extent was it to be an active financial gap-filler and to what extent an instrument, somewhat after the Skinner fashion, for helping to ensure also that the post-war reconstruction of industry took on the physical shape considered correct by a competent authority; if so, what authority? The Treasury, fearful of expensive and wrong-headed industrial interventionism by Whitehall, proved keen to maximise the role and authority of the reorganised BID. The Bank remained reluctant to go this far along the road but in the last resort was prepared to go a certain distance in order to head off the formation of a state-controlled finance corporation. These issues required further discussion, which extended over another nine months. Not until early in December 1944 could agreement be registered between the Bank and the

Government so that the foundation of the reconstructed BID, to be named the Finance Corporation for Industry could finally be negotiated with the insurance companies, the investment trusts, and the clearing banks.

After several weeks' reflection following Norman's collapse, Skinner sent a full note to Catterns on 7 March. 'BID reorganised', or FCI, was to have authorised capital of £50 million, of which £30 million would be issued and a smaller amount paid up initially. The shareholders would be the Bank, the insurance companies and the investment trusts, in equal proportions, but the Bank was to have ordinary and the rest preference shares. The FCI would be able to issue debentures, would be able to borrow from banks up to three times the issued preference capital, and could take up equities to a total equal to its ordinary capital. Its purpose was to provide money for the re-equipment, continuance, or reorganisation of industries or large industrial units when banking accommodation was inappropriate or the market was unable to provide capital for some temporary reason. It would work in collaboration with the Industrial Commission then under active consideration in Whitehall. It would not itself initiate schemes of reorganisation; these would emanate from HMG or from industry itself. Skinner again suggested that the new institution should also collaborate with trade associations, but this idea was again rejected by Niemeyer.

Conversations next took place between the Deputy Governor and Eady at the end of March. The latter saw a very large role indeed for the new institution and was reported as saying hyperbolically that it might be entrusted with all the executive action involved in organising the post-war reconstruction and providing the finance. Catterns, and even Niemeyer, seem to have succumbed reluctantly but to have begun to think of the company as the mainspring of industrial development post-war. This line of thought became linked to parallel discussions between the Treasury and the Bank about the Industrial Commission that had been suggested in the Report on Employment Policy. On inspection, this entity seemed to be an industrial organisation advisory council, whose practical utility was doubtful but which the Bank nevertheless saw as a useful umbrella under which the activities of the new corporation could be protected from ill-informed criticism. The Treasury was averse to providing the umbrella and thought the Bank could make one for itself.

Clay then brought matters down to earth in a trenchant minute dated 19 May, some five weeks after Catto had taken office as Governor. Eady, said Clay, was fearful of political intrusion into the work of a Whitehall agency and therefore very much in favour of a large FCI. But such an institution could not do all that would be needed; in some cases Government money would be essential. Since it was anyway a delusion to suppose that an FCI on Eady's lines could be non-political, the new corporation should be set up as a supplementary force rather than as the sole or principal agency for industrial reorganisation. It was simply not realistic to suppose that the Bank could be involved with industry across the board. On the same day, Skinner sent the new Governor a fresh and more detailed version of the scheme he had put forward in March. The corporation would have an industrialist in the chair and a board of industrialists together with nominees of the BIA and the AIT. Its manager would be supported by a lawyer, an accountant, and a technologist. In addition there would be an industrial advisory panel, one of whose members would be an economist.[5] The new Governor must have liked this plan, for it was sent to the Treasury on 25 May and discussed at a meeting held by Eady on the following day. The Deputy Governor, Niemeyer, and Clay attended from the Bank.

The Treasury found the suggestions attractive and sought to bend them further to its own purposes. Eady was disposed to seize on the proposed advisory panel as a preferable alternative to the Industrial Commission. For through the panel the corporation would be able to keep the needs of industry under constant review, and its assistance in individual cases would be given with due regard to the needs of the whole. In addition the Treasury now suggested that there might be Government representation on the board of the FCI and that, in particular cases, Government money might be contributed. Perhaps with an eye on which way the new Governor (fresh from the Treasury) might be inclined to go, Niemeyer and Skinner both recoiled at the Treasury's advances. The former would have nothing to do with any Government representation on the board. In choosing Directors, the Bank would keep the Government informed and listen to what they said but should give no public pledge in advance. Skinner shared Niemeyer's view, adding his own fear that the Bank might be in danger of agreeing that the FCI would initiate surveys and reorganisations when it ought to be concerned only to 'fill up holes in the financial structure'. This advice prevailed, but some weeks later Niemeyer and Skinner returned to the theme, this time on the question of the Industrial Commission. If it was to be an advisory body, then the establishment of the FCI could go ahead. If on the other hand it was to be a compulsory planning board, there would no hope of getting cash from the City and no FCI. The spectre of a compulsory planning authority then

[5] When the FCI was established in the following year, Clay was appointed a member of this panel.

seems to have faded away, for subsequent negotiations with Whitehall were confined to the difficult question of Government influence over appointments to the board. The President of the Board of Trade, Dalton, was especially keen that they be made in consultation with the Government, that there should be provision for at least one representative of 'labour' on the panel, and that there should be a commitment to close consultation with Whitehall on all matters of any importance. To this the Bank replied that while in practice it would keep the Treasury properly informed, the whole project would be prejudiced if the Government were to have a right of veto. Catto remained firm on this point, though convinced of the need to press ahead with the formation of both the new institutions. For the first time in his Governorship, but not the last, he got his way with Dalton.

Early in October 1944 the new Governor felt that his position was strong enough to write a letter to the Chancellor, Sir John Anderson. The letter was firm and convincing and its contents were designed to meet the legitimate concerns of Whitehall, as the Governor saw them, but to give no further ground. There was a need for new developments in industrial finance, especially to meet the needs of transition from war to peace. The first of these would be a company for the finance of small business, which the banks would be prepared to capitalise but which would be managed quite separately, by businessmen and by technical experts. The Bank itself would participate, but neither it nor any other single bank would exercise control. The company would be run on business lines and would not accept clearly uncommercial propositions. Next there would be a company for the finance of large industrial companies, in special cases. Discussions in the City led the Governor to believe that he could probably find the necessary £20–30 million of capital (giving a total lending capacity of £80–120 million[6]) though the Bank itself would need to make a substantial contribution. The company would have an advisory panel of personalities connected with both sides of industry. Both the proposed new institutions would have every incentive to run on the broadest possible basis consistent with reasonable commercial prudence. If not, they would die. They would nonetheless work in closest co-operation with the Government Departments concerned, most importantly the Board of Trade. Although their activities would at all times be fully related to Government policy in the national interest, they would have to be allowed to run on a commercial basis. Concluding, the Governor said he was most anxious to press ahead. Unless the new companies were quickly put into place, there would be

---

[6] The reader should adjust this for subsequent inflation. At 1990 values it amounts to some £1,200–1,800 million.

serious risk of financial difficulties in the transition. But before going any further the Bank must be given assurance by the Chancellor and by the President of the Board of Trade that the plans set out had their blessing and support.

There was a pause of a month before the Chancellor replied, in terms cleared with the Bank in advance, accepting and welcoming the Governor's proposals. Three comments were added, all acceptable to the Bank. Firstly, the Government itself might have to embark on special finance for industry in a few instances. Secondly, the Government hoped that the small-business institution would be prepared to assist new applicants as well as existing businesses. Thirdly, the Government wished every consideration to be given to the Development Areas.

The way was now clear for the Bank to complete its negotiations with the City. Whitehall had been successfully deterred from insisting that the new institutions should attempt too much, with an unacceptable degree of interference by Government; now, with his other face, Janus had to deter the banks, insurance companies, and investment trusts from insisting on too little.

Earlier in March 1944, after Norman had delegated the responsibility to him, the Deputy Governor had briefly resumed the discussions with the BIA about a reorganised BID. Catterns had stressed the desirability of the City rather than the Government finding money for post-war industrial finance, the likelihood that ordinary market channels would not always suffice, and the necessity to devise machinery for close liaison with Whitehall. Later in March Frazer of the BIA had taken soundings within the insurance industry and reported a favourable response, subject to negotiation on details. Catterns had also resumed the discussions with Crichton and the AIT. The response was sympathetic, but the Bank was warned both that £10 million would be a difficult target to meet and that the Scottish trusts would be awkward to handle. There the matter had rested until early the following winter when the discussions with Whitehall were being concluded. In the meantime the Bank had turned its attention to negotiations about the formation of the bankers' company for the finance of small businesses. The first step was to hold the meeting with the Chairmen of the Big Five clearing banks that had been held over since Norman's illness. This meeting took place early in March. Catterns deployed the arguments in favour of a new institution, emphasising that it would be a feature of post-war banking policy and not an instrument of Government. It was agreed to refer the matter to the Committee of Chief Executive Officers for a report on feasibility. Heading the Committee at this time was Lidbury of the Midland, an unusually commanding figure. The

Chairmen themselves appeared sympathetic; and two weeks later Campbell wrote to Catterns that he would like the banks 'to do this in a big way and a gracious way, rather than in a half-hearted grudging manner'. At the end of March there was a full meeting of the CLCB, at which the Deputy Governor presented the case for a new institution with substantial resources and with some participation by the Bank itself.

The views of two or three bank Chairmen on a matter of this kind sometimes fail to resemble those of their senior management; and the Bank was soon getting signals that this instance was to prove an example. In the middle of March Niemeyer circulated a minute arguing against an idea apparently current among the banks that, instead of combining in the way suggested by the Bank, each of the Big Five should form a separate small-business subsidiary. 'Instead of a unified effort', he wrote, 'we shall get five sheep wandering at random.' Individual subsidiaries would mean no independent Chairman, no general impulse to activity, and second-rate or uninspired administration. The subsidiaries would be 'run by bank managers and not by people who understand industrial finance'. A few days later Skinner entered the lists in opposition to another idea, namely that the Bank should not itself participate. 'If they [the banks] want to stand alone in this, they must be prepared to do so always and to run the risk that we might sometimes have to act alone for Government account. They would throw us towards HMG whatever their arguments.' In the end, and no doubt with the benefit of discussions behind the scenes, the banks dropped any such ideas. But in doing so they threw some bricks at the Bank. On 2 May the CLCB stated that, individually, the banks could provide fully and satisfactorily for long-term loans to small traders, but it recognised that a separate institution might be deemed essential by the authorities. On 9 May Campbell forwarded to the new Governor a memorandum by the Chief Executive Officers. The Bank, they said, was evidently being pushed by HMG.[7] They went on to rehearse familiar arguments that no gap existed in the financing of small business, but they advised that if HMG insisted then the banks should conform. In a final offensive flourish they said: 'This memorandum is presented through the intermediary of the Governor, for the consideration of the appropriate Minister.' The Bank found no difficulty in accepting this kind of treatment with constructive fortitude. Niemeyer, Peppiatt, Clay, and Skinner all advised the new Governor to take what was on offer and, as Niemeyer put it, 'leave the earlier stuff alone'. So the banks assembled in Threadneedle

---

[7] The Bank's position in this aspect of the affair had not been helped by Eady, who had lunched at the National Provincial on 10 February and indicated that Whitehall would take on the job if the banks refused.

Street on 11 May, said goodbye to Norman (*in absentia*), welcomed Catto, agreed in principle to the finance corporation for small businesses and instructed the Chief Executive Officers to get down to details. The latter met in the following month and, as a first 'detail', agreed that the Old Lady should be politely asked to participate as a shareholder. Subsequent negotiations throughout the summer covered a number of contentious matters. It was agreed that the Governor should appoint the first Chairman. In addition the banks were obliged to concede substantial modification of an ingeniously restrictive provision that they had proposed and by which applications to the new institution could only be made through the introduction of their existing bankers. There was also some familiar manoeuvring with the Scottish banks. Would they come in or would they form a separate company of their own? The Bank did not greatly care. Niemeyer, showing some disregard for the new Governor's origins, wrote that the Scots 'could be left to go to hell in their own way' provided their scheme was aligned with the English one. In the end they decided to come in.[8] By the end of October Catto could judge that the Industrial and Commercial Finance Corporation, as it had now been decided to call it, was complete except for its formal establishment, board appointments, and so forth. With Whitehall near to agreement with him about FCI, Catto now felt it was time to resume City progress with this latter project.

On 9 November 1944 The Governor saw Simpson and Frazer of the BIA. He outlined the latest version of the FCI and asked for £10 million. He was promised support and they came back a week later to say that the plan had been well received by the larger companies that they had now consulted. Only the Prudential was reluctant, but the Governor saw the Chairman of that company on the same day and recorded that he was quite satisfied. A month later Frazer was given the go-ahead for all members of the BIA to be approached; and early in the new year a letter sent out by its Chairman enclosed a note on the FCI that had been drafted in the Bank. Responses were favourable. An amount of £10 million was soon assured. As to the investment trusts, the Governor saw Crichton and two other representatives on 14 November and asked for £7½ million rather than £10 million. A week later they said that support from their

---

[8] Consideration was also given to setting up a parallel institution in Northern Ireland capitalised by the English and Scottish clearers. But the banks refused to put their capital behind Northern Irish business in this way, business that was in any case intermingled with that in Eire. They felt that if the Northern Irish authorities wanted a parallel institution for the Province it was for the banks in Northern Ireland to set one up for themselves.

London colleagues was good, but that there would be difficulties with the Scots. In this instance, because of their quantitative importance in the investment trust business, the Scots could not be left to go to hell in their own way and the Governor had to persuade his fellow countrymen to join him in the proposed venture. While embarking on this task, he sought the acquiescence of the clearing banks to their providing loans or advances to the FCI up to four times its issued capital. Unusually, he personally met the Chief Executive Officers, headed by Lidbury. They put forward a number of searching questions, mainly seeking assurance that the FCI's role would be commercial and that it would be supplementary to existing sources of funds for industry. They also warned that they might at times find difficulty in lending to the FCI if this were to mean either curtailing other lending or selling investments on a poor market. They seem to have been satisfied by the Governor's response, for on the following day there was a cordial exchange of letters with Lidbury.

On the advice of Crichton, Catto approached the Scottish investment trusts through Carlyle Gifford, who promised support and in turn advised that two or three representatives of the Edinburgh trusts should be invited to London to see the Governor in person. In this way, jealousy of the London trusts' more direct access to the Bank would be soothed. He later supplied three names and these were invited to the Bank through the intermediary of Crichton. The Governor saw them early in the new year and was promised their co-operation. Their record of the meeting, which was copied to the Bank and to their colleagues in Scotland, noted with approval that the Governor had referred to the duty of financial institutions 'of the country' and had not spoken of 'the City'. They also reported that the Governor had stressed that his proposals were in no way instigated by the Government and that there had been no threats from that quarter.

The Bank now felt that its position was strong enough to outflank remaining opposition north of the Border, for on 16 January 1945 Crichton circularised all members of the AIT, including the Scots, asking for support for the FCI. On 22 January he told the Governor that he was hopeful of £7$\frac{1}{2}$ million and on the 23rd the whole project was made public by the Chancellor of the Exchequer and by the Bank. The Scottish opposition then simmered for two months until, after a curious exchange between himself and Gifford,[9] the Governor received from the Scots a

---

[9] Possibly in order to warn him of what was coming, Gifford wrote to Catto on 9 March setting out some unattributed views in the form of a mock draft speech. This emphasized that the origin of the exercise had been talks between HMG and the Bank and that the Governor had then 'dutifully' set about Whitehall's business. Niemeyer considered this was 'cheek', to which the Governor replied: 'I agree, but possibly he means well.'

Report on dissenting views about the FCI. The opposition objected to being left out at the preliminary stages. They would have liked a round-table meeting with the Bank, the BIA, and the AIT. They were not satisfied that the FCI was really needed or, if it was, that it needed as much money as was being requested. Now they were presented with a *fait accompli*. They recognised they had a duty to cooperate in the public interest but they required assurances that the venture would be run on purely commercial lines, that it was not being promoted under pressure from the Government, and that it would not be subject to any more Government influence than any other company. The Governor sent an admonitory reply on 22 March and received an amende, with acceptance of participation, a few days later. The Scottish campaign was over.

Once the agreement to set up the two companies had been announced, the Bank immediately set about finding suitable Chairmen and agreeing other appointments to the two Boards. Attention was mostly focused on the FCI and by the end of January the Governor had assembled a long list of possible names from industry and from the City. From the start he favoured Lord Hyndley, a senior industrialist with special interest in the coal industry (Powell Duffryn), as Chairman. Hyndley had also been Commercial Adviser to the Department of Mines during most of the inter-war period and a member of the Court of the Bank since 1931.[10] He saw the Governor on 1 February and seems to have agreed to his name being put to the other shareholders. There was then a delay until the Articles of Association were agreed in detail, and it was not until the end of March that Hyndley's appointment was confirmed. He then secured the services of none other than Skinner, who agreed to become General Manager of the FCI and to leave the service of the Bank. Next Hyndley insisted that there should be a senior representative of organised labour on the Board. Despite opposition both from within the Bank and from the other shareholders, he made it clear that he would not serve as Chairman unless satisfied on this point. Appointment of a labour representative on the Advisory Panel, as a second best, would not suffice. He got his way. After some seven weeks of further consideration and negotiation, including a correspondence between the Governor and Sir Henry Tizard about a suitable scientist for the Board, its composition was announced on 22 May and included the name of Lord Westwood, a senior trade-unionist in the shipbuilding industry and at that time Chief Industrial Adviser to the Admiralty. In

---

[10] He resigned in May 1945 on taking up the Chairmanship of the FCI. Later, in 1947, he became the first Chairman of the National Coal Board.

addition there were three industrialists (including the Chairman), two eminent accountants, one scientist, one former Finance Member of the Government of India, and one member from the insurance world.[11]

Appointments to the ICFC were altogether easier. The Governor's only task was to appoint the Chairman, everything else being effectively left to Lidbury and his colleagues in the clearing banks. The Articles of Association were virtually completed by the end of March 1945 and some weeks later, following discussion in the Bank, Catto invited Sir Geoffrey Vickers to become Chairman. He declined, in part because he foresaw differences of attitude developing between himself and the banks. The latter, he felt, might take too narrow a view of the commercial objectives of the ICFC, at the expense of its 'public interest' aims. The Governor then turned to Lord Piercy, who accepted, and all was eventually announced late in July.

One small but lively problem remained. How was the FCI to meet its running costs before it had acquired sufficient income from the new business it hoped to attract? Income from the temporary investment of its paid-up capital would not be enough. Earlier, in April 1945, it had been suggested in the Bank that this question might conveniently be answered by selling to the FCI the controlling interest in the Lancashire Steel Corporation and the minority interest in Richard Thomas and Baldwin Ltd (held by the Bank through its subsidiary the Securities Management Trust). The Governor found this suggestion, which was most likely his own, to be a good one, but Niemeyer adamantly opposed it. He felt it would be wholly wrong for the Bank, having gone to all the trouble to set up the FCI and present it as a contribution of private finance to meeting immediate post-war industrial problems, to be seen making first use of the new company as a convenient receptacle for industrial assets that it had acquired pre-war and no longer wanted to keep. In the heat of the moment Niemeyer went so far as to refer to these assets as 'our junk'. This drew a sharp riposte from the Governor: 'This is nonsense, and not helpful...Let's not talk of selling junk. Indeed I did not know we had any junk. I have had it impressed on me how good these investments were.' But Niemeyer gave no ground, for his case was strong, and the matter was not pressed again until the autumn when he had to admit that the prospective nationalisation of the Bank made some difference to his argument. Eventually, a compromise was struck. In December 1945 the FCI was given a three-month option to buy the holding in Lancashire Steel

---

[11] The Governor remarked within the Bank: 'It seems to work out at four Englishmen, four Scotsmen (all in England), and one Jew. Could we do better for a Finance Company?'

while the Bank would retain its holding in Richard Thomas and Baldwin. In the event the FCI did not feel the need for its christening present and the option was never taken up.

Looking back at the end of 1945, Janus could have allowed himself some self-satisfaction. It can have been no secret anywhere that the wartime Government had been closely concerned with the foreseen problems of post-war industrial finance and anxious to secure the tangible support of the financial community towards the solution of those problems. To that end, as everyone seems to have known, a degree of pressure had been brought to bear on the City (and the Scots) through the usual channel. In responding to that pressure the Bank had had to take an initiative, which it then had to present as a City or private enterprise initiative of an almost spontaneous nature; and it had repeatedly to deny any pressure from Whitehall. Against taunts that it was the Government's errand-boy, the Bank could only remain silent, or issue unconvincing denials. In truth the Bank was responding not only to Whitehall pressure but also to its own analysis of the problem, and it was responding by itself constructing an initiative that it could and did sell to both its constituencies. If at some stage in the process an element of persuasive pantomime had to be employed, or endured, then that was all a necessary part of the job. At the end of the day some could perhaps claim that they had been misled, or that their understanding of what had been done or committed seemed rather different from the understanding of someone else. In complaining about a lack of round-table discussions, the Scots had a point to be made. In some different system, with a different Bank and different responsibilities, the whole approach to establishing the two corporations would perhaps have been clearer to everyone. But it might also have been less successful.

Throughout the two years since Churchill's broadcast in March 1943 the whole emphasis of the Bank's thought and action in the field of industrial finance had been the supposed needs of reconstruction and redeployment in the immediate post-war transition.[12] This emphasis on

[12] In memoirs written in the 1950s and printed privately after his death in 1959, Catto himself recalled this emphasis in the following terms:

'In addition to the many financial and economic problems of the time, there was a matter of special urgency to be dealt with on which the Bank had to give a lead. This was the problem of finance for industry as the war began to near its end. There had been much discussion between the Treasury and the Bank and in the public press on the subject, and particularly in regard to some method of dealing with what had come to be called, since the time of the Macmillan Committee, the Macmillan Gap. Plainly some permanent arrangements were needed to deal with these finance problems. Industrialists had made clear to me that plants had been run during the war at such excessive pressure that much rehabilitation and many renewals would be necessary, and that this applied universally throughout industry both in the large and small units. Capital would be required quickly to deal with this situation and I was asked whether at any rate temporarily the Bank of

what was thought to be an urgent priority enabled divisions of view within the Bank and within the City, about the proper long-term role (if any) of special financial institutions, to be left unresolved without prejudice to the successful foundation of the two new institutions themselves. As things turned out, however, the financial problems of industrial transition proved to be much less serious than everyone had feared. So as time went by, the questions about long-term role were the ones that came to the fore. In the case of the ICFC this did not really matter. Its shareholders did not behave in an oppressive manner and were anyway well content for the corporation to provide equity finance for small business (which the banks themselves had no wish to provide) in addition to long-term loans. Over the years the ICFC built up a considerable business, with a sizeable and expert staff and a branch network, which gave it a permanent place in the spectrum of financial intermediaries. For the FCI, by contrast, unresolved questions about long-term role mattered a great deal, especially because in the negotiating process of 1944–5 it had in the end been fashioned as a relatively passive institution that found it difficult actively to seek out business in competition with normal channels.

Over its first eight years the FCI built up a large loan book of some £60 million, or £900 million at 1990 values; but two-thirds of this represented special loans to steel companies, in large part made in market conditions that anticipated the nationalisation that took effect in 1951. The remainder was lent to a variety of companies, some of which were new and risky ventures and some of which (for example Petrochemicals Ltd) involved the FCI in substantial losses. In keeping with its passive constitution, the FCI had only a very small staff and effectively relied on the Board and the Panel for expert advice. Over the following two decades there were occasional and special opportunities for new business, but in general the FCI found little to do until it was merged with the ICFC in 1974 to form Finance for Industry Ltd. Those, like Niemeyer and Peppiatt, who all along regarded the FCI simply as a long-stop or occasional gap-filler, would not have been disappointed with this result. Lack of business simply meant lack of gaps; while in 1944 a failure to press ahead with the FCI would have provoked the Government into some ill-considered venture of its own. But Skinner and Kershaw would have been disappointed if they had come to judge, as many did, that the physical performance of British industry was inadequate; and indeed the more active and interventionist view was to

England would provide this very necessary finance. I replied that in the past the Bank on many occasions had come to the rescue of various companies in the national interest to tide over exceptional conditions, but what was now needed was something more definite than that, and on a larger and more permanent scale to meet the magnitude of the problem.'

Lord Catto, Governor 1944–1949

flourish in the 1960s and 1970s and bring about the rise and political fall of the 'state merchant bank', namely the Industrial Reorganisation Corporation and its subsequent but impermanent resurrection as the National Enterprise Board. Yet in 1944 Skinner himself was very nervous of the City taking interventionist responsibilities, preferring industry itself to indulge in self-intervention through trade associations. In practice there was probably no easily workable middle road between the passive City gap-filler, easily restrained by the sceptical views of its private-sector backers, and the Whitehall enterprise board. This remained true so long as it was thought that a special institution was the right vehicle both for supplying the necessary finance and for deploying the required advice and persuasion. Not until the late 1970s did the Bank, still resolutely playing the part of Janus, find the key that opened the door to the middle way. It did so by itself taking on the advisory and catalytic function, supported by a speedily reacquired expert knowledge, and relying upon particular banks and institutional investors to provide the financial counterpart case by case. Finance for Industry[13] remained and carried on good business as a gap-filler, but it was not the vehicle through which the Bank's middle-road industrial activities were pursued.

(c) FURTHER VENTURES IN THE PUBLIC INTEREST
The Steel Company of Wales: 1947

The episode recounted in the preceding section showed the Bank in negotiation with the clearing banks, insurance companies, and investment trusts. The principal merchant banks, comprising mostly membership of the Accepting Houses Committee (AHC), did not enter the picture at all. Although, along with the discount houses, they were closest to the Bank among the whole range of City institutions, they had little to contribute, either as principals or as organising intermediaries, to the formation of the FCI and the ICFC. This was not the case in the four further episodes now to be briefly discussed. In each they played a large or even central part, sometimes as disputants in a matter important enough in the public interest for the Bank to intervene, sometimes as confidential advisers, and sometimes as participants in special financial operations with which the Bank was concerned. These episodes were the financing of the Steel Company of Wales (SCOW) in 1947, the creation of the Commonwealth Development Finance Company (CDFC) in the winter of 1952–3, the denationalisation of the steel industry following the return of a Conservative Government in 1951, and the take-over of British Aluminium by Reynolds Metals and Tube Investments in 1958.

Early after the war the merchant banks were very much on the look-out for new business. It was not easy to get. Bill business was at a low ebb and

---

[13] Now renamed Investment in Industry, or 'three i's' for short.

slow to revive. New corporate issues, restricted both by the CIC and by the high level of corporate liquidity, proved fewer than at first expected. Corporate finance fees, in the sense now meant by the words, were few and far between. New ventures abroad were often likely to be hampered by exchange controls. Accordingly, there was likely to be keen if gentlemanly competition for such domestic new-issue business as there was. Financing the steel industry was a case in point. Large sums were likely to be needed in addition to ordinary banking accommodation, but the steel companies faced an uncertain, if profitable, future. Though not among the Government's first priorities for nationalisation, they were likely to meet that fate within five years unless the Labour Party lost office in the meantime. They were therefore a clear case for special financing through the FCI, whose Board gave plenty of preliminary thought to the problem. However, early in 1947 this did not seem so clear to those engaged in creating SCOW, a consortium company whose purpose was to carry out the reconstruction and modernisation of the Welsh tin-plate industry. The leader of the consortium was Richard Thomas and Baldwin Ltd (RTB). Its Chairman was Sir Ernest Lever who thought it might be possible, notwithstanding the uncertainty, to find a ready home for SCOW securities through the capital market. Barings, who had advised RTB in the past, disagreed and took the view that participation by the FCI would be essential. However, the promoters stuck to their opinion, did not even consult Lord Bruce (the new Chairman of the FCI), did not pursue matters further with Barings, and turned instead to Lazards who were prepared to try leading a syndicate of issuing houses to market the SCOW securities in the ordinary way, without the FCI. Prominent at the top of Lazards was its Chairman, the first Lord Kindersley. He was seventy-six and had recently retired from the Court of the Bank after no less than thirty-two years of service. Prominent at the top of Barings was 'ERP', Sir Edward Peacock. He too was seventy-six, had recently left the Court after twenty years' service, and had a formidable reputation as a shrewd investor. When approached by Kindersley in April 1947 to attend a meeting of seven houses (Barings, Hambros, Lazards, Morgan Grenfell, Rothschilds, Schroders, and Helbert Wagg) to discuss the SCOW financing, Peacock not only declined the invitation but informed the Governor he had done so. His reasons were that it was inadvisable to go ahead without the FCI, unwise to play down the risks of nationalisation, and anyway awkward for Barings as erstwhile advisers to RTB, the leader of the SCOW consortium.

Catto, a stripling of sixty-three who had himself been connected with Morgan Grenfell, reacted at once to the news received from Peacock. The Bank could not stand aside in face of a clear dispute between two leading merchant banks on a matter of general public interest, the more so when it involved two Nestors who were former members of the Court. Nor could the Governor, who had personally done so much to bring the FCI to life, easily accept that Bruce and his Corporation should be excluded from an exercise in which they seemed so well-suited to participate. He therefore set about resolving the dispute and ensuring that the FCI was brought in, without seeming to give orders and risk provoking a rebuff. He held a series of meetings with the houses concerned over a period of ten days; and it soon became clear that Morgan Grenfell and Rothschilds supported Peacock. Lazards then conceded. Bruce was duly consulted and asked to assist. His response was favourable and all was settled in outline at a meeting in the Governor's room that was attended by the FCI and five of the seven houses. There was unanimous agreement that the operation would require close co-operation between the issuing houses and the FCI and that the details should be worked out by a steering committee chaired by Bruce.[14] Catto had successfully provided a service as mediator and at the same time secured a solution in the public interest that was much to his taste. Not himself a true member of the City establishment, but with a rather wider breadth of commercial experience behind him than some of the other participants, he had brought his personality to bear on the problem with singular success.

The Commonwealth Development Finance Company: 1952

In the autumn of 1952, as preparations went ahead for the meeting of Commonwealth Prime Ministers to be held in London at the end of November, the subject of 'Commonwealth Development' came very much to the political fore as an integral part of the Collective Approach to convertibility and freer trade (see Chapter 8(b) above). The independent members of the Commonwealth all wanted to attract additional inflows of development capital, while the UK, at the centre of the Sterling Area, was closely interested in the development of additional non-dollar supplies of food and raw materials. Within the Sterling Area the outflow of UK private capital, notably to the 'old' Dominions, had been sustained at a high level since the war (some thought the level too high for the UK to bear). But in the summer of 1952 the idea gained ground, outside Whitehall, that there would be room for a special finance corporation in the City that would provide capital for sound long-term projects in Commonwealth countries,

---

[14] In the event, the members of the consortium took £15 million of equity, banks took £15 million of 3% first debentures (with the possibility of on-sale in the market), and the FCI took £35 million of convertible second debentures.

projects whose profitability in the short-term might not be sufficient to attract enough private capital in the ordinary way. The suggested corporation was sometimes seen as a Sterling Area complement to the IBRD. Lord Bruce scouted the idea of a Commonwealth Development Finance Corporation when speaking at the Annual General Meeting of the FCI in September. Earlier, Sir Ernest Oppenheimer and his sons had suggested to Bolton that Commonwealth central banks should put up equity capital for a Development Finance Corporation while the international mining companies would provide loan capital. The Governor, who talked with visiting Commonwealth officials and central banks during October, then began to think of a Commonwealth Reconstruction Bank sponsored by Governments and central banks. Its equity might come mainly from the Bank of England and its loan capital would come from all and sundry in the UK. This idea was further discussed by Beale, in consultation with Bolton, Mynors, Parsons, Kershaw and Haslam, an Assistant Adviser.[15] Cobbold next tried it out on the Chancellor, who found it a politically attractive alternative to a new Governmental institution and encouraged the Governor to pursue it in the City. The Reconstruction Bank was to be quite large (similar to the FCI), with £50 million of equity and borrowing powers of up to £150 million, the former to be subscribed by the Bank and other City institutions.

The Bank's outline scheme, though it might imply starting in a small way, was very ambitious. Moreover, its acceptability to other City institutions was likely to depend as much upon political enthusiasm for the Commonwealth as upon a rational conviction that the corporation would prove a good investment and would fulfil a real need that could not be met through ordinary channels. Moreover, the political timetable was very tight and the scheme would have to prove very acceptable if it were to be ready for announcement on 11 December, at the end of the Commonwealth Conference. Recollection of the time it took to get the FCI and ICFC off the ground suggested caution. Nonetheless the Governor decided to make the attempt within the short time available and once more turned for advice to Peacock, now aged eighty-two but little the worse for it. Unfortunately, the initial result on this occasion was a meeting between Bolton and Evelyn Baring at which the latter reportedly advised that the whole City would be glad to co-operate and that the Bank should go about raising the equity from insurance companies, investment trusts, mining finance houses, and the clearing banks. The merchant banks could assist

---

[15] *Haslam, Eric Percival (b. 1912)* Commonwealth Bank of Australia 1943–8. Entered Bank 1948, Assistant Adviser 1948–55, Adviser 1955–65, Adviser to the Governors 1965–72.

at a later stage by obtaining Commonwealth customers and piloting loan proposals to the Reconstruction Bank. This line of thought was not reliable, though likely to appeal to the large-minded Bolton whose experience in this type of activity was limited. Barings, in partnership with Morgan Grenfell, had recently entered a joint venture with Harris and Company in Toronto; and in common with several other merchant banks were keen to develop additional Commonwealth interests (for example, an interest taken by Rothschilds in the British Newfoundland Corporation). Accordingly their enthusiasm for a Reconstruction Bank was understandable, though the advice reportedly given to Bolton was incautious.

Relying on optimistic advice, the Bank next refined its plan. It provided this time for participation by Commonwealth central banks at a later stage and for the initial flotation to be managed by the six houses, including Barings, who had earlier managed an IBRD issue of sterling bonds in London. If the City would readily co-operate it would suffice for the Bank to let its support be known and for the rest of the work to be handled by the issuing houses. The Governor then consulted Hugh Kindersley. He was only mildly encouraging; and Cobbold, sensing difficulty, was deliberately and wisely cautious when reporting back to the Chancellor, saying he could not promise anything spectacular for the Conference. He then saw each of the six issuing houses, beginning with Peacock for Barings. He did not put forward a specific plan but suggested that the houses themselves should formulate one. While he was away on a brief visit to North America, the six merchant banks did their homework and came up with some very disappointing opinions. For a start they advised that the project would be too big for them to sponsor, would be inappropriate for a syndicate of only six houses, and would not be suitable for them to create if subsequently they were to put business proposals to it. The whole project would have to be sponsored by the Bank itself. Having concluded that there would after all be little City support for the equity of the proposed company, they reduced its suggested size drastically, to £10 million from £50 million, and advised that the Bank subscribe all but £2·5 million, which would be obtained from industrial, commercial, and mining companies. Even on this reduced scale, pressure would be needed to secure subscription of the £2·5 million. Peacock presented this unappetising fare first to Bolton and later to the Governor on his return from North America. He further advised that the Governor should himself begin by seeing the chairmen of a few of the largest British-domiciled multinational companies.

The houses' advice was now reliable and realistic. The Governor could therefore either drop the plan and disappoint Whitehall or press ahead and endeavour to raise as much as he could from industry and commerce. This would be a novel exercise and one requiring full use of his personal prestige. Never lacking in courage or pace, he decided to make the attempt. A list of over fifty companies was quickly compiled and on 1 December, with only ten days to go before the end of the Conference, he saw the Chairmen of Imperial Tobacco (Sir R. Sinclair), Shell (Sir F. Godber), Dunlop (Sir C. Baillieu), and Unilever (Sir G. Heyworth). The response was encouraging and a succession of other company Chairmen visited the Bank over the next few days with similarly encouraging results. By the end of the week the Governor was able to inform Whitehall that the omens were favourable and that a group was being formed to carry the whole project forward. On 11 December, coinciding with the final communiqué of the Conference and after customary prior notification of City institutions and Commonwealth central banks, he held a press conference. Explaining the purpose of the new institution, he announced that an organising group was being formed to bring it to life. The group was to be drawn from City interests and from industry and commerce. The announcement received a cautious welcome in the press.

Peacock chaired the organising group. Baillieu, Godber, Heyworth, Sinclair, and Stedeford (Tube Investments) were members along with representatives of the Accepting Houses Committee and the Issuing Houses Association. The Bank was represented by Mynors and Beale. On 16 December the Governor saw Peacock, handed him a list of those who had offered to subscribe, and requested him to bring the exercise to its intended conclusion. The group appointed a working committee for this purpose and in March 1953 the Commonwealth Development Finance Company (CDFC) was incorporated with an authorised capital of £15 million and borrowing powers of £30 million. Godber was Chairman and other Board members were Heyworth, Mynors, Duncan Oppenheimer (Chairman of British American Tobacco), Peacock, Sinclair, Stedeford, and R. E. Fleming (Robert Fleming and Company). Of the £15 million of authorised capital, £$8\frac{1}{4}$ million consisted of A shares and £$6\frac{3}{4}$ of B shares. The latter would all be subscribed by the Bank; the former by ninety-one industrial, mining, shipping, and banking companies. Ten per cent of both classes of shares were paid up at the outset; but no further call on the A shareholders could be made until the B shares had been paid in full. Thus although the total authorised capital, at £15 million, was somewhat larger than the £10 million originally suggested by the six issuing houses and although the Bank's ultimate liability was somewhat smaller, there was no doubt who was actually taking the lion's share of the risk until the CDFC had grown to full stature.

Over the first five years of its life the CDFC invested a total of £14½ million in twelve projects in eight countries. Its authorised capital was subsequently enlarged to £30 million, of which £26¼ million was issued and, by 1959, £7·3 million had been paid up (the B shares were by then 50% paid the A shares remaining at 10%). Born of the strong politico-economic currents of opinion prevalent throughout 1952, which seemed to make Commonwealth Development part of the answer to sterling's problems, the CDFC never found it easy to get worthwhile business. Opportunities were often either too risky or else well able to get finance through other channels. In 1952 City investment institutions apparently saw clearly enough that this was what would happen and accordingly discouraged Peacock and his colleagues from telling the Bank that they would readily subscribe to the equity. Industry and commerce were prepared to subscribe in small amounts under the leadership of multinationals with very large Commonwealth interests. But they cannot have found the experience very rewarding. As for the Bank, it could count itself rather fortunate to have escaped in 1952–3 without any loss of face. It had set itself to complete a difficult and politically sensitive task in very short order. Its initial thinking was too optimistic, over-reliant on particular merchant banking opinion, and lacking in direct contact with investor opinion. Fortunately, ERP was able to save the day with the novel idea of a trawl through industry and commerce, which the Governor was able to pursue with force and some worthwhile success. In such situations there was usually, though not always, a limited reserve of goodwill somewhere, a reserve that could be tapped by the Governor in a worthwhile cause with a public interest flavour. In this instance Peacock found it and Cobbold tapped it. The Bank had a service it wanted to provide in the public interest. The problem was to find a market for it, this time outside the City itself.

The denationalisation of iron and steel: 1951–1955

In November 1949 the Iron and Steel Act received the Royal Assent, but no vesting date was announced ahead of the General Election of February 1950. Notwithstanding the reduction in its majority to single figures and the likelihood of another dissolution before long, the Government then decided to go ahead. Vesting of the steel companies took place in February 1951. Unlike previous examples, the industry was not statutorily reorganised into divisions presided over by a Board. Instead, control passed to a state holding company, the British Iron and Steel Corporation, in whom the shares of the existing companies were vested. Initially, within

Edward Peacock ('ERP')
By courtesy of Baring Bros.

this framework of control, the previous corporate structure of the industry remained intact. It was therefore possible for the Conservative Opposition to consider reversing the whole process, by getting rid of the corporation and selling the companies back to private shareholders rather than by privatising the industry either as one company or as several new companies constructed for the purpose. It was even possible to contemplate returning the shares to their previous owners in exchange for the compensation stock paid to them.

The Conservative leadership was sympathetic. Though not prepared to contemplate unscrambling the nationalisation of coal, railways, gas, and electricity, it was prepared to consider the return of steel to private hands (and also the break-up of the new state monopoly of road hauliers). In these circumstances two leading figures in the industry before vesting, Ellis Hunter and Andrew Duncan, asked Lord Bicester and Edward Peacock (of Morgan Grenfell and Barings respectively) for advice. It was clear that City institutions would have a big job to do if the steel companies were to be sold back into private ownership. To provide the advice a Committee was set up under Archibald Forbes,[16] recently Chairman of the Iron and Steel Board. A draft Report was ready by the end of March 1951 and Peacock handed a copy to the Governor for information. It suggested resale of the former public companies in two or three separate offerings, starting with the simultaneous offering of the best-known firms, whose equity might total some £85 million. The issue would be underwritten in the City and former stockholders would receive preferential allotment. The size and difficulty of the operation, including the effect of any threatened renationalisation, was appreciated both by the Committee and by those who commissioned its work. Writing to Forbes on 29 March, Bicester advised great caution. No more should be said by the Conservative Party than a statement of general intent.

It was not the job of the Bank to give advice to the Opposition, except with the knowledge and consent of the Chancellor of the day. Early in May

---

[16] *Forbes, Archibald Finlayson*, GBE, (1903–90). Educated Glasgow University. Thomson McLintock and Co., Executive Director, Spillers 1935–60, Deputy Chairman 1960–5, Chairman 1965–8, President 1969–80. Director of Capital Finance, Air Ministry 1940, Deputy Secretary, Ministry of Aircraft Production 1940–3, Controller of Repair, Equipment, and Overseas Supplies and Director General, Repair and Maintenance, RAF 1943–5. Chairman, Iron and Steel Board 1946–9 and 1953–9, Director, Midland Bank 1959–62, Deputy Chairman 1962–4, Chairman 1964–75, President 1975–83, Deputy Chairman, CLCB 1968–70, Chairman 1970–2, Vice-President, British Bankers' Association (BBA) 1969–70, President 1970–2, Director, FCI 1950–3, Deputy Chairman 1961–4, Chairman, Central Mining and Investment Corporation 1959–64, Debenture Corporation 1949–79, Midland and International Banks Ltd 1964–76. Director, Shell Transport and Trading 1954–73, English Electric 1958–76, Dunlop 1958–76, etc. President, Federation of British Industries (FBI) 1951–3.

the Governor returned the Report to Peacock (while retaining a copy) without recorded comment, though he may have told him that the Bank was well aware of the difficulties. But should denationalisation ever come to pass, the Bank was likely to become involved at technical level as registrar of the steel compensation stock and as a possessor of the registers of the steel companies as of Vesting Day. Further, as an adviser to the Government it was likely to be involved in the planning of the various operations, including at first the drafting of the necessary legislation and at a later stage the formation of issuing-house consortia. Some forward thinking was therefore in order; and in the spring of 1951 Hawker, then Chief Accountant and head of the registrar function, together with Beale and Peppiatt all expressed grave doubts about the practical wisdom of attempting to unscramble in the way Forbes and his Committee had suggested. The proposed sell-offs would be too large for the market to handle and the political uncertainties too great. In addition, any plan for returning shares to their original owners would be so complicated as to be virtually impossible. Peppiatt's response was: 'The Opposition would be prudent now to accept a *fait accompli* and to confine themselves to promising that when returned to office they would so arrange the directions given to the Iron and Steel Board as to ensure that broadly speaking the industry ran itself, subject, of course, to any necessary overriding governmental supervision.' These views were to prove over-cautious. Even though it took two years after the Conservative victory in October 1951 for the necessary legislation to be adopted, the bulk of the industry was eventually returned to private hands. As an intermediary between Whitehall and the City, the Bank became involved at almost every stage and developed a very close relationship with the Iron and Steel Holding and Realisation Agency, the successor to the Iron and Steel Corporation.

In September 1951, following the dissolution of Parliament and against the contingency of a change of Government, the Governor asked Peppiatt to arrange for a scheme of unscrambling to be drafted by the Chief Cashier and the Chief Accountant. Early in October the Treasury became interested and Bridges asked for a talk with the Governor about steel. In the Bank, the senior officials concerned, together with Mullens and Company, did not alter their view that unscrambling, in the sense of attempting to re-market the shares, was scarcely a practical proposition. They went on to advise that no detailed scheme could be drafted without their first being given precise terms of reference by the policy makers in Whitehall. On 29 October, as the new Government took office, the Governor wrote to Bridges about steel and enclosed a note listing various points for discussion. For himself, he remained sceptical of the chances of a successful sell-off in the event that the Labour Party undertook to reverse it if returned to office at a later election.

The new Ministers, among whom was Duncan Sandys as Minister of Supply (responsible for steel), did not accept Treasury advice that a commitment to unscramble would be unwise. They agreed that it would not be possible to proceed by way of a simple Bill for immediate introduction; but they went on to ask for outline plans to be prepared for legislation establishing a new supervisory Iron and Steel Board and for a report on methods of returning the industry to private hands. It was hoped to bring legislation forward early in 1952. The Treasury, in the person of Bernard Gilbert, then assembled a working party with the Ministry of Supply and the Bank. The King's Speech at the opening of Parliament on 6 November included the passage: 'A Bill will be placed before you to annul the Iron and Steel Act with a view to the reorganisation of the industry under free enterprise but with an adequate measure of public supervision.' In the meantime the Governor had set about manoeuvring himself into the middle ground. On 5 November he saw Ellis Hunter and Andrew Duncan, who told him they were convinced that denationalisation was practicable. He also saw Peacock in order to explore 'the possibilities of handling the operation if it looked like coming to anything'. The next day he spoke to the Chancellor, repeated the difficulties he saw ahead, and asked whether he might form an exploratory City group to take things a step further. Butler asked him to stay his hand until there had been further discussion between Ministers. The Governor nonetheless saw Peacock on 12 November and discussed names for the suggested City group. Three days later he again saw Peacock, this time accompanied by Forbes. Anxiety was expressed about Labour threats to renationalise and it was agreed that the Governor should tell the Chancellor about these City worries. A letter was sent on the following day and that afternoon Cobbold spoke to Bridges and Butler and was given the go-ahead for the City group. It was later agreed with Peacock and Bicester that Mynors should chair the group, supported by Hugh Kindersley in his capacity as a Director of the Bank. The other members were George Erskine (Morgan Grenfell), Forbes, John Morison (Guest Keen & Nettlefold) and John Phillimore (Barings). The Group was to be an informal one: 'to advise the Governors with a view to any recommendations or suggestions they might see fit to make to the Chancellor'. The Governor would continue to consult Peacock and Bicester as necessary. At the end of November he explained matters to the Minister of Supply and agreed to see him again when the advice of the City group was available.

Mynors held six meetings of his Group and by mid-December a draft report had been prepared. It advocated the formation of a holding and realisation agency to whom the assets of the Iron and Steel Corporation would be transferred. The directors of the agency would be predominantly from the financial community and would be appointed by the Chancellor after nomination by the Governor. They would consult with a new statutory Iron and Steel Board, *inter alia* about the capital structure of the companies to be sold off. The shares would be marketed on the basis of the original compensation value of each company plus profits accumulated since vesting. The report contemplated a sell-off in several discrete operations, the first comprising eight or nine first-rank concerns and amounting to as much as £100 million. These multiple issues would be underwritten. Payment would be made in cash or in British Iron and Steel Stock (the compensation stock, subsequently renamed Treasury $3\frac{1}{2}$% 1979–81). Preferential allotment would be accorded to former holders of steel shares at Vesting Day. The report concluded by stressing that there would be a need for the utmost co-operation of all concerned, including institutional investors through their associations, the Stock Exchange, the Treasury, and the FCI (whose advances to the companies, prior to nationalisation, were still outstanding but would become repayable in August 1952). In addition, the report considered the renationalisation threat and wondered whether it would be possible for new shareholders to be given an option to sell to HM Treasury in defined circumstances.

The Governor accepted most of this advice but did not want to be committed to a method for calculating the selling prices of the various shares. Nor did he want to press for Bank nomination of directors for the realisation agency. He saw Butler and Sandys shortly before Christmas and went through the main points with them. He offered to keep the City advisory group in being, an offer that was warmly appreciated. His note of the conversation concluded: 'I stressed throughout that this operation bristles with difficulties and that undue optimism ... would be most unwise. While the City would be sympathetic and anxious to help, I thought it would be a mistake to think in terms of bringing undue pressure on underwriters or investors to take up more than they considered justifiable on general business grounds. I stressed again that the most important point of all is to achieve some working arrangement which has in fact a good chance of providing a durable basis for the steel industry.' The Governor maintained his robust attitudes when he saw Forbes early in the new year and was asked to give greater encouragement to Whitehall. He was particularly determined not to put up any suggestions about the amount of steel equity that it might be possible to issue. If Ministers were to put the Bill forward at all, he recorded: 'I thought they were bound to put it forward with conviction, but I was not going to let them do it on the basis of phoney figures provided by the Bank of England.' He did however agree to 'a little private talking' to a few institutional investors when the time was ripe.

Progress towards a new Act was much slower than Hunter, Duncan, and Forbes had hoped or than the King's Speech had suggested. A White Paper was not issued until just before the summer Recess of 1952 and the ensuing Bill did not get through the Commons until March 1953. It received the Royal Assent in May and came into force on 13 July. The first sale of shares was not made until October 1953, two years after the change of Government. Throughout, the Bank continued to advise the Treasury and the Ministry of Supply as required, and this included advice about appointments to the Board of the realisation agency. Mynors continued to work with a Whitehall Committee on the one hand and, when the time was ripe, with a City group on the other. Forbes continued his vigorous lobbying of the Bank, sometimes on matters a little beyond the financial. At one such meeting the Governor had to tell him firmly that he 'would have no views on the inclusion or exclusion of barbed wire, etc.', from the purview of the new Iron and Steel Board. During the period in 1952 before the White Paper was issued, Cobbold was urged to advise Ministers that delay would prejudice the eventual success of the whole operation; but he was unwilling to go that far, feeling it awkward to argue that a sale in the summer of 1953 would be so much more difficult than one in December 1952.

Once the White Paper was published, the Governor was approached by Sandys about the arrangements to be made for disposing of the nationalised companies. He asked for a few weeks in which to undertake some exploration in the City and the Bank. Early in September 1952 he obtained advice from Mynors and spoke with Peacock, Erskine, Forbes, and Morison individually. The latter was an eminent accountant, a Director of the FCI, a Director of Guest Keen and Nettlefold Ltd, and widely respected in the City. He was soon seen as a likely Chairman of the realisation agency. The Governor next took care to clear his lines with the Treasury. He wrote to Compton on 11 September, enclosing a note of the recommendations he was minded to send the Minister of Supply and asking whether the Chancellor would prefer him to talk to the latter alone 'or would rather himself have a talk with us together'. The reply was that the Chancellor would indeed prefer to host the meeting; and this was duly mentioned when the Governor wrote to Sandys on 14 September. His principal recommendation was that Morison be asked to take charge of all the preparatory work for the Agency, with a view to becoming its Chairman in due course. He would be given a small secretariat and would be in contact with the Departments concerned, the British Iron and Steel Federation, and the Iron and Steel Corporation. The Bank would arrange for City advice to be provided as required, at first mainly from issuing houses and later probably from institutional investors. From the Bank itself, Mynors would be asked to devote a large part of his time to assisting Morison over the first few months. When Cobbold discussed the plan with the two Ministers on 16 September, it was accepted. The Governor then obtained Morison's acceptance and the Treasury agreed to set up an interdepartmental committee to assist him. Finally, after several weeks delay, the Chancellor himself formally invited Morison to undertake the task, though his acceptance of the post of Adviser was not announced in the Commons until the new year. He was accommodated in Bank Buildings across the road from the Bank itself.

During the winter of 1952–3, as the Bill was going through Parliament, discussions between the Governor, Morison, the Treasury, and the Ministry of Supply were mainly concerned with further names for the board of the agency and for the new Iron and Steel Board. By the end of February, however, the time had come to get down to the mechanics of the sell-off, the first and vital question being: who actually brings the issues? Neither Morison nor Forbes thought the Bank should be the issuer. The responsibility should rest with the City issuing houses, some of whom had already begun preparatory work in the hope that they would act for their former clients. With the SCOW episode in mind the Governor then intervened, saying to Mynors, 'this is very tricky' and asking for a list of merchant banks and stockbrokers to issues by steel companies since 1935. Erskine agreed that the Bank should not be the issuer. Instead he suggested a syndicate of six or seven large houses, with the lead in each case going to the house with an existing connection with the company concerned. The Governor agreed with this and put it to Barings and Morgans. They accepted the need for a consortium, with the offers-for-sale being made by the Agency itself. The consortium would form the underwriting group and the Bank would be the receiving banker. The crucial element would be the insurance companies. How much steel equity would they take? The Governor then undertook to approach the BIA and arrange a working party that would work with the consortium. He would 'leave the two groups to work together in order to minimise the risk of the whole operation appearing to be a City huddle under the chairmanship of the Bank'. He also agreed to approach the investment trusts. The Bank was at this stage certainly playing a leading part. The Chancellor and his officials were kept informed, but Compton told the Governor they were content to leave the market side very much to him. The outline plans were set out in a letter to Butler dated 25 March, in which Cobbold was again careful not to promise too much. 'I think it proper to advise you once again that, because of the large figures involved and of the political complications, sale of the Agency's holdings will be a very difficult, and possibly a very long drawn-out, operation.'

The approach to the BIA came next. They were opposed to the idea of a special working party of general managers, no doubt smelling undue pressure and too high a public profile. They advised the Governor to speak to the Chairmen of the Prudential and the Pearl, both of whom agreed that normal market procedure should be followed. After taking soundings of the issuing houses individually, the Governor then went ahead with a meeting at the Bank on 9 April. Barings, Bensons, Hambros, Helbert Wagg, Lazards, Morgan Grenfell, Rothschilds, and Schroders were all represented. In his opening remarks the Governor said the sale of shares in iron and steel companies was a Government policy decision and it had to be made a success. There was need for a full City machinery to be used for this purpose, if only in the interests of the City itself. A broad framework needed to be established; the operation was not one for piecemeal attack, company by company, sponsored by individual houses. The outline plan was then put to the meeting and accepted. Rothschilds had reservations, but the rest agreed with the Governor that although the whole operation would be difficult, the market approach was still the right one. As to the Bank acting as receiving bankers, the Governor was not very keen. It might make the issue appear abnormal. The Bank was however bound to be involved to some extent because Government stock could be surrendered in payment for shares acquired. It was left that the consortium of eight houses should set up a working party of their own, consulting with the Bank when necessary.

Following this meeting, whose content was made known to the Chancellor by the Governor, further contact was made by the Bank with institutional investors. Ferguson of the BIA returned to say that although some insurance companies were alarmed lest the industry should acquire a controlling interest in steel, people generally were prepared to play and the climate was fairly good. The Governor also saw Carlyle Gifford of the investment trusts, who agreed that the operation was being mounted along the right lines. For their part, the issuing houses formed a working party under Erskine. The Mynors Group was regarded as terminated, its Chairman becoming available to advise Erskine as needed. The Governor then ended this particular round of consultations by asking the CLCB for their technical support. He added that the authorities might be willing to give dispensation from the guidelines on bank lending if the banks made temporary advances for the purchase of steel issues.

The membership of the Iron and Steel Holding and Realisation Agency (ISHRA) was announced on 10 June 1953. Morison was Chairman, Green (caretaker Chairman of the Iron and Steel Corporation) was his Deputy, and Whishaw of Freshfields was an ordinary member along with Oliver Franks, Thomas Chadwick, and A. C. Bull (the latter two being former officials of the Treasury and the Bank). The appointed day was 13 July. By then it was clear that there would be insufficient institutional support for a simultaneous issue of the shares of several of the largest companies. They would have to come one by one. There may also have been some worries about underwriting, for the Governor told Erskine on 16 July that the Bank might come in for up to £2 million if this would help complete an underwriting list.[17] After an initial sale of a private company to its earlier owners, preparations went ahead in September for the sell-off of a large public company, Stewarts and Lloyds, for some £18 million. The insurance companies[18] were expected to subscribe for about half of this. The Governor and Mynors were kept closely informed, both by Morison and by the issuing houses, and at the right moment expressed assent to the issue going ahead. Underwriting was completed without recourse to the SMT. The issue was announced on 25 October and, in the event, was oversubscribed. When it was all over, Cobbold sent congratulations to Peacock and Bicester. In his reply the former wrote: 'My partners all agree with me that the progress of arrangements for handling the stock and the great success of the first issue owe more to you than to anyone else.' ERP, at eighty-three, was not one who paid compliments lightly.

Further issues followed. The Bank continued its underwriting commitment but was never called upon to honour it. By the end of 1954 only RTB and SCOW, among the large companies, remained in ISHRA. For various reasons no early sale of these could be contemplated and in January 1955, at a meeting held by the Governor, the consortium was stood down. It was agreed that it would be reconstituted if RTB and SCOW came to the market and, after consultation with the Governor, for other

---

[17] The Bank was no stranger to underwriting Local Authority issues but would not ordinarily join the underwriting of a private issue. Earlier in 1952, following talks with Gilbert and Eady, it had been agreed that the Bank's subsidiary, the Securities Management Trust (SMT) was not debarred from a modest investment in steel. It had retained its interest in RTB right up to vesting in 1951. Underwriting a denationalisation issue, if done, would have been for SMT account.

[18] Attitudes within the insurance fraternity differed. Most wanted to be left to make up their own minds after having heard what the Bank had to say. Others, a minority, were in favour of concerted support, with each company taking its pro rata share.

issues in excess of £5 million if the house or houses directly concerned so requested. For the next few years the Bank continued its close relationship with ISHRA and maintained its concern with the financing of the steel industry. In the later 1950s it was prepared to put more money into the FCI in order to increase the corporation's capacity to lend to the steel companies for expansion and modernisation. But its main task was completed with the successful sale of Stewarts and Lloyds in 1953. Carrying out that task represented a classical operation in the style of Norman and his immediate successors, an operation performed in the City of those times and performable only in the City of those times. The Bank was acting both as an adviser to Government and as a kind of investment-banking overlord. The particular task was thought to be a difficult one. There were many, inside and outside Threadneedle Street, who thought it impracticable. But with a strong man at the centre, who commanded the confidence of the Treasury and the Chancellor at one end and the leading merchant banks at the other, it could in fact be done. Impressed by a display of firm and well-ordered intent, the principal investors rallied in support and all the fearsome difficulties fell away. Peacock was right when he said that the success of the first issue owed more to the Governor than anyone else. Besides paying a personal compliment, he was drawing attention to the vital nature of the service the Bank had to provide. Compared to the vast privatisation issues of the 1980s, in which the Bank played a much lesser part, the steel issues in the 1950s were quite small and the method by which they were brought was straightforward and technically quite simple. But so, in those days, were the issuing houses themselves. They needed a lead, from time to time a firm one, and they needed neutral ground that provided a focal point (a frequently used City term of that epoch) for collective discussion and decisions. They were lucky to have a Governor whose stamina measured up to the growing burdens of his office. However, favourable ground for classical operations in the Norman style was not to last for much longer. Competitive pressures and new practices were in the offing, as the final episode in this series of public-interest ventures was to show.

British Aluminium: 1958

During the winter of 1958–9, the British Aluminium Company (BA) were taken over by a company jointly owned by Tube Investments Ltd (TI) and by the American firm of Reynolds Metals. The take-over was strongly resisted by the Board of British Aluminium, who were in turn supported by a large and powerful group of London merchant banks and other financial institutions. Rivals to Reynolds Metals were the Aluminium Company of America (ALCOA), with whom British Aluminium entered a conditional agreement under which they would issue new equity to ALCOA giving that Company a 30% interest. Neither the take-over by Reynolds–TI nor the issue of shares to ALCOA could take place without Exchange Control permission. There were no purely exchange reasons for refusing such consent to either plan, both of which involved substantial inward investment; but formal consent was nonetheless required. This brought the Government into the fray, in part because of political considerations about foreign control of British industry, and in part because the nature of the rival schemes meant that merely giving consent to both, at the outset, would in practice favour the BA Board and ALCOA. Accordingly, the only way for the Government to preserve neutrality was to procrastinate, to delay consent until the fight was over and then give it to the winner. The fight was in fact a bitter one and the Government came under considerable pressure to abandon the neutrality that it wished to maintain. As an adviser to the Government, the Bank necessarily became involved. In addition, the Governor became worried about the intensity of the fight and the ill-feeling created by it. He therefore endeavoured to get the parties together in case an agreed solution could be found. This might have succeeded if legal advice had not intervened to declare withdrawal of the TI bid, at that stage, to be impossible. The Governor's initiative therefore came to nothing. Throughout he was careful to maintain a position of absolute neutrality on the merits of the rival schemes and also to avoid formal consultation with the Court, two of whose members (Kindersley and Hambro) were involved as advisers to BA.

Since the episode occurred several years before the Take-over Panel came on the scene, the battle was fought without any rules – beyond those enjoined by the Companies Acts and the Stock Exchange – and without an established code of conduct. It all began in the summer of 1958. BA was a company with heavy future commitments for expansion overseas and inadequate command over the necessary financial resources. Its market value was less than £30 million; its reserves were small. Its Chairman since 1951 was Lord Portal of Hungerford, aged sixty-five, Marshal of the Royal Air Force and a considerable public figure. Its Deputy Chairman was Geoffrey Cunliffe, aged fifty-five and a younger son of Lord Cunliffe, erstwhile Governor of the Bank. He had been working for BA for twenty-six years. Joint financial advisers to BA were Lazards and Hambros. Because it had valuable prospects and few resources, it was bound to attract the attention of large companies in North America that were anxious to expand their aluminium interests internationally and were in strong competition with each other. One of these was Reynolds Metals, a thrusting newcomer in the industry. Advised in London by S. G. Warburg and Company, not yet members of the Accepting Houses Committee, Reynolds decided to buy a stake in BA and in June or July of 1958 began buying it in the London market behind a nominee name.

The Bank was told by Lazards in July that BA were worried about this unidentified buyer, but nothing more was heard until early in November when Sporborg of Hambros approached the Permanent Secretary to the Board of Trade, Frank Lee, at Portal's request. It had now been disclosed to BA that Reynolds Metals and Tube Investments, through a jointly owned aluminium fabricating subsidiary in England, had acquired 10% of the BA equity. Advised by Schroders and Helbert Wagg for TI as well as Warburgs for Reynolds, they had recently asked Portal for a seat on the BA Board and for the development of a working partnership, but they had been rebuffed. They had then replied that they were prepared to make a take-over bid, to which Portal had made a non-committal response. At the same time, BA were in active negotiation with ALCOA about the plan under which the latter, through the issue of further BA shares, would acquire a 30% holding. There would then be a merging of interests between the two and an offer would be made to buy out the Reynolds' holding. Sporborg wanted the Government to be aware of what was afoot in view of the Exchange Control and CIC consents that might be needed. He was convinced that the ALCOA deal was the better alternative. Lee advised him that the Chancellor and the President of the Board of Trade should be approached as soon as negotiations with ALCOA were complete, Portal and Cunliffe being in New York for this latter purpose. There would be political sensitivity to an effective American control of BA. Lee reported all this to Makins at the Treasury and a meeting of officials was held on 14 November, with Parsons attending for the Bank. It was agreed that the ALCOA deal would need Exchange Control and CIC permission, whereas a Reynolds and TI take-over might not (but it was later established that it would). On 17 November Sporborg reported to Lee that a letter of intent, amounting to a conditional contract, had been signed with ALCOA. On 24 November the Chairman of TI, Ivan Stedeford, wrote to Portal making a formal offer to take over BA, half for TI shares and half for cash at 78/- per BA share. There was no response. On the following day he called on the Deputy Governor to explain what he was doing and to warn that he might have to publicise the existence of the bid if the board of BA kept silent. He was advised to talk to the Treasury, where responsibility for any necessary consents would lie.

The group of officials now saw that if consent were given to both the

ALCOA and the Reynolds–TI schemes, the result would be to validate the contracts contained in the former before the take-over by the latter could be properly mounted. BA and their advisers evidently appreciated this as well. Portal and Cunliffe, supported by a letter from the Transport and General Workers' Union, lobbied the Chancellor for approval of their plan. Shortly afterwards, however, Stedeford informed Makins that he would use his 10% stake to requisition a meeting of shareholders to discuss the Reynolds – TI bid if the board of BA continued to remain silent on the matter. Officials, with the support of the Bank, then advised the Cabinet that the shareholders of BA should be allowed to judge the rival merits of both plans. This was accepted and the parties were informed only that the Government was studying the matter and was not ready to reach a decision. On 4 December TI formally asked BA for the terms of the conditional contract with ALCOA and, instead of requisitioning a meeting, they publicly announced that they were making a bid for BA and that the terms would be conveyed to shareholders as soon as possible. Whitehall then let it be known in the press that the whole question should be left to the shareholders to decide. At this stage Parsons alerted the Governor to the storm that was blowing up, saying that the main line of Bank advice to the Treasury had all along been that they should attempt to hold the ring as fairly as possible between the two contenders. He also remarked: 'It rather looks as though the ineptitude by the BA board may put them in the position of either alienating their shareholders by entering into a conditional agreement with ALCOA in full knowledge of the fact that a Reynolds–TI bid was in the offing or being forced to accept the Reynolds–TI bid having ensured bad relations in advance.' The Governor bided his time. There was as yet no cause for him to intervene.

Over the following ten days, while the Reynolds–TI offer was communicated to shareholders, Portal and Cunliffe brought as much pressure to bear upon the Government as they could. They attacked what they said was the false neutrality of Whitehall, stressed their responsibilities to staff, customers, and associates as well as to shareholders, and argued that the future of all concerned in BA ought not to be decided by the prospect of a tax-free gain on a holding of shares. Since Ministers remained unmoved, BA and their advisers were obliged to adopt a different course. On 22 December Kindersley and Charles Hambro, both members of the Court, called on the Governor. They told him that whatever their intention, the Government was in practice favouring Reynolds–TI and they complained about the behaviour of Warburgs.[19] They also said that

---

[19] The grounds of the complaint were not recorded. Warburgs had themselves been keeping the Bank informed, as they thought fit, through Hamilton in Exchange Control.

a powerful City group was being organised in support of BA and that this would include a syndicate to acquire sufficient BA shares to block the Reynolds–TI plan. The Governor recorded: 'I said I thought it would be wise if, when these plans are definite, they would let me have a note which I could pass to Sir Roger Makins and Ministers before they read it in the press.' On the following day he was asked to warn HMG of the City group's ideas in case Whitehall took a prejudicial decision in ignorance of them. The message was duly transmitted to the Treasury.

Early on 31 December Kindersley and Hambro again called on the Governor. They brought with them an announcement by the City group,[20] timed for release that same evening. It contained an offer to purchase for cash one half of each holding in BA at 82/- per share, a price slightly above the Reynolds–TI offer, on condition that a shareholder accepting the offer did not sell any of the rest of his holding before 31 March 1959. The group's announcement also said that it already had support representing two million out of the nine million shares in issue. The offer did not apply to the existing holdings of Reynolds–TI. The Governor (who had earlier taken the precaution of a private word with Fraser of Helbert Wagg) anticipated that this move would simply provoke a counter-offer from the other side. He seems to have been repelled by the prospect of an all-out fight, for he told his callers he thought the situation ridiculous, damaging to the City as a whole and to everybody concerned. He expressed no view about the merits, which did not concern him. Nor was he concerned to attribute blame. But he felt he ought to try to get the parties together to see if a truce could be arranged, followed by round-table talks. He asked whether Kindersley and Hambro would meet Stedeford, under the Bank's auspices. They agreed to do this, as did Stedeford; and all three then met in the Bank after a second exhortation from the Governor. An hour later they told him that a truce might be possible and that they would work on it during the afternoon, with the aim of making an announcement for the following morning. They attached two conditions: firstly that they could indicate in the announcement that the Government would take no action pending the result of the round-table talks and secondly that they could say their meeting had been suggested by the Governor. The first condition was later cleared with the Treasury; the second presented no problem. The Governor also said that if the truce were agreed, he would be prepared to see Warburgs and discourage them from buying any more BA shares in

---

[20] Though impressive, the group was not overwhelmingly strong. It comprised: Robert Benson, Lonsdale; British South Africa Company; Guinness Mahon; Hambros; Lazards; Locana Corporation; Samuel Montagu; Morgan Grenfell; M. Samuel; Edward de Stein; Whitehall Trust. Notable absentees, apart from the advisers to Reynolds and TI, were Rothschilds and Barings.

the market on behalf of Reynolds. He next saw Portal and Cunliffe, who agreed to the procedure being adopted but warned that it would be extremely difficult to reach any compromise. Truce talks went on all afternoon, but lawyers then scuppered the plan by advising that the TI offer could not be withdrawn at this late stage. The City group therefore felt they were obliged to publish their own offer as planned. Kindersley, Hambro, and Stedeford nevertheless continued their talks and TI did agree not to buy any BA shares in the market for their own account. However, Stedeford added that he could not control Reynolds. The latter then recommenced their purchases as soon as the group's offer was known. The shares jumped to 84/-, above the City group's offer price.

On 1 January the Governor made a final attempt to secure a truce, on the basis that Reynolds would agree to stop buying. He also obtained some assurances for Whitehall that BA would remain under British control if the ALCOA deal were approved. But the attempt came to nothing. There was some degree of goodwill between the British adversaries, but there was no prospect of securing an agreement between ALCOA and Reynolds. The Governor concluded there was nothing further he could do and so informed the parties concerned as well as the Treasury. To the latter he remarked that he could only advise in a personal capacity as various Directors of the Bank were involved on one side. On the following day the *Financial Times* noted that the Governor had intervened to provide a meeting place where both sides could try to iron out at least some of their differences.

After a few more days of Whitehall lobbying, including an assurance by Stedeford that TI would always have not less than 51% of Reynolds–TI Aluminium Ltd, the issue was settled in the market. Reynolds and TI improved their offer and the former continued to buy in the market. The City group made no attempt to retaliate. By 7 January their rivals had passed the 50% mark. The Treasury would then have preferred that ALCOA gracefully withdrew; but the Governor advised them that feelings ran too high and that he would not himself attempt to negotiate such a withdrawal. If subsequent confusion was to be avoided this left the Government with no alternative but to give consent to the Reynolds–TI take-over and refuse the ALCOA deal. So the deed was done. Not long before the end Siegmund Warburg called on the Governor and offered to give his side of the story in view of the criticism of his firm in the City. But Cobbold told him he did not wish to get involved in the details; his only concern had been to bring the parties together.

The episode had established that there were strict limits to the part that the Bank could be expected to play in take-over battles and any associated disputes between the City interests that were involved. The Governor could keep himself informed and could advise the Treasury where appropriate and if advice were sought. If a real storm blew up, he could attempt, from a position of declared neutrality, to use both his personal authority and the status of his office to calm things down so that cooler heads were brought to bear. But his authority could not possibly run either to adjudication between adversaries or to enforcement of an adjudication. For one thing, he was not equipped either with a corporate finance division or a take-over secretariat with which to involve the Bank either in the merits of a particular case or in supervising the conduct of the parties concerned. In the BA affair he could not even go to the banking Directors on the Court for neutral advice; both were directly involved in it. Secondly, the customary authority of the Bank just could not be stretched so as to gain adequate acceptance of a necessarily controversial and somewhat arbitrary judgement in a highly charged atmosphere in which no accepted rules existed. For example, as the Governor told the Treasury at a late stage in the BA affair, he could not intervene to prevent an American company buying shares in a British one. He might try to lean on such a company's London advisers or agents only to find himself rebuffed or to find those agents replaced by others.

Cobbold's part in the BA affair was quite different to that which Catto was able to play eleven years earlier over the financing of SCOW; and it reflected the change in the City environment that had been brought about by the growth of competitive take-over activity. The solution of regulatory problems thrown up by such activity required the formation and adoption of acceptable rules and the construction of machinery for policing them. This was to happen in the 1960s. The Bank exerted its influence over that process, the more so because it was supported from Whitehall with credible threats of special new legislation. Thereafter it exercised some oversight. But that was the reasonable limit to its self-regulatory activity in this field.

(d) BANKING SUPERVISION

Old style

Throughout the period covered by this book the positive supervision of British banks was almost entirely confined to institutions for whom the Bank itself had come to assume ultimate financial responsibility. Since the Baring crisis of the early 1890s, it had in effect accepted such responsibility for the principal merchant banks. One sign of this, during the period covered by this book, was the Bank's willingness to buy their acceptances in the market without formal limit, the appearance of an excessive quantity or indifferent quality being a matter for discussion directly with the house concerned and not with the Discount Market. The principal merchant banks held accounts at the Bank and were members of the Accepting Houses Committee, an association formed in 1914 at the outbreak of war in view of the consequential difficulties with bills payable by firms in enemy countries. The Bank assisted the houses on that occasion, again in 1931 when the German Government imposed a standstill on payment of external commercial debt, and again in 1939. By the 1950s, in response to credit enquiries put to it as their banker, the Bank would invariably reply that the firm concerned was a member of the AHC and as such good for its engagements, irrespective of the actual condition of the house at the time. It followed that members of the AHC were in the last resort a liability of the Bank of England. If any one of them were to get into serious difficulty, the Bank would be obliged to protect its name and that of the City banking fraternity by arranging special loans or a change of ownership and control, either course being quite likely to need financial support from the Bank itself. In the end, even if it was only a very remote contingency, the Bank could be required to meet a deficiency and take the loss in the Banking Department.

The accepting houses, though numerous, were very small compared to the clearing banks. Meeting any of their losses, within reason, was within the Banking Department's capacity. But the assumption of ultimate responsibility clearly implied that for its own good as a banking undertaking, as well as in the public interest for good order in the banking system, the Bank had to protect itself by requiring the houses concerned to accept a measure of regular consultation and supervision. In addition, there were frequently a small number of merchant banks outside the AHC who aspired to membership, whether by straight admission or by acquisition of an existing member. These candidates, among whom in the 1950s were Warburgs, Rea Bros., and Philip Hill Higginson, had to establish themselves with the Bank and accept some supervisory guidance. For obvious reasons membership required the Bank's *nihil obstat*. It constituted the highest accolade that a merchant bank could receive,[21] and the senior houses occupied a kind of social and professional summit in the

---

[21] Rea Bros., headed by the redoubtable Walter Salomon, enquired what they had to do to become members of the AHC. They were told that a substantial part of their business would have to consist of acceptance facilities for third parties and that their bills would have to command the fine rate for a number of years. There was a catch-22 flavour to this and it was easier to gain membership by first establishing a good general reputation and then acquiring the business of an existing member. Walter, however, eventually won through on his own. Of German-Jewish birth and a fierce fighter in many causes, he deserves immortality for writing 'Human' on an official form, somewhere abroad, that asked to what race he belonged.

banking community, some way above the 'joint stock banks' – as the clearing banks were still called by their supposed superiors who had formerly been partnerships but most of whom were now limited companies themselves. In accordance with tradition the banking directors on the Court were still drawn exclusively from the accepting houses; as, frequently, were the Governors. Norman had come from Brown Shipley; Catto had had experience in Morgan Grenfell. In the future there would be Cromer from Barings and Richardson from Schroders. The special relationship with the Bank was accordingly far more than that of supervisor and supervised. It is unlikely that those words were ever used. It was more like a relationship between partners, each possessing some degree of control over the other. Perhaps symbolic of this was the action taken by the Governor in 1950 to ensure continuing close relations following nationalisation and the reduction in 1946 of the number of banking Directors on the Court. He arranged that he should himself take the chair every six months at a meeting of the AHC, no matter that it was a trade association in the private sector, each such meeting being preceded by a Court Room lunch, itself a rare honour.

Private and confidential knowledge of each house's affairs was ordinarily confined to the Governors and the Principal of Discount Office, the latter keeping the relevant files under lock and key in his own room. Annual discussions on the results and on the balance sheet often took place with the Governor personally; otherwise the main contact was with the Principal, who himself had direct access to the Governor and rightly regarded himself as the latter's personal adviser on all supervisory matters. These included capital adequacy, liquidity, the quality of acceptances, reconstructions and amalgamations, and diversification into new areas. It was all very informal. Capital or 'resources' was capital and reserves in the published accounts plus an allowance for hidden reserves, whose size was only elicited in discussion and not revealed in documents supplied. The concept of free resources (capital and reserves less investment in fixed assets and subsidiaries) was only just beginning to be used, as the houses began to acquire outside interests.

Until later in the 1950s, when some houses began bidding for money in the market at competitive rates (an innovation to which the Bank offered no objection despite complaints from the clearers), deposits were relatively unimportant and it was the ratio of acceptances to resources that attracted attention. The ratio desired by the Bank was around $3:1$; a ratio as high as $4:1$ was regarded as too high. This guideline accorded with best practice and as such was acceptable to the Bank in the absence of any good argument to the contrary. Acceptance business, though far less important to borrowers than earlier in the century, remained a valuable source of income to the houses. Acceptance commissions were normally uniform and remunerative; and some members of the AHC were occasionally tempted to overtrade a little. For example, Hambros and Brown Shipley were both warned by the Bank in 1950–1 because they exceeded the 3:1 ratio, the latter being told explicitly by the Governor to stop the upward drift in their acceptances. He did however also make it clear that he was not expecting a rapid and therefore embarrassing cut. On liquidity, there was an expectation that about one-third of deposits plus one-fifth of acceptances should be matched by liquid assets. Most houses kept well within these ratios, but in 1950, following a substantial bad debt, Erlangers were told by the Governors both to reduce their acceptances and to increase their liquidity.

The informal guidelines on capital adequacy and liquidity, guidelines deriving from evolved practice and experience rather than any set of articulated arguments, were complemented by guidelines about the generic quality of commercial bills. These emanated rather more from the Bank than from the market-place and were concerned with the purposes to which bill finance was put rather than the creditworthiness of the borrower, the latter being a matter for the acceptor to judge. In Threadneedle Street the view persisted that bill finance should be linked to the specific movement of goods and be self-liquidating. Periods longer than ninety days were justified only in special circumstances; anything longer was felt more suited to finance through overdraft. Early in 1951 the Governor reminded the AHC about the Bank's views on these matters and this was forcefully repeated a year later. But attempting to confine bill finance to genuine and identifiable self-liquidating transactions was a losing battle, particularly during the mid-fifties credit squeeze when borrowers were anxious to make full use of acceptance facilities. There was an impossible problem of identification. Large industrial companies with first-class names would obtain such facilities, often syndicated, draw bills directly on the houses concerned 'for value received', and mark them 'for exports' so as to soothe sensibilities in the Bank. Inland finance bills, if recognisable as such, were eligible at the Bank only in limited quantities, and an excess proportion in a parcel of bills purchased was returned to the brokers.[22] There was a similar limit on hire-purchase bills, partly on the

---

[22] In the early post-war decades the Bank never bought commercial bills in the course of day-to-day open market operations; it only bought Treasury Bills, whose volume vastly exceeded the former. But commercial bills were regularly acquired in small amounts as a means, not wholly reliable, of sampling the market. Each 'parcel' so acquired was inspected by a Deputy or Assistant Principal of Discount Office, who noted the contents

usual grounds of credit control. As to foreign finance bills, they were rejected outright by the Bank, though they might nevertheless be discountable in the market. In 1956 the Principal of Discount Office, Hilton Clarke, ruled that certain of Hambros acceptances were foreign finance bills, were accordingly ineligible, and were in respect of business that was anyway inappropriate for bill finance. He therefore advised that the bills should be kept off the market. They were embarrassing because they aroused comment in the market, where it was assumed that the Bank knew what was happening. But Clarke had to admit there was little he could immediately do if his warnings were ignored.

Reconstructions and amalgamations, the third area of supervisory activity, were not in this period provoked by losses and did not require any financial participation by the Bank. Special advances made to, for example, Schroder and Japhet on account of assets frozen in Germany in 1939 had been repaid by 1946.[23] But there were a number of new incorporations to which the Bank could have no objection. Antony Gibbs, William Brandt, Samuel Montagu, and Kleinwort were all converted to limited companies and by the early 1960s only Rothschilds, in splendid isolation, remained a private partnership.[24] Others went public; Kleinworts did so in 1952, M. Samuel and Company in 1960. The incidence of death duties was a prime influence and the Bank positively encouraged a widening of ownership in the interest of preserving the continuity and adequate capitalisation of the houses concerned. In other cases, where a house was already too small, it preferred either amalgamation or a fresh participation by a new corporate shareholder. The latter route, for example, was taken by Japhet with the Charterhouse group and by Arbuthnot Latham[25] with Pearl Assurance. The former route was taken by Erlangers with Philip Hill and by Seligman Bros. with Warburgs. The Bank sometimes favoured one solution rather than another. A new shareholder, Charterhouse for example, might be warned to take great care before venturing into a business very different from their own. Philip Hill, a firm mainly engaged in industrial financing and new issues, had been endeavouring to enter the acceptance business since 1951, but the Bank was doubtful about their City reputation and dissuaded them from doing so. They returned to the charge in 1955 and

and rejected, e.g., foreign finance bills. The parcel and the contract note then had to be presented to an Executive Director for his initial.

[23] Japhet had been required by Norman to cease acceptance business and to leave the AHC. In 1947 they were allowed to resume accepting and were readmitted to the AHC in 1952.

[24] The Bank had some difficulty in guessing how much capital they really had. On one occasion the Principal queried its adequacy, only to be met with the disarming response: 'Oh very well, how much would you like us to write in?'

[25] Not yet a member of the AHC but a long-standing private customer of the Bank, who took their bills at the fine rate.

were among the unsuccessful suitors for Seligman. They then began an acceptance business but found their Bills were not freely taken at fine rates. Finally, in 1959, they made a successful bid for Erlangers, to which the Bank offered no objection and which gained them inheritance of a seat on the AHC. Seligman Bros., the smallest of the houses, suffered a withdrawal of capital early in 1955, due principally to death duties. Another tranche of capital was due to be repaid in 1961. During 1955 approaches were made to them by Philip Hill, Samuel Montagu, Warburgs, the Colonial Trust Company of New York, and the Swiss Bank Corporation. The latter two were ruled out because foreign control would automatically compel resignation from the AHC, to which the Seligman family was strongly opposed. The Governor and the Principal did not think Seligmans' would get on with Samuel Montagu. As between Warburgs and Philip Hill, both thrusters in the post-war City, they inclined towards the former. Warburgs had for several years been contemplating entry into the acceptance business as a step to membership of the AHC. Unlike Philip Hill, they had received a green light from the Bank although they had not yet taken advantage of it. Siegmund Warburg had been granted an interview with the Governor in 1953 and had begun to discuss his annual figures with the Discount Office, indications that other doors might soon begin to open. Seligmans were therefore encouraged to continue negotiations with him and in May 1957 the merger agreement was signed. This enabled Warburgs to cease attempts to start an acceptance business on their own and instead to carry on and develop the existing business of Seligman. They were warned not to take eligibility for granted, nor automatic inheritance of Seligmans' seat on the AHC. The Bank did not want it thought that buying into the Committee was so straightforward. The Seligman people in the new firm should continue to have a say in the bill business, which should continue to be confined to areas the Bank considered suited to bill finance. Also, the balance sheet would have to remain satisfactorily liquid. On those conditions the Bank would be willing to take Warburgs' bills. The conditions were met and in due course the new firm inherited the vacancy on the AHC.

Finally there was diversification, a process that gathered pace in the 1950s and whose possible implications for the eventual soundness of the houses concerned were of obvious interest to the ultimate protector in Threadneedle Street. At home, the merchant banks began to set up unit trusts and investment trusts and to acquire interests in insurance and instalment finance. Overseas, the expansion of interests was usually in Commonwealth countries, especially Australia, Canada, Rhodesia, and South Africa. But there were also acquisitions in continental Europe and

South America. The Bank expected to be kept informed and habitually advised caution, its aim being to ensure that the bulk of the houses' assets was kept in the UK and liquid. During 1957, in a talk about a proposed investment in Switzerland, Samuel Montagu were sharply reminded of this aim; and were reminded at the same time that they should keep the Discount Office fully informed if they wished to go on being an accepting house. But the Bank seldom felt it necessary to go much further, except in the case of merchant bank investment in hire-purchase companies, where it made clear its dislike of such companies financing themselves by drawing bills on an accepting house that was also a substantial or controlling shareholder. In general, the principal merchant banks were a prudent lot and a motherly eye from the Bank on diversification was all that was needed.

Another set of institutions to which much the same fundamental considerations applied were the discount houses. The Bank's day-to-day central banking operations in the money market, then as now, were conducted either in the bill markets or by direct lending and were conducted exclusively with market intermediaries acceptable to it. As the chosen intermediaries, the discount houses always dealt as principals, financing their stock in trade by borrowing secured money from the banks, mostly at call or short notice. To make good a shortfall of borrowed funds on any one day they had the right to borrow from the Bank, a right attached to the possession of a Discount Account. The combination of good collateral (consisting largely, in those days, of paper that the Bank would buy) and access to the Bank continued to make call money with discount houses a desirable liquid asset for the banks, provided there was no remaining risk of loss. At least in theory, a sharp increase in interest rates, an imprudent investment in gilt-edged, a bad experience with trade bills, or a combination of these could so erode a house's capital as to render it insolvent. This would cause its money to be called and its assets realised, perhaps at some loss to the lenders. Such disorder could not possibly be tolerated, because the machinery of the whole market would be damaged and with it the ability of the Bank to conduct essential day-to-day central banking operations in the manner and the amount required. It followed that the Bank accepted financial responsibility for the discount houses and was willing to provide special and confidential assistance to an individual house through unsecured loans if capital became critically impaired. A merger with a stronger house might also be arranged. As with the accepting houses, supervision necessarily followed the assumption of financial responsibility and had to be acknowledged by the members of the Discount Market.

Financial responsibility could also justify the Bank's approval of restrictive practices designed to sustain the houses' profitability, such as the agreement by which the clearing banks stayed out of the Treasury Bill Tender, the practice by which the houses did not compete with each other at that Tender, and the practice whereby they set common prices for the on-sale of Treasury Bills purchased at the Tender or commercial bills discounted with them by accepting houses at the fine rate. Following an unavoidable depletion of resources caused by depreciation of their stock in trade after a sharp rise in Bank Rate, the Bank would go further and allow for a period a specially favourable resale margin on bills it bought direct from the houses. In return for these privileges and the degree of supervision that accompanied them, the discount houses were prevented by the Bank from applying a proportion of their profits to diversification of their business. They were also strongly discouraged from competing with the cartelised clearing banks by bidding for non-bank money at competitive rates.

In all these circumstances it was difficult for discount houses to run into serious losses through the conduct of their bill business. Though certainly a technically efficient piece of machinery for the conduct of the Bank's own operations and for the day-to-day adjustment of clearing bank liquidity, the Treasury Bill market had indeed taken on a stilted appearance that led some critics to query whether preservation of the discount houses was worth the cost. The conduct of gilt-edged business, however, was a different matter. Encouraged by the Bank to invest and trade in short-dated gilts in the interests of official debt management and allowed to raise capital to support this activity (see Chapter 5(b) above), houses could suffer heavy losses if wrongly positioned in adverse market conditions. By a liberal use of warnings and admonitions the Bank could usually prevent bond books from becoming altogether too large, a multiple of eight times resources being regarded as the prudent maximum. But it could not interfere with managerial judgements about the future course of market prices. Nor, in the 1940s and 1950s did the Bank find itself underwriting the houses' positions as an incidental consequence of well-known support operations undertaken to preserve an extreme marketability of gilt-edged during periods of downward pressure on prices. Such operations did not become an established practice until later in the 1960s (a practice that was itself terminated in April 1971). It was therefore quite possible in the fifties for an individual house to get into low water from losses in gilts. If necessary, the Bank could intervene in such cases to secure changes in management. It could also help the house's recovery by lending it unsecured money, thereby enabling it to avoid the full contraction of its business which the depletion of resources would otherwise compel, in the first instance through loss of the collateral margin required to support secured borrowing on the previous scale.

During the bear market in gilt-edged that persisted through much of 1955, but especially during the first six months, the capital resources of many houses were severely reduced by the fall in the market value of their bond books. In addition some houses were left holding bonds at a running loss. Over the year the resources of the market as a whole were reduced from £48 million to £30 million, a cut of no less than 37%. The inner reserves of four houses were extinguished and published reserves had to be protected by valuing bonds 'at or above market but below redemption value'. To help meet this situation the Bank had to allow one or two houses to trade for a time at up to sixty or seventy times their remaining capital, instead of the normal thirty-five to forty. In addition, as related in Chapter 10(c), the Bank reduced its margin on loans against Treasury Bills and very short bonds from 5% to 2%, a cut that was not rescinded until 1957. But at the same time Alexanders Discount and National Discount were instructed by the Principal to cut back their contingent liability on endorsements of commercial bills. He took the view that unless this were done the canon of two good British names in addition to that of the drawer would be breached. Finally, one house had to be given special help. Following the withdrawal of an unsecured deposit at the end of August 1955, the Bank placed £500,000 unsecured with Alexanders at 1% over Bank Rate. It was repaid after one month but the facility ran on until May 1956 when Alexanders realised the capital loss on a substantial part of their bond book, thereby relieving themselves of a running loss on the bonds previously held. Thereafter, though constricted by shortage of capital, they began to recover along with the rest of the market, whose aggregate resources had risen to £35¼ million by the end of 1956 and to £38¾ million by the end of 1957 despite the 7% Bank Rate in September of that year. However, both Alexanders and National were again over-trading during the last quarter of 1957 and were requested by the Principal to rectify this situation. Alexanders responded by cutting their final dividend. National did not respond and their Chairman had to be warned by the Governor. Both houses then benefited from the favourable conditions that prevailed throughout most of 1958.

Unlike the senior accepting houses, the discount houses were not great powers in the City land. Without undue effort they provided an essential but rather narrow set of specialist functions under the protection of the Bank. Within reason, they had to do as they were told. The Chairman and Deputy Chairman of the London Discount Market Association (LDMA) saw one or other of the Governors, accompanied by the Principal of Discount Office, every Thursday afternoon, after the weekly announcement on Bank Rate but ahead of the Treasury Bill Tender on Friday. At these meetings, once flexibility of rates had been restored in 1951, they could sometimes be given guidance in suitably guarded terms about the general direction in which the Bank would like to see Bill rates move or, if Bank Rate had been changed, where the Bank would prefer they settled. The market was expected to conform to such general guidance and never, for example, to run for cover by setting a Treasury Bill rate above Bank Rate. Within the guidance, however, there was room for free manoeuvre.[26]

Access to the Governors was ordinarily confined to these weekly meetings and confined to the subject described. Although on rare occasions the Governor might personally issue a warning to the Chairman of a house that was, for example, overtrading in bonds, there was no ordinary access by individual houses on supervisory matters. This was the province of the Principal of Discount Office, though if this official were thought to be behaving badly or unreasonably means would soon be found of ensuring that the Governor was warned and, if need be, that remedial action was taken. Most discount houses had friends in higher places in the City. Their contacts with the accepting houses and the clearing banks were necessarily very close and their lunch-time hospitality was dispensed with discernment.[27]

Beyond the accepting houses and discount houses supervision was minimal and regular supervision non-existent. Although there were no examples in the early post-war decades, it must have been presumed that if a clearing bank or a British overseas bank were to encounter serious difficulties, the Bank would be prepared to step in to secure a solution through arranged merger or some other reconstruction. Examples of such intervention had occurred in Norman's time, for instance the acquisition of William Deacons Bank by the Royal Bank of Scotland. But there was no presumption that the Bank itself had assumed financial responsibility for such institutions,[28] even though it might have had to help meet some part

---

[26] Its effect, if it would lead to an unwanted rise in the Bill rate, could sometimes be offset by the Bank itself tendering for Bills at a price higher than the market had tendered (and of which the Bank had advance information). The average rate at the Tender was thereby reduced.

[27] It was also dispensed liberally and usefully to senior officials of the Bank, though it was not until the mid-1960s that this began to be returned (with the Chief Cashier as host).

[28] The Bank's technical banking relationship with the clearing banks derived from its key function in the London clearing, a very different rôle to the one it performed with respect to the Accepting Houses. Nevertheless, from 1911 until 1972 the Governor held formal quarterly meetings with the CLCB at which he took the chair (and hosted a Court Room lunch). After 1972 the meetings were informal.

of the losses if a large bank were ever to become so insolvent as to be unsaleable without its losses being first stripped out. Nor could it be presumed that the Bank possessed the necessary financial resources to support such a responsibility. The 'Governor and Company' only commanded the relatively modest resources of the Banking Department. Application of Issue Department resources to banking rescues would have required the specific consent of the Treasury. Undeniably, a banking disaster involving the use of such public funds would have raised all kinds of questions about the absence of supervision and the need to ensure that it became adequate in the future. But in the early post-war period the contingency of such a disaster was exceedingly remote and there was no need to spend time preparing for one. There therefore continued to be no supervision over clearing banks or British overseas banks. The Bank did not even see their true profit and loss accounts on any regular basis. The Governor was consulted about a change of Chairman, but this was mainly as a matter of courtesy.

At the other end of the scale the Bank took no financial or supervisory responsibility for secondary banking institutions or, as it much preferred their being called, finance houses. These institutions, large and small, were in those days predominantly but not exclusively engaged in the provision of instalment credit, both to individuals and to industrial and commercial companies. As has already been related elsewhere, the use of financial controls to restrict their access to new capital and to banking accommodation had propelled them into deposit-taking, beginning in the late 1940s and accelerating in the mid-1950s. No comprehensive separate register of such companies existed, but the Bank could find out their individual repute, through customary channels of banking intelligence, if asked to do so. Before granting exemption from the Prevention of Fraud (Investments) Act to deposit-taking companies – on the grounds that the applicant was a banking undertaking – the Board of Trade would normally get an opinion from the Bank. But a favourable opinion about the nature of the business did not mean that the Bank accepted any responsibility for supervising it or ensuring its future viability. Moreover, before allowing a company to pay interest to depositors gross of tax – on the grounds that the applicant was like a bank and did not pay 'annual interest' – the Inland Revenue was not in the habit of consulting the Bank of England at all. Rather did the latter sometimes complain to the former after the event, that a kind of banking recognition had been conferred on a company that did not deserve it. But since it worked strictly within its own tax laws, repute was not really the Revenue's concern.

In all this grey area the Bank's main purpose was to put some brake on the increasing use of banking descriptions by small finance houses, descriptions that could easily mislead the public about the status of those using them. The use of banking words (e.g. 'bank', 'bankers', or 'banking') in the registration of new names under the Companies Acts could be effectively controlled by the Board of Trade, using advice from the Bank about whether a proposed name would be misleading. But the use of banking descriptions in text describing a company's business could not be controlled at all until the passage of the Protection of Depositors Act in 1963 (and then imperfectly); and in the 1950s the use of such descriptions, if challenged, could be plausibly supported by a display of minor statutory recognitions accorded by the Board of Trade or the Revenue. There was however one major legal recognition, namely exemption from the provisions of Schedule VIII of the Companies Act 1948. It enabled a banking company to maintain hidden reserves and was confined almost entirely to the clearing banks, the accepting houses, the discount houses, and the British overseas banks. With the strong support of the Bank, Schedule VIII exemption was withheld from finance houses by the Board of Trade.

So old-style supervision over finance houses or secondary banks, small or large, meant that the Bank positively avoided supervisory responsibility but attempted, with whatever means lay to hand, to restrain the indiscriminate use of misleading names and descriptions. In the absence of further legislation there was anyway nothing else that could effectively be done. The Bank had no comprehensive relationship with small secondary banks, though it kept in touch with the large finance houses, through the Finance Houses Association, on matters of mutual interest. Up to 1955 these did not include questions of banking-type supervision. There had as yet been no recent case of depositors losing their money. There was little public interest in the subject and there had been no troubles that might have led to a demand for the Bank's help. Apart from the effect of its advice to the Board of Trade, the Bank had little status or protection that it could properly confer or wanted to confer, no authority, and no sanctions that could be wielded in exchange for the comprehensive acceptance of supervision which secondary banks would find very irksome. The Bank of England Act, wholly silent on the supervisory function, could not be deployed over secondary banks, or so lawyers eventually advised. Anyway, it contained no provisions for enforcement. If anything more was to be done, it looked as if it would have to be achieved through fresh legislation that would impose statutory licensing and supervision. The story of the attempted legislation and its aftermath, essential to an understanding of later developments, must now be told.

The pursuit of new-style supervision – the Credit Trading Bill and after: 1955–1958

Late in September 1955, two months after the credit squeeze had been formally inaugurated by the Chancellor, the Governor spoke to Lord Limerick, Chairman of the FHA. Lombard Banking Ltd, members of the Association and prominent in motor vehicle hire-purchase, were advertising in the press for deposits. The Bank was concerned but was doubtful of its *locus standi* for objecting. Limerick went away to consider the matter and wrote a long private letter to the Governor a few days later. His principal argument was that the financial controls imposed on finance houses, through the CIC and the banks, were inequitable and should be removed in favour of exclusive reliance on hire-purchase terms control. Retailers, including the nationalised Gas and Electricity undertakings, were in practice less restricted in their access to finance; and members of the FHA had only about-one third of the hire-purchase market. He added firstly that advertising for deposits was not illegal and secondly that financial controls had for some years been encouraging the growth of small hire-purchase companies. 'Many of these', he wrote, 'are accepting deposits, it is believed, quite unrelated to their capital resources.' Removal of financial controls would make it unnecessary for finance houses to bid for these expensive deposits. This letter was passed to Peppiatt and the Chief Cashier for comment. O'Brien took advice from Jasper Hollom,[29] Hilton Clarke, and Maurice Allen before replying in a note devoted exclusively to the credit control aspect of Lord Limerick's argument. Following especially advice from Allen, he favoured retention of financial controls as a supplement to terms control, because they would act to restrain a widening of the hire-purchase market. But as a first step there should be a Board of Trade enquiry into the provision of hire-purchase. Possible future steps might be the licensing of all hire-purchase firms, the lowering of the £50,000 limit below which CIC consents were not required, and the imposition of some unspecified control over deposit-taking by hire-purchase companies.

At a meeting held by the Governor in mid-November 1955, at which there was agreement that financial controls had to continue, it was also mentioned that depositors in hire-purchase finance houses would be at

---

[29] *Hollom, Jasper Quintus, KBE (b. 1917).* Educated King's School, Bruton. Entered Bank 1936, Assistant Chief Cashier 1955–6, Deputy Chief Cashier 1956–62, Chief Cashier 1962–6, Executive Director 1966–70, Deputy Governor 1970–80, Director 1980–4. Chairman, Panel on Take-overs and Mergers 1980–7, Council for the Securities Industry 1985–6, CDFC 1980–6, President, Council of Foreign Bondholders 1983– .

considerable risk in the event of delay in the payment of instalments. The safeguarding of depositors should therefore form part of any enquiry that might be undertaken. A few days later J. Gibson Jarvie, the Chairman of United Dominions Trust and an old acquaintance of the Bank, wrote to the Governor. He was very worried to read the advertisements of small hire-purchase companies seeking deposits. 'I admit I am quite selfish in raising this point but I feel that as these companies are exclusively HP finance companies mostly dealing with small units, should they meet rough weather with any resulting scandal, a company even such as mine might suffer.' Something should be done, for example by prohibiting the seeking of deposits by companies capitalised at less than 'several millions'. In the Governor's absence, he was assured by the Deputy that 'this is a matter which is much in our minds'.

The next step was to draft a paper for submission to the Treasury. This was done by Hollom and Allen, in consultation with Clarke, and a final version was sent to Compton with the Governor's approval early in January 1956. After arguing in favour of maintaining financial controls and extending them so as to bring deposit-taking within their ambit, the paper noted that there might be some 200 small hire-purchase companies and continued: 'There is no official regulation of the liquidity maintained by finance companies to enable them to meet their depositors' withdrawals. The FHA has eleven members; in any event, so far as we are aware, it does not seek to establish practice relating to liquidity. Failure by one company to meet withdrawals might have widely spread effects on the trust placed in others. It is felt that on this ground it is desirable, even apart from the general problem of regulating hire-purchase finance, to ascertain the present position with respect to the acceptance of deposits by finance companies.' The paper advocated a Board of Trade enquiry, which might be followed by legislation providing for licensing, for a minimum liquidity ratio, and for minimum capital. An alternative approach, favoured by Discount Office, would be a self-regulatory one, through an expanded and strengthened FHA; but the paper doubted whether this would be feasible or effective. It could however be kept in mind in case its feasibility might be established by a threat of legislation.

Compton responded in a Minute to the new Chancellor (Macmillan) on 21 January, advising him that regulation of finance house deposit-taking was not for the immediate future. Much preparatory work would first be needed and should be set in hand. New legislation would certainly be required and the concerns licensed under it 'would then be subject to close regulation by the State as to the volume of their business and as to liquidity requirements'. Compton then commissioned an Assistant Secretary,

Shillito,[30] to begin preparatory work with the Treasury Solicitor and the Bank, the Board of Trade to be brought in later. O'Brien nominated Michael Thornton, then an Assistant to the Chief Cashier, to be the Bank representative. The exercise was slow to get going as the Board of Trade was slow to conduct a sample enquiry. It was felt that something more was needed than the meagre and impressionistic information then available before much useful work could begin.

But the pressure continued to mount. The Secretary of the Hire-Purchase Trade Association (HPTA), a club comprising retailers as well as finance companies, called on the Treasury during February to express worry about the soundness of small deposit-takers, to air uncertainty regarding the application to deposit-takers of the Prevention of Fraud (Investments) Act and the Control of Borrowing Act, and to scout the idea of self-regulation through the HPTA. The Treasury took note but offered no advice. Next, the Advertising Manager of *The Times* told Clarke that he was worried about accepting advertisements for deposits at high rates of interest by hire-purchase companies. He was advised that he would not go far wrong if he used the *Bankers Almanac* as a yardstick. The Agent at the Manchester Branch then reported that a 'medium-sized industrial banker' could get all the money it wanted at 8% for on-lending at 11%. He was followed by Lombard Banking, who publicly reported rapid growth in deposits and lending, prompting the Governor's expletive about 'sabotage' related in Chapter 10(e) above.

In the meantime there was another scent to follow. The Scottish banks were upset because one of their number, the Commercial Bank of Scotland, had acquired a hire-purchase subsidiary, the Scottish Midland Guarantee Trust Ltd, which was actively bidding for deposits and promoting its business. They complained informally to the Governor, who did not think he could intervene. The Bank then began to wonder whether the whole problem might be greatly reduced if the clearing banks themselves entered the hire-purchase field. The industry might then develop on a sounder basis, nearer to the Bank itself. But continuing direct control of credit would be an inhibiting factor and the authorities could hardly administer that control in such as way as to discriminate in the banks' favour. Opinion within the banks would probably be divided, some wanting to follow the Scottish example, others wanting to stick to existing practice. But the Governor, strongly supported by Niemeyer, closed this particular debate with a resounding 'No'. Caught up as he was in a difficult

---

[30] *Shillito, Edward Alan, CB (b. 1910).* Educated Chigwell and Oriel College, Oxford. Customs and Excise 1934–6, HM Treasury 1936–57, Under-Secretary 1951, Admiralty and Ministry of Defence 1957–69.

relationship with Whitehall over the credit squeeze, he noted: 'I am entirely opposed to the clearing banks going into HP business either directly or through subsidiaries and I shall continue to do everything I can to put obstacles in the way.' He continued to favour the business remaining in the hands of specialised institutions, which he thought should be made subject to statutory control.

Early in March Cobbold asked for a progress report on the Whitehall exercise. O'Brien had little to tell him, suggesting instead that an urgent study of the legislative possibilities should go ahead in advance of further factual evidence. The Governor agreed, spoke to the Treasury about it, and asked the Chief Cashier: 'Can we not produce what *we* should like to see and try it on them?' He got the immediate response that the urgent needs of credit control meant it was no good waiting for new primary legislation. Instead, the taking of deposits by banking undertakings should be brought within the purview of the CIC by amending the Control of Borrowing Order (issued under the Control of Borrowing Act) and the CIC exemption limit should be reduced from £50,000 and £10,000. But it soon emerged that bringing deposits at banking undertakings within the Control of Borrowing Order required amendment of the Act itself; while trying to bring about the desired result in another way, by adopting a very restrictive definition of 'banking undertaking', was fraught with difficulty. New primary legislation looked unavoidable and in mid-March Hollom submitted an outline that bore a striking but perhaps not altogether surprising resemblance to ideas current twenty years later, when Hollom was Deputy Governor, about the shape of a two-tier Banking Act. Powers should be taken to control the acceptance of deposits by anyone for any purpose, with provision for the exemption of various categories of deposit-takers (for example members of the BBA). Those not exempted would require a licence, would have to submit monthly returns, and would have to maintain prescribed minimum standards of capital adequacy and liquidity.[31] A conditional exemption could also be granted, for example, to members of an association that adopted and enforced adequate self-regulatory rules on capital and liquidity. There was no suggestion that the Bank should exercise the powers written into this proposed Act. These would be exercised by the Board of Trade, though no doubt with advice from the Bank. Hollom's ideas were readily accepted. They were tried out in Whitehall by the Governor and at the end of March Ministers decided against any legislative short-cuts and asked for plans to be prepared for a Bill to obtain direct powers for licensing either the activities of hire-

---

[31] Preliminary ideas for these were: capital and reserves to total borrowings, 1:3; liquidity (cash or Treasury Bills, etc.) 15%; minimum issued capital, £10,000.

purchase companies or all forms of deposit-taking at interest. The search for a workable Credit Trading Bill, as it was to be called, had begun.

An Interdepartmental Committee on Hire-Purchase Finance was set up with the Board of Trade in the chair.[32] The Treasury, the Scottish Office, and the Bank were the other participants, Michael Thornton representing the Bank *ad referendum* to the Chief Cashier and Hollom. Alan Whittome,[33] one of the occupants of 'Room Two',[34] was his alternate. It took over two months to agree terms of reference under which the Committee was both to review the credit control case for controlling the activities of all bodies granting hire-purchase credit and to review the supervisory case for extending some degree of control beyond deposit-taking hire-purchase companies 'to other forms of deposit-taking'. The Committee was also required to keep in mind the possibility of combining the proposed Bill with one that would put the regulation of hire-purchase terms on a permanent footing. The first meeting was held on 14 June, with the intention of producing an interim report within three weeks. Several papers were then submitted, including one by the Bank on the 'Technique of Control'. A draft Report was ready by 25 June and the final version was circulated on 4 July. By any standards, this was a quite extraordinarily short time in which to prepare vital ground for a Bill covering very complicated legal territory.

From the start, when terms of reference were being discussed, the Bank itself was none too clear in its mind whether the regulation of deposit-taking, for the protection of depositors rather than for credit control, should in principle cover all deposit-takers, as Hollom had suggested, or whether it should cover only deposit-taking hire-purchase companies. Though obviously concerned about the risk of failure among small finance houses, the Bank's more urgent interest lay in the extension of credit control. This is clear from the Governor's earlier interjections and from the tenor of the various papers circulated at the time. In Whitehall, however, it was the

---

[32] It was accepted that the Bill would be a Board of Trade responsibility, presumably because that Department was already responsible for the Companies Acts and the Prevention of Fraud Act.

[33] Whittome, Leslie Alan, Kt (b. 1926). Educated Marlborough and Pembroke College, Cambridge. Army 1944–8. Entered Bank 1950, Assistant Principal, Discount Office 1957–8, Assistant to the Chief Cashier 1958–9, Assistant Chief Cashier 1959–62, Deputy Chief Cashier 1962–4. Director, European Department, IMF 1964–87, Director, Exchange and Trade Relations Department, 1987–, Counsellor, 1980–.

[34] 'The Rooms', One and Two, were in a corridor situated above the suite occupied by the Chief Cashier and his Deputies. Room One was mainly concerned with preparation of the Bank's daily and weekly Books (including the Bank Return). Room Two acted as 'devils' for the Chief and the Deputies.

protection of depositors that was more in mind. In particular, the Board of Trade took the view that the Bill, or that part of it dealing with deposit-taking, could not obtain sufficient support unless presented as a measure for the protection of depositors. Not unnaturally therefore, it at first inclined to the view that the Bill should apply to all deposit-taking companies and not just to hire-purchase finance houses. The Bank at first agreed, but apparently only on the grounds that application to all would prove the most effective way of catching the hire-purchase companies. The plan earlier outlined by Hollom and approved by the Governor was sent to the Committee on 19 June in the Bank's paper on technique. However, the wisdom of including all deposit-takers, with exemption for banks proper, was doubted by Discount Office, whose Deputy Principal, P. J. Keogh, wrote: 'There is little on the record to suggest that the need to protect a small amount of deposits requires us to take this far-reaching step, and it is by no means certain that it will be a useful one.'[35] He feared difficulties for banks over exemption and suggested that inclusion of all deposit-takers in the Bill would require fuller justification than had so far been made. He was supported by both Clarke and O'Brien, the latter saying he was prepared to refer the issue to the Governors if the Whitehall discussions went the way the Bank itself had suggested in its note on technique.

As it turned out, there was no need for such referral and therefore no occasion for thorough debate on the vital issues Keogh had raised. For the Board of Trade itself suddenly and roundly declared that inclusion of all deposit-takers would be unworkable. Any comprehensive definition of 'deposit-taking' would catch not just banks and finance houses but a host of other traders for whom exemption could not be devised without in practice at the same time exempting hire-purchase companies themselves. The Board of Trade also declared that it could not sponsor a Bill for the protection of depositors that also included such credit control features as variable liquidity ratios. Both these dicta were accepted, the former because the Bank had by now no great objection and the latter because the Treasury was content to do so at this stage. The Committee therefore recommended both that the relevant part of the Bill be concerned only with the protection of depositors and that its scope should be confined to deposit-taking hire-purchase companies. Its Report estimated that there were in all some 800 such companies, with deposits totalling between £300 and £400 million. Though very ready to accept, without close questioning, the definitional difficulties regarding deposits, the Committee

---

[35] Ironically, James Keogh was fated to be Principal of Discount in the early 1970s and during the secondary banking crisis. By that time the ineffectual Protection of Depositors Act 1963, was in place, but nothing more.

had not gone on to consider whether the definition of a hire-purchase company might prove an equally formidable task. This was to prove a serious and irretrievable mistake.

Confining the Bill to hire-purchase companies had the incidental advantage that it would neatly dispose of the problem of statutorily defining a bank[36] for purposes of exemption. For the established banks did not at that time do hire-purchase business themselves and would anyway escape. Its disadvantage was that it would exclude novel kinds of secondary banking that might be emerging outside the hire-purchase field. But there was at yet insufficient hard evidence of this, even though the attractions of taking deposits to help finance property and investment business, frowned on by the CIC and hit by the credit squeeze, were obvious enough. In these latter activities, moreover, there could be greater temptations for people wishing to get round the Prevention of Fraud Act, as well as the provisions of the Companies Act relating to prospectuses, by obtaining deposits from the public without providing any worthwhile information about their businesses. Hitherto, in debates confined to hire-purchase companies, the main worry had been about over-trading, imprudent lending, and the resultant risk of systemic loss of confidence in finance houses. As it later turned out, however, the dangers prevailed mainly outside the field of hire-purchase and in the occurrence of fraud. It was this that eventually compelled the Government to sweep aside the supposed definitional roadblocks and legislate in 1963 for the protection of all depositors.

The first faint warning was heard in June 1956, just as the Interdepartmental Committee was about to start work. Early in June the Chancellor himself, not the Bank, became aware that 'The MIAS Group of Property and Investment Companies' was advertising for deposits. Macmillan spoke to Compton, who wrote to O'Brien asking for a report. This was supplied by Discount Office and sent to the Treasury. O'Brien remarked: 'The grandiose title of the concern is nothing more than a façade for a small group of insignificant firms.' He added that the advertisement was certainly misleading and would probably escape the Prevention of Fraud Act.[37] 'It is', he concluded, 'another example,

---

[36] One solution would have been to confine exemption to 'Schedule VIII' banks. But this could have been open to criticism as being undue protection of a privileged group. Schedule VIII banks were subsequently brought into the Bill in order to exclude their lending to hire-purchase finance houses from the definition of 'deposits' taken by the latter. But, unlike exemption, this gave no great privilege to the banks.

[37] The point was whether soliciting deposits fell foul of the prohibition on the selling of securities (other than by licensed dealers and various exempt categories) contained in the Act. It was soon established that it did not.

however, of the kind of development the new Committee on Hire-Purchase will doubtless have in mind when examining the case for licensing the taking of deposits in general.' The Committee may have had it in mind, but it was so persuaded of the immediate practical advantages of confining the Bill to hire-purchase companies that MIAS, and any others of that kind, escaped from the outset. The sequel came in 1958 when MIAS failed, amid considerable publicity, with deposits totalling some £620,000 (or around £6 million at current values), almost all of which was lost. The proprietor was subsequently convicted of fraud and sentenced to eight years' imprisonment.

In the middle of July Ministers accepted the Committee's recommendations and asked for heads of legislation to be prepared, remarking that they would not wish the definition of a hire-purchase company to be too widely drawn. It was hoped to introduce a Bill in the next Session, beginning in November, but there was no commitment to do so. The Governor did not like this uncertainty. By early August he had just emerged from his tussle with Macmillan and the banks over the prolongation of the credit squeeze and was also engaged in privately dissuading the Scottish banks from following the Commercial Bank and acquiring hire-purchase subsidiaries. Accordingly, he wrote to Bridges that his purpose was 'to urge most strongly that the necessary powers be taken as quickly as possible and that there should be no question of deferring this legislation until a later Session. Not only does the present position involve a gap in our arrangements for credit control (a gap which is naturally causing increasing resentment in other sections of the market) but it allows a position to develop where depositors might incur heavy losses.' He received a sympathetic reply; but at the end of October, when early drafts of the Bill were available, Thornton reported that Board of Trade officials were warning that its introduction might be postponed or dropped. However, the Queen's Speech at the opening of Parliament on 6 November, at the height of the Suez Crisis, contained the passage: 'A measure will be laid before you to replace the existing emergency powers in respect of hire-purchase and hiring agreements and regulate borrowing by hire-purchase finance companies.'

The next stage, alongside further drafting, was for the Board of Trade to consult the FHA and the HPTA. The latter was prepared to accept a capital adequacy ratio, provided it was lower for the larger companies than the smaller, but objected to a statutory liquidity ratio. The FHA would have none of either. Judging that their members comprised three-quarters of the market and had always conducted their business prudently, to the satisfaction of the clearing banks who provided part of their funds, they failed to see why they should be saddled with statutory ratios in order that these should also be imposed on the multitude of small companies whose growth was entirely due to official restrictions on ordinary business. As takers of time deposits financing assets that liquidated themselves in predetermined instalments, they particularly objected to a statutory liquidity ratio. They suggested instead that the Bill should adopt an approach similar to that governing building societies. There should be a Registrar of finance houses, who would be provided with detailed information by each company and would have powers to stop it taking deposits if it appeared to be behaving imprudently. Neither the Board of Trade nor the Bank were minded to accept these arguments. Nor did they think that Parliament would be prepared to grant sweeping discretionary powers to a Registrar. So the idea was mistakenly set aside and drafting proceeded on the lines previously agreed.

But difficulties soon began to mount. First of all the Treasury, with support from the Bank, returned to the charge about credit control and insisted that the power to set ratios be used to vary them for purposes of monetary policy. The Board of Trade, however, continued to argue that they should be prescribed only for prudential purposes and that successful presentation of the Bill would be prejudiced if it were seen to have a double intention. Next the Attorney General objected that the Bill as drafted would be inoperable because of imprecision about who would be caught by it and who would not. His objections were followed by some radical redrafting, after which he was content to allow the Bill to go forward to the Legislation Committee of the Cabinet. But the President of the Board of Trade disliked the Bill as it stood and recommended that it be dropped. The Chancellor, Peter Thorneycroft, recently promoted to the Treasury from the Board of Trade, continued to argue in its favour with support from his officials and from the Governor, but in mid-March 1957 the Cabinet dropped it from the legislative programme for the current Session. All that was left was some willingness to consider reviving it at a later stage if its blemishes could be removed. In reply to a Parliamentary Question, the President of the Board of Trade said the subject required further study before a Bill could be introduced and added that it raised questions of extreme complexity.

Some weeks earlier Thornton had minuted the Chief Cashier about the Board of Trade's opposition to the draft Bill. As the Bank's representative on the Whitehall Committee, he was closer to the action than anyone else in Threadneedle Street and had kept his superiors well informed throughout. The Board of Trade, he now wrote, had never been much more than lukewarm towards the proposal to regulate hire-purchase finance and had only agreed to participate in the exercise on the understanding that the Bill would be presented and justified in terms of the protection of depositors. It was bad enough to be saddled with discretionary powers to vary borrowing and liquidity ratios according to criteria that could not be at all clearly defined; 'but what really bothers them', he continued, 'is that a Bill to protect depositors ought not to stop at hire-purchase finance companies. To them the Bill seems to be balancing on a knife-edge, because it relies on drawing dividing lines – lines that are fundamental for us but almost invisible to them – between one kind of banker and another...They do not relish defending the view that a small finance company is more risky for depositors than a small bank, particularly as the danger is in any case a hypothetical one, none of the depositors having yet come to harm...and the position is made even harder to defend by the barely concealed efforts we have had to make to leave the banks untouched. These doubts cannot be answered without involving the second purpose of the Bill – to close a gap in credit control. Even this argument, however, hardly suffices to convince them because we are bringing only one small corner of the credit system under direct statutory regulation – and that at a time when everyone is thinking of relaxing the credit squeeze.'

The strength of these arguments must by now have been clear enough. Neither the Bank nor the Treasury had given sufficient thought to the whole subject at the outset, or indeed during the months of drafting that had ensued. Both wanted to stop an awkward though perhaps temporary gap in the apparatus of direct credit control. Both recognised the growing need for protection of depositors. But they were too ready to push these problems onto a Board of Trade that became more impressed by the legal and administrative difficulties as time went by and was, at the end, likely to possess a power of veto over the whole enterprise. For its part, the Bank was so steeped in old-style supervision and in an organisation suited to its administration that it had no means immediately to hand of mobilising its energies for the full elucidation and study of entirely new issues in the supervisory field. The Chief Cashier, his principal Deputy, and two juniors, all relatively inexperienced in this regard, were given the task of carrying out a policy laid down baldly by the Governor. But none of these officials, not even the Chief Cashier, had responsibilities for banking supervision (as opposed to operation of the credit squeeze). These latter belonged to the Principal of Discount Office and his Deputy, normally reporting direct to the Governors but sometimes also to Peppiatt, as a Home Finance Director whose own duties were somewhat ill-defined but who had earlier in his career been Principal of Discount. All these people were fully occupied with day-to-day business. Without a specific directive from the Governor, which was not forthcoming, they would be unlikely of themselves to get together and try to think everything through. On the key question of whether to confine the legislation to hire-purchase finance companies or to include all deposit-takers, there was nearly a referral to the Governors, but a sudden and overhasty declaration by the Board of Trade against including all deposit-takers, because of supposedly insuperable difficulties with definition of a deposit, seemed to dispose of the matter and no referral was made.

None of this meant that the resources did not exist anywhere in the Bank. After the Bill had been shelved, the Governor realised that further study was indeed required and that additional resources had to be brought to bear. He accordingly asked Laurence Menzies, now an Adviser to the Governors, to examine the issues in consultation with the Chief Cashier and to report. In the course of that examination Menzies also consulted the economic advisers, Allen and Fforde. Subsequently, the Deputy Governor intervened in the debate with a magisterial contribution that might have worked wonders if made a year earlier. As it was, the horse had already bolted and nobody in Whitehall was willing to try and lead it back.

Menzies reported back to the Governor during May 1957. He was inclined to look forward to some relaxation of the credit squeeze and to some rationalisation among the multitude of small finance houses. Impressed by the fate of the Credit Trading Bill, he saw that these future developments could provide an opportunity to bring the finance houses closer to the Bank. 'The ideal solution', he wrote, 'lies in close informal co-operation between the Bank and the finance houses.' There would be difficulties. Neither the FHA nor the IBA[38] were representative of all houses and co-operation would not be easy to secure. Nevertheless it might be preferred to threatened legislation or possibly to directives issued under the Bank of England Act. After noting that hire-purchase was now to be considered by the Radcliffe Committee, O'Brien was less sanguine about the prospects of useful progress by means of co-operation. Hawker, who had succeeded Peppiatt as Home Director in March, was sympathetic to Menzies but he too was doubtful if much progress was on the cards. Mynors was more optimistic but remarked: 'My first difficulty is that FHA and IBA will talk readily enough: but how get at the people we want to talk to, who are not their members?' The Governor, however, was thinking on the same lines as Menzies, was disinclined to let matters rest until Radcliffe had reported, and encouraged him to try his ideas out on the Treasury. This was done in a letter to Compton on 14 June which set out

---

[38] Industrial Bankers Association, a body representing providers of industrial instalment credit.

Cyril Hawker, Executive Director 1954–1962

the principles of a self-regulatory solution involving the adoption of suitable borrowing and liquidity ratios by members of the associations. The purpose of these would be the protection of depositors. Compton replied on 24 July, mentioning that the FHA, the IBA, and the HPTA had recently made another approach to the Board of Trade. They had argued strongly against ratios and in favour of a statutory Registrar with wide discretionary powers to stop a registered company from inviting further deposits. He objected to a self-regulatory solution both because of the non-member problem and because it would not lend itself to credit control as opposed to protection of depositors.

In the Bank a debate continued. Fforde argued against imposing variable ratio controls on finance houses on the grounds that they would cause a rise in hire-purchase charges, little reduction in hire-purchase business, and an increase in finance-house profits on which further growth would be based. He supported abolition of bank lending restrictions on finance houses and of the CIC control, so as to promote rationalisation and a decline in small deposit-takers. He also argued that the credit squeeze must be causing a resort to deposit-taking by finance companies outside the hire-purchase field. 'The longer an effective credit squeeze, in its recent form, is prolonged, the greater does this "grey market" become. We are chasing a Banking Act to deal with "banks" which have been created by restrictions on ordinary banks – well and good, but a bit odd.'' Menzies and O'Brien, meanwhile, took up Compton's suggestions and reverted to the idea of a Registrar, but suggested that the registered companies should then become subject to the Bank of England Act for supervisory purposes. The Treasury Solicitor, however, doubted whether the latter Act could be used in this way unless every company accepted deposits transferable by cheque. Talking to Makins, the Governor reserved his position on this point but said he proposed meanwhile to explore the possibilities of voluntary action.

At this juncture the Governor went on holiday and the Deputy Governor suddenly seized decisive control of the whole confusing debate in a note circulated to Hawker, O'Brien, Menzies, and Clarke on 30 August 1957.[39] The self-regulatory solution, using the Bank of England Act as a threat, would not work. 'It would never reach down to those companies whose activities are least easy to observe and most suspect.' The loyalty of the larger hire-purchase companies would therefore be subject to increasing strain. Furthermore the Treasury Solicitor doubted the propriety of using the Bank of England Act in this context. Among new legislative solutions, the idea of an Act that provided for registered hire-purchase companies to be subject to the Bank of England Act was not worth a moment's thought. 'It would throw doubt on the scope of this part of the 1946 Act which has never yet been tested. It would expressly give control (admittedly requiring the concurrence of the Treasury) to a body which is not directly responsible to Parliament, using methods for which it would have no formal duty to account and whose authority and competence in this direction have never been tested...If the Bank want to take this job on, the legislation should give powers to the Treasury which then used the Bank as its Agent, as with Exchange Control. The 1946 Act does not come into the picture at all.' The twin interlocking problems of legislation, he continued, were practicability and confusion of aim. As to the latter, the proper way to control the volume of hire-purchase, a growing activity that was here to stay, was through terms control. To import varying ratios as a means of such control was a nonsense and if nonetheless attempted they

---

[39] His subordinates often found Mynors very difficult to read. His behaviour when acting as Governor in August and September 1957 suggests a courageous man of strong views and a clear head who was capable of decisive action. These attributes were combined with great personal charm and a first-class mind. Yet in the ordinary course, either when acting as number two to Cobbold or in his earlier posts, he often gave the impression either of keeping his cards very close to his chest or else of great reluctance to disturb the conventions and ambience of Norman's Bank.

should be applied wholesale to any financial institution 'whose borrowing habits in particular circumstances are unwelcome. The last thing we want to do is to give the impression of protecting existing credit agencies against the competition of new agencies which meet new needs but did not go to the right schools.' The protection of depositors, by contrast, was much surer ground for legislation. There were respectable precedents in the insurance companies and building societies that should be followed. He therefore came down in favour of a statutory Registrar whose first task would be to gather regular information and who could then proceed to prescribe minimum standards of liquidity and capital adequacy, under discretionary powers. He would publish detailed reports annually. Mynors concluded: 'My guess is that subject to questions of definition, statutory powers of this kind are not unthinkable, and that they would result in a comparatively short time in the formation of a comprehensive trade association and in the consolidation of many of the mushroom companies. Once such an association were formed, co-operation on a voluntary basis would be conceivable, though still limited. In present conditions and until HP companies have been declared (on terms) respectable, I do not think it will get us anywhere.'

Although Clarke was very sceptical of Whitehall agreeing to legislate on the lines suggested, the Deputy was strongly supported by Hawker, O'Brien, and Menzies; and on 12 September he wrote direct to Makins, enclosing an abbreviated and, he said, personal version of his paper. Makins' reply was non-committal but not discouraging. With the Governor's assent, Mynors wrote again at the end of the month to argue further against using the Bank of England Act alongside registration and in favour of a Registrar with discretionary powers. But for all their wise common sense his proposals remained confined to hire-purchase companies, with all the attendant definitional and other problems encountered earlier with the Credit Trading Bill. Whittome, who had taken the subject over from Thornton and was now an Assistant Principal of Discount Office, pointed this out in the course of a note sent to Clarke on 30 September. So indifferent were vertical communications in the Bank at that time that he had not then seen copies of the Mynors-Makins correspondence, nor had he been asked to contribute in any way to their content. Yet in the course of his note to Clarke it was left to him to deploy the crucial argument: 'We should have to justify taking powers which only protect depositors in HP finance companies. We should be accused of leaving unprotected depositors in the minor banks and would-be banks, and at the other end of the scale the property speculators such as the MIAS group. Previously we have argued that we saw no need to make the Bill apply to the fringe banks, because even though they did not maintain the same cash and liquidity ratios as the clearing banks, they were, in the last resort, subject to the Bank of England Act. But such arguments never convinced the BOT. At the other end of the scale we argued that we should be happy to see the Bill apply to such people as the MIAS group, yet this raised many difficulties of definition and might lead us logically to protect all depositors.' Whittome went on to suggest a scheme for deposit insurance that would apply to all deposit-takers below a minimum size or, failing that, a Registrar with discretionary powers, arguing that a comprehensive scheme for depositor protection could attract general support and might not be subject to much evasion.

Whittome's powerful note was seen by O'Brien as well as by Clarke, and there is some evidence that during the winter of 1957–8 the Bank came round to the view that the legislation should not after all be confined to hire-purchase finance companies. But this was to no avail because by now the Government had lost interest in the subject. The Treasury did endeavour to put flesh on the Bank's new ideas, but in January 1958 Compton told Mynors that there was no hope of a Bill in the current session. In March the Governor raised the matter with the new Chancellor (Heathcoat Amory), saying he was worried lest failures of finance houses should expose the Government and the Bank to criticism for not legislating in advance of so clear a prospect. But the Chancellor was not optimistic, unless the problem could be met by a very short Bill, a most unlikely eventuality. In April Cobbold told O'Brien: 'I am beginning to doubt whether HMG will ever do anything about this. Should we therefore look at voluntarism again?' He was right; there was no longer any prospect of legislation in advance of a scandal that would compel its introduction. Voluntarism, moreover, did not now seem so feeble a course as hitherto. There was a genuine prospect, following the 7% Bank Rate of September 1957 and the concurrent onset of recession in North America, that the credit squeeze might be terminated. This would open up the possibility of the clearing banks acquiring interests in major hire-purchase finance houses while the large number of small houses would surely be reduced. So the Chief Cashier therefore encouraged the Governor to pursue a self-regulatory solution, pointing out that the FHA had earlier advocated legislation for a Registrar and might now be prepared to accept an analogous voluntary regime. The Chancellor was also encouraging; and at the end of April Cobbold told Makins he was going to explore things with the FHA and in due course withdraw his objections to clearing-bank participation in finance houses, a development that might help to 'clean up the industry'.

On 12 May the Executive Committee and the Secretary of the FHA were lunched in the Bank. At the ensuing informal meeting the Governor justified the restrictions of the credit squeeze while admitting that hire-purchase was here to stay and had a useful function to perform. He went on to express continuing concern with the protection of depositors and 'the distinct risks of trouble with some of the less solid institutions which I thought would be extremely damaging to the reputable part of the industry and very troublesome generally'. He then suggested that there should be closer contact between the Bank and the representative organisations of the finance houses leading to a comprehensive organisation that would develop codes of conduct along the lines of Lloyds or the Stock Exchange. His listeners seemed sympathetic and left to think it over. Greaves, their Chairman, accompanied by Gibson Jarvie, called back a few days later to ask whether members of the proposed organisation, come the end of the credit squeeze, could be given privileged access to clearing-bank accommodation. The Governor told them that conforming to a code of conduct might well attract favourable treatment from the banks on commercial grounds, but that no other means of discrimination would be feasible.

During the summer of 1958, while the credit squeeze was being terminated and the banks were acquiring substantial interests in finance houses, negotiations with the FHA continued. These were conducted by Hawker, Clarke, and Whittome for the Bank. Greaves and Jarvie represented the FHA. The latter did not want to enlarge their membership because they did not want to assume responsibility for supervising new members; nor did they wish to conform to specific ratios. They were however prepared at first to join a new comprehensive association whose members would conform to a 'best practice' that would be based upon the behaviour of the principal members of the FHA. They also agreed that regular returns should be collected and sent to the Bank. The Treasury was kept informed and in August Compton endeavoured to get the negotiations halted until Radcliffe had reported. It is unlikely he would have succeeded; but shortly afterwards the negotiations were halted by the FHA, using the new participations of the clearing banks in finance-house equity as an excuse. On 20 September Greaves bluntly informed Hawker that the banks' participations rendered 'control of our affairs' by the Bank of England redundant. That, for the present, was that; and it was left to Whittome, still Assistant Principal of Discount, to sum up. The FHA had eaten the carrot and escaped the stick. The Bank was left with its worries about small deposit-taking companies, MIAS included, having so far failed to make headway on either the legislative or the self-regulatory course.

There was no choice but to let the matter rest and reapproach Whitehall for legislation as and when some favourable opportunity arose.[40]

So it had all come to nothing. For a year or more prior to the rejection of the draft Bill by the Cabinet in March 1957 there had been a genuine opportunity to extend the boundaries of banking supervision. Everyone concerned, whether in Whitehall Departments or in the Bank, or indeed among the fraternity of finance houses, agreed that such extension was needed. The Government itself agreed and by the autumn of 1956 had every intention of legislating. But for good reasons the Credit Trading Bill had to be dropped and thereafter the window of legislative opportunity remained closed. In the aftermath the Bank had conducted within itself a useful if somewhat unmethodical debate. By the winter of 1957–8 this had sorted out many of the problems and pointed towards a workable legislative solution. But it was too late. Whitehall had lost interest and the sensible idea of establishing a Registrar of finance houses, with discretionary powers, continued to fall on deaf ears. Perhaps, as some in Whitehall had argued at an earlier stage, it would not anyway have commended itself to Parliament. Perhaps too the proposed exemption of at least the Schedule VIII banks would have proved awkward. But it has nonetheless to be concluded that the UK could have had a Banking Act in 1957. It would have been imperfect. It might have put responsibility for its administration in the wrong place. It would certainly have required amendment in the light of subsequent experience. But a great deal of the trouble and strife with secondary banking in the 1970s might well have been avoided. Experience with new-style supervision would have been gradually acquired, ready for confident application when needed.

In Whitehall, the Treasury had from the outset been too keen on closing gaps in the credit squeeze and too little concerned with the protection of depositors. The former was its departmental interest; the latter at this time was seemingly not. The Board of Trade was prepared to accept responsibility for the latter but wanted little to do with the former; though its misplaced concern with the definitional difficulties surrounding deposit-

[40] The failure of MIAS several months later had no systemic consequences; nor did the consequential prosecutions for fraud stir the Government into immediate legislation. However, heavy losses incurred by finance houses during the consumer credit boom of 1959, together with a scandal involving a building society, convinced the Treasury that something had to be done. First, in 1961, the Building Societies Act was tightened up. Next, in May of that year, the Board of Trade began to prepare a Protection of Depositors Bill that would provide for the regulation of advertisements for deposits and ensure that would-be depositors were supplied with better information. There would be no Registrar and no provision for effective supervision. The Bank acquiesced and it actively supported early passage of the Bill. It was eventually introduced at the end of 1962 and became law in July 1963. Banks, mainly the Schedule VIII variety, were exempt. The new and ineffectual Act was eventually replaced by the Banking Act 1979.

taking made it fall in with the ill-fated desire of the Treasury and the Bank to take legislative grip only of hire-purchase companies and not of secondary banking altogether. With the responsibilities in Whitehall uncertain or divided, the Bank had an unusual opportunity to exert decisive influence on the shape of legislation that it had itself taken the initiative in proposing. But its influence was indecisive and was if anything exerted towards driving up a legislative cul-de-sac. Only afterwards was it the wiser. The reason for this failure, as also for the parallel failure to debate the fundamental considerations of domestic monetary policy in sufficient depth, has to be sought in the organisation and method of the Home Finance and Supervisory functions.

Norman, it is reported, once opined that the Bank was a bank and not a study group. This adage was often repeated and much admired by many among the generation of officials at the top of the Bank in the forties and fifties. Correctly interpreted, it meant that the Bank should never let its eyes wander from the market-place, whether that be foreign exchange, money, gilt-edged, or banking practice. Wrongly interpreted, it was taken to mean that systematic thought and exhaustive debate were somehow not required and that a wisdom acquired from market experience was an adequate substitute for rigorous analysis. Put these ingredients into a very hierarchical system of management, into a staff mostly lacking in university training, and into an informality of discussion on matters of policy that was confined to a very few at the top and there had to result a tendency to make things up as one went along; admirable in the management of markets or talking to accepting houses, inadvisable when preparing legislation. In the episode just described it was a state of affairs that accounted for the Bank being represented in Whitehall by junior officials, two very able young graduates, who reported to a young Deputy Chief Cashier but who had no access to the Governors and never attended any meetings with them.[41] Their reporting was accurate and well judged, but though it provoked the Governor or the Chief Cashier to speak to the Treasury it did not provoke discussion and review in a group of officials, senior and junior, formed for the purpose. The Bank of those days did not like committees. O'Brien, an expert delegator, did his best but did not have the apparatus required. In later years, he was to do much to bring about change, even to the extreme of trying to convert an economist into a Chief Cashier; but in 1956 he was only beginning. The two Governors, who between them combined a wide range of talents, were both reared in Norman's Bank. It was a school that had served the Old Lady well enough,

[41] The clear recollection of both Michael Thornton and Alan Whittome.

but by 1958 it needed adjustment; just a little more study and not quite so much banking.

SOURCES

Bank files

C40/555	Chief Cashier's Policy File: Commonwealth Development Finance Co. Ltd (January 1951 – December 1957)
C40/721–4	Chief Cashier's Policy Files: Monetary Policy – Hire Purchase (April 1955 – December 1957)
C40/825–6	Chief Cashier's Policy Files: Nationalised Industries – Iron and Steel Denationalisation (January – October 1952)
C47/39–40	Discount Office (Markets Supervision) Files: Discount Market Annual Reviews (1937 – 73)
C48/2–3	Discount Office (Banking Supervision) Files: Accepting Houses Committee (January 1940 – November 1967)
C48/18 *et seq.*	Discount Office (Banking Supervision) Files: Accepting Houses
C48/397	Discount Office (Banking Supervision) Files: Accepting Houses Standstill Commitments and Summary of Balance Sheets (December 1938 – January 1957)
G1/125	Governor's File: Iron and Steel Denationalisation – Proposals for Formation of ISHRA (March 1951 – July 1953)
G1/126	Governor's File: Iron and Steel Denationalisation – ISHRA Operations (September 1953 – August 1965)
G1/179	Governor's File: British Aluminium Company Limited (July 1958 – January 1960)
G1/262	Governor's File: Miscellaneous Papers (1946–7)
G3/5	Governor's Diary (1952)
G3/57	Governor's Duplicate Letters (September – December 1952)
G14/54	Committee of Treasury File: Commerce and Industry – Finance Corporation for Industry (November 1943 – October 1973)
G15/1–3	Secretary's Files: Bank Rate Tribunal (September 1957 – September 1960)
SMT2/309–10	Securities Management Trust – Chairman's Papers: Industrial and Commercial Finance Corporation Ltd (1943–51)
SMT2/311–17	Securities Management Trust – Chairman's Papers: Finance Corporation for Industry Ltd (1943–55)

CHAPTER 12

ENVOI

At the time this was written, in the late autumn of 1989 and in the fifth decade since the statutory settlement of the Bank's place in the British Constitution, historical irony was plentiful. The Government of the day was under public criticism for too exclusive a reliance on counter-inflationary monetary policy and within that policy for its reliance on the short-term rate of interest to the exclusion of direct credit controls. Four decades earlier another Government had been under criticism, both private and public, for pursuing the exact opposite: too little use of monetary policy to combat inflation and within that policy an exclusive reliance on direct credit controls to the complete neglect of flexibility in short-term interest rates. The wheel had turned 180 degrees, yet the underlying problems of chronic inflationary undertow remained, so it seemed, unresolved. At this point in British monetary history the Constitutional issue, so neglected in 1945 and remembered infrequently ever since, suddenly came to the political surface. In part because of renewed pessimism about British inflation and in part because of growing interest in the future monetary constitution of the European Community, the question of central bank autonomy began to be seriously discussed.

In 1945 Robert Boothby quoted Abraham Lincoln to the House of Commons in support of the Bank's statutory subordination to the Treasury and to the Government of the day. Money was not only the prerogative of the government but also its greatest opportunity. In 1989, after forty-four years of use, the opportunity did not after all seem so attractive. Temptation looked a likelier description; and the substantial autonomy of the Bundesbank or the Federal Reserve System were beginning to attract envy from some surprising quarters in the United Kingdom. The discretionary management of money was still seen to be necessary, following the monetarist experiment with rigid targets for the money supply in the early

1980s; but management by successive Chancellors of the Exchequer, working within the short-term pressures of the British party political system, had not proved a great success. Might it not after all be better if the task were delegated to an autonomous institution that was given statutory responsibility for maintaining the stability of the currency? Thoughts of this kind were supported by rueful reminders that discretionary adjustments of British monetary policy quite often appeared to be prompted by the discretionary adjustments undertaken by a more autonomous central bank in Frankfurt.

The history of the Bank of England during the early post-war years, encompassing as it does the history of external and domestic monetary developments, contains little with which to mount a positive defence of the 1946 settlement and provides some support for the admonitory view expressed by Graham Towers in his letter to Keynes of September 1945:

> The half-way arrangement under which the central bank is neither a department of government pure and simple, nor directly responsible to the public for its actions, may contain the worst elements of both worlds.

In the late forties and fifties, as has been recounted in this book, the Bank continued its separate corporate existence, self-financing and with its own separate staff. It went on its way as a central bank run by central bankers and staffed accordingly. It thought as a central bank and it worked as one. Abroad it maintained and extended a wide and effective network of contacts and working relationships with international monetary institutions, with other central banks, and within other financial communities. Within itself it maintained traditional central banking attitudes towards inflation, excessive public spending, and external financial stability, attitudes made the more necessary by the international status of sterling and its chronically exposed position. At home the Bank's efficient relationships, regulatory or operational, remained almost entirely confined to those with financial markets and the financial community. Its relations with a wider public developed only slowly. Constitutional autonomy would have compelled a much quicker evolution. Likewise, it remained slow to develop the more elaborately structured economic and statistical services that modern central banking came increasingly to require and which an autonomous Bank could not have done without. At the same time the subordination of the Bank to the Treasury in matters of policy did not itself oblige the latter Department to develop the contacts or the services, in the domestic monetary field, that might in a different world have been undertaken by the Bank. In consequence they were left underdeveloped. Meanwhile, its subordinate status drove the Bank into further refinement of the art of a monetary adviser to Government whose advice was tendered almost entirely in private, to the probable detriment of public understanding of important policy issues. It also drove the Bank, an active and often ambitious institution, to enhance its part as an intermediary between Whitehall and the banking system, with little advantage to either. Civil servants and Ministers came to regard the banking system as a creature to be manipulated through the Bank in the interests of short-term macro-economic politics. Despite occasional public and private protests the banking system became used to accepting such manipulation, with damage to its own efficiency and to the services provided to its customers. Competitive forces and technological change were later to undermine these corporatist arrangements and to force deregulatory revolutions that produced great difficulties of their own. A different settlement in 1946 might have ensured more orderly progress and avoided the incidental damage of upheavals that were made unavoidable by the prolongation of defective policy technique.

But it is of course clear that no very different settlement was remotely possible. Even if the Conservatives had won the Election of 1945, some settlement would have had to be made and would have been little different in effect from the one enacted by the Labour Government. Lord Simon's declaration in the Lords, that since 1932 decisions of monetary policy belonged to the Chancellor of the Exchequer and that no other constitutional position was possible, perfectly expressed the conventional wisdom of the time. Everything pointed the same way, including Norman's own record in the later years of his Governorship; and the warning sent by Towers made no immediate impression on Catto or Cobbold.

A central bank condemned, even by its own choice, to be an adviser in private and an executant in public must be vulnerable to institutional frustration. Its vulnerability has to be the greater if it is a central bank of world renown working against intractable problems whose solution, or even sensible practical amelioration, depends so much on the decisions of other people whose preoccupations often derive from the month-to-month political process. Frustrations can lead to outbreaks of aggressive behaviour alternating with periods of acquiescence or boredom. Under Catto and Cobbold the Bank must often have suffered from frustration. But it seldom if ever gave way to bored acquiescence. Both those personalities, and their immediate subordinates, were made of stronger material. Indifferent advocates and communicators in Whitehall they may sometimes have been, but they never lacked tenacity. Apart from its relative passivity during the Dalton experiment in gilt-edged immediately following nationalisation, the Bank did not hesitate to keep pressing on the Treasury its view about the desirable shape of interest-rate policy and to keep resisting the Treasury's attempts to keep the banks in a veritable straitjacket of direct controls. On the external side, the Bank was even less of a quietist. Whether in the run-up to Bretton Woods, in the Loan negotiations with the US, in the period of the false dawn, in the four difficult years following the crisis of 1947, or in the prolonged struggle over the resumption of convertibility, the Bank was always one of the frontrunners. Its judgement may have been faulty at times, but its vigour was unquestioned.

As to outbreaks of aggressive behaviour, the Bank did at times indulge in sudden advocacy of far-fetched radicalism designed to break out of the cage in which sterling was confined by a combination of its exposed banking position and the exigencies of domestic political economy. Bolton in particular was prone to such outbreaks and to wishful thinking about sterling's place in Western Europe. But he was not the only one. Cobbold himself was another. A greater degree of statutory autonomy, carrying with it a duty of public explanation and a need to obtain public support, might have damped such symptoms. Yet in one vital respect the Bank's sense of anxiety and frustration brought it to a radicalism that was certainly very controversial at the time but may now look strategically well-judged. This was its conclusion that the restoration of external convertibility should not be undertaken without considerably more operational flexibility for sterling than that permitted by the Bretton Woods Agreement. A corollary was that the UK had to be prepared to act unilaterally, in the special interest of sterling, if it were to avoid endless accommodation to the interests of others, whether in North America or Western Europe. The Bank's advocacy on this score, of which the public knew relatively little, met with no lasting success even though it was shared by the Overseas Finance Division of the Treasury. It was profoundly damaged by the mishandled episode of February 1952; but the conclusion in this book is that the Bank was correct in its judgement and that the final contrary outcome in 1958 was not in the best interest of the UK. Frustration can stimulate good judgements as well as bad.

The warning contained in Towers' letter to Keynes was timely, but it went unheeded. Some features of the 'worst of both worlds' subsequently came to pass. But some did not. For this latter the Bank and its Governors, rather than Whitehall, must take the credit. Especially Cameron Cobbold, whose name features in every chapter of this history, must take the credit.

There is a story[1] of him returning to the Bank from an important meeting in Whitehall, sinking back exhausted into his chair, and exploding with the words: 'Well, I've failed.' True he often failed to get what he wanted. But he was a big man. He ruled the Bank with firmness and never ceased to argue fearlessly for what he believed was right.

[1] Related to the author by Alan Whittome.

APPENDIX A
THE BANK AND THE COMMODITY MARKETS

J. F. A. Pullinger

AT THE outbreak of war in 1939, Government contracts with suppliers of essential raw materials were negotiated and systems were devised for their allocation among consumers. There being no place for them in such a structure, the various UK commodity exchanges were closed. Controllers were appointed by the Ministry of Supply or the Ministry of Food and staff for their respective commodity controls were recruited, many from the trade. These controls paid commission to merchants and brokers for the physical operation of each allocation system. It was taken for granted that the commodity markets would be reopened when the war was over; it would merely be a question of deciding on the precise means of making the transition. By late 1943 it was recognised that exchange controls would continue in peacetime and that any reopening of markets could only be achieved within a framework that acknowledged strict limitation on the use of foreign exchange. In the Bank, however, markets for raw materials were seen to be not only an effective means of ensuring essential supplies for the reconstruction of the peacetime economy but also, to the extent that they could attract international trade, additional sources of foreign exchange earnings. Thompson-McCausland, reporting mainly to Siepmann, was responsible for much of the formulation of Bank policy in this area.

An early indication of the Bank's attitude came in a letter written in January 1944 from Thompson-McCausland to Frank Lee, then at the Treasury, in response to a request for guidance from the Ministry of Food. He suggested that the only formal controls needed would be those designed to restrain speculation and that these could be operated as part of the control of credit. Because there was already evidence of the willingness of the various market associations to co-operate with the Government in the enforcement of discipline on their members, their voluntary co-operation should be sought. Some months later it was agreed with the Treasury that reopening should be the objective and that work should be started on method and timing. The Ministry of Food, the Ministry of Supply, and the Bank were asked to contribute to this work.

A Bank paper setting out the principles of market co-operation with the authorities, market responsibility for members' behaviour, regular returns to Exchange Control, and a degree of freedom from import and exchange controls was then submitted to Whitehall. But the Ministry of Supply saw no early prospect of ending bulk purchase of rubber, tin, copper, lead, and cotton and suggested that the question of the reopening of markets under such conditions might be discussed at a joint meeting of the Treasury, the Ministry's Raw Materials Department, the London Metal Exchange (LME), and metal consumers. The Bank responded by arguing that the reopening of markets in the UK was more urgent than the Ministry seemed to think, because the Americans were already beginning to resume private trading and valuable business would accordingly be lost. It proposed a meeting with Whitehall Departments, so as to clear the way for action on individual markets, before any meeting with the trade. This advice, it seems, went unheeded.

Frustration was mounting in the Bank at the reluctance of anyone in the Treasury to take on the subject and it was with some relief that Thompson-McCausland received from Rowe-Dutton in the Treasury an extract from the *Daily Express* of 20 November 1944 headed 'Merchants Seek Restart of Commodity Markets'. A revision of his earlier paper was then considered at a meeting of the Bank's Defence (Finance) Regulations Committee and a sub-committee consisting of Mynors, Thompson-McCausland, and Beale was appointed to explore the technical problems involved. The paper went to the Treasury on 15 December and was discussed at a meeting chaired by Waley. Thompson-McCausland returned from this meeting lamenting that the Ministry of Supply saw any single difficulty as a bar to action. However, a further paper was requested and at a meeting with the Treasury on 5 January 1945 most of the Bank's suggestions were accepted. The Bank was then asked to work out a scheme in more detail, applying it to the zinc (and possibly copper) market. No approach to the trade was to be made. The Bank's sub-committee decided that zinc was unpromising because of the Imperial Smelting Corporation's near monopoly. But an important note entitled 'Proposed Arrangements for Operating the Copper Market in Conformity with Exchange Control Requirements' went to the Treasury in March.

In their final version these proposed arrangements formed the blueprint for the commodity schemes that were later, sometimes much later, to be applied to most of the more important commodities. A precondition was that the market should have its own organisation that accepted responsibility for members operating according to the scheme's provisions and was capable of enforcing discipline. Members of the market would be granted an open general licence to import and could hold the commodity abroad without Exchange Control permission. The commodity could be delivered only to registered consumers in the UK, to a market member, or to persons outside the UK. A register of consumers would be kept, based on established consumer interest confirmed by the market and those on the list would be subject to removal at the request of the Treasury. Consumers would submit to the Bank returns of purchases, stocks, consumption, and resale and would agree to observe stock limits. For residents of the UK, use of the three months' contract would be restricted to those with a 'legitimate interest' in the commodity in order to exclude purely speculative transactions. All transactions would be in sterling apart from those concerning commodities originating in the dollar area, for which non-resident buyers would be required to make payments in dollars. A limit determined by the Treasury would be imposed on the amount of foreign exchange locked up in stocks, market members making returns of stocks held. The Bank would inform the market of the total quantity and value of stocks and if the maximum were exceeded, the Treasury could examine individual returns and consider whether the market should be requested to take disciplinary action. A confidential return would be made to the Bank of forward commitments in foreign exchange. Arrangements for regular contact would be made, with periodic meetings to discuss problems arising in day-to-day operations and to consider the overall stock position from the point of view of the market and exchange control.

Waley's reaction to this prototype was that there would be endless opportunities for friction between consumers, the market, and the Bank. Keynes was consulted and disagreed. He thought the scheme could work but felt there should be less regulation. A market needed speculators, but the Bank's proposals appeared to exclude them. The Bank wrote again in April 1945. Combining an international commodity exchange with exchange control and rigorous economy of foreign exchange was not easy; but if it was to be attempted, something akin to the Bank's scheme would be required. A supporting letter from Cobbold in May finally goaded the Treasury into circulating the Bank's note to the Ministry of Supply, and it was there, at a meeting early in June with Metals Controllers, Treasury and Ministry officials, and the Bank team, that it was agreed after all that it might be possible to reopen the LME for trade in copper and that a working party should be set up with the LME, the Bank, the Treasury, and the Ministry of Supply. The Bank's scheme was explained at an exploratory meeting with the LME on 1 August. Only minor difficulties were foreseen and the Treasury went ahead with a draft paper for Ministers, concluding that it was worth making the effort to solve the remaining problems and seeking authority for substantive discussion with the LME. But with the change of Government at the end of July the topic fell victim to other preoccupations, including the Washington Loan negotiations. Momentum was lost and the prospect of reopening the copper market receded.

However, progress was being made on other fronts. The Ministry of Food had received an approach from Brazilian interests who wanted to develop their trade in coffee with the Continent through the UK. Hamburg and Amsterdam had taken the trade away after the 1914–18 war and this was seen as an opportunity to regain it. At a meeting at the Ministry in December 1945 the Bank could claim that the anti-speculative measures necessary in this type of trade had already been worked out. The Treasury agreed and were happy to allow the UK coffee trade to resell coffee of Latin American origin to continental countries for sterling, even though it had been bought for dollars. Following an approach from the Colombian Coffee Federation for similar arrangements Thompson-McCausland chaired a meeting of bankers and coffee merchants at which the Bank's proposals were explained.The Bank required a list of members of the Coffee Merchants Federation participating in the scheme and the names of their bankers, who would be given authority to approve payments abroad for coffee purchases against evidence of a contract. Participants were to send the Bank monthly statements and annual audited accounts of stocks.

Apparently the new Government was keen to make an early announcement in the House of Commons so as to demonstrate that its decision to keep the Liverpool Cotton Exchange closed should not be regarded as a precedent[1]. They accordingly approved the plan for coffee with the qualification that should the American Loan fail to get through Congress the decision should be reconsidered. On 8 May 1946 Rickatson-Hatt sent to City editors a Bank memorandum to the trade and an *aide-mémoire* to coincide with the announcement in the House of the re-establishment of entrepôt trade in coffee in London. The Bank held its first monthly meeting with representatives of the Coffee Trade Federation on 6 June. Siepmann, in the chair, stressed the novel character of the meetings. Never before in his experience had the Bank acted as intermediary between

---

[1] The decision was announced in the Commons on 18 March that centralised buying of Cotton would be continued as a permanent peacetime arrangement. The Cotton Control, set up in 1941 under wartime powers, was not considered an appropriate body to carry out this function and the Cotton (Centralised Buying) Bill, enacted in May 1947, gave rise to the establishment of the Raw Cotton Commission in December 1947.

HMG and a commodity market. Although the amounts traded were initially small, it was reported to the Ministry that the coffee merchants considered a satisfactory start had been made. But they pointed out that no real international market could be expected until the market was free to supply the home trade.

Progress was also being made towards reopening the London Rubber Exchange. Preparatory work with the Rubber Trade Association was begun in July 1946, Ministers by then confirming that bulk purchase of the commodity would be terminated. One of the first topics discussed with the Bank was disciplinary procedures. For at the first meeting with the Association on 21 August, attended by representatives of the Treasury, the Board of Trade, and the Bank, it was explained that the rules would have to be framed in such a way that undesirable speculation was firmly discouraged. To Thompson-McCausland, the Association's powers over its members looked Draconian and he feared lest it should turn itself into a star chamber working at the Bank's behest. Siepmann did not agree. The validity of his views on informal control depended on effective devolution of disciplinary control. He was not sorry to see established in a market association a regime more rigorous than the Bank really required.

Siepmann was equally insistent that self-regulatory rules should be the formal responsibility of the regulated and not the regulator. A request from Whitehall that the Rubber Association's rules be shown to the Board of Trade's Solicitor drew a sharp response. The scheme would rest on self-discipline. Although the Bank might see the rules in draft, it could not be committed to them. If anything went wrong, wrote Siepmann, 'we call the market to account. Either we say your rules are being broken (in which case you take disciplinary action) or your rules are unsatisfactory (in which case we ask you to put them right).' The Bank could not do this so effectively if it were involved in drawing up the market's instructions to its members. The Deputy Governor (Cobbold) then wrote to Whitehall that the Bank could not make the arrangements work unless the market itself were given full responsibility for ensuring that rules were observed. The Treasury's reply accepted the point but added that a sight of the rules would allow Departments to be satisfied that they sufficed to restrain undesirable speculation. To this, Siepmann replied that Board of Trade Solicitors were not competent to advise on the desirability or otherwise of speculation. However, the Board of Trade Solicitor did eventually see the Regulations and Bye-Laws of the Rubber Trade Association and was not satisfied with the disciplinary provisions. The President wanted the point cleared with the Rubber Trade Association before making his statement on the reopening of the market, but officials persuaded him to let the matter drop. Since there were no other outstanding problems of any importance, on 30 October 1946 the Chancellor and the President of the Board of Trade agreed to the reopening of the London Rubber Market. The Deputy Governor, Siepmann, Beale, Rootham, and O'Brien met the Association on 7 November. Its Chairman confirmed acceptance of the scheme and the market duly opened on 18 November, the first monthly liaison meeting taking place a month later with Siepmann again in the chair.

The Bulk Purchases Committee in Whitehall had also favoured reopening the LME; and at the end of June 1946 the Government agreed that, together with the Treasury and the Bank, the Ministry of Supply should prepare a report on the safeguards required. Thompson-McCausland pointed out to the Governor that the Bank's proposals for safeguards had been agreed with the Treasury nearly a year ago, in the abortive discussions about reopening the market in copper. Accordingly, the Bank was going ahead with the actual details of the exchange control arrangements. But the Ministry of Supply now had second thoughts. The supply position in non-ferrous metals had become tighter since the Bank's scheme had been drafted and it would be some time before the exchange could safely be opened. These comments drove the subject of the LME into the background, but the trade was not content to let things slide. In February 1947 representatives called on the Governor to ask if he saw any sign of the reopening of the LME. Enquiries then made at the Treasury elicited good intentions but nothing else, and in April the Deputy Governor could tell the LME no more than that the Bank had been keeping the matter alive in Whitehall.

The period of the great dollar shortage was beginning and the convertibility crisis was not far away. The distinction between dollar commodities (e.g. copper) and sterling commodities (e.g. rubber), according to whether or not the Sterling Area as a whole produced a surplus of any given commodity, was becoming a critical one for the Treasury. The drive to reopen markets slowed down accordingly. When the dollar shortage eased in 1950 and the reopening of markets returned to the agenda, progress was slowed once more by the reappearance of supply shortages caused by the repercussions of the war in Korea. Not until that situation had eased could progress be resumed and the remaining markets reopened.

However, alone among the non-ferrous metals tin was a sterling commodity and reopening the metal exchange for trading in tin therefore remained an active possibility, even though the supply position was tight and the metal was subject to international allocation. Although a detailed scheme, along the lines of that adopted for the rubber market had been worked out by the spring of 1948, the Treasury was apprehensive lest reopening the market should aggravate the problem of commodity shunting and the Ministry of Supply was still unwilling to cease bulk purchase of tin. Not until the autumn of 1949, after the devaluation of sterling, were these obstacles sufficiently overcome for the tin market to be reopened. It suffered in its early years from difficulties over the disposal of official UK stocks of the metal and later from the intervention of the US Government during the 'Korean' shortages. Monthly liaison meetings at the Bank, chaired by Siepmann, served not only as a useful outlet for market worries or complaints but also as a means of exercising official surveillance.

In the meantime, in response to Parliamentary Questions about the LME, the Government appointed a public Committee to enquire into the existing procedures relating to non-ferrous metals. Chaired by Sir Frederick Bovenschen, a retired Civil Servant, this Committee concluded at an early stage that reopening the markets in copper, lead, and zinc would be desirable provided the currency risks (direct dollar loss or indirect loss through cheap sterling) could be overcome by the Treasury and the Bank. In parallel with this public Committee, the Ministry of Supply chaired an official Committee that examined the merits of abandoning state trading in metals. The Bank was represented on both Committees by Thompson-McCausland, who endeavoured to argue that the risks of currency loss had to be set against gains that might accrue because sterling would be made more attractive by the reopening of international markets in London. The Bovenschen Committee reported in April 1949, after twenty-five meetings and having taken evidence from all the various interested parties. It favoured the reopening of the LME and the restoration of hedging facilities for the principal non-ferrous metals when the supply positions and the currency risks so permitted.

The tin liaison meetings provided opportunities for the LME to voice its wider aspirations for other metals. By March 1950 it was clear that the trade was turning its attention to copper, lead, and zinc, and at an LME committee meeting it was decided to approach the Ministry. The market soon narrowed its attention to lead, for which the supply situation had significantly improved over the past year, aiming for trade only in sterling, irrespective of origin. A scheme was drawn up and sent to the Governor. In May 1950 the Minister of Supply was asked in the House whether he would consider abandoning bulk-buying in view of the relatively plentiful supplies of lead from non-dollar sources. He replied that the abundance of lead might prove temporary and that he was not prepared to disturb the existing arrangements. Officials however were in fact contemplating a recommendation to reopen. Accordingly, at a meeting with the LME the

Minister shifted ground and emphasised that the Treasury would not consider opening any free market if there was a risk of it costing dollars. He urged the market to persist with a sterling scheme. In a discussion on lead at the tin liaison meeting in June Siepmann maintained that the Treasury now needed some prodding. The idea of a market operating on a sterling-for-sterling, dollar-for-dollar basis might be more acceptable.

At the end of July 1950 Siepmann reported that the Ministry had invited the exchange to resume discussions. Their response was a letter setting out the arguments against opening on a sterling-only basis. Siepmann then wrote to Brittain that although a limited amount of dollars would be put at risk, any loss would be more than offset by the advantages of reopening and thus encouraging foreign countries to look to London as a source of supply. To his mind the matter had passed from the Ministry of Supply to the Treasury and it was now for the Bank rather than the LME to take the initiative. However, the rest of August and part of September were taken up by the Korea-induced crisis in the tin market, a crisis triggered by the August announcement that the market should no longer rely on the Ministry being a continuous seller of cash tin.

Lead was again discussed at the tin liaison meeting in September when it was agreed that conditions were now favourable. But although a draft letter from the Exchequer to the Minister reached the Bank in October, it appears that no final letter was sent. Another threat to the tin market, namely an American call for the renewal of international allocation, had again driven lead into the background. But in February 1951 LME representatives called on Thompson-McCausland to report that they thought it feasible to operate a market in lead alongside an international allocation scheme. A voluntary embargo on tin exports had been surprisingly successful. However, it appeared that the Ministry had renewed fears on supply grounds. In July, due to increasing difficulties with the international procurement of raw materials, the Ministry of Materials was formed and the resulting reorganisation in Whitehall pushed lead into the background once more. However, with the change of Government at the end of October thoughts were directed more positively towards the restoration of private trading in commodities as the supply position eased and prices fell.

At a meeting at the Ministry of Materials, officials were commissioned to produce a note setting out the effect of reversion to private trade on UK dollar liabilities. They concluded that there should be no increase, possibly even some reduction, and that the timing of reopening should be carefully considered in relation to forthcoming talks in Washington. Officials in the Ministry were apparently in favour of reversion. Long in lead, they wanted to get out as part of the administrative economy campaign. The anticipated fall in the lead price would also give rise to financial loss. By January 1952 the exchange had met Ministry officials to discuss the question of reopening. They seemed to be in favour. Since lead was now in plentiful supply, the market was satisfied that conditions were ripe for resumption and its members were prepared to take on the Ministry's contracts and hold the necessary stocks. In May the Minister informed the exchange that it was the intention to reopen the market in lead as soon as the balance of payments position permitted. On 21 July the Chancellor agreed that, subject to arrangements being made to prevent currency evasion, the LME could resume trading in the metal. The Ministry of Materials would approach the Bank on the question of the necessary regulations. The LME duly opened for dealings in lead on a world-wide sterling basis on 1 October 1952, and the Bank's Metal Scheme was extended to zinc in January 1953 and to copper in August.

By January 1954 the Bank's commodity schemes had also been extended to the cocoa, copra, grain, sugar, and wool markets. Finally, legislation was introduced terminating the activities of the Raw Cotton Commission from 31 August 1954 and private trading in cotton futures on the Liverpool Exchange was to be resumed from May. To deal with the large volume of reports then coming in regularly from market members and commodity consumers a special office was set up in the Bank. It was the responsibility of this Commodities Office to supervise the operation of the schemes, to monitor and check on aggregates, to report to the Treasury, and to provide the secretariat for the market liaison meetings. Formed in 1954, the Office was disbanded in 1963 when responsibility for liaison with the markets passed to the Economic Intelligence Department.

These steps had made sterling a more useful international currency and the relaxation of exchange control entailed had, it seemed, no adverse effect. The schemes enabled the Bank to take up in another context a position between Whitehall and the Square Mile, to gain considerable knowledge and expertise in a field that was no longer within Whitehall's immediate ambit, and to play an increasingly leading part in the policy issues that were still to arise. Reopening free commodity markets, while preserving exchange control, had been an uphill task and the Bank's eventual success owed much to Thompson-McCausland's ingenuity, as well as to the tenacity and enthusiasm of a small group of people who ensured the smooth running of the schemes.

APPENDIX A

SOURCES

Bank files

ADM1/21 Commonwealth Central Bank Letters (September 1952 – August 1955)

EC4/103 Defence (Finance) Regulations: Commodities – Reopening of UK Commodity Markets After War (September 1943 – December 1945)

EC4/122 Defence (Finance) Regulations: Commodities – Proposals for Reopening London Metal Exchange (May 1944 – June 1948)

EC4/125–6 Defence (Finance) Regulations: Commodities – Reopening of London Rubber Market After War (January 1941 – April 1947)

EC4/133 Defence (Finance) Regulations: Commodities – Closure of Liverpool Market and Proposals to Reopen it After War (March 1941 – April 1951)

EC4/140–2 Defence (Finance) Regulations: Commodities – Revival of International Coffee Market in UK (December 1945 – September 1947)

EC5/12–13 Exchange Control Act: Commodity Schemes – General (February 1947 – May 1953)

EC5/66–71 Exchange Control Act: Commodity Schemes – Metals (June 1948 – July 1952)

APPENDIX B
EASTERN EUROPE

J. F. A. Pullinger

(a) THE BANK OF ENGLAND, THE BANK POLSKI, AND THE PLIGHT OF INDIVIDUALS

AT THE outbreak of war in 1939 all the central banks of Eastern Europe, including the State Bank of the USSR, had accounts at the Bank of England through which the ordinary business arising from their use of sterling as an international currency was conducted. These accounts remained open during the war, though business was greatly reduced or in some cases (e.g. Hungary) halted altogether. Immediately after the war day-to-day business started to recover as trade began to revive. This required proper contact with the central banks, if only to find out who their appropriate authorities and signatories were; and the Bank could not await full restoration of normal diplomatic and financial channels. With some of these customers contact during the war and at its end was a straightforward matter. Several Eastern European Governments and central banks had taken refuge in London, from where they had conducted their own war effort alongside their British allies.

Deriving from their pre-war experience, both Siepmann and Niemeyer maintained considerable interest in Eastern European affairs, and each had numerous contacts in the Finance Ministries and central banks concerned. They were supported firstly by C.A. Gunston, a pre-war specialist on Germany and Eastern Europe, who rejoined the Bank from the Army in 1946, and secondly by P.A. Pescud, who had joined the Bank in 1939 from the British Overseas Bank. The latter was particularly well versed in Polish affairs, spoke the language fluently, and had numerous acquaintances in that country. After Gunston's retirement in 1949 Pescud became the Bank's senior adviser on Eastern Europe. But for the previous four years it was Siepmann who was in effective charge of Bank policy in this area.

An institution with which the Bank was to forge particularly strong links in the war and which, in the throes of its country's submission to Communism at the end of the war, was to exercise the Bank's diplomatic skills to the full was the Bank Polski. Though privately owned, it was effectively controlled by the Polish State, who appointed its Directors. It held Poland's gold reserves and was responsible for the note issue. Within a week of the outbreak of war in 1939 the Board decided to send abroad one of their number, Zygmunt Karpinski, armed with a special power of attorney to conduct the Bank's affairs if this became necessary. Karpinski left Poland on 10 September and arrived in Paris on the 22nd. From there he wrote to Gunston explaining what had happened and asking for an assurance that the Bank of England would not execute any orders of the Bank Polski that originated in enemy-occupied territory. The Bank gave its assurance a few days later. Earlier, on 13 September, a telegram had been received from the Bank Polski (now situated in the town of Luck) advising London of Karpinski's departure and special powers.

Karpinski's letter to Gunston mentioned that the Bank's President had moved to Bucharest but that the whereabouts of its General Manager, Leon Baranski, were not yet known. Baranski joined Karpinski in Paris in December 1939 and wrote to Niemeyer telling him of the successful evacuation of the Bank Polski's gold and most of its stock of notes:

> After the departure from Poland of our Director Karpinski on the 10th September and the departure of our President, Mr Byrka, and Director of our Bank, Mr Nowak, on the 11th September, I remained in Luck (Volhynia) where I attended to the administration and further evacuation of the Bank's Treasury. Conditions were extremely difficult. Communications were completely paralysed by the enemy aircraft and trucks were the only means of communication available at that time. Due to the perseverance and sense of duty of our staff, we succeeded to export abroad a very large part of our assets, and almost our entire stock of notes. After having crossed the Rumanian frontier on the 17th September (practically under direct pressure of Soviet troops) with 45 trucks containing our shipment, I stayed for two months in Bucharest and after many difficulties arranged for the transportation to France of all the Bank's assets, with the exception of notes which for the time being must have been left in Bucharest.

The gold was stored in Paris until the spring of 1940, when the German advance compelled another migration. Some of the gold ended up in New York, some in Canada, and some in the Bank of England.

In June 1940 the Polish Government of General Sikorski moved from France to England and it was decided that Baranski should establish the Bank Polski in London. Siepmann responded by providing accommodation in the Bank of England for the General Manager and his staff. From there the Bank Polski went about its wartime central banking business. But the establishment in Poland of the Communist-dominated Lublin Committee in 1944 led to the issue of notes in liberated territory by a provisional authority called the Bank Naradowy Polski. In January 1945 this was formally established as a bank by the Lublin authorities, who were by then functioning as a Government in the ruins of Warsaw. The future of the Bank Polski at once became problematic and was to demand the close attention of Siepmann, Baranski, and others over the next eighteen months. The Bank's role was not made any easier by the designs of the Treasury on the Bank Polski's gold as a bargaining counter in any financial agreement.

In February 1945 Baranski informed Siepmann that the Polish Government in London were interested to know whether the Bank Polski would be prepared to provide the necessary financial resources in the event of withdrawal of recognition by the UK and the US and the consequent drying up of the sources from which they had hitherto financed themselves. Without reference to anyone, Baranski had made it clear that the Bank Polski's resources would not be available for that purpose and Karpinski, who had returned to London from the US, had supported him. Baranski then sought Siepmann's advice. Was it his duty to take the Bank Polski back to Poland if the opportunity arose, in spite of the fact that he felt unable to take his wife and family? Siepmann told him that he was faced with a cruel conflict of loyalties and that it would be an act of high patriotism on his part to associate himself with the future fortunes of the Bank at the cost of returning to Poland without his family. Although Siepmann did not think he could himself do it, he realised that Polish patriotism was something very special and said he would have great respect for the man who could. Baranski's main fear was personal isolation. Contacts with Poland, possible and frequent during the war, had already ceased.

In early March 1945 Baranski again called on Siepmann, this time to discuss a note he was preparing on the legal position of the Bank Polski. Siepmann told him that he thought that this was now a question for which the Allies should assume responsibility at Yalta and that Baranski would probably be better off if he subordinated his own decisions to those of the Allies. Shortly afterwards a letter about the legal position was sent to the Governor by Winiarski, Bank Polski's President. It was sent on to the Chancellor.

Early in July 1945 Ellis-Rees sent Siepmann details of the Bank Naradowy Polski's establishment and the appointment of Drozniak as its President; on the 16th Baranski told Siepmann that representatives of the

Bank Naradowy Polski were coming to see him and that Drozniak proposed visiting the Bank of England. Since neither the Treasury nor the Foreign Office objected to this visit, Drozniak, on Siepmann's suggestion, visited the Bank on the personal introduction of Baranski and was seen in the latter's presence. After the exchange of formal courtesies Siepmann volunteered that he felt that while the problems of the Bank Polski were not insoluble a great deal of time would be needed to resolve them. On 23 July Karpinski and Baranski called to say they had decided in principle to return to Poland. They were satisfied that the existence of the Bank Polski as a separate and independent entity was recognised by the Polish Government in Warsaw.

In August 1945 Baranski reported that Drozniak had informed his Government of the readiness of the Bank Polski to return to Warsaw. In the period immediately after the return the Bank Naradowy Polski would remain in charge of the note issue and the Bank Polski of the exchange reserves. There would then be a fusion of the two banks, which would involve the loss of identity of the Bank Naradowy Polski, not the Bank Polski. Drozniak, apparently, had agreed to this. Later in the month Drozniak and Baranski came to see Siepmann about the opening of a Bank Naradowy Polski account at the Bank. At Baranski's prompting, Siepmann emphasised the desirability of fixing a realistic rate of exchange for the zloty as soon as possible. Drozniak replied that the basis for doing so did not yet exist. Siepmann begged him to open the West windows first and not to try to calculate the extent of the draught until afterwards.

In September Baranski heard that the official view in Warsaw had turned right round and was now against the idea of fusion. Gold backing for the currency was deemed an outmoded concept and the new intention seemed to be to perpetuate the Bank Naradowy Polski and to allow Bank Polski to wither away. Siepmann asked Ellis-Rees in the Treasury for guidance. Should any formal or informal support be offered to Winiarski and Baranski in the event of their undertaking a journey that would bring them 'in the reach of the bear's teeth if it did not put them half-way down its gullet'? Ellis-Rees replied that if Baranski and Winiarski elected to go back to Poland, the Treasury would give them official support (and he was sure this was also true of the Foreign Office) since it would be in line with the British policy of facilitating the return of Poles to their own country to assist in the task of reconciliation within Poland. He was sceptical about the future of the Bank Polski, for the present rulers in Warsaw apparently had no intention of making use of such an institution. The Treasury, however, would be very reluctant to let the Bank Polski's gold go East until there was some financial agreement between London and Warsaw.

Before this advice had been received from the Treasury, two officials from the Warsaw Ministry of Finance visited London and walked in on the Bank Polski unannounced. They told Baranski that the Bank Polski must return to Warsaw and was in a state of 'factual liquidation'. Did they still intend to return to Poland? Baranski (in the absence of the President) replied unambiguously that he, for his part, still meant to return. Karpinski said the same. They were told that this would be reported to Warsaw and that the question would be taken up with Winiarski the following week. It was made clear that the Bank Polski would be liquidated on its return to Warsaw and that its officials would take whatever positions the Government assigned them. A lady who had accompanied the two officials and been cursorily introduced as a secretary, sat motionless, said nothing, and took no notes. Baranski said later that she had the cold eyes and expressionless face of the Party observer and that her hostility could be felt.

Ellis-Rees then wrote the Bank a second letter, in similar vein to the first. The Treasury would not feel justified in supporting Baranski if he decided to fight for the continued existence of the Bank Polski. On this, Siepmann pencilled: 'Guidance? Help?? Support???'. Shortly afterwards Ellis-Rees reported that the Foreign Office could not agree to take issue with the Warsaw Government 'if they decided to liquidate the Bank Polski or its employees'. The last three words were seemingly a slip but one that Siepmann did not allow to be forgotten.

On 1 October 1945 Winiarski and Baranski reported to Siepmann that the Warsaw decree establishing the Bank Naradowy Polski had expressly deprived the Bank Polski of its note-issuing powers, something that Drozniak had never disclosed. They further reported that the assets of the Bank Polski in Poland were now being administered by a body set up to deal with abandoned property. Siepmann replied that the Bank Polski would be allowed to continue its existence in London and to have the same rights as at present to dispose of its assets after consultation with the Bank. This met with Treasury approval. Baranski, however, could not agree with Siepmann that it was now up to the individuals concerned to decide whether or not to return to Warsaw. He still had formal responsibilities of which he would have to be divested before feeling free to decide. Siepmann then suggested to the Treasury that the assets of the Bank Polski in London be put into the custody of the Bank of England. The Defence (Finance) Regulations allowed this since the Bank Polski was a UK resident with respect to assets held in the UK. This would enable Baranski to return to Warsaw, with the continuing powers of a Bank Polski signatory but without power over the UK assets.

Later that month Ellis-Rees suggested that the Treasury should summon Baranski and explain the tasks assigned to a body that had been set up in July 1945 when the Polish Provisional Government in Warsaw was officially recognised, namely the Interim Treasury Committee for Polish Questions. Hitherto this Committee had relied on the close co-operation of the Bank Polski and the Bank of England. But if circumstances made it necessary for staff of the former to return to Warsaw, it had to be made clear that their assets could not go with them. The simplest course would be for the Bank Polski to hand them over to the Bank of England for custody and Siepmann predicted that Baranski would be happy to have his hand forced in this way. He later told him what was afoot and advised him to say nothing to his President until the latter had heard direct from the Treasury.

A letter from the Interim Committee went to Winiarski via Siepmann on 26 October. The Committee were concerned that their work might be hampered if a return of Bank Polski officials to Warsaw were to disturb arrangements governing the Bank's assets in London. If the staff did not return and if Warsaw disestablished the Bank Polski, its UK assets would become Polish assets, under the temporary control of the Interim Committee for use in eventual settlement of UK claims on Poland.

After some discussion behind the scenes, between the Treasury, the Bank of England, the Polish Embassy, Baranski, and Drozniak, a reply was sent by the Bank Polski to the Interim Committee. Their letter said that they wanted to return as a Bank and would therefore have to return with their assets, but that the attitude of the Treasury was making this impossible. Siepmann then advised Ellis-Rees that if the various Poles were all agreed that the Bank Polski should indeed return to Poland intact, with staff and assets, then the Treasury should agree to release its hold over those assets. If however Warsaw insisted on some other solution – the Bank without the staff or the assets without the Bank – then the Treasury should keep control of the assets. Towards the end of November Baranski reported that news from Poland was clearer. Bank Polski had been talking to Drozniak. As a result, the Bank Polski was prepared to confirm its previous willingness to be repatriated indivisibly, having been told privately that Warsaw would at any rate not want this to take place for six months. This left the way open for negotiations about the assets between the Treasury and Drozniak. In January 1946, however, relations between the Poles again deteriorated and the prospect of an orderly return of the Bank Polski and its assets to Warsaw receded. In February Winiarski was appointed to the International Court of Justice in the Hague. His term as President of the Bank Polski was due to expire at the end of March and he would take up his new post immediately afterwards. Siepmann then wrote to Ellis-Rees that although this decapitated the Bank, the torso would still have legal life and could continue to function for normal current business in the absence of a President. However the remaining directorate was unlikely to feel able to take decisions on fundamentals. One possibility was an effective liquidation through the exodus of personnel. For example, Baranski, who did not want to return to Poland, would be useful at the IBRD. Shortly afterwards, and somewhat to their surprise, Baranski and Karpinski were included in the Polish delegation (headed by Drozniak) to the inaugural meetings of the IMF and the IBRD at Savannah. Warsaw's intentions regarding the Bank Polski then began to clarify.

In early March 1946 Nowak, a Director of the Bank Polski, told Siepmann that increasing pressure was being brought to bear on their staff to return. Of the three directors and eleven staff only two expressed a willingness to return. Warsaw was not asking for the eleven but expected the Bank Polski to state which of their people were ready to return. Warsaw would take these and get rid of the rest. They did not want Baranski, but they did want Karpinski, to run the Foreign and Exchange Regulations Department of the Bank Naradowy Polski.

On 22 March Baranski wrote to Siepmann from Washington: 'I have been elected Executive Director of the Bank for Reconstruction by the votes of all the countries of East-Central Europe. Mladek [of Czechoslovakia] has been elected by the same votes for the Fund. It was probably for the first time that we worked as a group of nations of common race and with common interests and – what is very important – we came to the full agreement without any Russian help or action.' He said he would be going back to Poland with Drozniak for a few weeks. The latter would be appointed President of the Bank Polski, which augured well for eventual amalgamation with the Bank Naradowy Polski. His personal problems had found the best solution. 'I thank God the Almighty that they decided so.'

When Winiarski made his farewell visit to the Bank at the end of March, he asked Siepmann if Karpinski could take back to Warsaw the records and securities portfolio of the Bank and leave the gold behind. Siepmann reminded him that the assets of the Bank Polski had been taken into protective custody. As soon as the UK had made a satisfactory financial agreement with Warsaw, the assets could be at the free disposal of their owners, but not before. Baranski returned to London in late April and reported that the Directorate in Warsaw would now administer the derelict assets of the Bank in Poland. The intention was that the two banks would in some way be merged, but for the time being the Bank Polski would maintain an office in London. Of the eleven remaining officials about half would join the Bank in Warsaw and the other half would resign. Karpinski would remain in America for some time and on his return to Poland would become either a director of both banks or the Polish alternate at the IMF.

In point of fact none of the eleven staff were willing to return to Poland; and there was some resentment at the manoeuvres of Baranski and Karpinski. With nowhere else to turn Siepmann immediately took on the task of resettling as many as he could and helping with immigration problems. In July 1946 formal word came from Baranski that the London office was to be closed and in August the Foreign Office gave permission for the release of all Bank Polski's assets other than gold. An amount of £7 million in gold coin was held by the Bank on Bank Polski's account at the end of the war. In July 1947 £3 million was transferred to the Treasury under the terms of the Anglo-Polish Financial Agreement of 1947 and £2 million was transferred to the account of the Bank Naradowy Polski. The remaining £2 million was returned to the Bank Polski in Warsaw in 1948 and 1949.

The Anglo–Polish Financial Agreement of 1947 provided the occasion for a handsome gesture by the authorities in Warsaw and for a happy conclusion to the relationship between the Bank Polski and the Bank of England. Today, a fine set of crystal, each piece decorated with the Bank medallion in the form of Britannia, is brought out and used at Court functions for visiting royalty. The glass, specially made at a factory near Glatz in Lower Silesia and comprising several hundred pieces, was presented by Drozniak and Baranski to the Governor in 1947 in gratitude for the Bank's help and hospitality to the Bank Polski during the war.

This was by no means the last the Bank was to see of Baranski. Early in 1950 he became very worried about his future on the Board of the IBRD. It was likely that Poland and Czechoslovakia would leave the Fund and Bank. Even if they did not, it could not be assumed that he would be re-elected Executive Director. On his way to a meeting in Geneva he called on Siepmann and enquired about the possibility of a research post in the UK. Siepmann asked Clay if a fellowship at Nuffield College, Oxford, was a starter. But it was not. In May 1950 Poland left the Fund and the Bank and Baranski was ordered not to attend any more meetings. The following month he resigned and came to England, asking Siepmann to clear with the Home Office his and his wife's permanent residence in the UK. In September he was appointed Managing Director of the Ethiopian Development Bank, a post he held until August 1953 when he joined the Indonesian Planning Bureau as monetary and fiscal expert. In 1955 Bolton wrote to the Treasury about the naturalisation of Baranski and Mladek, but neither were allowed to become British subjects at that time. In 1966 Baranski, then Governor of the Central Bank of Kenya, called on Governor O'Brien for help with the maintenance of his residential status. He retired two years later and again sought naturalisation, again through

O'Brien. This was finally granted in March 1969 when he was seventy-four.

The Bank's concern for individual Eastern Europeans was not confined to personnel of the Bank Polski. Leopold Baranyai, President of the National Bank of Hungary, was imprisoned by the Germans in 1944 and when released managed to keep out of sight of the Russians. When he and his invalid wife arrived in England as refugees in 1947, Siepmann at once arranged for him to be given a room at the Bank and some interim historical work. Baranyai went to Germany in 1949 as adviser to the Bank Deutscher Länder, joined the staff of the IBRD in 1951, and returned to Germany in 1959 with a job in commercial banking. Another Hungarian, Maday, who had been a senior official in the National Bank, appealed to Siepmann for help in relief of the poverty he and his wife were then suffering. The Governor arranged for a food parcel to be sent every two months and this continued until Maday's death at the age of ninety in 1968. A third example had a Hungarian angle to it, but the person concerned was the world famous Russian dancer, Tamara Karsavina. In Petrograd in 1915 she married a young British diplomat, H.J.Bruce, who later (1931) became an adviser to the National Bank of Hungary. He returned to England at the outbreak of war and died in 1951, leaving very little for his widow. In 1955 Niemeyer was approached by a friend of Karsavina; and in recognition of Bruce's services to the National Bank of Hungary, the Bank agreed to pay her an annual sum to augment her meagre income. Payments continued until her death in 1978 at the age of ninety-three.

(b) THE CLOUDS OF DEBT DEFAULT: ONE STAR IN THE FIRMAMENT

Contact with East European countries was bound to become perfunctory and sporadic as the Iron Curtain fell and Stalinist domination became total. But interrelated questions of trade and debt, including pre-war commercial and bonded debt and wartime inter-governmental debt, remained key topics in a series of negotiations in which the Bank played a part. They were not questions to which there were ready answers. Either there was insufficient to export or the burden of debt was too great in any event. Even where significant levels of trade were achieved and where, in Yugoslavia's case, there was a strong political will to some form of agreement, default on debt could not be avoided for long.

Although most early post-war experience with countries in Eastern Europe was disappointing and frustrating, there was for some time one exception. This was Czechoslovakia. During the inter-war years, from its birth in 1920, that country had acquired well-developed international commercial and financial relationships. By 1938 the Czech Government and the City of Prague, together with Skoda, were among sterling borrowers in London. Ordinary servicing of these debts ceased in 1939 although British bondholders' sterling coupons continued to be met in full by the Czech Financial Claims Fund, out of Czech assets frozen in the UK and controlled by the Treasury. Servicing by the Czechs was resumed in 1946, albeit at reduced rates of interest; and at the time of the Communist take-over in 1948 there remained a large number of UK private and corporate holders of Czech sterling bonds. The Czech Government's indebtedness to the UK increased early after the war through the granting of a commercial credit of £5 million in 1945. Of all Eastern bloc economies Czechoslovakia was least damaged by the war; and in many respects Anglo–Czech financial relations possessed a normality that continued for as long as six years after the Communist take-over. The Czechs could point to a Monetary Agreement with the UK signed as early as November 1945 (replaced in 1949 by a Payments Agreement) and as late as the winter of 1953–4 they were the only member of the Eastern bloc (except the USSR) that had not defaulted on its debts to the UK.

The Anglo–Czechoslovak Trade and Financial Agreement of 1949 provided for the sterling bonds to continue to be serviced in full. The Agreement also provided for compensation to be paid to UK companies whose assets in Czechoslovakia had been nationalised. At some 50% of original claims the compensation was not ungenerous in the circumstances. By 1953, however, the country's external situation had deteriorated. Sterling liabilities for debt service and for compensation had become a significant burden and shortly before a review was to take place in 1954, under the terms of the 1949 Agreement with the UK, the Czechs defaulted on the last instalment of the 1945 commercial credit. Already, early in 1953, they had been slow to pay the penultimate instalment on the 1945 credit and the payment due under the 1949 Nationalisation Compensation Agreement. In May 1953, though still a member of the International Monetary Fund, Czechoslovakia devalued unilaterally and without consulting the Fund. There followed a long drawn-out debate before the Czechs were finally expelled from both the Fund and the Bank in December 1954, notwithstanding the wishes of the UK to preserve some semblance of good working relations across the Iron Curtain. The UK was also caught in the crossfire over the vexed question of Czech gold. The US, the UK, and France had been appointed arbitrators on questions relating to the restitution of gold. For political reasons the US refused to allow transfer to be made, while the Czechs persisted in claiming full compensation from the Bank of England for allegedly moving gold in March 1939 from a Czech account to a Reichsbank account.[1] This issue played a large part in negotiations held in 1956 following suspension of talks in 1954. It was symptomatic of deteriorating relations with the UK and contributed to their breakdown.

Since the 1949 Agreement provided for a review prior to its expiry at the end of June 1954, the Czechs invited HMG to send a delegation to Prague. The Treasury preferred London but was prepared to go to Prague as it thought these were the only negotiations with an Eastern bloc country that were likely to pay dividends. At the Treasury's request, Pescud became a member of the British delegation.

At the opening session on 18 May 1954 the UK delegates were received with a Marxist sermon from the Vice-Minister of Foreign Trade. It later became clear that the Czechs sought to imitate other Eastern bloc debtors and limit payment to an agreed percentage of exports. Pescud's account of his three-week stay in Prague, the first since 1949, gives some further insight into the reasons behind this changed outlook and why, in the end, the talks broke down with no agreement in sight. The economic situation, he wrote, was deteriorating. The previous year's currency reform had hit the peasants particularly hard, virtually confiscating their savings. The new controlled prices and the disappearance of the free market had discouraged agricultural production. In the towns many food items were scarce, although still free of coupon rationing. Too much manpower was employed in heavy industry, which was engaged in exports to the USSR at prices the Russians chose to pay. The average employee could provide barely more than food and shelter for himself. The artificial rate of exchange made Czechoslovakia extremely expensive for a visiting foreigner. There was a general atmosphere of gloom and depression. When they had the opportunity of expressing their true feelings, people asked: how long will it go on and can it end without war? The Czech officials concerned, he reported, were friendly but not particularly competent and had no plenary powers. Margolius, the Deputy Minister of Foreign Trade, who signed the 1949 Agreement, had since been tried and executed for

---

[1] This question, which properly belongs to the pre-war period, is not pursued further in this book. The gold was held on a BIS account at the Bank in London and instructions were received from the BIS to move it to another BIS account where assets were held for account of the Reichsbank. The Bank of England's action in effecting a transfer from one BIS account to another, on properly authenticated instructions from the BIS in Basle, was entirely legal. Although the Bank's action preserved the integrity of the BIS, it will forever remain controversial. The central bank of Czechoslovakia was being overrun. Czech assets in London had just been frozen by a rushed Act of Parliament, and the Bank was informally aware that the gold it transferred, though legally in Swiss ownership in London, was in practice being moved for benefit of the Reichsbank.

political offences. Caution on the part of the present negotiators was certainly understandable.

The talks were adjourned in June without agreement and default on inter-government indebtedness followed in July. Desultory overtures for renewal of talks came to nothing. In 1956, when the Czechs insisted on including the gold question on the agenda, any chance of significant progress was eliminated. It was finally agreed to defer further talks until 1958, by which time it was hoped the Czechs would have received their share in the distribution of the gold held by the Tripartite Gold Commission. However this was not forthcoming. Further talks in 1964 and 1974 were also abortive. In 1981 talks were resumed, and agreements reached with both the US and the UK led to the simultaneous transfer in February 1982 of tripartite gold to Czechoslovakia and of Czech sterling and dollar assets for debt settlement.

SOURCES

Bank files

ADM30/60	Museum and Historical Research: Gifts to the Bank (July 1920 – February 1977)
C43/392	Gold and Foreign Exchange: Relations with Central Banks, etc. – Post-war return of Bank Polski to Warsaw (January 1942 – May 1959)
C43/393	Gold and Foreign Exchange: Relations with Central Banks, etc. – Naradowy Bank Polski (March 1947 – September 1971)
C44/248	Overseas Central Banks' Accounts with the Bank: State Bank of the USSR (1935 – 1959)
G1/168	Governor's File: Dr Leon Baranksi (February 1950 – March 1969)
G15/377	Secretary's File: Charities – IKKA Gift Parcels Service (March 1954 – June 1968)
G17/2	Senior Officials' Personal File: Mrs T.Bruce, née Karsavina (May 1955 – October 1978)
OV110/6–7	Poland: Country Files (March 1940 – August 1948)
OV110/28	Bank Polski (May 1937 – February 1945)
OV110/29	Bank Polski and Naradowy Bank Polski (March 1945 – September 1947)
OV112/7–14	Czechoslovakia: Country Files (June 1939 – August 1960)
OV112/17–19	Czechoslovakia: Financial (including Trade) Relations with the UK (September 1945 – November 1953)
OV112/24	Czechoslovakia: Narodni Banka Ceskoslovenska (January 1939 – November 1949)
OV112/25	Czechoslovakia: State Bank of Czechoslovakia (March 1950 – June 1977)
OV112/29	Czechoslovakia: Miscellaneous – Foreign Debt (October 1945 – November 1953)

APPENDIX C
THE ANGLO–AMERICAN LOAN NEGOTIATIONS: THE US VIEWPOINT

Corinna Balfour

EXAMINATION OF the British sources on the Anglo–American Loan negotiations raises certain questions, as the American attitude often has to be surmised without direct evidence. The basic question is whether the approach proposed by Keynes would ever have been feasible from the American point of view or whether, given the American starting point, different tactics might have averted an outcome that, from the British side at least, was to have tragic consequences. What follows, therefore, is an attempt to look at the negotiations through American eyes to see how far the US documents shed any new light on the subject or confirm impressions already gained.

The question of financial assistance to Britain after the end of the Japanese war (Phase, or Stage, III) had been touched on in discussions on Lend-Lease in the autumn of 1944, but it was agreed that talks should be deferred for a later date. Morgenthau pointed out that the programme for Stage II would not solve Britain's long-term balance of payments problem and Keynes had agreed. In addition to making arrangements for Lend-Lease during Stage II, during the winter and spring of 1944–5 the US authorities were much preoccupied with a propaganda campaign for Bretton Woods and securing its passage through Congress.

The question was again raised by Judge Rosenman, an adviser to President Roosevelt, during a tour of Europe in the spring of 1945. In discussion with Keynes, Eady, and Harmer on 9 March Keynes noted Britain would be the only United Nation to emerge from the war with a 'seriously impaired' financial position, and he said that some way must be found to improve this position if an effective world economic structure of the kind desired by both Britain and the US was to be achieved. Keynes later suggested that conversations be held in Washington later in the year, saying that the post-war situation would call for a 'brain-wave' similar to the one the President had had in 1940 when Lend-Lease was evolved. A note addressed to Morgenthau on 19 April, passing on reports from the US Treasury representative in London, also stated that the British had made it clear informally that they did not wish to add to their foreign interest-bearing debt and that they wanted the Americans to devise some new way of meeting their needs for a very large amount of financial assistance in the post-war period.

Although no figures were mentioned at this time, the US authorities were therefore aware that Britain was likely to be seeking financial assistance after the end of the Japanese war. The idea that the British would be reluctant to borrow reappears in a memorandum by Clayton of the State Department to Vinson (then Director of the Office of War Mobilisation and Reconversion, but soon to become US Treasury Secretary) dated 25 June 1945. This memorandum noted that the British problem was the greatest barrier to rapid progress towards free multilateral payments and the relaxation of barriers to trade; it was therefore in the interests of the US to give Britain financial help. However, an outright gift would be 'quite unwise' and even a credit would need to have conditions attached to it that would ensure 'a sound advance towards our post-war objectives'. The credit could be for as much as $2–3 billion, repayable over thirty years, with an earlier repayment option. The amount should be sufficient to meet Britain's adverse dollar balance of trade under multilateral current payments. British reluctance to borrow suggested a low interest rate, $2-2\frac{3}{8}\%$, and a provision that Britain would not be considered in default in the event of a slump in world trade.

Clayton also suggested the conditions under which the loan might be granted. First, the dollar pool[1] should end on the granting of the loan and sterling proceeds of current transactions by UK non-residents should be convertible into dollars at the option of the holder for current transactions. Second, substantial funding of the abnormal wartime sterling balances should be required; in some cases (such as India and Egypt) substantial writing-down of the balances was justified. European and Latin American balances should be funded to a large extent. However, not all balances need be funded; Britain might be left free to repay agreed portions by exports during the transition years, as long as sterling was convertible. Third, Empire preferences should be eliminated, or at least substantially reduced. Fourth, Britain should continue with domestic import controls to cut down unnecessary imports and hence to reduce the strain on the balance of payments and the amount of financial aid required. Finally, Canada and others in a strong position should also give financial aid.

---

[1] The phraseology used here is that used by the Americans. In the use of such terms as the 'dollar pool' and 'blocked balances' it often reflects an incomplete understanding of how the Sterling Area worked.

This memorandum broadly set out the position the Americans were to take in the Washington negotiations. The first point of importance for the future negotiations was that assistance to the UK be in the form of a loan, not a grant, and that this loan be justifiable in terms of the benefits to the US. There is very rarely any suggestion that unequal sacrifice during the war could be a reason for financial assistance in 1945. The other major point was that conditions needed to be attached to the loan. The need for this arose from a fear that, despite acceptance of Bretton Woods, if left to herself Britain would maintain the wartime restrictions and trade would be channelled within the Sterling Area, thereby discriminating against American products. A possible devaluation of sterling would give the Sterling Area a further competitive advantage. Harry White subsequently explained in a speech in April 1946 that the continuation of the restrictions in peacetime 'would mean the existence of a Sterling Area economic bloc. Economic blocs mean discrimination against American trade, a greatly reduced level of world trade, and economic warfare, in place of peaceful, orderly, and mutually profitable commercial relations among nations.' In order that this situation did not occur sterling would have to be made convertible, and there would have to be some settlement of the wartime accumulated sterling balances and some reduction in, if not abolition of, Empire preferences. It was however recognised that if Britain was to remove the restrictions promptly a loan was necessary to allow the country to import fundamental needs while expanding exports. 'Thus, the proposed loan will help Britain back on her feet economically, and will make it possible for her to co-operate with us immediately in the creation of a world economy based on fair trade and currency practices and a minimum of restrictions on the flow of world commerce.' The conditions were used to justify the loan to the American public, who were in a less generous mood than after the First World War.

However, an earlier error of judgement in the public presentation of the case for a loan to the UK may have been a tendency to overemphasise the benefits the Bretton Woods Agreement would bring. The report of the Senate Committee on Banking and Currency, published in July 1945, did not deny that Britain would need financial assistance to meet the balance of payments deficit in the transitional period but stressed that the 'most important step in solving Britain's problem, as well as the exchange problems of most other nations, is the expansion of world trade and the revival of international investment'. The Fund and the Bank would play an important role in establishing the conditions necessary for such expansion; and only after there was assurance that they would be established would it be possible to decide what further steps would be necessary to solve Britain's problems. Interestingly, the report, while noting that settlement of the wartime accumulations of sterling was one of the problems that needed to be solved, did not feel it was urgent. The British were confident that they could deal with the problem and were entitled to every consideration in finding a workable solution.[2] The line taken in the report was part of a more general attempt to point out the deficiencies of the so-called key-currency approach. Harry White, however, went further by denying that a loan to Britain would help significantly with Britain's problem; it might merely burden Britain with dollar debt without making any real contribution towards balancing Britain's international payments.

The key-currency approach itself – expounded particularly by John Williams and also Alan Sproul of the Federal Reserve Bank of New York – concentrated on the relationships between the major currencies and saw the need to deal with the British problem as an essential prerequisite to currency stabilisation. It was suggested that the US make a large loan or grant to Britain on condition that the sterling–dollar rate be fixed and all British exchange restrictions be removed. As Sproul said in evidence to the Senate Committee: 'Unless we clear the decks with the British, I think any stabilisation we have will be a mirage, whether we have the Bank or the Fund or both. That, in my opinion, includes finally wiping out the debts of the last war, a liberal definitive settlement of Lend-Lease obligations, agreement and perhaps help on a programme of liquidating the blocked sterling balances, and agreement and help on meeting the deficit in the balance of payments in the immediate post-war years.'

The general American position was outlined to the British in talks between Clayton and Keynes in August 1945. On the British side, discussions were made more difficult by the recent change in Government, but Keynes was nonetheless able to give an estimate of the British balance of payments for the first three years after VJ Day and also express his own opinion – though he warned that he could not speak for Ministers – that current sterling should be made convertible and that the transition period should be brief. On the balance of payments deficit, Keynes gave a figure of £650–850 million for the first year (with £750 million the most likely), £500 million in year two and £200 million in year three, making some £1,500 million ($6 billion) over the three years. Clayton told the British that public opinion in the US seemed to be settling on the possibility of a $3 billion credit to the UK and that authority for such a credit on liberal

---

[2] In a letter to Brand of 11 July 1945 Keynes comments that 'Bernstein certainly did a grand piece of work' on the Senate Report. Since Brand apparently got him to strike out a reference to a figure of $4 billion for the aid required, he was perhaps able to put the UK viewpoint across in other ways as well.

terms might be achieved promptly if there was a fairly satisfactory overall commercial policy agreement. Some conditions would be necessary: the Sterling Area dollar pool was anathema to US exporters and it would be necessary to scale down and adjust the sterling balances. Keynes remarked that in terms of a figure for the loan, the important thing was to restore confidence in the convertibility of sterling and for there to be an adequate reserve if they were asked to make sweeping commitments; it was therefore not useful to talk about figures at the present time. In reply, Clayton reiterated the point that $3 billion was the figure in the minds of the US public (despite a $5 billion figure mentioned by Winthrop Aldrich).

The second meeting was more stormy. Keynes 'with typical abruptness' asserted that the British would not accept credits in which the new creditor (the US) would have priority over the existing creditors (the Sterling Area). Britain would have only a limited capacity to service debt and a solution whereby this would be entirely allocated to servicing the US credit would be 'indecent'. To this Clayton replied that the British would have to abandon that view if they wanted to discuss new money. Keynes again insisted that he and his colleagues wanted the same sort of economic world as the US, but he 'kept hinting and on several occasions virtually threatening that if the US was not "inspired" the British would probably choose a bilateralist course'. Both Keynes and Brand urged the US not to crystallise its views until the UK had made a full presentation. It was hoped that further talks could be held in September, but another difficulty was the British wish for trade and finance talks to be kept separate, an attempt resisted by the US. Finally Clayton, in response to a plea from Keynes for an 'inspired solution', said that while he had considerable sympathy with the view that bankers' solutions were not practicable, he (and the American public) were essentially 'realistic'; he would be frank and say that the British people should not expect to obtain assistance in the form of free grants.

These meetings gave the Americans some inkling of the difficulties to come. Clayton apparently believed that the British would come round to accepting a repayable credit, but to the US Treasury representatives in London this view seemed premature: Keynes still seemed to be hopeful of inducing the US Government to be much more generous than Clayton's initial offer, and there were continuing problems over the apparent British unwillingness to send a trade delegation at the same time as the talks on financial policy. Nonetheless there was some recognition of the importance of the talks for the US. The Ambassador in London, Winant, advised that this was the most important international economic problem facing the US.

The need to start the talks was increased by the abrupt termination of Lend-Lease, of which the British were informed on 20 August. Termination was opposed by the US Treasury and State Department. A note from Harry White to Secretary Vinson, dated 20 August, warned that if Lend-Lease were terminated either the three major Allies would be driven to seek aid from the US or there would be a tendency towards strengthening regional economic blocs. The abolition of Lend-Lease in the absence of other arrangements would be 'a serious blow' to the international economy.

The general US tactic seems to have been to wait for Keynes and the UK delegation to arrive and produce more information on which a recommendation could be made. At a meeting on 6 September, attended by Clayton, Vinson, and Marriner Eccles of the Federal Reserve Board, Vinson emphasised the need to make the financial arrangements conditional on British acceptance of satisfactory foreign trade policies. He also mentioned the necessity to develop a comprehensive lending programme (a role for the National Advisory Council) so that Congress could be presented with the complete picture of all foreign loans. Eccles raised the problem of justifying a large loan to Congress and also expressed worries that such a loan might have inflationary effects on the US economy, another criticism that was to recur in later discussion of the Loan. Clayton stressed that with the ending of Lend-Lease there would be ample capacity in the US economy to produce the kind of goods that would be demanded. He agreed that a satisfactory justification would have to be developed and suggested that it be based on the importance of stimulating a movement towards multilateral trade and on the role of foreign lending in promoting employment in export industries. He believed that the British genuinely wanted to move towards multilateralism, even though there were pressures to adopt a bilateral course; and he felt that every effort should be made to reach an agreement with the British to prevent this. Clayton warned that there might be difficulties in talking to the British in terms of a loan, for they had talked to him in London in terms of a grant-in-aid. At this, Vinson said that the proceedings would be considerably shortened if the British took this view, as the US would not consider a grant-in-aid.

There does seem to have been some activity in the US Treasury in August and September to devise a plan for aiding the UK and at the same time achieving some form of settlement of the sterling balances. However, there is no record of such a plan being discussed in the formal committees, though White seems to have mentioned some of his ideas to Keynes in early September, before formal talks began. In a note to Vinson of 31 August White began by emphasising the acute financial position of the UK following the end of the Japanese war and the termination of Lend-Lease. One major obstacle in the way of Britain emerging successfully from the present situation was the $12 billion or so of blocked sterling balances.[3] If this could be removed without imposing too great a strain on Britain's balance of payments, it would go a long way towards ensuring that England could be 'a strong positive factor in maintaining world prosperity rather than a possible drag and danger'. White's proposals would benefit the US and the world as a whole and would remove one of the most serious obstacles to an early resumption of multilateral trade and convertibility.

The plan envisaged some cancellation of the sterling balances (which would in part be a recognition of the high prices paid during the war). The US Government would take over all or part of the remainder for gold or dollars at a small discount, with the proceeds being split equally between the holders and the British Government. These balances would then be repurchased from the US beginning not later than 1950 in gold or dollars at the original price. The British Government would pay annually to the owners of the balances 2% of the nominal value of the sterling balances sold to the US, half in sterling and the other half in gold, dollars, or other acceptable currencies. The financial assistance likely to be needed might be $4–6 billion. In return, the UK would agree to eliminate exchange restrictions on current transactions within two years, to eliminate the Sterling Area dollar pool, and to revise downwards some of the British Empire tariffs regarded as unduly onerous. A further advantage for the US was that such a proposal would not set a precedent for giving financial assistance to other countries.

Keynes' initial presentation in September of the facts of the UK position and the suggested solution were in general well received on the US side and engendered an optimistic spirit amongst the US team, a spirit that really never left them. Clayton reported to the President on 24 September that considerable progress had been made in discussions with the British and that he was encouraged by their reasonable attitude. He also listed the concessions that the British had informally proposed: lifting exchange controls on all current transactions as from 1 January 1947; making all current sterling balances convertible and liquidating the Sterling Area dollar pool; progressive liberalisation of exchange arrangements over the next fifteen months; terminating the blocked-sterling system on 31

---

[3] White in particular virtually always refers to the 'blocked' sterling balances. In the case of Sterling Area countries the balances were, of course, freely transferable within the Sterling Area and transferable elsewhere for transactions conforming to policy agreed with London.

December 1946; and writing off $4 billion of the $12 billion sterling obligations, 10% of the remainder to be made convertible for current purposes and the remaining $7.2 billion to be funded at no interest and to be paid off in fifty annual instalments of 2% beginning after five years. A line of credit of $5 billion had been requested to meet the adverse balance of trade over the following three years. The concessions noted above are listed by Clayton and again illustrate a degree of confusion on the American side over what was being offered on the Sterling Area. Keynes in fact offered convertibility (in the Bretton Woods sense) for current transactions and releases from the sterling balances of Sterling Area countries from, say, the end of 1946. He also made it clear that the proposals for the sterling balances were illustrative rather than definite.

One important aspect of Keynes' presentation that did not go down well was the comparison of the war efforts of the UK and the US. The British were to be informed that this was a misunderstanding of the US psychology and that any publicity given to it would be on their own responsibility. The justification for the loan had to be forward looking; there was a need to extend sufficient financial aid to help the world get back on its feet and remain there. One of the main props of Keynes' plea for 'Justice' therefore fell away before he had begun to suggest solutions. The other feeling to emerge from Keynes' initial exposition was the need to get some more definite information from the British before any quantitative proposals could be made (this was expressed before the final meeting on 20 September).

Following Keynes' exposition the American side set to work to look at the UK figures for the balance of payments, and a technical sub-committee, under Treasury chairmanship, produced its own version. These estimates were far more optimistic than those of Keynes, reflecting Harry White's view that the reconversion of the UK economy from a wartime basis to exports would be very rapid (though some methods used to estimate export figures for 1946 were fairly crude extrapolations of changes that had taken place during 1945) and that the UK would take full advantage of the absence of competition from Germany and Japan. Another area of disagreement was over the price assumption used for imports in 1946; the UK figure of an increase of 5% over the previous year was thought to be too high. UK imports were predominantly of food, drink and tobacco, and raw materials; these were unlikely to be in short supply and prices might even fall. It was also felt that there would be scope for switching from high-cost to low-cost sources as shipping became available. The US estimate therefore allowed only for a 1.6% increase in prices. For 1947 and 1948 it was assumed that there would be some relaxation in import controls, though a degree of control would remain. The UK figures for invisible receipts were also felt to be too low. Overall the US estimate of the 'most probable' deficit for the first three post-war years (effectively the result of using mid-point range figures came to $3.3 billion, compared with the UK estimate of $4.87 billion.

It was assumed that the dollar deficit for 1946 might be met by dollars accruing to the Empire from the dollar pool, gold from British Africa, and the use of existing gold and dollar balances. The deficit with the rest of the world could be financed by increases in the sterling balances.

The sub-committee itself emphasised the conjectural nature of the figures; in addition a note from the Federal Reserve Board, the Commerce Department and the Foreign Exchange Administration (FEA) pointed out that the 1946 deficit was too optimistic because of the favourable assumptions about, in particular, reconversion. An amount of $2.7 billion was felt to be more probable. For the three-year period as a whole, it was felt that the figures seriously understated the UK position and envisaged a greater degree of import control than would be desirable. A figure of $4.2 billion for the three years would be preferable. A note from the State Department drew attention to the unsuitability of using the 'most probable' estimates. The UK figure of $5–6 billion was the upper limit, so the US figure on a comparable basis would be $4.6 billion. The amount of credit needed to give Britain a reasonable assurance of financing its deficit would then be about $4.5 billion.

Despite these notes of dissent, the figure of $3.3 billion did become the accepted estimate of the UK deficit for 1946–8. This was particularly unfortunate from the UK's point of view because it made it harder to justify a loan of even $4 billion on the basis of its being used to finance the deficit. A report from the 'technical men in the Treasury' sent on to Vinson by Harry White (9 October) proposed a credit of $4 billion, repayable over fifty years from 1950 at no or very low interest. About $2½ billion of this would go to finance the balance of payments deficit, with a further $2½ billion coming from the Sterling Area countries.[4] The remaining $1½ billion, together with $1 billion from Canada and South Africa and a fall in UK reserves of $½ billion would be used to purchase, at a discount, $5 billion of the sterling balances. It was assumed that the holders would prefer this solution to the British one of paying off the balances over fifty years at no interest. Of the remaining $8 billion of the balances, $4 billion would be cancelled, $2 billion would be freed as working balances, and $2 billion

---

[4] This figure was also referred to in an article in the *Baltimore Sun* of 11 October written on the basis of a document leaked by Bernstein, apparently without Harry White's knowledge.

would be offset against, *inter alia*, British foreign installations and war claims. Thus the entire problem of the blocked sterling balances would be eliminated in one go. Building on Keynes' illustrative figures, it took his proposals a stage further. It was assumed that such a scheme would be negotiable with the countries concerned. 'Without American assistance to Britain, the value of the $13 billion of blocked sterling claims against Britain is, on a realistic appraisal, almost nil.' The scheme again reflects Harry White's views that the existence of the sterling balances would hinder international trade and lead to the UK developing bilateral schemes (excluding the US).

Even inside the US Treasury not everyone accepted the optimistic view of Britain's prospects. Ansel Luxford and E.M.Bernstein, who worked with Harry White, both believed that the balance of payments estimate was too low. In response to the Treasury memorandum, Luxford put forward a note to Vinson, dated 12 October, in which he made three further suggestions. First, the Administration should make clear to Congress that it did not expect to be asking for other large sums as additional loans (other countries should make the use of the IBRD). Second, the loan would be more sound if it were $5 billion, as it should then be sufficient to meet Britain's balance of payments problem and also allow Britain to deal with the blocked sterling balances. Luxford was doubtful that the British could achieve the presumed 50% increase in exports over the pre-war level, and he also doubted whether the Sterling Area countries would be willing to hold $2 billion as working balances if Britain were still in deficit. Giving Britain a safety margin would be preferable to having to come back to Congress with a request for more aid. Finally, the loan should be interest-free. For, together with the further presumed increase in sterling balances, interest payments would amount to some $300 million a year for fifty years. An annual export surplus of that amount would be too much to expect on top of the increase in exports already assumed. The risks if Britain were unable to pay were greater than the amount gained in interest payments, and it was in any case hard to dress up the financial assistance as a commercial loan.

Once the reports from the Technical Committee were available the US side could get down to more detailed discussions of what could be offered to the British. This was covered at three meetings of the Financial Committee on 10, 11, and 17 October. It was quickly agreed that the assistance should be in the form of a line of credit rather than a loan, to be made available over a five-year period. There was little opposition to charging interest. Vinson, Eccles, and McCabe all emphasised the difficulties of getting acceptance of an interest-free loan. It was further agreed that payment of equal annual instalments, combining interest and amortisation, would be easier to understand. For a $1 billion loan, repayable over fifty years at 2%, the annual payment would be $31.8 million. Clayton proposed a five-year grace period, reducing the effective interest to 1.63%. The principle of a waiver was agreed, if not the details. The major problem was over the amount.

Substantive discussion on this did not take place until the third meeting, on 17 October, though Clayton had earlier said that he did not think the concessions they wanted could be obtained for assistance of less than $4 billion. By 17 October he was able to report that, from informal talks with the British since the last meeting, he had learnt that they had received instructions from London to ask for total assistance of $5 billion, $2 billion as grant aid and $3 billion as a fifty-year loan at 2%. This implied an annual service payment of $100 million a year, which was the most the British could accept. For Vinson this limit suggested that the loan must not exceed $3.1 billion, since annual interest and amortisation payments of $31.8 million per billion had already been agreed. He also felt that the commercial and other concessions to be obtained from the British should be established before the amount of aid could be determined; the British should not be allowed to set both the amount and the terms. In this he disagreed with Clayton, who felt the Committee should concern itself only with what the British would be willing to accept; he stressed that if sufficient assistance were not provided, the negotiations would reach an impasse that would prejudice the development of the world economy desired by the Americans. Vinson agreed that it was important to reach a favourable settlement, but he also said that its achievement necessitated an agreement that was acceptable to the US public.

Clayton himself favoured a figure of $4 billion, as the amounts that Canada ($500 million) and the Sterling Area ($1 billion) were expected to provide might not be forthcoming and the British might require a margin of safety. Since he also thought the British might be willing to make service payments of more than $100 million a year, he proposed that they should be on sliding scale rising from $100 million to $154 million. Wallace (Commerce) and Angell (FEA) agreed with this. However, Eccles doubted whether a $5 billion loan would be acceptable, given the figures produced by the Technical Committee. Both he and Vinson therefore went for $3½ billion, though Eccles suggested the figure might be increased to $4 billion at a later date if necessary. After discussion, Clayton concurred with an initial offer being made to the British of $3½ billion at 2% repayable over fifty years, if it was understood that the Committee would go to $4 billion if necessary.

This offer, duly made to the British on 18 October, was received with some dismay. Although Clayton (and Vinson) appeared to have had some idea of the important stage the negotiations had reached, they still appeared reasonably optimistic about the outcome. Towers, who was visiting Washington at Keynes' request, found that the Americans were rather too confident of their ability to dictate the terms of a financial settlement and insufficiently worried about leaving the UK in a weak position.

The American account of the same conversation notes that Towers was worried over the prospects for a large volume of world trade unless the US as well as other countries were willing to adopt an expansionist point of view at this time. Clayton, however, was confident that the current negotiations would lead to an agreement that would benefit both countries and result in increased world trade.

The offer of 3\frac{1}{2}$ billion and the discussion that led up to it also contrasts oddly with Keynes' reports to London about an informal meeting on 9 October – before detailed discussion of the amount and terms of the loan in the US Financial Committee – at which Clayton, in Vinson's presence, offered a loan of $5 billion. There are no minutes of the meeting, but the offer was also referred to by Clayton at a press conference on 10 October. Although Keynes said that the details of Clayton's proposals were not clear, it seems impossible that both he and Halifax should have misheard the amount Clayton mentioned. Keynes certainly took the $5 billion as the figure the US were assuming, despite being warned later by Harry White that it was not as firm as he had thought.[5] There is no reference to this offer in the records of the meetings of the Financial Committee and substantive discussions on the amount and terms of the loan only took place after 10 October. Therefore at best Clayton was making an offer without authority, though it seems unlikely that he can have been unaware of the significance of what he is reported to have said.

From this point on, from the American viewpoint, the negotiations with the British (after an interval while the delegation waited for briefing from London) centred largely on such questions as the form of the waiver clause, the definition, scope, and date of convertibility, the priority the new loan might take over other commitments, and whether it might be used to repay the sterling balances. On the last point it was agreed that repayment of the sterling balances should be made from sources other than the US credit; there is no indication that Harry White's ideas for the sterling balances were ever formally discussed. On the waiver, the main

---

[5] The total of $5 billion included $1 billion for 1945 and used a figure of $4 billion for the remainder of the period.

difficulties arose on the question of a reserves criterion, on which the US side finally gave way.

As far as convertibility was concerned, a draft discussed in November made the Americans realise that the British were now proposing that convertibility apply to the Sterling Area only. It was then confirmed that the US should insist that convertibility apply to all countries. Clayton said at a meeting on 13 November that he accepted the British arguments that arrangements could not be completed before 1946 and that it was necessary to accept the end of 1946. He also suggested that the convertibility date should be the date on which the British reached agreement with each individual country, but that this should be not later than the end of 1946. This was incorporated into the US draft agreement. At a later meeting on 25 November, Vinson reported that while the British agreed with the main American objectives, they felt that they could not agree to specific commitments to be carried out by specific dates because it would 'hamstring' them in their negotiations with third countries. (This was, however, before the major disagreement between the UK delegation in Washington and London over the separability of convertibility and the conclusion of agreements with Sterling Area countries, to which there seems to be no reference.) However the Americans stuck to a demand for a firm date and the only change eventually agreed was that it should be a year after the effective date of the Agreement rather than end-1946.

A further point that was to prove important later was provision for consultation. At Vinson's insistence the main clause providing for consultation was made to relate to the whole Agreement and any alterations would be subject to legislative approval. On the dates by which convertibility should be achieved, there was provision for extension after consultation and agreement, but, at a suggestion from Knapp of the FRB, provision was made for extension only in particular cases.

Argument continued on the US side over the amount of the loan, though the offer to the British remained at $3½ billion. Clayton continued to advocate $4 billion in order to achieve the concessions the Americans wanted. He felt that although the British would not necessarily use the full amount of the credit, they were being asked to revolutionise their payments systems and needed a reserve (particularly given the uncertainties of the balance of payments estimates). He was supported by Wallace and the Commerce Department. Vinson and Eccles, however, both felt that $3½ billion was sufficient and that a higher figure would be difficult to justify to Congress; other sources of finance (loans from Canada and the Sterling Area) were available. At a meeting on 8 November a motion to offer $4 billion was defeated, with State and Commerce in favour, the

Treasury and Federal Reserve Board against. At meetings at the end of the month Collado and Acheson represented Clayton (who was ill) and continued to argue for $4 billion; the issue was finally decided by the President, who split the difference at $3¾ billion.

A report sent to Winant in London says that the British appeared to be 'pleased' at the final offer of $3¾ billion, with $650 million for the Lend-Lease clean-up. Winant had been reporting from London on the British worries over the course of the negotiations. In a talk with Hall-Patch on 3 November he was told that the difficulties centred on the inadequate size of the proposed loan and the difficulties of servicing it. A conversation at the Foreign Office a few days later revealed that Bevin himself was clearly troubled about Britain's future and about the chances of getting the kind of world he wanted. He felt that unless the US were able to provide assistance on a sufficient scale to meet the British balance of payments difficulties, the future was not promising. Winant shared some of these worries, saying that he believed that 'the interests of security and the hope of restoring multilateral trade depend on success in the current negotiations'. However, although Vinson at one stage in late November spoke of the importance of the success of the negotiations, the warnings from London were not sufficient to induce the Americans to increase the amount of the loan significantly or to relax the conditions.

Starting from a stronger bargaining position (coupled with some tactical mistakes by the British team), the Americans were able to achieve broadly what they had set out to get in the negotiations, by giving (just) sufficient financial assistance coupled with the concessions they felt necessary if world trade and payments were to develop in the way they wished. As Clayton said in a press conference on 6 December, the agreement just reached 'would put Britain in a position to join in full partnership with us in bringing about a multilateral, non-discriminatory trading system throughout the world. This, in our opinion, is the consideration of the greatest value to the United States. It will open up the markets of the world to our goods and should lay the foundation for a period of expansion in production, consumption, and the exchange of goods and services, and a rising standard of living for all peoples everywhere.' Even Marriner Eccles, who, as he wrote to Sproul in January 1946, was 'not one to enter lightheartedly upon new commitments to foreign countries which would have the effect of increasing our national debt and creating further purchasing power to press upon our readily strained domestic economy', said that it was not a question of whether the US could afford to provide the help but whether, in their long-run interest, they could afford not to provide it.

From the American viewpoint it is very clear that Keynes' vision of 'Justice' was doomed to failure, as he had been warned by Brand and others. The Americans always saw the loan as a means of getting the kind of world they wanted and any appeal to equalising the sacrifice made in the war was ineffective if not counter-productive. It was also clear that the $5 billion loan Keynes asked for was taken as an opening bid, the Americans being unaware that this was the absolute minimum necessary to finance the balance of payments deficit forseen by London. On the basis of their own, extremely optimistic, forecasts the Americans were able to whittle down the amount of the loan. It seems evident that in any case the largest amount they were ever seriously prepared to contemplate was $4 billion.

The effect of reducing the amount of the loan was compounded by the fact that Keynes had offered convertibility of sterling within a year and some arrangements to scale down the wartime accumulated sterling balances without tying these concessions to the amount and conditions of the loan. The Americans therefore accepted these concessions even with a smaller loan and Keynes carried on the negotiations on that basis, without trying to play the ultimate bargaining card of breaking them off. The question of how far the Americans would have been willing to modify their position in order to save this situation never arose.

The error of judgement on the part of the American negotiators arose from a serious misunderstanding of how the Sterling Area operated (despite Keynes' explanations). It was therefore considered essential that sterling be made convertible (for current transactions) without undue delay and that some settlement be made of the so-called 'blocked' sterling balances in order that there should be no discrimination against American trade. These conditions would in any case have been difficult to achieve in the immediate post-war world, but in addition the Americans were extremely optimistic about the speed at which Europe would recover from the war. The so-called dollar shortage was simply not foreseen and therefore – on top of reaching a forecast of the UK balance of payments that was well below Keynes' estimates – no account was taken of demands from the rest of the Sterling Area and the unwillingness of other countries to accumulate sterling.

From a British viewpoint the American position might have appeared unimaginative, with Congress often being brought forward as an excuse for not giving the British the loan they asked for. It does appear that public opinion in the US was in general not in favour of a loan. A Gallup poll taken towards the end of December 1945 found that only 26% of those interviewed thought England needed a loan to get back on its feet (with

52% against) and 31% thought the loan would benefit the US as well (with 49% disagreeing). As a former member of the House of Representatives, Vinson was well placed to judge what would be acceptable. However, more than this was the inability of Keynes to cast his spell over his audience as he (though not all on the British side) had thought he would be able to. As Clayton had warned, late 1945 was a time for 'realism' rather than 'brain-waves' and Keynes' failure to realise this meant that the Americans were able to take full advantage of their stronger bargaining position and obtain the conditions they wanted, however difficult these would be to put into practice.

SOURCES

Bank files
   CBP376.02/3–4   USA: Anglo-US Financial Agreement Negotiations (October 1945)
   CBP376.02/1   USA: Anglo-US Financial Agreement Negotiations (December 1945)

State Department file 6611.4131/5–146
US Treasury files
Federal Reserve Bank of New York archives, file C261
Foreign Relations of the United States, 1945 Vol. 6
Report of Senate Committee on Banking and Currency
Harry White Papers, National Archives and Princeton University
Foreign Affairs, January 1945
Bank of Canada archives
Writings of J.M.Keynes

INDEX

Abbott, Canadian Finance Minister, and sterling devaluation, 293
Abdul Hardy Pasha, PM of Egypt, 257
Abell, Sir G. E. B.
  biog. note, 111
  and Parker Tribunal, 702
  as Private Secretary to Viceroy of India, 111
accepting houses, relations with Bank, 750–5
Accepting Houses Committee, 727
  and Bank rate change, 1951, 406
  and Commonwealth finance, 732
  formation, 750
Acheson, Dean
  and convertibility crisis, 1947, 148
  and Lend-Lease, 36n
  mentioned, 301
  and sterling devaluation, 274, 304
Agents, Branch, *see* Branch Agents
Agricultural Mortgage Corporation, 707
Aldenham, Walter D. G., Baron
  biog. note, 633
  chairman of CLCB, 632
  and credit restrictions, 632–4, 636, 652, 654
Aldrich, Winthrop
  and Anglo-American Loan negotiations, 811
  and sterling devaluation, 286
Alexanders Discount Co., 757
Allen, W. Maurice
  appointed Economic Adviser, 306, 373, 383
  author's recollections of, 383n
  and bank liquidity, 616
  and Bank Rate, 1952, 618–20; 1953, 621–2
  biog. note, 306

and credit restrictions, 638, 654–5; 630–1
and Credit Trading Bill, 771
and domestic monetary policy, 611
as Economic Adviser, 611
and exchange reserves, 1954, 627
and Exchequer financing, 617
and finance houses, 761
and fixed rate convertibility, 306
and floating rate convertibility, 311
and hire purchase, 762
and intervention in transferable, 523–4
and liquidity ratios, 629–30
and macro-economic policy, 636–7
and Monetary Organisation report, 661–5
and monetary situation, 1957, 675
note on current economic position, 1954, 625–6
and ratio controls, 383
and Robot, 466
views on monetary policy, 411
Alphand Plan, for European payments, 193–4
Aluminium Company of America, 744–9
aluminium industry, *see* British Aluminium
American Nile Corporation, 236
Amory, 1st Viscount, *see* Heathcoat Amory, Derick
Anderson, Sir Alan, and Bank of England Bill, 17
Anderson, Sir John
  and Bank of England Bill, 21
  chairs Ministerial group on IMF provisions, 59–60
  and finance for industry, 717–18
  and gilt market, 1944, 332
  and launch of FCI and ICFC, 704
  and Robot, 446n

823

Andes Agreement, with Argentina, 261–7
Anglo-American Loan, waiver of interest requested during Suez crisis, 560–1
Anglo-American Loan Agreement, 31–87
  assessment, 86–7
  'Brave New World', 63
  and Canadian Loan, 99
  Clause 7, 89–90
  Clause 8, 31, 157–8
  Clause 10, 90, 145
  and convertibility crisis, 1947, 141–63
  'Cruel Real World', 63
  negotiations, 73–87; US viewpoint, 807–22
  ratification, 95, 108
  'Sheer madness', 31, 85, 158
  and sterling balances of Australia and New Zealand, 102
  US terms accepted, 85
Anglo-American Mutual Aid Agreement, negotiations, 1942, 35
Anglo-Czechoslovak Monetary Agreement, 1945, 804
Anglo-Czechoslovak Trade and Financial Agreement, 1949, 804
Anglo-Egyptian Sudan, 121n
Anglo-Egyptian Treaty, 1936, 115, 119, 250
Anglo-Polish Financial Agreement, 1947, 802
Annual Report, Bank of England, publication of, 9, 24
Ansiaux, Hubert, 183, 189, 191
  and Belgian Monetary Agreement, 125
  at BIS meeting, 515
  biog. note, 125
  and Collective Approach, 493
  and European payments, 219, 532, 533
  and Operation Unicorn, 602
  and second Belgian Plan, 201–2
  views on convertibility, 1952, 479
  see also Ansiaux Plan
Ansiaux Plan, 172–93
  and Intra-European Payments and Compensations, 179–93
Anthony Gibbs, conversion to ltd. company, 753
arbitrage, in European Payments Union currencies, 495
Arbuthnot Latham, 753
Argentina
  meat, 103, 104, 106, 261–7
  payments agreement with, 250
  payments agreement, mentioned, 53
  railways, 103, 104, 105, 261–7
  second Monetary Agreement, 1949, 261–7
  sterling balances, 96; negotiations, 103–8
Armstrong, Sir William, and sterling devaluation, 299
Association of Investment Trusts, 710, 711, 721
Association of Pensioners of Austrian National Bank, 126
Atlantic Charter, 1941, 35
Atlantic Payments Union
  Cherwell's support of, 477, 478
  proposed, 470–1
Attlee, C. R., 1st Earl
  and Anglo-American Loan Negotiations, 76, 78
  and Argentinian sterling balances, 106
  and Stage III, 72
  and sterling devaluation, 295
Auboin, Roger,
  General Manager of BIS, 205, 206, 492n
Australia
  gift to UK as war contribution, 102
  gold reserves, 275
  sterling balances, 101–3, 417n
  views on sterling convertibility, 1952, 424
Avon, Earl of, see Eden, Sir Anthony

Babington Smith, Michael J.
  biog. note, 552
  and Suez crisis, 552
Baillieu, Clive L., Baron
  and Argentinian sterling balances, 261–7
  biog. note, 261
  chairman of Dunlop, 732
balance of payments
  1955, 524
  1956, 536–7
  1958, 566
  forecast, 1951, 393; 1953, 522
Balfour, Corinna, 'Anglo-American Loan Negotiations: the US viewpoint', 807–22
Balfour, Lord
  and Bank Rate change, 404
  consulted by Bank on bank advances, 363, 369
  and credit control, 1951, 409
Bamford, Sir Eric StJ., and Budget discussions, 1948, 361
bank advances
  1948–9, 359–70
  1951, 393
  1952, 410
  1955, 635

1966, 667
ceiling, 677–80
ceiling opposed by banks, 376–7
control over, use of in monetary policy, 406, 609–10
fall, 1952, 616
growth, 1947, 360; 1948, 363, 364; 1950–1, 616; 1951, 408; 1955, 632; 1957, 672
policy, 1948–51, 359–96
restrictions, 607, 632–93; 1939, 328; 1944–5, 328
bank deposits
1955, 637
fall, 1951, 408; 1955, 645
growth, 1948, 364; 1950–1, 389; 1952, 618
policy, 1948–51, 359–96
Bank Deutscher Lander, mentioned, 537, 572, 803
see also Bundesbank
Bank of England, governance and policy direction, 316–17
Bank of England Act 1946, 4–30
Clause 4(3), 679
and control over banking system, 18–19, 364
and finance houses, 773
Bank of England Bill
approved by Cabinet, 16
assets of Bank, net worth of, 22–3
City response to, 19
Clause 4(3), debated by House of Lords, 25–26; discussed in press, 19
Clauses 4(3) and (4), 11–16
Clauses 4(1) and (3), discussed by Court, 17
Committee stage, 24–5
draft heads of legislation, 7
passage through Parliament, 12, 20–7
preparation, 4–16
public response to, 18–19
Second Reading, 20–1
Select Committee, 21–4
submitted to Cabinet, 12
Third Reading, 24–5
Bank of France
and 1947 financial negotiations, 134–6
and cheap sterling, 244
and Collective Approach, 486
discussions with Bank of England, 1952, 457–61
and European payments, 1955, 533
lending rate cut, 623
mentioned, 171, 203, 215, 224, 286, 585
and Operation Unicorn, 597, 599

and suspension of convertibility, 1947, 136
suspension of foreign exchange dealings, 602
Bank for International Settlements
Basle meetings, 206, 486, 515, 520, 521, 593
and Czech gold, 805n
foundation, 178
proposed as agent for European payments, 178
Bank of Italy, 172, 186
Bank Lending Rate, 1953, 620
Bank Naradowy Polski, 797–802
Bank Polski, 795–803
Bank Rate
1945 Minute by Peppiatt, 323–4
change in associated with Robot, 446
change in consultation with Treasury, 6, 8
cuts, 592, 621, 622–3, 671
'leak', *see* Parker Tribunal
procedures for changes in, post-Radcliffe, 692
raised to $2\frac{1}{2}$%, 315, 404–6
raised to 3%, 404–6
raised to $3\frac{1}{2}$%, 521
raised to 4%, 447
raised to $4\frac{1}{2}$%, 526
raised to $5\frac{1}{2}$%, 545, 656
raised to 7%, 567, 571, 607, 684–7
raised to 8%, 607
restitution as instrument of monetary policy, criticisms, 412
rises discussed, 370, 374, 385, 386, 514, 523, 606, 643–4, 677
Bank Rate Tribunal, *see* Parker Tribunal
Bank Stock
dividend on, 8
exchanged for Government Stock on nationalisation of Bank, 10
Banker, The
and $2\frac{1}{2}$% Irredeemable, 353
and Bank of England Bill, 26
briefed on intervention in transferable, 526
and exchange reserves, 1954, 626
and gilt-edged market, 350
and liquidity ratios, 662
and sterling devaluation, 282
Bankers Almanac, and deposit-taking, 763
Bankers Industrial Development Company, 708, 709, 715
Banking Act 1979, 21, 777n
Banking Act 1987, 21
Banking Act
possibility of, in 1957, 700
two-tier, discussed, 764

banking institutions, secondary, *see* finance houses
banking statistics, 1946, 346
banking supervision, 749–79
banking system
  Bank's authority over, prior to 1939, 696
  Bank's control of, 1948–9, 359–96
  Bank's powers over, 21, 25–6
  Bank's powers over, under Bank of England Act, 18–19, 364
  Bank's statutory powers over, discussed during nationalisation, 9, 10–16
  fringe, *see* banking system, secondary
  beginning of, 658
banks
  asked to provide monthly figures of advances, 409
  and credit restrictions, 1952–8, 632–93
  foreign, as lenders, 609
  Irish, and Bank Rate change, 1951, 405
  liquidity ratios, 609, 614, 616–17
  relations with Bank of England, 609–10
  Schedule VIII, 777
  Scottish, and Bank Rate change, 1951, 405; and deposit-taking, 763; and finance for industry, 720
  Treasury control over, possible legislation, 680, 689
banks, British overseas, as lenders, 609
Banque de France, *see* Bank of France
Baranski, Leon, 796–803
Baranyai, Leopold, 803
Barclays Bank
  and cheap sterling, 239
  and finance for industry, 710
  mentioned, 638, 710
Bareau, Paul, 405n
Baring crisis, 749
  and Bank's powers over banking system, 21
Baring, Evelyn, and Commonwealth finance, 730
Barings
  and British Aluminium, 747n
  and Commonwealth finance, 731
  and SCOW, 728
  and steel denationalisation, 737, 741
Baumgartner, Wilfred S.
  and Bank rate rise to 4%, 447–8
  biog. note, 203
  and Collective Approach, 486, 490, 492
  and European payments, 203, 215, 533, 537
  and European Payments Union, 457–9
  and franc devaluation, 569, 676n
  friendship with Cobbold, *see* Cobbold, C. F.
  Governor of Bank of France, 585
  informed of end of Robot, 459
  offered Managing Directorship of IMF, 573n
  and Operation Unicorn, 596, 597, 598–9, 602
  and sterling convertibility, 515
  and sterling devaluation, 286
Beale, P. S.
  anxiety re Treasury interference, 403
  appointed Chief Cashier, 373
  at press briefing on Bank Rate change, 1951, 405
  author's recollection of, 628–9n
  biog. note, 112
  character and abilities, 614, 628–9
  and cheap sterling, 246
  as Chief Cashier, 613
  City career, 629
  and commodities, 786, 790
  and Commonwealth finance, 732
  and convertibility crisis, 1947, 152, 156
  and credit restrictions, 642
  and domestic monetary policy, 612, 614–15
  and European payments, 183–4
  and European Payments Union, 219
  and exchange reserves, 1954, 627
  and Indian sterling balances, 112–13, 114, 252n
  and interest rates, 1949, 374; 1950, 384
  member of Niemeyer's Committee on interest rates, 370
  member of Niemeyer's Committee on sterling–dollar exchange rate, 285
  paper on 'Inflation and Bank Rate', 401
  proposed package of financial measures, 1951, 401–2
  resignation from Bank and appointment as general manager of ICICI, 628–9
  and Robot, 434, 446
  and steel denationalisation, 736
Beaverbrook, Max, Baron, views on IMF provisions, 59, 60–1
Belgium
  bilateral trade negotions with, 1948, 191
  creditor of European Payments Union, 212
  and European payments, 533, 537
  external surplus, 171
  member of nucleus for Collective Approach, 471
  Monetary Agreement, 1944, 125–6

INDEX

and Operation Unicorn, 598, 601
payments agreement, mentioned, 53
plan for European payments, *see* Ansiaux Plan
Supplementary Financial Agreement, 1947, 134, 148
UK monetary disagreements with, post-war, 198n
Benelux, and Ansiaux Plan, 176
Bensons, and steel denationalisation, 741
Bernard, Sir D. G. M., 1st Bt
  appointed Deputy Governor, 372–3
  and Bank Rate change, 1951, 406
  biog. note, 218
  and cheap sterling, 226–7, 238
  and European payments, 215, 218
  and Robot, 446
Bernstein, E. M.
  and Anglo-American Loan Agreement, 810, 815n, 816
  and sterling convertibility, 506
Berthoud, Eric, Foreign Office, 439
Bevan, Aneurin, resignation, 312
Bevin, Ernest
  and Argentinian sterling balances, 265
  death, 312
  mentioned, 301
  and sterling devaluation, 298
Bicester, 2nd Baron, Randal Hugh Vivian Smith
  and Bank Rate, 1955, 644
  biog. note, 525
  and intervention in transferable, 525
  and steel denationalisation, 733, 737, 742
Birch, Nigel
  appointed Economic Secretary, 669
  chairman of Bank/Treasury Working Group on bank advances, 688
  and credit restrictions, 682, 688–90
  resignation, 567, 670
Bissell, Richard M. Jr.
  biog. note, 281–2
  and sterling devaluation, 281–2, 284, 293
Blessing, Karl
  biog. note, 596
  and Operation Unicorn, 596, 602
Board of Trade
  and Anglo-American Loan negotiations, 1945, 74
  and cheap sterling, 234
  and commodities, 789
  and Credit Trading Bill, 761–77
  and deposit-taking companies, 759, 760, 763–6, 768
  and Egyptian sterling balances, 258
  and European Payments Union, 456
  and finance companies, 658, 659
  and hire-purchase, 410–11
  and Indian sterling balances, 255
  and monetary trends, 1957, 687
  Order of 1952 revoked, 624
  and post-war finance for industry, 708, 710
  and Protection of Depositors Bill, 777n
  Report on Employment Policy, 711, 715
  represented on Working Party on convertibility, 470–1
  views on post-war financial and trade policy, 36
Board of Trade Solicitor, 789
Bolgert, M., 515
Bolton, Sir G. L. F.
  A Banker's World: the Revival of the City, 1957–70, quoted, 449n
  and alternative to Ansiaux Plan, 172–3
  and Anglo-Belgian Monetary Agreement, 125
  appointed Director of Bank, 88n, 163
  biog. note, 32
  briefs press on intervention in transferable, 525
  and central bank co-operation, 514, 515
  chairs meeting on post-EPU arrangements, 515
  character and abilities, 196
  and cheap sterling, 225, 227, 229, 233, 242, 246
  and Collective Approach, 480, 498, 499, 501
  and Commonwealth finance, 730, 731
  and convertibility, 309
  and convertibility crisis, 149, 150, 151, 153, 160, 161
  and devaluation, 279
  and discussions on post-war finance, 38, 39
  and European monetary agreements, 1945, 126–7, 128
  and European payments, 172, 181, 182, 187, 188, 189, 194, 195, 198, 199, 200, 218, 533
  and European Payments Union, 456, 513
  and exchange control, 296
  and exchange rate policy, 518
  and external crisis, 1951, 393
  and fixed rate convertibility, 311
  and floating rate convertibility, 310, 589–90
  and floating sterling rate, 296–7
  and foreign exchange policy, 1951, 410
  and forward exchange cover, 413

and freeze and offer plan, 273
and French financial reform, 457, 459
and IMF credit proposal, 1952, 453
and Indian sterling balances, 1948, 254, 256
member of Collective Approach Committee, 507
member of Committee on Post-War Domestic Finance, 705
member of Siepmann's Committee on Sterling Area, 88
member of UK delegation to Bretton Woods, 61
note on Economic and Industrial Crisis, 1947, 143–4
paper on European Central Bank Co-operation, 510–11
paper on post-war exchange control, 40–1
and proposed change in Bank Rate, 1945, 324
proposes enlargement of Sterling Area, 1949, 271
re-draft of Cobbold's paper on floating rate convertibility, 1952, 434–6
relations with Treasury, 242n
retirement as Executive Director, 546, 573
and Robot, 434, 469
and Sterling Area Working Party, 1955–6, 545–6
and sterling convertibility, 425–6, 429, 494–5, 540, 548
and sterling convertibility Stage II, 506–7
and sterling devaluation, 269–70, 274, 283, 284, 285, 293–4, 298, 299, 301, 304
and Suez crisis, 553, 556, 561
and Treasury Bill rate, 1953, 620
and unification of sterling, 504
view of sterling in Western Europe, 783
Boothby, Robert, 780
and Bank of England Bill, 21
Boscawen, John, 350n
Bovenschen Committee, 791
Boyle, Andrew, *Montagu Norman*, quoted, 14–15n
Boyle, Sir Edward, 545, 637
Branch Agents
annual meeting, 613–14
Manchester Branch, and finance houses, 763
quarterly reports, 658n
Brand, Robert H., 1st Baron
advice to Bank re Bank Rate leak, 702
biog. note, 67

and Justice, 67
and monetary policy, 614
and Stage III, 70
and Sterling Area policy, 426–7
Brave New World, *see* Anglo-American Loan Agreement
Brazil
coffee, 266
payments agreement, mentioned, 53
sterling balance agreement, 123n
bread, price increase after devaluation, 376
bread subsidies, 656
Brennan, Central Bank of Ireland, 447
Bretton Woods Agreement, 31, 32
Conference, 61
and European Payments Union, 205–6
and French Monetary Area, 224
Keynes architect of, 219
mentioned, 372, 627, 809, 814
provisions, 31, 153, 421, 438
ratification, 79
ratification delays possible, 81
and sterling devaluation, 299
Bridge, R. A. O.
biog. note, 186
and central bank co-operation, 514
character and abilities, 186–7
as Deputy Chief Cashier, 590n
and devaluation, 280
and European payments, 186–7, 188, 189, 194, 195, 201–4, 208, 209, 211, 212, 214, 216, 219
and Exchequer requirements, 1946, 349
and floating rate convertibility, 590
and Operation Unicorn, 602
and sterling devaluation, 290
and suggested EMF, 198
Bridges, Sir E., 1st Baron
and Anglo-American Loan Negotiations, 85
appointed Permanent Secretary to Treasury, 66n
at Treasury dinner, 655n
and bank advances, 373, 378
biog. note, 5
and Budget, Autumn 1955, 645
Chairman of National Debt Enquiry, 326
Chairman of Sterling Area Committee, 94
and cheap sterling, 242
and Collective Approach, 521
and convertibility crisis, 1947, 150, 156, 157
and credit restrictions, 640–3, 666
and dual lending rate, 1953, 620
and European Monetary Agreement, 535

and European payments, 199, 214
and European Payments Union, 1952, 455–6
and gilt market, 1946, 339
and independence of the Bank, 6
and interest rates, 1945, 329
and intervention in transferable, 523
and Monetary Organisation report, 665
and nationalisation of the Bank, 5
and NDO, 348–9
receives Bank paper on financial situation, 1951, 398
retirement, 529
and Robot, 434
and steel denationalisation, 737–7
and sterling convertibility, 431, 536, 548
and sterling devaluation, 271–2, 283, 291, 295
and Suez crisis, 551, 553, 554
British Aluminium, 743–9
mentioned, 698
British American Tobacco, 732
British Bankers Association
analysis of advances, 645
and credit restrictions, 642
Foreign Exchange Committee, 415
monthly figures provided to Bank, 653
British Honduras, cheap sterling trade, 247
British Insurance Association, 657
and credit restrictions, 640
and finance for industry, 710, 711, 718, 720
and steel denationalisation, 741
British Iron and Steel Corporation, 733–43
British Iron and Steel Federation, 740
British Iron and Steel Stock, 738
British Military Administration currency notes, *see* currency notes
British Newfoundland Corporation, 731
British Overseas Airways Corporation, 658
British Petroleum, nationalisation of in Iran, 312
British Railways Mission, Buenos Aires, 261–2
British South Africa Company, 747n
Brittain, Sir H.
biog. note, 5
Chairman of Working Party on convertibility, 470–1, 476
and cheap sterling, 238
and commodities, 792
and credit restrictions, 638, 644
and discussion of future nationalisation of Bank, 1943, 8
and European payments, 202–3, 203
and foreign exchange market, 415

and gilt market, 1944, 331–2
and interest rates, 1945, 328–9
member of National Debt Enquiry, 326
mentioned, 501
and nationalisation of the Bank, 5, 6
and Robot, 439
Brofoss, Governor of Norges Bank, 601
Brook, Brigadier Robin, appointed Director of Bank, 28
Brook, Norman, and Parker Tribunal, 701–2
Brown Shipley, 751
Bruce, Lord
and Commonwealth finance, 730
and SCOW, 728, 729
Budget
1945, 329
1946, 342–3, 357
1947, 355
1948, 362
1951, 389, 446
1952, 417, 433, 434–5, 447–8
1955, 531, 541, 645
1956, 660–1
1957, 568, 673–4
Budget discussions, Bank participation, 612
Building Societies Act, 777n
building work, postponement of new, 1951, 404
Bull, A. C. Discount Office, 370
Bundesbank
autonomy, 780
and European payments, 516
and Operation Unicorn, 600
Burgess, W. Randolph
and EPU, 489
and European Fund, 520
and sterling convertibility, 494, 508
and Suez crisis, 564
Butler, R. A.
appointed Chancellor of the Exchequer, 402
appointed Lord Privy Seal, 529
approach to Premiership, 1953, 620n
and Bank Rate change, 1951, 404–5
and Collective Approach, 485
and convertibility, 1952, 476, 477
and credit restriction, 632–93
and dual lending rate, 620
and foreign exchange reserves, 1951, 417
and IMF stand-by, 511
and intervention in transferable, 507, 523, 524–5
as Lord Privy Seal, 669
and Randall Commission, 502

request to banks re credit control, 1951, 409
retirement as Chancellor of the Exchequer, 653
and Robot, 434, 454, 455, 458, 463–9
and steel denationalisation, 737, 738
and sterling convertibility, 493, 498, 499, 504, 514, 520, 539; 1952, 423, 480
and Suez crisis, 564
Butskellism, 607, 627

Cabinet
 and Credit Trading Bill, 769
 discussion of Robot in, 443–444
 Economic Policy Committee, and interest rates, 1949, 374; and Robot, 468
 and sterling devaluation, 291
Cabinet Committee on External Economic Policy, 512n
Cabinet Office, Economic Section, *see* Economic Section
Caccia, Harold A., Baron
 biog. note, 559
 and sterling convertibility, 540
 and Suez crisis, 559–60, 564
Caine, Sir Sydney
 biog. note, 281
 and sterling devaluation, 281
Calvet, Pierre, 215
 Chairman of exchange rate policy assembly, 535, 537
 and Operation Unicorn, 600, 602
Campbell, Ronald, 258, 259
Canada
 and convertibility crisis, 1947, 148
 member of nucleus for Collective Approach, 471
 responsibilities for monetary policy, 1945, 14–15
 views on post-war exchange problems, 54–5
 views on sterling convertibility, 1952, 424
 see also Canadian Loan
Canadian Loan, 97–101
 1947 drawings, 158
 restriction on drawings, 1947, 148
 waiver of interest requested during Suez crisis, 560–1
Capital Issues Committee
 and bank lending, 609
 and British Aluminium, 745
 and credit control, 373, 410, 411, 657, 658, 673
 and Credit Trading Bill, 772
 and deposit-taking, 764

and finance houses, 761
and finance for industry, 707
guidance to, 389, 409
and hire-purchase, 624, 632
in WW2, 327–8
Catterns, B. G.
 advice to Catto on Bank's powers over commercial banks, 9
 biog. note, 3
 as Deputy Governor, 3
 and discussions on post-war finance, 38
 economic advice to, 322
 evidence to Ministerial group on IMF provisions, 59–60
 and finance for industry, 714, 715, 716
 and International Clearing Union, 45
 and Niemeyer Report, 321–2
 and problems of post-war period, 41
 retirement, 9n
Catto, T. S., 1st Baron
 A Personal Memoir and Biographical Note, quoted, 143–4
 agrees to remain as Governor after nationalisation of Bank, 8, 9, 18
 and Anglo-American Loan Negotiations, 80
 and Argentinian sterling balances, 107–8
 and bank advances, 362, 363, 366–8
 and Bank's statutory powers over banking system, 11–16
 biog. note, 2–3
 character and abilities, 2–3, 80n
 and convertibility crisis, 143–4, 146; explanation to Court, 159;
 diary, 156, 159
 and devaluation, 279
 and discussions with Treasury on Bank of England Bill, 17–18
 and finance for industry, 716, 720, 724–5n
 and French negotiations, 1947, 136
 and gilt market, 331–2
 and interest rates, 351–2
 and International Clearing Union, 43
 and launch of FCI and ICFC, 704
 and Morgan Grenfell, 751
 and nationalisation of the Bank, 7
 and proposal for two Deputy Governors, 10
 re-appointed Governor on nationalisation, 28
 relations with Dalton, 8n, 327
 relations with Treasury, 15
 and SCOW, 728–9
 speech to Court on eve of nationalisation, 28–30

INDEX

succeeds Norman as Governor, 2
and Towers' view of Stage III, 67
views on Anglo-American Loan, 62–3
central bank co-operation, 532
 exchange swaps, 567
central bank credit, rationing of, 693
Central Bank of Kenya, mentioned, 802
central banking legislation, constitutional issues of, 14, 15, 16
central banks
 briefed on Bank of England Bill, 16, 17–18
 Commonwealth, and Commonwealth finance, 731; informed of Bank Rate moves, 405, 447
 Commonwealth governors, and Suez crisis, 554
 consulted about sterling unification, 594–5
 duties re convertible sterling, 132
 Eastern European, 795–806
 informed of sterling devaluation, 299
 informed of unification of sterling and re-opening of gold market, 504
 non-sterling holdings, 1956, 548n
 overseas, Bank as adviser to, 13
 subscribe to gilt-edged funding, 1951, 406
Central Economic Planning Staff
 created, 359
 and Robot, 435
Ceylon
 delegation to Commonwealth Prime Ministers Conference, 1952, 483, 484
 gold reserves, 275
 objections to key currency approach, 478
 sterling balance agreement, 123n
 US underwriting of deficits proposed, 1949, 271–2
 views on sterling convertibility, 1952, 424
Chadwick, Thomas, member of ISHRA, 742
Chadwick, Treasury Accountant, 363
Chancellor of the Exchequer, authority re Bank Rate changes, 692
Charterhouse Group, 753
Chase Manhattan Bank, 235
Chase National Bank, mentioned, 286
Chatham House, *see* Royal Institute of International Affairs
cheap sterling, 167, 168, 273
 City use of, 697
 commodity shunting, 221–2, 234–5
 and exchange control 1948–51, 219–49
 problems of, 189

provides arguments for early convertibility, 249
recurrence of problems, 1949, 302
sale of sterling at discount, 222
see also under name of country
cheaper money policy, post-war, 327–59
Cherwell, Viscount
 and Atlantic Payments Union, 470–1, 477
 author's recollections of, 440n
 character and abilities, 441
 office represented on Working Party on convertibility, 470–1
 and Robot, 435, 437, 439, 441–3, 465
 and sterling convertibility, 449
Chester, Sir N.
 and amendments to Bank of England Bill, 12n
Chief Cashier, responsibilities of re monetary policy, 316
Chifley, Ben, PM of Australia
 and cheap sterling, 233
 and sterling balances of Australia, 101–2
China, private sterling balances, 242–3
Churchill, Sir Winston S.
 1943 speech on post-war economic plan, 705
 returned to office as PM, 312
 and EDC, 439
 friendship with Cobbold, 442n
 ill-health, 1953, 620n
 and nationalisation of the Bank, 7
 retirement as Prime Minister, 511, 530
 and Robot, 434–5, 444
City
 Bank's relations with, 4–5, 695–779
 and British Aluminium, 743–9
 and Commonwealth finance, 730–1
 and finance for industry, 704–27
 and steel denationalisation, 733–43, 737–43
Clarke, H. S.
 biog. note, 184
 and credit restrictions, 761
 and Credit Trading Bill, 774
 and deposit-taking, 763
 and European payments, 184
 and FHA, 776
 and Hambros, 753
 and hire purchase, 762, 766
Clarke, Sir R. W. B. (Otto)
 attitude to Europe, 453
 biog. note, 181
 and death of Keynes, 34
 and devaluation, 278
 and European payments, 181, 188, 190–1, 194–5

and European Payments Union, 488
and floating rate convertibility, 425n
mentioned, 501
and Robot, 436–8, 441
and Stage III, 70
and sterling convertibility, 1952, 427–30
and sterling devaluation, 383
Clay, Sir H.
and advice to Treasury re monetary policy, 317
biog. note, 38
and cheap money, 323
consulted on Baranski's future, 802
and discussions on post-war finance, 38
economic views, 57, 322
and finance for industry, 715–16, 719
and International Clearing Union, 41
member of Committee on Post-War Domestic Finance, 705
recruitment to Bank, 57
views on draft provisions of IMF, 57, 58
views on Keynes and White plans, 59
Clayton, William L.
and Anglo-American Loan Negotiations, 78, 79, 808, 810, 812, 817, 818, 822
biog. note, 71
and Stage III, 71
Clearing Union, Bank and Treasury views on, 198, 199
Cobbold, C. F., 1st Baron
and 2% Lending Rate, 1951, 408
advice to Catto on Bank's powers over commercial banks, 9
and alternative to Ansiaux Plan, 176, 177
and amendments to European monetary agreements, 133–5
and Anglo-American Loan Negotiations, 75, 82, 83
anxiety re Treasury interference, 403
appointed Deputy Governor, 3, 9, 28, 73
appointed Governor, 3, 366
appointed Lord Chamberlain, 567
and appointment of Jacobsson as Managing Director of IMF, 573n
as arbiter of Bank policy, 611
and bank advances, 1949, 368–9, 378
and Bank paper on financial situation, 1951, 398–401
and Bank Rate change, 1951, 406
and Bank's statutory powers over banking system, 1945, 10–11
and Bretton Woods Conference, 61
and British Aluminium, 743–9
and Canadian Loan negotiations, 98–100

character and abilities, 38, 231–2, 268, 375, 612, 783–4, 758n
and cheap sterling, 231–2, 237, 238, 239, 240, 242, 247
and Collective Approach, 490, 492, 499–500
and commodities, 787
and Commonwealth development, 483
and Commonwealth finance, 730–3
and convertibility crisis, 144, 147–8, 150, 151, 153, 155n, 156, 159–63, 168–9
and credit restriction, 1955–8, 632–93
and Credit Trading Bill, 761–77
and deposit-taking, 762–79
and discussions on post-war finance, 38
and discussions with Treasury on nationalisation, 8
and domestic monetary policy, 1952–8, 606–93
and Egyptian sterling balances, 114–23, 258
and European exchange rates, 1957, 570–2
and European Monetary Agreement, 535, 547
and European monetary agreements, 1946, 128
and European payments, 181, 182, 187, 189, 198, 200–18
and European Payments Union, 486
European visits, 1947, 171–2
evidence to Ministerial group on IMF provisions, 59–60
and floating rate convertibility, 310
and foreign exchange market, 414
and freeze and offer plan, 273
friendship with Baumgartner, 386
friendship with Churchill, 442n
and IMF quotas, 574–85
and IMF stand-by, 488, 530
and Indian sterling balance negotiations, 110–14
and industrialists, 665
and interest rates, 1945, 326, 338; 1946, 341–2, 351; 1948–51, 396; 1949, 372–4; 1950, 384–6; 1951, 390
and intervention in transferable, 523, 524–5
and liquidity ratios, 659–61
and Monetary Organisation report, 661–5
and National Debt Enquiry, 335n
and National Debt Office, 348
and Operation Unicorn, 585–605

paper on floating rate convertibility, 1952, 431–5
and Parker Tribunal, 701–3
and post-war exchange problems, 55
and post-war Sterling Area, 43
proposes package of financial measures to Butler, 1951, 402
relations with Bolton, 196
relations with Butler, 403–4
relations with Cripps, 403–4
relations with Dalton, 9n
relations with Gaitskell, 403–4
relations with Macmillan, 404
relations with Treasury, 612
and report of Niemeyer's Committee on interest rates, 372
request to banks re credit control, 1951, 409
retains Norman's Bank largely unchanged, 3
retirement as Governor, 567
and Robot, 431–67
and Seligman Brothers, 754
and Siepmann's exchange policy report, 50
and Special Deposits Scheme, 689–90
and Stage III discussions, 66–7, 68–9
and steel denationalisation, 736–43
and sterling balances, 268
and sterling convertibility, 422–3, 431, 475, 480, 508, 536
and sterling devaluation, 256, 268, 270, 282, 283, 287, 288, 390, 293–4, 295, 297–8
succession as Governor, 366
and Suez Crisis, 543–64
and unification of sterling, 504
view of sterling in Western Europe, 783
views on Chancellors, 660n
cocoa, commodity scheme, 793
Coffee Merchants Federation, 788
coffee trade, post-war, 788
Cohen, Lord, member of Council on Prices, Productivity and Incomes, 676n
Collective Approach Committee, 507
Collective Approach to convertibility of sterling, *see* sterling, convertibility
Colombian Coffee Federation, 788
Colonial Office
represented on Working party on convertibility, 470–1
and sterling balances, 95
Colonial Trust Co. of New York, 754
Commercial Bank of Scotland, 625, 763
Commissioners for the Reduction of the National Debt, 347n

Committee on European Economic Cooperation, agree to set up OEEC, 182
Committee of Inter-Allied Experts, 1942, 124
Committee of London Clearing Bankers
and Bank of England Bill, 16–17, 20
and bank lending, 1948, 363
and credit control, 409
and credit policy, 635, 637, 639, 650
and credit restrictions, 639–42, 656, 673, 679, 680, 682, 686, 688
and finance for industry, 709, 719
and foreign exchange market, 415
informed of Bank Rate change, 1951, 404, 405–6
and Parker Tribunal, 701
and steel denationalisation, 741–2
Committee on Post-War Domestic Finance, 320–1, 705–9
Committee on Sterling–Dollar Exchange rate, 1950, 285, 288–9, 290
Committee on Trade and Economic Affairs, US/Canadian, 506
Committee of Treasury
consulted on Bank Rate, 1955, 644
and intervention in transferable, 525
and liquidity ratios, 660
and report of Committee on Post-War Domestic Finance, 709
told of suggestions for altered constitution of Bank, 1944, 8
Commodities Office, 793
commodity markets
Bank of England and, 785–93
reopening, 697
commodity prices, rise as result of Korean War, 381
commodity schemes, 786–93
commodity shunting, 225–6
Commonwealth Air Training Scheme, 98, 100, 101
Commonwealth Bank of Australia, statutes of, 13, 14
Commonwealth Conference, 1952, 437
Commonwealth Development, programme proposed, 423
Commonwealth Development Finance Company
establishment, 699, 729–33
projected, 482–3
Commonwealth Development Finance Corporation, suggested, 730
Commonwealth Finance Ministers, meeting, July 1949, 293
Commonwealth Finance Ministers' Conferences, 422–5, 498, 502

Commonwealth Prime Ministers
  Conferences, 452, 477–92, 729, 730
Commonwealth Reconstruction Bank,
  suggested, 730
Commonwealth Relations Office, 423n
  represented on Working Party on
    convertibility, 470–1
Commonwealth Trade and Economic
  Conference, 1958, 592
Companies Act, 767
Companies Acts, registration of new
  names, 760
Competition and Credit Control, 610
Compton, Sir Edmund G.
  and bank figures, 632
  biog. note, 616
  and Budget, Autumn 1955, 645
  and Credit Trading Bill, 771–2, 773,
    775, 776
  and deposit-taking, 767
  and hire purchase, 762–3
  and Monetary Organisation report,
    661–5
  and monetary situation, 1957, 677
  and steel denationalisation, 739, 741
  and Treasury Bills, 616
Conolly, Frederick G.
  biog. note, 178
  and European payments, 178, 188–90
  and sterling convertibility, 1952, 480
  see also Conolly Plan
Conolly Plan, 185, 186–9, 195
Consols, 2½%, 376
Control of Borrowing and Guarantees Act
  1946, 763, 764, 327n
  origins of, 11–12
Control of Borrowing Order, 625, 764
Conversion Stock, 4%, 1957–8, 646
Conversion Stock, 4½%, 1962, 674
Conversion Stock, 3%, 1948–53, 356,
  357
convertibility, sterling, see sterling
Coombs, Herbert C.
  and Australian sterling balances, 101–3
  biog. note, 101–2
Copleston, E. R., 455
  biog. note, 455
  and Collective Approach, 480
copper
  market re-opened, 786, 791
  war-time position, 786
copra, commodity scheme, 793
cotton
  Egyptian, and sterling balances, 256
  war-time position, 786
Cotton (Centralised Buying) Bill, 788n
Cotton Control, 788n

Council of Europe, and European Payments
  Union, 509
Council on Prices, Productivity and
  Incomes, appointment, 676
Court of Directors
  appointment of, 7; discussed during
    nationalisation, 8
  approval of Bank Rate change, 1951,
    405
  and Bank rate, 611
  briefed on Bank of England Bill, 16–17
  composition of, 7, 9–10; after
    nationalisation, 28; changes discussed
    during preparations for
    nationalisation, 8
  Crown appointment of, 10
  deputation to Prime Minister, 1952, 444
  disqualification of Civil Servants as
    members, 10n
  letter from Governor to Treasury on
    behalf of, 631–2
  numbers of, 7
  and Parker Tribunal, 701
  views on Bank's net worth at time of
    nationalisation, 22
  see also Directors
credit control, 614
  1948–51, 396
  Bank group considers, 1949, 370–2
  machinery, 1951, 408–9
  selective, 1944–5, 327–9
  use of in monetary policy, 407
  see also ratio controls
Credit for Industry Ltd, 708
Credit Trading Bill, 761–77
Crichton, Association of Investment Trusts,
  710, 711, 721
Crick, Leslie F.
  biog. note, 600
  and Operation Unicorn, 600
Cripps, Sir R. Stafford
  appointed Chancellor, 355, 357
  and bank advances, 1949, 378
  and cheap sterling, 232, 233, 236, 237,
    238–9, 240
  and credit restrictions, 698
  and disinflation policy, 167
  and Egyptian sterling balances, 260
  and European payments, 191, 192, 194,
    198, 199, 204
  illness, 278, 294, 380
  and Indian sterling balances, 1948, 253
  request to Bank re bank deposits, 1948,
    362
  resignation, 312, 387
  and sterling balances, 1949, 268
  and sterling devaluation, 283, 284, 286,

287, 291, 292, 293, 295, 298, 299–301
and Transport Stock, 358
and Treasury Bill rate, 371
Cripps–Ansiaux Agreement, 182
Crookshank, Leader of House of Commons, 434–5
Crowther, Geoffrey
  editorship of *The Economist*, 407n
  member of Royal Institute of International Affairs study group, 426
  and sterling devaluation, 287
Crump, Norman, 526
Cunliffe, Geoffrey, and British Aluminium, 744, 746, 748
Cunnell, Rodney
  biog. note, 120
  visit to Egypt, 120, 121
Currency and Bank Notes Act, 2
currency notes, prepared during Suez crisis, 549, 552
Currency Pool, Treasury paper on, 1949, 200–1
Customs & Excise, 235–6
  and cheap sterling trade, 245
  form CD5, 243
  represented on Liaison Committee on cheap sterling, 242
Czech Financial Claims Fund, 804
Czechoslovakia
  debt, 804–6
  gold, 804–6
  monetary and trade agreements with UK, *see* Anglo-Czechoslovak Agreements

Dacey, W. Manning
  biog. note, 662
  and variable liquidity ratios, 662
Daily Express, and commodities, 786
Daily Herald, comment on Bank of England Bill, 19
Daily Mail, briefed on intervention in transferable, 526
Daily Telegraph
  briefed by Catto on Bank of England Bill, 18
  briefed on intervention in transferable, 526
  comment on Bank of England Bill, 19
Dalton, Hugh
  announces 2½% Irredeemable, 352
  appointed Chancellor of the Exchequer, 1945, 5, 70
  and Argentinian sterling balances, 106
  and cheap money policy, 327–59
  and convertibility crisis, 1947, 145, 146, 147, 156
  decides on nationalisation of Bank, 5
  Diaries, ed. J. A. R. Pimlott, reference, 292n
  and Egyptian sterling balances, 119
  and finance for industry, 717
  and gilt market, 1945, 338
  gives press conference on publication of Bank of England Bill, 18
  High Tide and After, quoted, 30n, 342n, 343n
  and Indian sterling balances, 108
  and interest rates, 326, 329, 330–70
  and nationalisation of the Bank, 6
  relations with Catto, *see* Catto
  relations with Cobbold, *see* Cobbold
  resigns as Chancellor, 355, 357
  and Stage III, 70–1
  and sterling balances of Australia and New Zealand, 101–3
  and sterling devaluation, 291
  tribute to Lord Catto, 7–8
Daltons, *see* Irredeemable, 2½%
Daniell, Sir Peter, 350n
  Goverment Broker, 647, 758n
Darby, Ainslie C.
  biog. note, 295
  and devaluation, 295
Darwish, *see* El-Darwish Bey
de Gasperi
  and OEEC, 487
  Premier of Italy, 193
de Gaulle, General
  and French economy, 595–6
  and new French constitution, 595
  and Operation Unicorn, 599
de Jong, Albert & Co., 234–5
Defence Aid, US, 308–9
defence expenditure, UK, during Korean war, 381
Defence (Finance) Regulations
  and assets of Bank Polski, 799
  in WW2, 327
Defence (Finance) Regulations Committee, 786
Denmark
  and European payments 1955, 532
  Monetary Agreement with, 126, 127
deposit-takers, risk of growth, 699
deposit-taking, by finance houses, 761–79
deposits, emergence of market in, 659
Deputy Governors, two suggested, 1945, 7, 8, 10
Deshmukh, Chintaman D.
  biog. note, 112
  and Collective Approach, 484

and Indian sterling balances, 112
and sterling convertibility, 1952, 431
Deutschmark, exchange rate, 1957, 569–72
Development Areas, 718
diamonds, cheap sterling trade in, 345
diary-keeping, habits of Norman, Catto and Cobbold, 282n
Directors
  involved in suspected Bank Rate leak, 700–3
  non-executive, and Bank Rate rise, 686n
  see also Court of Directors
Directors of Bank, Executive, numbers of, 10
discount houses
  capital and reserves, 645n
  operations in gilt market, 756–7
  relations with Bank, 755–8
Discount Market
  as lender, 609
  operations, 1951, 393
  and Treasury Bill rate, 329, 376
  wartime operations, 330
Discount Office
  and $1\frac{3}{4}$% Exchequer Bonds, 340
  and cheap sterling, 234–5
  and hire purchase, 762
  Principal, and accepting houses, 751, 753; banking supervision responsibilities, 770; and individual discount houses, 757, 758; and LDMA, 757–8; and merchant banks, 23; relations with City, 696; responsibilities of re monetary policy, 317
dollar earnings, London pool, 40
dollar pool, 815
dollar shortage, 141, 220
Dominions Office, briefs Bank on central bank statutes, 1945, 14
double tirage, 414, 415
Douglas, Lewis
  and convertibility crisis, 157
  and sterling convertibility, 494, 496
  and sterling devaluation, 285
Downie, Jack, 688n
Drozniak, President of Bank Naradowy Polski, 797–801
Dulles, Foster
  and Collective Approach, 489–90
  US Secretary of State, 481
  visit to NATO capitals, 486–7
Duncan, Andrew, 735, 737, 739
Dunlop, 732

Eady, Sir W.
  and 2% Lending rate, 1951, 408
  and Anglo-American Loan, 807
  and Anglo-American Loan Negotiations, 77, 82
  appointed Second Secretary to Treasury, 50
  and Argentinian sterling balances, 103–8
  and bank advances, 363, 378, 381
  biog. note, 5–6
  and Canadian Loan negotiations, 98–100
  chairman of Treasury meetings on European payments, 181–2
  character and abilities, 50
  and convertibility crisis, 145, 150, 151, 154n, 156, 157; summit of career, 159
  and credit control, 1950, 381
  and devaluation, 294
  and Egyptian sterling balances, 114–23
  and European payments, 173
  and finance for industry, 710, 711, 715, 716
  and gilt market, 1944, 331
  head of Home Finance Division, 359
  and Indian sterling balance negotiations, 110–12
  and interest rates, 1950, 388, 390
  member of National Debt Enquiry, 326
  Miranda Agreement, *see* Argentina, sterling balances
  and National Debt Enquiry, 335
  and nationalisation of the Bank, 5–6
  and ratio controls, 383
  relationship with Bank, 50
  and Stage III, 70
  and sterling balances, 92, 96
  and the White Plan, 52
Ebtehaj, Bank of Iran, 244
Eccles, Marriner, and Anglo-American Loan Agreement, 812, 816, 819, 820
Economic Adviser to the Governors, participation in discussions with Treasury, 318
Economic Co-operation Administration
  campaign for EPU, 302
  and European payments, 204
  rivalry with US Treasury, 284
  and sterling devaluation, 281–2
  UK mission, 1948, 279
Economic Intelligence Department, 793
Economic Secretary, post created, 359
Economic Section (of Cabinet, later of Treasury)

and balance of payments, 1947, 146
and bank advances, 366, 367
and bi-monthly economic reports, 362–3
and European payments, 198, 199, 204–5
member of working party on convertibility, 470–1
moves to Great George Street, 359
opposition to Collective Approach, 471
and ratio controls, 382
and regional Clearing Union, 198
and Robot, 435, 438, 465–6
and unification of sterling, 504
Economic Trends, 346n
Economist, The,
and 2½% Irredeemable, 353
and Bank of England Bill, 27
and Bank Rate change, 1951, 406–7
briefed by Catto on Bank of England Bill, 18
briefed on intervention in transferable, 526
and cheap money policy, 349
and sterling devaluation, 287
under editorship of Geoffrey Crowther, 407n
economists, Bank's attitude to and use of, 318–20, 383, 393, 434, 435–6
Eden, Sir Anthony
appointed Prime Minister, 530
character and abilities, 531
and Collective Approach, 1953, 489–90
and EDC, 439
Full Circle, quoted, 440n
ill-health, 620n
relations with Bank, 698
resignation as Prime Minister, 562, 669
and Robot, 440
and Suez crisis, 549, 552, 556, 557
Egypt
cheap sterling trade, 244, 256
Exchange Control, 120
monetary agreement with, prolonged, 1951, 273n
payments agreement with, 250, 251
political regime, 1949, 257–60
removal from Transferable Account Area, 550
sterling balances, 114–23, 250, 256–60; mentioned, 53, 62, 84, 96
subscription to IMF, 123
supplementary payments agreement, 1948, 250
see also Suez crisis
Egypt Committee, 544, 550, 552
Eisenhower, Dwight, President of US, 481

El-Darwish Bey, Mahmoud, and Egyptian sterling balances, 115–21
electricity, nationalisation, 646
electricity industry, and hire-purchase, 410
Ellen, ex-Union Discount, 401
Ellerton, Barclays Bank, 229, 233, 415
Ellis, Frederick, 405n
Ellis-Rees, Sir Hugh
biog. note, 127
and Collective Approach, 485–6
and European monetary agreements, 1945, 127–8
and European payments, 172, 173, 182, 183, 187, 188, 191, 195, 198, 200–1, 203, 532, 534
and European Payments Union, 216, 456
Minister to OEEC, 476
and negotiations with French Treasury, 1947, 135–6
and Poland, 797–800
and sterling convertibility, 479
and Swiss negotiations, 1947, 138
Emary Bey, and Egyptian sterling balances, 257, 260
Empire Letter, sent by Bank to Commonwealth central banks, 246
Employment Policy, White Paper, 1944, 438
Erhard, Ludwig, and Operation Unicorn, 597, 599
Erlangers, 753, 754
Erskine, George, 737
Etzel, German Finance Minister, 599
Europe, Eastern, 795–806
debt defaults, 803–6
Europe, Western, preparations for sterling convertibility, 132–41
European Account Area, proposed, 199
European Clearing Union, Bank's objections, 200
European Coal and Steel Community, 168
inception, 460
European Co-operation Administration, and European Payments Union, 212
European currency area, proposed, 172
European Defence Community, 439
treaty, 460, 461
European Economic Community, inauguration, 595
European Free Trade Area, negotiations, 585, 595, 597
European Fund, 600
suggested, 510–11
terms settled, 537

INDEX

European Monetary Agreement
  1955, 528–42; enforced, 566; origin of, 535; signed, 530
  1958, foreshadowed in 1953, 488 effected, 585
  provisions for European Fund, 600
European monetary agreements, 1942–6, 124–31
  assessed, 538
  text agreed by Council of Ministers, 537
European payments, 193–219
  Bank paper on, 1948, 199
  negative attitude in Bank to new initiatives, 185–8
  problems, 1947, 170–9
  settlement in gold, 517, 519, 522
European Payments Union, 193–219
  Bank assessment of, 212–14
  and Collective Approach, 493, 509
  credit, 1951, 417
  difficulties in 1952, 453–62
  discontinued, 566, 585, 597
  extended until June 1956, 537
  French debts, 595
  Managing Board, 515n; attitude to Collective Approach, 486; and convertibility, 479; and exchange rate policy, 519
  members consulted about sterling unification, 594–5
  Monetary Agreement with proposed, 456
  non-nucleus members, 480
  nucleus members, 480
  OEEC Interim Report on, 1948, 280
  opportunities for UK, 215–16
  outline approved, 211
  proposed special fund, 1953, 489
  quotas agreed, 211
  renewal, 1954, 510; 1956, 548
  report on renewal, 1955, 532
  success of, 215
  UK disengagement from under Robot, 436
European Recovery Programme, 172, 174, 180, 182, 308n
  Attlee government acceptance of, 277
  and European payments, 170, 175, 176
  receipts from, 358
  renewal debated, 283
  Special Aid provisions mooted, 176
  suggested, 149, 150, 151, 161
  suspension, 1951, 307
  US financial policy, 166–7, 179
  winding up suggested, 1949, 270
Evening Standard, and gilt-edged market, 647

exchange control
  Bank's administration of, 611, 696–7
  and British Aluminium, 744, 745
  and commodity markets, 785–7
  and Kuwait gap, 568
  and non-resident transactions, *see* cheap sterling
  post-war, 1941 paper, 40–1
  and Suez crisis, 550
  UK, 1946–7, 129–63
  see also cheap sterling
Exchange Control Act, 1946, 327n
Exchange Equalisation Account
  1947, 151
  Bank's management, 611
  currency exposure, 1950–1, 413–14
  establishment of, 2, 25
  and exchange control 1946–7, 130
  gold transactions, 130
  lack of statistics, 1946, 346
  loss in August 1947, 153
  and members of Sterling Area, *see* Sterling Area
  and Suez crisis, 558, 560
exchange policy
  Bank's post-war, 39–87
  key currency approach, 39, 53–4, 471
exchange rate policy, 1954–5, 518–20
exchange swaps, 514–15
Exchequer, 5% 1957, 674n
Exchequer and banking figures, 668
Exchequer Bonds, $1\frac{3}{4}\%$, 334, 339–40, 341, 358, 376
Exchequer financing, figures, 363
Exchequer Returns, 346
Export–Import Bank, 430, 482, 545, 560, 566, 569
Exter, John
  biog. note, 581
  and IMF quotas, 581–2

Falkland Islands, 265
Federal Reserve Bank of New York
  and cheap sterling, 240
  mentioned, 227, 238, 283–4, 447, 581, 810
  and UK credit, 1954, 503
Federal Reserve Board
  and dollar deficit 1946, 815
  mentioned, 812
Federal Reserve discount rate, 1954, 622–3
Federal Reserve System, autonomy, 780
Fforde, John S.
  and Credit Trading Bill, 771–3
  and IMF quotas, 577, 578
  joins Bank as Economic Adviser, 577n

member of Bank/Treasury Working
   Party on bank advances, 688
 and monetary situation, 1957, 675,
   677, 678–9
Figgures, Frank
 character and abilities, 206n
 and Collective Approach, 471
 OEEC Secretariat, 206–7
finance companies, and credit restrictions,
   658–9
Finance Corporation for Industry
 composition of first Board, 722–3
 consulted about credit restrictions, 653
 establishment of, 704–27
 mentioned, 316, 699
 merged with ICFC, 725
 and SCOW, 728–9
 and steel denationalisation, 738
 and steel industry, 743
finance houses
 bank's relations with, 759–60
 controls over, 411
 ratio controls, 772–3
 Registrar, suggested, 769, 773, 774,
   777
 use of controls, 699
Finance Houses Association, 760
 adaptation of, 700
 and credit restrictions, 640
 and Credit Trading Bill, 771, 772, 775,
   776
 and deposit-taking, 768–9
Finance for Industry Ltd,
 formed, 725
 progress, 726
Financial News, mentioned, 322
Financial Times, The,
 advice to Bank re Bank Rate 'leak', 702
 and Bank of England Bill, 27
 briefed by Catto on Bank of England Bill,
   18
 briefed on intervention in transferable,
   525n
 and British Aluminium, 748
 and cheap sterling, 237
 and credit restrictions, 626
 and floating rate rumours, 1952, 448
 and NDO purchases, 349
 and special funding operation, 445
 and sterling convertibility, 538
Finebel, 457n
 announced by French, 301
 and European payments, 196
 sponsorship of Alphand Plan, 193–4
Fisher, John L.
 biog. note, 226
 and blocked sterling suggestions, 427

 and cheap sterling, 226, 241
 and Cobbold's plan for floating rate
   convertibility, 434
 and convertibility, 309, 311
 and exchange reserves, 1954, 627
 and foreign exchange market, 414
 and freeze and offer plan, 273
 and IMF stand-by, 1955, 530
 and monetary situation, 1957, 675
 possible authorship of 1952 paper on
   convertibility, 431n
 and Robot, 434
Fleming, R. E., 732
Fletcher, Walter, 236
Forbes, Sir Archibald F.
 biog. note, 735
 and steel denationalisation, 735, 739
Foreign Exchange Administration, 815
Foreign Exchange Committee, US, 240
foreign exchange market, re-opening, 279,
   412–17
foreign exchange policy, 1953–4, Stages I
   and II, 498–542
foreign exchange reserves
 UK, 1949, 285n; 1949–50, 302; 1950,
   379, 389; 1951–2, 417; 1952, 429,
   451; 1954, 625–7; 1955, 524, 543;
   1956, 535–6, 555, 558, 560; 1957,
   571, 674; 1958, 568, 592; 1958,
   517n, 566, 568, 592; effect of Suez
   crisis, 563
Foreign Office,
 and Egyptian sterling balances, 259
 and European Payments Union, 456–7
 and French monetary situation, 1952,
   461
 and OEEC, 476, 477
 represented on Working Party on
   convertibility, 470–1
 and Robot, 439, 468
Foreign Operations Administration, 486–7,
   506
Four Wise Men, 661–5
 supplementary report, 672
Fournier, M., 501n
franc, French, devaluation, 224, 569,
   598–9, 601–2; discussed, 458–9
France
 cheap sterling trade, 224, 225, 244
 and EDC, 439
 and European Fund, 601
 and European payments; 1955, 532,
   533; plan for Second Category
   Compensations, 185–6
 Fourth and Fifth Republics, 595
 member of nucleus for Collective
   Approach, 471

Monetary Agreement with, 1944, 126;
  negotiations to amend in 1947,
  133–6
 and Operation Unicorn, 596–604
 payments agreement, mentioned, 53
 sterling balances, 1947–8, 224–5
 and Suez crisis, 558n
France, Arnold
 biog. note, 501
 and unification of sterling, 508
Franco-Italian-Benelux Union, *see* Finebel
Franks, Oliver, Baron, 174, 271
 and cheap sterling, 239, 240
 and credit restrictions, 650, 666,
  679–80
 Deputy Chairman of CLCB, 661n
 and liquidity ratios, 661
 member of ISHRA, 742
 speech to Lloyds Bank shareholders,
  576
 and sterling devaluation, 282, 283,
  285–6, 299n
 at Treasury dinner, 655n
 see also Franks Plan
Franks Plan, for sterling balances, 271,
  274
Fraser, Peter, PM of New Zealand, 101
Frazer, British Insurance Association, 710,
  711, 718, 720
Free Trade Area, discussions, 587, 588
French Assembly, rejection of EDC Treaty,
  513
French Monetary Area
 and cheap sterling trade, 225n
 and membership of International
  Monetary Fund, 224
Frère, Maurice
 biog. note, 171–2
 discussions with Cobbold, 1947, 171–2
 and European payments, 201, 533
 and sterling devaluation, 286
 and visit from International Monetary
  Fund, 284n
Fuhrmann and Co., 243
Funding $2\frac{3}{4}\%$ 1957, 674n
funding operations, 1957, 671
Funding Stock, $2\frac{1}{2}\%$ 1956–61, 357–8
Funding Stock, 3% 1966–8, 386–7
Funding Stock, $3\frac{1}{2}\%$ 1992–2004, 671–2
furs, cheap sterling trade in, 225
Fussell, Reserve Bank of New Zealand, and
  Robot, 463

Gaillard, Felix, and European Payments
  Union, 457–8
Gaitskell, Hugh,
 1951 Budget, 312
 appointed Chancellor of the Exchequer,
  387
 and Bank of England Bill, 21
 character and abilities, 209n, 387
 and credit restrictions, 640, 698
 deputises for Cripps, 380
 and European payments, 209, 211
 and floating rate convertibility, 310
 and floating rate sterling, 296
 and forward exchange markets, 413
 and interest rates, 1951, 388, 390–3
 and ratio controls, 1950, 382
 and sterling devaluation, 294
 and Treasuring Bill rate, 371
Gallagher, W. N., and Parker Tribunal,
  701–2
Gampell, Sydney, 405n
gas, nationalisation, 646
Gas Boards, and hire-purchase, 410
General Agreement on Tariffs and Trade,
  539
 and Collective Approach, 471
General Election
 1945, 5
 1950, 272, 274, 312, 371, 380
 1951, 394, 398
 1955, 530–1, 534
Germany, Federal Republic of,
 creation, 1949, 193
 and EDC, 439
 and European payments, 1955, 532,
  533
 member of nucleus for Collective
  Approach, 471
 and Operation Unicorn, 598, 601
Gibson, George, appointed Director of
  Bank, 28
Gifford, Carlyle
 and finance for industry, 721
 and steel denationalisation, 741
Gilbert, Bernard William
 biog. note, 507
 chairman of Collective Approach
  Committee, 507
 and credit restrictions, 651
 and exchange policy, 521
 and steel denationalisation, 737
 and sterling convertibility, 536; 1956,
  548
gilt-edged funding, 1951, 406
gilt-edged market
 assessed by Committee on Post-War
  Domestic Finance, 706
 performance 1951–2, 445
 use of in monetary policy, 324–6,
  327–59, 609, 646–9
 wartime, 330–1, 333

Glasgow Local Authority stock issue, 647
Glendyne, Lord, 350n
Godber, Sir F., chairman of CDFC, 732
gold market, London
　re-opened, 504
　re-opening proposed, 434, 495–6
Gold Standard
　revival and demise, 2
　use of term in Bank, 1949, 209n
Goodenough, Barclays Bank, 710
Gordon, Lincoln, 481
Goschen, H. K., 69n
Government Broker
　and NDO purchases, 348
　operations, 1946–7, 348, 349–50
　responsibilities of re monetary policy, 317
　activities in WW2, 330
government financing, absence of statistics, 1946, 345–6
Government Stock, exchanged for Bank Stock, *see* Bank Stock
Governor
　authority re Bank Rate changes, 692
Governors
　appointment by Prime Minister and Chancellor, 7
　term of office, 10
Grafftey-Smith, Sir Anthony P.
　biog. note, 152
　and convertibility crisis, 1947, 152
　and Egyptian sterling balances, 260
　and European payments, 184, 188, 199, 202, 219
grain, commodity scheme, 793
Grant, A. T. K.
　biog. note, 109
　and sterling balances, 109
Great Universal Stores, and hire-purchase, 410
Greaves, Finance Houses Association, 776
Greece, debtor of European Payments Union, 212
Green, Maurice, Deputy Editor of *The Times*, 657
Gregory, Sir Theodore
　biog. note, 96
　and Indian sterling balances, 96
Grunfeld, H., 236
Guaranteed Stock, 646–7
Guaranty Trust Co. of New York, 228, 235
Guardian, The, briefed on intervention in transferable, 526
Guest Keen & Nettlefold Ltd, mentioned, 737, 739
Guindey, Guillaume, 177

Guinness Mahon, 747n
Gunston, C. A., and Eastern Europe, 795, 796
Gurney, H. W.
　biog. note, 228
　and cheap sterling, 228
Gutt, Camille
　biog. note, 283
　and sterling devaluation, 283, 284, 287

Halifax, Viscount, 818
　and Anglo-American Loan Agreement negotiations, 73n, 74, 80, 81
Hall, Robert
　and bank lending, 363–6
　biog. note, 278–9
　and credit restrictions, 638, 641, 642–3, 687
　and devaluation, 278, 279, 283, 287, 290
　and floating rate sterling, 296
　head of Economic Section, 359
　and IMF quotas, 577, 582–3
　and Monetary Organisation report, 661–5
　and Robot, 435, 439
　and sterling convertibility, 429, 449, 512
　The Roberthall Diaries, quoted, 435n, 438n
Hall-Patch, Sir Edmund L.
　and Anglo-American Loan Agreement, 820
　and Anglo-American Loan Negotiations, 82
　biog. note, 82
　and European payments, 174
　and sterling convertibility, 1954, 508
　and sterling devaluation, 284
Hambro, Sir Charles, 245
　and Bank Rate, 1955, 644
　and British Aluminium, 744, 746, 747, 748
　and cheap sterling, 245
Hambros Bank
　and British Aluminium, 744, 745, 747n
　and cheap sterling, 245
　and foreign finance bills, 753
　and SCOW, 728
　and steel denationalisation, 741
Hamilton, Cyril R. P.
　biog. note, 183
　and British Aluminium, 746n
　and European payments, 183, 198
　and IMF stand-by, 1955, 530
　and unification of sterling, 587

Hammarskjold, Dag H. C.
  biog. note, 139–40
  and European payments, 203
  and Swedish monetary negotiations, 1947, 139–40
Hanbury-Williams, Sir John
  biog. note, 366
  in deputation to PM, 444
  offered Governorship of Bank, 366–7
Harcourt, Viscount
  biog. note, 559
  and Suez crisis, 559–61, 564
Harriman, Averell, and sterling devaluation, 281–2, 293
Harrod, Roy
  and credit restrictions, 626
  and Hanson-Gulick proposals, 45n
  The Life of John Maynard Keynes, quoted, 36n, 95
  views on post-war Sterling Area, 43
Haslam, Eric P.
  biog. note, 730
  and Commonwealth finance, 730
Hawker, Sir Cyril
  appointed Home Finance Director, 573, 771
  biog. note, 569
  and Credit Trading Bill, 771, 773, 774
  and European exchange rates, 1957, 569
  and FHA, 776
  and monetary situation, 1957, 677
  and steel denationalisation, 736
Heasman, Roy E.
  biog. note, 184
  and European payments, 184, 516
  and floating rate convertibility, 589
Heathcoat Amory, Derick,
  appointed Chancellor of the Exchequer, 567, 586
  and Bank Rate changes, 692
  and Credit Trading Bill, 775
  and Operation Unicorn, 598, 603
  and sterling convertibility, 587
  and unification of sterling, 592–3
Helbert Wagg
  adviser to Tube Investments, 745, 747
  and SCOW, 728
  and steel denationalisation, 741
Henderson, Hubert
  biog. note, 36
  paper on post-war finance, 1941, 36, 37–8
  and sterling devaluation, 282
  views on draft provisions of IMF, 57, 58
Henning & Co., Messrs I., 245
Heyworth, Sir G., 732

hire-purchase
  credit restrictions, 658
  relaxation of controls, 1954, 624
  restrictions of finance, 1955, 632–3
  terms raised, 1955, 526
hire-purchase finance, controls, 410–11
  see also Credit Trading Bill
Hire-Purchase Finance, Interdepartmental Committee, *see* Interdepartmental Commtitee
hire-purchase market, 1955–8, 761–79
Hire-Purchase Trade Association, 763, 768
  and Credit Trading Bill, 772
Hobson, Sir R. Oscar, 525n
  and Bank Rate, 656
  biog. note, 19
  briefed on Bank Rate change, 1951, 405n
  and credit restrictions, 370, 626
  and nationalisation of Bank, 19
Holland
  cheap sterling trade, 225–6, 227, 228, 233, 236, 240–1, 245, 246–7
  debtor of European Payments Union, 212
  and European payments, 532–5
  member of nucleus for Collective Approach, 471
  Monetary Agreement with, 126, 127
  and Operation Unicorn, 598, 601
  Supplementary Financial Agreement, 1947, 134
Holland-Martin, E., Executive Director
  advice to Governor re nationalisation, 9
  advice to Treasury re monetary policy, 317
  biog. note, 9
  and convertibility crisis, 1947, 156
  and gilt market, 1944, 331
  member of Committee on Post-War Domestic Finance, 705
  sends Norman copy of Bank of England Bill, 18
Hollom, Jasper Q.
  biog. note, 761
  and credit restrictions, 761
  and deposit-taking, 764, 765
  and hire-purchase, 762
Holtrop, M. W.
  biog. note, 233
  and cheap sterling trade, 233
  and sterling devaluation, 284
home finance 'story' instituted, 373
Hong Kong, private sterling balances of residents, 243n
Hongkong & Shanghai Trading Corporation, 236

INDEX

Hopkins, Harry, and Lend-Lease, 36n
Hopkins, Sir R. V. N.
  appointed Permanent Secretary to Treasury, 50
  biog. note, 8
  chairs National Debt Enquiry, 326
  and discussion of future nationalisation of Bank, 1943, 8
  and gilt market, 1946, 339
  and interest rates, 1946, 351
  and post-war financial discussions, 36
  relations with Norman, 8
  retirement as Permanent Secretary to Treasury, 66n
  and Robot, 446n
  and Treasury paper on post-war economic policy, 1941, 42
Hudson's Bay Company, 225
Humphrey, George
  and Collective Approach, 489–90
  and exchange crisis, 1956, 545
  and IMF stand-by, 506
  and Randall Commission, 502
  Secretary of US Treasury, 481
  and sterling convertibility, 494
  and Suez crisis, 560–1, 564
  and US tariffs, 513
Hungarian central bank, 795
Hunter, Ellis, 735, 737, 739
Hyndley, Lord, appointed chairman of FCI, 722

Iliff, W. A. B., 115, 119, 121
Ilsley, Canadian Finance Minister, and Canadian Loan negotiations, 99–100
Imperial Smelting Corporation, 786
Imperial Tobacco, 732
India
  delegation to Commonwealth Prime Ministers Conference, 1952, 483, 484
  dollar expenditure, 1948, 251–2, 253–4
  gold reserves, 275
  monetary partition of, 251
  objections to key currency approach, 478
  payments agreement with, 250; 1948, 251–6
  sterling balances, 108–14, 250, 251–6; mentioned, 53, 62, 84, 96
  US underwriting of deficits proposed, 1949, 271–2
India Office, and sterling balances, 95
Indian currency, proposed devaluation, 1946, 92
Industrial Bankers Association, 772
  and Credit Trading Bill, 771

Industrial and Commercial Finance Corporation
  consulted about credit restrictions, 653
  establishment of, 704–27
  loan book, 725
  mentioned, 316
  merged with FCI, 725
Industrial Commission, proposed, 711, 715
industrial companies, approached re expenditure cuts, 657, 658
Industrial Credit and Investment Corporation of India, establishment, 628
Industrial Development Corporation, proposed, 708
Industrial Finance Corporation, proposed, 707
industry, finance for, see Finance Corporation for Industry; Industrial and Commercial Finance Corporation
Industry Reports, to Governors, 658n
Inland Revenue, 759, 760
insurance companies
  and Commonwealth finance, 730
  and finance for industry, 718
  and steel denationalisation, 742
  Treasury anxiety about, 657
Interdepartmental Committee on Hire-Purchase Finance, 765–8
interest rates
  high, associatd with 1920s and 1930s, 371
  as instrument of monetary policy, 314–70, 407, 607, 608, 614
  long-term, post-war, 330–70
International Bank for Reconstruction and Development, 483, 583
  inaugural meeting, 801
  Indian borrowing from, 1948, 253
  US proposals for, 49
International Clearing Union
  proposed, 37, 39–49, 51, 54
  US views, 49
International Development Association, 583
International Monetary Fund
  Article V, 578
  Article VII, 574, 577, 578
  Article VIII, 33, 69, 166, 169, 175, 218, 249, 277, 540
  Article XIV, 33, 75, 83, 180, 223
  Article XIV, 65n
  and Collective Approach, 471
  draft provisions, 56–7, 58–60, 61
  early development, 58
  Egypt's subscription to, see Egypt
  inaugural meeting, 801

843

increase in UK quotas, 1958, 566
Indian drawing on, 1948, 253, 254
passivity, 56
Scarce Currency Clause, 311
stand-by, and convertibility, 510–13
and sterling devaluation, 282
UK drawing on during Suez crisis, 555–64, 592
UK drawings after Suez, 566
UK quotas, 573–85, 593
US proposals for, 49
views on European payments, 203–4
White Paper, 1944, 61
see also White Plan, The
International Monetary Fund/GATT Committee of Twelve, 482
International Trade Organisation 1946 conference, 74, 81
Intra-European Payments and Compensations, 179–93
  agreement signed, 184
  changes to plan, 188
  progress towards, 1945, 79
  proposed, 71n
  defects of agreement, 185
  scrapping of, suggested, 194, 270
  Treasury's opposition to liberalisation, 285
investment trusts
  and Commonwealth finance, 730
  and finance for industry, 718, 720–1
  Scottish, and finance for industry, 718, 720–2
  and steel denationalisation, 741
  see also merchant banks
Iran, UK relations with, 1951, 312
Iraq, sterling balance agreement, 123n
Ireland, Northern, and finance for industry, 720n
iridium, cheap sterling trade in, 236
iron and steel, denationalisation, 699, 733–43
Iron and Steel Act, 1949, 733, 737
Iron and Steel Board, 735, 736, 739
  formation, 738
Iron and Steel Corporation, 736, 740, 742
  transfer of assets, 738
Iron and Steel Holding and Realisation Agency, 736, 738
  close association with Bank, 742–3
  membership, 742
iron and steel nationalisation, compensation stock, 738
Irredeemable, $2\frac{1}{2}$% ('Daltons'), 339–55
Irving Trust, 235
Isner, H. J., 235

Israel
  attack on Egypt, 1956, see Suez crisis
  political situation, 1949, 257
Issue Department
  and $1\frac{3}{4}$% Exchequer Bonds, 340
  holdings, 1946, 353n
  holdings of Daltons, 379
  purchases, 1946, 354
  purchases of Daltons, 356
  stocks bought by Government Broker, 330
  underwriting arrangements, 1950, 387
  operations in WW2, 332
Issuing Houses Association, and Commonwealth finance, 732
Italy
  cheap sterling trade, 223–4, 225, 243–4, 247
  and European payments, 1955, 532, 533
  and Operation Unicorn, 598, 601
  Payments Agreement, 1947, 224
  sterling balances, 204

Jacobsson, Per
  appointed Managing Director of IMF, 573
  asks Norman about nationalised Bank, 30
  diary quoted, 548n
  and economists in BIS and IMF, 320n
  and European exchange rates, 1957, 571–2
  and illness of Cripps, 277n
  and IMF quotas, 574, 577, 582, 594
  and interest rates, 1950, 386
  and Operation Unicorn, 602–3
  and sterling convertibility, 492
  and UK IMF stand-by, 597
  and unification of sterling, 592, 593
Janus
  Bank likened to, 20
  Norman portrayed as, in mosaic, 20
Japanese sterling, 247
Japhet, special advances to, 753
Jardine Matheson and Co., and Parker Tribunal, 700, 702
Jarvie, J. Gibson
  and Credit Trading Bill, 776
  and hire-purchase, 762
Jay, Douglas
  advocates financial controls, 1949, 376
  appointed Economic Secretary, 359
  and bank advances, 369
  Change and Fortune, reference, 292
  character and abilities, 359–60
  and devaluation, 294

and Exchange Equalisation Account, 413
as Financial Secretary, 413
and floating rate sterling, 296
and monetary policy, 1948–9, 360, 361, 362
Johnson, W. J., 116
Jordan, UK relations with, 1949, 257
Jowett, Lord, and Bank of England Bill, 26, 27

Karpinski, Zygmunt, 796–8, 801
Karsavina, Tamara, 803
Keller, Dr, 138
Keogh, P. J., 766
Kershaw, R. N.
  biog. note, 38–9
  character and abilities, 321n
  and Commonwealth finance, 730
  and convertibility crisis, 1947, 150
  and gilt-edged market, 1946, 356
  and Indian sterling balances, 109
  member of Committee on Post-War Domestic Finance, 705, 707
  member of Niemeyer's Committee on sterling–dollar exchange rate, 285, 288, 290
  member of Siepmann's Committee on Sterling Area, 88
  and proposed Money Equalisation Account, 323
  and Purchase Tax, 321n
  and Sterling Area negotiations, 1946, 94
  and sterling convertibility, 1951, 421–2, 423
Keswick, Sir William
  consulted on Bank Rate, 644
  and Parker Tribunal, 700–1
key currency approach, *see* exchange policy
Keynes, J. M.,
  and Anglo-American Loan Negotiations, 73–87, 807–22
  and Anglo-American Loan Agreement, 31–87
  attends inauguration of IMF, 95
  attends Savannah Conference, 340, 342
  Bank's criticisms of proposals for international monetary objectives, 33
  and Belgian Monetary Agreement, 125
  and Bretton Woods Agreements, 31
  at Bretton Woods Conference, 61–2
  and Canadian Loan, 97–8
  character and abilities, 32, 34
  and commodities, 786
  and convertibility crisis, 1947, 162

death, 31, 34n, 95
defence of Anglo-American Loan Agreement, 92
delegation to Washington, 1945, 32–3
dislike of Bank's 1941 views on Sterling Area, 43
election to Court, 41
and European monetary agreements, 1946, 128–9
exhaustion from Anglo-American Loan negotiations, 84
and Government's borrowing programme, 1946–7, 340–1
leads UK delegation to Bretton Woods, 61
member of National Debt Enquiry, 326
monetary theories criticised by Thompson-McCausland, 323
and nationalisation of the Bank, 14–15
paper on post-war finance, 36–7, 62
and Pierpoint Morgan tankard, 75
proposals for International Clearing Union, 37
relations with Bank during Bretton Woods and Anglo-American Loan discussions, 31–87
and Stage II, 64
and Stage III, 64–73
and Sterling Area negotiations, 93–5
views on IMF draft provisions, 60–1
visit to US in 1941 re Lend-Lease, 36
Khan, Liaquat Ali, and Indian sterling balances, 109, 111
Khashaba Pasha, 260
Kindersley, Hugh K. M., 2nd Baron
  advice asked by Bank, 401
  and Bank Rate, 1955, 644
  and British Aluminium, 744, 746, 747, 748
  and Commonwealth finance, 731
  and intervention in transferable, 525
  and Parker Tribunal, 700–2
  and steel denationalisation, 737
Kindersley, R. M., 1st Baron
  and Bank of England Bill, 17
  biog. note, 17
  retirement from Court, 728
  and SCOW, 728
King, Wilfred
  biog. note, 350
  and exchange reserves, 626
  and gilt-edged market, 350, 353
  and intervention in transferable, 526
  and special funding operation, 445
Kleinwort
  conversion to ltd. company, 753
  flotation, 753

Knoke, Werner
  and cheap sterling, 227
  and sterling devaluation, 283
Korean War
  economic effects of, 169, 302, 305, 371, 380–1, 394, 790–1
  effect of on commodity prices, 245
Koszul, Bank of France, 515
Kuwait Gap, exchange control, 568–9

Lancashire Steel Corporation, 723, 724
Lazards
  and British Aluminium, 744, 745, 747n
  and Parker Tribunal, 700, 701, 702
  and SCOW, 728, 729
  and steel denationalisation, 741
lead
  market re-opened, 793
  post-war trade, 792–3
  position in WW2, 786
leads and lags, commercial, 414–15, 416
Lebanon, sterling, 243
Lee, Sir Frank G.
  biog. note, 67
  and British Aluminium, 745
  and commodities, 785
  and IMF quotas, 577
  member of Collective Approach Committee, 507
  quoted, 449–50n
  and Stage III, 67
Leeper, Reginald W. A.
  and Argentinian sterling balances, 103, 104, 105
  biog. note, 103
Leith-Ross, Sir Frederick W.
  biog. note, 116
  and Egyptian sterling balances, 116, 120, 121, 257n
  and Suez crisis, 551
Lend-Lease, 807, 812, 813, 820
  Anglo-American discussions, 35, 36n
  termination, 31, 72
Lever, Sir Ernest, and SCOW, 728
Liaison Committee on cheap sterling, 242, 246
Lidbury, Midland Bank, 718–19, 721
Limerick, Lord, and FHA, 761
Linlithgow, Lord, consulted by Governor on bank lending, 363
liquidity ratios, variable, 651, 660
lira, free market depreciation of, 223–4
Lithiby, John S.
  biog. note, 124
  and convertibility crisis, 1947, 152
  and European payments, 172, 174, 175, 182, 183, 203
  and European Payments Union, 457
  member of Committee of Inter-Allied Experts, 124
  and negotiations with Bank of France, 1947, 135–6
Liverpool Cotton Exchange, 788, 792
Liverpool stock issue, 647
Lloyds Bank
  and finance for industry, 710
  mentioned, 363, 372, 650n
Lloyds Bank Review, 662
Local Authority loan conversions, 1946, 349, 350
Local Loans, 1946, 353
Local Loans Fund, 353n
Locana Corporation, 747n
Lomax, Commercial Counsellor, Argentina, 265, 266
Lombard Banking Ltd, 658, 761, 763
London clearing banks
  and bank lending, 393–4
  briefed on Bank of England Bill, 18
  and Commonwealth finance, 730
  and credit control, *see* bank advances, restrictions and credit control
  and finance for industry, 718–20
  meetings with Home Finance Director, 373
  paper on bank advances, 1949, 377–8
  requested to limit bank advances, 1949, 369
  see also Committee of London Clearing Bankers
London Discount Market Association, 654n, 757–8
  informed of Bank Rate change, 1951, 405
  and Parker Tribunal, 701
London Metal Exchange, and re-opening of commodity markets, 786–92
London Rubber Market, re-opened, 789, 790
Loombe, Claude E.
  biog. note, 116
  and Egyptian sterling balances, 116, 121, 122, 257
Lublin Committee, 797
Lucius, *see* Thompson-McCausland, L. P.
Lundgren, Swedish representative at BIS meeting, 515
Luxford, Ansel, 816
Lyttelton, Oliver, Baron
  and floating rate convertibility, 425n
  and nationalisation of the Bank, 7

M3, 365n
M. Samuel and Company, flotation, 753

MacDonald, Malcolm, and Canadian Loan, 98
MacDougall, Donald
  biog. note, 435
  Don and Mandarin: Memoirs of an Economist, quoted, 435n, 441n, 448n, 470n
  and Robot, 435, 442, 465
  and sterling convertibility, 449, 478
Mackay, Baron, 596
  biog. note, 596
Mackenzie King, William L., PM of Canada, and Canadian Loan, 98
Macmillan Committee, 1931, 724n
Macmillan Report, 1931, 708
Macmillan, Rt. Hon. Harold
  appointed Chancellor of the Exchequer, 529, 651, 653
  appointed Prime Minister, 562, 669
  character and abilities, 655
  and credit restrictions, 655–92
  and deposit-taking, 762, 767
  directorship of IMF, 573n
  economic views, 653–4
  and floating rate convertibility, 587, 589
  and hire-purchase restrictions, 632
  introduces Premium Bonds, 545
  and liquidity ratios, 659–61
  and Operation Unicorn, 597
  relations with Bank, 698
  relations with Eden, 531
  and sterling convertibility, 637, 548
  and Suez crisis, 544–64
  and unification of sterling, 592
macro-economic management, and monetary policy, 411
Maday, National Bank of Hungary, 803
Makins, Roger (Lord Sherfield)
  biog. note, 454
  and British Aluminium, 745–7
  and credit restrictions, 685
  and Credit Trading Bill, 744, 745
  and European exchange rates, 570
  and European Payments Union, 454, 489
  and monetary situation 1957, 677
  and Operation Unicorn, 597, 602
  and sterling convertibility, 587
  and Suez crisis, 554, 556, 564
  transfers to Treasury, 529
  and unification of sterling, 586, 593
Mansergh, Professor, 426
Marget, Federal Reserve Board, 582
Marjolin, Robert
  biog. note, 187
  and Collective Approach, 486
  and European payments, 187–8, 195, 509, 511
Marshall Aid and Plan, *see* European Recovery Programme
Martin, William McChesney, Jr.
  appointed Chairman of Federal Reserve Board, 481
  and Bank Rate rise to 4%, 447
  biog. note, 307
  and sterling convertibility, 494
  and UK plans for convertibility, 1950, 307
Mathesons, and Parker tribunal, 701
Matthai, Dr, 254
Maudling, Reginald
  and intervention in transferable, 523–4
  and Operation Unicorn, 597
Mayer, René, Prime Minister of France, 486
Meade, James, 43
  and cheap money, 323
  member of National Debt Enquiry, 326
Menichella, and Operation Unicorn, 602
Menzies, Sir Lawrence J.
  biog. note, 122
  and Credit Trading Bill, 771, 773, 774
  and European exchange rates, 1957, 569
  and IMF quotas, 577, 578
  and IMF stand-by, 529, 530
  and monetary situation, 1957, 675
  and sterling convertibility, 1953–4, 495
  visit to Egypt, 122
Menzies, Sir Robert, PM of Australia
  and Robot, 462, 463
merchant banks
  and Commonwealth finance, 730–1
  overseas expansion, 754–5
  post-war position, 727–8
  setting up investment trusts, 754
  setting up unit trusts, 754
Messina Conference, 529
metals, non-ferrous, post-war enquiry, 791
Metals Controllers, 787
MIAS Group of Property and Investment Companies, 767–8, 774–5, 776, 777n
Middle East, cheap sterling trade, 228
Middle East currencies, proposed devaluation, 1946, 92
Midland Bank
  and finance for industry, 709, 718
  investments, 667
  liquidity, 637–8
  mentioned, 363, 718
  and Suez crisis, 552
mining industry, and Commonwealth finance, 730

848   INDEX

Ministry of Defence
   and Egyptian sterling balances, 259
Ministry of Economic Affairs, 357
Ministry of Food
   and Argentinian sterling balances, 263–4
   and coffee trade, 788
   and gift of Argentinian meat, 106n
   operations in WW2, 785
Ministry of Supply
   and commodities, 787, 790, 791
   and steel denationalisation, 740
   operations in WW2, 785, 786
   Working Party with Bank on steel denationalisation, 737
Miranda, Miguel
   and aftermath of convertibility crisis, 1947, 158
   and Argentinian sterling balances, 103–8, 262–5
   character and abilities, 265–6
   death, 265
Monckton, Sir Walter, 245
monetary agreements, European, *see* European monetary agreements
monetary policy
   Bank's responsibility for, 1920–45, 15–16
   Bank's team under Cobbold, 372–3
   domestic, 1945–51, 314–98; 1952–8, 606–93; lack of, in early post-war period, 314–16
   proposals, 1945, 324–6
   responsibility for, Bank and Treasury, 407; discussed during passage of Bank of England Bill, 25
Monick, Emmanuel, 136, 171
Moody's Economic Service, 322
Moonshine, *see* Operation Unicorn
Morgan Grenfell, 259
   and British Aluminium, 747n
   and Commonwealth finance, 731
   and SCOW, 728, 729
   and steel denationalisation, 737, 741
   see also Catto, T. S.
Morgenthau, Henry Jr.
   and Anglo-American Loan Agreement, 807, 808
   biog. note, 33
   hostility of US banking industry to, 33
   and Lend-Lease, 36n
   and the White Plan, 51
Morison, John, 737, 739, 740
   appointed chairman of ISHRA, 742
Morrison, Herbert S.,
   and convertibility crisis, 1947, 159

   as Foreign Secretary, 312
   as Lord President, 357
Mountbatten of Burma, Earl, 112
Mullens & Co, 349–50, 647n
   and iron and steel denationalisation, 736
Mullens, Sir Derrick, Government broker, 647
Munro, Sir R. G.
   biog. note, 67
   and Commonwealth development, 423n
   and Stage III, 67
Mutual Security Administration, 481
   re-named, 486–7
   see also Foreign Operations Administration
Mynors, Sir Humphrey C. B. Bt.
   as Acting Governor, 680–3
   appointed Executive Director, 373
   and bank deposits, 364–5
   and bank figures, 632
   and bank lending, 372
   and Bank Rate, 618, 621–2, 623
   briefs Governor on overseas central bank statutes, 13
   briefs press on intervention in transferable, 525
   chairman of City group for steel denationalisation, 737–8
   character and abilities, 773n
   and commodities, 786
   and Commonwealth finance, 730, 732
   and convertibility crisis, 1947, 149, 150, 152
   and credit control, 381
   and credit restrictions, 672, 678, 679, 680–3
   and Credit Trading Bill, 773–5
   as Deputy Governor, 613
   and domestic monetary policy, 612
   drafts papers for Governor on external and internal monetary prospects, 398
   as economist and Adviser to Governors, 318, 320n, 322
   and European exchange rates, 1957, 569
   and European payments, 172, 175
   and European Payments Union, 213, 215
   and Exchequer requirements, 1946, 349
   and freeze and offer plan, 272
   and IMF quotas, 579n
   and interest rates, 374, 376, 384, 390
   member of Bank/Treasury Working Group on bank advances, 688n
   member of Committee on Post-War Domestic Finance, 705

INDEX

member of Niemeyer Committee on Sterling–Dollar exchange rate, 285, 288–9, 290
member of Niemeyer's Committee on interest rates, 370
member of Siepmann's Committee on Sterling Area, 1945–6, 88
and monetary situation, 1957, 677
and nationalisation, 9
and Operation Unicorn, 597, 603
and proposed change in Bank Rate, 1945, 324–5
and ratio controls, 383
and Robot, 434, 446
and steel denationalisation, 739
and sterling convertibility, 421–2, 539
and sterling devaluation, 274, 282, 283, 290
and Suez crisis, 553, 561
and Treasury Bills, 616
views on monetary policy, 411

Nahas Pasha, 257
Nasser, President, 551n
 and nationalistion of Suez Canal Company, 550
National Advisory Council on International Monetary and Financial Problems, 281
 and sterling devaluation, 284, 293
National Bank of Belgium, 125, 130, 133, 148, 158–9, 171–2, 219, 284n, 286
National Bank of Egypt, 116–17, 120, 121, 257n
 subscription to gilt-edged funding, 1951, 406
National Bank of Hungary, mentioned, 803
National Bank of Pakistan, subscription to gilt-edged funding, 1951, 406
National City Bank of NY, 235
National Debt, Commissioners for the Reduction of, *see* Commissioners
National Debt Enquiry, 1945, 326
 report, 335
National Debt Office
 holdings, 1946, 353n
 market purchases, 1946–7, 347–57
 operations, 1946, 346–7, 354
 purchases of Daltons, 356
 statutory position, 347n
 operation in WW2, 330, 332, 347
National Defence Bonds, 343n
National Defence Stock 1954–8, 629n
National Discount Co., 757
National Health Service, prescription charges, 312, 389

National Insurance funds, in WW2, 330
National Provincial Bank, 20
 mentioned, 633, 719n
National Savings, 345, 629
National Savings Bank, in WW2, 330, 331
National War Bonds, 617, 646
 $1\frac{3}{4}\%$, 331–2
 $2\frac{1}{2}\%$ 1949–51, 1954–6, 333, 380
 $2\frac{1}{2}\%$ 1952–4, 331
nationalisation of Bank, *see* Bank of England Act, 1946
nationalised industries
 Bank's involvement in stock issues, 380n
 borrowing, 667
 investment programmes cut, 656
Nehru, Braj Kumar, 113
Nehru, Pandit
 and Indian sterling balance negotiations, 109, 110, 111
 and Indian sterling balances, 254
Netherlands, The, *see* Holland
Netherlands Bank, 233
 mentioned, 596
New York, cheap sterling trade, 228, 234–5, 238
New York Times, and cheap sterling, 246
New Zealand
 gift to UK as war contribution, 102
 gold reserves, 275
 sterling balances, 101–3, 417n
 views on sterling convertibility, 1952, 424, 425
News Chronicle,
 and Bank Rate, 656
 briefed on intervention in transferable, 525n
 and credit control, 370
Niemeyer, Sir O. E.
 advice to Catto on Bank's powers over commercial banks, 9
 advice to Treasury re monetary policy, 317
 and Argentinian sterling balances, 104, 263
 and Bank of England Act, Clause 4(3), 24
 and bank lending, 1948, 361
 and Bank Rate, 324–6, 618
 biog. note, 9
 briefs press on Anglo-American Loan Agreement, 108n
 chairman of Committee on Post-War Domestic Finance, 320–1, 705–9
 chairman of Committee on Sterling–Dollar Exchange Rate, 285, 288–9, 290

850 INDEX

chairman of group considering credit control, 370–2
character and abilities, 321n
and convertibility crisis, 1947, 156
and deposit-taking, 763
and devaluation, 279
and European payments, 182, 185
and finance for industry, 716, 719, 720, 723, 725
and gilt market, 1944, 331
and illness of Cripps, 277n
and interest rates, 1949, 374; 1950, 384–6
and launch of FCI and ICFC, 704
and liquidity ratios, 660
member of CIC, 327
and National Bank of Egypt, 116
and National Debt Enquiry, 335–7
and Robot, 446, 465
and Special Deposits, 677n
and sterling devaluation, 278, 290
Treasury views of, 337–8
Nivison & Co., 350
Nokrashi Pasha, 115, 120, 122, 257
Norges Bank, mentioned, 601
Norman, Montagu C.,
and Brown Shipley, 751
and establishment of FCI and ICFC, 704–5
and finance for industry, 707–14
as Governor during WW2, 1–3
illness, 714
and Keynes' plans for post-war sterling area, 44
meeting on post-war financial problems, 1941, 41–2
opinion of nationalisation of Bank, 30
personality, 2, 15
receives copy of Bank of England Bill, 18
relations with Whitehall, 1
retirement, 2
toasted by Court on eve of nationalisation, 30
and Treasury proposals for post-war financial policy, 1942, 47–8
use of economic advisers, 318
North Atlantic Treaty, 257
Norway
debtor of European Payments Union, 212
Monetary Agreement with, 1945, 126, 127
and Operation Unicorn, 601
Nuri Es-Sa'id, 259

O'Brien, Leslie K.,
and 1957 deficit, 675
appointed Chief Cashier, 629
appointed Deputy Chief Cashier, 248n
and Baranski, 802–3
biog. note, 212–13
character and abilities, 778
and cheap sterling, 237, 238, 240, 241, 242
and commodities, 790
and credit policy, 634–5, 636, 638, 644, 646, 647, 651, 652
and credit restrictions, 630–1, 632–93, 761
and Credit Trading Bill, 769–77, 773, 774
and deposit-taking, 763, 764
as Deputy Chief Cashier, 613
and European exchange rates, 1957, 569
and European Payments Union, 212–13, 213n, 215, 216
first meeting with Macmillan, 653
and hire-purchase finance, 766
and liquidity ratios, 651
and Monetary Organisation report, 661–5
and monetary situation, 1957, 677
and ratio controls, 650
Office des Changes, France, 244
Official Committee on Sterling Area Negotiations, 1946, 93, 94
oil, see Suez Crisis
Operation Gearcrash, see sterling, convertibility crisis, 1947
Operation Unicorn, 585–605
approach, 585–95
and France, 595–605
Oppenheimer, Duncan, 732
Organisation for European Economic Co-operation
attitude to visit from International Monetary Fund, 284
Council, and sterling convertibility, 493
Currency Pool proposed, 199
and European Payments Union, 1952, 454; 1956, 534, 535
Fourth Annual Report, 485
Ministerial Group, 512
origins of, 182n
Payments Committee, 186
report on European Payments Union see European Payments Union
and sterling convertibility, 479
UK involvement, 476
Overby, Andy
Director of International Monetary Fund, 204
and European payments, 1956, 534

INDEX

Overseas Financial Policy in Stage III, paper, 65-6
  'Justice', 65, 66, 67, 70, 74, 75, 79, 80, 87, 814, 821
  'Sheer Madness', 85, 158
  'Starvation Corner', 65, 66, 67
  'Temptation', 65, 66, 85, 158, 418, 420
Owen, John G., 532

Paish, Professor, 426
Pakenham, Lord, and Bank of England Bill, 26
Pakistan
  delegation to Commonwealth Prime Ministers Conference, 1952, 483, 484
  gold reserves, 275
  objections to key currency approach, 478
  sterling balances, 250, 417n
  US underwriting of deficits proposed, 1949, 271-2
Palestine, sterling balance agreement, 123n
Paris Committee for European Economic Co-operation, 174
  Payments Subcommittee, 177; reports, 174-5
Parker Tribunal, 700-3
  mentioned, 567, 573
Parsons, Sir Maurice H.
  appointed Assistant to the Governors, 629
  appointed Executive Director, 546, 573
  at Sydney Conference, 502-3
  biog. note, 248
  briefs press on Operation Unicorn, 602
  and British Aluminium, 745
  character and abilities, 546n
  and cheap sterling, 248
  and Collective Approach, 484, 489-90
  and Commonwealth finance, 730
  and European payments, 1955, 533
  and European settlement, 1955, 531-2
  and exchange rate policy, 519
  and IMF quotas, 574, 576, 577, 578, 579, 581, 582
  and IMF stand-by, 530
  and market management, 591-2
  and Operation Unicorn, 597
  opposed to sterling devaluation, 546
  possible authorship of paper on convertibility, 431n
  and Revised EPU, 509-10
  and Robot, 434
  and sterling convertibility, 586; 1956, 548

  and sterling convertibility Stage II, 506
  and Suez crisis, 553, 561
  and unification of sterling, 587, 593-4
Payton, Stanley W.
  biog. note, 596
  and Operation Unicorn, 596
Peacock, Sir E. R.
  and Bank of England Bill, 17
  chairman of Barings, 318
  chairman of organising group for CDFC, 732
  and Commonwealth finance, 730, 731, 733
  retirement from Court, 318
  and Robot, 446
  sounds out Towers as possible Governor, 1944, 14n
  and steel denationalisation, 736, 737, 742, 743
Pearl Assurance
  and Arbuthnot Latham, 753
  and steel denationalisation, 741
pepper, cheap sterling trade in, 225, 236
Peppiatt, Sir K. O.
  anxiety re Treasury interference, 403
  appointed Executive Director, 373
  at press briefing on Bank Rate change, 1951, 405
  and bank advances, 632; 1954, 623
  and bank lending, 635
  and bank liquidity ratios, 617
  and Bank Rate, 323-6, 618, 623-4
  biog. note, 237
  briefs press on intervention in transferable, 505
  character and abilities, 317-18
  and Cheap Money, 323
  and cheap sterling, 237
  and control of credit base, 1951, 407-8
  and credit restrictions, 645, 659, 667, 761
  and domestic monetary policy, 612, 614-15
  and exchange reserves, 1954, 627
  and finance for industry, 711, 719-20, 725
  and freeze and offer plan, 273
  and gilt market, 331-4, 349, 356
  as Home Finance Director, 612-13, 770
  improves links with commercial banks, 373
  and interest rates, 341-2, 374, 384-6, 388
  member of Committee on Post-War Domestic Finance, 705, 707
  member of Niemeyer's Committee on interest rates, 370

and money supply, 635
  note on gilt-edged operations, 648–9
  questioned by Treasury about bank lending, 360–1
  and Robot, 446
  and steel denationalisation, 736
  Treasury ignorance of, 1945, 318n
Peron, Eva, 265, 266
Peron, Juan, 261, 267
  and Argentinian sterling balances, 103, 105
  elected President of Argentina, 96
Peruvian sterling, 247
Pescud, P. A., and Eastern Europe, 795, 805
Pethick-Lawrence, Lord
  and Bank of England Bill, 25
Petrochemicals Ltd, 725
Philip Hill, 753, 754
Philip Hill Higginson, 576
  and AHC, 750
Phillimore, John G.
  and Argentinian sterling balances, 263, 265, 266
  biog. note, 263
  and steel denationalistion, 737
Phillips, Frederick
  biog. note, 50
  as Treasury Representative in Washington, 50
Piercy, William, 1st Baron
  appointed chairman of ICFC, 723
  appointed Director of Bank, 28
  and Bank of England Bill, 26
  biog. note, 26
  in deputation to PM, 444
Pinay, Antoine, 585
  and European Payments Union, 457, 458
  and French economy, 595–6
  government, 459–60
  mentioned, 486
  and Operation Unicorn, 599
Pitman, Isaac
  and Bank of England Bill, 21
  opinion of Norman, 21
  retirement as Director of Bank, 28
Pitt, William, the Younger, 444
Playfair, Sir Edward W.
  and cheap sterling, 237, 244
  and European payments, 173–4, 175, 187, 213, 215, 237
  mentioned, 501
Plowden, Edwin, N., Baron
  An Industrialist in the Treasury, quoted, 435n
  and bank lending, 363–4

biog. note, 289–90
  head of Central Economic Planning Staff, 359
  and Robot, 435, 439, 465
  and sterling convertibility, 1952, 449
  and sterling devaluation, 289–90
Poland
  financial agreement with, *see* Anglo-Polish Financial Agreement
  financial arrangements 1939–47, 795–802
  Polish government in exile, 795–803
Pollen, J. A. Chairman of BIA, 657–8
Portal of Hungerford, Lord
  and British Aluminium, 744, 745, 746, 748
Portsmore, Frederick J.
  biog. note, 479
  and Collective Approach, 493
  and IMF quotas, 574
  and sterling convertibility, 1952, 479
  and unification of sterling, 593
Portugal, Monetary Agreement with, 1945, 126, 127
Post-War Domestic Finance, Committee on, *see* Committee on Post-War Domestic Finance
Postal Savings Fund, 344, 346, 347
Posthuma, Professor, 515
Powell Duffryn, 722
Powell, Enoch
  appointed Financial Secretary, 669
  resignation, 567, 670
Powell, Frederick F. J.
  and Argentinian sterling balances, 103, 104, 263
  biog. note, 103
  and convertibility crisis, 1947, 152
Premium Bonds, 545
Preston, L. T. George
  biog. note, 192
  and European payments, 192
  Principal of Dealing and Accounts Office, 590n
Prevention of Fraud (Investments) Act, 759, 763, 767
Profit and Loss Account of Banks suggested publication, 8–9
Protection of Depositors Act, 760, 766n, 777n
Prudential Assurance, 720
  and steel denationalisation, 741
Public Record Office, 564
Pullinger, J. F. A.
  'Eastern Europe', 795–806
  'The Bank of England and the Commodity Markets', 785–93

INDEX

Purchase Tax, 321n

Radcliffe Committee on the Working of the Monetary System
  appointment announced, 672
  approval of bank controls, 610
  and Bank Rate procedure, 692
  foreshadowed, 655
  and hire-purchase, 771
  mentioned, 573
  paper on 'Alternative Techniques', 692–3
  preparation of evidence, 674, 691
  and procedure for Bank Rate change, 702–3
  questions to be considered by, 683–4
  terms of reference, 567
Radcliffe, Lord
  and Bank of England Bill, 22–3
  chairman of Committee on the Working of the Monetary System, 22n
railways, nationalisation stocks, 353, 355, 357, 358
Raisman, Jeremy, and Indian sterling balances, 251–3
Randall Commission, 494, 502
  report, 503
Rao, Narahari, 110, 113
Rasminsky, and sterling convertibility, 503
ratio controls, 381–4, 396, 650, 772–3
  Special Deposits, 610
Raw Cotton Commission, 788, 792
Raw, Rupert G.
  biog. note, 569
  and European exchange rates, 1957, 569
  and monetary situation, 1957, 675
  and Operation Unicorn, 601
Rea Bros., and AHC, 750
Reconstruction Committee of the War Cabinet, 48
requests, *see* credit restrictions
Reserve Bank of India
  mentioned, 112, 251, 254
  statutes of, 14
  subscription to gilt-edged funding, 1951, 406
Reserve Bank of New Zealand, statutes of, 13, 14
Reserve Bank of South Africa, statutes of, 13
Reuben, S. S., 236
Reuters, 286, 624
  briefed on intervention in transferable, 526
Revenue Bonds, suggested, 669
Reynolds Metals, 743–9

Rhodesia
  views on sterling convertibility, 1952, 424
Ribon, J. G., 234–5
Richard Thomas & Baldwin Ltd
  and FCI, 723, 724
  leader of SCOW consortium, 728
  membership of ISHRA, 742
Rickatson-Hatt, J. B.
  at press briefing on Bank Rate change, 1951, 405
  Bank's Press Officer, 286n
  biog. note, 18
  handles press enquiries on nationalisation, 18
  and launch of FCI and ICFC, 704
Rickett, Sir Denis H. F.
  appointed Second Permanent Secretary, 595
  biog. note, 508
  and Operation Unicorn, 602
  and sterling convertibility, 508–9
  and Suez crisis, 553–5
  and unification of sterling, 593
Rifai, Dr, and Egyptian sterling balances, 257
Robarts, David J.
  and bank lending, 633
  biog. note, 633
  Chairman of CLCB, 661n
  and credit restriction, 637, 638, 639, 640, 654, 672, 679, 679–80, 686, 666n
  and liquidity ratios, 661
Robbins, Professor Lionel
  and Anglo-American Loan Agreement negotiations, 74
  Autobiography of an Economist, quoted, 32, 36, 36n
  and bank advances ceiling, 679
  and credit restrictions, 688, 689, 690
  member of National Debt Enquiry, 326
  member of Royal Institute of International Affairs Study Group, 426
  and monetary policy, 670
  opinion of Keynes, 32
  and post-war Sterling Area, 43
  and Robot, 446n
Robert Benson, Lonsdale, and British Aluminium, 747n
Robert Fleming & Co., 732
Roberthall, Baron, *see* Hall, Robert
Robertson, Professor Sir Dennis
  and Cheap Money, 323
  invited to become Economic Adviser, 282, 383n

member of Council on Prices, Productivity and Incomes, 676n
and Monetary Organisation report, 664n
and sterling devaluation, 282
Robot and Robot II, *see* sterling, convertibility
Roll, Eric, Baron
  biog. note, 479
  and OEEC, 479–80
Rooms One and Two, 765n
Roosa, Robert V.
  biog. note, 581
  and IMF quotas, 581
Rooth, Ivar
  and Bank Rate rise to 4%, 447
  biog. note, 140
  and Collective Approach, 482
  and Robot, 464, 468
  and sterling unification, 504
  and Swedish monetary negotiations, 1947, 140
Rootham, Jasper StJ.
  alternate on Working Party on convertibility, 470–1
  biog. note, 153
  and commodities, 790
  and convertibility crisis, 153
  and European exchange rates, 1957, 569
  and monetary situation, 1955, 675
  and Operation Unicorn, 600, 601
  and revised EPU, 509
Rosenman, Judge, 807
Rothschilds
  and British Aluminium, 747n
  and British Newfoundland Corporation, 731
  as private partnership, 753
  and SCOW, 728, 729
  and steel denationalisation, 741
Rowan, Sir T. Leslie
  biog. note, 239
  chairman of Working Party on International Payments Problems, 579
  and cheap sterling, 239, 240
  and Collective Approach, 480, 484, 493
  and EPU, 454
  and European exchange rates, 572
  and European payments, 532, 534
  and European Payments Union, 456, 458
  and exchange rate policy, 518, 520
  and foreign exchange market, 414, 415
  and IMF quotas, 574, 576, 582, 583
  and intervention in transferable, 522–3
  joins Vickers Ltd, 595
  member of Collective Approach Committee, 507
  and Operation Unicorn, 594
  paper on 'Can the UK Pay its Way?', 529
  paper on 'Why Convertibility?', 529
  and re-opening of gold market, 504
  resignation from Treasury, 595
  and sterling convertibility, 307, 422, 427–31, 508–9, 512, 536, 538, 541, 543, 586
  and Suez crisis, 550, 551, 553, 554, 559, 561
  and unification of sterling, 588, 589, 592
  in Washington, 272
Rowe-Dutton, Sir Ernest
  and Anglo-American Loan Negotiations, 77, 85n
  appointed Third Secretary to Treasury, 180
  biog. note, 141–2
  and commodities, 786
  and convertibility crisis, 141–2
  and European payments, 180–1
  and floating rate sterling, 296
  and payments problems, 1947, 249–50
  and sterling devaluation, 279
Rowland, Archibald, 109
Royal Bank of Scotland, 758
Royal Charter, new, granted to Bank in 1946, 28
Royal Exchange Insurance, and Parker Tribunal, 700, 701
Royal Institute of International Affairs, 450
  paper on Sterling Area policy, 426–7
rubber
  cheap sterling trade in, 225, 235–6
  post-war trade, 789–90
  position in WW2, 786
  see also London Rubber Exchange
Rubber Trade Association, 789, 790
Rueff, Jacques, French economist, 595

Sadd, Clarence, and finance for industry, 709, 710, 711
St Laurent, L. S., and Canadian Loan negotiations, 99
sale and lease-back transactions, 657
Salomon, Walter, and AHC, 750n
Salter, J. Arthur, 1st Baron, 450
  biog. note, 424–5
  opposition to Robot, 425n
  and Robot, 439
  and sterling convertibility, 1952, 424–5, 426

INDEX

Samuel Montagu, 629, 747n
  conversion to ltd. company, 753
  proposed investment in Switzerland, 755
  and Seligman Brothers, 754
Sanderson, Basil, 1st Baron, in deputation to PM, 444
Sandys, Duncan, 737, 738, 739
Saulnier, Chairman of Council of Economic Advisers, 579
Savings Bonds
  3%, 1960–70, 331; 1965–75, 333
Sayers, R. S.
  Financial Policy 1939–1945, reference, 330n
  invited to become Economic Adviser, 383n
  quoted on successor to Norman, 14n
Schrijver, A. L., 234–5
Schroders
  adviser to Tube Investments, 745
  and SCOW, 728
  special advances, 753
  and steel denationalisation, 741
Schuman Plan, *see* European Coal and Steel Community
Schuman, Robert
  biog. note, 301
  French Foreign Minister, 460
  kept in ignorance of devaluation, 301
Scottish Midland Guarantee Trust Ltd, 763
secondary banking crisis, 766n
Securities Management Trust, 723, 742
Seligman Brothers, 753, 754
Serial Funding Bonds
  1¾%, 617, 629n
  2¼%, 675
  3%, 646
Serial Funding operation, 614
Serial Funding Stock, 1¾%, 406, 672n
Sevres Agreement, 554
Shackle, George, economist, 43
Shammah, M., 236
Shell Petroleum, 732
Sherfield, 1st Baron, *see* Makins, Roger M.
Shillito, Edward A.
  biog. note, 763
  and deposit-taking, 762–3
Shone, Terence, 110
Sidki Pasha, 115
Siepmann, H. A.
  appointed Executive Director of Bank, 88n
  biog. note, 38
  Chairman of Committee on Sterling Area, 1945, 88–92
  and cheap sterling, 226–7, 229–31, 236, 237, 241–2, 244–5, 246, 247

Committee on Post-War Exchange Policy, 38, 50
Committee on Sterling Area, Report, 129–31
  and commodities, 785, 788, 789, 790, 791, 792
  and convertibility crisis, 142, 143, 144; chairs action group, 152–3, 154–5; unpleasant climax to Bank career, 163, 196
  and discussions on post-war finance, 38
  and Eastern Europe, 795, 795–9
  and Egyptian sterling balances, 121, 258–9
  and European monetary agreements, 1945, 128
  and European payments, 172, 180, 181, 189, 218
  and exchange control, 696
  and freeze and offer plan, 273
  and Indian sterling balances, 109
  and International Clearing Union, 41
  and proposed blocking of sterling balances, 269
  and proposed Money Equalisation Account, 322–3
  relations with Treasury, 242n
  Report on Loan Agreement and Sterling Area, 108–14
  and Stage III discussions, 69n
  and sterling area negotiations, 1946, 94
Sikorski, General, 796
silver, cheap sterling trade in, 236
Simon, Viscount, 25, 328, 782
Sinclair, Sir R., 732
Skaug, Norwegian Minister of Commerce, 601
Skinner, Ernest H. D.
  appointed General Manager of FCI, 722
  biog. note, 704
  and FCI and ICFC, 704
  and finance for industry, 715, 716, 719–20
  member of Committee on Post-War Domestic Finance, 705, 706–8
Snyder, John, Secretary to US Treasury 230, 270, 274n
  and cheap sterling, 230
  and sterling devaluation, 281, 282, 286, 293
Society of Motor Manufacturers and Traders, 625
South Africa
  and Anglo-American Loan Agreement, 97
  gold, 496
  membership of Sterling Area, 496

856 INDEX

Southard, Frank A., Jr.
  biog. note, 280
  and sterling devaluation, 281–2, 282, 293, 299
Spaak, Paul-Henri, 176, 191, 533
Spain, Monetary Agreement with, 1945, 126
Special Deposit scheme, 670–1, 677n, 689–91
Special Deposits, see ratio controls
Sporborg, H. N., 745
Sproul, Allan
  and approach to US re sterling convertibility, 1952, 481
  and Bank Rate, 1954, 630
  and Bank Rate change, 405, 447
  biog. note, 19
  and cheap sterling, 242, 243
  and Collective Approach, 492
  critical of UK policy, 307
  and key-currency approach, 810
  queries Bank of England Bill, 19–20
  and sterling convertibility, 492–3, 496, 498–9, 503, 508, 512, 513–14
  and sterling devaluation, 294, 298
  and unification of sterling, 504
Stamp, A. Maxwell (Max)
  biog. note, 452–3
  and IMF, 452–3, 530, 578
  and monetary situation, 1957, 675
  paper on 'International Payments', 575
  resignation from Bank, 576, 584
  and sterling convertibility, 546–8
  supports World Central Bank, 575–6
Stassen, Harold, visit to NATO capitals, 486–7
State Bank of the USSR, 795
statistics, financial, paucity of pre-Radcliffe, 345–6
Statistics Office
  post-war functions, 318–19
  preparation of Industry Report, 658n
Stedeford, Sir I., and British Aluminium, 732, 745, 746, 747, 748
steel, denationalisation, see iron and steel, denationalisation
Steel Company of Wales, 727–9
steel industry
  finance, 728
  loans from FCI, 725
sterling
  'back-door' convertibility, 505–28
  Bank's duty to maintain value of, 14
  cheap, see cheap sterling
  convertibility of, 1957–8, 566–605; and Anglo-American Loan negotiations, 74–84, 819; Bank's attitude towards, 1948–55, summarised, 221; and Collective Approach to, 451–543; crisis, 1947, 141–63; during Stage III, discussed, 64–73; and floating exchange rate, 309–11; 427–31, 586–9; interdepartmental working party on, 1952, 470–1; new approach to 1951, 309–12; plans for, 1946–7, 129–63; and Robot, 431–67; suspended, August 1947, 136, 139, 141–63
  current-account transferability, Bank's hopes of in 1943, 53
  devaluation, 167–8; Cabinet agree on necessity, 294; carried out, 299–300; decision taken, 298; discussions leading up to, 267–304; foreign governments informed of; general realignment of exchange rates, 301
  External Accounts, 602
  fixed-rate convertibility, 427–31
  floating rate v. dollar, 296, 297
  floating-rate convertibility, 427–31; discussed, 309, 310
  inconvertible, management problems, 167
  intervention in transferable introduced, 505
  reconciliation with European Payments Union, 210, 219
  resident, 53
  and Suez crisis, 553–64
  transferable, liberalisation of, 1953–54, 492–505
  unification see Operation Unicorn, 504, 506
  unification of official and transferable, 585, 602
Sterling After the War, report on, 52–3
Sterling Area
  balance of payments, 1950, 245
  Bank's views on post-war position, 1941–2, 35–48
  and Collective Approach, 471
  and devaluation, 301
  dollar earnings, 221
  Indian membership of, 1948, 251–2
  members sell foreign currency to Exchange Equalisation Account, 275
  plans for, under Robot, 436–7
  post-war arrangements, differences between views of Bank and Keynes, 63–4
  post-war planning for, 34
  Siepmann's Committee on, 1945–6, see Siepmann, H. A.

sterling balances in, *see* sterling balances
US misunderstanding of, 813, 821
US views of, 40
Sterling Area dollar pool, 808, 811, 813
Sterling Area Negotiations
 Official Committee on, see Official Committee
 paper by Keynes, 92–93
Sterling Area Working Party, 1955–6, 545–6
sterling balance agreements, appraised, 123–4
sterling balances, 1947–51, 249–67
 and Anglo-American Loan Agreement, 813–14
 Australia, 90, 91
 Bank's plans for post-war management, 1942, 50–1
 blocking suggested, 268–9, 426–31
 determination of strategy for, 1946, 88–95
 Egypt, 90, 91, 92
 Eire, 90n, 91
 freeze and offer plan, 272–3
 general policy towards, 95
 growth, 1951–2, 417
 India, 90, 91, 92
 Iraq, 90, 91
 New Zealand, 90, 91
 plans for post-war arrangements discussed, 1942, 35–48
 renewed problems in 1949–50, 305
 South Africa, 90, 91
 in Sterling Area, 96–102
sterling liabilities, UK, December 1945, table, 91
Stevens, Sir John M.
 appointed Executive Director, 573
 and Argentinian sterling balances, 265–6
 biog. note, 265
 and IMF quotas, 576, 578
 and Operation Unicorn, 597, 598–9, 600, 602, 603
Stevenson, Sir Matthew
 biog. note, 237
 chairman of Liaison Committee, 242
 and cheap sterling, 237, 238
Stein, Edward de, 747n
Stewarts and Lloyds, sale, 742, 743
Steyn, Dr, South African Finance Ministry, 496
Stock Exchange
 Chairman informed of Bank Rate change, 1951, 405
 and steel denationalisation, 738

stockholders of Bank, compensation of at nationalisation, 7
Suez Canal, 115, 116
Suez Canal Authority, 552
Suez Canal Company, 117
 nationalisation, see Suez crisis
Suez Crisis, 543–64
 Bank's lack of early knowledge, 549–50
 effect on economy, 544
sugar, commodity scheme, 793
Supplies and Services (Extended Purposes) Acts, 410–11
Sveriges Riksbank, mentioned, 139, 140
Sweden
 creditor of European Payments Union, 212
 Monetary Agreement, 139
 and Operation Unicorn, 598, 601
 sterling balances, 204
 Supplementary Monetary Agreement, 139
Swinton, Lord
 and Bank of England Bill, 25–6
 and credit control, 1951, 408n
Swiss National Bank, and suspension of convertibility, 1947, 136
Switzerland
 and European payments, 532, 533, 537
 Monetary Agreement, 126, 127, 136–8
 and Operation Unicorn, 598, 601
 Supplementary Monetary Agreement, 137–8
 UK tourist allowance, 138
Syria, sterling, 243

take-overs, Bank's intervention, *see* British Aluminium
Tangier, cheap sterling trade, 225, 228, 245, 247
Tansley, Geoffrey, H.
 biog. note, 260
 and Egyptian sterling balances, 260
 and OEEC Report, 1948, 280
 and sterling devaluation, 282, 283
 and Suez crisis, 551
tea, cheap sterling trade in, 225
Tether, Gordon, 405n, 525n
Texaco, 544
Thailand, cheap sterling trade, 225
Thompson-McCausland, L. P. (Lucius)
 alternate member of Collective Approach Committee, 507
 attitude to Europe, 453
 and bank lending, 1948, 365–6
 biog. note, 32
 character and abilities, 322
 and cheap sterling, 225, 232, 241, 247

INDEX

and Collective Approach, 480, 499, 501
and commodities, 785, 786, 789, 792
and convertibility crisis, 150, 152–3, 154, 156
and discussions on post-war finance, 38
and European exchange rates, 1957, 569
and exchange rate policy, 519
and fixed rate convertibility, 311
and floating rate convertibility, 310–11
and freeze and offer plan, 271
and IMF Fund stand-by, 488, 530
and IMF quotas, 577, 578–82, 583, 584
impact of economic advice, 318
and Keynes' conduct of Anglo-American Loan Negotiations, 80
and macro-economic policy, 636
member of 1943 delegation to US, 32
member of Niemeyer's Committee on interest rates, 370
member of Siepmann's Committee on Sterling Area, 88
member of Working Party on convertibility, 470–1
and monetary situation, 1957, 675
monetary theories, 675n
paper on Cheap Money, 323
possible authorship of paper on convertibility, 431n
and post-war financial arrangements, 51–2
and revised EPU, 509–10
and Robot, 469
seconded to Treasury, 1943, 56–7n
and Stage III, 67–8
and sterling area negotiations, 1946, 94
and sterling convertibility, 418–20, 421, 506–7, 514
and sterling devaluation, 1949, 270
and Treasury 'planners', 494
and White Plan for sterling balances, 77
Thorneycroft, Peter
appointed Chancellor, 562, 669
character and abilities, 670
and credit restrictions, 632–93, 673–93
and Credit Trading Bill, 769
and European exchange rates, 1957, 570–2
and IMF quotas, 582
and Parker Tribunal, 701–2
resignation, 567, 586, 670
Thornton, Michael
biog. note, 668
and Credit Trading Bill, 769
and deposit-taking, 763, 765
assists Chief Cashier, 668n

lack of access to Governors, 778n
and seasonal deficits, 668–9
Thornton, Sir R. G.
biog. note, 638
and credit restrictions, 638, 652
Thorold, Sir Guy F.
biog. note, 574
and IMF quotas, 574, 583
and Operation Unicorn, 597
and unification of sterling, 593
Times, The
advice to Bank re Bank Rate 'leak', 702
and Bank of England Bill, 18, 26–7
and deposit-taking, 763
and intervention in transferable, 525n
letter from bankers, 636–7
letter to, from CLCB, 409
and sterling devaluation, 287
mentioned, 657
tin
market re-opened, 791
post-war trade, 790–1
war-time position, 786
Tomlinson method, 183n
Towers, Graham
biog. note, 14
and Canadian Loan, 97–8
considered as successor to Norman, 14–15n
and convertibility crisis, 1947, 148
and nationalisation of the Bank, 14–15, 781–3
offered Managing Directorship of IMF, 573n
and post-war exchange problems, 54–5
queries Bank of England Bill, 20
and Stage III discussions, 66–7
and sterling convertibility, 506
and sterling devaluation, 293
and unification of sterling, 504–5
Trade and Payments Committee, 202
Trades Union Congress, and wage-freeze, 289n, 292, 376
Transferable Account Area
Belgian sterling accumulations, 159
Egyptian membership of, 256–7
extension of, 1950, 308
Italian membership, 224
proposals, 1954, 495
proposed extension, 284
and Suez crisis, 550
Transport Stock, 3%, 1978–88, 358
travel allowance, overseas, cut, 1951, 404
Treasury $3\frac{1}{3}$% 1979–81, 738
Treasury $3\frac{1}{2}$% Stock, 1979–89, 661
Treasury, HM
1947 reorganisation, 359

and appointment of Governors, 7
and Argentinian sterling balances, 103–8
assumes ownership of Bank, 27–8
attitude to Europe, 453
and Bank Rate rise, 1951, 398–410
and Bank's report on sterling balances, 1946, 92–3
Bank's statutory subordination to, 780
and Bretton Woods Conference, 64
and British Aluminium, 745–9
and Canadian Loan negotiations, 98–100
and cheap money policy, 327–59
and cheap sterling, 219–49
and Collective Approach to sterling convertibility, 468–528
and commodities, 786–93
considers devaluation, 1949, 267
and convertibility crisis, 1947, 141–63
and credit restriction, 1955–8, 632–93
and deposit-taking, 762–79
discussions with bank on nationalisation, 8
Economic Policy Committee, and Robot, 468
Economic Section, *see* Economic Section
Egypt Working Party, 551
and Egyptian sterling balances, 114–23, 257–60
and European exchange rates, 1957, 570–2
and European payments, 170–219, 193–219
and European Payments Union, lack of enthusiasm, 216
and exchange control, 696
Finance Division, reorganisation of, 159, 359
and finance for industry, 710–17
Home Finance Division created, 359 and credit restrictions, 667
independence of Bank from, discussed during nationalisation, 6–7
and Indian sterling balances, 108–14, 251–6
Interim Committee for Polish Questions, 800
and International Clearing Union, 44–5
and monetary policy 1945–51, 314–98
and Operation Unicorn, 585–604
Overseas Finance Division, created, 359; and European Monetary Agreement, 535; joins Bank in advocacy of resumption of external convertibility, 1952, 169; relations with Bank, 611; and Robot, 435, 436, 437, 448–9, 465–7, 469
Overseas Finance Section, and Collective Approach, 480; views on European payments, 204
paper on External Monetary and Economic Policy, 1942, 44–8
paper on Post-war Monetary and Economic Policy, 1941, 42
paper on sterling devaluation, 288
planning European monetary agreements with Bank, 1944, 124
and Poland, 797–800
powers over Bank given to at nationalisation, 10
represented on Liaison Committee on cheap sterling, 242
responsibility of Bank to, under Bank of England Act, 13–16
and Robot, 431–69, 464–7
statutory powers of direction over Bank, 611
and steel denationalisation, 736–43
and sterling balances, 95–6
and sterling balances of Australia and New Zealand, 101–3
and sterling convertibility, 1952–5, 475–528
and sterling devaluation, 267–304
and Suez crisis, 543–64
and suggested EMF, 198
views on post-war financial and trade policy, 36
Working Party on sterling devaluation, 271, 272, 274
Treasury Bill rate
1945, 328–9
1951, 394, 406
1952, 447, 448
1953, 620
increase discussed, 1951, 401, 402
Treasury Bill Tender, 756
Treasury Bills
1946, 345, 346
1950–1, 389, 390
1954, 629
substituted for Treasury Deposit Receipts, 375
yield, 1949, 376
Treasury Deposit Receipts, 689, 691
1946, 345
1950–1, 389
objections to revival, 635, 651
rates, 1945, 329
reduction in quantity, 1949, 375
Treasury Solicitor, 773
and deposit-taking, 763

860 INDEX

Treasury/Bank Working Party on monetary policy, 670
Treaty of Rome, 529, 548, 585, 600
Trend, Burke St J.,
  biog. note, 381
  and ratio controls, 381–3
  talks with Chief Cashier, 408
Trinder, Manager of Union Discount, 408
Trinidad Leaseholds Ltd, 544
Tripartite Agreement, 39, 45, 501n
Tripartite Gold Commission, 806
Trustee Savings Banks, funds, 1946, 346–7
Tube Investments, 743–9
  mentioned, 732
Tuke, A. W.
  and Bank Rate change, 404; 1951, 405–6
  and credit control, 1951, 409
Turner, C. W. St John
  and Anglo-Swiss negotiations, 1947, 137–8
  biog. note, 137

Ullman & Co., 235
Unicorn, see Operation Unicorn
Unilever, 732
Uniscan, 196
unit trusts, see merchant banks
United Dominions Trust, 762
United Nations, General Assembly, and Suez crisis, 555, 560
United Nations Relief and Rehabilitation Administration, 126n, 141
United Nations Security Council, and Suez crisis, 555
Uruguay, sterling balance agreement, 123n
US
  and Anglo-American Loan Agreement, see Anglo-American Loan Agreement
  Argentinian trade with, 262
  attitude to European payments problems, 179, 190, 193
  attitudes to floating sterling rate, 297
  and Collective Approach, 481–92
  commercial banks, proposed financial assistance from, 420–1
  and EDC, 439
  external policy, 1949, 269
  financial assistance to UK, see Anglo-American Loan Agreement
  member of nucleus for Collective Approach, 471
  rearmament during Korean war, 380–1
  Republican Administration takes office 1953, 475, 486
  and sterling devaluation, 283
  and Suez crisis, 556–63
  views on UK plans for convertibility, 1950, 307, 308
  see also European Recovery Programme; Lend-Lease
US Commerce Department, 815
US Congress
  and Anglo-American Loan negotiations, 807–22
  debates on renewal of European Recovery Programme, 283
  and sterling devaluation, 283
US Senate, Committee on Banking and Currency, 809–10
US State Department, and Anglo-American Loan Negotiations, 33
US Treasury
  and Anglo-American Loan Agreements, 33, 51, 59, 68, 71, 76, 77, 79, 84–7
  and cheap sterling, 229–30
  and convertibility crisis, 1947, 141–63
  rivalry with ECA, see Economic Co-operation Administration
  and sterling devaluation, 282
US Treasury Stabilisation Fund, 482

Van Zeeland, Belgian Foreign Minister, 195
Vickers Ltd, 595
Vickers, Sir Geoffrey, 723
Vinson, Frederick. M.
  and Anglo-American Loan Negotiations, 76, 78, 79, 86, 808, 812, 815, 817–19
  appointed Secretary of US Treasury, 1945, 68–9
  biog. note, 68–9
Vivian Smith, Randal Hugh, see Bicester, 2nd Baron
Vocke
  Bank Deutscher Lander, 572
  President of Bundesbank, 516
Von Mangoldt
  Bank Deutscher Lander, 537
  and Operation Unicorn, 597

wage freeze, voluntary, after devaluation, 376, 379
wages policy
  1949–50, 305
  Bank opinion on, 1949, 289
Waight, Leonard, and Egyptian sterling balances, 257–60
Waley, Sir David S.
  biog. note, 93

chairman of Committee of Inter-Allied Experts, 124
chairman of Payments Subcommittee, 175, 177
and commodities, 786
criticism of Keynes, 1946, 93
and European monetary agreements, 1946, 128
and sterling area negotiations, 1946, 94
and sterling balances, 1946, 108
and sterling convertibility, 1946, 132
Wall Street Journal, comment on Bank of England Bill, 19
Wansbrough, George, appointed Director of Bank, 28
Warburg, S. G. & Co., 236–7
  and AHC, 750
  and British Aluminium, 745–7
  and Seligman Brothers, 753
Warburg, Siegmund, 236–7
  and British Aluminium, 748
  and cheap sterling, 237, 238
  discusses annual figures with Discount Office, 754
Wardington, Lord, Lloyds Bank, 710
Watson, Guy McO.
  and Argentinian sterling balances, 104
  biog. note, 104
  and European Payments Union, 216
  and French negotiations, 1947, 134–5, 136
  and Revised EPU, 510
  and Swiss negotiations, 1947, 138
Ways and Means Advances, 347, 349
Westminster Bank, mentioned, 632
Westwood, Lord
  appointed to Board of FCI, 722
White, Harry D.
  and Anglo-American Loan Agreement, 809, 812, 814, 815, 816, 818
  biog. note, 39
  and Stage III, 71
    US plan for sterling balances, 1945, 76–7, 78
  and the White Plan, 51, 52–62
White Weld, 235
Whitehall Trust, 747n
Whitehead, Sir Edgar, 423n
Whittome, L. Alan
  as Assistant Principal, Discount Office, 774

biog. note, 765
and Credit Trading Bill, 774–5
and FHA, 776
and hire-purchase finance, 765
lack of access to Governors, 778n
William Brandt, conversion to ltd. company, 753
Williams Deacons Bank, 758
Williams, Professor John H.
  biog. note, 39
  exponent of 'key-currency approach', 39, 810
  and sterling convertibility, 503
Wilson, Horace
  discussions with Norman, 1941, 44
  retirement, 50
Wilson, Rt. Hon. Harold, resignation as President of Board of Trade, 312
Wilson Smith, Sir Henry
  appointed Second Secretary to Treasury, 182
  biog. note, 182
  and cheap sterling, 225, 232, 238
  and Egyptian sterling balances, 260
  and European payments, 182, 187, 191, 195, 198, 199, 211
  and Exchange Equalisation Account, 413
  head of Overseas Finance Division, 359
  and Indian sterling balances, 254, 255, 256
  and sterling devaluation, 283, 286, 287, 295, 299
Wincott, Harold, 405n
Winiarski, Bank Polski, 798–800
Wood, Kingsley, opinion of Towers, 14n
wool
  cheap sterling trade in, 225, 243–4
  commodity scheme, 792
Woolton, Lord, Minister of Reconstruction, 711, 712, 714
World War 1, debt settlement, 80, 81

Yugoslavia, debt, 803

zinc, post-war trade, 791
zinc market, re-opening, 786
Zurich
  cheap sterling trade, 228, 247
  gold market, 495